THIRD EDITION

INTERNATIONAL MARKETING
A Global Perspective

Hans Mühlbacher   Helmuth Leihs   Lee Dahringer

THOMSON

Australia · Canada · Mexico · Singapore · Spain · United Kingdom · United States

THOMSON

International Marketing: A Global Perspective, Third Edition

Hans Mühlbacher, Helmuth Leihs, and Lee Dahringer

Publishing Director	**Publisher**	**Development Manager**
John Yates	Jennifer Pegg	Anna Herbert
Production Editor	**Manufacturing Manager**	**Editorial Assistant**
Emily Gibson	Helen Mason	Natalie Aguilera
Typesetter	**Production Controller**	**Marketing Manager**
Photoprint, Torquay, Devon	Maeve Healy	Leo Stanley
Cover Design	**Text Design**	**Printer**
Land-Sky Ltd	Design Deluxe, Bath, UK	G. Canale & C., Italy

Brief contents

Brief Contents

Contents

PART I Strategic analyses   1

Part II Basic strategic decisions

8 Intended strategic position

Part III Building and sustaining the intended global position   449

11 International product management   452

Each student who embarks on a course in international marketing brings with him or her a rich view of the world and marketing that was acquired within that student's particular domestic culture. Nevertheless, to be successful as an international marketing practitioner, the student must open his or her worldview to permit a thorough analysis of opportunities in other cultures. A major goal of this book is to broaden the way business students view international markets and marketing in order to encourage such an expanded view.

Despite widespread global marketing rhetoric, most marketing managers view world markets from a multinational perspective, as a series of discrete markets that are basically different. Yet worldwide opportunities and challenges presented by recent events – the integration or association of middle and eastern European countries into the European Union, the further increasing liberalization and deregulation of world trade, the impressive economic growth of China that fuels the development of the Asia Pacific area, the economic integration of Latin America, and the economic strength of the North American market – require marketing management approaches successfully dealing with global competitors and suppliers in global markets. Most important, international marketers require a **global perspective** to compete successfully.

The text does not argue that a marketer should sell the same thing, the same way, everywhere. But a company that believes it *must* overhaul its marketing mix for each separate country market errs as much as one that applies only domestic marketing solutions to international marketing problems.

This text discusses current challenges of international business and the impact of different perspectives of management on business behavior. It illustrates the driving forces of international business in the early 2000s: the limited growth in domestic markets of highly developed economies, rapid technological change, increasing global competition, and the global access to resources.

Whatever perspective management takes, leaders of the firm have to answer four fundamental questions:

1 Should the company conduct international operations and is it able to do so?

2 What markets should be served?

3 How much of the firm's resources should be spent for what purpose?

4 How is the firm's competitive advantage to be built and sustained?

The text presents a decision-oriented framework to answer those questions.

International Marketing: A global perspective is written for the student who is interested in international business and who has completed a principles of marketing course. Thus, some knowledge is assumed on the part of the student, as basic concepts are applied internationally.

Philosophy

The underlying assertion of this book is that *any firm – regardless of size – can compete globally.* Success is a function of perspective, opportunity, motivation, knowledge, skills, and luck. International opportunities are plentiful. The challenge for today's marketing manager is to identify those opportunities as they fit the capabilities available to the firm, to develop an appropriate marketing strategy, and to build and sustain competitive advantages in cooperation with other members of the firm as well as external partners.

Approach and organization

The book's three sections, as illustrated in Figure P.1, make the global approach to international marketing accessible to the student.

Building on an introduction to the factors **motivating** a marketing manager to enter international markets:

- Part I looks at the **strategic analyses** to be conducted in assessing potential markets and the competitive position of the firm in those markets.

- From that assessment, Part II takes the student through the process of taking **basic strategic decisions** that guide the application of marketing tools. Managers must develop an intended strategic position, determine general rules of business behavior, and decide on the allocation of resources across markets, time, and organizational subunits.

- Part III then discusses the process of implementing strategic decisions by **building and sustaining** the global position through product management, distribution, sales and logistics, market communication, and price management. The book ends with a discussion of how the results of various analyses and decisions on different hierarchical levels of decision making may be summarized into an international marketing plan.

To develop and implement a global marketing perspective successfully, an international marketer must be systematic in dealing with opportunities and threats. This book presents a systematic approach to global marketing decision making. Part I, for example, which deals with assessing potential markets, addresses the important issues in the same logical order used by a global marketer. While the marketer first examines its business mission and philosophy to determine the relevant product market and the characteristics to be looked at, it then assesses those characteristics in the economic, political and legal, and cultural environments of various country markets. Then, local product markets are more closely analyzed in a small group of attractive country markets. Finally, the firm's competitive position is evaluated by comparing the company's capabilities concerning the success factors in each market to the potential of important competitors.

Why you should use this text

The turn of the century has been economically, socially, and politically turbulent. Fundamental changes continue across the world. Although any textbook can rapidly become outdated due to the speed of those changes, this book will remain useful because it provides a structured approach for *analyzing* dynamic changes. The student is responsible for remaining up to date with world affairs. Both the analytical framework, which addresses such issues, and the global marketing perspective in this book will be valid in rapidly changing environments. Perhaps the global approach is necessary not only to help a firm become aware of changes and their impact, but also to help it adjust successfully to such changes, which is the key to long-term survival.

FIGURE P.1 *General framework for global marketing*

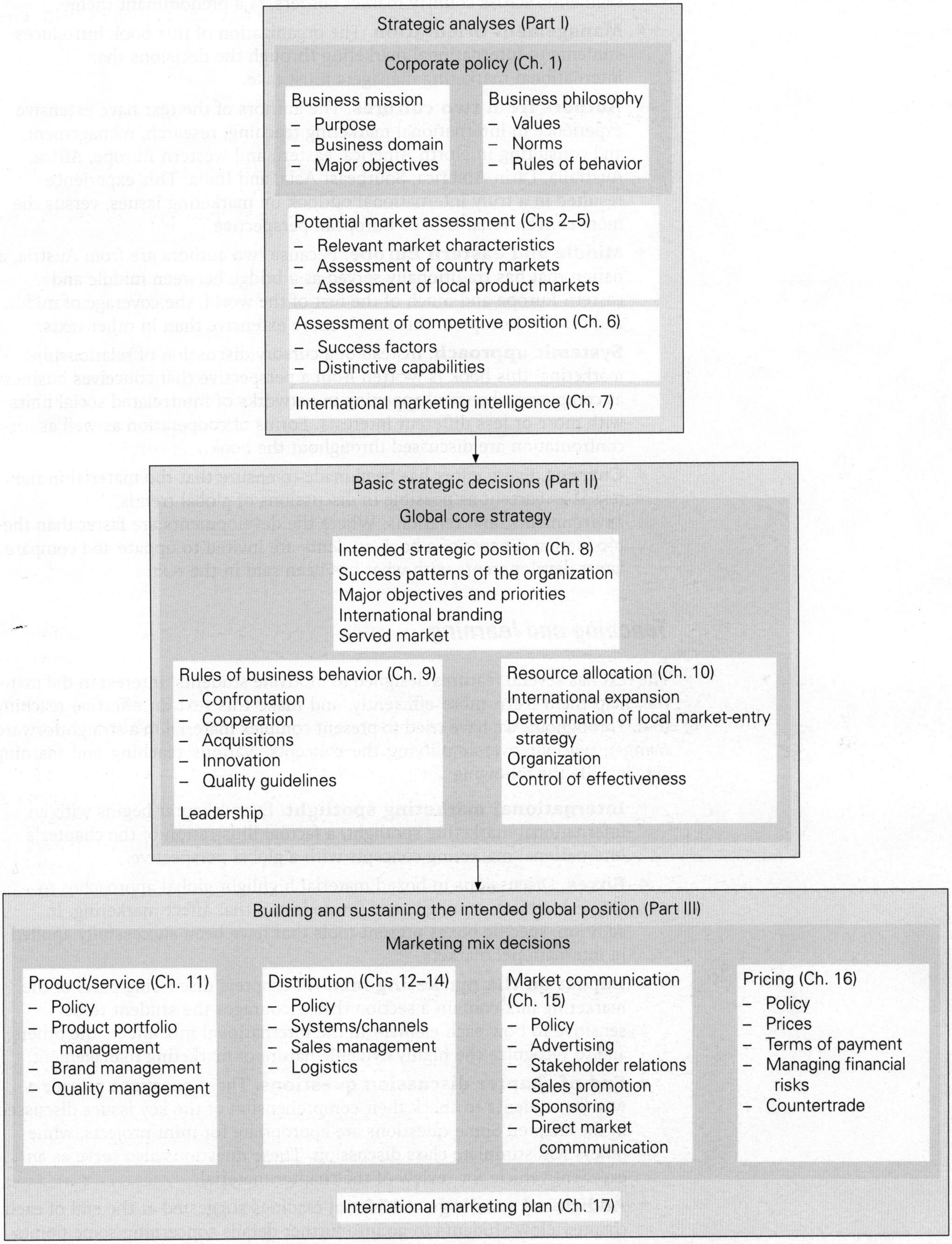

Strategic analyses (Part I)

Corporate policy (Ch. 1)

Business mission	Business philosophy
– Purpose	– Values
– Business domain	– Norms
– Major objectives	– Rules of behavior

Potential market assessment (Chs 2–5)
– Relevant market characteristics
– Assessment of country markets
– Assessment of local product markets

Assessment of competitive position (Ch. 6)
– Success factors
– Distinctive capabilities

International marketing intelligence (Ch. 7)

Basic strategic decisions (Part II)

Global core strategy

Intended strategic position (Ch. 8)
Success patterns of the organization
Major objectives and priorities
International branding
Served market

Rules of business behavior (Ch. 9)	Resource allocation (Ch. 10)
– Confrontation	International expansion
– Cooperation	Determination of local market-entry
– Acquisitions	strategy
– Innovation	Organization
– Quality guidelines	Control of effectiveness
Leadership	

Building and sustaining the intended global position (Part III)

Marketing mix decisions

Product/service (Ch. 11)	Distribution (Chs 12–14)	Market communication (Ch. 15)	Pricing (Ch. 16)
– Policy	– Policy	– Policy	– Policy
– Product portfolio management	– Systems/channels	– Advertising	– Prices
– Brand management	– Sales management	– Stakeholder relations	– Terms of payment
– Quality management	– Logistics	– Sales promotion	– Managing financial risks
		– Sponsoring	– Countertrade
		– Direct market commmunication	

International marketing plan (Ch. 17)

To support this approach, this text offers several unique features:

- **Global perspective**. The horizontal search for strategically equivalent segments, across country market borders, is a predominant theme.

- **Management orientation**. The organization of this book introduces students to international marketing through the decisions that international marketing managers must take.

- **Authors from two cultures**. The authors of the text have extensive experience in international marketing teaching, research, management, and consulting in North America, eastern and western Europe, Africa, Australia, Latin America, Southeast Asia, and India. This experience resulted in a truly international outlook on marketing issues, versus the more conventional U.S. or European perspective.

- **Middle and eastern Europe**. Because two authors are from Austria, a nation that has traditionally served as a bridge between middle and eastern Europe and much of the rest of the world, the coverage of middle and eastern Europe in this text is more extensive than in other texts.

- **Systemic approach**. Instead of a cursory discussion of relationship marketing, this book is written from a perspective that conceives business as complex exchanges happening in networks of interrelated social units with more or less different interests. Forms of cooperation as well as confrontation are discussed throughout the book.

- **Current**. Every effort has been made to ensure that the material in the text is as current as possible in discussions of global trends, environments, and relations. Where the developments are faster than the production process of a book students are invited to update and compare latest developments with what has been said in the text.

Teaching and learning

The text has several features designed to motivate students' interest in the material, help them learn more efficiently, and make this text an effective teaching tool. Throughout, we have tried to present complex material in a straightforward manner, without oversimplifying the concepts. Various teaching and learning aids include the following:

- **International marketing spotlight**. Every chapter begins with an international marketing spotlight, a factual illustration of the chapter's international marketing concepts with a global perspective.

- **Boxes**. Discussions in boxed material highlight global approaches to cultural, ethical, strategic, and future issues that affect marketing. In addition, specific boxes present tools that have been successfully applied in international markets.

- **Impact on the marketing mix**. All chapters discussing parts of the marketing mix contain a section that encourages the student to be sensitive to how each element in the international mix affects the others, and to recognize the highly dynamic nature of marketing management.

- **End-of-chapter discussion questions**. These questions provide a way for students to check their comprehension of the key issues discussed in the chapter. Some questions are appropriate for mini-projects, while others will stimulate class discussion. These questions also serve as an excellent vehicle for review of the chapter material.

- **Additional readings**. Additional readings suggested at the end of each chapter allow students to go into further details concerning some points of special interest discussed in the chapter.

- **Useful internet links**. At the end of each chapter there is a list of internet links helping students to find access to additional study material and to the business organizations mentioned in the chapter.
- **Artwork, photos, and maps**. Each chapter contains artwork, tables, figures, maps, or photos that supplement and illustrate the chapter discussion.
- **Supplementary teaching material**. An instructors' manual, PowerPoint presentation pack and internet resources, inclding cases for discussion, are available to adopters of *International Marketing: A global perspective*. These materials are designed to provide assistance to the instructor in several ways:
  - to provide valuable and time-saving support material and resources for the instructor
  - to make teaching the course using this text even easier
  - to help in the preparation of lectures and discussion sessions with the students.

Internet resources to accompany the text can be found in the resources area of the Thomson Learning website at www.thomsonlearning.co.uk/muhlbacher3. The website includes continuously updated support material for lecturers and students including overviews of each chapter in the book, links to useful international marketing sites on the world wide web and PowerPoint slides to download directly from the site.

A note about Wikipedia

The multilingual, web-based, free-content encyclopedia Wikipedia has been suggested as a resource for further investigation in this text. In general, academic research discourages the use of encyclopedias as a main research source. When consulting Wikipedia in particular, be aware of any issues arising from its open nature:

> Articles in Wikipedia are regularly cited by the mass media and academia, who praise it for its free distribution, editing, and diverse range of coverage. Editors are encouraged to uphold a policy of "neutral point of view" under which notable perspectives are summarized without an attempt to determine an objective truth. But Wikipedia's status as a reference work has been controversial. Its open nature allows vandalism, inaccuracy, and opinion. It has also been criticised for systemic bias, preference of consensus to credentials, and a perceived lack of accountability and authority when compared with traditional encyclopedias.

> *Source: http://en.wikipedia.org/wiki/Wikipedia, 3 November 2005*

Acknowledgments

All textbooks are the result of a team effort. In this case, with parts written on two different continents, it is especially true. But no textbook will be successful without professional support, encouragement, and input from academic colleagues around the world. The authors and the publisher would like to thank the following individuals who helped us to make this edition even better than the second edition.

Robert Bradshaw
De Montfort University

Susan Bridgewater
Warwick Business School

David Chesley
Dearne Valley Business School

Geraldine Cohen
Brunel University

Ian Fillis
University of Stirling

David Gillingham
Coventry University

Said Al-Hasan
University of Glamorgan

David Kilburn
Bournemouth University

Jorma Larimo
University of Vaasa

Michael McDermott
University of Strathclyde

Anja Moessmer
University of Innsbruck

Connie Nolan
Canterbury Christchurch University

Charles Pahud de Mortanges
University of Liege

Christian Pinson
INSEAD

Milton Pressley
University of New Orleans

Stuart Rooks
Oxford Brookes University

Eylette Roux
Ecole Supérieure de Sciences
Economiques et Commerciales
(ESSEC)

Bodo Schlegelmilch
Vienna University of Economics
& Business Administration

Marilyn Stone
Heriot-Watt University

Jon Swift
University of Salford

Jeryl Whitelock
University of Bradford

Hildegard Wiesehoefer-Climpson
University of Derby

Van Wood
Virginia Commonwealth University

The authors would also like to thank the various people involved in the production and design of the text: Jennifer Pegg, Publisher; Anna Carter, Development Manager; Emily Gibson, Production Editor; and Melinda and Nick Welch from Design Deluxe.

THIRD EDITION

INTERNATIONAL MARKETING
A Global Perspective

Hans Mühlbacher, Helmuth Leihs, and Lee Dahringer

Visit the supporting website at **www.thomsonlearning.co.uk/muhlbacher3**
to find further teaching and learning material, including

Students

- MCQs to test your learning

- Links to useful company, news, and other relevant sites

- Exam tips

Lecturers

- Instructors' manual – Including how to teach from this text, answers
  to discussion questions, and analysis of case studies in the text and
  on the students' side of the site

- Downloadable PowerPoint slides

- Mini case studies

- Full-length cases allowing more detailed study

Supplementary resources
Exam View®
This testbank and test generator provides a huge amount of different
types of questions, allowing lecturers to create online, paper, and local
area network (LAN) tests. This CD-based product is only available from
your Thomson sales representative.

Virtual learning environment
All of the web material is available in a format that is compatible with
virtual learning environments such as Blackboard and WebCT. This
version of the product is only available from your Thomson sales
representative.

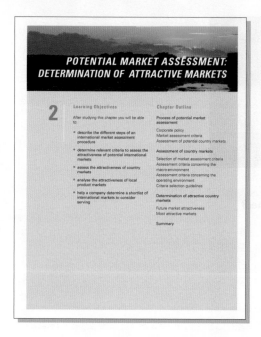

Learning objectives and **Chapter outlines** are listed at the start of each chapter, highlighting the core coverage that you should have acquired after studying each chapter

International marketing spotlights represent factual illustrations of the chapter's international marketing concepts that are shown within a global perspective

Toolboxes outline the successful tools that have been implemented in international markets

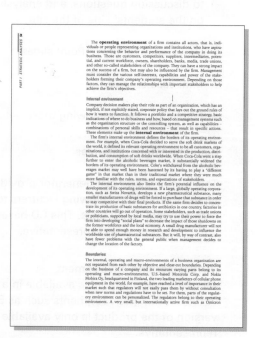

Key concepts are highlighted throughout the text, alerting you to the core concepts and techniques

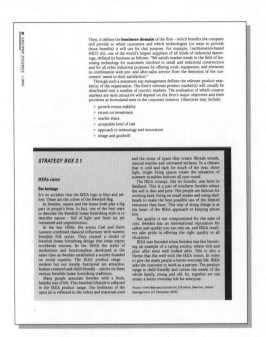

Cultural boxes, Strategy boxes, Ethics boxes and **Future issues boxes** are distributed throughout the text and highlight global approaches to cultural, ethical, strategic, and future issues that affect marketing in the business environment

Summaries at the end of each chapter briefly review the main concepts and key points covered

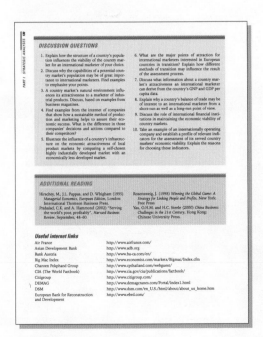

Discussion questions allow revision of the main issues and concepts learned within the chapter that can be used for self-study or within tutorials and seminars
Additional readings are suggested at the end of each chapter to help you find out more details
Useful internet links, listed at the end of each chapter, direct you to additional study material and business organizations included within the chapter

PART I
STRATEGIC ANALYSES

A strategic approach to global business is closely related to marketing analyses and decisions. For international marketing analyses and decisions to be effective and efficient, they need to follow a specific sequence, which is called the international marketing decision process (see Figure I.1). This process is based on the company's statement of corporate policy, which defines the business mission as well as business policy. The business mission identifies in general terms product markets to be served and major objectives to be reached. The business philosophy determines the core values and norms of behavior to be followed.

Strategic analyses

The international marketing decision process starts with a series of strategic analyses. Their major purpose is to check whether the decisions made in defining corporate policy may be successfully implemented. Only if the outcome is positive does corporate policy become the "constitution" of the firm. If strategic analyses show that some statements of corporate policy cannot be successfully implemented or that the firm could do better than stated in corporate policy, the respective statements will be reformulated.

Strategic analyses start with an assessment of potential country markets. The relevant parts of their economic, technological, social, cultural, political, and legal environments as well as the parts of the operating environment that are of importance to the local product markets have to be carefully analyzed to determine the most attractive markets.

From this assessment, the success factors in the most attractive markets – the major capabilities needed to be successful – are derived. They serve as the basis for a comparison between the company's potential to serve those markets, and the related potential of its most important competitors. The comparison with major competitors will help the firm find out whether it can excel in any of the

FIGURE I.1 *International marketing decision process*

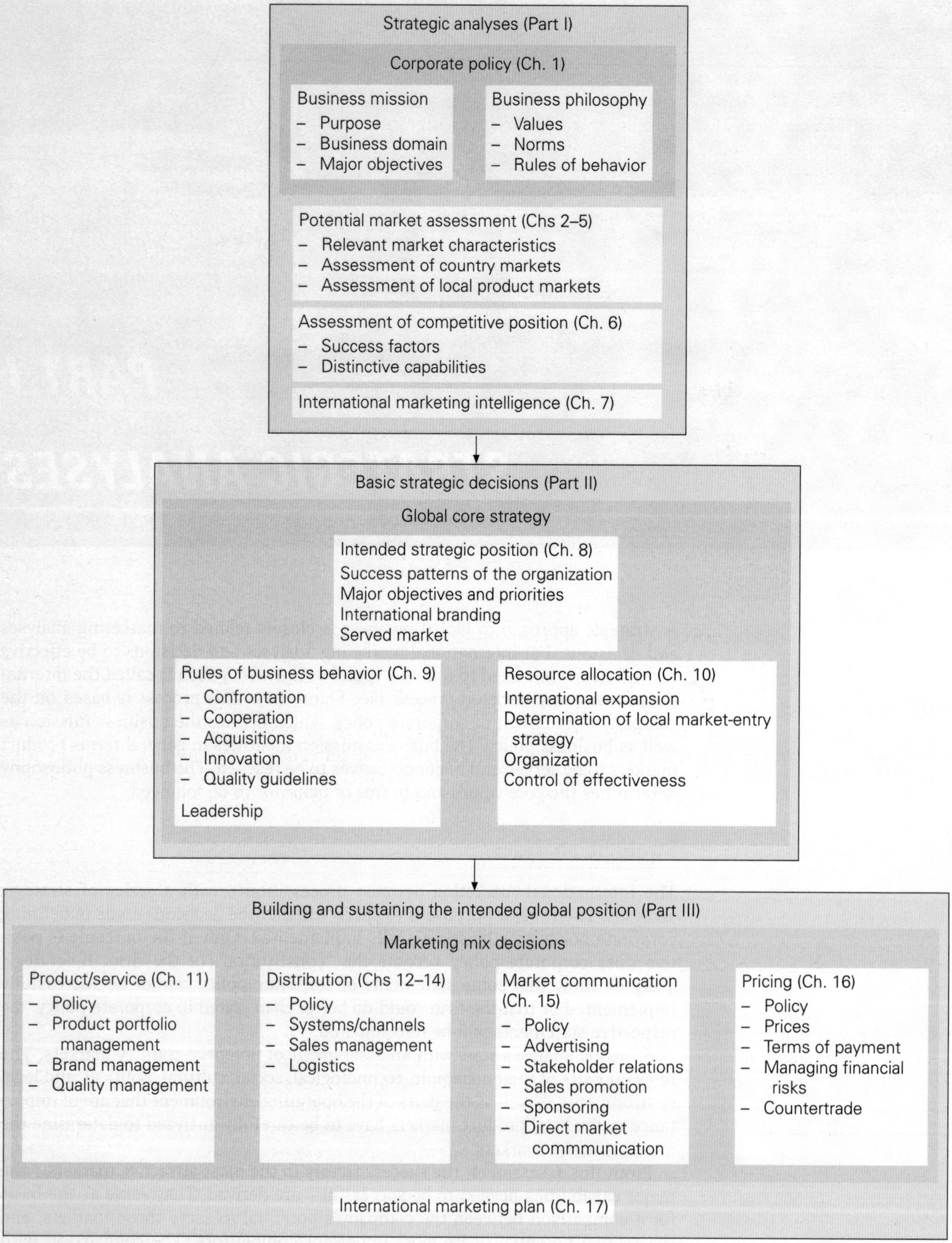

Strategic analyses (Part I)

Corporate policy (Ch. 1)

Business mission
- Purpose
- Business domain
- Major objectives

Business philosophy
- Values
- Norms
- Rules of behavior

Potential market assessment (Chs 2–5)
- Relevant market characteristics
- Assessment of country markets
- Assessment of local product markets

Assessment of competitive position (Ch. 6)
- Success factors
- Distinctive capabilities

International marketing intelligence (Ch. 7)

Basic strategic decisions (Part II)

Global core strategy

Intended strategic position (Ch. 8)
Success patterns of the organization
Major objectives and priorities
International branding
Served market

Rules of business behavior (Ch. 9)
- Confrontation
- Cooperation
- Acquisitions
- Innovation
- Quality guidelines

Leadership

Resource allocation (Ch. 10)
International expansion
Determination of local market-entry
  strategy
Organization
Control of effectiveness

Building and sustaining the intended global position (Part III)

Marketing mix decisions

Product/service (Ch. 11)
- Policy
- Product portfolio
  management
- Brand management
- Quality management

Distribution (Chs 12–14)
- Policy
- Systems/channels
- Sales management
- Logistics

Market communication
(Ch. 15)
- Policy
- Advertising
- Stakeholder relations
- Sales promotion
- Sponsoring
- Direct market
  commmunication

Pricing (Ch. 16)
- Policy
- Prices
- Terms of payment
- Managing financial
  risks
- Countertrade

International marketing plan (Ch. 17)

success factors. Further, the firm can identify which, if any, success factors it is lacking, which would prevent it from fully serving a market. Distinctive competences can be detected.

For example, an Italian furniture manufacturer, such as Poltrona Frau, may find the Scandinavian living room furniture market to be among the most attractive options. To be a successful contender there, a marketer needs to rise to Scandinavian expectations concerning design and weight, as well as do-it-yourself potential. Through an assessment of its own capabilities the Italian firm may discover that it can easily meet the design and weight factors, but has no experience in the production or marketing of do-it-yourself furniture. In comparing its capabilities to the major competitors, the company may find that the most important Danish and Swedish competitors have an advantage in the do-it-yourself area, whereas the Italian firm has an edge in creative design.

Basic strategic decisions

Based on the firm's competitive advantages, that is, those distinctive competences that can be transformed into customer benefits, management will then determine the global core strategy of the firm. This process will be discussed in Part II of the book.

The core strategy determines what development direction the firm should take and how this development should be achieved. The core strategy must contain information on:

- intended strategic position (Chapter 8)
- rules of business behavior to be followed (Chapter 9)
- resource allocation (Chapter 10).

The intended strategic position (Chapter 8) determines the major objectives of the organization, which have been defined as intentions earlier on in the international marketing decision process as part of corporate policy. Based on the strategic analyses accomplished in the following, those objectives can now be formulated in a more precise manner and priorities can be fixed.

In addition, the intended identity of the business organization has to be determined. It is not only salient for the development of a shared understanding of staff; it concerns the purpose and the major characteristics of the organization they are members of. Organizational identity also provides the basis for global branding. For example, depending on the identity to be reached the company may strive for having one global brand covering all its activities or become the home of various brands having their own identities.

Objectives and intended international branding also have a strong influence on selection of the served market(s), that is, the product and country markets to be served as well as the technologies (i.e. ways) to satisfy the current and potential expectations and aspirations of customers and other stakeholders in those markets.

The intended strategic position provides the basis for the determination of rules of business behavior – the way the organization and its subunits will behave in the served markets to reach the intended identity and fulfill their mission (Chapter 9). An important part of an organization's business behavior is competitive behavior, that is, rules concerning how the firm will behave in its contacts with stakeholders in the selected markets. Choices range from a frontal attack on any competitor, to cooperative agreements that not only allow peaceful coexistence but also the exploitation of mutual strengths, achieving synergy. Microsoft, for example, frontally attacks any rival in its major product markets, but cooperates with the most powerful marketers of PCs, such as IBM, Dell or Compaq, to increase the benefits to its customers. The rules of business behavior also comprise policies concerning:

- growth through mergers and acquisitions as well as cooperation norms concerning:

- innovation and communication behavior of the firm

as well as general quality guidelines.

How well the rules of business behavior are accepted and fulfilled by the members of a business organization largely depends on the behavior of its leaders and their ability to handle needs for change. The influence of leadership on the implementation of the rules of business behavior, therefore, will also be discussed in Chapter 9.

Having defined the intended global strategic position of their organization and the rules of business behavior to reach that position, management has to determine how it wants to allocate the limited resources of the company (Chapter 10). The way resources are deployed across processes and organizational subunits as well as across markets and technologies in time influences the success of the organization. Therefore, as Chapter 10 will describe, management determines the path of international market expansion of their organization. Closely related to the intended strategic position and the rules of business behavior, a market-entry strategy has to be determined. It contains the positioning in each of the local markets to be served as well as the selection of appropriate market-entry modes. Positioning includes the selection of customer group(s) to be served and how the firm wants to be attractively differentiated from the most important competitors. HILTI's global strategic position, for example, involves offering high-quality, high-priced fastening solutions employing the latest technology to all construction businesses throughout the world. Nevertheless, management has to decide on specific local positioning in individual country markets in the light of attractive customer segments, competition, and the aspirations of important stakeholders.

Intended global strategic position and intended position in a chosen country market determine the way in which the market is entered. If the company decides to enter more than one new market, market-entry timing becomes an issue. Depending on such factors as available resources, technological advantage or ease of imitation, management will have to select one of the options from a stepwise procedure to a simultaneous rollout.

Resources not only need to be allocated across markets and technologies but also inside the organization. Organizational structures and processes must be shaped to enable the company to plan, implement, and evaluate its international marketing decisions. Depending on the selected structure and the shape of their core processes companies will be more or less well adapted to their international business.

Finally, the effectiveness of resource allocation needs to be controlled in the light of the intended global strategic position as a basis to make the business organization learn and continually improve.

Building and sustaining global position

Based on the global core strategy of their company, managers of business units can develop coherent sub-strategies. The goal of those sub-strategies is to make a contribution to building and sustaining the intended global position of the firm. Decisions and actions regarding the marketing mix are an essential part of business unit strategies. The marketing mix is organized around:

- product and services management (Ch. 11)

- distribution, including sales management and logistics (Chs 12–14)

- market communication (Ch. 15)

- and pricing (Ch. 16).

The contribution of these elements to building and sustaining the intended global strategic position and how the more specific product and country market positions are determined will be discussed in Part III of the book.

The basic strategic decisions taken by top management serve as guidelines for those decisions. HILTI's headquarters, for example, developed a policy for each element of the marketing mix, such as a corporate design handbook and HILTI services guidelines. Country market managers, however, are given enough flexibility in setting prices, establishing product characteristics and service levels, and managing market communication to adapt to local market conditions.

All the analyses made and the decisions taken in the international marketing decision process are summarized in an international marketing plan. This plan also indicates what and how much resources are to be spent for what purpose, and how the planned activities are to be financed. The international marketing decision process will be the guideline for the sequence of chapters in this book. This process should make sure that all members of a company work towards attaining agreed-upon objectives.

CHALLENGE OF GLOBALIZATION

1

Learning objectives

After studying this chapter you will be able to:

- discuss the pros and cons of trade liberalization

- explain the most important dimensions of economic integration

- explain the major forces driving the globalization of business

- explain the specifics of a global business perspective

- differentiate between a multinational and a global approach to international marketing

INTERNATIONAL MARKETING SPOTLIGHT

Red Bull

In 2007 Red Bull, the globally distributed energy drink, will celebrate its 20th year of existence. Despite a loss of sales of one-third in the important German market due to the German government's introduction of a deposit system, total yearly sales growth is still above 15%. The U.S., U.K. and Southeast Asian markets helped boost sales to 1.5 billion cans up from 200 million in 1997.

On 1 September 2003, Fleming Sundo, Danish citizen and a former top manager at Kellogg's, took over responsibility for daily operations as chief operating officer at Red Bull, headquartered in Fuschl near Salzburg, Austria. Dietrich Mateschitz, inventor of Red Bull and 49% owner of the company will keep the title of chief executive officer for at least another 7 years. This is in agreement with the contract signed with his 51% partners: Chaleo and Chalerm Yoovidhya, father and son from one of the richest families in Thailand.

"Mr. Red Bull," Dietrich Mateschitz, will focus on strategic issues. He takes a global perspective on busi-

ness. In an interview on the occasion of Mr. Sundo's introduction he said: "There is only one market, that is the world. We have started 15 years ago without any tradition. From zero on we have gone for global positioning – global brand philosophy, global pricing, global media plans. Traditional companies in our country have seen themselves as pioneers when they exported to neighboring Germany. May be this is one of the reasons why Austria does not have a great number of global consumer brands."

2005 Jordan International Rally

Source: Adapted from "Strategien statt Tagesgeschäften", *Der Standard*, 9–10 August 2003, p. 2

The focal question of this chapter is: What are the challenges of globalization to management?

Globalization of trade

Historical development

The history of world trade is one of exotic products coming from faraway lands to customers eager to buy something new. The southern islands of the Philippines, for example, were the center of a trading hub throughout Southeast Asia in the 4th century. Camphor from Borneo, cloves from the Moluccas, and parrots from New Guinea were all traded in the area. Today, a "typical European consumer" may wake up to an alarm clock made in Korea, drink coffee imported from Columbia, drive a Volvo from Sweden, listen to rock and roll recorded in the U.S., wear shirts from Guatemala, let the kids play on a PC manufactured in China, using software produced in India, while keeping track of the time with a Swiss watch. From the early days of barter between neighboring communities to today's large-scale international trade, the result has been the same: Customers have been provided with more and different goods at lower prices than would have been possible if international trade had not occurred.

According to a study by the Organization for Economic Cooperation and Development (OECD) (see Table 1.1), the global economy has been growing for 200 years, following a period of 300 years of stagnation. In 1820 Asia was the most important region in the world in terms of production. It contained 70% of the world's population and produced 58% of its total goods. With growing industrialization Europe took the lead because traditions and bureaucracy impeded the economic and social changes needed in Asia. The world wars in the first half of the 20th century resulted in industrial dominance by the U.S. Today East and Southeast Asia have become the most economically dynamic region of the world again. And Europe is in danger, this time, of experiencing a setback due to too much bureaucracy and social inflexibility.

The OECD, a Paris-based organization – including 30 members representing more than two-thirds of total world production – focuses on the planning, co-ordination, and intensification of economic cooperation and development. With active relationships with some 70 other countries, Non-Governmental Organizations (NGOs), and civil society, it has a global reach. The members of the OECD represent only about 20% of the world population, but they account for up to four-fifths of aid to industrially developing countries.

Members of the OECD are Australia, Austria, Belgium, Canada, Czech Republic, Denmark, Finland, France, Germany, Greece, Hungary, Iceland, Ireland, Italy, Japan, Luxembourg, Mexico, Netherlands, New Zealand, Norway, Poland, Portugal, Slovak Republic, South Korea, Spain, Sweden, Switzerland, Turkey, U.K., and U.S.

The OECD is active in all economically and socially relevant sectors, such as trade, agriculture, fishing, sea transportation, energy (IEA = International Energy Agency), capital markets and capital transfers, taxation systems, labor force, and policies concerning: development, environmental protection, education, science, technology, industries, and city and regional development.

The OECD produces about 250 publications a year, including economic and social issues from macroeconomics, to trade, education, development, science, and innovation. Of particular interest to international marketers are analyses and forecasts of the economic and social status of member countries. They can be found under "Country Surveys/Reviews/Guides" on the home page of the OECD.

TABLE 1.1 *Organization for Economic Cooperation and Development (OECD)*

Objectives	Planning, coordination and deepening of economic cooperation and development
Members	Australia, Austria, Belgium, Canada, Czech Republic, Denmark, Finland, France, Germany, Greece, Hungary, Iceland, Ireland, Italy, Japan, Luxembourg, Mexico, Netherlands, New Zealand, Norway, Poland, Portugal, South Korea, Spain, Sweden, Switzerland, Turkey, U.K., U.S.
Activities	In all economically and socially relevant sectors, such as trade, agriculture, fishing, sea transportation, energy (IEA = International Energy Agency), capital markets and capital transfers, taxation systems, labor force, policies concerning: development, environmental protection, education, science, technology, industries, city and regional development
Publications	About 250 a year, including analyses and forecasts of the economic and social status of member countries

The members of the OECD represent only 20% of the world population, but they account for more than two-thirds of total world production and up to four-fifths of aid to industrially developing countries.

Source: Baratta, M. (ed.) (1995) *Der Fischer Weltalmanach 1996*, Frankfurt a.M.: Fischer Taschenbuch Verlag, pp. 859f

In 1820 the world population had reached 1 billion but rose to reach about 6.5 billion in 2005. Despite this enormous growth in population, average per capita income had multiplied by eight, from $650 in 1820 to $5,120 in 2001. Four major driving forces have been fundamental to this development:

- *technological change* which was led by the U.K. until 1913 when the U.S. took over the leading position followed by Germany and Japan
- *accumulation of capital* needed to finance the development of new products and increased productivity in production and marketing processes
- *human resources* allowing faster implementation of new technologies based on increasing levels of education, specific skills, and more efficient management
- *liberalization of trade* leading to more competition, which has been a strong driver for productivity gains and improvements in the quality of products and services.

By 2003 world trade had reached a total of $9,220 billion. Of this amount, 63% was contributed by the most highly industrialized nations of western Europe, North America and Japan. They are called the "triad". With some 900 million consumers, less than one-fourth of the world's population, these 20 nations account for about 70% of the world's **gross national product** (GNP) also called **gross national income** – a measure of a country's total domestic and foreign economic value added by the residents of the country.

In 2003 the leading countries in world trade were the same as in the previous years: the U.S., Germany, Japan, France, and the U.K. The tremendous economic development of the People's Republic of China (PRC) made it rank third with a very strong upward trend (Table 1.2). The next ranks were filled by the other big western industrialized countries: Italy, the Netherlands, Canada, and Belgium. Only Hong Kong (reintegrated into China in 1997, but counted as a separate economic unit) had managed to squeeze in at rank 11. The following ranks of the list impressively demonstrated the consolidated position of Southeast Asian countries in world trade. The Republic of Korea, Singapore, and Taiwan had established themselves as equally important in exports and imports as Spain, and substantially stronger than Sweden or Switzerland and Australia. They contributed the most to the more than 30% share of world trade held by developing economies in 2003. Together with Indonesia, Malaysia, and Thailand, which had also been developing rapidly economically in the last decade, they are referred to

TABLE 1.2 *Leading countries in world trade 2003*

In 2003 the U.S. and Germany were still the leading countries in world trade.

Rank 2003	(1994)	Country	Imports in billions ($) 2003	(1994)	Annual percentage change	Rank 2003	(1994)	Country	Exports in billions ($) 2003	(1994)	Annual percentage change
1	(1)	U.S.	1,303.1	(689.1)	9	1	(2)	Germany	748.3	(414.5)	22
2	(2)	Germany	601.7	(370.1)	23	2	(1)	U.S.	723.8	(512.7)	4
3	(11)	China	413.1	(115.7)	40	3	(3)	Japan	471.8	(387.9)	13
4	(4)	U.K.	390.8	(220.0)	13	4	(11)	China	437.9	(121.0)	34
5	(5)	France	390.5	(217.9)	19	5	(4)	France	3,867.7	(220.7)	17
6	(3)	Japan	382.9	(266.5)	14	6	(5)	U.K.	304.6	(196.0)	9

Source: WTO, International Trade Statistics 2004, www.wto.org/english/news_e/pres.5_e/pr411_e.htm

as the "newly industrialized countries" (NICs) of East and Southeast Asia. In 1950–2001 income per head increased fivefold in these countries. Even the financial crisis in most of the NICs in 1997/98 and the economic recession in Japan only slowed growth to a more sustainable level.

Only 0.5% of international trade is contributed by the economically less developed countries (LDCs) of Africa and Asia. In over 40 of those countries, GNP per capita decreased in the early 2000s, often due to political instability, a high national debt, and disease. Picture 1.1 illustrates the uneven level of economic activity in the world.

As a result of increasing international trade, buyers around the world – especially in the most economically developed markets, but also a growing number of consumers in the newly industrialized countries – have become accustomed to being able to obtain goods that have been produced in many other nations. In the past decade, soaring growth rates in the Pacific Rim, for example, have created a new class of urban, professional women with money to spend on designer goods. Customers all over the world want to obtain the best products at the best possible prices. Hence, to be successful today, most businesses must be able to market to, and to satisfy, customers in a global marketplace. Ethics box 1.1 illustrates one of the potential problems caused by this development.

Trade liberalization

Trade liberalization has advantages and disadvantages depending on the perspective one takes.

Advantages of trade liberalization

Trade liberalization has contributed positively to several global issues.

PICTURE 1.1 *A picture of the world taken by a satellite during the night impressively shows the uneven economic development of various parts of the world*

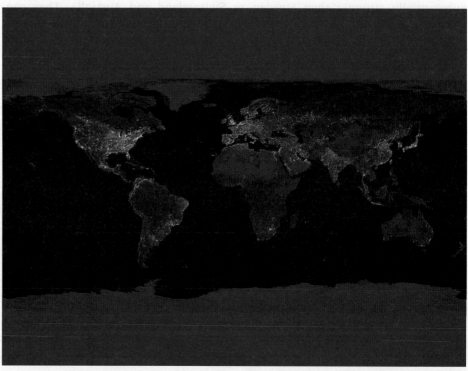

Source: Jeff Rosensweig, Emory University

Increase in customers' choices at lower prices When there are barriers to trade, whether natural or artificial, customers' choices are limited and they end up paying higher prices or being forced to accept lower quality. For example, until 1993 India was a closed market for cars. As a consequence, the average vehicle there was 20 years old and technologically unsophisticated. Because domestically produced cars did not have to compete with imports, Indian manufacturers did not use the latest technology in styling or engineering. In 1996 Maruti was the country's only well-established modern carmaker. Jointly owned by the Indian government (18%) and by Japan's Suzuki (54%), Maruti had a 75% share of the new-car market, selling cars based on 1970s technology. In 1998, Tata Motors started producing passenger cars called Indica. Their electronic and air-conditioning systems come from Germany, airbags from Sweden. All the rest is produced in India. But because of the international marketing experience accumulated by their headquarters, management of Tata Motors was able to sell Indicas in Italy, Portugal, Spain, and the U.K. In 2004, about 50 million Indians had enough income to buy a car. The size of the new-car market reached 1 million. Imported cars from Europe, such as middle-class Škoda, were considered as high-standard automobiles. In 2005, because of the opening of Indian markets to outside competitors, Renault announced a joint venture with Mahindra and Mahindra, the No. 4 Indian car manufacturer, to assemble 50,000 "Logan" cars yearly from 2007 on. And BMW, exporting cars to India, considered a direct investment.

Continual improvement of productivity As the Future issues box 1.1 shows, barriers to trade also run counter to continual improvement of productivity.

If productivity can be increased without losing jobs the wealth of a country increases.

ETHICS BOX 1.1

Exploitation financed Taylor's terror

The toppling of President Taylor's terror regime in Liberia from power started in July 2003 when the UNO imposed an embargo on Liberian timber. Consequently, Oriental Timber Corporation, a company related to Joseph Wong and his Global Star Company headquartered in Hong Kong, refrained from further cutting the rainforest in the southeast of Liberia. Taylor was stripped from his major sources of income beside blood diamonds, which could not be sold any longer either because of strict controls.

It all began in 1999: The Dutch businessman, Gus van Kouwenhoven, bought five concessions for cutting timber from the Liberian government. His negotiation partner representing government was the brother of President Taylor. Because of lack of maps nobody could say exactly how big the conveyed area really was, but estimates are between 2.5 and 4 million hectares of rainforest, the last big forest in Western Africa.

Because van Kouwenhoven could not manage operations on his own he cooperated with the Oriental Timber Corporation (OTC). OTC erased about 100,000 m³ of timber per month, which represents about 4,500 hectares (= 45 million square meters) of rainforest: Where OTC had passed through with its machines and own security people, villages were burned, fields left behind, not even bushes were left.

European and US timber purchasers were impressed by the efficiency and reliability of OTC's business. In addition, OTC's prices were comparatively low, allowing western customers to profit from the exploitation of nature.

In 2000, President Taylor personally cashed at least $186 million from OTC. His private wealth was estimated to reach $2 billion at that time. Human rights organizations claim that the weapons Taylor needed to keep his terror regime alive were also delivered by OTC.

Source: Adapted from Plott, G. (2003) "Raubbau finanzierte Taylors Terror", *Der Standard*, 9–10 August, p. 4.

FUTURE ISSUES BOX 1.1

Going nowhere fast

Companies such as Sony, Toshiba, and Toyota have made Japan famous as the place where people always make things better, cheaper, smarter. Management tools and techniques invented here – just-in-time manufacturing, total quality management, continuous improvement, kanban manufacturing – have been imitated all over the industrialized world. Certainly, Japan's leading export manufacturers deserve this reputation. They are highly productive compared to their international competitors. But they are quite few in number. Together, they make up only 10% of the country's workforce and 10% of its GDP.

Although Japan's showcase export companies have redefined competitiveness and economic advantage worldwide, the country's far larger domestic sectors – construction, retailing, agriculture, healthcare, and financial services, among others – have languished. Shielded from competition by government subsidies, tariffs and protectionist policies, the nation's domestic suppliers have hardly changed, let alone improved, for decades. According to the Japan Productivity Center

for Socio-Economic Development, a government-affiliated research center, Japanese workers are 40% less efficient than Americans. In other industrially advanced countries, for example, mom-and-pop shops are niche operators, accounting for only 19% of retail employment in the U.S. (measured by hours worked) and 26% in France. But in Japan, mom-and-pops are the rule not the exception, making up 55% of the retail labor force.

On the one hand, industrial lobbies dedicated to preserving the status quo have tremendous sway over politicians. And, on the other, there is no doubt that increasing competition in the domestic economy will bring high unemployment (at least in the short term) and the chance of social unrest. As its population is aging dramatically (see Figure 1.1) in the decades ahead, Japan's productivity crisis may become even more significant, as far fewer workers will have to perform even more work even more efficiently to maintain the same standard of living.

Layers of increased costs are passed on to Japanese consumers, who face one of the world's highest costs of living, which in turn depresses demand. The Japanese economy may not rebound until the performance of domestic business organizations begins to significantly improve.

Source: Adapted from Frederick, J. (2002) "Going nowhere fast", *Time Magazine*, 9 December, 160 (22)

Growth of national wealth Historically, increasing trade liberalization has contributed strongly to the growth of the wealth of nations. World trade, for example, has grown 23 times since 1950. In 1820 only 1% of total production was exported; 14% went to other countries by the end of the 1990s (see Figure 1.2). International trade was the driver for growth in **gross domestic product** (GDP), the measure for total domestic economic value added claimed by the residents of a country.

Opening up of new markets Where once many national markets were difficult to enter because of natural or artificial barriers, liberalization of world trade has opened up new markets in almost all regions of the world. The most important institution concerned with the rules of world trade is the World Trade Organization (WTO).

The 146 WTO members have agreed to reduce trade barriers among themselves. They respect the **most favored nation clause**, which stipulates that favorable tariff and trade agreements between two member countries must also be applied to all other members. Exceptions are allowed for developing countries and import restrictions on volumes in case of severe problems concerning a country's balance of payments. WTO watches over members' compliance with the following basic rules:

- *reciprocity,* that is, equivalency of trade policy actions between WTO members

FIGURE 1.1 *Age structure of Japan vs Mexico*

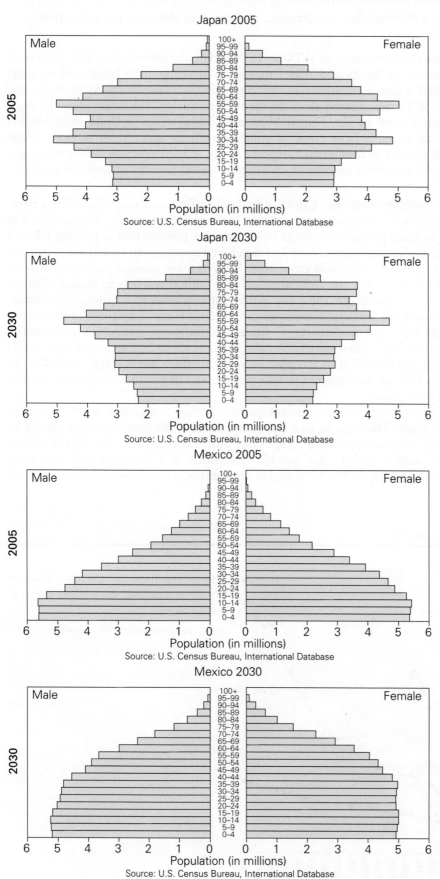

The population of Japan is over-aging. A decreasing number of younger people will have to be highly productive in the future to ensure the general standard of living. In comparison, Mexico's demographics represents a very large reservoir for the future workforce. Today, a smaller number of people have to be very productive to finance the education of the young generation.

Source: Jeff Rosensweig, Emory University

- *liberalization* in terms of reduction of tariffs and non-tariff barriers, such as local technical norms making imports very difficult
- *non-discrimination*, in particular, realization of the most favored nation clause.

Since the foundation of WTO in 1948 (originally known as GATT, or General Agreement on Tariffs and Trade) members' meetings have been used on more than half a dozen occasions to negotiate multilateral reductions in tariffs and non-tariff barriers among all of the member countries. The latest round of negotiations, started by the Fourth Ministerial Conference in Doha in November 2001, discussed a large range of subjects such as agriculture, services, trade-related aspects of intellectual property rights, transparency in government procurement, electronic commerce, and market access for non-agricultural products.

Rising unemployment rates Critics of trade liberalization charge that it has a negative influence on employment rates in the highly industrialized countries. The move to open economic systems has initiated a process that is putting 1.5 to 2 billion workers in economically less developed countries into worldwide product and labor markets over this generation. Most of these workers currently earn less than $3 a day, while the approximately 250 million workers in western Europe and the U.S. earn about $85 a day. With relatively modern technology, the workforce in less industrialized countries can produce from 75 to 100% of the output of their western counterparts. Considering the major difficulties of manufacturers in highly industrialized countries brought about by the 90 million workers in Japan and the NICs in the past 30 years provides some insight into the difficulties that can be expected to take place in the highly industrialized countries in the years ahead.

In any country there are non-competitive sectors and companies that are hurt by free trade. The logic of free trade requires that displaced workers should be retrained to move into more competitive business activities – but this is accomplished neither simply nor quickly. Therefore, a substantial and increasing number of people in the most highly economically developed countries run the

FIGURE 1.2 *International trade drives GDP growth*

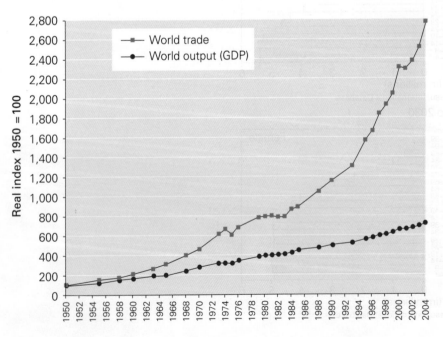

International trade was the major driver for growth in economic value added over the last 50 years.

Source: Jeff Rosensweig, Emory University

risk of not being able to profit from the greater choice and lower prices resulting from trade liberalization.

Exploitation A further critic of the effects of trade liberalization is the potential exploitation of poor countries by the richer ones. If wages in LDCs are kept low and working conditions are far below the level in highly developed economies, mainly the capital owners of internationally operating companies will profit. Even at slowly increasing standards of living the workforce does not get an adequate share. This point is discussed later in Future issues box 1.2.

Economic integration

Economic interdependency

The remarkable level of world trade today has led to an economic environment in which all countries are economically interdependent. Even the U.S., which represents the biggest national market of the highly industrialized countries, is far from being self-sufficient. The country imports, for example, almost all its VCRs, bananas, and coffee. Japan, which has become famous for its export power in previous years, depends on imports for 90% of its energy needs. More farmland in the U.S. than in Japan is used to feed the Japanese. Table 1.3 gives an overview of the interdependencies of the leading nations in world trade. The countries depend on trade with each other to help their citizens to achieve and to ensure a high standard of living.

Table 1.3 shows that some of the economically strongest countries in the world, such as the U.S. or the U.K., tended to run trade deficits in the early 2000s, whereas others such as PRC, Japan, Germany, or France achieved trade surpluses. Because of its trade deficits in goods since the middle of the 1970s and despite its earlier role as the world's leading supplier of capital, the U.S. has become the world's leading debtor nation (see Figure 1.3). The imbalance was offset somewhat by a surplus in services, such as tourism and consulting fees. Japan, PRC and some oil-producing countries have become big investors in the U.S. They own much of the U.S. debt in bonds. Because these bonds produce interest payments, the U.S. income balance also tends to turn into a deficit.

In reaction to the recognized interdependence of their national economies, governments of the seven industrially leading nations (Canada, France, Germany, Italy, Japan, U.K., U.S.) have installed the "G7" series of meetings between prime ministers, presidents, and ministers of finance. As from 1998 onwards, Russia has been accepted (because of political reasons) as a new member of G7, to make it "G8". G8 governments have the objective to cooperate closely in managing the development of the global economy, to foster stability of currency exchange rates, and to master problems of high unemployment rates.

International economic cooperation

Economic integration is reinforced by economic cooperation among countries. Cooperation can take the form of bilateral or multilateral arrangements, ranging from simple agreements on tariff reduction to full-scale political integration (see Figure 1.4).

Bilateral agreements The simplest cooperative agreement is the **bilateral agreement**, a pact between two countries concerning trade in one or a few product groups. The purpose of the agreement is to reduce or even abolish barriers to trade. Bilateral agreements often serve as the basis for trade between countries with restrictive conditions, such as:

- *non-convertible currencies*, that is, currencies that cannot be freely exchanged against each other (as in the Commonwealth of Independent States (CIS)

TABLE 1.3 *Structure of international trade of leading nations*

The table shows exports and imports of leading trading nations with their major trading partners

U.S. 2003

	Export $714 billion	Import $1263 billion	Major trading partners	Export	Import
Capital goods	43%	24%	Canada	24%	18%
Consumer goods	12%	26%	Mexico	14%	12%
Food products	7%	4%	Japan	7%	9%
Automotive products	12%	17%	PR of China	4%	11%
Industrial materials	23%	23%	U.K.	5%	3%
			Germany	3%	5%

Germany 2003

	Export €661.6 billion	Import €532 billion	Major trading partners	Export	Import
Automotive	20%	11%	France	11%	9%
Chemicals	14%	11%	U.S.	9%	7%
Machinery	12%	11%	U.K.	8%	6%
Electrical and electronic	11%	11%	Netherlands	6%	8%
Food products	4%	7%	Italy	7%	6%
Information technology	5%	6%	Belgium/Luxembourg	5%	5%
Fuel	—	7%	Austria	5%	4%
			PR of China	3%	5%
			Japan	—	4%
			Total EU	56%	55%

U.K. 2003

	Export £188 billion	Import £234 billion	Major trading partners	Export	Import
Machinery and transportation	42%	43%	Germany	11%	17%
Manufacturing goods	24%	30%	U.S.	15%	10%
Chemicals	17%	11%	France	10%	9%
Fuel	9%	5%	Netherlands	7%	7%
Food products and livestock	3%	7%	Belgium/Luxembourg	6%	6%
			Ireland	6%	4%
			Italy	5%	5%
			Japan	—	5%
			Total EU	80%	78%

Japan 2003

	Export ¥54.55 trillion	Import ¥44.36 trillion	Major trading partners	Export	Import
Transportation equipment	24%	—	U.S.	25%	15%
Electrical appliances	24%	—	PR of China	12%	20%
Machinery	20%	32%	South Korea	7%	5%
Automotive	17%	—	Taiwan	7%	4%
Chemicals	8%	8%	Hong Kong	6%	—
Metals and metal products	6%	4%	Germany	4%	4%
Fuel	—	21%	Singapore	3%	—
Food	—	12%	Thailand	3%	3%
Textiles	—	6%	U.K.	3%	—
Raw materials	—	6%	Indonesia	—	4%
			Australia	—	4%
			Total EU	15%	13%

France 2003

	Export €401.9 billion	Import €382.6 billion	Major trading partners	Export	Import
Investment goods	24%	21%	Germany	14%	17%
Semi-finished products	30%	31%	Germany	15%	17%
Investment goods	23%	21%	Spain	10%	8%
Consumer goods	15%	17%	Italy	9%	9%
Automotive	15%	17%	U.K.	8%	7%
Food products	9%	10%	Belgium/Luxembourg	8%	7%
			U.S.	7%	6%
			Total EU	53%	60%

PR of China 2003

	Export $438.4 billion	Import $412.8 billion	Major trading partners	Export	Import
Textiles	18%	3%	U.S.	21%	8%
Electrical and electronic	10%	19%	Hong Kong	17%	3%
Information technology	10%	5%	Japan	14%	18%
Office machinery	14%	6%	South Korea	5%	10%
Machinery	5%	13%	Germany	4%	6%
Chemicals	5%	12%	Netherlands	3%	—
Shoes	3%	—	U.K.	3%	—
Raw materials	—	19%	Taiwan	2%	12%
			Total EU	17%	13%

Source: Adapted from Baratta, M. (ed.) (2004) *Der Fischer Weltalmanach 2005*, Frankfurt a.M.: Fischer Taschenbuch Verlag

FIGURE 1.3 *Trends in the shift of U.S. current account to deficits*

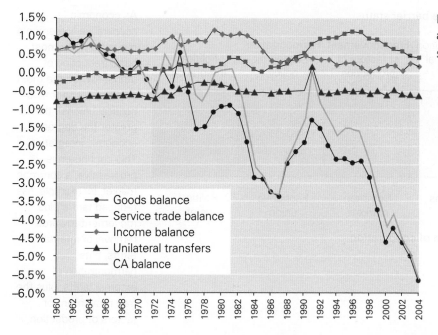

Because of big deficits in trade the U.S. has accumulated very high debt.

Source: Jeff Rosensweig, Emory University

– a group of countries including Armenia, Azerbaijan, Belarus, Georgia, Kazakhstan, Kyrgistan, Moldova, Russia, Tadjikistan, Turkmenistan, Ukraine, and Uzbekistan – formed in 1991 after the dissolution of the Soviet Union)

- *centrally controlled economies*, that is, economies with no or very few official free market exchanges where a central planning bureaucracy determines and controls all official flows of goods and capital (as in the Democratic Republic of Korea or in Cuba)

- *lack of hard currency*, that is, a national currency that is not accepted as a unit of payment by international suppliers (as in most developing countries of Africa, Asia, and Latin America but also in many countries of the former Soviet Union). For example, a bilateral barter clearing agreement has been signed between the governments of Iran and Ukraine in which Iranian oil and gas have been exchanged for weapons, metal scrap, refined products, chemicals, and machinery.

There is a tendency for industrialized nations to sign bilateral agreements among themselves. One such agreement is the Free Trade Area Treaty between the U.S. and Israel, which was signed in April 1985, providing for the eventual elimination of virtually all barriers to trade between the two countries. It has also been the first trade agreement ever to cover explicitly a full range of services, including transportation, travel, tourism, communications, banking, insurance, construction, accounting, education, law, management consulting, computer services, and advertising. Since the failure of the WTO World Trade Conference in Cancun, Mexico, in 2003 the U.S. government has signed several bilateral agreements with countries such as Chile or Singapore to improve trade conditions.

Multilateral agreements In 1994 the free trade accord between Canada and the U.S., which had taken effect in 1989, was enlarged to a **multilateral agreement** (regulating trade among more than two countries). Canada, Mexico, and the U.S. agreed to build a free trade area, called the **North American Free Trade Association (NAFTA)**, in 15 years.

FIGURE 1.4 *A continuum of different forms of economic cooperation*

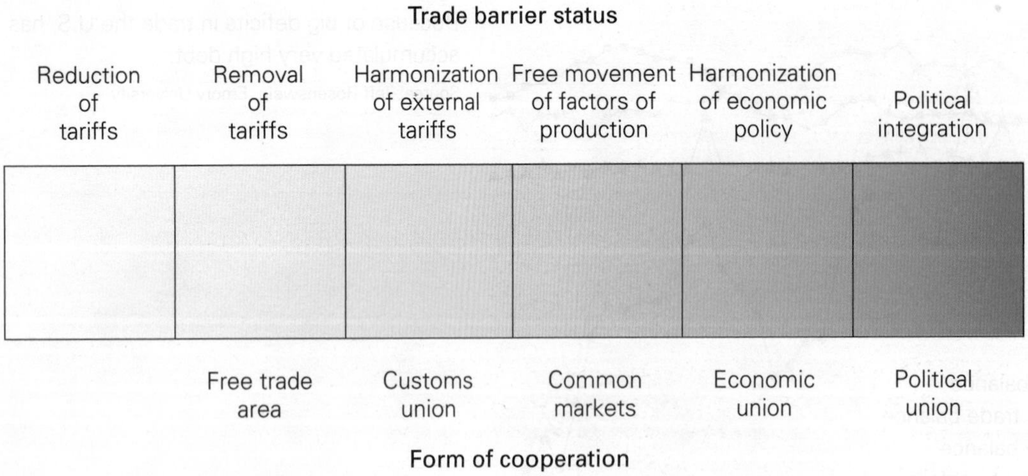

Trade barrier status

Reduction of tariffs	Removal of tariffs	Harmonization of external tariffs	Free movement of factors of production	Harmonization of economic policy	Political integration

| | Free trade area | Customs union | Common markets | Economic union | Political union |

Form of cooperation

As economic cooperative agreements move from the most basic (reduction of tariffs) toward the most complex (economic or political unions), the greater the degree of economic integration. This continuum is progressive; a common market, for example, has reduced tariffs plus movement towards removal of internal tariffs, plus harmonization of external tariffs, plus the free movement of factors of production.

Free trade area A **free trade area** removes all formal impediments to trade for a specified group of products. However, the individual countries maintain independent policies with regard to non-members. For example, a company based in a non-member country faces different barriers to entry with each NAFTA member. NAFTA came into effect on 1 January 1994 and has since become the most important free trade agreement in the world. NAFTA created a market with what is now more than 420 million consumers (Table 1.4).

NAFTA has produced positive effects for the respective economies. Mexico, for example, has expanded its exports of goods to the U.S. from $52 billion to 136 billion in the year 2000. In 2002 Mexico reached a trade surplus of $27 billion with the U.S. In the U.S., household brand manufacturers, such as Zenith Electronics or Smith Corona, shifted production to Mexico (partly from Southeast Asia) to take advantage of low wages. Large numbers of apparel makers also moved. Wal-Mart entered a joint venture with Cifra, Mexico's largest retailer, to open wholesale clubs in Mexico City. Compaq Computer, Lotus Development Corp., and Microsoft opened subsidiaries in Mexico City. Franchises, including McDonald's, Pizza Hut, Baskin-Robbins and Athlete's Foot, spread fast. Overall employment was growing, and even employment lost to Southeast Asia was won back to North America because wages in important industries in Hong Kong, Singapore, Taiwan, and Malaysia were up to twice as high as they were in Mexico.

But all three countries took big risks as well. It was clear from the beginning that U.S. workers in important industries would suffer. More than 70,000 low-skilled workers in the U.S. lost their jobs because of plant relocations or import competition involving Mexico and Canada. Mexico opened its agricultural market to more efficient U.S. farmers. In 2003 the tariffs remaining on about 30 agricultural products, such as rice, chicken, or pork were abolished. A significant number of the still 24 million Mexican laborers have already been driven off the farms. And there will be many more. But in the last 15 years, between 18 and 20 million people in the U.S. have experienced unemployment at some point each year. The number of "displaced workers" – those who lose their jobs as factories close or their positions are abolished – totals 3.5 to 5.5 million every two years, and these losses stem from a wide variety of causes, such as fierce competition in the electronics or retail industry. Meanwhile, the cycle of regeneration goes on: From January 1994, when NAFTA came into effect, to the end of 2001 the number of people employed in the U.S. has risen by an average of about 200,000 each month.

As a response to NAFTA and similar developments in Europe, Asian countries also started working on free trade agreements. Brunei, Indonesia, Malaysia, Philippines, Singapore, Thailand, and Vietnam decided to defend their economic future by creating an Asian free trade area, called the **Association of Southeast Asian Nations (ASEAN)**, in 1993. As a first step, tariffs on 15 groups of manufactured goods were cut. Cambodia, Laos, and Myanmar were

TABLE 1.4 *Comparison of economic data of NATFA members*

	U.S.	Canada	Mexico
Population in millions (2002)	288.369	31.362	100.819
GNP in million $ (2002)	10,383,100	714,327	637,203
Per capita income in $ (2002)	35,400	22,390	5,920
Average inflation rate 1990–2001	2%	1.5%	18.2%
Jobless (2003)	6%	7.6%	2.8%

The U.S. clearly dominates NATFA in economic terms.

Source: Adapted from Baratta, M. (ed.) (2004), *Der Fischer Weltalmanach 2005*, Frankfurt a.M.: Fischer Taschenbuch Verlag

accepted as members later. A really powerful Asian free trade area must include Japan and China, however. Therefore, negotiations have been started with PRC to create the most highly populated free trade area in the world, with 1.7 billion consumers and an accumulated GNP of $2 billion by 2010. In the meantime, Brunei, Indonesia, Malaysia, the Philippines, Singapore, and Thailand created a specific free trade area called the **Asian Free Trade Association (AFTA)** in early 2002.

The **Asia-Pacific Economic Cooperation Forum (APEC)** was founded in 1989. In addition to the members of ASEAN today it contains: Australia, Canada, Chile, PRC (including Hong Kong), Japan, Mexico, New Zealand, Papua-New Guinea, Peru, Russia, South Korea, Taiwan, and the U.S. In November 1995 the members of APEC signed the "Osaka Action Agenda", an agreement to abolish the barriers to trade among their countries in 15 years.

Because of the wide differences in the stage of economic development reached by the various members of APEC, the establishment of entirely free trade is particularly difficult. Despite the fast economic development of its neighbors, Japan's lead in everything from technology to finance to living standards is still considerably greater than the edge Germany ever enjoyed in Europe. So is the lead of countries such as Singapore or South Korea compared to Myanmar.

In Africa, the **Common Market for Eastern and Southern Africa (COMESA)** was created in 1994. It contains 20 members, nine of which have successfully founded the COMESA free trade area: Djibouti, Egypt, Kenya, Madagascar, Malawi, Mauritius, Sudan, Zambia, and Zimbabwe.

The NAFTA agreement has triggered a trade boom and spawned similar market-opening pacts throughout Latin America. The Andean countries of Bolivia, Colombia, Ecuador, Peru, and Venezuela signed an agreement, called the **Andean Pact**, to establish a free trade area, which is planned to become a common market of 100 million inhabitants. With effect from 1 January 1995 Argentina, Brazil, Paraguay, and Uruguay set up a free trade area called **Mercosur** (Chile, Bolivia, Peru, Ecuador, Colombia, and Venezuela are associated members), with about 250 million consumers, which represents 60% of Latin America's GNP. Since 1 January 2000 Mercosur is a customs union (with the exception of sugar and cars).

Customs union A **customs union** has the characteristics of a free trade area, but in addition the members establish consistent tariff policies vis-à-vis non-members. Examples of such an agreement are the **Southern African Customs Union**, which includes the Republic of South Africa (the dominant member), Botswana, Lesotho, and Swaziland, as well as the customs union between the **Economic Cooperation Organization** (which brings together Iran, Pakistan, and Turkey) and the three former Soviet republics of Azerbaijan, Turkmenistan, and Uzbekistan. An exporter to any of these countries will receive the same tariff treatment. This has the effect of creating a larger market with a shared "tariff wall".

Common market Caribbean countries and territories, such as Antigua, Bahamas, Barbados, Jamaica, Haiti, Surinam, Trinidad and Tobago founded **CARICOM**, the Caribbean Community and Common Market. A **common market** is formed when member countries, in addition to removing tariffs between them and harmonizing their tariff policies vis-à-vis non-members, remove all barriers to the free movement of production factors among them. For example, capital can be transferred without any restriction, workers can freely choose their jobs throughout the common market, there is free trade in services, and factories can be built in those member countries that seem best to the companies.

The **European Union (EU)** is the most familiar example of a multilateral agreement resulting in such a common market. Members of the European Union as of May 2004 are Austria, Belgium, Cyprus, the Czech Republic, Denmark,

Estonia, Finland, France, Germany, Greece, Hungary, Ireland, Italy, Latvia, Lithuania, Luxembourg, Malta, the Netherlands, Poland, Portugal, Slovakia, Slovenia, Spain, Sweden, and the U.K. (see Map 1.1). The EU is the most populous market in the industrialized world, with a total population of over 450 million. It represents the largest concentration of purchasing power in the world.

Other European countries have reacted to the new situation. Iceland, Liechtenstein, Norway, and Switzerland have signed an agreement with the EU that created a free trade area called the **European Economic Area (EEA)**. The economic situation for suppliers and customers located in the EEA is similar to that in the EU, but the political autonomy of its members is not diminished. Bulgaria, Croatia, Romania, and Turkey have gained associate status. They have also applied for membership of the EU.

Economic union In the Maastricht Treaty (and later in the Amsterdam and Nice Treaties) the members of the EU agreed to harmonize their tax and subsidy policies as a precondition for the unification of their fiscal and monetary policies. Theoretically, the result has been an **economic union**, in which member

MAP 1.1 *Member states of the European Union*

Source: www.nationsonline.org/oneworld/small_europe_map.htm (10 May 2004)

nations are fully integrated economically. Half of them have a common currency, called the **euro**, as of 1 January 1999. Table 1.5 contains some economic criteria set in the Maastricht Treaty that have to be fulfilled by countries wanting to take part in the common currency.

In the discussion of the pros and cons of a unified European currency, there has been a tendency to focus on lower transaction costs, because the euro would end currency conversion and hedging costs. For example, Hoechst Marion Roussel, the pharmaceuticals unit of Germany's Hoechst, has been able to save tens of millions of German marks each year on hedging against European currency shifts. KLM Royal Dutch Airlines has saved on bank charges by closing as many as possible of the firm's 80 bank accounts in different currencies, each with its separate charges.

But these benefits, while useful, are marginal. Much more important for companies operating internationally is the potential for a strong euro contributing to a stable economic environment with low inflation and interest rates. The cost of corporate capital is reduced, which encourages investment.

It has been clear from the very beginning that some EU members will not be able to join the eurozone or will not want to participate in the euro because they are either unable to fulfill the fixed criteria or have particular political reasons not to join. For most of the new members that joined the EU in 2004, participating in the euro would result in a terrible shock for their economies, which are not yet as productive as their western partners. As the reunification of the former two parts of Germany has shown a monetary union among economically uneven partners can have disastrous effects on the weaker economy. Some of the new members such as Slovenia, for example, have reached a very promising level, while others are still doing their "homework" (see Strategy box 1.1).

The U.K. does not want to participate in the euro, mainly for political reasons. Neither does Denmark or Sweden, despite the fact that they would be able to fulfill the criteria for participation. It may not be appropriate for those countries to join. But whether those countries are in or out, companies with operations in the single currency area, or trading with partners in that area, found many aspects of their business affected. Competitive strategy, pricing, financial systems, treasury operations, tax arrangements, terms of payment, procurement, and other contractual arrangements all needed to be reviewed. For example, in Siemens' medical equipment division, prices for complex products such as X-ray scanners

TABLE 1.5 *Convergence (Maastricht) criteria for participation in the EU Single Currency Area*

For a country to become a member of the European Monetary Union the following criteria have to be fulfilled:

- Country's inflation rate does not exceed past year's average inflation rate of the best three EU countries by 1.5%

- Minimum two years' participation of the national currency in the established exchange mechanism without self-proposed devaluation (= remaining inside the fluctuation zone relative to the euro allowed by the EMS: e.g. for the Danish crown this is +/– 2.25%)

- Nominal interest rate for long-term government loans does not exceed the past year's average rate of the best three EU members by 2%

- Net deficit of all public budgets in the country does not exceed 3% of GDP

- Total public debt of the country does not exceed 60% of its GDP

still continue to vary from country to country, reflecting the high proportion of final price levels due to installation and service costs, which are determined by local wage rates and other factors. Prices for smaller, more easily transportable products such as hearing aids, by contrast, had to be harmonized to a great extent.

Political union The most advanced form of economic cooperation is a **political union**, in which the agreement between the signing parties results in a new country. A recent example may be the reunification of Germany. Today, however, most governments believe that they would have to give up too much political sovereignty if they were to enter into such an agreement. The difficulties with establishing a generally accepted constitution of the European Union may be an example of this state of mind. Political unions, therefore, are likely to be formed infrequently.

It is important to note that none of the existing arrangements falls neatly into any of these categories. The European Union, for example, is a full customs

STRATEGY BOX 1.1

Malta plans to become a role model for new EU members

Malta is in a mood of new start. With a land surface of only 316 square kilometers and a population of 390,000 inhabitants, the island republic is the smallest newcomer in the European Union as of 1 May 2004. Because of its strategic location in the middle of the Mediterranean Sea the group of islands has been a landing place for Phoenecians, Punes, Romans, Byzantinians, Sarazenes, Normans, Turks, French and British during the last 3,000 years. They all left their traces, which make Malta a cultural tourist target of first rank. But government also plans to turn it into a role model for other newcomers in the European Union. By decreasing budget deficit and public debt quickly government intends to be ready for the euro in 2006.

The share of new debt of GDP was decreased from 11% in 1998 to 5.2% in 2002 and 4.5% in 2003. It will be further diminished by significantly reducing tax evasion, by achieving economies in public spending, and by reforming the pension system. The age of retirement is to be increased from 61 to 65. Privatization was started with Malta's airport, which was sold to Vienna Airport. Next were Air Malta (the national airline), Sea Malta (the national shipping company), the ferry lines between the islands belonging to Malta and the water as well as energy supply organizations of the country.

Inflation rate (1.3% in 2003) as well as the stability of the country's currency are under close control. And the jobless rate is lower than the EU average.

Environmental pollution and traffic are still pressing points to be resolved. But even in this respect the government plans to turn its island into a role model. Careful separation of waste is to be introduced. As a first step, dumping rubble on Maghtab, the country's dust heap, is no longer allowed. New sewage treatment plants are to be built. But government has decided to wait for EU funds before starting heavy investments in these ambitious projects.

Source: Adapted from Kness-Bastaroli, T. (2003) "Malta will sich zum Musterschüler in der EU mausern", *Der Standard*, 15, 17 July; "Malta – kultureller Schmelztiegel und historischer Vorposten Europas im Mittelmeer", *Euronews*, 2 March, p. 6

Valletta as seen from Tigne Sliema Malta   © Pixmedia/Alamy

union, a well-developed common market, a still only partially developed economic union, and a rather weak political union. Moreover, there is no automatic progression from agreements on tariff reductions to full-scale political union.

Political and social dimensions

Economic integration, of course, also has political and social dimensions. For example, if cold-rolled steel is manufactured in South Korea by Pohang Iron and Steel (POSCO), one of the world's largest steelmakers, at a cost lower than in Taiwan and Japan it can be sold in Pittsburgh at a lower price than steel actually manufactured there. This affects employment rates in both the U.S. and Korea. So does the fact that more Japanese cars than cars made by Swedish manufacturers are sold in Sweden.

Social and ecological "dumping" With unemployment rates increasing in western Europe, more and more politicians accuse other countries of **"social"** and **"ecological dumping,"** that is, selling their products at very low prices based on much lower costs due to a lack of social and ecological standards comparable to those in western Europe. Politicians increasingly ask for internationally agreed and controlled social standards for the workforce, as well as internationally enforced norms of environmental protection. Ethics box 1.2 shows that such demands cannot easily be dismissed as long as consumers in highly industrialized countries have not become sensitive to unethical practices in less developed countries.

Cultural "imperialism" Films and TV programs produced in the U.S. are exported throughout the world. Sales of U.S. TV programs to Europe alone were worth more than $2 billion in 2003. Such activity is controversial, of course. Critics charge that the high pressure of the U.S. entertainment industry not only endangers the production of films and TV programs in other countries but also risks destroying the cultural identity of other nations in favor of a general

ETHICS BOX 1.2

200 million children as work slaves

They work in coalmines in Brazil, on carpet looms in Pakistan and Nepal, in leather factories in India, in the fields of Senegal, and in the sex salons in Thailand. Millions of children, starting at age 3, are exploited as work slaves all over the world. Following an estimate of the International Labor Organization (ILO), headquartered in Geneva, more than 200 million children are forced to work, many of them in dangerous activities. Only very few violations of human rights are as unanimously condemned as child labor, but nevertheless the outcome remains bleak.

Child labor is not a side issue: it is a major problem for society. Only a reduction of the difference in wealth between the rich and the poor countries of the world can help to resolve it. Global information campaigns can contribute to higher awareness of the problem in the highly industrialized countries. They should make governments, entrepreneurs, top managers and consumers more conscious in their decisions concerning who to do business with and what not to buy.

Why should animals in the highly industrialized countries be better protected against abuses than children in the less industrially developed parts of the world? If families there need additional income to survive, why can we not ensure that the parents earn enough money? Is it to keep the prices of consumer products imported from these countries as low as possible? Do we want to further improve our material standard of living at the expense of child slavery?

Americanization. The global spread of fast-food restaurants has been attributed to that kind of influence. Culture box 1.1 gives an impression of how strong the resistance to foreign cultural influences can be in some countries.

Foreign capital ownership Foreign investment also still tends to be controversial, such as the purchase of CBS Records by Sony, or foreign investment in French wine facilities, which were seen as undermining the gastronomic traditions of France. In Hungary, critics complained that the boom of foreign investments at the end of the last century has created an industrial two-class society. The capital flow focused on those industries that promised the fastest and most profitable development: food, tobacco, alcoholic beverages, and automotive as well as electrical machinery, and construction. Industries in need of new capital to survive in international competition, such as iron and steel or chemicals, were avoided by foreign investors.

Despite all charges, foreign investment is increasing in every highly industrialized or fast developing country. Depending on the available skills and resources as well as their prices in a country, foreign capital is invested in different domains. For example, as a reaction to the more liberal legislation concerning biotechnology in the U.S., and taking into account the high level of specialized skills as well as the global competitiveness of the industry, Swiss pharmaceutical firms invested heavily in pharmaceutical, chemical and biotechnological research and development in the U.S.

Exploitation of the poor The controversy over world trade has a further dimension. Many critics charge that economically developed nations are exploiting developing ones (see Future issues box 1.2). Criticism centers on the less developed nations' limited ability to accumulate capital needed for the production of goods to export (owing to high interest rates on loans), except for low-value-added

CULTURE BOX 1.1

Domino's survives India's food fight

In the culture wars over American fast food coming to this land of curry, fried chicken has been taken hostage – but not pizza. Local governments shut the two Kentucky Fried Chicken restaurants in India – one in New Delhi and another in Bangalore, in the south. Court orders allowed them to reopen, but anti-western activists ransacked the Bangalore outlet in what was called an act of civil disobedience. The storming of the outlet invoked a symbol held dear in this predominantly Hindu nation – the cow. The protesters distributed a leaflet stating they wanted to "save the country's cattle wealth".

The criticism of American fast food, hurled from both political left and right, begins with nutrition but extends to anxiety about the threat to traditional lifestyles as western products and tastes seep into a newly opened economy.

But Domino's Pizza, which opened a small restaurant in one of New Delhi's upscale neighborhoods, has quietly served pizzas and Cokes to a curious stream of housewives, executives and students. "We've not had any trouble," said Gita Agarwal, a manager at Domino's headquarters in India. "It's an Indian company."

The rights to open Domino's franchises in India belong to the Bhartia family of industrialists better known for chemicals and fertilizers. Opening on New Year's Eve with almost no advertising also seems to have helped Domino's escape confrontation with fast-food critics. Domino's has respected Hindu reverence for the cow by omitting pepperoni, the beef-based topping popular with Americans, from its menus in India. Vegetarian offerings precede non-vegetarian ones on its menu, also in keeping with Indian customs.

Source: Adapted from Cooper, K.J. (1996) "Domino's survives India's food fight", *International Herald Tribune*, 12 March, p. 14

products such as raw materials, for example coffee beans or iron ore. This means, critics say, that the value added in terms of profits and higher wages all stays (on purpose) in the more economically developed countries. Others argue that if less rich countries sell whatever products they have, they can earn money to develop other industries, which do contribute greater profit margins. This in turn would lead to their citizens becoming wealthier, and able to buy more products from their own suppliers in addition to imports from more highly developed economies. Thus in the long run, everyone should win.

Driving forces of international business

Theoretical explanations

Economists have provided some theoretical explanations for the described evolution of international business. The most well known are the theory of comparative costs and the related concept of international product lifecycles or international investments.

Comparative costs

In simple terms the theory of comparative costs suggests that each country, owing to its available resources and the efficiency of their use, has or can develop specific advantages compared with other countries. If each country specializes in

---

FUTURE ISSUES BOX 1.2

Are the rich exploiting the poor?

Critics charge that trade liberalization has only enriched the rich at the disadvantage of the poor. As proof they show that "the west", that is western Europe, North America, Australasia, and Japan, increased their income per inhabitant fourfold in 1950–2001, whereas the per capita income of the rest of the world only tripled during the same period. Thus, during this era of trade liberalization and fast growth of world trade the gap between the industrially most developed countries and the rest of the world has been widening. It is now particularly wide between the richest and the poorest few, which are mainly in Africa. The question is, can this problem be resolved?

Supporters of liberal trade say yes, by further decreasing the barriers to trade that still exist. And they cite the countries in south and east Asia, including the world's most populous countries, China and India, as examples to follow. Excluding Japan, in 1950–2001 income per capita in those countries has grown fivefold. The countries have lived under many different forms of government, have followed many varieties of economic policy, but have all succeeded in raising living standards rapidly over long periods. None of them, perhaps except Hong Kong, has followed the laissez-faire formula criticized by anti-globalists. Rather, they liberalized some markets in order to stimulate competition, internally and from imports; and they ensured that imports of most basic commodities and components faced few barriers. They adopted liberal trade partly, selectively, and, mostly, gradually.

The result is that the gap between the most industrially developed countries and the countries in east and southern Asia when measured as the distribution of individual incomes has narrowed considerably. Some large parts of the poor world are pulling themselves out of poverty. But the problem is that others are not. These others include some countries in Asia, such as Pakistan, Afghanistan or Bangladesh, and some in Latin America. Most notably, however, they include most of Africa. Home to 13% of the world's population, the continent accounts for a mere 3% of world GDP. Incomes have stagnated or even declined, and life expectancy is falling.

Source: Adapted from "Liberty's great advance", *The Economist*, 28 June–4 July 2003, pp. 4–7

products and services it can produce or perform comparatively better than others, and exchanges them for products and services in which other countries have advantages, all exchange partners will profit. The standard of living will increase in all economies.

Economic reality shows, however, that resources as well as their efficient use underlie a dynamic process, which leads to continual changes in comparative advantages and, as a consequence, continuing changes in production sites. For example, because of the technical expertise required, the production of TV sets first started in the U.S. and Europe. From there most of the production sites went to Southeast Asia, where mass production costs for labor-intensive production were much lower. But production was not lost for western countries forever. On the one hand, economic success led to increasing labor costs in countries such as Japan, Taiwan, Hong Kong, or Singapore. On the other, the fierce cost competition from those countries led to heavy restructuring of industrial organization and processes in Europe and in the U.S. As a result, some of the production came back to the highly industrialized countries, because there existed a sufficient number of highly trained workers who could ensure the expected level of high-quality output. With the opening of the Chinese economy to foreign investment, this trend has changed again. Today an increasing amount of consumer durables sold in western countries is produced by Chinese-owned companies. Haier Group Company, for example, the fifth largest manufacturer of consumer appliances in the world, has the largest market share in the global refrigerator business.

International product lifecycle

International product lifecycle theory claims to explain the process of dissemination of innovations across countries. Following this theory, an economically developed country that possesses the ability to provide a new way of satisfying customer needs, that is, a product or service innovation, will try to profit from the resulting advantages by selling the new product or service to other countries. Soon other economically developed countries will follow. They will create their own production capacities for the new product or service. Next, the less developed countries will follow when they have gained the needed production know-how in one way or another. Finally, more and more of the economically advanced countries, which, in the meantime, have lost their comparative advantage to the less developed countries, will start importing the product or service from their former customers.

This process can be visualized by three overlapping lifecycle curves (see Figure 1.5). They show the development of the innovation in the three types of

FIGURE 1.5 *International lifecycle of innovations*

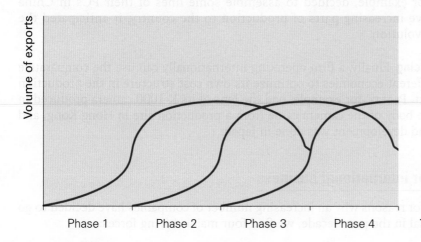

The volume of exports of an innovation follows a lifecycle curve. The growth rate of exports starts declining when exporters from lower cost countries enter the market.

country, the innovating country, the highly developed early followers, and the less developed late followers.

Phase 1 starts with the export of the local innovation to other markets. Phase 2 is characterized by relative stability. Demand in the markets served so far continues to grow, but is increasingly satisfied by local production. In phase 3 the exports of the innovator start decreasing. Demand for the new good in the less economically developed countries is rising, but is increasingly satisfied by the production capacities installed by the early followers. Finally, in phase 4, the picture changes completely. The product or service is no longer an innovation. It has become common to an extent where companies in economically less developed countries are able to provide a, perhaps simplified, version at very low cost.

One example of such a process seems to be the semiconductor industry. The production of semiconductors first started in the U.S. Germany, France, the U.K., and Japan followed, before Hong Kong and Taiwan took over. Today semiconductors are produced in PRC, Indonesia, and Malaysia.

The duration of each of the phases may vary. High tariffs or transportation costs, high production volumes needed to be cost efficient, high capital investment intensity, or patents can extend the cycles. Culture-dependent innovations may not even experience the process described at all because no demand for the product or service can be created in other markets.

For individual firms in highly industrialized countries it is important to notice that the international product lifecycle does not mean that firms will automatically go out of business after some time. There are at least three ways to counteract the theoretically prescribed path.

Differentiation First, international imitators will have a much harder time if the company does not offer an average product or service for "everybody," but steadily improves its specific know-how for the service of defined customer segments. Differentiation potentials not only exist in the core product or core service itself but concern the entire "product" delivered to clients. Polypropylene granules for the production of plastic goods can be fairly easily imitated, for example. But it is much harder to develop the specific application know-how needed for the production of granules for recyclable dashboards for passenger cars. In particular, the personal relationships that will be built with specialists from the automotive industry, resulting in mutual trust and personal commitment, will be more difficult to "imitate." Internationally successful companies continuously search for opportunities to build and sustain competitive advantages through differentiation.

Dislocation Second, a company can follow the described international lifecycle of innovations by moving its own production sites from one region of the world to another, depending on the phase in the lifecycle. When Hewlett-Packard, for example, decided to assemble some lines of their PCs in China and to move increasing parts of production to the country, it anticipated the expected evolution.

Global sourcing Finally, a firm operating internationally can use the comparative costs of different economies to optimize its own cost structure in the production of a product. Pentax, for example, had the lens of its K-1000 camera produced in Taiwan, the body of the camera came from a production site in Hong Kong, and research and development was done in Japan.

Stimuli for international business

Searching for reasons why an increasing number of companies have decided to go international in the past decade, we find four major driving forces:

- relative saturation of many markets in highly industrialized countries, which causes serious limits to local growth
- technological changes, which have largely facilitated communication and transfer of knowledge across national borders
- increase in competition, locally as well as internationally, which forces companies to globalize their business perspective
- resource procurement wherever it seems most readily available.

Limited growth in domestic markets

In order to remain financially healthy, most companies must grow. However, many product markets in industrialized countries are saturated. Diversification into new areas of business as a growth alternative is always risky. The most viable way to grow may be to enter foreign markets. For example, AmorePacific, the largest cosmetic manufacturer of South Korea, decided to go abroad because of the limited growth potential in its domestic market. After establishing itself in the less saturated neighboring China market, the company introduced its "Lolita Lempicka" branded perfume in the highly competitive French market. The success in France allowed AmorePacific to enter other lucrative markets in Europe and the U.S.

International business is not only a route to growth but also a necessary means to survival. In Europe, stagnant growth, local competitive pressure, and the need to reduce costs have made non-domestic business a must for many firms. For example, Austria-based Linz Textil Holding AG, one of Europe's four largest manufacturers of yarns, was forced to invest in joint ventures in the Czech Republic, in spite of its high investments in the latest production technology, to stay internationally competitive. Carrefour SA, the French retail chain and inventor of hypermarkets, started its internationalization as early as the 1970s, when it opened its first hypermarkets in Brazil. Now it is involved in most countries of the EU and in the U.S., but is also progressing in Latin America and in Southeast Asia.

U.S. companies have been successful in diversifying into emerging markets in Asia and Latin America. Critics charge that, in contrast to Europe, in the U.S. only a small number of companies still account for almost all exports. Only about one in ten small and middle-sized companies in the U.S., for example, exports. By one estimate, there are at least 30,000 small U.S. companies that have export potential but are not conducting business in foreign markets. Although U.S. exports totaled $693.5 billion in 2002, only about 7% of the country's GDP was derived from export. Much smaller Germany had exports of over $612 billion, some 30% of its GDP. The validity of such comparison is questionable, however, because an average of about 65% (from 58% for the U.K. up to 80% for Belgium) of international trade of European countries is done with their EU partners. Taking into consideration that the U.S. consists of a considerable number of states (theoretically doing business with each other), for a better comparison only exports of European countries to non-European (or at least non-EU) destinations should be compared to U.S. exports. A comparison of "corrected" export shares shows that the EU members hold about 15%, compared to the U.S. with about 10%, and Japan about 8%.

Technological change

Important drivers for international business are technological improvements and change in the areas of transportation and communication. The number of direct airline connections inside Europe, to Asia, and from many different points in the U.S. to overseas destinations has dramatically increased while ticket prices have substantially decreased. Low-priced transport supports the development of international business.

Low air ticket prices offered by companies such as Ryanair or easyJet have contributed strongly to increased international leisure travel. More and more consumers have physical contact with new products and services in countries they have chosen as vacation destinations. They learn about different customs and consumption patterns, and develop a demand for so far unknown products and services in their home country. Demand for Greek restaurants, French cheese, Italian pasta, Australian wine, Mexican beer, Thai food, and Caribbean music, for example, was strongly supported by the vacation experiences of satisfied consumers once they had returned home.

The portable phone and the internet have revolutionized the way business is conducted. An internal memo with attachments can be shared by email with all managers around the world at the same time, for example. Such connections have improved the international logistics and shipment of goods. Benetton, for example, does not need to produce most of its products in advance and keep them in stock to be able to deliver to its outlets worldwide in time. Having online computer connections to their shops, they know at any time which products are bought in what numbers, sizes, and colors, and are therefore able to guide their production according to the latest market response information. By getting real-time information via satellite data transmission on the location of their trucks or other transportation vehicles, shippers know at any time of the day where in the world their shipments are. Data transfer for accounting and financial systems can also be made at any time, across national boundaries. Even information bases such as disease analysis information databanks are shared by hospitals around the world.

The internet provides real-time information to even very small firms and to consumers. A fast increasing number of companies use internet services for advertising purposes as well as for direct selling. Companies such as Amazon.com or eBay have extended their services to consumers around the world.

Satellite TV has also changed the way business is conducted, for example advertising. Commercials broadcast in England may be seen throughout Europe, increasing the need to understand cultural differences and the effects of communication standardization. Perhaps more importantly, satellite television has significantly changed how quickly people receive information about significant events around the world. This in turn probably changes the way they view not only world problems, but also consumption opportunities and the solutions they think should be pursued. Walt Disney Co., for example, operates 24 Disney-branded cable and satellite channels in 67 countries outside the U.S. When they launch a new film, millions of children in all these countries are exposed to the same popular icons and want their parents to buy them. This is made possible by the widening international reach of retailing giants such as Wal-Mart Stores Inc., Toys "Я" Us Inc., or Carrefour SA, which between them have opened more than 2,500 stores outside their home markets.

Global competition

For many firms, the primary driving force to start international business is competition. Both local and national firms are confronted with foreign competitors in their home markets. For instance, more than 70% of all goods produced in the U.S. are facing direct competition from non-domestic sources. For example, consumer electronics firms based in PRC, Taiwan, and South Korea sell their products in the U.S. market. Global competitors often manage to put local manufacturers under high competitive pressure or even drive them entirely out of the market.

Basically, competition can be local, regional, or global (see Figure 1.6).

Local competition Competition is local when the companies serving a country market are all based in that market. Industries can be domestic only when the need they serve does not exist in other countries or when legal barriers prevent foreign competitors from entering a country market. Firms from other countries will either not have the specific skills and know-how to satisfy the local need, or will be held off by the existing barriers. Examples are many less industrially developed countries, which try to protect their vulnerable industries through barriers to foreign competition – or some local personal services markets, such as hairdressing.

What may happen in a market, which was closed to foreign competition and is suddenly opened up, is well illustrated by Chile's long-distance telephone market. In 1995, all restrictions on entry into the long-distance business were removed at one stroke. More than half a dozen Chilean companies jumped into the fray, along with three U.S. firms: Bell South, SBC, and Bell Atlantic. As a result, the price of off-peak calls from Chile to the U.S. fell from $1.50 a minute just before competition began to about 25¢ a minute – the lowest in the world for international long distance at that time. The phone companies were bombarding the country with ads touting low prices. Barely more than a year before free competition was allowed, Entel, once Chile's state-owned long-distance carrier had 100% of the market. Less than a year after market liberalization its share was 40%.

Regional competition Competition is regional when competitors serving a country market come from different neighboring countries. This was the case in most markets of highly industrialized countries until limits to growth made governments liberalize international trade and technological changes allowed competitors from all over the world to enter most of those country markets. For example, in the European shoe market Italian manufacturers competed against German, French, and local producers in the respective country markets. In recent years, brands have stayed European, but a substantial volume of shoes is manufactured in eastern Europe, Southeast Asia, and Brazil.

FIGURE 1.6 *Globalization of competition and industries*

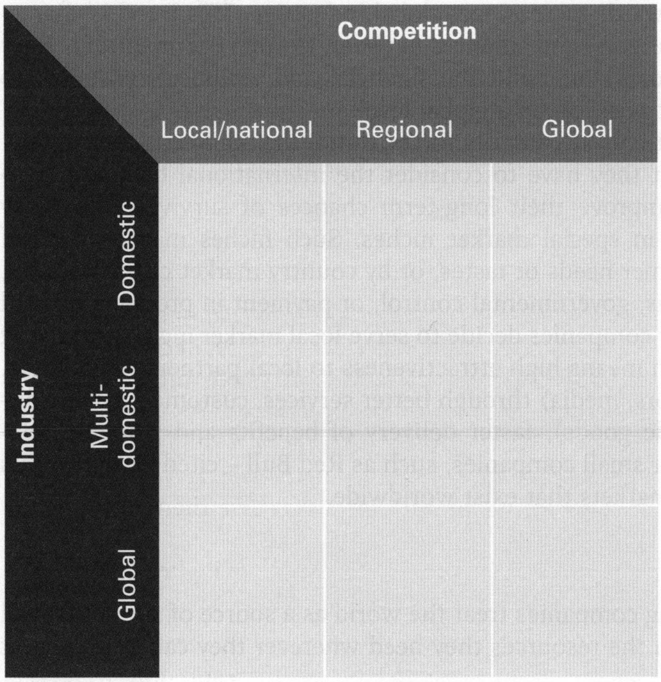

A company may be active in a purely domestic, a multi-domestic or a global industry. In each of those industries a company may face local, regional, and global competition.

Global competition Competition is global when the companies competing for customers in a country market come from all over the world. This is the case for an increasing number of products, such as consumer electronics, food products, cars, machinery, electrical engines, and pharmaceuticals, as well as industrial engineering, bank or insurance services, especially in the highly developed industrial countries.

Global competition in a product or service category of a country market does not automatically mean that the industry to which the product or service belongs is also global. It might be multi-domestic.

Multi-domestic industries In a **multi-domestic industry**, competitors in each country can come from all over the world, but owing to differences specific to each country market, the relative competitive position of a competitor is largely independent of its competitive position in other countries. In a multi-domestic industry a firm can choose to remain domestic or become multinational, applying different strategies depending on local market conditions. Mr. Maucher, the former president of Nestlé, for example, followed the guiding principle that "every business is local." He therefore, insisted on local adaptations of strategies for all brands, even globally marketed ones such as Nescafé. Other companies, such as Austria's VAI, one of the three world-leading firms in metallurgical engineering, perceives the needs of its customers to be regionally differentiated to an extent that regionally adapted strategies seem to be justified.

Global industries In recent years a growing number of industries have become global in their competitive scope, that is, a firm's competitive position in one country is significantly influenced by its position in other countries. Examples of **global industries** include commercial aircraft, computers, pharmaceutical products, consumer electronics, watches, clothing, tourism, insurance, and banking. In a more global industry, the firm that wants to survive must develop an integrated worldwide strategy for all of its operations. The potential success of Dell personal computers or Microsoft software in Europe, for example, depends on its market position in other parts of the world, in particular the U.S. The same applies to the watch market. A brand that does not reach an important position in the U.S. will find it difficult to be successful in the rest of the world.

Most industries are somewhere between multi-domestic and global. However, there is a clear trend towards increasingly global industries. This trend is characterized by takeovers, mergers, and alliances between (former) competitors. They seek to reduce their costs and build the financial and technical resources to strengthen their market position on a global level.

Smaller companies are not necessarily forced out of the market as their industry becomes global. But they have to consider the international business environment in order to improve their long-term chances of survival. They may discover opportunities in special market niches. Such niches may be defined either by specific customer needs or tastes, or by country market characteristics, such as legal restrictions, governmental control, or payment in products instead of money. Many smaller companies decide to serve local market niches by relying on "local charm," which means high attractiveness to local partners (customers, intermediaries, regulators, media) through better services, customer-specific differentiation (tailor-made goods), faster delivery of benefits and personal relationship building. Other small companies, such as Red Bull – cited earlier in this chapter – go for niche markets that exist worldwide.

Access to resources

Internationally operating companies treat the world as a source of supply as well as demand. They obtain the resources they need wherever they can buy them at the best price.

Technological know-how Technological know-how gained in different parts of the world is quickly applied to new products. Cooperation with firms in other countries can reduce costs and increase management knowledge, further enhancing the competitiveness of global firms relative to others.

For example, Germany's Siemens AG and French–British GEC Alsthom are fierce competitors in the European and North American markets. Nevertheless, the two companies decided to cooperate in marketing their high-speed trains ICE (intercity express) and TGV (train à grande vitesse) in Asia, in particular China and Taiwan. For that purpose they founded a marketing agency, called "Euro Train," on a joint venture basis, without placing any capital. Its purpose is to submit tailor-made offers to the Asian clients, using the parts best suited of both train systems, and to improve their competitive position against Japanese competitors. Nevertheless, China decided in favor of the Japanese Shinkansen train offered by a Japanese–Chinese alliance between Kawasaki Heavy Industries and Nanche Shifang.

Less expensive raw materials, capital, and labor In many industries the rate of innovation is not very dramatic. As a consequence, domestic as well as global competition for market share often boils down to a race for lower prices. Hence, opportunities to reduce costs and/or increase efficiency are welcome. Again, the internationally operating firm has an advantage. It has access to lower priced sources of raw material, capital, and labor. For example, Fujitsu, in order to become the No. 2 PC maker in Japan, overhauled its supply network, dumping locally made parts in favor of foreign components that were 20 to 30% less expensive. Manufacturing spare parts or even entire products in low-wage countries allows global firms to engage in intensive price competition against domestic firms in many markets.

Access to sources of R&D Research and development can be conducted wherever the necessary resources in terms of brainpower, technological know-how, and capital are located. Companies such as Hoffmann-La Roche, a Swiss pharmaceutical manufacturer, increasingly locate their research centers near to centers of intellectual excellence such as university departments specializing in their domain of research. Proximity not only furthers research cooperation but also facilitates hiring the best graduates. Other firms choose sites where companies doing research in the same field are located, such as Silicon Valley in California or Sophia Antipolis in the south of France. Most international companies procure research and development services from specialized firms or institutions in various countries. For example, in addition to purchasing business software from U.S. vendors, American Express obtains high-quality software at a lower cost from a supplier based in India.

Balanced resource investments To attain and maintain global competitiveness, however, it is not enough simply to keep abreast of technological developments. Serving more than one country market allows the firm to balance resource investments in some markets against resource surpluses in others. Moreover, when a competitor attacks it in its home market, a globally competitive firm would be able to mount a counter-attack in the competitor's own domain.

Business response to the challenge

Perspectives of international business

A firm does not have to be a global giant like Mitsubishi or Boeing to look for business opportunities and watch for potential threats outside its local environment. What counts most is the managers' view of their firm's markets. One classification of potential views is EPRG: ethnocentric, polycentric, regional, geocentric.

Ethnocentric perspective

Ethnocentric managers see the domestic market as most important, reacting defensively to international markets, if at all. They feel certain that their markets are too small and too specialized to be entered by global competitors. Or they put their faith in economic, political, and legal barriers to entry by foreign firms. But is the current success and future profit potential of any business organization really independent of developments in other parts of the world? Even the owner of a pharmacy in Llandudno, Wales, needs to take a more global view. From the prices of the products sold in the store to the rate of interest on the mortgage, many elements of day-to-day business reflect the impact of decisions made in London, Tokyo, or New York.

Polycentric perspective

Polycentric managers see international markets as being multi-domestic. This leads them to cater strongly to each individual market's tastes and preferences. Polycentric managers want their company to be seen as an "Australian" company, a "German" company, and so on. Probably increasing the company's local attractiveness, this approach also increases the complexity of the organization, makes it less cost competitive and impedes a company-wide mutual learning process.

Regional perspective

Managers with a regional orientation focus on a clearly limited "product market," which is defined by specific benefits delivered to a group of customers by the use of certain technologies (ways to provide those benefits) within a geographic or perhaps culturally homogeneous region. In serving the product market, the firm seeks opportunities for coordinating and possibly standardizing procurement, production, and marketing. National boundaries and differences are respected, but are not of primary importance. For example, a firm like Wolford, the leading manufacturer of up-market fashionable women's tights in Europe, has for years focused its marketing activities on western Europe. They concentrated production in Bregenz, Austria; communicated with their customers, intermediaries and shareholders by staging events that attracted media interest all over western Europe; used the same packaging and similar shop displays in all countries; and distributed their products in under 48 hours from a warehouse at their production site. Only later has the company started to change its outlook to become geocentric. It has been opening up a growing number of "Wolford Boutiques" in the metropolitan areas of the U.S., in Japan, Russia, and Singapore. For Hong Kong and PRC it has entered a distribution agreement with a local partner.

Geocentric perspective

Managers with a geocentric view are continually seeking out opportunities for procurement, production and marketing coordination, and standardization in a worldwide product market, independent of country borders. Managers of the more than 118-year-old Coca-Cola Company, headquartered in Atlanta, Georgia, for example, consider most of the product markets of their 300 brands to be global. In 2003 the company earned about $20 billion in revenue from customers all over the world consuming 14,200 drinks per second. It used 180 currencies to do business. Management coordinated the activities of their bottling and distribution partners in all countries of the world except Cuba, Iraq, and North Korea, gave them marketing support and assured quality control. The product formula of Diet Coke, for example, its positioning and advertising are uniform across all served country markets despite the 650 different languages used. The brand name varies slightly owing to various legal regulations. In some western European countries, the word "diet" has medical implications. So Coke Light or another name is used instead of Diet Coke. The artificial sweetener and package also differ in some countries. In Asia, smaller portions are offered to consumers. In Mexico, the small glass bottles are returnable. Promotional programs are localized, such as Coca-Cola's educational grants made through the Palestinian Authority and donations to environmental causes in Spain. Despite those variations, while the Coca-Cola Company is based in the U.S., it earns 80% of its profits from international sales and clearly has a geocentric view of its markets.

Major decisions

Confronted with the increasing globalization of trade and the driving forces of international business, entrepreneurs, and top managers who have overcome an ethnocentric perspective of business have to answer four fundamental questions:

- Should our company expand its business international or not?
- Which markets should be served and in what sequence?
- How much of our resources should we spend for what purposes?
- How should we build and sustain our firm's competitive advantages?

Figure 1.7 shows that the answers to these questions will depend on external and internal stimuli facing a company's decision makers, their personal motives, and the major objectives of the company agreed on by the dominant management group in the firm.

Level of international business

External and internal stimuli serve as triggers for decision-making processes concerning the first question: Should the company expand its business internationally or not?

External stimuli include unsolicited orders from foreign customers, perceived market opportunities, competitive pressures in the home market, or government programs to encourage exports. Honda, for example, today the leading

FIGURE 1.7 *Factors influencing managers' internationalization decisions*

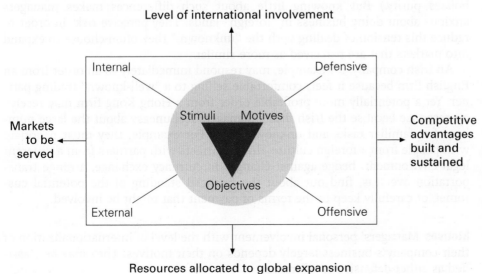

The level of a company's international involvement, the choice of markets to be served and the resources allocated to global expansion as well as the building and sustaining of appropriate competitive advantages depend on external and internal stimuli facing the company's decision makers, the personal motives of those managers, and the major company objectives agreed on by the dominant management group in the firm.

manufacturer of motorcycles, once found competition by Yamaha so strong in its Japanese home market that it decided to enter the less competitive markets of Europe and the U.S. in order to grow. The design of Louis Vuitton luggage, its high-quality/high-prestige image, and the attractive architecture of their stores in France, for example, resulted in so many Japanese tourists buying their products that the firm decided to open stores in Japan. Sales to Japanese customers world-wide account for about 30% of the company's total sales.

Internal stimuli may include unique products, strong marketing skills, or excess capacity in the areas of production, finance, marketing, or management. When Apple first marketed its Macintosh, for example, the product had superior graphic facilities. Customers in communication business around the world were eager to use them for their work. Those early adopters served as the spearheads for the company's entry into the global business market.

Perception and interpretation A company's top managers are confronted with those internal and external stimuli. But each manager is likely to have different knowledge and skills, varying experiences and differing personal motives, which make them more or less sensitive to the stimuli and lead to different reactions. Human decision making is never based on objective criteria but on subjective interpretations of information stored in memory and data gathered from the environment. Decision makers have to decide what information is useful and what can be ignored. What managers think to be relevant in a given decision situation is determined by:

- *their cognitive frameworks*, that is, their "theories" and assumptions about the environments
- *the methods they use* to observe and analyze those environments
- *the affective assessment* of their findings
- *their personal involvement* with the decision that needs to be taken.

Consequently, management's reactions to international business opportunities are not always governed by business strategies, profit and loss evaluations, or capital-budgeting schemes. Often they are based on **psychic distance**, that is, the perception of differences (psychological distance) between foreign and domestic markets. "Going international" exposes managers to unknown environments, such as different buyer behavior. Management may have heard of important differences, such as different symbolic meanings of color. (For example, white is the color of mourning in many African cultures. There, products packaged in white boxes do not sell as well as they do in the U.S., where white symbolizes purity.) But knowing little about such differences makes managers anxious about doing business in "foreign" lands. They perceive risk. In order to reduce this tension of dealing with the "unknown," they often choose to expand into markets that are perceived as more similar.

An Irish company, for example, may respond immediately to an order from an English firm because it feels comfortable selling to a "well-known" trading partner. Yet a potentially more profitable order from a Hong Kong firm may receive no response because the Irish firm's managers feel uneasy about the large number of unfamiliar tasks and unknown risks. For example, they must negotiate with people from a foreign culture, draft contracts with partners from a different legal environment, hedge against changes in currency exchange, arrange transportation overseas, find out about the financial standing of the potential customer, or carefully keep to the terms of payment that might be involved.

Motives Managers' personal involvement with the level of internationalization of their company's business largely depends on their motives. They may be classified as either defensive or offensive.

Defensive motives may be, for example, to focus on protecting domestic market share from a foreign competitor or to ascertain a satisfactory level of company value added, sales, or profit. When defensive motives dominate, management is reluctant to become involved in international business. Some managers will even react negatively to the idea. They may be generally reluctant to change, taking a position of "wait and see," follow traditional lines of business, being satisfied with their local business success, or fear the additional stress of international business and the risks involved, owing to their lack of specific knowledge.

Offensive motives lead to aggressive and systematic efforts to locate or respond to global opportunities. An offensive motive would be, for example, to attack foreign competitors in their strongest market. As the level of information and experience increases, perceived risk decreases and companies generally enter more dissimilar ("riskier") markets. More innovative managers appreciate the long-term growth potential that results from international business and the resulting opportunities to develop new capabilities (technologies, expertise, experience) and new products. Instead of reacting passively to stimuli from external or internal environments, more experienced, but also more entrepreneurial types of company decision makers will proactively consider non-domestic business opportunities as part of their firm's strategic decision making.

Market selection

When management has decided to internationalize the business of their firm, the question arises as to which markets to serve and in what sequence.

Because this decision will bind the company's resources for a substantial amount of time, the risk involved is high. Management needs to undertake a market assessment procedure that allows them to evaluate carefully the attractiveness of different product and country markets.

However, the choice of new markets in internationalizing the business of a firm will only lead to success when the company possesses or can build competitive advantages in those markets. They must be able to offer a benefit to potential customers that is more attractive to them than what those customers have experienced before. Consequently, management will need to find out the specific capabilities (= bundles of related skills and resources) needed to be successful in each of the markets it has shortlisted for potentially serving, and to compare their company's strengths and weaknesses to those of its major competitors concerning those capabilities.

Resource allocation

The resources of a company, even the world's largest, are not unlimited. As there are always a greater number of attractive market opportunities around the world than can be pursued, management has to answer the third major question: How much of our resources should we spend for what purpose?

In answering this question, management has to find a balance between choosing too many markets, which inevitably leads to a lack of sufficient resources in some or each of the served markets, and deciding on too small a number of markets, keeping the firm from efficiently exploiting its opportunities. Depending on a number of factors such as relative size of its home market, competitive situation there compared to other markets, degree of globalization of competitors, growth objectives set by corporate policy, or kind and importance of competitive advantages, management will determine the allocation of company resources.

The Jefferson Smurfit Group, an international paper and packaging concern based in Ireland, for example, decided that its Asian expansion plans proceed in a "phased approach." The company made its first direct investment in Asia with privately owned Singapore-based New Toyo to form Smurfit Toyo, which makes folding cartons. Additionally, Smurfit formed a joint venture in China where it bought a linerboard mill near Shanghai. The goal was to become familiar with these markets before making any major financial commitments.

The available choices for a company that has decided to do international business range from achieving a substantial market share in a niche existing in a number of country markets to dominating one or more global product markets. Firms such as Japan's Panasonic, one of the world's leading marketers of consumer electronics, Stockholm- and Zurich-based ABB, the giant electrical products and engineering company, or Kodak, the U.S.-based world leader in photographic material, have sufficient resources to master a full range of capabilities and technologies. They can efficiently serve an extended range of product markets in all country markets in need of their products and services. Panasonic, for example, may serve different groups of consumers looking for various kinds of audiovisual home entertainment. Or ABB may offer different problem solutions for various customer groups in the field of electrical installations. Both strive to dominate global markets.

At the other extreme, a highly specialized company with limited resources but strong competitive advantages in its field of competency, such as Austrian RSB-Roundtech, may decide to serve a regional or global market niche. RSB-Roundtech, specializing in formwork for round constructions such as egg-shaped digesters, water towers, telecom towers, or funnels, with a personnel capacity of only 100, is active in most highly industrialized countries including Japan and the U.S., but also in countries such as Cameroon, Korea, Indonesia, Malaysia, and Zaïre.

Building and sustaining competitive advantage

Distinctive competences of a firm that can be transformed into customer benefits can be regarded as competitive advantages to be sustained by reinforcing actions. But competitive advantages are not available to a company forever. In addition, negative differences need to be reduced to a level where they do not jeopardize market success. Management, therefore, has to answer a fourth important question: How to build and sustain the firm's competitive advantages?

When analyzing the markets of eastern Europe, John Brown, a U.K. industrial engineering firm, for example, found that it was not competitive on one of the major success factors: long-term relationships with decision makers or influencers. But they had other competitive advantages such as self-developed and referenced technologies. Since building the needed strength to serve the eastern European markets seemed to take too much time, management searched for a partner interested in entering a joint venture. They finally entered a joint venture with the chemical engineering division of VAI, the Austrian metallurgical engineering firm, which was searching for a partner with the strengths of John Brown.

International marketing

International marketing is the application of marketing orientation and marketing capabilities to international business.

Marketing orientation

Marketing may be described as a bundle of management skills and resources, often referred to as **marketing capabilities**. These capabilities allow a business organization to understand, develop, and maintain exchange relationships with individuals, groups, and organizations in order to reach the objectives of the organization. International marketing capabilities support a company in searching for appropriate markets, in building and sustaining competitive advantages in those markets, and in managing the relationships with all important stakeholders belonging to those markets.

By way of contrast, marketing can be viewed as a basic approach to doing business, termed **marketing orientation**. Marketing-oriented managers focus in a systematic way on the management of their business organization's exchange relationships with stakeholders in the operating environment. Marketing orientation is characterized by:

● a systems perspective, emphasizing the interrelatedness among the organization and its various stakeholders in a market

● an exchange perspective, interpreting all interactions among the stakeholders (including the firm) in a market as episodes in an ongoing complex exchange that needs to be balanced

● a value perspective, focusing the mind of all members of a business organization on the values or benefits to be mutually provided in the continual exchanges with stakeholders

● a process-oriented approach to all decisions and actions of the organization.

Systems perspective

The long-term success of a company depends on a continuous influx of resources from raw materials through capital, manpower, and information to regulations that become transformed in the company into resources such as products, information, dividends, or skilled labor, and flow back out to all kinds of customers and other stakeholders interested in getting them. To make sure that this two-way flow of resources takes place in quantities and qualities needed for the attainment of the company's objectives, mutually satisfactory relationships with all suppliers and customers of those resources have to be established and maintained. The marketing orientation, therefore, includes a systems perspective. That is, marketing-oriented managers hold the conviction that the company's well-being depends on relationships with customers and other stakeholders that fulfill certain minimum levels of expectations and do not interfere with each other.

For example, a new liquid fertilizer increasing farm production may represent an attractive solution to a customer problem. But at the same time it may create living conditions near the company's production facilities difficult to accept because of air pollution, or may come close to violating government regulations, perhaps by exposing workers to dangerous fumes. In such a case, the company may be well advised not to start production of that product.

Exchange perspective

Lasting customer and stakeholder relationships can be established and maintained only if all the partners in the relationship are willing and able to contribute in a way that each partner subjectively benefits from the relationship in a direct or indirect manner. Marketing orientation, therefore, includes an exchange perspective. That is, marketing-oriented managers hold the conviction that the establishment and maintenance of relationships needed for long-term business success has to build on balanced exchange relations between two or more partners.

A Fiat Stilo, for example, is exchanged between a customer and a Fiat dealer. The exchange takes place only as long as the customer believes that she will gain something (for example, reliable transport, fun driving, attractive styling, good resale value, social acceptance) at least as valuable as the value of what she brings to the exchange (for example, money, trust in the dealer and the brand, positive word of mouth, social status). The dealer will sign the contract only if he thinks that he will gain at least as much (for example, money to keep his business running, good reputation attracting more customers, follow-up business when servicing the car) as he gives away. Some of those benefits on both sides cannot be achieved from the simple dyadic exchange relationship between the customer and the car dealer. Others, such as family members enjoying the car, friends interested in its performance, or reliable service personnel working for the dealer, have to play their role in the exchange to fulfill some of the expectations (such as social acceptance or reputation).

Value perspective

Both partners need to have a good reason to establish and maintain an exchange relationship. The best reason is when the potential partner offers a solution to an actual or potential problem (the satisfaction of a need) that is more attractive than other solutions offered. The attractiveness of a problem solution depends on the subjectively valued benefits it is able to provide. The third perspective of marketing orientation, therefore, is the value perspective. Marketing-oriented managers hold the conviction that balanced exchange relationships between a company, its customers, and other stakeholders cannot be established and maintained unless the company personnel involved in those relationships are aware of the actual and potential problems (needs and aspirations) of their exchange partners and offer them solutions which seem more beneficial to them than other options.

Thus, the first question to ask when analyzing a potential relationship is not what the company can gain from the deal, but whether it can make a substantial direct or indirect contribution towards solving the problems faced by its exchange partner. If so, then sales and profits or other benefits for the company result.

Process-oriented approach

To be able to consider the various stakeholders involved in a system of complex exchange when making decisions and to manage the multitude of daily actions in a way to provide attractive value to all the interested exchange partners, the members of a business organization need to closely coordinate their activities across all functions. Marketing-oriented managers, therefore, understand that all members of a business organization, independent of their specific role, are part-time marketers.

They organize their company in a process-oriented manner to make everyone partly responsible for providing superior value to the stakeholders needed for company success.

Marketing orientation requires that the company's personnel adhere to the four perspectives on a long-term basis. One of a manager's most important duties is keeping track of current relationships with customers and other stakeholders, anticipating future developments, and assessing their implications for the firm. While present success is a result of past efforts, it is no guarantee of success in the future. Future success can be achieved only by preparing for likely changes in the company's relationships with stakeholders, that is, in the nature of the problems it will be called on to solve and the expectations concerning the problem solutions.

Repsol, a Spanish manufacturer of granules for the production of plastic wrapping materials, which has been concentrating on compound technology for special applications in the food industry, may find, for example, that consumers' growing environmental concerns will force governments to raise recycling standards in the coming years. To prepare for new specifications from customers and to preempt competitive entry in its markets, the company will broaden its focus to include the recycling potential of its material in time.

In international business, the conditions for establishing and maintaining mutually satisfying relationships with customers and other stakeholders may differ from one country market to another. But the ground rules of relationship management remain the same all over the world. Therefore, marketing orientation is a universal approach to international business conduct when long-term success is a major objective. Marketing-oriented managers, contrariwise, may adhere to one of two basically different approaches to international business: a multinational or a global approach.

Multinational marketing

In multi-domestic industries, international marketing has traditionally concentrated on differences between product markets in countries that had previously been assessed to be attractive business environments. For example, many managers of companies located in neighboring countries, such as Denmark, the Netherlands, or Switzerland, have found Germany to be a very attractive business environment, because of its political stability, its economic wealth, its highly developed infrastructure, and the number of potential customers compared to the domestic market. They decided that their company had to do business in Germany before they had analyzed the state of the product market they were planning to serve in that country. This did not seem to be a problem to them because they thought they knew that differences were abundant and had to be considered by developing a specific marketing strategy. The result was a multinational approach to marketing that concentrated largely on country markets, developing a distinct marketing strategy for each market.

Global marketing

Many companies face fierce competition in increasingly global industries. In their search for synergy and learning potential across international activities, they find their individual and industrial customers having increasingly differentiated aspirations, which result in country market segments becoming smaller and smaller. That said, international differences among such narrowly defined country market segments still exist, but in serving them, substantial parts of a marketing strategy can be kept the same across geographic market boundaries.

The result is a global approach to international marketing. Rather than focusing on country markets, that is, differences due to the physical location of the customer groups, managers concentrate on product markets, that is, groups of customers seeking shared benefits or to be served with the same technology, emphasizing their similarities regardless of the geographic areas in which they are located. The location continues to be important, of course. Cultures still vary considerably, transportation difficulties plague successful international marketing, and laws and regulations vary. But a global approach to international marketing considers such constraints, real as they may be, after first examining what the most attractive product markets for the company are and where in the world groups of customers that fit into those product markets can be found.

For managers who adopt a global marketing approach to international business, the critical point is not whether countries are more or less similar and buyers are the same everywhere, but to what extent shared customer aspirations and similar marketing infrastructure (distribution system, logistics, media, norms, regulations) exist in different nations. If they do, the company can develop a relatively standardized marketing strategy to appeal to those needs. It serves a global product market. For example, it can offer the same high-tech, high-quality camcorders to video "freaks" around the world.

However, a global approach to international marketing does not ignore differences among local market segments. These differences are taken into account when implementing the marketing program. Beefeater Gin, for example, can be positioned as the authentic English (exclusively London-distilled) gin for people of discernment worldwide. It can have the same premium quality (alcohol content) and taste, and use the same bottle, label (including the Beefeater Yeoman) and premium pricing strategy. It can be sold via wholly owned distributors, and distribution can be focused on hotels, bars and restaurants all over the world. Country market differences still exist and have to be accounted for. For example, sales personnel in the various countries do not react to the same sales incentives. Barkeepers in Chile were offered vouchers for children's school clothes and goods, an incentive that would be considered ridiculous in Germany. Sponsorships must embrace different kinds of sport to have the same effects. For example, in the U.K., Beefeater sponsored the Oxford vs Cambridge boat race, in Thailand, deep sea fishing competitions, and, in Spain, American football games. But, in general, the focus of Beefeater's marketing management is on a specific group of customers that exists worldwide and not on local differences.

Experience curve effects

The most powerful argument in favor of a global product market approach is the opportunity to benefit from experience curve effects (see Figure 1.8). This concept has two dimensions: increased efficiency due to size effects and increased effectiveness due to experience (accumulated know-how) effects.

Increased efficiency is more easily attained by larger than by smaller companies – if costs for increased coordination needs and substantially rising transportation costs are kept under close control – and by serving a global rather than a local product market. Because of their greater size, Paris-based Cartier, a marketer of high-prestige accessories, for example, can more easily profit from reduced average production, marketing, or administration costs per watch or piece of jewelry sold than its competitor Poiray, also a Paris-based manufacturer of fine jewelry, which targets women in major capital cities all over the world who can afford to wear expensive contemporary jewelry. But even this smaller firm, by

---

FIGURE 1.8 *Experience curve effects*

The experience curve shows the decrease of cost per unit when the cumulative production volume in units increases.

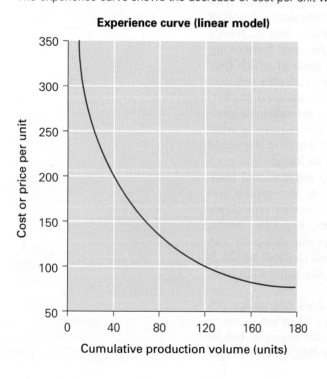

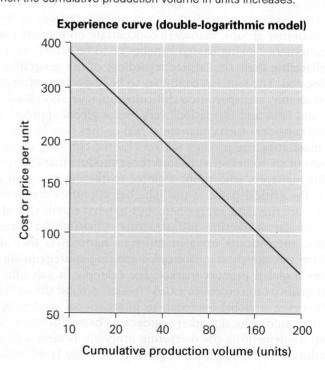

totally standardizing the packaging of its products, display materials, advertising visuals, and catalog layout, can profit from marketing efficiency effects.

Increased effectiveness occurs when a company "learns by doing." The second time a worker or manager does a job, he or she usually does it better than the first time, thereby becoming more effective. Similarly, when a company enters its second foreign market using what it learned when it entered its first such market, it should be more effective. Companies such as Wal-Mart, the largest retailer in the world, that offer their services in a product market spread over many country markets, benefit from both dimensions of the experience curve. Because of their high sales volume and the resulting purchasing power, they can procure products and capital at lower costs. They can distribute their administration overheads across a higher total turnover, and can transfer the experiences gained in one country market to other markets.

Global market analysis

A second argument in favor of a global product market approach to international marketing is the opportunity to find new and sufficiently large market niches through global market analysis. A marketer of a line of cosmetics, such as Guerlain, a member of the French Groupe LVMH, which holds a number of internationally well-known luxury brands such as Christian Dior, Louis Vuitton and Moët Hennessey, for example, might not find a single country market (except the U.S.) big enough to be served by an adequate marketing program and provide a sufficient return on investment. But it might be able to identify a target market consisting of high-income, fashion-conscious women above 40 in several countries (for example Brazil, China, the EU, India, and the U.S.). This "global" product market is much larger than a single domestic market. A marketing mix with highly standardized product features, distribution system, pricing strategy, and promotion activities emphasizing the French style of classic fashion could appeal to this target market. Thus, it offers a greater opportunity to take advantage of experience curve effects in production, administration, and marketing.

Summary

In the past 200 years the world economy has continually grown. Growth and accumulation of material wealth were not equally distributed across countries. Differences are mainly due to:

- different levels of education, skills, and know-how of a country's population
- accumulation of capital for production purposes instead of consumption
- speed of technological development and its implementation in new products and processes
- extent of liberalization of trade inside the country as well as with international partners.

Liberalization of world trade has triggered major impulses for the development of the world's economy. In recent years international trade has been growing significantly faster than most national economies. Trade liberalization has been achieved on different levels. On the one hand, deregulation of country markets has opened up new opportunities for national and international business, while, on the other, international agreements on the reduction of tariffs and non-tariff barriers have become very popular in most parts of the world.

Such agreements do not happen by chance, however. One of the major driving forces for liberalization of international trade has been the limited growth potential in the home markets of companies based in the highly industrialized countries. And tremendous technological changes – in particular in communication technologies – have only added to that effect.

Many industries in a world with decreasing barriers to international business have changed from a multi-domestic to a global state. Not only do we find the same competitors in most country markets of the world, but their competitive position in each market also depends on their position in others. That is, in order to be successful in a world of global business, a company – of whatever size – must assess opportunities and threats on an international level, and must develop a strategy that takes into account its strengths and weaknesses compared to competitors potentially based all over the world.

The critical element for success in international business is not so much the size of a company as an approach or business perspective of top management that seeks to do business where it can be done with the greatest success. Managers of locally operating companies who have overcome an ethnocentric perspective of international business must decide whether their firm should go international or not. Each company operating internationally has to determine which markets should be served and in what sequence. Because the resources of a company are not unlimited management needs to determine how to allocate the resources in such a way as to maximize potential success across the product and country markets served. For that purpose a plan has to be developed indicating how competitive advantages should be built and sustained in those markets.

A strategic approach to international business is needed to ensure a steady flow of resources to and from the company. The critical aspect of such an approach is to manage relationships with customers and other important stakeholders of the firm in a way that satisfies their expectations. Building and maintaining relationships is the major focus of marketing. International marketing is the application of marketing orientation and marketing techniques to international business.

There are two different ways in which marketing managers can approach international business:

- a multinational approach that focuses largely on country markets, developing a distinct marketing strategy for each market
- a global approach that occurs when a company's managers focus on product markets, emphasizing their similarities regardless of the geographic areas in which they are located.

The most powerful argument in favor of a global approach to international marketing is the opportunity to benefit from experience curve effects. These include increased efficiency due to size effects and increased effectiveness due to experience effects. The size effects result from decreasing fixed costs per unit sold. Increased effectiveness occurs when a company "learns by doing."

The described analyses and decisions needed for a strategic approach to international business constitute the international marketing decision process, which will be discussed in the following chapters.

DISCUSSION QUESTIONS

1. What are the pros and cons of trade liberalization from an economic, political, and social point of view? Gather some recent material from newspapers and trade magazines to substantiate your points.

2. What are the major international agreements on economic cooperation? How have they been developing in the past three years? What are their most important plans for the coming five years?

3. Look for two examples of companies that have gone international in the past three years. What were their major reasons for doing so?

4. What are the latest technological changes facilitating international business? What impact do they have on how business is conducted?

5. What are the major reasons why an increasing number of industries develop from multidomestic to global?

6. Find two recent examples of companies doing business in globalizing industries. How do those companies react to globalization?

7. Suppose your company is based in Oslo, Norway, and manufactures fish smoking equipment for the home market. A Brazilian firm inquires about your company's products. Prepare a script for a roleplay in which you (1) play the role of a manager having mainly defensive motives, and (2) play the role of a manager having mainly offensive motives in reaction to this inquiry.

8. What are the major decisions a company's management has to take when considering international business? Find examples from business magazines to illustrate each of the decisions.

9. What are the basic convictions underlying marketing orientation? Why are they important for international business success?

10. What is the basic distinction between multinational and global marketing? What are the consequences of each of the two perspectives to a firm?

ADDITIONAL READINGS

Donaldson, T. and L.E. Preston (1995) "The stakeholder theory of the corporation: concepts, evidence and implications", *Academy of Management Review*, 20, 65–91.

Hirschey, M., J.L. Pappas, and D. Whigham (1995) *Managerial Economics* (European Edition), London: International Thomson Business Press.

Kaku, R. (1997) "The path of Kyosei", *Harvard Business Review*, July–August, 55–63.

Lachelle, N. (2003) "The human face of globalization: plant closings and life transitions",

Journal of Fashion Marketing and Management, 7(2) 163–81.

Schlegelmilch, B.B. (1998) *Marketing Ethics: An International Perspective*, London: International Thomson Business Press.

Svensson, G. (2002) "Beyond global marketing and the globalization of marketing activities", *Management Decision*, 40(6), 574–83.

Troiano, J. (1997) "Brazilian teenagers go global – sharing values and brands", *Marketing and Research Today*, August, 149–61.

Useful internet links

ABB (Asea Brown Boveri)	http://www.abb.com/
AmorePacific	http://www.amorepacific.com/index.jsp
APEC (Asia-Pacific Economic Cooperation)	http://www.apecsec.org.sg/apec.html
ASEAN (Association of Southeast Asian Nations)	http://www.aseansec.org/
Business Knowledge Centre	http://www.netmba.com/
CARICOM (Caribbean Community)	http://www.caricom.org/
Cartier	http://www.cartier.com/

CIS (Commonwealth of Independent States)	http://www.cisstat.com/eng/cis.htm
	http://www.cis.minsk.by
Coca-Cola	http://www.coca-cola.com/
COMESA (Common Market of Eastern and Southern Africa)	http://www.itcilo.it/actrav/actrav-english/ telearn/global/ilo/blokit/comesa.htm
	http://www.comesa.int
Compact	http://www.compact.org/
The Economist	http://www.economist.com/
EFTA (European Free Trade Association)	http://secretariat.efta.int/Web/legaldocuments/
EU (European Union)	http://europa.eu.int/
G7/8	http://www.g7.utoronto.ca/
GEC Alsthom	http://www.marconi.com/
Gross national product worldwide	http://www.scaruffi.com/politics/gnp.html
Groupe LVMH	http://www.lvmh.fr/
Hewlett-Packard	http://www.hp.com/
Hoffmann-La Roche	http://www.roche.com/
IEA (International Energy Agency)	http://www.iea.org/
International Herald Tribune	http://www.iht.com/pages/index.php
Louis Vuitton	http://www.vuitton.com/
Marketingteacher	http://www.marketingteacher.com/
MERCOSUR (Mercado Común del Sur)	http://www.mercosur.org.uy/
NAFTA (North American Free Trade Agreement)	http://www.nafta-sec-alena.org/
Nestlé	http://www.nestle.com/
OECD (Organization for Economic Cooperation and Development)	http://www.oecd.org/home/
Pentax	http://www.pentax.com/
Red Bull	http://www.redbull.co.uk/
RSB-Roundtech	http://www.rsb-roundtech.com/
SACU (Southern African Customs Union)	http://www.dfa.gov.za/foreign/ Multilateral/africa/sacu.htm
VAI (Voest-Alpine Industrieanlagenbau)	http://www.vai.at/
Wikipedia (free encyclopedia on the EU)	http://en.wikipedia.org/wiki/European_Union
Wolford	http://www.wolford.com/
WTO (World Trade Organization)	http://www.wto.org/

POTENTIAL MARKET ASSESSMENT: DETERMINATION OF ATTRACTIVE MARKETS

2

Learning objectives

After studying this chapter you will be able to:

- describe the different steps of an international market assessment procedure

- determine relevant criteria to assess the attractiveness of potential international markets

- assess the attractiveness of country markets

- analyze the attractiveness of local product markets

- help a company determine a shortlist of international markets to consider serving

Chapter outline

Process of potential market assessment

Corporate policy
Market assessment criteria
Assessment of potential country markets

Assessment of country markets

Selection of market assessment criteria
Assessment criteria concerning the macro-environment
Assessment criteria concerning the operating environment
Criteria selection guidelines

Determination of attractive country markets

Market exclusion procedure
Future market attractiveness
Most attractive markets

Summary

INTERNATIONAL MARKETING SPOTLIGHT

RSB-Roundtech

RSB-Roundtech is a global player in a rather narrow product market niche: The company plans and produces formwork material for circular structures, such as water towers, sewage treatment plants (digesters), telecom towers, windmill shafts, or biogas production plants. It handles the formwork on construction sites all over the world and provides technical assistance to local construction contractors. The company, headquartered in a village close to Lake Constance in the industrial triangle between Austria, Germany, and Switzerland, employs no more than around 100 people. It has subsidiaries in Germany, Hungary, Japan, and Switzerland.

Because of its small size – there are only about 20 people working in headquarter offices in Hard – the right choice of markets to be actively focused and served by the firm is of particular importance. The major problem management has encountered is that every country market plays to a different tune. Economic indicators of country market level of industrial development, wealth, or urbanization alone have proved to be no valid criteria for estimating potential success.

The northern parts of Italy, for example, are highly industrialized, densely populated and wealthy. But there is a severe lack of sewage treatment plants. As a consequence, rivers heavily pollute the Adriatic Sea, a major summer tourist destination. The Italian government provided a substantial budget to resolve this problem. But instead of investing in sewage treatment plants administrators gave the money to the hotels at the shore of the Adriatic Sea to build swimming pools for their clients.

Based on a per capita income assessment, by way of contrast, the People's Republic of China would

Egg-shaped digester tanks of the Deer Island sewage treatment plant on Boston harbor   © Michael Dwyer/Alamy

not be an interesting market. But government and local administrators decided to build egg-shaped digesters because they are a symbol of highly industrialized countries. The major problem for RSB in China is to find the right local partners who strongly influence the selection of the supplier.

In densely populated Singapore, the land is so expensive that building the most modern digester costs only about 15% of what a developer can earn by selling the land economized in comparison to a normal sewage treatment facility. Coastal areas in Australia are also highly urbanized. But there is still so much land that sewage treatment companies could easily afford staying with the old space-consuming technology. However, an engineer read about egg-shaped digesters and wanted to use that technology. By chance, he found RSB at a fair in Kuala Lumpur and a successful business relationship was started.

The focal question of this chapter is: How can a business organization select a number of assessment criteria to determine the attractiveness of potential country markets in an effective and efficient way?

Process of potential market assessment

The world is made up of a variety of potential markets, country as well as product markets. Limited resources, however, mean that no company can serve all potential markets in the world in such a way that customers are satisfied and the firm's objectives are achieved. The company must select the most appropriate markets. It might focus on one product market and serve it in many different geographic areas, but it might also decide to serve various product markets in a small group of selected geographic areas. Because of the great number and diversity of markets to choose from, the task of assessing the markets' attractiveness and selecting the most interesting ones is rather complex.

To be meaningful, the assessment of potential markets must be based on detailed and continually updated information. But the great number and diversity of markets prevents gathering and analyzing the vast amount of data needed for a detailed simultaneous comparison of all potential markets at a reasonable cost. Further, at a given point in time, not all potential markets will be attractive to a firm. Management must, therefore, find a way to pre-select the most attractive markets in a quick and low-cost manner, and gather relevant and precise data that leads to an accurate evaluation of this restricted number of potential markets (see Figure 2.1).

Corporate policy

Assessment of potential markets is based on a business organization's corporate policy. In the statement of corporate policy top management has made a first choice of which markets the company should serve. A corporate policy includes the company's vision, mission, and business philosophy.

The mission statement begins by defining the general purpose of the company – the vision of its founders or top managers (see Strategy box 2.1 for an example).

FIGURE 2.1 *Process of potential market assessment*

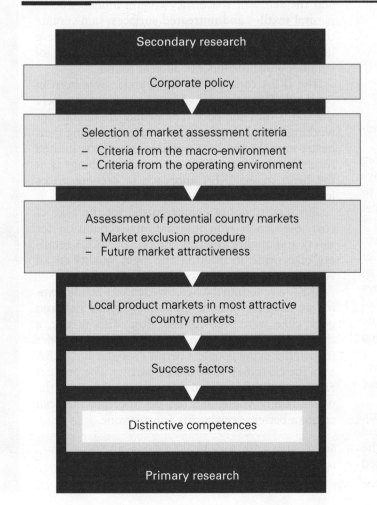

The assessment of potential markets is based on the firm's corporate policy. The mission statement defines the product market(s) to be served as well as the major objectives and their priorities. The business philosophy defines central values and rules of behavior to be followed. By applying criteria derived from corporate policy, country markets are classified to narrow their number to the markets of greatest attractiveness. Then the local product markets in the most attractive geographic areas are individually analyzed for their potential. Before company management can decide which markets should be served, how, and in what sequence, it has to consider the competitive position of the firm in each of the attractive markets. Success factors have to be determined for each of the pre-selected markets. A comparison between the major competitors and the firm on those success factors reveals distinctive competences, which can be transformed into competitive advantages. As the process moves forward, the emphasis on research shifts from secondary (desk research) to primary (field research), as the marketing manager needs increasingly precise data for market evaluation.

Then, it defines the **business domain** of the firm – which benefits the company will provide to which customers and which technologies (or ways to provide those benefits) it will use for that purpose. For example, Liechtenstein-based HILTI AG, one of the world's largest suppliers of all kinds of industrial fastenings, defined its business as follows: "We satisfy market needs in the field of fastening technology for customers involved in small and industrial construction and for all other industrial purposes by offering tools, equipment, and elements in combination with pre- and after-sales service from the detection of the customers' needs to their satisfaction."

Through such a statement top management defines the relevant product market(s) of the organization. The firm's relevant product market(s) will usually be distributed over a number of country markets. The evaluation of which country markets are most attractive will depend on the firm's major objectives and their priorities as formulated next in the corporate mission. Objectives may include:

- growth versus stability
- return on investment
- market share
- acceptable level of risk
- approach to technology and innovation
- image and goodwill

STRATEGY BOX 2.1

IKEA's vision

Our heritage

It's no accident that the IKEA logo is blue and yellow. These are the colors of the Swedish flag.

In Sweden, nature and the home both play a big part in people's lives. In fact, one of the best ways to describe the Swedish home furnishing style is to describe nature – full of light and fresh air, yet restrained and unpretentious.

In the late 1800s, the artists Carl and Karin Larsson combined classical influences with warmer Swedish folk styles. They created a model of Swedish home furnishing design that today enjoys worldwide renown. In the 1950s the styles of modernism and functionalism developed at the same time as Sweden established a society founded on social equality. The IKEA product range – modern but not trendy, functional yet attractive, human centered and child friendly – carries on these various Swedish home furnishing traditions.

Many people associate Sweden with a fresh, healthy way of life. This Swedish lifestyle is reflected in the IKEA product range. The freshness of the open air is reflected in the colors and materials used and the sense of space they create: Blonde woods, natural textiles and untreated surfaces. In a climate that is cold and dark for much of the year, these light, bright living spaces create the sensation of summer sunshine indoors all year round.

The IKEA concept, like its founder, was born in Småland. This is a part of southern Sweden where the soil is thin and poor. The people are famous for working hard, living on small means and using their heads to make the best possible use of the limited resources they have. This way of doing things is at the heart of the IKEA approach to keeping prices low.

But quality is not compromised for the sake of cost. Sweden has an international reputation for safety and quality you can rely on, and IKEA retailers take pride in offering the right quality in all situations.

IKEA was founded when Sweden was fast becoming an example of a caring society, where rich and poor alike were well looked after. This is also a theme that fits well with the IKEA vision. In order to give the many people a better everyday life, IKEA asks the customer to work as a partner. The product range is child friendly and covers the needs of the whole family, young and old. So, together they can create a better everyday life for everyone.

Source: Adapted from www.ikea-usa.com/ms/en_US/about_ikea/our_vision/heritage.html (15 December 2003)

- establishment of a specific working climate within the organization
- independence versus cooperation as a general approach to business.

For example, when Austrian Doppelmayr, the world-leading producer of ski lifts, chairlifts and cable cars, assessed Asian markets for potential investment in a production site, they had to bear in mind their corporate mission. The objectives formulated in that mission demand:

- application of the latest technology in the products and production processes of the firm
- a cost structure that allows lower production costs than the major competitors
- a consolidated corporate real growth rate of an average 10% a year
- exceptional use of foreign capital for the purpose of interim financing only
- capital flows from subsidiaries to the headquarters.

Because objectives are not always consistent – a high growth rate goal may conflict with a goal restricting the use of foreign capital, for example – the mission statement indicates which priorities should be pursued. In the case of Doppelmayr, the mission statement allows interim financing by foreign capital when growth cannot be exclusively financed by the firm's cash flow.

Depending on the intended degree of internationalization the firm will either: *keep its business local*. If the firm's corporate mission contains the objective of keeping the business local, management has no need to assess the attractiveness of potential markets. It must continually screen the global business environment, however, to make sure that its local competitive advantage can be sustained. Developments in other local parts of the same product market have to be followed in order to prevent unpleasant surprises from competitors intruding into the home market. Breitschopf, an Austrian producer of kitchen furniture, for example, has to watch for the development of its product market in other European country markets. From there, competitors, such as German Bulthaup or Italian Boffi, launch new designs that quickly penetrate the Austrian home market and strongly influence customer expectations.

Or it may *try to expand a local business to a regional one and later one of global size*. If the firm's corporate mission contains the objective of internationalizing the business from a local market base, country markets will have a prominent position in managers' minds. This will occur despite the fact that every market assessment procedure has to start from the definition of the firm's business. Characteristics relevant to the attractiveness of geographically limited product markets have to be determined. A company that wishes to grow quickly, for example, will choose country markets in which its product market is large enough and has sufficient purchasing power to support a high growth rate. A company that prefers more stable development, or slower growth, may look for country markets where its product market is in later stages of development.

Or, it will *do business on a global level*. If the company has adopted a global perspective of international marketing, management will think primarily in product market terms – serving cross-national customer segments with particular values (benefits). Specific characteristics of geographic sub-markets will only be used for the purposes of adaptation of marketing mixes and resource allocation decisions. For example, firms such as Boeing, Compaq, or Whirlpool serve certain segments of a global product market. They use information about different technical standards for product adaptation in country markets. Information on local customer activities or on legal restrictions on financial transfers affects decisions on how much resources to deploy in which geographic area.

The **business philosophy** formulates the basic values and rules of behavior a company wants its personnel to respect inside the organization and in contacts with external stakeholders. Those values and norms may lead management to avoid certain country markets. For example, 93% of all Fortune 1000 firms have formulated corporate ethics codes, which in many cases are part of their business philosophy. Those ethics codes lead company managers to rate country markets lower in attractiveness, for example, where bribes are needed to complete business deals. This is the case in most of the economically less developed countries of Africa, Asia, and South America. Ethics box 2.1 gives an example of the parts of such a corporate ethics code that are relevant for country market assessment.

Market assessment criteria

To allow a comparison of geographic sub-markets' attractiveness, characteristics relevant to business success in the selected product market(s) have to be assessed. Such characteristics can be found in the macro- and operating environments of the country markets. Market selection will also be strongly influenced by the internal environment of the firm (see Figure 2.2).

ETHICS BOX 2.1

ABB's ethical standards

Business ethics
Guidelines
Conflicts of interest

ABB employees shall avoid entering into any situation in which their personal or financial interests may conflict with those of the ABB Group.

No ABB employee shall seek or accept any payment, personal gift or entertainment which might reasonably be believed to influence business transactions or which are not within the bounds of customary business hospitality.

Confidentiality and protection of assets
Insider trading
Bribery and corruption

No ABB company or employee shall offer or provide an undue monetary or other advantage to any person or persons, including public officials or customer employees, in violation of laws and the officials' or employees' legal duties, in order to obtain or retain business.

Intermediaries

Agreements with consultants, brokers, sponsors, agents or other intermediaries shall not be used to channel payments to any person or persons, including public officials or customer employees and

thereby circumvent ABB policies regarding bribery and corruption. These agreements are strictly subject to the requirements set forth in the corresponding Group directive.

Political contributions

Contributions to political parties or committees, or to individual politicians, should not in principle be given. Any exceptions to this rule must be cleared in advance with Group Function Legal and Compliance (GF-LC).

Antitrust compliance
Disclosure and records
Lender's and export credit compliance
Violations of corporate policies

Each employee is responsible for ensuring that his or her conduct and the conduct of anyone reporting to the employee fully complies with the policies governing the company's business dealings. Compliance, both personal and by subordinates, will be a factor in periodic performance appraisals. Violations of our policies will result in appropriate action, up to and including, discharge from employment. An individual or individuals may also face civil or criminal penalties.

Responsibility and implementation

Source: http://search.abb.com/library/ABBlibrary.asp?Document ID=BUSETH05EN&LanguageCode=en&DocumentPartID= &Action=Launch

Courtesy of ABB Ltd

Macro-environment

A company's macro-environment is generally defined as the political, legal, economic, ecological, social, cultural, and technological dimensions of the universe in which the operating environment of the firm is embedded. Whereas the macro-environment of a company strongly influences the structure and state of its operating environment, individual members of the operating environment are restricted in their influence on the development of the macro-environment.

Management has to determine and analyze the relevant dimensions of their firm's macro-environment. For example, when Zuegg, the Verona-based leading Italian manufacturer of fruit juice and second-largest marketer of jam in the country, planned its expansion to other European markets, it had to study legislation concerning food preparation, product declaration, packaging, and recycling. The potential impact of culture, in terms of consumption patterns, country of origin prejudices, or ecological awareness was considered. Trends in economic and demographic development, such as the unemployment rate, distribution of purchasing power, or ageing of the population, were analyzed, and the effects of changes in the technological environment concerning transportation, warehousing infrastructure, and media studied.

(Chapters 3 to 5 will discuss the dimensions of the macro-environment in terms of their effects on country market attractiveness.)

Operating environment

By using easily available data concerning the relevant dimensions of the macro-environment, the great number of available country markets is reduced to a small set of highly attractive markets, which have to be analyzed in more detail. This more detailed analysis uses evaluation criteria related to the firm's operating environment such as purchasing power of potential customers, intensity of competition, or availability of skilled labor force.

FIGURE 2.2 *Types of business environment*

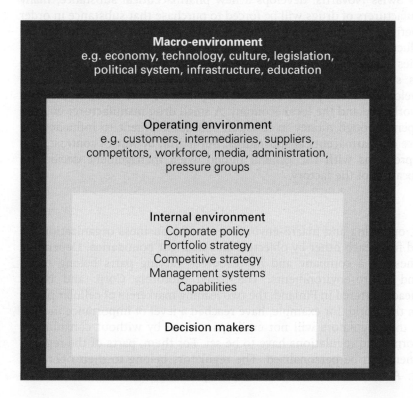

The decision makers of an internationally operating company live in their firm's internal environment, which is embedded in the operating environment of the company's global product market, which, in turn, is influenced by the global macro-environment.

The **operating environment** of a firm contains all actors, that is, individuals or people representing organizations and institutions, who have aspirations concerning the behavior and performance of the company in doing its business. Those are customers, competitors, suppliers, intermediaries, potential, and current workforce, owners, shareholders, banks, media, trade unions, and other so-called stakeholders of the company. They can have a strong impact on the success of a firm, but may also be influenced by the firm. Management must consider the various self-interests, capabilities and power of the stakeholders forming their company's operating environment. Depending on those factors, they can manage the relationships with important stakeholders to help achieve the firm's objectives.

Internal environment

Company decision makers play their role as part of an organization, which has an implicit, if not explicitly stated, corporate policy that lays out the ground rules of how it wants to function. It follows a portfolio and a competitive strategy, basic indications of where to do business and how, based on management systems such as the organization structure or the controlling system, as well as capabilities – combinations of personal skills and resources – that result in specific actions. These elements make up the **internal environment** of the firm.

The firm's internal environment defines the borders of its operating environment. For example, when Coca-Cola decided to serve the soft drink markets of the world, it defined its relevant operating environment to be all customers, organizations, and institutions concerned with or interested in the production, distribution, and consumption of soft drinks worldwide. When Coca-Cola went a step further to enter the alcoholic beverages market, it substantially widened the borders of its operating environment. Coke's withdrawal from the alcoholic beverages market may well have been hastened by its having to play a "different game" in that market than in their traditional market where they were much more familiar with the rules, norms, and expectations of stakeholders.

The internal environment also limits the firm's potential influence on the development of its operating environment. If a large, globally operating corporation, such as Swiss Novartis, develops a new pharmaceutical substance, many smaller manufacturers of drugs will be forced to purchase that substance in order to stay competitive with their final products. If the same firm decides to concentrate its production of basic substances for antibiotics in one country, factories in other countries will go out of operation. Some stakeholders, such as trade unions or politicians, supported by local media, may try to use their power to force the firm into developing "social plans" to decrease the impact of those shutdowns on the former workforce and the local economy. A small drug manufacturer will not be able to spend enough money in research and development to influence the worldwide use of pharmaceutical substances. But it will, by way of contrast, also have fewer problems with the general public when management decides to change the location of the factory.

Boundaries

The internal, operating and macro-environments of a business organization are not separated from each other by objective and clear-cut boundaries. Depending on the business of a company and its resources varying parts belong to its operating and macro-environments. U.S.-based Motorola Corp. and Nokia Mobira Oy, headquartered in Finland, the two leading marketers of cellular phone equipment in the world, for example, have reached a level of importance in their market such that regulators will not easily pass them by without consultation when new norms and regulations have to be set. For them, parts of the regulatory environment can be personalized. The regulators belong to their operating environment. A very small, but internationally active firm such as Omicron

Electronics, the leader in the global market niche of test sets for protective relays, transducers, and energy meters for electrical utilities and industry, can hardly directly influence parts of the regulatory environment by building personal or organizational relationships. For them, legislation is part of the given macro-environment.

The internal and operating environments of a firm may overlap. Increasing numbers of cooperative agreements, such as clusters of small companies working together in the supply of complex industrial services and deepening relationships between companies to improve their competitive position in globalizing industries, have reinforced this trend. Management increasingly often has to consider (parts of) internal environments of partner firms when taking decisions. For example, Airbus and Boeing, the two companies dominating the aircraft business, want to deal with a minimum number of supply partners. Thus, middle-sized suppliers such as FACC, LMI Aerospace, or Latecoere, need to cooperate in aircraft development subprojects to be recognized by their potential customers. In the end, only one of them will get the contract, but may be forced by the customer to give part of the contract away to the "competing cooperation partner."

Assessment of potential country markets

As a result of applying the selected criteria, the company possesses a shortlist of country markets ranked according to their attractiveness. For example, the high level of education of the available labor force in India has led investors from the software industry to transfer some of their capacities to that country. Another example is Japan's Shiseido, one of the world's leading marketers of perfumes. The available infrastructure in perfume development and production as well as the global reputation of the French perfume industry have made this company invest in a production site in France.

Assessment of country markets

To systematically assess the geographic sub-markets of their firm's global product market(s), managers need to select assessment criteria that are relevant to the business domain of the company (see Figure 2.3). Political risk may be a relevant characteristic, for example, if the firm's business demands local investment to be run successfully. It may be rather irrelevant, however, if the company intends to sell products to customers who do not need any after-sales service.

Which criteria are the most relevant will vary from one business to another. For a marketer of engineering services, for example, the technical norms to be followed in the country, the level of technology the country has reached, the available infrastructure, and the availability of a well-trained construction labor force may be of importance. In contrast, a firm from the fast-food industry might consider factors such as disposable household income, the availability of reliable food suppliers, the level of urbanization, or habits concerning dining out.

The information gathered on these criteria is then compared in a market exclusion procedure to find a small number of currently attractive country markets. For this group of markets, potential future changes in factors influencing their attractiveness are assessed. They will further reduce the number of attractive geographic areas in which the local product markets are to be analyzed in detail.

Selection of market assessment criteria

Assessing the attractiveness of potential country markets on a global level is a complex task. Nevertheless the cost of data gathering and the time for decision making must be kept reasonably limited. Therefore, in a first step managers will choose only those characteristics of the macro- and operating environments that:

- are relevant to their product market(s)
- can be evaluated through secondary research
- have an exclusive impact on the number of markets to be considered.

For example, the different marketing strategies of local competitors will not be considered at this stage of the process, because gathering this information will demand some primary research. But the level of economic development, the quality of local infrastructure, the number of major competitors present in the market, the price level that can be reached, or the number of potential customers may be relevant criteria in assessing the attractiveness of country markets. These data can be gathered from secondary sources. Primary sources of information are used only at later steps of the assessment process when the amount of needed data is reduced because the most attractive country markets have already been determined and only a small number of remaining local product markets have to be evaluated in detail.

Assessment criteria concerning the macro-environment

Criteria for the assessment of country markets can be most easily found in their macro-environment. For the sake of speed and cost of decision making, therefore, managers tend to use the criteria discussed in the following subsections.

Geographic proximity

The location of country markets is often used as a basis for evaluation. Minimal physical distance most often results in low psychological distance, which in turn

---

FIGURE 2.3 *Assessment of country markets*

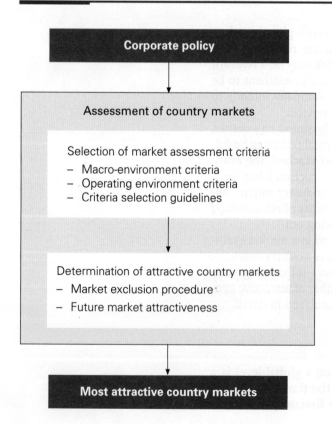

Based on corporate policy, management determines criteria from the macro-environment and the operating environment of the business unit for assessing the attractiveness of potential country markets. Following a market exclusion procedure the future attractiveness of the most attractive markets is estimated. In the remaining most attractive markets the firm's competitive position is to be determined.

leads to a perception of lower market-entry risk. Thus, a U.S. firm may perceive the Mexican market as being less risky than the New Zealand market, even if this is not the case.

Classifying countries along geographic lines sometimes makes sense. For example, if the costs of transporting a product are high relative to production costs, the company may decide to export only to neighboring countries; this helps to explain the high level of U.S.–Canadian trade. However, a different market-entry technique, such as direct investment, may be appropriate for a more distant market and yield considerably higher long-term profits.

It is tempting to argue that markets located in the same geographic area are likely to share cultural traits and geographic conditions, and that they should therefore be grouped together as a potential target market. But geographic proximity does not guarantee that two target markets will be similar. To cite just one example, Austria, the Czech Republic, and Hungary have a long history of joint political and similar cultural development. A closer examination of these countries, however, reveals that these nations differ considerably in social structure, economic conditions, language, infrastructure, and natural resources. Therefore, treating them as a single target market would not result in a reliable evaluation of their potential or lead to the best marketing decisions.

Grouping countries according to geographic proximity is rarely enough for market assessment purposes, but it does have some value. A geographic grouping makes it easier for the company to organize its structure and activities. Multinational companies such as Heineken or Exxon-Mobil, for example, structure their divisions according to geographic market clusters. Netherlands-based Heineken, the world's fourth largest brewery firm after Belgium's InBEV, Anheuser-Busch (U.S.) and South African SAB-Miller, has grouped its business into the Americas, western Europe, central and eastern Europe, Africa and the Middle East as well as Asia Pacific.

Therefore, two groupings of countries or geographic zones will be looked at in more detail: Latin America and east Asia. They are of special interest because of their supplies of critical raw materials, their fast developing economies, and their changing political and economic environments. Another geographic area, central and eastern Europe, which has aroused much interest in companies in recent years, will be examined in Chapter 3.

Latin America For decades, Latin America's economic development model was based on "import substitution," under which imports were not just discouraged, but often prohibited. But the "lost decade" of the 1980s, a decade of stagnation, inflation and debt, has led Latin America to discard its old model and look to free trade and free enterprise. Governments of the most important countries are pursuing remarkably similar free market policies, including trade liberalization, privatization, and fiscal discipline. In parallel, most countries in the subcontinent have returned to the democratic fold. Seen from that perspective, Latin America, with a booming population of 400 million, represents a market region with an interesting potential for international marketers. Not all countries are moving at the same speed, however.

Mexico Mexico, with a population of about 100 million, is the forerunner. Because of its membership in NAFTA, the economy grew at about 3% a year in the last decade. Exports to the U.S. have nearly tripled from 1994 to the present day. Metal products, machinery, and equipment reach close to 80% of total exports, 89% of which go to the U.S. Inflation had dropped from a previous 160% a year to an average of 18% over the last decade with a significant downward tendency. Tariffs inside NAFTA were dropped for most products. Communication and transportation infrastructures have improved.

But still about one-quarter of the Mexican population works in agriculture (compared to the U.S. and Canada where only 2% of the population still remain in the agricultural sector), which produces only 4.4% of its GDP. Some one-third of the Mexican government's revenues (7% of the country's export earnings) comes from Petróleos Mexicanos (Pemex), the state-owned oil company. About 10% of the population are illiterate. The average Mexican has only a sixth-grade education, and a rather low number of people have college degrees. An

MAP 2.1 *Latin America*

Source: www.lib.utexas.edu/maps/americas/latin–america.gif (6 May 2004)
Courtesy of the University Libraries, The University of Texas at Austin

improvement of the education system, key to both competitiveness and population control, is still under way.

But if properly recruited, trained, and motivated, Mexican workers can be as productive as their U.S. counterparts. Top executives at Ford, Procter & Gamble, Thomson, and Philips Electronics all rave about the quality of their workforces in Mexico. Nevertheless, Mexico's assembly-for-exports industry, dominated by U.S. investors, has seen tremendous job losses in the early 2000s. From 1.3 million jobs in late 2000, by only three years later 300,000 jobs had been lost. Scientific-Atlanta, a manufacturer of TV-top cable boxes in Ciudad Juarez, for example, laid off more than 4,000 workers between 2000 and 2002, while sending more and more work to China. In 2003, however the company rehired about 1,500 people as it sought to shorten its delivery lines.

Average per capita income of Mexicans has grown from around $3,700 in the middle of the 1990s to more than $5,500. The bases for a mass market for consumer products and services have been laid. The long pent-up demand for quality goods and services in areas such as cars, cosmetics, computers, consultancy, canned goods, clothes, and cellular phones represents an attractive business potential.

Brazil Brazil is the largest Latin American country, with an improving infrastructure and an average rate of economic growth of around 3% in the last decade. Brazil is one of the world's leading exporters of agricultural products. But it also has export-oriented automotive, metal, and chemical industries. Aracruz Celulose, for example, is one of the world's most efficient pulp producers. But Brazil also exports many consumer goods, for example, it is the largest exporter of shoes to the U.S. International tourism has also been significantly increasing. The number of tourists visiting the country rose from fewer than 200,000 at the end of the 1980s to more than 5 million in 2000.

The country's biggest problem is its high percentage of impoverished people (approximately 30% of the population of about 170 million do not have more than the equivalent of $1 a day for their living expenses). So far, the payoff from privatization and trade liberalization has gone to the higher income classes. Immediate costs are paid by the working and middle classes: companies go out of business, and workers lose jobs as firms try to become more productive. An estimated 25,000 Brazilians are still forced to work under conditions of virtual slavery. The country may face tremendous social difficulties if people do not get their share of progress.

Argentina Argentina is a typical example for the up and down economy many Latin American countries have experienced in the last 20 years. With its large agricultural sector, Argentina is among the world's most competitive suppliers of grain, soybeans, and beef. It tops the Latin American list of GDP per capita and boasts one of the most educated workforces.

After a period of strong GDP growth in 1997, starting in 1998, Argentina was hit by a combination of domestic and external factors. They included the 1998 Asia crisis, a weakening currency of neighboring Brazil, a global economic slow down after 11 September 2001, a decrease in foreign investments and increasing interest rates on loans. The economy entered a period of recession, which led to a severe financial crisis. While GDP decreased by 4.4% in 2001, it dropped by 10.9% in 2002 at an inflation rate of 26% (after three years of deflation). Only since 2003 has a certain political stabilization of the country contributed to stabilization of the economy. Even today, however, 50% of the population live below the poverty line, and 25% are unable to nourish themselves sufficiently.

Chile In contrast, Chile's growth rate of 6.3% from 1990 to 2001 – despite a recession in 1999 – beats every country in east Asia except China. The country has a market-oriented economy characterized by a high level of foreign trade.

Chilean companies are the export stars of the subcontinent, shipping copper, lumber, fruit, and even software. Chilean firms are also finding lucrative niches. Fósforos Chilenos, a matchstick manufacturer, for example, sells millions of ice cream sticks to the U.S. and is serving the Japanese chopstick market. Chile's winemakers have successfully conquered market shares in western economies. As a result, Chile's per capita income was $4,250 in 2002 up from $3,600 in 1994. The country signed a free trade agreement with the U.S. after having signed a trade pact with the EU in April 2002.

Together, these countries (including Venezuela) account for more than 90% of Latin American exports of manufactured goods. Their growth in basic industries such as steel, machinery, pulp and paper, gas, hydroelectric power, and home appliances is based on imports of capital, machinery, materials, and intermediate goods. They are attractive markets if governments can secure economic and social stability. Future issues box 2.1 discusses some pros and cons of a free trade area tying together North and South America. Despite economic reforms, and while the broad move towards private enterprise is unlikely to be reversed, governments will still come and go, and rules may change. The inevitable ups and

FUTURE ISSUES BOX 2.1

One America

Imagine: A free trade zone stretching from Port Barrow, Alaska, to Patagonia, tying all the nations of the Americas in a web of commerce and democracy. One America.

At the end of 2005 such a free trade area will be reality if the Free Trade Area of the Americas (FTAA), which was envisioned in summer of 1994 at a meeting of the trade ministers of 34 North and South American countries, comes into existence. With a population of nearly 800 million it will be the largest free trade area in the world. The entire region has a GDP of $13 trillion and $3.4 trillion in world trade. By way of comparison, the 25 member EU has 454 million people, GDP of $9.7 trillion and $1.9 trillion in world trade.

Before FTAA can take off, barriers to trade and investment are to be lifted. Free trade throughout the Americas, proponents argue, would channel investment and technology to Latin nations, radically restructuring their economies, and give U.S. firms a head start in capturing business there. Latin American imports were more than $110 billion in 2001. The U.S. could expect to supply $45 billion of those imports. Until 2010 the U.S. plans to export more to Latin America than to Japan and Europe together. Optimists hope that through this trade expansion more than 2 million additional jobs will

be created in the U.S. In Latin America free trade would gradually lift millions from poverty.

But U.S. opponents deride a hemispheric bloc as a nightmare. They argue that NAFTA is already degrading blue-collar wages, health, and environmental standards throughout North America because Mexico's wages are still low and its environmental enforcement lax. A hemisphere-wide trade pact, giving U.S. businesses a choice of poor countries in which to set up business duty free, would depress standards even more. The result would be high unemployment rates in the U.S. and a lower standard of living.

Latin American opponents charge that the heavily subsidized U.S. agricultural sector, such as soybean growers, would destroy large parts of the Latin American agriculture: A potential disaster for all countries heavily depending on that part of their economy, such as Argentina or Brazil.

There is no certainty of success in the FTAA negotiations. What each country wants most from the FTAA are concessions that the other is most reluctant to yield. Brazil, in its role as a spokesperson for the economically developing countries and co-chair of the final negotiations will have a significant influence. The divergent views of the two co-chairs, Brazil and the U.S., in the final stages of the negotiations may be too much for a successful conclusion of the FTAA on the present timetable.

Sources: Adapted from Weigel, K.G. (2003) "World trade", Troy, July, 16(7), p. 44

downs, while frustrating to European and U.S. managers, have been a particular turnoff to the cautious Japanese. They are not as well represented as in other areas of the world, leaving important markets to their competitors.

East Asia In the first half of the 1990s, south and east Asia experienced the fastest economic growth in the world. Overall GDP growth in the Asia Pacific region from Kazakhstan in the west to the Pacific island states in the east, excluding Japan, was 7.9% in 1995 and stayed at that level in the following year. Forecasts were that by the year 2000 the economies of east Asia – spanning from Japan to Indonesia – would almost certainly equal the GNP of the U.S. and total about four-fifths of that of the EU. But in 1997 Southeast Asian countries were sharply hit by banking, currency, and foreign debt crises at the same time. Economists estimate that bank bailouts cost taxpayers in Indonesia, Thailand, and South Korea an amount equal to 20% or more of one year's gross domestic product. Lost economic output equaled another 30% of one year's GDP in Indonesia, less in Thailand and South Korea.

Overall economic growth between 1990 and 2001 was reduced to 5.6% in South Korea, 3.7% in Thailand, and 3.6% in Indonesia (Table 2.1). Since 2000 the economies have stabilized. The region is back on a less steep growth path: around 6% a year. Enduring economic stability will depend on the stability of the currencies and the financial sectors.

Most nations in this area of the world practice a brand of capitalism – even if it is called a "socialist market economy" such as in the People's Republic of China – that combines industrial policy with freewheeling competition. In Singapore, for example, the government runs many industrial companies, including Singapore Technologies Group, which has joint ventures with such companies as Xerox and Pratt & Whitney.

The most dynamic economies beside China have been the newly industrialized countries (NICs) of east Asia, which first included Hong Kong (handed back to China in 1997), Singapore, South Korea, and Taiwan. Thailand and Malaysia started their development later but since then have attracted much interest. Despite the financial crisis, the NICs remained highly competitive, export-oriented manufacturing countries. Low wages, long working hours, and strong

TABLE 2.1 *Comparison of east Asian countries*

Country	Population in millions	Population urban %*	Adult literacy %	GNP per capita $	GDP average growth rate 1990–2001	Inflation average 1990–2001
China	1,287.626	37	m 92/f 78	960	9.7	6.2
Indonesia	211.716	42	m 92/f 82	710	3.6	15.8
Malaysia	23.802	58	m 91/f 83	3,540	6.2	3.6
Philippines	79.944	59	m 95/f 95	1,030	3.5	8.2
Taiwan	22.521	92	n/a	12,588	3.6	–0.1
Thailand	61.613	20	m 97/f 94	2,000	3.7	3.9
Singapore	4.164	100	m 96/f 88	20,690	6.7	0.9
South Korea	47.640	82	m 99/f 96	9,930	5.6	4.5
Vietnam	80.424	25	m 95/f 91	430	7.6	13.8

Note: Database 2003; * Database 2002

Source: Adapted from Baratta, M. (ed.) (2004) *Der Fischer Weltalmanach 2005*, Frankfurt a.M.: Fischer Taschenbuch Verlag

Despite their economic success stories, east Asian countries differ greatly in population size, urbanization, income, growth rate, and inflation.

MAP 2.2 *East Asia*

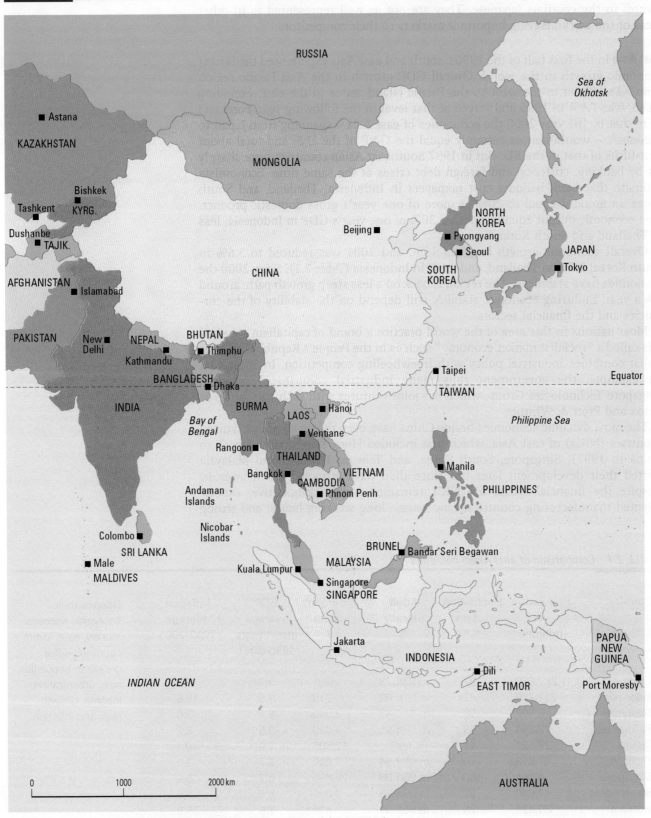

Source: www.lib.utexas.edu/maps/middle_easr_and_asia/wast_asia_pol (6 May 2004)
Courtesy of the University Libraries, The University of Texas at Austin

management have been the basic ingredients of their success. Political stability and market-oriented public policies have been top priorities. All the NICs import technology and consumer products. South Korea, for example, was the fourth-largest importer of U.S. farm products in the 1990s. But food products only reached a share of 4% of total imports in 2001, whereas machinery, electro-technical, and transportation equipment imports accounted for 35%.

The major problems of these countries are still a partial lack of modern infra-structure and an increasing lack of a highly educated workforce. In its *Asian Development* outlook, for example, the Asian Development Bank stated that Thailand and Malaysia are not producing the university graduates that their level of economic development suggests they need. The lack of a qualified workforce steadily increases production costs and demand for capital goods. In 1996, for example, car workers' wages in South Korea were already higher than those in Scotland.

In reaction to this development, an increasing amount of manufacturing has been transferred to neighboring countries with lower wages, such as China, Indonesia, or Vietnam, or even back to parts of Europe. In 2003, the world's top memory chipmaker Samsung Electronics, for example, announced that it would move most of its PC manufacturing operations to Suzhou, China, in order to increase its competitiveness against rivals such as Hewlett-Packard and Dell. Around 60% of Samsung's home appliances and more than two-thirds of its digital media products were already produced abroad in 2003. Other Korean com-panies relocating to China include LG Electronics, the country's biggest home appliance maker, which built a plasma display panel module plant in Nanjing, China, and Hyundai Heavy Industries, the world's biggest shipbuilder, which has built an excavator plant in China. Korean companies operating in China pay local workers about one-tenth what they pay their Korean workers.

On closer examination, the east Asian countries turn out to be quite different in basic economic structure, as the following shows.

South Korea South Korea has become one of the 15 largest industrial nations in the world. The country's economy is characterized by a few very large indus-trial conglomerates, called "chaebols," which, in the 1970s, were selected by gov-ernment to prosper and grow. They were granted all kinds of preferential treatments. In 2003 there were four chaebols accounting for close to two-thirds of the country's GDP and employing over half a million South Koreans: Hyundai, Samsung, Daewoo, and LG Electronics.

The financial crisis of 1997/98 hit the country very hard. Economic reforms were needed. To attract foreign capital, the government decided to privatize eight publicly owned companies in 1998, and to open up its own markets further. Despite the fact that the chaebol economy was not really changed, the country's economy recovered quickly, with growth rates of 10.8% in 1999 and 9.2% in 2000. After a short fallback in 2001, led by consumer spending and exports, growth in 2002 was an impressive 6.2%, despite the weak global economy.

Taiwan In contrast, the economy of Taiwan is characterized by a host of small and medium-sized privately owned companies with highly skilled workers and a high level of technical expertise. The companies are extremely flexible in their response to changes in customers' needs, but vulnerable to low-price competition from neighboring developing countries. In spite of the high barriers against imports erected by its government to protect the domestic economy, Taiwan has become a viable market for high technology. The high surpluses in its trade balances, in particular with the U.S., forced the Taiwanese government to open up its markets.

Compared to most of the neighboring countries, Taiwan remained largely untouched by the financial crisis of 1997/98. The Taiwan dollar's (TWD) close link to the U.S. dollar was given up during the financial turmoil. But, owing to the country's high currency reserves and very little external debts, the TWD stayed quite stable. Its devaluation was around 15%. Industry production, external trade, inflation, and unemployment rates did not show any alarming changes.

Because of its high percentage of exports to the U.S. (20%) and its strong reliance on exports of electronic products and information technology (32%) the country was more strongly hit by the economic downturn in the U.S. and the worldwide crisis of the electronics and information technology sectors. After a loss of 3.3% of GNP in 2001, the economy started to grow again in 2002 at a pace of 3.5%. Taiwan's companies continue to be important investors in the neighboring People's Republic of China, Malaysia, Thailand, the Philippines, and Vietnam. More than 50,000 Taiwanese firms have set up plants in the Peoples' Republic of China to make bicycles, handbags, sporting goods, consumer electronics, and much else that can no longer be manufactured competitively in Taiwan. Taiwanese investors have committed an estimated $60 to 100 billion to the mainland. About 600,000 Taiwanese citizens permanently work there.

People's Republic of China PRC represents a special case. It is by far the most populated country in the world (1.3 billion). With a GNP of about $960 per capita in 2002 it is the second-largest economy in the world. Since economic reforms began in 1979, China's GDP has averaged growth rates of 10% annually between 1990 and 2001. After 15 years of negotiations, China finally became a member of WTO at the end of 2001. ASEAN members have given it market economy status (dominant share of private enterprise, legal certainty). But this status has not been accepted by the U.S. and the EU yet. China's volume of exports reached $438 billion in 2003, representing more than one-quarter of global trade expansion that year, and producing a surplus over imports of $26 billion. Despite those very impressive figures, and the fact that the country dominates certain product markets such as textiles, China still does not account for more than 5% of total international trade.

Since 1990 foreign investments have increased every year. In 2002, China (including Hong Kong) attracted $66 billion in direct investments, second only to Luxembourg, which is a special case because foreign capital mainly goes to financial institutions (see Table 2.2). This is five times the amount of foreign investments in eastern Europe. In the same year, more than 150,000 companies with foreign capital – two-thirds of which were joint ventures, the rest wholly foreign-owned subsidiaries – accounted for half of China's external trade (against 5% in 1988) and employed about 10% of China's active urban population. Such economic success mainly resulted from two factors:

- economic liberalization, which allowed small private enterprise
- the set-up of so-called special economic zones along the coastline (Map 2.3), which offer preferential treatment to foreign investors (Table 2.3).

Guangdong Province, which borders Hong Kong, was the first to develop special economic zones. Today it is the most open, thriving economy in the People's Republic. It combines Taiwan's technology and financial power, Hong Kong's international marketing skills, and China's vast supplies of land, workers, and ambition. Hong Kong companies employ more than 3 million workers in thousands of factories in Guangdong Province, more than triple the number of workers in Hong Kong itself. In Guangzhou, the provincial capital (known in the west as Canton), more than 85% of households have refrigerators, and 90% have TV sets. Nevertheless, labor costs in China are still among the lowest worldwide.

One very special economic zone is Hong Kong. In 1898 the U.K. leased the "New Territories," most of today's Hong Kong, from China for 99 years. Under the terms of this contract, Hong Kong was handed back to China in 1997. But the two were already economically linked before that. Since 1978 Hong Kong had

TABLE 2.2 *Direct investments in the world (in $ billion)*

Country	Investments		Receptions	
	2002	2001	2002	2001
Belgium/Luxembourg	167,361	100,646	143,912	88,203
U.S.	119,741	102,764	30,030	143,978
France	62,547	92,974	51,505	55,190
U.K.	39,703	68,037	24,945	61,958
Japan	31,481	38,333		
Canada	28,793	36,642	20,595	28,809
Netherlands	26,270	48,514	29,182	51,244
Germany	24,534	42,079	38,033	33,918
Spain	18,456	33,093	21,193	28,005
Hong Kong	17,694	11,345	13,718	23,775
Italy	17,123	21,472		
Switzerland	11,787	17,300		
China			52,700	46,846
Ireland			19,033	15,681
Brazil			16,566	22,457

Source: Adapted from Baratta, M. (ed.) (2004) *Der Fischer Weltalmanach 2005*, Frankfurt a.M.: Fischer Taschenbuch Verlag, p. 595

TABLE 2.3 *Special economic zones*

The economic policy adopted by the Chinese government for the special economic zones along the country's coastline is quite different from the policy applied to interior areas:

1 The ownership structure of companies located there comprises state-owned, collectively owned and privately owned companies. Foreign investment may be in joint ventures or in totally foreign-owned firms

2 Policies are designed to provide incentives to foreign investors and to facilitate their entry:

- companies with foreign investment pay a reduced corporate income tax of 15%

- manufacturers with an operational period of more than 10 years are exempt from corporate income tax for the first 2 years when they start making profits and are taxed at half the rate between the third and the fifth year

- companies possessing advanced technologies may profit from an extension of another 3 years paying only half the income tax

- firms exporting more than 70% of total sales are eligible for a reduced income tax rate of 10%

- exported products (with some specified exceptions) are exempt from export duty and value-added tax

- equipment, raw materials and office supplies for own use that have to be imported are exempted from import duty and value-added tax

3 Local administrations are given more freedom to govern their local economies according to the needs of investors

invested more than $80 billion in China. With more than $16 billion of investment, however, China had become the biggest investor in Hong Kong, leading Japan and the U.S. Hong Kong will remain a special region, keeping its economic, social, and parts of the legal system as well as its autonomy for another 50 years. In June 2002 the Beijing government signed the Closer Economic Partnership Arrangement with the administration of Hong Kong. It provides for the abolition of a great number of product-related taxes and eases the entry of mainland companies to the territory.

Despite the serious economic crisis encountered in 2001 Hong Kong has at present the second-largest per capita income in east Asia, after Japan and before Singapore. It runs the busiest container port in the world. More than 30% of China's international trade transits via Hong Kong. The territory represents a major manufacturing center for watches, electronic consumer goods, toys, fashion fabrics, printing, and design. With approximately 160 banks, it is the world's third-largest center of financial transactions, behind New York and London; banking represents more than one-fifth of Hong Kong's GDP.

Its current economic problems are mainly due to:

- increasing competition from neighboring special economic zones in China. Foreign investment is increasingly going directly into those areas instead of via Hong Kong. To fully appreciate the importance of that issue: in 2001

MAP 2.3 *Special economic zones*

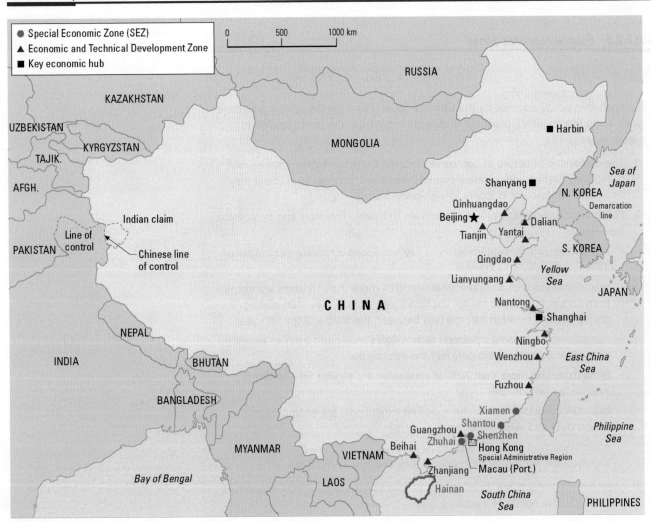

Source: www.china4visitors.com/maps/china-special-ec97-272k.jpg

direct foreign investments in Hong Kong reached a level of €378 billion, that is 256% of its GDP

- the SARS health crisis in 2003. Retail sales and tourism income slumped dramatically
- the low value of the yen having significantly decreased the inflow of wealthy Japanese tourists.

Despite social problems and bureaucratic impediments (see Future issues box 2.2), political uncertainties and cultural differences, China's market potential is extremely attractive to most international marketers. The fast economic development results in a rising demand for consumer goods, in particular foreign brands. For example, forecasts for the automotive market run at 6 to 10 million passenger cars in 2007. Companies such as Volkswagen with its Santana plant in Shanghai, Mary Kay Cosmetics Inc., which offered pink mobile phones as sales incentives when it opened its Shanghai office, or Motorola, which invested in a pager, cellular phone, and semiconductor plant in Tianjin were among the first to profit from

---

FUTURE ISSUES BOX 2.2

Explosion of social inequalities

In China the state-owned industrial sector has traditionally assured employment and social security cover for a large part of China's salaried employees. For years, it has been kept afloat shielded from competition by subsidies. Nevertheless, it had been losing the ability to pay full wages and pensions. Now, the Communist Party Congress has voted laws concerning bankruptcy, the dissolution of conglomerates and "transparency" in the top governance structures of big companies. By doing so the Congress has tackled one of several urgent economic problems China has to resolve in order to further raise its level of economic development:

1 The country has become famous for its notorious budget deficits. Coupled with high growth rates, they trigger increased inflation rates (6.2% average inflation between 1990 and 2001) that wipe out much of the improvement in people's standard of living. The government says that further spending is needed to finance the country's ongoing rural development, agricultural restructuring and social security projects. In the past 5 years, spending on social welfare has increased ninefold and spending on agriculture and education has doubled. But the government still struggles to collect revenues due from provinces, businesses, and individuals.

2 The consequences of ending the "Iron Rice

Bowl" policy of providing cradle-to-grave job security, which, in combination with widening differences in living standards between urban and rural areas as well as between provinces in the south and others in the north and center of China, could lead to social unrest. From 80 to 100 million surplus rural workers are adrift between the villages and the cities. Some 8 million additional people enter the workforce every year. Hope for millions of Chinese workers and consumers comes from economic developments similar to the southern provinces in northern cities such as Dalian, Quingdao, Changchun and Tianjin, or Chonqing and Wuhan in the center (see Map 2.4).

3 The lack of efficiency of its state-run enterprises that still lose money. The banking system has been weakened by the continued accumulation of bad debts, while the development of collective and private sectors is constrained by limited access to bank financing. Yet, the expansion of this sector is important for job growth to pick up in smaller companies and services, and to halt the rise in unemployment and informal labor.

4 Insufficient infrastructure in most parts of the country combined with the deterioration in the environment, notably air pollution, soil erosion, and the steady fall of the water table, especially in the north.

If the problems of social inequality are not reduced to a level acceptable to the less privileged part of the population, the fragile social cohesion of China may break.

that development. Fashion marketer Tom Tailor, as another example, plans to open up to 50 shops together with their joint venture partner Chinatex. Strategy box 2.2 describes how changes in the external and internal environment of a firm may put success in China at risk.

Natural environment

Evaluating country markets according to their natural environment, that is, climate, mineral resources, water supply, or other resources, may help identify markets with differing attractiveness. In some industries, such as tourism, climate plays a major role in market assessment. In tropical areas, like Papua New Guinea, climatic conditions necessitate special treatment and storage techniques to ensure proper conditions of food and water supply for tourists. Mountainous areas, like the Andes, may lack adequate transportation infrastructures. And countries that are rich in natural resources such as oil (Nigeria), productive farmland (Colombia), or iron ore (Australia) have a better chance of increasing

MAP 2.4   *The great difference between coastline and interior*

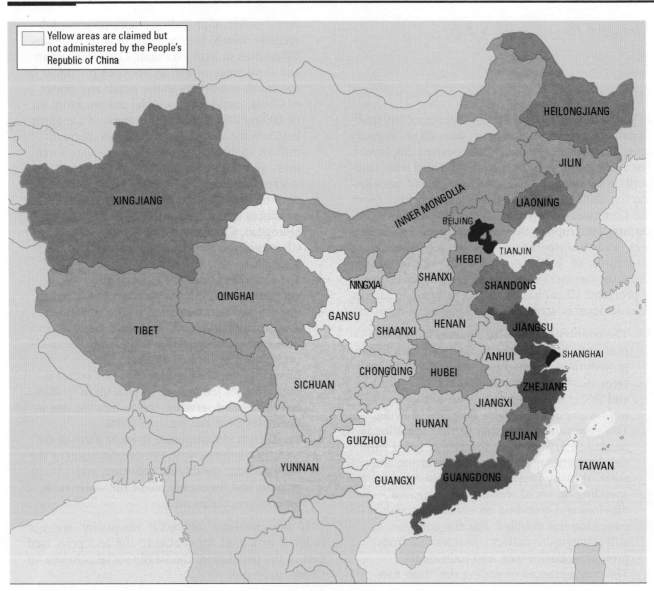

Source: www.en.wikipedia.org/wiki/Image:GDP_per_capita_China_2002.png

the purchasing power of their citizens than do countries that lack such resources. Even so, using these criteria alone is not much more effective than using geographic proximity alone; the resulting rank order of attractive markets overlooks the complexities of business systems that largely determine market attractiveness.

Political system

A country's political system may be an important criterion for the assessment of market attractiveness under the following conditions:

- business opportunities depend on the political system
- the firm's business requires big investments, such as in the oil business, which may be jeopardized by political instability
- business is done directly with the political authorities of the country.

Venezuela is an example of the strong influence of political instability on the attractiveness of a country market. Venezuela is a member of OPEC. Oil and gas constitute 80% of its exports, most of which go to the U.S. The country has used its oil income to underwrite industrial development. As a consequence, until the end of the last century the country seemed to be on an upward track. But tremendous inequalities of wealth led to the election of Hugo Chávez Frias to the presidency. Since then, political unrest has heavily hurt the country's economy. In the first quarter of 2003 GNP decreased by 29%.

STRATEGY BOX 2.2

Motorola's China challenge

With more than 240 million cell phone users, China is the world's largest mobile phone market. Motorola has long enjoyed the top position in handset sales there. Motorola's lead in the market is now shrinking, however. While still No. 1, the company is slipping. The local suppliers such as TCL and Ningbo Bird are making inroads, with stylish phones that are more in tune with the tastes of fashion-conscious Chinese consumers. Even more worrisome for Motorola, the Chinese competitors are no longer simply assembling phones based on parts they have purchased abroad. Instead, they are increasing their in-house research and development efforts. TCL, for instance, has sharply cut its purchases from French Wavecom, and has more than doubled its staff of R&D engineers.

As competition grows, China is no longer the dynamic market it once was. Growth is slowing to around 10% a year, from much higher double-digit rates during former years. A particular challenge for the company is the location of that demand. The three big and prosperous metropolitan areas – Beijing in the north, Shanghai in the east, and the Pearl River Delta in the south – are close to saturation. Now companies need to be looking more to smaller cities and the countryside for growth. That is where local competitors have a big advantage. They have well-developed distribution networks in these areas.

More than their counterparts at many other multinational companies, Motorola executives have long realized the importance of cultivating close ties with Chinese officials. CEO Christopher Galvin himself traveled frequently to China, meeting everyone from top government officials to the executives at vendors in Guangdong province. As a result, telecom analysts say that Communist Party cadres view the company with far less suspicion than they do other U.S. outfits. With the resignation of Galvin and the loss of Timothy Chen, the head of its China operations, who has gone to run the Microsoft business in China, the big question is, will Motorola be able to find new people who can keep those relationships going?

Source: Adapted from Einhorn, B. (2003) "Motorola's China challenge", *Business Week Online*

...ng the political system or situation as a criterion for assessing market ...eness presents several problems:

...classification of a country's political system is sometimes very ...lt. For example, how do you rank the levels of democracy in ...a, compared to those in Argentina, Thailand, or Ukraine?

...untry markets could be compared and grouped according to their ...itical systems, those systems may generate quite different ...es.

...in countries with relatively similar political systems and ide- ...nditions may differ significantly. For example, Cuba, North ...China are ruled by communist parties, but their economic ...the resulting business opportunities are quite different. Because ...ralized economy, **North Korea** does not have any private firms or ...gn investments from western nations. Its people are starving.

In contrast, **Vietnam** introduced *doi moi* (renewal) in 1986. At that time the country suffered from a very low GNP per capita that did not grow, a high inflation rate, and unstable currency. Since then:

- it has opened export-processing zones (e.g. in Ho Chi Min City, Hanoi, and Da Nang)
- taxes on profits of companies with foreign capital owners are limited to 15%
- profits may be repatriated
- foreigners are allowed to buy state-owned firms or to invest in wholly owned subsidiaries.

Since government has passed its Foreign Investment Law in 1987 more than 4,100 foreign direct investment projects worth $40 billion in registered capital have flowed into Vietnam. In 2003 approximately 2,100 such projects were in various stages of progress across the country. Small private enterprises flourish. In 1996, the per capita income in Vietnam did not exceed $240. But the economy has been growing at an average rate of 7.6% between 1990 and 2002 (the U.S. trade embargo was lifted in 1994). Growth rates are expected to grow around 7% until 2006. The inflation rate in 2003 was down to 3% and the currency was stable. The country is a member of ASEAN, the east Asian economic cooperation agreement. It campaigned to become a WTO member in 2005. Because of warnings that without a modern legal and public administration system in place, Vietnam's transition to a wealthy economy will run into trouble, government has taken regulatory measures such as enforcing the Enterprise Law or amending the Corporate Income and Value-Added Tax laws. Still, greater efforts need to be made on the governance agenda for the public and private sectors.

Legal system

A country's **legal system** determines the rules that govern the conduct of business in that country as well as the norms and standards that products and services have to fulfill. Because there is no international business law system, international marketers must consider the consequences of different "rules of the game" in various potential markets.

Country markets may be rated according to whether their legal systems are based on common or code law. But even when two countries belong to the same group of law systems, they may have very different regulations governing business activities. The U.K., for instance, regulates advertising more strictly than does the U.S. Thus, comparing the legal systems of country markets in general terms will not provide the precise information necessary for a full assessment of opportunities in the attractiveness of those markets. By the same token, norms and regulations specific to the business of the firm, such as the prohibition of alcoholic beverages or of wholly foreign-owned subsidiaries, as well as the imposition of import licenses, may quickly lead to the exclusion of a country market from further analysis.

Cultural and social influences

The cultural and social environment of any country strongly influences customers' needs, tastes, and expectations. The social organization of a society influences disposable income and purchasing processes. For example, who makes the decisions in the purchase of a family car? Do the children influence the choice of model, do Mom and Dad play an equal role, or does one family member dominate product choice? Education and living conditions influence product choices as well as the communication methods available to marketers. While many cultural and social characteristics play a role, here we will focus on those that are often used in the preliminary classification of markets: language and religion.

Language A nation's language (or languages) affects the way in which marketers communicate with customers and other important stakeholders in their market. The use of brochures, advertising, packaging, or training manuals, for example, is greatly simplified when the same language can be used in different country markets.

There are some drawbacks to assessing the attractiveness of markets according to their dominant language, however. Grouping together countries in which the dominant language is derived from Latin, for example, would result in a heterogeneous set of markets including Argentina, France, Italy, Peru, and Romania. Even sorting out the Spanish-speaking group, including countries such as Honduras, Mexico, Spain, and Venezuela would result in a group of very dissimilar markets. Thus, although language must be considered in assessing country markets (because the firm may have no potential to communicate effectively in this language), it cannot be used by itself as a basis for evaluating their attractiveness.

Religion Religion is an important cultural element in most societies. Many kinds of behavior, including buying behavior, are based on religious beliefs. One might think that markets in which Christianity is the dominant religion differ significantly from markets in which Hinduism, Buddhism, Islam, or Animism is dominant. Therefore, in some cases religion may represent an important criterion for determining the attractiveness of markets. For example, a New Zealand producer of lamb or a Central American producer of fruit juice might find markets highly attractive where other meat or alcoholic beverages are avoided for religious reasons, such as Saudi Arabia.

Yet a closer examination of countries with the same dominant religion reveals enormous differences between markets. In Bangladesh and India, Pakistan and Saudi Arabia, El Salvador and Italy, high percentages of the population belong to the same religion. But each market must be treated very differently, owing to other distinctions. Thus, like language, religion is an element that needs to be considered, if it is relevant to the firm's business, but it is not by itself a viable criterion for evaluating the attractiveness of markets.

Level of economic development

There are more than 190 countries in the world, and their levels of economic development range from very low to very high. Assessing market attractiveness on this basis results in groups of markets with comparable average purchasing power, demand for industrial products, and development of infrastructure. Several approaches can be used in evaluating country markets according to economic development.

Gross national product/income per capita The simplest approach is to use gross national product (GNP) or gross domestic product (GDP) per capita as a basis for classification. This results in a rank order of 10 affluent countries, with per capita GDP over $24,000, and at the other extreme, 10 countries that belong to the lowest income category, with per capita GDP below $180 (see Table 2.4).

As Chapter 3 will discuss in more detail, classifying markets on the basis of GNI or GDP alone, however, can be misleading. For example, oil- and gas-producing countries, such as Qatar, or city-states, such as Singapore, have very high national incomes and small populations. This results in a high per capita GNP figure ($27,500 for Qatar and $21,500 for Singapore in 2001), so these nations are in the same income group as Canada, Italy, or the Netherlands. However, their level of economic development is not directly comparable.

Complex indicators Inconsistent data make it even more important not to rely on one single economic criterion to assess country markets. More complex economic approaches can be used. Income measures can be combined with other characteristics of country markets such as:

- social class structure
- national resources
- environmental conditions
- level of technological sophistication

TABLE 2.4 *Poorest and richest countries 2002*

Country	GDP per capita 2002 ($)	Population in million
Democratic Republic of Congo	90	51.580
Ethiopia	100	67.218
Burundi	100	7.071
Sierra Leone	140	5.235
Guinea-Bissau	150	1.447
Liberia	150	3.295
Malawi	160	10.526
Eritrea	160	4.297
Niger	170	10.743
Tadjikistan	180	6.265
Netherlands	23,960	16.144
Sweden	24,820	8.924
U.K.	25,250	59.229
Iceland	28,590	0.284
Denmark	30,290	5.374
Japan	33,550	127.150
U.S.	35,060	288.369
Norway	37,850	4.538
Switzerland	37,930	7.290
Luxembourg	38,830	0.444

A comparison between the 10 most affluent and the 10 poorest countries in the world in terms of gross domestic product reveals a tremendous difference.

Source: Baratta, M. (ed.) (2004) *Der Fischer Weltalmanach 2005*, Frankfurt a.M.: Fischer Taschenbuch Verlag, p. 591

Der Fischer Weltalmanach 2005 © Fischer Taschenbuch Verlag in der S. Fischer Verlag GmbH, Frankfurt am Main 2004

- current infrastructure
- level of education
- cultural and behavioral variables

to create a more realistic picture of the markets in question. This approach results in groups of countries ranging from highly economically developed to economically very undeveloped (LDCs = less developed countries).

Although evaluating country markets according to more complex economic indicators can be useful in the early stages of market assessment, the marketer must be aware of specific differences between markets that may be obscured by aggregate economic data. A firm that assesses developing countries as potential markets should keep in mind that there is a big difference between the well-educated and affluent members of a society and its workers, unemployed, and rural poor. Even if many urban dwellers in developing countries have the same low income as the rural population, there are significant differences between the consumption patterns of the two groups. Thus, differences in income, age, and educational level within a population together with the environment they live in give rise to different lifestyles that must be taken into account in marketing consumer products or services to developing countries.

Another factor that has to be considered is the dynamics of economic development. In the early 2000s countries like Thailand and Malaysia had not yet achieved high per capita income. Yet their populations are not only numerous but also skilled and industrious. Low wage levels, relative political stability, and industrialization programs in these countries produced respectable economic growth rates. Economic development similar to Singapore and Taiwan, their very successful neighboring countries, was under way. As a result, these countries represent markets that should not only be considered as low-cost production sites.

In 2002 **Malaysia**, for example, had already reached a higher annual GDP per capita ($3,540) than Turkey ($2,490) or South Africa ($2,500) at average growth rates of 6.2% a year since 1990. It is trying to move its economy from commodity exports to manufacturing. A large Panasonic plant near Kuala Lumpur airport produces about 1 million color TV sets a year for the Japanese market, for example. The company has also established the "Panasonic R&D Centre Malaysia" for the development of digital networking multimedia software.

At first, the use of more complex economic indicators seems to result in useful classifications for the purposes of market assessment. For example, it might be assumed that the highly industrialized countries represent a homogeneous target market for prestigious consumer durables, high-tech industrial products, and expensive services. A closer look, however, reveals that such a classification is still oriented too much toward national averages. There may be some homogeneous product markets such as for designer shoes or vinyl extruders, but what does such a classification of countries do for a marketer of ravioli or security services?

High-income nations differ in a variety of ways. Sweden's social class structure, for example, is very different from that of the U.S. (see Figure 2.4), while Japan is characterized by a system of economic cooperation that is unparalleled in either Sweden or the U.S.

Other attempts to assess the attractiveness of country markets based on their level of economic development lead to similar results. The group of nations that need technology transfer and open markets, rather than massive foreign aid, to further develop their economies, for example, includes countries such as Brazil, Morocco, or Oman. They are similar in certain respects of their economies, but goods desired by consumers in Oman are so different from those desired by consumers in Brazil or Morocco that this grouping is of limited value to marketers of consumer goods. Contrariwise, machinery and transport equipment, chemicals and cereals needed in Morocco may not be very different from those needed in Bangladesh, which depends heavily on foreign aid.

Cooperative agreements

Independent of the product market it serves, every company assessing the attractiveness of country markets must know whether the countries involved have signed cooperative agreements with others. Each type of economic cooperation has different effects on the conduct of business and the nature of competition. The following effects on international marketing can be expected:

1 *Larger markets* accompanied by opportunities for mass production, mass marketing, and more efficient use of resources. As a result, industries will increasingly move toward duality, with a few major international competitors involved in most of the product market segments at one end and small competitors focused on one segment (or a niche) at the other end. The publishing industry in Europe, for example, is already dual with a few international communication media groups (such as Pearson, Hachette, and Bertelsmann) and smaller publishers, more or less specialized.

2 *Higher income* in the cooperating markets, which in turn stimulates internal trade and creates opportunities for external suppliers of industrial goods, consumer goods, and services. When Latin American Mercosur was founded in 1995, for example, trade among the four member countries – Argentina, Brazil, Paraguay, and Uruguay (Bolivia and Chile only joined Mercosur as associated nations in 1996) – was growing very quickly. In 1997 the joint GDP of Mercosur members reached $1,208 billion. And companies adapted quickly. BASF, the German chemicals giant, for example, had production facilities for the same products in most of those countries, because of closed borders. In reaction to the creation of Mercosur, they reorganized production to avoid the duplication of products.

But external suppliers also find increased business opportunities. From the initiation of the European Common Market 1992 program in 1985 to the end of 1991, when the common market was not yet in place, the U.S.–EC trade balance, for example, moved from a $23 billion deficit in 1985 to a surplus of $17 billion in 1991.

3 The *possibility of direct investment*, to avoid tariff and non-tariff barriers and to profit from the increase in internal trade. Extended tariff barriers may result if the members of a cooperative agreement abolish all tariffs among themselves, but keep tariffs for non-members. Such a decision would automatically give a cost advantage to companies located inside the "tariff wall." Non-tariff barriers include quota regulations and administrative hurdles. During the negotiations between the EU, Japan, and the U.S. on the liberalization of international telecommunications markets, for

---

FIGURE 2.4 *Social strata: U.S. and Sweden*

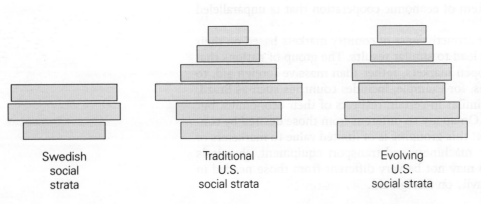

Swedish social strata

Traditional U.S. social strata

Evolving U.S. social strata

Sweden and the U.S. have traditionally had a similar social class distribution (although the U.S. has a lower class that is larger than its upper class). Due to factors such as dual career households as well as governmental taxation policies, the U.S. distribution seems to be changing: Upper and lower classes are increasing, while the middle class is shrinking.

example, a goal of the U.S. negotiators was the abolition of restrictions on foreign ownership of telecommunications infrastructure in Belgium, France, and Spain.

4 An *increase in the number of mergers, acquisitions, and alliances* initiated by firms inside as well as outside cooperative agreements. In the wave of cross-border transactions following the creation of Mercosur, for example, Indufren, an Argentinian autoparts maker, has sold half of its capital to two Brazilian companies, Cofap Cia. Fabricadora de Pecas and Freios Varga SA, so all three companies can gain better access to the other country's auto industry. In the European brewing industry, as another example, Heineken and InBEV have taken strong positions across Europe by acquiring local breweries or even substantial competitors such as Brau Union AG (acquired by Heineken), a major player in central and eastern Europe.

Acquisitions may help foreign firms ensure that a local subsidiary avoids the negative effects of cooperative legislation that might confront a "pure" foreign firm. Such subsidiaries are also able to take advantage of subsidized research programs within a cooperative agreement, which would not be available to the foreign firm on its own.

Economic cooperation among countries does not mean, however, that customer expectations, tastes or behavior become unified. Even if international comparative studies on consumer lifestyles show a tendency to similar segments, which exist across country borders, the contextual situation varies considerably from one country to another, and therefore customer behavior may also vary. This can lead to people in different countries doing the same thing for different reasons; but equally it can lead to people in different countries doing different things for the same reason. Despite increasing similarities inside economically cooperating regions, customer habits, norms and standards, infrastructure, the educational level of the labor force, and the level of salaries as well as taxes will stay different over a substantial amount of time. Closer economic cooperation mainly intensifies competition, allows companies to profit from regional cost and regulatory differences, and makes international business easier, but it does not allow companies to choose a country market without closer examination of its specific environments.

Assessment criteria concerning the operating environment

Besides criteria concerning the macro-environment, international marketers may use criteria concerning the operating environment relevant to their business to assess the attractiveness of country markets. Again, to make the assessment process fast and cost efficient, criteria demanding secondary data will be preferred to criteria necessitating primary research.

Structure of the operating environment

An important factor influencing a country market's attractiveness may be the structure of the local operating environment. The company should know who, besides potential customers and competitors, are the major stakeholders in its product market, what interests they have, and what influence they can exert on market processes. The marketer will find it easier to build customer relationships if the structure of customers, intermediaries, and other buying decision influencers, such as media, consultants or administrators, in the country market to be assessed is comparable to the structure in currently served markets.

Substance of local product market

The substance of a local product market is determined mainly by:

- size, that is, the number of customers
- their purchasing power or investment expenses
- their creditworthiness
- rate of growth.

Size A product market's size may be expressed in terms of sales, measured in some standard unit such as tons, or in terms of value (currency unit volume); the latter is referred to as market volume (see Toolbox 2.1).

Rate of growth The rate of growth can be viewed as an indicator of the product's lifecycle stage. Early stages are associated with greater potential, growing market volume, and an improving return on investment. Later stages are characterized by stagnant or declining sales accompanied by low potential return on investment for new entrants to the market. For example, compact disc sales grew rapidly in Europe in the early 1990s. Many marketers were entering the market, their sales were rising rapidly, and their profits were increasing. But when market growth slows, as in CD markets at the end of the 1990s, marketers will be faced with lower profits as they increase promotion but lower prices in an attempt to keep sales active.

Besides the local product market's current growth rate, the company should consider potential additional sales that may be generated through its specific

---

TOOLBOX 2.1 Estimating market volume

There are different ways to estimate the volume of a geographically defined product market. If neither the number of customers nor their purchasing power can be determined from available statistics, total exports of similar products from the most important industrialized countries may provide a simple estimate of market volume. However, such an estimate does not account for exports from the country in question or for the activity of domestic competitors. Management can compare the size of industries in served country markets to the approximate size of the same industries in a potential market. Relating those figures to the market share attained in served markets and expressing market share in terms of total sales leads to a rough estimate of the market volume in the potential market.

If the company is internationally active in business-to-business markets and management has some indications about the approximate size of customer industries in a potential market compared to served markets, it can estimate the volume of the potential market based on the company's market share achieved in served markets expressed as share of the firm's total sales.

For example, when a Luxembourg-based producer of small electrical motors, which is active in EU markets, wants to estimate the market volume for its products in Brazil but cannot get any reliable national statistic for this special product market, management can proceed as shown in Table 2.5. They take Portugal as a basis for comparison, because it is the industrially least developed of its served EU markets. First, they list industries that are potential clients of their products, such as manufacturers of do-it-yourself tools, pumps, food, and chemical products. Then they evaluate the size of those industries and the competitive position of their company in the respective product market segments. The firm's market shares in the different parts of the Portuguese product market are then expressed as shares of total sales of small electrical motors in Portugal. Multiplying the result of a comparison of the size of relevant industries in Portugal and Brazil by those sales figures finally leads to a (very rough) estimate of the probable size of the product market in Brazil.

If more market data are available, more complex indicators can be used to estimate market volume. The volume of the market for disposable nappies, for example, can be estimated from the number of babies born per year, minus deaths, weighted by average household income. Although such a simple indicator does not take into consideration consumption behavior or the activities of competitors, it will give the marketer a good estimate of the approximate size of the market.

marketing mix. As described in Toolbox 2.2, the potential of total sales in a market is never totally exhausted. By applying gap analysis, the marketer can determine the firm's potential to expand the current total sales volume in this

TABLE 2.5 *Estimating market volume*

Industry	Industry size and firm's competitive position in served market	Market share[1] in %	Total sales[1]	Industry size in potential market	Estimate of product market volume
DIY tools	Small, strong position	40	.....	3x bigger?	.....
Pumps	Small, weak position	15	.....	???	.....
Food	Big, strong position	60	.....	7x bigger?	.....
Chemical	Small, strong position	35	.....	5x bigger?	.....

Comments

[1] In product market related to served industry

TOOLBOX 2.2 **Gap analysis**

The assessment of gaps between the current treatment of markets and the aspirations of the various stakeholders reveals potentials for increasing the total sales volume of the market (see Figure 2.5).

The current volume of total sales achieved by the firm and its competitors may be increased through a stimulation of use (usage gap), an expansion or intensification of distribution (distribution gap), or an improvement of the product line (product line gap). By analyzing the gaps in a country market and their extent the marketer may estimate the potential additional sales to be generated through a specific marketing mix.

FIGURE 2.5 *Gap analysis*

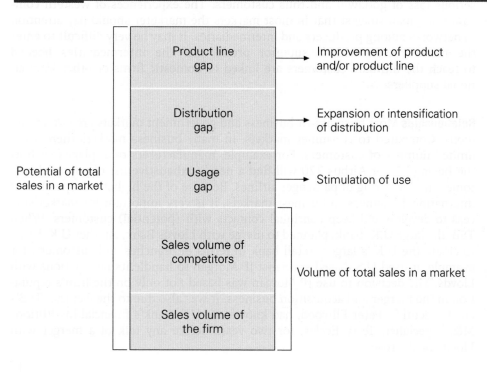

market. Even such a rather complex approach to the estimation of market substance, however, will not reveal regional concentrations of potential customers, local customs regarding product use, and other special market characteristics.

Accessibility of local product market

Accessibility refers to the marketer's ability to reach the potential customers in a country market effectively. To be successful, an international marketer must be able to reach the customers by means of communication and distribution.

The accessibility of local product markets strongly depends on the availability of appropriate distribution channels and transportation, communication infrastructure, suppliers, and labor force as well as legal measures and administrative procedures.

Distribution channels A marketer needs to obtain information about available intermediaries, including their:

- organization
- negotiation power
- capital equipment
- relatedness to competitors of the firm
- approach to doing business
- level of information
- portion of the market
- product range.

If no appropriate intermediaries exist, international marketers may have to invest considerably to enter a new country market effectively. The special conditions faced by marketers in LDCs have already been described. But even in highly industrialized countries there may be special problems to overcome. For example, in Japan it is unusual to transfer business from one intermediary to another. There, close inspection of potential intermediaries is more important than in other countries, such as Germany, where such changes can be made without a serious loss of goodwill and thus customers. The experiences of western companies in Japan suggest that in most markets the marketer should pay attention to networks among producers and intermediaries. It may be very difficult to enter the market, even with a superior product, if the intermediaries needed to reach the ultimate customers are linked to domestic firms or other international suppliers.

Relationships Most business-to-business and government markets are not anonymous. Compared to consumer markets, in many business markets there are a limited number of customers. For example, manufacturers of airplanes such as the Boeing 777 or Airbus 320 will find a nearly exhaustive list of potential customers in any listing of passenger airlines. Because of the higher transparency of international business-to-business markets, it is very important for market success to develop and keep continual contacts with (potential) customers. When TSB, the large U.K. bank, planned to merge with Lloyds Bank, another U.K. bank, to create the U.K.'s largest retail bank in terms of branches and customers, for example, it used U.S.-based specialist JP Morgan to handle its negotiations with Lloyds. The decision to use JP Morgan was based not only on the firm's reputation in the merger and acquisition business. It was also due to the fact that TSB's chief executive, Peter Ellwood, had known the U.S. bank's financial institutions M&A specialist, Terry Eccles, for two years before any talk of a merger with Lloyds Bank arose.

Close customer contacts are based on local presence. Some form of strategic partnership or direct investment may be necessary to gain access to local public administration/government markets. Inside the EU, public administrations are forced to call internationally for tenders and treat EU member firms equally, independent of their nationality. But well-covered "buy national" tendencies persist.

Suppliers When evaluating potential suppliers of services, parts, or systems, management should consider:

- size and number of such firms
- potentially available substitutions
- importance of supplied service or good to their firm's product
- importance of their firm as a customer of the suppliers
- threat of potential forward integration (when the supplier gains control of the next level of distribution, towards the customer) by the supplier.

Like intermediaries, suppliers may be linked to certain competitors. Companies such as Ford, Honda, and Volkswagen commonly sign long-range contracts with (or even hold equity shares in) their suppliers. These may be producers of metal sheets (such as Thyssen-Krupp, the largest supplier of this product category in Europe), electrical systems (for example, Germany's Bosch), air-conditioning equipment (for example, Webasto, headquartered near Munich), or entire cars (such as Canada's Magna producing models for Daimler-Chrysler and BMW). The suppliers conform strictly to the customer's product specifications and may profit from its technical and financial assistance.

Even in such cases, however, supply risks should be evaluated. If a manufacturer relies on just-in-time delivery of parts, disruptions of supply can be very expensive. Quality is also critical. Local suppliers in China, Indonesia, or

Many auto firms have strong links with suppliers

© Aravind Teki/iStock

Vietnam, for example, may seem attractive because of the low wage rates in these countries. But they do not always have the skilled labor force necessary to deliver consistently high-quality parts for sophisticated products.

Labor force The number of potential employees seeking a job and – more importantly – their level of education and skills have a direct impact on a company's potential success in the market. So does the existence of strong labor unions. In the 1990s, many joint ventures in eastern Europe, for example, experienced serious trouble because of the lack of personnel with the management training expected in their western counterparts. Cultural factors must also be considered. Western companies that have established sales and service offices or subsidiaries in Japan, for example, have found to their great dismay that few Japanese like to work for foreign companies. And if they are ready to do so, they expect substantial increases in salary.

Legal measures and administrative procedures Legal measures such as restrictions on import licenses or advertising can be effective barriers to entry in a market that would otherwise seem attractive to the company. For example, because of its enormous population and entrenched smoking habits, the Chinese market looks very attractive to every tobacco products marketer. However, legal restrictions on tobacco advertising – China has adopted total bans on all forms of tobacco promotion, including posters and magazine ads – reduce this attractiveness. They force marketers to creatively circumvent the bans. BAT, as an example, not only sponsored the great China bicycle race, which allowed it to be in all major media, but also endowed a chair at the China Europe International Business School in Shanghai.

Responsiveness of local product market

Responsiveness refers to whether potential customers and intermediaries in a market will react favorably to the company's offer. First guesses may be wrong in this respect. For example, Shredded Wheat has never become well accepted in the French market because it is too "British." Yet the very "American" McDonald's, despite first guesses that such a style of eating, alien to French habits, would never be accepted by local customers, has become a big success in France.

To avoid the risk of guessing, it seems reasonable to determine first the most important factors that influence a market's responsiveness. However, such an analysis may require primary research that may be too expensive for many smaller firms at that stage of international marketing decision making. To get a low-cost but reliable estimate of how responsive potential customers in a market might be to the company's offer, international marketing managers can evaluate current direct or indirect contacts with customers from that market. Fasti, a small Austria-based firm manufacturing special machines to dehydrate plastic granulates, for example, when assessing the attractiveness of Far Eastern markets, analyzed some business deals that had been solicited from customers in those markets. The firm also analyzed how much business it did already in Far Eastern markets through indirect customer contacts, that is, via manufacturers of plastic extrusion machines located in Europe and the U.S.

Other indicators of the responsiveness of a local market may be:

● *cultural or political prejudices*, which strongly influence the image of the international marketer's home country. In many European markets, for example, products manufactured in Germany, such as passenger cars or machinery, profit from a cultural prejudice that attributes particular technical skills and superior reliability to Germans

● *level and kind of a country's predominant international commercial relations.* These can be a good indicator of market responsiveness. If potential customers in a market are used to having business contacts with suppliers from the marketer's home country, it will be easier to approach them.

Intensity of competition

Product market attractiveness also depends on the intensity of competition in the market. Therefore, the major current and potentially arising competitors, their number, market position, competitive strategy, and expected reactions to the market entry of a new contender have to be determined. A competitor's reactions will depend on the new firm's strengths, weaknesses and strategy, as well as the competitor's view of the threat posed by the new firm. The impact of competitive reactions on the company's success will depend on their intensity and speed. The marketer, therefore, should analyze the predictable reactions of competitors to find out if entry to a potential market is attractive or not (see Chapter 6 for an intensive discussion).

Profitability

If a local product market is substantial, accessible, and responsive to a marketer's product and the intensity of competition seems to be acceptable, the product market has to be checked for its potential profitability. The estimated income generated by closing a deal effectively with an individual customer has to be compared with the estimated costs it would take to arrive at that point plus the costs of performance delivery. A product market should not be considered attractive until this analysis has been finished with a positive outcome. Market dynamics have to be considered, however. Italy-based Generali, one of Europe's international insurance companies, for example, accepted substantial losses in Hungary from 1990 to 1994. But as one of the very few insurance companies that invested in this newly opened market, it achieved a comfortable market share position, which allowed it to transfer its first earnings to headquarters in 1995.

Criteria selection guidelines

Corporate objectives and priorities can be used to guide the decision of what criteria are most relevant for assessing the attractiveness of potential markets.

Return on investment

If a company seeks a high return on investment, it must select markets in which it can achieve a leadership position, in which demand is high in relation to supply, and in which customers have sufficient purchasing power. Therefore, the size of competitors present in the market, the ratio of market potential to market volume, and the economic wealth of potential customers will be relevant criteria for market attractiveness.

Level of technology

Companies that give a high priority to technological innovation tend to favor country markets characterized by high levels of technological sophistication, such as Japan, where customers seek technical solutions that require significant research and development. Other companies prefer markets in which their level of applied technology fits the needs of the targeted customers. Thus, traditional producers of hand scythes located in the area south of Steyr (Austria), may not find enough customers in EU markets any longer, but may be very interested in potential markets in sub-Saharan Africa. Relevant market assessment criteria in those cases might be the level of technological sophistication reached in a country, the quality of its infrastructure, or the availability and quality of higher education institutions.

Global identity and goodwill

Companies that rely on their global identity and the goodwill of intermediaries, customers and suppliers will look for markets in areas where their home country or company name has already earned a positive reputation. A Danish marketer of food products such as yoghurt, cheese, pork, or bacon, for example, will focus on markets where Denmark is known as a country that manufactures high-quality food. It will not consider markets in which Danish products are avoided for ideological, political, or religious reasons. In such cases, managers will find criteria such as volume of imports, amount of political influence on individual firms, legal restrictions concerning the product market, or influence of religion on purchase decisions relevant for the assessment of market attractiveness.

Level of independence

Finally, the organization's priorities regarding independence or strategic cooperation may also influence the relevance of characteristics for the evaluation of country markets. A company such as IBM may want to maintain total control over its special technical know-how. It will not consider country markets in which wholly foreign-owned subsidiaries are prohibited and joint ventures can only be started if the transfer of the entire production know-how is guaranteed, as is the case in some developing nations. Contrariwise, a small company with limited financial resources might look for country markets where strong potential co-operation partners are located. They can help speed up the increase of the global product market share held by the firm. Therefore, both companies might find it useful to apply criteria such as legal regulations concerning activities of foreign firms or the importance of competitors in the country market.

Determination of attractive country markets

Market exclusion procedure

As the assessment of country markets progresses, markets are classified by the chosen criteria to narrow their number to the markets of greatest attractiveness (Figure 2.6). The exclusion procedure consists of:

1 a stepwise application of knockout criteria
2 or a grouping of markets into homogeneous clusters and a subsequent ranking of the remaining markets through a scoring model.

Stepwise market exclusion

When excluding markets step by step, the marketer applies evaluation criteria, which allow the immediate exclusion of country markets if they do not reach a given standard. For example, a producer of cellular communication equipment, such as Sweden-based Ericsson, may exclude large parts of sub-Saharan Africa from further investigation because it lacks the needed infrastructure. From the remaining markets, some may have technical norms (they use a specific communication technology) that the company is unable or does not want to fulfill. The reduced number of markets is further diminished when all country markets are deleted where legal restrictions, such as state monopolies or the requirement of import licenses, make market entry extremely difficult. Finally, the list of potential markets may become even shorter if Ericsson's top management has set ethical standards that do not allow serving certain markets.

The major advantage of this market exclusion procedure is its simplicity and speed. The use of assessment criteria that lead directly to the elimination of a number of country markets is appropriate, if the criteria are:

- directly related to the corporate policy of the firm such as ethical standards

• or represent critical features of the chosen product market such as the level of electrical supply infrastructure for a marketer of refrigerators.

There are several disadvantages to be considered, however.

The *application of knockout criteria* tends to support market assessment dependent on the firm's current strengths and weaknesses. Even very promising markets will not be further considered if, currently, the firm does not possess the needed skills and resources to serve them successfully. For example, when RSB-Roundtech, introduced earlier in the chapter, assesses the attractiveness of international markets in the field of sewage treatment plants, they may use "current customer relations" and "available language skills" as part of the assessment criteria. The result may be a restricted choice of markets: the potentially attractive U.S. market will not be considered further, because the company does not have any relations with customers there, and all Portuguese-speaking countries are ruled out because of lacking language skills.

The *stepwise use of assessment criteria* does not consider trade-offs between different market characteristics. For example, the quality of available telecommunications and transportation infrastructure in Ukraine might not be up to the level of neighboring Poland, but labor costs are lower. If both factors are of importance to a firm, such as a Korean manufacturer of cars considering investing in Europe, it is important to use them simultaneously when comparing the attractiveness of the markets. Market clustering based on a set of assessment criteria is an appropriate solution.

Market clustering

The procedure used in market clustering consists of the following steps:

1 Splitting the global product market into groups of geographic sub-markets in a way that the resulting clusters are more homogeneous than the global market as a whole.

FIGURE 2.6 *Determination of attractive country markets*

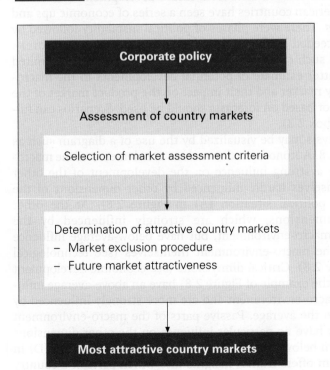

As the assessment process of country markets progresses, markets are classified by the chosen criteria to narrow their number to the markets of greatest attractiveness.

2 Describing the "typical" member in each cluster.

3 Evaluating the attractiveness of each cluster.

4 Choosing the most attractive clusters for further analysis.

Country markets will be most effectively clustered with criteria that consider the specifics of the served product market. Characteristics often used include:

- product-related purchasing power of potential customers
- product market growth rate
- profit generation potential
- transferability of funds
- number and size of competitors (intensity of competition)
- availability of intermediaries
- local subsidies readily available to the company.

Assessment and market selection in such a case depend on strategic considerations, not just on easily accessible, general data about the macro-environment of potential markets. For example, Japanese and U.S. companies, such as Dell Computers, entered the markets of the European Community via Ireland. They did so because wages are relatively low and the Irish government offered high subsidies for new industrial plants.

The country markets that fulfill the set conditions will remain in the group of attractive markets to be further investigated. If the number of these markets is still too big to allow a quick and cost-efficient analysis of details, a scoring procedure can be used to rank the markets according to their relative attractiveness. Only for the high ranked markets will future developments be estimated.

Future market attractiveness

In many instances, the decision to serve a country market commits the firm's resources for a considerable amount of time. Therefore it should not be based on the current attractiveness of a market alone but should also consider potential changes in market attractiveness that arise from future developments.

For example, Latin American countries have seen a series of economic ups and downs in the last 20 years. There were phases of political instability followed by economic expansion, succeeded by financial problems and subsequent recovery. Forecasting techniques in such cases are either unreliable or have a very limited time horizon. To get a better estimate of potential developments in the macro-environments of a country market and their impact on the product market of the firm, a technique that is not based on forecasts should be used. Scenarios can fulfill this demand (see Toolbox 2.3).

The results of this analysis may be visualized by the use of a diagram such as the one shown in Figure 2.8. Autonomous dimensions are elements of the macro-environment, which have a strong influence on the development of the other dimensions but are themselves hardly influenced by other dimensions of the macro-environment (see political situation (A) in Figure 2.8). At the other extreme are reactive dimensions, which are strongly influenced by the other dimensions of the macro-environment, but have below-average influence on the development of the macro-environment themselves (see technological development (B) in Figure 2.8). Critical dimensions (see economic development (E) and legislation (C) in the example of Figure 2.8) have an above-average influence on the rest of the macro-environment and are more strongly influenced by the other dimensions than the average. Passive parts of the macro-environment are those dimensions that have no particular influence on the other dimensions and are influenced by them below average (see the existing infrastructure (D) in Figure 2.8). Such a diagram offers fruitful insights into which parts of a country market's macro-environment – the critical and autonomous dimensions – are to be more closely watched than others.

When a time horizon is fixed for the analysis (one possibility would be to take the time needed to enter the market plus 5 years), potential future developments with respect to each factor of influence on each dimension of the macro-environment can be formulated. They describe the potential extreme states of development of the factors at the time horizon. For example, the development of photovoltaic technology may come to a complete stop because there are no results that can be commercialized, or, at the other extreme, may have reached a point where every household can produce the energy they need during daytime.

TOOLBOX 2.3   The scenario technique

The scenario technique is a strategic planning technique. It uses systems analysis to identify the relationships between the essential dimensions of the macro-environment that influence the company and its operating environment. For a U.S. manufacturer of electric power plants, for example, important dimensions of the U.K. macro-environment may be the political situation, technological development, legislation, existing infrastructure, and the development of the economy. Each of these dimensions must be specified by relevant factors of influence on the company's product market. Relevant factors of technological development concerning the market for electrical power plants may be, for example, the development of anti-pollution equipment, security technology for atomic power stations, and the further development of photovoltaic technology.

The dimensions of the firm's macro-environments are interdependent. This complexity

is reduced to a matrix showing the degree to which the dimensions of the macro-environment (represented by the factors of influence) interact. That is, the matrix shows to what extent the dimensions actively influence the developments in the country market's macro-environment, or to what extent they are influenced by other dimensions (Figure 2.7). For that purpose, the influence of each dimension on each other dimension is estimated on a scale from 0 (no influence at all) to 3 (very strong influence). When the lines of the matrix are summed, each sum expresses the influence of the respective dimension on all the others in the macro-environment. The sums of the columns stand for the potential of the rest of the macro-environment to influence the respective dimension.

Source: Adapted from Probst, G.J.B. and P. Gomez (1989) *Vernetztes Denken, Unternehmen ganzheitlich führen*, Wiesbaden: Gabler, p. 11

FIGURE 2.7   *Matrix of interrelationships among macro-environment dimensions*

Potential of influence on → of	A	B	C	D	E	Sum A (influence)
A						
B						
C						
D						
E						
Sum B (potential of being influenced)						

When the potential states of all factors of influence are analyzed for their best logical fit, the two most highly consistent scenarios can be chosen which describe the two most different potential pictures of the macro-environment at the time horizon. The scenarios can be compared to the current situation and the country market's attractiveness under each scenario can be assessed.

The scenario approach helps to avoid focusing too much on country markets that are only attractive in the short run. The firm becomes alert to potential developments, such as changes in customers' basic values, countries' financial stability, or the development of new technologies that may have a strong impact on the attractiveness of a market.

Most attractive markets

Having analyzed the attractiveness of its product market in various country markets, marketing managers can rank the markets according to their attractiveness. To finally be able to decide which markets to serve, however, a comparison has to be made between the capabilities a firm needs to be successful in those markets and the extent to which the company possesses those capabilities compared to its major competitors. How to do such a comparison efficiently will be the subject of Chapter 6. The following Chapters 3 to 5 will provide a more detailed discussion of the impact of economic, technological, political, legal, social, and cultural factors on global marketing decision making and execution.

FIGURE 2.8 *Pattern of influences in the macro-environment*

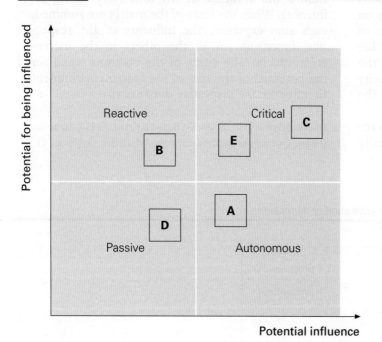

Summary

For a company that regards the entire world as a marketplace, there are many potential markets. In order to restrict the number of options to markets worth further investigation, the international marketer should go through an international market assessment procedure. Such a process of increasingly precise data collection and analysis starts with a

- definition of the product market in the company's corporate policy statement. From this definition, as well as from the company's objectives and priorities
- criteria for market assessment can be derived. Focussing on characteristics of the economic, technical, political, and legal, as well as cultural and social, dimensions of the macro-environment that are relevant for the company's product market
- country markets can be assessed and ranked according to their attractiveness.

The final ranking of country markets, however, will also depend on the viability of local product markets.

The operating environment of the company in each potential country market must be investigated. Customers are evaluated on the basis of substance, accessibility, and responsiveness. The interests, structure, quality, and potential influence of important stakeholders, such as intermediaries, suppliers, or the workforce need to be considered. Together with the intensity of competition in the local product market, they influence the potential profitability of serving a particular country market.

Scenarios of potential future developments in the macro-environment can help to evaluate potential changes of market attractiveness. The resulting short-list of most attractive country markets serves as an input to the next step of the analysis: the determination of the international marketer's competitive position in those attractive markets.

DISCUSSION QUESTIONS

1. What basic market exclusion procedures do you know? Describe their rationale and compare their pros and cons.

2. What sources of market assessment criteria can be used by a marketing manager? What are the differences between them?

3. Why is geographic proximity of a market an assessment criterion very popular with managers? Discuss its pros and cons, giving examples you have found in newspapers, magazines, and the internet.

4. Compare the latest developments in Latin American markets to the information given in this chapter. What changes have occurred? Choose a company doing business in Latin America and discuss the impact of those changes on its business.

5. How does the level of economic development influence the attractiveness of a country market? Find examples of companies to illustrate your points.

6. What information concerning the attractiveness of a local market can be derived from GNP (GDP) per capita figures? Illustrate your points by the use of examples you have found in newspapers or the internet.

7. Compare the latest developments in east Asian markets to the information given in this chapter. What changes have occurred? Choose a company doing business in east Asia and discuss the impact of those changes on its business.

8. Choose a product you are interested in and develop an estimate of the market potential and market volume of that product in a country in Europe, in Asia, in Latin America, and in Africa. Indicate what sources of information you have used, what indicators you have applied, and the pros and cons of your approach.

9. Interview managers from three internationally operating firms about the criteria they use to assess the attractiveness of international markets. How does this compare to what you have read in this chapter?

10. Ask the same managers to describe the market assessment procedure used in their companies. Discuss your findings in the light of what you have read in this chapter.

ADDITIONAL READINGS

Agarwal, J. and T. Wu (2004) "China's entry to WTO: global marketing issues, impact, and implications for China", *International Marketing Review*, 21(3), 279–300.

Bridgewater, S. (1995) "Assessing the attractiveness of turbulent markets: the Ukrainian experience", *Journal of Marketing Management*, November, 11(8), 785–96.

Ninov, N. (2004) "Determining market size: sources of market information on the web", University of Virginia Darden School Foundation, Charlottesville, VA.

Rahman, S.H. (2003) "Modelling of international market selection process: a qualitative study of successful Australian international businesses", *Qualitative Market Research: An International Journal*, 6(2), 119–32.

Tessun, F. (1998) "Air traffic – quo vadis? Scenarios for the next twenty years", *Marketing and Research Today*, November, 229–43.

Useful internet links

ABB (Asea Brown Boveri)	http://www.abb.com/
Airbus	http://www.airbus.com/prehome.asp
Aracruz Celulose	http://www.aracruz.com.br/en/
Boeing	http://www.boeing.com/flash.html
Doppelmayr	http://www.doppelmayr.com
FTAA	http://www.ftaa-alca.org/alca_e.asp
Generali	http://www.generali.it/
Heineken	http://www.heineken.com/
HILTI AG	http://www.hilti.com/
Hyundai Heavy Industries	http://www.hhi.co.kr/Korea/Default.asp
IKEA	http://www.ikea-usa.com/ms/en_US/about_ikea/our_vision/heritage.html
Mercosur	http://www.mercosur.org.uy/
Motorola Corp.	http://www.motorola.com/
Nokia Mobira Oy	http://www.nokia.com/
Novartis	http://www.novartis.com/
OPEC	http://www.opec.org/home/
RSB-Roundtech	http://www.rsb-roundtech.com/
Samsung	http://www.samsung.com/
Wikipedia (the free encyclopedia)	http://en.wikipedia.org/wiki/Image:GDP_per_capita China_2002.png
Zuegg	http://www.zuegg.it/ita/dd.htm

POTENTIAL MARKET ASSESSMENT: ECONOMIC ENVIRONMENT

3

Learning objectives

After studying this chapter you will be able to:

- explain how a country's population, natural environment, and technical resources influence its economic attractiveness to international marketers

- illustrate the influences of a country's economic system on its economic wealth

- discuss the use of various indicators of economic wealth for the evaluation of a country market's economic attractiveness to an international marketer

Chapter outline

Assessing the economic environment

Bases of economic wealth

Population
Natural environment
Technological resources
Economic system

Economic wealth indicators

National income
Balance of payments
Exchange rate
Foreign investment ratio

Economic viability profiles

Summary

INTERNATIONAL MARKETING SPOTLIGHT

Karmet Steel

When London-based LNM Group, one of the world's three biggest steelmakers, bought Karaganda-based Karmet, Kazakhstan's largest steel plant, for about $1 billion in the fall of 1995, the KGB came along with it, at no extra charge. The intelligence agency had set up shop in the Karmet steel plant in the 1940s, when Stalin built the mill as a work camp. When the plant was sold to the British firm, more than a dozen agents refused to leave their electronically sophisticated corner office.

For LNM, ousting the KGB may have been the least of its worries. The company faced a tough test on the Kazak steppe, on the edge of Siberia. Following some failed government attempts to sell the plant to its managers, Kazakhstan's most important industrial asset, and the source of 10% of its gross domestic product was near collapse in the summer of 1995. Yet while Karmet lingered near death, its managers lived like kings. On Lenin Avenue, across from the plant, Karmet's former directors built a lavish guesthouse complete with several restaurants, a massage parlor, and a disco. The company spent $1 million on armchairs alone. Hundreds of Karmet's employees came to work drunk. (After taking over, Ispat fired about 100 people a week for coming to work drunk and others for allegedly cheating the company by getting paid for two jobs but working only one.) There were at least 10 management layers (as one new manager put it: "Everyone has got his assistant and his assistant and his assistant"); and the biggest customer was broke.

Because LNM was the first Karmet owner in years to have any money, it was quickly viewed as a soft target. Soon after the new owner had taken over, a man claiming to represent a society for the blind asked the company for donations. If Karmet would donate steel, he said, the society could resell it and raise money. After the company agreed, 68 other societies for the blind turned up.

But the worst problem was the dearth of orders. In the former Soviet Union Karmet's steel was used to make half of all tin cans produced in the country. With that demand almost gone, Karmet had to sell about 90% of the plant's products outside the Commonwealth of Independent States. Today, production has climbed from 2.2 million tons in 1995 to over 5.2 million tons. Most of this goes to China. Karmet wants to ship more there, but it is thwarted because the railway gauges, which are different in China, create a bottleneck. Trains loaded with steel must stop at the border, where the load is shifted onto a train that can run on Chinese tracks.

Kazakhstan, the last of the former Soviet republics to declare its independence, desperately needs Karmet to work. Karaganda is a poor, isolated region. Employing roughly 50,000 workers, the revitalized plant is the region's key engine of economic development.

Source: Adapted from Pope, K. (1996) "Blast from the past, troubled Kazak mill is testing the mettle of British steelmaker", *Wall Street Journal Europe*, 2 May, pp. 1 and 6; Balakrishnan, P. (2003) "L.N. Mittal: the king of steel", rediff.com, 27 September

The focal question of this chapter is: What are the relevant dimensions of the economic environment of the company's served product market, how are they shaped in the geographic markets under consideration, and what impact do they have on the attractiveness of those markets?

Assessing the economic environment

The macro-environment of a company strongly influences the structure and state of its operating environment, which, together with the firm's resources and capabilities, determines its potential success. The economy of a country is a major part of each company's macro-environment. It is a complex system of interdependent local, regional, and international forces. Besides purely economic factors such as the economic system or the current industrial sectors, a modern economy is characterized by:

- skills and flexibility of its population
- available infrastructure and level of technology
- level of relative ecological balance.

These factors constitute essential bases of a country's economic wealth.

A marketer serving international markets or planning to go international is confronted with a greater number of economic environments. Therefore, when considering which country markets' operating environments to analyze more closely or how much of the firm's resources to invest in which of the currently served country markets, the international marketer will have to run through a sequence of analytical steps as follows (Figure 3.1):

1 The *marketer has to determine the characteristics of the economic environment* that are relevant for the company's business domain. For example, a producer of food products such as Very Fine Products Inc., a Littleton, Massachusetts-based juice manufacturer, may define the economic system, population size and age structure, disposable household income, level of urbanization, climate, transportation, communication and distribution infrastructure, the currency exchange rate, and the country's level of economic development as important characteristics of the economic environment.

2 Having determined the relevant factors of influence, the marketer will need to analyze *their current state in the country markets under consideration.*

FIGURE 3.1 *Analyzing the economic environment*

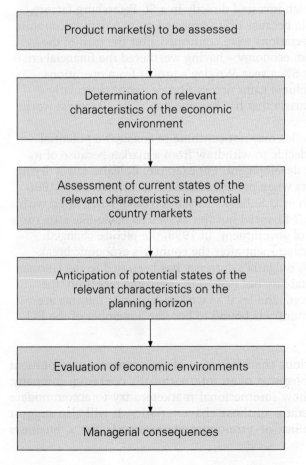

In analyzing the economic environment of the firm, the marketer first has to determine which factors are relevant to the product market(s) the company is serving. Then the current state of international, regional, and local factors of influence can be assessed and their potential states on the planning horizon anticipated. From the results of the analysis, managerial consequences concerning the further treatment of the analyzed country markets may be drawn.

A full evaluation of the impact of those factors on the potential success of the firm will only be possible, however, if the following point is considered.

3 *Management must also try to anticipate the potential states of the relevant factors on the planning horizon.* For example, economic factors such as 10 years' economic stagnation and reduced tariffs helped to increase significantly Japanese purchases of imported food in the 1990s. Recession has fostered innovations in the traditional distribution system of the country. Discount retailing, convenience stores, and direct-delivery services have grown. Such developments, helping non-Japanese food marketers to enter the market, will not be dropped when the economy starts booming again. Because of international agreements, tariffs can be expected to stay low in the coming years. The exchange rate of the yen to other currencies is more volatile, however. International marketers who had based their success mainly on the strong yen in the first half of the 1990s have found themselves driven out of the market when the dollar appreciated strongly in 1997/98.

4 *An evaluation of the economic environments in the country markets of interest* considering their current states and their potential developments, allows the marketer to decide how to "manage" those environments. That is, management will be able to find ways of specifically reacting to the expected developments. It may decide to invest in a market with an interesting future potential, which currently would not be attractive enough. For example, Russia in 1996 had an inflation rate around 35%, gross domestic product had been falling since 1991, its economic reform had remained a patchy process, and the task of making privatized factories efficient and internationally competitive had only just begun. Nevertheless, companies such as world-leading chewing-gum maker Wm. Wrigley Jr. Co., which invested directly in a St. Petersburg factory, decided in favor of Russia because of its expected more positive economic development. Their expectations were confirmed after the turn of the century when the Russian economy – having weathered the financial crisis of 1998 – grew by about 6% a year. Wrigley's profits from operations increased due to solid volume gains across Europe, with particularly strong performance in Russia that has become one of its 10 largest world markets.

In other cases, companies may not continue to consider a potential country market or may decide to withdraw from a market because of its unsatisfactory economic development. For example, Bulgaria saw a drying up of foreign investments when privatization was at a standstill in 1996. Interested investors such as U.S.-based Texaco retreated when faced with a jungle of bureaucratic and financial hurdles as well as mafia-like structures up to the highest levels of government. In 1998, the picture changed: Following a change in government after the country's economic break-down in winter 1996/97, Bulgaria's currency has been tied to the German Mark. Macroeconomic stability has helped to overcome recession, the national budget is balanced, and legal as well as economic reforms are slowly under way. The country is bound to become a member of the EU in 2007.

This chapter will discuss various characteristics of the economic environment that may be relevant to the business of an internationally operating company. It will provide examples of how international marketers try to accommodate the current and anticipated status of those characteristics. It will also suggest a way to evaluate the viability of economic environments for a business organization.

Bases of economic wealth

The economic wealth of a country is based on its human, natural, and technical resources. These resources affect a country's ability to produce globally competitive goods and services and to offer a viable market for such products. The human resources of a country are the most important factor of influence on its economic wealth. Factors such as:

- population composition and distribution
- degree of urbanization
- the available capabilities in a country's population

that are based on the level of education, skills, flexibility and mobility of people, determine how well the natural resources of a country can be used and how far the country's technical resources are developed.

Natural resources and geographic features, such as topography and climate, are a second important basis of economic wealth.

Technological resources available to a country, such as energy, transportation, communications, and commercial infrastructure, also have a strong impact on its economic wealth.

Finally, the skillful use and maintenance of all available resources also determines a country's level of economic development. How resources are used is largely influenced by the economic system of the country. The better this system allows building and using the bases of economic wealth in a sustainable manner, the more economically attractive the country will be for an international marketer.

Population

The size of a potential local product market is a key element in its viability. Therefore, the total population of a country and its growth rate are of interest to many international marketers. Besides these two factors, the distribution of age groups and the degree of urbanization may have a strong impact on market attractiveness. The degree of urbanization represents concentrations of potential customers. The distribution of age groups in a country is closely related to the demand for certain products, to the availability of labor, and to potential economic problems if there is an imbalance between young and old people.

Size and growth

Many international marketers are interested in rapidly developing product markets in China and India. The two countries together represent some 70% of Asia's population (about 2.4 billion consumers) and close to 40% of the population of the world. The higher population also helps to explain why the U.S., the EU and multinational cooperative agreement areas like the Mercosur have so much appeal to many international marketers. Clearly, the size of the population and its rate of growth affect a society's ability to progress economically and provide for the future.

The **population growth rate** is defined as the increase in a country's population during a period of time, expressed as a percentage of the population at the start of that period. It reflects the number of births and deaths during the period and the number of people moving to and from a country. Sheer population size without purchasing power is not economically meaningful. Sometimes population growth outpaces economic growth. This is a particular problem in developing countries, notably those in Africa (Table 3.1). Even when those countries experience positive economic growth, their per capita economic growth is low or even negative owing to the rapid rate of population growth.

The population gathers for a festival in Asakusa, Tokyo, Japan

© Lawrence Karn/iStock

TABLE 3.1 *Most fertile countries in the early 21st century*

Country	Population in million (2002)	Fertility rate (2001)	GDP per capita growth in % (2000–2001)
Niger	11.4	7.2	4.2
Somalia	9.3	7.0	n.a.
Afghanistan	28.0	6.8	n.a.
Angola	13.1	6.6	0.3
Burkina Faso	11.8	6.4	3.1
Chad	8.3	6.3	5.5
Malawi	10.7	6.2	−3.5
Mali	11.4	6.2	−0.9
Yemen	18.6	6.1	0.0
Democratic Republic of Congo	51.6	6.1	−7.1
Uganda	24.6	6.1	2.0
Burundi	7.1	5.9	1.3
Congo Republic	3.7	5.9	0.1
Liberia	3.3	5.9	2.6

Fertility rate = Births per female inhabitant capable of childbearing

Source: Baratta, M. (ed.) (2004) *Der Fischer Weltalmanach 2005*, Frankfurt a.M.: Fischer Taschenbuch Verlag, pp. 502–512.

Der Fischer Weltalmanach 2005, © Fischer Taschenbuch Verlag in der S. Fischer Verlag GmBH, Frankfurt am Main 2004

Increasing fertility in many countries means decreasing economic wealth for the individual. Exceptions are mainly due to special resources or political influences.

Within a society, it is often the economically poorest classes that exhibit the highest population growth rates. From the standpoint of the individual, there may be strong economic reasons for having a larger family. In countries where no general social security system exists to help support elderly people who can no longer support themselves, and where people do not have the income to save for their retirement during work life, the more children one has, the greater are one's chances of living relatively comfortably in old age.

Religious beliefs can also contribute to higher birth rates. For example, according to Hindu doctrine, funeral rites must be performed by the eldest son if a dead parent is to progress to the next life. Families are thus encouraged to have several sons, to ensure that the rites will be carried out properly. Regardless of the motivation, however, the results are similar: Larger families reduce per capita income.

Countries with close to half of their population under the age of 15 have a major drain on their economic resources owing to the "non-productivity" of so many young people. Brazil, as an example from Latin America, must balance the need to create more than 1 million new jobs a year to absorb the increase in population that needs to work against the need to pay the interest on its foreign debt. Many other nations with high population growth rates, including Bolivia, Nigeria, Côte d'Ivoire, Djibouti, El Salvador, Guatemala, Guinea-Bissau, Kenya, and Zimbabwe, face similar economic dilemmas. Ironically for the international marketer, markets that are growing very fast in terms of number of consumers are usually those that are increasingly unable to afford the marketer's products (see Figure 3.2).

Immigration

Population growth may be due not only to a high reproduction rate but also to immigration. For example, in a decade between 5 and 10 million people immigrate into the U.S. An analysis by the Center for Immigration Studies conducted in 2002 showed that more than 33 million immigrants live in the U.S. Between January 2000 and the end of 2002 more than 3.3 million legal and illegal immigrants entered the country. Given the slowing rate of population growth

FIGURE 3.2 *Per capita real GDP growth rates diverge*

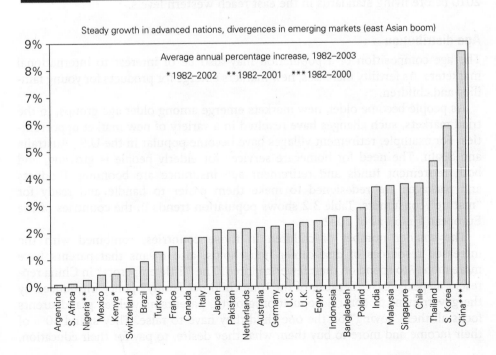

Steady growth in advanced nations, divergences in emerging markets (east Asian boom)

Average annual percentage increase, 1982–2003

*1982–2002   **1982–2001   ***1982–2000

Real per capita GDP shows a rather steady growth in all industrially developed countries. In emerging markets there are significant divergences depending on population growth, natural resources, and economic policies.

Source: Jeff Rosensweig, Emory University

overall, this new inflow represented close to 40% of total population growth for the last decade. In 2004, immigrants accounted for about 12% of the total population, the highest percentage in 70 years. The large majority of the immigrants came from Asia and Latin America, changing the distribution of different races that constitute the U.S. population. Currently, there are already more Hispanic U.S. citizens than African U.S. citizens. For the international marketer, this means the creation of new markets or the growth of traditionally less important niches. For example, media in Spanish have a much higher reach, or Asian food producers are faced with an increasing market potential.

Some immigrants bring considerable job skills and even investment capital. Many entrepreneurs come from immigrant groups, and of the immigrants of the 1990s the percentage of male workers who are college graduates is slightly higher than for native-born U.S. citizens. But such high proportions of immigrants also have political consequences, as they compete for jobs as well as resources for education, social, and medical care with those already in the country. In the U.S., the poverty rate for immigrants and their U.S.-born children (under 18) is two-thirds higher than that of natives. One-third of immigrants do not have health insurance – 2.5 times the rate for natives. And immigration accounts for virtually the entire national increase in public school enrollment over the last decade.

When the economy is growing slowly, if at all, considerable political backlash may occur. This has been the case in Europe where extreme right-wing parties have gained considerable shares of votes in prosperous countries such as France, Germany, Italy, Belgium, or the Netherlands. There, governments have tried to absorb immigrants – economic as well as political refugees fleeing because of political and economic problems in some former communist countries, such as Albania, Bosnia, Croatia, Serbia, or Romania, as well as in African countries including Algeria, Morocco, Rwanda, Liberia, or the Congo.

Perhaps the most extreme example is Germany, which not only had to overcome the economic difficulties of its now integrated but former communist eastern part, but is also the most preferred destination, after the U.S., of immigrants from all over the world. Germany has spent $1 trillion on revamping the economy of the formerly communist East Germany from reunification in 1990 to the early years of the new century. That is almost 10 times the amount the West has promised to Russia, though East Germany has just one-tenth of Russia's population. Moreover, Berlin expects the torrent of funding to continue until 2010 before living standards in the east reach western levels.

Age distribution

The age composition of a population may also be of interest to international marketers. As fertility increases, new markets emerge for products for young families and children.

As people become older, new markets emerge among older age groups. In the triad markets, such changes have resulted in a variety of new market opportunities. For example, retirement villages have become popular in the U.S., Australia and Spain. The need for homecare services for elderly people is growing, and both retirement funds and retirement age insurance are booming. Products and packages are redesigned to make them easier to handle and ready for "mature" consumers. Table 3.2 shows population trends in the countries of the European Union as of 2002.

The smaller number of children in those countries, combined with the increased resources of dual-career households, also means that parents have more money to spend on their fewer children. The "little emperors" in China represent a special case. Because of the "one child per family" policy introduced by the government to control population growth, parents as well as grandparents focus all their "loving" on the one child they have to raise. They spend 30% of their income and more to buy them what they desire, to pay for their education, and to see them become successful in the future. The increasing amount of pocket-money those children have makes them a very interesting market for products targeted to more and more precisely defined segments of children and youth.

The maturing of the population in the economically most advanced markets not only leads to new product markets, but also presents significant problems to their societies, which should not be ignored by international marketers. In Japan, for example, economists are worried that there will soon not be enough workers to support the retired generation – traditionally, retired people in Japan live with their families. In Hong Kong, where some 80% of the companies listed on the stock exchange are controlled by a single family, "mom and pop" multinationals are finding it increasingly difficult to continue to do business run by family members as leaders retire, and fewer sons and daughters are available to take their place.

The worry in most western European countries is who will work to generate the retirement funds needed for a longer living population. Currently, most people retire at around 60 years of age and live until around 80. That is, they want to receive retirement payments for approximately half as long as they have been active in production processes during their working life. In addition, for example, in France three people held a job for every retired person in 1970. In 1990, that ratio had fallen to 2.3, and came down to be less than 2 to 1 in the early 2000s.

TABLE 3.2 *Population trends in the European Union*

Country	Population in 2002 000s	Population growth in % 1980–2002	% of population above 65 years in 2002
Austria	8,048	0.3	15.9
Belgium	10,333	0.2	16.7
Cyprus	765	n.a.	11.9
Czech Republic	10,210	0.0	13.8
Denmark	5,374	0.2	14.9
Germany	82,495	0.2	16.8
Estonia	1,358	−0.4	15.0
Finland	5,199	0.4	15.2
France	59,485	0.4	16.1
Great Britain	59,229	0.2	16.0
Greece	10,631	0.4	19.0
Hungary	10,159	−0.2	14.6
Ireland	3,920	0.6	11.1
Italy	57,690	0.1	18.7
Latvia	2,338	−0.4	15.1
Lithuania	3,469	0.1	14.0
Luxembourg	444	n.a.	14.9
Malta	397	n.a.	12.3
Netherlands	16,144	0.6	13.8
Poland	38,626	0.4	12.3
Portugal	10,177	0.2	15.2
Slovakia	5,379	0.3	11.4
Slovenia	1,964	0.1	14.6
Spain	40,917	0.4	16.9
Sweden	8,924	0.3	17.5

Since the 1990s, population growth rates in the European Union have been below reproduction level. The share of those above 65 is dramatically increasing.

Source: Adapted from Baratta, M. (ed.) (2004) *Der Fischer Weltalmanach 2005*, Frankfurt a.M.: Fischer Taschenbuch Verlag

As a result, the current social security systems simply cannot afford to continue as they are. Politicians and also company managers are urged to find ways to ensure the level of individual wealth in the years to come (Figure 3.3).

In other words, the future of highly industrialized countries may hold a most challenging major market for international marketers – there will be more old people, perhaps with less money, and fewer young people more preoccupied with financially ensuring their retirement. Certainly not only new goods and services and altered marketing campaigns will be necessary if this scenario comes true. The entire concept of pricing, credit, and the viability of certain product markets may be called into question.

Urbanization

The term **urbanization** refers to the proportion of a population that lives in cities. The degree of urbanization in a society is of interest to international marketers because it represents concentrations of potential customers. In addition, despite all the faults of urban agglomerations, they are centers of industrial productivity and economic growth. For example, Metro-Manila is characterized by a concentration of economic, social, and political activities, as evidenced by the presence of 90% of the biggest companies in the country, all major newspapers, all main television stations, and 60% of the country's non-agricultural labor force. The area serves as the distribution center for exports and capital goods. It is the Philippines' center for non-primary goods production, providing almost

FIGURE 3.3 *Comparison of age pyramids in industrially developing and highly developed countries 1985 and 2025*

Indicator	1985		2025	
	More developed regions	Less developed regions	More developed regions	Less developed regions
Population (thousands)	1,114,785	3,729,162	1,248,954	6,656,285
Male population (thousands)	539,588	1,897,357	605,461	3,355,239
Female population (thousands)	575,197	1,831,805	643,493	3,301,047
Population sex ratio (males per 100 females)	93.8	103.6	94.1	101.6
Percentage aged 0–4 (%)	7.0	13.5	5.1	8.6
Percentage aged 5–14 (%)	14.4	23.6	10.6	17.1
Percentage aged 15–24 (%)	15.7	20.5	11.2	16.1
Percentage aged 60 or over (%)	16.4	6.6	27.5	12.8
Percentage aged 65 or over (%)	11.6	4.2	20.8	8.6
Percentage aged 80 or over (%)	2.3	0.5	5.4	1.4

Many industrially developing countries experience high birth rates compared to industrially developed countries. While the latter have increasing difficulties in financing their retirement systems, the former need high economic growth rates to avoid substantial unemployment.

Source: United Nations, Department of Economic and Social Affairs, Population Division (2005). World Population Prospects: The 2004 Revision Population Database; www.esa.un.org/unpp (June 2005)

one-half of the total national output in manufacturing, commerce, and services. In addition, about 90% of internal revenue collection for the entire country is taken from Metro-Manila and almost 80% of the Philippines' imports enter through the ports of the City of Manila.

As the same example shows, however, despite the cited economic performance, too rapid urbanization can lead to high unemployment, harsh living conditions, and frequent episodes of political and social unrest. Other examples are Ciudad de México (Mexico City), São Paulo or Al-Qahira (Cairo), the most urbanized areas of their countries. They have such high population growth rates that their population could double every 20 years. Much of this growth results from rural–urban migration – people moving away from poor rural areas in search of better opportunities. Whereas in 1970 less than 20% of the world's population lived in urban complexes, in 2000 it was 47% and estimates are that from 2007 on more than half of all people will live in cities. Jobs cannot be created fast enough to absorb this rapid increase in the urban workforce. Ghettos of extremely poor people become larger and larger, and the percentage of people working in the informal sector (mainly self-employed work without any social, retirement or medical care security) increases.

European urban agglomerations experienced the same phenomena during the period of capitalist industrialization in the early 1800s. In contrast, Japan and the U.S. have histories of slow but steady urbanization. Their active and growing economies, coupled with a lower rate of urbanization, have allowed them to better absorb new urban dwellers and workers without a dramatic increase in unemployment. Nevertheless, today every big urban agglomeration is characterized by a duality: ghettos of poor and often unemployed people with largely low levels of education and a center with skyscrapers, bank offices, and luxury boutiques.

It may come as a surprise to discover that Australia (together with Taiwan) is the world's most urbanized country, with more than 90% of its close to 20 million people living in urban areas. For the international marketer, this is of particular interest because urban and rural dwellers often have different consumption patterns. In the U.S., for example, Sears Roebuck built a tremendous business by catering to the rural population through catalog sales. But, as an increasing proportion of the population moved to the cities, Sears found it necessary to follow its customers; it changed its product offerings and placed more emphasis on stores in suburban shopping centers.

Urban dwellers in different countries are more likely to have similar consumption patterns than urban and rural consumers within the same country. For example, urban women in Algeria, Argentina, Brazil, Morocco, and Peru have more similar consumption patterns with regard to cosmetics than do urban and rural women within any one of those countries. In industrially developing countries, such as India, international marketers are often unable to reach consumers outside urban agglomerations. In China, urban dwellers represent only 37% of the population. Yet that market contains around 450 million potential customers and is rapidly increasing.

Capabilities

Besides the size of a country's population combined with the purchasing power of those potential customers, which is, in turn, influenced by the age structure of the population and the society's degree of urbanization, the intellectual capability of a country's population has a significant influence on its wealth. Because such capabilities are to some extent based on the available knowledge, the nature of a country's educational system is of interest to international marketers. It affects:

- literacy rate, that is, the proportion of the population that can read and write
- generally accepted rate of change
- level of available technology
- number of highly educated people in the workforce
- marketing mix that will be most effective for a country.

In Sweden, for example, the literacy rate is virtually 100%, and all students start English as a foreign language in the first grade, compared to Niger, where the literacy rate does not reach 20%. Swedish workers who are familiar with printed materials will not only react to print advertising campaigns, but they also have no difficulties working with machinery provided with user information in English. In Niger much knowledge is passed along through family and kinship groups. Most consumers there cannot be effectively reached through print media, and most user instructions for the workforce need to be given through drawings. Because the educational system of the country provides less information about other cultures, the majority of customers in Niger can also be expected to have a lower tolerance for change than customers in Sweden, which, in turn, will influence the rate at which new products of international marketers are accepted.

The educational system also affects the level of local technological know-how an international marketer can take advantage of. For example, manufacturers of highly sophisticated software for industrial robots and control systems, such as Japan's Oki or Germany's Siemens, choose the locations of their research and development units according to the availability of advanced teaching institutions and research laboratories. Oracle, the world's second-largest software company after Microsoft Corp., expands its activities in Bangalore and Hyderabad, both in India. They are not only attracted by the relatively low paid English-speaking graduates available there, but also by their excellent level of training.

Future issues box 3.1 discusses potential future problems in a society where adolescents have a negative attitude concerning certain fields of education. But

FUTURE ISSUES BOX 3.1

Preferences of Japanese students

Japan's population curve will soon resemble a lollipop. In the first decade of this century the number of people in their 20s will decline by 4 million. By contrast, the proportion of people over 65, for whom the young generation will have to care, is expected to swell from 17% of the population in 2000 to a quarter of the population in 2015. The birth rate, around 1.3 children for every woman, is so low that Japan's labor force will begin shrinking.

It is assumed that young people will have to be more efficient and innovative than their parents in order to carry this enormous burden. But will they?

A survey of junior high school students compared 4,800 Japanese students with their peers from 37 other countries. Just 9% of Japanese students said

they had positive or strongly positive feelings toward math, compared with 35% of U.S. students and 45% of Singaporeans. Japanese students were ranked 37 out of 38 nations surveyed for their interest in math and 22 out of 23 countries for their interest in science.

Significantly, however, Japanese students ranked near the top for their actual skills in both math and science. In math they ranked 5 after Singapore, South Korea, Taiwan, and Hong Kong. In science, they ranked 4 behind Taiwan, Singapore, and Hungary.

What young people's negative attitudes mean for the future of Japan's labor force and economy is the subject of debate. But the underlying question is disturbing: What happens when a country famous for its world-class electronics and cars loses interest in math and science?

Source: Adapted from Fuller, T. (2001) "Work hard? Young Japanese have other ideas", *International Herald Tribune*, Bangkok, 11 April, pp. 1, 7

education is not the only factor influencing capabilities. Skillfulness, diligence, and flexibility, as well as the mobility of people, have an impact, too. They are mostly based on the prevailing local culture and will therefore be discussed in Chapter 5.

Natural environment

The natural environment of a country market represents an important source of potential wealth for its population. Natural resources, such as minerals, water and waterpower, oil, coal or gas, and the country's climate and topography are major determinants of the economic structures and interdependencies of a local economy. The Netherlands, for example, is rich in natural gas but has limited mineral resources. Therefore, it has had to depend on international trade to build and sustain its economy – exports and imports account for over 50% of the Netherlands' GNP. Because natural resources are "given" by nature, in most countries they have been exploited for the profit of individuals, firms, or society. The fact that they are limited has largely been overlooked. Only recently have voices demanding a sustainable world economy based on a sustainable use of the natural environment become more prominent and got some attention.

Natural resources

The oil wells of the North Sea have made a major contribution to the economic success of the U.K. and Norway. They might even be a major reason why the U.K. can afford to follow a rather independent policy inside the EU and why Norway was able to refuse EU membership without suffering any significant economic disadvantages. In addition to their oil industry, the two countries have a long-standing tradition of other industries that profit from the countries' oil income and also substantially contribute to their economic wealth.

Some countries are overly dependent on the use of a single resource. Chile, for example, frequently suffered economically because too much of its GNP was derived from copper mining. When the world market price of copper fluctuated, so did Chile's GNP. When good substitutes for copper were developed, such as high-quality plastic pipes used in construction, Chile's economy faced difficulty. To resolve that problem, Chile has diversified its economy by increasing its exports of grapes, timber, fish, and wine. This policy has somewhat improved the balance of Chile's economy, but, nevertheless, more than one-third of the country's total exports is still copper.

Topography

Topography affects a country's economic wealth in fundamental and enduring ways. Topographic features like rivers, waterfalls, mountain ranges, and beaches constitute resources, such as natural trade routes or sources of energy, but can also be viewed as products. The Netherlands, for example, is located at the mouth of the River Rhine. Rotterdam is the second busiest port in the world, and the country is crisscrossed with canals and rivers bustling with commercial traffic. Half of the exports and imports that move through the Netherlands are on their way to and from Germany, France, and Switzerland (all three border on navigable parts of the Rhine). Goods can be shipped to the Netherlands for distribution throughout Europe, or for export to the rest of the world, via Rotterdam.

Topography as a product is illustrated by the examples of the beautiful Maldive Islands off the southwestern coast of India, which attract almost half a million tourists per year, leaving more than $300 million worth of tourist income annually, and the coast of Thailand which – together with the cultural treasures of Bangkok – makes tourism a very big foreign currency earner of the country. Niagara Falls, located on the border between the U.S. and Canada, is a source of electric power for both countries as well as a famous tourist destination.

Topography may also be a major constraint on a country's economy as well as for international marketing. It has a major impact on the cost and ease of distributing an international marketer's products. A firm wanting to transport its products from the coast of Brazil westward to Peru will find that the only efficient way to do so is by air. The surface route up the River Amazon and across the Andes Mountains would take many weeks and expose both travelers and products to considerable risk. The Andes thus act as a topographic constraint on both domestic and international business. So does the Sahara Desert in the northern part of Africa. Many other examples of topographic conditions as economic constraints can be given. The lack of water supplies, or the presence of rivers that flood regularly, influences the location of agricultural processing plants. Countries with no coastline, such as Botswana, Nepal, or Switzerland, must rely on the ports of neighboring countries to export goods by sea.

Climate

Climate is a part of a country market's natural environment that is closely linked to the country's economic development and functioning. The importance of climate as a potential source of economic wealth is illustrated by the ability of Central American countries to produce tropical fruits for export to countries where they cannot be grown, because of different climatic conditions. Economic constraints resulting from climatic conditions are illustrated by monsoon winds and rain that hamper business in countries like Bangladesh, India, or Pakistan through flooding, mudslides, and washed-out railroads. And in Siberia, where natural resources are plentiful, the extremely cold climate makes it difficult to exploit them.

For the international marketer, climate has a great deal to do with market viability. Consumers living near the equator prefer different food products to those living in milder climates. Heat and humidity result in lower levels of production, and therefore income, particularly in countries with limited energy for climate control and poorly developed infrastructure systems.

Patterns of consumption and production are, of course, influenced by many other factors besides climate. For example, ownership of in-home air conditioners in Brisbane, Australia, is estimated at 10–20%. In New Delhi, where the heat and humidity are so oppressive that they severely limit economic activity, the proportion of homes with air conditioners is even lower. Yet in Atlanta, Georgia, where the climate is far milder than that of either Brisbane or New Delhi, 80% of the homes are air conditioned. Obviously, cultural norms, economic resources, and many other factors affect the purchase of goods such as air conditioners. Nevertheless, it remains true that the natural environment of a country market has an important impact on the market's viability.

Impact on country market viability

How strong the influence of natural resources, topography and climate can be on the economic development of countries and their viability for international marketers is impressively illustrated by the countries in the Middle East. The rich, oil-producing countries of the Middle East, for example, include Kuwait, Oman, Saudi Arabia, and the United Arab Emirates. They have per capita income of more than $18,000, $9,000, $8,000, and $9,000 respectively. Their rather stable governments are encouraging industrialization by importing high-tech industrial goods, turnkey plants for food production, packaging, plastic and metal treatment, and construction material, as well as maintenance contracts and industrial services.

Those Middle Eastern countries constitute a generally promising market for industrial goods. There are also markets for many consumer goods, provided that they are not prohibited by Islamic religious principles. However, because of small populations these markets are limited. In spite of their substantial capital resources, these countries are still developing economically. Their topographic and climatic conditions, combined with a rather uneven distribution of wealth, are not supportive of faster development. For example, attempts to increase agricultural production by using substantial underground supplies of sweet water for irrigation purposes have largely failed owing to the hot and dry climate.

Turkey, as another example, offers a market that is growing in importance. Turkey has achieved relative political stability, and its liberal economic policies have encouraged foreign investment. In recent years growth rates of GDP averaged 3.5%. Growth has been mainly due to private business success in the areas of communication, tourism, textiles, and transportation. Turkey's location between Europe and Asia as well as at the Bosphorus, the entrance to the Black Sea, enables it to engage easily in trade with countries on both continents. Its beautiful shores and the Mediterranean climate attract increasing numbers of tourists. After the goal of free convertibility of the Turkish lira had been reached, the country also succeeded in signing a customs union agreement with the EU in 1995 (which excludes the free trade of agricultural products and the free movement of Turkish workers). Negotiations to become a member of the EU were started in 2005.

Sustainability

In using resources from the natural environment of a country market for their business purposes, international marketers need to take care of the **sustainability** of their activities. That is, they must be aware that a business will only be successful over a long period if it does not destroy its own bases (see Ethics box 3.1). For example, the 18 countries located around the Mediterranean Sea have based much of their economic development on increasing tourism. But tourists come to those countries not only because of the warm and sunny weather, and the low-priced hotels and good food – many of them also want to enjoy swimming in the sea. If tourism and related activities pollute the Mediterranean to an extent that swimming becomes dangerous for the tourists' health, they will go somewhere else. Tourism managers, therefore, need to be concerned with organizing their businesses' activities in a way that does not destroy one of its bases.

Technological resources

Besides the human and natural resources available in a country market, the technological resources in that market may influence its attractiveness. Managers of internationally operating companies need to be attuned to differences between the technological environment of their home country and those of their various country markets. A lack of technological resources may make it difficult to sell the marketer's product and to satisfy customers. For example, when U.S. computer manufacturers first came to China, they were eager to close a sale. But they did not know that air conditioning was not readily available there. As a result, their computers, which at that time required a temperate environment, did not perform as expected.

Differences in technological development may also offer opportunities to market a firm's product. Thus, Austria's VA Industrial Services has been successful in marketing training programs and management assistance in advanced steel production methods and maintenance of steel production plants to industrially less developed countries. There, new steel plants had been constructed and run up to full capacity use by the suppliers, but local managers and personnel lacking the needed experience were not able to sustain that production level. Many plants were running at no more than 30% capacity. VA Industrial Services assisted the plant owners by training their personnel in subjects such as work organization, proper use of the machinery, and maintenance.

As the example shows, international marketers must consider not only the level of technological development in a society, which is represented by factors such as the available infrastructure (for example, a container terminal for the shipment of products or the existence of a digital phone system for communication with sales people). They must also be aware of the concept of technology that is *characteristic* of that society.

Infrastructure

A country's infrastructure is the transportation, energy, communication, and commercial systems available to its population and industries. For international marketing to be possible, a certain infrastructure has to be in place or needs to be installed in a country market:

- The *level of development of a country's infrastructure* affects the extent to which its natural resources can be used. Alaska's vast oil reserves could not be used until the Alaskan pipeline was built. The water that powers turbines to generate electricity in northern Canada would be economically useless if there were no electrical system to transport power to industrial sites in the south.

- The level of development of a country's infrastructure also determines how well its *human resources can be developed and used*. Modern research and medical centers, for example, only function at the highest level if the

ETHICS BOX 3.1

Sustainable business?

Many international marketers are not sufficiently aware of the dangers to the natural bases of their income in what they are doing or how they do it. For example, Thai prawn farming companies, such as a business unit of Charoen Pokphand, successfully export their products all over the world, in particular to Japan and the U.S. Prawn farming in Thailand takes place in the coastal mangrove forests. The problem is that the chemicals used in farming are highly polluting, as is the waste left behind. Many farms are abandoned after a few years, when the land ceases to be cultivable. Prawn farming has resulted in the clearing of about two-thirds of Thailand's coastal mangrove forests, the breeding grounds of the prawns.

In Somalia, the strong market for charcoal in the Gulf countries and Saudi Arabia led to large-scale and environmentally damaging logging. Charcoal is made from acacia trees that are 50 to 500 years old. Charcoal replaced livestock as Somalia's main export following the livestock ban imposed by the Gulf states in September 2000. A bag of charcoal could sell for $10 in Saudi Arabia. Intensive lobby-

ing and education by an NGO called the Horn of Africa Relief and Development Organization caused the export of charcoal to be banned in some parts of Somalia, leading to an 80% reduction in exports. To eliminate the domestic need for charcoal, Horn Relief promotes the use of solar cookers.

Sustainable production and marketing of goods and services may increase costs, but not necessarily. In many cases it provides increased customer satisfaction and secures increasing returns on investment. For example, Costa Rica's small-scale coffee farmers are spurning chemicals to win customers, at better prices, from the swelling ranks of organic coffee drinkers in Europe and North America. The 20% premium is not the only reason for going organic. The local coffee growers' cooperative also worries that the modern arsenal of fertilizers, pesticides and herbicides kills the ground cover that prevents erosion. Organic methods mean a lot more work, and it takes time to switch to them. But growers such as Coocafé, a consortium set up by small cooperatives in Costa Rica, is helped by "fair trade" companies that buy the coffee at a usually guaranteed premium over world market prices and sell it without intermediaries under such brand names as CaféDirect in the U.K., Equal Exchange in the U.S., and Max Havelaar on the European continent. Demand for organic coffee in rich countries is expanding and far from saturated.

available infrastructure allows instant international communication. Complicated medical operations, for instance, are carried out by a team of specialists in one place, but this team may be in online visual contact with specialists in other countries who assist with their know-how and expertise when it is needed.

● *Infrastructure also determines whether international marketers can reach their potential markets.* A large target market with adequate buying power is of little value if goods and services cannot be sold to customers because of a lack of transportation infrastructure, energy shortage, faulty communications, or a lack of financial institutions.

Transportation infrastructure Transportation infrastructure is particularly important to international marketers. Managers from triad markets often take for granted the availability of distribution systems made up of good roads, railways, waterways, and air cargo systems. But western Europe, Russia, and China have different gauges (railway track widths), for example. To transport a load of electrical appliances from Lyon in France to Xian in China by rail, France's SEB would twice have to unload freight cars at borders and reload the cargo onto cars that fit the other gauge. Similarly, roads and dependable trucking lines are not equally available throughout the world. The freeways in the U.S. may have their counterparts in the *autostrade* in Italy, but on a freeway near Hanoi truck drivers may encounter cyclists transporting coal for their homes and pigs from neighboring farms crossing the road. In some parts of eastern Europe, dirt roads still connect one village to another, and these may be difficult to pass in rainy seasons, when the roads turn into mud.

Communication infrastructure Communication infrastructure has become a major factor of influence on the economic wealth of a country. For instance, Singapore, the very dynamic newly industrialized country with the second-largest per capita income in Asia behind Japan, prides itself on being ahead of the technological game. Its economic success relies on a state-of-the-art communication infrastructure. More than 90% of homes are cabled for services such as the internet and interactive television. About 20% of Singapore's 3 million inhabitants already use those services.

Owing to global competition between the suppliers and countries involved, the development of communication infrastructure in the highly industrialized and newly industrializing countries has been extremely fast. Global networks using satellite transmission, digital telephones, and email permit daily communication among far flung business units of an internationally operating company.

Economically less developed countries are experiencing an ever widening gap between themselves and the industrially more developed parts of the world. In some African, Asian, and Latin American countries, telephone connections with other countries are easier, faster, and clearer than connections within the same country. The home office of an international marketer may be able to communicate with the local representative, but that representative may not be able to communicate easily with local customers.

Commercial infrastructure The commercial infrastructure of a country market relevant to an international marketer contains the available distribution channels (which will be discussed in Chapter 12), market research (see Chapter 7) and market communication agencies (see Chapter 15), logistics service providers (see Chapter 14), and financial institutions. How important the existence of a well-functioning commercial infrastructure may be for an international marketer is illustrated by the following example.

After 13 years of talks, Nestlé was finally invited into China in 1987 by the government of Heilongjiang Province to help boost milk production in the region.

Capitalizing on its experience in Sri Lanka and India, Nestlé opened a powdered milk and baby cereal plant in 1990. Then it had a choice: Use the severely over-burdened local trains and roads to collect milk and deliver finished goods, or create its own infrastructure. The latter was a lot more costly but would ulti-mately be more dependable. So Nestlé began weaving a distribution network known as "milk roads" between 27 villages in the region and the factory collec-tion points, called chilling centers. The farmers, pushing wheelbarrows, pedaling bicycles, or on foot, followed the gravel roads to the centers where their milk was weighed and analyzed. Then the area managers organized a delivery system using vans dedicated to carrying Nestlé products. Nestlé hired retired teachers and gov-ernment workers to serve as farm agents, bringing Swiss experts to train them in rudimentary animal health and hygiene. Once this system was in place, the business took off.

A country's financial institutions are of interest to an international marketer because they affect customers' purchasing power and the availability of capital. Table 3.3 listing the world's top banks in 2005 shows that they are located in Japan, the U.S., France, Switzerland, and the U.K. National banking systems, like the Federal Reserve System in the U.S., or the European Central Bank located in Frankfurt, Germany, contribute to economic stability by regulating the money supply and banking operations. If the money supply grows too quickly, the result may be inflation; if it grows too slowly, the economy may stagnate. The major task of a national or regional banking system, therefore, is to opti-mally balance the money supply for the economy. This can be done through policies that govern:

- interest rates
- amount of money in circulation
- lending practices of banks, savings and loan associations, and other financial institutions.

In former centrally controlled economies such as in eastern Europe, the bank-ing system was an entirely regulated monopoly in the hands of government. The central bank had the monopoly for short-term credits, some special state-owned banks were responsible for long-term credits, and a bank for external trade held the monopoly for all currency issues as well as export/import financing. To trans-

TABLE 3.3 *World's top banks*

Bank	Total assets in $ billion	Country	Net profit in $ billion in 2004
Mitsubishi UFJ Financial Group	1,788	Japan	—
Citigroup	1,484	U.S.	17.04
Mizuho Financial Group	1,305	Japan	3.85
BNP Paribas	1,228	France	5.80
J.P. Morgan Chase	1,157	U.S.	4.46
UBS	1,115	Switzerland	6.51
Bank of America	1,110	U.S.	14.14
HSBC	1,034	Switzerland	8.77*
Sumitomo Financial Group	968	Japan	3.12
RBS	811	U.K.	6.59*

The size of available banks to a certain extent expresses the economic standing of the market where the bank is headquartered.

* Result at 31 December 2003
Source: Bohineust, A. (2005) "Fusion bancaire géante au Jappon", *Le Figaro économie*, 19–20 February, p. v

form that system into a market-oriented banking system following the example of western industrialized countries was no easy task. In Russia, for example, after 1991 about 2,500 banks were formed. Following the country's liquidity crisis in 1995, 300 of them lost their licenses and many more went out of business because of bad credits, the loss of returns from currency fluctuations, inflation and treasury bonds, luxurious bank buildings, and simply inexperience. As a consequence, international marketers doing business with Russian partners are well advised to seek information about the reliability of those partners' banks before signing any contract.

Because of such worries concerning banks in eastern Europe, some western European banks, such as Austrian-based Bank Austria, an affiliate of German Hypo-Vereinsbank, were highly successful in expanding their business to those economies in transition. EU companies building their business in central and eastern Europe were happy being able to rely on their financial partner without much risk analysis.

Some countries do not have a national banking system. In those countries the money supply is potentially unstable, a situation that can result in high inflation rates. Thus, the existence of a national banking system may be a sign of a relatively stable economy, but it is by no means a guarantee – too many other factors determine the extent to which an economy is stable over time.

Concept of technology

Besides the current and developing infrastructure in a country market, an international marketer assessing a market's attractiveness needs to consider the predominant concept of technology in the society being analyzed. Concepts of technology can vary considerably from one country market to another and may demand entirely different marketing mixes to assure long-term success. The significance of such differences can be seen in the following example.

Steyr Daimler-Puch sold 200 trucks to the Sudan where transportation had traditionally taken place on the back of camels (or on trains, as long as the British administration looked after the maintenance of the system). Two years later, when the supplier wanted to sell more trucks, sales calls were unsuccessful. The customer considered the quality of the trucks to be far below the expected level. No further order would be placed. When the truck manufacturer's salespeople tried to find out why the customer was so dissatisfied, they were informed that none of the trucks was any longer in service. The truck drivers, unfamiliar with the concept of preventive maintenance, had failed to change the oil, or otherwise maintain the trucks. When the trucks broke down, the drivers left them where they had stopped, and returned to transportation by camels, a technology that they understood and knew how to maintain.

Economic system

The economic system of a country is its specific combination of the bases of economic wealth discussed so far. Depending on the level of industrial development, the shares of different industrial sectors of the economy will vary. So will the ownership of the means of production, depending on the market orientation of the governing political forces.

Industrial sectors

Industrial sectors are categories of economic activity, such as mining, manufacturing, agriculture, wholesale and retail trade, construction, transportation, and business and personal services. In general, countries with a high proportion of their GDP coming from agriculture have less per capita income than those with high proportions coming from manufacturing or service sectors. Countries in which a single industrial sector dominates the economy are referred to as a

monoculture. Usually, monocultures rely on a commodity such as coffee or copper (see Figure 3.4). Because prices of commodities have strong cycles, monocultures are at the mercy of the world market price for the commodity.

In assessing the attractiveness of potential country markets, the international marketer must consider such factors of economic instability. They may present a market opportunity, when the marketer's product or service provides a potential remedy for the country's problem. For example, a supplier of fruit juice and canning plants may find fruit monoculture markets attractive. In most cases, however, strong imbalances in the industrial sectors of a country market diminish the attractiveness of its product markets.

Another potentially important factor for an international marketer interested in a country market is the existence and importance of an **informal sector** of the economy. In industrially developing countries, the informal sector is characterized by a large number of small-scale production and service activities that are individually or family owned and use labor-intensive and simple technology. The usually self-employed workers in this sector have little or no formal education, are generally unskilled and lack capital resources. Moreover, workers in the informal sector do not have any job security, lack decent working conditions and have no retirement security. Their motivation is usually to obtain sufficient income for survival. As many members of the household as possible are involved in income-generating activities, including women and children, and they often work very long hours. Most inhabit shacks that generally lack electricity, water, drainage, educational, and health services.

To better understand the functioning of many (rapidly) developing economies, it is important to note that the informal sector is closely connected with the formal – mainly urban – sectors. Many formal sectors depend on the informal sector for low-priced inputs to their own production. The informal sector in fact subsidizes the formal sector by providing basic inputs at very low prices maintained through the formal sector's economic power (the informal sector depends on the growth of the formal sector for a substantial portion of its income and clientele) and its legitimacy granted by governments.

FIGURE 3.4 *Commodity dependency*

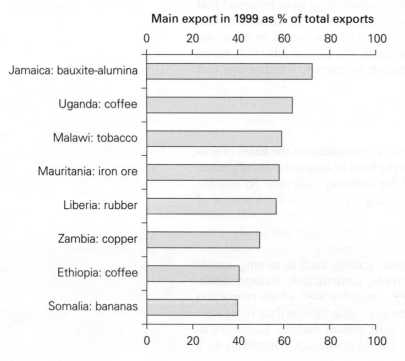

Main export in 1999 as % of total exports

Jamaica: bauxite-alumina
Uganda: coffee
Malawi: tobacco
Mauritania: iron ore
Liberia: rubber
Zambia: copper
Ethiopia: coffee
Somalia: bananas

Some countries strongly depend on one sector of industry and its exports. These are called monocultures. Historically, a monoculture is economically more unstable than a more balanced economy.

Source: Adapted from Baratta, M. (ed.) (2003) *Der Fischer Weltalmanach 2004*, Frankfurt a.M.: Fischer Taschenbuch Verlag

The informal sector not only exists in industrially developing economies, however. In southern and eastern Europe the informal sector takes the form of an underground economy. The estimated sizes of those hidden sectors compared to the countries' official GDPs run up to 25%, improving the officially available government statistics concerning the economic standing of those economies. Compared to Luxembourg, the U.S., and Switzerland, the world leaders in per capita income, where the size of the informal sector does not exceed an estimated 5%, an international marketer interested in serving markets with a substantial informal sector must consider its potential impact on local competition. Italy, for example, is the European champion in sales of pirated CDs. Estimates are that Italy would have no public deficit if the informal sector paid the same percentage of income and value-added taxes as the formal sector.

Economic decision making

Economic systems vary considerably in their approaches to economic decision making. The economic systems associated with socialist or communist political systems traditionally rely on central decision making to allocate scarce resources, to meet industrial as well as consumer demand according to the priorities of society. In capitalist and Islamic economic systems, market forces predominantly guide economic development. The U.S. is generally considered to have a highly free market, yet its economic policies in effect establish production quotas for some agricultural products, limit automobile imports, and protect domestic manufacturing in such areas as steel, textiles, and shoes. Their liberalized telephone market is significantly biased by the norms imposed by a regulating body.

Most economies lie somewhere between the two extremes of centrally planned versus free market economy. They are considered "mixed" economies, because they are guided partly by market forces and partly by centralized decision making.

Centrally controlled economies International marketers interested in investing in more centrally controlled economies need to inform themselves carefully about the specific legal regulations of those countries.

The Republic of North Korea may have been the most centrally controlled economy in the world in 2004. All production facilities have traditionally been in the possession of government. Because of the breakdown of its international trade relationships with eastern European countries, Cuba was forced to take some cautious steps in the direction of a somewhat more market-driven economy. Joint ventures with foreign companies are allowed. Foreign firms may establish wholly owned subsidiaries after government checking on a case-by-case basis. Cubans may possess foreign currency, and the peso is convertible. Since the middle of the 1990s, farmers and craftspeople have been allowed to sell their products in private markets.

The People's Republic of China calls itself a "socialist market economy." It is encouraging private investments and enterprise, and is actively attracting private foreign investments. Nevertheless, five-year plans are still fixed by the National People's Congress dominated by the Communist Party, a Central Planning Committee is discussing and making decisions about new projects, and a substantial part of China's industry remains state owned. Attempts to close the state-owned firms with the highest deficits led to unemployment rates in urban areas of around 15% and in rural areas of up to 25%.

Economies in a state of transition Until 1989, all countries in eastern Europe were centrally controlled economies. Their foreign trade was a state monopoly. Traditionally, only official foreign trade organizations (FTOs) were authorized to make international purchases and sales for these nations. FTOs had to conform to annual and five-year plans that were developed, supervised, and administered by the nation's ministry of foreign trade. FTOs received direction about product requirements and specifications, even the number of items to be produced, from an office of central planning.

Since 1989 the political as well as the economic environments in this part of the world have changed dramatically. The Soviet Union was dissolved and split into 15 sovereign states, 11 of which (Lithuania, Latvia, and Estonia had left the USSR earlier, Georgia has been participating since 1993) agreed to form the Commonwealth of Independent States (CIS) in December 1991. Table 3.4 shows the membership, population, and GDP details of CIS countries. In 2002, the GDP per capita of most members was still significantly below the level of the early 1990s. Only Armenia, Azerbaijan, Georgia, Kazakhstan, and Russia had been able to restore their level of economic activities.

The example of Russia may be an illustration for the problems the members of CIS have to resolve. More than a decade after the dissolution of the Soviet Union, the Russian Federation is still struggling to establish a modern market economy and achieve significant and lasting economic growth. Russia saw its economy contract for five years, before it achieved a slight recovery in 1997, which was followed by a financial crisis in 1998. This crisis culminated in a 60% depreciation of the ruble, a debt default by the government, and a sharp deterioration in living standards for most of the population. Since then, the economy has picked up speed. Growth rates reached an average of more than 5%, despite the ruble's real appreciation back to the level of 1998. These data along with a government effort to advance lagging structural reforms have raised business and investor confidence over Russia's prospects. Yet, the country remains heavily (80%) dependent on exports of commodities, such as oil, gas, metals, and timber. The weak banking system, corruption, local and regional government intervention in the courts, and widespread lack of trust in institutions add to a strong need for modernization of Russia's industrial base. Culture box 3.1 gives some additional insights concerning the situation prevailing in Central Asian members of the CIS.

The Council for Mutual Economic Assistance (CMEA, also called COMECON) was broken up in September 1991. Bulgaria, Hungary, Czechoslovakia, Poland, and Romania started to trade on world market terms. The CMEA had accounted for 70 to 80% of its members' exports and imports. Furthermore, owing to central planning, industrial production of many goods had been centralized at certain locations. Because of the sudden loss of their former market relationships, the economies of all former CMEA member countries suffered from substantial difficulties. In 1991 Hungary, for example, lost two-thirds of its exports to its former partners in the CMEA.

In the three central European countries (now there are four, because Czechoslovakia was split into the Czech Republic and Slovakia), production output fell by 40% between 1990 and 1992, real wages plummeted, unemployment climbed, and inflation rose to hitherto unknown heights. The real income of Czechs in 1991, for example, was 24% less than in 1990. Official unemployment figures in Hungary in 1992 were around 12%. But from the middle of 1992 on, some indicators showed an improvement. For example, despite the worst drought for decades, Polish GDP rose slightly; the collapse in industrial output had ended. A turnaround came into sight. As from 1994 on, all the economies were growing. Since then, the four countries have seen tremendous changes in their economic structures. In 1997, for example, about 80% of Hungary's GDP already came from private enterprises (see Strategy box 3.1). Using different approaches, all four central European countries managed to be prepared for joining the European Union in May 2004.

Starting in 1990, the Hungarian government had handed over small service companies, such as restaurants and shops, to their employees, while 5% of industrial firms were privatized through management buyouts. Today, only very few companies, such as the atomic power plant Paks, the state forests and some

TABLE 3.4 *Members of the Commonwealth of Independent States*

Country	Population in million	GNP per capita ($)	GNP per capita ($)
	2002	1993	2002
Armenia	3.1	660	790
Azerbaijan	8.2	730	710
Belarus	9.9	2,870	1,360
Georgia	5.2	580	650
Kazakhstan	14.9	1,560	1,520
Kyrgyzstan	5.0	850	290
Moldova	4.2	1,060	460
Russia	144.1	2,340	2,130
Tadjikistan	6.2	470	180
Turkmenistan	4.8	1,390	950*
Ukraine	48.7	2,210	780
Uzbekistan	25.3	970	310

* Database 2001

Source: Adapted from Baratta, M. (ed.) (2004) *Der Fischer Weltalmanach 2005*, Frankfurt a.M.:
Fischer Taschenbuch Verlag; Baratta, M. (ed.) (1995) *Der Fischer Weltalmanach 1996*,
Frankfurt a.M.: Fischer Taschenbuch Verlag

The Commonwealth of Independent States (CIS) is an association of 12 countries, which until 1991 belonged to the USSR. It is dominated by Russia controlling more than half of the economic activity.

CULTURE BOX 3.1

At the crossroads

Central Asia is strategically placed at the crossroads between Europe and China, Russia and Iran. Throughout its history, trade between east and west moved through Central Asia along the famed Silk Road, bringing development and prosperity. But from the times of Scythes and Mongols to the Russians, this special location was also bringing war and devastation.

In Central Asia, the Turkic nomads met up with the Muslim and Persian world. Turkish and Persian cultures and languages blended to form a strong local identity. Although Central Asia shares a common history and similar culture, there are plenty of differences among its constituent parts. There is a cultural split between nomads from the steppes and mountains, mainly Kyrgizs, Kazakhs and Turkmens, and the sedentary, mainly urban Uzbeks and Tadjiks who settled in the river basins of Transoxania. This split was responsible for distinct cultural, religious, and political identities.

The cultural split, however, ignores borders. Today's Central Asian states are Soviet creations, which, before 1991, had no history as separate, independent countries. After decades of Soviet rule and careful manipulation of language and history, they suddenly found themselves independent, but without anything much to hold them together. They all have large ethnic minorities.

Since independence, the individual Central Asian states have made different political and economic choices, which have meant that the contrasts between them are now quite striking. Kazakhstan and Kyrgyzstan have embraced noticeably more ambitious economic reforms than the rest of the region. Kazakhstan, with its large Russian minority and more developed economy, feels far more European than its neighbors. In terms of natural resources, mainly oil and gas, Kazakhstan's and Turkmenistan's relative wealth contrasts with Kyrgyzstan's and Tadjikistan's poverty.

Source: Adapted from Lambert, C. (2003) "At the crossroads", *The Economist*, 26 July, pp. 3–4

special agricultural units, stay in full public ownership. In some others, government has kept a 25% share with veto rights.

In the beginning Hungary was most successful in attracting foreign direct investment. This may be partly due to privatization by bidding with tenders and sales to the highest bidders. A big part of Hungary's productive assets, including energy providers and public telecommunications, were sold through bidding. But, privatizations also occurred through the stock exchange. By the end of 1996 there were already 32,000 firms with foreign investment out of a total of around 150,000 companies in Hungary. Foreign direct investments, mainly from Germany, the U.S., France, and Austria, began dominating some sectors of Hungarian industry. The sugar, tobacco, car, lighting equipment, and

STRATEGY BOX 3.1

Economic transition in central European countries

Since 1990 much of the economic development in central Europe has been heavily influenced by privatization and foreign investment. Privatization has been financed through joint ventures with or the purchase of equity stakes in companies through foreign investors. Estimates are that around $100 billion of foreign direct investment has flowed into central and eastern Europe (see Table 3.5) in 10 years. The development was slowed where inefficient publicly owned

large companies were kept from going out of business mainly for employment reasons.

A relatively new phenomenon is cross-border investments by one country in transition in another. At 4% of Slovene FDI stock, for example, companies headquartered in the Czech Republic have invested in Slovenia as much as investors from the U.S., or the U.K. Slovenes and Bulgarians have invested capital into the banking, industrial and food processing sectors in Macedonia. Hungarian investors in Serbia or Czechs in Romania are common.

Source: Adapted from European Bank for Reconstruction and Development; UNECE 2002; Vakin, S. (2003) "Eastward, ho – foreign direct investment in central and east Europe", palma@unet.com.mk, 26 January

TABLE 3.5 *Foreign direct investment in central and eastern Europe (CEE) ($ billion)*

Foreign direct investment inflow into CEE declined from a record $31 billion in 2002 to a low of $21 billion in 2004. This was almost entirely due to the end of privatization in the Czech Republic and Slovakia.

Country	Foreign direct investment					CUM FDI		Ratio FDI to GDP (%)	
	1994	1995	2001	2002	2003	Until 1996	Until 2001	1995	2001
Bulgaria	0.10	0.98	0.17	0.9	1.4	0.45	1.4	0.8	1.3
Croatia	0.98	0.81	1.5	1.1	1.7	0.58	5.3	0.5	7.4
Czech Republic	0.75	2.53	4.9	8.5	2.6	6.61	15.3	5.6	8.6
Hungary	1.15	4.45	2.4	2.8	2.5	13.27	27.1	10.2	4.6
Poland	0.54	1.13	6.9	4.1	4.2	4.96	45.2	0.9	3.9
Romania	0.34	0.37	1.1	1.1	1.6	1.43	5.3	1.0	2.9
Slovakia	0.18	0.18	0.32	4.0	0.6	0.77	1.7	1.1	1.6
Slovenia	0.13	0.17	0.5	1.87	0.3	0.73	3.4	1.0	2.7

Source: UNCTAD, FDI/TNC database (www.unctad.org/fdistatistics)

refrigerator industries, for example, are dominated by one or more foreign-owned companies.

In the Czech Republic, where at the beginning of 1993 the private sector accounted for only about 15% of GDP, mass privatization began as an attempt to create a nation of shareholders. Every adult got a voucher that could be used to bid for shares in state firms at auctions. The first auctions, which ended in December 1992, transferred 2,000 firms with a book value of $7 billion to the public. The next round sold off another 1,500 firms. By 1998, 5,780 out of 6,284 state-owned firms had been formally privatized in this way. The Czech Republic reached a level of 68.4 private companies per 1,000 inhabitants, a level not only far beyond the neighboring countries in transition, but also above the EU level. To channel the multitude of shares, however, government encouraged the development of investment funds. Nearly three-quarters of Czech vouchers were invested by 400 such funds, many set up by publicly owned banks. Most of those funds had no industrial management experience. They did not pay attention to the necessary restructuring of the companies. At the end of the century, therefore, a substantial number of the companies privatized through the voucher system were in economic difficulties. The success of privatization – more than 75% of the country's GDP comes from private firms today – was based on additional auctions, tenders, management and employee buyouts, and direct sales to foreign investors.

In former East Germany, reunited with its western brother state, the "Treuhandanstalt," a government agency, took over all the publicly held firms, sold the better ones to private investors, closed the worst, and tried to improve the situation of the remaining ones so that they could sell them. They finished their work in 1996, but could not help leaving the eastern part of Germany with too much concentration in the construction industry and a lack of internationally competitive firms. The radical change in economic decision making forced on former East Germany's economic system as well as the fast introduction of the West German mark also had significant social implications. Unemployment increased drastically, since private firms, forced to compete on world markets, could not continue to support the large workforces previously employed by the publicly owned companies. Unemployment went up to more than 20%. In 2004 it still remains at that high level in some parts of former East Germany, despite a great number of people "employed" in retraining programs and in part-time jobs.

Of all the countries of former Yugoslavia, Slovenia has managed the transformation process best. The Slovenian tolar became convertible in 1995. In 1996, one-third of all 1,359 former state-owned companies were entirely privatized. In 2002 the long-deferred privatization of the banking sector took place. With a GDP per capita of $10,370 in 2002 the country had managed to come very close to the GDP per capita of Portugal. Figure 3.5 shows the economic development of the new central European members of the EU as well as eastern European candidates for membership compared to the average development of the 15 members of the EU before the enlargement in May 2004. GDP growth is impressive, inflation has come down substantially, and unemployment rates are similar with the exception of Poland and Slovakia.

Mixed economies Most governments allow private investments in parallel with public investments. In countries with economically liberal traditions, public investments mainly focus on technical and social infrastructure projects that do not attract enough private interest to be carried out. In most countries of western Europe and in industrially developing countries such as Indonesia, governments have also tended to hold stakes in business firms that are of some public interest. For example, the government of the Netherlands, before privatizing their shares, was the owner of the Koninklijke PTT Nederland (the postal and telecommunications company), the public utilities companies, and the Dutch railways. It held shares in KLM (the Dutch airline now merged with Air France, partly owned by the French government), Schiphol Airport in Amsterdam, and DSM (a chemicals group).

Overall, privatization of public investments has been in progress during the 1990s. In the EU, electricity and gas suppliers as well as railway companies, telecommunication and postal services will have to be privatized before 2010. This privatization process increases the opportunities for international private investors. So far Portugal and Austria have been the most active privatizing countries after the U.K. Companies such as Portugal Telecom, the cement maker Cimpor, Electricidade de Portugal, the tobacco monopoly Tabaqueira, the petroleum group Petrogal, and the Banco Fomento & Exterior were privatized. The revenue from privatization mostly went towards canceling public debt and thereby reducing the budget's debt-servicing costs.

The extent to which a country market's economy is governed by free market forces is important to an international marketer. A market-led economy generally offers an international marketer more opportunities. The degree of market orientation affects a firm's ability to reach target markets in other countries.

Economic wealth indicators

As discussed earlier, when assessing the attractiveness of a country market's economic environment, the international marketer needs to establish a list of evaluation criteria against which to systematically compare potential and served markets. The chosen criteria should be relevant to the product market(s) of the company and indicative of the economic standing of the country. In the following, some potential evaluation criteria are presented.

FIGURE 3.5 *Economic development of central and eastern European economies 2002–2006*

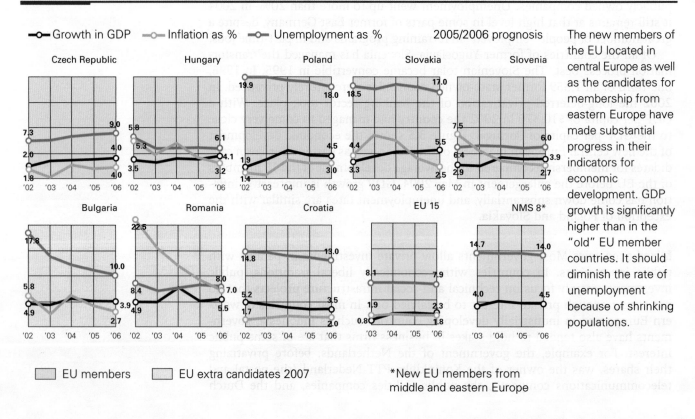

The new members of the EU located in central Europe as well as the candidates for membership from eastern Europe have made substantial progress in their indicators for economic development. GDP growth is significantly higher than in the "old" EU member countries. It should diminish the rate of unemployment because of shrinking populations.

National income

A country's level of production of goods and services may be considered an indicator of its economic wealth and attractiveness as a potential market. The level of production is traditionally expressed through the country's GNP – the World Bank now uses the term gross national income (GNI) or gross domestic product (GDP) per capita. Depending on the firm's product market, one or the other may be a better indicator of a country market's attractiveness. For example, cement producers and companies active in the public transportation sector might prefer GNP because it is more closely related to the potential of their product markets.

Gross national product

In general, the higher the level of economic development, as measured by GNP, in a country market, the more economically viable it is likely to be. As Chapter 1 has illustrated, most of the highly industrialized countries are located in Europe. They are joined by Canada, Japan, and the U.S. Australia, Israel, New Zealand, and Singapore can also be classified as highly developed in economic terms. Large numbers of customers with sufficient economic resources make these strong potential markets.

Most of the world's poorest countries in terms of GNP are located in sub-Saharan Africa (see Figure 3.6). Countries such as Burkina Faso, Burundi, Chad, Ethiopia, Mozambique, Malawi, Mali, Rwanda, Sierra Leone, Somalia, the Sudan,

MAP 3.1 *Sub-Saharan Africa*

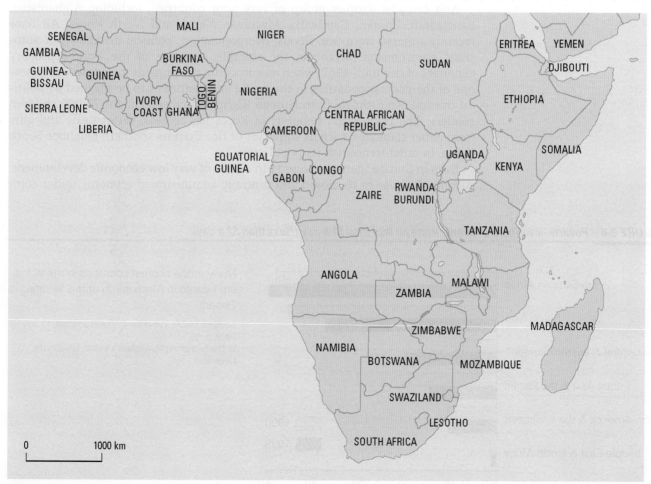

Source: *World Atlas*

and Tanzania repeatedly experience devastating droughts, as well as civil strife and enormous refugee and health problems. Today they are the largest recipients of foreign assistance. Their stagnant economies lack almost all the resources necessary for development: capital, infrastructure, trained industrial and agricultural workers, and political stability. To do business in such countries, the marketer must identify the country's most urgent needs, develop specific solutions, assist in financing, train personnel, and maintain products.

For example, Peter Dyk, an Austrian producer of grain mills, discovered that farmers in the Sudan have a need for small transportable mills with little energy consumption. The mills should not only treat wheat, corn, sorgum, and other local grains, but should also be able to eliminate bugs and the grains of other plants during the milling process. In contrast to competitors' products, the mills Peter Dyk developed can be maintained on site by technically skilled Sudanese. The sales results in this market have encouraged the firm to look for other markets in LDCs.

Even countries such as Cameroon, which produce commodities of a certain value such as crude oil, coffee, cocoa and cotton, experience only little economic development because of their inefficient government-related firms, high budget deficits and political instability. Even in Uganda (coffee accounts for more than 60% of its export revenues), lauded as an example for others to follow in the past decade, where economic reforms and strong fiscal policies lead to GDP growth at an average rate of 6.8% between 1990 and 2001, income per capita is still below $250. Many of those countries have not managed to diversify their economies away from commodities. They have not done enough to foster small firms and women are often marginalized. Strategy box 3.2 discusses some recipes offered by observers of how to reduce poverty in the most deprived countries.

Asia contains another group of very poor countries, including Afghanistan, Bangladesh, Bhutan, Cambodia, Myanmar, Nepal, and North Korea. All have recently suffered from war, floods, overpopulation, political instability, or autocratic governments. Myanmar, for example, was one of the world's primary exporters of rice until 1962, when an autocratic government took power. It is now one of the poorest countries in the world and continues to be plagued by political turmoil. An estimate from Human Rights Watch talks about 70,000 children soldiers. The Democratic Republic of Korea has to seek barter deals and gifts from richer countries, such as shiploads of rice from its southern neighbor South Korea, in order to nourish its population.

Even in Europe there is a country in a state of very low economic development: Albania. Because of its closed and centrally administrated economy under com-

---

FIGURE 3.6   *Poverty line: Share of people living on less than $1 a day (*less than $2 a day)*

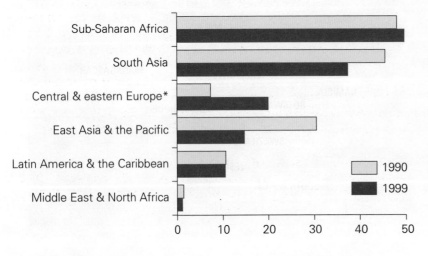

Many of the poorest countries in the world are located in Africa south of the Sahara Desert.

Sources: UNDP; World Bank; *The Economist*, 12 July 2003, p. 68
© The Economist Newspaper Limited, London (18 December 2004)

munist rule and its subsequent political instability, the country's GNP shrank substantially between 1980 and 1997. In the early 1990s the budget deficit reached 50% of GNP. Industrial production equipment is up to 60 years old. More than 70% of the population work in agriculture. Because of corrupt governments and civil war in the middle of the 1990s, things got increasingly bad. In the late 1990s the survival of Albania's population depended on massive aid from western Europe. But nevertheless, the country provides interesting opportunities. It has rich mines of copper, nickel and chromium, its own sources of crude oil, unused waterpower, and beautiful coastlines on the Mediterranean Sea. After the turn of the century the two biggest political parties stopped fighting. Since then, a certain stabilization took place. Inflation slowed from an average of 34.4% in the 1990s to around 5% today. In 2003 the EU started negotiations with the Albanian government to help the country in coming closer to standards needed for EU membership. The wage level has reached $40 to $60 a month.

The potential for conducting profitable international business in these countries seems very low. Low income, restrictive legislation, and poor infrastructures present major obstacles to marketing in these countries. Why, then, should international marketers be interested in these markets at all? The answer lies in both

STRATEGY BOX 3.2

Poverty reduction programs

The *Human Development Report* published by the United Nations Development Program (UNDP) states that in the 1990s income per capita fell in no fewer than 54 industrially developing countries. Even though these years were celebrated as times of reform and hope, the Human Development Index – a statistic summarizing health, longevity, education, and standards of living – fell in 21 countries during the decade.

The report calls for substantial public investment in social and physical infrastructure to remedy problems such as over-dependence on commodities, lack of small private firms, or marginalization of women. This is not very likely to be a valid recipe for African and Asian countries with very low public budgets and high debt.

Other sources call for help from the most economically developed countries and point at the fact that between 1990 and 2001 aid from 23 members of OECD's Development Assistance Committee fell from 0.33% to 0.22% of GDP. And they offer trade liberalization as a way out of the negative development.

In contrast, some specialists in development economics point at some systemic "resistance to change" by those in power in the least developed countries and also by the poor themselves. Most of the poor live in a kind of rural subsistence economy based on food crops and livestock. To shift to cash crops would immediately endanger their subsistence in case of failure. From their point of view, it is the responsibility of the government to distribute goods and services in the form of aid programs as a way to share some of the prosperity of the city people with them.

A key to rural development seems to be the problem of land ownership rights and legal security. In countries where most people own the land they cultivate, such as the northern part of Thailand, rural productivity is much higher than in countries where land ownership is not clear or even non-existent. People must feel safe from abuse of power by local elites and corrupt government officials. They must be safe from land expropriation without adequate compensation and from resettlement against their will.

As the World Bank's Development Report *Attacking Poverty* (2000/2001) emphasizes, without the rule of law, people's participation in the development process, and transparency and accountability, in most cases economic aid rather tends to delay changes because it is simply used to fill the most obvious gaps. The report states that the development of reliable political and administrative institutions goes hand in hand with economic growth.

Source: Adapted from Luther, H.U. (2002) "Resistance to change – why poverty reduction programmes did not work", D+C Development and Cooperation, No. 3, May/June, pp. 22–3; "Years of plenty?", *The Economist*, 12 July 2003, p. 68

current and future opportunities. Many markets in highly industrialized countries are almost, if not entirely, saturated. Developing economies with the natural and human resources to overcome periodic financial and political crises are therefore becoming interesting target markets. To be successful in these markets, companies will have to take a long-term view. They must:

- be willing to train local residents
- facilitate technology transfer
- be adept at cultivating relationships with local firms and influential individuals.

Sometimes governments attempt to attract the participation of non-domestic firms by providing financing for projects with potentially high sales volumes. Opportunities may also arise because many LDC governments want technology from more advanced economies. But technology transfers do not occur in a single step. Rather, there is a multistage flow of technology and managerial expertise between countries at different levels of economic development. Brazil, China, India, and Korea import significant amounts of advanced technology. At the same time, they are playing a significant role in the transfer of technology to developing countries. For example, Indian firms have cooperated with German, Finnish, and Swiss engineering firms such as DEMAG (steel plants) or Jacob Poeri (paper mills) in industrial projects throughout the developing world.

GDP per capita

The **GDP** is the monetary value of all goods and services that have been produced in a country during a year for consumption, investment or governmental purposes, not taking into account the value of products and services produced by agricultural and industrial organizations for their own purposes. GDP per capita is an assessment criterion preferred by international marketers that are more interested in individuals' purchasing power in the countries under consideration, such as manufacturers of consumer products or service providers. However, when applying this criterion in the comparison of country market attractiveness, managers should be aware of the manifold problems related to that measure.

Traditionally, for comparative purposes GDP measured in local currency has been converted into U.S. dollars at currency market exchange rates. However, exchange rates are influenced more by the economic situation of a country. Therefore, a conversion of GDP per capita at market exchange rates in general understates the true purchasing power in developing economies relative to more industrially developed countries. An international marketer wanting to make meaningful comparisons needs to use *purchasing power parities* for conversions. Purchasing power parities take into account the difference in price levels among countries.

Because price levels in industrially developing countries are traditionally rather low, their GDP per capita in U.S. dollars increases compared to conversions at currency market exchange rates. A calculation of the World Bank shows, for example, an increase in GDP per capita for Vietnam from $430 to $2,700 when purchasing power is taken into account.

The problem for the international marketer is to determine the proper purchasing power parities. A theoretically proper approach would be to construct a basket of goods and services available in all countries under consideration, to determine the local prices for that basket, and then to calculate multipliers that equalize the prices of the identical baskets across countries. Because it is rather difficult to define a standard basket of goods and services across different country markets, less sophisticated approaches have been proposed. One is the Big Mac Index illustrated in Figure 3.7, which gives the currency exchange rates that result in hamburgers costing the same in each country.

In addition, both GNP and GDP figures represent national per capita averages. However, bimodal distributions of income are quite common in many industrially less developed and developing countries. That is, a very small part of the population controls most of the income of the entire country, setting a trap for GDP per capita which is calculated as a (then meaningless) mean across the entire population. Because of strong imbalances in the distribution of income and wealth, there may exist a group of potential customers with important disposable income. For example, India (per capita GNP around $300) has a middle class that consists of about 200 million people, growing at about 5% a year, who have consumption expectations comparable to southern Europeans. One percent of the population of approximately 1.1 billion is very rich even by North American standards and lives in a small number of urbanized areas (as illustrated in Strategy box 3.3). This market might therefore be as attractive to a French producer of prestigious perfumes as, for example, Spain, which has a significantly higher per capita income.

A similar statement holds true for industrial goods. In India, to continue the same example, the manufacturing sector is developing rapidly. In recent years Indian firms, such as Larsen & Toubro, an Indian multinational corporation with subsidiaries in the U.S., Asia, and Europe, have become increasingly competitive

FIGURE 3.7 Big Mac index

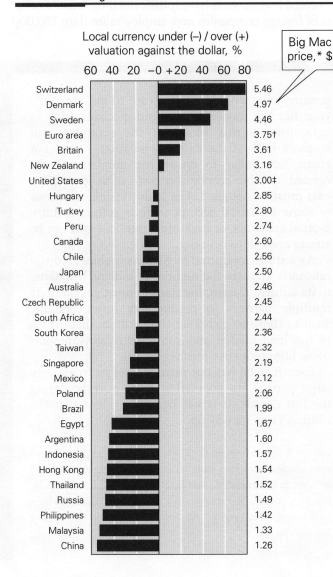

The Economist's Big Mac index offers a light-hearted guide to whether currencies are at their "correct" levels. It is based on the theory of purchasing power parity (PPP) – the notion that a basket of identical traded goods should cost the same in all countries. The Big Mac PPP is the exchange rate that would leave hamburgers costing the same in each country as they do in America.

* At market exchange rate (December 13th)
† Weighted average of member countries
‡ Average of four cities

Source: The Economist (using McDonald's data) 18 December 2004
© The Economist Newspaper Limited, London (12 July 2003)

in such markets as machinery, computer software, and railroad construction. Consequently, there is a growing market for industrial goods. The number of businesses where import licenses are needed was greatly reduced, and foreign participation in Indian companies was fully liberalized. In 34 industries, such as metallurgy, telecommunications, or laboratory equipment, foreign joint venture partners are allowed to hold 51% of shares. Infrastructure is a problem. The bigger firms, both foreign and Indian, invariably have their own generators and dedicated satellite links, which allow them to bypass creaking telephones and power lines. All this specific information, which strongly influences the attractiveness of the country's product markets, is not provided through a simple evaluation using GDP data.

But income distribution may also need to be more closely considered by international marketers interested in highly developed economies, such as the U.S. where the middle class is shrinking. For example, in the early years of the 20th century, South Carolina built a formidable manufacturing base in the textile industry, which thrived by consuming Dixie's cotton crops. But after decades of textile dominance, South Carolina began an economic transformation in the 1960s. It diversified by aggressively courting outside investments, including investment by foreign companies. The inflow of overseas capital increased in the 1980s, when the state won the symbolic capstone of the international trend: a sprawling BMW plant near Greenville, which the German company has been expanding over the years. Foreign investments have transformed the state's economy. American subsidiaries of foreign companies now employ more than 100,000

STRATEGY BOX 3.3

India shining?

Noida, a quarter-of-an-hour drive from New Delhi, via a brand new toll bridge, represents the well-to-do part of India's society. At 11am the Centrestage Mall with its steel and glass façade opens to a crowd quickly filling its seven floors of boutiques, restaurants, coffee shops, and cinemas. A great number of young people stand in line to go see one of 13 films (seven of which are American) in an ultramodern multiplex movie theater. This is the India where 2 million mobile phones are sold every month, 1 million additional cars a year, and which has 100 billion in foreign currency reserves. The consumption spending of the urban middle class of India has raised the country's growth rate to 10.4% at the end of 2003.

Two hours from Lucknow, the capital of India's most populated state, Uttar Pradesh, a village called Sandinagin represents the other side of India: There are 300 million Indians earning less than $1 a day. India is home to half of all hungry people in the world, and 20% of the population have no access to safe drinking water. In order to effectively diminish poverty, India would have to create 10 million jobs a year. But the modernization and mechanization of agriculture – this sector of the economy still employs 60% of the entire population – does not create new jobs. To create the number of jobs needed, durable economic growth of at least 8% a year must be obtained. The highly visible successes of some industrial sectors such as software, automotive assembly, or back-office services will not be strong enough to help out.

As a study conducted by McKinsey shows, to significantly increase the number of Indians belonging to its affluent classes, the country must get rid of its multiple barriers to productivity improvements, such as those to increased competition, distortions in the land market and subsidies to government-owned unproductive businesses.

Even if India has not managed yet to free a very large part of its population from poverty during the last decade, it is has become evident that the country is on its way up.

Source: Adapted from Fr. C. (2004) "'India Shining', un slogan pour classes moyennes dans un pays qui abrite la moitié des affamés de la planète", *Le Monde*, 21 April, p. 4; Lodovico, A.M. Di, W.W. Lewis, V. Palmade, and S. Sankhe (2001) "India – from emerging to surging", *McKinsey Quarterly*, No. 4: *Emerging Markets*, pp. 28–50.

South Carolina workers, almost 9% of the South Carolina workforce. The new manufacturing sector is producing Fuji film, Michelin tires, Hoechst fibers, and BMW cars for sale to Americans and for export as well. Average annual salaries in the state have risen some 38% in one decade, and the average manufacturing hourly wage has risen 33%. These figures mask a costly, offsetting erosion in textiles and related businesses. About half of the losses stem from technological advances that raise productivity; the rest relate to low-priced imports. Thus, if one part of South Carolina's population is thriving, another part is suffering.

Balance of payments

Countries, like firms and individuals, need to keep track of their transactions. The account that records all the economic transactions that take place between a country and other countries over a period of time is the **balance of payments**. This account is divided into several categories, including:

- one or more capital accounts (recording all financial transactions)
- and the current account, commonly known as the **balance of trade**, which keeps track of the country's exports and imports of goods and services.

By definition, the balance of payments must balance – it cannot be either a credit or a debit. But within the balance of payments account any given category, such as the balance of trade, can be either positive or negative. In the last decade, for example, the U.S. balance of trade has been notoriously negative, whereas during the same years the trade balances of Japan and Germany have been positive. In the short run, a country may be able to offset a negative balance of trade by borrowing, using savings, selling off assets, and the like. But in the long run, it is not possible for a country to sustain a negative balance of trade without jeopardizing its economic wealth (see Ethics box 3.2). This is particularly true, if a country's government runs budget deficits of enormous size, such as the U.S. (see Figure 3.8).

A negative balance of trade can have many causes:

- One is that *not enough companies engage in exporting*. For example, most big companies in the U.S. do not emphasize the extension of their exports. They prefer delocalizing their production by investing in emerging economies such as China. From there, the products produced at a by far lower cost are imported to the U.S. and Europe at a by far higher margin.
- A second reason for a country's negative balance of trade may be that *its companies are not internationally competitive enough* (because of high labor costs, lack of technology, high taxes, inadequate industrial structures, etc.).
- Another reason may be *an overrating of the country's currency*, which makes its products and services too expensive to export, while imports from other countries are relatively low priced.
- Finally, a *government's budget deficit* may be an important factor leading to a negative balance of trade. The U.S. government, for example, not unlike many European governments, supports its budget deficit by borrowing from other countries. This borrowing makes it possible to maintain consumption at high levels, which results in a negative balance of trade (and in net imports of capital because of the higher returns of investments).

An international marketer interested in the economic outlook of a potential country market may analyze the country's balance of trade and the government's budget deficit as a percentage of GDP for both short-term and longer term effects.

In the short run, a country's trade deficit indicates that the market is open to imports. In the longer run, the market may become less attractive because of decreasing economic wealth. The impact of budget deficits on the economic future of the country can be estimated from the country's public debt expressed as a percentage of the country's exports.

Ireland is a good example of what government budget discipline may do for economic health. In 1987 Ireland's economy looked a mess. Inconsistent growth and years of loose fiscal policy had pushed the ratio of gross government debt to GDP to 115%; among EU countries, only Belgium was more deeply indebted. But policy was then tightened, and the budget deficit brought down well below 3% of GDP. In combination with substantial development funds financed by EU partners this has helped to make the Irish economy grow at an average of 7.7% throughout the 1990s, that is, significantly faster than the EU average.

Exchange rate

The **exchange rate** of a currency is its price in terms of another currency. Fluctuations of exchange rates may have a dramatic effect on the success of an

---

ETHICS BOX 3.2

A reverse Marshall Plan?

Since World War II U.S. aid and credits – under the label of the Marshall Plan – have significantly contributed to the reconstruction of war-torn Europe. According to figures published by the International Monetary Fund in 2002 the U.S. absorbed 75.5% of all the savings in the world. And this was not a singular event. Is there a reverse Marshall Plan in effect? Does it make economic sense and is it ethically proper that the less economically developed countries of the world finance the economically most prosperous and, in particular, the U.S. through their savings?

The term world savings addresses the sum of funds immobilized for more than a year. This sum represents about $700 billion that pass durably among countries every year. Some countries are net capital exporters: Japan, China, Germany, and France in decreasing order of importance. Surprisingly for many, China, the praised paradise for foreign investors, comes out second as net capital exporter. China primarily buys U.S. treasury bonds, and these purchases are higher than the total of all foreign investments in the country per year.

Other countries are net capital importers. In Europe this is, for example, true for Spain, the U.K., Italy, and Portugal. But their capital imports are minimal compared to the tremendous amount of foreign capital fueling the U.S. economy. In 2002, the U.S. net imported about $528 billion to finance its deficit in the trade of goods and services. Or seen from another perspective, the country's military budget of $379 billion in 2003 was entirely covered by foreign credit.

Classic economic theory on diminishing marginal returns seems to teach us that capital will be invested in emerging countries because the potential gains there are the highest (starting from a lower level). And this is the basic reason given for the free circulation of capital in the world, which supposedly leads to greater wealth of all. In the same way that free exchange of goods is supposed to lead to an optimum for all because every country will specialize in what it is best able to do. But these theoretical considerations are countered by real events. The U.S. economy attracts most capital because it is able to provide the highest returns. The questions remain: Are those high returns:

- the effect of superior productivity levels, efficiency of the workforce, and its organization compared to the rest of the world (why is it then that the U.S. has such a high trade deficit?)

- or does the free movement of capital favor the strongest in terms of technology and military power, because these two factors determine the confidence of investors?

Source: Adapted from Robin, J.-P. (2003) "Les États-Unis prélèvent 75% de l'épargne mondiale", *Le Figaro économie*, 11 September, p. x

international marketer and a destabilizing effect on world trade. When the value of the euro rose for example from $1 = €0.85 in 2003 to €1.32 in 2004 this increase of more than 50% severely hurt European exports.

Contrariwise, when currency exchange rates are entirely fixed, currencies can only be bought or sold at specific rates that do not vary. This again may create global economic strains as described in Future issues box 3.2. Part of the huge U.S. trade deficit problems stem from the fact that the Chinese yuan and other east Asian currencies are pegged to the dollar. Currency fluctuations cannot adjust for differences in competitiveness. Governments can change currency rates, but abrupt changes may lead to a shock for their economies. Compared to the minute-by-minute fluctuations of floating exchange rates, fixed exchange rates offer the advantage of predictability to business firms that need to exchange currencies.

When induced by market forces, exchange rate fluctuations may have short-term or longer term causes. Short-term fluctuations stem from the very complex offer and demand structure of the international currency market:

- An individual consumer changing currency for vacation or other consumption purposes acts as a buyer or seller.
- So do large corporations, buying and selling foreign currency for international trading purposes.
- So do investors, trying to profit from different interest rates across country markets.
- So do commercial banks and brokers, serving their clients.
- So do central banks, intervening to reach macroeconomic goals such as decreasing inflationary pressures.
- Or speculators, who buy and sell foreign currencies in anticipation of their changing future value.

FIGURE 3.8 *The twin deficits and the U.S. dollar*

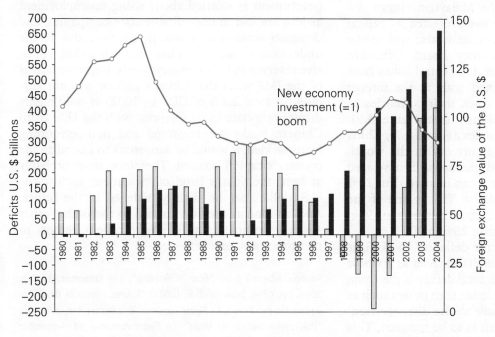

Federal government budget deficit — Foreign exchange value of U.S. $
U.S. current account (broad trade) deficit

The U.S. balance of trade has been notoriously negative. But since the turn of the century the trade deficit as well as the federal government budget deficit have seen tremendous increases. The effect on the value of the U.S. dollar is demonstrated by the blue line in the figure.

Source: Jeff Rosensweig, Emory University

Longer term fluctuations are the result of a country's growth, balance of payments, and inflation rates.

Inflation is an increase in prices in an economy that results in a decline in real purchasing power for customers in that economy. Inflation increases the prices of factors of production, which results in increasing costs. Increased costs are reflected in higher prices of goods and services. Their international competitiveness is reduced. Exchange rate fluctuations are in theory supposed to offset that effect of inflation exactly. Devaluation of a currency should increase exports, because export prices will be lower.

Because fixed exchange rates may prevent international business transactions, most governments let their currencies' exchange rates fluctuate to a certain extent. To keep exchange rate fluctuations at a level that is manageable by international business, and to promote international monetary cooperation, the International Monetary Fund (IMF) has been established. Toolbox 3.1 describes its purpose and functioning in more detail.

Independent floating

Independently floating currencies, such as the U.S. dollar, the euro, the U.K. pound, the Japanese yen, or the Swiss franc, can be bought, held and sold like any other commodity. This helps to ensure the availability of foreign currencies for conducting international transactions, but it can also result in an "overvalued" or "undervalued" currency (compared to the economic status of the country),

FUTURE ISSUES BOX 3.2

Fear of floating?

The Chinese yuan and the Malaysian ringgit are pegged to the U.S. dollar and protected by capital controls. The Hong Kong dollar is also tied to the greenback through a currency board. Officially, other Asian currencies float, but central banks have been intervening on a grand scale in the foreign exchange market to hold down their currencies as the U.S. dollar has weakened (see Figure 3.9). According to the Big Mac index (Figure 3.7), China has the most undervalued currency in the world. Using more sophisticated methods, Swiss-based UBS bank reckons that the yuan is more than 20% undervalued against the dollar. This is one of the reasons why exports of industrial products made in China increased by more than 25% in 2003.

The biggest bilateral trade deficit of the U.S. is with China ($103 billion in 2002). Asia as a whole accounts for half of the U.S. total deficit. If the Asian currencies are fixed to the dollar, then others such as the euro or the yen will have to rise disproportionately if the U.S. trade deficit is to be trimmed. This fact has made the U.S. and Japanese governments as

well as some western European governments lead a campaign in favor of a free-floating or at least appreciated yuan.

But there are some arguments against such a decision. Asian governments worry that appreciating currencies might hurt their exports. The Chinese government is worried about rising unemployment as jobs are lost in unprofitable state companies, and deflation remains an issue. In addition, due to the undervalued yuan, China has been able to build massive reserves in U.S. treasury bonds. Representatives of the IMF warn that China's current account surplus (in total 2.2% of GDP in 2002) is only highly disproportionate in its relations with the U.S. Until Chinese banks are reformed and non-performing loans tackled, it would be dangerous to liberalize the country's capital account. Therefore, most probably at best, the yuan's band of movement against the U.S. dollar may be slightly widened in the future. And, as long as the yuan is tied to the dollar, other Asian governments will have excellent reason to resist changes, too.

Source: Adapted from "Fear of floating", *The Economist*, 12 July 2003, pp. 65–6; Marchand, S. (2003) "L'Apec rejette la flexibilité demandée par Bush", *Le Figaro économie*, 6/7 September, p. iv; and "Polémique autour du yuan", *Le Figaro économie*, 11 September 2003, p. x

because market mechanisms are strongly influenced by personal perceptions of central bank governors, currency traders, investors, and speculators.

For example, since 2003 the U.S. dollar has been undervalued compared to the euro (estimates run between 15 and 30% depending on the actual exchange rate). The U.S. government and the U.S. Federal Reserve take joint action to keep the value of the U.S. currency down in order to decrease the country's large deficit in the balance of trade. American companies enjoy a certain price advantage.

Stepwise and block floating

Some currencies, such as the Swedish krona and the Danish krone, do not fluctuate freely against each other. The currency exchange rates are allowed to fluctuate "stepwise" around fixed exchange rates to the euro in a predetermined percentage. If two currencies arrive at the upper and lower end of their allowed zone of fluctuation, the national banks involved must buy and sell the respective currencies to stabilize their exchange rates.

Foreign investment ratio

In theory, foreign investment is simply capital flowing from one country to another according to the country's relative advantage. That is, in the absence of artificial barriers such as tariffs, investment funds can be expected to seek the highest real rate of return. Therefore, with increasing liberalization of global

FIGURE 3.9   *Crawling tigers*

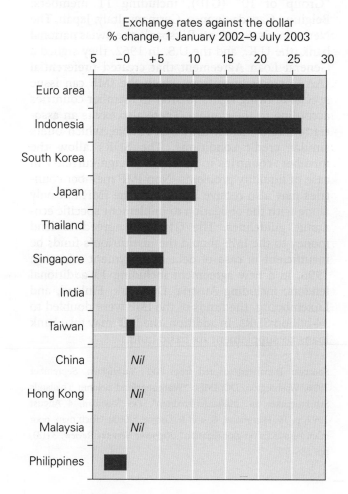

Exchange rates against the dollar
% change, 1 January 2002–9 July 2003

The currency exchange rates of most newly industrialized countries in east Asia have been rather stable against the U.S. dollar in the last years. In contrast, the euro saw a spectacular increase in its value against the U.S. dollar.

Source: *The Economist*, 12 July 2003, p. 65
© The Economist Newspaper Limited, London (12 July 2003)

trade, foreign investment expressed as a percentage of GDP in a country under consideration becomes an increasingly valid indicator of the market's economic attractiveness.

Financial institutions

Because the economic situation in many industrially less developed countries around the world is not promising enough to attract international direct investment, international financial institutions play an important role in funding investments needed for economic development. The most important institutions are international banks and funds:

- World Bank
- European Bank for Reconstruction and Development
- Asian Development Bank and Fund

TOOLBOX 3.1   International Monetary Fund

Established in 1944 at the Bretton Woods Conference, along with the World Bank, the International Monetary Fund today is a special organization of the United Nations Organization. Its major objective is to promote international monetary cooperation through information and consultancy, to stabilize currency exchange rates, to establish and maintain a multilateral payment system for trade, to reduce barriers to foreign exchange transactions, and to support a balanced expansion of world trade (along with the World Trade Organization). The IMF acts as a lender of last resort to countries that are unable to pay the interest on their external debt by providing foreign currency loans.

For example, in August 1997, Thailand agreed to privatize important state-owned companies, to reform its taxation system, and to stop paying subsidies to firms that are close to bankruptcy in exchange for a loan of $8 billion from the IMF together with Japan's Export–Import Bank which should refill the country's foreign exchange reserves. The country at that point had an external debt of around $100 billion, and its currency, the baht, had been devalued against the U.S. dollar by more than 20% in one month, leading to problems in servicing the external debt. In addition, the accord fixed a maximum inflation rate of 7%, and a maximum budget deficit of 7% of Thailand's GDP. In exchange, the IMF offered to stabilize the baht, in relation to the U.S. dollar, at a level not more than 15% below the exchange rate before the exchange rate crisis struck.

Despite such successful actions the IMF has not been able to avert crises from Mexico in 1994–95 to Argentina in 2001–2002, with the east Asian crisis of 1997–98 and the Russian crisis of 1998 in between. In fact, some commentators have even argued that the policies of the IMF have made conditions worse rather than better.

As of 2003 the IMF had 184 members. The regular fund of IMF is financed by quota subscriptions of those members. The major financiers are the "Group of 10" (G10), including 11 members: Belgium, Canada, France, Germany, Italy, Japan, The Netherlands, Sweden's Riksbank, the Swiss national bank, the U.K., and the U.S. In 1962, they signed a General Loan Agreement that created preferential (AAA) credit lines from which the IMF can issue special drawing rights (SDRs) to member countries according to their quota. There also exists an association agreement with Saudi Arabia, which offers similar credit conditions. The SDRs allow the member countries to purchase foreign currency in case of liquidity problems. Non-IMF member countries may also receive loans from the IMF, but only along with the obligation to implement specific economic guidelines. The G10 also agreed to lend money to the IMF should the institution's funds be insufficient in case of debt and payment crises. In 1996, in a new agreement including 13 additional lenders, including Austria, Denmark, Finland, and Luxembourg, the funds of the IMF were doubled to 34 billion SDRs. In addition, the IMF may take bank loans to supplement its basic fund.

Sources: Translated/adapted from IWF Nachrichten, September 1996, Washington, DC: IMF; "Währungsfond belohnt Thailands Strukturpaket mit Milliardenkrediten", Der Standard, 4 August 1997, p. 15; Hammond, C. and R. Grosse (2003) "Rich man, poor man: resources on globalization", Reference Services Review, 31(3), pp. 285–95

TOOLBOX 3.2   Model for an economic viability profile

The model suggested here is rather simple. It contains data and evaluations concerning the internal economic status of a country market, its foreign debt position, and the country's status in international trade.

To gain 100 points (the best evaluation) for a criterion specified target figures must be reached. The number of points given to a country for any criterion depends on the value that the respective indicator reaches in that country. The result of such an analysis is one figure that can be compared across countries (see Table 3.6).

In addition, to be managerially meaningful, such profiles and comparisons need to be established on an ongoing basis. Table 3.7 shows how the basic economic data of a country market may change over time. The conclusions of an international marketer concerning a country market's economic viability should, therefore, be taken in the light of time series data. To better understand their meaning, they need to be further supplemented by information concerning the political and legal environments as well as the cultural specifics of the country. These will be discussed in the chapters that follow.

TABLE 3.6   *Economic viability profile*

Criteria	Indicator	Weight	Target
Growth rate	Change of real GDP		≥ + 5%
Level of development	GDP per capita		≥ USD 10,000
Inflation	Inflation rate	40%	≤ 2% > 0%
Investments	Investments as % of GDP		≥ 30%
Fiscal policy	Net budget deficit as % of GDP		≤ 3%
External debt	Public external debt as % of export		0%
		30%	
Debt repayment	Repayment of external debt as % of exports		0%
International trade	Balance of trade as % of GDP		≥ 5%
		30%	
Liquidity	Foreign exchange reserves as % of imports		≥ 100%

Source: Adapted from Schicklgruber, W. (1991) "Die Beurteilung des Länderriskos" report, April, Vienna: Länderbank, p. 6

TABLE 3.7   *Development of selected economic indicators in the Czech Republic*

Indicator	2001	2002	2003	2004 estimate	2005 forecast
Real growth (%)	2.6	1.5	3.1	3.7	3.5
Inflation rate (%)	4.7	1.8	0.1	2.9	2.1
Total exports ($ billion)	40.5	45.5	56.5	74.5	91.6
Total imports ($ billion)	42.0	47.1	58.6	75.7	92.5
Balance of trade ($ billion)	−5.1	−3.0	−2.8	−1.8	−1.3
External debt ($ billion)	22.4	27.0	34.9	39.0	44.0
Debt service ratio (in % of export revenue)	14.8	9.0	8.1	6.7	6.0
Foreign exchange reserves ($ billion)	14.5	23.7	26.9	29.0	32.0

The development of some economic indicators in the Czech Republic over a period of 5 years illustrates the importance of observing time series to make meaningful conclusions.

Source: Adapted from Schrick-Hildebrand P. (2004) "Tschechische Republik – Länderanalyse," IKB Deutsche Industriebank AG, p. 3

- Inter-American Development Bank
- African Development Bank and Fund
- Islamic Development Bank.

The Appendix to this chapter illustrates their major objectives and functioning. The international marketer should be interested in the activities of these financial institutions because they provide business opportunities in otherwise economically unattractive markets.

International stock and debt markets

In the highly developed economies, private institutions, such as pension funds and insurance companies, are important capital sources. They operate via international stock and debt markets, which present an opportunity for international companies to find the lowest interest rate for loans or the highest stock price for equity issues. For example, the Tokyo Stock Exchange has grown to be second only to the New York Stock Exchange. Since the mid-1980s, more foreign than domestic companies have been newly listed in Tokyo. In fact, the international growth of stock markets has changed the corporate financial picture considerably. More and more often, companies in industrial countries are going directly to financial markets, meaning that commercial banks are being replaced by other sources of funds.

Economic viability profiles

When the international marketer has gathered the relevant data the economic environment of various country markets can be comparatively evaluated. The comparison is largely facilitated by developing profiles of economic viability. Toolbox 3.2 shows an example of such a model. Of course, each company will need to construct a profile relevant to the specific product market(s) it is targeting.

Singapore's economic success relies on state-of-the-art communication infrastructure

© Jeannette Meier Kamer/iStock

Summary

The economy of a country is a major part of each company's macro-environment. Generally, it is the first dimension to be studied in assessing the attractiveness of any country market. As a first step the international marketer has to decide which characteristics of the economic environment are relevant to the company's business. Having determined the relevant factors of influence, the marketer will need to analyze their current state in the country markets under comparison and to anticipate their potential states on the planning horizon.

If a market does not contain enough customers with the purchasing power to buy the product, it is not economically viable:

- The degree of urbanization in a society is of interest to many international marketers because it represents concentrations of potential customers and strongly influences distribution needs.
- The capabilities to be found in a country's population have a significant influence on the country's wealth. The educational system and the skills and flexibility of the population may therefore be important factors to be considered.

The natural environment of a country market, its resources, topography, and climatic conditions, represent an important source of potential wealth for its population. In using resources from that natural environment for their business purposes, international marketers need to take care of the sustainability of their activities. That is, they must be aware that a business will only be successful over a longer period if it does not destroy its own bases.

Besides the human and natural resources available in a country market, its available and emerging technological resources may influence its attractiveness. For international marketing to be possible, a certain energy supply, transportation, communication, and commercial infrastructure has to be in place in a country market. In addition, an international marketer needs to consider the predominant concept of technology in each of the societies analyzed. Technological resources and technology concept may demand entirely different marketing mixes to ensure long-term success.

The economic system of a country is its specific combination of human, natural, and technological resources. Depending on the level of industrial development, shares of different industrial sectors of the economy will vary. So will ownership of the means of production as well as economic decision making, depending on the market orientation of the governing political forces.

To finally assess the attractiveness of a country market's economic environment, the international marketer needs to establish a list of evaluation criteria against which to systematically compare potential and served markets. The economic literature suggests some general indicators of economic wealth:

- national product
- balance of payments
- exchange rate
- foreign investment ratio.

The chosen criteria should be:

- relevant to the product market(s) of the company
- indicative of the economic standing of the country
- applicable across all country markets to be compared.

If the economic analysis yields positive results, the international marketer may continue the evaluation process by examining the political and legal as well as the cultural environments of the country markets.

DISCUSSION QUESTIONS

1. Explain how the structure of a country's population influences the viability of the country market for an international marketer of your choice.

2. Discuss why the capabilities of a potential country market's population may be of great importance to international marketers. Find examples to emphasize your points.

3. A country market's natural environment influences its attractiveness to a marketer of industrial products. Discuss, based on examples from business magazines.

4. Find examples from the internet of companies that show how a sustainable method of production and marketing helps to assure their economic success. What is the difference in those companies' decisions and actions compared to their competitors?

5. Illustrate the influence of a country's infrastructure on the economic attractiveness of local product markets by comparing a self-chosen highly industrially developed market with an economically less developed market.

6. What are the major points of attraction for international marketers interested in European countries in transition? Explain how different methods of transition may influence the result of the assessment process.

7. Discuss what information about a country market's attractiveness an international marketer can derive from the country's GNP and GDP per capita data.

8. Explain why a country's balance of trade may be of interest to an international marketer from a short-run as well as a long-run point of view.

9. Discuss the role of international financial institutions in maintaining the economic viability of country markets.

10. Take an example of an internationally operating company and establish a profile of relevant indicators for the assessment of its served country markets' economic viability. Explain the reasons for choosing those indicators.

ADDITIONAL READINGS

Hirschey, M., J.L. Pappas, and D. Whigham (1995) *Managerial Economics, European Edition,* London: International Thomson Business Press.

Prahalad, C.K. and A. Hammond (2002) "Serving the world's poor, profitably", *Harvard Business Review,* September, 48–60.

Rosensweig, J. (1998) *Winning the Global Game: A Strategy for Linking People and Profits,* New York: Free Press

Yau, O.H.M. and H.C. Steele (2000) *China Business: Challenges in the 21st Century,* Hong Kong: Chinese University Press.

Useful internet links

Air France	http://www.airfrance.com/
Asian Development Bank	http://www.adb.org
Bank Austria	http://www.ba-ca.com/en/
Big Mac Index	http://www.economist.com/markets/Bigmac/Index.cfm
Charoen Pokphand Group	http://www.cpthailand.com/webguest/
CIA (The World Factbook)	http://www.cia.gov/cia/publications/factbook/
Citigroup	http://www.citigroup.com/
DEMAG	http://www.demagcranes.com/Portal/index1.html
DSM	http://www.dsm.com/en_U.S./html/about/about_us_home.htm
European Bank for Reconstruction and Development	http://www.ebrd.com/

Fischer Weltalmanach	http://www.weltalmanach.de/
Human Development Reports	http://hdr.undp.org/reports/default.cfm
Hypo-Vereinsbank	http://www.hypovereinsbank.de/pub/io/engl/home_engl.jsp
infoBASE Europe (European News Service)	http://www.ibeurope.com
Information on the Commonwealth of Independent States (CIS)	http://en.wikipedia.org/wiki/Commonwealth_of_Independent_States
Information on the Council for Mutual Economic Assistance (CMEA, also called COMECON)	http://en.wikipedia.org/wiki/Comecon
International Bank for Reconstruction and Development (IBRD)	http://www.worldbank.org/
International Centre for the Settlement of Investment Disputes (ICSID)	http://www.worldbank.org/icsid/
International Development Association (IDA)	http://www.worldbank.org/
International Finance Corporation (IFC)	http://www.ifc.org/
International Monetary Fund	http://www.imf.org/
Islamic Development Bank	http://www.isdb.org/
KLM	http://www.klm.com/corporate_en/
KPN Netherlands	http://www.kpn-corporate.com/eng
Larsen & Toubro Limited India	http://www.larsentoubro.com/
LNM Group / Mittal Steel	http://www.lnmnv.com/Company/Profile.htm
McKinsey	http://www.mckinsey.com/aboutus/whatwedo/
Mitsubishi UFJ Financial Group	http://www.mtfg.co.jp/english/
Mizuho Financial Group	http://www.mizuho-fg.co.jp/english/
Multilateral Investment Guarantee Agency (MIGA)	http://www.miga.org/
New York Stock Exchange	http://www.nyse.com/
Online information on countries	http://www.your-nation.com
Oracle Corporation	http://www.oracle.com/
Organisation for Economic Co-operation and Development (OECD)	http://www.oecd.org/
Texaco	http://www.texaco.com/
UNCTAD (United Nations Conference on Trade and Development)	http://www.unctad.org/wir
United Nations Development Program	http://www.undp.org/
United Nations Population Division Home Page	http://www.un.org/esa/population/unpop.htm
VA Industrial Services	http://www.vatech.at/
World Bank	http://www.worldbank.org/
World Bank Publications	http://publications.worldbank.org/ecommerce/
Wrigley	http://www.wrigley.com/

The richer economies of the world have established financial institutions to support the economic development of countries with a lower level of economic development.

World Bank Group

The World Bank Group is based in Washington, D.C. It consists of five closely associated institutions: The International Bank for Reconstruction and Development (IBRD), the International Development Association (IDA), the International Finance Corporation (IFC), the Multilateral Investment Guarantee Agency (MIGA), and the International Centre for the Settlement of Investment Disputes (ICSID), which have a common president and are organizationally integrated. Their common objective is to support the economic and social development of their less developed member countries by providing financial aid and consultancy as well as some help in getting support by third parties. IBRD and IDA, both heavily involved in fighting poverty, play a major role in the coordination of foreign aid, that is, in the coordination and financing of development programs for individual countries.

IBRD was established at the currency and finance conference of the UNO in Bretton Woods in 1944 and has been operative since June 1946. Its members are most countries of the world. The IBRD (and IDA) is mainly capitalized by the U.S. (16.4%), Japan (7.8%), Germany (4.5%), France and the U.K. (4.3% each). It provides loans to middle-income economically developing countries throughout the world (against interest payments or governmental guarantees) if private capital for productive investments is not available at adequate rates. It also provides technical assistance to aid in development across a variety of projects, including water supply, infrastructure development, population planning, industrial development, and tourism, and provides loans for measures to improve a country's industrial structure (Figure 3.10). Funds are mainly generated through borrowing in international capital markets.

IDA provides long-term (35–40 years with a 10 years' grace period) loans at no interest, and grants to the countries with the lowest per capita GDP (below $875) for projects reducing poverty, improving economic structures, and protecting the environment. IDA depends on contributions from wealthier member countries for most of its financial resources.

IFC supports private productive enterprise in industrially less developed countries through partly (usually 25%) financing investment projects without government guarantees at market conditions (if sufficient private capital is not available at reasonable conditions), as well as through provision of investment capital (giving takeover guarantees), technical assistance and consultancy.

Established in 1988 MIGA has the main objective of supporting foreign private direct investments in economically developing member countries by providing guarantees for non-commercial risks such as currency transfer limitations, expropriation of assets, war, or civil disturbance. Guarantees are given for 15 years for up to 90% of the investment, limited to a maximum of $50 million per project. MIGA also provides technical assistance to help developing countries promote investment opportunities and uses its legal services to smooth possible impediments to investment.

ICSID provides facilities for settlement – by conciliation or arbitration – of investment disputes between foreign investors and their host countries.

Inter-American Development Bank

The Inter-American Development Bank (IDB), located in Washington, D.C. and established by 19 Latin American countries and the U.S. in 1959 (today 27 Latin and Central American members, the U.S. and Canada as well as 17 European countries, Israel and Japan), has the main objective of supporting the economic and social development of the less industrially developed members in this part of the world by providing project loans to governments or against governmental guarantees, supporting industrial sector adaptation programs, and helping in foreign debt reduction programs. The fight against poverty, the improvement of environmental protection, and modernization of the members' industries are of primary importance.

In addition to the Bank, the IDB Group consists of the Inter-American Investment Corporation (IIC) and the Multilateral Investment Fund (MIF). The IIC, an autonomous affiliate of the Bank, was established to promote the economic development of the region by financing small and medium-scale private companies. The MIF was created in 1992 to promote investment reforms and to stimulate private-sector development.

African Development Bank Group/Asian Development Bank

Both banks based in Abidjan, Côte d'Ivoire, and Manila, Philippines, respectively, focus on similar development needs as the World Bank in the most deserving countries of their respective regions.

FIGURE 3.10 *IBRD/IDA lending by sector 2002*

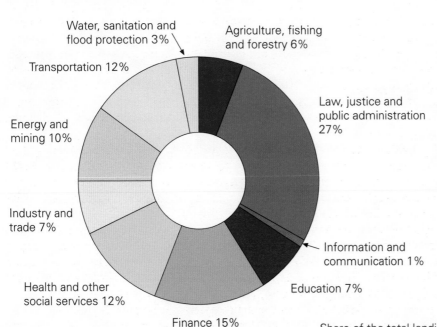

The International Bank for Reconstruction and Development provides technical assistance to aid in development across a variety of projects, including water supply, infrastructure development, population planning, industrial development and tourism, and provides loans for measures to improve a country's industrial structure.

Source: World Bank Group (2002) *Working for a World Free of Poverty*, p. 19
International Bank for Reconstruction and Development/The World Bank

Share of the total lending of $19.5 billion

Islamic Development Bank group

The Islamic Development Bank (IDB) was founded by the members of the Organization of Islamic Countries in 1974. It supports the economic development and social improvements of member countries and other Muslim communities conforming to sharia worldwide. Loans for 15 to 25 years are made for infrastructure projects such as education centers or irrigation projects, free of redemption for the first three to seven years. In addition the bank engages in equity financing of industrial and agricultural projects, leasing, and part payment sales in international trade.

European Bank for Reconstruction and Development

The 60 members of the European Bank for Reconstruction and Development (EBRD), including the EU and the EIB (European Investment Bank) founded the bank in 1991 with its main purpose to support a balanced development of the former communist countries in central and now mainly eastern Europe as well as central Asia. Countries adhering to a multiparty democratic political system, a market economy and a pluralistic society receive help through the financing of investments in infrastructure projects as well as the restructuring of industrial sectors.

Source: Adapted from World Bank Group (2003) *Working for a World Free of Poverty*, Washington, D.C.; Baratta, M. (2004) *Der Fischer Weltalmanach 2005*, Frankfurt a.M.: Fischer Taschenbuch Verlag

POTENTIAL MARKET ASSESSMENT: POLITICAL AND LEGAL ENVIRONMENT

4

Learning objectives

After studying this chapter you will be able to:

- discuss the importance of political and legal environment stability to a firm

- explain the effects of a government's political objectives on an international marketer's business

- illustrate various forms of non-tariff barriers encountered in international marketing

- discuss the impact of different political objectives on governments' investment policies

- explain the influence of legal restrictions on the attractiveness of different country markets

- develop a list of criteria to evaluate the company-specific exposure to political risk in different country markets

Chapter outline

Analyzing the political and legal environment

Political system

Political system stability
Form of government
Parties and interest groups

Major political objectives

Political sovereignty
National prestige and prosperity
National security
Protection of cultural identity

International trade policy

Export/import policy
Investment policy
Trade sanctions

Legal environment

International business law
Regulation of competition
Regulations concerning the marketing mix

"Managing" the political and legal environment

Assessing political risk
Management decisions

Summary

INTERNATIONAL MARKETING SPOTLIGHT

Competing on legal grounds

In 2003, Deutsche Post, a listed company controlled by the German government, had a bitter regulatory dispute with its main competitors in the U.S., United Parcel Service Inc. and FedEx Corp. Until July 2003 Deutsche Post owned a 25% stake in Miami-based Astar Air Cargo Inc., a freight-carrying airline then called DHL Airways Inc. Deutsche Post sold its stake but still 90% of Astar's business was generated by Deutsche Post's DHL unit. When the Germans acquired the ground operations of Airborne Inc., Seattle, to become the No. 3 express courier in the U.S., the two major competitors asked for a ruling of the U.S. Department of Transportation. They argued that Deutsche Post continued to control Astar, violating a U.S. law that bars foreign-owned and foreign-controlled airlines from carrying freight or passengers within the U.S. The threat to Deutsche Post consisted in that they would be forced to find a new carrier, a potentially costly and time-consuming undertaking.

Deutsche Post countered that its relationship with Astar was similar to the airline deals of UPS and FedEx in Europe. UPS contracts out intra-European flights to Star Air, a subsidiary of Maersk A/S of Copenhagen. UPS is Star Air's main customer. The planes carry the UPS logo and are painted in its trademark brown. Chief Executive, Klaus Zumwinkel, declared his company prepared to strike back with a move that could hamper the European operations of FedEx and UPS looking abroad for growth. He said that the company had asked the European Commission to consider whether a Danish airline that serves UPS exclusively should meet the same standards UPS is trying to impose on Deutsche Post's U.S. airline partner.

David Bolger, a spokesperson for UPS, said that Deutsche Post made illogical, improper comparisons: "UPS isn't a government-controlled entity. Deutsche Post is." FedEx asserted that it followed all EU regulations.

"We've only just arrived in the U.S. and have been confronted with political issues to an unbelievable degree," Mr. Zumwinkel said, noting that UPS has been allowed to operate its European hub from Cologne in Germany for two decades without facing such scrutiny. And he added: "If our partners lose their license because they're allegedly under the control of an evil foreign ruler – one who, by the way, studied in the U.S., is a big fan of the U.S. and who worked there for McKinsey – then we would simply look for other air-freight carriers," adding that he would "regret it, because a lot of jobs at our partner airlines would be lost."

Source: Adapted from Kartnitschnig, M. (2003) "Deutsche Post girds for battle; German delivery firm asks EU to impose restrictions on rivals UPS and FedEx", *Wall Street Journal*, 6 October, A14

The focal question of this chapter is: What are the relevant dimensions of the political and legal environment of our served product market, how are they shaped in the geographic markets under consideration, and what impact do they have on the attractiveness of those markets?

Analyzing the political and legal environment

The political systems of the countries served or being considered by an international marketer are an important part of the firm's macro-environment. A multitude of more or less powerful groups of stakeholders from inside but sometimes also outside a country's borders influences:

- who governs the country
- what policies the government follows
- what legal regulations result from those policies.

Most companies are not able to influence their political and legal environment directly but their opportunities for successful business activities largely depend on its structure and content. A marketer serving international markets or planning to do so, therefore, has to carefully assess the political and legal environments of the current or potential markets to evaluate their attractiveness and derive potential consequences. Such consequences may be:

● resource investments
● adaptations of competitive strategy
● development or acquisition of specific capabilities
● policies and actions
● divestments.

The first step in assessing the political and legal environment of country markets is to determine which *characteristics of that environment are relevant to the product market(s)* of the company (Figure 4.1).

For Airbus Industries, the U.K., French, German, and Spanish manufacturer of Airbus jetliners headquartered in Toulouse, France, for example, the political climate between its home governments and the governments of potential customers' countries can have a determinant effect on sales. For some years after China cracked down on the democracy movement in 1989, France had taken a clear position concerning human rights in China. As a consequence, it took Airbus years until China's Premier Li Peng visited Paris, to finalize a contract for 33 Airbus planes. The deal could only be struck because at the same time, the

FIGURE 4.1 *Assessing potential markets: Political and legal environment*

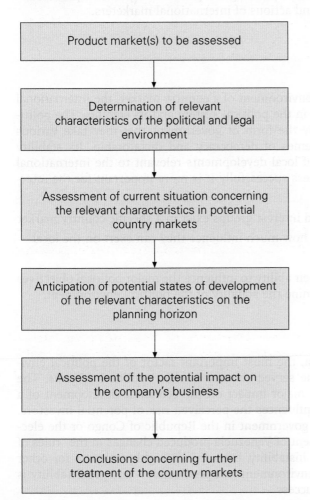

In assessing the political and legal environment of potential markets the marketer first has to determine factors relevant to the product market(s) the company is serving. Then the current situation concerning international, regional, and local factors of influence can be assessed and their potential states of development on the planning horizon anticipated. From the results of the analyses the potential impact of the political and legal environment on the company's business can be assessed. Finally, conclusions concerning the further treatment of the analyzed country markets may be drawn.

U.S. government came close to taking sanctions against China in an attempt to make it reduce piracy of software, CDs, and other products. China's government believed that Boeing, the largest U.S. exporter and fierce competitor of Airbus Industries, could influence the U.S. government's policy if it found out that its business interests were at stake.

Having determined the relevant factors of influence from the political and legal environment, the marketer may *analyze their current state in the country markets* under consideration. To fully assess the potential impact of the relevant factors on the success of the firm, their *potential states of development at the planning horizon* will need to be anticipated. For example, in 1995, when the U.S. had not yet established full diplomatic relations with Vietnam, U.S.-based companies from capital intensive industries, such as Mobil Oil or Unisys Corp., were hurt by not having access to U.S. Export–Import Bank financing, Private Investment Corp. guarantees, risk insurance, and other subsidized credits. From that point of view, Vietnam would have been a very unattractive market. But because the establishment of full diplomatic relations in the not too distant future was highly probable, those companies still considered the market as interesting.

An *evaluation of the impact of the current state and future potential development* of all relevant characteristics of the political and legal environment in the country markets under consideration will allow the international marketer to decide how to "manage" those environments. That is, the company's management will decide *how to react to the expected development*. It may, for example, decide to withdraw from a market, to search for a local business partner to improve its situation, or to invest heavily in order to profit from a promising development.

This chapter will discuss various political and legal factors that may be relevant for the business of internationally operating companies and give examples of how they influence the decisions and actions of international marketers.

Political system

When analyzing the political environment of a country market, the international marketer is mainly interested in the political system and its stability. The political system is characterized by the form of government that may take various forms between the two extremes of democracy and dictatorship. Its stability influences the predictability of local developments relevant to the international marketer. But for doing business successfully it is more important for the international marketer to know:

- what political parties and interest groups exist in a specific country market
- what their goals are and how much influence they can exert on the local government.

Such interest groups and their ability to influence the major political objectives of government strongly determine the stability of the political environment.

Political system stability

For the international marketer, the most important factor of the political environment is the stability of the served country markets' political systems. The level of instability can have a major impact on the economic development of a country or region because it influences the perceived risk of potential investors. Events like the change of the government in the Republic of Congo or the election of Hugo Chávez as president of Venezuela produced changes in the "rules of the business game." Political instability, even if it is highly welcome for other reasons, makes the business environment less predictable – and predictability is a key to long-term business success.

Form of government

Forms of government differ in the extent to which they permit political participation by the general population. Democracies provide opportunities for the population to take an active role in the formulation of governmental policies. Although they vary greatly in the actual forms of their political mechanisms, Denmark, Thailand, Mexico, Tunisia, Canada, and Australia, for example, consider themselves as democracies. Countries such as the Netherlands, the U.K., and Japan are also constitutional monarchies. Each has a royal head of government with limited and specified roles. In addition to performing important ceremonial roles, Queen Elizabeth II of the U.K., for instance, can convene parliament, reads the government's policy statement, and may ennoble meritorious persons (following the suggestions of government). But she does not rule by holding centralized power, in contrast to the royal heads of absolute monarchies, like the King of Saudi Arabia.

According to the 2002 United Nations Human Development Report (UNHDR), 81 countries have taken "significant" steps towards democracy, with 33 military regimes replaced by civilian governments. Of the world's around 200 countries, 140 now hold multiparty elections. That may not make them democratic. In sub-Saharan Africa, 42 out of 48 countries have held multiparty elections since 1990, but most have simply allowed a rotation of plundering governments. Many of the other new "democracies" have not gone beyond elections: An independent judiciary, equality before a well-enforced rule of law, and constitutional limits on the abuse of political power are still missing. Eighty-two countries may be considered to be full democracies in that sense, and those are home to 57% of the world's population.

Observers from western democracies tend to attribute the extent of political stability in a country to the country's form of government. However, as a number of examples show, the form of government and political stability are not directly related. For example, when the communist regime in Serbia was replaced by a more democratically constituted government political stability decreased in the country. The centrally controlled power of the former dictatorship with rather stable civilian and military structures deeply entrenched in the local society was replaced by the weak power of political parties who started fighting each other. The result was that the old government structures were not entirely abolished but did not function as before and the newly established structures did not have the power to impose new rules. The resulting political instability slowed efforts to rebuild the country's economy following a market-oriented model (see also Future issues box 4.1).

By the same token, the examples of authoritarian regimes in China and Vietnam as well as of semi-authoritarian governments in Singapore and Malaysia (those countries only have pseudo-elections) show that stable political environments may allow fast economic progress in the sense of a market-oriented economy. The remaining question is how far economic market development can go without changes in the political system of a country. The examples of South Korea and Taiwan seem to point in the direction of increasing pressures to introduce more democratic structures when the economic welfare of large parts of a country's population increases.

In Indonesia, as another example, President Suharto's dictatorial government oversaw unprecedented growth over three decades. But his policies also ignited popular discontent bubbling to the surface. Rampant corruption, nepotism, economic inequality, and political oppression became flashpoints for disgruntled workers, the urban unemployed, and muzzled intellectuals. All this led to riots which in turn resulted in Suharto being forced to resign in May of 1998 and a certain reluctance of international marketers to invest further in Indonesia. In 2001 Mrs. Megawati Sukarnoputri was elected president. But despite Jakarta's glistening office towers, American steak houses and young millionaires, about 27% of Indonesia's population (about 60 million people) still live in poverty.

In the face of radical political changes, for instance, the situation after the U.S. invasion of Iraq in 2003, even government bureaucracy is unable to continue operating. Sometimes, when such changes take place, opportunities to conduct business increase. For example, when the apartheid system in South Africa was ended and Nelson Mandela became president, the economic sanctions on the country were lifted. The new government created a reconstruction and development plan, a policy framework for ushering the black population into the economic mainstream. The plan called for various public and private initiatives in land reform, as well as training and capital formation designed to redress the economic scars left by decades of apartheid. New business opportunities arose even for small international marketers. In the U.S., the National Minority Business Council in New York developed a strategic program for minority- and women-owned enterprises interested in establishing a beachhead in the South African market. The NMBC program matched up South African companies with American partners, developed a cooperative in South Africa to facilitate trade opportunities in the NMBC's absence, and worked with local small business assistance centers.

Parties and interest groups

Political parties are important factors of influence on a country market's political environment because they channel public opinion into the formulation of government policies and laws. Even communist regimes, which traditionally install a dominant political party and severely limit opposition to that party, use political polls to obtain information about the attitudes and concerns of members of society.

Political parties

Knowledge as to which political parties exist in a country and how powerful they are is important to an international marketer since the role that foreign businesses are allowed to play in a given country market is influenced by the

---

FUTURE ISSUES BOX 4.1

Government and political stability in the Middle East

Most countries in the Middle East do not have democratic governments in the sense of western democracies. When doing business in those countries a very important question is: Who are you dealing with? Is it the right member of the right tribe?

Because of the difficult ecology in that part of the world for hundreds of years people had to rely on tribes, clans, and religious groups to ensure their survival. As a result, the political influence of single families or tribes is significant. King Abdullah of Jordan, for example, is the 44th generation after Mohammed. Leaders such as the former president of

Iraq, Saddam Hussein, or Arafat, the former leader of the Palestinian people, are the institutions; compared to western societies where the institutions, such as the British Houses of Parliament, are the leaders.

Increased education and the information revolution through the free press and internet lead to changes and some questioning of the current situation. But a democratic government system as in Europe or the U.S. will not be implemented easily. Even if elections take place, parliaments are installed and governments elected, tribes and their leaders will use the system to keep their position largely untouched. There is no separation of powers.

Source: Adapted from Stein, K. (2003) *The economy of the Middle East: Cauldron for change, challenge, and opportunity*, Atlanta, GA: Emory University Press; and Stein, K.W. (2003) "Ein Bagdader Frühling?", *Die Welt*, 26 May

philosophies of those parties. For example, the Greens, a rather small but vocal political party in Germany, have taken a strong stand on environmental issues. They work very hard to defeat any business activity that they believe will contribute to environmental pollution or destruction such as nuclear power, unnecessary road transportation, and packaging, CO_2 emissions, or overfishing. Their long-term effect has proven to be quite important even before they became part of the ruling coalition government in the early 2000s. Not only have they influenced German politics and law making by forcing the other parties to adopt most of the points brought onto the public agenda, but they have succeeded in spreading their influence through like-minded political parties throughout Europe. And there is a pan-European green group in the European Parliament in Strasbourg.

The Greens/European Free Alliance represents a well-organized grouping at the EU Parliament
© allOver photography/Alamy

Unions

Strong influences on a country's political decisions may also come from unions. In France, Italy, or Germany, and in contrast to the U.K., for example, unions have an influence on what is politically feasible or not. For many years, the Austrian political system was a special case. There, the Chamber of Workers and Employees, the Chamber of Commerce, and the Chamber of Agriculture (workforce, companies, and farmers are compulsory and paying members of these organizations) formed what has been called a "social partnership," a forum for discussion and political decisions, which influenced the local government's decision making. As a positive consequence, the time lost due to strikes in Austria per year was counted in seconds, compared to countries such as France, where unions and management act more as adversaries than as partners. This in turn leads to a situation where any significant negotiation between representatives of management and personnel is introduced by a warning strike. As a negative consequence of "social partnership," any changes in government policies on regulations concerning Austria's economic environment were rather slow and taken in small steps.

Special interest groups

Special interest groups may play a very important role in particular product markets. Internationally organized environmentalists such as Greenpeace, for example, have not only exerted considerable pressure on companies such as Esso or Shell, but also on governments. As a reaction to strong campaigns against the clearing of thousands of square kilometers of tropical forests, various European governments, for example, considered bans or restrictions on imports of tropical wood. When the exporting countries threatened to retaliate by banning imports from those countries, most European governments withdrew their intended regulations. Environmentalists found other solutions. For example, they started cooperating with big Swedish firms, including AssiDoman and Stora, to develop timber "certification" schemes. The idea behind certification schemes is to encourage consumers to buy products made from environmentally sound wood by giving such products a label or a stamp of approval. The Swedish firms, which together own about 40% of the country's forests, discussed what exactly they needed to do to get their wood certified under the auspices of the Forest Stewardship Council, an international coalition of lobbyists and firms. In the U.K., more than 60 big buyers of forest products, including DIY chain B&Q, pledged not to buy uncertified wood products after 1999.

Figure 4.2 illustrates how special interest groups may influence legislation in the U.S.

Lobbyists

Lobbyists also influence the international marketer's political environment; more than 7,000 lobbyists and foreign agents for over 200 interest groups and countries are registered in Washington, D.C., and it is estimated that perhaps twice that many are active. In Brussels, the headquarters of the European Union, about 4,000 people are employed for lobbying purposes; 200 companies are directly represented, while others use about 100 law firms that try to influence EU regulations or about another 100 consultants. More than 30 countries or regions have their own representations. Together they spend around $3 billion a year for lobbying purposes. The influence of lobbyists on European and U.S. politics depends on the lobbyists' professionalism, the quality of their arguments, their knowledge about which person to contact for what purpose, and the number as well as the importance of the supporters they are able to mobilize.

An example of effective lobbying is Swiss-based Novartis. At the end of the 1990s Novartis was in the 15th year (the end) of the patent of its market-leading pesticide in the U.S. American competitors were preparing to launch their generics. At the same time, public administration decided to reduce the volume of pesticides used in the U.S. by 50%. When they announced their decision, the lobbyists of Novartis approached the responsible agency (EAD) telling them that they had developed a similarly poisonous product, but only 50% of the volume was needed for the same effect. They asked for speeded-up approval to support the objectives of the agency. When Novartis got the fast approval they suggested the old product be decertified. By doing this, the agency put out of business all the American companies that were preparing to enter the market with their generics.

Major political objectives

Depending on the people in power, their view of the world, and whose interests they mainly follow, governments may have very different objectives. Some general objectives seem to be relevant for almost all governments, however. Those objectives include:

- maintenance of political sovereignty
- enhancement of national prestige and prosperity
- national security
- protection of cultural identity

Political sovereignty

Like many other creatures, humans feel the need to manage and control a certain territory around them to assure their existence. Humans form states in order to

FIGURE 4.2 *Potential development of an issue in U.S. public attention*

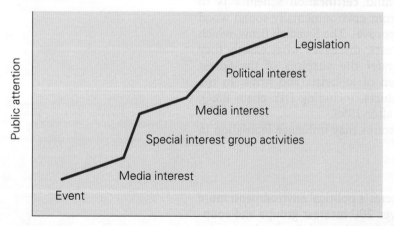

Special interest groups, such as the National Federation of Independent Businesses or the National Rifle Association, may have a significant influence on legislation in the U.S. All they need to do is to launch a specific event raising media interest that makes their issue reach public attention. If the special interest group uses public attention for additional activities, they may manage to raise even more media coverage. If there is enough media coverage to make it risky for politicians *not* to react, they will quickly pick up the issue and initiate legislation.

manage and control a political territory and its economy. Maintaining the political sovereignty of those states has traditionally been a major goal of all governments. So-called "nation-states" were formed. But because of expansion or splitting, changing borders, and the immigration or emigration of people, the term is misleading today.

Nation-states

Most nation-states have more than one nation inside their borders. The U.S. is a very impressive example. Despite long-term domination by its Anglo-Saxon population, there are many other nationalities present in the country, from native Indian tribes to Africans, Hispanics and Asians, and all sorts of European. But the great majority believe themselves to be part of one "nation." In other countries, such as China, Russia, Belgium, and the U.K., there is more than one nationality too, but they do not believe they belong to the same nation. Such perceived differences may lead to terrorism, such as in Spain, by the Basque separatists called ETA, or in Turkey, where the Kurd organization called PKK fights for autonomy, or to outright warfare, such as in Chechnya. In total, close to 3,500 groups of people describe themselves as a "nation." But there only are about 200 nation-states. This discrepancy has led experts to predict continued problems in terms of smaller groups of people, determined to apply the doctrine of self-determination to their own group – leading to considerable political instability throughout the next decades.

Nationalism

Nationalistic feelings and their consequences have strong effects on the business of international marketers. In the U.S., a marketer can count on the pride of most customers in being "American." In Bosnia, where Serbs, Croats and Bosnian Muslims fought each other, many international marketers that had invested there not only lost their capital, but – more important – their business partners and many customers.

Several recent trends, such as the increasing liberalization of world trade and the resulting globalization of an increasing number of industries, have worked against nationalism and have strongly decreased the ability of a country's government to control its own economy. But, even within the EU, political fragmentation occurs. The Danes, for example, first voted against the acceptance of the Maastricht treaty, which should establish closer political integration. The Danes only accepted the treaty after they had been granted some exceptions, which left more sovereignty with their government. The U.K. and Sweden did not join "Euroland." Austria, Ireland, and Sweden have maintained their status of political neutrality. Together with Denmark they hold the status of mere observers in the western European Union (defense system), and the U.K. did not sign the Schengen Treaty, which ties the internal security measures of members more closely together.

Cooperation vs sovereignty

Governments are faced with a dilemma: To keep their country's industries internationally competitive or to help them develop faster they need to promote economic cooperation or even integration, but they do not wish to give up their political sovereignty. This dilemma results in a constantly changing political environment, which may be detrimental to the business of international marketers.

National prestige and prosperity

The objective of governments to further or maintain their country's international prestige leads to results very similar to those of nationalism. In its more peaceful form, the struggle for national prestige often results in protecting or subsidizing national industries, with the consequence of distorted competition. For example, foreign companies complain about the Chinese government's tactics in cutting healthcare costs. The government maintains lists that define those drugs that the state will pay for. If consumers want drugs that are *not* on the list, they must pay out of their own pocket. Many foreign drug makers note that the lists contain few foreign products. They claim the lists are a disguised form of protectionism.

Prosperity

A major objective of most governments is national prosperity, to increase the standard of living of the country's population, or to increase the personal wealth of the members of government, their families and friends. Traditionally, a country's prosperity depended to a substantial degree on the availability of natural resources, such as iron, coal or water supplies. As discussed in Chapter 3, the prosperity of modern industrialized countries depends on the international competitiveness of their industries.

Competitiveness

The competitiveness of a country's industries partly depends on the level of local labor cost compared to other countries. Therefore, the issue of minimum social standards in global competition has become pre-eminent. Canada, France, and the U.S. are major advocates of imposing minimum social standards on all 146 member states of WTO. They state that there is no fair global competition if child labor and the forced labor of prisoners are not banned and if minimum wages as well as freedom of association are not guaranteed. Industrially developing countries such as Indonesia, Malaysia, and Singapore protest such claims as the latest attempt by highly industrialized economies to protect themselves against less expensive products and services.

Competitiveness today is not only based on low labor cost. It is largely based on:

- a country's infrastructure
- population capabilities.

The capabilities a country's industries can rely on depend on the level of education and adaptability of the workforce as well as the level of available technologies.

For that reason, Bill Clinton, when first elected president of the U.S., announced his strong emphasis on further improving the educational system of the country. George W. Bush followed suit by signing the No Child Left Behind Act in 2002. The Swedish government, after having turned around the national budget to result in no more deficits, substantially increased their spending for educational purposes in 1998. From an international competition point of view, such actions are overdue because in the mid-1990s a higher proportion of students in Asia were taking courses in applied sciences and engineering than in the U.S.

National security

To ensure national security, many countries not only build up armed forces, thereby creating large markets for weapon manufacturers, but many governments are also anxious to be able to acquire the weapons they need inside their own borders. Recent examples are countries such as Iran or North Korea striving to develop their own nuclear arsenal. Despite the existence of the western European Union for national security reasons, governments of member countries such as France or the U.K. do not want to see technologies leave the country. Therefore, France's government, for example, decided that Thomson-CSF should be merged with Dassault Electronique and the military telecommunications unit of Alcatel.

Together they are still rather small compared to their U.S. competitors such as Lockheed Martin or Raytheon. With some exceptions, such as British BAE SYSTEMS, which merged with Marconi Electronic Systems, the former defense electronic business of U.S.-based General Electric Company (GEC), the political sensitivities of defense prevent cross-border alliances that might be economically meaningful.

Protection of cultural identity

Each society has its specific rules of conduct, which are transmitted from one generation to the next by socialization. Changes of rules that occur over time lead to more or less conflict between generations or interest groups. But when members of a society perceive that changes of behavioral norms come from outside, resistance is usually strongest (Culture box 4.1). The example of resistance against fast-food restaurants by some religious groups in India has shown how sensitive governments react to such "foreign attacks on the cultural identity of their people."

Such reactions are not limited to developing countries. European countries strongly resist attempts by the U.S. to open up markets for entertainment products and education. Because of the dominance of U.S. producers, they fear too much of an influence on the culture of their societies. A total "Americanization" of life is definitely not what most European governments want.

International marketers must be careful, therefore, to know exactly how far they can go, for example, in standardizing goods and services, distribution activities, and – most important – market communication.

International trade policy

The prevailing political interests in a country market and the major political objectives of the governing forces determine the policies of government. The **international trade policy** of a country's government is a set of laws and rules that regulate the flow of goods and services across a country's borders. This policy provides a framework for exports, imports, and foreign investment and therefore needs to be more closely analyzed by the international marketer.

CULTURE BOX 4.1

Portraying Malaysian identity

In 2003 the Culture, Arts and Tourism Ministry of Malaysia asked hotel managers in the country to take more care portraying the Malaysian identity to tourists. Their staff should use six aspects of the Malaysian identity:

- greeting by placing the right palm firmly on the left side of the chest while giving a slight bow
- wearing traditional Malaysian costumes

- adding local flavor to their interior decorations
- employing in-house cultural troupes
- offering friendly hospitality
- playing Malaysian music.

A spokesperson of the ministry complained that up to 80% of the hotels in Malaysia were not implementing any of the six aspects of the Malaysian identity. For hotels unclear of what to do, the ministry came up with 14 items of clothing costing RM 14,000 that could be used to display seven different types of cultural costume.

Source: Adapted from Ganesan, V. (2003) "Portray Malaysian identity, hotels told", *New Straits Times*, 30 July

Export/import policy

All countries control exports and imports to some degree, providing both barriers to trade and support for certain domestically as well as foreign produced goods and services.

Export/import assistance

Governments use various ways to encourage trade between their country and attractive partners.

Political relations One way to encourage trade between two countries is to use political relations as a means to establish contacts between companies from both countries. The German Economy Ministry, for example, brought the leaders of 125 medium-sized Chinese companies to Bonn to meet with German counterparts.

Financial assistance Another way to stimulate and assist exports is to provide financial assistance either directly or indirectly. The People's Insurance Co. of China (PICC), for example, is the country's agency responsible for the export credit insurance sector. PICC's more than 40 subsidiaries nationwide offer comprehensive export credit insurance and guarantees, export documentation insurance, and foreign investment insurance. German Hermes Bank provides long-term low-interest rate loans ("soft loans") to companies bidding for projects in industrially developing countries. Without such loans, many projects would not be financially viable, for either customers or suppliers. The U.S. Export–Import Bank (Eximbank) provides financial support to U.S. exporters that allows those exporters to charge competitive prices. The Japanese approach of identifying key industries and then developing an export policy for those industries has proven particularly effective. The Japanese External Trade Organization (JETRO) has been so successful in implementing an aggressive export promotion policy that the Japanese government has asked it to help marketers in other countries increase their exports to Japan.

Tax refunds Governments may also support international marketing of their industries by refunding domestic taxes to exporters. This policy is often found in countries that rely heavily on exports. Value-added taxes on supplies are commonly refunded to domestic producers, giving them an advantage over competitors from countries with sales taxes that are not refunded. Another commonly rebated tax is the duty on items such as component parts for machinery intended for re-exportation. The U.S. government applies lower tax rates to profits generated through exports by permitting the creation of foreign sales companies (FSCs). These are corporations that are not located in a U.S. customs zone. An FSC is allowed to export products and pay little or no income tax on those sales, thereby increasing its profits or price competitiveness considerably.

Tariff preferences Sometimes governments support imports of particular goods or services. The EU and Japan as well as the U.S. have import support programs that offer tariff preferences for selected products from industrially less developed countries, in order to stimulate their economies. In the agricultural sector this preferential treatment of the poorest countries has stirred up fierce resistance from other countries such as Argentina, Brazil, Egypt, or India, which have filed a complaint of unequal treatment at the WTO.

Normally, when the products that have been treated preferentially are viewed as fully competitive, they no longer qualify for import support and the tariff structure is changed. In India, a company that exports at least 80% of its products is considered an "Export-only unit" (EOU). Such EOUs are allowed to import raw materials without paying tariffs. In addition, all goods purchased in India by such companies are exempt from taxes during the first eight to 10 years of the company's existence. In the first five years after their establishment, EOUs do not pay taxes on profits left in India. Profits transferred outside the country are subject to a 20% tax.

Trade barriers

Barriers to trade include tariffs, non-tariff barriers, and trade embargoes or sanctions.

Tariffs Tariffs have traditionally been used as barriers to international trade. They either protect domestic industries by raising prices to non-competitive levels or compensate for subsidies by governments to their exporters. In the last decade of the 20th century, international trade liberalization has led to a significant reduction of tariff barriers. But they still exist. In 2003 India had an average tariff level on industrial goods of 58.7%, compared to Brazil with 30%, and an average of 4.1% and 3.9% in the EU and the U.S., respectively. From time to time, both the EU and the U.S. use tariffs on specific products to protect their related industries. The U.S. government, for example, imposed special tariffs on steel imports, because a lack of investments had resulted in the steel industry being far from globally competitive. The Cairns Group consisting of 20 big exporters of agricultural products such as Australia, Brazil, Canada, China, Egypt, and India, representing two-thirds of the world population, has in particular demanded market-opening measures from Europe and the U.S. for their agricultural products.

Non-tariff barriers **Non-tariff barriers** to international trade are government laws, regulations, policies, or practices that protect domestic producers from foreign competition. Because trade liberalization has progressed through WTO and international economic cooperation agreements, governments are using non-tariff barriers to protect some of their countries' industries that they think are unable to endure free international competition. Table 4.1 lists some of the most popular non-tariff barriers applied.

Arbitrary product classification Sometimes international marketers are confronted with an unpredictable manner in which a country's tariff administration classifies its products. Such arbitrary product classification may strongly affect the tariff status of the export product. In India, for example, international investors are officially supposed to pay a 20% import duty on equipment. But because of imprecise legal regulations, in reality, the tariff ends up being not 20% but whatever the customs inspector wants it to be on the day the firm's products arrive.

TABLE 4.1 *Popular non-tariff barriers to international trade*

Non-tariff barriers to international trade
Arbitrary product classification
Import quotas
Import license requirements
Export license requirements
Discriminatory government procurement contracts
Port-of-entry requirements
Local content requirements

Governments are very creative when it comes to the invention or virtuous use of non-tariff barriers to protect their countries' industries from international competition. This list contains some of the most popular non-tariff barriers in international trade.

Import quotas These are quantitative restrictions on imports that may be expressed as individual units imported or as a total value of imports. Such quotas are commonly imposed on an annual basis. An exception was the 30-year-old quota system established by the members of WTO to regulate the amounts of imported textiles from manufacturing countries. It was abolished as from 31 December 2004. Forecasts had been that China's share of the global textile market, which had a volume of about €400 billion in 2004, would increase from 16% in 2003 to up to 50% in some years. From January to April 2004, however, textile imports from China to the EU rose fivefold. Under great pressure from the European textile industry the EU Commission threatened to reintroduce quotas as a legitimate defense if the Chinese government would not take measures to restrict their textile exports.

Before the Czech Republic and Slovakia became members of the EU in 2004, Austria imposed import quotas on cement from those countries, decreasing over the years. The reason given was that unrestricted low-priced imports would destroy the Austrian cement industry. It needed some time for restructuring, in particular because competition was "unfair" considering that the Czech and Slovakian firms did not have to obey the same cost-driving regulations concerning environmental protection as their Austrian counterparts.

One effect of such quotas is that international marketers try to make their deals during the first months of each year, before the quota is met and all imports cease. Promotion, inventory, and financing have to be managed accordingly. Another effect is retaliation by the affected country's government. They also impose quotas on certain products until the first mover steps back from its erected barriers.

Import license requirements These may exist in the form of restrictions on the number of foreign companies allowed to enter a country market or without limitation on the number of firms but with the obligation to apply for an import license for each business contract. Owing to bureaucratic delays, it may take years to obtain the right to import. For example, Dornier, the German manufacturer of weaving machines, had to prove that no producer in India could make the same kind of machine in order to receive an import license. To circumvent this restriction, which would have forced the company to disclose its technological know-how in a country where intellectual property rights are not well protected, Dornier decided to enter into a joint venture with an Indian producer.

In service industries, government permission may be needed to operate in a country market. For example, Econet, a Zimbabwe-based telecommunications firm in which Telecel International, a U.S. firm, had a 40% stake, was all ready to start operations in 1996. It had built a base station and switching center in Harare, the capital of Zimbabwe; it had $3 million of mobile phones sitting in warehouses or containers; and 5,000 subscribers had already signed up. Yet the Zimbabwe government did not stop trying to prevent it from operating. Econet had already won two court cases: the first eliminated the government's claim to a monopoly on all telecoms; the second upheld Econet's claim to be able to install a cellular network under the constitutional right to freedom of expression. Not content, President Mugabe issued a proclamation in February 1996 making it illegal for anybody to operate a cellular network without state permission. Econet's foreign contractors, fearing imprisonment, stopped working; Telecel International withdrew its stake.

License requirements may even exist inside a country. In China, for example, at some time the local administration of Shanghai imposed huge "license fees" on Citroën cars from Hubei province to protect the locally made Volkswagen Santana, which monopolized the taxi fleet. The Shanghai government owns a stake in the VW joint venture.

Export license requirements Most goods need no license to be exported from their country of production. But exports of some products that might affect national security or are in limited supply are controlled. For example, exports of products and technologies related to nuclear power are restricted because of concern about the proliferation of nuclear weapons. For such sensitive goods, or goods exported to politically sensitive countries, a validated, written export license must be obtained after appropriate governmental agencies, such as the Departments of Commerce and Defense in the U.S., have been consulted.

Such policies allow suppliers from other countries that do not prohibit such trade to gain contracts they would not have obtained otherwise. For example, the Iranian government wanted to finish construction of two nuclear power plants that German suppliers had begun building at some time. When neither western industrialized countries nor Japan were ready to allow any of their firms to bid for the contract because of fears that the Iranians could use the radioactive material from those power stations for military purposes, the Russian nuclear power industry stepped in and finished the plants. They have maintained strong business relationships since then.

Discriminatory government procurement contracts Discriminatory government procurement contracts discriminate against foreign suppliers in bidding for government contracts. Such a policy reflects the desire to spend public funds in the domestic economy. In industrialized countries, the large volume of public expenditures makes the economic impact of such barriers to international suppliers significant. For example, "Buy America" rules oblige the U.S. Defense Department to purchase many kinds of defense equipment at home. Even when a foreign weapon is chosen, it must be made in the U.S. In the EU, discrimination against suppliers from other EU member states is illegal. Another example of such illegal discrimination would be the use of bidding deadlines that are too short to be met by suppliers from another country.

Port-of-entry requirements Sometimes imports to a country are only allowed when using a specific harbor or airport or a specific customs office. In most cases, such port-of-entry requirements are accompanied by taxes or levies that are placed on the use of those facilities. The official purpose of such regulations has traditionally been to finance the development of transportation infrastructure and to streamline bureaucratic infrastructure for specific customs purposes. However, the taxes often endure well past the time necessary to offset the original capital cost, are often higher than operating costs would indicate, and centralized customs activities are located in places where international marketers have logistical disadvantages. The French government, for example, some time before the EU made such actions impossible, centralized all customs activities concerning the import of consumer electronics at Poitiers, a city in the middle of France, well away from any port or border.

Local content requirements Such requirements are typically expressed as a certain percentage of a product's total value added that must be produced in the host country to get an import license or to avoid high tariffs. For example, before its commitment to the WTO the Thai government required local content of more than 50% for pickup trucks and passenger cars. Tenders for the construction of industrial plants or for big infrastructure projects in industrially developing countries, as another example, generally contain such local content clauses. They are intended to force some technology transfer, to provide some degree of domestic employment, and to improve the country's balance of payments position. Local content requirements may be fulfilled, for example, by the local acquisition of component parts, the use of local construction services, or local product assembly. But because local suppliers in many cases may be less reliable than suppliers in the international marketer's home market, it may be necessary to bring those suppliers to the new market as part of the total operation.

Investment policy

A government can either support or deter foreign investment. A country's **investment policy** consists of all general rules that govern legislation concerning domestic as well as foreign participation in the equity or ownership of businesses and other organizations of that country. All products that need a great deal of customer participation in their production process, such as most services, cannot be exported, that is, produced in one country and consumed or used in another country. A hotel, a telecommunications network or a retailing outlet, for example, must be located where their customers want to use them. Suppliers of such services are therefore more concerned about the investment policies of governments in the potential country markets than about those governments' international trade policies.

A government's policy towards investment reflects its market orientation. Each policy will be located between the two extremes of no private investment and only private investment. Consequently, international marketers assessing various country markets for their attractiveness will need to consider the governments' policies concerning foreign direct investments, subsidies, takeovers, and general operating conditions.

Foreign direct investments

Foreign direct investment occurs when a company invests in a subsidiary or joint venture with a partner firm in a foreign market. An example is Nissan's $660 million investment in an automobile assembly plant in Smyrna, Tennessee. In contrast to financial investments in stocks, bonds, or funds deposited in a bank, which are generally left alone by the investor, foreign direct investment entails some degree of control by the investor.

In Europe, there is substantial competition among countries for foreign investors to improve the competitive position of the countries' industries. Slovakia, for example, has introduced a 19% flat income and corporation tax. Together with low wages and relative political stability, that decision turned the country into a very strong contender for foreign investments. After Peugeot of France has decided to invest €700 million in a car assembly plant at Trnava, Hyundai of Korea will invest a similar sum in the eastern part of the country. Foreign investments in the eastern European countries have injected much needed capital for improving the technological level of production facilities. Since the early 1990s, for example, foreign investors have pumped €3,500 per capita into the Czech Republic. Foreign investments also served to improve company and brand reputation and to establish greater credibility with customers and financiers.

Governments may become nervous when investments under foreign control become important. Even in the U.S., for example, there is some concern about the economic impact of foreign multinational corporations, such as Japanese automakers or European food producers. In the case of Nissan's assembly plant in Tennessee, maintenance of the company's traditional supplier relationships had a dual impact. First, new jobs were created as Nissan's Japanese suppliers developed production facilities near the new plant to meet Nissan's "just-in-time" delivery requirements. Second, U.S. parts suppliers were excluded from these special arrangements, and a larger portion of automobile industry profits went to foreign investors. Some politicians claim that this pattern represents "creeping colonialization"; others maintain that the jobs created by foreign investment are important to the economy.

Governments of industrially developing as well as highly developed countries (see Strategy box 4.1) encourage foreign investment in an attempt to *increase employment and domestic economic growth*, but, at the same time, they are anxious to *control foreign investor influence on the local economy.*

Malaysia, for example, allows only companies that export 50% or more of their production to be up to 100% foreign owned. In Indonesia, Pertamina, the state-owned petroleum company, is an automatic partner in every oil and gas project under a system that calls for sharing production after foreign developers of fields have recovered their costs.

Problems may arise when radical shareholder value-based decisions lead to the closing of subsidiaries without appropriate social plans for the personnel concerned. For example, French Renault announced the shutdown of its Vilvoorde production plant in Belgium without prior negotiation of a social plan with personnel representatives. The announcement not only provoked negative reactions from most parts of Belgian society as well as demonstrations in the streets of Paris, but also a ruling of the European Court in Luxembourg declaring the Renault decision illegal.

One of the most effective deterrents to foreign investment in a country is the non-existence of clear regulations, too complicated or unstable regulations, and the very slow handling of bureaucratic work related to those regulations (see Strategy box 4.2).

Subsidies

Subsidies are payments made by local authorities (governments of states, provinces, or cities) and regional institutions, such as the EU administration, to local and international firms in an attempt to improve either the competitive position of the firm or the attractiveness of a location to the investor. When governments subsidize local companies it is mainly to keep those firms in existence.

STRATEGY BOX 4.1

Georgia Quick Start

The Georgia Department of Technical and Adult Education has implemented a program called Quick Start to attract foreign investors to Georgia. Companies from 31 different countries have welcomed the offer of the agency to develop and execute training solutions for every aspect of their operation.

Quick Start offers to start with a comprehensive study of the tasks to be accomplished in the foreign investor's facility. The project study often takes place overseas at a plant that mirrors the proposed site in Georgia, one with a similar operation so that job details can be assessed. After capturing the process, Quick Start offers cooperation with the Georgia Department of Labor Recruitment to find the right people for the jobs to be executed. Agency specialists design and execute a training curriculum for those people. The curriculum not only prepares them for their specific job but provides them with increased sensitivity for the culture of their new employer. Georgian workers are assisted in understanding the Japanese, German, Korean, French, and Hispanic cultures. Additionally, each program has its counterpart to acclimate expatriates to the local culture. Comparing and contrasting U.S. culture with the culture of the other country, the training addresses communication styles, traditional business interactions, realities about stereotypes, and cultural values and customs.

The importance of working proficiently with international firms is evidenced by their economic impact. The U.S. Commerce Department reports that, in 2002, international companies contributed $29.7 billion of investment in Georgia. And, in the same year, there were nearly 125,000 employees working in international facilities in Georgia.

The EU has forbidden any subsidies that lead to a distortion of competition in an industry. Nevertheless, member countries such as Italy, Greece, and Spain have managed to keep their national airlines alive through subsidies.

Governments offer subsidies to international marketers to *attract their direct investments*. Again, the EU has made subsidies that distort international competition illegal. Companies that have received such aid to their investment are forced to pay back the amount received. But there are various areas inside the EU, so-called E1 areas, that are considered economically less developed than the rest such as the greatest part of eastern Poland. In such areas, limited subsidies may be given to firms ready to invest. There may even be additional subsidies available from EU development budgets.

Where no direct subsidies are allowed, governments have found indirect ways to attract interesting international marketers. There is a kind of race among European governments as to which country is able to provide the *most attractive taxation system* to its own industries, but in particular to international investors. For some time Ireland was the champion, but other governments such as in Slovakia have managed to follow them closely. As a result, taxes on capital and capital revenue have steadily decreased in Europe over recent years. Social

---

STRATEGY BOX 4.2

China–India: The fight for economic leadership in Asia

The temptation to compare them is great. Their population size of 1.3 and 1.1 billion respectively is relatively similar. Their average economic growth over the last 10 years has been about 7.5% for China and 6% for India.

Nevertheless, China is increasingly seen as a major competitive threat. Its export prowess is frightening manufacturers and factory workers not only in the U.S. and Europe, but everywhere from Malaysia to Mexico. India – despite its impressive success in call centers, software firms, and pharmaceutical factories – is viewed as a less formidable competitor. The Chinese have order, discipline, modern telephones, and roads (at least in coastal areas). The Indians have democracy, administrative red tape, lousy infrastructure, more poverty (25% compared to 10% in China) and slower growth.

China's success and global reputation reflect the huge foreign investment in factories, buildings, and machinery. Foreign direct investment in China is more than 15 times that of India. The Chinese government does everything to do away with barriers caused by the old communist apparatus: Private enterprises are privileged monopolies and foreign investments are preferentially treated.

India does not inspire the same confidence in foreign investors. Many urgently needed reforms – such as a modification of the fiscal system, the liberalization of telecommunication, transportation, energy, and other markets – are blocked by political fights and public administration. Even farmers are not allowed to sell their products freely. Intermediaries appointed by government fix their prices. Furthermore, India still very much depends on monsoon rainfalls. Agriculture contributes 25% to GDP and gives work to two-thirds of the population.

The question is: Will India be able to close the gap with China over the next 20 years so that more of its people prosper? Comparing growth and saving rates in China and India, an interesting picture emerges. China as a nation saves about 40% of income, India saves about 24%. Adding foreign investments to those saving rates, India is much more effective, reaching an average growth of 6% compared to about 7.5% for China. A huge amount of capital in China is wasted, particularly investments made by the Chinese government. Consequently, if India can raise its saving and foreign investment rate modestly, its growth rate may rise substantially. Reforms to increase the confidence of foreign investors become even more urgently needed.

Source: Rodier, A. (2003) "Chine–Inde: bras de fer pour la suprématie en Asie", *Le Figaro*, 10 September, International 3; Wessel, D. (2003) "India could narrow its economic gap with China", *Wall Street Journal*, 24 July, p. A2

security payroll taxes on the other hand may become a major obstacle for future investments (see Future issues box 4.2).

A special case is so-called *"tax havens"* such as the Bahamas, the Channel Islands, Liechtenstein, and Monaco. Because they have low corporate tax rates, companies establish subsidiaries in such countries – they are sometimes no more than a "letterbox" – and use transfer pricing to remit as much profit as they can to the low-tax rate subsidiary. That is, they charge licensing and consultancy fees, for example, or they play the role of the international sales headquarters buying products at very low prices from the production subsidiaries of the firm. Of course, governments in the other countries that such companies are serving attempt to tax these funds.

Economically developing countries may not possess enough free capital for direct payments. They subsidize foreign investments by offering *tax breaks* over substantial amounts of time, or the provision of energy and water at a subsidized rate. The Taiwanese government used tax breaks, government shareholdings, low-interest loans, and R&D grants to encourage high-tech startups. Similarly, the Chinese government is now offering semiconductor companies favorable tax treatment (see Table 4.2). However, international marketers should keep in mind that capital invested and taxes are two important factors of influence on their market choice, but not the only ones to be considered.

FUTURE ISSUES BOX 4.2

Coming battle over social security

In 2011 the first baby boomers in the U.S. will reach 65. This flood of new retirees will present an opportunity to international marketers, which are prepared to offer them adequate products and services. But indirectly the increase in retirees poses a serious threat to future (foreign) investments: Unless it is reformed, the U.S. social security system will switch from an annual surplus to a deficit on a cash flow basis around 2017 and will become insolvent around 2041. If Congress waits until then, they will either need to cut social security benefits by over 25%, to raise social security payroll taxes from 12.4 to over 18% or to finance social security in another way. A substantial cut of social security benefits would strongly reduce the purchasing power of an increasing share of the population. Raising social security payroll taxes would mean an increase in the portion directly paid by employers from 6.2% to over 9% of wages. To keep the U.S. industry internationally cost competitive and to be able to further attract foreign investment, the Bush administration plans to privatize social security. This solution puts the entire capital risk on the shoulders of future retirees.

Sweden is a European example of how such problems may be handled in time without hurting the interests of either investors or employees. From 1960 to 1990 the ratio of workers to retirees in Sweden declined from 3:1 to 2:1. During the 1990s Sweden responded by slowing the growth of traditional social security benefits to reflect increased life expectancy. It also created mandatory personal accounts to provide a modest portion of social security benefits.

Maintaining its 18.5% rate for social security payroll taxes, Sweden credited 16% to unfunded accounts for each worker and transferred 2.5% to personal retirement accounts (PRA) for each worker. These latter funds may be invested by the worker in a broad variety of funds meeting government qualifications. On retirement, the value of the investment in the PRA is converted by the worker into a fixed or variable annuity.

Blue-collar and white-collar workers can make additional contributions to a private defined-contribution plan to the extent that their earnings exceed a specified amount. Below that amount, workers' contributions are typically used to help finance a private defined-benefit retirement plan.

Source: Adapted from Pozen, R.C. (2002) "Arm yourself for the coming battle over social security", *Harvard Business Review*, November, pp. 52–62

Takeovers

In contrast to subsidies to attract foreign investment, local governments sometimes take over foreign-owned firms. Such takeovers can take the form of confiscation, expropriation, or domestication.

Confiscation takes place when a company's assets are taken over without any compensation payment. In cases of *expropriation*, the government taking over the business operation offers some kind of compensation. In most cases, however, the compensation is too little, too late. *Domestication* may take the form of the forced sale of a dominant part of the firm to locals, the placement of local personnel in leading hierarchical positions, and/or the forced procurement of local supplies.

Expropriation and domestication affect a firm in very different ways. With expropriation, the company suddenly loses all control over its assets. With domestication, the firm usually has enough time to manage the transfer of ownership or dominant influence in a systematic way.

Since competition has become increasingly global, most governments have understood that their countries' economic well-being at least partly depends on international investments. Because such investments will not take place under the continual threat of potential government takeovers, this kind of hostile intervention has become very rare. In some countries led by dictators and a small group of people in power that splits most of the country's wealth, the risk of takeovers may still exist. For example, the government in Zimbabwe has introduced legislation that no longer allows the ownership of land by companies. This means that agricultural firms with foreign capital majority ownership can no longer exist.

Operating conditions

Another important factor of influence on direct investment decisions is the operating conditions in a country market. Governments have a significant influence on those conditions. For example, before the economic crisis hit Southeast Asia, the minimum wage for an autoworker set by the Thai government was 10,000 baht a month, at that time about one-tenth the wage in Japan. Engineers earned up to 15,000 baht a day. Benefits included family medical care, free bus transportation to and from work, a uniform, lunch, and 12 days' vacation. Any

TABLE 4.2 *Tax breaks for chip makers*

Value-added tax	6%	The Chinese government tries to attract investments in the semiconductor industry by offering favorable tax treatment.
Regular tax		
* First two years of profitability	0	
* Next three years of profitability	15%	
Depreciation		
* Mechanical equipment	3 years	
* Electronic equipment	3 years	
Materials (incl. value-added tax)	0	
Equipment (incl. value-added tax)	0	

Source: Chun Chen, A. and J.R. Woetzel (2002) "Chinese chips", *McKinsey Quarterly*, No. 2, p. 26

potential foreign investor assessing the attractiveness of a country must gather such information to come up with a rational evaluation of given opportunities versus problems to be encountered.

Trade sanctions

Besides the more long-term and stable political orientation expressed through laws and regulations, the international trade of and with a country is also influenced by much more spontaneous intergovernmental relations. They are often reactions to specific events that are difficult for the international marketer to anticipate. But they may have a significant impact on its business opportunities.

The U.S., as the world's leading military and economic power, has in recent years increasingly used trade sanctions in an attempt to punish governments whose policies or actions the U.S. government perceives to be hostile. For example, the shooting down by Cuban military forces of a private U.S. airplane that had intruded into Cuba's territory led to the Helms-Burton Act, designed to punish U.S. as well as foreign companies "trafficking" in property confiscated after the 1959 Cuban Revolution. An action has to be initiated by aggrieved U.S. individuals or companies. The D'Amato Act, also signed in 1996, bans U.S. and companies from other countries dealing with Iran (because the Iranian government allegedly supports international terrorist activities). The act involves the U.S. government: The president is required to impose at least two out of six sanctions on any company that invests more than $40 million a year in the gas and petroleum industries of Iran.

The question is whether such sanctions really do what their authors expect them to do. They surely drive most U.S. companies out of the sanctioned country markets. For example, U.S. federal authorities charged equipment maker Case Corp. with violating U.S. law by participating in the sale of excavators and other heavy construction machinery from Case's foreign affiliate in France for use in Libya's great manmade river project. This $25 billion venture, begun in 1984, is the Libyan government's effort to pump some 2 million cubic meters of water daily from an aquifer beneath the Sahara Desert more than 1,000 miles north to the Mediterranean coast. The network of underground pipes and reservoirs is an attempt to become more self-sufficient in food production and lessen Libya's reliance on imports. But from 1986 to 2004 U.S. citizens and companies were prohibited from performing "any contract in support of industrial or other commercial or government projects in Libya."

The withdrawal of Case Corp. and other U.S. companies from the sanctioned country markets results in business opportunities for other firms. Some companies are handed contracts on a plate while the offending government goes unpunished. For example, only one week after Bill Clinton had signed the D'Amato Act, the Islamic Republic of Iran signed a deal, supposedly worth more than $20 billion over 23 years, to sell natural gas to Turkey. The deal does not contravene the new U.S. rules, the Turks may argue: It is not investment, merely trade.

Legal environment

When government policies are turned into formal rules and regulations, they are known as laws. The **legal environment** of a company is the set of laws and systems that enforce those laws, established by a society to govern its members' behavior. When international marketers are assessing the political and legal viability of potential markets, it is important that they consider certain aspects of the legal environment relevant to their product market. The generally most important considerations will be discussed in the following subsections.

International business law

There is no international business law in a formal sense. Traditionally, courts, laws, and regulatory agencies have been national, not international, in scope. No agreed on regulations have existed that can be always applied to international business relations. Current laws vary considerably, sometimes in what seem to be quite ridiculous ways. For example, it is illegal to send soap to Paraguay through the U.S. mail. Even the terms under which parties to a contract can be released through an "act of God" differ considerably in different countries. This distinction is important, because an "act of God" normally releases a party from having to fulfill the terms of a contract. Thus, a labor strike might be viewed as an "act of God" in some countries but not in others, where strikes are considered predictable and manageable.

There are some treaties and agreements among countries that provide frameworks and guidelines for business relations, but, by and large, the international marketer must work with different legal systems in different local markets.

In view of the many differences, it is very important for a company that plans to internationalize its served markets to employ international legal counsel. Culture box 4.2 gives an example of how cultural differences may influence the perception of proper conduct.

Legal systems

A country's legal system determines the rules that govern the conduct of business as well as the norms and standards that goods and services have to fulfill. A major reason for differences among national legal systems is their legal heritage. Australia, Canada, New Zealand, the U.K., the U.S. and some other countries have legal systems based on common law, which is an outgrowth of English law. Code law, which is found in many countries with no Anglo-Saxon traditions, is based on Roman law. Islamic law is based on the Koran and the Sunna. To further complicate matters, many countries have more than one set of laws. In code law countries as well as in the U.S., for example, laws may be commercial, civil, or criminal. In most common law countries, such distinctions are not made.

Common law Under common law, precedent is critical in resolving any given issue. In reaching a decision, the court will examine existing laws and regulations, customary procedures, and previous cases dealing with similar issues.

Code law Under code law, in contrast, formal laws spell out precisely what constitutes proper behavior, although sometimes some interpretation is required.

An example of the potential impact of these differences on international marketing can be seen in the case of rights to brand names and other intellectual property such as patents or publishing rights. Under common law, prior use is the most significant determinant in deciding who has the right to use a specific brand name. But under code law, whoever registers a brand name first controls the rights to it. Thus, in a code law country, a company that uses a brand name first does not necessarily have the legal right to continue doing so. Anyone could register the same name. A company that wants to enter a market in a code law country might have to purchase the rights to its "own" brand name or even operate under a different brand name.

Socialist law The legal system of socialist countries is based on a different view of society. In societies based on capitalism, each individual has the freedom to pursue his or her best interests, and legal regulations are made to indicate the rules of the game. The central principle underlying socialist law, in no matter what country, although it varies in the degree applied, is that the needs of the larger society dominate individual needs. For example, in a strongly socialist country, for example North Korea, no private ownership of means of production and intellectual products is allowed, compared to China where private ownership of production resources has been made legal but private intellectual property is not very well protected.

Islamic law Islamic law, or shariah ("God's rules"), is a form of code law. Its major distinguishing characteristic is that it is directly based on religious interpretations of the Koran and the Sunna. Even more than a code system, Islamic law governs all dimensions of human behavior, and is extensively concerned with

CULTURE BOX 4.2

Flirting with danger

When Swedish pharmaceutical company Astra AB learned about wide-ranging sexual harassment allegations against the chief executive of its U.S. subsidiary, the company suspended him and two top-ranking managers. But Mitsubishi Motor Manufacturing of America Inc., faced with charges of pervasive sexual harassment by the U.S. Equal Employment Opportunity Commission, has maintained that the agency is wrong and mounted a full-scale public relations campaign to discredit complainers, even paying employees to picket the EEOC offices to protest the suit.

In strikingly similar circumstances, two companies operating in the U.S. have reacted very differently to harassment charges, a perilous area in which laws and societal norms are exposing companies to significant liability.

Both companies lacked a clear and strong written policy on harassment. They reflected a poor understanding of the legal, financial and public relations liabilities involved in the issue in the U.S. Astra's three-paragraph policy was so brief that it failed to even define sexual harassment. While Mitsubishi's policy included an adequate definition and statement of management's philosophy, the policy suffered from a failure to discuss social functions. What may have been the reasons?

A cultural gap is partly to blame. In polite Japan, people do not talk much about the underside of a paternal working society, where young women in particular are expected to suffer in silence from sexual harassment from their seniors. A pat on the bottom from the boss, awkward questions about one's love life, and persistent requests for a date from older male colleagues are all part of the workplace obstacle course. In 2000 Japan introduced laws for the first time forbidding sexual harassment. What sexual harassment in Japan probably is not, is being asked about personal details. Japanese resumés often contain quite a lot of personal data. Conservative managers usually want to know all about a job candidate's family, husband, and other details.

In Europe, studies show that up to 50% of women and 10% of men have experienced some type of sexual harassment at work. But national estimates vary widely. They range from an estimated 11% in Denmark and 17% in Sweden, to 54% in the U.K. There is still a lack of agreement on what amounts to sexual harassment. With the exception of France and Italy, the level of awareness and importance attached to the issue is not very high. Therefore, the European Commission has approved a directive that came into force in 2005. Under this new law, employers will be forced to prove, in response to an employee's complaint about sexual harassment, that they had taken all possible measures against it.

But even the most outrageous acts do not bring settlements on a par with the U.S., largely because most European judges and juries do not grant the kind of huge awards for "pain and suffering" seen in the U.S. Still, those familiar with European countries point out that the legal situation notwithstanding, European women do not let the men walk all over them. It is less handwringing and more "right-back-in-your-face, buddy". The apparent difference stems in part from the fact that Europeans are far more reluctant than Americans to go to court. Instead, Europeans tend to resolve such workplace issues through negotiations between trade unions and employers.

Source: Johannes, L., J.S. Lublin, B. Coleman, and V. Reitman (1996) "Flirting with danger: sex harassment cases trip up foreign firms operating in the U.S.", *Wall Street Journal Europe*, 10–11 May, pp. 1, 6; Lloyd, T. (2003) "Sexual harassment in interviews", www.japantoday.com, 11 October

defining moral conduct. Pakistan, for example, introduced legislation in early 1991 that would make the Koran the supreme law, and bring all aspects of life, including social codes and civil liberties, under the law of Islam.

Two concepts in Islamic law directly affect international marketers, especially of financial services. They are based on the prohibition of gambling in the Koran. One is *riba*, which prohibits unearned profits. A common interpretation is that interest cannot be charged. Instead, "fees" paid by a borrower are charged in order to compensate the lender for its services. The second concept is *gharar*, which prohibits unanticipated gain or profit. Thus, contracts with organizations that operate under Islamic law must be very careful to spell out all outcomes and expectations.

Agreements and conventions

It would be easier, of course, if there were a standard legal system that applied to all countries. But for that purpose, governments would have to give up considerable political sovereignty. Nevertheless, faced with the reality of growing economic interdependence, many countries have signed multinational agreements and conventions to give some degree of consistency to the international legal environment. One of the great values of the EU, in fact, is the ongoing attempt to standardize laws and regulations among members. The European Commission has produced some hundreds of directives that have been more or less quickly transformed into national law by the member states' legislators, but which lead to a certain standardization of laws and regulations across the EU.

Legal agreement among countries may be *bilateral*, such as the agreement between France and the U.S. that helps prevent double taxation of firms and personnel doing business in both countries. Or they may be part of a *multilateral* understanding like the Paris Convention, which established a patent-filing process that covers patent applications in 80 countries. If an application is filed in one member state, that company has priority over companies filing similar applications in all member countries for up to 12 months. Other multilateral conventions and agreements dealing with property rights are illustrated in the Appendix to this chapter.

Extraterritoriality

A particular aspect of a firm's international legal environment that can give rise to problems is the extraterritoriality of national law: The laws of the home country govern the operations of a company, including its subsidiaries or sales offices located in another country. Extraterritoriality creates a double legal standard. A practice that is legal in a host country may be illegal in the home country. To take just one example, in Hong Kong it is legal to discuss prices with a competitor; in the U.S. it is not. Thus, international marketers must be concerned not only about having to operate under more than one legal system but also with the fit between different systems.

Court system

Just as there is no international business law, there is no international court system. The International Court of Justice, located in The Hague in the Netherlands, provides a forum in which countries can air their political grievances. And the European Court in Luxembourg applies uniform legal standards to all members of the EU. Member countries now follow the European Court's interpretations in applying national law. This court is thus functioning as a supreme court for the EU.

Such situations are unusual, however. More commonly, the problems caused by the lack of international business law are confounded by the lack of courts to hear international cases.

Host country courts often exhibit bias against foreign companies, particularly in countries where nationalism is running high or there is a history of exploitation by multinational companies. A company that loses a case in a host country court has little recourse. About all it can do is attempt to influence intergovernmental relations in the hope of getting the ruling overturned. Only large firms with ample resources are in a position to exercise such influence.

Regulation of competition

Deregulation of markets

Governments differ in the extent to which they regulate competition. Following the examples of the U.K. and the U.S., all industrially developed countries have begun to deregulate their markets. That is, governments tend to decrease the number and specificity of regulations concerning competition. For example, EU governments agreed to open the electricity and gas as well as telecommunication, railroad, and air transportation industries to competition. Customers are allowed to choose between competing suppliers. The infrastructure still stays in the hands of single firms. This should help avoid problems of breakdowns, such as in the U.S. electricity supply, or of underserviced railroad tracks causing major accidents such as in the U.K.

When governments are more or less forced to agree with international deregulation but do not accept its impact on local industries, they try to find loopholes in the deregulation agreements. For example, the deregulation of air travel in Europe as of April 1997 has given European airlines the opportunity to fly between any two cities in the European Union. But at Europe's major slot-controlled airports, governments can limit the number of slots to keep competition out. Airlines cannot buy and sell slots without approval. As a reaction, large carriers such as British Airways have acquired airlines based in Paris largely for access to their slots.

In Hong Kong it is legal to discuss prices with a competitor

© mika makkonen/iStock

Examples from the telecommunications business show that large companies such as U.S.-based AT&T, Germany's Deutsche Telecom, or British Vodafone are often better equipped to move quickly into recently deregulated markets. They have the resources needed to acquire smaller firms or business units of other firms in international markets or to set up joint ventures with local partners. Small and medium-sized companies such as Telecom Austria may find international niche opportunities (e.g. in eastern Europe), or can form a joint venture with an internationally operating partner, such as Telecom Italia.

Antitrust controls

Deregulation of markets only leads to increased competition if the new players in the industry are prevented from taking a dominant position that allows them to control the market. Antitrust commissions in the deregulating countries, therefore, are having a close look at every merger or acquisition that risks resulting in market dominance. For example, in 1999, Montreal-headquartered Alcan, the aluminum giant, gave up an intended merger with French Pechiney because the European antitrust agency had asked it to sell its 50% share in the aluminum mill of Norf, Germany. They did allow the purchase of Swiss Algroup, which was accepted with less significant restructuring demands. Only in 2003 did Alcan come back with a new offer to take over Pechiney. Because of emerging competition from China and Russia, the antitrust agency now had a harder time believing that a merged firm could wield excessive market power.

In another case, Brazil's Administrative Council of Economic Defense, known as Cade, started investigating U.S.-based Colgate-Palmolive's $1 billion acquisition of the Brazilian Kolynos oral-care business after rival Procter & Gamble filed a complaint questioning whether Colgate should be allowed to dominate 79 per cent of Brazil's $400 million toothpaste market. The approval of the deal came 20 months after the acquisition. But it included restrictions that required Colgate to make cumbersome changes. Cade said that Colgate, which had acquired Kolynos as a fast way to expand its business in the potentially lucrative Latin American market, must either stop selling toothpaste under the Kolynos brand in Brazil for four years, or license the Kolynos toothpaste trademark to another company for 20 years.

Dumping

Selling products in other country markets below cost or below domestic prices, called **dumping**, can give rise to legal problems for an international marketer. Dumping is similar to predatory pricing, which has long been outlawed by U.S. antitrust legislation. Both practices are aimed at capturing market share, injuring competitors, and, in the long run, giving the company a high degree of market control. Companies ranging from Japanese computer chip manufacturers to U.S. agricultural concerns have been charged with dumping products into other country markets. The number of antidumping cases involving Chinese companies has soared in recent years, with the EU and the U.S. accounting for most of them.

It is not difficult to bring charges before a commission that hears dumping cases, such as the U.S. Treasury Department, but it is often difficult to prove such charges. The definition of cost, such as marginal versus average cost, may be central to the case. Thus, accusations often focus on the difference between the price of the imported good and its price in the home market.

Charging competitors with dumping can also serve as a means of gaining information about the structure of their added-value chain and product technology, or simply holding them off the market for some time. For the international marketer accused of dumping in such cases, the biggest problem is to prove that no dumping has taken place without disclosing too much information on new product technology.

Regulations concerning marketing mix

The most important part of a country's legal environment from an international marketer's point of view is legislation concerning the company's marketing mix. Each element of the marketing mix is subject to legal regulation. Some of the most important aspects are discussed below.

Protection of industrial property rights

An important concern of every international marketer is the protection of industrial property rights, or corporate assets that have the potential to generate funds, such as brand names, trademarks, patents, copyright, and technology. No uniform international legal code addresses this issue, although there are several multinational agreements in this area. The most important is the **Trips Agreement** signed by the members of WTO. It covers the trade-related aspects of intellectual property rights, which extend to software, films, literature, trademarks, and other expressions of creativity. This agreement makes disputes in this area subject to adjudication by the world trade body.

Patent protection An important problem is patent protection. For example, in August 2003, after a long struggle, WTO member governments broke their deadlock over intellectual property protection and public health. They agreed on legal changes that make it easier for poorer countries to import lower priced generics made under compulsory licensing if they are unable to manufacture the medicines themselves.

Trademark protection **Trademarks** may be graphic signs, that is, words, names of persons, pictures or slogans, as well as the design and packaging of a product, that can be used to differentiate goods and services of one supplier from another. Figure 4.3 shows one of the oldest international trademarks and its development over the last 270 years.

The loss of a trademark may have devastating effects on the sales and profits of a firm. If the Coca-Cola Company, for example, lost its trademark, any soft drink maker could bottle a sweet, brown carbonated beverage under the Coca-Cola name. The effect the loss of a brand name can have is illustrated by Swiss Emmental cheese. Cheese is Switzerland's oldest export product, and it remains the top agricultural export. The Emmental Valley, situated along the Emme River, has been the heart of Switzerland's cheese-making industry since the 15th century. But imitations of Swiss-made Emmental cheese, which may freely be called "Emmental cheese" are generating a large hole in sales in export markets. The Germans, the French, and the Dutch all produce less expensive versions of Emmental, in bigger factories, and with pasteurized milk, which is cheaper to buy and to transport. And, in the U.S., any cheese that resembles Emmental can be called Swiss cheese. The only trademark distinction the Swiss have held onto is the label, with "Emmenthaler Switzerland" printed next to a man blowing an Alpenhorn. Imitations have caused a sharp decline in cheese prices.

The European Commission has published a list of 41 "European regional high-quality products" for which it demands exclusivity of their trademark. The list contains, for example, Portuguese porto (port wine), French sauternes (white wine), and Greek uozo (an alcoholic beverage produced from the bark of a tree growing on the isle of Chios). No uniform international legal code addresses the issue of brand protection, although there are several multinational agreements in this area.

European unification has produced a new and improved system for protecting trademarks throughout the EU with a single application and registration. The application for a community trademark (CTM) must be drafted in one of the EU languages plus a secondary language from one of the five official languages of the EU, English, French, German, Italian, and Spanish. A CTM may be obtained from the Harmonization Agency for the Common Market located in Alicante, Spain, assuming there is no opposition to the process. Because there are more than 3 million registered trademarks in the EU, the applying firm must make sure that its requested trademark has not already been registered by another firm. The initial CTM application period is 10 years from the date of filing the application.

FIGURE 4.3 *Trademark of the Staatliche Porzellan – Manufaktur Meissen*

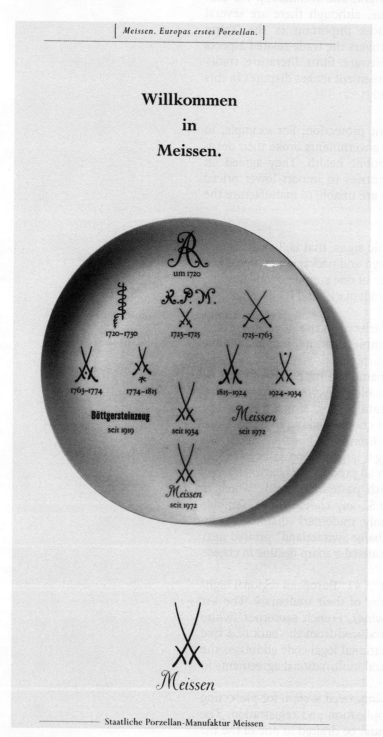

Meissen. Europas erstes Porzellan.

Willkommen

in

Meissen.

Staatliche Porzellan-Manufaktur Meissen

In 1723 the porcelain factory of Meissen, Germany, which was the first to produce fine porcelain outside China, chose two crossed swords as its trademark. Since then the trademark has been kept largely unchanged, only being adapted to suit the more graphic taste of the times.

The CTM registration procedure takes at least four months. The process is available to nationals of the EU countries, countries that are parties to the Paris Convention, and other countries granting reciprocal rights. A CTM applicant is not required to have a commercial establishment in the EU. One of the most significant advantages of the CTM lies in the "leveraged use principle." The proprietor of a CTM must prove use within five years of registration. However, the trademark proprietor can maintain rights throughout the EU by proving genuine use in just one member country. This allows staged introduction of their trademark across the EU.

Counterfeiting Even improved international systems of trademark application and registration do not help to resolve the major international problem related to the protection of brand names and trademarks: counterfeiting. **Counterfeiting** is the intentional production or sale of a product under a brand name or trademark without the authorization of the holder of that name or trademark. It is difficult to estimate total corporate losses due to counterfeiting. But an estimated 10% of products sold worldwide are phony, and almost any brand that sells well becomes unfair game. The International Anti Counterfeiting Coalition has calculated such losses at $200 billion a year, and that is only for U.S. manufacturers.

The pirate captains of the underground economy typically hail from places like China, South Korea, Vietnam, Bulgaria, Italy, or Russia. They work as a loosely intertwined network of importers and distributors, often living in the U.S. or Europe and using connections overseas to procure counterfeits. Italy is the uncontested leader in European counterfeited product manufacturing and sales. Piracy in Italy has more than doubled since the early 1990s, to levels comparable with those in China. An estimated 95% of Bulgaria's CD production is illegal knockoffs for sale throughout Europe.

Counterfeits account for half or more of total sales in many developing countries. But even firms from economically developing countries, such as Ghana-based Printex, which produces colorful African fabrics that are the staple of Ghanaian fashion, have to fear textile pirates from China, Pakistan, Nigeria, India, or the Ivory Coast. Yet in many of the countries of Asia and Latin America where piracy is worst, such as Pakistan or Mexico, sales of international brands – both legitimate *and* fake – are still quite small. Consumers in the U.S. and Europe buy counterfeit products in countless places – small discount stores, flea markets, street vendors' carts, and, occasionally, chains whose honest supply managers do not realize the counterfeit. Covert retailing is on the rise, such as Tupperware-like parties for phony Rolex watches, Louis Vuitton bags, or Porsche design spectacles. The U.S., which buys 30% of all the world's annual sales of recorded music, accounts for more than 10% of pirated sales value. Americans have the questionable distinction of spending more on pirated music than any other country apart from Russia.

Retaliation Even when conventions and agreements exist, protection of industrial property rights is difficult and expensive. In addition to law enforcement actions, an option available to international marketers is retaliation. For example, Cartier of Paris retaliated against a Mexico City retailer that was selling other manufacturers' products under the Cartier name in an international event. The company publicly gathered piles of faked Cartier watches and jewelry. Cartier's CEO personally gave the sign to a steamroller, which smashed them in front of invited international journalists. Potential customers all over the world were informed of that event and became much more prudent in buying products bearing the Cartier label, and counterfeiting of this trademark sharply decreased in the following years.

Packaging

The international marketer has to consider local legal regulations concerning:

- packaging material
- package design
- kind and amount of information to put on it.

In Australia, Aim toothpaste, after spending $5 million on a promotional campaign, had to change its package because it was ruled to be too similar to that of a competitor. The number and intensity of legal regulations concerning the reusability of packages and their recycling potential has been increasing significantly in the European Union.

Many countries have different regulations concerning how product ingredients are to be listed and the manner in which promotional material is presented on labels. Cigarette labels, for example, have to include statements ranging from Japan's rather mild warning, "Don't smoke too much," to Oman's much stronger statement, "Smoking is a major cause of cancer, lung disease, and diseases of the heart and arteries," to France's no holds barred, "Smoking kills."

Regulations on ingredient listing are not automatically less demanding in countries with a lower level of industrial development. In Saudi Arabia, for example, there is a nomenclature for food products to be respected in addition to the list of ingredients, the net filling weight, name and address of the producer, production and latest consumption date to be indicated on the package. The entire information has to be given in Arabic as well as English.

The differences in legal regulations make it particularly difficult for an international marketer to standardize packaging across country markets. Venezuela, for example, prescribes the indication of prices on the package, whereas in Chile this practice is illegal, as is recommending retail prices to intermediaries.

Product liability

Product liability is a producer's or intermediary's responsibility (independent of contractual obligations) for any personal damage or damage of a good (that is not the product itself) incurred by a person through a defective product. Legal systems vary considerably in their treatment of product liability. The strict liability laws found in the U.S. are often a source of surprise and alarm to international marketers planning to enter this market for the first time. For example, in 1990 Dr. Gore paid $40,750 for a new BMW which, he later discovered, had been damaged and repainted before he took delivery. Feeling cheated, Dr. Gore sued BMW for the $4,000 reduction in his car's value, plus punitive damages based on the fact that BMW had sold 983 such "refinished" cars in America over a 10-year period. An Alabama jury awarded Gore his $4,000, along with a huge $4 million award in punitive damages (later reduced to a $2 million by the state's supreme court and, finally, rejected by the U.S. Supreme Court).

Fearful of such lawsuits, companies whose products might be a target simply avoid the U.S. market. For instance, Axminster Electronics, a small British firm whose devices help prevent cot death by monitoring a baby's breathing, does not sell in the U.S. because it cannot secure product-liability insurance. Manufacturers of small private aircraft have similar insurance problems.

Product safety laws also vary from one country to another. When sales of the pesticide DDT were banned in the U.S. for safety reasons, for example, such sales continued to be legal in most industrially developing parts of the world. U.S. manufacturers of DDT found themselves unable to sell the product in their own country, but they were able to exploit a ready export market – whatever ethical standards such behavior may express. Ironically, as U.S. food imports increased, more contaminated produce was purchased in stores in the U.S. because of the relatively relaxed controls on pesticide use in food-exporting countries.

Even similar product use situations may be subject to different product-liability interpretations. Thus, theme park rides that are considered safe in Queensland, Australia, are not subject to the same level of crowd control as similar rides in theme parks in Texas. By U.S. standards, such rides may be dangerous. Eliminating the product-liability hazard in this case would require more equipment and personnel, which would increase costs and affect profits.

The European Commission has created a range of common standards for various products, from kidney dialysis machines to food coloring. However, when it comes to safety, the rules specifically allow countries to prohibit imports that threaten "public security." That has caused trouble for exporters both inside and to the EU. Dormont Manufacturing Co., a U.S.-based producer of hoses that hook up household appliances to gas outlets, for example, once sold those in outlets freely throughout Europe. Since national safety specifications were written by committees often dominated by domestic producers, the company needs individual approval in each country, because hoses are crucial to the safe operation of gas appliances.

Regulation of advertising

Legal regulation of local advertising may concern the use of media, comparative and other claims, advertisements for specific product categories, advertisements addressing children, and the use of language as well as agency–client relationships. For example, tobacco advertising is entirely banned in countries such as Canada, China, New Zealand, Norway, and Thailand. It is still permitted in Cambodia and Laos. The U.S. has imposed tighter tobacco advertising restrictions, and the European Commission has voted a directive urging legislators of member countries to make tobacco advertising unlawful by August 2005.

Japan prohibits direct advertising of drugs to consumers. Therefore, indirect drug advertising in Japan typically involved generic newspaper ads, the distribution of leaflets about treatable conditions, and the sponsoring of meetings for doctors where highly reputable local doctors noted the growth in the number of patients suffering from certain conditions and discussed ways of treating them. Finland limits TV ads for fruit juices and mouthwash, while Belgium has forbidden spots for heating and insulation devices. Italy bans ads for diet products, daily newspapers, and consumer magazines from state television. Greece requires car advertisers to mention emission levels.

How important clear regulations may be to avoid abuse of potential customers is shown by the example (see Ethics box 4.1) of firms using the internet to address children. Having said that, the diversity of regulations from one country to another represents a major hurdle for international marketers in developing international campaigns. The difficulty of developing an advertisement that can be used across countries in view of existing restrictions is illustrated by the example of a TV spot for the launch of a new low-fat chocolate bar in Europe. It was planned to introduce the product in five countries, Belgium, Denmark, France, Germany, and the U.K., using the following claims: "Does not make you gain weight," "A treat after class that does not cut appetite," "Contains only one-third of the calories of other chocolate bars." The campaign could not get started because in Belgium dietary claims are not allowed in advertising. In Denmark, advertisements that make nutritional promises are forbidden. In France, advertising to children is illegal. In Germany, a comparison with other products was not allowed, and in the U.K. sweets may only be presented as snacks.

In view of such a multitude of different regulations, the European Commission has made efforts to unify advertising regulations. As a result, for example, comparative advertising has been authorized, provided that certain conditions are met. Comparative advertising is legal for goods and services, which are in fact comparable. The comparison must relate to one or more "essential, pertinent, verifiable and representative characteristics," of which price is one. The text does not allow confusion over names, distinctive trademarks or brand names; it also bans "knocking copy."

In some countries there are constraining legal restrictions on agency–client relationships. South Korea, the second-largest advertising market in Asia, for example, has traditionally barred foreign agencies from the country. In response, agencies like Ogilvy & Mather have developed "technical consultant" agreements with Korean agencies. These agreements enable the Korean agencies to serve their clients more fully. In the Ogilvy example, Korean agencies can offer global advertising support to their own clients. Such agreements also permit greater coordination of the advertising used in Korea with that used in the rest of Asia.

Restriction of sales promotions

The use of sales promotion tools may be constrained by the laws in some of the served country markets. Laws against price discrimination may prevent the use of price-offs, for example. In the case of contests and sweepstakes, legal issues constitute the largest implementation problem. In the U.S., for example, a sweepstake that requires proof of purchase is considered an illegal form of gambling. In Malaysia, contests are allowed, but they must involve games of skill and not of chance.

ETHICS BOX 4.1

Mining kids online for information

As millions of kids go online, marketers are in hot pursuit. Eager to reach an enthusiastic audience more open to pitches than the typical adult buried in junk mail, companies often entertain children online with games and contests. But to play, children frequently are required to fill out questionnaires about themselves, their families, and their friends – valuable data to be sorted and stored in marketing databases.

For example, the website of Jelly Belly offers visitors free samples of jelly beans – so long as they spill the beans about their name, address, gender, age, and where they shop. In 1997, the fine-print disclaimer revealed what might be done with this personal data: "Anything you disclose to us is ours. That's right – ours. So we can do anything we want with the stuff you post. We can reproduce it, disclose it, transmit it, publish it, broadcast it, and post it someplace else."

Such behavior rattled many privacy advocates, who are pushing for new regulations. Critics say online come-ons aimed at kids are particularly insidious, and fret that the internet could erupt into a frenzy of online infomercials toying with children's minds. They call for the same kinds of protections that now restrict television advertising geared to kids. But some experts question whether a raft of new legislation is the right answer, rather than simply extending current rules on fraudulent and deceptive practices to the online market. The U.S. and the EU have reached an agreement on internet privacy issues. The rules provide safe-harbor status for companies that receive permission from customers to sell or otherwise transfer their information to other companies, and give access to such data to the relevant customer.

Being asked for a statement Rob Muller, manager of marketing at Herman Goelitz, said the Jelly Belly legal disclaimer "was intended to be somewhat tongue-in-cheek ... to entertain, not intimidate." He added that the company has no intention of selling or renting out personal information on users, but was issuing a warning for internet users at large. In the meantime Jelly Belly has a privacy statement posted as follows: "You can be sure all of your personal information is treated as strictly confidential and will not be sold or rented for any reason. We use this information to send you a sample and to better understand our customers. If you are under 18 years of age, please obtain parental permission before completing this survey."

Source: Adapted from Sandberg, J. (1997) "Marketers mine kids on-line for information: alarmed privacy advocates push for new regulations", *Wall Street Journal Europe*, 10 June, p. 12; www.jellybelly.jellybelly.com/surveyNew/survey_intro.asp

Taxes also affect the choice of sales promotion tools. For example, in Sweden liquor products are subject to high sales taxes that substantially raise the price to the consumer. A costly sales promotion item, such as a commemorative decanter, would not be feasible if it were to raise the price of an already expensive product beyond a level that consumers find acceptable.

Price regulations

At one time or another almost every country's government has engaged in some form of price control. In countries with highly inflationary economies it is common to find price controls on food and beverage products. Some countries, such as Ghana, controlled the manufacturer's profit margin, which has the effect of controlling the price paid by the consumer. South Korea forced international marketers, such as U.S.-based Whirlpool, to label their products with the price at which they entered the country. That price does not include internal transportation costs, or the mark-ups of intermediaries. In the EU and the U.S., antitrust laws limit international marketers' discretion in setting prices for intermediaries. Some countries, such as Germany and Norway, have fixed book prices, insisting that free competition, as in the U.K., the Netherlands, and Sweden, would drive many booksellers out of business and discourage investment in publishing less popular books. France prevents stores from selling goods at a loss. Retailers must charge their customers at least what they were invoiced by the supplier. International marketers must make sure that they are informed about such country market specifics before evaluating the attractiveness of doing business in a market.

Regulation of distribution and sales

The legal environment affects the distribution channels available to international marketers. Door-to-door selling, for example, is prohibited in France. In Australia, a customer can send liquor anywhere in the country via a system similar to that used by florists in the western industrialized countries, but in the U.S. most states do not allow the sale of liquor in that manner. Finland, Norway, and Sweden traditionally restricted most alcoholic beverage sales to state-owned shops. When Sweden and Finland joined the EU, they had to drop state monopolies on the import and wholesale distribution of alcohol.

The legality of agreements between manufacturers and distributors can also differ considerably under different legal systems. For example, tying contracts specify that a retailer must buy all of a manufacturer's products in order to buy one particular product line. Although such contracts are illegal in the U.S., in other countries they are not only legal but may signify the culturally desirable existence of a long-term relationship. Similarly, the establishment of exclusive territories for intermediaries is prohibited by antitrust laws in the U.S. In contrast, it is an accepted practice in Europe and Latin America.

Regulations concerning opening hours of retail shops may have a significant influence on the profit potential of international retailers. In 2004, for example, in Austria, Germany, and Switzerland all shops had to be closed on Sundays. Austria and Switzerland only allowed shops in tourist areas and in airports or train stations to keep their doors open on Sundays. In Italy retailers were allowed to open on eight Sundays from January to November and on all Sundays in December. The Czech Republic and Hungary gave total freedom to their retailers. They may stay open 24 hours, seven days a week.

The U.S. government has stepped in with rules to curb fraud in telephone selling. The Telemarketing Sales Rule requires telephone salespeople to tell consumers promptly that they are making a sales call, the nature of the products or services offered, and in the case of prize promotions, that no purchase is necessary to win. Market researchers are exempt from those rules.

Regulation of business relationships

Legislation that deserves special attention by international marketers concerns the regulation of appropriate business relationships. What are considered corrupt practices may vary from one country market to another. For example, the Foreign Corrupt Practices Act in the U.S. forbids bribery of foreign public officials, allows payment for services (known as "grease," because it lubricates business transactions), and stipulates criminal penalties for violators. In other countries, where public administration personnel partly live on additional payments or gifts from their clients and where business relations are less functional than in North America, legislation concerning corrupt practices may be much more relaxed.

"Managing" the political and legal environment

Assessing political risk

A company operating internationally or a firm on its way to internationalization would prefer stable, friendly and predictable political and legal environments in the country markets to be served. But this ideal is rarely found. Thus, international marketers must develop a monitoring tool to be able to evaluate the degree of the company's exposure to political risk in all served and potential markets (see Toolbox 4.1).

TOOLBOX 4.1 Assessing political risk

List of assessment criteria

The development of a list of risk assessment criteria may be a simple way to go. In establishing the list the marketer will need to start from the definition of the company's business domain in the corporate policy statement. From there it may determine factors concerning the state and potential development of the economic and political/legal environment of the company's product market that are relevant for evaluating the firm's (potential) risk exposure. Table 4.3 gives an example of what such a list could look like.

Scoring model

In transforming such a list of risk evaluation criteria into a scoring model, the international marketer develops a company-specific tool for political risk assessment. In the scoring model each risk evaluation criterion receives a weight according to its importance for the product market of the company. Then the geographical markets under consideration are evaluated along the selected criteria. The sum of scores for each market indicates its estimated political risk.

One major problem with scoring models is that assessment criteria should be selected in a way to be independent of each other. A look at the list given in Table 4.4 shows how difficult it may be to fulfill this demand. Attributing weights to interrelated criteria, however, may lead to strongly biased results.

Buying risk assessment data

A faster but perhaps less managerially relevant way to assess the political risk in country markets under consideration is to buy risk assessment data from specialist consulting firms, such as the *International Country Risk Guide* (*ICRG*) published by Political Risk Services, IBC U.S. Table 4.4 gives the ranking of creditworthiness established semi-annually by *Euromoney*, one of the most well-known service organizations carrying out international risk analyses on an ongoing basis.

The *Euromoney* country risk assessment uses nine categories that fall into three broad groups: Analytical indicators, credit indicators, and market indicators. The weighted scores are calculated as follows: The highest score in each category receives the full mark for the weighting; the lowest receives 0. In between, figures are calculated according to the formula: Final score = weighting / (maximum score – minimum score) × (score – minimum score). The country risk ranking shows only the final scores after weighting.

The categories are:

Political risk (25%). *Euromoney* polled risk analysts, risk insurance brokers, and bank credit officers. They were asked to give each country a score of between 0 and 10. A score of 10 indicates no risk of non-payment; 0 indicates that there is no chance of payments being made. Countries were scored in comparison both with one another and with previous years. Country risk was defined as the risk of non-payment or non-servicing of payment for goods or services, loans, trade-related finance and dividends, and the non-repatriation of capital. This category does not reflect the creditworthiness of individual counterparties in any country.

Economic performance (25%). Based (1) on GNI (Atlas Method) figures per capita and (2) on results of *Euromoney* poll of economic projections.

Debt indicators (10%). Calculated using these ratios from the World Bank's World Development Indicators 2004: Total debt stocks to GNP (A), debt service to exports (B); current account balance to GNP (C). Developing countries that do not report complete debt data get a score of 0.

Debt in default or rescheduled (10%). Scores are based on the ratio of rescheduled debt to debt stocks, taken from the World Bank's World Development Indicators 2004. OECD and developing countries that do not report under the debtor reporting system (DRS) score 10 and 0 respectively.

Credit ratings (10%). Nominal values are assigned to sovereign ratings from Moody's, Standard & Poor's and Fitch ratings. The higher the average value, the better. Where there is no rating, countries score 0.

Access to bank finance (5%). Calculated from disbursement of private, long-term, unguaranteed loans as a percentage of GNP. Source: The World Bank's World Development Indicators 2004.

Access to short-term finance (5%). Takes into account OECD consensus groups (Source: ECGD) and short-term cover available from the U.S. Exim Bank and Atradius UK.

Access to capital markets (5%). Heads of debt syndicate and loan syndications rated each country's accessibility to international markets.

Discount on forfaiting (5%). Reflects the average maximum tenor for forfaiting. Countries where forfaiting is not available score 0.

TABLE 4.3 *Potential criteria for assessing political risk*

1 General risks
- Border conflicts
- Alliance commitments or alliance shifts
- Embargoes/international boycotts
- Position of the host government vis-à-vis the company's home government
- Civil war/(selective) terrorism
- Stability of legal regulations

2 Company-specific risks
- Expropriation/domestication
- Selected boycott
- Operating restrictions
- Special fees and taxes not levied on domestic firms
- Restrictions on profit remittance

TABLE 4.4 Country risk ranking 2005

		Country	Total score	Political risk	Economic perform-ance	Debt indicators	Debt in default or rescheduled	Credit ratings	Access to bank finance	Access to short-term finance	Access to capital markets	Discount on forfaiting
March 2005	September 2004											
1	2	Norway	100	25	25	10	10	10	5	5	5	5
2	3	Switzerland	99.45	24.69	25.00	10.00	10.00	10.00	5.00	5.00	5.00	4.77
3	1	Luxembourg	99.15	25.00	24.38	10.00	10.00	10.00	5.00	5.00	5.00	4.77
4	4	U.S.	99.10	24.90	24.43	10.00	10.00	10.00	5.00	5.00	5.00	4.77
5	5	Denmark	96.93	24.12	22.81	10.00	10.00	10.00	5.00	5.00	5.00	5.00
6	6	Sweden	95.63	24.69	21.18	10.00	10.00	10.00	5.00	5.00	5.00	4.77
7	7	U.K.	94.58	24.76	20.05	10.00	10.00	10.00	5.00	5.00	5.00	4.77
8	9	Finland	93.55	24.52	19.26	10.00	10.00	10.00	5.00	5.00	5.00	4.77
9	10	Austria	93.52	24.77	18.99	10.00	10.00	10.00	5.00	5.00	5.00	4.77
10	8	Ireland	93.43	24.59	19.07	10.00	10.00	10.00	5.00	5.00	5.00	4.77
			93.43	24.48	19.01							
175	167	Micronesia (Federated States)	22.54	12.87	7.17	0.00	0.00	0.00	0.00	2.50	0.00	0.00
176	165	Namibia	22.23	12.20	4.87	0.00	0.00	0.00	0.00	2.50	1.50	1.16
177	171	Burundi	21.77	4.00	1.27	5.33	10.00	0.00	0.00	1.17	0.00	0.00
178	179	Somalia	20.35	3.13	6.05	0.00	10.00	0.00	0.00	1.17	0.00	0.00
179	176	Liberia	18.52	1.92	4.59	1.17	10.00	0.00	0.00	0.83	0.00	0.00
180	182	Democratic Republic of the Congo (Zäire)	18.16	4.32	2.67	0.00	10.00	0.00	0.00	1.17	0.00	0.00
181	181	Cuba	14.07	2.81	8.43	0.00	0.00	0.00	0.00	2.83	0.00	0.00
182	178	Marshall Islands	10.47	6.51	2.45	0.00	0.00	0.00	0.00	1.50	0.00	0.00
183	185	Afghanistan	3.66	0.73	2.10	0.00	0.00	0.00	0.00	1.17	0.00	0.00
184	184	North Korea	3.25	0.00	2.09	0.00	0.00	0.00	0.00	1.17	0.00	0.00
185	183	Iraq	1.85	0.55	0.47	0.00	0.00	0.00	0.00	0.83	0.00	0.00

Source: *Euromoney*, March 2005, 36(431), pp. 136 ff

Management decisions

Having comparatively evaluated the risk involved with the political and legal environment of the potential and currently served country markets, the management of an internationally operating firm will first have to decide which markets to avoid. The remaining markets can be ranked according to the risk they represent and decisions may be taken on how to handle the risk in the most attractive markets.

Basically an international marketer has two non-exclusive options for reducing the risk from its markets' political and legal environment. It may primarily rely on *reducing financial exposure* by insuring the firm's activities against political risks, minimizing fixed investments in the served country markets, raising local capital, or producing only parts of the products' value added in one country.

Contrariwise, the international marketer may focus on *building and maintaining strong relationships* with the most important stakeholders in each country it serves. For that purpose the firm may cooperate with local investment partners, employ local executives, financially support public institutions and interests, or make its products an inevitable "must" in customers' eyes.

All these possibilities will be further discussed in Parts II and III of the book concerning the international marketer's basic strategic decisions and the building and sustaining of its international market position.

Summary

Most companies are unable to influence the political and legal environment of their markets directly but their opportunities for successful business conduct largely depend on the structure and content of that environment. A marketer serving international markets or planning to do so, therefore, has to assess carefully the political and legal environments of the markets served or under consideration to draw the appropriate managerial consequences.

The first step in assessing the political and legal environments of country markets is to determine which parts or characteristics of those environments are specifically relevant to the product market(s) of the company. Generally, the most important factor is the *stability of the served country markets' political systems*.

The *form of government* has some impact on the extent of political stability in a country, but the two are not directly related.

The *power structure of interest groups* most strongly influencing local policies has a larger impact on political stability. Political parties channel public opinion into the formulation of government policies and laws. The role that foreign businesses are allowed to play in a given country market is influenced by the philosophies of those parties. Strong influences on a country's political decisions may also come from unions, special interest groups, and lobbyists.

Depending on the people in power, their view of the world and whose interests they mainly follow, governments may have very different objectives. Some general objectives relevant for most governments include:

- maintenance of political sovereignty
- enhancement of national prestige and prosperity
- national security
- protection of cultural identity.

The prevailing political objectives of the governing forces in a country market determine the policies of government.

The international trade policy of a country's government provides a framework for exports, imports, and foreign investment and therefore needs to be closely analyzed by the international marketer. All countries control exports and imports to some degree, providing both barriers to trade and supports for certain domestically as well as foreign-produced goods and services. One way to encourage trade between two countries is to use *political relations* as a means to establish contacts between companies from both countries. Another way to stimulate and assist exports is to provide *financial assistance* either directly or indirectly. Governments may also support the international marketing of their industries by *refunding domestic taxes to exporters*.

Sometimes governments support imports of particular goods or services from industrially less developed countries through *tariff preferences*. A government may also support or deter international business through its *investment policy*.

Barriers to trade include *tariffs*. International trade liberalization has led to a significant reduction of tariff barriers. Therefore, governments have been increasingly using *non-tariff barriers* to protect some of their countries' industries that they think are unable to sustain free international competition. *Trade embargoes or sanctions* are mainly used for political purposes.

The legal environment of a company determines the viability of potential local product markets. Generally important considerations are the kind of legal

system, agreements and conventions the country's government has signed that are relevant for the company's product market, and a country's regulation of competition.

Finally, legislation concerning the *potential use of marketing tools* needs to be closely analyzed.

Having determined and analyzed the current state of the relevant factors of influence from the political and legal environment, the marketer needs to anticipate their potential states of development at the planning horizon to evaluate the potential impact of the political and legal environment on the success of the firm. A comparison of the environments' impact in the various geographical markets will allow the marketer to decide how to "manage" those environments.

DISCUSSION QUESTIONS

1. Describe a current political trend in your home country that effects international marketers based in your country. What implications do you see?

2. Why is political stability so very important for international marketers? Find a recent example to underline your points.

3. How can the change of major political objectives in a country have an impact on the potential for success of an international marketer?

4. Take the example of a small company you know of and discuss how it can profit from the export support activities of your country's government, administration, and related organizations.

5. What are the impacts of the absence of a body of international business law on an internationally operating firm? Find current examples for your points.

6. Why would some smaller companies opt for less deregulated and liberalized markets? Discuss the consequences they have to bear.

7. Why is dumping a controversial issue in international marketing? What can international marketers do about it?

8. What relationship do you see between antitrust controls and the deregulation of markets? Whose interests are involved? Discuss.

9. What can an international marketer do to protect its industrial property rights? Find examples from business newspapers.

10. Take the example of a company you know and develop a list of country risk evaluation criteria. Explain why you selected the criteria on your list.

ADDITIONAL READINGS

Baum, H. (ed.) (1997) *Japan: Economic Success and Legal System*, Berlin: Walter de Gruyter.

Castro, J.O. de and K. Uhlenbruck (1997) "Characteristics of privatization: evidence from developed, less-developed, and former communist countries", *Journal of International Business Studies*, 28(1), 123–43.

Keillor, B.D., T.J. Wilkinson, and D. Owens (2005), "Threats to international operations: dealing

with political risk at the firm level", *Journal of Business Research*, 58(5), 629–35.

Morash, E.A. and D.F. Lynch (2002) "Public policy and global supply chain capabilities and performance: a resource-based view", *Journal of International Marketing*, 10(1), 25–51.

In addition, read the *Wall Street Journal Europe* or *The International Herald Tribune*, *Le Monde*, *Neue Zürcher Zeitung*, *Corriere de la Sierra*, or *The Economist*.

Useful internet links

Airbus Industries	http://www.airbus.com/
ALCAN	http://www.alcan.com/
Alcatel	http://www.alcatel.com/
Astra AB	http://www.astrazeneca.com/article/11148.aspx
B&Q	http://www.diy.com/
BAE Systems	http://www.baesystems.com/
BMW	http://www.bmw.com/
Cairns Group	http://www.cairnsgroup.org/introduction.html
Colgate-Palmolive	http://www.colgate.com/
Community Trademark (CTM)	http://oami.eu.int/
Dassault Electronique	http://www.dassault.fr/
Deutsche Post	http://www.deutschepost.de/dpag?check=yes&lang=de_EN&xmlFile=828
DHL Airways Inc.	http://www.dhl.com/
Dornier	http://www.lindauer-dornier.com/english/index.htm
Econet	http://www.econet.co.zw/
Equal Employment Opportunity Commission	http://www.eeoc.gov/
Eximbank	http://www.exim.gov/about/index.htm
FedEx	http://www.fedex.com/us/tracking/
General Electric Company (GEC)	http://www.ge.com/en/company/companyinfo/
Georgia Department of Technical and Adult Education	http://www.dtae.org/
Greenpeace	http://www.greenpeace.org/international/about
Information on the Helms-Burton Act	http://www.earlham.edu/~pols/ps17971/weissdo/HelmsB.html
International Country Risk Guide (ICRG)	http://www.icrgonline.com/
International Court of Justice	http://www.icj-cij.org
International Trademark Association (INTA)	http://www.inta.org/info
Japanese External Trade Organization (JETRO)	http://www.jetro.go.jp/
Libya's great manmade river project	http://www.pubs.asce.org/WWWdisplay.cgi?9804924
Lockheed Martin	http://www.lockheedmartin.com/
Maersk A/S	http://www.maersk.com/
Marconi Electronic Systems	http://www.marconi.com/
Mitsubishi Motor Manufacturing of America Inc	http://www.mitsubishi-motors.com/corporate/about_us/e/index.html
National Minority Business Council	http://www.nmbc.org/
Nissan	http://www.nissanusa.com/0,,,00.html
Novartis	http://www.novartis.com/
Ogilvy & Mather	http://www.ogilvy.com/
Paris Convention	http://www.bitlaw.com/source/treaties/paris.html
Peugeot	http://www.peugeot.com/fr/default.htm
Procter & Gamble	http://www.pg.com/
Raytheon	http://www.raytheon.com/
Renault	http://www.renault.com/gb/home/accueil.htm

Schengen Treaty	http://www.auswaertiges-amt.de/www/en/willkommen/einreisebestimmungen/2
Thomson-CSF	http://www.ventures.thomson-csf.com/
U.S. Department of Transportation	http://www.dot.gov/about_dot.html
United Nations Human Development Report (UNHDR)	hdr.undp.org/
UPS	http://www.ups.com/
World Intellectual Property Organization (WIPO)	http://www.wipo.org/treaties/index.html
World Trade Organization (WTO)	http://www.wto.org/

Berne Convention

The Berne Convention created a union of nations in 1886 to protect literary and artistic works. Seventy-four nations are members of the union, including most European countries and some Asian, African, and Latin American nations. The principal non-members are the U.S., Russia, and China.

The convention stipulates:

1 A work whose country of origin is in the union receives the same protection by other union members as is conferred on works of that country's nationals.

2 The enjoyment of protection in countries other than the country of origin is automatic and subject to no registration formalities.

3 The protection of an author's work does not rest on whether it is protected in his home country.

The Berne Convention is administered by the World Intellectual Property Organization (WIPO) in Geneva, a specialized agency of the union.

Universal Copyright Convention (UCC)

The United Nations Education and Social Council (UNESCO) administers this major copyright convention, established in 1952. The purpose of the convention is to link countries with high levels of copyright protection, from the Berne Convention, with those of limited protection, as well as to secure the membership of the U.S. in an international copyright system. The UCC seeks to protect the rights of authors of literary, scientific, and artistic works. UCC member nations are required to accord the same protection to foreign works as to their own.

International Convention for the Protection of Performers, Producers of Phonograms, and Broadcasting Organizations (Rome Convention)

This convention originated in 1964 and is jointly administered by the International Labour Organization (ILO), UNESCO, and WIPO. Only 23 nations have joined; Germany and the U.K. are its leading members. This convention, like the Berne and UCC conventions, requires the same protection for foreign as for national works. The convention seeks to protect performances, sound recordings, and broadcasts, but not films, which are protected by the Berne and UCC conventions.

Convention for the Protection of Producers of Phonograms against Unauthorized Duplication of their Phonograms (Geneva Convention)

Adopted by an international meeting in 1974 in Geneva, there are 36 member nations. Three important nations who signed this convention, but not the Rome Convention, are France, Japan, and the U.S. This convention seeks to limit record piracy, that is, duplicating records without permission. The convention requires that member nations protect sound-recording producers from other member nations against duplication and importation for distribution to the public. As with the Rome Convention, if the nation's domestic law prescribes formalities prior to protection, these are fulfilled if all authorized duplicates issued to the public bear the "P" notice.

Convention Relating to the Distribution of Program-carrying Signals Transmitted by Satellite (Satellite Convention)

This convention was established at Brussels in 1974 and is administered jointly by UNESCO and WIPO. Seven nations are members. The convention seeks to prevent satellite piracy or the transmission and distribution of "poached signals" to unlicensed audiences. Member states are to prevent unauthorized distribution of a signal in their territory.

Multilateral Convention for Avoidance of Double Taxation of Copyright Royalties (Madrid Convention)

Established in 1979, only four states have signed this convention. It does not require compliance with certain minimum standards of protection; rather, it prescribes a model bilateral agreement for member nations to prevent double taxation.

Hague Agreement Concerning International Deposit of Industrial Rights

This convention enables an international application for design protection to be regarded as the equivalent of a national application. Membership is restricted to Paris Convention members. The agreement is effected by deposit of a sample registered at WIPO by a national of a member state. That deposit is then regarded by all member nations as if the formalities of the domestic laws of those nations have been met.

Paris Convention for Protection of Industrial Property

The basic principle is national treatment for patents and trademarks for all member nations. The principal advantage of the convention is that it allows persons who have sought protection (registration) in one member nation priority in another member nation for six months for trademarks and one year for patents.

Nice Agreement Concerning the International Classification of Goods and Services for the Registration of Marks

This provides a system of common classification of goods and services to use in the registration of trademarks. It does not bind member nations who may use it, or not, as they wish.

Trademark Registration Treaty

With only five members, this treaty provides for the international registration of trademarks.

Patent Cooperation Treaty (PCT)

This treaty is an agreement to provide for international cooperation in patent law and, especially, procedures to obtain patent protection. It was established in Washington, D.C., in 1970 and has 32 members, including the U.S., Russia, U.K., and France. It is administered by the WIPO.

Principal features include:

1 An application filed in one's national patent office will extend to as many PCT countries as the applicant may designate.

2 The application is researched and findings are sent to each designated national patent office.

The PCT thus facilitates examination of a patent in a national office, although it does not prescribe what each nation's substantive patent law should be.

International Patent Classification (Strasbourg Agreement)

This agreement was established in 1971 and has 27 member nations. It seeks to have a universal system of patent classifications and certificates. This is aimed not at the patent law of a nation, but to facilitate its administration.

Source: Adapted from Ricketson, S. (1984) *The Law of Intellectual Property*, North Ryde, NSW: Law Book Company; and Lahore, J. (1977) *Intellectual Property Law in Australia*, Sydney: Butterworths; World Intellectual Property Organization www.wipo.org/treaties/index.htm

POTENTIAL MARKET ASSESSMENT: CULTURAL ENVIRONMENT

5

Learning objectives

After studying this chapter you will be able to

- illustrate the impact of culture on individual and organizational customer behavior

- give an overview of cultural factors having an impact on international marketing

- explain the necessity of international marketers adapting to cultural differences

- discuss marketing's influence on culture

INTERNATIONAL MARKETING SPOTLIGHT

Generation slump

Their heroes are athletes and actors, comedians and television personalities. They tell pollsters they dislike math and science and they aspire to become television announcers, musicians, athletes, beauticians, and video game creators. At the bottom of the list are politician, business executive, and banker.

They change their jobs frequently, more often than their parents in a lifetime. Graduates are postponing career choices and marriage, taking time to travel, dabble in temporary work and just hang out. The word "freeter," a combination of "free" and the German word *Arbeiter*, or "worker," is now commonly used in Japanese society. It describes young people who do not commit to one line of work, change jobs frequently and will not, even if unemployed, take up a decent job if they do not like it.

Many color their hair blond and orange. On the streets of Tokyo walking beside the legions of salarymen in dark suits rushing to fill 14-hour work days are wild-haired, brightly dressed young people, some of them with platform shoes and artificial tans. On occasion, flustered, older Japanese have been known to refer to these younger people as *uchu jin*, or space aliens.

As a generation they do not yet have a name. But young people in Japan might as well be called generation slump: For the past 10 years they have lived in the shadow of the country's deepest postwar economic recession, a decade that has left many of them disillusioned and apathetic.

One economist popularized the term "parasite singles" to describe young people who are content to live off their parents well into their 20s and beyond. But perhaps most significantly, young people are rejecting their parents' job choices and heavily structured lifestyles.

They are not "hungry." Despite the country's economic troubles, members of generation slump have had some of the most pampered lives in Japan's history. They reaped the benefits of being the children of one of the world's richest countries. Because they came from small families, they were often doted on and given large allowances. A survey of teen trends found that older teens, aged 18 and 19, spend on average $100 a week on leisure-related things, some of the money coming from an allowance provided by their parents.

Yet, despite these apparently cushioned lives, one of the hallmarks of generation slump is malaise. A survey found that half of the 4,800 Japanese teenagers polled said they were unhappy and only 50% said they "liked themselves." Just 47% said they believed they would have happy families, and only 34% of Japanese students said they foresaw themselves playing an active role in society in the future.

It goes without saying that the economic success or failure of young people in Japan is crucial for both the nation and the world: Generation slump will soon carry the burden of supporting the world's fastest aging society.

Source: Adapted from Fuller, T. (2001) "Work hard? Young Japanese have other ideas", *International Herald Tribune*, Bangkok, 11 April, pp. 1, 7

The focal question of this chapter is: What cultural dimensions are particularly relevant for our served product market(s), how are they shaped in the geographic markets under consideration, and how do they influence the attractiveness of those markets?

Influence of culture on international marketing

Marketing managers are focusing on exchanges of more or less tangible products with business partners who are more or less personally involved in the exchange. The exchange may be a single transaction or take place as part of an ongoing relationship between the exchange partners. In any case, the initiator of the exchange has to know who its preferred exchange partners are. A precise idea of what needs to be offered to them and how to make the exchange happen in a manner satisfying both parties is critical for business success.

Understanding potential business partners and their open as well as latent expectations means understanding the reality in which they subjectively live. This personal view of the world determines the business partners' goals, decision making, and behavior. People's subjective perceptions of reality depend on their cognitions and cognitive structures, which they have acquired to a great extent through experience during enculturation and acculturation. **Enculturation** is the process by which individuals become a member of their culture. That is, they learn what a member of the group they belong to (or want to belong to) accepts as normal, necessary, reasonable and plausible facts, behavior and actions, values, and social relations. As a result, both organizational buyer and consumer behavior are strongly influenced by the cultural environment in which those persons have been raised.

Acculturation is the process of learning about a new culture. This might occur when people adopt some language, values, customs, and beliefs when coming in real or virtual contact with another culture. Such contacts occur, for example, when students go to study abroad, when business people extensively travel to foreign countries, but also when people participate in an interest group on the internet, or when they are subject to intensive market communication campaigns from business organizations of foreign cultures.

For an international marketer to be successful in a multicultural environment, managers need to carefully analyze the relevant cultural environment of potential markets. The first step in assessing the cultural environment of a country market is to determine which parts or characteristics of culture are relevant to the product market(s) of the company (Figure 5.1). Having determined those relevant

Business relations are largely governed by cultural context
© Dynamic Graphics Group/Creatas/Alamy

factors, the marketer may analyze their current state of development in the country markets under consideration. To fully assess the potential impact of the relevant factors on the success of the firm, their potential changes will need to be anticipated based on current trends.

An evaluation of the impact of the current state and future potential development of all relevant characteristics of the cultural environment in the country markets under consideration will allow the international marketer to decide how to "manage" those environments. That is, management will decide how to react to the expected development.

This chapter will first describe the various layers of consumer culture and business culture. Then, characteristics of cultures that may be relevant for the business of internationally operating business organizations will be discussed, and examples given of how they may influence decisions and actions of international marketers. A look at the need for adaptations to cultural differences as well as marketing's influence on culture concludes the chapter.

A definition of culture

Culture may be defined as the standards of beliefs, perception, evaluation, and behavior shared by the members of a social group. Some authors even define culture as "the collective programming of the minds" that distinguishes the members of one group of people from another.

FIGURE 5.1 *Assessing potential markets: Cultural environment*

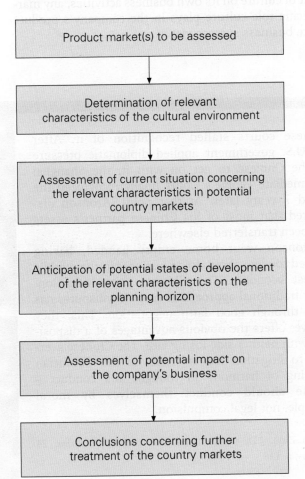

In assessing the cultural environment of potential markets the marketer first has to determine factors relevant to the product market(s) the company is serving. Then the current state of those factors of influence can be assessed in various country markets, and their potential states of development on the planning horizon anticipated. From the results of the analysis the potential impact on the company's business can be assessed. Finally, conclusions concerning the further treatment of the analyzed country markets may be drawn.

Markets, companies, and exchange relations exist inside such cultural contexts. Culture affects people's tastes, preferences for colors, and attitudes towards product classes. For example, Dutch children often eat chocolate shavings on buttered bread for breakfast. Children in the U.S. frequently have fried eggs. Indian children may have a paratha with chillis, and Malays have rice. All are culturally acceptable and appropriate within their culture, but seemingly strange in others. How exchange relations come to exist, how business partners communicate with each other, how they negotiate, perceive each other, or terminate business relations largely depends on the cultural environment. Culture box 5.1 gives an example that illustrates how strongly business behavior is influenced by cultural factors.

The example also shows that a (potential) business partner's interpretation of the international marketer's behavior depends on expectations of proper conduct, which, in turn, depend on the cultural background of the business partner. For example, *amae* is an important value of Japanese culture that stresses mutual goodwill, complaisance, and kindness in personal relationships. Because of *amae*, Japanese managers tend to perceive detailed contracts, such as those to which U.S. businesspeople are accustomed, as signs of distrust.

Even business behavior, down to details such as the proper way to present a business card, is determined by culture. North Americans and Europeans, for example, most often present a business card informally, between two fingers. They may turn the card over and take notes on the back. In Japan, a business card is an extension of the person – to be handled carefully and respectfully, with both hands. It is laid on the table and only put in one's pocket, or written on, after the meeting is over and the guest has gone.

In fact, all behavior occurs within the framework of a culture. Thus, in order to adequately assess the impact of culture on its own business activities, any marketer must determine the specific role culture plays in the company's product markets. Culture may influence business success via:

CULTURE BOX 5.1

Confucian confusion

Robert Aronson is a U.S. engineer and businessman, owner of Revpower, based in Fort Lauderdale, Florida. He signed a joint venture agreement with the Shanghai Far East Aero-Technology Import & Export Corp. to develop a battery factory. Revpower would provide the know-how and distribute the product. The Chinese partner would organize the plant. Two years later the Chinese imposed a price hike of 40% on Revpower, purportedly because of higher utility costs. In reaction Aronson terminated the contract and started arbitration proceedings in Stockholm.

Aronson won a $5 million award, which, with interest, came to $8 million. But Aronson's award could be enforced for only 6 months, and the Chinese courts stalled recognition of it. After the U.S. government applied diplomatic pressure on the Chinese to get on with it, the Shanghai Intermediate People's Court finally recognized the award 7 years later. At that point, Aronson discovered that most of his Chinese partner's assets had been transferred elsewhere.

Aronson went home empty handed, having learned too late about doing business in the world's hottest economy. The Chinese abhor litigation. Their traditional approach to resolving disputes has been through good faith negotiation. This, they believe, offers the obvious advantages of a disposition with neither side losing face. The Chinese aversion to litigation has its roots in the Confucian teaching of harmony in thought and conduct – people should conduct themselves by moral example, not legal compulsion.

Source: Zirin, J.D. (1997) "Confucian confusion", *Forbes*, 24 February, p. 136

- *consumer culture*, that is, the cultural factors determining consumer decision making and behavior
- *business culture*, that is, all cultural factors influencing business behavior.

In international marketing the situation is further complicated because cultural differences among customer and stakeholder groups may lead to different perceptions and behavior even in similar product markets. Indeed, in the search for similar product markets that exist across countries' boundaries, it is very important that the international marketer understands the cultural differences and similarities that exist.

Consumer culture

Consumers have specific cognitions and related emotions based on their learning experiences. These cognitive systems make consumers perceive their environment, evaluate alternative sequences of behavior, interpret actions of others, and behave in individual ways. But all humans are social individuals. That is, to survive they need social contacts with other humans (in particular in early childhood). As a consequence they gather in groups.

Social learning

Much learning takes place in groups of people such as the family, peers, occupational or ethnic groups, and religious communities. Such social learning results in shared cognitions of the individuals belonging to a specific group. Cultures develop. For example, most of the basic values and norms of behavior that individuals take for granted, that is, what they think is basically good or evil, what is desirable and what to avoid, are learned in the family during childhood. Some additional values and many of the norms and patterns of behavior people follow during their lives are learned in groups of peers, that is, groups of people of the same age, sex, occupation, interests, or religion. Aspiring to membership of groups that serve as references adds to this cultural learning (see Figure 5.2).

Subcultures

Groups of people with strongly shared values and cognitions, common consumption preferences or habits may constitute **subcultures** in a society. In the U.S., for example, there are numerous subcultures owing to the many different ethnic groups, religious denominations, and regional societies that exist in the country. Each in its own way influences the conduct of business as well as consumer and buyer behavior. For example, Campbell's sells different flavors of tomato soup depending on the region of the country. Tomato soup sold in Montana is not as spicy as that sold in Texas.

FIGURE 5.2 *Layers of consumer culture*

Consumer culture contains various layers: Personal culture is part of reference group cultures, which, in turn, are part of a national culture.

International subcultures

It is important for international marketers to understand their customers' personal values and accepted norms of behavior in order to market to them properly. At the same time, marketers must search for groups with shared cognitions that result in shared views of the marketer's offerings and in similar product-related behavior, to simplify their task. Such groups may even exist across country borders, either because the borders are not indicative of demarcations between ethnic groups or nations, or because international media, travel, and education have led to the development of similar consumer subcultures.

For example, in Europe some trends have crossed country borders. Green awareness, interest in health and fitness, home orientation, creative use of leisure time and female careerism can be detected in all markets of central and western Europe at different levels and in different manifestations. Future issues box 5.1 describes technological advances that contribute to the development of internationally similar consumer behavior.

As examples from sports-related, fashion, fast-food and entertainment sectors show, international marketers themselves may be able to induce the creation of new consumer subcultures, such as Diesel jeans wearers, roller bladers (Roller Blade is a brand of Head), Burton snowboarders, Red Bull drinkers, Apple users, multimedia addicts, or fans of pop stars like Kyle Minogue, Bruce Springsteen, or Elvis Presley (even 30 years after his death). Members of such international subcultures do not need to meet and to know each other to develop shared values and cognitions. The brand they feel they belong to, the personality they adore, the activity they are highly involved with or media reports about the common theme of interest are the center of communication from where consumption-related norms and patterns of behavior spread all over the world (often supported by communication on the internet). Following those consumption patterns helps

---

FUTURE ISSUES BOX 5.1

Globalization of consumption patterns

Just picture this: After a busy day at your business school, you decide to unwind at one of the city's numerous cafes. While sipping your macchiato, you switch on your notebook or personal digital assistant, and the range in front of you is almost limitless: Listening to your favorite music via an MP3 player, chatting, sending emails, browsing websites, transferring payments, downloading a movie, or, if you are one of those workaholics, drafting out a paper or a business proposal for the next day.

Connecting is smooth, easy and, above all, hassle free. The cafe you have selected is equipped with a WiFi, short for wireless fidelity, network. As of April 2003 more than 500 Starbucks outlets have been equipped with a WiFi network. And WiFi will be installed in another 4,000 outlets all over the world by the end of 2005. Since March 2003 McDonald's

has also started to equip their worldwide outlets with WiFi. During the test phase at 10 McDonald's outlets in New York, free one-hour connections were provided with the purchase of an extra value meal.

WiFi fever has also caught on in Australia. Brisbane International Airport is equipped with a wireless network. The initial success with passengers wanting to overcome the boredom prior to boarding has prompted Optus, the provider, to build installations in more than 500 locations. Among those locations are other airports, seaports, cafes, convention centers, hotels, apartment buildings, and campuses.

WiFi is only possible using wireless enabled equipment, such as a notebook computer with a wireless card. By the end of 2002 about 20% of notebooks manufactured had WiFi accessibility. The phenomenally high speed of WiFi has created a close attachment or "addiction" among consumers. All sorts of multimedia have been made possible and more realistic, including 3D games.

Source: Adapted from Gunarto, W. (2003) "WiFi: A prominent 'third' place", *Jakarta Post*, 6 October

individual consumers to perceive themselves as members of a highly desirable group.

Caution must be taken, however, not to overemphasize the apparent similarities that an international subculture implies. Even within international subcultures, marketing adaptations may be necessary because national culture specificities do not entirely lose their influence. For example, advertising campaigns for international rock stars are still localized according to the media habits of concertgoers. The international success of the film *Babe*, as another example, was partly due to the translation of the soundtrack into different local accents, which gave the film additional interest.

Local cultures

In a backlash against trade liberalization and economic integration, nationalism is once again gaining popularity around the world. While the political and economic implications of this development have been discussed in Chapter 1, nationalism also brings increased support for local cultures, not necessarily national ones. In Spain, for example, this localization movement has resulted in the region of Catalonia, and speakers of Catalan, gaining such strength that Catalan was one of the four official languages, along with English, French, and Spanish, at the 1992 Olympic Games in Barcelona. The 6 million people in Spain who use Catalan regularly, out of some 40 million Spanish citizens, must effectively be treated as a subculture of the national Spanish market.

National cultures

Because of the many combinations of potential learning experiences, individual consumers show wide variations in beliefs and behavior. Despite those differences among individuals and cultures of groups constituting a society, the members of a society have some common values, norms and patterns of behavior indicating that they belong to a bigger cultural group, traditionally called a *nation*.

As described, there is a rich and complex diversity within national cultures. But a perspective on what is important within such cultures is useful to international marketers in assessing the attractiveness of potential markets as well as in building marketing mixes that will appeal to customers belonging to a national culture.

When discussing national cultures, one must be careful to avoid the two common traps of stereotyping, and equating the country with national culture.

Stereotyping A **stereotype** is a conventional, usually oversimplified, and often negative view of other cultures; for example, "the Japanese workaholics who think that they are superior to everybody else, cannot do anything individually, and are fervently macho."

Equation of country with national culture So-called "nations" such as the U.S., Iran, China, or Russia contain a variety of national or ethnic cultures owing to the heterogeneity of their populations. The fact that they live together in one big country may lead to some shared values, norms, and patterns of behavior, but it is rather overstated to talk about one national culture.

Bearing in mind those potential traps, general descriptions of what is important within a national culture may be useful to international marketers if the culture of one ethnic group dominates a country. For example, a general description of Australians might include that they typically avoid open displays of achievement. This is known as the "tall poppy syndrome" (the tallest flower in the field is the first to get cut down). Australians have combined this reluctance to achieve, or at least to seem to *over*achieve, with a strong support system for society. Further, they very much enjoy leisure time activities, travel extensively during longer vacations than average U.S. citizens take, and are very active in outdoor sports such as tennis, sailing, or swimming. They have been described as "laid back" owing to this somewhat leisurely approach to life. The considerable Australian love of the outdoors, nature, and exercise results in adults drinking substantial amounts of milk. It is drunk for lunch, as a snack, and in times when, for example, a soft drink is more likely the product of choice in Europe. Marketers have reacted by offering milk in many flavors, including chocolate, strawberry, mango, and lime.

General descriptions of national cultures can be made more systematically in order to serve comparative purposes if they are based on an analytical framework. Perhaps the most well-known analytical framework for national cultures has been developed by the Dutch social scientist Geert Hofstede, based on research into the values and beliefs of 116,000 IBM employees from 66 countries. Table 5.1 describes the five dimensions of culture empirically identified by Hofstede: Individualism, power distance, uncertainty avoidance, competitiveness (which he calls masculinity), and time perspective (which he calls longterm orientation).

The problem with the identification of political boundaries as cultural separators is that this is arbitrary at best. Countries may contain various clearly different ethnic cultures. The population of Malaysia, for example, consists of 66% Malays, 26% Chinese, and 8% Indian. They have different religions, values and norms of behavior. Due to history and migration, there are often a number of cultural groupings within a country, resulting in countries like Australia, Canada, and China becoming multicultural marketplaces.

In addition, Asian cultures seem to have a certain tolerance for ambiguity. There are no two irreconcilable forces of either or. Many Asian cultures tend to see changing sides of the same phenomenon. For example, Confucianism deals with human relationships, Taoism with life in harmony with nature, Buddhism with people's immortal world, and Hinduism has many gods to choose from. In some countries people follow the philosophies of several cultures. Asian cultures show respect for hierarchy, age, and authority and modify reactions accordingly. In a negotiation situation, for example, Chinese may display both an "individual face" of one to one reasonableness and a "group face" of inflexibility. Asian cultures are also characterized by the "yin yang" principle. There simultaneously are elements of female and male. Country typologies based on Hofstede's criteria may be strongly misleading, therefore, and should be treated with sensitivity.

Business culture

Just as culture influences personal consumption patterns and buyer behavior, it also largely determines accepted business behavior. Not knowing the rules of the game puts any player at a disadvantage; not knowing the rules of the business game in a country market means that a foreign competitor is at a disadvantage compared to local business.

Layers of business culture

As in consumer culture, there are different layers of business culture (see Figure 5.3).

National cultures Internationally operating companies conduct their business and are managed inside national cultures, one of which traditionally dominates. In most cases this is the national culture of the headquarters' location. The national culture determines the values that influence corporate behavior. But business conduct is also influenced by industry standards of behavior, which are more specific than national cultures, and, in regional or global industries, may extend across national cultures.

1 Individualism

Individualism is the degree to which individuals are integrated into groups. Individualism is high when the ties among individuals belonging to a social group are loose. Individuals are ready to start new relationships that are not very deeply entrenched, however. Highly individualistic cultures find people responding to opportunities on a personal level. There is a strong belief that every individual is supposed to take care of herself, and an emphasis on individual achievement and initiative. In such cultures, goods and services helping to mark a consumer's difference compared to others should be well received.

When individualism is low, social relationships are characterized by strong ties. They take longer to be established, but are more enduring. Members of cohesive in-groups protect each other. There is a common belief that the unfortunate deserve sympathy. In such cultures an international marketer may want to understate market-dominating positions. In exchange for protection by the group, all group members are expected to be absolutely loyal. Company personnel focus on team and organizational achievements, but are less inclined to cooperate across organizational borders.

2 Power distance

Power distance relates to how members of a national culture view distribution of power; for example, how much less powerful members of a social group expect that power is distributed equally, how easy it is for people with different backgrounds to relate to each other, or how easy upward social mobility is. Power distance tends to be high for Latin, Asian, and African societies. In India, for example, there is considerable difference between people's status, and movement upward is rather difficult. In lower power distance societies upward mobility is much easier to achieve, and thus goods and services promising to support upward mobility are well received.

3 Uncertainty avoidance

Uncertainty avoidance is the extent to which members of a culture feel comfortable or uncomfortable in unstructured situations. Unstructured situations are novel, surprising, and different from usual, and therefore unclear or unpredictable to individuals. Cultures dominated by uncertainty avoidance tend to be highly regulated, having complex rules and regulations in terms of proper behavior (such as safety and security regulations), and try to avoid risk taking. Low uncertainty avoidance cultures operate in the opposite manner.

4 Competitiveness ("masculinity")

The competitiveness of a national culture is the extent to which individuals perceive social relations as a kind of competition (for all kinds of resources and rewards) as opposed to focusing on mutual benefits. Less competitive cultures, such as those existing in Scandinavia, tend to focus on solidarity. They are concerned with the social security of their members, attractive working conditions, and fairness. More competitive-oriented societies tend to emphasize personal achievement, challenging tasks, performance, and purposefulness.

5 Time perspective ("long-term orientation")

Time perspective is defined as the way members of a culture tend to approach decision making in consumer as well as business activities. They may have a dynamic, future-oriented mentality, including persistence, hard work, thrift, and shame. At the opposite extreme, a culture may be characterized by a static mentality focused on the past and present, emphasizing reciprocation, "face" and tradition. These values encourage keeping within well-known and well-accepted boundaries. In China, for example, saving "face" is very important. Saving face involves preserving a person's dignity and social status whatever the person does. As a result, western-quality fashion designs are very successful with affluent Chinese consumers eager to wear a symbol of their status, and Chinese managers tend to continue investing in product development even after serious questions about project viability arise.

Source: Adapted from Hofstede, G. (2001) *Culture's consequences: Comparing values, behaviours, institutions and organisations across nations*, London: Sage

Industrial cultures In national cultures, values prevail, whereas industrial cultures are mainly characterized by practices related to business conduct in the industry. For example, car manufacturers, independent of the location of their headquarters, follow certain (unwritten) rules of how to compete (or not to compete) against each other and when to announce and show new car models.

Corporate cultures Each company is a social organization or group. As such, companies develop cultures specific to their organizations that are called organizational or *corporate* cultures. Those organizational cultures are embedded in the national and industrial cultures. That is, they are based on the values dominating the national culture and, in most cases, incorporate the norms of industry behavior. In addition, an organizational culture contains rituals, heroes, and symbols that make the firm unique (Figure 5.4):

- *Rituals* are common activities such as business meetings, initiation workshops for new entrants, or jubilees that serve the purpose of spreading shared norms of behavior and conveying a feeling of belongingness.
- *Heroes* are profiles of ideal persons, alive or dead, in the history of the firm that serve the same purpose.

FIGURE 5.3 *Layers of business culture*

Business culture contains various layers: Embedded in the national culture are industrial cultures, organizational cultures, and functional/professional cultures.

FIGURE 5.4 *Manifestations of organizational culture*

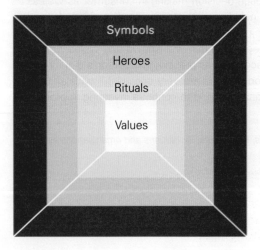

Based on values that characterize the national culture dominating the firm, a company's organizational culture contains rituals, heroes, and symbols.

- *Symbols* may be a specific company language, its logo or possessions. Those symbols have meaning only for the people working for the company or having some kind of relationship with the firm.

The management of values shared and of norms of behavior accepted by the members of the organization becomes increasingly important with the extent of the company's internationalization. When people with increasingly diverse cultural backgrounds are hired by expanding firms, organizational culture can provide a common framework of how to do business. Employees of Atlanta-based Delta Airlines (in Georgia), for example, know about the great importance of customer service to the company's success, whether they work in Tokyo, Berlin, or Cincinnati. Organizational norms of behavior even provide some assistance with highly controversial cross-national cultural problems such as ethics. The ethics code of Delta Airlines clearly indicates, for all employees of whatever nationality, what business conduct is undesirable.

Functional cultures Inside each business organization, people fulfill different functions. Because those functions require specific training, which results in shared experiences, a common specialized language and a shared way of reasoning, membership in a functional group leads to the development of a functional or professional culture. For example, product managers of Procter & Gamble from all over the world may have more norms of business behavior in common than a product manager and a finance manager in Copenhagen who also work for Procter & Gamble.

Values, norms, and patterns of behavior individually accepted by a person as guiding rules for his or her life are also important to international marketing managers when making decisions about who should perform which marketing task. For example, in western societies people with a high need to achieve usually make the most successful sales representatives. Internationally active personnel must also possess a sense of humor and adventure, sensibility to differences, a readiness to accept such differences as different and not necessarily as bad, and an ability to relate to others, all of which will contribute to success.

Cultural diversity

The cultural diversity of employees potentially offers a strategic advantage to business firms. International activities for U.S.-based Procter & Gamble, for example, have been run for a considerable time through its office in Geneva, Switzerland. The employees there come from around the world, not just from Switzerland, the U.S., or from Asia. Working in English, the only common language of all employees, in a French-speaking environment, each employee brings their own personal cultural background to corporate decisions. This width of view enriches decision making and may lead to better decisions than, for example, if the same decision had to be made by managers from one national culture. One major hurdle to overcome, however, is the potential conflicts in a culturally diverse team because of misunderstandings due to verbal and non-verbal communication blunders. Marketing decisions taken by such teams are more likely to capture the advantages of international standardization, while making necessary adjustments to local cultural issues, which, if ignored, would spell marketing disaster.

Business manners

Manners are social codes of conduct. Like personal manners, business manners and practices vary considerably from one culture to another. And like ignorance of personal manners, insufficient attention to business manners may impede the establishment of trusting business relations. For example, in China great embarrassment would result if one party to a business relationship failed to bring a gift for the other. Small gifts, not available or made in a nearby country, would seem critical for success. But large gifts will just prove embarrassing to the host, and will not produce the expected reaction of impressing them. Gift wrapping is also especially important. And proper formalities should be observed. Giving the gift in private, and not expecting it to be opened in the presence of the giver, will avoid embarrassing both the guest and the host. Chinese consider opening gifts in front of the giver, as is customary in France, for example, as rude.

In Japan, floral arrangements have become the business gift of choice, partly as a response to Japanese executives traveling so much that they found it difficult to continue their traditional gift-giving habits. But even the type of flower chosen may lead to difficulty, such as giving white chrysanthemums in Europe, which are generally considered a bad omen because they are associated with funerals.

But knowledge concerning business manners goes beyond knowing how to handle gift giving or shaking hands, of course. It would include general training on how to behave in business contacts with partners from other cultures. Table 5.2 contains a selection of "dos" and "don'ts" for some European countries, seen from a (partly outdated) U.S. perspective.

U.S. businesspeople, in particular, find themselves at a disadvantage in other business cultures, mainly because they have little (conscious) experience concerning other cultures or training for international appointments. In many ways this lack of cultural training is somewhat ironic, for in the U.S., great cultural diversity does exist. However, one dominant business culture glosses over such cultural diversity in the main.

Culture has an impact on formality and readiness to compromise in business negotiations   © Brand X Pictures/Alamy

Business negotiations

Business negotiation in Europe and North America is defined as the process in which two or more persons, as representatives of their organizations or organizational units, come together to discuss common, complementary, and conflicting interests in order to achieve an agreement that will benefit each party. In Japanese, the most common term for negotiation is *kosho*, which implies fighting, conflict, verbal debate, and strategy.

Negotiation is something managers do constantly, usually in a familiar cultural setting and thus most often without thinking about how they are behaving. But, as the difference in the implied meaning of the term shows, culture shapes negotiation in much the same way it shapes all behavior. For example, Russians traditionally negotiate by moving the discussion upwards through the organizational hierarchy. At each level the negotiator involved wants to gain a concession of some kind. Sellers who offer major concessions early in this process are likely to lose a lot of money, or may not make the sale at all. Table 5.3 gives some examples of cultural differences in conflict handling, straightness, readiness to compromise, priority of organizational versus personal objectives, emotionality, formality, and relationship building.

Within a culture there is a shared frame of reference as to what verbal and nonverbal cues during a negotiation process mean, and what they imply in doing business. In international negotiations the lack of such a common frame of reference may result in erroneous interpretations of meaning and mistaken reactions. For example, if a sales representative from San Francisco, California, notices that the people to whom she is trying to sell something in Dallas, Texas, do not smile at all during the sales presentation, the salesperson would probably interpret that behavior as "the potential customers are not happy; they won't buy." The same nonverbal behavior in another cultural environment, however, may have a very different meaning. Not smiling during a sales presentation can mean that those listening are paying serious attention to the salesperson's ideas. If the sales representative reacts there as she is likely to do in the U.S., for example, by telling a joke, the listeners may consider themselves insulted. International business negotiations, therefore, should be carefully prepared and planned. (Chapter 13 will elaborate this issue in some more detail.)

TABLE 5.2 *Protocol dos and don'ts*

When is the right time to act friendly? Or reserved? It is tough to know which stance to take without doing your homework first. In 1990, Dorothy Manning of *International Business Protocol* suggested adhering to the following dos and don'ts when in these respective countries. Find out if those rules of behavior are still valid more than 15 years later. What has changed?

Great Britain

DO hold your fork (tines pointed down) in the left hand and your knife in the right hand throughout the meal

DO say please and thank you – often

DO arrive promptly for dinner, 10 minutes late is acceptable, but 10 minutes early is not. And if invited to a British person's home for victuals, DO bring a gift for the lady of the house, but DON'T bring white lilies; they are a bad omen

DO make appointments well in advance. The British are religious about keeping their calendars

DO offer your "mates" (friends) a cigarette when pulling one out for yourself, but DON'T smoke until after the toast to Her Majesty's health

DON'T ask personal questions. The British protect their privacy

DON'T gossip about royalty

DON'T stare in public

DON'T wear striped ties lest they are copies of British regimentals

France

DO be punctual for appointments. DO shake hands (a short, quick pump) when greeting, being introduced and leaving. Only close friends kiss cheeks

DO address all women over 21 as *madame*, whether they are married or not

DO dress more formally than in the U.S. Elegance is *de rigueur*

DON'T expect to complete any work during the French two-hour lunch

DO ask your host to recommend something from the menu

DO keep your hands visible at all times

DO eat everything on your plate

DON'T smoke before eating or between courses

DON'T chew gum

DON'T try to do serious business during *les vacances* (the vacation season from mid-July until the end of August)

Italy

DO write business correspondence in Italian for priority attention

DO make appointments between 10am and 11am, or after 3pm

DO meet for a strictly social lunch or dinner and nightclubbing with Italian associates and spouses

DO stand when an older person enters the room

DO observe the *passeggiata* – dress in your finest and stroll on the piazza between 6pm and 8pm to see and to be seen

DON'T eat too much pasta, as it is not the main course

DON'T get drunk. Drinking wine is a ritual; expect constant refills

DON'T hand out business cards freely. Italians don't use them much

Spain

DO write business correspondence in English, unless your Spanish is impeccable

DO take business lunches at 2.30pm and dinner at 9pm or 10pm. Be prepared to dine until midnight, later if chatter flows

DON'T feel offended when interrupted in conversation. Your host is not rude, but interested

DON'T expect punctuality. Your appointments will arrive 20–30 minutes late

DON'T make the American sign for 'okay' with the thumb and forefinger. In Spain, this is vulgar

DON'T pay for a male colleague's lunch if you are a woman

DON'T discuss bullfights

DO talk about American lifestyle, sports, and politics

Greece

DO be prompt, but DON'T expect punctuality from your hosts

DO distribute business cards freely so people will know how to spell your name

DO eat appetizers with your fingers. DO eat a great deal

DON'T be surprised or offended if the Greeks ask personal questions; it is a sign of interest

DON'T expect to meet deadlines. A project takes as long as the Greeks feel is necessary

DON'T discuss Turkey or Cyprus

DON'T risk insult by waving with an open palm. To wave hello, raise the index finger while keeping the palm closed

DON'T address people by formal or professional titles. The Greeks want to be closer than that

Source: "Protocol Dos and Don'ts", *TWA Ambassador*, October 1990, p. 69

Business relationships

Depending on the cultural background, managers tend to feel to different degrees the necessity of building and maintaining close relationships with stakeholders from the firm's operating environment, such as suppliers, intermediaries, customers, administrators or media, as well as with its personnel.

Communication context The varying importance given to relationship building in different cultural environments is partly due to the importance of the communication context in those cultures. In some cultures messages are explicit; the spoken or written words carry most of the information. In other cultures, part of the information is contained in the verbal portion of a message, but the remainder is in the context, that is, the setting, atmosphere, the status and power of communicators, gestures, and other nonverbal communication. Thus, cultures can be ranked on a continuum from "high context" at one end to "low context" at the other. Figure 5.5 ranks various national cultures from the standpoint of reliance on the communication context.

Managers from high-context cultures prefer doing business with people who are known and have a high status. To get to know new potential business partners, they use pre-negotiation or pre-transaction rituals, such as business visits by varying delegations, sightseeing tours, or dinners including heavy drinking. Managers from high-context cultures have a lack of haste: Time spent in building business relationships is not seen as diminishing efficiency. Informal, personal agreements are much more important than contractual, formal agreements.

TABLE 5.3 *Cultural differences in business negotiation behavior*

Culture has an impact on conflict handling, readiness to compromise, goal orientation, predominance of organizational or individual objectives, emotionality, formality, and importance of personal relations in business negotiations.

Conflict handling

French, German, and U.S. negotiators prefer direct confrontation when conflicts of interest exist. In other cultures, such as the Japanese or Chinese cultures where it is important to let all negotiators keep "face", potentially explosive negotiations are handled with respect and modesty. In the Middle East conflicts of interest are not subject to negotiations between business delegations. Conflicts are handled by middlemen who are fully trusted by both sides.

Readiness to compromise

Readiness to compromise is perceived as a signal of democratic attitudes, of goodwill and "fair play" in the U.S. In many Latin American countries, making concessions to negotiation partners is positively valued as signaling honor, integrity, and grandeur. In Russia, however, a concession is perceived as a weakness: To give in to a demand means losing control over one's own will and giving in to the will of the other.

Goal directedness

Japanese prefer a negotiation style called *haragei*, in which all aspects of a problem are discussed again and again in order to gain a "holistic" view of the issue. North Americans, in contrast, prefer to "come to the point" immediately, because they want to negotiate in an "efficient" and "systematic" way. This strive for efficiency is interpreted as pushiness by negotiators from other cultures. It also leads to starting negotiations at levels close to what the negotiators plan to achieve, whereas in countries such as Brazil or China as well as in Arab countries negotiators love to haggle and, therefore, start negotiations with exaggerated positions.

Organizational versus individual objectives

Western European, Japanese, and U.S. negotiators feel primarily obligated to reach their companies' objectives. In contrast, Indian negotiators tend to focus on the realization of their individual goals such as power, prestige, or personal satisfaction.

Emotionality

Latin Americans and negotiators from countries around the Mediterranean tend to show their emotions during negotiations. Brazilians talk at the same time and touch their negotiation partners. Arabs raise their voices. More harmony-oriented cultures, such as many Southeast Asians, prefer to keep respect and coolness. Chinese negotiators even allow for longer periods of absolute silence and wordless reasoning during negotiations. This is very difficult to accept for negotiators from western industrialized countries who are used to a constant flow of discussion.

Formality

U.S. negotiators are most characterized by informality and equality in human relations. Titles have no place in mutual addresses, and the negotiation partner is preferably called by his or her first name. This leads to misunderstandings on the part of central European or Asian negotiators who are used to highly formal addresses with titles. They consider negotiation partners using their first names as wanting to express their personal closeness and not to be overly tough. In Japan the status of the interacting persons dictates the flow of negotiations. And in Arab cultures social interactions follow strict rules, which have to be known to foreign negotiators who want to be successful.

Personal trust

In countries where individualism dominates, such as in the U.K., the Netherlands or the U.S., personal trust does not play an important role for starting serious business negotiations. It is expected to develop during negotiations. Sometimes close personal relationships are even considered as a barrier to achieving business goals. In contrast, personal relationships play a major role in highly collectivist countries, such as Brazil, Japan, Malaysia, or Thailand. Personal trust is a precondition to serious business negotiations in countries such as China or Mexico where the legal system is not considered as an efficient or socially acceptable shelter against cheating.

Sources: Graham, J.L. and R.A. Herberger (1983) "Negotiators abroad – don't shoot from the hip", *Harvard Business Review*, 61, July–August, pp. 160–68; Herbig, P. and H.E. Kramer (1992), "Do's and don'ts of cross-cultural negotiations", *Industrial Marketing Management*, 21, pp. 23–31; Leung, K. and Wu, P.G. (1990) "Dispute processing: A cross-cultural analysis", in R.W. Brislin (ed.) *Applied Cross-Cultural Psychology*, London: Sage

Managers feel most comfortable in their own cultural environments. A particular approach that works very effectively at home, however, could turn into major problems abroad. For example, in Germany, Scandinavia, and the U.S., business negotiations may be started without having established a personal relationship beforehand. Negotiators rely on their competence and experience. The results of the negotiation process are laid down in detailed contracts. A personal relationship between business partners may develop over time when a one-time transactional exchange turns into repeated relational exchanges. Businesspeople acquainted with such a culture may encounter major problems when they come to China, South Korea, Japan, or Arabic countries for the first time. There, a certain level of personal trust needs to be established before meaningful business negotiations can be started. That is, personal relationship building comes before business negotiations. For that reason, negotiations between potential business partners who have not had previous contact are slow and ritualistic. By way of contrast, specifying the results of the negotiation in an extensive contract does not seem very important.

Family ties and friendship Besides the importance of the communication context, the importance a culture attributes to family ties and friendship strongly influences building and maintaining business relationships. The Chinese, for example, are well known for their strong family ties in business. For instance, when a European marketer of spices wants to buy raw materials in Malaysia, it may first get in contact with a Chinese wholesaler in Singapore. Not content with the prices asked by the wholesaler, the procurement manager may travel to the plantations where the spices are harvested. A Chinese owns or at least runs them. When the manager has negotiated a contract at an acceptable price, shipment has to be arranged. And again, the manager encounters a Chinese entrepreneur. By the time the spices have arrived in Europe, they cost more than the wholesaler in Singapore would have charged. One thing has become evident: The entire chain of production and logistics, including intermediaries, is dominated by the Chinese. But more important, they are either members of a single large family or very loyal friends. For the customer, it is often less expensive and time consuming to rely on their entire business network than to try, in vain, to establish their own supply chain.

Similar situations have been encountered by western marketers when entering the Japanese market. There, the distribution system traditionally not only contains many more layers than in western industrialized countries, but it is also rather difficult to get access to distribution partners because of their long-term and very close business relationships with local suppliers.

Internal relationships

The success of international marketing largely depends on the quality of relationships with the firm's external stakeholders. But marketing managers also need to make sure that internal relationships allow the implementation of

FIGURE 5.5 *"High-context" vs "low-context" national cultures*

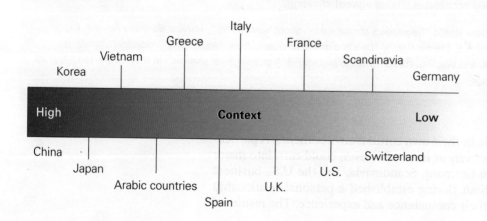

Depending on their reliance on cues from the situational setting, the characteristics of the people interacting, and all kinds of nonverbal cues for the interpretation of a verbal message, national cultures may be ranked on a continuum from "low-context" to "high-context" cultures.

strategies and actions. Companies in Europe trying to profit from the EU freedoms by expanding their business to neighboring countries must be particularly concerned about cultural differences concerning the conduct of business, because differences in management abound:

- *German managers* emphasize creativity, professional competence and coordination skills as key ingredients of organizational success. They tend to view the firm as a network of individuals who make appropriate decisions based on their professional competence and knowledge.

- *U.K. managers* favor interpersonal skills and the ability to influence others and negotiate effectively. They tend to view the firm as a network of relationships among individuals who get things done by influencing each other through communication and negotiating.

- *French managers* view the ability to organize and control as particularly critical. For them, the firm is a pyramid of differential levels of power to be acquired or dealt with. Success depends on the ability to manage power relationships effectively and to "work the system."

- *Italian managers* rely very much on hierarchical power, subordinates waiting to get orders from their leaders. But to keep the shop running, Italian managers, more than the rest, know how to informally maintain flexibility in bureaucratic structures.

When managers with such different views have to cooperate in one firm, considerable emphasis on personal relationship building may be needed to avoid major conflicts.

Business ethics

Every culture, ethnic, industry, organizational or functional, establishes a set of moral standards for business behavior, that is, a code of **business ethics**. This set of standards influences all decisions and actions in a company, including, for example:

- what and how to manufacture (or not)
- what wages are appropriate to pay
- how many hours personnel should work under what conditions
- how to compete
- what communication guidelines to follow.

The poster shown in Figure 5.6, for example, seemed totally appropriate to Luciano Benetton, the owner and manager of the Italian knitwear maker. But it stirred up a lot of conflict even with Benetton's franchise partners in countries such as Germany. For that reason, in 2003 Benetton launched a new campaign called "Food for Life," jointly realized with the World Food Program, a UNO agency.

Which actions are considered right or wrong, fair or unfair, in the conduct of business and which are particularly susceptible to ethical norms is heavily influenced by the culture in which they take place. For example, North American firms tend to emphasize ethical standards concerning internal issues, in particular fair treatment of personnel, whereas European companies tend to focus on ethical standards concerning the firm's relationships with its external stakeholders and the natural environment.

Perhaps the most common ethical issue faced by international marketers is how to handle corruption. Paying large or even small sums of money to administrators is considered unethical in many countries. Such behavior is almost always illegal, unless it is considered as what U.S. legislators term "grease" or money that "lubricates" decision making. The fine and, in many cases, not clear distinction between bribery and grease shows how difficult it can be for an internationally operating manager to meet differing ethical standards in a multi-cultural environment. Different cultures use different terms, such as *baksheesh* in Arabic, *mordida* in Mexico, *chai* in East Africa, *dash* in Nigeria, *omaggi* in Italy, *on* in Japan, and give them different, culture-dependent meanings. For example, *mordida* in Spanish literally means "the bite" which is more of a "gift" or a "consideration." The English word "bribe" would translate as *sobornar*.

In general, U.S. criticism concerning bribery is met with the response that U.S. managers have a very simplistic view of the world, based exclusively on their culture. Other cultures view such activities as gifts, considerations among friends who need each other's support and help. Ethics box 5.1 goes into more detail concerning culture-specific views of corruption.

Some countries, such as India, are well known for "requiring" small payments if customs officials are to allow goods to enter the country. While this may indeed be a bribe and illegal, the ethics of that country seem to allow it (at least to a certain extent). The company is then left with a problem:

- Do they bribe the official?
- Do they cooperate with a local partner who pays the proper amounts to the right people in time?
- Do they wait for normal clearance and let their products sit in the customs warehouse for a considerably longer time?

Fees and commissions paid to a firm's foreign representatives or to consultant firms for their services are a particular problem – *when does the legal fee become a bribe?* One reason for employing a foreign representative or consultant is to benefit from his or her contacts with decision makers, especially in a foreign administration. If the representative uses part of the fee to bribe administrators, there is little that the firm can do. For example, Munich-based Siemens, the Japanese firms Marubeni and Tomen, the U.K.'s BICC, and Italy's Pirelli were barred from all public orders in Singapore until 2001 because of corruption accusations. The consultant Lee Peng Siong had paid bribes to Choy Hon Tim, vice-president of the state-owned utilities concern PUB, to obtain secret information concerning

FIGURE 5.6   *United Colors of Benetton*

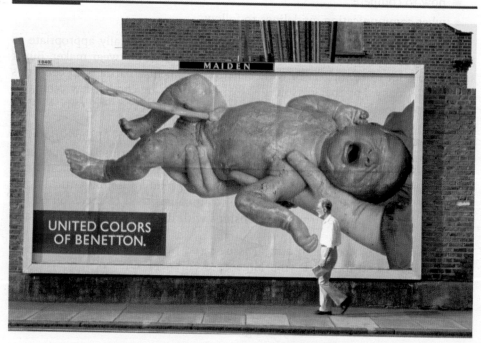

public projects. Siemens had used this consultant in a public power plant project, but they denied having paid any bribes.

Recent studies by the World Bank have found that corruption in many parts of the industrially developing world is "endemic," "systemic," and "pervasive," the norm rather than the exception. It is considered to be a leading cause for the failure of development programs in sub-Saharan Africa and other parts of the world, despite the investment of more than $1 trillion over the last 30 years. Since most aid is given as loans, the wasted funds burden the countries with unproductive debt.

Corruption is, of course, not the only ethical issue involved when a company is engaged in international marketing activities. Other ethical issues, such as child labor, working conditions on a par with slavery, intellectual property theft, environmental protection, and faked sales will be discussed throughout the book. Each chapter contains special ethics boxes discussing an issue related to the content of the particular chapter.

ETHICS BOX 5.1

What is corruption?

The word corruption comes from the Latin verb *rumpere*, meaning "to break." What is broken in the case of corruption is a moral or social norm of behavior, or, more often, administrative rules. To be broken, those administrative rules must be precisely formulated and transparent. A second element of the term corruption is that the administrator breaking the rules receives a favor in return for him/herself, the family, friends, his/her clan or party, or another social group. In addition, this favor in return must be seen as a direct "quid pro quo" for a special act of breaking a rule. This simple description of corruption shows that there are many sources of problems with "corrupt practices" in different cultural environments.

For example, in many countries legislation leaves tax allowances or granting import licenses to the decision of administrators. They are free to decide if an investment is "essential" or the import of a good is "necessary" for their country. The administrators are often the only authority to interpret the given cases. The greater the room for discretion, the greater is the opportunity to use it for personal purposes. Seen from that point of view, the easiest way to avoid corruption is to establish precise and restrictive regulations for administrative decisions. But experience has shown that often it is precisely too many regulations that are the breeding ground for corruption because of the resulting lack of transparency.

When social relationships in a society tend to be close, it may be rather difficult to establish proof of a direct "quid pro quo." There are too many exchanges going on among the people belonging to the closely knit social network. Delayed compensations, such as a substantial gift when the daughter gets married, and indirect reciprocity – that is, the establishment of balance in an "exchange" across a multi-person network – may inhibit the establishment of a provable corruption case. There does not even need to be direct contact between the people involved. Social norms ensure that the administrative decision maker gets adequate recompense in time.

And finally, social norms concerning reciprocation may be different from one culture to another. In an Indian village, for example, an attempt to establish an administration that works according to the (western) dissociation principle that personal relationships are not allowed to make any difference in administrative decision making would collide with the highly accepted social norm that family and friends come first. People expect administrators to treat their family and friends in a preferential way even if such behavior demands the breaking of administrative rules. A person refusing to act according to this dominant social norm would break that norm and be ousted. This may be one of the reasons why anticorruption reforms in some industrially developing countries demanding personal distance were broken before they had really started.

Source: Tanzi, V. (1995) "Korruption, Regierungsaktivitäten und Märkte", *Finanzierung & Entwicklung*, December, pp. 24f

Analyzing the cultural environment

Most managers, no matter where they are from, are culturally conditioned as to proper personal and business behavior. But once cultural borders are crossed, the rules change to a set of unknown ones, which are often difficult to understand. Confronted with other cultures, the secure knowledge of how to behave, how others behave, and how to market to them disappears. Therefore, an international marketer assessing the attractiveness and viability of country markets needs to establish a list of cultural factors that may influence the behavior of potential customers and important stakeholders in the firm's product market(s). Based on that list, information can be gathered and used for a decision on:

- which markets to consider further
- how to adapt to the local culture
- how to influence it.

Determining relevant factors of influence

To determine which parts of the considered country markets' cultural environments have the most influence on the company's business, international marketing managers need to analyze their product market(s). Starting from the dimensions of what to offer, to whom and how, the marketer may determine cultural factors of influence on each of the dimensions. Depending on cultural characteristics, the benefits may be more or less relevant in different countries, the applied technologies may have different meanings, and the target customer groups may be more or less substantive.

Self-reference criterion

When searching for important factors of influence from the cultural environment, the international marketer must be careful not to fall into the trap of the **self-reference criterion**, that is, the unconscious application of one's own cultural experience and values to a market in another culture.

Consider the following example. A U.S. marketing manager analyzing the Egyptian market would find that elaborate sales contracts play a very minor role in that country. Applying the experience from the home market, the manager would evaluate doing business in that market as rather risky, because there is no "reliable" system of legal contracts and courts for cases of litigation. In Egypt, however, giving one's word commits one to an agreement. This behavior stems from the religious values of Islam, in which God holds people responsible for keeping their word. An Egyptian who has never done business with U.S. salespeople before and has never heard or read about their business habits would be shocked by a request for a written contract. Such a request would be considered an insult to a Muslim's honor. Both the U.S. and the Egyptian manager, unconsciously applying their own cultural experiences, would arrive at erroneous interpretations of the situation.

Application of the self-reference criterion to the analysis of cultural factors of influence can never be entirely excluded. Every individual interprets their environment based on former experiences. But, considering this as a given and the dangers of taking erroneous decisions, the international marketer may take some precautions:

- One is to let a foreign TV team produce a video about the firm's product market in its home country and show it to the managers analyzing other country markets. By recognizing what people from other cultures view as important characteristics of their product market and how they interpret them, managers can learn what to look for when assessing foreign cultural environments.

- Establishing multicultural teams for the process of country market assessment diminishes the danger of making conclusions based on one cultural view. In addition, the use of more than one language in such a team may lead team members to new insights, because the use of different terms may evoke different meanings.

- If such a multicultural team gets the opportunity to scrutinize their judgments by doing some of their work in the countries under consideration, awareness of potentially incorrect interpretations of cultural influences will become even stronger.

List of evaluation criteria

The final list of evaluation criteria for the cultural environments to be considered will be specific to the company and its product market(s). There are some general factors, however, that in most cases will be relevant for international market success:

- values and norms of behavior
- education
- language
- aesthetics
- social organization.

They will need to be considered by internationally operating companies. Education has already been discussed in Chapter 3. The potential impact of the other factors on international marketing is discussed in the following subsections.

Values and norms

An important indicator of culture is the values shared by individuals within a given social group or society. A **value** is an enduring belief that a specific mode of conduct or end state of existence is personally or socially preferable to alternative modes of conduct or end states of existence. Values influence customers' perceptions. They underlie social **norms**, that is, accepted rules, standards and models of behavior, that direct the search for information and alternatives in a buying decision process, and influence consumption as well as usage behavior. Therefore, an international marketer wanting to initiate and maintain exchange relations with specific customer groups needs to know the dominant values of its potential customers (relevant to the served product market) in each of the country markets under consideration.

Values potentially having an important impact on customer behavior are:

- based on religious beliefs
- concern work, achievement, and wealth
- related to risk taking and change
- related to consumption in general.

These values will be discussed in the following.

Religion

The dominant religious values in a society determine many other values and norms of behavior. Morality, etiquette, gender roles, and attitudes towards individual achievement and social change are all derived from religious values. Thus Confucianism in China, Shintoism in Japan, Islam in the Middle East, Africa and parts of Asia (see Map 5.1), Buddhism and Hinduism on the Indian subcontinent, and Judeo-Christianity in western Europe, North and Latin America as well as parts of east Asia have a strong influence on norms of behavior in those societies.

Toolbox 5.1 contains an example of how norms of acceptable behavior have to be accounted for in international marketing research.

Religion may help to boost international trade. For example, a good deal of the growth in international business of Utah, the U.S. state located in the Rocky Mountains, can be traced to the pervasive influence of the Mormon faith, formally known as the Church of Jesus Christ of Latter-day Saints. For more than a century, the Mormons have been sending their young overseas, mostly 19-year-old men dispatched for two-year stints in missions. Many of those young men go into business on their return, capitalizing on language skills and contacts developed over the years. For example, Evans & Sutherland Computer Corp. designs display systems for flight simulators. A cadre of former Mormon missionaries can speak Mandarin Chinese with the Taiwanese airforce, give presentations in German to visitors from Germany, and speak Hebrew with Israeli customers. But the Mormon faith also has its drawbacks in international business. In many Asian societies, for example, drinking at night over dinner is critical to smooth business relationships. Mormons do not drink liquor. Neither do strict Mormons drink tea or coffee, because they are stimulants.

Some conservative religious subcultures resist the quick introduction of new products. The Amish in the U.S., for example, do not use electricity or motor vehicles in their everyday life, which is dominated by agriculture. Muslims and Jews shun pork; Hindus refuse to eat beef.

But even in societies where active participation in organized religion is not high, the influence of religious values should not be underestimated in assessing the importance of this cultural element. The importance of success and achieve-

MAP 5.1 *Religions of the world*

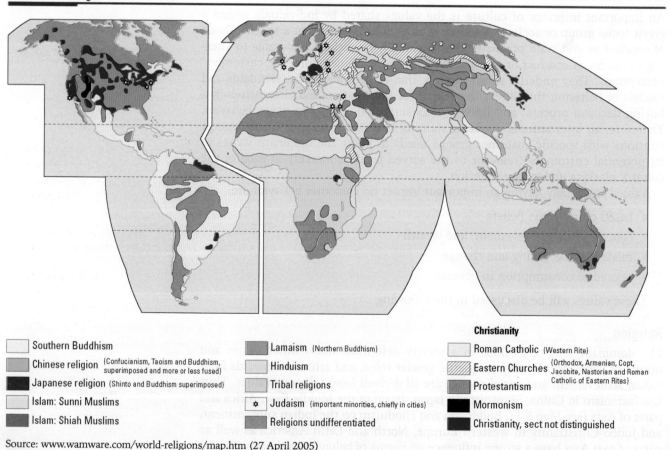

		Christianity
Southern Buddhism	Lamaism (Northern Buddhism)	Roman Catholic (Western Rite)
Chinese religion (Confucianism, Taoism and Buddhism, superimposed and more or less fused)	Hinduism	Eastern Churches (Orthodox, Armenian, Copt, Jacobite, Nastorian and Roman Catholic of Eastern Rites)
Japanese religion (Shinto and Buddhism superimposed)	Tribal religions	Protestantism
Islam: Sunni Muslims	Judaism (important minorities, chiefly in cities)	Mormonism
Islam: Shiah Muslims	Religions undifferentiated	Christianity, sect not distinguished

Source: www.wamware.com/world-religions/map.htm (27 April 2005)

ment goals differs among countries depending on the extent to which their dominant religions value individual economic achievement. For instance:

- societies with a dominant Protestant faith have traditionally been richer than others, partly due to the high value attributed to individual economic achievement which is considered a sign of having God's blessing
- Islamic societies (with the exception of oil-rich countries), contrariwise, have traditionally been rather poor. This is partly due to the religious belief that wealth is to be used to satisfy basic needs in moderation. Thus, material richness does not entail higher status or merit.

Many other patterns of behavior, such as gift giving at certain times of the year, are based on religious beliefs. They must be understood by international marketers in the process of evaluating the attractiveness of country markets.

Work, achievement, and wealth

Different cultures have different perspectives on work, achievement, and wealth. For example, Asian followers of Confucianism do not make a clear-cut distinction between work and play like that contained in the western ideas of "weekend" and "Sabbath." Such differences are not only reflected in the values and norms of consumers, they also have an impact on how business is conducted.

Importance of agriculture One significant factor in a society's perspective on work is the historical importance of agriculture in that society. Countries that are known to have a strong work ethic and motivation to succeed may owe these values to an economy historically based on agriculture. In such societies, hard work is less a moral issue than a prerequisite for survival. Even when its economy

---

TOOLBOX 5.1   **Doing focus group research with women in the Arab Gulf**

In the Arab Gulf one has to be particularly careful to take into consideration the prevailing socio-cultural conditions when formulating the research objectives. Too often the attempts made by researchers to better understand what makes consumers "tick" are hindered by the embedded "kindness" of the Gulf culture. People in this region of the world are generally inclined to overstate their positive opinions and neutralize any negative opinions for fear of offending the person they are conversing with.

Conducting qualitative research with women in the Arab Gulf, however, is particularly challenging. Given the prevailing norms, it is often impossible to approach them for an interview. To organize successful focus group interviews, the focus group moderator, for example, must be female and have a personality to which the participants can relate. Most preferably the moderator is of a similar age and the same nationality as the respondents.

The recruiting practices followed in inviting female respondents to participate in focus group discussions are crucial. Unless the researcher carefully and discreetly screens the respondents before starting the research, discussions may be conducted among respondents of very similar demographic and social background. Too often, invited women express the desire to bring along another "eligible" woman (either a close friend or a relative).

Female focus groups should always be held in the casual and non-threatening settings of a private home. One-way viewing facilities or the videotaping of the discussion is highly inappropriate, particularly among local Arab women.

The discussion of sensitive personal or societal issues is very difficult in female focus groups. But this is also true for men.

Because of the large extent to which societal norms and expectations shape the provided responses, the person in charge of analyzing the transcripts should be preferably female with a good understanding of the social background and culture of the respondents.

Source: Adapted from Eid, N.C. (1999) "Market research with women in the Arab Gulf countries", *Marketing and Research Today*, pp. 52–7

becomes less dependent on the production of crops, the society may continue to value hard work. This may be true of an entire society or a prominent minority group, such as the Indians in Uganda, who are noted for their achievements in distribution and commerce.

Value of work How long people work is only one measure of the value of work in a society, but it does provide a basis of comparison. For example, compared to Japan and the U.S., but in particular compared to the newly industrialized and rapidly industrially developing countries of Southeast Asia, western European countries have lower weekly and yearly working hours. Western Europeans work about 25% less than U.S. citizens. They have a 35- to 38-hour week and enjoy 4–6 weeks' paid vacation compared to typically 2 weeks in North America. Over the years, U.S. businesspeople have learned not to schedule major business trips to Europe during July, August, or the end of the year, because their European partners or customers are likely to be on vacation during those months.

Change of values Like other cultural elements, values concerning achievement and work change over time (see Culture box 5.2). With increasing wealth, readiness to work hard and for long hours has declined in Japan. The same seems to be the case in South Korea, where an attempt by government and business firms

CULTURE BOX 5.2

Changing values in Asia?

Internationally operating firms, media, political liberalization, and increasing wealth together may be able to give rise to substantial changes of values in Asian societies. For example, Asian teens seem to have increasingly more individualistic rather than collectivistic values. They are more focused on personal growth rather than community growth, more focused on personal advancement rather than community advancement, both psychological and financial.

A study conducted in the end of 2001, interviewing 200 teens and 400 adults in each of 11 Asian markets, aimed at discovering how Asian teens and their parent generation rank personal values found that youth between the ages of 13 and 19 ranked values such as individualism, ambition, and freedom significantly higher than did adults between 40 and 65. For example, out of the total 57 values to be ranked in order of importance by the two groups, teens placed freedom at 12, while adults placed it at 23. Again, ambition found more favor with the young, ranking it at 16, while the older group placed it at 40.

The development of a hard work-intensive consumption subculture in a traditionally contempla-

tive cultural environment seems to be in sight. In India, for example, an increasing number of young people are rushing to make their way up. Today, India's middle class is about 200 million, a little more than 20% of the entire population. Fifty years ago, when India became a sovereign state, only 10 million, or 3% of the population could be regarded as middle class. The fast change in business and consumer behavior only started in the early 1990s when India somewhat liberalized its international business relations.

Asked about their models in life, the kids of the Indian success generation often mention the biggest U.S. firms in their sector of industry. They are ready to work very hard to achieve their goals: 12 to 15 hours a day. Hard work, stress, and job pressure are regarded as positive. To make money and to spend it are the most important activities of the early 2000s. One of the dominant rules is: Each one for him- or herself and against all others. Nothing is given, but everything may be achieved.

Sociologists call them the "ego generation," suffering from the give-me-more syndrome: More success, more money, more pleasure, more sensuality.

Source: Adapted from Parmar, A. (2002) "Global youth united", *Marketing News*, 28 October, 36, 1–2; Kungsawanich, U. (2001) "Sex, lies, and Generation Y", *Bangkok Post Outlook*, 11 April, pp. 1, 3; Voykowitsch, B. (1996) "Leben auf der Überholspur", *Der Standard*, Reportage, p. 3

to diminish production costs by increasing working hours has led to violent mass strikes.

Risk taking and change

A society's or a subculture's potential for change is strongly related to their members' flexibility. Flexibility, that is, the readiness to accept new, altered or different values and norms of behavior, is heavily influenced by education that takes place largely through the family and in school.

Tradition-oriented societies In tradition-oriented societies, family ties are very important. They tend to teach their children to do as their ancestors did, to be respectful of their parents' view of the world, and to accept the existing order. In such cultures, changes in values and patterns of behavior take much time. An international marketer will be better off adapting its goods and services and how they are offered to the way traditionally accepted by customers in those cultures.

Education in school School education may also have a strong impact on flexibility. Where the understanding of different reasoning patterns and value systems is emphasized, the chances that people are open to change are much better than in school systems where one view of the world – obviously the "right" one – and the mastery of subjects through knowledge of concepts prevail.

Acceptance of change The extent to which change is accepted in a culture affects the speed of product acceptance. Norms related to acceptance of change are often rooted in religious traditions, but they are influenced by the living conditions and material culture of a society. More economically advanced countries are usually characterized by greater acceptance of change than economically less developed countries. However, there are differences in the speed of adoption of new lifestyles and products within the group of most wealthy countries and their societies.

For example, baby boomers (that is, the generation now in their 50s) in Japan are a far less interesting target group than their peers in the U.S. Unlike their American counterparts, there were few rebels. Largely content to absorb their parents' values, Japan's baby boomers immersed themselves in their jobs. Growing up in a devastated postwar Japan, boomers did not always have a car. Therefore, they grew up aspiring to purchase a fancy sedan – and still do so. In contrast, the next generation grew up having a car and treating it as an appliance. They led the development of demand into minivans and sport-utility vehicles. They are the first demographic slice where more than 50% of women have a driver's license.

Change of habits A useful approach to the analysis of consumers' and organizational buyers' readiness to change their consumption, buying or user habits may be to examine the elements that influence the acceptance of an innovative product within a culture. Table 5.4 lists product characteristics that influence the diffusion of innovations and indicates whether they encourage or inhibit them. Such information can help international marketers understand the likelihood of acceptance of or resistance to their products in a country market under consideration.

The value of this approach can be seen in the example of marketing microwave ovens internationally. Microwaves sell well in all countries where the rate of women taking an active part in the official workforce is high. To many consumers in the U.S. and in western parts of Europe, the advantage of the product is easy to communicate: It saves time and does not demand that all family members eat at the same time. In countries where the buying decision makers do not usually do the cooking themselves, because they are mostly males or because they are affluent enough to afford a cook, such as in many Latin American countries, communicating the product's relative advantage compared to conventional cooking may be rather difficult. Sales of microwave ovens are likely to be lower, even among consumers in similar income groups. The international marketer will need to find other advantages of its product that are relevant to the local culture, perhaps prestige or energy savings.

Risk taking For more affluent consumers, the financial risk of poor product performance is relatively lower than is true for low-income consumers. They may be more inclined to experiment with new offers from international marketers. But financial risk is not the only factor influencing customers' readiness to change. For example, Germany, Europe's largest country and one of the most affluent countries in the world, had only 11.6 million (up from 3 million in 1996) Visa cardholders (Visa was the market share leader together with Eurocard) in 2004, compared with 13.6 million (up from 11 million in 1996) in the less affluent U.K. and 36.8 million in Spain. Germans prefer to pay their bills with debit cards, bank transfers, and, most of all, cash. German customers tend to pay their credit card bills immediately rather than using the borrowing privileges. That means banks have to make their money almost exclusively on fees charged to merchants, instead of on interest paid by consumers. Such behavior may be associated with a deep-seated value that debts are an evil accompanied by all kinds of risks.

Perceived risk In analyzing those risks potentially inhibiting international marketing success, the concept of perceived risk, which is cross-culturally valid, appears to be useful: When faced with a choice situation, both consumers and organizational buyers perceive varying levels of risk due to two factors.

1 they may be uncertain whether the chosen object will meet their objectives
2 they may be concerned about the consequences of the object's failure to meet those goals.

Depending on their goals and the potential consequences of failure, customers may perceive the following kinds of risk:

TABLE 5.4 *Product characteristics affecting product diffusion*

Product characteristics can either encourage or inhibit the rate at which a product is adopted by a social group.

Relative advantage (encourages)	Degree of product superiority
Ease of testing (encourages)	Degree to which the product can be tried at low financial, personal, and social risk
Ease of communications (encourages)	Degree to which relative advantage can be quickly and easily understood
Compatibility (encourages)	Degree to which product use is consistent with current consumption patterns
Complexity (inhibits)	Degree to which the customer finds the product difficult to understand

Source: Based on Rogers, E.M. and F.F. Shoemaker (1971) *Communications of Innovations*, 2nd edn, New York: Free Press, pp. 22–3

- physical (harmful to health)
- functional (non-performance)
- psychological (negative effect on self-image)
- social (embarrassment in front of others)
- financial (loss of money)
- time (time wasted in product search)
- environmental risk (consumption/use of the product causes harm to the environment).

International marketers can employ the concept of perceived risk in understanding buyer and consumer behavior in different cultural environments. However, they must be aware that customers can reduce perceived risk in different ways across national cultures and subcultures. Strategy box 5.1 illustrates how international marketers may be confronted with perceived physical and environmental risk and what they can do about it.

STRATEGY BOX 5.1

Of greens and American beans

Monsanto, a U.S. chemical and biotechnology company, had difficulties persuading Europeans to buy its new, genetically engineered soybeans. The company's beans are engineered to be resistant to Roundup, a herbicide that accounts for around half of Monsanto's operating profits, and that kills normal soybeans.

U.S. consumers have barely batted an eyelid at the product's introduction. In Europe, environmentally and health conscious consumers have argued that the new soybeans have not yet been properly tested and that the plant's genes could cause unforeseen problems in future. In May 2000, as a spokesperson for European consumers, the Prince of Wales said on the BBC: "Above all, we should show greater respect for the genius of nature's designs, rigorously tested and defined over millions of years. This means being careful to use science to understand how nature works, not to change what nature is, as we do when genetic manipulation seeks to transform a process of biological evolution into something altogether different." As a result, the German subsidiaries of both Nestlé and Unilever, the two European food giants, decided not to use genetically modified soybeans in their main products. And a host of European food retailers asked for the new beans to be kept apart from ordinary ones, so that consumers can choose whether or not to eat them.

The EU banned genetically manipulated food from its markets in 1997. Imports were forbidden in 1998. In July 2003, EU agriculture ministers followed a decision of the European Parliament opening the market for genetically altered products under the condition that they are clearly marked. Monsanto has said that this would be impractical and costly. In 2005 U.S. corn exporters were complaining because they were not allowed to sell their corn, which was still not adequately marketed in EU markets.

One of the few successful biotech foods in Europe is a genetically engineered tomato invented by Zeneca, a British firm. The tomato, which went on sale in early 1996, has captured 60% of tomato paste sales in big British supermarket chains – but only after an intensive campaign to make consumers aware of its safety and benefits. Moreover, consumers have been presented with a choice between the old and new style tomato paste.

The conclusion from the two companies' experience is, first, that it pays to spend time and energy educating consumers before introducing a largely new product. And, second, that it is easier to introduce genetically engineered food when it is simple and cheap to distinguish it from unmodified products.

Source: "USA rufen WTO im Streit mit der EU um Genfood zu Hilfe", Der Standard, August 2003, p. 19; Roush, R. (2002) "Europe reverses position to support genetic engineering", GENTECH Archive, 28 January; "Of greens and American beans", The Economist, 4 January 1997, p. 62

Product adoption Independent of the ethnic culture, there are always some individuals who are more inclined to adopt new ways of thinking and behaving than others. For an international marketer assessing the attractiveness of various country markets, it may be of interest, therefore, who the potential innovators are in the firm's product market in a country, what purchase power they represent, and how much influence they have on the behavior of the remaining potential customers.

A useful framework for such an analysis is the product-adoption process described in Toolbox 5.2.

One major advantage of applying the product-adoption framework to cultural analysis is that it forces the marketer to consider the specific characteristics of potential buyers along with cultural influences on them. Early adopters tend to be relatively abstract in thinking and forward looking in orientation. But early adopters are also influenced by their ethnic culture, the subcultures they belong to, and the industry and company cultures. For that reason, a potential early adopter of Finmet (a new process for steel production) in China will have different characteristics from an early adopter of the same technology in Russia. Those differences might make it more or less difficult for an international marketer of metallurgical engineering such as VAI to introduce the new process technology there. The resulting assessment of market attractiveness will also be different.

TOOLBOX 5.2   Product-adoption process framework

Individual customers are differently inclined to buy new goods and services. Knowing the adopter categories in a company's local product market, and their characteristics, helps the international marketer to assess the attractiveness of the country market.

The product-adoption process framework classifies potential customers into five categories: Innovators, early adopters, early majority, late majority, and laggards (see Figure 5.7).

Customers may not belong to the same category for every product. Early adopters of the latest production equipment, ever eager to cooperate with suppliers in the development of such equipment, may be much more reluctant to buy the latest office equipment or marketing consulting services, for example. Therefore, the customer groups in the framework have to be researched for each product category separately.

Source: Rogers, E.M. (1995) *The Diffusion of Innovations*, 4th edn, New York: Free Press, p. 262

Reprinted with the permission of the Free Press, a division of Simon & Schuster

---

FIGURE 5.7 *Product-adopter categories*

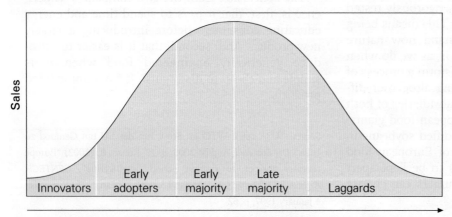

Individual customers are differently inclined to buy new goods and services. Knowing the adopter categories in a company's local product market, and their characteristics, helps the international marketer to assess the attractiveness of the country market.

Source: Rogers, E.M. (1995) *The Diffusion of Innovations,* 4th edn, New York: Free Press, p. 262.
Reprinted with the permission of the Free Press, a division of Simon & Schuster

Consumption

Basic values concerning the importance of material possessions (to "have" something) versus ideal possessions (to "be" something) strongly influence the consumption patterns in a country. In materialistic societies or subcultures, people express their self-image, their status, and their success in life by the goods and services they buy and consume.

Pleasure seeking Pleasure seeking is positively valued in most affluent societies and in affluent subcultures of less industrially developed countries. Buying trips may be a means of entertainment for consumers. German consumers, for example, are seeking pleasure when they buy fashion. In Europe, they are second only to Italian consumers in hedonism. A great part of their leisure time is taken up in finding clothes that fit them well and products that they enjoy. U.S. consumers, in comparison, are traditionally looking more for comfort and simplification of everyday life. Time-saving goods and services are attractive to them. Many Germans plan their buying trips ahead, whereas U.S. consumers tend to be more spontaneous. They buy when they are in the right mood. Wealthy Indian, Iranian, or Tunisian consumers take planes for buying and leisure trips to big European and U.S. cities. Business travelers to Tehran, for example, may encounter women boarding the plane wearing a *chador* (the black Persian women's dress that covers the entire body, including her face), disappearing into the toilets, and coming back to their seats wearing the latest western fashion clothing, before the plane has taken off from Tehran airport.

Importance of services The most affluent parts of society in the EU countries are less concerned with material possessions; these have become a matter of course to them. Services have increasingly taken their place. A study conducted among affluent women in France, Germany, and Italy, for example, showed that they are very interested in taking care of themselves by going to the hairdresser or a beauty parlor, playing sport, or going on a diet. Even more important to them is having time for themselves: going on vacation or away for the weekend, artistic activities, drawing or writing, meditation, yoga and psychotherapy, or simply doing nothing. There are differences between the various nationalities. French women leaders are more interested than other European women in culture, reading, writing and drawing. Italians like to shop more than other nationalities. German women consider that taking care of oneself equals doing nothing.

Health and nutrition With increasing wealth, consumers also become more concerned with health and nutrition issues. This concern creates numerous opportunities for international marketers. However, it should be borne in mind that different cultures define health differently, and these differences affect the types of products that can be marketed successfully in a given culture. For example, U.S. consumers spend around $100 billion a year, or one-third of their total food-store expenditure, on low-calorie, low-cholesterol foods. This is considerably more, both in total and as a proportion of food purchases, than is spent on such products in any other country. Greeks, Italians, and Spanish eat considerably more fruit and vegetables than other consumers in western industrialized countries, and have a significantly lower rate of heart attacks than the U.S. and northern Europe.

Savings Even consumption versus saving rates are influenced by culture. U.S. culture largely supports the "pursuit of happiness" (guaranteed to every U.S. citizen by the country's constitution), which – from a materialistic point of view emphasizing short-term orientation – means consumption. As a result, saving rates in the U.S. are three times smaller than in Japan, where longer term orientation supports saving and self-sacrifice for the long-term good. This leads to economic consequences, as discussed in Chapter 3.

Communication

Differing values between the cultures of potential customers and the culture of the marketer are not the only source of many problems in international marketing. A second very important factor of influence on business success is the existence or non-existence of shared symbols. **Symbols** are abstract characters that represent ideas, feelings, and other contents of communication. The message transmitted by a particular symbol or a combination of symbols, however, often changes from one ethnic culture to another. For example, snakes symbolize danger in Sweden. In Korea, they represent wisdom. A Korean company that uses a snake as its corporate symbol should expect some difficulty with its public image when entering the Swedish market.

Communication may be:

- *direct*, during social interaction
- *indirect*, through the use of media.

It may use verbal, para-verbal, and nonverbal expressions. In Korea, for example, there exists the concept of *kibun*, which is very important for interpersonal communication, but is unknown in western cultures. Kibun means something like "feeling" or "mood." And Koreans know that they should interact in a way that addresses the "kibun" of their partner if they want to build a relationship or keep it going.

Language

The most important symbols of human beings are their language. Language is much more than a formal written and oral structure of symbols that permit communication. It is an essential element of culture. Understanding another language not only allows one to conduct business in that language but, perhaps more important, it also provides some insight into the social organization, the values, and the way of thinking of those who speak it. Even if a great number of businesspeople in the world speak English to the extent that they can come to a deal, therefore, an international marketer should not rely on knowledge of English alone.

There may be even some resistance to the "English takeover." The Academie Française is fighting the introduction of more and more English terms into the French language. English is not allowed to squeeze out Portuguese in Brazil, either. São Paulo's Abril media group, for example, started a commercial online service in Portuguese in 1996. In Japan, despite students studying English for eight years, many people think that personal computers are advanced enough to run good *kanji* character programs easily.

Verbal expressions Verbal expressions may be hard to translate into another language, because the cultural frames of reference are not compatible. The Spanish *mañana* or the Arabic *bukara*, for example, are traditionally translated into the English word "tomorrow." But their real meaning is something like "sometime in the future." This difference in meaning may result in an important misunderstanding when it comes to carrying out projects "in time" in countries speaking Spanish or Arabic. The Japanese *hai*, as another example, is literally translated into the English affirmative "yes." Its meaning, however, is more like "yes, I have understood" than "yes, I agree." When negotiating with Japanese business partners, this slight difference may result in major misunderstandings concerning the progress of mutual consent.

Multilingual markets From the international marketer's perspective, a complicating factor related to language is that few countries are monolingual. In most countries several dialects are used, and in some countries several languages are spoken, often reflecting entirely different cultures or subcultures. Switzerland, for instance, has four major language groups: French, German, Italian, and Romansch. And despite the fact that the people speaking those languages founded Switzerland some centuries ago, even today they represent clearly different ethnic cultures.

The dominant languages spoken in India are Hindi (about 30% of the population) and English as the country's official language. Fourteen other languages, such as Bengali and Marathi (both about 8% of the population), are recognized across regions. Besides many others, such as Nepali or Mizo, that are recognized as official local languages, there are many languages that are not officially recognized. An international marketer who wants to reach more than the well-educated population of India, therefore, may be forced to communicate in many different languages.

MAP 5.2 *Selected major language groups of the world*

The languages of the world are quite diverse. This map illustrates major language groups in the world, and shows how widely diverse a geographic area those languages cover. What it does not illustrate, however, is how concentrated those languages are. English, for example, is the first language of some 320 million people. Hindi (Indo-Aryan group), one of the major languages of northern India, is spoken by about the same number of people, but within a significantly smaller geographical area.

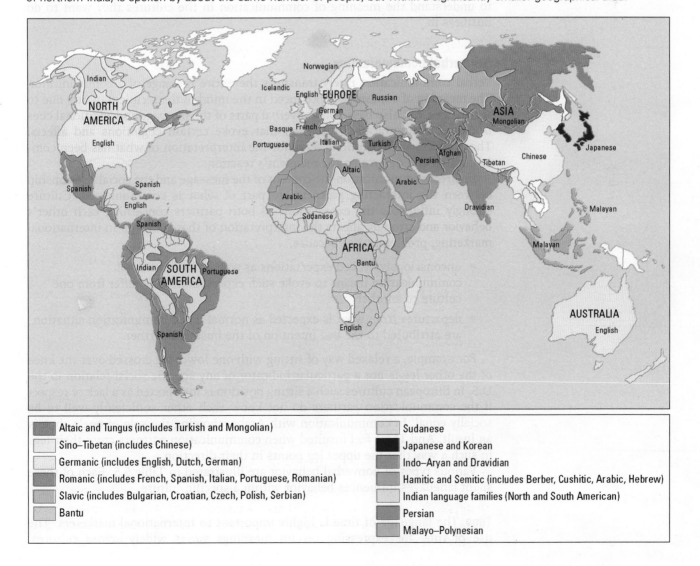

■ Altaic and Tungus (includes Turkish and Mongolian)	■ Sudanese
■ Sino–Tibetan (includes Chinese)	■ Japanese and Korean
■ Germanic (includes English, Dutch, German)	■ Indo–Aryan and Dravidian
■ Romanic (includes French, Spanish, Italian, Portuguese, Romanian)	■ Hamitic and Semitic (includes Berber, Cushitic, Arabic, Hebrew)
■ Slavic (includes Bulgarian, Croatian, Czech, Polish, Serbian)	■ Indian language families (North and South American)
■ Bantu	■ Persian
	■ Malayo–Polynesian

Differences in meaning Even a single language spoken in more than one country may have differences. Too often, businesspeople in countries that share a language are not prepared for communication difficulties. For example, when a U.S. participant in a business meeting suggests "tabling a motion," the mover wants to postpone discussion; but U.K. participants will think that the person wants to begin discussion. In Australia, the suggestion of a U.S. manager to have "regular meetings" would lead to some surprise. North Americans use the term to mean normal, or acceptable: for example, "regular coffee." In Australia, the word is used in a different way. The closest Australian equivalent to "regular guy," for example, would be "mate."

Para-verbal communication

Para-verbal communication, that is, how speakers intonate their sentences and modulate their voices, is also culture specific. It leads to certain interpretations of the communication content or the communication situation. For example, the typical extent of pitch modulation of an "educated speaker" in the U.K. is negatively loaded in other cultures. It is interpreted as a signal of the speaker's affectedness. In some African and Arab cultures, the volume of voice is used to regulate the sequence of speakers: the one who speaks loudest has the greatest chance of being listened to. In Europe, simultaneous loud speaking by a group of people is interpreted as an indicator of dispute. The personnel of international marketers need to be trained in the proper interpretation of such signals in order to be able to understand the meaning of communication in the cultures they want to do business in.

Nonverbal communication

Verbal communication rarely transmits the entire message of a communicator. The meaning of a message is produced in the mind of the recipient, partly due to verbal cues, but also based on nonverbal parts of the message and additional cues from the communication situation that evoke certain cognitions and affects. Those affects and cognitions serve for the interpretation of what has been communicated and determine the recipient's reactions.

In direct communication the content of the message and the social relationship between the interacting partners are part of what is communicated. Culture strongly influences the expectations of both partners concerning each other's behavior and strongly affects the interpretation of that behavior. In international marketing, problems arise because;

- unconsciously evoked expectations as well as the nonverbal communication means to evoke such expectations may differ from one culture to another
- departures from what is expected as normal in a communication situation are attributed to the bad intention of the business partner.

For example, a relaxed way of sitting with one lower leg crossed over the knee of the other leg is not a particular indicator of any specific social relation in the U.S. In European cultures such a sitting position is interpreted as a lack of respect if the communication partners do not know each other sufficiently well to be socially equal. In communication with Arabs, showing the sole of one's shoe is an insult. And Thais feel insulted when communication partners cross their legs in such a way that the upper leg points in their direction.

Various types of nonverbal behavior are illustrated in Table 5.5. Each of these silent languages influences behavior within a specific culture.

Time The language of time is highly important to international marketers. The use of time for expressing certain meanings varies widely across cultures.

Indonesians, for example, show respect by arriving "late" for a meeting. This once caused the president of a Dutch company some considerable difficulty. Expecting visiting Indonesian guests to be punctual (the Dutch way of showing respect), he was put off by the tardiness of his visitors.

Similar misunderstandings can occur over the speed with which a meeting should approach the business topic or how long negotiations should take. For example, trying to force Japanese negotiators to reach an early decision is not only difficult but rude; it ignores the need of Japanese team members to reach a consensus before reacting to a proposal.

Space The concept of language of space is illustrated by how close to one another people stand or sit. Arabs, for instance, prefer to stand quite close to the person with whom they are speaking – uncomfortably close by North American standards. When a Canadian or U.S. manager automatically steps back to a more comfortable distance, he or she inadvertently offends the Arab business partner.

Similarly, in some cultures such as the Chinese, waiting in line means standing close together and jostling towards the front. U.K. managers, who come from a culture where one is expected to wait one's turn without crowding, may be driven crazy "crowding in line" in front of a Shanghai airport checkin counter.

Signs Finally, identical nonverbal signs may have different meanings. For example, when potential business partners in Bulgaria shake their heads they mean "yes," rather than the "no" as would be assumed by communication partners from western Europe. The trouble is that Bulgarian managers who have

TABLE 5.5 *Silent languages*

Nonverbal communication accounts for a large amount of information received by a potential customer or a stakeholder. International marketers must take care to learn a culture's silent languages when conducting business in another country market.

Time	Appointments
	Deadlines
	Scheduling of people and events
Space	Size of office
	Location of office
	Furnishings
	Conversation distance
Things	Material possessions
	Interest in latest technology
	Personal connections versus material symbols of status, power, and respect
Friendship	Friends versus self as social insurance for times of stress and emergency
Agreements	Rules of negotiations based on laws, moral practices, or informal customs

Source: Hall, E.T. (1960) "The silent language in overseas business", *Harvard Business Review*, May–June, pp. 87–96

experience of western business partners might know about that difference and use shaking of the head in the sense of their western counterparts. Reliance on that nonverbal communication, therefore, would be rather ambiguous.

Context relatedness

The trap of using the self-reference criterion to interpret a communication or a situation is even more dangerous when confronted with nonverbal or para-verbal communication than with verbal communication. A manager traveling to another country expects differences in spoken language and even in some observable behavior. Differences in silent language are much less obvious. Nonverbal communication is largely unconscious, but has a strong emotional impact.

Much of the difficulty has to do with the extent to which communication partners rely on the context for determining the meaning of what is said or done. Businesspeople from east Asian and Arabic countries, for example, derive much of what is meant to be said from the communication context. Confronted with businesspeople from North America or the Germanic parts of Europe, who rely more directly on the spoken words themselves, emotional misunderstandings are commonplace.

But this problem may also arise in indirect communication. In cultures relying strongly on communication context, advertising campaigns are often highly visual and mood setting. How something is presented is as important, often more important, than specifically what is said. Japanese TV commercials, for instance, can be relatively informative with the inclusion of certain product information categories, such as packaging and performance. But they clearly avoid mentioning product benefits, guarantees and safety. Japanese marketers' media communications tend to be more intuitive, subjective, and human relations oriented, while marketers from Anglo-Saxon and Germanic cultures tend to be more logical, data and procedure oriented. Stressing company reputation is a more effective way to transfer the intended "feelings" to customers in Japan than detailing specific product attributes and quality. Directly addressing why somebody should buy the product, as is common in much of western advertising, would be perceived as an insult to the customer's intelligence concerning making a sound judgment. Japanese advertisers are also reluctant to use comparative advertising, which connotes a confrontational practice to denigrate competitors unfairly.

Intercultural training

Because of all the cited differences in communication, only intensive training may help internationally active marketing people to avoid major blunders in direct as well as indirect communication with potential customers. Such training must incorporate:

- cultural self-awareness, making marketers aware that one's own thinking and behavior are culture bound
- cross-cultural awareness, making them aware of culture-specific differences in the thinking and behavior of others
- communication awareness, making them aware of the limits of mutual understanding in cross-cultural communication even after intensive training.

The training should not be limited to knowledge transfer. To make it effective there must be important segments of practical experience training. Internationally operating firms such as German-based chemical firms Bayer and Hoechst or French Merlin-Gerin, a producer of switching panels, for example, train their employees in nationally mixed seminars and workshops to let them directly experience the cultural differences in working style, delegation of responsibilities, communication, and handling of time.

This intercultural training has shown that German managers, for example, perceive the French style of doing more than one thing at once as less serious. In contrast the French criticize their German counterparts for tending to stick to their plans even in unforeseen situations. French managers have a more paternalistic style of leadership than Germans who prefer a more team- and facts-oriented style. When French managers make presentations in a way in which brilliant formulations are as important as proper facts, German managers think that they take too long to say very little. But French managers feel they are being treated as beginners when their German colleagues go into details of facts and related background information.

Aesthetics

Colors, forms, shapes, sounds – all that is considered attractive or unattractive in a given culture – constitute the aesthetics of a culture. They affect customers' responses to product, shop, and office design as well as labeling and packaging, and they help define what communication is appropriate in a country market. Therefore, the degree of potential product and communication standardization across country markets is strongly influenced by the local customers' aesthetic preferences.

Meanings

Aesthetic preferences and the meaning of aesthetic expressions may be very different. For example, when John Player, the English cigarette brand, was to be introduced in Hong Kong, Marlboro was the leading brand there at the time, and John Player was positioned to compete directly against it. One of John Player's distinctive brand characteristics was its black box with gold trim. At the time, black dresses were the leading fashion item in many markets, including Hong Kong. Player's advertising agency decided that the best time for the product launch would be the Chinese New Year. An extensive introductory campaign was designed and executed. Samples were distributed, coupons were provided, and an expensive advertising campaign was undertaken. The result was disastrous. Not only did the product not sell well, people took the free sample packages to stores and traded them in for their usual brand. John Player had inadvertently violated the association of the color black with bad luck and bad fortune. The timing of the launch made matters worse. At a time when people were in a happy, festive mood, they were especially sensitive to the negative connotations of the color black. The fact that black was popular among fashion-conscious consumers did not help John Player in its appeal to the mass market. Fashions are temporary and change rapidly. Underlying aesthetic preferences are enduring and change very slowly. John Player's marketer mistook one for the other and paid the price – market failure.

In Mexico, as another example, the color of one's underwear assumes added significance as a new year begins. Wearing yellow briefs or panties on New Year's Eve is traditionally believed to bring good fortune, while wearing red unmentionables is thought to bring luck in love.

International subcultures

Owing to the existence of subcultures, there are also international product markets in which very similar aesthetic preferences exist. Music, for instance, is particularly likely to have cross-cultural appeal. Jazz musicians such as Wynton Marsalis tour the world; for a long time the rock group ABBA was one of Sweden's leading exports; and an Australian entrepreneur signed an exclusive contract to sell the recordings of Moscow-based Melodiya throughout the Asia Pacific Rim. The design of accessories such as Gucci bags, Étienne Aigner leather goods and Poiray jewelry, as well as the design of sporting goods such as Alfred Dunhill golf equipment, also seems to be attractive to customers all around the world. In assessing the attractiveness of various potential markets, the international marketer therefore has to consider carefully how the aesthetic features of its products may be received by the targeted customers.

Social organization

Social organization provides the framework of a culture. It includes virtually every aspect of how people live together from day to day, the assignment of social tasks, and how and why people join together to meet their shared needs. Because the social organization of a society is so basic in terms of what consumers and organizational buyers are expected to do or not to do, information on social organization is extremely important to international marketers.

An example of this can be seen in the definition of what constitutes a household and how many households there are in a potential market. In the U.S., for example, a "typical" household is a nuclear family – one or two parents and their children. In Europe, the Mediterranean countries – Greece, Italy, Portugal, and Spain – have higher proportions of family households and fewer one-person households. Scandinavian countries are more likely to have more non-family households and more one-person households. In Kenya, a typical household is an extended family – a nuclear family plus grandparents, aunts, uncles, and cousins.

Other aspects of social organization that are important to marketers are the roles people play within households and organizations, and the social groups to which they belong.

Social roles

Through defining social roles, culture largely determines who influences, makes and carries out purchasing decisions, as well as who actually uses goods and services. People's roles include their privileges and their responsibilities towards other people. Each one plays many roles in society – child, parent, sibling, student, worker, boss – and each of these roles causes needs and expectations potentially important to international marketers. For example, a woman playing the role of:

- a mother may buy consumer products for her children
- a partner to her husband may have the last word in the purchase of a family car, home furniture, or household appliances
- a procurement manager in a firm may be responsible for buying production raw materials and office equipment
- a host when inviting friends to go out for dinner needs to decide what restaurant to go to.

The complexity of social organization and the stability of social roles and relationships are related to a society's level of technological and economic development. For example, in Zimbabwe, women are almost excluded from participation in meaningful economic activities as owners or creators of wealth. Men have an entrenched absence of positive attitudes towards women and their capabilities. Women's status is reflected in the fact that a mere 18% of gross national income accrues to the rural population, comprising 64% of Zimbabwe's population – the majority of whom are women. In high-density urban areas women are no better off. Most of them work in cross-border trading, micro-manufacturing and vending. But the money they earn goes to supplement their husband's or family's income. They are unable to generate wealth for themselves. With an average take-home pay for urban dwellers of less than $50 per month compared to the basic cost of living of more than $65 per month, survival is the ultimate concern. Where social roles are strictly defined on the basis of gender and change in social roles is taking place very slowly, if at all, the international marketer needs to understand those roles in order to predict buying and consumption behavior.

In more economically advanced countries, social roles and relationships tend to be more ambiguous and dynamic. In the U.S., for example, gender roles have been rapidly evolving toward more individualized and less predictable forms. In Japan, where social norms based on Confucianism have long emphasized seniority among family members and the dominant role of the male, the level of well-being and happiness of the wife was considered second in importance to the well-being of other family members. In the workplace, female attractiveness was a highly appreciated trait. But Japanese women are increasingly dismissing the belief that women must remain at home and take care of the children. Since the 1990s the number of married women working in business organizations in metropolitan areas has exceeded that of married women working in the home.

The changing roles of women, in turn, are generating other types of change throughout society. For example, 70% of American women of working age are employed outside the home and need services such as childcare and household products that save time.

Social groups

When people join together formally or informally to reach shared goals and to meet shared needs, they create social groups. People's behavior in business situations is strongly affected by their previous experiences in such social groups: in the family, at school, and in different kinds of peer groups. In order to understand the behavior of (potential) customers and stakeholders in another country, managers of internationally operating companies should therefore acquire some knowledge about families and social relationships in their target markets.

Family From a cultural point of view, the family is the most powerful social group in any society. Within the family children learn what is important, what to believe and how to behave, including what needs are socially acceptable and how to satisfy those needs in the marketplace. As the discussion of values has shown, variations in the process and outcome of enculturation inside the family from one culture to another can have significant impacts on international marketing.

Peer groups As children grow up and go to kindergarten and school, they become members of peer groups, which have an increasing influence on their view of the world and their behavior. Such peer groups play the role of **reference groups**, that is, a number of related persons to whom an individual looks for guidance regarding behavioral norms. This guidance does not have to come from the group members themselves. They may follow the role model of a person highly attractive to them, such as a film or pop star; or they gather around the use of certain branded objects which give them the opportunity to differentiate their group from others and, simultaneously, to experience shared identity with the other users of the brand.

Individuals need not necessarily be members of their reference groups. Reference groups may also be:

- *anticipatory* (groups to which a person would like to belong)
- *dissociative* (groups the person would not like to belong to).

Reference groups are particularly important for international marketers in the case of products that are socially visible, unfamiliar to the buyer, or expensive.

"Managing" the cultural environment

Having identified the most important factors of influence from the cultural environment on the firm's business and having analyzed those factors, the international marketer is able to take decisions about how to react to the results of the analysis. On the one hand, less attractive markets will not be considered further. For example, marketers of industrial plants who cannot afford large time overruns in their projects because of capacity and capital resource restrictions may decide to put at the end of their list of attractiveness countries where respecting time limits is not part of the cultural heritage of customers and local stakeholders. On the other hand, in the more attractive markets, marketing management must decide to what extent adaptations to the given cultural specifics are needed.

Adapting to cultural differences

Marketing practices in a country are culturally dependent, and what works in one country market does not necessarily work in another. Adaptation of the marketing mix is needed in many cases when the target customers belong to different cultural environments. Countries where women's major role is defined as home-making, for example, are more often served by distribution systems that include bargaining. Arguing about the price of products requires that considerable time be spent shopping. Where women are more likely to have a career outside the household, time becomes more precious – a constraint on bargaining. In those cultures, fixed prices are more common.

Obviously, adjusting to cultural imperatives, such as language to ensure communication, is a must. But adjusting to other cultural elements that are not critical for success only adds expense and detracts from economies of scale and scope. Therefore, the international marketer must carefully analyze the cultural imperatives that exist in the served product and country markets and only adapt to those. Not only the application of marketing tools may need to be changed. Even the categories of thinking may be so essentially different from one society to another that the entire marketing approach may need to be adapted.

Marketing's influence on culture

Increasingly, international marketing managers must be aware that culture not only influences their decisions, but that their decisions and actions influence culture as well.

Agent of change

International marketers act as agents of change within a culture. For example, most of rural Indonesia, the most populated Islamic country in the world, used to be beyond the reach of the cash economy. However, the situation has changed. Leading the way were women's toiletries and cosmetics. At the end of the 1990s, more than half the women in the country's four most populous rural provinces used face powder, half used lipstick and body lotion, and one-third used sanitary pads. Foods and beverages also have their attraction. More than half of the rural population buy candy and around one-third purchase biscuits. Sixty percent drink mineral water and about 40% consume bottled soft drinks.

After decades of buying poor-quality goods from state-run factories, Chinese consumers and private industrial buyers almost always preferred foreign-made or foreign-branded goods and services when they had a choice after the Chinese market was opened to foreign suppliers. Capitalizing on that prejudice, an increasing number of companies have adopted foreign-sounding names or trademarks. In the meantime, foreign goods have been adapted so much to specific

Chinese expectations and Chinese marketers have developed their quality to such a level that an increasing number of Chinese customers prefer buying from local (less expensive) suppliers.

Cultural imperialism

Marketers conducting business across cultures should be clearly aware of the effect their activities have on local cultures and consider the rebounds such effects may have on their own business success. U.S.-based multinational corporations, not only in east Asia, have sometimes been accused of "cultural imperialism." For instance, in preparing the opening of Euro Disney (near Paris) in 1992, Euro Disney's first chairman proudly announced that his company would "help change Europe's chemistry." The French ridiculed the park as a "cultural Chernobyl." It took a series of adaptations such as renaming the park "Disneyland Paris" and the addition of some special attractions to make the park profitable and the most frequented "monument" of France.

Global vs local cultures

In the long run, as more country markets are opened up to international business, the rate of cultural change induced by international marketers will increase. As a result, more product markets will become global. The further developed this globalization becomes the more standardization of business activities will be possible. The processes of cultural change and standardization reinforce each other. Thus, international marketers are contributing to the sharing of ideas, values, and behavior among cultures. At the same time, and as a reaction, local subcultures are becoming stronger. They open up business opportunities for local marketers, but also for international marketers that have enough flexibility to adapt to the local specifics.

Summary

Culture, defined as the standards of beliefs, perception, evaluation, and behavior shared by the members of a social group, strongly influences the behavior of organizational buyers as well as consumers. Consumers learn the most important values governing their behavior during childhood in their families before they become members of peer groups and are attracted by reference groups from which they take additional standards of

behavior. Consumers participate in subcultures and they are members of ethnic (or national) cultures.

Business people are also members of a national culture that strongly influences the basic values they share with others. In addition, they follow norms of behavior that are part of the industrial culture to which their company belongs. Each company develops an organizational culture, that is, a set of behavioral norms specific

DISCUSSION QUESTIONS

1. Use examples to illustrate how different layers of culture may influence the behavior of consumers.

2. What layers of business culture have the strongest impact on businesspeople's behavior? Support your points with some empirical evidence from the literature.

3. Find examples of international subcultures from the internet. How have they developed? How can they be used for international marketing purposes?

4. What role does the self-reference criterion play in international business ethics? Is there more than one set of ethical standards? Discuss.

5. Illustrate the difficulties in intercultural communication. What can an international marketer do about it?

6. What do differing work ethics have to do with international marketing? Give examples for the points you list.

7. Compare the role of women in your country to their role in another culture of your choice. Use the internet as an information source. How do the different roles affect women's behavior as consumers and as businesspeople?

8. Take an example of a firm you know and try to establish a list of cultural factors that this company would need to consider in assessing new country markets to be served. Explain your choice of factors.

9. Take an example of a company from your home market and a foreign country market where you find information about its cultural specifics on the internet. Based on that information, what adaptations of the company's marketing do you suggest?

10. Discuss the potential influences of marketing on culture. What are your conclusions concerning the impact of international marketing?

ADDITIONAL READINGS

Asgary, N. and M.C. Mitschow (2002) "Toward a model for international business ethics," *Journal of Business Ethics*, 36(3), 239–46.

Lin, X. and St.J. Miller (2003) "Negotiation approaches: direct and indirect effect of national culture", *International Marketing Review*, 20(3), 286–303.

Srnka, K.J. (2004) "Culture's role in marketers' ethical decision making: an integrated theoretical framework", *Academy of Marketing Science Review*, 1.

to the firm. All those values and norms, potentially combined with a functional culture, influence the behavior of potential business partners and stakeholders in international marketing.

Consumer culture and business culture both need to be thoroughly analyzed by an international marketer in order to:

- choose the most attractive markets
- determine the proper level of adaptation of marketing activities in each of those markets.

To reduce the amount of analyses to be conducted to a minimum, the international marketer must determine a list of cultural factors specific to its product market(s), which are most important for business success. Those factors may be specific values, and may relate to verbal and nonverbal communication, education, aesthetics, or the social organization of society.

They are used to evaluate the attractiveness of a country market's cultural environment. Based on that evaluation, the potential country markets may be ranked and the most attractive ones will be considered further. Later in the process of strategic international marketing, the acquired knowledge concerning the cultural environment of the company will be used to "manage" this environment. Decisions will be taken as to what extent to adapt to cultural specifics and to what extent to try to influence the cultural environment through marketing activities.

(The tools an international marketer may apply in the analysis of country markets and how the analytical process can be conducted in a rational as well as cost-efficient way will be discussed in Chapter 7.)

Useful internet links

ABBA	http://www.abbasite.com/start/
Academie Française	http://www.academie-francaise.fr/
Alfred Dunhill	http://www.dunhill.com/
Bayer	http://www.bayer.com/page52.htm
Benetton	http://www.benetton.com/
Business Behavior	http://www.worldbiz.com/
Delta Airlines	http://www.delta.com/
Étienne Aigner	http://www.etienneaigner.com/
Euro Disney	http://www.disneylandparis.com/uk/introduction.htm
Evans & Sutherland Computer Corp	http://www.es.com/
Global Corruption Report	http://www.globalcorruptionreport.org/
Global Market Information Database	http://www.euromonitor.com/gmid.asp
Gucci	http://www.gucci.com/
Hoechst	http://www.hoechst.com/
Hofstede's Five Dimensions of Culture	http://www.geert-hofstede.com/
International Business Etiquette and Manners	http://www.international-business-etiquette.com/
International Business Protocol	http://www.business-protocol.com/
Market Research Resource List	http://www.library.cornell.edu/johnson/library/faq/market_research.html
Marubeni	http://www.marubeni.com/company/index.html
McDonald's	http://www.mcdonalds.com/corp.html
Melodiya	http://www.melodiya.ua/
Merlin-Gerin	http://www.merlingerin.com/
Monsanto	http://www.monsanto.com/
Nestlé	http://www.nestle.com/
Pirelli	http://www.pirelli.com/en_42/
Poiray	http://www.poiray.com/
Procter & Gamble	http://www.pg.com/
Siemens	http://www.siemens.com/

Tomen	http://www.tomen.co.jp/aboute/index.html
Unilever	http://www.unilever.com/company/ourcompany/£
VAI	http://www.vai.at/
WiFi	http://www.wi-fi.org/OpenSection/index.asp
Zeneca	http://www.astrazeneca.co.uk/

OPERATING ENVIRONMENT ASSESSMENT: FIRM'S COMPETITIVE POSITION

6

Learning objectives

After studying this chapter you will be able to:

- assess a company's success factors in the most attractive international markets

- analyze major competitors' strengths and weaknesses concerning those success factors

- assess a company's potential to do business in the most attractive markets

- determine the distinctive competences of the company

- explain the concept of competitive advantage

- distinguish different ways of determining competitive advantages

Chapter outline

Assessing the competitive position

Success factors in international marketing

General factors of influence on international marketing success

Determination of success factors

Competitor analysis

Structure of the competitive environment

Barriers to market exit

Determination of distinctive capabilities

Assessment of corporate policy

Assessment of core strategy

Assessment of management systems

Assessment of operations

Competitor information sources

Profiles of strengths and weaknesses

Summary

INTERNATIONAL MARKETING SPOTLIGHT

Grohe Water Technology

With total sales of about $770 million, German company Grohe Water Technology is the market leader in Europe and among the world's top three fitting manufacturers, together with Masco from the U.S. and Japan's Toto. The company markets all kinds of fittings for residential and non-residential purposes, installation and flushing systems as well as water management systems. Grohe started its internationalization process by founding sales subsidiaries in Austria, France, and Italy in the 1960s. A second wave of internationalization during the 1970s gave birth to sales subsidiaries in Belgium, the Netherlands, Spain, the U.K., and the U.S. Until the mid-1990s, manufacturing sites were exclusively located in Germany. Since 1987 company sales have grown by an average of 10% a year all over the industrialized world, resulting in tripled total sales in 10 years.

Before Grohe's top management determined the firm's global strategy for the second half of the 1990s, they formed a special taskforce of marketing people and technicians to conduct a thorough analysis of the global $8 billion product market served by the firm and its most important competitors. Market analysis revealed an increasing concentration of retailers, a rising number of private labels, the emergence of new price-driven retail channels, increasing internationalization of key competitors, stagnant demand in core markets, and a polarization of demand. High-end and low-end product segments had been growing while the middle segment had virtually disappeared.

Competitors could be divided into two strategic groups following two basic strategies: (1) fitting specialists, such as Hansa, Kludi, Oras, and Moen,

and (2) all-in suppliers, offering everything for the bathroom, such as Ideal Standard, Roca, Masco, Kohler, and Toto. Fitting specialists suffered from increasing density of competitors, a fragmented competitive structure, and rather narrow markets. All-in suppliers had to master very complex logistics problems which were not entirely counterbalanced by synergy effects. End users showed some resistance to the idea of getting everything from one supplier.

Part of the "water technology" range
© Carl Kelliher/iStock

As a consequence, Grohe's top management decided to position the firm as a system supplier of sanitary technology. Because end users have a rather low involvement with the firm's products, Grohe concentrated on its relationships with planners and installation companies. Those customers were offered compatible product systems, access to new fields of technology, and an enhanced service level. Production sites were started in Canada, Thailand, and Portugal. Companies possessing some additional know-how have been acquired to further strengthen Grohe Water Technology's position as a system supplier. The product range was split into two groups under the brand names of GROHEtech (for the mass market) and GROHEart (for the high end). Annual pre-tax profits of around 12% have shown that careful market assessment and a close examination of competitor strengths and weaknesses pay off.

The focal question of this chapter is: **What is the competitive position of our business organization in the most attractive geographical markets and does it have any differentiating capabilities to rely on?**

Assessing the competitive position

To get a fairly unbiased picture of the attractiveness of potential country markets, the firm needs to assess those markets independently from the perspective of its own resources and capabilities. When the most attractive country markets have been defined, the company must determine whether it can serve them successfully. Potential success depends on the fit between the firm's capabilities and the success factors in the markets. Success factors are the capabilities that a company needs in a market to distinguish itself attractively from its competitors – seen from the potential customers' and most important stakeholders' point of view – and to be able to turn challenges from the market's macro-environment into opportunities. Figure 6.1 provides an overview of the process that leads from the identification of the success factors in a potential market to the determination of the company's competitive advantages in that market. Competitive advantages are the result of a company's distinctive competences based on capabilities that are demanded by a market and its macro-environment and that competitors cannot easily match, except at high cost and/or over an extended period.

First, the success factors in each potential market have to be determined. Then, an assessment of the firm's potential related to these factors compared to its competitors can be conducted. This process will lead to an understanding of the capabilities that are crucial for success and that differentiate the company from its competitors. Management can use positive differences (= strengths) as distinctive competences to build and sustain the firm's competitive advantages. It will work on negative differences (= weaknesses) to overcome their potential impact on the success of the firm. In this chapter, the process of how to determine the success factors in a market, how to assess a firm's competitive position, and how to derive competitive advantages will be described and discussed in detail.

Success factors in international marketing

To determine its potential for success in a market, a company has to find out if it will be able to differentiate itself attractively from the major competitors at a profit. For that purpose, management must, first, identify the specific capabilities needed to successfully serve the market, and, second, compare the current state of their firm concerning those capabilities to the characteristics of the major competitors.

FIGURE 6.1 Determination of a firm's competitive position

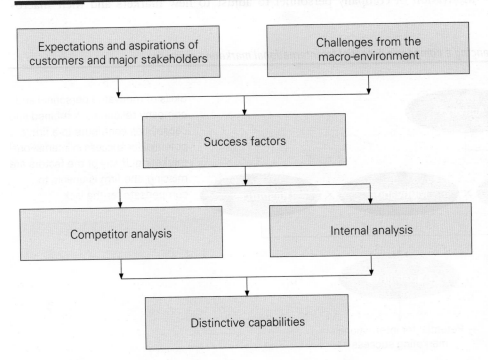

The competitive position of a firm in a market depends on its distinctive capabilities, that is, on the strengths and weaknesses of the company compared to its major competitors. Distinctive capabilities are determined by a comparative analysis between the company and its competitors. This analysis should concern the success factors, that is, the capabilities needed by a firm to be successful in a given market. Success factors can be derived from customers' and major stakeholders' expectations and aspirations as well as from present and future challenges from the macro-environment of the market under consideration.

General factors of influence on international marketing success

Figure 6.2 shows some general factors that influence a company's potential for international marketing success.

Capabilities

Overall, the internal factors that determine a company's potential for international marketing success can be called the capabilities of the firm. **Capabilities** are the specific blend of the skills of its personnel times their motivation to apply those skills in ways desired by top management times the availability of appropriate resources. If either personnel skills or motivation are not internationally oriented and up to competitive standards, or if the firm's resources are insufficient or inadequate, the resulting capabilities will not lead to the achievement of company goals. Thus, when analyzing a firm's potential for international marketing success, a manager must look at all of the three dimensions.

Skills

International marketing success depends on how closely the skills of the company's personnel match the expectations and aspirations of customers and other important stakeholders in the market. A person's skills are a blend of knowledge and the ability to apply this knowledge appropriately. Managers and employees with distinctive skills such as production know-how, product development skills, or extensive experience in relationship building may truly set a company apart from its competitors, who will have a hard time acquiring the skills at short notice.

Taittinger, a French producer of high-quality champagne, for example, possesses specific production know-how that has allowed it to be one of the most prominent brands in the world. Because the small number of the company's cellarers personally transmit their know-how from one generation to the next, the know-how specific to the brand does not leave the company, making it difficult for competitors to imitate their product quickly.

Motivation

Company personnel must be motivated to apply their skills internationally. Motivation of company personnel to adjust to new markets and their macro-

FIGURE 6.2 *General factors influencing a company's potential for international marketing success*

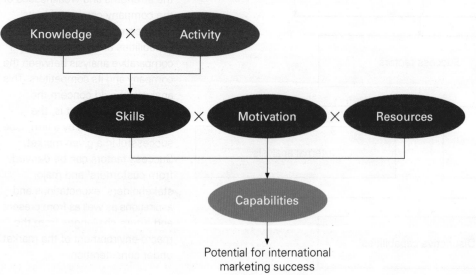

Skills of motivated personnel and company resources combined into capabilities contribute to a firm's potential for success in international marketing. If any of the factors are missing, the firm is unable to compensate for the lack.

environments is based on the dominating values and social norms that form the firm's corporate culture. An appropriate culture may be lacking, for example, if the compensation system does not reward foreign assignments, or worse, if it acts as a disincentive in terms of opportunities for promotion. That may be the case when managers returning from international assignments find that somebody else has taken their former position and they are offered an inappropriate position instead.

Resources

International marketing success also requires appropriate resources. Company resources that are of major importance for successful internationalization include financial, technological, production, information, and organizational elements.

Determination of success factors

Strengths and weaknesses concerning available resources, personnel skills, and motivation should be analyzed in terms of the firm's corporate policy, corporate strategy, management systems, and operations. However, any general analysis of a company's strengths and weaknesses includes two practical problems: the large number of potential characteristics to look at and the choice of criteria to evaluate them. Both problems can be resolved by first determining the success factors in the market. On the one hand, they indicate which characteristics of the firm and its major competitors should be analyzed, and, on the other, the level of competence to be achieved on each of the important characteristics.

Core factors

When searching for the success factors in a market, a company has to make a clear distinction between success factors and core factors (Figure 6.3). **Core factors** are the capabilities a company needs to be considered as a relevant supplier by the customers and other important stakeholders in this market, and to prevent present and future challenges from the macro-environment from becoming a threat. A Brazilian producer of pharmaceuticals unable to provide the medical test information required in order to be accepted by the British medical administration will not be able to participate in that market, for example. Thus, the competitors in a market will usually not differ regarding those capabilities. To attract Scandinavian summer tourists, for example, an area must be able to guarantee sunshine. Italy, Greece, and Tunisia, competing for those tourists, can satisfy the demand, but they do not differ from each other regarding that

---

FIGURE 6.3 *A firm's core and success factors*

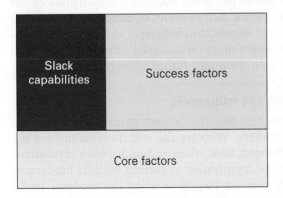

The total capabilities of a firm can be distinguished into core factors, success factors, and slack. Core factors are the capabilities a company needs to be considered as a relevant supplier by the customers and other important stakeholders in this market, and to prevent present and future challenges from the macro-environment from becoming threats. Success factors are the capabilities a company needs to be considered as an attractive supplier by the customers and other important stakeholders in this market, and to be able to turn present and future challenges from the macro-environment of this market into opportunities. All other capabilities can be regarded as slack.

Source: Grunert, K.G. and C. Ellegaard (1993) "The concept of key success factors: Theory and method", in M.J. Baker (ed.) *Perspectives on Marketing Management*, vol. 3, Chichester: John Wiley & Sons, pp. 245–74

characteristic. The decision of Scandinavian customers on what country to select for their summer vacation depends on other factors, the so-called success factors.

Success factors

Success factors are the capabilities that a company needs in a market to distinguish itself attractively from its competitors – seen from the potential customers' and most important stakeholders' point of view – and to be able to turn present and future opportunities from the macro-environment of this market into opportunities. Business success will depend on how the firm scores on these factors compared to its major competitors.

Ways to determine success factors

When determining the success factors in attractive potential markets, some managers rely on their past experience.

Past experience In the ever changing environment of international markets, however, past experience is likely to be quickly outdated and it is dangerous to generalize from one country market to another. French Gervais-Danone, for example, knows from its U.S. experience that a big budget for national consumer advertising is very important for getting enough shelf space in supermarkets all over the country. But will that also be true in China? It may be much more important there to use networking skills, that is, to build up personal and maybe financial relationships, to obtain the desired shelf space.

Consultants Experienced consultants may have extensive knowledge based on work with numerous and diverse companies. They may transfer their experience across business domains in a very productive manner. Such individuals are in a relatively good position to determine general success factors for international marketing. However, because current and potential expectations of customers and other important stakeholders vary in different product and country markets, attempts to define general success factors across markets have achieved high levels of attention but not much enduring success in international marketing.

Customer expectations and aspirations The best way to determine the success factors in a potential market is to identify the expectations (concerning the satisfaction of needs) and aspirations (concerning the solution of problems) of the (potential) customers and important stakeholders in the markets under consideration and to derive the capabilities a company needs to fulfill those aspirations and expectations (Figure 6.4). Because of the diversity of aspirations and expectations in most cases, segments of customers and related stakeholders have to be formed before the success factors in each of those segments can be derived. In addition, the marketer needs to define the most important dimensions of the macro-environment as well as the specific factors on these dimensions the future development of which might present significant challenges to firms doing business in those segments. The challenges must be analyzed concerning the capabilities a firm needs to be able to turn them into future opportunities.

Determination of decision makers and influencers

The first step in determining the success factors in a country market is to find out who is driving the product market there: Who are the real decision makers significantly influencing what is exchanged, how, when and under what conditions? Is it the direct exchange partners the organization is serving with its product, or the exchange partners' customers who are buying or using the product? In the case of RSB-Roundtech, the Austrian marketer of formwork material for circular structures, the real decision makers may be the government or the local administration taking the investment decision, the engineering firm responsible for the applied technology, or the main contractor who selects the subcontractors.

Longitudinal analysis To be managerially relevant, the analysis of decision processes and potentials of influence in a market needs to be done in a longitudinal way. A longitudinal analysis looks at an emerging process over time. That is, management may analyze a purchase decision-making process as a series of episodes with potentially varying players of changing roles and influence over time. To allow in-depth understanding of how business in the relevant product market of a country is done, such a longitudinal approach to customer decision making should include post-purchase episodes in which the customers co-create value by product consumption or usage as well as communication about the product. Such an analysis tends to be rather complex. But if a country market is relatively new and highly important to a company the information gained about the functioning of the product market clearly outweighs the resources spent.

FIGURE 6.4 *Determination of a firm's competitive position*

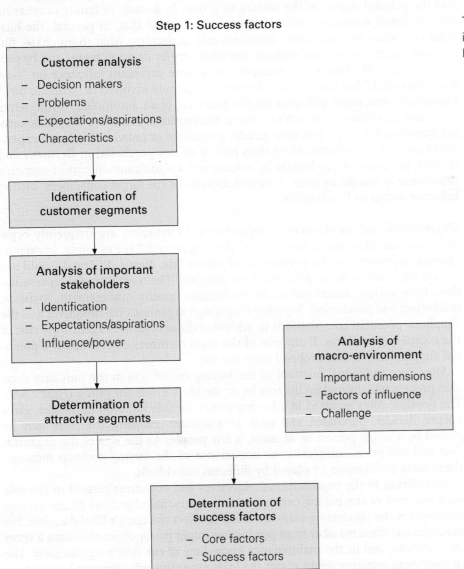

Step 1: Success factors

Customer analysis
- Decision makers
- Problems
- Expectations/aspirations
- Characteristics

↓

Identification of customer segments

↓

Analysis of important stakeholders
- Identification
- Expectations/aspirations
- Influence/power

↓

Determination of attractive segments

Analysis of macro-environment
- Important dimensions
- Factors of influence
- Challenge

↓

Determination of success factors
- Core factors
- Success factors

To assess a firm's competitive position in a market, core and success factors have to be determined first.

Real decision makers The real decision makers – whatever position they may have inside or outside the value chain – are to be considered the "customers." Further analysis of a country market first focuses on these most important players. For example, if a pharmaceutical company, such as Swiss Novartis, plans to launch a new slimming agent, they have to determine who their customers are. A quick and superficial response would be: the consumers of the new drug. But if the agent needs to be prescribed by medical doctors and is to be sold through distributors delivering to pharmacies, the real decision maker could be one of those. Presumably doctors have a significant influence on drug consumption and in particular the brand choice of their patients, even if the consumers of the new slimming agent pay and consume it. Pharmacists may stock and, at least informally, promote the new drug. But they may also boycott it. Therefore, the marketer of pharmaceuticals needs to carefully analyze the decision processes concerning his offer, before deciding on whom to focus as the "customer." All other members of the business system are more or less important stakeholders, even if they include those who are directly served by the company.

The real decision makers in a market may be consumers, business organizations, or institutions.

Consumers Consumers' buying processes may be individual or may involve a group of persons, mostly family members or friends, depending on the product and the cultural norms of the society or group. In a study of family purchasing roles in Saudi Arabia, for example, researchers found that, in general, the husband continues to play a more dominant role in deciding what to purchase. But in Saudi Arabia, as in most nations, the roles vary by decision stages and by product category. Husbands, for example, are a more dominant influence on "how much to spend," but husbands and wives together are involved in "when to buy." Husbands exert more influence on the purchase of an automobile, while wives dominate decisions on women's clothing. International marketers should be careful, however, not to project their gender prejudices or individual cultural experiences onto other cultures. More than half of all ties purchased in Germany and Austria, for example, are bought by women and a significant amount of women's underwear is bought by men. A careful analysis of the target consumers' buying behavior seems to be advisable.

Organizational customers Organizational customers are frequently organized into multifunctional teams called "buying centers." For example, when purchasing aluminum for the production of yogurt lids, Nestlé do Brazil would use a team approach in making the purchase decision. The team includes representatives from various functional areas: production, quality management, logistics, marketing, and purchasing. Together they weigh organizational objectives and the suppliers' potential contributions to achieving those objectives against the cost of the competing products. If any one of the team members objects about a potential supplier this firm is dropped from the list.

How each individual member of the buying center acts in the purchase decision process will depend on the role he or she plays inside the group (Figure 6.5). The possible roles involved in a buying center include initiator, influencer, gatekeeper, decider, purchaser, and user. In a smaller company, the roles may be played by a single person or, at most, a few people. As the size of the organization and the price, complexity, or importance of the buying decision increase, these roles are likely to be played by different individuals.

In addition to the organizational objectives and objectives related to the role each member of the buying center plays, the personal objectives of the various members of the purchasing team are likely to affect the team's final decision. For example, the team member from production might prefer offers that have a short delivery time and fit the maintenance know-how of the firm's service crew. The procurement manager might prefer the least expensive offer because bonuses are dependent on capital spent, and a member of top management might focus on references provided by the competing suppliers. There might also be a power struggle between some members of the group, based on personalities.

When serving globally active organizational customers, the problem of multiple roles and objectives may be complicated still further. In addition to having potentially different personal and corporate objectives, role players may come from different cultures or be located in different companies belonging to the firm. A marketer selling to Procter & Gamble's European headquarters, based in Geneva, Switzerland, may face a buying center whose members are American, French, Irish, and Taiwanese. Although the negotiations would be conducted in English, the cultural background of each member and specific career experiences in different parts of the firm would result in a complex matrix of roles, objectives, and cultures that is very difficult for the international marketer to handle.

Customer problems, expectations, and aspirations

When the drivers of a market are determined and their purchase decision-making processes are researched, in the next step, needs and expectations of buying decision makers and important decision influencers that are relevant to the business of the company have to be assessed. At this point the marketer should bear in mind that potential customers can only identify expectations related to objects they know about. Innovative solutions to customer problems are rarely found from customer needs they describe themselves. Therefore, the analysis should focus on:

- (potential) problems the customers need to be solved
- customer aspirations concerning potential problem solutions.

For example, because of the rising environmental and personal health concerns of their customers, hairdressers in Denmark may need hair styling products with reduced negative impact on the environment and the condition of hair. They will only accept a new problem solution offered by French L'Oréal, however, if L'Oréal offers to inform their customers about the improved features of the new product through adequate market communication and if the margin they can earn stays roughly the same. Toolbox 6.1 describes a technique that may help the marketer in researching customer aspirations.

FIGURE 6.5 *Business customer buying centers*

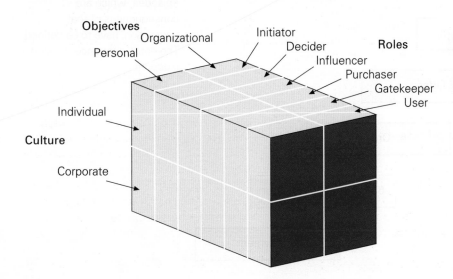

The multi-person, multifunctional purchasing situation that international business-to-business marketers face is characterized by the different objectives and roles that are involved as well as by the potentially different individual, cultural, corporate, and national culture backgrounds of the buying center's members.

TOOLBOX 6.1   Sequence-oriented problem identification

Sequence-oriented problem identification includes, first, "blueprinting" the sequence of steps that make up an exchange process from its preparation to its consequences seen from an exchange partner's perspective. Second, exchange partners are asked to provide accounts of critical incidents they may have experienced in each step of the exchange process.

Blueprinting is a term borrowed from movie production where a story to be told is split up into a series of scenes that can be filmed apart from each other. In a similar manner, blueprinting an exchange process means defining a series of episodes from the first direct or indirect contact between potential exchange partners to an intended transaction and following episodes that are consequences of that transaction (see Figure 6.6). Such a blueprint may be established through in-depth interviews with stakeholders reporting their view of "typical" exchange processes of the interesting kind. Blueprints may also be drawn by people inside the company having extended experience with the kind of exchange process under investigation.

With the help of a blueprint, a sample of (potential) stakeholders is guided through the entire exchange process in face-to-face, personal interviews. Respondents are requested to give an account of their experiences during the various episodes in individual exchange processes. Emphasis is placed on any particularly negative or positive incidents related to these episodes. The oral reports of interviewees are recorded, transcribed, and content analyzed. The evaluation of the recorded incident reports results in the detection of process elements creating particular satisfaction or dissatisfaction among stakeholders. These elements determine the value stakeholders perceive to gain when being offered the specific kind of exchange.

Source: Adapted from Botschen, G., L. Bestieler and A.G. Woodside (1996) "Sequence-oriented problem identification within service encounters", *Journal of Euromarketing*, 5(2), 19–52

FIGURE 6.6   *Example of a blueprint*

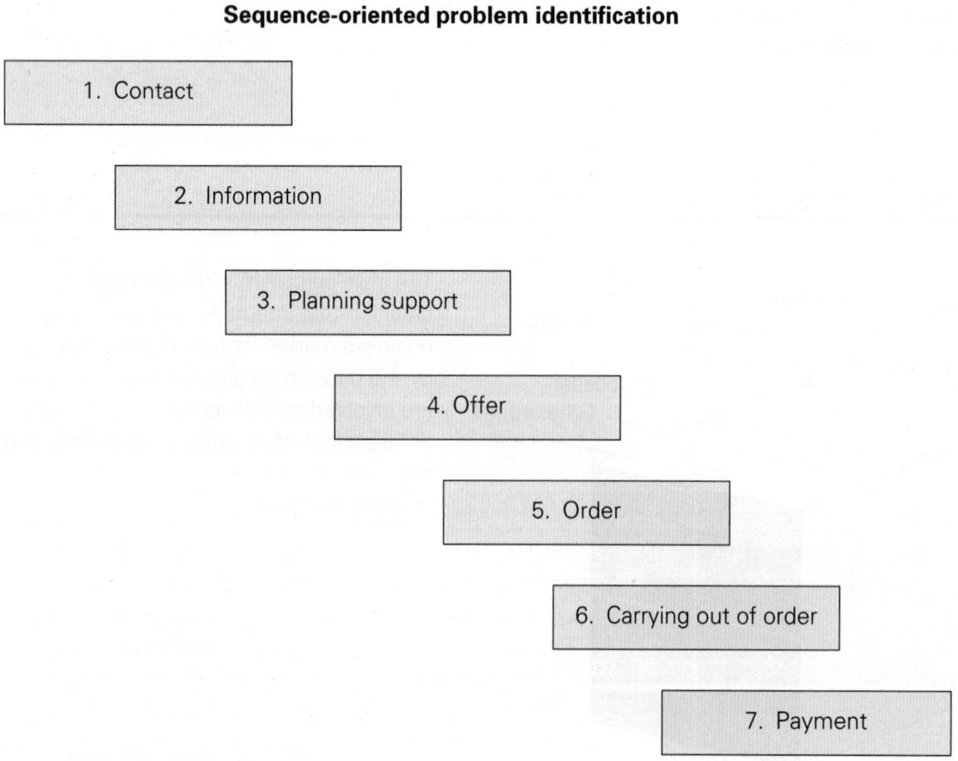

Sequence-oriented problem identification

1. Contact
2. Information
3. Planning support
4. Offer
5. Order
6. Carrying out of order
7. Payment

For the purpose of sequence-oriented problem identification a series of episodes from the first direct or indirect contact between potential exchange partners to an intended transaction and following episodes, which are consequences of that transaction, have to be defined. The entire sequence is called a blueprint.

Customer characteristics

The diversity of customer expectation and aspiration makes most international marketers group their potential customers in a country market into more homogeneous segments. Marketers may choose to segment their customers either by the benefits they are seeking or the characteristics that are relevant to the customers' market behavior.

For example, characteristics such as location in cities versus in villages, the occupational structure of their clients, the turnover of the shop, or the competitive differentiation of the firm (traditional vs highly fashionable, cheap vs sophisticated) can be relevant to the behavior of hairdressers. Because benefit segmentation of customers demands more sophisticated primary research techniques to gather the data (for an example see Toolbox 6.2) and, in addition, may result in segments that are difficult to reach, most marketers prefer to use customer characteristics for segmentation purposes. The choice of segmentation criteria is crucial for the homogeneity of the resulting segments in terms of similarity of expectations and aspirations, which, in turn, strongly influences the quality of marketing decision making based on those segments.

TOOLBOX 6.2   Laddering

The laddering technique is based on means–end theory that hypothesizes people doing things, such as buying a product, because that action leads to positive consequences that, in turn, positively contribute to reaching attractive values or goals. Goals are considered the ultimate source of choice criteria that drive exchange behavior.

Personal oral or pencil-and-paper interviews are conducted in which, first, features of an exchange offer that seem important to each individual respondent are determined. For that purpose, questioning techniques such as dual comparison or triadic sorting can be applied. The individually important features are the basis for the laddering interview. In its oral version, this interview starts by picking up one of the features and asking the respondent why this feature seems important to her. As Figure 6.7 shows, the interviewee may respond by mentioning another feature of the exchange offer, but she may also mention a consequence resulting from the feature. By asking the same question: "Why is this important to you?", over and over again until the respondent is no longer able or willing to give a reason, the person is "laddered" up to the goals underlying the importance of the specific feature. Then the question sequence starts again at another feature of the exchange offer found to be of importance to the respondent.

In the written version of the laddering interview respondents are asked first to note up to a maximum of five important attributes of the product under investigation in boxes aligned one above the other. Then the respondents are asked to write short statements about why they consider each of the listed attributes important into boxes next to the first column of boxes. The laddering goes on with asking why the noted reasons are important to the respondents, and so on.

The data gathered by oral or written interviews are transcribed and content analyzed. Content analysis of the interviews is based on a codebook containing a categorization scheme developed by three researchers. For the purpose of developing the codebook additional data concerning the exchange context (for example, usage, exchange situation, personal environment) may be of help in interpreting and categorizing responses. Based on the categorization scheme the researchers independently analyze the data and compare their findings. If there are differences, the researchers discuss the reason for these differences, and if needed ask another researcher for help as a kind of mediator. This process results in means–end chains for each of the respondents.

The next step is to aggregate the results across all respondents (see Figure 6.8). Traditionally, a data matrix is established in which all identified attributes, consequences, and values act as the row and column elements. The cells of the matrix contain the frequency with which a particular column element is mentioned after a particular row element, aggregated across respondents and ladders. Usually

FIGURE 6.7 *Ladder from attributes via consequences to goals*

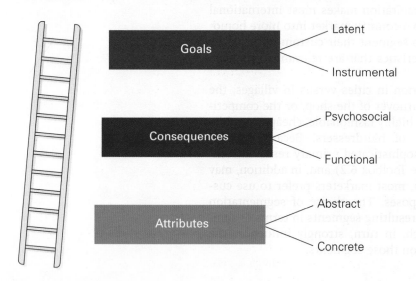

only direct linkages between elements are entered. Finally, to allow better interpretation of the results, a map is constructed depicting the most important linkages in a graphical way. This hierarchical value map not only shows the dominant contents of the exchange partners' means–end chains but also indicates the cognitive relations among various concepts and the strength of those relations.

When using this technique in an international study, the researcher may compare the hierarchical value maps between countries to find out important differences. But because customers in a country market most probably belong to different segments, the researcher may also look for similar segments, that is, customers with similar means–end chains across country markets. For example, Geiger, an Austrian manufacturer of ladies' apparel, asked their Austrian, German, and Italian customers to compare them with the products of major competitors. A comparison of findings in the three countries showed that Geiger could standardize its products, as well as distribution and pricing policy, but had to adapt its basic promotional message to the expected benefits in each country. Italians were more interested in fashionable styles, for example, than Germans, who expected enduring quality for a satisfactory price.

Source: Adapted from Botschen, G., and A. Hemetsberger (1998) "Diagnosing means–end structures to determine the degree of potential marketing-program standardization", *Journal of Business Research*, June, 42(2), pp. 151–5

Identification of customer segments

In most cases the use of a hierarchy of segmentation criteria will be appropriate. The customers of the biggest European steelmaker French Arcelor, for example, might be segmented using the industry they belong to (automotive, durable consumer goods, machinery, construction), their annual consumption of steel, the quality standards they impose, and the intensity of customer service they require, in that order. Because there is no single best way of segmenting a universe of potential customers, alternative solutions should be considered.

Segmentation will result in a number of customer groups that are not equally attractive to serve. Only the most attractive customer segments should be considered in the further steps of product market analysis. But to arrive at a meaningful determination of segment attractiveness, the most important stakeholders and competitors in each of the segments need to be identified and analyzed first.

Analysis of important stakeholders

The stakeholders of a business organization may have interests that are supportive or averse to the goals of the organization and they may have more or less power to carry them through. For example, a German engineering firm that has developed a highly effective plant for the burning of industrial toxic waste may have identified the attractive-looking segment of chemical and pharmaceutical plants in Switzerland. The attractiveness of this segment is very much diminished, however, if green activists together with the media (via public administration) have the power to keep decision makers in the segment from buying. Therefore, the attractiveness of a customer segment will be raised or diminished by the importance of such stakeholders.

To identify the most influential stakeholders, an exhaustive list of all organizations, institutions, and people participating in the business is drawn up. Then, in order to assess their power to influence the business system, a matrix such as the one used for the analysis of interrelatedness of macro-environmental dimensions (see Chapter 2) is developed. It shows the interrelationships between the members of the operating environment as well as the direction and strength of each relationship. For example, in a country such as France, unions may play a much greater role in the market for textiles than in Portugal, where their role may be more important than in Indonesia. The positions of all stakeholders – from passive to autonomous – can be defined and the most important players as well as their specific interests identified.

The identification of the most relevant competitors will be discussed later in this chapter. Their market position and competitive behavior also has a substantial influence on the attractiveness of segments.

FIGURE 6.8   *Example of a hierarchical value map*

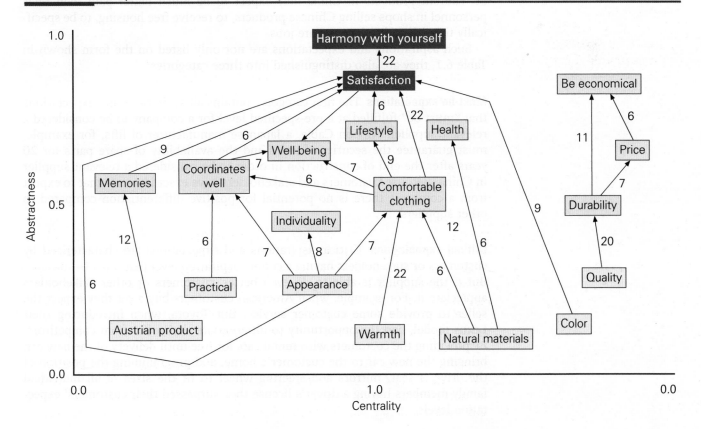

Determining the most attractive segments

For the evaluation of segments, a scoring procedure may be applied. This procedure will evaluate segment:

- substance (for example, volume and growth)
- accessibility (for example, entry barriers and intensity of competition)
- responsiveness (for example, urgency of need, innovativeness, and cultural prejudices)
- profitability (for example, attainable margins, price sensitivity, and net present value of segment investments).

Because a scoring procedure uses a broader base of information and does not rely on estimations of future streams of income, in most cases the results of such a scoring procedure are more reliable than the calculation and comparison of net present values of investments in building and maintaining successful business relationships with the customers in each segment.

Deriving core and success factors

The profile of expectations and aspirations of customers and important stakeholders varies from one attractive segment to another. Therefore, the capabilities needed to fulfill those expectations and aspirations will also vary. Table 6.1 shows a form that helps managers to go through a formal process of deriving core and success factors for each market segment.

First, managers need to list the customer group and most important stakeholders in the given market segment. They have specific aspirations and expectations concerning companies doing business in the market and the outcomes of their activities. Potential customers of Yves St. Laurent in China, for example, expect their products to be easily distinguishable from ordinary clothes, to help express wealth and success, but also to be affordable (for them) and to have a certain level of fabric quality. Additionally, employees in shops selling Yves St. Laurent products in China may expect to be much better paid than sales personnel in shops selling Chinese products, to receive free housing, to be specifically trained, and to have secure jobs.

Such aspirations and expectations are not only listed on the form shown in Table 6.1, they are also distinguished into three categories:

Must-be expectations The first category contains all aspirations and expectations that "must be" fulfilled at a pre-specified level for a company to be considered a relevant supplier. Nippon Cable, a Japanese manufacturer of lifts, for example, must guarantee the security of users and the availability of spare parts for 20 years after the end of construction in order to be considered a relevant supplier in China. Because customers and stakeholders have exact ideas of what to expect from a company, there is no potential for positive differentiation compared to other suppliers.

Critical expectations Critical aspirations and expectations are characterized by customers or stakeholders having a certain aspiration level that must be fulfilled. But if the supplier is able to do even better, customers or other stakeholders appreciate it. For example, when American customers buy a car they expect the seller to provide some customer service. But Toyota, when introducing their Lexus model, had the opportunity to differentiate their offer from competitors. By providing the customers with rental cars for free until delivery of the new car, bringing the new car to the customer's home, and programming the position of the driver's seat, mirrors and steering wheel to fit the sizes of all individual family members having a driver's license they surpassed their customers' expectation levels.

May-be expectations Potential customers and important stakeholders may not be consciously aware of "may-be" expectations. They have the related needs or interests, but they do not know about the potential solution. Such a situation occurs when a company plans to market a product or service that is an innovation to the customers or contains innovative features. The fulfillment of may-be expectations may not have any impact on customer satisfaction but it may also lead to customer excitement.

Having split the aspirations and expectations of customers and other important stakeholders into the three categories, the marketer may also want to attribute an importance weight (seen from the stakeholder perspective) to each. Higher weights would point to greater importance for the firm to possess the capabilities needed to satisfy the respective expectations.

TABLE 6.1 *Determination of core and success factors in a market segment*

Depending on the level of pre-specification, the aspirations and expectations of customers and other important stakeholders in a market segment fall into three categories: Must-be, critical, and may-be. Importance weights seen from the customer and stakeholder perspective can be given. Capabilities a company needs to fulfill expectations belonging to the "must-be" category, as well as to prevent challenges from the macro-environment from becoming a threat, are core factors. Capabilities needed to fulfill expectations belonging to the "critical" and "may-be" categories as well as capabilities needed to turn challenges from the macro-environment into opportunities are success factors.

Stakeholders	Aspirations and expectations			Importance weight	Needed capabilities and resources	
	Must-be	Critical	May-be		Core factors	Success factors
Customers	ISO 9001			5	Certificate	
		Simultaneous engineering		4		Team of technicians know-how Online connections
	Just-in-time delivery			5	Production planning and control system	
		Flexible reaction to change in production needs		5		Warehouse at customer production site
			Amount and kind of products in stock	2		System of transportation Stock management system Relative cost position
		Personal treatment		3		Commitment of personnel to customers
	Pre-specified quality			5	R&D capabilities Quality assurance system	
Consultants		Latest level of information		4		Relationships with consultants
Public administration	Adherence to pollution regulations			5	Quality assurance system R&D capabilities	

In the next step the capabilities a company needs to fulfill the listed aspirations and expectations are derived.

Core factors Capabilities needed to satisfy expectations belonging to the "must-be" category are classified as "core factors." The company must have them to be considered a relevant supplier. Magna International, the Canada-based supplier of automotive parts and systems, for example, must have a production planning and control system as well as a distribution logistics system that allows exact delivery to their clients in the automotive industry. The state of each control panel, for example, in the process from its order to the end of production and its position in the logistics chain to the customer must be traceable.

The list of core factors in a market is completed by the capabilities the firm needs to prevent current and potential challenges from important dimensions of the macro-environment from becoming a threat. For example, if the political and economic situation in a country is not entirely stable, as in some Latin American countries, the company will need specific capabilities, such as establishing informal relationships with influential people as well as hiring and integrating local management, to stay in business over time.

Success factors Capabilities needed to satisfy aspirations and expectations from the "critical" and "may-be" categories are success factors. They allow the company to be attractive to the stakeholders in the market and to differentiate itself from major competitors. For example, to provide their Lexus customers in the U.S. with the extended services just described, Toyota needed to have a fleet of cars to rent (for free) to the customers for some time, to have a car seat supplier with the electronic and technical know-how to produce programmable seats, and to hire well-trained, highly motivated personnel in sufficient numbers to ensure home delivery of the new cars.

Additional success factors are capabilities the firm needs to turn current as well as potential future challenges from important dimensions of a market's macro-environment into opportunities. If the population of a country is increasing significantly, as for example in India, and the per capita income is steadily growing, a success factor for a consumer products manufacturer such as Wilkinson, the U.K. globally established shaving products firm, might be to have a distribution system which tightly covers all urban areas where young and educated people live. For producers of telecommunications equipment, such as Sweden's Ericsson, the development of technical standards is of great importance. For them a success factor in a market such as India might be their ability to influence norm-setting bodies.

Competitor analysis

To assess their firm's potential for success in the most attractive segments of highly attractive country markets, management first has to determine if the company possesses the needed core factors. If those basic capabilities exist, the company's relative strengths and weaknesses can be determined. That is, to what extent the company possesses the success factors compared to its major competitors. For practical purposes, the assessment starts with competitor analysis to avoid too much of a biased perspective toward factors where the company has its strengths.

To be able to complete a strategically useful competitor analysis, the marketer first has to determine the structure of its competitive environment, that is, the relevant competitors and their membership in strategic groups, as well as barriers to market exit (Figure 6.9).

Structure of the competitive environment

Relevant competitors

In order to analyze competition, the marketer has first to decide on the definition of a relevant competitor. Competitors may vary depending on whether the product market is considered to exist globally, regionally, or locally. Marketers in the same industry may define their markets differently. For example, the owner of a private hotel called Zum Bären in Bern, Switzerland, may consider his market being restricted to business travelers from Switzerland while the management of Ritz-Carlton hotels defines its market as travelers from all over the world.

The most important competitors will be firms that supply similar goods. Besides existing competitors, there may be a threat of upcoming competitors. Important firms which have not served the market so far might consider doing so in the future. The marketer must therefore have a closer look at potential candidates and existing barriers to entry.

But relevant competitors may include not only domestic or international suppliers of similar goods. Marketers of substitute goods, that is, any organization supplying products or services that satisfy the same customer need, must be considered as potential competitors. From this broader perspective, for example, Red Bull, the energy drink made in Austria not only competes against other energizing drinks but may also compete against Diesel shirts.

New competitors may arise from the development of a new technology. A marketer of fuel, such as Shell, might see important competitors emerge when the production of electrical energy through photovoltaic is developed to be highly efficient. It may feel the need to follow the development of this technology closely and to consider companies working in that field as potential important competitors. In the case of Shell, the company has entered the new technology themselves. The company's photovoltaic systems have been successfully marketed in many parts of the world, including Africa, China, India, and South America.

FIGURE 6.9 *Determination of a firm's relative competitive position*

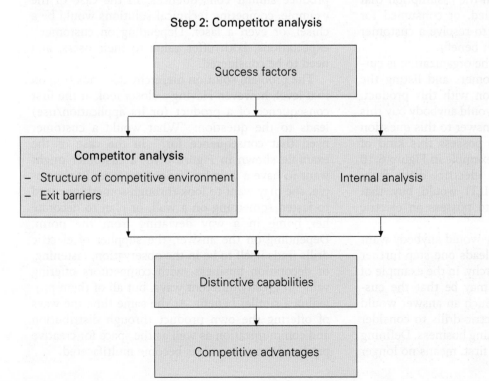

Step 2: Competitor analysis

Success factors

Competitor analysis
- Structure of competitive environment
- Exit barriers

Internal analysis

Distinctive capabilities

Competitive advantages

Competitor analysis starts with an assessment of the competitive environment in attractive segments of specific country markets and existing barriers to market exit.

But competitors might also emerge from a change in customer behavior. If an increasing number of people tend to avoid heating their homes during the cold time of the year by spending extended vacations in warmer regions of the world, Shell will be confronted with major competitors from the vacation services industry. Therefore, the determination of major competitors is not only a task that demands thorough analysis of the industry to which the firm belongs, but also a screening of the environment in search of potential substitute problem solutions that might become a threat to the firm. Toolbox 6.3 describes a simple tool that may be helpful in that respect.

Strategic groups

Not all suppliers of similar products or services in a market are automatically potential competitors of an organization. Strategic groups with differing relevance to its competitive position may exist. **Strategic groups** may be defined either in terms of the behavior or of cognitions of their members. That is, a strategic group either consists of a group of organizations serving a given market by following a similar core strategy, or of a group of organizations in which the dominant decision makers have similar mental models of the market environment.

Similar core strategies The similarity of core strategies is observable by scope, that is, what the organizations do (based on what capabilities) in terms of their business domain, the served market segments, their differentiation, and geographic extension, and by resource deployment, that is, how they do it.

TOOLBOX 6.3   Problem solution hierarchy

Developing a problem solution hierarchy may help to open up the view of managers from a narrow product-oriented to a broader value-oriented perspective. The tool is based on the assumption that products are not used, applied, or consumed for their own sake, but in order to resolve a customer problem or to gain a customer benefit.

Starting with the product the organization is currently providing to the customers and listing the products in direct competition with this product, the question is asked: "Why would anybody buy this product?" The most simple answer to this question is that the person wants to possess this kind of product. Accordingly, as the example in Figure 6.10 shows, customers of an electric drill from Black&Decker, Bosch, or HILTI would buy that product because they want to possess an electric drill.

Asking the question: "Why would anybody want to possess such a product?" leads one step further in the problem solution hierarchy. In the example of the HILTI drill, the answer may be that the customer needs to drill a hole. Such an answer would lead the manufacturer of electric drills to consider itself as being in the hole-making business. Defining the business as hole making, first, means no longer

thinking in terms of products but of their consequences; and, second, opens up the perspective of competitors offering other technical solutions that produce similar consequences. In the case of the example, competing technical solutions would be a chisel, or even a laser. Depending on customers' expectations, both offer value to their users, and need to be considered.

The problem solution hierarchy does not stop on that level, however. Having a closer look at the first consequence of a product (or its application/use) leads to the question: "What would a customer need that consequence for?" In the case of the example shown in Figure 6.10, a customer might want to have a hole for various reasons: For example, she may want to look through something, need to fasten something on a wall, or plan to decorate her home in a way deviating from the norm. Depending on the answer, the supplier of electric drills finds itself to be in the observation, fastening, or decoration business, with competitors offering value in greatly different ways, but all of them providing a similar benefit. At the same time the ways of offering the own product through distribution and communication as well as the space for creative product innovation ideas become multifaceted.

In the German car market, for example, Mercedes, BMW, and Audi tend to base their competitive strategies on high quality combined with differentiation. They form one strategic group compared to the carmakers from South Korea, Kia, Hyundai, and Daewoo, which form another strategic group relying mainly on cost/price leadership. The first group defends its position through intensive R&D, technological pioneering, and exclusive image, whereas the second group optimizes its cost position through high production volumes, rationalization, low wages, and lean management.

Similar mental models Senior executives of companies that present similar products or benefits to the stakeholders in a particular market to a varying extent share views about the boundaries of the market, that is the competitive domain. In addition, they more or less agree concerning the legitimate competitive process inside that domain. For example, some top executives in the air travel industry implicitly agree that their market is global, low cost is essential for price competition to fill air plane capacities, and growth by acquisition and strategic alliances is the way to attractive profitability. Some others believe that there are regional markets in which superior service, punctuality, and attractive connecting flights with major carriers allow them to demand significantly higher prices. These mental models of senior executives about the relevant market environment strongly influence their strategic decisions and the behavior of their firms through the way of implementing those decisions. In turn, company performance resulting from that behavior strongly influences the executives' mental models. In the air travel example, both mental models may lead to business success and may, therefore, be continually reinforced.

The similarity of mental models of key decision makers may be measured by analyzing their cognitive maps. For example, content analysis of company publications, such as presidents' letters to shareholders published in annual reports, interviews in trade magazines, or home pages on the internet may provide the data for analysis.

FIGURE 6.10 *Example of a problem solution hierarchy*

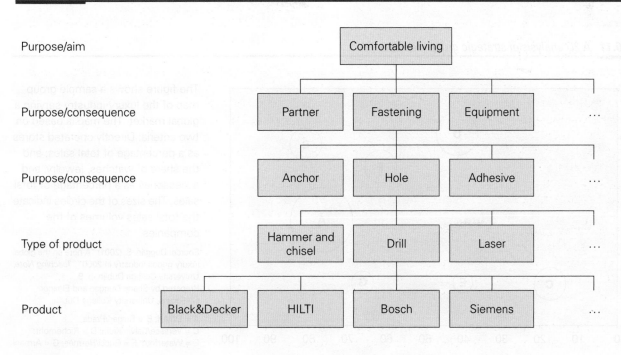

Criteria driving competition Detecting cognitive maps may turn out to be a heavy task. The determination of strategic groups from a behavioral or a cognitive perspective tends to produce similar results because mental models, strategic decision making, resource allocation, and organizational performance influence each other. Therefore, managers tend to define strategic groups in terms of criteria driving competition in the analyzed market. The criteria will depend on the business domain. However, it is important that they are strategically decisive and represent mobility barriers for the members of any strategic group, that is, they do not allow an easy and fast switch from one group to another. Such criteria may be, for example:

- central benefit offered by the supplier
- market segments the company is focusing on
- extent of integration of various steps in the value chain
- intensity of cooperation with partners
- expenditures in R&D
- level of integration of the distribution system.

Competitors are described by the selected criteria. The descriptions are used as data for defining the strategic groups. There are basically two ways of forming the groups:

- a graphic analysis using two essential criteria
- cluster construction through cluster analysis or factor analysis based on a larger number of criteria.

Figure 6.11 shows an example for a 2D graphical analysis.

Competitive structure

Having determined the current strategic groups in the markets under consideration, management can focus their further analysis on the groups that seem most relevant for assessing the relative competitive position of the own organization. Because the boundaries of strategic groups may not be as clear cut, and the core

---

FIGURE 6.11 *A 2D analysis of strategic group membership*

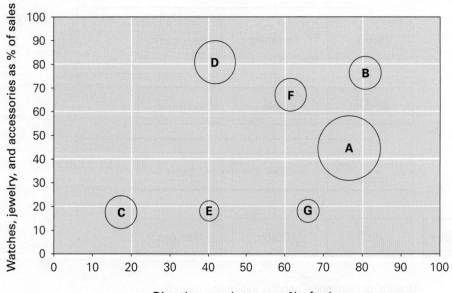

The figure shows a sample group map of the luxury industry serving a global market. The map is based on two criteria: Directly operated stores as a percentage of total sales, and the share of watches, jewelry, and accessories as a percentage of total sales. The sizes of the circles indicate the total sales volumes of the companies.

Source: Duggan, S. (2001) "A note on the global luxury goods industry in 2000", *Teaching Note*, University College Dublin, p. 9
Prepared by Shane Duggan and Eleanor O'Higgins, University College Dublin

A = LVMH; B = Bulgari/Prada;
C = Versace/Calvin Klein; D = Richemont;
E = Waterford; F = Gucci/Hermès; G = Armani

strategy of the organization not as fixed by available capabilities as theoretical concepts are asking for, it may be necessary to look at more than one strategic group per market.

To determine the most important competitors in those strategic groups their competitive structure will be analyzed. The **competitive structure** of a strategic group may be defined in terms of *the number of its members.* The number of competitors management considers belonging to a strategic group may be less reliable than the number of (potential) suppliers customers consider relevant. To check for potential differences in perception, management may analyze the customers' consideration sets for the specific good or the benefit to be provided, that is, they may try to find out the top ranked suppliers in the minds of potential customers (see Figure 6.12).

The *size* of the most important competitors can be estimated from such data as the number of employees or the annual sales volume. These figures should be evaluated carefully, because they are influenced by the nature of the product or service and the production technology used. The number of people working for a shoe manufacturer in Brazil, for example, may be similar to the number working for a competitor in Italy. But this does not mean that the companies are the same size, because the two firms may employ different production technologies. In many cases, therefore, it will be necessary to estimate competitors' production capacities.

Members of a strategic group are not totally uniform. Despite their similar strategic orientation they try to establish individually different positions in the minds of (potential) stakeholders. Thus, management may be interested in what **position** the members of the relevant strategic group effectively have achieved. Among others, multidimensional scaling, correspondence analysis, and policy capturing as described in Toolbox 6.4 are potential tools to be used for that purpose.

The **market shares** of competing firms are a measure of their competitive strength (in the past). They indicate what portion of total sales volume or share of voice (for non-profit organizations) in the market has been captured by each competitor. They may also be viewed as indicators of competitors' strategies. A large market share points toward cost leadership in profit-oriented markets, whereas smaller shares may be a result of niche strategies, that is the

FIGURE 6.12 *Consideration sets*

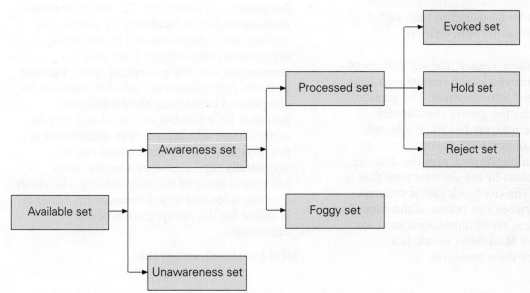

Customers are not aware of all available suppliers of a specific benefit. They only have stored information concerning some of the suppliers they are aware of. Only a small number of those suppliers are considered attractive enough to be selected in a buying situation. These companies belong to the evoked set of the customers. They are the most important competitors.

Members of a strategic group are supposed to have a certain position in the perceptual space of actual and potential stakeholders. This perceptual space is, in general, multidimensional. That is, stakeholders make up their minds about (potential) suppliers or their offers along various assessment criteria that are related to each other and may interact.

There are a number of methods to determine the position of competing members of a strategic group in the perceptual space of stakeholders. These methods can only be applied to companies, or their offers, that stakeholders know of. This knowledge is either based on direct experience or has developed indirectly through media or personal communication or through observation. The available methods use data on the perceived potential of suppliers or their offers to fulfill stakeholder expectations or data on their perceived similarity. In the following the basic approaches of multidimensional scaling, correspondence analysis, and policy capturing will be outlined.

Multidimensional scaling

In multidimensional scaling (MDS), stakeholders are asked to indicate their perception of similarity or dissimilarity of the members of a strategic group or their offers. The obtained similarity data can be used to determine the configuration of the competitors in the perceptual space of the stakeholders. The method follows a certain sequence of steps:

1   *Measuring similarity perceptions.* Similarity measurement is based on the assumption that stakeholders compare (potential) suppliers according to implicit dimensions, which are to be detected without asking directly. Similarity perceptions can be measured by rank ordering or by rating, until a full rank order is established.

2   *Selection of a distance measure.* The similarities of competitors perceived by the respondents have to be transformed into distances. The greater the dissimilarities the greater the distance. Thus, a distance measure has to be selected from a number of potential choices.

   The Euclidian metric measures the distance between two points by the shortest way, that is a straight line. The city-block metric measures the distance between two points as the sum of absolute distances on all dimensions used for comparison. The Minkowski metric is a generalization of these measures.

3   *Determination of the graphical configuration.* In a space of minimum dimensionality, MDS tries to find a configuration of points that represents the dissimilarity of competitors as closely as possible. That is, the rank order of distances among the competitors in the space should reflect their rank order of dissimilarities.

4   *Determining the number of dimensions.* The number of dimensions used for the graphical configuration should represent the number of dimensions used by stakeholders in the comparison of competitors. In most cases researchers may have some hypothesis of how many dimensions stakeholders use in making comparisons, but they do not really know.

   Some criteria to resolve that problem are the measures of stress and of data compression, as well as the ease of interpretation of the outcome. The stress criterion indicates how badly a configuration fulfills the condition of reproducing the original rank order. The improvement of stress by adding another dimension is exponentially decreasing. If the achieved increase in stress becomes marginal, the researcher should refrain from adding another dimension.

   Data compression, indicated by the data compression coefficient Q, improves with a decreasing number of dimensions used for the graphical description of distances among a certain number of competitors to compare. Coefficient Q should be greater than or equal to 2.

5   *Interpretation of dimensions.* The interpretation of dimensions can be facilitated by statistically rotating the dimensions and by projecting expectations respondents have used for comparison into the perceptual space. For that purpose, respondents are asked to evaluate the competitors concerning their fulfillment potential for a number of critical and may-be expectations, which have been determined in a previous study. Each expectation can be statistically represented as a vector in the perceptual space of the respondents. The closer a vector is located to a dimension the better it is suited for the interpretation of the dimension.

MDS has the advantage that:

- researchers do not need to know the relevant evaluation criteria of stakeholders beforehand
- the assumption that evaluations are made on a metric level of data is avoided
- results are not influenced by the selection of evaluation criteria and their verbalization.

Disadvantages to be considered are:

- the large number of competitors to be compared in order to derive meaningful results (for a 2D configuration to be meaningful an input of comparison data concerning at least nine competitors are needed)
- extent of data to be gathered
- difficulty of interpreting the meaning of the dimensions of the perceptual space.

One particular problem may be the assumption that stakeholders compare all competitors along the same criteria. Part of successful competition is to try to impose exactly the contrary. But uniqueness of values offered to the stakeholders would mean that there is no common perceptual space.

Correspondence analysis

Like MDS, correspondence analysis also depicts the objects to be compared as points in a space, and their graphical distance is a measure of closeness in the perception of respondents. In contrast to MDS, however, the number of competitors to be compared has no lower limit. Competitors or their offers are not directly compared with each other. Each of the competing organizations is evaluated individually concerning their potential for fulfilling a list of expectations, determined in a preceding study. There is also no limit to the measurement level of data. That is, nominal data can be used as input to correspondence analysis.

The graphical results produced by correspondence analysis not only provide the positions of the competing organizations in the perceptual space of respondents, they also depict the position of the fulfillment levels of each expectation in the same space. Therefore, interpretation of results is much easier than with MDS (see Figure 6.13).

Data are gathered by first presenting a list of competing organizations or products to the respondents asking if they know any of them. Then respondents are asked to evaluate the potential of organizations/products they know of for fulfilling the expectations given on another list. The answers result in evaluation tables for each expectation containing the evaluations of all competing organizations/products known to the respondents.

Each cell value in the tables is transferred into a chi-square value. The chi-square values are treated in a way resembling exploratory factor analysis,

FIGURE 6.13   *Example of a perceptual space resulting from correspondence analysis*

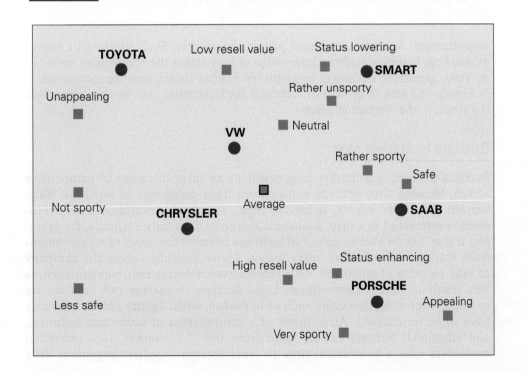

producing dimensions in relation to which competitors/brands as well as levels of expectation fulfillment are located. The more dimensions extracted from the data, the more precise the graphical representation will reproduce the data. But, at the same time, the managerial interpretation of the graphical result becomes more difficult.

The graphical analysis of the data indicates:

- what expectations are perceived as closely related to each other (those expectations have similar frequency profiles of fulfillment across competitors)
- what competitors are perceived as belonging to the same group
- what groups of competitors are characterized by which bundles of expectation fulfillment.

The number of dimensions to be used for the graphical representation of relationships in the data depends on the percentage of total variance explained by each of the dimensions and their chi-square values. The number of dimensions finally used should allow explanation of a minimum of 80% of total variance.

A major weakness of correspondence analysis compared to multidimensional scaling is that its results can only be reliable to the extent that the list of expectations presented to the respondents contains all relevant expectations and their respective levels.

Policy capturing

Policy capturing starts from the assumption that individuals when making a decision, are governed by an underlying judgment "policy," that is, a cognitive model, which allows them to integrate the various pertinent items of information into a single judgment. The method's objective is to uncover that cognitive model.

The first step of the procedure involves personal interviews with customers. They are asked to think of their purchasing objectives and then to identify as many supplier criteria as they can that might in any way reflect effectiveness or ineffectiveness in achieving the objectives. The purpose of this step is to generate a fairly exhaustive list of all potential assessment criteria that might be used by any purchasing decision maker to evaluate potential suppliers and their offers.

The next step involves the isolation of those criteria that are actually used by purchasing decision makers in their assessment of suppliers and their offers, and the relative weightings of those criteria. This can be accomplished by having respondents make evaluations regarding various potential suppliers. With the ratings of those suppliers as dependent variables and the measures of the assessment criteria as the independent variables, multiple (stepwise) regression can be used to determine which criteria have been used in the ratings, as well as the weighting factors of those criteria.

organizations' focus on a selected part of the market. Such conclusions can be misleading, however, without knowledge of how stable the competitive situation is. Thus, growth or decline in competitors' market shares must be monitored.

Finally, the rate of growth or technical sophistication may be used to analyze the *structure of a competitive group*.

Barriers to market exit

Barriers to leaving a market may result in an intensification of competitive action, because they prevent competitors from going out of business. Such barriers can be economic, technical, legal, social, or emotional. If a government is interested in a firm, a national airline such as Italy's Alitalia, for example, it may not be able to go out of business because the country's government finds ways to subsidize its heavy losses. Those subsidies allow the company to stay in price competition with foreign competitors. Exit barriers such as this result in biased competition. Legal barriers to market exit may be, for example, high litigation costs such as in France, when agency agreements may have to be terminated. An example of a combination of economic, technical, and emotional barriers can be cited from the U.S. market. U.S. industrial customers take a substantial time to trust foreign suppliers regarding their willingness to stay in the market and to ensure spare parts delivery. But when a foreign company's products are accepted, the company must be aware that it will be extremely hard for them to find a comeback to the market once they have left it. In the evaluation of potential markets, therefore, an international marketer must include such barriers.

Determination of distinctive capabilities

Having determined the structure of the competitive environment the marketer must gather information concerning the strengths and weaknesses of the most important competitors relative to the success factors in the various market segments. When competitor analysis is completed, the next step is to add data from internal analysis to allow a comparison of the extent to which the firm and its competitors possess the success factors needed in an attractive market segment.

The information for competitor as well as internal analyses may be found in corporate policy and the core strategy. It may concern management systems and operations (Figure 6.14).

Assessment of corporate policy

Corporate mission

The corporate mission defines the business domain. It limits the market considered as relevant, restricting the number of potential customers and

FIGURE 6.14 *Determination of a firm's competitive position*

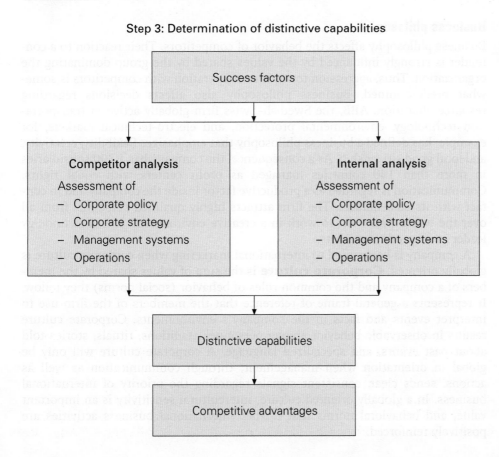

Having analyzed the structure of the competitive environment the marketer can assess the capabilities of the major competitors related to the success factors in the most attractive market segments. Comparing them to the firm's capabilities allows the determination of distinctive capabilities.

(seemingly) relevant competitors. For example, if a competitor defines its product market as sweatbands for European women who ski, the size of the market is different than if it is defined as sweatbands for European women involved in sports in general. Depending on this definition, the competitor will either not respond to the market entry of a new company with sweatbands for summer sports or take action to limit the success of the new entrant.

The major goals and priorities stated in the corporate mission influence the competitive strategy of a competitor as well as its organizational structure and its information, planning, and leadership systems. A competitor striving to become a global player will tend to have a more complex organization than a local competitor, whereas competitors with a locally focused mission will defend their market niche more fervently than global competitors with many other markets to which they allocate their limited resources.

Internally, top management's ability and willingness to lead the company in its international marketing effort is the most important factor determining the potential for success. Companies have much higher proportions of non-domestic sales when their top managers have a global perspective. These companies are even more successful than competitors that enjoy advantages in such areas as products, distribution systems, and capital. If they are to have a global perspective, top managers should have experience with more than one culture. Such experience may come from family socialization, education, business experience, or intercultural training.

For the company to be internationally competitive, top management must be committed to providing the necessary resources throughout the organization. For example, it must establish support facilities at headquarters such as a customer, intermediary, and supplier databank or a small staff for the analysis of potential acquisitions. Additional travel budgets are needed. And because it may take longer internationally than in the home market to achieve financial success, top management must take a long-range view of financial matters.

Business philosophy

Business philosophy affects the behavior of competitors. Their reaction to a contender is strongly influenced by the values shared by the group dominating the organization. Thus, aggression towards or cooperation with competitors is somewhat predetermined. Business philosophy also affects decisions regarding resource allocation. ABB, the Swedish–Swiss firm globally active in transportation technology, environmental protection, and electro-technical markets, for example, has defined a business philosophy that emphasizes flexibility, creativity, and local good citizenship. As a consequence, the company has 1,300 subsidiaries in more than 140 countries managed as profit centers with equal rights. Communication is regarded as a productive factor inside the company and in contact with its stakeholders. The firm attracts highly qualified personnel from all over the world who want to work in a creative environment. It is a technology leader in its product markets.

A company is best suited to international marketing when corporate culture is globally oriented. **Corporate culture** is the sum of values shared by the members of a company and the common rules of behavior (social norms) they follow. It represents a general frame of reference that the members of the firm use to interpret events and facts in the company's environments. Corporate culture results in observable behavior among personnel, traditions, rituals, stories told about past events, and specialized language. A corporate culture will only be global in orientation when management, through communication as well as actions, sends clear, consistent signals regarding the priority of international business. In a globally oriented culture, intercultural sensitivity is an important value, and behavioral norms that further international business activities are positively reinforced.

Diversification

The degree of **diversif**
petitor is serving, will
ing the market. Divers
Samsung or Daewoo, v
to cars and consumer e
businesses. They are a
competitor even when
specialized competitor:

Internationalization

Each competitor is cha
internationally active
entering their "home"
market. Such "cross-s
biggest Italian produce
share in the French ar
Thyssen-Krupp) and F
saturating the Italian r

Local competitors r
strong personal ties ir
tionships. The Spanisl
It has a high local ma
relationships. But bec:
tinations, Iberia has to
and providing superio

If a competitor spre
markets, it will suffer
and be easily attacked
why Allied Domecq a
Pedro Domecq and ha
decided to reshape th
the U.K.-based firm v
on such well-known
Baskin-Robbins, and

If a competitor's re
country markets, "**ov**
on the one hand, doe
on the other hand, wi
in the served market
entrant may expect ir

In many companie
Sometimes it is basec
duct lines during rec
first served" or even
Since an internation
than a domestic firn
Heuristics allow mar
riences, and, in a s
extremely short tim
understood or not re
is sharply diminishe
ences obtained in ar
if the manager igno
quality of the decisic

Assessment of core strategy

A **core strategy** broadly defines the direction in which an organization wants to develop and outlines how this development is to be achieved. For example, a competitor such as Korea's Samsung may have decided to become the most well-respected market leader in consumer electronics. Other competitors have decided to be specialists in one or more market niches, such as Gucci, the Italian marketer of fashionable women accessories. Others strive to be technological leaders, such as Fuchs, a small German engineering firm in the field of electrical arc furnaces for steel production, or are content with being a "me-too" follower, such as Ali Corporation, the PC producer from Taiwan.

In analyzing the core strategy of competitors as well as of the own company, management must check:

- length of integrated value chain
- configuration of business activities
- degree of diversification
- spread of international activities
- competitive behavior.

They are the result of available capabilities and how resources have been allocated in the company so far.

Value chain

An important point of interest is the length of the value chain covered by a competitor, that is, how much of the entire production and marketing process from the procurement of raw materials to after-sales customer service is handled by the competitor. For example, when Mercedes, based in Stuttgart, Germany, started developing the Swatch car together with the Swiss Swatch company, they decided not to produce it themselves. Mercedes planned to concentrate on the development, Swatch on the design and marketing of the car. In the meantime Mercedes, now Daimler-Chrysler, has taken over marketing the car, but production in a plant located in France is still delegated to other companies such as the European branch of Canada's Magna International.

Conventional wisdom is that competitors covering a shorter part of the value chain can develop an enhanced innovation potential from focusing on their specialties. They need fewer assets and profit from a smaller and more stable number of personnel, which is not only easier to manage but also represents a lower amount of relative fixed costs. Practical examples show, however, that some companies are most successful by integrating large parts of the value chain because it allows them to provide highly attractive customer benefits based on a closely controlled bundle of processes needed for their production.

In the internal analysis, the marketer should, therefore, analyze which sequence of processes is needed for producing its product or service in the most attractive way for customers and other important stakeholders by looking at the good in terms of a bundle of features with related effects. Management can then determine what the company is able to do better than its competitors. Figure 6.15 gives an example of how conceiving a product as a bundle of effects related to certain features can help in developing highly competitive offers. By concentrating on the **core competences**, that is, by focusing on the processes the company does best (and which provide most attractive customer and stakeholder benefits), the marketer can develop and defend a strong competitive position.

For example Selva, a Bolzano-based company (in Italy), is very successful in the high-style furniture business. When analyzing the core competences of his company related to European markets, Josef Selva found that their relative strengths resided mainly in marketing activities, that is, defining international customer segments, designing attractively styled furniture, and promoting and

Competitive behavior

Finally, the company must assess the competitive behavior of the major players in the market. Some competitors seek confrontation others are ready to cooperate where both parties can win. Microsoft, for example, attacks any competitor trying to do business in what it considers to be its market. Germany's chemical giant BASF and U.S.-based DuPont, by way of contrast, decided to cooperate in an equal share joint venture to produce and market materials for nylon manufacturing in Asia. Although they are competitors in other markets, they decided to invest in what they intended to be a long-term engagement in the Asian nylon markets.

One competitor may be highly innovative, leading technological development in the industry. Others may rely on their ability to quickly follow any innovator with an improved version of the product. A third category of competitors may acquire smaller firms that have developed interesting problem solutions. AT&T, for example, having decided to dump its phonemaking and computer businesses, bought shares of smaller firms in its move to become a global media company. To avoid civil engineering projects in wireless communication, it

FIGURE 6.15 Featu

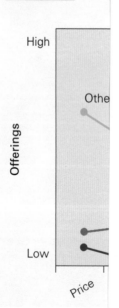

FUTURE ISSUES BOX 6.1

On your marks, get set – phone!

With Mexico's long-distance telephone market set to open fully in 1997, competitors were taking aim at Téléfonos de México (Telmex). While the company had some serious flaws, its strong market position, dominance in local phone service, and $10 billion investment to create a modern digital network made it a formidable opponent.

At stake was a fast growing telephone market. Even with Mexico's stagnant economy, local and long-distance volume was expected to grow from $6 billion to close to $9 billion by 1999. The question was how much share Telmex would lose to its new competition. The company was expected to retain a near monopoly on local service for years. Competitors seemed likely to gain substantial market share on long distance calls due to their expected low international rates.

Of Telmex's seven announced rivals, Avantel – a joint venture between U.S.-based MCI Communications and Mexico's largest bank, Banamex – was the strongest. The other main challenger, Alestra – originally a joint venture between AT&T and Mexican industrial conglomerate Alfa – got a big boost through its merger with a group that included Telefónica de España, Bancomer, Mexico's No. 2 bank and GTE.

Telmex had been slow to take its competitors seriously. The company also was having trouble living down a reputation for dismal service before privatization in 1990. But Telmex was now offering some hot new services, including internet access, a high-speed data network, and videoconferencing.

At the end of 2002 nearly 6 years after it was first exposed to competition, Téléfonos de México looked like soon finding itself all but alone in the marketplace again. The company had an iron grip on more than 70% of the domestic long-distance market and almost all of the local market. Telmex and its mobile phone daughter, America Movil, accounted for 82% of total sales by fixed-line and mobile operators in Mexico. Their closest rival in terms of sales, Iusacell, reaped just 3.7%. Alestra held roughly 9% of the long-distance market and slightly more in data services, and, in addition, was in a severe financial crisis. WorldCom wanted to sell its stake in Avantel to raise money – with no success.

Telmex said it did not want to be left alone. "Having competition helped us become a better company and helped consumers," said Mr. Arturo Elias, the company's spokesman. Some industry analysts agreed, betting that Alestra, Avantel and Iusacell will all ultimately succeed. But will their wishes come true?

Source: Malkin, E. (1996) "On your marks, get set – phone!", *Business Week*, 6 May, p. 54; Torres, C. (1996) "New phone rules in Mexico to allow strong competition", *The Wall Street Journal*, 29 April, p. A18; Luhnow, D. (2002) "Telmex's long, strange trip – facing rivals, firm is unfazed: can Mexican upstarts compete?", *Wall Street Journal*, 26 November, p. A.22

bought McCaw Cellular. Its acquisition of DirecTv helped avoid having to launch their own satellites.

Assessment of management systems

Management systems are the infrastructure of a company's operations needed to coordinate its function effectively and efficiently. With internationalization increasing, a company's management systems have to be able to cope with greater complexity of (new) environments and market interrelatedness. Managers must determine how well the current management systems of their competitors as well as their own organization fit international business realities:

- Will they be able to cope with new environments?
- What changes may occur without much managerial influence?
- What changes will have to be strategically managed?

An information system, for example, may need to contain online connections with all the warehouses and retail outlets to allow simultaneous stock management of products around the globe, thereby reducing the danger of stockouts in one place and shelf warmers in another. For example, the Italian clothing manufacturer Benetton can tell at any time what products are in stock in its warehouses (and have been sold) by model and size. There are plans to incorporate radio frequency identification chips into the clothes during manufacturing that are imperceptible to the consumers. Entire boxes containing clothes of varying styles, colors, and sizes can be scanned, and the information uploaded to Benetton's inventory tracking system. This information not only helps production planning, but also allows shipments between warehouses when different customer preferences lead to shortages in one area of the world, compared to an overstock in another. Because more than 90% of their sales come from franchise operations, however, the electronic tracking of global retail sales is less easy.

Organization

A firm's organization is characterized by its structure and processes, that is the interactions occurring among the elements of this structure. Accordingly, the international marketer may compare:

- organizational focus
- layers of hierarchy
- integration among functions

of the major competitors to its own company.

Organizational focus The organizational structure of a competitor expresses the company's strategic emphasis and its priorities. Competitors that are organized around functions usually emphasize production. When distribution of products seems strategically important to the company, top management may structure the firm regionally. Liechtenstein-based HILTI, for example, has structured its worldwide operations in the fastening business along geographic lines. There are regional headquarters responsible for their business in the local markets. The growing importance of brand management to the success of many firms has led them to restructure their organizations around brands. For example, the French luxury brand group LVMH is organized into five different sectors: wine and spirits, fashion and leather goods, perfume and cosmetics, watches and jewelry, and selective retailing. Each of the sectors contains brand companies such as Louis Vuitton, Guerlain, Moët&Chandon, Fendi, TAG Heuer or Sephora. Increased customer orientation leads competitors to organize around customer groups or around projects. W.L. Gore & Associates, Inc., the U.S. firm, which became famous owing to Gore-tex, for example, has organized its entire company along product market and project lines.

Layers of hierarchy If the organizational structure of a competitor has many layers of hierarchy, it will have higher costs than "lean" competitors with a flat structure. The lines of communication in the company will also be longer and, as a consequence, decision making is slower. The firm will react to changes in the market, such as the entrance of a new competitor, with a time lag. This is one of the reasons why most EU governments have taken such a long time to deregulate their telecommunications, air and rail transportation, as well as energy markets. They did not want to see their national firms being overrun by more cost efficient and faster foreign competitors.

Functional integration Functional integration of competitors is hard to assess from outside the company. But some hints, such as the speed of innovation, the level of quality management, or the extent of management training programs can be used as indicators. A competitor that conducts training programs on an ongoing basis can adjust to new challenges much faster than competitors that lack such programs.

If the internal analysis of the marketer reveals a lack of mutual support and understanding among different parts of the company, effective interaction in international business will not be possible. Problems existing in domestic markets such as salespeople promising customers impossible delivery dates, procurement managers minimizing inventory levels at the cost of production interruptions, and production managers optimizing use of machinery without regard to delivery requirements must be resolved before the company attempts to operate internationally. Otherwise, business will almost inevitably be lost to competitors where process-oriented decision making and project work of interfunctional teams is part of daily routine.

Planning

A company's **planning system** consists of all the people formally involved in the organization of planning, the planning process itself, and the planning tools employed. Its major purposes are to:

- define the "right" goals and objectives for all parts of the company
- develop strategies, policies, and actions to achieve those goals and objectives
- allocate the company's resources accordingly.

If a competitor lacks a planning system, it might have difficulties in systematically matching success factors in any foreign market. Its business is based on the experience of influential managers or mere chance. Contrariwise, if the formal planning system of a competitor becomes too complex and sophisticated, it leads to inflexibility in market behavior. For example, if the local manager of a franchise firm in Japan, such as Kentucky Fried Chicken, has to contact headquarters for minor decisions concerning the size and outfitting of stores as well as price actions to counter the market entry of a new competitor, such as Texas-based Churches Fried Chicken, decision making will take far too long to fend off the entrant effectively.

To fulfill the demands of international marketing, the firm's planning system should not be restricted to a simple budgeting system. Budget figures, even when based on careful planning of activities, do not reveal anything about underlying strategies. The problems listed in Table 6.2 show that highly budget-driven planning renders centralized coordination of actions more difficult and synergy among different parts of the company is unlikely to occur. Top management's ability to manage international marketing effectively is limited.

Corporate objectives should be realized by all local operations. This may not be the case if the budget for the promotion campaign of Cav. G.B. Bertani, a winery located in Verona, for the southeastern part of the U.S., for example, is a simple projection from the Atlanta-based distributor's budget for last year plus an increase to account for inflation. But even if the budget is based on the distributor's activity plans, it may not reflect the Italian winery's objective of providing outstanding quality. A company with a planning system based on corporate objectives, basic assumptions concerning the development of international business environments, and clearly defined policies to be followed by local employees or business partners is better prepared to enter and be successful in international markets.

The organization of the planning process will also influence the firm's competitive position. If strategies exist only in the minds of top management, as is the case in many small and even medium-sized companies, marketing success will largely depend on chance. Companies that have established a formal planning procedure for their local business, with specific responsibilities for its execution assigned to members of the organization and set dates for the achievement of the different steps in the process, will be better off.

Information

A firm's information system predominantly serves the purpose of coordination. The marketer completing a competitor analysis will therefore be interested in how the major competitors resolve the problem of coordinating all the activities in their organizations and the resulting consequences. At one extreme, decision making is decentralized and coordination is achieved through information flows between organizational subunits. Webasto, the German supplier of sunroofs and air-conditioning equipment for cars and buses, for example, has largely independent production plants in various countries near their customers' factories. To coordinate their activities in the fields of product development, marketing and personnel, the headquarters has initiated regular meetings of the local managers where they exchange information on successful and less successful operations and develop joint projects.

TABLE 6.2 *Problems faced by companies that rely exclusively on a budgeting system*

Lost opportunities for profit Meaningless numbers in long-range plans Unrealistic objectives Lack of actionable market information Interfunctional strife Management frustration Proliferation of products and markets Wasted promotional expenditures Pricing confusion Growing vulnerability to environmental change	While budgets are important planning devices, over-reliance on budget-driven planning means too much attention is paid to numbers, and not enough to the dynamics of international business.

Source: McDonald, M.H.B. (1982) "International marketing planning", *European Journal of Marketing*, 16(2), p. 10

Reproduced with permission, Emerald Group Publishing Limited

The other extreme is centralization of decision making and standardization of activities. Depending on the success factors in a market some coordination mechanisms in between the two extremes will be more successful than others.

A company's potential for international marketing is greater when an effective information system for its domestic business is in place. Therefore, in assessing the distinctive capabilities of their organization marketers have to look at the way information is currently *gathered*. Most companies have standardized processes such as quality control, cash management and managerial accounting, which produce important internal management data. However, these processes may not be appropriate for the new potential markets. Financial accounting, for example, follows different rules in the U.S. than in Norway. Further, the systems may not be sophisticated enough to allow effective control of international activities. For example, the firm should be able to identify costs per customer, order and product, as well as costs per country and product market. Only if the company can determine its financial status and its profitability in any given market at any given point in time is it well equipped for international competition.

Marketers should also look at the way information is *disseminated*. The internationalization of marketing will be hampered if customer information only exists in the minds of salespeople and customer service personnel, because there is no system in place to summarize this information and then to distribute it to research and development, logistics or production managers. In the complex environment of international markets, any attempt to develop a marketing strategy or to implement consistent product or communication policies will be impossible if the company's management cannot rely on timely and precise customer information from all markets.

And, finally, marketers need to look at the way managers make *use* of available information. Problems may arise if relevant information is available to the decision makers but they do not use it. Sales managers, for example, may think that they know enough about the market without going through all the "paper" on their desks. Research and development managers may believe they know the customers' problems better than the customers do and therefore ignore market information. If such conditions exist, the company's management will need to change their minds before potential markets can be successfully entered.

Leadership

There is a strong relationship between a company's management style and its decision-making processes. When assessing the firm's distinctive capabilities, management should determine whether its decision-making processes are designed in a way that allows the following.

Timely and flexible responses to opportunities in new market environments Business decisions are riskier and seem to be more complex in foreign markets. There is less information and it is less certain. In addition, the potential for conflict is increased. For example, in a European champagne-producing firm such as Veuve Clicquot, based in Reims, about to reinforce its business in the U.S. market, the marketing manager may be enthusiastic about the market's size and growth potential. She will try to attract support from all the firm's managers for serving this market. The national sales managers for France and Germany, the company's main markets so far, however, may worry about production capacity restrictions. They will tend to assure delivery to current clients by evaluating the U.S. market less optimistically.

Technical quality and acceptance of decisions Speedy and flexible decision-making processes are desirable. Simply making snappy decisions in response to environmental stimuli does not result in immediate action, however. The decision must be implemented. If decisions are based on consensus, the individuals involved are more committed and generally the decisions can be implemented faster. But decision effectiveness not only depends on consensus. Effectiveness also depends on the technical quality of the decision, and the desired learning effect from decision making, that is, the development of technical and managerial skills of personnel. As comparative international studies have shown, there is no one best decision-making style. Processes ranging from highly autocratic to highly participative or democratic can be equally effective, depending on the particular decision situation.

Adaptation to cultural differences Because objectively similar situations will be subjectively perceived in varying ways across cultures, managers should be able to adapt the decision-making process not only to their own interpretation of the given situation but also to the perceptions of local personnel.

Successful companies in the Scandinavian industrialized nations tend to have a management style that stresses autonomy and entrepreneurship. Formal rules are kept to a minimum, and there is relatively little social distance between people at different levels of the hierarchy. For example, at IKEA, the international Swedish furniture retailer, nobody wears a tie and employees have the right to disregard the management structure when they feel it is necessary to do so. This management style, however, will work only when employees at all levels mutually respect each other, when responsibilities are accepted by each individual, and when there is a high degree of trust between personnel and managers.

People in the Middle East assume that successful leaders impose their will on the firm. Managers in Indonesia, Malaysia, the Philippines, and Thailand also favor an authoritarian style, whereas those in Singapore and Hong Kong tend to be less authoritarian. In the Latin countries of Europe, such as in France, Italy, or Spain, managers and personnel have highly personalized hierarchical relationships dominated by authority and power. As examples of highly successful companies from these countries show, such as Michelin, the French dominator of the world tires market, or Ferrero, the Italian candy company, such a different style of management need not make a firm less competitive in international markets.

Many publications have advocated the Japanese style of management as a recipe for global success. As Culture box 6.1 describes, there is much myth around Japanese leadership and it can be doubted that copying the Japanese management style would lead to the international success of firms headquartered in other parts of the world. But the success of Japanese companies shows that their management style is well suited to international marketing under social conditions found in Japan's society.

Depending on the country market under consideration and on the location of the headquarters of a competitor, their leadership styles will vary. Which style of leadership is most effective will depend on the market environment.

It may also be important to know what incentive systems the competitors in a market use. Again, cultural differences play a major role in which incentives are most acceptable. For example, a system of bonuses that rewards individual achievement may be appropriate for a Canadian or U.K. salesforce, but it is less appropriate for salespeople based in Korea, Malaysia, or Taiwan. Employees in those countries tend to favor group rewards and recognition over rewards for individual behavior. In Japan and PRC, job security is an important motivator. There, salespeople are more willing to perform when they are offered security than when they are offered a monetary bonus. In the Netherlands good interpersonal relations are a strong motivator, and employees disapprove of performance-oriented competition.

Assessment of operations

Finally, the search for distinctive capabilities will focus on the operative level. The procurement potential, the level of available product and process technology, marketing know-how, innovation behavior, and financial resources as well as the skills and motivation of the personnel may be sources of relative strengths and weaknesses in a market segment.

Procurement potential

In general, companies with experience in international procurement are stronger competitors in international marketing. They have better chances of balancing currency exchange rate and price differences than their counterparts with only regional purchasing experience. A European firm that serves the U.S. market will have much less trouble with a decreasing dollar value of the company's sales, for example, if it purchases substantial amounts of raw material, parts or systems in countries that belong to the dollar area, such as Southeast Asia, Latin America, and the Middle East.

Technological potential

To determine its competitive position concerning research and development capacities in an attractive market, the company needs to take an inventory of its major competitors' technological potential. This potential can be indirectly assessed through the number of patents, licenses, or copyrights. But an increasing number of firms in industries with shortening innovation cycles, such as software production or mechanical engineering, no longer register patents because they fear signaling the latest developments to their competitors and giving them enough details to innovate around the patent. Therefore, in addition to

---

CULTURE BOX 6.1

The myth of Japanese management style

Japanese management style is highly valued in many western publications. Enthusiastic authors mention as its main elements: Bottom-up decision processes involving all members of the company; goals, values and strategies made highly transparent to workers and employees to create motivation and identification; groups as the smallest functional unit, enhancing creativity, communication, and responsibility; and a long-term strategically oriented human resource policy aiming for the generalist who has succeeded in many different functions.

In reality, the human resource policy of Japanese companies is based on the principle of seniority. Salary, advancement, and fringe benefits predominantly depend on the age of a person. Japanese companies are extremely hierarchically oriented. Status

symbols, such as titles and privileges, play a central role for Japanese managers. Collaborators are led in a much more authoritarian way than in western companies.

People from more hierarchical levels are involved in decision-making processes, indeed, but they do not necessarily have any influence. German workers have more opportunities to effectively influence decisions taken in their companies than their Japanese colleagues. Working in groups has many advantages, but it also diminishes individual initiatives and risk taking. The high level of achievement is not so much due to a higher level of meaningfulness of work in Japanese companies as to a mixture of traditions, group pressures, and financial coercion.

The undoubted advantage of Japanese management style is its long-term perspective in personal planning as well as personal development.

Source: adapted from Sonnenborn, H.-P. and M. Esser (1991) "Japan II: Führen in einer fremden Welt – das Beispiel BMW", *Harvard Manager*, 3, pp. 109–15

patents, licenses, and copyrights, it is worth taking a closer look at the competitors' product and process technology.

Product technology Product technology affects customers' perceptions of the relative benefits provided by a product compared to competitive offerings. When digital displays were introduced by the Japanese watch manufacturers Casio, Hatori Group (Seiko), and Citizen quickly followed by their Hong Kong competitors, Swiss analog watches looked old fashioned. They risked being reduced to the very high priced and traditional segments of the world market. But ETA, a Swiss watch movement supplier, developed a very light, thin, waterproof, shock-resistant analog watch powered by an inexpensive 3-year battery with a face and strap made of durable colorful plastic. This stylish and attractive watch became a world success under the brand name Swatch.

"Too little" technology may result in problems for the marketer. For example, Hirsch Bracelets wanted to sell their leather watchstraps to major watchmakers in Japan such as Citizen or the Hatori Group. The Austrian managers in research and development, as well as production, were convinced their product had the highest levels of tearing and perspiration resistance, as well as color constancy and anti-allergy features, in the world. All their European and American customers so far had been satisfied. But Japanese watchmakers required much higher technical specifications (already provided by the local suppliers of metal straps). For 3 years Hirsch's Japanese sales manager tried to convince potential Japanese customers that their specifications were exaggerated and had no practical value. During that time the firm did not sell even one strap. Only when the company's management understood that its product had to meet customers' expectations, and not vice versa, did sales start to grow.

But a company also needs to avoid putting "too much" technology into the product. The most well-known PC makers such as Compaq face the problem that their PCs are too sophisticated, and as a consequence too expensive, for the great majority of potential customers looking for machines simply to play games or to use internet services.

Bracelets need to meet customer expectations   © Frank Pathol/iStock

Process technology The kind of technology used in the production process of a good or service has a strong impact on a company's capacity, production flexibility, cost structure, and productivity (the cost per unit produced). Production capacity and flexibility influence a competitor's ability to adapt to changing market demands, as well as to react to the entry of a new firm in its market. In the example given earlier, the ability to produce and market Swatch was largely dependent on a unique process technology developed at ETA.

Production capacity High capacity results in lower costs per unit, but only when the capacity is filled. It needs high investments in production facilities, which represent a barrier to exiting a market when it becomes less attractive. Therefore, a competitor with high production capacity will defend its market share with much energy and a tendency to lower prices.

By the same token, the company's production must have enough capacity to properly handle orders expected from the new markets or must be able to find a way to outsource them to reliable suppliers. If additional investment in machinery, equipment or storage capacity is needed, the timing of market entry is affected. So, too, is the cost per unit produced – it may increase because of higher investment costs, but it may also decrease because of gains in productivity.

For service firms, capacity problems may arise through the inability to acquire sufficiently skilled personnel in the numbers needed to ensure service quality or because of a lack of available locations. For example, the competitive position of gas-distributing firms such as Netherlands-based Royal Dutch Shell or London-based BP in central and eastern Europe very much depends on their ability to acquire the best locations for gas stations. Again, the competitive position in an attractive market can be at risk by delayed entry or personnel acquisition and training costs.

Production flexibility The flexibility of a competitor's production system determines the speed with which it can make changes in the physical characteristics of a product or its package. A highly flexible competitor, when confronted with a more competitive international marketer may choose to escape competition and a potential price war by altering its product lines.

Car manufacturers have made use of computer-aided manufacturing (CAM) to enable customers to "compose" their own cars. But even greater flexibility is possible. On the one hand, computer-aided design (CAD) allows customers and manufacturers to jointly design custom products. On the other hand, the level of general qualification of workers is of major importance for production flexibility. Competitor analysis therefore also has to consider the availability of a qualified workforce at all hierarchical levels.

Cost structure A competitor's production flexibility is related to its cost structure. Both determine the variations it can pursue in general marketing strategy. For example, when French Renault increases the number of robots in its plants, the cost per unit produced will decrease as long as robots are more productive than skilled workers. Fixed costs as a share of total costs will increase as variable costs decrease, because of the need for fewer workers. Renault can either lower the price of its cars, increase the margin for its dealers, or make higher profits, which can be reinvested to further increase productivity or develop the market.

But higher fixed costs can have major disadvantages. One is that the company needs a bigger market to be profitable. Therefore, the competitor is more vulnerable to negative economic developments in other parts of the world. In our example, Renault is vulnerable to economic stagnation in the U.S. that results in economic problems in Asia and Latin America. Additionally, the firm is faced with much higher barriers to leaving a market. If a car model produced by robots is not successful, Renault will probably encounter financial difficulties.

Marketing know-how

If local competitors are still developing their marketing know-how, as in most LDCs, a firm from a highly industrialized country entering their markets will have an advantage. Its marketing experience and reputation as an internationally operating firm is often a relative strength. For example, when Canadian Alcan, the second largest aluminum producer in the world, entered the Brazilian market its reputation as a world leading company with a very strong market position in highly developed economies was an important issue in attracting local customers.

If the firm can clearly differentiate its products from those of competitors in a way that matches the needs of customers better than other product offerings, it can justify higher prices. In other words, marketing know-how can have a decisive impact on a company's competitive position when the product is equivalent in technical quality to competing products and production costs are higher. For example, perfumes can be produced in parts of the world where production costs are far less than in France. The technically testable quality of such perfumes is equal to the quality of French products. But, nevertheless, French companies have acquired so much specific marketing know-how that their brands are successful competitors in the global perfume markets.

But it is not only marketing mix skills that determine marketing success. In many cases building and maintaining relationships with intermediaries and final customers, and also with other important stakeholders in the market, are as important. Competitor analysis, therefore, must include the search for and evaluation of formal and informal networks among companies and their stakeholders in the markets under consideration.

Such networks exist in every industry. Denmark, for example, has long been a European center of the pork and bacon industry thanks to a network of pig farms, abattoirs, and processing plants (see Strategy box 6.1). In Vicenza, in northern Italy, the jewelry business is strongly related to a host of specialized services: banks used to the paperwork involved in handling precious metals, security services, gemologists, and others all helping to support the jewelers in a network. In the Veneto and Emilia Romagna regions of Italy, there is a network of designers and suppliers specializing in motocross engines, which serves firms such as BMW. And the Japanese economy is a formidable example of how firms can be interrelated with government agencies.

STRATEGY BOX 6.1

To be or not to be – the Danish pork and bacon industry

By May 2004 eight central and eastern European countries as well as Cyprus and Malta had become members of the European Union. The enlargement has provided new business opportunities for the Danish food industry. In the short run the new member countries imported more pig and pork products, estimated to be 800,000 to 1,200,000 tons by 2007. The Danish food industry intends to make the best of this opportunity to expand in the European market.

Given the size of the country, it is extraordinary that Denmark has so far maintained its position as the world's largest exporter of pork. In 2002 total production amounted to 1.9 million tons, and 1.6 million tons were exported to more than 130 countries across the world. Inside Europe, Germany and the U.K. are the most important markets. Overseas, Japan is the frontrunner with imports of Danish pork reaching a record level of 240,000 tons in 2002.

Despite low pig prices and fierce competition from low-cost producing countries such as Brazil and Canada, Danish pork remains very competitive on the world market. Farmers have found a renewed emphasis on efficiency and improved management. Despite low prices investment has remained at a high level throughout the business. Farmers are investing heavily to turn the competitive disadvantage of very strict Danish animal welfare, environmental, and food safety legislation into a product advantage in the marketplace.

The number of sows living in confinement-free systems exceeded 50% in 2003 and will exceed 70–80% within the next five years. Transportation is another important issue. More than 90% of Danish finishers spend under two hours on the road to the slaughterhouse. Danish Crown has completed a new slaughterhouse, technologically the most advanced in the world. TiCan, the other major player in the business, has invested in new "clean" slaughterhouse and processing facilities.

Food safety standards in Denmark have been enhanced in recent years. Antibiotic growth promoters were removed from production by 1 January 2000, on the initiative of the pig producers. This significant change in production systems has been widely applauded by the consumers. The Danish program to control salmonella at all stages of production is being copied by a number of countries.

If Denmark is to continue to carry additional costs in delivering improved results on animal welfare, food safety and environment, it is crucial that the producers and the food industry are equipped with the best know-how and management skills. In this field, the Danish Bacon & Meat Council, the National Committee for Pig Breeding, Health and Production and the Danish Meat Research Institute – all part of the same organization – are important performance drivers. The strength of the industry is a well-integrated infrastructure based on the cooperative system. The pig farmers own the slaughterhouses and the meat processing companies. This unique structure provides an opportunity for a fully integrated chain from the farm to table and guarantees tracing between the companies and their producer members.

Source: Adapted from Lundholt, A.B. (2003) "To be or not to be – we aim to be", press release 28 May 2003

Finance

Without appropriate financial management, effective international marketing cannot occur. International marketing places a greater strain on the firm's financial resources than domestic marketing does. For example, the government of Saudi Arabia charges a non-refundable fee or bond of up to $100,000 for the right to bid on certain large projects.

The most important aspect of financial management from the standpoint of international marketing is the degree to which top management is able and willing to make substantial investments that will not yield immediate return. Jürg Zumtobel, the former owner of Austrian Zumtobel Licht AG, one of the three leading providers of light systems in the world, for example, decided to open sales offices in a number of promising markets, even though it would take up to 5 years for the investments to become profitable. To take such a long-term view the company must have healthy financial statements, a reasonable debt-to-equity ratio, sufficient cash flow, consistent growth in revenues and profits, and capital owners who do not go for the quarterly profit.

Financial resources can be internal or external funds available to the firm. The financial resources of the major competitors strongly influence their ability to react to actions of the marketer and the way they will react.

Allocation of working capital As a company becomes more international and invests in more subsidiaries around the world, the use and allocation of working capital (current assets minus current liabilities) becomes more complex. Internationally operating competitors can transfer funds internally through loans, equity capital, transfer-pricing mechanisms, or other financial transactions between subsidiaries. Thus they have considerable financial flexibility. This often results in a lower cost of funds, compared to a purely domestic competitor.

Ownership structure The ownership structure, that is, the number and quality of individuals or organizations holding equity in a competitor, also influences its behavior in the market. In general, multiple ownership results in additional capital. Private ownership, in contrast, may mean a higher tolerance of risk. If a competitor is partially or totally owned by a government, it may have access to funds even in economically disastrous situations where private owners would not support the business as fully. A recent example is the large amounts of capital spent by the Swiss government to keep their national airline (Swiss Air and later on Swiss) alive. If the competitor is part of a financial network of interrelated firms such as many Japanese companies, it may have advantages in building relationships with suppliers, intermediaries, and final customers.

Commercial banks Commercial banks are still a major source of corporate funds. In analyzing competitors' financial resources it is important to know that commercial banks operate quite differently in different countries. In Europe and Japan, they may underwrite security issues, and buy and sell bonds and equities on their own account. German banks, for example, have long dominated the corporate sector by acting simultaneously as creditors, supervisors, and shareholders to many companies. They may not perform these activities in the U.S., where these functions are performed by investment banks. When a commercial bank holds an equity position in one of its customers, the relationship between the bank and the customer will usually be more supportive.

When the international marketer's financial resources are limited, it must recognize that it cannot enter markets in which financing of activities via bank loans is impossible and cooperation with local business partners is not feasible. A company with a substantial cash flow can choose from a wider array of potential markets. It can afford to look at those markets as investments with different payoff periods and varying potential returns.

Personnel

Skilled personnel are a significant factor for a company's competitive position in international markets. Personnel does not mean only top management. Acknowledging top management's importance to the development of a company and therefore to competitor analysis, highly skilled workers and employees can make a substantial contribution to market success. Take the example of Japanese competitors. Despite high labor costs they have gained an important share of many industrial and consumer markets, to a large degree because of the globally known "Japanese quality." This quality standard in turn can only be provided because of the well-trained and highly motivated workforce in the country.

Language skills and cultural sensitivity Lack of personnel with the necessary language skills and intercultural experience is often a major obstacle for small and medium-sized firms that wish to market their products in other parts of the world, even when the products are well suited to the potential markets. Many U.S. and also European firms based in the major language areas (English, French, German) lack personnel with foreign-language skills. They tend to select markets in which they can communicate easily. This is one reason why, for example, Austria conducts about 32% of its exports with neighboring West Germany compared to about 4% with France and 4% with the U.K., whereas Belgium, split into a French- and a Flemish-speaking part, conducts about 20% of its exports with Germany compared to about 17% with France, 12% with the Netherlands and 9% with the U.K. Although this approach is understandable from a practical point of view, it does not necessarily result in optimal market choices.

Experience in non-domestic markets Another potential constraint is lack of experience in non-domestic markets, coupled with lack of knowledge about how to conduct business in those markets. Finding initial business contacts, closing a deal, and delivering the product or service may seem to be either insurmountable hurdles or, at the other extreme, without any difficulties, "similar to the home market." Both attitudes are dangerous.

Customer service potential Even when personnel with the necessary skills and experience are available to contact customers and close deals, the problems of providing training, technical assistance, or maintenance services to customers may remain. Intermediaries are often unable to perform these tasks satisfactorily. If the firm does not have qualified personnel to perform needed services, it will be forced to refrain from entering markets where the services are needed.

All these problems could be overcome by adding new staff with appropriate skills or by engaging outside consultants. But most smaller companies are unwilling to invest in new personnel before they are assured of success in the new market; the risk seems too great. Consultants can help companies enter foreign markets and establish business contacts there, but the company will still lack skilled personnel to conduct business in the new markets on a regular basis.

Attitudes and prejudices The attitude of personnel towards the company's plans for serving new international markets is crucial to its competitive position. Training in language and cultural issues can be provided to those who need it. But the company must have enough people who are willing to undergo training if it is to take advantage of international opportunities. In Europe, many employees, despite well-developed language skills, are unwilling to leave their own country for an extended period. They are reluctant to exchange a familiar environment for a strange one. Only high salaries can motivate them to spend some time in a foreign market. This attitude acts as a major constraint on companies' international activities.

If employees have marked prejudices concerning specific markets, or if they are not ready to cooperate with people from other regions, the company may have to refrain from entering such markets.

Competitor information sources

The ways of obtaining information about major competitors range from the illegal activity of industrial espionage to the acceptable, and universal, practice of using salespeople to monitor competitors' public actions in the field (see Ethics box 6.1). Management has to find the most efficient way of gathering the information needed for the evaluation of competitors' strengths and weaknesses in the specific market, without leaving the ethical path of research.

Some firms disassemble the products of their competitors, like for example Xerox did with Canon copiers. Others enter joint ventures to obtain information on their competitors' manufacturing techniques, such as GM and Toyota, or set up an office in their major competitors' home country, as IBM did in Japan, to have current information on what competitors are doing there. (Chapter 7 will mention more examples of competitor information sources.) Companies that have instituted formal intelligence programs, such as Eastman Kodak or Gillette, have an advantage over others that do competitor research on an ad hoc basis.

Profiles of strengths and weaknesses

Having finished the assessment of the firm's characteristics related to the success factors in the most attractive potential markets, the marketer can establish

---

ETHICS BOX 6.1

The Wade system for judging sources of information

Ethical

1 Published material and public documents such as court records
2 Disclosures made by competitors' employees, and obtained without subterfuge
3 Market surveys and consultants' reports
4 Financial reports and brokers' research reports
5 Trade fairs, exhibits, and competitors' brochures
6 Analysis of competitors' products
7 Legitimate employment interviews with people who worked for competitor

Arguably unethical

8 Camouflaged questioning, and "drawing out" of competitor's employees at technical meeting

9 Direct observation under secret conditions
10 False job interviews with a competitor's employee (i.e., without real intent to hire)
11 Hiring a professional investigator to obtain a specific piece of information
12 Hiring an employee away from the competitor to get specific know-how

Illegal

13 Trespassing on a competitor's property
14 Bribing a competitor's supplier or employee
15 "Planting" your agent on a competitor's payroll
16 Eavesdropping on competitors (e.g., via wiretapping)
17 Theft of drawings, samples, documents, and similar property
18 Blackmail and extortion

* The numbers in the list are ranked in degree of ethicality of legality.

Source: Adapted from Wade, W. (1965) by P.E. Murphy, and G.R. Laczniak (1992) "Emerging ethical issues facing marketing researchers", *Marketing Research*, 4(2), p. 8

profiles of the company's and its major competitors' strengths and weaknesses which can be compared to each other.

A profile of strengths and weaknesses lists the success factors and indicates how well the capabilities available to a firm fit them. Figure 6.16 gives an example of a strengths and weaknesses profile of a competitor in the metallurgical engineering business in an LDC market. This profile reveals that the competitor can provide a number of references, has easy access to cheap loans, and enjoys high mobility of personnel. By the same token, the counterpurchase capabilities, which are important for market success and relations with government are less well developed. Importance weights for the different success factors may be derived from the form shown in Table 6.1. They provide additional information about the appropriateness of the structure of competitors' and the company's capabilities.

As Figure 6.17 shows, ideally a company's capabilities and the success factors in a market fit together perfectly (Case 1). At times, however, a company's capabilities are not relevant to a particular market. For example, the sophisticated distribution know-how of a producer of frozen foods such as Iglo, a brand of Unilever, may not be relevant in a market that lacks an adequate transportation and storage infrastructure, such as Moldova (Case 2). Contrariwise, even if the

FIGURE 6.16 *Profile of a major competitor's strengths and weaknesses*

Competitor: Lurgi										Market: Angola
Success factors	Importance weight	Strength							Weakness	
References	1	2	3	4	5	6	7	8	9	
Counter purchase capability	1	2	3	4	5	6	7	8	9	
Access to cheap loans	1	2	3	4	5	6	7	8	9	
Relations to government	1	2	3	4	5	6	7	8	9	
Training facilities	1	2	3	4	5	6	7	8	9	
Project management experience	1	2	3	4	5	6	7	8	9	
Mobility of personnel	1	2	3	4	5	6	7	8	9	

The marketer must evaluate to what extent each of the major competitors possesses the success factors in a market segment.

FIGURE 6.17 *Fit between company characteristics and success factors in a market segment*

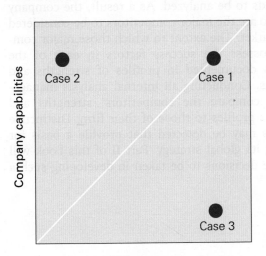

Before a company decides to pursue a market opportunity, it needs to determine whether it has the necessary company strengths to turn that opportunity into a viable business. The line that runs from the lower left to the upper right represents a match between company capabilities and success factors in the market.

Case 1 Swedish turnkey plant supplier for electronic communication equipment, and the Nigerian government, which is interested in improving the country's communication infrastructure with locally manufactured equipment

Case 2 European producer of frozen foods with sophisticated distribution know-how, and the Moldovan market, which lacks a sufficiently reliable transportation and storage system.

Case 3 Brazilian market for atomic power generation equipment, and a French manufacturer, which lacks technical personnel who speak Portuguese

Brazilian market for atomic power generation plants appears to present a major opportunity for a French firm such as Electricité de France (EDF), the firm will not be able to respond to the opportunity if it lacks technical personnel who speak Portuguese which is a success factor in this market (Case 3). In short, a market opportunity cannot be translated into a specific business opportunity unless the company's characteristics match the most important success factors in the market. Where the match is strong, the company possesses a strength; where it is weak the company has a weakness or the firm's capability is not relevant to the market.

Possession of certain strengths is not, in itself, enough for success in international markets. If major competitors are equally able to match the same success factors, a distinction in the market becomes more difficult. Therefore, the profile of a company's strengths and weaknesses has to be compared with the profiles of its major competitors. This should lead to a list of success factors that the firm matches better than its competitors. In this case, the company possesses distinctive capabilities.

If distinctive capabilities only exist in specific market segments they can be used to be successful there. If such capabilities attractively distinguish the company in a greater number of segments and across country markets the marketer can rely on those capabilities in the development of a global strategy. Apple Computer, for example, has been well known for its superior know-how in the development of user-friendly computer surfaces and for its product design ideas. User friendliness and attractive design are success factors in all markets where personal computers are mainly used by creative people for visualization purposes. Apple has built its globally successful strategy on these distinctive capabilities.

Summary

To assess its competitive position in the most attractive segments of the most attractive country markets, a company must conduct a thorough analysis. To keep time and costs at the lowest potential level, the analysis will have to be focused on the success factors. Success factors are the capabilities a company needs to fulfill the critical and (relevant) may-be aspirations and expectations of customers and other important stakeholders in a market. Those capabilities may relate to corporate policy, corporate strategy, management systems, and operations of a firm.

Additionally, success factors are the capabilities a company needs to turn challenges stemming from the development of the macro-environment in the considered markets into opportunities.

To determine capabilities distinguishing the firm from its competitors in a way that is highly attractive to the customers and other important stakeholders the competitive environment in each of the market segments needs to be analyzed. As a result, the company knows who are the major competitors to be considered in each market. The extent to which those major competitors possess the success factors in each of the markets is documented in profiles of strengths and weaknesses. Conducting an internal analysis management can compare the competitors' strengths and weaknesses profiles to those of their firm. Distinctive capabilities may be detected that provide a basis for developing its global strategy. Part II of this book will discuss the decisions to be taken in developing such a strategy.

DISCUSSION QUESTIONS

1. What specific criteria can a manager use to determine whether a company has the potential to be a successful international marketer?

2. Discuss the usefulness of deriving success factors in a market from the aspirations and expectations of customers and major stakeholders as well as present and future challenges in a market.

3. Why is top management's commitment crucial to the firm's success in international marketing?

4. Describe the position in the value chain, the configuration, diversification, and competitive behavior of an internationally operating firm. Gather information from all sources available to you, and indicate what sources you have found.

5. How do the information system, planning, control, and resource allocation affect a company's potential to succeed in the global marketplace?

6. What role does the company's ability to provide product-related services play in determining its potential for international marketing success?

7. What elements of research and development influence a firm's potential for success in global markets?

8. What role does the cost structure of production play in a company's ability to compete internationally?

9. "Personnel aren't really important in determining whether we should go into a non-domestic market. After all, we can hire someone in that country." Do you agree or disagree with this statement? Why or why not?

10. Find an internationally operating firm and interview them about how they determine the company's competitive position in international markets.

ADDITIONAL READINGS

Barney, J. (1991) "Firm resources and sustained competitive advantage", *Journal of Management*, 17(1), 99–120.

Day, G.S. and R. Wensley (1988) "Assessing advantage: a framework for diagnosing competitive superiority", *Journal of Marketing*, April, 52, 1–20.

Hunt, S.D. and R.M. Morgan (1995) "The comparative advantage theory of competition", *Journal of Marketing*, April, 59, 1–15.

Mahoney, J.T. (1995) "The management of resources and the resource of management", *Journal of Business Research*, 33, 91–101.

Prahalad, C.K. and G. Hamel (1990) "The core competence of the corporation", *Harvard Business Review*, May–June, 79–91.

Stalk, G., P. Evans, and L.E. Shulman (1992) "Competing on capabilities: the new rules of corporate strategy", *Harvard Business Review*, March–April, 57–69.

Warner, M. and P. Joynt (eds) (2002) *Managing Across Cultures: Issues and Perspectives*, 2nd edn, London: Thomson Learning.

Yau, O.H.M. and H.C. Steele (eds) (2000), *China Business: Challenges in the 21st Century*, Hong Kong: Chinese University Press.

Useful internet links

ABB	http://www.abb.com/
Alitalia	http://www.alitalia.com/
Arcelor	http://www.arcelor.com/
AT&T	http://www.att.com/
BASF	http://www.corporate.basf.com/en/
Black&Decker	http://www.blackanddecker.com/
Bosch	http://www.boschappliances.com/

BP	http://www.bp.com/
Daewoo	http://www.daewoo.com/
Diesel	http://www.diesel.com/
DuPont	http://www.dupont.com/
Electricité de France (EDF)	http://www.edf.com/
Ericsson	http://www.ericsson.com/
Gervais-Danone	http://www.danone.com/
Gore-tex	http://www.gore-tex.com/
Grohe Water Technology	http://www.grohe.com/
Hansa	http://www.hansa.de/com/index.html
HILTI	http://www.hilti.com/
Iberia	http://www.iberia.com/
Ideal Standard	http://www.ideal-standard.co.uk/
Kludi	http://www.kludi.de/index.php3?lang=e
Kohler	http://www.kohler.com/corp/welcome.html
L'Oréal	http://www.loreal.com/_en/_ww/index.aspx
Lexus	http://www.lexus-europe.com/
LVMH	http://www.lvmh.com/
Magna International	http://www.magnaint.com/
Masco	http://www.masco.com/corporate_information/index.html
Michelin	http://www.michelin.com/
Moen	http://www.moen.com/index.cfm
Nippon Cable	http://www.nipponcable.com/index02.htm
Oras	http://www.oras.com/
Roca	http://www.roca.es/contents/aboutroca/home_eng/index.htm
Royal Dutch Shell	http://www.shell.com/
Samsung	http://www.samsung.com/
Selva	http://www.selva.com/
Taittinger	http://www.taittinger.com/
Thyssen-Krupp	http://www.thyssenkrupp.de/en/index.html
Toto	http://totousa.com/toto/whoweare.asp
Unilever	http://www.unilever.com/
Veuve Clicquot	http://www.veuve-clicquot.com/
Webasto	http://www.webasto.com/
Wilkinson	http://www.wilko.co.uk/
Yves St. Laurent	http://www.ysl.com/
Zumtobel Licht AG	http://www.zumtobel.com/com/en/index.htm

INTERNATIONAL MARKETING INTELLIGENCE

7

Learning objectives

After studying this chapter you will be able to:

- describe decisions to be taken and tools to be used in international marketing research

- design and run through the steps of an international marketing research project

- handle the specifics of international comparative studies in a sensitive way

- assess cultural biases that influence reactions to research techniques as well as the interpretation of research results

Chapter outline

The intelligence system

Information gathering
Knowledge management

International market research process

Defining the research problem

Research question
Unit of analysis
Timing
Organization
Preliminary budget

Assessing information needs and availability

Dimensions of the research problem
Information available within the firm
Information from outside sources

Designing and conducting research

Secondary research
Primary research
Sampling
Analytical plan
Research budget and schedule

Interpreting and presenting results

Interpretation
Presentation

Organizing for marketing research

Centralized research
Decentralized research
Selecting a research agency

Summary

INTERNATIONAL MARKETING SPOTLIGHT

Yahoo!

Yahoo! began as an idea, grew into a hobby, and turned into a full-time passion. The two developers, David Filo and Jerry Yang, PhD students in electrical engineering at Stanford University, started their guide in April 1994 as a way to keep track of their personal interests on the internet. During 1994 they converted Yahoo! into a customized database designed to serve the needs of thousands of users who began to use the service through the closely bound internet community. Over the years it has become a very strong brand.

It has also developed a well-functioning marketing intelligence system. Although the marketing research function is positioned within the marketing team, it also supports sales, communications, business development, distribution and production. In the flat organization everybody is integrated, and research has to support the entire company.

A lot of research is conducted both online and offline using both qualitative and quantitative approaches – user surveys, brand tracking of image and awareness, pre- and post-advertising measurement, as well as advertising development. Cooperation with panel-based measurement companies allows looking at users' behavior in more detail in terms of time spent on Yahoo! sites, pages per user, and other useful data. An important part of research work is to find out what people want to use Yahoo! for, so that it can be provided in the most user-friendly way. The ways in which people are using the internet are developing all the time, and Yahoo! needs to be ahead in understanding the trends. The right products have to be available to customers at the right time.

Specialist experts in human/computer interaction – "usability engineers" – are constantly conducting fieldwork to investigate the overall appeal of the company's site, and how easy people find it to use. These tests are done in usability labs, as well as on site. As this work is done in close contact with production, the findings can be put into use immediately.

Source: Adapted from Vangelder, P. (2000), "Yahoo!", *ESOMAR Research World*, 4 April, p. 22

The focal question of this chapter is: **How can relevant data be determined, gathered, treated, and disseminated in a way to enable informed decisions and actions of all members of an internationally operating organization?**

The intelligence system

International marketing requires a company-wide intelligence system that significantly contributes to the coordination of activities. The importance of an intelligence system to a company is comparable to the importance of the central nervous system to the human body. The central nervous system comprises a structure of cells, nerve tracts relating them, and processes taking place in and between them, to gather information from inside and outside of the body, as well as to process, evaluate, and disseminate that information in the body. In a similar way, a company's intelligence system consists of a structure containing elements such as people, data files, reports, analytical tools, and PCs, which are related to each other in a network. In addition, an intelligence system contains information processes through which internal and external information is gathered, evaluated, processed, and distributed among all members of the company, as well as important stakeholders in the external environment. The major difference is that a company's intelligence system consists of formal as well as informal structures and processes. The formal part of an intelligence system is quite easy to manage compared to the informal part, which is as important for successful decision making but less evident, in particular in companies comprising a variety of national cultures.

A company's intelligence system has to keep the members of the company informed about relevant developments, such as new EU legislation on national quality standards or the signing of an agent's contract with a partner firm in Kuala Lumpur. It also has to inform the firm's stakeholders about all relevant company events, such as the introduction of a new product or the hiring of a new sales manager in the Mexican subsidiary. Such an intelligence system will be used to:

1 monitor the international macro- and operating environments

2 monitor performance in different product markets and geographical areas

3 help the firm make strategic decisions, such as decisions about market expansion or divestment

4 assess resource allocation decisions and their impact on the company's overall success

5 exchange and integrate experiences gained by different parts of the company

6 communicate information about the firm and its products, activities, and achievements to relevant stakeholders.

Information gathering

Any company gathers information in more or less systematic ways, whether the firm serves local or global markets. However, for an internationally operating company the information-gathering activities must be more formalized.

Selectivity

For the gathered information to be relevant the information requirements of different business units, management levels, and stakeholders must be determined and satisfied. An overly general system of monitoring the firm's environments would not only be too expensive for most internationally active companies, it would also overburden the company's personnel with information requests. There is widespread feeling among operating managers that the reporting required by headquarters is excessive and that reported information is only partially utilized. Many country managers view the home office as a place where uninformed people frame irrelevant, time-consuming questions. This is particularly so when highly standardized reporting procedures are uniformly applied to all organizational units independent of their stage of development or of their economic, cultural, and regulatory environments.

For example, when St. Louis-based Kentucky Fried Chicken founded a local sales subsidiary in Japan to learn about the different environment and to build a customer franchise in the new market, the local manager regarded it as bureaucratic nonsense when he had to report as extensively and in equal detail as his colleagues who were responsible for the mature U.S. home market. Similarly, the local national managers of U.S. Corning Glass Works had some difficulty to understand, why their headquarters insisted that they had to submit accounting information in English according to the American accounting system format, even though these procedures were not allowed in their countries and therefore useless to the subsidiaries. Therefore, the formal information-gathering process must be highly selective and must be regarded as useful for both local units and corporate headquarters.

Flexibility

At the same time information gathering of an internationally operating company will have to be more flexible than is necessary when serving only local markets.

Because of the greater environmental variety, a wider range of information-gathering techniques is needed.

Managers of international businesses must gather information from a much greater variety of potential sources. The best information concerning customer expectations, for example, may come from salespeople in the U.K., agents in Saudi Arabia, consultants in Taiwan, suppliers in Spain, or a government agency in Japan. Management needs to apply considerable creativity concerning new information sources they are not familiar with, or that are of little importance in the domestic market. In order to find and select the best information sources, the relevant stakeholders in the company's international operating environment have to be known. Besides those important players the most influential dimensions of the relevant macro-environment have to be specified. If no one in the firm has any experience in this regard, it may be useful to hire a consultant to get started.

Harmonization of procedures and methods

Because of the multitude of information sources and the great variety of information available at many different levels of detail, an intelligence system cannot fulfill its objectives when international marketing research is carried out on a study-by-study basis. The information flow from external sources has to be continuous and be based on a great variety of sources from personal conversations, to internet screening, and reading business literature. Harmonization of procedures and methods applied wherever possible, increase the efficiency and effectiveness of data collection and analysis.

Positive working environment

Finally, a positive working environment within the firm is vital to successful international information gathering. Such an environment will not only ease feedback between managers and employees, but it will also encourage experienced employees to stay with the firm longer. The company benefits from increased experience curve effects. Such positive working environment can be reinforced by taking local knowledge and requirements seriously. Central staff at Royal Dutch Shell in Rotterdam (the Netherlands), for example, try to understand the information-gathering approaches of local operating companies and research firms and to see if their approaches would be beneficial to follow more broadly. Although many information-gathering issues may be international ones, for example the launch of a new passenger car motor oil, ownership and implementation of information must be local. Shell, therefore, ensures that information gathering reflects the local or cultural considerations as much as possible.

Knowledge management

Databanks

Integration of data on different levels of decision making, for example for salespeople, product managers, or business unit managers increases their information value. A great part of formally available internal and external data that are routinely collected is usually consolidated in an object-oriented databank, that is, an information system that stores and retrieves information by objects instead of relations. The potential manipulation of data at any level of aggregation makes the system totally responsive to the requirements of specific decisions. For example, sales can be analyzed by country, product, or important customers across countries as well as by product sold to specific customers in selected countries. Such a system not only permits managers to take well-informed decisions by tracking changes in the firm's environments over time but also to avoid wasting budgets for information stored in other parts of the firm. The biggest problem is to keep the databank updated. There need to be clear rules of what data have to be loaded by whom and when to make sure that stored information stays strategically and operationally relevant.

Tacit knowledge

Beside formal information there exists much informal knowledge and know-how in a company and at business partners, for example at intermediaries, suppliers, or service firms. It is stored in the minds of the members of the organization as well as in shared values, assumptions, and experiences. Routine behaviors that members of the firm automatically select each time a task arises are a typical example. They are strongly influenced by group, ethnic, and corporate cultures and can persist tenaciously even in the face of negative performance feedback.

This becomes particularly a problem when a firm operates in a foreign cultural environment. When Japanese carmakers, such as Toyota, first opened factories in the U.S., expatriate Japanese managers, for example, used long wooden sticks to tap American factory workers on the head to get their attention. This habit, perfectly acceptable in Japan, resulted in an escalating cycle of resentment and violence in a U.S. factory before it was abandoned.

Values, assumptions, experiences, and rules of behavior are passed on through:

- special recruitment
- training
- role models
- job rotation
- stories and traditions.

Mazda, for example, selected a group of 3,500 American workers for its new Michigan plant from an applicant pool of 96,500 partly on the basis of performance in interpersonal dramas. During a 10- to 12-week training period new recruits were continually monitored as to their abilities to sustain new performance roles. The emphasis was on learning how to become part of an interactive, reciprocal team that performed according to a carefully written and rehearsed script.

How important this "soft" part of a firm's intelligence system is to its international success is underlined by the fact that firms such as IBM, Procter & Gamble, or Unilever have a policy of rotating managers through various jobs and moving them around the world, especially early in their careers.

Information dissemination

Systematic distribution of relevant information to managers results in more co-ordinated decisions throughout the company. However, too much information is not only costly, it also reduces managers' interest in using available information. Therefore, new information should not be automatically distributed. It should be available to decision makers when they need it.

Availability This objective is not always easy to fulfill. Because of local differences and changes in information requirements central information managers rarely know the exact information needs of their colleagues in the firm's operating units spread across the world. In addition, managers in an internationally operating company are often located in several different time zones.

A PC network linked to a central database that gives managers of all levels and functions in the company access to information they need for their decisions can be of great help. The information needs to be presented in a way easy to incorporate into the daily operation of business, and adequate analytical tools must be installed which allow simple handling. Nokia, the Finnish company leading the world cellular phone market, for example, has an in-house team conducting analyses, looking at both original studies and secondary data. The team provides fast information updates by email, SMS, WAP, and the intranet. All the studies are to be found in the database in a well-organized way, although there is a security matrix, which means they can only be accessed by people for whom they are intended.

Expert systems that produce evaluations of decision alternatives under a range of operating environment scenarios can strongly expand the usefulness of information accessible to management. These systems stimulate the decision makers' thought processes improving their decisions.

Texas Instruments enabled engineers in Dallas to remotely operate giant testing machines at assembly plants in the Philippines that hunt for flaws deep within multimillion-circuit chips. The U.S.-based engineers could actually reprogram the computer-controlled production line by the time the morning shift arrived the next day in the Philippines. Special software lets operations managers distribute new orders to whichever factory needs the work at the moment. The result: Texas Instruments with fewer delays has improved on-time delivery from 77% to 96% in 4 years.

Special occasions Even fully integrated and best managed intelligence systems cannot assure that managers will actively search for available information as a basis for their decisions. Therefore, information should flow to managers not only when they ask or search for it, but also when unforeseen events affect their area of responsibility. Computer technology permits a management-by-exception approach to information dissemination, which is particularly important for international organizations. Critical events have to be specified in a joint process involving managers and information system specialists. Procedures for access to and distribution of information, and presentation formats for fast and easy communication, must be developed.

Cross-cultural experience of system managers

The personnel responsible for the intelligence system in an internationally active firm must be able to effectively communicate across geographic, organizational, group, and individual boundaries. They must be aware of contextual settings on both sides of each boundary. They therefore need cross-cultural experience in addition to information-processing expertise.

For example, consider the seemingly simple introduction of a new sales order form in a global consumer goods company. A form that serves the computer staff's needs may not be accepted by all the subsidiaries. Even if one country finds it useful, it may not reflect the sales approach used in another country. The personnel responsible for the intelligence system should be regularly assigned to functional units in different countries to learn about their specific information needs.

Adoption by potential users

Cross-cultural experience of intelligence system managers may not be sufficient, however. It seems to be even more important that the potential providers to and users of the system adopt it as their system. When top management of John Wiley & Sons, a mid-sized publisher of technical and scientific books headquartered in the U.S., decided to adopt a common hardware and software platform for its international business, it chose to replace first the systems that supported the core business process: order processing, distribution, warehousing, publishing support, and fulfillment activities. The replacement process was started in Singapore, the location of the company's smallest office. The implementation team then took the Singapore system and transplanted it first to Australia, and then to the U.K. When implementation was scheduled to start in the company's main market, the U.S., both the business and information technology groups of employees initially resisted the concept. To overcome this resistance eight representatives of the various user departments, from the manager level down, were invited to travel to the U.K. to see the system. Their British business peers gave a system demonstration. After a weeklong review in which the American guests could use the screens and see how easily modifications could be made, they decided to go with the new system. One business manager who initially resisted became so convinced of the new system's superiority that he volunteered to market it to his peers in the U.S.

International market research process

International marketing intelligence is characterized by the fact that the firm is operating or plans to do business within a number of different environments. To interpret their past and potential future development properly as a basis for strategic and tactical decisions, the firm needs to establish international market research processes that cover all important parts of those environments and the relationships among them. Data about the firm's external environments, the economic, political–legal, cultural–social environments, the product market, and the industry in which the firm operates, as well as the firm's internal environment, the corporate policy, management systems, and capabilities relevant to international marketing have to be systematically gathered and analyzed. They need to be selectively distributed to the decision makers in time.

The following discussion focusses on the planning and implementation of international marketing research processes (see Figure 7.1). It discusses the adaptation of techniques successfully applied in domestic marketing research to the more complex international environments and introduces some additional methods.

International marketing research starts with the definition of the research problem. From there, the information needed to answer the research questions can be defined and its availability inside or outside the firm can be determined. Before research can be started, an effective, efficient and flexible data-gathering procedure must be carefully planned, including what questions to raise, when, and where to find the right information sources. In international marketing research, only a particularly careful and culturally sensitive interpretation of findings can produce valuable information for decision makers. The presentation of results has to be planned in terms of selected content, amount of information, and timing in order to have an impact on management decision making.

FIGURE 7.1 *International marketing research process: Overview*

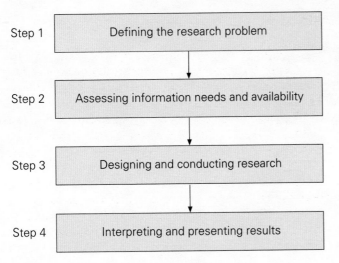

Step 1	Defining the research problem
Step 2	Assessing information needs and availability
Step 3	Designing and conducting research
Step 4	Interpreting and presenting results

An international marketing research process starts with the definition of the research problem. Based on an assessment of information needs and availability, the international research project can be designed and conducted. To make the research findings useful for management purposes, they need to be carefully interpreted and presented to the target audience.

Defining the research problem

Successful international marketing research requires a systematic and thorough approach. Lack of planning in this area can easily lead the company to the wrong markets or to make bad decisions about the right markets. Such mistakes can be costly and even cause managers not to pursue international opportunities.

One of the most serious, and yet most common, mistakes made in international marketing is to begin studying a promising market without adequate planning. Careful planning not only helps prevent research blunders but also ensures that better results are achieved within the firm's budget and time constraints.

Research question

Any planned international marketing research begins with the definition of the problem the firm is trying to solve. This is by far the most important step of the research process. The care and accuracy with which this step is carried out largely determines how useful the research results will be. Figure 7.2 presents the elements of this step.

The research problem should be defined as (a) research question(s). A classic example of poor problem definition in international marketing research is a study concerning spaghetti consumption in different countries conducted by *Reader's Digest*. The study concluded (falsely) that West Germans eat more spaghetti than do Italians. The researchers erred in measuring only sales of packaged spaghetti. Italians buy much of their spaghetti fresh and in bulk, from local pasta shops, and they consume considerably more spaghetti (about 28 kilos a year) than West Germans (about 5 kilos a year). By defining the research question incorrectly, that is, as how much packaged spaghetti the consumers buy rather than how much spaghetti they *consume*, the researchers reached a false conclusion.

FIGURE 7.2 *International marketing research process, step 1: Defining the research problem*

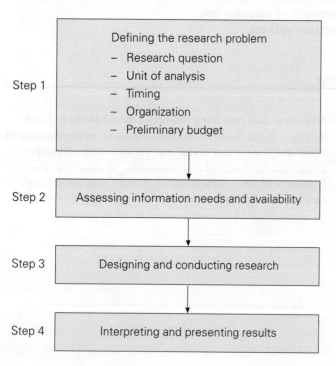

The definition of an international marketing research problem contains a formulation of the research question and a definition of the unit of analysis, as well as basic information on project timing, organization, and budget.

Preliminary information

As we can conclude from this example, management needs some preliminary information about international markets, such as the relevant decision makers, business habits or consumption patterns, to be able to define the research question(s) properly. Without such information, the problem will be treated as in the domestic market. To gather preliminary information about potential markets, the marketing researcher may read professional journals or talk with managers of other companies that serve the targeted market. Suppliers located in that market are another cheap source of valuable information.

It may also be helpful to visit major trade fairs or exhibits for the company's product in the market region to be researched. Major trade fairs include, for example:

- ISPO (for sporting goods) in Munich, Germany
- New York International Gift Fair
- International Fair in Frankfurt, Germany (the biggest consumer goods fair in the world, with over 4,400 participating firms from about 60 countries)
- Hanover Fair in Germany (the biggest industrial goods fair in the world)
- Première Vision in Paris (for fabrics, textiles, and accessories).

They provide the marketing researcher with numerous opportunities to observe and talk with competitors, suppliers, distributors, and customers; to gather brochures, catalogs, reports, reference lists, and technical specifications; and to participate in cocktail parties and experts' talks and presentations. Information on trade fairs and exhibits can be obtained through local chambers of commerce and local embassies as well as via the internet.

Strategic decisions

In international marketing, research questions may relate to strategic as well as tactical marketing decisions. Strategic decisions are mainly concerned with the allocation of scarce resources over more than one product or country market. They should ensure the overall success of the firm instead of local optimization.

Market development decisions Market development decisions concern:

- where to invest
- where to hold a competitive position
- where to retreat from.

A small producer of highly specialized glass treatment machinery, for example, may not have enough cash flow to finance research and development while maintaining a presence in every potential market. The market research questions that have to be answered in that case are, for example:

- Which markets are more attractive than others?
- In what sequence should they be entered?
- What specific treatment do they need?
- How much emphasis should be put on the penetration of one of these markets before entering the next?

Market-clustering decisions Market-clustering decisions concern whether there is a chance to form clusters of similar product markets, independent of national boundaries that allow a standardization of the marketing mix or whether adaptation has to take place.

Positioning decisions Finally, marketing research has to help the firm's management define how to position the firm itself or one of its business units or product lines in the international target markets. For example, a tour operator such as Wagons-Lits, based in Brussels, will not leave the decision of how to position the company and its product lines in each country to the local managers. Because the firm's customers may be in contact with a number of different offices, it is very important that they act uniformly. Market research will provide information about the strategies of local, regional, and global competitors to help Wagons-Lits develop a competitive and consistent international market position.

The research question should reflect the nature of the marketing problem to be solved. If the problem is a strategic one, the question that the research attempts to answer must be framed in strategic terms, not as a tactical question. Strategy box 7.1 gives an example of a strategic research problem and its formulation as research questions by the Nissan Motor Company.

Tactical decisions

Tactical decisions relate to the marketing mix for a particular product market or a special target segment. Marketing research can supply information concerning different expectations of various customer groups and their levels of satisfaction with current products. Marketing research can also provide information on brand awareness and image, the usual terms of delivery and payment, the price of competing or substitute offers, appropriate outlets, and the availability, and usage pattern of advertising media in each market.

For example, U.S.-based Whirlpool Corporation, which after the acquisition of Philips' appliance business has become the largest appliance company in the world:

- regularly tests new products, interviewing people to determine their reaction to the product and brand
- has set up simulated stores to see how people react to products and different messages from salespeople
- sends mystery shoppers into a series of retail stores to find out exactly what the salespeople are saying and doing

---

STRATEGY BOX 7.1

Global marketing research by the Nissan Motor Company Limited

The Nissan Motor Company has production bases located in more than 20 countries. For customers in these many nations to be fully satisfied with the performance of their cars, it is necessary to observe carefully and arrive at a full understanding of the customer from the initial stages of product planning and strategy.

Nissan first started with exporting cars designed for the Japanese market. Then they took factors related to the U.S. and European markets into consideration, but designed mainly for the Japanese market. The resulting product matched none of the markets. As a consequence they installed the so-called "lead country system." Special attention was focussed on the major target markets and manufacturing vehicles to match the needs and requirements of those markets.

In the latest phase Nissan has been seeking to base its strategy on a global perspective. This global perspective is based on a strategic research effort that attempts to compare the perception and attitudes of car users in the triad to identify the common and differing elements in these three areas. The research questions are phrased like this: "Do Japanese, U.S., and European customers have the same values and the same demands regarding functions and performance of their cars?" "If there are differences, what are the reasons for those differences?" They do not consider tactical elements such as: "How should the gear shift and the front lights look to be equally attractive to the customers in the triad countries?"

- conducts telephone interviews to measure brand awareness and brand image
- tracks progress using traditional financial data like sales, market share, and performance compared to budget and the previous year.

Research brief

Effective problem definition may require the participation of the firm's decision makers as well as that of research specialists. The team approach has the added value of keeping key individuals informed and involved in solving the research problem and eventually using the findings.

To define the problem fully and accurately, the team must address not only the general content of the problem, but also specific elements. This has to be done in writing. A useful way to document the thinking involved in defining the problem is to develop a research brief or preliminary proposal to be submitted to management for approval. The research brief states:

- the research problem,
- research objectives (benefits that will be realized)
- potential costs of making a decision without the information to be obtained from the research.

The brief also defines:

- the unit of analysis
- the timing of the research
- who will be responsible for the project
- a preliminary budget.

This document serves as a framework for the research project and also provides a basis for deciding whether to proceed with the research.

Unit of analysis

The **unit of analysis** is the smallest source of information that will be used to answer the research questions. For example, a research project that aims to compare total consumption patterns for fast food in Singapore, South Korea, and Thailand will use the country as the unit of analysis. However, if the goal is to measure specific brand preferences within each country – for example, the preference between McDonald's, Kentucky Fried Chicken, and local street kitchens – the unit of analysis will be the individual consumer.

Country market perspective

Traditionally, the country has been the most common unit of analysis for international marketing research. The advantage of this approach lies in the fact that most information available on the environment (cultural, social, demographic, economic, legal, and political) is organized by country. In addition, it is still common for the international salesforce, the internal sales department, or the firm's subsidiaries to be organized according to national boundaries.

Although this approach is convenient, it is not always effective. Its chief disadvantage is that data describing a whole country give an impression of homogeneity that may mask considerable diversity. Italy, for example, consists of the highly industrialized, wealthy north, and the less developed, relatively poor, rural south. These two areas have differences in income distribution (although rich and poor people are found in both areas), marketing infrastructures, and, to a lesser extent, culture.

Product market perspective

Research projects that use country data for purposes of comparison often fail to discover the best business opportunities. Such opportunities are more likely to be recognized if the unit of analysis is based on a product market perspective. A product market is composed of organizations or individuals. Units of analysis may be, for example, firms, buying centers, households, or individuals. They face similar problems, seek similar benefits or display similar response patterns, but they do not necessarily share the same nationality. By starting with a product market perspective, the marketer gains the advantage of being able to compare target segments regardless of size and geographic boundaries and to cluster them into homogeneous supranational markets.

The major disadvantage of using a product market perspective to define the unit of analysis lies in subjective influences in defining product market boundaries. The perspectives and ambitions of managers have a significant impact on the research design and findings. For example, if a manufacturer of downhill skis, such as French Rossignol, defines its market as wealthy, experienced skiers in the Rocky Mountains area of the U.S. who ski for fun, the research project to discover their purchasing behavior will be very different from a project with a similar research problem, where the manufacturer defines its product market as all the people in industrialized nations who like to spend their leisure time in winter doing outdoor sports. The impossibility of an objective definition of product market boundaries should not discourage researchers from using that perspective, however. Marketing research could even help to find the most promising definition of the product market to serve. It simply emphasizes the need to define clearly the problem underlying the research project.

Selection procedure

Because the costs of data collection often rise as the size of the unit of analysis is reduced, it is important that researchers be clear about the level of detail needed. An easy trap to fall into, especially in an international context, is assuming that more information is needed, in more detail, than is really necessary. A practical way of choosing the unit of analysis may be to follow a stepwise procedure. This starts with an exact definition of the potential product market to be served. Then the most attractive geographic areas are determined, and finally the adequate unit of analysis for the product market in those areas is chosen.

For example, a Dutch manufacturer of durable plastic pipes for use in building construction may want to explore international product markets. But the firm may not be large enough to expand simultaneously from one country market to all potential markets. To cope with such limitations, it should focus on product markets for plastic construction supplies in a carefully selected geographic area, such as Scandinavia, and take a closer look at construction supply wholesalers (as the unit of analysis) there.

Timing

Timing is an especially sensitive issue in the development of a research brief. Thorough international research projects often take more time than many firms believe they can afford. Before embarking on a full-scale research project, therefore, it is important to determine the latest possible date on which the results of the research could contribute to decision making.

Similarly, it is important to determine the latest date on which one might begin the research process in order to produce results based on the most recent information available.

These two factors obviously pose a dilemma. The marketing researcher will have to find a reasonable compromise that relies on thorough planning, paired with personal experience.

Organization

The assignment of responsibility for a research project depends not only on the specific problem to be explored but also on the size, resources, and experience of the firm.

Strategic decisions

Research for strategic purposes is usually conducted by members of the firm. The export manager, a marketing researcher or a business unit manager, for example, could take over the direction of the project. Small firms and those with little international experience may prefer to consult with experts outside the firm.

If a company plans to become active in a region where it has no experience and to assign a new manager to the region, the firm should assign the research responsibilities for this new market area to the chosen manager. Knowing that strategy, resource deployment and actions will be based on the findings of the research project, the manager will be much more motivated to produce reliable and relevant information than a marketing research specialist who is less involved.

Tactical decisions

In industrial marketing most of the international research for tactical decisions will also be done by members of the company. They have the technical expertise needed for research concerning their products, which is not usually available from external organizations. In addition, the number of distribution channel members, potential customers, and important competitors is rather restricted in many industrial product markets. Therefore, little or no field organization is needed for data gathering.

In international marketing of consumer products and services, only a few companies have enough personnel and specialized knowledge to conduct marketing research projects for tactical purposes in an effective and efficient manner. They may be able to define the specifications for the research design. But in most cases they do not have a field organization to run interviews on an international level, or they are not familiar enough with local environments and languages to avoid misunderstandings and misinterpretations. If they cannot satisfy their information need via the internet, they therefore rely on external marketing research organizations. The choices they have, and related advantages and disadvantages, will be discussed later in this chapter.

Preliminary budget

A tentative budget should be drawn up based on the research questions, a preliminary understanding of what information is needed and at what level of detail, and a consensus about timing, organization, and what the firm's management is willing and able to spend. This is only a preliminary budget. Assuming that the proposal goes forward and the project moves into the next stage, a more detailed budget and a full research design are developed to guide the remainder of the project.

Assessing information needs and availability

A research brief is seldom specific enough to serve as a detailed research plan. But the defined research questions point to the second step of the research process: assessing information needs and availability (see Figure 7.3). This requires that the researchers define more clearly the dimensions of the research problem. The list of those dimensions allows researchers to find out what information is available inside the company and what information must be gathered from external sources. It also provides guidance for developing the research design and final budget.

Dimensions of the research problem

In international marketing, the specific dimensions of a research problem depend on the research objectives, product markets, geographic areas of interest and targeted market segments. Table 7.1 illustrates the dimensions of a research problem that were defined by a European manufacturer of spectacle frames interested in entering the fast developing South Korean market. Note that this outline only focusses on one country; other geographic areas might be included, and target segments within each would probably be identified. Different research dimensions for each segment may result. The researcher can use the list of dimensions as a checklist, which will be further refined during the research process. Its first use is to identify information available within the firm.

Information available within the firm

Before looking elsewhere, the researcher should determine what data are available within the firm. The value and scope of such information vary with the firm's size, experience, and policies. McDonald's, for example, considers itself an experience-based company with business units in different stages of development and a flat management structure in which managers can learn from each other by picking up the phone and discussing issues with people at all levels throughout the world.

Statistics

Relevant information can often be derived from accounting records, especially sales and cost figures. The most valuable internal statistical data for marketing purposes are summarized in Table 7.2. Internal statistics can help the marketing manager judge the effectiveness of various strategies and tactics. The spectacle-

---

FIGURE 7.3 *International marketing research process, step 2: Assessing information needs and availability*

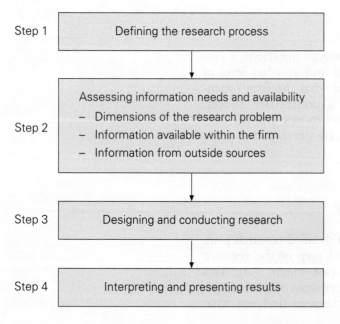

Step 1 — Defining the research process

Step 2 — Assessing information needs and availability
- Dimensions of the research problem
- Information available within the firm
- Information from outside sources

Step 3 — Designing and conducting research

Step 4 — Interpreting and presenting results

To assess information needs and availability, international marketers first need to specify the dimensions of the research problem. Then they can determine what information is available within the firm and what information has to be gathered from outside sources.

frame manufacturer described earlier, for example, may examine data on orders, sales, and profits or losses for exports to other markets and conclude how large the market volume and market share would have to be in South Korea to be profitable. In order to overcome comparability problems caused by different rules of bookkeeping and cost accounting as well as tax legislation in various countries, firms operating in more than one legal environment must apply standardized systems that are used exclusively for internal purposes.

The increased use of scanning in retail outlets in highly industrialized countries has provided retailers and cooperating manufacturers of consumer goods with an extremely valuable internal source of information. It not only allows logistics and the variety of goods on offer to be optimized, it also provides information on issues such as price sensitivity, reactions to product presentations, and the purchasing patterns of customers.

Databanks

Some firms, in particular smaller ones and those whose interest in international marketing is relatively recent, may have internal data for only a limited market area. In more experienced and sophisticated firms with more complex information and control systems, up-to-date databanks may already exist. They

TABLE 7.1 Dimensions for assessing the South Korean market for spectacle frames

Environment	Political/legal	Role of government	Restrictions on capital flows
		Political stability	Price regulations
		International trade policy	Restrictions on ownership
		Trademark protection	Regulation of competition
	Cultural/social	Business ethics	Norms and values
		Negotiation customs	Attitudes towards foreign products
		Networks	Aesthetics
		Resolution of disputes	Consumption patterns
		Social structure	
	Economic	Growth of GNP	Population development
		Rate of inflation	Communication systems
		Balance of trade and payments	Transportation systems
		Currency and banking	
Product market	Structure	Potential	Imports/exports
		Volume	Development
	Consumers	Buying power	Lifestyles
		Buying and usage behavior	Preferences
		Product-specific physiological characteristics	
	Intermediaries	Number	Size
		Reliability	Buying habits
		Margins expected	
	Competition	Number	Size
		Market share	Profitability
		Apparent strategies	Positioning
		Product lines	Distribution policy
		Price levels	Promotion policy

will contain not only general information on market development, but also on customer, intermediary, supplier, and competitor behavior, based on reports from sales, maintenance and service people, procurement personnel, subsidiary managers, distributors, or professional journals. Findings from other research projects that are relevant to the research problem at hand may also be available in the databank.

Information from outside sources

Having gathered internal data, the researcher may need to obtain additional information from external sources. The question is how to obtain this information at a reasonable cost and in a timely manner. There are basically two ways of obtaining data from sources outside the firm: primary research and secondary research.

Secondary data

For reasons of cost, time, and problems in data collection, firms often attempt to satisfy their information needs by using **secondary data**. They gather and analyze data that have already been published by or are available from an existing source. Secondary data are most valuable in assessing the attractiveness of markets about which management has little knowledge. They are regularly used to:

- identify country or product markets that merit in-depth consideration and to
- monitor changes in the international environment.

Secondary data enable the researcher to:

- roughly evaluate the risk associated with operating in a specific market

---

TABLE 7.2 *Internal statistics for marketing research*

Order statistics
Offers made
Orders accepted (by delivery time)
Cancellations of orders (including reasons why)
Order structure (size of orders, costs per order, number and size of
    orders per customer and per salesperson)

Sales statistics

Sales (pieces, value)		Market segment
Average prices		Channel of distribution
Price cuts/bonuses	per	Sales area
Terms of payment		Product (line)
Promotion costs		Customer

Profit and loss statistics

Profit and loss structure (including absolute and relative contributions to gross margin)	per	Order Product (line) Customer Sales area Channel of distribution Market segment

Order, sales, and profit and loss statistics of a company may provide useful information for an international marketing researcher.

- determine the likely costs of alternative modes of operation and different marketing strategies
- forecast probable returns associated with operating in the market under study.

Secondary data provide information quickly and cheaply. But the researcher must be aware that in most cases they have been collected and analyzed for purposes that differ from the firm's research objectives. Such data can be used to reduce the amount of information that must be newly obtained through studies initiated by the firm, thereby reducing the amount of time and money needed to complete the project. Most research problems can be addressed using secondary data, but require primary data for precision at the end of the research process.

Primary data

Primary data are new or as yet unpublished data collected and analyzed by the firm. They provide specific and targeted information for a given research problem. Such data may come from customers, intermediaries, competitors, suppliers, or experts in a particular field. It is most useful during an in-depth analysis of product markets, because it helps to identify the behavior, needs, and benefits sought by customers in those markets. The feasibility and cost of obtaining primary data vary considerably with the product category and the geographic area.

According to the ESOMAR 2003 Research Prices Study on worldwide research prices the U.S. is the most expensive country overall for market research, closely followed by Japan. For example, on average, a typical survey will cost more than one-third extra to conduct in the U.S. or Japan than it does in the U.K., France, or Germany. The six project index ranges from 242 for the U.S. and 230 for Japan as the most expensive countries to 37 for India and 29 in Bulgaria as the countries where research is cheapest.

Designing and conducting research

Figure 7.4 presents a two-step approach to research design and implementation, beginning with secondary research and following up where necessary with primary studies. The characteristics and difficulties of both steps in carrying out international marketing research will be discussed in the following subsections.

Secondary research

Secondary or desk research is the gathering and analysis of data that have already been published by or are available from existing sources. The cheapest sources of secondary data are census and other statistical reports published by government agencies, such as the U.S. Department of Commerce or the European Commission in Brussels, and by specialized agencies such as trade associations, chambers of commerce, research institutes, and banks.

Production statistics

Production statistics on product categories are available for all industrialized countries. Together with other statistics they help the marketing researcher to estimate market volume, the degree of saturation, and the level of local production. Production statistics are published with varying frequency, from monthly, as in western industrialized nations, to every few years or not at all, as in some developing countries. In using production statistics for marketing research the marketer has to be careful, because:

1 *Not all production facilities are included in the statistics.* Small firms are frequently not included. If the industry the marketer is interested in is

characterized by a multitude of small family businesses, as is the case with the European textile industry, production statistics would lead to erroneous conclusions.

2 *The way products are classified may vary from one country to another*. It is important, therefore, to study the product lists accompanying production statistics thoroughly or to ask for specific information at the office that publishes them.

3 *The product categories may contain a different number of products*. Smaller countries often use broader product categories than big ones. TV sets, for example, are in a category of their own in some countries, whereas in others they belong to the consumer electronics category.

4 *An industry may contain only a few producers, whose data are not published for competitive reasons*. For example, when an industry in an EU market is controlled by very few companies – such as aerospace and air traffic control industries – no production data are published, because they would provide too much information to foreign competitors.

5 *The value of the products in the statistics may have been calculated in different ways*. Some of the calculations contain only the production costs; others include sales or value-added taxes; and others consider market prices.

6 *The structure of the statistics may follow different international trade codes*, as shown in Table 7.3. The marketing researcher used to a particular domestic code may be misled.

Consumption statistics

Statistics on a country's consumption of consumer products are usually organized according to the major purpose of consumption or usage. For example, in the furniture category the statistics may be grouped into living room, bedroom,

---

FIGURE 7.4 *International marketing research process, step 3: Designing and conducting research*

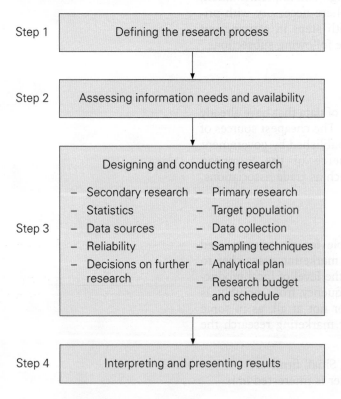

International marketing researchers first try to gather the needed information from secondary sources. Primary research provides more specific information that cannot be gathered from those sources.

kitchen, and so on. Unfortunately, such statistics exist only for the highly industrialized nations.

Import/export statistics

Import and export statistics contain data on the volume, value, and destination of a country's imports and exports. They allow insights into the global flow of products and services. The major country markets for a specific product, as well as the most competitive areas in a global product market, can be determined. The statistics show the degree of saturation of demand through local versus non-domestic production. Therefore, they are the single most valuable source of information for a preliminary evaluation of a country's market attractiveness. But, as with production statistics, there are some problems with import and export statistics that a researcher should bear in mind:

1 *Different product classification codes are used from one country to another.* In many countries not belonging to common markets such as EU or NAFTA, product classification codes are adapted to the customs classification applied by the national government. As a result the same product may be found in different classification groups from one country to another. A simple electrical motor may be counted in the categories of "electrical motor" or "drive unit for screens" depending on its application.

2 *Exports and imports are valued differently.* Exports are usually valued without international freight or insurance costs added at the export harbor, for example, whereas import figures usually contain those costs.

3 *Statistics are published at different intervals.* For example, companies such as EUROTAX publish figures on European car registrations indicating the obtained market share to car makers and dealers. As those customers are interested in short-term trends, EUROTAX publishes the statistics monthly. In other countries, figures on car registrations published by official statistics agencies are only available once a year. They are not made available before the middle of the following year or even later. The data will therefore vary considerably in timeliness.

4 *Data are sometimes unreliable.* In researching small or economically less developed markets, the marketer may find the import data published by their administrations to be unreliable. The export statistics of the most developed industrialized nations generally provide more reliable information on imports in those markets.

Other statistics

Tax statistics for industrialized countries, in particular sales and value-added tax statistics, are organized by industry and product categories. They allow the assessment of the number and size of potential customers, intermediaries, and competitors. Other statistics, such as construction, transportation, and agricultural statistics, are not only of interest to marketers in these fields, but also

---

TABLE 7.3 *International trade codes for product classification*

SIC	Standard International Classification (U.S.)
SITC	Standard International Trade Classification (UNO)
BTN	Brussels Tariff Nomenclature
NIMEXE	Harmonized nomenclature of international trade of EU members

In international markets, products may be classified following different trade codes.

provide information on a country's stage of industrial development, its general economic situation, and its infrastructure.

Secondary data sources

There is a great variety of secondary data sources available to the international marketer.

Embassies and consulates of country markets They provide access to a wide variety of references on business conditions and opportunities. Often a staff member, such as a commercial attaché, commercial officer or economic secretary, is available to provide specialized assistance. They have access to databanks, names of firms interested in business contacts, industry publications, address and telephone books, catalogs on industrial suppliers, and annual reports of potential customers. From these sources, information can be gathered on market conditions, potential intermediaries, and competitors. Schedules of international promotion programs are also available; they provide perspective on which industries are particularly important to the respective governments.

Public agencies Valuable sources of information are public agencies such as patent offices or registration authorities. For U.S.-based firms the U.S. Department of Commerce's Global Market Surveys furnish detailed information on, for example, market shares, product use, repeat purchase rates, and competitive activities in key markets for selected products. For other countries, specialists known as country desks can provide the latest government import–export statistics for their country.

In PRC a valuable source of information for foreign firms is the Economic Information Department (EID) of the computer center of the Ministry of Foreign Trade and Economic Cooperation. Its market research section, for example, furnishes information on investment opportunities and cooperation partners. The China Trade and Commercial Service Co., another department, provides credit ratings of firms, and the Compass (China) International Information Service Co. manages a databank of manufacturers and products and furnishes a directory of industry and commerce.

Some countries have governmental commercial delegations in the researcher's country of interest. Danish companies interested in doing business in Japan or the Netherlands, for example, can contact JETRO (Japanese External Trade Organization) or the Dutch Trade Commission for valuable secondary information. These organizations, plus trade organizations sponsored by industries in the country of interest, also help companies to establish direct contacts with potential partners. In addition to government agencies, other organizations regularly compile and publish reports that are useful in international marketing research. Table 7.4 illustrates some of these sources.

Chambers of commerce Chambers of commerce and trade commissions regularly ask consultants to study particular markets. (Addresses of chambers of commerce and trade commissions can be found in address or telephone books and on the internet.) Unfortunately, they usually concentrate on one country market. An international product market perspective is missing. When using industry reports from such sources, the marketing researcher must bear in mind that in many countries there is no obligation to belong to a trade commission. Therefore the data only cover the members of the organization.

Research institutes A number of research institutes, such as the Institut für Weltwirtschaft of the University of Kiel and the Institut für Wirtschaftsforschung in Hamburg, Germany, regularly publish reports on global economic topics. Market research companies and information services, such as American Dun &

Bradstreet or German Schimmelpfeng, offer purchasing power maps, analyses of the economic structure of specific regions, reports on the development of an entire industry, and information concerning the financial reliability of potential customers and intermediaries.

Foreign business departments Foreign business departments in banks, insurance companies, and forwarding agents provide information on market risks, terms of payment, and transportation and insurance problems in different countries.

Internet The fastest way to collect secondary data is through the internet and electronic databanks. A great number of databanks are available for online use, and their number is still growing. Table 7.5 contains some examples of interesting databanks.

Approximately 75% of databanks are located in the U.S., another 20% are in Europe, and the remaining 5% are in other parts of the world. Although most databanks charge fees for accessing the data, these costs are minimal compared to what a firm would have to spend to collect the information on its own. A carefully planned online search can reduce data collection costs even further.

Media News agencies, broadcasting networks, and specialized publishers such as *Euromonitor* regularly publish data on industry structure, firms, brands, and sources of information. Trade journals contain information on market development, new products, and competitors. Newspapers like *The Wall Street Journa*, *The Economist*, *Frankfurter Allgemeine Zeitung*, *Neue Zürcher Zeitung*, *Asiaweek*, *Le Monde* and *Le Figaro* offer detailed analyses of environmental factors, specific features of country and product markets, and the latest news on suppliers, competitors, and intermediaries.

Libraries Public libraries often contain non-technical but nonetheless valuable sources, such as country yearbooks, economic atlases, and tourist guidebooks.

Personal contacts Finally, personal contacts with international suppliers, domestic suppliers of complementary services or products, customers who have

---

TABLE 7.4 *Selected reports published by international organizations*

Organization	Publication
United Nations	*United Nations Yearbook, Trade and Development Report, World Investment Report, State of World Population*
United Nations International Development Organizations	*Trade by Commodities*
OECD	*OECD in Figures*, country reports, online library (e-books, e-periodicals, and interactive statistical databases)
International Monetary Fund	*World Economic Outlook, Annual Report, Global Financial Stability Report*, country reports
World Bank	World tables, *World Development Report, Doing Business in 20—, Global Economic Prospects*
EU	Reports on countries, economic and financial affairs, employment and social affairs

International organizations publish many reports that contain useful information for international marketing researchers.

business experience in the market under consideration, or even competitors can be very helpful in the interpretation of information about environmental influences, specific business behavior, consumption patterns, competitors, and potential intermediaries. Contacts with companies with subsidiaries in the target country may provide similar information.

Reliability

To be reliable, secondary data should have been rigorously gathered, must not be outdated, and need to be comparable.

Rigor of data collection To establish the comparability and usefulness of secondary data, the researcher must locate the original sources. In addition, the researcher must make sure that the data collection and analysis procedures that were used in producing the secondary data meet the standards of the current project. In other words, using someone else's sloppily collected data will not save money and time; in the long run, the information will have to be collected again in a more effective manner.

Timeliness of data Timeliness is another factor that must be considered. The data may be too old to be relevant for the current research problem. This would be the case, for example, when in 2005 a marketer interested in Austria finds census data gathered by Statistik Austria (the national statistics agency) that is 5 years old, and an informative country report published by OECD that is 4 years old. Because the country is neighboring some of the new member countries the enlargement of the European Union as from May 2004 this has produced significant changes in the economic environment. The particular product market of the firm may also have changed in the meantime. New competitors may have entered the scene, generating changes in price structures but also producing income effects through direct investments.

Data compatibility Finally, the researcher should be aware that secondary data may not be fully comparable because:

TABLE 7.5 *Examples of databanks on the internet*

- BOS (Business Opportunities Services), a cooperation of the biggest European banks dedicated to the arrangement of international commercial exchanges
- COMEXT-EUROSTAT, a time series of import/export data from the European Community
- ECONOMIST, a source of latest data on economic developments all over the world
- Euro-Select, containing funds of all European countries and the EU
- EVIS (Environmental Information System), containing 2,500 firms, 10,000 procedures, technologies and offers
- NIKKEI Economic, a source of economic statistics on Japan
- TED (Tenders Electronic Daily), which contains all tenders in EU member countries as well as tenders from the U.S., Japan, Israel, Norway and Switzerland and those in other countries that are funded by the EU or the European Investment Bank
- WARC.com, a source of material published by the Market Research Society

1 *The criteria used for grouping data into statistical categories are different.* For example, an area classified as urban in Japan has at least 50,000 inhabitants, whereas in Sweden and Norway the same term means an area with a population over 200.

2 *The categories in the statistics to be compared have been given different widths.* For example, occupational statistics in the U.S. use different age categories from the same statistics in Italy.

3 *The categories are defined too broadly.* For example, if a marketer of ball bearings for ski lifts wants to determine the market volume in France, production and import–export statistics won't help if the statistics only contain a category for all metal parts in ski lift equipment.

4 *The data come from different units of analysis.* Two datasets about the projected markets for computer paper forms in Switzerland and Spain, for example, would not be comparable if the first dataset came from domestic manufacturers and the second from a survey of users.

To overcome some of these potential problems, ESOMAR, the European-based world association of marketing researchers, has launched a working party on "Harmonization of Demographics," which presented very promising results for western Europe. But convergence in the shape of published statistics is progressing rather slowly.

Decisions on further research

After the firm has gathered and analyzed secondary data, it must decide whether further research is necessary. It may turn out, for example, that the research problem has to be redefined in the light of newly gained insights. The marketing researcher may also use the data and the list of research issues to determine what additional information has to be gathered. Consider again the example of the European spectacleframe manufacturer. Based on secondary data, the firm may have decided that the South Korean market is attractive. But it may still need to know more about the lifestyles and preferences of South Korean consumers, as well as their attitudes towards foreign products. It may also want to find out more about potential intermediaries and the marketing strategies of competitors in the South Korean market. These kinds of information can seldom be obtained in any other way than through primary research.

The decision whether to go on to primary research or not will be based on estimates of how much research is still needed and what it will cost to obtain the desired information. If, for example, secondary data account for 75% of the information needed by management at 10% of the estimated research budget, the remaining 25% of information may not be worth the additional expense required to obtain it. In most cases, however, management will not be able to avoid gathering information through primary research, in order to fine-tune the firm's marketing mix.

Primary research

Primary or field research is the collection and analysis of new or as yet unpublished data. It promises the most specific and targeted information possible for a given research problem. But it is also costly and time consuming. Researchers used to studying domestic environments may face new problems. For example, statistical data for a reliable sampling frame may be missing. There may be the need to translate questionnaires into different languages. Moreover, in many parts of the world there are no service organizations to assist in the collection of data.

Because of such problems, careful planning of a primary research project for international markets is particularly important. Different types of research design, that are exploratory for aid in problem definition and initial insights, descriptive for examining patterns of market behavior, and causal for determining what stimulus leads to what behavior, may be used to help answer the questions of market behavior: what, when, by whom, and how much. The research plan must specify:

- objectives and scope of the study
- what techniques will be used for data collection, analysis, and interpretation.

On the basis of this plan, a budget and schedule for carrying out the research can be established, and personal responsibilities for different parts of the project can be assigned.

Target population

The appropriate target population for a research study depends on what management is trying to learn and what is likely to be the best source of this information. For example, researchers who want to learn about the attitudes and expectations of intermediaries who handle high-technology communications equipment will try to obtain data from wholesalers, retailers, and even independent sales representatives in that industry. The marketer of an expensive consumer product may try to get information directly from affluent consumers in a number of countries. A marketer of machine tools will be mostly interested in decision makers such as purchasing specialists, production managers, technical directors, and top management.

Depending on culture-specific management structures and decision-making styles, the right choice of target population in industrial markets may be different from one country market to another. In consumer product marketing, the relevant target population may also change from one country to another. In the U.S. and western Europe, for example, family car purchases are strongly influenced by women and children. Therefore, they are part of the target population if consumer preferences for different cars are to be determined. In Saudi Arabia, religious guidelines and a patriarchal family structure do not usually permit the inclusion of women in the target population for research on car purchases.

Sometimes the firm may want to obtain information from more than one target population. For example, a vacation destination in Switzerland such as St. Moritz, will be interested in its image with both travel agents and travelers. The researcher will also have to decide if information on a topic has to be gathered in all potential markets and from all the potential partners, or if research findings from one area are representative for others. However, even if the budget is restricted and the markets under consideration seem to be similar, as would be the case for the Scandinavian markets, for example, researchers have to be careful in making generalizations. A Finn would not appreciate being classified as being similar to a Swede.

Data collection techniques

Once researchers have determined the best potential sources of information, they must select the most appropriate method for collecting the data. The best data collection technique is a function of what has to be found, who has to be contacted, the size of the sample, and how the members of the sample can be reached. There are basically three ways to get information from primary sources:

1 observation
2 experiments
3 surveys.

Observation Observation is a means of collecting information without asking questions. A French manufacturer of sunroofs, for example, can hire an agency to observe the advertising campaigns of its three most important competitors in all the EU markets. It can also gather information on potential intermediaries in the Italian market by observing the number of customers they have, their business behavior, and their service capacity at the Ravenna trade fair.

The biggest advantage of observation is that it is not obtrusive. It is most appropriate when a behavioral sequence (e.g. information seeking, buying behavior in stores, or usage behavior concerning a product) largely unknown to the decision makers in a company is to be explored; or when direct methods (experiments and surveys) might affect the way subjects behave or respond. Another advantage is less danger of researchers imposing a cultural frame of reference on the units of analysis than there is with, for example, standardized questionnaires. The problem associated with observation, however, especially in an international context, is that the observer must understand what he or she is seeing well enough to interpret it.

A North American food packaging expert scanning the European environment for new opportunities might notice that Dutch grocers stock milk in containers no larger than one liter. She might conclude that Dutch households do not consume enough milk to warrant the use of larger containers, such as the half-gallon and gallon jugs that are widespread in the U.S. However, on seeing several shoppers purchase two liters at a time, she might conclude that there is a market for larger containers in the Netherlands. Neither of these conclusions would accurately reflect the milk consumption and shopping habits of Dutch families. Dutch consumers place a high value on freshness, shop every day (often by bicycle), and own small refrigerators. These factors combine to make one-liter cartons and bottles highly suitable for the Dutch market.

Experiments Experiments can be used to causally test the potential impact of a given marketing decision. A supplier of international travel tours, such as Germany-based TUI, might test a new arrangement with an airline carrier, such as Indonesia's Garuda Air, on a limited number of destinations, for example the flights from Frankfurt to Bali, to project how the target market will respond to the offer.

Although in theory experimental techniques are applicable to all markets, in international marketing it is often difficult to control the experiment's reliability. Ideally, an international researcher has two experimental groups: one in which the experimental variable is manipulated while all other variables are held constant, and another in which no variables change at all. The researcher can then measure the impact of the experimental variable. Such conditions are even more difficult to establish in international research than in domestic test marketing because experiments are attempted in different cultures. Even laboratory tests cannot rule out certain cultural elements. For example, cultural differences in attitudes towards authority affect perceptions of spokespeople in different countries. In India, a country where authorities play an important role, the behavior of the person who conducts a test will have much more influence on the reactions of respondents than in Sweden, which is characterized by low authority differences.

Test markets for consumer products deliver information about customer reactions and enable managers to identify appropriate adaptations of the marketing mix before product launch. In international marketing the problem of determining representative test markets is hard to resolve. Belgium and the Netherlands, for example, are often used as test markets for Europe. They cannot be considered representative of the entire EU. But experience has shown that the results from a test in those markets provide information that is useful for marketing purposes in western Europe in general and are more than worth the cost of the test.

Researchers may confront technical problems. For example, it may be impossible for France-based Thomson Consumer Electronics to compare the effects of the same advertising approaches in France, Greece, and Sweden because of media differences and the inability to control the behavior of competitors. In addition, the introduction of new products in international markets must be increasingly fast to be successful. When Philips introduced its DCC music system, for example, it had to do it in all the triad markets at once because Sony threatened to introduce its Mini-Disc system at the same time. There was no time left for extensive market testing.

Highly intangible and integrative products may be tested through trial demonstrations at company-owned locations. Japan's Sega Enterprises first opened two test centers called Joypolises in their home market before they opened Segaworld, a vast videogame arcade, in London, followed by another one in Sydney supposed to be followed by dozens of others around the globe.

Because of the significant level of concentration in many industrial markets, international market tests are difficult to establish. A market test would be equal to a product launch. Nevertheless, before introducing the product on an international level, the business-to-business marketer should let a small group of closely cooperating customers try the product, at least in the lead market. If there are improvements to be made, they can be carried out without losing the trust of potentially dissatisfied international customers. If the product works as expected, the customers who tested them may be used as references.

In cases where product tests are not feasible, as for example in the construction industry, product tests need to be replaced by the participation of lead customers at defined steps in the product development process. A manufacturer of plants for burning toxic waste may build a plant at its own expense, to prove the promised benefits and to test the reactions of potential customers, and environmentalist groups.

Surveys A third means of gathering primary data is to ask questions. Survey research is conducted for the purpose of gathering information that is difficult or impossible to collect in any other way, such as the attitudes and knowledge of respondents. How structured the survey should be depends on the amount of knowledge the researchers already have about the target population and the product market under study. Basically, the less that is known, the more important it is to use an open-ended approach to data collection. Exploratory or pilot studies are very useful in identifying issues that can be addressed later in more structured surveys. Group interviews have become most popular for that purpose in Europe and the U.S. The importance attributed to focus groups versus in-depth interviews differs widely across countries, however.

By the same token, when there is considerable knowledge about the research issues, a highly standardized and structured approach is more suitable. The marketing researcher can choose between verbal and visual surveys, or a combination of the two, depending on the research problem, the units of analysis, and the advantages and disadvantages of each technique.

Group interviews can be an effective method of gathering information on consumer knowledge and attitudes
© BananaStock/Alamy

Mail surveys Mail surveys can be effectively used in many industrial marketing research projects. The costs of administering a mail survey appear to be low on a per-unit basis. But, in addition to problems that are well known from domestic surveys (such as varying levels of literacy), in an international context there are additional limitations on this approach. Motivation to respond may be even lower than in the domestic market, and mail surveys may suffer from inadequate or unreliable postal services. In some African countries, for example, mail delivery is so unreliable that mail surveys are useless. In India, the postal service claims to deliver mail anywhere in the country within two days, but recipients may not be able to read the questionnaire because of language differences – there are 15 major languages in India!

Telephone surveys Telephone surveys, like mail surveys, can be used effectively in international industrial marketing research and sometimes in consumer research. Almost all firms have telephones, and relevant respondents can be identified by means of a few preliminary questions. Multi-regional studies can be conducted from a single location, saving time and money and increasing the response rate, because of the higher motivation to respond to international telephone calls. The main drawback of telephone surveys in industrial marketing research is the anonymity of the interviewer. Respondents may be concerned about revealing information that competitors could use, or reluctant to respond fully because of work pressures. As a result, only a limited amount of information may be obtained. In Japan, however, cooperation levels of business respondents reach 60 to 80% (higher than in western countries).

Compared to the U.S., where telephone surveys are popular, European marketing researchers are on average less inclined to use this method of gathering primary data. Limited ownership of private telephones in many other areas of the world, such as China, Indonesia, the Philippines or Thailand, restricts the feasibility of telephone surveys for consumer research, except among the most affluent consumer groups. Yet, taking China as an example, telephone penetration in the big cities exceeds 40%. In Hong Kong, carrying out telephone research is very well accepted. Participation is comparable to responses in Europe. In many cultural contexts, such as in PRC and Latin America, there is a strong reluctance to respond to strangers and respondents may be unaccustomed to lengthy telephone conversations.

Computer-aided surveys Computer-aided surveys may be useful in conducting specialized research on consumer behavior. This approach is limited to industrially developed countries where people are familiar with keypads or keyboards and video screens. Automated interviews, in which respondents answer questions posed on the computer screen, produce lower error rates, and fewer biases than other survey techniques. Visual aids make them easy to use, and the computer can register the response time of interviewees as well as the responses themselves.

Internet interviews are particularly suited for research purposes where the participation of highly involved customers in a clearly defined international product market is sought. For example, when Swarovski, the Austria-based crystal company, wanted to get some fresh ideas for the design of crystal tattoos, they offered a toolkit to interested consumers allowing them to create their personal tattoos. Many consumers from all over the world participated intensively in a very short time span. The consumers created a range of ideas that were adopted by the in-house designers and became saleable designs.

Personal interviews Personal interviewing is the most expensive survey method, but it is also the most cost effective. This is because high response rates, a flexible interview situation, and the ability to address complex issues in face-to-face studies all result in higher quality data. In Europe face-to-face interviews clearly account for the majority of survey expenditures but their share is decreasing.

In areas where postal services are poor, illiteracy rates are high and telephones are not available, personal interviews are mandatory. However, in some cultures interviewers may encounter suspicion. For example, in Latin America, they may be perceived as tax inspectors. In Russia, people are concerned that interviewers might cooperate with burglars because they ask questions about possession of consumer goods. Thus, care must be taken in the selection of interviewers. The social class and language of the interviewer and the target group should be matched.

Panel research Most survey research is done on an ad hoc basis, but continuous research has won an important share of national and international research budgets. ACNielsen's Nielsen/NetRatings, for example, has panels in 30 countries, covering some 90% of the worldwide internet audience, including all major markets in Europe, Asia Pacific, Latin America, the Middle East, and Africa. In Europe continuous research accounts for close to half of total market research expenditures. The importance of omnibus surveys is also increasing. Ipsos, for example, offers panel-based omnibus surveys such as:

- Ipsos U.S. Express, a telephone poll of 1,000 adults fielding twice a week
- Ipsos Insta-Vue, a monthly mail-based omnibus survey that provides access to 250,000 households
- Ipsos Global Express, quarterly interviewing 500 people in each of 50 countries
- Capibus Europe, weekly interviewing 1,000 individuals in France, Germany, Italy, Spain, and the U.K.
- Eastern European Omnibus, conducting monthly face-to-face interviews with 1,000 adults in Bulgaria, Czech Republic, Hungary, Poland, Romania, Russia, and Ukraine
- Asian Omnibus, doing the same amount of face-to-face interviews in China, Hong Kong, India, Indonesia, Korea, Malaysia, Philippines, Singapore, Taiwan, and Thailand on a monthly basis.

Ethical issues In survey research, ethics play an increasingly important role. Because there are so many researchers with greatly varying self-interests concerning the results of their work and their usage, respondents have become increasingly skeptical. There is a growing trend for legislative restrictions on the publication and even on the conduct of surveys. Restrictions have been proposed in Greece and Ireland, for example, and legislation has been enacted in countries like France, Italy, Portugal, and Spain. As a reaction, professional associations of marketing researchers such as ESOMAR and the Market Research Association (MRA) have developed and published guidelines on the proper conduct of surveys, including:

- "Conducting marketing and opinion research using the internet"
- "Guideline on interviewing children and young people."

MRA expects members to follow principles of honesty, professionalism, fairness, and confidentiality to guard the interests of the public and the clients in order to promote good business practices. MRA's Code of Data Collection Standards consists of the responsibilities of respondents, clients, and data collectors not only to one another, but also to the general public and business community. The Appendix to this chapter contains parts of the ICC/ESOMAR International Code of Marketing and Social Research Practice that sets out the basic principles which must guide the actions of those who carry out or use marketing research.

Validity and comparability

The greatest challenge in conducting survey research in an international context is to obtain valid, reliable, and comparable data. Culture box 7.1 describes some of the problems that can occur even when doing international comparative marketing research in neighboring countries. Researchers must check the validity of each variable measured in the different geographical areas. That is, they must make sure that the survey instrument really measures what it is intended to measure.

Triangulation One way to improve the validity of a research design is to use triangulation. If marketing researchers can afford to apply at least two data collection techniques which are as different as possible and, therefore, contain different sources of error, they can make sure that similarities or differences in the gathered data are not due to the research design, rather than market differences. For example, to assess the purchasing behavior of consumers in a street market in Hong Kong, a researcher may use open-ended interviews, observation by video cameras, and analysis of ethnographic documents. Only if the outcomes of the three data collection techniques converge should results be interpreted.

Equivalence Even if validity is assured, comparability or equivalence of findings is a concern. When comparing product markets in dissimilar countries in order to assess their attractiveness or to find opportunities to standardize parts of the marketing mix, comparability of the data has to be assured. Comparability should be established for the research process as well as for content. For example, respondents must interpret the stimuli (for example, questions, items, or pictures) used in data collection in the same way and interviewees' responses to these stimuli must have the same meaning in the markets to be compared.

If, for example, a survey on radio listening behavior in Belgium using the same method for radio audience measurement shows that the Flemish-speaking Belgian spends 219 minutes with radio on an average day but the French-speaking Belgian only 113 minutes, the finding may be due to real differences in

CULTURE BOX 7.1

Cultural problems with survey instruments

When Young & Rubicam developed a measurement tool to define lifestyle segments across all member countries of the EU they encountered the following problems:

- *Influences of language differences* When translated from one language to the other sometimes questions underwent a subtle but significant shift of emphasis even though the intention was to make them exactly equivalent. For example, the English statement: "There are times when it is right to disobey the law" got another nuance when it was translated into French: "Il y a des fois où désobéir aux lois est une bonne chose." The French "une bonne chose" is far less strict than the English notion of "right."

- *Ethnocentric bias* Even when correctly translated, the same question meant different things in different cultures because people interpreted the meaning of terms and concepts, and gave answers, relative to the norms of the culture in which they exist. Some cultural differences were differences of fact. Agreement with the statement "We drink more wine at home these days," for example, clearly implied different things in the wine-drinking

country of Greece compared to the same response in the U.K.

Other cultural differences were variations in generally accepted beliefs, or customs. Using the two statements: "Religion plays an important part in my life" and "I go to Church very regularly," for example, to get some measure of how religious people are, produced non-comparable results. In the U.K. 75% of people claimed to be religious, because it is the socially acceptable thing to do, yet in reality it is not a religious country (less than 10% of people regularly go to church). In Italy the situation was reversed. About 55% of people regularly go to church, yet only about 30% of people claim to be religious (going to church in Italy has a strong social function).

- *Cultural response patterns* A third important influence of culture on responses to questions and statements Y&R encountered was national traits in the way people answer questions, even when they do have exactly equivalent meanings in every country. For example, Italians like extremes, and mark towards the ends of any semantic scale; Germans are more restrained, and mark towards the middle. Comparison of sample means between the two countries would lead to erroneous conclusions.

Source: Williams, J. (1991) "Constant questions or constant meanings? Assessing intercultural motivations in alcoholic drinks", *Marketing and Research Today*, 19(3), August, pp. 173f

behavior but also to different reactions to the measurement instrument. Even a similar difference in Switzerland (the German–Swiss listen for 170 minutes but the French–Swiss for 113 minutes) does not allow us to conclude that there is a cultural difference in radio listening behavior due to the French culture. The different cultural background may simply lead to different interpretations of the questions or the responses. We would need an observation of overt listening behavior to validate the results. Tool box 7.1 discusses the various dimensions of equivalence that have to be considered in cross-cultural marketing research and indicates some techniques to be applied for assuring equivalence on those dimensions.

The problem of potential miscommunication between researcher and respondent is particularly prominent in international marketing research. On the one hand, the data collection form has to be translated into other languages and dialects in a way that exactly transmits the intended content. This may be difficult with new technical terms, which may not even exist in the other language. Even if the translation is perfect, the researcher may find that respondents in the countries under consideration have different levels of education. For example, in Vietnam the use of scales is particularly sensitive, as only very easily understandable scales can be used, and each questionnaire has to be very carefully tested several times to ensure that the questions are fully understood by everyone.

Content, phrasing, and presentation of a question may result in different responses. In one country it may be appropriate to formulate a question in an

---

TOOLBOX 7.1 Equivalence

Three different levels of equivalence have to be taken into account in international marketing research: construct equivalence, measure equivalence, and sample equivalence.

Construct equivalence requires that a concept is relevant and has the same meaning across countries and contexts. Three types of construct equivalence can be distinguished:

- functional equivalence, which refers to a concept serving the same purpose across cultures

- conceptual equivalence, referring to a construct occurring in all the countries under investigation and being expressed in the same way

- category equivalence, which refers to a concept (subjectively) belonging to the same class of objects or activities across countries.

Once data have been collected, construct equivalence across cultures and contexts can be statistically assessed by computing the internal consistency of a measure and applying confirmatory factor analysis to check for dissimilarity in the data structure. However, for practical purposes this is too late. Effectiveness demands that a cross-culturally reliable and valid measure must be developed *before* an international study is conducted. Therefore, in a

preliminary phase of the research project differences in definition, in relevant domains and in formulation have to be determined by checking nomological networks as well as convergent and discriminant meanings of the construct compared to similar concepts. Qualitative data collection techniques such as in-depth interviews or projective techniques can be used to identify elements common across respondents from various cultures in contrast to culture-specific elements.

Measure equivalence requires that the measure used to operationalize a concept or construct measures the same content across cultures. To achieve measure equivalence calibration, translation and score equivalence must be given.

- Calibration equivalence refers to equivalence in measurement units. "Level of education," "household income," or "company size" may be difficult to measure equivalently across countries, for example, because of differences in the educational and taxation systems as well as in the importance of the number of staff to the "size" of a firm.

- Translation equivalence is given if the measurement tool is interpreted similarly by respondents in different countries. Translation and

abstract, verbal manner. In another country the same question may have to be communicated through visual means. There may be culturally based differences in the meaning of a question that lead to non-comparable responses between people from different countries (for example, "to be outstanding" means "not to stand out" in China).

On the other hand, in order to obtain comparable results, it may be necessary to use different approaches in different areas. The most important thing is to ensure the equivalence of the survey instruments used in each culture. That may lead the researcher to abandon the spurious security of having the same questions in all geographic areas. What has to remain constant is the socio-cultural significance of the questions used.

For example, energy-saving household behavior may need to be measured in different ways in Norway and the U.S. In the U.S., people who are highly motivated to save household energy may install insulating materials in the walls, floors, and attics of their homes. But in Norway, where heating costs have traditionally been higher, homes may be insulated as a matter of course. There, a high level of energy-saving behavior might be represented by the purchase of an energy-efficient heating system. Under such conditions, the use of a standardized data collection form would result in astonishment or little understanding from respondents in one of the countries.

The marketing researcher must understand even slight cultural differences between countries and target groups. More than with domestic research,

back-translation by bilingual translators will be needed. But verbatim translation is less important than adequately conveying the same meaning. Carefully pre-testing each question or item concerning the meaning it evokes with respondents in the countries under investigation is required before a measure can be seriously taken.

- Score equivalence exists if the observed scores on the measures in the various countries express the same meaning. Score equivalence at the individual level can be tested by confirmatory factor analysis for repeated measurements of a construct. It yields individual scores corrected for lack of score equivalence. These scores can be used in subsequent analyses.

  But there can also be a lack of score equivalence due to cross-cultural differences in response style, such as acquiescence bias, extreme responding, or social desirability. Observed scores may be purged from response style biases by regressing the raw summated scale scores on response bias indices or by determining culture-specific thresholds that need to be surpassed by a measure to be interpreted.

Sampling equivalence refers to the equivalence of the information collected from the drawn

samples. It is not about obtaining samples with the same features of participants in different countries. Sampling equivalence depends on an adequate definition of the target population in each country, the availability of reliable sampling frames. What can be considered an adequate target population in each country depends on the research question(s).

One way to find equivalent samples is to make them broad enough to cover all potential influences of subcultures, that is, to draw probability samples of the entire target population. Because reliable sampling frames are missing in many countries of the world, however, probability samples of sufficient size cannot be drawn.

Therefore, other solutions are the selection of matched samples in the countries under investigation, that is, to draw specific samples representing similar subcultures in the geographical areas to compare (for example, Bolivian nurses compared to Argentine nurses); or the selection of typical representatives for the phenomenon under investigation in each of the cultures.

Source: Douglas, S.P. and E.J. Nijssen (2002) "On the use of 'borrowed' scales in cross-national research. A cautionary note", *International Marketing Review*, 20(6), pp. 621–42; Steenkamp, E.M. and F.T. Hofstede (2002) "International market segmentation: issues and perspectives", *International Journal of Research in Marketing*, 19, pp. 185–213

qualitative investigations to gain better insights into each culture and careful pre-testing of international data collection methods are necessary.

Sampling

When the data collection technique has been established, the researchers must decide how to go about selecting particular respondents for observation, experimentation, or surveying. First, a sampling frame has to be established. Then a sample of appropriate size can be drawn by the use of a sampling technique that accounts for the given research problem and the reliability of the sampling frame.

Sampling frame

A sampling frame is a list from which elements of the target population can be identified. Researchers in western industrial nations can choose from a variety of reliable sampling frames – mailing lists, telephone books, voter registration lists, motor vehicle registration lists, the *International Business and Company Yearbook*, and so forth. However, many traditional sources are becoming limited because of privacy and data protection legislation.

In many industrially developing countries there are few reliable sampling frames for either industrial or consumer target markets. Census data may not be available or recent enough to use. (India, for example, does not have an accurate count of its total population.) The reliability of the few lists that are available may be limited by such problems as unusual housing situations (such as people living on houseboats or out in the open), rapid changes in small business ownership, and a high proportion of family-owned businesses. These problems not only make it difficult to compare markets but can actually prevent researchers from reaching sources of information. Under such conditions, different sampling techniques may be needed to obtain appropriate samples.

Sampling techniques

The method used to select potential respondents from a sampling frame is the sampling technique.

Probability sampling With a reliable sampling frame, the researcher can choose a probability sample, in which each member of the population has a known chance of being drawn into the sample. When detailed sampling frames are not available, the marketing researcher may use a cluster sample. For example, Mumbai in India, might be divided into equal-sized units or neighborhoods. A random sample of these units would then be drawn. Within these clusters, every member or every household would be included in the survey. But even with this technique problems may arise. For most developing countries, no reliable city maps are available. They are drawn by hand and nobody really knows how many people live in which neighborhood.

Probability samples are more elegant from a theoretical point of view. The absence of a reliable sampling frame and other practical reasons, such as the educational level of respondents or simply their reachability, often lead international marketing researchers to draw a non-probability sample.

Convenience sampling Convenience sampling allows the researcher to choose respondents who are readily available, such as people in a marketplace in Indonesia or production managers in Bolivian companies.

Judgment sampling Judgment sampling is often used for industrial marketing research. With this technique the researcher chooses "experts" or "typical" representatives of a product or country market that allow fast and cost-efficient data collection at an acceptable level of reliability.

Because of their sensitivity to many sources of bias, such as high non-response rates, unreliable sampling frames and interviewer influences, the reliability of different sampling techniques varies with the market environments. It is not reasonable, therefore, to apply one standard technique independent of research areas and product markets (see Culture box 7.2). An intelligent adaptation of the sampling technique to the specific circumstances encountered in the markets will greatly improve response rates, quality of data, and the price/benefit relationship of the research project.

Even large international companies, such as Cincinnati-based Procter & Gamble, which are well known for their high levels of process standardization, allow for different local standards of field work in countries such as China compared to Canada. Their main objective is to gather comparable data. Quantitative studies in highly industrialized markets are harmonized to a much greater extent than qualitative research that is mainly used in the initial stages of playing with an idea, to explore a specific usage situation, or for understanding customer language.

Sample size

The quality of research results depends not only on the instrument used to collect data and the sampling technique employed, but also on the size of the sample. The size and structure of samples depend on the firm's information needs, characteristics of the target market, and research budget.

Sample size is partly a function of the diversity in the population to be sampled. Samples with 50 units of analysis may be sufficiently large when the statistical universe is quite homogeneous. In areas where the population to be surveyed is not well known, the degree of variability may be difficult to determine. For example, there are no census data for Ho Chi Minh City. To allow for possibly high variability among households, a larger sample would be required.

CULTURE BOX 7.2

Sampling in the Arab Gulf

In the Arab Gulf a random sampling technique such as knocking on every nth door is simply not feasible. Apart from being socially unacceptable, knocking on the door of a household is guaranteed not to provide an equal chance to all household members to participate in any survey.

Consequently, for gathering data from males non-probabilistic sampling at their place of work or at other suitable locations, such as coffee shops, parks, or public areas is used.

In countries where it is socially acceptable, interviews with women can be conducted in high-traffic areas such as shopping centers, supermarkets, or parks. This practice is most acceptable in the more liberal countries of the Arab Gulf and less so in countries such as Saudi Arabia. Where interviews with women in central locations are possible, the researcher should be careful in selecting the sites: Particular shopping centers or supermarkets quite commonly are frequented by specific nationalities.

For interviews with women in the more conservative countries, most commonly "snowballing" is a quite successful technique. When selecting respondents by that technique, each contact being made is asked for an introduction to some of her own acquaintances. Provided these acquaintances meet the eligibility criteria, they are then asked for an interview. To avoid the potential problem of conducting a large number of interviews among a very narrow circle of relatives and friends, it is best to set a cap of two acquaintances from each respondent. Moreover, after having conducted interviews with a certain number of given contacts, it is preferable for interviewers to move to a new region or neighborhood altogether.

Source: Adapted from Eid, N.C. (1999) "Market research with women in the Arab Gulf countries", *Marketing and Research Today*, May, p. 55

In such instances, exploratory studies with small samples may help researchers gain a better understanding of the population to be studied.

Toolbox 7.2 describes how multistage sampling can help diminish the cost of a sample.

In any case, inexperienced researchers will find it useful to rely on the services of international marketing research organizations, such as ESOMAR, or internationally operating marketing research firms (see Table 7.6) to find equivalent samples.

Analytical plan

An important part of the research design is the plan for analyzing the data. This involves determining which data are needed for which purpose, as well as which tools will be used in their analysis. For example, if the research is designed to find out how consumers in Canada and Mexico respond to one packaging design compared to another, the analysis plan must include a way to group and compare the responses of consumers to each design. Specifically, the plan has to specify if the researchers want to compare the average response of users of one design with the average response of users of the other design for each country, or if they want to identify groups of consumers in both countries for whom brand recognition is important. The statistical techniques to be used will depend on this decision. By answering these types of question in the research design before data gathering has started, researchers ensure that information will be collected in an appropriate manner and that irrelevant and unnecessary (and therefore costly) information will not be sought. The tools used to analyze the data collected in international marketing research do not differ from those used in domestic research.

Research budget and schedule

The cost of each activity included in the project must be estimated. If the firm has a fixed research budget, the project must be designed to meet the constraints imposed by that budget. If the budget is based on the costs of the planned

---

TOOLBOX 7.2   Multistage sampling

On the practical side, since most research budgets are fixed, trade-offs must be made between the number of areas that can be studied, the size of the sample in each area, and the amount of data collected from each respondent. Even where larger samples are appropriate, their cost may be considerably reduced by using a multistage sampling technique. Such an approach was used by TRM, an Austrian manufacturer of cast-metal parts, when it studied the feasibility of enlarging its mould construction department to serve all potential users of industrial moulds in Germany, Switzerland, Italy, and Austria. In the first stage, a probability sample of potential customers was drawn from addresses provided by trade commissions. Telephone calls were used to find out which companies and which individuals

within these companies should be included in the second stage. The individuals identified in this way were mailed questionnaires designed to gather additional information about potential customers. The responses to the questionnaires were used to identify a third sample of individuals who were interviewed personally, to get more details about how to approach new customers successfully.

Such a multistage sampling procedure keeps the costs of research lower than those associated with one-step projects. Contrariwise, it takes more time to implement and the errors committed at each stage accumulate over the duration of the project. Unfortunately, there is no general recipe for how to draw perfect samples in international marketing research.

activities, the marketing researcher should compare these costs with the profit the company may lose if management makes poor decisions because of the lack of information.

Estimating a budget for international marketing research can be difficult. The costs of doing comparable studies vary in different countries, even in the same part of the world. As an example, Table 7.7 shows the average price index for six research projects. Because of such variations, many marketing managers may prefer to establish the project budget in stages and review expenditures at the end of each stage. When this approach is used, the stages need to be outlined in the research brief.

TABLE 7.6 *World top 25 market research companies*

Research agencies now provide a link around the world to help international firms in their marketing research processes.

2002 rank	Organization	Website	Parent country	Number of countries with subsidiaries/ branch offices	Global research revenues ($ in millions)
1	VNU NV	www.vnu.com	NL	81	2,814.0
2	IMS Health Inc.	www.imshealth.com	U.S.	75	1,219.4
3	Kantar Group	www.kantargroup.com	U.K.	62	1,033.2*
4	TNS (formerly Taylor Nelson Sofres plc)	www.tns-global.com	U.K.	54	908.3
5	Information Resources Inc.	www.infores.com	U.S.	20	554.8
6	GfK Group	www.gfk.com	Germany	51	528.9
7	Ipsos Group SA	www.ipsos.com	France	35	509.0
8	NFO World Group Inc.	www.nfow.com	U.S.	40	466.1
9	Westat Inc.	www.westat.com	U.S.	1	341.9
10	NOP World	www.nopworld.com	U.K.	6	320.0
11	Synovate	www.synovate.com	U.K.	46	317.6
12	Arbitron Inc.	www.arbitron.com	U.S.	2	249.8
13	Maritz Research	www.maritzresearch.com	U.S.	4	183.3
14	Video Research Ltd.**	www.videor.co.jp	Japan	4	152.0
15	Opinion Research Group	www.opinionresearch.com	U.S.	6	132.7
16	J.D. Power and Associates	www.jdpa.com	U.S.	5	132.1
17	Harris Interactive Inc.	www.harrisinteractive.com	U.S.	3	120.9
18	NPD Group Inc.	www.npd.com	U.S.	11	115.5
19	INTAGE Inc.**	www.intage.co.jp	Japan	2	105.4
20	Dentsu Research Inc.	www.dentsurresearch.co.jp	Japan	1	62.0
21	AGB Group	www.agb.com	Italy	19	61.1
22	Wirthlin Worldwide	www.wirthlin.com	U.S.	4	54.2
23	Abt Associates Inc.	www.abtassociates.com	U.S.	3	53.8
23	Market & Opinion Research International	www.mori.com	U.K.	2	53.8
25	Lieberman Research Worldwide	www.lrwonline.com	U.S.	1	52.7

* Estimated by top 25   ** For fiscal year ending March 2003

Source: Honomichl, J. (2003) "Top 25 global research organizations", *Marketing News*, August, 37(17), August, H4

Listing activities on which budgets are based also serves to help schedule the project and control its implementation. International marketing research projects are usually complex, taking place across many countries and using agencies that have a variety of skills and capabilities. In order to ensure that the job is done within the budget and on schedule, the activities list is used as a planning tool for these projects.

In order to control expenses and the efficiency of the firm's marketing research activities, the unit within the company which will bear the expense of the research needs to be determined. If the information is used to support strategic decision making, the costs may be assumed by top management or the appropriate business unit. If the findings are to be used in making tactical decisions the corresponding organizational units such as a category management team or a regional sales unit may have to bear the cost of the study. A marketing research unit that operates as a separate cost or profit center that supports all of the firm's marketing research efforts may have its own budget.

Interpreting and presenting results

Figure 7.5 illustrates the final stage of the international marketing research process. The data that have been collected and analyzed must be interpreted and presented in a form that will help improve management decisions.

Interpretation

The interpretation of research results requires a healthy skepticism because of the potential for errors in data collection and analysis, especially when data have been collected under varying circumstances. For example, there may be substantial biases in the answers to attitude questions because of cultural differences. In

TABLE 7.7 *Average price indices for six different research studies*

2003 research price overall index			
	Average index		Average index
U.S.	242	Italy	92
Japan	230	Brazil	88
Sweden	180	Mexico	84
U.K.	170	Greece	81
Australia	166	Portugal	77
France	158	Czech Republic	76
South Africa	157	China	70
Germany	152	Turkey	70
Belgium	138	Poland	52
Netherlands	137	Russia	50
Hong Kong	123	Ukraine	48
Finland	116	Argentina	47
Spain	115	India	37
Austria	105	Bulgaria	29
South Korea	96		

The price of a marketing research project can vary greatly depending on the country in which it is conducted. But there is a wide variation in prices quoted by different research agencies in a country.

Source: ESOMAR (2003), *2003 ESOMAR Prices Study*, Amsterdam
© Copyright 2003 by ESOMAR® – The World Association of Research Professionals

some societies, it is quite common to express one's opinion openly; in others, however, understatement is more common or people are reluctant to express their attitudes to strangers. If researchers want to compare answers given to the same questions in two such different environments, they need to correct for biases due to the typical response styles of the respondents. This can be achieved by normalizing or standardizing the gathered data.

Normalization

In normalizing data the researcher assumes that respondents of all countries use extreme scale values equally. Respondents in one country are, however, expected to be more positive about a construct than respondents in another country. Therefore only corrections for differences in mean are applied by setting each country's mean to zero, and expressing differences in terms of standard deviations.

Standardization

When the researcher has good reasons to assume that respondents from one culture are both more likely to give positive answers and to use more extreme values on the scales, these effects have to be removed before valid comparisons can be made. By setting the countries' means to zero and standard deviations to 1, that is, by standardizing the data, comparability can be achieved.

Cultural understanding

The interpretation of data gathered on an international level demands a high level of cultural understanding. In international marketing research there is the constant danger of selective perception due to cultural biases, that is, a tendency to believe that other people perceive (or should perceive) things in the same way oneself does. Many Anglo-Americans are at the disadvantage that they have greater difficulty in recognizing that bias because they are only able to read or talk in one language. What is not said or published in English does not exist in "their" world. This problem can derail an otherwise well-designed and well-executed research project. The probability of correctly interpreting data can be improved by ensuring that at least one person who interprets the data from a particular region is well acquainted with the culture and business customs of that region.

FIGURE 7.5   *International marketing research process, step 4: Interpreting and presenting results*

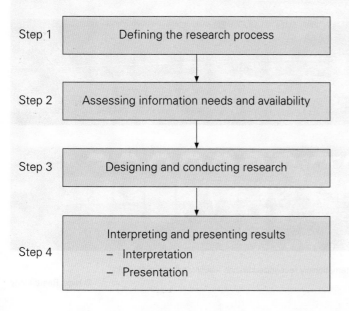

Findings of international marketing research projects need careful interpretation and well-prepared presentation to management decision makers.

Step 1 — Defining the research process

Step 2 — Assessing information needs and availability

Step 3 — Designing and conducting research

Step 4 — Interpreting and presenting results
- Interpretation
- Presentation

Presentation

The findings of a research project are a "product" that, like any other product, deserves its own marketing strategy. The findings should be presented in a fashion that meets the needs of different "customers" within the company. Because there are many different customers of research findings, with different degrees of technical and cultural expertise, it is almost always necessary to prepare both a written report and oral briefings.

Research report

The purpose of the research report is to explain to those who did not participate in the research exactly what problem was studied, how it was studied, what the results were, and how the researchers believe the results should be interpreted. The report should make a case for using the results of the research. The report should also be easy to understand. An extremely detailed and precise report is not best under all circumstances. Strategic and tactical decisions need different degrees of detail in information. Furthermore, high-level managers shy away from long reports. They prefer short summaries of the most important facts, backed by verbal and visual presentations where the managers can ask supplementary questions of special interest to them. Product managers, by way of contrast, often need very detailed market information for their tactical decisions.

Presentation of findings

The shared commitment developed through a team approach to preparing the research brief can be reinforced through proper presentation of the findings. A preliminary presentation of the findings can be made to the team that helped generate the research brief. They can be asked for suggestions regarding revision or expansion of the findings. After the recommended changes have been made, the team may be willing to "sponsor" the reporting of the research to the rest of the organization. This approach can result in a sense of shared ownership of the research. It can be especially important when the results of the research indicate a need for changes in the way the organization conducts business.

Marketing research is vital to internationally recognized brands – such as these soft drinks

© Nigel Reed/Alamy

Organizing for marketing research

The way a firm organizes its research reflects its overall structure.

Centralized research

Highly centralized companies are likely to centralize their marketing research, particularly strategic research activities. At Procter & Gamble, for example, market research is an integral part of each of seven business units based on categories: fabric and homecare, babycare, feminine protection, tissue towels, healthcare, beauty care, and food and beverage. Market research provides each business unit with specific consumer and market knowledge. The basic idea is that a mother in London is not so different from a mother in Tokyo, so baby-care research can be similar worldwide. An expert group can coordinate global studies.

Decentralized research

Firms that decentralize management decision making, by way of contrast, especially those that delegate tactical decision making to local organizations, are likely to have decentralized marketing research. The advantages of decentralized marketing research are:

- more intimate knowledge of markets
- greater appreciation of differences among markets
- potential for greater control over the implementation of research.

French Groupe Danone, for example, has formed a network of research experts working for the marketing teams in different countries. The whole team, including research managers and executives, is only about 24 people spread over Europe, the U.S., Hong Kong, and New Zealand. Their role is to help marketing managers with their expert knowledge to take better decisions. Coordination and learning are achieved through international meetings where experiences are exchanged between marketing research personnel and international research agencies.

Potential disadvantages include:

- ineffective communication with the home company
- lack of comparability of information gathered in different research projects.

To overcome such difficulties, central coordination is useful to ensure agreement on research objectives. However, as in any other marketing activity, central coordination of research leads to higher costs and more delays.

Selecting a research agency

A small firm is unlikely to have a formal marketing research department. Usually, only one or a few people are responsible for research and are part of another unit, perhaps the marketing department. For larger projects, therefore, such firms have to rely on outside agencies and experts. But even large consumer products companies, such as Groupe Danone, ranking third in Europe's food industry, concentrate their in-house marketing research activities on the key elements of research: at the beginning:

- helping marketing teams to move from the marketing problem to the market research problem
- helping them select suitable suppliers for specific problems, to understand and choose the best proposals

● helping them work through the data-gathering instrument.

At the end, Danone's marketing research people have a very important role in understanding and interpreting the results.

Whirlpool Europe, too, has established the principle of putting as much as possible out to research agencies, and to let marketing researchers function as enabling managers rather than as a data-processing house. All the companies mentioned here aim for a restricted number of external service suppliers, who:

● act as partners
● are involved in the company
● fulfill their processing and analytical standards
● can add value with their understanding.

When considering hiring an outside organization to carry out a research project, management has three alternatives from which it may choose. These exist in all of the industrially developed countries and in many developing ones. First, there are research agencies based in the geographic area of interest. They have expertise on the local environment, as well as the ability to cope with problems of language and concept translation. For an example of such an agency, Figure 7.6 shows the internet advertisement of Orient Pacific Century. The difficulties associated with using such agencies include finding reliable ones and coordinating their activities.

The second alternative is to select a research firm that specializes in the industry in question. Computer Technology Research Ltd, for example, is a U.K. market research firm specializing in studies such as the development of RISC technology or the spread of workstations, all concerning the computer industry. Such firms are more likely to understand the research issues related to that industry, and may have experience in carrying out studies in many different parts of the world.

A third option is to contract with a reliable internationally operating research agency or chain of cooperating agencies to manage the entire project. The customer deals with only one office, located in the home country.

The needs of customers who do business at an international level have led some agencies to become international themselves. The Gallup Organization, for example, has subsidiary operations in 20 countries, covering 75% of the world's GNP. These are owned and managed by Gallup. The operations are directed by nationals of each country. Other research firms have signed multilateral cooperative agreements, thereby building worldwide chains of research agencies, such as U.S.-based International Research Associates or WalkerInformation Global Network, a network of 25 individual research agencies spread around the globe and working closely together (Figure 7.7). Others have merged on a global level. For example, by merging, Dun & Bradstreet and AC Nielsen have formed the largest market research firm in the world, called D&B Marketing Information Services.

Toolbox 7.3 presents a checklist for evaluating market research agencies.

But even with the help of outside experts, marketers may have difficulty carrying out primary research in some parts of the world. In developing countries in Asia and Africa there are relatively few market research organizations. In Southeast Asia the biggest weakness is the problem of "too much, too quick." Research tends to be seen as just another business, without the professional and ethical standards that set it apart in industrially more developed countries. Agencies may be technically weak and their staff needs further training. In addition, some governments, especially in China, Myanmar, and Vietnam, see marketing research as threatening. This, plus Islam's attitude to family life, means permission for surveys is required in Indonesia and the government bans all surveys in the protracted runup to elections. Future issues box 7.1 gives an example

FIGURE 7.6 *Orient Pacific Century*

Market Research	Brand Research	Asian Market Strategy	HR Strategies	Team Building	Recruitment Services	Clients & Projects

Orient Pacific Century is a specialist Asian focused **market research** and **brand research** firm assisting both international and Asian business with business, marketing, & brand strategy.

Our strategic research division specialises in **market research, brand research, brand strategy & Asian business strategy**, backed by a world-wide field research capability in both qualitative and quantitative research including **focus group research, consumer surveys, on-line surveys, mystery customer** & **feasibility analysis**.

Our Publishing Division publishes the **Asia Pacific Management Forum, Asian Business Strategy** & **Street Intelligence Ezine, Asia Market Research** dot com and **Branding Asia** dot com.

ENQUIRIES

You may send Requests for Proposals or Quotations (RFPs or RFQs) directly via email to opc-enq@orientpacific.com. You can also make enquiries from our Enquiry Form, contact page.

Head Office:
Plaza 138, Suite 21-01
138 Jalan Ampang, 50450 Kuala Lumpur, Malaysia
Phone: 603 2732 8827
Fax: 603 2732 8826
Email: opc-enq@orientpacific.com

THE ORIENT PACIFIC CENTURY ADVANTAGE

- Strong track record of successful market research & brand research projects for the world's leading brands, companies, and government agencies
- Region wide field research: Japan, China, Singapore, Malaysia, Thailand, Indonesia, Indo-China, South Korea, Taiwan. Also international field work & data collection for testing Asian products and services worldwide
- Reliable & fast data collection; Valid research analysis
- Market research techniques developed and refined specifically for Asia
- Original brand research analysis methods developed over 10 years and used with some of the world's leading brands, developed specifically for Asian consumer markets
- Integrated back-translation
- English speaking International Market Research Directors based in Asia for over 10 years
- Local language field researchers, supervisors and focus group moderators
- Responsive phone and email support after hours for clients in all time zones
- Personal phone and email communication direct with senior and principal researchers

INSTANT ANSWERS!

- **Chat to us now!:** To discuss how we can help you right now or to discuss your RFP or RFQ
- See our latest news

MARKET RESEARCH & DATA COLLECTION

We provide reliable and highly valid data collection, from focus groups, telephone interviews, depth interviews, field/street intercepts/interviews and structured observational methods.

Our methodologies are state of the art, and supported by our R&D program which has resulted in powerful unique methods for analyzing and making sense of raw data, especially that collected in Asia. These relate to market share estimation, identifying target market segments, life-style & market segmentation, customer satisfaction, needs & perception, and competitive positioning.

We cover **Japan, China, South Korea, Singapore, Malaysia, Thailand, Indo China, Indonesia, India**, and the **Philippines** with our own field forces and field supervisors and/or long established partners. We also undertake field research in all countries for international projects with proven results over several major international and regional projects.

BRAND RESEARCH

Our brand research services are specifically tailored for questions relating to competitive branding and brand positioning including brand recall and recognition, integrity, switching, image and many other metrics, especially tailored for Asian consumer markets. These have been used to establish or develop global brands in Asian markets or Asian brands in international markets. They pay particular attention to different market segments and evaluate the need for sub brands or modified brand value statements in each. Our R&D efforts have resulted in unique and tested methods for brand research and strategy in Asia.

ASIAN MARKETING STRATEGY

OPC maintains a strong record helping develop market strategy and brand strategy in Asia for USA and European multinationals as well as Asian governments and companies.

More Information & Services:

- Latest Company News - Overview
- Market Research Overview
- Market Research Services by country
- Clients and Recent Projects
- Strategy and Market Research Consultants
- Join our Field Research Force
- Strategic Marketing Questions addressed by OPC Market Research
- Asian Business Strategy Articles
- Recruitment Services
- Asian Team Building, Training, & Human Resource Management

PAN ASIA CHINA JAPAN KOREA SINGAPORE MALAYSIA THAILAND
ASIAN BUSINESS & MARKET ENTRY STRATEGY MARKET RESEARCH BRAND STRATEGY & RESEARCH
CONSUMER RESEARCH ADVERTISING TESTING FEASIBILITY RESEARCH

Source: www.orientpacific.com

FIGURE 7.7 *WalkerInformation Global Network*

Customer Loyalty
Measuring your critical relationships

Which customers are most important? Will they continue to work with you? What do they really think of your company? In today's global economy, measuring these critical relationships is more important than ever.

Members of the Walker Global Network are equipped with world-class proprietary research tools and methodology for measuring and managing these critical business relationships. The WGN is a network of more than 20 prominent research companies serving more than 75 countries. Each partner is expertly trained—projects are conducted with amazing consistency whether they are across your region or around the globe.

Not just good research, Walker Information's tools are known for being *practical*—reporting systems to assist you in enhancing your business performance and setting strategic goals for the future. You can receive ongoing customer metrics so you can address problems before it is too late.

Employees, suppliers, and other stakeholders are important too. And all are part of the WGN tools to measure and manage relationships that matter.

So contact a partner today and learn more about your customers.
Or visit our website: www.walkerinfo.com/wgn/

WALKER
GLOBAL NETWORK

Argentina	Cyprus	Greece	Korea	Poland	Spain
Australia	Czech Republic	Hong Kong	Kuwait	Puerto Rico	Taiwan
Brazil	Ecuador	Hungary	Malaysia	Romania	Thailand
Canada	Egypt	India	Morocco	Russia	Venezuela
Chile	Finland	Indonesia	Netherlands	Saudi Arabia	UAE
China	France	Israel	Peru	South Africa	UK
Colombia	Germany	Japan	Philippines	Singapore	US

Source: www.walkerinformation.com/globalnetwork/

TOOLBOX 7.3 — Selecting a research agency

1 Basic information about the agency

(a) How long has it been in business as a research company? Is market research its only (or at least its main) business, or is research just an element in a wider range of non-research activities such as marketing/management consultancy or direct marketing?

(b) If it belongs to another company or a group of companies, how independently does it operate?

(c) Is it part of any international research chain or association? If so, how close are the links?

(d) What clients has it worked for during the last 2 years or so, and on what types of project? Which ones does it work for regularly? (Although an agency is obviously restricted by confidentiality requirements in the information it can give, it will often be able to provide some general picture of its clientele and the type of work it carries out for them.)

(e) Are there any potential conflicts of interest that might need to be sorted out?

(f) How much practical experience does the agency have of tackling specific types of research problems or markets, or of using particular research methods?

(g) How firmly is it committed to following the accepted codes of professional practice in marketing research – both ESOMAR and national codes? What are its links with professional bodies in the field?

(h) Are its security/confidentiality procedures acceptable?

2 Information about the agency's staff

(a) What are the professional training, qualifications, and experience of the agency's staff – both senior management and further down the organization?

(b) How experienced are they in dealing with marketing and other relevant non-research issues as distinct from research techniques as such?

(c) What specialist skills (psychologist, statisticians, etc.) can the agency call on – either within the agency or on a regular basis from outside?

(d) Who would be responsible for looking after the client's own project(s)? Is it possible to meet them?

(e) Are there any potential problems of communication? In particular, do the key people (in client and agency) adequately understand a common language? If there are possible difficulties, how could they be dealt with effectively?

3 Information about the agency's facilities and operating procedures

(a) What procedures does the agency follow in setting up a research project? What form does a research proposal normally take?

(b) What kind of field organization does the agency use – its own or a separate supplier? Either way:

- How large and widespread is the interviewing force?
- Are specialist interviewers available if required (e.g., for interviewing executives or professional people)?
- How are interviewers selected and trained?
- What briefing are they given on specific projects?
- How and to what extent are they supervised? What are the qualifications of the supervisors?
- What quality and accuracy checks are applied to the fieldwork?
- Can the client see interviewers in action (in conformity with the ESOMAR Code requirements)?
- [if relevant] Is the agency prepared to accept independent checks on the quality of the fieldwork?

(c) What types of sampling method does the agency customarily use?

(d) How does the agency handle its data processing (internally or subcontracted)? Either way:

- What editing, coding, data entry, and processing procedures are used?
- What quality of staff are used, and how are they supervised?
- What quality and accuracy checks are applied?
- Can flexible and/or more sophisticated forms of analysis be provided when required?
- Are checks of statistical significance routinely applied to the findings wherever relevant?

(e) What form of reporting does the agency normally use? Can it provide tabulation only/written summary of results/interpretation of the findings/recommendations for action, as required? Is it possible to see examples (allowing for possible confidentiality problems)?

(f) Does the agency give presentations of the findings, if required? If so, what form do these take? Are they charged for separately?

(g) Does the agency offer any special research facilities (e.g., a telephone research installation, test room or laboratory, test shop, special testing equipment)?

(h) Does the agency offer any special proprietary research systems (e.g., for testing advertisements/packaging, market modeling, or prediction)?

(i) What are the agency's normal accounting and charging procedures? What billing systems does it normally follow?

(j) What contractual and other legal arrangements are customary with the agency?

Note: not all these questions will be relevant to every enquiry about an agency. Also, it will often be sensible in connection with a specific survey to go in greater depth into certain issues (e.g., the agency's sampling and interviewing approach on surveys among business).

Source: ESOMAR (1992) "Guidelines on selecting a research agency", Doc.E.4, Amsterdam, pp. 4f

that shows how the marketing research industry may still be restricted in countries where strong industrialization trends exist.

In Latin American countries, consumer surveys are available only for urban areas. In addition, it may be difficult to establish a field research staff with enough training to produce reliable interviews. The cheapest and most effective way of getting information in such cases may be to design the research around secondary data and add interviews with carefully selected experts in the markets of interest. The marketer may visit each market to verify the interpretation of secondary data and the insights gained from expert interviews.

FUTURE ISSUES BOX 7.1

Regulation of marketing research in the PR of China

Regulations in China require that only agencies approved by the State Statistical Bureau (SSB) can conduct survey research and no research that competes with SSB's own research activities is allowed. Agencies must obtain a permit for research (renewable each year) and every project, including questionnaire and methodology must be submitted for approval; any substantive changes require new approval.

One particularly problematic requirement is that the research agency must provide the SSB with the final report for review and approval before it can be provided to the commissioning entity. This means that the company that paid for a survey might not ever see the results. Even if it does, the perceived risk of leakage of commercially sensitive information has already led some companies to cancel or delay market research projects.

It will be interesting to see how long it may take until such regulations, which are based on the worldviews of an ideologically closed society, are thrown over by the necessities of a fast modernizing economy.

Source: ESOMAR (2000) "New regulations in PR of China affecting marketing research", *ESOMAR Research World*, March, 3, p. 11

Summary

The intelligence system of an internationally operating company has to provide for:

- a multitude of information sources from inside and outside the firm
- a great number and variety of data at many different levels of detail to be gathered continuously
- the difficult task of treating those data in a manner appropriate to their culture-specific meaning
- effectively disseminating the resulting information to the right people with various cultural backgrounds in time.

International marketing research is best carried out in an integrated fashion embedded in the company's intelligence system.

Marketing research projects start with a definition of the research problem. While sometimes neglected, this is the most important step in the research process. The care and accuracy with which the research question is specified, the unit of analysis is determined, the timing and organization of the project are laid out, and a preliminary budget is set up largely determines how useful the research results will be. Therefore, a written research brief containing all these elements is prepared by a team of people concerned with the research problem and submitted to a decision maker for approval.

In the second stage of the research process, the research team must outline all the dimensions of the research problem. This outline is used to identify information that might be available within the firm and then to determine what information needs must be met from outside sources.

The consequent step is data collection. The researchers will first attempt to solve the research problem through the use of secondary research. Secondary data are inexpensive and often easy to obtain. If secondary research cannot provide enough information to solve the research problem, the firm may decide to carry out primary research. This will mostly be the case when precise data are needed for tactical decisions in an attractive market. Primary research starts with a definition of the target population. Then the most appropriate method for collecting the data has to be selected.

In most international research projects, some kind of sampling will have to take place. With a reliable sampling frame, the researchers can choose an appropriate probability sample. In its absence, convenience or judgment samples will have to be accepted. Such a sample will not fulfill the demands of probability statistics, but it may be more cost effective than a probability sample.

To determine the final research budget, the cost of each activity included in the project must be estimated. The list of activities needed for budget estimation can also be used for preparing and monitoring the research schedule. The budget is related to the organization of market research.

In many cases the company may decide to hire a research agency to carry out the project. Research agencies may

- be based in the geographic area of interest
- specialize in the industry in question
- be international agencies with branch offices or partners in a number of countries.

The data that have been collected and analyzed must be interpreted and presented in a way that is most useful to decision makers. When preparing the written report and oral presentation, researchers should bear in mind that the findings of a research project are a "product" that should be "packaged" and communicated in a fashion that meets the needs of different "consumers" within the company.

DISCUSSION QUESTIONS

1. How does international marketing research differ from domestic marketing research?

2. How does the choice of the unit of analysis affect the results of marketing research?

3. "An international marketing research project must have the latest in-depth market data to be of any value to a marketing decision maker." Do you agree with this statement? Why or why not?

4. How can information available within the firm help in an international marketing research project?

5. What are some of the problems associated with using secondary data in international marketing research?

6. When should primary research be conducted?

7. Why is it important to determine the target population before conducting primary research?

8. What special problems may be encountered in obtaining a sampling frame for international marketing research?

9. What types of agency may be employed to conduct an international marketing research project? What trade-offs are associated with each type?

10. What is an international marketing information system?

ADDITIONAL READINGS

Craig, C.S. and S.P. Douglas (2000) *International Marketing Research*, 2nd edn., Chichester: John Wiley & Sons.

Diamantopoulos, A. and B.B. Schlegelmilch (1997) *Taking the Fear Out of Data Analysis – A Step-by-Step Approach*, London: Dryden Press.

Leonidou, L.C., and M. Theodosiou (2004) "The export marketing information system: an integration of the extant knowledge", *Journal of World Business*, 39, 12–36.

Malhotra, N.K. and B.C. Bartels (2002) "Overcoming the attribute prespecification bias in international marketing research by using non-attribute-based correspondence analysis", *International Marketing Review*, 19(1), 65–79.

Marketing and Research Today, The Journal of the European Society for Opinion and Marketing Research, Amsterdam.

Scholl, N., S. Mulders, and R. Drent (2002) "On-line qualitative market research: Interviewing the world at a fingertip", *Qualitative Market Research: An International Journal*, 5(3), 210–23.

Steenkamp, J.-B.E.M. and H. Baumgartner (1998) "Assessing measurement invariance in cross-national consumer research", *Journal of Consumer Research*, 25, 78–90.

Steenkamp, J.-B.E.M. and F.T. Hofstede (2002) "International market segmentation: issues and perspectives", *International Journal of Research in Marketing*, 19, 185–213.

Useful internet links

ACNielsen	http://www.acnielsen.com/
Asian Omnibus	http://www.ipsos-insight.com/about/
Asiaweek	http://www.asiaweek.com/asiaweek/
BTN Tariff Nomenclature (EU)	http://www.eurunion.org/legislat/customs.htm
Bureau of Economic Analysis	http://www.bea.doc.gov/
Capibus Europe	http://www.ipsos.fr/CanalIpsos/english.asp
COMEXT-EUROSTAT	http://www.fd.comext.eurostat.cec.eu.int/xtweb/
Corning Glass Works	http://www.U.S.Corning_Glass_Works.com
Danone	http://www.danone.com/
Dun & Bradstreet	http://www.dnb.com/us/

Eastern European Omnibus	http://www.ipsos-insight.com/about/
The Economist	http://www.economist.com/
ESOMAR	http://www.esomar.org/
Euromonitor	http://www.euromonitor.com/
European Union	http://www.europa.eu.int/
EUROTAX	http://www.eurotax.com/
Le Figaro	http://www.figaromagazine.fr/magazine/
Frankfurter Allgemeine Zeitung	http://www.faz.net/s/homepage.html
Gallup	http://www.gallup.com/
Garuda Air	http://www.garuda-indonesia.com/
Hanover Fair	http://www.hannovermesse.de/homepage_e?x=1
IBM	http://www.ibm.com/
Institut für Weltwirtschaft Kiel	http://www.uni-kiel.de/ifw/ifwinfo_e.htm
International Code of Marketing	http://www.ibfan.org/english/issue/code01.html
International Fair Frankfurt	http://www.messefrankfurt.com/
International Monetary Fund	http://www.imf.org/
IPSOS	http://www.ipsos-insight.com/about/
ISPO	http://www.ispo.de/englisch/
JETRO (Japanese External Trade Organization)	http://www.jetro.go.jp/
John Wiley & Sons	http://www.wiley.com/WileyCDA/
Kentucky Fried Chicken	http://www.kfc.com/
Market Research Association (MRA)	http://www.mra-net.org/about/index.cfm
Mazda	http://www.mazda.com/
Le Monde	http://www.lemonde.fr/
Neue Zürcher Zeitung	http://www.nzz.ch/english/index.html
New York International Gift Fair	http://www.nyigf.com/
NIKKEI Economic, Japan	http://www.nikkeieu.com/needs/
NIMEXE (harmonized nomenclature (EU))	http://europa.eu.int/comm/taxation_customs/customs/customs_duties/tariff_aspects/harmonised_system/index_en.htm
Nissan	http://www.nissanusa.com
OECD	http://www.oecd.org/
Orient Pacific Century	http://www.orientpacific.com/
Philips	http://www.philips.com/index.htm
Première Vision Paris	http://www.premierevision.fr/en/home/home.php
Procter & Gamble	http://www.pg.com/
Quirk's Marketing Research Review	http://www.quirks.com
Reader's Digest	http://www.readersdigest.co.uk/
Research Magazine	http://www.research-live.com/
Royal Dutch Shell	http://www.shell.com/
Schimmelpfeng	http://www.schimmelpfeng-forderungsmanagement.de/
SIC (Standard International Classification (USA))	http://www.nextlinx.com/global_content/traderefs/acronyms.shtml
SITC (Standard International Trade Classification (UNO))	http://unstats.un.org/unsd/cr/registry/
State Statistical Bureau (SSB)	http://www.stats.gov.cn/english/

Statistik Austria	http://www.statistik.at/
Swarovski	http://shop.swarovski.com/is-bin/INTERSHOP.enfinity/
TED (Tenders Electronic Daily)	http://www.tenders.com/
Texas Instruments	http://www.ti.com/
Thomson Consumer Electronics	http://www.thomson.net/EN/Home
Toyota	http://www.toyota.com/
TUI	http://www.tui.com/
United Nations	http://www.un.org/
United Nations International Development Organization	http://www.unido.org/
U.S. Department of Commerce's Global Market Surveys/Economic Information Department (EID)	http://www.commerce.gov/
Wagons-Lits	http://www.wagons-lits-shop.com/
Walker Global Network	http://www.walkerinfo.com/globalnetwork/
Wall Street Journal	http://online.wsj.com/public/us
WARC.com	http://www.warc.com/
Whirlpool Corporation	http://www.whirlpool.com/
World Bank	http://www.worldbank.org/
Yahoo!	http://www.yahoo.com/
Young & Rubicam	http://www.yr.com/

APPENDIX: ICC/ESOMAR INTERNATIONAL CODE OF MARKETING AND SOCIAL RESEARCH PRACTICE

1. Marketing research must always be carried out objectively and in accordance with established scientific principles.

2. Marketing research must always conform to the national and international legislation which applies in those countries involved in a given research project.

3. Respondents' cooperation in a marketing research project is entirely voluntary at all stages. They must not be misled when being asked for their cooperation.

4. Respondents' anonymity must be strictly preserved at all times. If the Respondent on request from the Researcher has given permission for data to be passed on in a form which allows that Respondent to be personally identified:

   a) the Respondent must first have been told to whom the information will be supplied and the purposes for which it will be used, and also

   b) the Researcher must ensure that the information will not be used for any non-research purpose and that the recipient of the information has agreed to conform to the requirements of this code.

5. The Researcher must take all reasonable precautions to ensure that Respondents are in no way directly harmed or adversely affected as a result of their participation in a marketing research project.

6. The Researcher must take special care when interviewing children and young people. The informed consent of the parent or responsible adult must first be obtained for interviews with children.

7. Respondents must be told either at the beginning or end of the interview if observation techniques or recording equipment is being used, except where these are used in a public place. If a Respondent so wishes, the record or relevant section of it must be destroyed or deleted. Respondents' anonymity must not be infringed by the use of such methods.

8. Respondents must be enabled to check without difficulty the identity and bona fides of the Researcher.

9. Researchers must not, whether knowingly or negligently, act in any way which could bring discredit on the marketing research profession or lead to a loss of public confidence in it.

10. Researchers must not make false claims about their skills and experience or about those of their organization.

11. Researchers must not unjustifiably criticize or disparage other Researchers.

12. Researchers must always strive to design research, which is cost-efficient and of adequate quality, and then to carry this out to the specifications agreed with the Client.

13. Researchers must ensure the security of all research records in their possession.

14. Researchers must not knowingly allow the dissemination of conclusions from a marketing research project, which are not adequately supported by the data. They must always be prepared to make available the technical information necessary to assess the validity of any published findings.

15. When acting in their capacity as Researchers the latter must not undertake any non-research activities, for example database marketing involving data about individuals which will be used for direct marketing and promotional activities. Any such non-research activities must always be clearly separated and differentiated from any organization, which carries out marketing research and the conduct of any marketing research activity.

16. These rights and responsibilities will normally be governed by a written Contract between the Researcher and the Client. The parties may amend the provisions of Rules 19–23 below if they have agreed to this in writing beforehand; but the other requirements of this Code may not be altered in this way. Marketing research must also always be conducted according to the principles of fair competition, as generally understood and accepted.

17. The Researcher must inform the Client if the work to be carried out for that Client is to be combined or syndicated in the same project with work for other Clients but must not disclose the identity of such Clients.

18. The Researcher must inform the Client as soon as possible in advance when any part of the work for that Client is to be subcontracted outside the Researcher's own organization (including the use of any outside consultants). On request the Client must be told the identity of any such subcontractor.

19. The Client does not have the right, without prior agreement between the parties involved, to exclusive use of the Researcher's services or those of his organization, whether in whole or in part. In carrying out work for different Clients, however, the Researcher must endeavor to avoid possible clashes of interest between the services provided to those Clients.

20. The following Records remain the property of the Client and must not be disclosed by the Researcher to any third party without the Client's permission:

    a) marketing research briefs, specifications and other information provided by the Client

    b) the research data and findings from a marketing research project (except in the case of syndicated or multi-client projects or services where the same data are available to more than one Client).

    The Client has however no right to know the names or addresses of Respondents unless the latter's explicit permission for this has first been obtained by the Researcher (this particular requirement cannot be altered under Rule 16).

21. Unless it is specifically agreed to the contrary, the following Records remain the property of the Researcher:

    a) marketing research proposals and cost quotations (unless these have been paid for by the Client). They must not be disclosed by the Client to any third party, other than to a consultant working for the Client on that project (with the exception of any consultant working also for a competitor of the Researcher). In particular, they must not be used by the Client to influence research proposals or cost quotations from other Researchers.

b) the contents of a report in the case of syndicated and/or multi-client projects or services where the same data are available to more than one Client and where it is clearly understood that the resulting reports are available for general purchase or subscription. The Client may not disclose the findings of such research to any third party (other than to his own consultants and advisors for use in connection with his business) without the permission of the Researcher.

c) all other research Records prepared by the Researcher (with the exception in the case of non-syndicated projects of the report to the Client, and also the research design and questionnaire where the costs of developing these are covered by the charges paid by the Client).

22. The Researcher must conform to currently agreed professional practice relating to the keeping of such Records for an appropriate period of time after the end of the project. On request the Researcher must supply the Client with duplicate copies of such Records provided that such duplicates do not breach anonymity and confidentiality requirements (Rule 4); that the request is made within the agreed time limit for keeping the Records; and that the Client pays the reasonable costs of providing the duplicates.

23. The Researcher must not disclose the identity of the Client (provided there is no legal obligation to do so), or any confidential information about the latter's business, to any third party without the Client's permission.

24. The Researcher must on request allow the Client to arrange for checks on the quality of fieldwork and data preparation provided that the Client pays any additional costs involved in this. Any such checks must conform to the requirements of Rule 4.

25. The Researcher must provide the Client with all appropriate technical details of any research project carried out for that Client.

26. When reporting on the results of a marketing research project the Researcher must make a clear distinction between the findings as such, the Researcher's interpretation of these and any recommendations based on them.

27. Where any of the findings of a research project are published by the Client the latter has a responsibility to ensure that these are not misleading. The Researcher must be consulted and agree in advance the form and content of publication, and must take action to correct any misleading statements about the research and its findings.

28. Researchers must not allow their names to be used in connection with any research project as an assurance that the latter has been carried out in conformity with this Code unless they are confident that the project has in all respects met the Code's requirements.

29. Researchers must ensure that Clients are aware of the existence of this Code and of the need to comply with its requirements.

PART II

BASIC STRATEGIC DECISIONS

The preceding part of the book has shown how the attractiveness of international markets can be assessed and how a comparison with major competitors will help a company identify whether it can excel on any of the success factors in the most attractive markets (Figure II.1).

Based on corporate policy, the assessment of potential markets, and distinctive competences, management can determine the core strategy of the organization. That is, it decides what direction of development the firm should take and how this development should be achieved. The core strategy must contain information on:

- intended strategic position (Chapter 8)
- rules of business behavior to be followed (Chapter 9)
- resource allocation (Chapter 10).

The intended strategic position (Chapter 8) determines the major objectives of the organization, which have been defined as intentions earlier on in the international marketing decision process as part of corporate policy. Based on the strategic analyses accomplished in the following, those objectives can now be formulated in a more precise manner and priorities can be fixed.

In addition, the intended identity of the business organization has to be determined. It is not only salient for the development of a shared understanding among staff concerning the purpose and the major characteristics of the organization they are members of. Organizational identity also provides the basis for global branding. For example, depending on the identity to be reached the company may strive for being one global brand covering all its activities or the home of various brands having their own identities. Objectives and intended international branding have a strong influence on the selection of markets to be served and technologies to be applied for that purpose.

FIGURE II.1 *International marketing decision process*

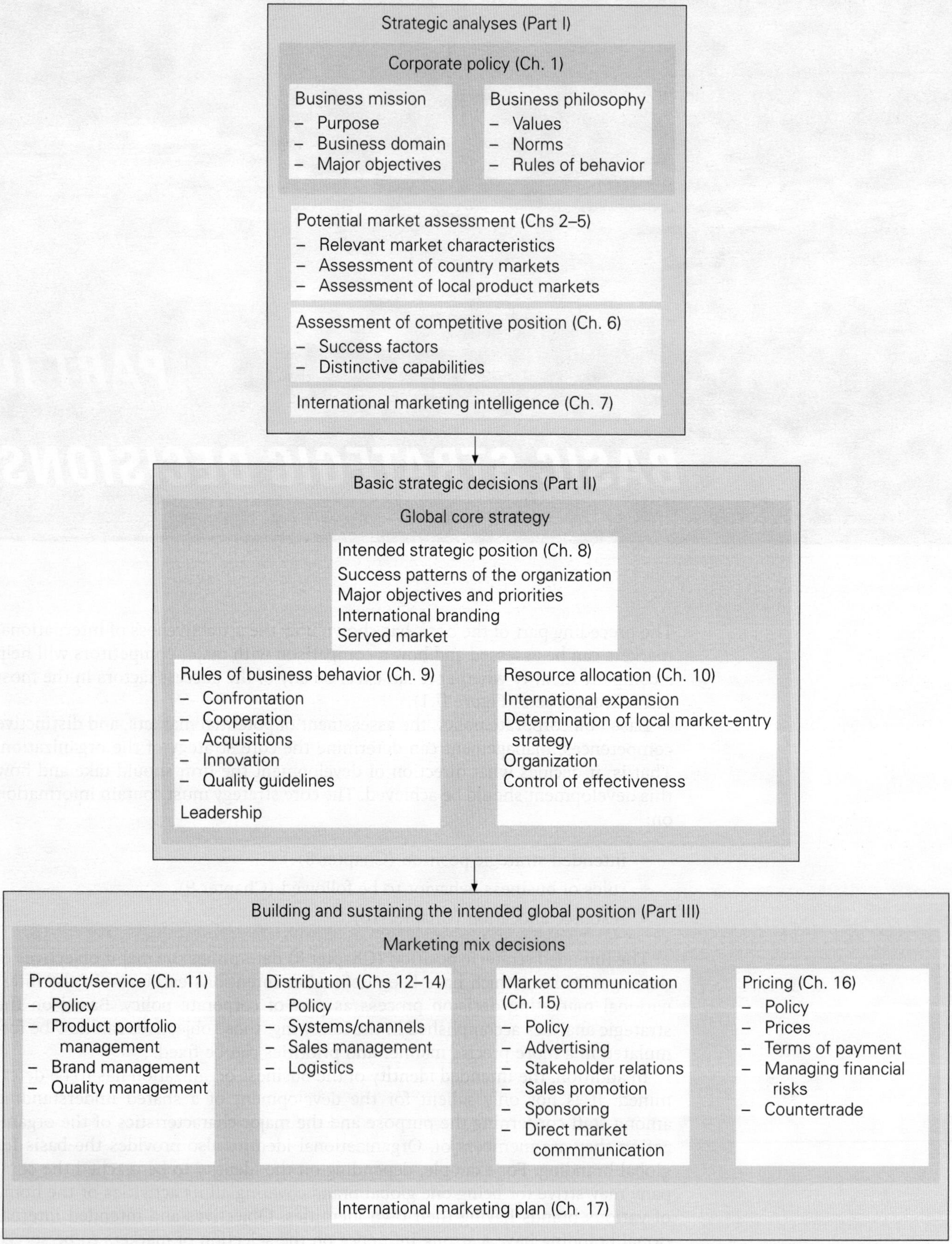

Strategic analyses (Part I)

Corporate policy (Ch. 1)

Business mission
- Purpose
- Business domain
- Major objectives

Business philosophy
- Values
- Norms
- Rules of behavior

Potential market assessment (Chs 2–5)
- Relevant market characteristics
- Assessment of country markets
- Assessment of local product markets

Assessment of competitive position (Ch. 6)
- Success factors
- Distinctive capabilities

International marketing intelligence (Ch. 7)

Basic strategic decisions (Part II)

Global core strategy

Intended strategic position (Ch. 8)
Success patterns of the organization
Major objectives and priorities
International branding
Served market

Rules of business behavior (Ch. 9)
- Confrontation
- Cooperation
- Acquisitions
- Innovation
- Quality guidelines

Leadership

Resource allocation (Ch. 10)
International expansion
Determination of local market-entry
  strategy
Organization
Control of effectiveness

Building and sustaining the intended global position (Part III)

Marketing mix decisions

Product/service (Ch. 11)
- Policy
- Product portfolio
  management
- Brand management
- Quality management

Distribution (Chs 12–14)
- Policy
- Systems/channels
- Sales management
- Logistics

Market communication
(Ch. 15)
- Policy
- Advertising
- Stakeholder relations
- Sales promotion
- Sponsoring
- Direct market
  commmunication

Pricing (Ch. 16)
- Policy
- Prices
- Terms of payment
- Managing financial
  risks
- Countertrade

International marketing plan (Ch. 17)

The intended strategic position provides the basis for the definition of rules of business behavior – the way the organization and its subunits will behave in the served markets to reach the intended identity and fulfill their mission (Chapter 9). An important part of an organization's business behavior is competitive behavior. Choices range from a frontal attack on any competitor, to cooperative agreements that not only allow peaceful coexistence but also the exploitation of mutual strengths, achieving synergy. The rules of business behavior also comprise the policy concerning growth through mergers and acquisitions as well as cooperation, norms concerning the innovation and communication behavior of the firm as well as general guidelines concerning quality.

How well the rules of business behavior are accepted and fulfilled by the members of a business organization largely depends on the behavior of its leaders and their ability to handle needs for change. The influence of leadership on the implementation of rules of business behavior will, therefore, also be discussed in Chapter 9.

Having defined the intended global strategic position of their organization and the rules of behavior that are supposed to help reaching that position, top management has to determine how they want to allocate the limited resources of the company (Chapter 10). The way they deploy those resources across processes and organizational subunits as well as across markets, technologies, and in time influences the success of the organization. Therefore, as Chapter 10 will describe, management determine the path of international market expansion of their organization.

Closely related to the intended strategic position, the fixed rules of business behavior, and the planned path of international expansion, a market-entry strategy has to be determined. It contains the positioning in each of the local markets to be served as well as the selection of appropriate market-entry modes.

Resources not only need to be allocated across markets and technologies but also inside the organization. Organizational structures and processes must be shaped to enable the company to plan, implement, and evaluate its international marketing decisions. Depending on the selected structure and the shape of their core processes companies will be more or less well adapted to their business and path of internationalization. By discussing those resource allocation decisions and the control of their potential impacts Chapter 10 will provide the basis for all international marketing mix decisions to be addressed later in Part III.

INTENDED STRATEGIC POSITION

8

Learning objectives

After studying this chapter you will be able to:

- explain the foundations of successful international competition

- discuss the impact of major objectives on the behavior of managers

- explain the importance of branding to international business success

- discuss issues to be considered in determining an international brand architecture

- explain the factors influencing intended and actual brand meaning

- use portfolio analysis for the selection of markets to be served

Chapter outline

Intended global strategic position

Success patterns of the organization

General sources of competitive advantages
Foundations of successful competition
Company-specific competitive advantages

Major objectives and priorities

Market leadership
Growth
Profitability
Stakeholder value

International branding

Need for branding
International brand architecture
Intended brand meaning
Brand interest group

Served markets

International portfolio analysis
Market/product portfolios
Technology portfolios
Selection of markets and technologies

Summary

INTERNATIONAL MARKETING SPOTLIGHT

Nestlé refines its strategic position

Nestlé is the world leader in food manufacturing. It has a yearly cash flow of around €700 million. In 2004, sales in nutrition reached €5 billion (including branded active ingredients). The goal is to reach €10 billion in nutrition by 2010, to decrease costs by €4 billion per year by 2006, and to push for 5–6% currency-adjusted overall annual sales growth.

To reach those objectives and to ensure its leading position in the future, Nestlé had to refine its global strategic position. Two big changes dominate the picture: an increased focus in product markets served and a reorganization of the group.

Instead of a defining itself as a food and beverage company Nestlé has decided to focus on health, nutrition, and wellness. In the early 2000s, Nestlé acquired the pet food giant Ralston Purina, the frozen-food company Chef America Inc., and a controlling stake in Dreyer's Grand Ice Cream Inc., all three based in the U.S. After having filled some gaps in terms of product market as well as country market coverage, future growth is to be achieved mainly internally, based on Nestlé's in-house R&D. Additional growth should come from joint ventures, such as the cooperation with L'Oréal in the area of nutricosmetics that resulted in a nutritional supplement called Inneov to improve the health of skin. Unlike companies such as Unilever, which have sold off a substantial number of brands to

focus on a relatively small group of more profitable brands, Nestlé plans to further improve performance while maintaining a large and diverse portfolio inside the defined product markets.

Instead of having a decentralized structure with many individually managed middle-sized firms spread across most countries of the world, in the future, Nestlé wants to behave more as a group. Country managers have traditionally been given a wide leeway on everything from purchasing to capital investment. For example, each ice cream factory was ordering its own sugar. Now, everything below customer visibility is managed in a more centralized manner. Most purchasing is handled by regional units, fewer and bigger factories do the manufacturing, and services such as treasury, administration, and legal services are managed on a regional basis.

Nestlé head office – taking control © picturesbyrob/Alamy

Source: Adapted from Matlack, C. (2003) "Nestlé is starting to slim down at last", *Business Week*, 27 October, p. 56; Szemeliker, L. (2004) "Der Riese Nestlé stellt sich neu auf", *Der Standard*, 12/13 June, p. 25

The focal question of this chapter is: How can a business organization determine an intended global strategic position?

Intended global strategic position

Corporate policy was the starting point for the international marketing decision process (Figure 8.1). In its corporate policy the company has defined the business mission and philosophy. An important part of the mission is the business domain. The business domain describes the relevant product market of the organization and its geographic limitations. Inside this given framework, management can assess the current state and potential future developments of the relevant market. In most cases the assessment will show that the relevant market is not homogeneous. There are several sub-markets in both customer benefit as well as geographic terms. For the most attractive of those markets distinctive capabilities of the firm may be determined. If there are such distinctive capabilities, management can build the core strategy of their organization on them.

The **core strategy** – in larger companies it is called corporate strategy – is a more detailed and precise version of corporate policy transforming general strategic intentions into decisions concerning:

FIGURE 8.1 *International marketing decision process*

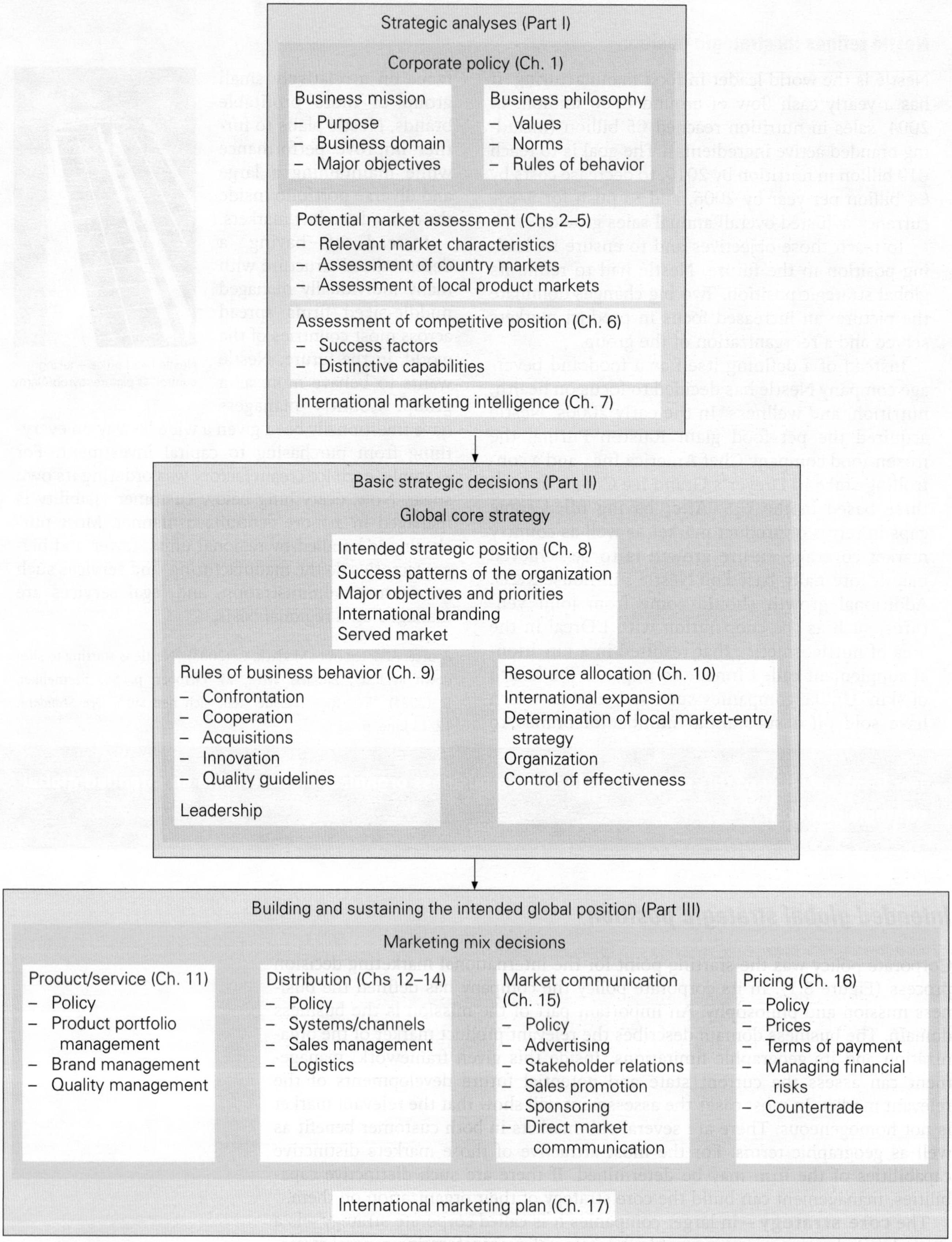

Strategic analyses (Part I)

Corporate policy (Ch. 1)

Business mission
- Purpose
- Business domain
- Major objectives

Business philosophy
- Values
- Norms
- Rules of behavior

Potential market assessment (Chs 2–5)
- Relevant market characteristics
- Assessment of country markets
- Assessment of local product markets

Assessment of competitive position (Ch. 6)
- Success factors
- Distinctive capabilities

International marketing intelligence (Ch. 7)

Basic strategic decisions (Part II)

Global core strategy

Intended strategic position (Ch. 8)
Success patterns of the organization
Major objectives and priorities
International branding
Served market

Rules of business behavior (Ch. 9)
- Confrontation
- Cooperation
- Acquisitions
- Innovation
- Quality guidelines

Leadership

Resource allocation (Ch. 10)
International expansion
Determination of local market-entry
  strategy
Organization
Control of effectiveness

Building and sustaining the intended global position (Part III)

Marketing mix decisions

Product/service (Ch. 11)
- Policy
- Product portfolio
  management
- Brand management
- Quality management

Distribution (Chs 12–14)
- Policy
- Systems/channels
- Sales management
- Logistics

Market communication (Ch. 15)
- Policy
- Advertising
- Stakeholder relations
- Sales promotion
- Sponsoring
- Direct market
  commmunication

Pricing (Ch. 16)
- Policy
- Prices
- Terms of payment
- Managing financial
  risks
- Countertrade

International marketing plan (Ch. 17)

- objectives
- served market
- rules of behavior
- resource allocation.

In determining the objectives of their organization and the markets to be served, management refines and details the mission of the organization. That is, it specifies the intended strategic position. How this position is to be reached is determined by the rules of behavior and resource allocation. This chapter will discuss the issues to be addressed in formulating the intended strategic position of an internationally operating organization.

To be able to formulate meaningful objectives and select the markets to be served, management must first determine the success patterns of their organization in the past, and then reinterpret them according to current and future challenges in the international markets considered serving. A newly created business organization will have to determine its major capabilities and assess how it can help establishing a sustainable success position in international markets.

Market leadership, growth, and profitability (or contribution to the mission of the organization) may be the most prominent objectives formulated by managers of all kinds of organizations. These objectives serve the more basic goal of long-term survival. An organization's survival can best be ensured, however, by providing attractive value to all of the relevant stakeholders. Therefore, a high level of stakeholder awareness and an attractive meaning to at least the most influential stakeholders in all served markets must be a prominent objective of any business organization.

Influencing the meaning of the company, one of its business units, a product line or a product to its stakeholders, needs carefully coordinated management of stakeholder experiences at all touch points. This is called **branding**. Management of an internationally operating organization needs to decide intended objects of branding, that is, the brand architecture of the whole organization. For example, the company may strive for developing one global (corporate) brand covering all its activities or may decide to be the home of various (product) brands having their own distinctive meanings. Management must also decide the intended meaning of those objects to the stakeholders.

Objectives and branding have a strong influence on the markets an organization decides to serve. Management will select the markets and the technologies to be used in serving them according to the fit between the success factors in the most attractive potential markets, the capabilities of their organization, the objectives to be reached, and the intended meaning of the organization's brands. This chapter will discuss the issues raised in the sequence given.

Success patterns of the organization

The core strategy of a business organization is guided by a vision of how the organization, as a whole, will create and generate value for its stakeholders to achieve its own objectives. To be successful this creation and generation of value must be based on competitive advantages the organization possesses or can build up and is able to sustain for some time.

General sources of competitive advantages

Depending on the degree of internationalization of its business, an organization has access to different general sources of competitive advantage. A globally operating company may derive competitive advantages from qualities that are not available to firms with a regional or domestic focus, such as the following.

Efficiencies of global scale and volume

A global scale of business can lead to significant gains in production efficiency and sales volume that can be transformed into customer benefits. Global efficiencies of scale allowed Asian manufacturers of VCRs, for example, to make their products at lower costs and sell them at more competitive prices than was possible for U.S. manufacturers serving only the regional market. As a consequence, U.S. manufacturers no longer produce VCRs.

Transfer of experience, ideas, and successful concepts

A globally operating company is also able to transfer experience, ideas, and successful concepts from one country market to another. McDonald's country managers in Europe, for example, regularly meet to compare products and promotional ideas, but also to discuss how to avoid waste, and whether such ideas might be appropriate in other markets. Faster knowledge transfer and learning result in superior customer benefits through lower prices and improved product and service features.

Global reputation

Globally active companies often have a stronger reputation than can be achieved by domestic companies. As travel and communication across national boundaries increase, this potential is likely to grow. To take the same example, McDonald's, which is active in many country markets, enjoys a higher reputation for product quality in Australia than does the domestic Hungry Jack, an affiliate of BurgerKing, which was unable to use its better known name in Australia because of legal registration problems.

Transfer of resources between business units

Globally operating companies can transfer resources between business units in different parts of the world. These resources may include:

- personnel (such as experienced production managers)
- funds (global organizations usually have a lower capital cost than domestic firms)
- superior market information.

Firms such as Kraft-Jacobs-Suchard, the Swiss-based chocolate and coffee manufacturer belonging to Philip Morris, transfer their managers to operations in which their specific know-how is required, for example, in the growing markets of eastern Europe, and profit from the capital transfer capacity of their company to respond quickly to market opportunities wherever they occur.

Exploitation of local advantages

One might expect that globally operating companies are less well situated than local firms to exploit local advantages, such as closeness to the market and working with distributors on a personal basis. However, domestic marketers, especially those located in small country markets, are often underfinanced, lacking in well-qualified management, and not highly competitive in nature. The additional resources available to global marketers, coupled with a more professional marketing orientation, may make them better prepared to seek out and exploit local advantages.

Ability to provide global services

Increasingly, customers in industrial and consumer markets are looking for more complete products, including pre- and post-sale services. Despite greater distances such services may be performed more efficiently or more fully by global marketers. For example, the car industry does not accept more than 2 hours' standstill of a machine. Germany's Trumpf, the world leader in industrial lasers, therefore, provides a 24-hour standby service to customers of their bending machines. Each machine is connected to Trumpf via the internet. The subsidiaries in Pasching, Austria, in Farmington, Connecticut, and in Singapore take turns in service standby. Service engineers at those places can see what is going on in each machine sold worldwide. Diagnosing the reasons for problems has become a core competence besides mechatronic know-how. Additionally, customers can order spare parts around the clock directly via the computer screen integrated into each machine.

Foundations of successful competition

Successful competition is always based on providing superior value to customers and other important stakeholders. Superior value can be built on cost leadership, on a superior product (including services) a company is able to provide, on time leadership as well as on special capabilities in building and sustaining relationships.

Cost leadership

A company striving for cost leadership does everything necessary to have the lowest costs per unit marketed and to either pass this advantage on to their customers through low prices or to their shareholders through high profitability. For example in March 2003 Japan's Toyota announced the best result of the entire car industry in the last 10 years. At a time when General Motors reached an operating margin of 1.5%, Ford operated at a loss, and DaimlerChrysler U.S. lost substantial shares of the market, Toyota announced an operating profit of 8.3%. This success was very much based on a consistent cost leadership policy. In 2002 costs were diminished by $2.5 billion. Kaizen, six sigma, total quality management, total productive maintenance, and zero-defect programs have traditionally been central to Toyota's management. So have waste reduction programs at all points in the value generation process, from ending overproduction, to minimizing waiting times, movements, transportation, storage, warehousing and scrap, to optimizing machining. While U.S.-based automakers tend to diminish their costs by outsourcing highly paid jobs to suppliers and pressing them for low prices, Toyota follows another path. Suppliers are strongly involved in the development of new models. They are expected to come up with suggestions as to how to continually lower the costs of components.

A manager of a manufacturing firm who wants to base the company's future success on cost leadership must be aware that the costs a firm incurs largely depend on its production volume and the number of products (product lines) in its program. Figure 8.2 shows that owing to economies of scale, an increase of production volume of a single product leads to a decrease of costs per unit (doubling the volume may lead to cost decreases of 15–25%). At the same time, any increase in the number of products produced and marketed increases the costs of inventory, storage, transportation, and overhead. Experience shows, for example, that cutting the number of products by half may increase productivity up to 30% and decrease costs by around 17%. This leads to a cost curve of the shape shown in Figure 8.2.

From there we can conclude that large, mass-producing firms such as Matsushita, Philips, Siemens, or Alcatel can make maximum use of economies of scale and accumulated experience in all functional areas. Because of their broad range of products, however, they run the risk of lower productivity than smaller more focused competitors. To achieve reductions of product program costs, the firms have to reduce the variety of their own production. They seek partnerships with more focused suppliers and cooperative ventures. In the automotive industry, for example, Japanese car producers buy 70% of their products from suppliers

FIGURE 8.2   *Cost curves depending on production volume and program size*

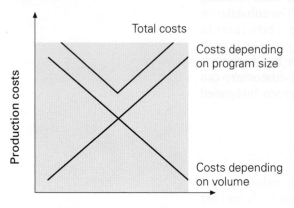

Increasing production volumes and decreasing program size lead to reduced costs per unit

---

FUTURE ISSUES BOX 8.1

Is Wal-Mart too powerful?

With more than $250 billion revenues Wal-Mart Stores Inc. is the world's largest company. It is three times the size of the No. 2 retailer, France's Carrefour. Every week, about 140 million shoppers visit Wal-Mart's more than 5,000 stores. Wal-Mart operates close to 2,000 stores in 10 countries. If the company can maintain its 15% growth rate, it will top $600 billion in 2011.

At Wal-Mart, "everyday low prices" is more than a slogan. Over the years, Wal-Mart has relentlessly wrung tens of billions of dollars in cost efficiencies out of the retail supply chain, passing the larger part of the savings along to shoppers as bargain prices. Because other retailers must also make price cuts to compete the "Wal-Mart effect" has contributed to suppress inflation and increase productivity of suppliers year after year.

However, Wal-Mart's seemingly simple and virtuous business model is fraught with perverse consequences. For example, America's largest private employer is widely blamed for the sorry state of retail wages in the U.S. On average, Wal-Mart sales-clerks earned $13,861 a year in 2001. At the time, the federal poverty line for a family of three was $14,630. The employee turnover rate still exceeds 40%.

Additionally, Wal-Mart controls a large and rapidly increasing share of the business done by many U.S. and overseas consumer products com-

panies: for example, close to one-quarter of Del Monte Foods and Revlon cosmetics, but also close to 20% of Procter & Gamble's turnover. Were Wal-Mart ever to go into a tailspin, the effect on the economy would be traumatic.

There is no question that the company has the legal right to sell only what it chooses to sell. But Wal-Mart's cultural gatekeeping has narrowed the mainstream for entertainment offerings while imparting to it a rightward tilt.

Certainly, the supercentering of the U.S. and in the following of Europe and the fast developing economies of Southeast Asia can be expected to result in huge savings at the cash register. On average, a Wal-Mart supercenter offers prices 14% below its rivals'. However, those everyday low prices come at a cost. As the number of retail outlets shrinks, more shoppers will have to travel farther from home. The rush for lower and lower prices leads to bypassing middlemen and buying finished goods and raw materials from low-cost manufacturers. With a global workforce of about 1.5 million, Wal-Mart plays a huge role in wages and working conditions worldwide. Its hard line on costs has forced many factories to move to low-wage countries. Jobs get increasingly lost in the countries where, supposedly, Wal-Mart customers are located. How long will the spiral of lower prices, lower wages, fewer jobs last until it breaks?

Source: Adapted from Bianco, A., W. Zellner, D. Brady, M. France, T. Lowry, N. Byrnes, S. Zegel, M. Arndt, and R. Berner (2003) "Is Wal-Mart too powerful? Low prices are great. But Wal-Mart's dominance creates problems – for suppliers, workers, communities, and even American culture", *Business Week*, 6 October, p. 100

they have close relations with. Partnerships with suppliers and competitors permit a firm to maintain a large product program at lower costs and provide access to technology and management expertise that would otherwise not be available.

Non-dominant firms, whether large or small, may cater to special market needs, concentrating their resources in a narrow field where they can dominate competition. Focusing on a small range of products allows them to market higher volumes and to produce at lower costs per unit. An example of a smaller company successfully focusing on a special market to gain economies of scale is Portugal's Corticeira Amorim, which controls a large share of the country's cork manufacturing. Amorim makes 70% of the world's cork floorings, about 15% of the world's wine corks (the world uses about 25 billion corks a year) and almost 95% of the cork-based gaskets Portugal produces to seal engine joints. To further improve its cost position the company has been buying up cork distributors in almost 30 countries and distributes for smaller Portuguese producers.

Companies – large or small – relying on cost leadership may have great success with their customers or their shareholders. As Future issues box 8.1 shows, however, this success may create problems to other stakeholders and, finally, to the customers themselves.

Superior product

The success of a business organization may be based on its capability to provide a bundle of special benefits to customers or other important stakeholders. Californian Silicon Graphics, for example, sells mostly to companies that need to create complex 3D images. Its machines, which animated the dinosaurs in the film *Jurassic Park*, dominate Hollywood's computer graphics industry.

Competition based on superior exchange offers to customers and stakeholders uses the company's potential for differentiation from competitors through higher attractiveness of core product characteristics. In this case customer preference is not achieved through lower prices but through higher perceived value of the product. Media centers offered by Philips or Microsoft, for example, replace old stereo equipment, VCR, and computer in one case. In a similar vein to eliminate cables disliked by consumers, Hewlett-Packard builds digital camera docks into the tops of its home-use desktop PCs. Strategy box 8.1 gives an example of how marketers in the same industry can differentiate from each other by offering superior value through product characteristics providing different benefits.

The example in Strategy box 8.1 also shows that the provision of superior value by product characteristics is often based on technological leadership. Nintendo has accumulated great experience in videogames, whereas Sony is a major player in the development of consumer electronics. Technological leadership can be the main source of competitive advantage in business-to-business industries. Picogiga, a French semiconductor manufacturer, for example, is the global market leader in gallium arsenide wafers used to make chips for cellular phones and digital TVs. They build their success as much on strong R&D as Lernout & Hauspie, a Belgian speech translation company, which produces software that helps computers translate written text in one language to speech in another.

Superior value is not only produced by features concerning the function of a product.

Services Services provided before, during, and after purchase decision making can be decisive for customer preference. For example, the Genius Bars in Apple Stores have strongly contributed to their customers' level of satisfaction since the first store opened in Washington in 2001. At any of the more than 100 Apple-owned retail stores in the world, customers receive free face-to-face support by "Geniuses" – Apple's term for its in-store technical support staff. Other computer retail stores have technical support counters, too. CompUSA or Best Buy even have traveling teams of support staff who make house calls. But those services are not free.

Metso, the Finnish world leader in industrial paper-making equipment and procedures, to cite an example from the business-to-business world, produces machines that are more than 110 meters long and come at a price of about €150 million. Those machines are not only capable of transforming wood into coils of paper or cardboard, they are also equipped with electronic sensors and a computer connected to the internet, which allow diagnosing problems (that may occur very quickly) from a maintenance center in Finland. The cost of service teams' traveling can be reduced, and, in many cases even removed, and machine availability can be largely increased.

Symbolic values These may be even more important as sources providing superior value, since they are difficult for competitors to imitate. Take the example of Chanel. For close to 100 years now the luxury brand based in Paris has managed to remain one of the top five brands and an uncontested reference in the minds of consumers interested in top-end clothing. Coco Chanel's designs – later followed by the designs of Karl Lagerfeld – have always been an expression of the rejection of the "typical" female fashion of the time, as created by Pioret in the 1920s and Dior in 1950s. With its emphasis on the functionality of all details, Chanel created fashion for upmarket professional women.

Time leadership

Time leadership is a way of competing successfully by being faster than competitors in every respect, from new product development through production to delivery. A series of examples of successful companies such as Benetton or

---

STRATEGY BOX 8.1

Nintendo vs Sony

For 15 years Nintendo had a monopoly in portable game consoles. Having sold 180 million Game Boys, the Japanese firm launched a new product called DS at the end of 2004 to sustain its supremacy in the market. But, for the first time, Nintendo's omnipotence was challenged by the arrival of Sony in this very profitable niche of the video market. Sony launched its portable PSP in December 2004, 10 years after it had successfully introduced PlayStation in the living rooms of consumers all over the world.

The two big rivals tried to attract customers in a clearly differentiated manner: Nintendo has put all its experience and development capabilities into the "playability" of the new product. To make playing games more easy and intuitive the DS is equipped with two screens (one touchscreen), a pen- and hand-writing recognition, a microphone, and voice recognition. An automatic wireless connection system among DS facilitates playing in groups and increases potential variations and experiences. In addition, the European version, launched in March 2005 offering 14 games (with 20 more in development), was able to read all games available for PlayBoy (more than 550).

In contrast, Sony tried to make their PSP more than a tool for playing video games. The PSP is conceived as a portable digital leisure device. It integrates a memory card to record the games played but also to load digital pictures, readers for numerical music, mini-DVDs to watch movies, and multiple connection capacities.

By providing superior value to different consumer segments in the same market, Nintendo and Sony together hope to increase the total market volume for videogames.

Source: Adapted from Macke, G. (2005) "Nintendo veut asseoir sa suprématie dans les consoles de jeux portables avec la sortie de la DS", *Le Monde*, 29 January, p. 19

Motorola indicates the importance of time leadership to successful strategic positions in the most economically developed regions of the world.

Benetton, the Italian fashion house based in Treviso, for example, was first to have online connections between its shops and a central logistics unit in Italy. This central unit is informed about stock movements and developments in demand wherever they occur. Because their knitwear is produced and stocked without being dyed, the greatest variety and quick response are ensured without uncontrollable risk. The products are dyed in the colors and numbers needed, and sent out by overnight delivery to the shops.

Motorola's U.S. production plant for cellular phones takes orders by computer connections with sales outlets and delivers the products in the following 48 hours. Such speed and flexibility were achieved by expanding just-in-time principles to the entire value chain. Tasks that were not required for ultimate customer benefit were eliminated. System response time was further reduced by doing things in parallel instead of sequentially. Work is done in small batches, eliminating idle or dead time wherever it existed.

To be faster than competitors in any respect needs perfect management of value creation and generation processes. Processes are more difficult to copy than products. To establish and maintain:

- a highly sensitive market information system
- fast and continuous product and process innovation (often) in close cooperation with suppliers and customers, in small steps and through multifunctional teams
- a highly flexible production process with partly autonomous groups of workers
- just-in-time delivery
- short production runs
- total quality management

needs people having the know-how, being ready for continual organizational learning, and a management that is able to provide an inspiring context. Under such conditions a high diversity of products can be quickly and reliably delivered at low cost compared to competitive offers.

But to be faster than competitors in only one aspect may also improve the strategic position in particular of smaller companies. At the turn of the century, Fortune Oil, a small Hong Kong company, for example, tried to do what much larger oil companies had not managed to do: create a wide network of gas stations in China. While urban Chinese were used to paying a premium for branded consumer products, gasoline was still just gasoline to most people. Service stations were run by a patchwork of local operators, many with links to state-owned refineries. Fortune hoped to implant itself before China opened its market to the big multinational competitors.

Stakeholder relationships

The increased importance of being fast in many industries should not lead management to neglect the fourth basic dimension of business success: reliable relationships, that is, a network of positive personal and institutional relations with all the important stakeholders in the relevant business system. Examples of industrial business and service firms in highly industrialized regions of the world as well as experience from Arab, Asian, and African countries demonstrates how companies can very successfully build their market position on personal and institutional relationships with important stakeholders. Toolbox 8.1 describes how a world-leading company in the business-to-business sector uses customer relationship management tools to further build and sustain its competitive position in a highly dynamic market.

In most cases it costs less to keep current customers than to continuously build new customers. Because relationship management strongly depends on personal contacts, the firm's customer contact personnel need permanent training. But they must also be highly motivated through having satisfying relationships with the company themselves. In this respect, the standing of the firm in its local environment plays a significant role.

IBM, for example, follows a policy of good local citizenship. On the French Riviera, where they have located their European research and development center, the company sponsors the kindergarten, schools on all levels, local festivals, concerts, and even the restoration of historical buildings. Such behavior has not only been attractive to IBM's highly trained international workforce who were assured of living in a culturally pleasant environment where their children could

---

TOOLBOX 8.1   Customer relationship management tools and services

Datacon Technology AG, one of the world's leading producers of die-bonding machines (machines mounting chips on substrates that go into all kinds of electronic devices), has based much of their business success on technological leadership and customer relationship management (CRM). The tools and services they use in CRM are shown in Figure 8.3.

For key accounts, defined as internationally operating firms that are leaders in their specific markets, Datacon offers specially designed machines. Volume purchase agreements guarantee standardized pricing and fixed conditions if an agreed volume is bought in a certain period. Management meetings with key accounts prepare joint developments and serve the purpose of exchanging and adapting roadmaps.

Datacon uses its own salesforce wherever possible. Salespeople are increasingly working as consultants. They help customers establishing useful networks, for example with research institutes or suppliers. Distributors are only used where language and culture are an issue, such as in Scandinavia for language reasons and in Japan for cultural reasons.

Datacon has been very successful with joint new product developments often subsidized by public institutions. Machines are customized to market specifics and to customer production lines. A productivity package offers preventive maintenance, service and repair, application support as well as an extended hotline (24 hours 7 days a week). In the so-called application lab customers can develop new products on machines at Datacon headquarters. There is no mandatory buying. Machine use is paid on a daily basis. Thus, customers do not need to buy a new machine for developing samples for their own customers.

On the financial side, the 4-year advanced leasing program offered to customers includes replacement of the machines after 2 years. Smaller clients are offered financing services for their investment. And even rental machines are provided to established customers who need increased production capacity for short time periods.

Market communication includes traditional trade shows, but also a customer area on the website that includes spare part service and hot mails concerning technical as well as commercial issues.

CRM software constitutes the communication tool for international information exchange. It serves for documentation, planning of resources, controlling, and marketing analyses. Two essential parts of that software are the Contact Book and the Business Opportunity Manager.

The Contact Book contains addresses, products, personal information, and the structure of customers' buying centers. The Contact Book is fed by the salespeople who use the book as a tool for preparing their calls.

The Business Opportunity Manager contains data concerning potential customer projects. Salespeople, service personnel, and project managers feed in information on the contact history with the customer, about competition, forecasts, basic information for resource planning, and controlling, as well as general documentation concerning the project.

In addition, Datacon runs customer satisfaction and customer enthusiasm analyses. Satisfaction analysis concerns the performance of the equipment and of service personnel. It compares Datacon with its competitors and looks at year-to-year trends. Customer enthusiasm analysis tries to find out what inspires the customers and what is required from Datacon to be perceived as being more attractive than competitors.

have an excellent education, but also to local administrators who in reaction largely facilitated the firm's business in the region. Culture box 8.1 further illustrates how important close relationships with stakeholders may build success for international businesses.

Non-dominant firms may build highly successful relationships on a local basis, taking advantage of distinctive competences in specific country markets. Such companies may rely on close contacts with commercial and administrative stakeholders leading to government preferences for purchasing from specific suppliers. But they may also build on trusting personal relationships with key local personalities such as "market mammys" in West Africa or *bazaari* in Iran who can have strong influences on business deals in developing economies. A number of small embroidery manufacturers located in Austria's most western province of Vorarlberg, for example, have developed substantial competitive advantage through cultivating their relationships with local intermediaries and administrators, such as customs officers, in West African countries. Developing and maintaining such contacts demands specific knowledge of cultural and political conditions in a country and flexibility in responding to changes.

Combination of sources

Successful competition, whether local, regional or global, can be based on cost leadership, superior products, time leadership, or reliable relationships. To be successful a company must have a competitive advantage from at least one of the discussed sources. For example, Hong Kong's very successful apparel makers Toppy, Esprit, and Theme all share something that Japanese apparel makers lack: cost competitiveness. Most of the clothes are made in China, and each of the three firms designs, produces, and markets its wares itself. In Japan, they are displayed alongside DKNY, Max Mara, and Calvin Klein, but they sell for half the price of the New York brands. They possess another plus that Europeans and Americans cannot match: a grasp of the fashion sense of oriental women. Their colors are not overly bold, and the widespread use of materials like silk appeals to Asian customers.

FIGURE 8.3 *CRM tools and services at Datacon Technology AG*

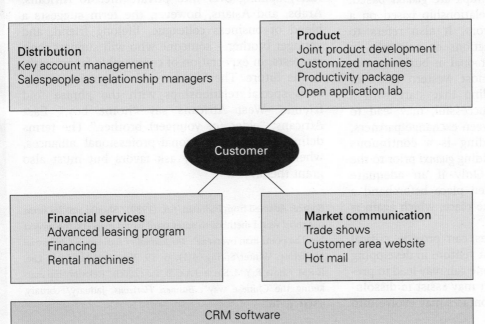

Customer relationships are best managed using various tools from the areas of distribution, product, price, and market communication management. For coordination purposes those tools need to be based on CRM software.

The best performers are likely to be driven by strategies that combine competitive advantages based on efficiency in terms of cost and time and on stakeholder orientation, finding its expression by superior value as well as strong relationships.

Swiss-based Basler Insurance, one of the biggest insurance companies in Europe, for example, after having largely improved its cost position by restructuring organizational processes, which also led to substantial gains in speed of new product development in reaction to market needs, has discovered that the most important factor for long-term success in its markets is the establishment and maintenance of close relationships with customers.

Company-specific competitive advantages

A company can identify its specific sources of competitive advantage by running through its list of distinctive capabilities for the markets under consideration. For example, it is critical for a producer of optical frames and sunglasses, such as Austrian Silhouette, who wants to establish a subsidiary in China, to be able to establish firm relationships with members of the business system, such as retailers or transportation companies, in order to ensure timely distribution. Because the firm has long-term experience in building such relationships in Hong Kong, Taiwan, and Japan, it possesses a distinctive capability that can be transformed into a competitive advantage compared to other suppliers from western countries.

CULTURE BOX 8.1

Relationship building for success in world markets

In China business relationships are *guanxi* based. *Guanxi* means a personal relationship based on a continual exchange of favors. It also refers to drawing on broader connections or networks in order to secure favors in personal or business relationships. In contrast to most western views of business relationship building that start with a transaction, and, if it is successful, may lead to a personal relationship between exchange partners, Chinese relationship building is a continuous process that begins with building *guanxi* prior to the first business exchange. Only if an adequate exchange of favors has taken place beforehand a business transaction can take place, which again is embedded in ongoing *guanxi*.

Well-placed local notables can provide critical assistance in early stages of a venture in developing markets. One influential phone call may lead to preferential treatment. One visit may assist in dissolution of a bottleneck. Such contacts may evolve into both mentors and allies, guiding newcomers through social or commercial minefields that could prove fatal were they attempted on their own.

The term "ally" means something different to non-U.S. residents than it does to most U.S. citizens. In U.S. corporate circles, business alliances are usually limited to specified commercial matters, rarely spilling over into private life. To Africans, Arabs, and Asians, however, the term suggests a blend of business colleague, lifelong friend, and younger brother – someone who will support their interests, in expectation of comparable favors within the future. The Chinese address participants in such special relationships with the phrase "old friend." West Africans say "home boy," East Africans, "elder (or younger) brother." The terms define composite personal/professional alliances, wherein each side may ask favors but must also grant them.

Source: Adapted from Fadiman, J.A. (1989) "Should smaller firms use third world methods to enter third world markets: the project head as point man overseas", *The Journal of Business and Industrial Marketing*, Winter/Spring, 4(1), p. 19; Yau, O.H.M., J.S.Y. Lee, R.P.M. Chow, R.Y.M. Sin and A.C.B. Tse (2000) "Relationship marketing the Chinese way", *Business Horizons*, January/February, 43(1), p. 16

Distinctive capabilities may become competitive advantages if the firm can successfully transform them into benefits for potential customers or relevant stakeholders. The distinctive capability of highly flexible low-cost production, for example, can only become a competitive advantage when it is transformable into low-priced customized products. Customers and stakeholders will have a high propensity to develop preferences and long-term relationships with the provider of such benefits if they are highly attractive to them.

Competitive advantages are strongest when they are based on capabilities unique to the firm, that is, when they cannot be easily duplicated. The family ties of owners and managers of Taiwanese and Hong Kong-based companies with business people from the People's Republic of China, for example, give them a competitive advantage over U.S. companies in obtaining joint venture contracts with Chinese firms.

A marketer should not overlook, however, that competitors might develop capabilities quite quickly through acquisitions, mergers, or cooperation.

A competitive advantage only exists if the customers and stakeholders are ready to value the offered benefits by adequate exchange reactions such as paying a good price or providing goodwill. Sometimes a company does not have a particular distinctive capability in a market that looks highly attractive. In such cases it must develop differences between itself and its competitors. Such differentiation may take the form of:

- providing creative solutions to previously unsolved problems
- applying new technologies
- developing customer benefits that are not currently offered
- simply promoting or distributing in a new way.

Major objectives and priorities

Most companies, whether large or small, globally or locally active, formulate objectives such as market leadership in terms of sales, growth, and profitability. Table 8.1 shows the objectives McDonald's set in April 2003 to increase the firm's attractiveness to shareholders.

Market leadership

Market leadership makes top managers and financial analysts dream. It is a reflection of power in comparison to competitors but also in the relationship with stakeholders. A market leader is supposed to impose the rules of the game.

Where market leadership objectives may lead to is best illustrated by the example of the agrifood industry. As a reaction to the enormous concentration of purchasing power in food retailing, all big companies in the agrifood industry, that is Nestlé, Unilever, Kraft, and Danone, focus their forces to become the leader or at least No. 2 in a certain sector. They abandon activities that do not help them reach that goal. In 1996, French Danone started with recentering its activities around fresh products, water, and biscuits. Well-established brands such as Carambar or Kronenbourg were sold. In 2000, British–Dutch Unilever followed by starting to eliminate 2,000 brands, such as Banania, Benco, and its cheeses, to focus on the remaining 400 brands such as Lipton (tea) and Miko (ice cream). American Kraft Foods focuses on chocolate (Suchard, Toblerone), coffee (Maxwell, Carte Noire), and biscuits, where it became world leader by acquiring Nabisco in the year 2000. Suisse Nestlé, the traditional leader in coffee (Nescafé) put all its financial forces into becoming the leader in pet food and ice cream. They acquired Ralston Purina and Dreyers in the U.S. Today, there are two majors in every sector of the agrifood industry: Nestlé and Danone in water, Nestlé and

Kraft Foods in coffee and chocolate, Unilever and Nestlé in ice cream, and Kraft Foods and Danone in biscuits. Behind those giants, there is a great number of smaller companies that have the option to focus on specific local or regional niches, to cooperate or merge themselves, or to be acquired.

Growth

Closely related to market leadership, growth is a very prominent objective and a major driver of international marketing. Most top managers and financial analysts think that a company cannot survive without growing. But there are some examples that show a different picture. Glenwood, Illinois-based Landauer Inc., for example, produces badges for hospital personnel who measure radiation. They charge around $45 a year per person for a badge, collect them monthly, and test for exposure. Landauer has more than 50% market share in the U.S. More than 1.3 million people wear their badges worldwide. The company has selected a very small niche of the hospital supply market that, in addition, needs specialized logistics to be properly served. That has kept bigger companies from acquiring Landauer, but has also kept Landauer from branching out. Instead, the company pays its profits out to the capital owners.

Following growth objectives in new country markets may end up in fierce competition occurring in current markets. For example, Huawei and Zhongxing (ZTE) are two major Chinese companies operating in the global telecommunication business from mobile telephone infrastructure to sophisticated optique fiber equipment. Huawei conducts more than 25% of its business outside China and reports growth rates of 30% annually. The company has signed contracts in Algeria, Indonesia, Russia, and Thailand; but also in Uzbekistan and Zimbabwe. ZTE, having supplied equipment to Algeria, Kuwait, Pakistan, and Russia plans to reach sales of $10 billion by 2008 by largely increasing its international business. Those companies have profited hugely from technology transfers by western companies such as Alcatel, Ericsson, Lucent, and Motorola, which sought

TABLE 8.1 *Objectives set by McDonald's in 2003*

In 2003 McDonald's embarked on a new strategic course, reflecting a fundamental change in the approach to growing the business. Instead of adding new restaurants, the emphasis is on building sales at existing restaurants.

Objectives

- To attract new customers
- To encourage existing customers to visit us more often
- To build brand loyalty
- To create enduring profitable growth

Targets

- Improve trends in comparable sales and margins and create momentum toward sustainable, profitable performance during 2003 and 2004
- Achieve annual system-wide sales growth of 3–5% in 2005 and beyond
- Achieve annual operating income growth of 6–7% starting in 2005
- Achieve annual returns on incremental invested capital in the high teens in 2005 and beyond

Source: McDonald's revitalization plan (2003), www.mcdonalds.com

cooperation partners to enter the promising Chinese market. For example, in order to firmly install itself in the third-generation mobile telephone market in China, Siemens decided to invest $100 million in a joint venture with a Chinese partner in 2004.

Profitability

Profitability is the basis for survival of any privately owned company. The problem is that it can be measured in a variety of ways, and that each way of measurement results in different incentives to the members of a business organization. For example, *return on investment* tends to decrease the willingness of responsible managers to invest in R&D, but also in building a company-owned distribution system. *Return on sales* tends to increase the focus on margins compared to the growth of market share. *Return on capital employed* tends to reinforce outsourcing trends.

Depending on the specifics of the product market and the state of development of a company's international operations those tendencies may have positive or negative impacts. If a company-owned distribution channel is highly important to tightly control customers' experiences with the company, or if vertical integration is the only way to keep important know-how from becoming available to competitors, top management should carefully consider what profitability objectives to select.

Difficulties may arise if business development in different country markets demands adapted behavior. For example, if one of the markets is in a stage of growth, gaining market share may be more important compared to a rather flat market, where attractive margins may be of interest. Using the same profitability measure would be counterproductive in such a case.

Finally, management should not forget that market leadership, growth, and profitability are largely influenced by the capabilities of their organization, but in the end depend on the satisfaction of stakeholders with what the organization is doing.

Stakeholder value

The implicit but major objective of most all organizations is to ensure long-term survival. The best way of ensuring survival is to continuously increase the value of the organization (compared to others) to its stakeholders. If the stakeholders possessing the resources an organization needs for its survival perceive the organization as providing attractive benefits to them those stakeholders will help the organization survive by

- repeating purchases
- providing positive relationships
- positive word of mouth.

For such an ideal situation to occur, the organization must be known to the stakeholders and have an attractive meaning to them. That is, a high level of stakeholder awareness and an attractive meaning to at least the most influential stakeholders in all served country markets must be a prominent objective of any business organization. The fulfillment of other objectives, such as market leadership in terms of sales, growth, and profitability, is a logical consequence of high awareness and attractiveness to stakeholders.

Focusing only on stakeholder awareness, for example by strongly communicating a brand name, does not fulfill the objective. High levels of awareness combined with a negative meaning would lead to disaster. Influencing the meaning of the company, of one of its business units, or a product to stakeholders, needs coordinated management of stakeholder experiences at all touch points strongly led by top management. This is called *branding*.

International branding

Need for branding

Branding is central to creating and generating stakeholder value. **Branding** refers to all activities of an organization that focus on influencing the value of the organization to stakeholders. **Brands** are social representations jointly constructed by organizations, their customers, and other stakeholders in an ongoing communication process. Brands consist of three closely interrelated elements (as shown in Figure 8.4)

Brand interest group

A **brand interest group** is a social entity of individuals and organizations more or less intensively communicating in a brand related direct and indirect, verbal, and nonverbal manner. Members of such a brand interest group may be the supplier of a product or service, who communicates about its organization, about a business unit or one of its offers, the staff of this supplier, the customers and sympathizers, the intermediaries and their staff, and all kinds of other stakeholders such as journalists or consumer protection agencies.

The members of the brand interest group contribute their experiences, knowledge, expectations and evaluations to a real and virtual public discourse concerning a brand object.

Brand meaning

Brand meaning consists of collective knowledge and evaluations continually emerging from communicative processes among the members of a brand interest group. Because it is jointly elaborated, brand meaning is conventional wisdom concerning a brand object. As such it is taken for granted.

Brand meaning is consensual, but not uniform. Each individual member of the brand interest group holds part of the collective knowledge and evaluation system. These individual parts overlap. The brand has the same essence (= core) for all members of the brand interest group. But a great variety of time and context related cognitions and related effects are distributed across members (= periphery). Therefore, various subversions of the same brand meaning exist depending on the specific context. For example, Hennessey is a prestigious French cognac to be consumed at festive occasions. But for French consumers it

---

FIGURE 8.4 *Brands as social representations*

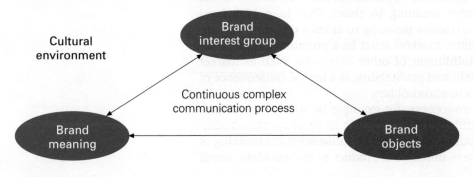

Cultural environment

Brand interest group

Continuous complex communication process

Brand meaning

Brand objects

Brands are social phenomena. Mutually shared meanings concerning brand objects are continually emerging from an ongoing complex communication process among members of a brand interest group.

is a special treat after a good meal, whereas U.S. consumers perceive it as a cocktail drink before dinner.

Brand objects

Brand objects are the material manifestations of the meaning of a brand. Brand objects can be a product, but they can also be an organization, a shop, or people. For example, when a consumer enters a retail outlet of Sephora the layout of the shop, the staff, and the products will stimulate a clearly different brand meaning from when the same person visits an outlet of the Body Shop.

How brands develop depends on the cultural environment in which the social interactions concerning the brand objects take place. In international marketing there are so many varying cultural environments that there are no universal rules to follow for brand management. But there are some questions to be asked in a sequence that can be followed independent of the environment:

1 What should the brand objects be?
2 What is the current meaning of those brand objects
   - to the members of the organization
   - to the current stakeholders of the organization?
3 What should the meaning of those brand objects be to members of the organization as well as the stakeholders in the various country markets to be served?
4 What needs to be done to make the appropriate brand meanings develop?

International brand architecture

Brand objects are the object of consumption or use. For example, Disney Worlds in the U.S., in France, and in Japan are visited by millions of customers every year who personally experience the Disney brand together with many others. At the same time, brand objects are the simplified visual representation of the brand in terms of a symbol. By using that symbol, the members of a brand interest group can communicate to themselves and with others. For example, Rolex, Porsche, Ungaro, or Bang & Olufsen are examples of brands that customers all over the world use for communication purposes.

Some product categories, such as commodities, seem rather alien to branding for many international marketers. Success stories such as Outspan Oranges, Chiquita Bananas, and Lycra fibers have proved the contrary. Ingredient branding may even improve the attractiveness of a consumer product to customers all over the world. For example, PCs are more easily sold when the buyers know that the product has "Intel inside." Sports textiles that have a little booklet attached explaining how Gore-tex has been used to make the product wind and water resistant without keeping perspiration inside are more attractive to many consumers. In addition, such branding decreases the dependence of the former commodity supplier on its direct customers.

Even if, in very rare cases, the product of the international marketer does not seem to lend itself to branding, there is a need to formulate branding objectives for the organization as a whole. Stakeholders continually make direct or indirect experiences with the organization. They make sense of those experiences by attributing a meaning to them and communicating about it. Consequently, the company has a brand meaning independent of management's decision to explicitly think about brand building and actively try to influence it or not. Therefore, when determining the intended strategic position of their organization international marketers do not need to decide if they should bother with branding. They rather have to decide what they would like to be brand objects.

Brand architecture is the result of that decision process. To avoid confusion inside the company and among stakeholders, brand architecture establishes clear roles, relationships, and boundaries for brands. It determines the hierarchical levels in the organization at which brands are to be established and managed, that is, from the level of the whole company, across business units, down to product lines, and products; the geographic extension of those brands, that is, if they are to be established and managed worldwide, regionally, or only locally; and the scope of brand objects, that is, the range of objects a brand is allowed to cover: the entire company, a business unit, a product line, or only a product.

Types of brand architecture

Depending on what the brand objects should be, management can decide between one-firm branding, house branding, endorsed branding, and separate branding.

One-firm branding Also called monolithic branding or branded house strategy, this consists of focusing all branding activities on the firm level. Examples from all sorts of industries abound. Nike, Samsung, Crédit Suisse, or Siemens have used the synergy effects of a strong corporate brand on a worldwide level. Table 8.2 shows that in 2003, the majority of the 10 most powerful brands in the world were corporate brands.

A **corporate brand** allows cost reduction in markets where product lifecycles have shortened to an extent that the costs of continually launching new product brands in the market can hardly be recovered. More important, a corporate brand increases the attractiveness of the entire company to shareholders, employees, distribution partners, suppliers, public administrations, and other potentially important stakeholders. It helps building trust, loyalty, and even commitment.

For example, Sony has a reliably high level of competence in its field and high product quality based on intensive care for details. This holds true for stereo equipment as well as TV sets and computer games. Corporate brands like Harley-Davidson have been able to attract members of their interest group in a way to make them even feel part of a community. They like to virtually communicate with each other and even personally spend some time together.

A well-managed international corporate brand allows consistent appearance to a great number of stakeholders. For companies involved in marketing closely

---

TABLE 8.2   *Top 10 most powerful brands 2003*

Rank	2003 brand value in billion $	2002 brand value in billion $
1 Coca-cola	70.45	69.64
2 Microsoft	65.17	64.09
3 IBM	51.77	51.19
4 GE	42.34	41.31
5 Intel	31.11	30.86
6 Nokia	29.44	29.97
7 Disney	28.04	29.26
8 McDonald's	24.70	26.38
9 Marlboro	22.18	24.15
10 Mercedes	21.37	21.01

Source: "Special report: The 100 Top Brands", *Business Week*, 4 August, 2003

To be rated in the contest a brand must have a brand value greater than $1 billion, it must derive at least one-third of its sales from outside the home country, have significant distribution throughout the Americas, Europe, and Asia, and must have publicly available marketing and financial data.

related product lines, running businesses that share a common technology or rely on very similar core competences, building a consistent corporate brand may seem rather easy. General Electric, for example, markets from aerospace products and electric generators to medical equipment, all relying on engineering skills under its GE name. The more different products are delivered by a business organization in an increasing number of culturally diverse markets, the more difficult it may become to influence brand-related communication of stakeholders in a way to help in creating and reinforcing an unambiguous meaning. But as the examples of Disney or Virgin show, consistency is only needed for the core elements of the brand. As long as the central core of brand meaning is not jeopardized, the corporate brand may have different meanings in different environments without any detriment.

House branding When the expectations of customers and other important stakeholders vary significantly from one usage situation to another, house branding may help in profiling different bundles of a company's activities and may increase the perceived competence of the corporate brand at the same time. **House branding** uses the name of the company in a prominent role but adds business unit or product(line) names to them. For example, the French automaker Renault helps distributors, consumers and journalists differentiating product profiles by calling its models "Mégane," "Safrane," "Espace," or "Twingo."

Endorsed branding The international marketer uses **endorsed branding** when product names are in the foreground and the corporate brand is used to indicate their origin. Examples may be "Smart – a brand of DaimlerChrysler" or adding Nestlé to Buitoni, Maggi, or KitKat to reinforce the sub-brands by the strong corporate origin.

Electrolux, the world's largest producer of kitchen, cleaning, and outdoor appliances, has grown through acquisitions and therefore has a very large and diverse portfolio of brands. For years, those brands were behaving independently, depleting resources, giving rise to both internal and external confusion, and increasing costs. Given this, there were four issues that Electrolux's management found to be important to develop internally: a brand policy, common goals for the brands, a common language, and common measurements for brand performance. The company decided for an endorsed branding strategy, using Electrolux as an endorser standing for quality, leadership, and trust. The number of brands was reduced in order to create bigger and stronger brands that are attractively differentiated but still support each other. Brand positioning was refined to converge globally; leaving to the local managers the burden of proving that their local situation demands adaptations departing from the worldwide intended brand meaning, and not the other way around.

Separate branding Many internationally operating companies target various customer segments that expect different benefits, which need to be provided through different capabilities building and maintaining relationships with varying stakeholders. In such cases, management tends to separate branding. **Separate branding** relies on the corporate brand in its relationships with the financial community, the public administration, and sometimes, potential employees, but develops independent appeals for customer segments and related stakeholders. For example, the U.S.-based international fashion retailer Gap has three successful brands: Banana Republic, Old Navy, and Gap, each having a distinct profile attracting different groups of customers.

A separate product brand may develop such a strong meaning that the corporate source is no longer of importance. This is the case of Nivea, Pampers, or Dove. As companies such as Procter & Gamble have experienced, however, separate branding may lead to an ever increasing number of product brands with decreasing market shares at increasing complexity costs. Thus, British Unilever has decided to eliminate 1,200 local brands from its portfolio to focus on 400 brands. In addition, as the example of Seat, Škoda, Audi, and VW all belonging to Germany's Volkswagen AG shows, there is a danger of cannibalization among product brands if the products are not differentiated enough because of cost cutting reasons.

Global vs local brands

When determining the brand architecture of their organization, managers must decide the geographic extension of brands. Brands may be global, regional, or local.

Global brands Perceived quality and status are among the most important factors driving customer preference for global brands. Global brands, such as Chanel's "No. 5," boost worldwide brand recognition. What is called a global brand depends on the perspective. For a brand to be effectively global from a customer/stakeholder point of view its essential positioning has to be consistent across the world, resulting in a universally shared meaning of the brand's core concept. To achieve that goal, brand name, design, packaging, distribution, pricing, and communication at all touch points with (potential) customers and other stakeholders must provide the stimuli needed for creating a similar brand meaning. Because of culture-dependent differences in the interpretation of stimuli this will be rather difficult to achieve with a standardized marketing program.

In most cases, however, customer preference for global brands has not been the primary reason for companies to opt for global brands. Most companies consider a brand being global when worldwide brand related activities are highly standardized. Globally active companies, such as Accor, the French hotel group (Atria, Coralia, Ibis, Mercure, Novotel, Suitehotel) use the same product-related cues, such as brand name, logo, packaging, or product design, in all their served country markets in an attempt to significantly lower their costs.

Business logic states that global brands – in that sense – provide economies of scale and scope in new product development, purchasing, manufacturing, logistics, and marketing. By standardizing its brand-related activities, Avon, the world's biggest direct-sales cosmetics maker active in more than 120 countries, has been able to improve quality, reduce the number of suppliers, and cut costs. This and other economies, such as uniform ingredients and packaging, mean that gross profit margins on Avon's global brands have been higher than those of its other lines.

Global brands allow higher speed to market, and a concentration of communication budgets. Therefore, L'Oréal focuses on 16 brands worldwide. Procter & Gamble, having had 300 brands in eight product categories in the early 2000s, tries to increasingly focus on a few world brands such as Ariel, Pampers, Pantene, or Pringles. However, P&G's decision to eliminate Dash, its leading detergent brand in Italy, and to replace it by Ariel, the European leader, resulted in significant market share losses and reduced profitability. Management had to rethink that decision.

Most internationally operating companies are aware of the difficulties related to the global establishment and maintenance of a brand. Acquiring established local or regional brands is often a less risky policy because the great majority of new brand names fail to catch on with consumers. This was a major reason behind South Korean L. G. Electronics Inc.'s decision to buy a controlling stake in Zenith Electronics Corp., the U.S. manufacturer of TV sets. Similar objectives lay behind Sara Lee's takeover of brands such as Delial (sun protection), Natreen (sweetener), Satina (body care), and Quenty forty (cosmetics) from Bayer, the German chemical giant. But such a policy inevitably leads to a portfolio of many different local brands in what may be the same product categories. Companies having acquired various local brands, therefore, try to initiate a process of brand globalization by making their visual identities converge, before they change anything else.

For an effectively global brand – in terms of shared brand meaning – to be successfully established the existence of a global product market is required. That is, there must be customer segments in each of the served country markets that are quite similar concerning their product-related needs or at least do not have contradictory needs. The lack of such homogeneous international product markets may be one of the reasons why, despite the economic advantages of globally standardized branding, a great number of brands are still local.

Local brands Local brands exist in one country or in a limited geographical area. Table 8.3 shows the split of 744 European brands from 12 product categories in the food sector of the U.K., France, Germany, and Italy into local versus international brands. The long tradition of thinking in terms of national markets as well as cultural differences between managers may have contributed to that finding.

Strong local brands have traditionally benefited from a high level of awareness and attractiveness in their markets. Due to a custom approach to local stakeholders trust in local brands tends to be high. L'Oréal, for example, having discovered the customer retention potential of local brands has decided to pursue a combination of local and global branding. Instead of globally using only the Maybelline brand that is very strong in the U.S., they market Gemey-Maybelline in France and Jade-Maybelline in Germany.

Despite the fact that management has given priority to the company's six strategic worldwide brands, including Nescafé and Buitoni, the example of Nestlé shows that a company can be very successful by developing local or regional brands. They may even be focused on a part of a multicultural country market, such as the most southern parts of the U.S., which are populated by many Spanish-speaking consumers. Local brands are particularly advisable where more

TABLE 8.3 *International vs. local brands per product category in France, Germany, Italy, and the U.K.*

Product category	Number of brands	Number of local brands (% of total)	Number of international brands (% of total)
Alcohol	153	61 (40)	92 (60)
Chocolate	124	53 (43)	71 (57)
Beer	119	70 (59)	49 (41)
Yogurt	72	45 (63)	27 (38)
Mineral water	45	26 (58)	19 (42)
Frozen goods	38	24 (63)	14 (37)
Chewing gum	36	16 (44)	20 (56)
Fruit juice	36	29 (81)	7 (19)
Coffee	36	25 (69)	11 (31)
Ice cream	34	17 (50)	17 (50)
Soup	26	12 (46)	14 (54)
Pasta	25	19 (76)	6 (24)
Total	**744**	**397 (100)**	**347 (100)**

There is still a substantial number of local brands in many consumer product categories.

Source: Schuiling, I. and J.-N. Kapferer (2004) "Executive insights: real differences between local and international brands: strategic implications for international marketers", *Journal of International Marketing*, 12(4), p. 104

differences than similarities exist between country markets in the benefits provided by a product. In 2000, Coca-Cola decided to give more freedom to local subsidiaries. They are now permitted to develop advertising campaigns to local consumers, and may even launch new local brands.

Regional brands Regional brands make sense where:

- cultural similarities among neighboring markets exist
- the same language can be used in brand communication
- the same media are used by the customers across borders
- there is intensive cross-border traffic.

Decision criteria

What kind of brand architecture an international marketer selects will depend on a number of criteria that have to be considered.

Complexity of business systems If the relevant product market contains a number of attractive sub-markets with varying stakeholders having varying power and potentially conflicting interests, separate business unit or product branding may help smoothing contradictions in market appearance.

Risk of negative spill-over effects In high risk businesses, such as parts of the chemical industry, running all activities under one single name may lead to negative spill-over effects when there are technical problems in a part of the business or in a certain country market. Negative spill-over effects may also arise in consumer businesses, however. Today, negative news about a company or a product that is known to an internationally spread out brand interest group are diffused via the internet in an extremely short time. Tommy Hilfiger, for example, was falsely accused of having made racist statements on a TV show in the U.S., which led to a global reduction of sales.

Potential for brand extension If the meaning of an existing brand has a rather abstract core it is easier to extend to other businesses or products than if the core is very much product fixed. In western Europe, for example, Danone stands for dairy products and the brand covers all kinds of such products. In the U.S. it is also used for bottled water because the brand's meaning is not so strongly related to one product category.

Cultural embeddedness If a brand can have a core meaning that easily crosses cultural frames of reference, it can be built globally. Red Bull's intended core meaning, for example, is to vitalize the body and the mind. This is interculturally expressed by the slogan "Red Bull gives you wiiings" and by events called "Flugtag," which are called the same thing all over the world and undertaken in all countries to make the interest group experience the meaning of Red Bull and fuel brand-related public communication.

Speed of change in business models and company structure The actual brand structure is continually changing both shaped by and evolving in response to changes in the external environments (e.g., new regulations, new competitors, changing structure of distribution channels or customer expectations) and the internal environment, for example, because of acquisitions or spin-offs. Some companies, such as in the fields of biotechnology or information technology, have the mission of developing and then selling off businesses. Danish NKT, for example, sold its Giga subsidiary to Intel. Other firms, such as Austria-based construction materials giant Wienerberger mainly grow and stay profitable by acquiring other businesses. For such companies, separate branding of business units for customers, distribution, and supply partners as well as media might be as important as building and sustaining a strong corporate brand for the financial community, politicians, public administrations, and unions.

Intended brand meaning

Having determined the intended brand objects, management can turn its focus to the intended meaning of those objects. If the company is not a startup the marketer must first assess the current meaning of the brand objects to the members of the organization, and to the current stakeholders of the organization. Then, management can determine what the meaning of the brand object should be to the stakeholders in the various country markets to be served. The intended meaning will be the goal to be reached by all experiences provided to stakeholders at touch points with the organizational unit responsible for the brand object.

Identity

The intended meaning of a brand can only be reached in an effective manner if the responsible organizational unit knows what it would *like* the meaning to be. Therefore, the intended identity of the brand has first to be determined. **Identity** can be defined as the way in which a social unit describes itself based on its interactions with others. Members of a business organization have a social identity. They possess mutually shared knowledge about the characteristics of the group they belong to and how it is differentiated from others. They also share evaluations determining the value of membership to the group.

In a similar manner, members of an organizational unit responsible for a brand have a certain self-perception concerning the brand. Because identities have a strong impact on the behavior of group members the establishment and reinforcement of a strong brand must start with an assessment of this self-perception.

The leading idea

As Figure 8.5 shows, the starting point of any brand assessment – independent from what the brand object is – is its leading idea. The **leading idea** defines the purpose of the brand, giving sense to its existence. For example, Alberto Alessi the owner of Italy's famous design company, defines the leading idea of his company as: "We are mediators between the so-called market place, that is people's dreams, and the best Italian artists in design. We are an industrial research lab for design."

The leading idea can be strongly related to a product or a service, to its function, or a technology. But leading ideas formulated in terms of problem solutions or a bundle of stakeholder benefits are better suited for brand extensions into other country and product markets. For example, Germany's Webasto has formulated the leading idea of its corporate brand as "We provide well-being in driving."

If there is no pre-formulated leading idea readily available the marketer may analyze the products and services constituting the brand object, looking for the central benefits provided by the brand object and the major values having governed the provision of the brand object so far; the patterns of former success, looking for typical processes that have generated the central benefits and transferred the major values in the past (the founder of Marriott Hotels, for example, took great care to personally control and reinforce service processes once having made his company known on all continents); symbols and signs related to the brand object used in the past as vehicles of symbolic interactions between the company and its stakeholders, and also among stakeholders (for example, Apple has used its design that stands out from other PC makers to symbolize its individuality, originality, and difference to the big business mainstream); the personality of the leader such as Steven Jobs, Estée Lauder, or Richard Branson. Entrepreneurial leaders often are strong personalities, not only highly visible to the public but also marking the internal environment of a company. The values leading their behavior as well as the central benefits they want to provide to stakeholders may be central to what can be the leading idea of a brand.

Self-perception

The leading idea is the starting point of the development of any strong brand. To make it materialize, however, the people creating and generating the brand object must understand the leading idea and make it become their frame of reference for operations. That is, the meaning of the brand to the members of the organizational unit must be in line with the leading idea of the brand.

To see if there is a gap, the actual internal brand meaning needs to be researched. Information can be collected through team meetings, focus groups, the observation of processes, document analysis, or an interactive website. Information gathering may focus on the perceived personality of the brand, that is, the interests and goals it is pursuing, its needs and constitution, tradition and heritage, capabilities and competences as well as its temper; the values and norms governing brand behavior (for an example see Ethics box 8.1) and self-projection, that is, how the brand as a person would see itself. For example, the self-projection of Ralph Lauren could be: I am American. I belong to the elite. I have style and taste.

From the leading idea interpreted through the self-perception of the members of the responsible organizational unit arises the intended identity of the brand.

FIGURE 8.5 *Brand identity and brand meaning*

Based on a leading idea brand management can determine an intended identity of the brand object. By managing self-expressions at the touch points with relevant stakeholders in a way that considers their expectations, stakeholder perceptions may be influenced to result in a fit between the intended and actual brand meaning.

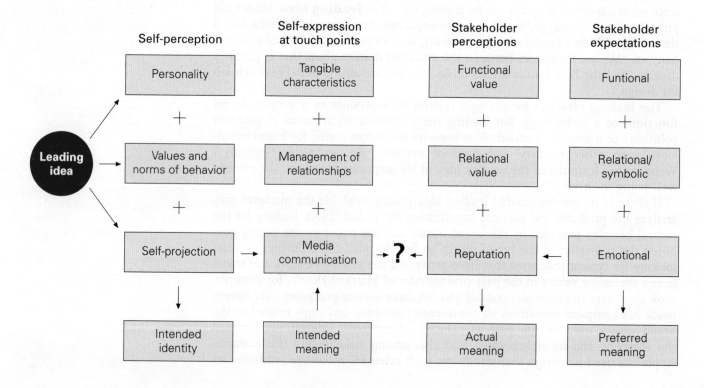

The **intended identity** defines what the people participating in the generation of the brand object would like the brand to be.

Stakeholder perceptions

An assessment of the actual meaning of the brand to the relevant stakeholders can serve as a benchmark to the intended brand identity. Perceived functional value, relational value, and brand reputation influence the attraction of a brand to stakeholders. All stakeholders have different expectations, varying social relations, and live in diverse environments. The assessment of actual brand meaning must consider such differences. Shell, for example, not only regularly researches customers' perceptions but also seeks feedback from investors, distribution partners, suppliers, or activists through surveys, focus groups, and its web-based "Tell Shell" program.

If there is too much of a gap between the vision of brand managers and the current perceptions of the members of the brand interest group trouble may arise. For example, when British Airways decided to globalize the brand by repainting its aircraft and removing the Union Flag from the tailfin a cabin crew strike broke out. Business-class travelers, informed by a furious press, threatened to change suppliers.

Self-expression at touch points

A comparison of the intended meaning and the actual meaning of the brand to the stakeholders will show what needs to be done at the touch points of the

ETHICS BOX 8.1

Levi's global sourcing guidelines

Can a company priding itself on enlightened attitudes towards employees at home turn its head when some of its foreign contractors abuse their workers? Should western companies justify paying near starvation wages because that's what the market will bear?

While U.S.- and European-owned factories in places such as China, Indonesia, and Thailand are often well run, some independent contractors and suppliers there and in other countries provide working conditions that are dismal even by third world standards. At least that's what Levi-Strauss found. The company, which makes most of its jeans and shirts overseas, investigated its several hundred foreign contractors and has discovered that some of them treat their workers badly. According to Levi, its contractor in Bangladesh was routinely using child labor, for example. One contractor on the island of Saipan, a U.S. territory near Guam, allegedly refused to pay employees back-wages, often worked them 11 hours a day, seven days a week, and paid below the local minimum wage.

Levi not only terminated that contract, a company taskforce worked for 3 years on developing "global sourcing guidelines" for doing business abroad, which reflect Levi's shared values. They contain "business partner terms of engagement," among them: Suppliers must provide safe and healthy conditions that meet Levi's standards and must pay workers no less than prevailing local wages. Laborer's work week is limited to 60 hours. Company inspectors make surprise visits to ensure contractors tow the line. The Bangladesh outfit has stopped using children.

The second part of the guidelines deals with country selection standards, which focus on political or social instability, dangers to company employees, a country's impact on brand image, and human rights abuses. The company had suspended business dealings in Peru because it felt that employees were in danger from terrorist activity. When the danger subsided, Levi's lifted the suspension. Subcontracts in Myanmar and China were phased out because of flagrant human rights abuses.

Source: Dumaine, B. (1992) "Exporting jobs and ethics", *Fortune*, 5 October, p. 10; Beaver, W. (1995) "Levi's is leaving China", *Business Horizons*, March–April, pp. 35–40

organizational unit with its stakeholders to help the intended brand meaning emerge. At the touch points stakeholders directly or indirectly experience:

- the tangible characteristics of the brand
- how personal relationships are managed
- how the organization communicates via the media.

Thus, companies like Dior, the inventor of brand licensing based in Paris, have reintegrated most of the activities covering their brand name. Hermès, Cartier, Louis Vuitton, and Chanel have even bought many manufacturers of their products. And Hermès sells all of its 20,000 products, except perfumes and tablewear, in its more than 150 Hermès shops, which are designed by the same architect to increase the presence of Hermès's brand identity.

What stakeholders experience strongly depends on how the intended brand identity translates into actual behavior of the suppliers of the brand object. Internal branding becomes very important. That is why Lego, the Danish toymaker, invited several thousand managers and employees from all over the world to participate in workshops called "pitstops." At these workshops the participants shared their dreams for the company and themselves, building support for the brand in the process. In so-called "dream-outs" participating employees were invited to interactive, real-time problem solving. For example, one of those dream-outs improved the distribution channels in the U.S.

Brand interest group

Impact on brand meaning

In international marketing brand meanings may not only differ due to varying frames of cultural reference, but also due to differing stakeholders participating in the brand-related discourse. Brand meanings are socially constructed. When selecting the markets to serve, therefore, the marketer has to consider the stakeholders potentially interested in the defined brand objects.

For example, the meaning of Amnesty International in China will be different to its meaning in Sweden, simply because of different treatment by the media and government officials. Similarly, Red Bull has meanings that vary between Denmark and France, where it is not allowed to be marketed because of health reasons, and other countries, such as the U.S. or Thailand, where it can be openly consumed in bars and is sold in supermarkets. For young consumers in Denmark and France it is a very special drink that needs to be purchased in another country and, therefore, is a means to contest imposed rules. It is consumed for special occasions. In countries where Red Bull can be freely purchased it is rather perceived as an energizer used to get a "kick" whenever needed.

In addition, the meaning of a brand and therefore its attractiveness to potential customers may depend on who is interested in the brand. If in certain country markets, for example, Rolex gold watches are worn by pimps to show off, this may have a particular impact on the meaning of the brand. If Greenpeace, as another example, is mainly supported by long-haired young activists who try to gain awareness for their cause by breaking generally accepted rules of behavior, the meaning of the brand to the majority of the population will differ from a situation where Greenpeace is supported by well-respected politicians and influential media.

Impact on competitive advantage

There are strong reasons to closely consider the members of a brand interest group in potential markets. They may be key to establishing and sustaining competitive advantage:

- *The meaning of a brand serves as a heuristic.* The members of a brand interest group – whether they are positively or negatively attracted by the brand – interpret brand-related stimuli in a way that reinforces the meaning of the brand. Subjective quality perceptions and interpretations of experiences concerning strong brands make it very difficult for competitors to imitate successful marketers.

- *Brand objects are used for symbolic interaction.* Because the meaning of a brand is consciously shared by many people it is hard for individuals to opt out. Only if a critical mass of customers and other stakeholders have substantially differing experiences the resulting social discourse will change the meaning of the brand.

- *A strong brand provides competitive advantage not only in relations with customers, but with all stakeholders.* A strong brand continually reinforces emotional bonds not only with and among customers but with all stakeholders taking part in brand-related social interactions.

Served markets

To decide which markets should be served, management must simultaneously examine the attractiveness of potential product and country markets and the firm's competitive position in the markets under consideration. Management will try to focus the activities of the firm on the most attractive markets. At the same time, it has to consider the firm's ability to build on or develop competitive advantages in those markets. Swiss-based Zurich Financial Services, for example, has the priority of increasing earnings power by maintaining a consistent policy of focusing on selective growth. It is active in non-life and life insurance, reinsurance and asset management, benefiting from one of the industry's most global networks, an expanded position in the U.S. market through acquisitions, a sharply focused approach to customers, and product innovation.

International portfolio analysis

A potential method to simultaneously analyze the attractiveness of markets and the competitive position of the firm (its business units, product lines, or products) in those markets is portfolio analysis. Portfolio analysis provides an overview of:

- how the firm has allocated its resources so far
- what opportunities exist
- what threats have to be faced.

For internationally operating companies, portfolio analysis is more complex than for a domestic business, because it must provide for additional units of analysis. International portfolio analysis starts at the corporate level, where country and product markets, as well as available technologies, must be compared; proceeds to the business unit level, where for each of the units on the corporate level the related customer segments and product lines can be analyzed; and goes down to the product line level, where for each product line and customer segment the related portfolio of products can be assessed (see Figure 8.6).

For example, a firm such as Nike, the U.S. marketer of sports footwear, will start a global portfolio analysis on the corporate level where it will not only compare different product markets, like low-priced sports fashion for young consumers, footwear for fashion-conscious sports amateurs, or expensive high-tech solutions for sports professionals, but must also consider the attractiveness of the country markets it currently serves and compare its competitive position there to potential other markets.

FIGURE 8.6 *Interrelations of portfolio categories*

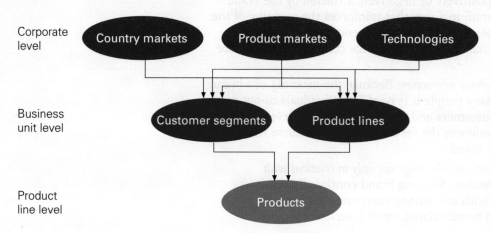

Corporate
level

Business
unit level

Product
line level

Portfolio analysis can take place on different levels of a company: Corporate, business unit, and product line. On each level the analysis can focus on different units: Product markets, country markets, or technologies on the corporate level; customer segments and product lines on the business unit level; and products on the product line level. Essentially, the portfolio decisions taken on an upper level have an impact on the portfolio of the level below.

Figure 8.7 shows how a portfolio comparing country markets with regard to market attractiveness and relative competitive position can be used in a defined product market (for example, low-priced sports fashion for young consumers):

- to determine where the company has acted successfully
- to seize opportunities in attractive areas
- to find out where it has allowed competitors to establish strong positions before it acquired appropriate market shares.

By comparing the current portfolio of country markets to opportunities, management can determine whether the company is overcommitted in less attractive markets, leaving highly attractive markets untapped. In Figure 8.7, for example, Belgium and Denmark represent attractive markets that need more attention compared to Canada.

FIGURE 8.7 *Portfolio of country markets*

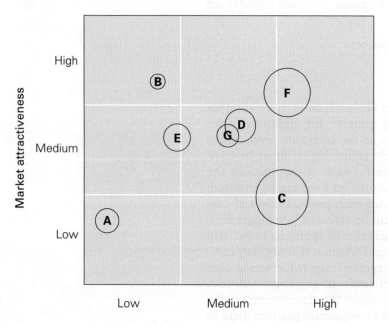

Portfolio analysis can be used to determine market priorities. In this figure the firm has mapped the attractiveness of country markets compared to the firm's competitive position. Thus France is its best market, but Denmark merits attention because it is large in size. However, the firm's competitive position in Denmark is only fair.

Note: Circle sizes are proportional to market share in a country market. Letters represent country markets: A = Austria, B = Belgium, C = Canada, D = Denmark, E = Spain, F = France, G = Greece

In addition, the company can analyze different levels of technology (such as complete automation vs hand assembly) used to produce its shoes. At the business unit level, customer segments, such as high-school kids wanting to express their protest against parents, young single professionals wanting to work out on weekends, or middle-aged women interrupting their time at home with their small children to perform some exercises in a spa, will be compared concerning their attractiveness and the firm's competitive position in each country market or in a product market. The portfolio position of product lines, like sporty leisure shoes or healthcare shoes for small children, can also be analyzed per country or product market, or related to a certain production technology. And, of course, Nike will assess the product mix of every product line, such as running, walking or tennis shoes, as well as the product mix for each customer segment.

Market/product portfolios

Besides the higher number of units of analysis compared by portfolio analysis, international firms have to consider more factors for the determination of their markets' and products' positions in the portfolio. Factors such as:

- political and financial risk
- transferability of funds
- taxes and subsidies
- potential for standardization

influence the portfolio structure. They have to be introduced to the comparison to increase the information level of the analysis. A highly profitable market can be threatened by political unrest, religious upheavals, or restrictive laws concerning business. For example, trade between Ireland and the Lebanon, although profitable, may be less attractive owing to insecurities concerning the Lebanese government and administrative barriers in the form of import restrictions. Such factors can be accounted for in the development of the scale that is used to measure attractiveness. But they can also be explicitly considered in the way the portfolio is designed.

Figure 8.8 shows an example of how portfolio analysis can compare profitability to political risk in various country markets.

Possessing a balanced portfolio is of no help to the firm if the funds generated in one market or by one product (line) cannot be freely transferred to another. For example, if an agricultural products company such as Charoen Pokphand based in Bangkok has cash cows in the Philippines, Indonesia, and China but is not allowed to transfer funds from there to its newly started business units in eastern Europe, the international business strategy will be handicapped. To check this situation, the transferability of funds earned in different regions of the world can be introduced into the assessment (see Figure 8.9).

Technology portfolios

An internationally operating firm must decide which technologies to hold in its portfolio to contribute adequately to the resolution of its customers' problems. To take informed decisions, management can assess the attractiveness of each available technology for the product and country markets as well as customer segments and product lines under consideration and compare it to the firm's relative strengths in those fields of technology.

Figure 8.10 shows that the attractiveness of a technology is defined by its potential for customer problem solution and diffusion. The problem solution potential of a technology depends on its scientific and technical potential for further development as well as the amount of time and development risks until the technology is ready for application.

FIGURE 8.8 *Political risk/profitability portfolio of country markets*

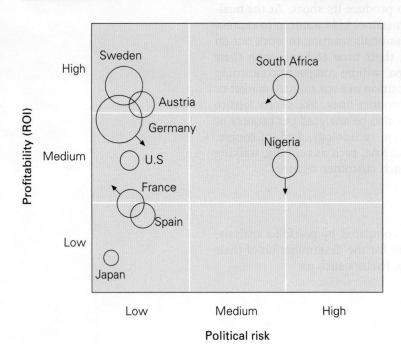

The profitability of a country market can be mapped against an issue that affects the attractiveness of profitability – in this example, political risk.

Note: Circle sizes are proportional to potential country market sales. Arrows indicate the expected direction of change in country market positions in the coming three years.

FIGURE 8.9 *Portfolio combining country market attractiveness/competitive position analysis with international transferability of funds*

Market attractiveness/ competitive position	International transferability of funds		Region
	High	**Low**	
High attractiveness/ strong competitive position		●	Pacific Rim
	●		EU
	●		NAFTA
High attractiveness/ weak competitive position		●	Pacific Rim
	●		EU
	●		NAFTA
Low attractiveness/ strong competitive position		●	Pacific Rim
	●		EU
	●		NAFTA
Low attractiveness/ weak competitive position			Pacific Rim
	●		EU
			NAFTA

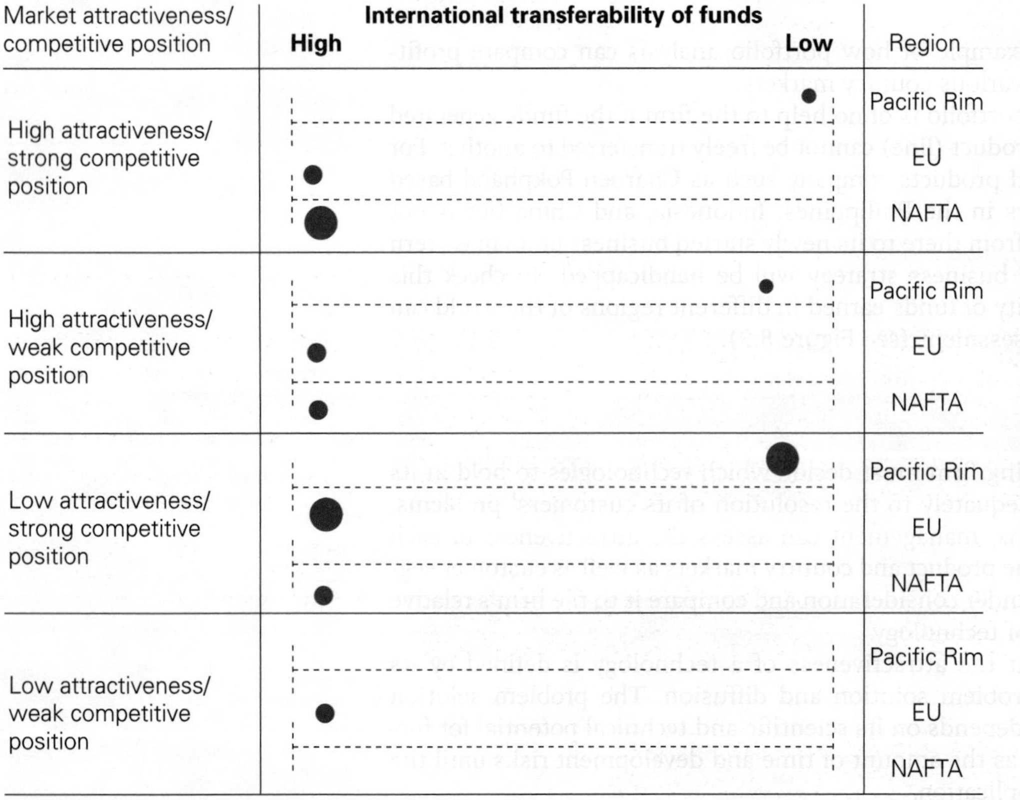

Portfolio analysis is used in this figure to help the firm analyze the relationship between its product lines' position in a market attractiveness/competitive position portfolio, and its ability to transfer funds, by major regions. In the given example, most of the sales of "stars" are in the NAFTA and EU, where the company can transfer funds. "Cash cows" have their highest sales volume in the Pacific Rim where transferability of funds is restricted. But future growth of "question marks" and further development of "stars" depend on available funds. The firm faces severe funding limitations.

Note: Circle sizes are proportional to share of total sales

Micro-mechanics, for example, is a field of technology, which not only has enormous potential for future application in toys but also in medicine, such as the treatment of effects from high levels of cholesterol. Japanese researchers have been working on its development for 25 years. They have made significant progress but no application with a strong economic impact has resulted so far.

A technology's diffusion potential is determined by its:

- general customer acceptance
- benefits provided compared to alternative technologies.

For example, microbiological cloning is a technology with great potential for further development. A company such as U.K.-based pharmaceutical manufacturer Glaxo that holds this technology in its portfolio, however, must be aware of the risks it takes concerning legal regulations or resistance from environmentalists in certain country markets such as Germany.

The relative strength of the firm in a field of technology depends on the company's potential for:

- differentiation from competitors
- implementation of the technology in the firm (see Figure 8.11).

The potential of a company to differentiate itself from competitors in a field of technology is determined by:

- (technology-specific) know-how available to the firm relative to its competitors
- the opportunity to become a technology leader in the field.

The potential for implementation depends on:

- the fit of the technology into the existing competitive strategy of the firm
- availability of complementary technologies in the organization.

For example, if a laser technology for cutting purposes fits the competitive strategy of being a technology leader in cutting problem solutions and the firm possesses the engineering know-how to construct the relevant machinery, the potential for successful implementation of this technology in the company is very good.

FIGURE 8.10 *Factors influencing the attractiveness of a technology to a firm*

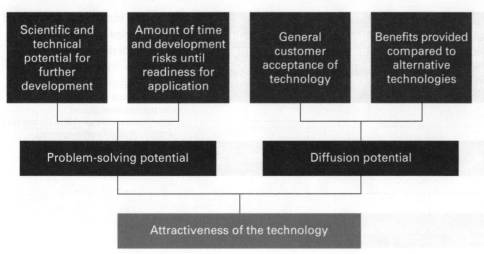

The attractiveness of a technology to a firm is determined by its potential to solve customer problems and its diffusion potential.

Source: Adapted from Specht, G. (1994) "Portfolioansätze als Instrument zur Unterstützung strategischer Programmentscheidungen" in H. Corsten (ed.) *Handbuch Produktionsmanagement*, Wiesbaden: Gabler; p.105

Selection of markets and technologies

Based on market/product portfolios and the firm's technology portfolio, management can take decisions on which markets to serve with which products applying which technologies. Product-market, customer segment, and product line portfolios assist in focusing the firm's expansion. The technology portfolio has to be considered in all of those decisions because it gives some information on the sustainability of competitive advantages in the delivery of superior products and services. DaimlerChrysler, for example, is No. 1 for premium vehicles. To achieve and sustain this market position DaimlerChrysler has consistently increased its focus on passenger cars and commercial vehicles. The company has sold off

DaimlerChrysler has withdrawn from the space technology business   ©Lars Lentz/iStock

FIGURE 8.11 *Factors influencing relative strength of a firm in a field of technology*

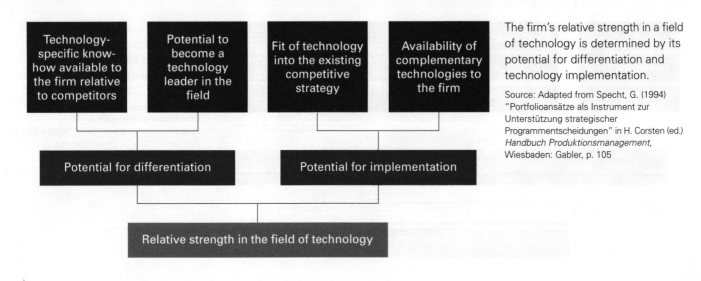

The firm's relative strength in a field of technology is determined by its potential for differentiation and technology implementation.

Source: Adapted from Specht, G. (1994) "Portfolioansätze als Instrument zur Unterstützung strategischer Programmentscheidungen" in H. Corsten (ed.) *Handbuch Produktionsmanagement*, Wiesbaden: Gabler, p. 105

Technology-specific know-how available to the firm relative to competitors | Potential to become a technology leader in the field | Fit of technology into the existing competitive strategy | Availability of complementary technologies to the firm

Potential for differentiation | Potential for implementation

Relative strength in the field of technology

numerous business units outside the core area of the worldwide automotive business, such as the European Aeronautic, Defense and Space Company (EADS) or the railway engineering subsidiary Adtranz.

When using the described portfolios for decision making, however, managers should bear in mind that these techniques provide some structured insights into a field of complex interdependencies but they do not provide rigid formula-based decisions. Management's choice of markets does not only depend on economic considerations concerning the attractiveness of markets, customer segments, and product lines compared to the competitive position of the firm in those units of analysis. The personal interests of managers, general evaluations based on the values formulated in the corporate policy statement, and branding intentions can play a decisive role.

Basic options

Management must decide whether to:

- keep the status of the current portfolio
- increase the extent of the firm's international activity
- change the focus on particular markets.

For example, lift makers like Finnish Kone have virtually no control over general demand for their products. When the construction industry is putting up new buildings it needs lifts; when it is not, as was the case in North America and Europe in the mid-1990s, then demand disappears. Shrinking demand in one part of the world may be offset by rising demand in another. In the fast developing markets of Asia, skyscrapers are sprouting up all over cities such as Shanghai or Kuala Lumpur, each with a battery of lifts to be built by firms such as Kone. The lift makers react by shifting more of their resources to those new markets.

Decisions will be guided by the ground rules concerning the extent of internationalization laid down in the firm's corporate policy. If the major competitors are all active on a global scale, as is the case in the commercial aircraft, computer or watch industries, geographic market restriction may turn out to be fatal. Contrariwise, in cases such as the furniture industry, where most business is local, the example of IKEA shows that a greater than average extent of internationalization can be very successful. They started internationalizing their business by supply agreements with factories in eastern Europe and opening stores all over western Europe and later on in the U.S. and Asia at a time when their competitors concentrated on local business opportunities.

In developing a portfolio, the company can choose between four basic options: product market penetration, geographic expansion, product market development, and diversification (see Figure 8.12).

FIGURE 8.12 Basic portfolio options

	Current country markets	New country markets	
Current products	Product market penetration	Geographic expansion	Basically, a company can be involved in a current or a new country market, with current or new products.
New products	Product market development	Diversification	

Product market penetration

The highest degree of resource concentration occurs when the firm decides to penetrate a product market in a limited number of country markets that it already serves. This results in production and marketing experience curve effects, which permit the firm to lower prices and increase quality at the same time. The result is increasingly loyal customers.

Markets that are in an early stage of development require a greater investment of resources. When, for example, Eindhoven (Netherlands)-based Philips first introduced compact discs, a large budget was necessary to train sales personnel both within the company and in stores that would sell the new product, and to communicate the benefits of the new technology to customers through advertising and promotion campaigns. If the market has high growth potential, such an investment is justified, because it will establish a strong competitive position before other firms enter the market.

Product market penetration allows using different tactics, including the following.

Product line stretching When stretching its product line, a company, which has successfully served a small segment of the market in the past, gradually adds new items to the current product line in order to reach a broader market. Japanese car producers, for example, started their market penetration in Europe with inexpensive, middle-sized cars. From there they first stretched their product line to small cars, then started offering bigger and stronger cars. Their latest move has been to challenge European competitors with luxury and sports car models.

Product proliferation When the company opts for **product proliferation**, it introduces as many different models or product types as possible at each point in the product line. Casio, the Japanese calculator and watch manufacturer, for example, introduced a variety of hand calculators, with different functions, features, and designs to cover the expectations of most customer segments in the product market, from low-priced calculators for everyday purposes to highly sophisticated devices for special applications.

Product improvement When the company continually augments the capabilities and reliability of its products, extends warranties and services related to the products, and is quick to apply improved technologies, it has chosen the tactic of **product improvement**. For example, Komatsu, the Japan-based competitor of Caterpillar in the market for earth-moving and construction equipment has taken a significant market share by continually raising the quality of its products, which allowed an extension of warranties, and by extending the range of its products' application through improved technologies.

Product market penetration involves a trade-off: The more the firm limits the number of country markets it serves, the more opportunities it gives competitors to build up their presence in other markets. Japanese companies, for instance, strengthened their competitive positions in Southeast Asia before entering the U.S. market. They were not challenged in these markets by U.S. competitors, who at that time focused their activities on European markets.

In addition, too strong a focus on a product market in a limited number of country markets may reduce potential success. For example, although Ford Tractor operations had experienced varying profitability, cash flow, and market share by product type (such as light versus heavy tractors), some of their greatest opportunities were due to wide potential profit variations across market areas.

Geographic expansion

Expanding operations to new geographic areas is most appropriate when the firm is relatively small and has developed an innovative product for which patents offer little protection or when the advantage of a firm's new product can be matched by competition in a fairly short time. For example, Austria-based Omicron, a very small firm specializing in electronic testing equipment, after having developed an innovative test set for protective relays, transducers and energy meters for electric utilities and industry, expanded globally in three years by cooperating with Germany's Siemens AG, which let them use their distribution network.

Geographic expansion is especially appropriate if the lifecycles of the company's products in different markets are similar, as is often the case for industrial goods and consumer durables in developed economies, including the newly industrialized countries. At the limit, a company is not even obliged to sell its innovative products in its current markets before entering new ones. If other markets are better suited to the new product, the firm should start there. For example, Matsushita, the Japanese consumer electronics giant, exported its color TV sets to the U.S. five years before it introduced them at home; its managers did not believe that the Japanese market was ready for the new product.

Geographic expansion is also appropriate:

- when important competitors are opening up new markets
- when opportunities in new markets will be available for only a short time.

These characteristics are often found in high-tech industries like computer technology and advanced circuit technology. The speed with which new computer chips, for example, can be matched by competitors means that they are marketed globally as quickly as possible to take advantage of product superiority for as long as possible.

Geographic expansion also becomes necessary when intense price competition in slow growing markets leads to diminishing profit margins. To achieve higher sales volume, the company introduces its products in markets where few product modifications are required.

Product market development

Following the basic option of **product market development**, a company allocates its resources to a limited number of country markets and focuses its operations on the development of new product markets in these areas. This approach is appropriate if:

- the company is well established in its country markets
- the company lacks the motivation, ability, or knowledge to adapt to a new environment
- the currently served product markets have matured
- new product markets are growing fast.

For example, one out of three small firms in Japan's consumer electronics industry, which had delivered product parts to the big names such as Sony or Hitachi, and were hit by those firms' exodus offshore, started developing new products.

Diversification

Diversification may be attractive when:

- served markets stagnate
- new product markets in new geographic areas generate a high return on investment
- there is high growth potential.

Körber/Hauni, world-leading German manufacturer of cigarette machines, for example, was confronted with a stagnating market in the late 1980s when smoking became less popular and cigarette machines more efficient. While

Körber/Hauni clearly defended its leadership in this market, it also entered into a quick and active diversification program. The company founded Hauni Elektronik, which launched a breakthrough innovation in the field of oxygen production from normal air. E.C.H. Will, another result of diversification, established a world market share of 90% for cut-size sheeters (machines that cut small pieces of paper for items such as passports and checkbooks).

There are two dangers associated with diversification, however:

- *Entering a new product market in an unknown geographic area is risky,* especially when it involves a technology that is new to the firm. The new business may have only few aspects in common with current operations, so the firm may benefit very little from synergy.
- Even if the company is able to overcome this problem, competitors may choose a more focused portfolio strategy and dominate the markets in which the *firm does not have the experience needed to develop strong competitive advantages.*

For example, it may seem attractive to Cathay Pacific, the Hong Kong-based airline, to invest in a hotel chain in Australia because tourism from the U.S., Japan, and Europe is increasing there and customers can be flown in on the company's jets. But Cathay Pacific may find itself confronted with U.S. or European competitors specializing in global hotel management, which possess long-established relationships with international tour operators and travel agencies. It may also be confronted with Australian competitors, which are better entrenched in the intricacies of Australian regulations and have a stronger lobby when it comes to construction and operating permissions.

Successful balance

A company will be most successful in international marketing if:

- it has a balanced mix of product and country markets, as well as technologies with different cash flow positions and resource requirements
- it serves an attractive mix of customer segments at different stages of product adoption with product lines that contain products at different stages of maturity.

That is, the situation of the company is at its best when management can be sure that

- some parts of the firm's portfolio provide the resources needed by others for their positive development
- choice of market and technology portfolios provides for a balance of business cycles in industries as well as regions of the world.

For example, Japan's Sony Corp. cannot count on its TV sets always selling well and being highly profitable. A portfolio of product lines is needed to spread the market risk. Forseeing profits decline as its TV sets move through the product lifecycle, Sony needed new products to help maintain sales and cash flow. Thus over time, Sony developed hi-fi towers, the Walkman, the Watchman, compact discs, video cameras, mobile phones, laptops, videogame players, DVD players, and multimedia wifi equipment. Because investments needed to be in the forefront of technological development are substantial, Sony decided to serve only one broad product market: consumer electronics. But again, to spread the risk of this decision and to profit from given opportunities, it developed a global portfolio of country markets in which it serves different customer segments, such as teens buying their first stereo equipment mostly to play pop music or lovers of classical music who are ready to spend substantial amounts of money to own the best recordings and to enjoy perfect sound reproduction.

Summary

A globally operating company may derive competitive advantages from qualities that are not available to firms with a regional or domestic focus, such as:

- efficiencies of global scale and volume
- transfer of experience, ideas, and successful concepts
- global reputation
- transfer of resources between business units
- exploitation of local advantages
- ability to provide global services.

Successful competition is always based on providing superior value to customers and other important stakeholders. Superior value can be built on:

- cost leadership
- a superior product (including services)
- time leadership
- special capabilities in building and sustaining relationships.

Attractive stakeholder value can be more easily attained if the company has a consistent market appearance that:

- arouses high levels of awareness
- is easily recognizable
- is positively valued by the stakeholders.

Coordinated activities of an organization that focus on influencing the value of the organization to stakeholders are called branding. Brands are social representations jointly developed by organizations, their customers, and other stakeholders in an ongoing communication process. Brands consist of three closely interrelated elements:

- brand interest group
- brand meaning
- brand object(s).

To avoid confusion inside the company and among stakeholders, brand architecture determines clear roles, relationships, and boundaries for brands in a decision process that determines:

- the hierarchical levels in the organization at which brands are to be established and managed
- geographic extension of those brands
- range of objects brands are allowed to cover.

Depending on what the brand objects should be, management can opt for:

- one-firm branding
- house branding
- endorsed branding
- separate branding.

Brands are local if their geographical extension is limited to one country or a specific geographical area. Strong local brands have traditionally benefited from a high level of awareness and attractiveness in their markets. For most companies global branding means that a highly standardized marketing mix is used in all served country markets to achieve economies of scale and scope. For a brand to be effectively global, however, its core meaning would need to be very similar across country markets. That is, brand-related activities need to be adapted according to local frames of reference.

What kind of brand architecture an international marketer selects will depend on a number of criteria, such as the:

- complexity of business systems
- risk of negative spill-over effects
- brand extendability
- cultural embeddedness
- speed of change in business models and company structure.

Having determined brand architecture, management can turn its focus to the intended meaning of the designated brand objects. The starting point of any brand assessment is the leading idea of the brand. To make the leading idea materialize, the people involved in the creation and generation of the brand object must understand the idea and make it become the frame of reference of their operations. Therefore, the marketer must:

- assess the current meaning of the brand objects to the members and the current stakeholders of the organization
- determine what should be the meaning of the brand object(s) to the stakeholders in the various country markets to be served
- implement actions at the touch points with stakeholders that help the intended brand meaning emerge.

Brand meaning is socially constructed. Therefore, in international marketing brand meanings may not only differ due to varying frames of cultural reference, but also due to differing stakeholders participating in the brand-related discourse. Thus, when selecting the markets to serve the marketer has to consider the stakeholders potentially interested in the defined brand objects.

To decide which markets should be served, management must simultaneously examine the attractiveness of potential product and country markets and the firm's competitive position in the markets under consideration.

International portfolio analysis is a method potentially fulfilling that purpose. Based on market/product portfolios and the firm's technology portfolio, management can decide which markets to serve with which products applying which technologies. The country market portfolio will help determining the geographic focus.

A company will be most successful in international marketing if:

- it has a balanced mix of product and country markets, as well as technologies with different cash flow positions and resource requirements
- it serves an attractive mix of customer segments at different stages of product adoption with product lines that contain products at different stages of maturity.

That is, the situation of the company is at its best when management can be sure that:

- some parts of the firm's portfolio provide the resources needed by others for their positive development
- choice of market and technology portfolios provides for a balance of business cycles in industries as well as regions of the world.

DISCUSSION QUESTIONS

1. What is the content of an internationally active firm's intended global strategic position? What is it needed for?

2. What are the general sources of competitive advantage a globally operating company may use that are not available to firms with a regional or domestic focus? Discuss by using examples you have found on the internet.

3. What are the bases on which an international marketer can build superior customer value? Explain by using examples from the same industry.

4. Find an example of how a small company might follow a global niche strategy to survive when faced with larger global competitors offering lower prices.

5. Why do distinctive competences of a firm not automatically transfer into competitive advantages? What are the consequences for the international marketer?

6. Contact an internationally operating organization of your choice and ask them for their major objectives. Are they rank ordered according to

their priority? What is their impact on the behavior of the organization in its market(s)?

7. Discuss the factors an international marketer should consider when determining its brand architecture. Show the impact of those factors by providing examples found in trade magazines, business pages of newspapers, or the internet.

8. How can an international marketer determine the intended meaning of the whole company compared to the meaning of a product/service offered in a number of country markets? What information is needed, how can it be gathered?

9. Why is global portfolio analysis more complex than domestic portfolio analysis? Give examples of a locally and an internationally operating company you have found reading a trade magazine.

10. Contact a company doing international business and ask them about their intended global strategic position. Do they have a written statement, and, if not, why not? What are their objectives in the markets they serve? What is their brand architecture?

ADDITIONAL READINGS

Hooley, G., J. Saunders, and N. Piercy (2004) *Marketing Strategy and Competitive Positioning*, 3rd ed., Harlow: Pearson Education Ltd.

Keller, K.L., B. Sternthal, and A. Tybout (2002) "Three questions you need to ask about your brand", *Harvard Business Review*, September, 80–86.

Schuiling, I., and J.-N. Kapferer (2004) "Executive insights: real differences between local and international brands: strategic implications for international marketers", *Journal of International Marketing*, 12(4), 97–112.

Souiden, N. (2002) "Segmenting the Arab markets on the basis of marketing stimuli", *International Marketing Review*, 19(6), 611–36.

Vallaster, C. and L. de Chernatony (2005) "Internationalisation of services brands: the role of leadership during the internal brand building process", *Journal of Marketing Management*, 21, 181–203.

Useful internet links

Accor	http://www.accor.com/
Alcatel	http://www.alcatel.com/
Apple Computer	http://www.apple.com/
Bang & Olufsen	http://www.bang-olufsen.com/
Basler Insurance	http://www.baloise.ch/
Benetton	http://www.benetton.com/
Burger King	http://www.bk.com/
Business Horizons	http://www.elsevier.com/wps/find/journaldescription.cws_home/620214/description£description
Business Week	http://www.businessweek.com/
Carambar	http://www.carambar.fr/
Cartier	http://www.cartier.com/
Casio	http://www.casio.com/
Caterpillar	http://www.cat.com/
Cathay Pacific	http://www.cathaypacific.com/
Chanel	http://www.chanel.com/
Chiquita Bananas	http://www.chiquita.com/
Coca-Cola	http://www.coca-cola.com/
Corticeira Amorim	http://www.cai.amorim.com/
Crédit Suisse	http://www.credit-suisse.com/en/home.html
DaimlerChrysler U.S.	http://www.daimlerchrysler.com/dccom
Danone	http://www.danone.com/
Datacon Technology	http://www.datacon.at/
Disney Worlds	http://disney.go.com/home/today/index.html
Dreyers	http://www.dreyers.com/
Electrolux	http://www.electrolux.com/
Ericsson	http://www.ericsson.com/
Estée Lauder	http://www.esteelauder.com/
European Aeronautic, Defense and Space Company (EADS)	http://www.eads.net/
Ford Motor Company	http://www.ford.com/

Fortune Oil	http://www.fortuneoilandgas.com/
General Electric	http://www.ge.com/en/
General Motors	http://www.gm.com/
Glaxo	http://www.gsk.com/
Gore-tex	http://www.gore-tex.com/
Hermès	http://www.hermes.com/
Hewlett-Packard	http://www.hp.com/
Hitachi	http://www.hitachi.com/
Hungry Jack	http://www.hungryjacks.com.au/
IBM	http://www.ibm.com/
IKEA	http://www.ikea.com/
Intel	http://www.intel.com/
Komatsu	http://www.komatsu.com/
Kraft Foods (former: Kraft-Jacobs-Suchard)	http://www.kraft.com/default.aspx
Kronenbourg	http://www.brasseries-kronenbourg.com/
L G Electronics	http://www.lge.com/
L'Oréal	http://www.loreal.com/_en/_ww/index.aspx
Landauer Inc.	http://www.landauerinc.com/
Lipton	http://www.liptont.com/
Louis Vuitton	http://www.vuitton.com/
Lucent	http://www.lucent.com/
Lycra fibers	http://www.lycra.com/
Marriott Hotels	http://marriott.com/marriott/
McDonald's	http://www.mcdonalds.com
Metso	http://www.metso.com/
Microsoft	http://www.microsoft.com/
Motorola	http://www.motorola.com/
Nestlé	http://www.nestle.com/
Nike	http://www.nike.com/
NKT Cables	http://www.nktcables.com/
Nintendo	http://www.nintendo.com/
Omicron	http://www.omicron.at/
Outspan Oranges	http://www.outspanfresh.co.uk/
Philip Morris	http://www.philipmorrisinternational.com/
Philips	http://www.philips.nl/
Porsche	http://www3.porsche.com/
Porsche Design	http://www.porsche-design.com/
Procter & Gamble	http://www.pg.com/
Ralston Purina	http://www.purina.com/
Red Bull	http://www.redbull.com/
Renault	http://www.renault.com/
Samsung	http://www.samsung.com/
Sara Lee	http://www.saralee.com/
Siemens	http://www.siemens.com/
Smart	http://www.smart.com/

Sony	http://www.sony.com/
The Body Shop	http://www.thebodyshop.com/
Toblerone	http://www.toblerone.com/
Tommy Hilfiger	http://www.tommy.com/hilfiger/
Toyota	http://www.toyota.com/
Trumpf	http://www.trumpf.com/
Ungaro	http://www.ungaro.com/
Unilever	http://www.unilever.co.uk/
Volkswagen	http://www.vw.com/
Wal-Mart	http://www.walmart.com/
Wienerberger	http://www.wienerberger.com/
Zenith Electronics	http://www.zenith.com/

RULES OF BUSINESS BEHAVIOR

9

Learning objectives

After studying this chapter you will be able to:

- describe different types of confrontation with competitors

- discuss the pros and cons of international cooperation vs acquisitions

- explain the need for coordination and flexibility

- understand the importance of quality norms to the branding of a company

- explain the role of leadership in the implementation of the intended global strategic position

- evaluate the pros and cons of various ways of establishing organizational control

Chapter outline

Rules of business behavior

Confrontation
Cooperation
Acquisition
Innovation
Quality guidelines

Leadership

Role models
Human resource development
Reinforcement
Conflict resolution
Managing change

Organizational control

Centralization
Standardization
Socialization

Summary

INTERNATIONAL MARKETING SPOTLIGHT

The Gore philosophy

W.L. Gore & Associates is a privately owned company consisting of 50 manufacturing sites in all industrialized countries, employing about 7,000 people and generating sales of more than $1 billion with double-digit growth rates. The company has four independent divisions active in the fields of textiles, electronics, medical, and industrial products.

To govern this multifaceted organization and to sustain a global identity top management has developed the Gore philosophy. During its first month of membership in the Gore organization each new member gets one week of intensive training concerning this philosophy. The philosophy is a set of rules based on the firm's most central values:

1 *Commitment* to self-selected "projects," that is (new) tasks in addition to the main function. To take on commitments and accomplish the tasks successfully is a precondition for a career in the firm.

The Gore-Tex XCR glove for snowboarders.
©imagebroker/Alamy

2 *Waterline/trust.* Encouragement to be innovative, to take carefully considered risks without hurting the long-term financial success and the reputation of the firm (= waterline).

3 *Freedom/self-organization* to grow with a task, to enhance individual capabilities, and to be reinforced by colleagues in the process of personal enhancement.

4 *Fairness* to each other, to customers, suppliers, and other stakeholders. Whoever consciously commits illegal action – even if it is part of the local business culture – is fired.

The focal question of this chapter is: **What general framework of rules of behavior needs to be established and reinforced to facilitate the realization of the business organization's intended global strategic position?**

Rules of business behavior

Implementing the intended strategic position, that is, realizing the decided way of attractive differentiation from local, regional, or global competitors, is a more difficult task for the managers of a company than determining that position. To establish a "monopoly" in the minds of customers and to reach the major objectives of the firm, top managers must balance their *desire for predictable behavior in each business unit* to ensure global efficiency and cross-market learning, and the *need for flexibility and responsiveness to local environments*.

The values and norms of behavior laid down in the statement of corporate philosophy are to be formulated in a more precise manner. Top management has to develop guidelines for the behavior of all members of their organization in all of the served markets (see Figure 9.1).

Depending on its basic values and resources, its market power compared to major competitors, and challenges in the external environments, the business behavior of a company can be more or less aggressive. It may emphasize:

● confrontation with competitors
● cooperation with partners.

At first sight, confrontation seems to be the rule. Management should not overlook, however, that market competition in most cases is not a zero-sum game. A firm cannot only win what it takes away from its competitors. In many

FIGURE 9.1 *International marketing decision process*

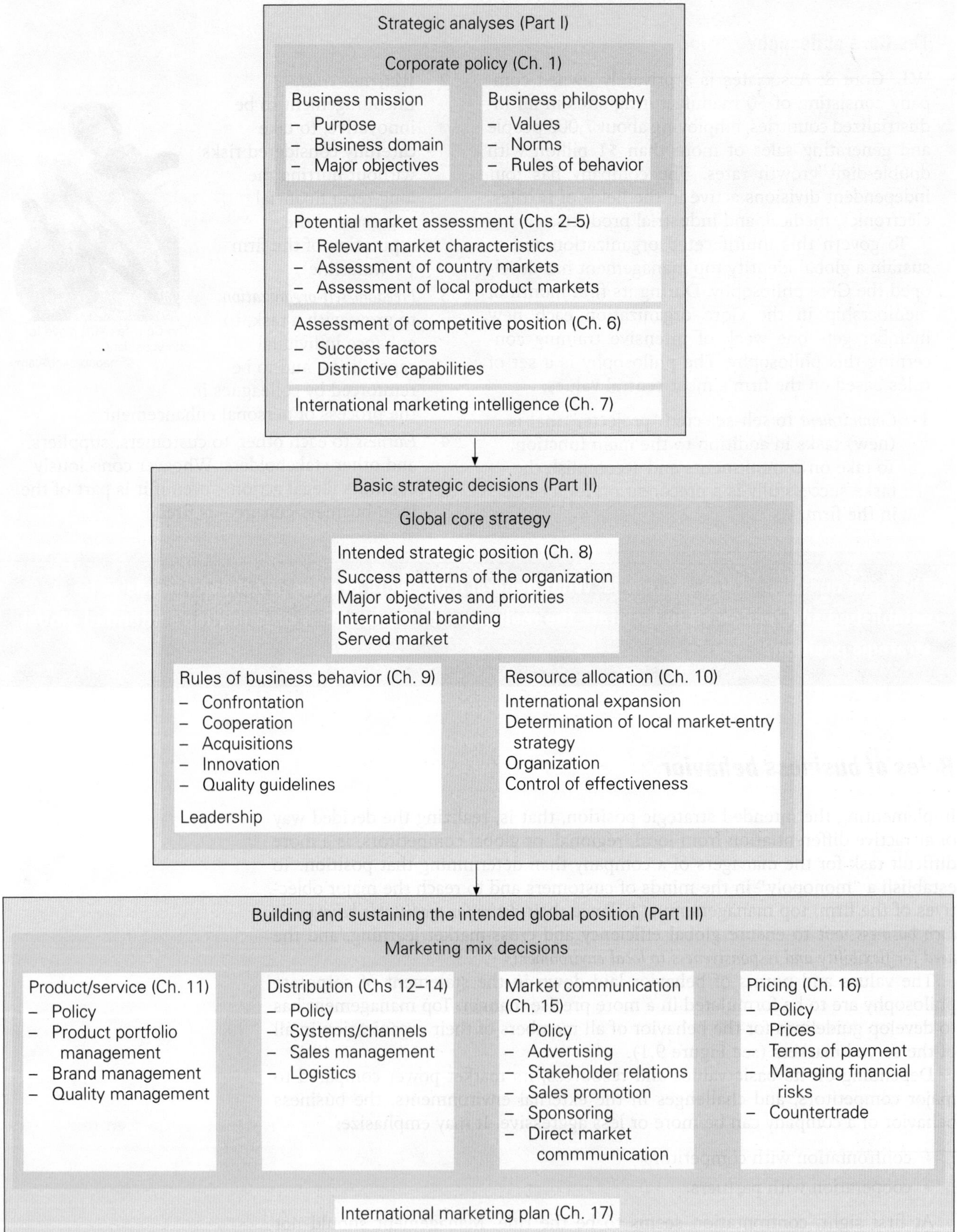

Strategic analyses (Part I)

Corporate policy (Ch. 1)

Business mission
– Purpose
– Business domain
– Major objectives

Business philosophy
– Values
– Norms
– Rules of behavior

Potential market assessment (Chs 2–5)
– Relevant market characteristics
– Assessment of country markets
– Assessment of local product markets

Assessment of competitive position (Ch. 6)
– Success factors
– Distinctive capabilities

International marketing intelligence (Ch. 7)

Basic strategic decisions (Part II)

Global core strategy

Intended strategic position (Ch. 8)
Success patterns of the organization
Major objectives and priorities
International branding
Served market

Rules of business behavior (Ch. 9)
– Confrontation
– Cooperation
– Acquisitions
– Innovation
– Quality guidelines

Leadership

Resource allocation (Ch. 10)
International expansion
Determination of local market-entry
 strategy
Organization
Control of effectiveness

Building and sustaining the intended global position (Part III)

Marketing mix decisions

Product/service (Ch. 11)
– Policy
– Product portfolio
 management
– Brand management
– Quality management

Distribution (Chs 12–14)
– Policy
– Systems/channels
– Sales management
– Logistics

Market communication
(Ch. 15)
– Policy
– Advertising
– Stakeholder relations
– Sales promotion
– Sponsoring
– Direct market
 commmunication

Pricing (Ch. 16)
– Policy
– Prices
– Terms of payment
– Managing financial
 risks
– Countertrade

International marketing plan (Ch. 17)

cases sophisticated definitions of target customers and benefits provided to them allow the creation of "new" product markets.

Because such behavior largely depends on a firm's potential for innovation and acquisition, the rules of business behavior must also contain guidelines concerning product and process innovation as well as acquisition behavior.

Whether a company can impart its intended meaning to stakeholders depends on the experiences those stakeholders have at all kinds of touch points with the firm and its representatives. Therefore, quality guidelines need to be formulated that govern the company's personal and impersonal external contacts. Those guidelines should include product quality standards as well as market communication standards. The quality of external contacts to a great extent depends on the ability of management to make their own staff adopt the intended identity of the firm and become committed to its implementation.

Strong and coherent leadership is needed for that purpose. Managers will need to be convincing role models in playing themselves to the given rules of behavior. They will have to passionately train their people concerning the central values of the organization and how they are consistently turned into stakeholder experiences. They will have to continually reinforce adequate staff behavior, and manage change in a conscious manner.

Finally, to keep track of the efficiency and effectiveness of organizational processes management has to install organizational control. That is, any globally operating firm must find a balance between tendencies towards:

- centralization
- standardization
- socialization.

In the following all these points will be discussed in some detail.

Confrontation

The rules of business behavior must, first, contain statements on when and how to seek confrontation versus cooperation with competitors but also with suppliers, intermediaries or other important stakeholders. A firm with local, regional, and global competitors in its product markets may choose among a variety of ways of confronting them. These include frontal attack, flanking, encirclement, and bypassing.

Frontal attack

Frontal attacks are appropriate for large companies or groups of cooperating firms with substantial resources and a significant competitive advantage in their product concept or its delivery. There are three types of frontal attacks: limited, price based, and value based.

Limited frontal attack When the company limits its attack to a specific customer group and tries to win these customers away from competition, it is launching a **limited frontal attack**. Anheuser Busch, the big U.S. beer company, for example, might compete against Danish Carlsberg for exclusive supply contracts with top restaurants in major Italian cities. A limited frontal attack requires a great deal of attention to the specific needs of the targeted customers, in order to convince them of the superior benefits to be derived from the product and the related services.

Price-based frontal attack **Price-based frontal attacks** rely on product and service features that are similar to those of competitors, offered at a significantly lower price. This strategy was used in France by U.K. Cable & Wireless, U.S. West, and Germany's Veba, when together they launched the third mobile phone network on an initiative of their French partner, Bouygues. Their prices offered for international calls to Belgium, Germany, the Netherlands, and the U.K. were lower than the prices of existing competitors for calls using the normal earth-bound phone network. However, price-based attacks are risky. They work only when customers do not view price as indicative of quality and competitors are unable or unwilling to lower their prices further. The company must be willing to cross-subsidize its efforts or be a cost leader. In most cases, price competition leads to a generally lowered price level in the market with no or not much advantage for the attacking firm.

Value-based frontal attack A **value-based frontal attack** relies on product or service differentiation through characteristics other than price. The nature of the difference is determined by the company's distinctive capabilities. The firm may use a competitive advantage in research and development, for example, to constantly improve its products. One such firm is the plastics division of U.S.-based Allied Corporation, which starts with a rather simple, basic product – plastic granules – and adapts it for different applications of international customers such as manufacturers of yogurt cups or car dashboards. In general, a value-based frontal attack can succeed only when customers and intermediaries in the distribution system perceive the firm's product as more attractive than competitors' offerings.

Flanking

Flanking is a way of confrontation focusing on a specific, often just emerging segment of a larger product market. It is chosen by companies that do not have the resources to attack established competitors head-on or that do not want to take the risk of spending the resources needed for a frontal attack. They use flanking to build a position that will permit direct competition in the other parts of the product market later on.

Geographic flanking With **geographic flanking**, the firm chooses geographic areas in which major competitors are weak or non-existent and offers products that are similar to those that competitors sell in comparable product markets elsewhere. For example, in Mexico more than 95% of all tortillas are produced and sold in little shops licensed by the government. These outlets are virtual monopolies in their neighborhoods, with a captive market. In part, the reason is cultural: Mexicans like their staple fresh. But, more important, Mexico subsidizes small tortilleras with low prices on corn flour, making it possible to sell corn tortillas for less than the real production cost. Thus, equipped with modern baking technology, Mexican Grupo Industrial Maseca has chosen the U.S. market to launch their mass-produced, packaged tortillas, honing their marketing skills for the day when Mexico's tortilleras will no longer be subsidized.

Segmented flanking With **segmented flanking**, the firm enters a segment of a larger product market that is not served by major competitors or in which customers are dissatisfied. When Honda entered the U.S. market with its motorcycles, for example, it initially concentrated on small "transportation" devices. Domestic firms such as Harley-Davidson continued to focus on larger sports motorcycles because they believed that the transportation market was limited. Honda was able to gain market experience, establish its name, and generate local cash flow. Eventually, after consolidating its initial position, it started developing other market segments from this platform. Honda gradually introduced larger motorcycles that competed directly with local competitors' models.

The success of segmented flanking depends on the company's ability to identify shifts in the market that will allow it to enter and develop a particular segment faster than potential competitors. The segment must be large enough to repay the effort. Both forms of flanking assume that competitors will not take notice of the firm's actions or see any reason to intervene in its chosen markets. Success can be achieved more easily when the entire product market is growing or the potential size of the emerging market segment is unclear. Under such conditions competitors do not fight for sales volume in a market niche, and dominant firms in the market do not consider the new entrant a major threat to their position.

Market encirclement

With **market encirclement**, the firm tries to attack its major competitor in as many ways as possible. It offers product lines to customers in almost every segment of the entire product market. The company applies product line stretching and product proliferation simultaneously, as Japan's watchmaker Seiko has done in the watch market. They introduced a diversity of watch models (under varying brand names) in all price categories except the most expensive. Because the firm was able to satisfy all or most of the needs of potential customers in the given product category, intermediaries had less need to associate with other suppliers.

To be successful, encirclement requires that the firm spends large amounts of resources over a long period. It must gain sufficient market share to repay the large investment. Competitors should be unable or unwilling to invest similar large amounts of resources to defend their markets. This may not be the case if the firm encounters dominant competitors ready to defend their position.

Bypassing

Relatively small companies that are unable to confront major competitors in the international marketplace may choose bypassing as an adequate way of confrontation. They can either satisfy customer needs in product markets that are not served in a comparable manner by any competitor, or enter country markets for current products that no important competitor has yet served. In both cases the company needs adequate marketing experience and know-how.

Product bypassing In the first case of **product bypassing**, the firm may develop a new version of a traditional product or service, thereby opening up a new product market with little competition. For example, the French tire manufacturer Michelin first entered the U.S. market with its radial tire and focused on customers, such as fleet owners, who needed long-lasting tires. At that time, Goodyear and other producers of bias-ply tires established in the U.S. market believed radials could damage their profitable replacement market. Therefore, they did not follow Michelin's move, but decided to ignore their new competitor's early efforts in an attempt to avoid giving radials a stamp of approval. The success of their French competitor forced them to follow later when they had already lost substantial parts of the market.

Geographic bypassing In the case of **geographic bypassing**, the firm may concentrate on minor markets. Small firms that face strong competition in developed economies may seek opportunities in less developed countries. Although such markets may be difficult to enter, once established the firm may secure a quasi-exclusive position in the market. Thus, Merloni Refrigerators has signed a government procurement contract to meet the total need for refrigerators in a small, less economically developed country.

Cooperation

Confrontation avoidance

Confrontation can be avoided by defining "new" product markets, changing the "rules of the game" or entering strategic partnerships.

Defining "new" product markets A company can avoid direct confrontation by creating a "new" product market, that is, by defining target customers and benefits provided to them in a highly sophisticated manner. For example, Japanese Bandai Digital Entertainment, instead of seeking head-on confrontation with PC manufacturers, unveiled Pippin, a stripped-down Macintosh developed with Apple that looked like a videogame machine, offered internet access and CD-ROM, and plugged into a TV set. Bandai sold parents on Pippin's educational benefits accessible through the net while pitching kids on games. Its price was closer to VCR than PC prices. The company created its own new market.

Potential customers either do not perceive well-positioned companies and products as directly comparable to each other or they appreciate having a choice between various offers for different purposes. All stakeholders in the market may subjectively profit.

Changing the "rules of the game" Direct confrontation will also be successfully avoided when a company does not blindly imitate the way its competitors behave in a market but bases its actions on a thorough analysis of the business system and how customer value can best be created. By changing some "rules of the game" the firm may establish a "new" market with less competition.

U.S.-based PC maker Dell, for example, has found that experienced business clients and knowledgeable consumers looking for the most cutting-edge PC models know what they want – and therefore, are ready to order hardware over the phone or internet. Dell decided to build to order, rather than run up big inventories of various finished systems like most PC firms (35 for Dell versus 110 days for Compaq Computer). They first created a mail-order market. Now, Dell sells mostly through the internet.

Entering strategic partnerships The globalization of markets and the increasing speed of technological developments as well as international market introductions of new products forces even traditionally fervent competitors to enter strategic partnerships. For example, more than 25 major car and truck companies worldwide have joined together in over 300 strategic partnerships. Peugeot and Fiat as well as Ford and Volkswagen have joint ventures where minivans are produced and sold under the brand names of each of the partners. Renault, Europe's fourth-largest producer of heavy trucks, cooperates with MAN, Germany's second-largest heavy truck maker, and in another business with General Motors to develop and market light commercial vehicles called panel vans.

Many small and medium-sized companies that wish to become international marketers possess the required technical know-how to offer attractive products and services. But they lack the international experience or financial and personnel resources to confront their competitors in many markets simultaneously or to acquire businesses to reach the competitive advantages needed for success. In the U.S., for example, about 250 mostly large companies account for 80% of exports. But there are at least 20,000 small and medium-sized firms that produce products that could boost their revenues by being offered internationally. Cooperation may allow companies to enter more markets, faster, cheaper, and with a broader product line than if they tried it alone.

Forms of cooperation

When international business experience or financial or human resources are lacking, a company can supplement its strengths with those of partners through cooperation, such as business clusters, supply agreements, licensing agreements, joint ventures, and the use of strategic alliances even with competitors.

Business clusters Aprilia, the Italian motorbike company, based in Noale near Venice, and nearby Nordica, which has established itself as a world leader in ski boots, are European examples of firms using "network" manufacturing in business clusters that allow even very small supplier firms to profit from internationalization. Neither Aprilia nor Nordica manufactures a single component. Instead, they work closely with hundreds of suppliers specializing in the production of parts where they can reach economies of scale and profit from experience. The firms' own resources go into design, assembly, and international marketing.

Supply agreements and original equipment manufacturing (OEM) Firms that want to gain access to markets in Asia, the Community of Independent States (CIS), and Latin America may have to establish cooperative agreements with local supply organizations. Hughes Rediffusion Simulation Ltd of the U.K., for example, has joined Mikoyan Design Bureau, the Russian builder of MiG fighters, and GosNIIAS, a Russian avionics integration organization, to develop, co-manufacture and market training and simulation systems for Mikoyan military and civil aircraft.

Joint ventures Energia, a Russian aerospace firm based in Kaliningrad, has established a joint venture with middle-sized German Kayser-Threde GmbH to secure access to sources of capital. The advanced technology equipment and industrial know-how of the Russian partner helped the German firm to become a major provider of remote sensing services to customers in Asia, western Europe, and North America.

Larger companies can also profit from cooperation. Nike, the Oregon-based footwear company, entered into a manufacturing joint venture with Alpargatas SAIC, Argentina's largest shoe and textile company. The deal has given Alpargatas access to Nike's advanced shoe-making technology while Nike has got factory space and a ready-made salesforce for the Argentine market.

DVD / VHS machine: companies profit from cooperation   © Judith Collins/Alamy

In a great number of cases combinations of various forms of cooperation are needed to be internationally successful. The problem is that on a global business level there is strong competition for the best partners in each industry. Decisions have to be taken rather quickly when the need for cooperation or an attractive opportunity arise. Therefore, to assist the implementation of the firm's intended strategic position top management of an internationally operating company has to formulate rules defining under which circumstances to cooperate, in what way, and with what kind of partners.

Strategic partnerships

Strategic partnerships or strategic alliances are a special type of cooperative behavior. They involve two or more organizations, in which the combined strengths of the partners permit each to perform better in international markets. One or all partners contribute marketing knowledge and skills, production technology, manufacturing competency, and access to financial resources and distribution channels.

Reasons There are several reasons for forming strategic partnerships.

Economies of scale and experience curve effects These can be gained faster and more efficiently through a strategic partnership than through the efforts of a single firm. Alliances of airlines such as SkyTeam (31% share of world market), Star Alliance (25%), or One World (see Table 9.1 for the members of those alliances), for example, were formed to coordinate their passenger and freight business on a global level, to use the cost advantages of code sharing (joint flight numbers for computer reservation systems), and to increase customer loyalty through joint frequent flyer programs. Sharing information, logistics, and booking systems allows significantly reduced costs for all partners.

Limited resources for adequate R&D The research and development investment needed to remain competitive on a global scale may be beyond the financial resources of a single organization, but become feasible through the establishment of a strategic partnership. St. Petersburg-based Klimov, Korea's Hala Group, and the Korean Institute of Science and Technology, for example, have joined forces to develop a 1.5-megawatt ground-based electrical power and heating station. The technology developed by Klimov and the Russian Central Turbine and Boiler Institute has significantly contributed to lowering the R&D expenses of this project.

Remaining independent For an increasing number of firms facing global competition the only way to remain independent is to enter strategic partnerships. This apparent contradiction is explained by the fact that, given global competition and the cost of resources, single organizations may not be able to generate enough cash flow to operate independently. Alliances make it possible to obtain resources and share experience with partners without acquiring or being acquired by others. Californian Oracle Corp., for example, was joined by Apple Computer, IBM, Netscape Communications, and Sun Microsystems for the development of an internet device called NC that combines the functions of telephones, televisions, and computers in one simple unit at a price below $1,000.

Establishing a new business model Some businesses could not even exist without strategic partnerships. Internet firms such as Amazon.com, but also brick and mortar firms such as Dell or Lego could not do their business via the internet without having formed strategic partnerships with internationally operating logistics firms that provide the physical distribution network needed for delivering their products to the customers.

Additional reasons for establishing strategic partnerships are to:

- enter new markets
- gain access to distribution systems
- maintain technological and manufacturing competency
- monitor the activities of competitors
- keep abreast of technological development.

TABLE 9.1 *The three big airline alliances*

SkyTeam	Star Alliance	One World
Aero Mexico	Air Canada	American Airlines
Aeroflot	Air New Zealand	Aer Lingus
Air France	All Nippon Airways	British Airways
Alitalia	Asian Airlines	Cathay Pacific
Continental Airlines	Austrian Airlines	Finnair
ČSA Czech Airlines	bmi british midland	Iberia
Delta Airlines	LOT Polish Airlines	Lan Chile
KLM	Lufthansa	Qantas
Korean Air	SAS	
Northwest Airlines	Singapore Airlines	
	Spanair	
	Swiss International Airlines	
	Thai Airways	
	United Airlines	
	Varig	

Three alliances dominate the global air traffic market. Airlines have formed these alliances to gain economies of scale and experience curve effects.

Risks As with any competitive behavior, there are risks associated with strategic partnerships. Often failure to foresee differences in corporate cultures may place the partnership at risk. Change of business domain may cause other problems to occur as the partnership pushes one, if not both, of the new partners into areas in which it has no previous experience. Still another problem with establishing a strategic partnership is the cost of a one-way flow of technology. If guarantees are not established and strictly enforced, an organization might share technology only to find that it faces additional competition from its supposed partner.

Success factors

Finding the right cooperation partner(s) For finding the right cooperation partner(s), interested firms should develop a profile of characteristics expected from an ideal partner, based on the intended global portfolio and assessment of the firm's versus the competitors' distinctive capabilities in the targeted markets. Based on the profile of characteristics sought, the company can either start a search process on its own or use foreign trade organizations or consultants to find the right partner(s).

Shared and mutually understood objectives Strategic partnerships must have shared and mutually understood objectives if they are to succeed. Partners that seek short-term profits will have problems with partners that are more concerned with long-term gains in market share. Similarly, organizations that are looking for marketing assistance may have difficulties with partners that prefer technical solutions.

Respect for cultural differences Strategic partners must understand and trust each other. When Californian Robert Mondavi established a partnership with Chile's Errazuriz to form their Caliterra winery, they started off based on the trust between the two business leaders. But they overlooked the importance of establishing a broader program allowing decision makers on both sides to learn to accept the specifics of the other culture. A real dialogue between the partners was never established and the partnership broke up after only a relatively short time.

Other attributes of successful strategic partnerships include a careful study of the market to serve jointly and sharing equity.

Skills and resources The skills needed to ensure international competitiveness through strategic partnerships are similar for large and small firms.

Patience in negotiating with partners from different cultures U.S. executives, in particular, seem impatient with international standards. In the U.S. "time is money," but in China, for example, "time is eternity." Chinese partners will not take any cooperation decision before they have established a trustful relationship with their potential partners. And when the decision is finally taken, the signing of the contract to the Chinese is the signal for starting detailed negotiations.

Complementary capabilities Success in a strategic partnership occurs when each partner brings to the alliance a strength that the other partner lacks. The best partners might be those that do not have a dominant share of the market or are not even in the industry. U.S.-based Corning Glass, for example, cooperates with over 14 different alliance partners in Europe, Asia, and Latin America to learn of potential improvements in designing and manufacturing different glass- and ceramic-based products, to penetrate new markets, and to share the risks of technical development. With Novartis of Switzerland it focuses on medical diagnostics. The partnership with Siemens concentrates on fiber optics. The alliance with NGK Insulators of Japan produces ceramics for catalytic converters and pollution control equipment.

Small and medium-sized firms that would like to take advantage of international market opportunities can also establish partnerships. In strategic alliances between middle-sized firms, one partner may, for example, produce (part of) the product while the other sells it under its well-established brand name. Smaller firms can also run a sales office together, one bringing in its existing office facilities, the other an additional product line to be sold through the same distribution channels (improving the distribution of overheads across product lines).

Acquisition

The globalization of markets has produced a great number of acquisitions. The reasons for those acquisitions are diverse. So is their level of success.

Reasons for acquisitions

There are various reasons for acquiring other companies. Sometimes management wants to acquire skills and resources needed to reach the intended strategic position in very short time. In other cases the intention is to add resources to reach global standards of efficiency or adequate R&D potential. Other acquisitions are simply motivated by the

- struggle for a dominant market position
- avoidance of a hostile takeover
- need to have an interesting "growth story" to present to financial analysts.

Instant presence During the process of assessing potential international markets, management may find very attractive product or country markets that the company cannot serve adequately because of missing capabilities. Instead of leaving those markets to competitors that are in a better position or starting to build up the needed strengths, management may decide that the markets are of great importance to the firm and speed is the key to attain an attractive strategic position. In such a case, acquisition gives the company the opportunity to build a presence instantly.

Germany's Robert Bosch GmbH, located in Stuttgart, the first company to offer ABS (anti-lock braking systems) for cars, for example, was confronted with the demand of its major car manufacturing clients to deliver and service entire product systems instead of only electronic parts to improve braking systems. It therefore acquired 24 brake-making factories in Europe, Latin America, and the U.S. as well as shares of joint ventures in China, India, and Korea from U.S.-based Allied Signal Inc. With this acquisition Bosch became one of the four largest brake-making firms in the world, together with U.S. competitors Teves and Kelsey-Hayes and the U.K.'s Lucas.

Global size The pressure to match global standards of efficiency and financial resources available to market and product development also contributed to an increasing number of mergers. Particularly in Europe, many firms in industries such as airlines, autos, banking, and media, which have traditionally avoided international mergers, could not contend any longer with local markets. For example, French multimedia company Infogrames Entertainment, and Ocean International Ltd, a similar privately held U.K. company whose catalog of simulation, adventure, and arcade software games was complementary to that of the French company merged in a move that created Europe's biggest entity in the multimedia industry. In the airline industry, Air France acquired KLM and Lufthansa bought ailing Swiss.

Dominant market position Other companies acquire (shares of) firms to reach a dominant market position (see Strategy box 9.1). For example in the retailing sector, Watson, the world's largest duty-free operator, which is part of Hong Kong-based Hutchison Whampoa, successively acquires big cosmetics chains worldwide. In 2005 it took over the European market leader Marionnaud, which at that time had about 9,000 employees and 1,280 outlets.

As a reaction to such concentrations in retailing, manufacturers also tend to improve their market position through acquisitions. After having acquired French Clairol SA in 2001 and German Wella in 2003, for example, Procter & Gamble announced the acquisition of Boston-based Gillette, one of the world leaders in mouth hygiene, body care products and batteries, in early 2005. This acquisition made Procter & Gamble the world's biggest consumer product company with sales above $60 billion. It strengthened the firm's bargaining power in the negotiations with media companies as well as retailers such as Wal-Mart.

Acquisition management

Most acquisitions accomplished in the last 10 years have not reached expectations published beforehand. This may be due to inappropriate management of one or the other part of the acquisition process. To be successful in acquiring other businesses, a company must:

- constantly survey its markets for potential acquisition candidates
- properly assess the attractiveness of the targets

STRATEGY BOX 9.1

L.N. Mittal: The King of Steel

There is only one question left to ask about billionaire Lakshmi Mittal: When will he become the King of Steel?

Mittal was born in Sadulpur, Rajasthan. At the age of 26 his father sent him to Indonesia to oversee the family's steelmill now called Ispat Indo. In the late 1980s, Mittal moved into acquisition mode. He bought mills in Trinidad and Canada. In 1992, he snapped up the loss-making Sibalsa Mill in Mexico for $220 million. The 20-year-old facility was originally built by the Mexican government for around $2 billion. Lakshmi Mittal parted company with his father in 1995. That year he made his riskiest and most ambitious buy. The giant Karmet steelworks in Kazakhstan was reckoned to be a gamble. Since then, he has never let an opportunity pass. In 1998, bidding $1.4 billion for U.S. rust belt giant Inland Steel he consolidated the firm's strong base in North America.

Then Mittal shifted focus to western Europe and bought plants in Ireland, France, and Germany giving him a stronghold in the market for long products. Since 2000 he has moved from Algeria, where he took a 70% stake in a mine now called Ispat Annaba, to South Africa, where Mittal bought 47% of Iscor, to Romania and the Czech Republic. There he bought run down nationalized companies such as Sidex and Nova Huta that were being privatized – and that other steelmakers did not want to touch. In each he managed to increase productivity significantly. At Ispat Sidex in the Czech Republic, for example, production climbed from 3.04 million tons to 3.65 million tons, only one year after it was acquired. Once a plant is taken over, a crack team is brought in that always includes large numbers of Indian executives. Most have been handpicked from the Steel Authority of India. They are willing to work 7 days a week in the most remote locations. After working in places such as Rourkela and Bokaro, they also know everything there is to know about rusty state-run enterprises.

Mittal has a remarkable eye for a bargain and has figured the art of turning around rundown steelmills. In addition, he is willing to walk away from a deal if the price is not right. His investments per ton have always been rather low throughout his career as a takeover artist.

Source: Adapted from Balakrishnan, P. (2003) "L N Mittal: The king of steel", rediff.com business, 27 September, pp. 1–5

- take the appropriate approach to initiating the acquisition
- carefully orchestrate the integration of the acquired firm into its own organization.

Because of the complexity of such processes in an internationally operating company, top management has to define general rules of behavior concerning all these steps. Japanese-owned ICL, for example, has a special planning group called Acquisition Group, which studies and evaluates targets on a global basis. Toolbox 9.1 describes how part of such studies might be done.

How difficult integration processes can be is illustrated by Renault's acquisition of 36% of the capital of Nissan, the second largest Japanese car manufacturer in 1999. Six months after his arrival Carlos Goshn, the new CEO, presented his "plan of revival" for Nissan, which at the time carried a debt of €20 billion: 30% reduction of working capital, shutdown of factories, layoff of more than 20% of personnel, sale of a great number of participations in Japanese firms. The Japanese were shocked by this plan that stood in total contrast to Japanese industrial culture. Carlos Goshn worked hard to explain his ideas, tried everything to convince his Japanese collaborators, and invested time and resources in management training. And it worked. After two years, Nissan became one of the most profitable automakers in the world. Nissan's stock market value climbed to reach three times the value of Renault. Carlos Goshn became a legend.

TOOLBOX 9.1   Acquisitions need not be a loser's game

Making smarter acquisitions begins with understanding customer profitability. Most acquiring companies will not have profitability data on the target's customers. In some industries, such as financial services or phone services, companies routinely possess and may even publish data such as number of customers, customer acquisition costs, and churn rates. Combining those average figures with the experience of the acquirer, market surveys, or data of consultants provides at least a rough idea of a target candidate's customer profitability. In other industries, estimating customer profitability may be extremely difficult. However, the internal data needed may become available in the due diligence process.

Crunching the numbers then, is a straightforward exercise:

Step 1: Measure product and service profitability, taking into account all costs, including capital costs. This means going well beyond the gross margin measures that many companies use. Subtracting capital charges from net operating profit after tax yields economic profit. Companies often find that, when they allocate capital appropriately, many of their products and services turn out to be unprofitable.

Step 2: Once true economic profitability of products and services is known, it is important to find out which customers buy which ones. This analysis will provide a preliminary understanding of customer profitability. Gathering these data is easy if customers pay by credit card or are otherwise identifiable. But even if customers pay in cash, useful information can be gathered by observing customers on a sample basis.

Step 3: From the preliminary estimate of customer profitability subtract all customer-specific costs. Again, gathering the data is easier for business-to-business companies that can exactly identify their customers and calculate their cost by order or project. In other cases data must be estimated by the use of samples of customers.

Step 4: Finally, all the costs in the business that have not been assigned already – for example, overhead costs for the CEO's jet or capital costs for the headquarters building – must be divided up and accounted for in the customer profitability figures.

This analysis will give the acquiring firm valuable information on what companies or parts of companies to buy and which to leave alone.

Source: Adapted from "How to measure the profitability of your customers", *Harvard Business Review*, June 2003, 81(6), p. 74

Innovation

When a company is confronted with global competitors, low-cost production, international sourcing, and international marketing may not be sufficient for success. The firm's innovation behavior may become a major factor in reaching the intended global strategic position. Innovation processes include product innovation as well as process innovation.

Management must decide whether the company or a business unit should be a pioneer, an innovation leader, or a follower in its industry.

Related to this decision, a general rule must be formulated concerning the firm's intended rate of innovation, that is, how fast product and process innovations should follow each other and be transferred into changes in the company's offer to the market. All strategic decisions concerning the firm's innovation behavior are influenced by management's attitude toward risk and the organization's capabilities, current market position, and orientation toward innovation.

Product innovation

Product innovation involves:

- *developing new solutions to customer problems*, for example, a new technology to produce irrigation water from sea water
- *making current products more useful*, such as developing portable phones that have multimedia properties
- *adding new services*, for example, introducing banking by phone or online
- *challenging the total product portfolio*.

When production costs are high because of high labor costs (sometimes even lean production does not resolve the problem), a company that does not want to transfer production to low-wage countries may concentrate on product innovation for special international market segments. In doing so, it may have to give up large parts of the market, in particular if its products are priced too high for most customers.

Wolford, the Austrian producer of high-quality bodies, tights, swimsuits, and underwear, for example, has concentrated its innovation on high fashion and the production technology for seamless products allowing top management to concentrate production in Bregenz, a location where labor costs are eight to ten times higher than in the neighboring Czech Republic. Wolford cannot compete with the price of tights marketed by Sara Lee, which are targeted to the mass market. The company focuses its activities on an up-scale market, which is estimated to represent only 3% of the total market. But in doing so, Wolford has gained a reputation as European fashion leader.

Companies located in countries with high labor costs may also find opportunities to grow in markets where a lower level of product technology (and, hence, a lower price) is better suited to customers' needs. For example, Dornier, a German manufacturer of weaving machines, found that its products were too sophisticated and expensive for most Latin American customers. It started a second-hand machinery market for those customers, adapting used machines the company has to take back from customers who buy new equipment in highly technologically developed markets.

Even intensified product innovation may not protect the firm against situations in which high-tech, high-quality products become the industry standard. In such cases the company must turn to new product markets, provide new customer benefits, or develop new technologies to regain a competitive advantage. An example of this approach is AT&T, formerly the only international U.S. telephone company. As a reaction to market deregulation and difficulties in differentiating its services from those of competitors in the telecommunications market, AT&T decided to compete in the multimedia market. Since then it has systematically acquired or started cooperation with firms having the appropriate know-how and the physical distribution systems needed.

Process innovation

Process innovation means changing the way processes such as production, new product development, or product delivery are conducted. In mature product markets, where rates of real product innovation are low and cost pressures are high, process innovation can be a significant means of gaining and sustaining competitive advantage by reducing the costs of generating customer value and making processes faster and more flexible.

The restructuring and reorganization of procurement, production, and distribution processes adds value for the customers who get their products and services earlier or just in time.

In many cases, product and process innovation have to be pursued simultaneously. For example, the Smart car, which is marketed by DaimlerChrysler, contains new technical solutions in its realization and is entirely produced by a network of cooperating suppliers.

Role in innovation process

Management must decide what role the firm should play concerning innovation processes in its product markets. Basically, there are two ways to behave:

1 strive for innovation leadership
2 reach for attractive market positions as an innovation follower.

Innovation leadership Innovation leadership is not necessarily the same as **pioneering**. Pioneering firms are the first to introduce a new solution to a customer problem in the market. They have the opportunity to:

- develop market know-how earlier than their competitors
- enjoy customer loyalty
- influence the direction of technological development
- set industry standards
- experience high rates of market share growth leading to effective performance.

But they also experience all the difficulties of introducing an innovation such as:

- high development costs
- quality problems
- legal constraints
- customers' misperceptions
- intermediaries' reluctance concerning new products.

Innovation leadership is not so much characterized by being first to market but by some managerial factors, which help a firm to profit from the opportunities of a pioneer and to reduce its disadvantages.

Vision of the mass market To be or to become an early leader in a new product category, a company must have managers who are able to envision the full potential of the new product. They need to develop the vision of a broad international mass market. Only the sales volume of such a market can provide the economies of scale and experience needed to overcome startup problems such as high costs, limited features, or missing distribution.

For example, Ampex pioneered the video recorder market in 1956 and was the leading supplier for several years. At $50,000 each, initial recorder sales were limited. RCA and Toshiba, the only competitors, were way behind, so Ampex had almost a monopoly in sales and R&D. However, the company's managers did little to improve quality or lower costs. Instead, they sought to reduce Ampex's dependence on video recorder sales, and pursued diversifications such as audio products and computer peripherals. In contrast, at JVC, Yuma Shiraishi, manager of video recorder development, asked his engineers to develop a machine that could sell for $500, while using little tape and retaining high picture quality. It took JVC engineers 20 years to realize the goal. But when their efforts were successful in the mid-1970s, JVC's video sales went from $2 million to almost $2 billion in the following 15 years.

Managerial persistence   When deciding on what innovation behavior guidelines to formulate for their company, management should be aware that most successful products are not the immediate result of technological breakthroughs but the fruits of small, incremental innovations in design, engineering, manufacturing, and marketing over extended periods. They only exist because management maintained a commitment to the product over a long period of slow and continual progress. For example, VAI, one of the world's top two metallurgical engineering firms based in Austria, developed COREX. This direct reduction technology for iron production largely reduces the costs and environmental stress of the process. It took the company more than 12 years from the first technical solution to the point where customers around the world started to accept the new technology as a feasible alternative.

Financial commitment   As the examples show, it can take significant time to overcome R&D as well as marketing odds of innovations. Therefore, the management of a company wanting to be an innovation leader must be able and willing to commit substantial finances to last through this struggle.

Relentless innovation   Finally, management must be aware that innovation is an ongoing process of continual product and process improvement that will not take place in a large bureaucracy, when people are satisfied with their first success, or when management fears undermining current market success through the cannibalization of established products. IBM, for example, stymied its development of minicomputers and workstations to protect mainframe sales, even though competitors kept making inroads into the mainframe market. When they finally decided to put more energy into the development of this product category, they were slow to bring out new products because of their bureaucratic approval process.

To maintain a leadership position, the company must continually develop and implement new technologies or acquire them through licensing, strategic partnerships, or acquisitions. To keep their leading position in the market of high-powered lasers and bending machines, Germany's Trumpf, for example, has formulated innovation and quality leadership to be more important than cost leadership. The company continually invests 6–7% of its sales in R&D projects. Sometimes this share is as much as 15%.

Innovation follower   An innovation follower may be able to avoid the mistakes made by the innovation leader. It may also have lower research and development costs (in effect, lowering fixed costs) and may therefore be able to match the innovator's low costs. But to be in a position to become market leader, to set standards and influence the development of the industry, the firm must hold a dominant position in a product category related to the new product, as for example Coca-Cola in the soft drinks market. Such a position allows it to leverage assets such as name recognition, an existing distribution network, production facilities or managerial expertise.

Merck, a producer of pharmaceutical products, successfully pursues the role of an innovation follower. Operating in many different markets where it faces primarily local competition, it can use its global distribution network to quickly introduce the products, services or ideas of its more innovative, but localized, competitors in the markets where they are not present.

Rate of innovation

For both product and process technology, the company's rate of innovation compared to the rate for the industry is of major concern. A company's rate of innovation is heavily influenced by various factors.

Traditions in home market German automakers, for example, preferred not to change their models too often, not only in order to communicate an image of reliable quality and craftsmanship, but also to let their products develop a strong visual image in the minds of their relatively conservative customers. This strategy was of advantage in European markets. In the U.S., in contrast, customers are interested in fast product changes and in east Asia they expect continual product improvement. There, the quality of a company's offerings is judged partly on the basis of the firm's rate of product innovation.

Domestic customers' basic values Owing to the different expectations of their customers, Japanese companies had learned to be much faster in new product development than their European (and U.S.) competitors. The higher speed allowed them to swamp the markets with new products or product features. Such continual product innovation in small steps can lead to significant advantages over competitors. Japanese manufacturers of air conditioners, for example, after a few years of small but continual product innovation steps were seven to 10 years ahead in product technology compared to their U.S. competitors. But higher speed can also lead to economic trouble as experienced by Mazda. The company once had six models, selling about 1 million cars. In 1996, when Ford took over a majority stake in its shares, Mazda was offering 29 models but selling the same number of cars. The increased complexity of their range had dramatically decreased the firm's profits.

One way of overcoming the problem of different innovation rates expected by customers in different parts of the world is to split the world market into customer segments on the basis of innovation orientation and to develop different strategies for each segment. In many cases, however, this approach entails higher costs than selling to a unified market. Another way out is to offer customized flexibility in many different product features.

Computer-aided production planning and production flexibility can enable customers to design individualized products. In the case of cars, for example, the customer can specify such features as color, power, interior equipment, and "options" such as sunroof or air conditioning.

Speed of innovation processes inside the company In general, an internationally operating firm should be able at least to meet the latest standard of technology in its field. To be able to compete successfully in global markets, the company may undertake any of the following steps:

- *Monitor trade journals*, patent and research reports, and attend international conferences and seminars on relevant technological issues.
- *Establish and maintain product as well as process innovation teams*, supported by recognized organizational commitment, with a knowledgeable team leader and members from all relevant disciplines in the company who are rewarded for the success of the teamwork.

- *Enter into agreements with research organizations* that give the company access to recent research and the right to bring the resulting innovations to market.
- *Hire specialized engineering firms.*
- *Engage in cooperative research projects with partners* (such as lead users, intermediaries, suppliers, designers, or competitors) that have complementary expertise.
- *Acquire new technologies through licensing or acquisitions.*

If a company cannot be among the innovation leaders in its industry, it does not necessarily lack international market potential, but it faces greater difficulty, and must choose its target markets with more care. Most Latin American markets, for example, are not sufficiently technologically developed to use the latest generation of weaving machines. Workers lack the necessary skills, raw materials do not meet the specifications met by materials in highly industrialized markets, maintenance capabilities are lacking, and the machines are too expensive. As a result, there is a large market for simpler machines and second-hand equipment in Latin America, which can be provided by companies that are not among the technological leaders in the industry.

Quality guidelines

The implementation of an intended strategic position needs the formulation and reinforcement of rules specifying adequate behavior at all touch points of the business organization with its customers and other stakeholders. All contacts should strongly support the development of the intended brand meaning.

For example, Giorgio Armani, the famous Italian designer and owner of a luxury products firm bearing his name, closely controls every kind of market communication of his company. Subsidiaries from all over the world have to clear their planned activities with headquarters in Milan. Armani runs a great number of directly owned retail shops, and he has bought his former license partners to ensure close control over product quality.

Contacts at touch points may be personal through company staff or representatives such as agents, service providers, or the personnel of retailers, or impersonal, when customers and other stakeholders come in contact with company products or promotional media such as advertising, sponsoring activities, or the internet. Contacts may be direct when stakeholders personally get in touch with personnel, representatives, products, or communication media of the international marketer. But they may also be indirect through hearsay, word of mouth, or reports in the media.

In any case, the quality of those contacts determines the perceptions of customers and other stakeholders. The level of satisfaction or even enthusiasm with the company, a subunit or one of its offers as well as the meaning of the corporate brand and its sub-brands will result from contact experiences. Lasting cognitive structures can only develop in the stakeholders' minds when their brand-related experiences are consistent over time. Thus, guidelines for total quality management need to be formulated and a TQM program installed.

Total quality management is based on in-depth knowledge of customer and other stakeholder expectations as well as the intended meaning of the corporate brand and its sub-brands. Value creation processes, such as new product development, market communication campaigns, or the build up of a distribution system, and value generation processes in all parts of the company, such as logistics or production have to be analyzed, remodeled according to customer/stakeholder satisfaction and branding objectives, and continually monitored along continuous improvement standards (see Toolbox 9.2). Most evidently, product quality and market communication standards play a prominent role in total quality management.

Product quality standards

Increasing global competition has resulted in a continual increase in expected quality standards. Superior product quality based on:

- higher attraction of processes involving customers
- superior material features of the total product
- uniqueness of its immaterial features

is a major platform for international marketing success. This is particularly true in country markets where local suppliers have not systematically invested in the quality of their products. For example, the success of Japanese department stores in countries such as Australia may be partly due to the more intense efforts of their managers and personnel to deliver superior customer service.

TOOLBOX 9.2   **SYNCHRO**

SYNCHRO is the name of the production system installed at all production units of Germany-headquartered Trumpf Werkzeugmaschinen, a manufacturer of machine tools, lasers for production machinery, high-frequency, and electrical tools. SYNCHRO is a methodology for systematically detecting and avoiding waste. It aims to optimize the company's products and services, the speed and efficiency of production, innovation in value generation, and the motivation of staff.

SYNCHRO follows three principles:

- We only produce what is ordered and do it just in time.
- For that purpose we need secured processes generating flawless quality.
- The basis of any improvement is the knowledge and creativity of all our people.

Those principles translate into guidelines for the organization of production processes (Figure 9.2).

FIGURE 9.2   *SYNCHRO quality system*

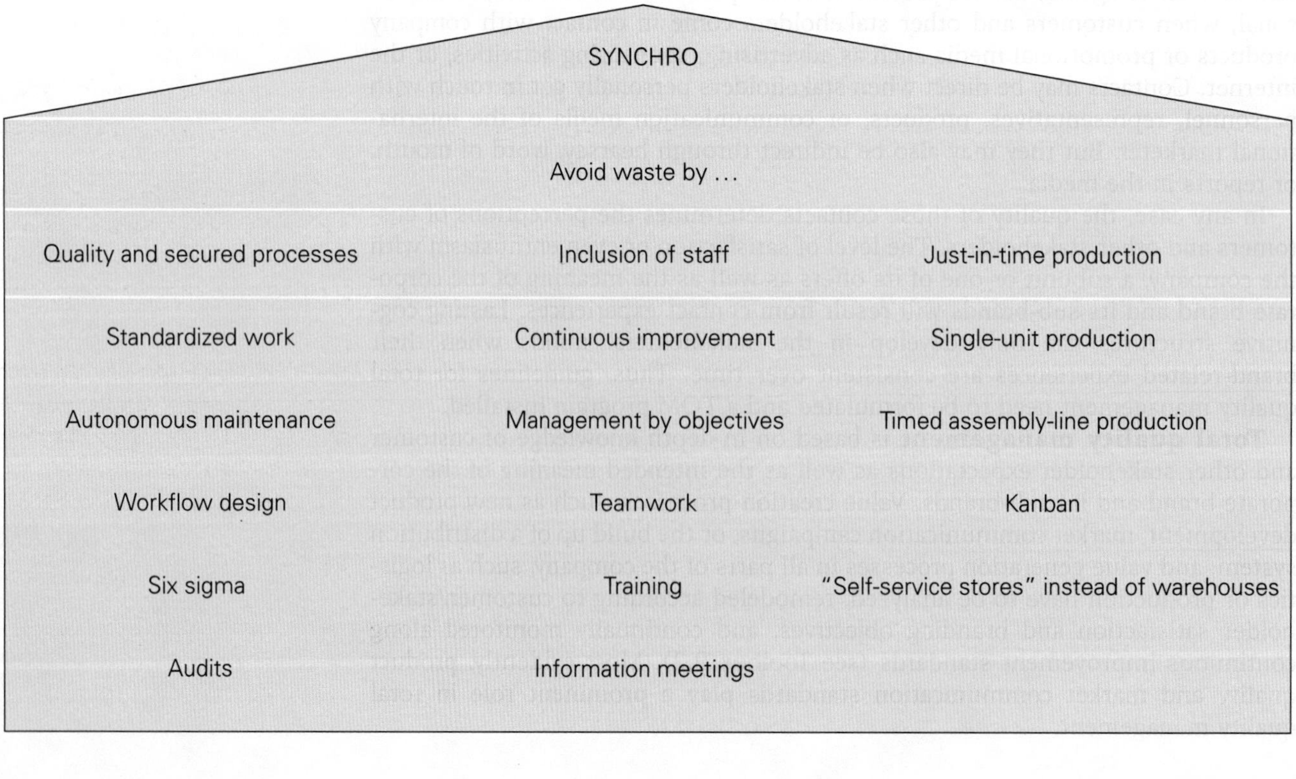

SYNCHRO		
Avoid waste by …		
Quality and secured processes	Inclusion of staff	Just-in-time production
Standardized work	Continuous improvement	Single-unit production
Autonomous maintenance	Management by objectives	Timed assembly-line production
Workflow design	Teamwork	Kanban
Six sigma	Training	"Self-service stores" instead of warehouses
Audits	Information meetings	

Therefore, the development, formulation, and control of product quality standards is a substantial part of a total quality management program. For example, when U.S.-based Motorola started semiconductor assembly in China, they trained their personnel intensively in the concepts of "total customer satisfaction" and "six sigma." Within six months, Chinese line operators had achieved six sigma output quality – fewer than four defects per million units.

To effectively help reaching the intended strategic position of an internationally operating organization, product quality standards need to be based on profound knowledge about how customers and other important stakeholders assess the quality of the kind of products offered.

Customer quality assessment Business and government customers all over the world want to be sure that the purchased products make the expected contribution to their own customer value generation process. Consumers want to buy safe products that perform in the expected way. However, depending on a product's level of immateriality and of customer integration in the value creation and generation processes, it is more or less difficult for a customer to assess beforehand if a given product will perform as expected (see Figure 9.3).

Level of product immateriality The result of a firm's value generation process is a product. A product can be a good, a service, an idea, an organization, a person, or a combination of these, depending on what is marketed to the potential customers. In any case a product is more than what the customer can touch or see.

A product can have more or less tangible attributes. A vacation in a New Zealand ski resort, for example, contains elements such as the slopes, the hotel room, and the food in the restaurants. All of these can be physically experienced. At the same time the total vacation product also consists of intangible elements such as the friendliness of service personnel, the waiting time at the elevators, or the kind of "people around." Even a physical product, such as a Hewlett-Packard printer, has some immaterial features, for example its ease of use or its brand name, which stands for a certain reliability of the supplier and professionalism of

FIGURE 9.3 *Impact of product immateriality and level of customer integration on quality perception and management*

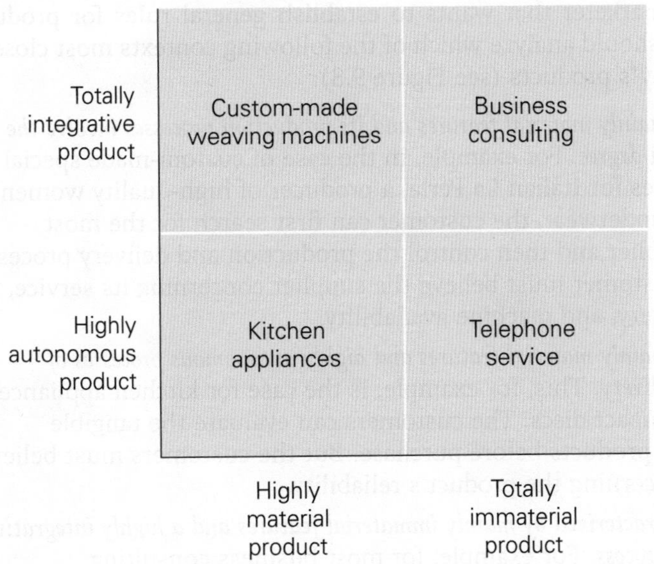

The higher the level of customer integration in a product's process of value generation, the more intensive is the customer's experience with that process and consequently, the closer the marketer comes to controlling the quality of personal contacts.

The higher the level of immateriality of a product the more difficult it is for customers to make sure that the quality of the product will be as expected before they take the buying decision. Therefore, the marketer must take particular care over the adequate design of quality signals.

The more autonomous the value generation process and the more material the product, the more customers will base their quality judgment on material features. The marketer has to focus on assuring that quality.

the user. But there need not be any material results of a company's value generation process. Telephone service provided by a company such as France Telecom, for example, does not have any material features provided to customers.

Level of customer integration The customer of a product may be more or less integrated in the value creation and value generation processes of an organization. The integration of the customer can take the form of intensive personnel involvement, for example, when a specialist at Ochsner Hospital in New Orleans, Louisiana, transplants a kidney to a Brazilian customer. For many products, physical customer contact is limited to the initial phase of product development and production or to the last phase of the customer value generation process. For example, the production process of a kitchen machine by French SEP does not involve future customers at all. They are only indirectly integrated in the value creation process through consumer research during the design stage and become directly involved at the very end of the value generation process, when they buy the machine at a retailer, bring it home, and use it.

Customer integration can also take place by the contribution of an object, such as a PC in the case of Otten, an Austrian producer of printed textiles, when using the hotline of its international production software provider. In other instances, customers provide a right or some information to the value generation process. For example, when the Boston Consulting Group gets an order to develop a new organizational structure for Basler Versicherungen, one of the biggest internationally operating Swiss insurance companies, the outcome of its work largely depends on the information provided by the company's personnel.

Customer integration may occur in any phase. For instance, the procurement manager of a food production company, such as U.S.-based Kraft Foods, which specifies the material to be used in the production of plastic trays, participates in the purchasing process of the supplier. The U.K. buyer of a Motorola portable phone, who indicates the color of the phone and the specific features expected when ordering the phone via the internet, is partly integrated in Motorola's production process. A French customer of Sweden's furniture giant IKEA is integrated in the company's marketing process when she describes the family's living room, the family size, structure, and living habits to the salesperson, picks up the bought furniture, transports it to her home, and sets it up there. Even for consumer products produced and marketed to a global mass market, such as Sensodyne toothpaste or Pampers nappies, for which autonomous processes dominate the customer value generation, at least some communication has to take place in the final phase between the customer and sales personnel or a computer.

An international marketer that wants to establish general rules for product quality management should analyze which of the following contexts most closely describes the company's products (see Figure 9.3):

- *The product has mainly material features and its production processes involve the customer to a high degree.* For example, in the case of custom-made special weaving machines for Italian La Perla, a producer of high-quality women's swimsuits and underwear, the customer can first search for the most appropriate supplier and then control the production and delivery process. However, the customer must believe the supplier concerning its service, spare parts delivery, and machine availability.

- *The product has mainly material features and highly autonomous processes of production and delivery.* This, for example, is the case for kitchen appliances, furniture, or compact discs. The customers can evaluate the tangible features of such products before purchase. But the customers must believe the supplier concerning the product's reliability.

- *The product is characterized by mainly immaterial features and a highly integrative value generation process.* For example, for most business consulting activities, the customer must first rely on signals provided by the supplier, such as references or the reputation of their personnel, to take the purchase decision. Having decided to buy, however, the customer can influence the production and delivery process of the product.

● *The product is generated in a highly autonomous way and has mainly immaterial features.* In the case of international telephone services, for example, the customer must exclusively rely on the promised performance of the product. Signals, such as reputation, warranties, or the friendliness of personnel, are the only means of quality assessment.

Formulation of standards International marketers will have to define their product quality standards for the processes and features that are accessible to the customers. Depending on the contexts just described, those may be integral parts of the product or peripheral cues used as indicators of product quality. For example, Robert Kuok, one of Asia's richest overseas-Chinese tycoons and the owner of the Shangri-La luxury hotel chain that runs hotels in China, Fiji, Indonesia, and the Philippines, is said once to have lectured his hotel managers on what sort of fruit they should have in the rooms.

Because the quality expectations and quality perceptions of customers may vary in an international context, the international marketer needs to carefully analyze what influences those expectations and perceptions. On that basis, quality standards can be formulated that are to be followed throughout the company (see Toolbox 9.3). A general guideline may read as follows:

> The quality of our products concerning the processes and features central to the intended customer benefit has to be oriented at the highest standard demanded across all served country markets.

For a marketer of watchstraps, such as Geneva-based Golay & Guignard, this might mean, for example, that the level of perspiration and tearing resistance of its products would have to fulfill the standards expected by its Japanese watch-making customers. But the variety in the color and design of the straps would have to fulfill different expectations of consumers in Italy and France, and the quality of delivery service and after-sales services would be oriented according to German standards.

Product liability Because not all marketers are similarly aware of the importance of product reliability, product liability legislation has been introduced in all highly

---

TOOLBOX 9.3 **Quality certification**

To assure business and administrative customers of the purchased product's contribution to their own customer value-generation process, quality certification has become the rule in many product markets.

International norms, such as European ISO 9000 and 14000, define quality as the controlled compliance with exactly defined company-specific and documented processes of customer value generation. They force the supplier to rethink its processes starting from the customer benefit and to document all processes related to the firm's products. Customers of certified companies are assured that their suppliers conform to the stated processes. They are not assured, however, of receiving a specific quality pre-specified by a neutral institution. In case of problems with the performance of a purchased product, the source of the defect can be found by analyzing the related documentation.

International marketing managers either have to make manuals developed inside the firm during a quality certification process part of their international product policy statement or they need to formulate a policy of which quality certification – if any – to go for.

industrialized countries to protect consumers from unsafe products. **Product liability** is the responsibility of a product's supplier or intermediary to cover damage to the life, health, or property of a customer or a third person that is caused by the performance of the product during consumption or use. Fines in such cases may reach a level many times over the total annual sales of the company involved.

Because product liability legislation is not as severe in some countries as in others, the international marketer has to determine which country's legislation to take as the level to use as an international standard and if certain countries' standards cannot be met, which country markets to avoid serving.

Market communication standards

Indirect stakeholder contacts will hardly be manageable by the international marketer. But direct communication – whether it involves personal or impersonal contacts – may be managed in a way to maximize the consistency of customer and other stakeholder experiences. The quality of direct contacts consequently will influence the content and emotional character of indirect contacts. Therefore, international marketers need to define a set of rules guiding the communication behavior of all members and representatives of their organization independent of where they are located and what functional area they belong to.

Internal branding The marketer must make sure that all people representing the company in direct personal contacts with stakeholders fully understand and adopt the intended meaning of the brand. That is, internal branding programs need to be established in order to develop and implement the appropriate rules of behavior.

The top management of Rodenstock, the Munich-based manufacturer of optical products, for example, has developed a description of its brand's most important characteristics. Those characteristics should mark the identity of the brand as perceived by the firm's customers. To make this perception become reality, managers from all international parts of the company as well as employees and workers have been intensively informed about their brand's identity. They were invited to workshops where they discussed their potential contribution to achieving this identity and what coordinated actions need to be set in motion to ensure consistency of customers' brand-related experiences across country markets.

Brand manuals In order to keep local brand adaptations in a certain range that is needed to create similar meanings in different country markets, companies operating internationally develop brand manuals. Such manuals specify which parts of brand appearance have to be standardized across country markets, for example, logo, package color, design of machines or of company offices and buildings, and which parts are open to local or customer-specific adaptation, for example, visual and verbal creation of a certain meaning. Brand manuals may also contain guidelines concerning brand extensions or ingredient branding activities. That is, they indicate what kinds of products may be launched under a certain brand name, or they specify the type of customers who may be allowed to use the name of the supplier as part of their own communication campaign and the conditions of that use.

In companies with a longstanding tradition of local autonomy, the process of developing and implementing brand management guidelines can take a while. For example, it took Germany's Henkel AG 5 years to develop and implement its first international "Manual of packaging design and brand identification." Other companies prefer to give their local subsidiaries more freedom of action. U.S.-based Colgate, for example, defines its Colgate brand as a global brand to be introduced first in all international markets as the "flagship" of the company. Around this leading brand, local managers can introduce local brands with differentiated customer benefits to address specific customer segments.

Conflict handling Conflicts may arise between the company and its local stake-holders, such as governments, unions, special interest groups, or trade organiza-tions. For example, Germany-based Continental, one of Europe's leading tire producers, decided to stop the profitable production of passenger car tires in their Austrian Semperit AG factory and to transfer the latest technology production equipment to the neighboring Czech Republic. There, wage levels are only about one-eighth of those in Austria. Continental's top management was only interested in maximizing profits by improving the firm's geographic alloca-tion of resources. But they encountered strong resistance by local unions and gov-ernment. The local interest groups saw the willful destruction of a well-functioning factory to which government had given substantial subsidies a few years earlier to bring the level of productivity to the highest international standards. Consumers reacted by buying fewer Semperit tires now made in the Czech Republic. Market communication standards should contain rules of how to handle such conflicts in order to avoid major damage to the firm's reputation.

Market communication standards may also contain guidelines on how to handle potential conflicts between manufacturers and retailers. Big retailers like to use established brands of manufacturers' products as low-price customer attraction devices. For example, in 2001 Levi Strauss, the San Francisco-based clothing giant, sued U.K. supermarket chain Tesco PLC for selling Levi's jeans at cut-rate prices. Levi did not want its products sold in grocery stores, as these did not meet its criteria for retail outlets. At that time, Levi preferred authorized dealers, such as department stores and approved retail outlets, where staff are specially trained to sell a wide range of "genuine" Levi apparel and there is the "optimum service presentation" to match the brand's image. Tesco was not part of those distribution channels. Levi refused to supply Tesco with jeans. Undeterred, Tesco located a consignment of 45,000 pairs of men's jeans from what it described as an official supplier in Mexico. It put them on sale in 128 of its supermarkets at $49 each, compared with $85 at an official Levi's store in London. In an official statement Levi insisted that the company does not dictate retail prices. If Tesco changed its retail environment the supermarket chain could be supplied. In the meantime, Levi Strauss has launched a new product line called Signature that is sold at Asda in the U.K., Carrefour in France, Wal-Mart in Germany, and ... Tesco in the U.K.

The way the international marketer wants request for private-label supplies to be handled is another important subject for regulation. In most of the highly industrialized countries manufacturer brands have given way to retailing labels. However, this is not only due to action taken by retailers. Many manufacturers have reinforced the trend by actively expanding their sales through no-name pro-duction. For example, Quadro, a knitwear firm in Italy's Tuscany, manufactures more than 600,000 pieces of knitwear for stores in the U.S., about one-third of which goes to the Limited chain. Italy's two biggest textiles groups, GFT and Marzotto, are both very active in private-label men's clothing. Marketing man-agers of both international manufacturing and retailing companies will have to define their general course of action in such an environment.

Business sustainability

With customers' increasing environmental consciousness and the decreasing reserves of natural resources, the sustainability of a firm's business may become part of its international quality standards. Sony, the Japanese manufacturer of consumer electronics, for example, has a guideline that calls for developing TV sets in a way that makes them last for 40 years. In order to keep those products attractive to customers despite technical progress, new technologies are to be loaded into the TV sets from disk. Rank Xerox in Holland has set a goal of reach-ing a reutilization rate of 80% for its products. This rate has been reached by developing a highly modular product design where parts with longer lifecycles than others can be reused. For the U.K.'s Unilever, environmentally sound and sustainable products have such importance that they have published environmental reports. The first contains a policy statement, which can be found in Ethics box 9.1.

Need for continuity

The establishment and consistent management of a brand needs *perseverance*. Strong Japanese brands, such as Sony, Toyota, or Canon, have taken years to develop their global position. It also needs *patience*. Both the use of pricing tools and fast changes in market communication to increase market shares rapidly have proven to be detrimental to a brand's lasting success.

Companies that are not able to ensure a high level of continuity in their brand-related actions across countries, for personnel or financial reasons, will have a hard time establishing their intended international brand. Table 9.2 contains the names of the 14 best selling brands in Europe in 1995. They were all still successful in 2005. From the years of their first appearance on the market, however, one can conclude that consistent brand management not only strongly contributes to short-term success but also to the longevity of international brands.

Leadership

Leadership in an internationally operating company means having to develop and maintain a set of rules and processes that lead all members of the organization to:

- strive for global-scale efficiency and competitiveness
- remain sensitive to demands of the local environments
- be ready to learn from successful experiences of others in the organization

independent of their relatedness to an ethnic culture, a functional area, or a business unit.

People from different cultures live in different worlds of social reality. Different perceptions of social reality result in different motivation, decision making, con-

---

ETHICS BOX 9.1

Unilever environment report: The policy

"Unilever is committed to meeting the needs of customers and consumers in an environmentally sound and sustainable manner, through continuous improvement in environmental performance in all our activities.

"We ensure that our products and operations are safe for the environment, while we seek to build environmental performance into our innovation strategy.

"We aim to reduce waste, conserve energy, examine reuse and recycling throughout our business

and exercise the same concern for the environment wherever we operate.

"Our policy reflects our commitment to the International Chamber of Commerce Business Charter for Sustainable Development. It reflects our emphasis on those issues outlined in the Charter, which we regard as current priorities.

"We also fully support the principles for environmental protection set out in the OECD Guidelines for Transnational Companies, and will contribute to meeting the increasing number of international conventions on environmental protection."

Source: Glaskin, M. (1996) "Catalyst for Action", *Unilever Magazine*, 2(100), pp. 16–18

flict resolution, personnel development, and organizational change. For example, in Japanese companies, a decision will not traditionally be made until all employees involved have had a chance to express their views and a solution is found that enables them not to be socially disregarded. In some European countries, by way of contrast, top management may decide to release personnel to increase productivity, without paying any attention to what it may mean to the working climate in their company. They regard shareholder value as more important (and it often increases when management takes "downsizing" decisions).

National boundaries do not necessarily indicate distinct differences between leadership practices. As Chapter 5 has shown, countries group together into clusters that share similar cultural values, and leadership practices are often similar within each cluster. For example, in Australia and the U.S., identity is placed in the individual. There is a strong belief that everybody is supposed to take care of themselves. Individual achievement and initiative are emphasized. Managers in both countries tend to reject interlocking group structures in favor of systems, which focus on individual accomplishment and self-interest. Culture box 9.1 shows that important cultural differences may exist even between neighboring countries such as the U.S. and Mexico that result in leadership problems having negative effects on the people and firms involved.

Role models

People learn much of their behavior through imitation. Managers serving as role models are, therefore, extremely important for a positive motivation among employees to work and act in a way that makes stakeholders experience the intended meaning of the corporate brand or a specific sub-brand. If leaders consistently demonstrate behavior that can be related to business and personal success, many of their employees will try to imitate them. For example, if a top manager such as Peter Brabeck, the CEO of Nestlé, regularly visits customers to stay in close contact with the market, the firm's product managers and R&D managers will feel they should go regularly into the field, too.

TABLE 9.2 *Top 14 brands in Europe 1995*

Brand	Product category	Sales volume in billion $	Year of market launch
1 Coca-Cola	Soft drink	3.59	1886
2 Ariel	Detergent	1.45	1968
3 Pampers	Nappies	1.36	—
4 Barilla	Pastas	1.105	1877
5 Jacobs	Coffee	1.07	1895
6 Nescafé	Coffee	0.94	1938
7 Danone	Yoghurt	0.82	1919
8 Whiskas	Pet food	0.79	1959
9 Pedigree	Pet food	0.59	1963
10 Langnese	Ice cream	0.57	1935
11 Persil	Detergent	0.555	1907
12 Fanta	Soft drink	0.55	1958
13 Pepsi Cola	Soft drink	0.525	1898
14 Milka	Chocolate	0.505	1892

Source: "Top 100 Marken in Europa", *Werbung & Print*, December 1995, p. 9

According to a study by Nielsen, the top selling brands of consumer products in 14 European countries in 1995 are international brands, most with a high degree of standardization. None of them is less than 15 years old, showing that well-managed brands are not subject to short-term lifecycle curves.

International brand building and brand management have proven to be particularly successful when senior managers make it part of their personal responsibilities and strategic plans. Examples such as Ralph Lauren, CEO of his company, not only have the ability, authority, and incentive to ensure that the intended brand meaning is being delivered consistently across the firm's active and passive communication activities, but they personally represent the brand. This personal attachment makes it easier for all people inside and outside the company who are involved in the implementation of brand-related activities to develop a common understanding of the brand's meaning. This common understanding, in turn, is the condition for creating a strong, clear and rich brand identity.

Human resource development

The development of human resources is one of the most important functions of leadership. For international marketing purposes, it entails:

- improvement of skills
- encouragement of self-enhancement
- internal branding
- preparation for non-domestic assignments.

Improvement of skills

In an internationally operating organization managers and personnel must be systematically prepared for new tasks in a more complex world. For example, if they are not in the office or on the factory floor, U.S.-based Motorola employees are at school. Each employee trains a minimum of 40 hours annually. Training and Education Center staff work directly with managers, tailoring the courses to their specific issues.

CULTURE BOX 9.1

Clash of cultures

"In Mexico, everything is a personal matter," said Ken Franklin, manager of an assembly plant at Ciudad Juarez's giant Bermudez Industrial Park just across the border of the U.S. "But a lot of U.S. managers don't get it." And Fernando Duenas, Federal Express's local manager who was born in Ecuador added: "You are constantly fighting the mañana syndrome."

The culture clash between U.S. managers and Mexican workers has been most evident in the *maquiladora* program. Maquiladoras are Mexican assembly plants that manufacture finished goods for export to the U.S. Most maquiladoras are owned by U.S. corporations. In 2002, some 3,600 plants employed approximately 960,000 workers. The problems in maquiladoras are rooted in the fact that the border plants generally fall under the control of U.S. corporations' domestic divisions, rather than their international ones. Less sensitive to the special problems of operating abroad, the domestic division chiefs usually selected maquiladora managers based on their skill in production rather than human relations.

The gulf between the Mexicans and Americans at maquiladoras results in a heavy turnover of both labor and management. A less publicized problem has been the rapid burnout of American managers along the border. Even premium payments do not keep American managers in the border factories for a long time.

Source: Adapted from Moffett, M. (1992) "Culture Shock", *Wall Street Journal*, 24 September, p. R13; www.encyclopedia.com/html/m1/ maquilad.asp (4 May 2005)

Self-enhancement

Training not only improves skills. It can also be used to encourage self-enhancement of personnel as well as managers. The problem-solving and innovation potentials of all members of the organization have to be developed. Supported by one of the most ambitious, well-funded employee training programs in the U.S. (more than four times the national average), Motorola pushes employees to continually redefine themselves and how they do their job. Adaptability and flexibility in reasoning and action are part of the training program. Leadership skills are improved.

Internal branding

Self-enhancement of personnel is not enough to justify substantial expenses for training programs. However, such programs may serve the additional purpose of "internal branding." That is, values central to the intended identity of the organization or one of its subunits can as well be intensively explained and transmitted as ways of behavior expressing those values. IKEA managers from a certain hierarchical level upwards, for example, get specific training in Sweden, where they learn about the founder of the company, the basic values driving his business ideas, and also about the cultural background of Sweden.

Preparation for non-domestic assignments

Strategically meaningful and personally rewarding headquarters and non-domestic service assignments need to be supported by a human resource development system that identifies and moves appropriate employees across business units or national borders. Typically, Japanese companies have more specialized training programs to prepare managers for non-domestic assignments than do U.S. and European firms. These programs include language training, career training, field experience, and graduate programs abroad. Japanese companies also enjoy a higher success rate of managers in non-domestic assignments.

Poor human resource planning may be the major reason for the high failure rate to be found among U.S. business expatriates. That is, U.S. managers often have to be recalled to headquarters or dismissed from the company because of their inability to perform effectively in a foreign country. Managerial inventories such as Unilever's, including detailed profiles of the best managers from all parts of the company, regardless of nationality, may help to lower such failure rates.

There exist widespread objections by managers and personnel to international transfers. Language deficiencies as well as limited mobility play a major role. In southern Europe, for example, family ties are a strong reason against leaving a local job. In other parts of Europe they are less pronounced, but marketing managers and personnel who are transferred often feel that they risk being forgotten "out there" in their new assignments. Clear career paths, based on a management development plan, should exist to assure employees that they will not be forgotten or necessarily passed over for promotion.

It is rare that a smaller company has the resources to undertake personnel development on such a scale. It will need external consultants, coaches, and training institutions to build up personnel for successful international marketing. But top management, no matter the size of the firm, should be aware that lasting success in globalizing markets will not be possible without investments in personnel development.

Reinforcement

Human resource development will only be effective in the longer run if appropriate behavior of staff is systematically reinforced. Performances that help the company achieve its goals and sustain its intended identity should be rewarded through appropriate compensation packages and job assignments. The internationally operating firm faces the difficult task of developing a consistent performance appraisal system and compensation system that can be accepted by all the personnel from a variety of cultures.

IBM, for example, striving to become the world leader in network-centric computing, a market estimated at $1,000 billion in 1998, installed a system of feedback talks for all its 200,000+ people, which permitted them to access a databank of 10 million different capabilities. Managers can use the databank to form successful project teams. If certain capabilities cannot be found inside the firm, management can hire new people. Because top management considers teams as extremely important if the company is to reach their ambitious goal, 30% of the variable part of the income of people working for IBM has been made dependent on the collective results of the teams they belong to. How well such a system will work depends on its acceptance by people from very different cultures who work for the company.

U.S. managers, for example, are used to one bonus per year and promotions based on achievement. Their Japanese counterparts receive bonuses at least twice a year, and whether they are promoted depends a great deal on their seniority and their capabilities in the long run. Japanese managers have budgeted amounts to spend on entertainment after work. German managers prefer fringe benefits like the use of a company car for non-business purposes. A company that is serving international markets with personnel from various cultural backgrounds must be ready and able to accommodate its incentive system to cultural differences without arousing conflicts in its different local units.

Conflict resolution

Conflicts in an international organization are different from, and often greater than, conflicts in domestic firms. Not only do functional interest groups hold markedly different beliefs concerning the appropriateness of particular goals and strategies, but local managers may disagree with central staff concerning the strategic importance of business units, resource allocations among them, and the interpretation of market situations. Different meanings assigned to a company's actions are due not only to different interests but also to cultural differences.

Business units and local subsidiaries often feel undervalued by top management. Some European Black&Decker managers, for example, could not see that centrally directed highly standardized marketing was needed as a defense against Japanese competition, because their subsidiaries dominated the consumer power tool markets in Europe. They resisted corporate strategic change, because they thought its impact was to threaten their individual power.

Leaders of an internationally operating firm must be able to cope with the entire range of potential conflicts. Table 9.3 contains various approaches to conflict management. Some managers aggravate conflicts by denying their existence. Others try to resolve conflicts by replacing employees or managers who resist

TABLE 9.3 *Approaches to conflict management*

Structural approaches	Process approaches	Mixed approaches
Common goals	De-escalation	Rules
Reward system	Confrontation	Liaison roles
Regrouping	Collaboration	Taskforces/teams
Rotation		Integrator roles
Separation		

Managers of internationally operating firms must choose an appropriate conflict management approach depending on the specific situation.

direction, as was done in the Black&Decker case. Managers who perceive such replacements as losses of important management know-how or experience may seek to resolve or even avoid conflicts with improved information and greater participation by the people concerned. Such managers should be aware that collective decisions tend to unfold in an incremental manner from processes of negotiation and compromise among participants living in different social realities and holding various self-interests. They often depend more on the partisan values and power of the interest groups involved in the process than on rational analysis. Thus, such decisions are easier to implement but they will not be of the highest potential quality.

There is no universal best way of resolving conflicts. In China, Korea or Japan, for example, direct and open conflicts are to be avoided. Consequently, managers from those countries tend to either use authority to suppress open conflicts or to resort to private coordination. The best way of conflict resolution for any given situation depends on both the objective features of the situation and the interpretations of different cultural and interest groups.

Successful international marketing managers have to be able to apply the most appropriate conflict management technique specific to the situation to safeguard the long-term interests of the company.

Managing change

Because a company is a "partly open" system, it is subject to external influences as well as internal processes. Both lead to marginal but constant change. That is, the organization – its structure and processes – continuously adapt to environmental developments in small steps. Such ongoing changes are not strategically managed, however, and therefore they do not automatically lead to an optimum result for the firm. If a misfit develops between the organization and its business environment because of important changes, such as occur when a company goes through different phases of internationalization, management intervention may become necessary. The firm may have to replace organizational structures, internalized policies, and rules of behavior with new ones.

For example, when Austrian Grass AG, one of the leading manufacturers of furniture fittings in the world, established a production company in the U.S. and sales offices in France and China, it found that centralized planning and control did not lead to the expected results. It therefore founded a holding company, which acted as a coordinating agency. As a result, the firm's information system became much more important. The leadership system had to be adapted to the different motivations of managers and employees in the various countries. When Grass AG was taken over by the German assembly specialist Würth Group in 2004 the holding company stopped its business activities.

The successful accomplishment of such changes depends on significant learning processes of organizational members. Re-socialization processes of that kind are difficult to manage. They may require a great amount of time, patience, energy, skills and money. Also, management must be able to tolerate uncertainty and ambiguity, and must be willing to learn new attitudes and rules of behavior. Developing and sustaining an appropriate corporate culture is especially hard when international business grows fast. Robert Epstein, the founder of Sybase, a U.S.-based company producing software for computer networking, personally spent 6 months working in the company's Paris sales offices for that very reason.

The problems of managing organizational change are manifold under any circumstances. They are even more complex in a cross-cultural business environment. Communication, sources of change, the conceptual ability and participation of personnel, and management's involvement in and commitment to the change process all may differ from one business environment to another. Certain tools of organizational and personnel development may be difficult to apply because of labor union resistance, the general educational level, social structure, or traditions in a society. For example, U.S. journal articles on easing internal change frequently advise managers to include the personnel who will be affected by change in company planning to reduce their resistance to the change. This advice may be appropriate for most organizations in the western industrialized countries, but it may be of no value in parts of the world where more authoritarian processes are common such as in India.

Small and medium-sized companies with successful local business traditions but lacking experience in non-domestic marketing are likely to find that they cannot globalize their business all at once. Rather, they must manage a continuous process of organizational change leading to a corporate culture that favors international marketing, changing management systems to accommodate the higher complexity of international business, and attracting or developing the needed number of skilled people.

Organizational control

An internationally operating company that wants to reach the goals of global efficiency and competitiveness, flexibility, and responsiveness to local market environments, as well as inter-unit organizational learning, must be able to control the firm's output, that is, the efficiency of organizational processes, as well as the behavior of the firm's organizational entities, that is, the effectiveness of ongoing processes.

For that purpose it has to find a balance between centralization, standardization, and socialization tendencies (see Figure 9.4). Centralization is best suited for output control. Standardization can be used for both output and behavioral control. For the latter the global marketer will be better off using socialization mechanisms, however. Behavioral control is less direct and less costly than output control, and it permits a longer time horizon.

FIGURE 9.4 *Equilateral triangle of global business management*

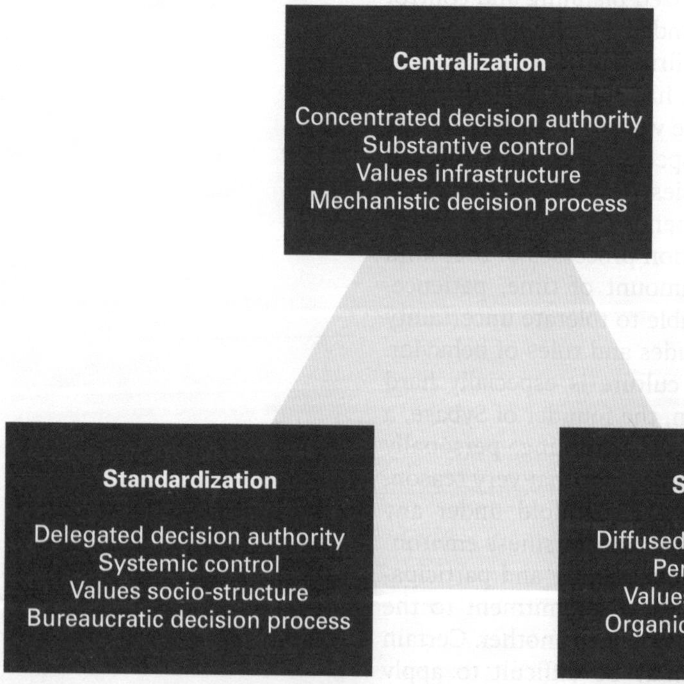

Centralization

Concentrated decision authority
Substantive control
Values infrastructure
Mechanistic decision process

Standardization

Delegated decision authority
Systemic control
Values socio-structure
Bureaucratic decision process

Socialization

Diffused decision authority
Personal control
Values superstructure
Organic decision process

To achieve maximum global efficiency and competitiveness, flexibility, and responsiveness to local market environments, as well as inter-unit organizational learning, the management of a firm operating internationally must find a balance between centralization, standardization, and socialization processes.

Source: Adapted from Sullivan, D. (1992/3) "Organization in American MNCs: The perspective of the European regional headquarters", *Management International Review*, 32, p. 248

Centralization

Centralization means concentration of decision authority at the firm's head office and direct intervention in the operations of business units. Local units adapt the global corporate strategy to their domestic environment after receiving approval from headquarters. For example, at Armani no subsidiary is allowed to start any market communication activity without having asked for approval from the Milan headquarters.

Control can be very specific and limited to the short term (for example, the annual budgeting systems, with monthly reporting, used by many U.S. firms). It can be implemented vertically across the organizational structure, with the home office imposing identical roles, functions, and responsibilities on all organizational elements at the same hierarchical level.

Centralization leads to:

- rather mechanistic decision procedures worldwide
- equalizing the influence of business unit managers on the planning process
- using standardized criteria to evaluate performance.

Pros

Centralization becomes increasingly feasible as managers in the home office gain more global experience and as standardized procedures and rigid structures reduce the complexity of the operations for which they are responsible.

Centralization has positive effects when reaching and sustaining an intended global brand meaning of the company is of major importance to the success of the firm. In addition, improved transportation and communication allow easier evaluation and correction of performance of widely dispersed business units.

Cons

The major argument against centralization is that each organizational unit in the global company is itself a complex organization existing in a particular environment. If every decision or action must be cleared with a higher level, reaction time is slowed and resources are wasted. Control exerted through strict budgets generally requires a great deal of time for the process of coming to mutual agreement on the appropriate figures. Responsiveness to demands in the local environments is low.

Similar treatment of local business units in different states of development might unnecessarily:

- restrict the flexibility of those in the market entry stage
- not give enough strategic guidance to those in their stage of growth
- not be interactive enough to allow for quick information sharing and transfer of successful innovations between local units in their stage of maturity.

Standardization

Standardization is the formalization of tasks and decision procedures to be performed in different parts of the company to ensure similar performance processes and comparable results. Leadership, information, planning, and control processes such as conflict resolution, quality control, new product development, or managerial accounting are formally prescribed (usually in a manual), to be followed by all members of the organization. The more decentralized decision authority is in an internationally operating firm, the more top management will tend to standardize the processes by which its business units are managed.

Philips, the Dutch electrical and electronics giant, for example, has an investment project manual that helps assure top management that investment calculations for different projects are derived in the same manner and therefore can be compared to each other. The result are rather bureaucratic decision processes following identical rules without any tributes to the specifics of a decision situation:

- *Standardization* helps increasing global-scale efficiency in a decentralized organization.
- *Cross-market learning* is difficult because the standardized rules hinder innovation.
- *Flexible reaction* to local demands is only possible as long as the decisions and actions fit into the given system of standards.

Socialization

Socialization is the process of instilling and reinforcing basic values and behavioral norms in members of an organization in a way that leads to a common set of values and accepted rules of behavior. If socialization is strong the employees of the company will act in a predictable manner consistent with the general goals of the firm, even if decision authority is spread out all over the globe. Control ski exerted on a personal behavioral level. Socialization can be achieved through integration, enculturation, or acculturation.

Integration

Integration is the building of a tight network of interrelationships among the elements (individuals or groups) of a social system. The stronger the integration of a firm's organizational units, the less output control is needed to ensure the implementation of strategies and plans. For example, when top management increases the flow of products, resources, and information among local units, those units will recognize the need for coordinating their actions.

Enculturation

Enculturation takes place if top management succeeds in promoting company-wide understanding of, and commitment to, its intended global strategic position. In that case, the superstructure of shared values, goals and rules of behavior leads to informal agreement, information sharing, and cooperation among all parts of the company. Less emphasis on a formal structure, such as a sophisticated multidimensional matrix organization, and less formal control processes will be necessary. At Zara, the Spanish fashion company, for example, all shop managers, regardless of their national or cultural heritage, are trained the "Zara way" (according to the defined company culture). The training takes at least 2 weeks but it may take as long as needed to make the individuals firmly share the company's rules of business behavior. Zara's leaders believe this improves intra-company communication and leads to similar management behavior throughout its global operations.

Acculturation

Acculturation is a process where two or more groups of people with different cultural background learn to understand and accept those differences. As a consequence they tend to take over parts of the other culture that seem to be more effective or efficient. Such acculturation processes may occur in global business when friendly mergers and acquisitions take place. They need strong, participative, and interculturally experienced leadership to be started and continually encouraged.

For example, when Italian Leitner acquired French Pomar to create the second largest supplier of ski lifts in the world, top management very quickly formed project teams with members from both organizations. Those teams were put in charge of projects important to the entire organization, such as the development of new products. In working in those teams French and Italian members learned to understand the different approaches of the former competitors. They quickly understood the potential contribution of the so far "foreign" team members and learned to appreciate it. Over time, the behavior of team members tended to converge.

Behavioral consequences

Because of the multitude of informal networks resulting from socialization processes, inter-unit learning is largely facilitated. Global-scale efficiency may result but is not ensured. Responsiveness and flexibility to local specifics might be reduced.

When Volvo, the Swedish automotive company, tried to replicate its successful Swedish retail organization in France, for example, it did everything to socialize its dealers according to the company's culture. Because of its own strong enculturation it overlooked, however, the fact that it created an oasis of relative egalitarianism and close personal relationships in a cultural environment that did not give those values as much support. As a result, Volvo was never able to be as successful in France as in Sweden.

In conclusion, we can say that an internationally operating firm's organizational control should represent a compromise between top management's desire for predictable behavior in each business unit to ensure global efficiency and cross-market learning, and the need for flexibility and responsiveness to local environments.

Summary

Having determined their organization's intended global strategic position, management has to define a set of basic rules of business behavior that are to be followed by all members of the organization in order to reach the set goals as well as the intended global identity. Those guidelines will have to specify expected behavior in terms of:

- confrontation
- cooperation
- acquisition
- innovation
- quality guidelines.

Such rules of behavior intend to provide a general frame of reference that guides the decision making and actions in all parts of the company wherever they are located. But rules will not be followed if strong leadership is missing. In order to assure the impact of rules on organizational life, leaders have to:

- be consistent role models
- actively care for human resource development
- continually reinforce appropriate behavior
- resolve conflicts in a way adapted to differences in the cultural background of actors
- manage change in a culturally sensitive but strategically conscious way.

The success of leadership is strongly dependent on appropriate organizational control. The top management of an internationally operating firm will, therefore, have to find the proper balance between centralization needs, standardization of management systems, and socialization processes.

DISCUSSION QUESTIONS

1. What are the basic goals to be achieved by shaping an internationally operating company's rules of business behavior?

2. When and why can cooperation be more effective for an international marketer than confrontation?

3. Have a look at some newspapers such as the *International Wall Street Journal* for reports about acquisitions. What do they report before the deal is struck and what do they say after? Is there anything to be learned?

4. Find an interesting community on the internet and analyze their exchanges in terms of new product ideas. To what extent can this be a useful source for an international marketer?

5. Take an internationally operating company of your choice and analyze all available data about their market communication behavior. To what extent is it consistent over time?

6. What has total quality management to do with global branding? Illustrate with an example of your choice.

7. Find examples in business magazines that demonstrate the influence of a company's leadership on the international success of the firm. What are your conclusions?

8. Why is an international marketer so concerned with organizational change? What does that mean to you?

9. What factors need to be considered to ensure organizational control is accepted by managers in all parts of the company instead of becoming a bureaucratic nightmare?

ADDITIONAL READINGS

Chen, M. (2004) *Asian Management Systems, Chinese, Japanese and Korean Styles of Business*, 2nd edn, London: Thomson Learning.

Hooley, G., J. Saunders, and N. Piercy (2004) *Marketing Strategy and Competitive Positioning*, 3rd edn, Harlow: Pearson Education Limited.

Koopman, A. (1991) *Transcultural Management – How to Unlock Global Resources*, Cambridge, MA: Blackwell Publishers.

MacMillan, I.C., A.B. van Putten, and R. Gunther McGrath (2003) "Global Gamesmanship", *Harvard Business Review*, May, 63–71.

Veludo, M., D.K. Macbeth, and S. Purchase (2004) "Partnering and relationships within an international network context", *International Marketing Review*, 21(2), 142–57.

Useful internet links

Air France	http://www.airfrance.com/
Amazon.com	http://www.amazon.com/exec/obidos/subst/home/
Asda	http://www.asda.co.uk/
AT&T	http://www.att.com/
Bandai Digital Entertainment	http://www.bandai.com/
Black&Decker	http://www.blackanddecker.com/
Boston Consulting Group	http://www.bcg.com/
Bouygues	http://www.bouygues.fr/us/index.asp
Cable & Wireless	http://www.cw.com/
Carrefour	http://www.carrefour.com/english/homepage/index.jsp
Clairol SA	http://www.clairol.com/
Colgate	http://www.colgate.com/
Compaq	http://www.compaq.co.uk/

Continental	http://www.conti-online.com/generator/www/com/en/continental/portal/general/home/index_en.html
Dell	http://www.dell.com/
Dornier	http://www.lindauer-dornier.com/
Encyclopedia.com	http://www.encyclopedia.com/html/m1/maquilad.asp
Federal Express	http://www.fedex.com/
Fiat	http://www.fiat.com/
Gillette	http://www.gillette.com/
Giorgio Armani	http://www.giorgioarmani.com/
Goodyear	http://www.goodyear.com/
Grass	http://www.grass.at/
Grupo Industrial Maseca	http://www.gimsa.com/swfi/index.html
Harley-Davidson	http://www.harley-davidson.com/
Harvard Business Review	http://harvardbusinessonline.hbsp.harvard.edu/b02/en/hbr/hbr_home.jhtml
Henkel AG	http://www.henkel.com/
Honda	http://www.honda.com/
Hutchison Whampoa / Watson Duty Free	http://www.hutchison-whampoa.com/eng/retail/retail_asia/nuancewatson.htm
Infogrames Entertainment	http://corporate.infogrames.com/
International Chamber of Commerce	http://www.iccwbo.org/
JVC	http://www.jvc.com/
Kelsey-Hayes	http://www.hayesbrake.com/
Klimov	http://www.klimov.ru/
KLM	http://www.klm.com/
Lego	http://www.lego.com/
Levi Strauss	http://www.levistrauss.com/
Lucas	http://www.lucas.co.uk/
Lufthansa	http://www.lufthansa.com/
MAN	http://www.man.de/index.php?id=130
Management International Review	http://www.management-revue.org/
Marzotto	http://www.marzotto.it/
Merloni Refrigerators	http://www.merloni.com/
Michelin	http://www.michelin.com/
Netscape	http://www.netscape.com/
Ocean International	http://www.oceaninternational.co.uk/
Ochsner Hospital	http://www.ochsner.org/
OECD	http://www.oecd.org/
One World	http://www.oneworldalliance.com/
Oracle	http://www.oracle.com/
La Perla	http://www.laperla.com/
Peugeot	http://www.peugeot.com/
Rank Xerox	http://www.xerox.com/
Robert Bosch GmbH	http://www.bosch.com/
Robert Mondavi	http://www.robertmondavi.com/
Rodenstock	http://www.rodenstock.com/

Seiko	http://www.seikousa.com/
Semperit	http://www.semperit.com/
Shangri-La hotels	http://www.shangri-la.com/en/
SkyTeam	http://www.skyteam.com/EN/index.jsp
Star Alliance	http://www.star-alliance.com/
Sun Microsystems	http://www.sun.com/
Swiss	http://www.swiss.com/
Sybase	http://www.sybase.com/
Tesco PLC	http://www.tesco.com/
Teves	http://www.conti-online.com/generator/www/us/en/continentalteves/continentalteves/general/home/index_en.html
VAI	http://www.vai.at/
Veba	http://www.eon.com/
Volvo	http://www.volvocars.com/
W.L. Gore & Associates	http://www.gore.com/
Wella	http://de.wella.com/
Wolford	http://www.wolford.com/
Würth Group	http://www.wurth.com/
Zara	http://www.zara.com/

RESOURCE ALLOCATION

10

Learning objectives

After studying this chapter you will be able to:

- discuss various issues related to international market expansion

- explain the importance of local positioning for the choice of an appropriate market-entry mode

- discuss the general advantages and disadvantages of different market-entry modes

- develop a list of market and company-specific criteria for the evaluation of market-entry modes

- describe the decision process leading to the choice of a certain market-entry option

- evaluate the impact of various organizational structures on the implementation of the intended strategic position

- discuss ways of controlling the effectiveness of resource allocations

Chapter outline

Resource allocation

International expansion

Spread of resources
Scheduling international expansion

Determination of local market-entry strategy

Decision-making approaches
Typical market-entry situations
Positioning in local markets
Market-entry modes
Evaluation criteria
The decision process

Organization

International marketing manager
International marketing department
National subsidiary structure
International division structure
Global structures
Organizational processes

Control of effectiveness

Summary

INTERNATIONAL MARKETING SPOTLIGHT

Trumpf Maschinenbau

Trumpf Maschinenbau, the German machine tool manufacturer located near Stuttgart, has a tradition of starting a new business in a new country market with the help of an export house. This market-entry mode allows them testing opportunities at no capital risk. But it also means that they have no control over marketing activities concerning their products and their identity. Therefore, when the Brazilian market they had entered first through an export house responded positively, Trumpf selected a distributor to represent them in the country. The distributor also took care of after-sales service. When the market share was growing further sales became voluminous enough to cover the cost of establishing a sales subsidiary. To keep the capital risk as low as possible, after-sales activities were left to the former distributor. It turned out, however, that customer relationships and trust in the machinery business largely depend on fast and reliable service. Therefore, Trumpf had to integrate after-sales service into the subsidiary. Finally, Trumpf's share of a dynamically developing market reached a level that caused the company's top management to add a production site to their subsidiary in Brazil.

In Taiwan, market entry took a somewhat different development. It also started off with an export house, followed by a distributor later on. But here the representative was kept on because of his excellent relationships with customers and stakeholders and, further, to demonstrate the trustworthiness of Trumpf. Both are extremely important values in Chinese markets. To increase their control over direct contacts with customers, however, Trumpf took over all after-sales service activities. Later on, they built up their own distribution network to support the Taiwanese representative in its market approach.

With increasing customer globalization Trumpf is faced with the demand from headquarters for a consistent level of service all over the world. This cannot be handled without close control over standards in business behavior. Trumpf has to establish a centralized key account management. Contrariwise, local representatives of the global key account customers want to be treated personally in the culturally specific way they are acquainted with. Therefore, local representatives or sales subsidiaries need to keep in close contact. Conflicts concerning the coordination of their activities or the calculation of commissions are unavoidable.

Trumpf Maschinenbau technology at work © Rene Mansi/iStock

The focal question of this chapter is: How should the resources available to the organization be allocated internally and externally and how should the effectiveness of this allocation be controlled?

Resource allocation

When top management has decided the intended strategic position of its organization in global markets and when it has fixed a set of basic rules of behavior to be followed in implementing that position the decision makers must determine how much of the available resources should be spent for what purpose and when (see Figure 10.1).

First, top management has to decide the intended manner and speed of international expansion. There are various options in terms of market expansion and

FIGURE 10.1   *Determining the intended global strategic position, step 5: Resource allocation*

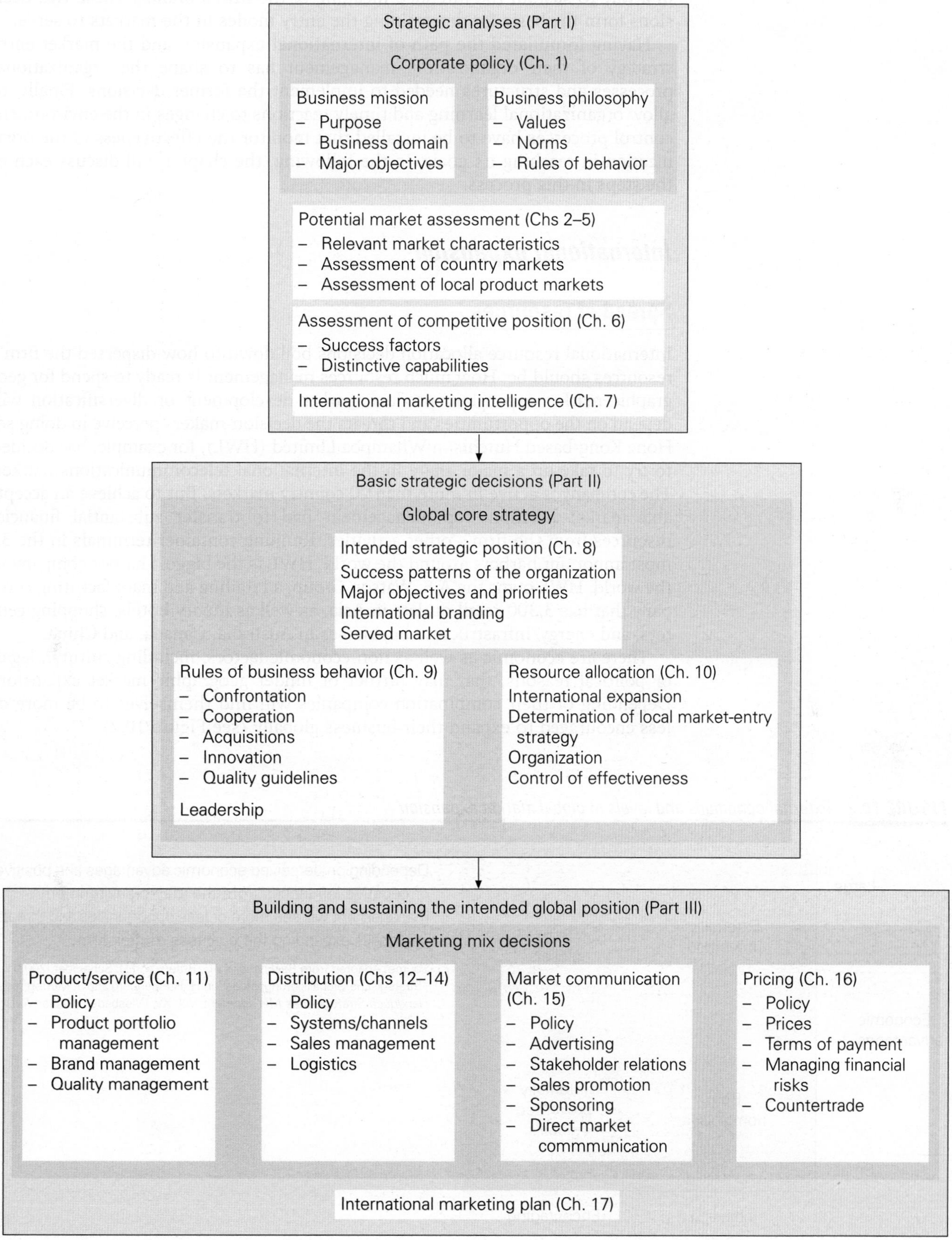

Strategic analyses (Part I)

Corporate policy (Ch. 1)

Business mission
- Purpose
- Business domain
- Major objectives

Business philosophy
- Values
- Norms
- Rules of behavior

Potential market assessment (Chs 2–5)
- Relevant market characteristics
- Assessment of country markets
- Assessment of local product markets

Assessment of competitive position (Ch. 6)
- Success factors
- Distinctive capabilities

International marketing intelligence (Ch. 7)

Basic strategic decisions (Part II)

Global core strategy

Intended strategic position (Ch. 8)
Success patterns of the organization
Major objectives and priorities
International branding
Served market

Rules of business behavior (Ch. 9)
- Confrontation
- Cooperation
- Acquisitions
- Innovation
- Quality guidelines

Leadership

Resource allocation (Ch. 10)
International expansion
Determination of local market-entry
  strategy
Organization
Control of effectiveness

Building and sustaining the intended global position (Part III)

Marketing mix decisions

Product/service (Ch. 11)
- Policy
- Product portfolio management
- Brand management
- Quality management

Distribution (Chs 12–14)
- Policy
- Systems/channels
- Sales management
- Logistics

Market communication (Ch. 15)
- Policy
- Advertising
- Stakeholder relations
- Sales promotion
- Sponsoring
- Direct market commmunication

Pricing (Ch. 16)
- Policy
- Prices
- Terms of payment
- Managing financial risks
- Countertrade

International marketing plan (Ch. 17)

timing. When a preliminary schedule has been fixed, the positioning of the organization in each of the served product and country markets has to be determined in a way to sustain the intended meaning of the firm's brands. These two decisions form the basis for determining the entry modes in the markets to serve.

Having formulated the path of international expansion and the market-entry strategy of their organization, management has to shape the organizational processes and structures needed to implement the former decisions. Finally, to allow organizational learning and timely reactions to changes in the environment control processes have to be installed that monitor the effectiveness of the organization in reaching its goals. In the following, the chapter will discuss each of the steps in this process.

International expansion

Spread of resources

International resource allocation decisions boil down to how dispersed the firm's resources should be. How much resources management is ready to spend for geographic market expansion, product market development or diversification will depend on the opportunities and threats the decision-makers perceive in doing so. Hong Kong-based Hutchison Whampoa Limited (HWL), for example, has decided to try to take up a major share in the international telecommunications market. The company is active in more than 20 country markets. But to achieve an acceptable market position, top management had to transfer substantial financial resources from the firm's other activities: Running container terminals in the 32 most important harbors around the world, HWL is the biggest harbor company in the world. HWL owns the A.S. Watson Group, a retailing and manufacturing company that has 3,300 retail outlets in Asia, as well as luxury hotels, shopping centers, and energy/infrastructure businesses in Australia, Canada, and China.

There are economic as well as non-economic factors, including cultural, legal, or political reasons, that may further or hinder geographic market expansion. Depending or their combination companies will find themselves to be more or less encouraged to expand their business globally (see Figure 10.2).

FIGURE 10.2 *External conditions and levels of global market expansion*

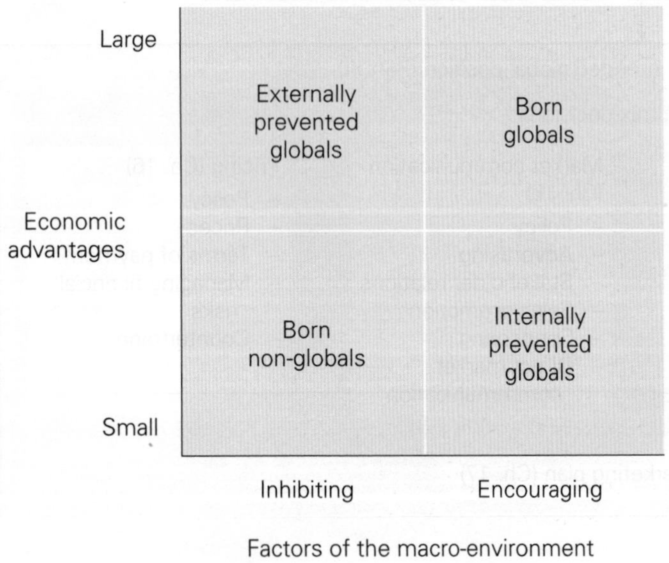

Depending on perceived economic advantages and positive or negative influences from the macro-environment management will see more or less opportunities and threats in globally expanding the business of their firm.

Source: Adapted from Backhaus, K., C. Braun, and H. Schneider (2003) "Strategische Globalisierungspfade" in H. Hungenberg and J. Meffert (eds) *Handbuch Strategisches Management*, vol. XV, Wiesbaden: Gabler Verlag, p. 75

Born globals

Some companies do not internationalize their business incrementally but global-ize their market activities soon after inception. Such firms may be confronted with a very competitive or a very small domestic market that forces them to look for business opportunities abroad. They may not even have substantial sales in their domestic market. FACC, an Austrian supplier of aircraft parts, for example, has virtually no domestic market but delivers to every important producer of air-craft and to major suppliers of that industry in the world.

If a company operates in a product market where continually shortening pro-duct lifecycles add to high R&D costs and fierce price competition, such as in many parts of the IT industry, reaching large sales volumes fast becomes a must. This can be achieved by focusing on one product market and serving this market on a global level.

Internally prevented globals

For some companies it would not make economic sense to expand their number of served country markets quickly given their current business model. They either expand their geographic market coverage step by step or have to change the served product market(s).

For example, Swiss Winterhalter Gastronom produce dishwashers for hospi-tals, hotels, and canteens that vary widely insofar as customer expectation about these products is concerned. The complexity of their product lines made geo-graphic market expansion look somewhat difficult and non-profitable. But in serving its domestic market only, the firm was restricted in its growth potential. Therefore, top management decided to focus business on one customer segment, that is hotels, and serve that market globally.

Externally prevented globals

Some companies may have difficulties to geographically expand their served market quickly because of cultural or political–legal reasons. If cultural differ-ences prevail, a company may either try to educate potential customers in buying and using their product or adapt the product to the specifics of each country market. Each of the alternatives takes time. McDonald's, for example, when it opened its first outlet in Moscow, explained to Russians who were queueing, how to order a meal. In China, they showed Chinese customers how to handle a ham-burger. Additionally, they allow for some small adaptations in the menu.

Obstacles to geographic market expansion are greater when political or legal barriers exist. A single company is less able to make such barriers disappear. Therefore, geographic market expansion is either impossible, such as in the case of public monopolies in energy industries, or demands creative solutions. German Lufthansa, for example, has significantly enlarged its number of served destinations by joining other carriers in Star Alliance.

As the case of Körber/Hauni has shown, diversification is an alternative solu-tion for management that wants the company to internationalize business. But again, international expansion through diversification is a matter of careful com-parison of market attractiveness with resource and capability needs for market entry; and this is a process that should be undertaken step by step.

Born non-globals

Finally, some companies may be faced with cultural, legal, and political barriers to geographic market expansion. For them, difficulties of expanding their geo-graphic market coverage may seem so enormous and barriers to foreign competi-tors on entering this domestic market so high that management may decide to keep business local. In such cases, growth through market penetration or product market development will be management's choice.

Balance of spending

In deciding how many country and product markets to serve management must consider the dangers of overspending and underspending.

Overspending Focusing all the available resources on a small number of country markets may lead to competitive pressure when competitors do the same. For example, some producers of food products in Denmark, France, Greece, and Italy have traditionally concentrated their international activities on serving the German market because it is the biggest country in the EU and consumers' purchasing power looks attractive. The result is fierce price competition for shelf space in German supermarkets.

Limiting the company's activities to a small number of product markets may also result in overspending of resources. For example, Friedrich Grohe AG, the Germany-based leading supplier of fittings in Europe, recognized that their focus on one product market led to an overspending of resources in distribution, customer services, and personnel development. To spread their resources over a broader range of markets, the company acquired DAL and AQUA, the leading brands in flushing systems and electronic water management in Germany, and introduced them in their international markets. The cost of the highly qualified global customer service organization was split between the three brands, procurement of materials was centralized, and a complete sanitary system could be offered to international intermediaries thus improving their market position.

Underspending Some European companies, such as PSA Peugeot Citroën, the second-ranked manufacturer of passenger cars and light commercial vehicles, have failed in the U.S. market largely because of *under*spending. The French government wanted Peugeot (at that time a state-owned company) to export to a market that would bring hard currency back to France. At the same time the firm planned to build a network for global exports, starting with France's former colonies. As a consequence, Peugeot had no resources to do more than distribute the cars its factory was already producing. Their budget for product development did not allow redesigning some models to U.S. customers' expectations such as power windows and seats, air conditioning, or controls at familiar locations. The firm's dealer and service systems were not dense enough to seem reliable to potential customers. Their promotion budget did not produce enough national visibility and clear-cut positioning to make the firm a real contender.

Serving too broad a range of product markets may lead to a loss of overall competency, since resources will be spread too thinly among research and development, engineering and customer service, or salesforce training and support.

TABLE 10.1 *Scheduling the international expansion*

Scheduling international expansion

Form of expansion
- Concentric expansion
- Platform expansion
- Focused expansion

Timing

When taking strategic resource allocation decisions, management has to fix a schedule for the firm's international expansion.

Technologies

Product markets are characterized not only by specific benefits provided to certain customer groups but also by the technologies applied to produce the intended benefits. An internationally active firm, therefore, must decide how much of its resources to allocate to the development of new technologies compared to the maintenance of current technologies.

Questions such as "How much time and money should be spent on the development of a new product technology?" or "Should current production facilities be expanded, or should new plants with newer equipment be built?" have to be answered. In 1992, for example, when the enormous growth potential of the telecommunications industry became evident, Finland's Nokia Mobira Oy decided to focus on telecommunications. They not only sold their computer division to the U.K.'s ICL but also got rid of their other low-value-added commodity product businesses, including the original paper products group.

Scheduling international expansion

Few companies can enter all potentially viable markets at once. Depending on their home market, the available resources, their experience with international business, and the nature of the business environment they face in the domestic and new markets, they will choose an appropriate form of expansion into the local markets: concentric expansion, platform expansion, or focused expansion (see Table 10.1). This decision is strongly related to the timing of entry into the markets.

Concentric expansion

Many small companies successfully start their concentric expansion from a strong competitive position in the home market and enter neighboring markets or markets perceived to be similar to the home market first, gradually expanding their marketing activities from those markets to their respective neighbors. A Norwegian firm, for example, might enter Sweden and Denmark before attempting to expand to Germany. (See Map 10.1.) The similar or neighboring markets are used as bridges to more "distant" markets. **Bridging** is similar to a market rollout campaign, in which the company uses its experience in a particular market segment to gain a competitive advantage in similar segments.

Resources are allocated to well-defined product markets. The company continually seeks to increase its penetration of the markets it is currently serving and continually sustains its competitive advantages in those markets. Expansion is regarded as a long-term process.

The main problem with this approach is that neighboring markets are not necessarily the most attractive ones. Moreover, competitors can gain a dominant position in other markets before the company reaches them. In addition, the firm may develop a false sense of security, underestimating the difficulties of entering neighboring markets simply because they seem familiar.

Platform expansion

In global product markets of technologically advanced industries such as computers, machine tools, and consumer electronics, a company must quickly attain a sizeable share of the global market in order to remain competitive. Companies in such industries may choose a platform expansion strategy. This approach involves starting out simultaneously in the technologically advanced triad markets and then expanding to other markets. Thus, IBM has used its U.S., Canadian, Japanese, and EU markets as platforms from which it entered other markets in Latin America, Asia, and Europe.

This strategy may seem to be appropriate only for large companies, but smaller firms can either build a network of cooperative partners or utilize the services of a global trading house. A Canadian manufacturer of movable gas barbecues used a similar approach adapted to its company size. When the firm decided to enter the attractive German market, it also decided to expand from there to the neighboring German-speaking markets (Austria, Switzerland, parts of northern Italy), in order to take advantage of possible synergies.

Focused expansion

Companies of any size operating in an industry in which physical distances are relatively unimportant (such as small consumer goods like shavers or large industrial products like ship cranes) may choose a focused expansion strategy. In this approach, starting from the product market the company serves, the marketer examines the most promising country markets, regardless of location, entering local markets according to their level of attractiveness.

Market-entry timing

International expansion must be precisely timed for maximum success and should be based on a commitment to long-term goals.

MAP 10.1 *Concentric expansion*

A Norwegian firm following a concentric expansion schedule would probably move first into Sweden, Finland, and Denmark before moving into Germany or the rest of western Europe

Bonduelle, the French producer of canned and deep frozen vegetables, for example, has the goal to be one of the major players in the markets of central and eastern Europe. The firm started expansion through exports to the Czech Republic in 1991, followed by Hungary a year later, and Poland in 1993. Slovakia and Russia were entered in 1994. After this period of commercial implantation, Bonduelle started local production to overcome the high costs of transportation and tariffs. Following 2 years of leadership through management contracts, the company bought a factory in Hungary and another one in Poland.

Part of timing is the decision on how long it may take before an investment in a new market becomes profitable. Management should not withdraw immediately if success cannot be achieved in a short time. International marketing is, to a large extent, a learning process. Only if a pre-specified reasonable amount of time has passed without success should management withdraw from a market.

Determination of local market-entry strategy

Once a company's management has identified the intended path of international expansion, it must decide how to conduct business in local or regional markets. Management must develop an entry strategy (see Figure 10.3). Depending on the size of the company's business, an intended position of the firm, a business unit, a product line, or a product has to be determined as well as an appropriate entry mode for each local market. A **market-entry mode** is the general way the company plans to enter a new country market, for example through selling its goods to an importer or through direct investment in a production facility and a distribution system.

A company's market-entry strategy should not be confused with its distribution policy. It has to be developed before distribution decisions can be taken. The decision of kiwi fruit growers from New Zealand to enter the U.S. market through an import agent, for example, left to the importer the decision of how to distribute the fruits to the consumers in the U.S. Unilever's decision to acquire the ice cream operations of the Hungarian state-owned dairy company VMTV, however, gave the company the opportunity to develop its national distribution system in the country.

The development of a market-entry strategy depends not only on market factors but also on available production capacities, personnel, and financial resources. It is an organizational learning process. Therefore it involves managers from all functional areas of a company. Because it is based on market analyses and strongly influences marketing operations, however, marketing managers should have a major influence on the decisions to be taken.

FIGURE 10.3 *Development of a market-entry strategy*

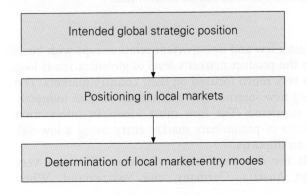

A market-entry strategy consists of decisions concerning the positioning of the firm (product line or product) in the chosen local markets and the local market-entry modes.

Decision-making approaches

In developing a market-entry strategy managers can be observed following one of three approaches.

Naive approach

Only one potential entry mode is considered. For example, a marketer might do all international business through local wholesalers in the served markets because experiences with this mode of market entry were satisfactory when the firm exported its products for the first time. This rule greatly simplifies the task for the decision makers, but very often misses attractive opportunities and leads to inappropriate solutions.

Pragmatic approach

The company starts serving local markets with a low-cost entry mode, and if it is successful changes to a more risky and costly alternative. For an example see the International marketing spotlight at the beginning of this chapter.

The advantage of this rule is that it saves the time and cost of analyses and it takes low first-entry risks. Its biggest disadvantage is that the company might fail to identify other solutions with much higher potential for fast and lasting market success and it may encounter high costs for the change of market-entry mode.

Strategic approach

In taking a strategic approach, decision makers first identify feasible modes of market entry, then critically evaluate them through comparison against criteria significant for reaching the intended market position, and finally select the solution which seems most appropriate.

Despite the problem that information concerning a new business environment is always somewhat superficial, this rule leads to higher performance than the first two mentioned. There is no one best market-entry mode through which to internationalize a firm's marketing activities. Neither are there any logical steps to be followed from one market-entry mode to another in the course of increasing internationalization. In the remainder of the chapter, therefore, we assume that this approach will be used in making market-entry strategy decisions.

Typical market-entry situations

Information concerning the relevant operating environment in a new country market in most cases can only be superficial for an observer from outside. After entering the market in some way, more detailed information becomes available that may result in the need for an adaptation of the chosen entry mode. The quality of information available to the firm will depend on the degree of globalization of the product market and the level of internationalization of the firm. Figure 10.4 shows that there are four typical situations with which a company seeking entry in a new country market can be confronted.

Early starters

An "early starter" has no or just a few and unimportant relationships with business partners abroad. Because the product market's level of globalization is low, potential competitors are also very much focused on their country markets. The level of information concerning new international markets directly or indirectly available to management is restricted. The firm must invest in information gathering that can take the form of preliminary market entry using a low-risk entry mode such as selling to an importer.

For example, in the 1990s the European market for stove tiles was very regional, mainly focused on Austria, Germany, and Switzerland. When

Sommerhuber, the Austrian market leader, decided to serve new international markets, it first had to invest in basic information-gathering activities. Focus group interviews with potential customers, semi-structured interviews with architects, designers and developers, and extensive talks with potential intermediaries as well as administrators, trade media representatives, and financial institutions in the new country markets were conducted.

Late starters

A "late starter" is surrounded by internationally active suppliers, competitors, and intermediaries. The size of the firm largely determines how market entry will take place. Small firms will need to focus on entry modes that allow close relationships with customers in niche markets. Larger firms can buy market share through modes of entry that need substantial investment such as participation in or acquisition of local firms.

Operating in the global product market of motorcycles, for example, with international competitors such as Honda, Yamaha, and BMW, the Hong Kong Ek Chor Investment Co., a Thai corporation, established a joint venture with Shanghai Automobiles Industry Co. for the production of component parts and motorcycles in China.

International among others

When the company is an "international among others," it has substantial international business experience in a global product market. Its further expansion into new country markets does not imply any significant changes in the core strategy of the firm. Management can use the firm's position in other markets to leverage its entry into the new market.

For example, Air Liquide, an internationally present French producer of industrial gas, has joined the globally active Japanese trading house Sumitomo in the creation of two production plants for industrial gas in Tianjin, in the northeast of China. The plants produce oxygen, azote, hydrogen, and argon for Toyota and Motorola factories in the area – two companies with which business contacts existed already in other countries.

FIGURE 10.4 *Typical market-entry situations*

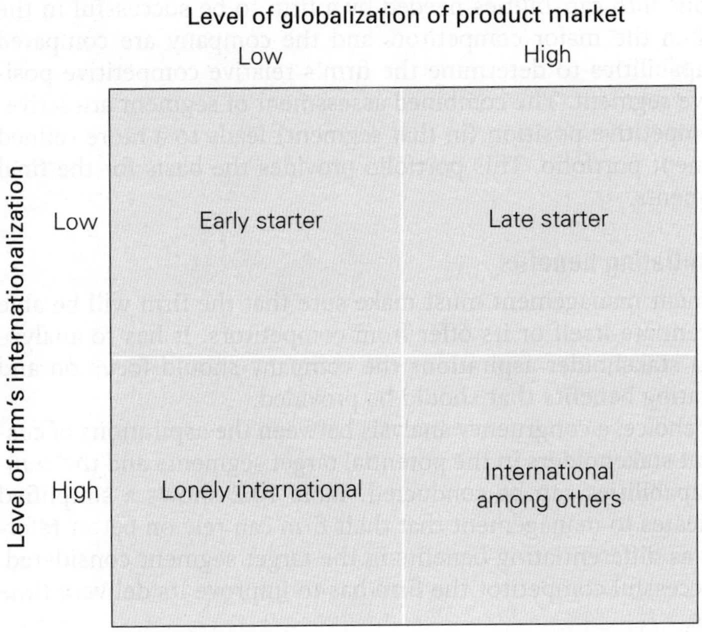

Level of globalization of product market

	Low	High
Low	Early starter	Late starter
High	Lonely international	International among others

Level of firm's internationalization

Depending on the level of globalization of its product market and the extent of its own internationalization, a company seeking market entry in a new country market can be confronted with four typical situations.

Source: Johanson, J. and L.G. Mattsson (1992) "Network positions and strategic action – an analytical framework" in B. Axelsson and G. Easton, *Industrial Networks – A New View of Reality*, London: Routledge, pp. 205–217
Reproduced with permission.

Lonely international

A "lonely international" is a firm with highly international business activities in a rather locally structured product market. It can use its position in and experience from other country markets to facilitate entry into a new geographic market. Nevertheless, because the company is confronted with local stakeholders who are not used to international suppliers, it will need to invest more time and capital in information gathering and relationship building than an "international among others." There may be traditions of business conduct or long-established close business relationships in the new market that make successful entry very difficult even for internationally experienced firms. For example, most of the problems foreign firms encountered when they first tried to enter various product markets in Japan or China were due to a lack of understanding of such networks.

Positioning in local markets

One important premise for selecting a market-entry mode is the determination of the firm's intended position in the new country markets (Figure 10.5). Entry into a new country market is always a learning process during which a firm continually commits resources in smaller or larger steps to establish an intended position. The intended position may be determined through a strategic positioning process. In this process, management defines a company (product line or product)-specific set of benefits that is attractive to selected target customers, is at least acceptable to important stakeholders in the market, and at the same time positively differentiates the firm (its product line or product) from competitors.

The process starts at the intended global strategic position of the firm and develops an intended position for each local business unit, product line or product, considering the specific conditions of the local markets.

The positioning process uses all the local market information gathered and analyzed for the evaluation of potential markets (Chapters 3–5) as well as concerning the distinctive capabilities of the firm (Chapter 6) and adds more detailed information about the country-specific product market where it is needed.

Selection of target market segments

As described in Chapter 5, for the purpose of selecting market segments, the marketer refers to the expectations and aspirations of the customer decision makers and most important stakeholders in each segment and transforms those aspirations and expectations into capabilities needed by a firm to be successful in the market segment. Then the major competitors and the company are compared concerning those capabilities to determine the firm's relative competitive position in each attractive segment. The combined assessment of segment attractiveness and relative competitive position (in that segment) leads to a more refined evaluation in a segment portfolio. This portfolio provides the basis for the final choice of target segments.

Selection of differentiating benefits

For each target segment management must make sure that the firm will be able to attractively differentiate itself or its offer from competitors. It has to analyze which customer and stakeholder aspirations the company should focus on and define the differentiating benefits that should be provided.

To make a careful choice, a congruency analysis between the aspirations of customers and important stakeholders in the potential target segments and the company's distinctive capabilities can be conducted. Table 10.2 shows a simplified example, which indicates to management that their firm can rely on better references and low price as differentiating benefits in the target segment considered. However, to be a successful competitor the firm has to improve its delivery time and training services.

FIGURE 10.5 Local positioning process

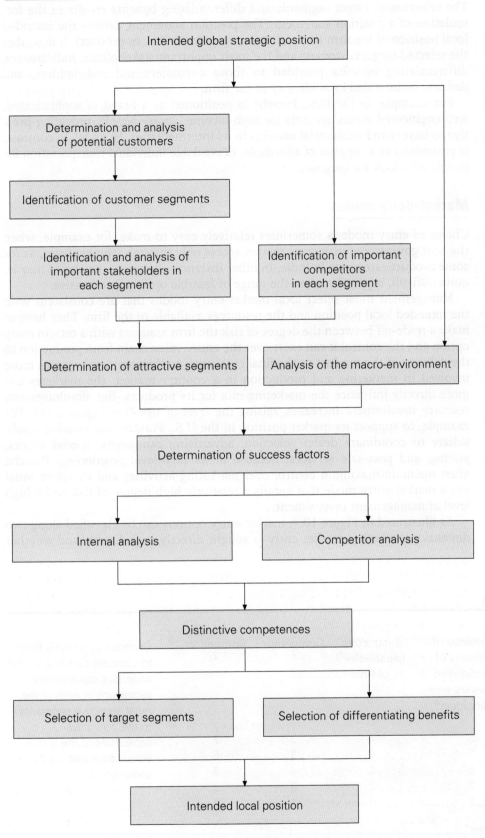

Based on the intended global strategic position attractive customer segments can be identified in the local market. From their expectations, the expectations of other important stakeholders, and challenges from the relevant parts of the macro-environment success factors in the local market can be determined. Comparing the strengths and weaknesses of the firm and its major competitors concerning those success factors leads to the detection of distinctive competences. These are the bases for a final selection of segments to target and differentiating benefits to offer. The intended local position is the intended perception of the firm by customers and other stakeholders, based on their experiences at contact points.

Source: Adapted from Mühlbacher, H., A. Dreher, and A. Ritter (1994) "MIPS – Managing Industrial Positioning Strategies", *Industrial Marketing Management*, 23, pp. 278–97

Intended local position

The selection of target segments and differentiating benefits results in the formulation of a position statement. The position statement defines the intended local position of the firm (its business unit, product line, or product). It describes the selected target customers and the most important stakeholders, indicates the differentiating benefits provided to those customers and stakeholders, and defines the intended local identity of the firm.

For example, in the U.S., Porsche is positioned as a brand of sophisticated, well-engineered status symbols for high-income, sporty people, providing prestige to buyers and substantial margins to its intermediaries. Hyundai, in contrast, is positioned as a supplier of affordable, dependable individual transportation for people who look for bargains.

Market-entry modes

Choice of entry mode is sometimes relatively easy to make, for example, when the host government may grant market access only through joint ventures, as for some product categories in India. In other instances, however, the choice may be quite difficult, especially when the range of feasible options is extensive.

Management must select local market-entry modes that are consistent with the intended local position and the resources available to the firm. They have to make a trade-off between the degree of risk the firm assumes with a certain entry option and the control it can exert over the entire value chain from production to the delivery of the product to the final customer. As the company becomes more involved in marketing and production in a country market, the marketer can more directly influence the marketing mix for its products. But simultaneously resource involvement increases, raising the level of risk (see Figure 10.6). For example, to support its market position in the U.S., Porsche has founded a subsidiary to coordinate dealer selection, advertising campaigns, special events, pricing, and post-sale services. Because of its high-level positioning, Porsche must maintain maximum control over marketing activities and therefore must use a market-entry mode that entails a relatively high degree of risk and a high level of management involvement.

As illustrated in Figure 10.7, market-entry options can be classified along two dimensions: whether market entry is sought directly or indirectly and whether

TABLE 10.2 *Congruency analysis*

Customer and important stakeholder aspirations	Importance of fulfillment of aspirations to customers and stakeholders[a]	Distinctive capabilities[b] of firm	Competitor 1	Competitor 2
References	5	4	3	2
Innovative technology	3	5	3	5
Low price	5	5	4	3
Short delivery time	3	2	5	3
Training of staff	2	1	4	2

[a] 1 = unimportant [b] 1 = very weak
3 = important   3 = average
5 = very important 5 = very strong

Congruency analysis helps to compare customers' and important stakeholders' aspirations in each of the most attractive segments to the distinctive capabilities of the firm versus its major competitors.

FIGURE 10.6 *Alternative market-entry modes: Involvement, risk, and control*

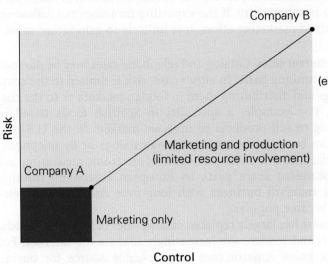

As the company becomes more in marketing and production in a country, the risk and control of the organization increase. For example, Company A is involved in marketing only – its risk and control are low. Company B, involved in marketing and production with extensive capital, has assumed higher risks to gain greater control in the local market.

they involve marketing activities only or both marketing and production in the host market.

In the following, the whole range of options, from casual exporting to establishing a foreign subsidiary, and the advantages and disadvantages of each are discussed from the perspective of a marketing manager.

Indirect entry, marketing only

The market-entry mode that offers the lowest level of risk and the least market control to an expanding firm is indirect entry involving marketing activities only. There are several variations on this approach.

Casual exporting For example, when Professional Training Systems, based in Atlanta, Georgia, a company specializing in the production of DVDs, receives an

FIGURE 10.7 *Market-entry modes*

	Indirect entry	Direct entry
Marketing only	Casual exporting Catalog and telephone sales Export management companies Export trading companies	Import houses Wholesale and retail purchasing groups Public trading agencies Foreign sales representatives or branch offices
Marketing and production — Limited capital	Licensing Franchising Production or management contracts	
Marketing and production — Extensive capital		Joint ventures Direct foreign investment

Market-entry modes can be classified according to whether they require indirect or direct involvement on the part of the firm, and whether they involve marketing activities only or both marketing and production. Note that a direct entry strategy for marketing and production has to involve extensive capital, while indirect market entry never involves extensive capital.

unsolicited order from a customer in Spain and responds to the request on a one-time basis, it is engaging in casual exporting. However, just as risk is minimized in this approach, so too is opportunity. If the exporting firm does not follow up the contact with a sustained marketing effort, it is unlikely to gain future sales.

Catalog, telephone, and internet sales Catalog and telephone sales may be pursued on either a casual or a continuing basis. In either case, risk is limited to the costs of producing the catalogs and distributing them in foreign markets or to the cost of the telephone calls. For example, a specialist in Scottish foods based in Edinburgh uses a catalog to sell products to up-scale markets in the U.S. But even industrial goods can be sold internationally via catalogs or by telephone. Balzers AG and Wild Leitz AG, two Swiss producers of electronic measuring and guiding devices, sold standard spare parts to European customers through catalogs and conducted standard business with long-time customers by telephone until e-business became popular.

In recent years e-business has largely replaced catalog sales of industrial goods. But also consumer goods and services are increasingly sold via the internet. For example, most students know Amazon.com as a valuable source for buying books. And many of them book their vacation travel through the internet.

Export management company Export management companies function like external export departments. They assume most or all of the company's risk of market entry. Often such companies perform all the services necessary to sell the exporter's product in a foreign market. A popular arrangement is for the export management company to buy the product from the manufacturer; however, some companies perform an agency role and do not take title to the goods. Export management companies vary in other ways, too. They handle different product lines, and the completeness of the service provided varies. Regardless of these differences, they are all located in the same country as the producing firm and provide a relatively risk-free means of entering foreign markets. The manufacturer, however, does not have any access to foreign market information. It is not able to react flexibly to changes in market demand or to innovate based on knowledge about customer problems.

Trading company A trading company buys products or acts as an export agent. Additionally, it imports, invests, manufactures, or engages in countertrading (the trading of goods for other goods, instead of money). Trading companies may operate in several country markets and handle a variety of products, or they may specialize in a single industry or product market.

For example, the Shanghai Lan Sheng Corp. imports whatever raw materials and production equipment for manufacturing balls, bags, sportswear and sports shoes are not available in the country, runs sports shoes factories in the Pudong New Area and in Shenzhen, and produces golf balls. It is also active in hotels and shipping. Shanghai Lan Sheng works as an export agent for several hundred factories and close to 100 joint ventures in six Chinese provinces. It markets Chinese products – partly under well-known brands such as U.S. Wilson for golf balls and Japanese Ace for bags – all over the world.

Perhaps the best known trading companies are the *sogo shosha* of Japan. Their worldwide operations, combined with an information network that provides market knowledge and links to capital resources throughout the world, make them major trading organizations in a number of markets. Over time sogo shosha have reached beyond their traditional functions and have become involved in direct global investment (see Chapter 12).

Export group An export group is a cluster of manufacturers with similar production programs or complementary product lines that cooperate to enter international markets. The cooperating firms stay legally and economically independent, but transfer all or most of their export activities to a central export unit that does business either in the name of the individual manufacturers or on its own account. We have already seen examples of very successful export groups such as the small firms with complementary product lines grouped around international marketers like Nordica or Selva, all located in northern Italy, who do the international marketing of their production partners on their own account.

The advantages of such a cooperation agreement are the significant reduction of costs and risks that small companies with no international experience have to bear and the much improved market information flow compared to other forms of indirect exports.

Problems occur in export groups with similar production programs when bigger orders have to be split among members of the group who are potential competitors or when group members start following different basic strategies.

For example, the Stubaitaler Werkzeug Genossenschaft, a cooperative of small, independent producers of metal tools from drills through pliers and chisels to highly sophisticated equipment for mountain climbing located in the Austrian Alps, got into trouble when some of their members decided to specialize in high-quality special-purpose tools at high prices while others preferred to stick to their traditionally produced product lines, which can only be sold at low prices. Such differences in opinion about the most successful competitive strategy and the fear of another group member getting too much business are the main reasons why most export groups do not last for a very long time.

Direct entry, marketing only

Direct entry involving only marketing occurs when the firm becomes directly involved in marketing its products in the host market. In general, this approach represents a stronger commitment to global markets than indirect approaches. It also entails greater risk for the firm, because it requires that more corporate resources be invested outside the home country.

However, the results are often well worth the risk. In the following, the common direct-entry modes for marketing purposes in industrialized countries will be discussed. Culture box 10.1 gives an example of how complicated things can become in industrially less developed countries.

CULTURE BOX 10.1

"Sponsors" in Saudi Arabia

A "sponsor" in Saudi Arabia is any Saudi person or firm that entertains business or private relationships with a foreigner or foreign company. The Saudi term for sponsor is "kafil" which means guarantor. It stems from the legal regulation that any foreigner who wants to get permission to stay in the country has to name a Saudi citizen who guarantees that the person will leave the county after finishing the task.

The relationship between the Saudi and the foreigner can take various forms. The sponsor may be the person who invited the foreigner to business talks. He can be an agent, an employer, or a joint venture partner. But he may also be a person who lends his name to a foreign company interested in doing business in the name of the sponsor.

Thus, the term sponsor is very popular but not precisely defined. A marketer getting in contact with a potential "sponsor" is therefore well advised to clarify carefully the legal relationship hidden behind the term before entering into a contract. The term should not be used for specifying the function of a business partner in Saudi Arabia at all.

Source: Adapted from Ehlert, D. (1992) "Der Sponsor und andere rechtliche Möglichkeiten einer Kooperation in Saudi-Arabien", *Internationale Wirtschaft*, 7 May, p. 8

Export department Expansion into international markets often begins with hiring an export manager or the establishment of an export department. This is not actually a form of market entry; rather, it is an internal response to the need or desire to move into new country markets or regions. Located within the home organization, the export department is responsible for:

- international sales and possibly shipping
- advertising
- credit evaluation
- other activities related to operating in foreign markets.

Export departments may be organized either by geographic area or product lines such as casting products, construction material, and molding products of a steel exporter.

The chief disadvantage of export departments is their domestic base. Despite the fact that employees of export departments may regularly visit their foreign customers, it is hard for them to maintain close enough contacts to react quickly or obtain sufficient information about trends in international markets.

Import house Perhaps the simplest form of direct marketing-only entry is selling to an import house. An import house, based in the host country, provides marketing services through which products are sold either to intermediaries or directly to the final customers. The exporter needs only to sell its products to the import house.

Philip Morris sells its cigarettes to Mitsui, for example, and R.J. Reynolds to Mitsubishi, both using import houses to serve the Japanese market. Because control over local marketing activities passes to the import house, the exporter loses the ability to determine how its products are marketed in the host country. But this loss of control is offset by a lower level of business risk.

Wholesaler In a similar manner, the sale may be made to a wholesaler, independent distributor, or retail purchasing group in the served country market. Normally, such business partners serve a number of retail outlets within the host country or a specific industry.

Compared to a wholesaler, a distributor normally carries fewer product lines and therefore focuses more of its interests and resources on the products of the manufacturer. For example, Liechtenstein-based Ivoclar-Vivadent, a world-leading manufacturer of products for dentists and dental laboratories, sells its products through wholesalers and mail order firms specializing in dental products. To improve the information level of customers about their products, they have additional local representatives who do not sell products but counsel (potential) clients concerning the benefits derived from the product.

Agent (sales representative) To use foreign sales representatives is one way management can improve the company's reactivity to market trends while maintaining a relatively low level of risk. Sales representatives are not employed by the home organization. They are independent sales agents working on a commission basis. Dodwell, for example, represents Brinton carpets, Christie's contemporary prints and Mars petfood, as well as Pitney-Bowes office machinery in Japan. Sales representatives may focus only on selling or act as a total foreign sales department for the home organization.

A well-run system of sales representatives can provide the foundation for a successful long-term export program. The potential disadvantage is shown in the example of Dodwell just cited: a sales representative may represent more than one firm or one product line and, therefore, may not focus appropriately on the development of market share for products that are harder to sell or that provide less sales margin.

Representation office The simplest form of actual market presence for an exporter is achieved through a representation office. It does not have an individual legal status, is not allowed to do direct sales, and is not taxed. The person representing the firm in the local market has to:

- make contact with potential customers and other important stakeholders
- maintain current relationships
- gather market information and disseminate it to people in the home base for whom it might be relevant.

In comparison to all other modes of market entry discussed so far, a company opening representation offices has much closer contacts with the local market, its needs, and developments.

The major disadvantage of representation offices comes from the fact that one person is rarely able to hold equally good contacts with all potential customers if the company sells to different product markets. A representative for Elk, an Austrian manufacturer of prefabricated homes, in Switzerland might find it difficult, for example, to simultaneously build up relationships with architects, developers, decision makers of construction firms, and private customers. For complex technological products such as mechanical equipment or engineering, the representative may not be able to go into enough detail to gather all relevant information for the home company or to negotiate with potential customers.

Branch office When a representation office is staffed with more personnel (normally employees of the home organization) to cover the local market more intensively, and when the unit is officially registered, it becomes a branch office. If it is even organized as a formal unit according to the legislation of the host country it is called a **sales subsidiary**. In Italy, for example, sales subsidiaries most often take the form of Società per Azioni (SpA) or Società a responsabilità limitata (Srl.).

One advantage of this option is that in addition to performing the relationship-building, maintaining, and information function, branch office staff may perform other marketing activities, such as sales, customer service, warehousing, or even joint product development with customers. They also participate in the home organization's planning of its international marketing efforts and are much easier for the home organization to lead than independent sales representatives.

Friedrich Grohe, the German sanitary fittings company, for example, established branch offices in Poland and in Singapore. Grohe Polska, located in Warsaw, has a training facility where Polish plumbers are supported through technical and management seminars. Grohe Pacific in Singapore has announced a design award recognizing modern design and environmental protection, which has created much interest in the Pacific region.

The greatest disadvantage is the high fixed cost of sales subsidiaries. Strategy box 10.1 gives an example of a company that has taken the very popular way of starting its international activities with sales representatives or a branch office and, as the market grows and the company gains experience, establishing more extensive operations in the host market.

Indirect entry, marketing and production

There are three indirect market-entry modes that involve production with limited capital involvement: licensing, franchising, and production or management contracts. For organizations that want to establish a market presence rapidly with limited capital risk, licensing and franchising are especially popular.

Licensing Industrial property rights, including rights to technology, patents, processes and trademarks (registered brand names), may be licensed to an organization in the host market. Ralph Lauren, for example, has a licensing agreement with Onward Kashiyama and Seibu Department Stores to serve the Japanese market.

A marketer that wants to serve a bigger number of country markets simultaneously, but does not have enough resources to build up the required production and marketing capacities, may pass on its technological know-how to partners in those markets. An example is the arrangement of San Miguel, a Philippine beer brewer, with Mt. Everest Breweries of Nepal to produce and market San Miguel beer in Nepal.

A firm that is focused on services, the Disney Company, for example, may license a trademark, say, Mickey Mouse, to several companies in foreign markets, thereby permitting the production and marketing of Mickey Mouse products in those markets as long as they:

● observe certain rules of behavior

● pay a license fee or otherwise compensate their partners.

Licensing allows companies with small capital resources to exploit competitive advantages if they are either legally protected or difficult to imitate quickly at short notice. In addition, companies with little international experience can profit from their local partners' marketing know-how. Licensing may also be regarded as a source of additional profits if spin-off technologies are not to be used by the firm itself or if the company is not interested in international business.

The capital risk associated with licensing is relatively low. At the same time, however, the profit potential of this market-entry mode is lower compared to

STRATEGY BOX 10.1

Cerberus

Swiss-based Cerberus AG, world market leader in fire detection installations, is a good example of how market-entry modes may be changed depending on the stage of the product market lifecycle.

The company started in 1941 with an innovative idea of how to automatically detect fire in its early stages. Extraordinary growth over many years led to a monopoly position in the market for nearly 20 years. Because of restricted financial resources, the young entrepreneurs first decided to focus their installation business on Switzerland. Then, they entered France through a joint venture with Guinard. As the rest of the world quickly recognized the importance of the invention, licensing agreements and sales representative contracts were signed with firms such as Siemens (for Germany, the Netherlands, and Austria), Ericsson (for Scandinavia), Sielte (for Italy), Thorn-EMI (for the U.K.), Nohmi Bosai (for Japan), and Baker Industries (for the U.S.). Cerberus became the world leader in the production of early warning detectors.

When semiconductors were developed in the early 1960s Cerberus quickly changed to this new technology, but it could not prevent the rise of competitors from Japan and the U.S. Growth rates declined in the 1970s. Contractual agreements with the different partners increasingly became a drag on the firm's further development because they prevented Cerberus from direct contacts with their end customers.

In 1982 Cerberus decided to serve the product market for fire security installations on a global scale. To be able to provide all the services needed for successful business, existing contracts had to be cancelled and wholly owned subsidiaries to be installed. Wherever possible, the business organizations of previous partners were acquired, as, for example, in Scandinavia. In the U.S. the licensing partner was taken over, and in Italy and the U.K. new subsidiaries were founded.

At the end of 1990 Cerberus had 15 subsidiaries with 80 branch offices. Some 61% of its employees worked outside of Switzerland.

Source: Adapted from Hug, L. (1991) "Globale Marktentwicklung am Beispiel Cerberus", *Management Zeitschrift*, 60(2), pp. 45–8

alternatives with more intensive involvement in the local markets. Moreover, the home organization must retain some measure of control to ensure that quality standards are maintained and corporate or sub-brand identity are not hurt. If later inconveniencies are to be avoided, the object and content of the licensing agreement should be precisely specified in the contract. The danger that a license partner improves the licensed technology and becomes a major competitor cannot be excluded.

Franchising The reasons for franchising are similar to those for licensing – the organization wants to enter a foreign market quickly with a limited degree of risk and a minimum of capital involvement. Whereas licensing may embrace all forms of industrial property, franchising is usually limited to the use of trademarks and the associated marketing strategy. In addition, the franchisees get counseling and help in the management of their business. They can profit from the experiences of all other franchise partners. If the trademark has a high degree of market awareness and the brand has proven to be attractive, access to capital is facilitated.

The franchiser may sign individual contracts with a number of partners per country market. St. Louis-based Kentucky Fried Chicken, for example, has more than 400 franchised outlets in Japan, not more than 10 of which are owned by a single partner. Or the franchiser may prefer a master franchise, that is, a single contract with a general franchisee in a country market or region. The master franchisee in turn, sells franchises in that market. Ziebart International Corp., based in Troy, Michigan, has established an automotive aftermarket business specializing in products and services for detailing, accessories, and protection. Using master franchisees that have taken over the organization and control of sub-franchise relationships in their country, the company is present in 44 countries all over the world.

The major attraction of franchising as a market-entry mode is due to the combination of the advantages of an internationally operating firm and small privately owned local businesses. *Franchising strikes a balance between adapting the marketing mix to local conditions and maintaining a high level of international standardization.* Stefanel, the Italian fashion franchiser, for example, delivers its products to all partners, controls the appearance of shops, and runs internationally standardized advertising campaigns. The franchisees deliver useful market information to the Italian partner and run sales promotion campaigns that are specifically tailored to their local environments. The franchising organization tends to be more directly involved in the development and control of the marketing mix, while the franchisee is more involved in the execution of that strategy in the host market.

Franchising permits rapid market expansion with relatively little capital risk (the franchisee invests some of its own capital). Many successful examples, from restaurants, such as Ponderosa Steakhouse; hotels, such as Ibis or Scandic Crown; employment and travel agencies; computer or language training, such as New Horizons Computer Learning Centers or Berlitz; to cleaning services or print shops, such as AlphaGraphics, have reached high levels of international customer awareness because the provided customer benefit is accepted by the targeted segments across countries and the competitive advantage can be sustained against imitators because of its perceived uniqueness. But because the franchisee is directly involved in running the business, *franchising offers less control by the home organization* than would be possible if it owned the foreign organization. Indeed, sometimes control must be reclaimed by the home organization. For example, McDonald's has had a stormy relationship with some of its 240 franchisees in France, owing to concerns about the maintenance of corporate standards.

Before choosing this market-entry mode the firm's decision makers should check the legal situation in the local markets. Otherwise, antitrust legislation and product liability regulations could lead to negative surprises.

Production contract Production contract partners in host countries do not pay any fee, but get paid for their performance. In many cases the production partners only receive the minimum know-how needed to accomplish their job. A fashion marketer, such as Swedish H&M, only transmits its designs to production contractors in China and delivers the fabrics to be used. Nevertheless, it cannot avoid similar designs manufactured in other Far Eastern production facilities very quickly appearing on the European and U.S. markets. Therefore, relentless and fast design changes are important in such businesses.

Japanese companies often seek closer cooperation with partners in production contracts. Such cooperation may range from information about the latest production technologies to the joint development of production know-how. Strategic partnerships may result. In any case the internationally operating firm markets the products itself.

Management contract Increasingly, companies are actively seeking management contracts in foreign markets. A management contract allows the firm to be involved in the management of a business organization. Energy corporations like Aramco, for example, provide technology, skills and experience to countries in the Middle East that have oil fields but lack the management capacity to develop them. Hotel management firms sign contracts with governments such as in China or Russia that want to develop their tourism industry faster than they can manage on their own.

Engineering and construction contracts in economically less developed countries often include a management contract stipulating that the leader of the consortium or the general entrepreneur will continue to manage the operation for a certain period at a specified fee. Such contracts are called **turnkey contracts**. The plant is built, started up, and run at the risk of the constructor. For the time specified, he also takes care of the training of workers and employees as well as the maintenance of the plant.

Direct entry, marketing and production

For financially strong companies that want to keep control over their international activities and consider the markets to be served as sufficiently attractive to justify the capital risk, direct investment options seem to be the market-entry modes to choose from. The company may:

- make venture capital available to an innovative partner in the local market
- establish a new firm together with a local or international partner
- participate in or acquire a firm in the market to serve
- or start up a subsidiary.

Venture capital If a company detects an innovative firm working on promising developments in the international markets it wants to enter, it might decide to offer venture capital to this firm. Innovations are risky, and firms working on such high-risk projects normally find it difficult to attract a sufficient amount of capital from traditional sources such as banks or stock markets. Making such an investment:

- gives the funding company a "window" on the market
- keeps the marketer informed on research and development through its links to innovative firms
- avoids full commitment to those firms and their local product market, thereby reducing overall risk.

Joint venture As capital involvement increases, the level of risk and the need for control also increase. Yet many companies are still willing to share control in order to share or diversify risk. A frequently used market-entry mode that shares both risk and control is the joint venture. A partnership between home- and host- or third-country firms is formed, usually resulting in the creation of a new firm.

For example, McDonald's Russia is a Canadian–Russian joint venture. Having started with their first outlet opening in Moscow in January 1990 McDonald's operated more than 100 restaurants by 2005. Because obtaining quality inputs on a timely basis was very difficult in Russia in the early 1990s, the joint venture comprises a farm to raise cows for beef and grow potatoes for French fries. The company also invested $45 million to build McComplex, a state-of-the-art food processing plant. This plant runs a meat production line, a dairy, a potato processing plant, garnish and cheese lines, a bakery, pie and liquid products lines, and houses a quality assurance laboratory and a distribution center.

A joint venture often combines the market knowledge and skills of the host-country firm with the production or technical capabilities of the company that wants to enter the market. For example, in 2003 the Chinese province of Shanghai hosted 58 joint ventures in the automotive industry. The largest ones were dominated by VW and DaimlerChrysler. A company not present in Shanghai faces very low odds when it comes to trying to enter the Chinese automotive market. The foreign firms, such as AVL List, which installed a test and development plant for engines and simultaneously sponsored a chair at Tongji University in Shanghai, transfer their technology. The Chinese partners bring other critical resources to the partnership, such as low labor costs, access to scarce natural resources, and important stakeholders in the business system, or the avoidance of negative national prejudices.

Joint ventures are not only sought by firms in need of a partner based in the market to be entered. Globally active companies, like French Air Liquide and U.S.-based Prax Air, the leaders in the industrial gaz market, also join forces. The two companies have built a joint production plant in the chemical park of Caojing, south of Shanghai. Matsushita Electrical Industrial Co. of Japan and Siemens AG of Germany have completed a joint venture to produce electronic parts in Austria, France, Germany, and Spain.

The selection of an appropriate partner is critical to the success of a joint venture. To avoid a disaster the partners need to understand each other well, should have jointly analyzed the feasibility of the project, coordinate their goals, regulate foreign currency issues, and must have determined management responsibilities.

A carefully chosen partner can significantly contribute to the success of a joint venture. Austria-based Lenzing AG, the world's biggest producer of viscose fibers, for example, entered a joint venture with an Indian partner to construct and manage a plant in Indonesia. The success of the joint venture is based on the technical know-how of the Austrian firm, but also to a substantial extent on the capability of the Indian partner to lead the Indonesian workforce in a sensitive way.

Acquisition The acquisition of a firm in the market to enter provides an opportunity to serve the targeted customers much faster and more efficiently than through the other entry modes discussed so far.

Along with the firm itself, the buyer also acquires its experience and its network of relationships with customers, intermediaries, and other important stakeholders (see Toolbox 10.1). For example, faced with automakers increasingly bent on global expansion that prefer to have suppliers following them rather than seek local suppliers in new markets, U.S. and European suppliers, such as Delphi Automotive Systems or Tyrolit, are turning to international acquisitions to keep up with their customers.

Multinational corporations often prefer acquisitions to other market-entry modes because they help to:

- gain access to new skills or technologies quickly
- move along the experience curve more quickly
- establish a strong position in a new country or regional market.

South Korea's Daewoo, for example, wanted to buy the French Lotus Group. It was fended off amid fears that Daewoo would scare off other automakers that work closely with Lotus's design studio.

Acquisitions are a mode of market entry focusing on the fast expansion of market share. However, decision makers should not overlook the fact that different organizational as well as ethnic cultures may lead to conflicts in management that can potentially use up the time lead achieved through acquisition. Acquisition candidates, therefore, should be evaluated concerning their:

- economic attractiveness
- positions in the local business network
- quality of management systems
- values and norms dominating management behavior.

There are also cases where legal restrictions limit the internationally operating firm to taking shares in its partner in the market to enter. For example, Deutsche Telekom, the German phone company, which considered the U.K. market key to its aspirations to become a global player and did not see other ways to enter

---

TOOLBOX 10.1   Acquisitions in the U.S.

When acquiring a U.S. firm to smooth market entry, the first thing to make things easier is to create a U.S. limited liability company (LLC) under the law of the state of Delaware. This state has a very flexible corporate law that allows companies to be registered even if they are headquartered elsewhere. An LLC is not taxed at the entity level. It can be formed in a day and be structured as the founder likes. There is no need to specify its purpose, neither is there a minimum capital requirement. There is only a registration fee to be paid.

In the next step, a thorough investigation of the buying object – called due diligence – needs to be conducted. It will concern legal, economic, technical, and environmental issues. Then, the newly created acquiring firm can either buy:

- assets of a company (asset deal)
- stock of a corporation (share deal)
- or merge with another company.

An asset deal can concern tangible and intangible assets, such as contracts, trademarks or patents. The buyer only gets what he agrees to take. The danger is that an important asset can be overlooked. But, by the same token, no liabilities are taken over,

such as underfunded pension funds or sexual harassment problems of former owners.

The faster solution is to buy stock. It is more easily done and results in less discussion. But the risk is more important because all the liabilities are automatically taken over.

Before making the deal, antitrust legislation needs to be looked at in the country of the buyer and in the U.S. If the buyer is headquartered in the European Union, EU legislation is also relevant. Any deal at a purchase price above $50 million needs to be filed to the U.S. antitrust authorities. A market study on the competitive situation after the deal must be included. A related problem to be considered is the definition of the market. The narrower the market is defined the higher will be the probability that FDC regulations on antitrust are infringed.

If the authority makes what is called a "second request," there may be 60 to 80 lawyers working for months to answer all the specific questions of the administration. Thus, the procedure becomes extremely expensive. The buyer, therefore, may agree with the seller not to consider the deal any further if there is a second request.

the market, considered buying the U.K.'s Cable & Wireless. Because of possible U.K. government objections to a foreign company taking over the sensitive international communications services that Cable & Wireless handled for the U.K., Deutsche Telekom launched a bid for only part of the firm.

Subsidiary Establishing a wholly owned subsidiary for production and marketing purposes usually means hiring host-country personnel. Cultural differences will inevitably lead to leadership problems that can never be completely resolved. Initially, U.S. managers, for example, impress European superiors with their "efficiency"; French employees, for their part, have problems dealing with the "efficiency" of their German superiors; American women may consider as sexual harassment what their Japanese superiors view as normal male behavior.

By the same token, examples like Japanese car factories in the U.S. or U.S. production plants in China show that intensive training and appropriate focus on the development of organizational culture can do a lot to ensure the quality standards of the headquarters. General Motors' gearbox factory near Vienna and Sony's compact disc production facility near Salzburg, both in Austria, even provide examples showing that the quality and output expectations of the investors can be surpassed by foreign subsidiaries. This may be one of the reasons why the most successful middle-sized German companies prefer founding subsidiaries to the acquisition of companies.

IBM in Japan, Nestlé in Australia, Toyota in the U.S. and Pfizer in Ireland are but a few large companies that have decided to take this approach. They have taken the risk to become subject to protectionist policies and more backlash than either domestic companies or joint ventures. Large-scale foreign investment is controversial in many countries. Ethics box 10.1 describes a situation where restrictions are defensible because investors try to escape environmental laws in their home countries.

Many countries, such as those in eastern Europe or the industrially fast developing nations in Southeast Asia, actively solicit direct investments. Such investments allow a company to show potential customers and other stakeholders that they are serious about their commitment and are determined to stay. For example, German automakers have spent nearly $1 billion building up dealer, supply, and service support networks in Japan. When BMW entered the Japanese market, its initial investment was several times higher than the amount required running what was then a very small operation. The company used the heavy investment as a selling point to dealers, banks, and potential customers. Today BMW has its own highly visible and prestigious building in Tokyo, a symbol of its continued commitment. Volkswagen Audi Nippon built an import facility in a deepwater port, which includes an inspection center, a parts warehouse, and a training center.

Evaluation criteria

The criteria on which a business organization bases its decisions about market-entry modes may be classified into five categories:

- issues specific to the organization
- characteristics of the served product market
- product considerations
- conditions of the local operating environment
- macro-environment.

As with the various market-entry modes, there are several evaluation criteria within each of these categories (see Table 10.3); all applicable criteria should be used in a specific case.

Issues specific to the organization

The following issues specific to a company have an impact on the attractiveness of available market-entry modes.

Objectives Company objectives strongly influence the firm's decisions concerning market-entry modes. For example, a company that wants to "be number one or two in every market" it serves would probably choose a direct market-entry mode. To achieve and hold a market leader position, it usually needs to tightly control the marketing of its products in the served markets. As the example of IBM shows, in such situations the company is likely to establish a joint venture or a subsidiary. At the very least, a corporate sales office is required.

Firms that view international sales as an "extra" and only pursue follower positions in their non-domestic markets, however, are more likely to select an indirect market-entry mode. A firm that wants to test a market or to start a

---

ETHICS BOX 10.1

The race to the bottom

Current debates over globalization have produced a seemingly simple and intuitive conclusion: Unfettered globalization triggers an unavoidable "race to the bottom" in labor and environmental standards around the world. Companies tend to invest in the country or location where they can earn the highest return. Strict labor laws or rigorous environmental protection lower profits by raising the costs of production. Multinational corporations will therefore engage in regulatory arbitrage, moving into countries with lax standards. Fearing a loss of their tax base, governments in countries with high standards have little choice but to loosen their regulations to avoid capital flight. Governments of less industrially developed countries usually having lower or no standards will avoid establishing improved regulation to attract investments.

There are some examples, such as the discussion in western Europe about increasing working hours without reimbursement, decreasing the number of holidays and making working time totally flexible, that point in this direction. But there are other examples that show the contrary: Shandong Province's Weihai High-Tech Industrial Development Zone in China is particularly attractive to foreign high-tech businesses specializing in electronic information, biomedical engineering, electromechanical products, new materials, and energy because of its clean natural environment. The development area also attracts businesses that in their home countries

have difficulties in maintaining production facilities because of dangerous environmental pollution. Early in 1996, a U.S. businessman hoping to establish a high-tech firm in Shandong Province's Weihai High-Tech Industrial Development Zone with an investment of $7.6 million was rejected because his products contained radiation.

Similar rejections have taken place involving more than a dozen projects in the 1990s. For example, a company with 20,000 employees, which wanted to invest 100,000 yuan, was rejected because its projected production procedures would have produced unacceptable high levels of pollutants. As a result, Weihai's environment, which is particularly well suited for manufacturing electronic products, is being protected.

As a matter of fact, labor regulations in export-processing zones (EPZ) do not reach the standards of highly industrialized countries. There are countries, such as Bangladesh and Zimbabwe, that have attempted to preempt competitive pressures by exempting their EPZs from regulations covering labor standards. And the number of EPZs has rapidly grown from 845 (22.5 million workers) in 1997 to more than 3,000 (43 million workers) in 2003. However, there are positive signals. Governments in some countries, including the Dominican Republic and the Philippines, actually established labor standards in their EPZs where none previously existed.

Source: Adapted from "Weihai Toush On Pollution", *Beijing Review*, 25–31 March 1996, p. 27; "Ces zones franches qui bafouent le droit du travail", *Le Figaro*, 11 September 2003, p. 6; Drezner, D.W. (2000) "Bottom feeders", *Foreign Policy*, November/December, pp. 64–70

long-term sales growth trend can use an exporting approach or appoint sales representatives.

Rules of business behavior The firm's rules of business behavior in many cases exclude some market-entry modes and favor a number of others. They may even dictate certain entry modes. Small firms often define their rules of business behavior in terms of their home market. In the U.S., most lack an export orientation. At best, they might engage in indirect market-entry modes, such as casual exporting. In contrast, because their home market is so restricted, many small companies in Switzerland believe that their survival depends on regular exporting. Therefore, they tend to choose direct market-entry modes.

Other companies want to have their production concentrated "at home" and tend to see a "natural" development of their market-entry modes from exports (to import houses, wholesalers, or distributors) to direct-entry modes such as sales subsidiaries. Such companies refer to the pragmatic rule of choice between market-entry modes. They do not even consider immediate direct entry into a new market to build a strong market position quickly, to overcome entry barriers, or to improve their competitive cost position.

TABLE 10.3 *Evaluation criteria for market-entry modes*

Criteria	Elements	
Issues specific to the organization	Objectives Rules of business behavior Level of influence needed Control of value chain Personal resources Financial resources Acceptable capital risk	Each criterion listed in the table influences the attractiveness of market-entry options, and all should be considered for inclusion in a market-specific catalog of evaluation criteria.
Characteristics of the served product market	Availability of information Market resistance Market volume Product market lifecycle	
Product considerations	Level of customer service Product usage	
Conditions of local business environment	Competition Distribution channels	
Macro-environment	Geographic distance Stability Currency risks Level of technological development Infrastructure Political situation Legal restrictions Trade restrictions Cultural environment	

Level of needed influence Another important issue is the level of influence on intermediaries and customers a firm needs to have in order to successfully market its product or service. If the company wishes to influence customers directly and is unable to do so from its home base, direct-entry modes are called for. ETA, the Swiss inventor of Swatch watches, for example, after some unsuccessful trials with local sales representatives, recognized that mass marketing its watches to target customers in the U.S. and Europe was impossible without securing some direct influence on the local marketing activities, such as choice of outlets or market communication activities. Thus, top management decided to open sales subsidiaries in all major markets.

Control of value chain The need to control the flow of resources also influences market-entry decisions. A company that needs to be vertically integrated from raw materials through to distribution to be competitive should probably use a direct marketing- and production entry mode. Foreign copper companies in Chile, for example, want to control copper mining, extraction, and processing into a semi-finished product. They therefore invest directly in mining, melting, and processing activities.

Personnel resources Management personnel that have worked on an international business level for years can choose more direct market-entry options. They are experienced and therefore better able to manage the higher risk associated with those entry modes.

Without properly trained and internationally experienced personnel, however, an organization is well advised to avoid high-risk, high-control entry modes. Well-managed small companies often have only the number of highly qualified personal they need to be successful in their domestic market. Even if additional capacities cannot be built up quickly enough, such companies may still be successful in foreign markets. Some indirect market-entry modes, such as using a trading company or signing a licensing contract, but also simple kinds of direct entry, such as selling to an importer, allow the company to use external personnel with the necessary skills and experience.

Financial resources For many small and middle-sized firms, the amount of capital involved in the choice of a market-entry option is crucial. Even very dynamic entrepreneurs cannot seriously overdraw the financial resources of their companies. Indirect market-entry options with fewer capital needs will seem more attractive to them. The global expansion undertaken by companies such as Hertz or Novotel would not have been possible had the home organization had to provide all the necessary capital.

Small companies may find that the only way to enter a major market, such as the U.S., that requires extensive marketing support is to sell through an export group or a trading company. Such business partners are able to bundle several products that may be profitably sold as a group. Or the home organization may wish to sell to an import house or a purchasing group that performs similar services in the market to be entered.

Acceptable capital risk The degree of capital risk a company is willing to accept is largely determined by its core strategy. Together with the amount of capital required to finance market entry, it is often central to the market-entry decision. Franchising is popular, for example, because it allows a company to expand quickly and to share capital risk with firms in the local markets.

Even larger companies that are well equipped with financial resources or have access to external capital will tend to choose cooperative forms of direct market entry, such as joint ventures, when the business environment is not entirely stable or entry requires expensive marketing campaigns, strong local networking, or high capital spending on plant and equipment.

Characteristics of the served product market

The attractiveness of a market-entry mode also depends on the characteristics of the served product market.

Availability of information Because of its close link with market influence and control, the availability of information is an important factor in market-entry decisions. When in-depth market information is needed for local success but is difficult to obtain, the most attractive alternative is a direct, marketing-only-entry mode, or it may be a direct marketing- and production entry mode with capital involvement. In both of these cases a local partner is needed, either because it possesses the required information or because it is better able to gather the information than a foreign organization would be.

For example, a Canadian manufacturer of maple syrup planning to enter the Malaysian market would be well advised to form a joint venture with a Malaysian partner. Food preferences are quite different in Malaysia than in Canada, and a local partner could provide the information needed for successful product adaptation. At the same time, because market information is not as readily available in Malaysia as in Canada, a local partner may be the only viable source of information.

Market resistance The greater the market's resistance to a product, the greater the need for a market-entry mode that gives the organization direct control over local marketing activities. Microwave ovens, for example, met with fairly strong resistance in Puerto Rico and the U.K., owing to cooking habits and social norms that were not consistent with the benefits offered by the marketers of the product. Microwave oven manufacturers must undertake appropriate marketing efforts to carefully reposition the product. To make sure that marketing tools were properly applied in the local markets, the manufacturers had to choose direct market-entry modes.

If the product is likely to diffuse rapidly through the market, decision makers can opt for an entry alternative that leaves great parts of market control to the intermediary in the host market.

Market volume The market volume (or market potential) can also influence the choice of market-entry mode. In large markets, especially those with strong growth rates, direct investment is more easily justified than in small markets with low or stagnating growth rates. One of the reasons U.S. and Japanese companies have made major investments in Europe is that the EU represents an even larger market than the U.S. Before the economic integration provided by the EU, national markets in Europe were mostly entered by less financially risky methods, such as exporting.

Some products can find high-volume markets outside the triad markets. The macro-environments of those markets, in many cases, are less attractive, however. They suggest entry modes that minimize capital risk. For example, foreign firms generally prefer to export their products or sell them to wholesale or retail purchasing groups rather than establish subsidiaries in the Democratic Republic of Congo, an African country with more inhabitants than Poland. In their view, the level of economic activity in the Congo is too low and the political environment too unstable to justify direct investment. International marketers should not forget, however, that more direct involvement in such markets might encourage a process of development, improve the market situation, and strengthen their own position in the country.

Stage in product market lifecycle Just as the marketing mix changes at each phase of the product lifecycle, attractive market-entry modes also change depending on the phase of the local product market lifecycle. For product markets in the early (introductory) phase of the lifecycle, indirect market-entry techniques are often preferred. But if the local product market is highly attractive it may be wiser to invest directly in the early stages, gain product and brand awareness, and thereby gain market share quickly while raising barriers to entry by competitors. Japanese and Korean firms, in particular, employ this approach with great success.

High-growth product markets often require direct market-entry approaches because in such cases the firm usually wants to manage and control the local marketing of its product as closely as possible.

Companies planning to enter a local product market in the *mature phase of its lifecycle* will have to choose an alternative which, on the one hand, ensures the firm's intended competitive position and, on the other hand, generates the expected cash flow to be spent in markets in earlier stages of their lifecycle.

Companies already present in a market often change their entry mode over the product market lifecycle. Strategy box 10.1 gives an example of the Swiss company Cerberus, which has followed such a stepwise change. In the mature phase of the market they tend to extend the direct approach followed during the growth phase, so that the product will maintain its market position and profit margin for as long as possible. During the decline phase of the product market, the firm may switch back to an indirect approach, decreasing the costs as sales fall, if it plans to slowly draw back from the market.

Product considerations

The characteristics of a product influence not only the speed of its diffusion in a new market, but also the choice of market-entry mode.

Level of customer service The greater the level of customer service needed to support a product, both before and after the sale, the more the preferred market-entry option will be one that allows significant influence on the behavior of the local business partners. The chosen entry mode must enable the home organization to control the quality of services provided by their own employees or those of their local partners. Direct investment may seem to be the best solution, but is not absolutely necessary.

Caterpillar, the Peoria, Illinois-based manufacturer of machines and diesel engines, is an example of a company that is committed to worldwide service excellence but chose to enter most markets without capital involvement. They closely cooperate with independent dealers around the world who are long-established members of their communities and therefore have close ties to local customers and stakeholders. They advise customers on the selection and application of a product, financing, insurance, operator training, maintenance and repair, and help in deciding when it makes economic sense to replace a machine. Through extensive training and involvement of dealers in product design and delivery, service and field support, and the management of replacement part inventories, Caterpillar has managed to develop a common understanding of what it takes to provide superior customer service.

Product usage Product usage affects the degree of control needed in particular markets. Industrial goods normally make entry modes involving direct marketing or production (often with capital involvement) more desirable than consumer goods. But also an advertising agency, for example, that wishes to serve major global corporations must be directly involved in the markets its clients seek to reach. For example, London-based Saatchi & Saatchi Advertising has undertaken a series of multinational joint ventures and acquisitions in an effort to offer efficient and effective advertising to corporate clients throughout the world.

Conditions of the local operating environment

The conditions of the local operating environment not only influence the attractiveness of a market but also the choice of market-entry mode.

Competition Management must assess the competitive situation in broad terms, to name but a few, of:

- size
- intensity
- relative market share
- rate of growth
- interweaving with other stakeholders
- technological sophistication.

Each of these aspects of competition affects market entry in different ways. For example, foreign companies entering the car market in the U.S. face intense competition. In this situation it is more effective to "buy" market share through affiliation with a firm that is already in the market than to enter the market alone and build market share slowly. Mercedes Benz used this approach when it affiliated with Chrysler to get better access to the U.S. market.

Distribution channels The attractiveness of different market-entry modes is strongly influenced by

- available distribution channels
- level of interrelationships of their members
- company's distribution objectives.

For example, local partnerships seem to be a good choice when the distribution system is complex and its members have long-lasting personal ties as well as mutual capital involvement, as is the case in Japan.

Direct investment in distribution systems may be necessary when marketing objectives cannot be met using existing distribution systems. For instance, in the case of a local market where food products usually pass through several levels of wholesalers and retailers before reaching consumers, it might be appropriate for a firm that wants to market perishable products to invest in a new distribution channel. Also, when a firm wants to lower distribution costs it might establish a more efficient channel.

An indirect entry technique may be used when entering a market in which the distribution system is sophisticated and accepts new entrants easily, as is the case in Hong Kong.

Macro-environment

Characteristics of the macro-environment affect the final selection of a market-entry mode by eliminating some options and making others more viable. Besides the geographic distance of the local market, evaluation criteria from the macro-environment are economic, technical, political, legal, and cultural factors.

Geographic distance The geographic distance between the home market of a firm and its targeted country market can affect the market-entry decision. Most managers tend to choose indirect market-entry modes for distant markets because they perceive increasing risks with increasing distance. But this is mainly an emotional reaction to such "foreign" markets.

A Finland-based company, such as Polar Electro Oy, the world's leading producer of heart rate monitoring, registering and evaluation equipment, entering the New Zealand market would probably use some low-risk direct market-entry mode, such as a wholesaler or a sales representative. Given the distance between the two countries, some 8,000 miles, such a decision would pass most control (including market information sources) to the host-country organization. A branch office, such as Polar Electro Deutschland GmbH, contrariwise, would ensure direct contact with local customers and facilitate contacts with importers in neighboring countries such as Leuenberger Medizin Technik in Switzerland.

The impact of distance has been reduced by advances in telecommunications. Fax messages and emails are conveyed as easily between Scandinavia and New Zealand as they are within either country. Nevertheless, distance still creates a gap in face-to-face communication that cannot be fully overcome by video-conferences. If personal contacts are crucial for market success, the choice of market-entry mode should consider that fact independent of geographic distance.

Economic and political stability In countries with unstable economic or political environments, most companies prefer joint ventures to wholly owned subsidiaries. This was proved after the fall of the Iron Curtain in central Europe where most international involvement in the early 1990s was through joint ventures. The share of more direct forms of capital investment has been growing since the mid-1990s when the economic and political stability of countries such as the Czech Republic, Hungary, and Poland was assured.

Political situation The political situation in a market to enter influences both the choice and the success of a market-entry mode. Whereas companies that wanted to do business in the Soviet Union had a rather restricted range of choice to enter the market (either selling to public trading agencies or establishing joint ventures with one of those agencies), they have a much broader set of choices now to enter product markets in Russia. Positive political relations between two nations, such as those between Australia and the U.K., permit a free decision among market-entry alternatives.

Currency risks Currency risks, such as quick changes in the value of currencies, decrease the attractiveness of direct marketing and production entry modes. For example, a profit margin of 10% of gross sales can be eliminated by a more than 10% currency devaluation in the host country. Profit would be increased, of course, if the exchange rate were to shift the other way. Market entry by means of direct production permits the firm to avoid the impact of rapid changes in exchange rates through reinvesting profits and improving the long-term performance of the company.

Level of technological development When entering a technologically sophisticated market like Sweden, an inventor of a new crank mechanism for bicycles may be able to transfer its technology directly into the market. This might be done without capital involvement, through a licensing arrangement between the inventor and a Swedish firm. In a market with a lower level of technological sophistication, direct marketing-only alternatives or even indirect marketing-only entry modes may seem preferable because appropriate use of the technology in local production might possibly not be ensured. In Argentina, for example, a sales representative or an import house might be used for the same new product.

Some technologically less developed countries, however, impose the creation of joint ventures with local firms. The goal is to improve the technical know-how of host-country managers and personnel as well as to get hold of the latest machinery. Only if the product is very complex and cannot be ordered at any other supplier, as in the case of a Cray Computer, might the host country allow the company to export to its market.

Infrastructure A country's infrastructure can act as either a resource or a constraint in the evaluation process of market-entry options. A French vacation company such as Club Méditerranée, developing a vacation resort in Sierra Leone, will have to use a market-entry mode that entails capital involvement. It will probably need to build roads to transport tourists to the vacation site. It may also have to build its own electrical power plant and house its employees. But when entering the Portuguese market the same company could use an indirect technique, because the infrastructure there is far more highly developed.

Legal restrictions Legal restrictions on the choice of market-entry mode may be motivated by economic concerns (public or private), as when a host country requires local firm participation in business conducted by a foreign company like in Saudi Arabia, or government participation in specific businesses such as in weapon deals.

Legislation may restrict foreign investment for market entry. U.S. advertising agencies, for example, have been denied any role other than non-equity affiliation in Korea. In countries with publicly owned companies, those firms often hold exclusive rights for the production and distribution of certain products or services.

Trade restrictions Trade restrictions control or limit trade within a country or between that country and others. India, for example, has very tight restrictions on imports of automobiles, including low import quotas and a high tariff on each vehicle, as well as on many industrial goods. Exports to this country are very much complicated by the procedures governing the receipt of an import license. The exporter must prove that no Indian competitor exists that could provide similar products. The government introduced this rule to make as many potential exporters as possible transfer their technology to India by entering the market through joint ventures with Indian partners.

Sometimes high trade restrictions in an otherwise attractive market make direct foreign investment the most appropriate entry technique. In the U.S., for example, increased protectionism, coupled with the devalued dollar and a sizeable market have resulted in increased direct foreign investment by Asian and European manufacturers.

Cultural environment The local success of an internationally operating company can strongly depend on its capability to adjust to the cultural environment. If a Caribbean fruit producer usually negotiates with purchasing agents of powerful retail organizations and relies on those organizations for marketing its products to the target customers in EU markets, it may encounter difficulties when trying to enter east Asian markets the same way. There, most food products are sold by small retailers in open markets. The market-entry mode must be adapted to the cultural environment of each local or at least regional market.

A society that is characterized by a high level of ethnocentrism is probably best entered through a management contract, licensing, or a joint venture. In contrast, Japanese electronic firms entering the U.S. are probably better off maintaining their home-country identity. Because American consumers believe that Japanese manufacturers produce higher quality products, a market-entry mode that keeps the Japanese name visible probably makes the most sense.

The decision process

An attempt to assess the attractiveness of each potential market-entry mode for each country market to be served would not only require masses of information that would be hard to acquire but would also consume considerable management time. The resulting high costs and the loss of time would a priori decrease the competitiveness of the firm. A less extensive approach to choosing an adequate market-entry mode, which leads to satisfactory results, is described in Toolbox 10.2. It contains the following steps:

- establish a set of "knockout" criteria that have to be satisfied by an entry mode in order to be feasible
- reduce the great number of alternatives to a small set of feasible entry modes
- critically evaluate those entry modes and rank them into an order from which the best placed entry mode that can be implemented in the existing macro-environment will be chosen.

In the decision process described in Toolbox 10.2, analytical work is reduced to a realistic volume without leaving the decision to the gut feelings of management or taking it on the basis of "successful traditions." Management does not

TOOLBOX 10.2 Selecting market-entry mode

Step 1: Establish a set of knockout criteria

The establishment of K.O. criteria for local market-entry modes is based on the firm's objectives. If the company wants to minimize its financial risks, for example, market-entry modes that entail high capital involvement, such as establishing a subsidiary with production and marketing, would be excluded. "Needed capital equipment" becomes a K.O. criterion in the pre-selection of entry options. If the company strives to gain the highest degree of control over market information flows and the marketing of its products to the final customers, criteria such as "Access to market information" and "Influence on local markets" will have significant influence in the pre-selection process.

Step 2: Apply criteria related to organizational identity

All market-entry options that survive this first reduction step will then be checked according to criteria related to:

- intended brand meaning of the organization
- fundamentals the firm plans to compete on
- major benefits to be provided to the customers
- rules of business behavior fixed in the core strategy.

From there, important criteria for the selection of market-entry modes can be deduced. For example, if cooperation with potential competitors is not allowed, all entry alternatives that rely on such cooperation, for example licensing or joint ventures, are to be excluded from further investigation.

Step 3: Apply criteria related to the intended position in the local market

The small set of feasible entry modes quickly determined by this approach then undergoes a critical evaluation through comparison against criteria related to the intended local market position. Factors such as:

- control required over resources
- market resistance to be expected
- current market volume
- or capacity to secure a high level of customer service

may play a prominent role in the evaluation process. Table 10.4 gives an example of how the evaluation process can be formalized.

The result is a rank order of theoretically feasible market-entry modes according to their potential contribution to the intended local position of the firm.

Step 4: Assessing the implementation potential

Once this ranking is established, the remaining shortlist of entry options is assessed concerning the implementation potential of each mode in the macro-environment of the local market. The procedure starts with the entry mode ranked first. If this most preferable option cannot be chosen because of problems in the macro-environment, such as missing infrastructure or too high currency risks, the next ranked option is assessed until a market-entry mode is identified, which not only comes up to the standards of the intended global strategic position, but also to intended local position, and demands of the local macro-environment.

make a final decision until all available information on the effects of potential market-entry modes has been considered. In effect, this approach forces management to continually re-evaluate criteria and options from different perspectives. Each local market-entry analysis might, therefore, result in a different entry mode decision even if the intended position in the markets is the same.

Organization

With the broadening of markets that occurs as a result of internationalization, a new organizational structure may become necessary. That is, resources not only need to be allocated to the served product and country markets, but additionally, have to be carefully allocated to organizational processes and units. For example, in order to reduce complexity and costs the German–Japanese computer manufacturer Fujitsu Siemens decided to restructure its European business in terms of regional clusters. Spain and Portugal, the Nordic countries, Austria and Switzerland as well as eastern Europe each represent such a cluster. Back-office functions such as finance, logistics or marketing management are centralized for each cluster.

Management has a range of organizational structures, each with its own strengths and weaknesses, to choose from.

International marketing manager

In small companies just starting to go international, organizational structure seems of minor concern, because one person or a few can handle all of the elements just mentioned. In most cases, however, international marketing responsibilities should not be given to someone whose main job lies in the domestic area.

TABLE 10.4 *Evaluation of feasible market-entry modes*

Evaluation criteria	Feasible entry modes				Comments
	Branch office	Sales subsidiary	Fran-chising	Joint venture	
Needed personnel resources	4	3	5	2	
Neded capital equipment	4	3	5	1	
Influence on local market	3	4	2	5	
Access to market information	3	4	3	5	
Level of customer service	2	4	4	5	
Intensity of competition	1	2	3	4	
Market volume	5	3	4	1	
Capital risk	4	2	5	1	
Distribution system	2	2	4	5	
Trade restrictions	3	4	5	5	
Total points	31	31	40	34	

Scale: 1 = very bad
3 = satisfactory
5 = very good

When the decision makers have established a shortlist of feasible market-entry modes, they can evaluate the remaining options by comparison against evaluation criteria relevant for the intended local position of the firm on a scale that might range from 1 to 5. The entry options are then ranked according to the number of points they are assigned. To keep the evaluation procedure understandable and verifiable for other managers in the firm, a comment column should be used to indicate why the scale points were attributed as given.

This person will rarely focus on the more complex and, certainly at the outset, often less rewarding job of starting an international business.

Small companies, therefore, are well advised to begin their internationalization process by hiring an international marketing manager. The appointment should be made before the company has analyzed potential markets in detail and before marketing strategies, programs, and activities are determined. The new manager should report directly to top management.

The international marketing manager should have administrative and management ability in addition to selling skills, and she or he should be thoroughly familiar with the company's product, procedures, and personnel.

Specific markets may restrict the number of applicants who might be successful. For example, if the targeted markets are located in Southeast Asia or Arab countries, the manager will probably have to be male, because business partners in these areas are generally not prepared, or even willing, to deal with female business executives.

International marketing department

As the international business grows, the firm may first add an assistant to the international marketing manager. The assistant will:

- gather, update, and present information on specific markets and their relevant environments
- help in executing decisions
- organize international meetings
- take over much of the administrative work.

From that nucleus an international marketing department may develop along with increasing business volume and complexity. Regional managers may be assigned specific geographical territories when the company has expanded its business to a range of different market areas. Regional managers:

- call on distribution channel members
- introduce new products to them
- train their sales representatives and personnel
- monitor competitors
- keep in touch with key customers.

When the size of the company's international business grows further, sales offices, joint ventures, or subsidiaries may be useful. At this point, top management usually decides on one of the following two structural options.

National subsidiary structure

If national sales offices or subsidiaries report directly to top management, without intermediate levels such as the international marketing manager or regional managers involved, a **national subsidiary structure** exists. This structure is often referred to as a "mother–daughter relationship." Because this structure allows for direct influence by top managers, it is particularly popular with privately owned and managed small and middle-sized European firms. Figure 10.8 shows the example of the organizational structure of Friedrich Grohe Group, the leading German firm in the European sanitary fittings market.

However, when an international business increases further in size, this form of organizational structure loses most of its attraction. Concentrating international issues in the hands of one or a few people results in an inefficient use of top management's time. Top management becomes increasingly unable to properly treat the vast amount of information and to maintain corporate growth.

FIGURE 10.8 *National subsidiary structure of Friedrich Grohe Group*

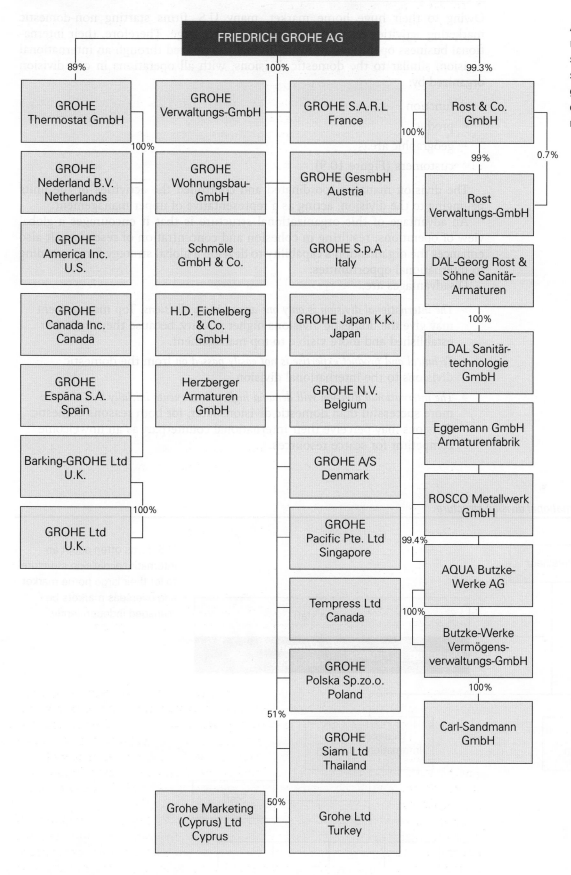

A firm that adopts a national subsidiary structure gives each subsidiary manager a great deal of control over the subsidiary's marketing activities.

International division structure

Owing to their huge home market, many U.S. firms starting non-domestic marketing activities have already been relatively large. Therefore, their international business operations were traditionally organized through an international division, similar to the domestic divisions, with all operations in one division organized by:

- function
- product
- geographic areas
- customers (Figure 10.9).

The division manager coordinated and controlled the activities of the units belonging to the division, acting as a representative of upper management.

An advantage of this organizational structure is that it encourages a global view of operations, resulting in cohesion and concentration of resources. It also enhances the organization's capability to develop a global strategy for responding to international opportunities.

Disadvantages are:

- *The international division is only one among many divisions.* Top management may give the domestic divisions higher priority, because they are better established and more visible to top management.

- *Technical and product expertise is not easily passed on* from the domestic divisions to the international division.

- *The international division will demand higher investments initially* but may be more successful than domestic divisions later; for both reasons domestic divisions may perceive their international counterpart as an unwelcome competitor for scarce resources.

FIGURE 10.9 *International division structure*

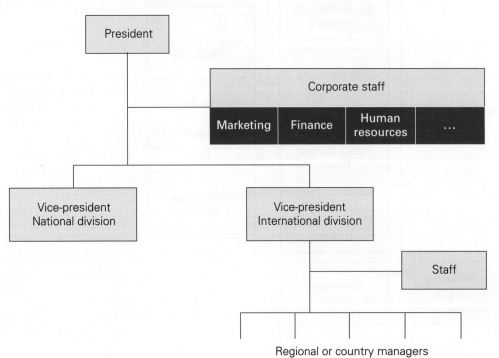

U.S. firms often adopt an international division structure to let their large home market and overseas markets be managed independently.

Global structures

The international division structure has proved to be useful as a transitory state for many firms on their way to globalization of business activities. Eventually, however, global structures emerge, equalizing domestic and foreign operations so that the distinction between the two is no longer reflected in the company's structure. A firm has a **global structure** when its organization is based on:

- major functions
- geographic areas
- product markets

regardless of its home base. Additionally, customer-centered organizational units may be found in companies that deal with a restricted number of important customers or customer groups that need to be treated individually.

Functional structure

Firms with narrow, highly integrated product lines designed to satisfy similar needs across a number of country markets (for example, producers of basic chemicals) often choose a functional structure (Figure 10.10). Knowledge and experience are concentrated, diminishing operating costs. The biggest disadvantage of a functional structure is its inability to flexibly react to regional market differences as top management tends to lose touch with local conditions.

Geographic area structure

Where differences among country markets demand adapted operations, a firm may organize its activities according to a geographic area structure (Figure 10.11). With a geographic area structure, the company can readily respond to stakeholder demands. Economies of scale are achieved within regions.

Regional units of an international company can be treated as strategic business units. For example, a global catfood producer such as Master Food may establish SBUs serving Latin America, the EU, and the U.S. These organizational units could be further split into local businesses and brands (for example, Whiskas in Brazil). Tasks and responsibilities are differentiated among business units.

FIGURE 10.10 *Global functional structure*

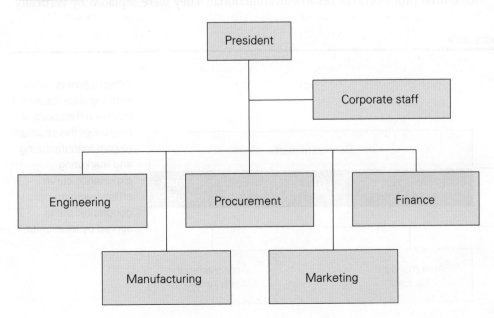

Global firms with narrow product lines that serve similar customers with similar needs across country markets may choose a global functional structure.

Business unit managers are given full responsibility. For managers to be able to bear that responsibility, SBUs must have strategic autonomy, that is, managers must be able to take decisions independently of decisions taken in other SBUs of the company; and success and failure must be unequivocally attributable to individual SBUs.

Strategic autonomy should exist without losing potential synergy effects among the SBUs. With synergy, the whole is greater than the sum of its parts. That is, information gathered in one SBU might help another to launch a new customer problem solution more quickly than its competitors. So would the development of a new technology in one SBU, which may help developing new products or improving productivity in another. A company that synergistically manages multiple geographic SBUs has greater potential for success than the individual SBUs would otherwise generate.

Managing an internationally operating company with geographic SBUs:

- decreases the complexity of a company's business
- simplifies the allocation of available resources to current or potential business activities
- allows direct attribution of success
- allows faster detection of flops and mistakes (with less doubt).

This leads to enhanced motivation of personnel. However:

- international product coordination is inhibited
- functional efforts are duplicated, increasing costs overall.

For example, PerkinElmer, the Connecticut-based scientific instruments manufacturer, used to maintain divisions in the U.K. and Germany. They went their separate ways on R&D, manufacturing, and marketing until functions were concentrated at single locations that were best able to handle them. Actually, the firm is organized in a product division structure.

Product division structure

In a product division structure (Figure 10.12), most often product responsibilities are centralized in corporate headquarters.

When Bonduelle, a French company specializing in canned and deep frozen vegetables had gone through an expansion to central and eastern Europe (Czech Republic, Hungary, Poland, Russia, and Slovakia), the former geographically structured profit centers became dysfunctional. They were replaced by vertically

---

FIGURE 10.11 *Geographic area structure*

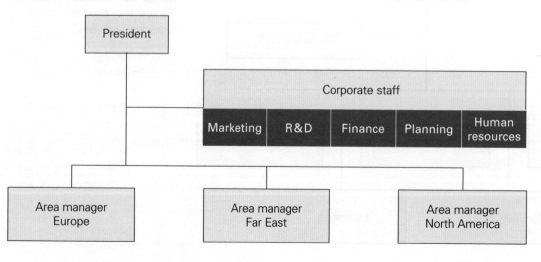

When a firm is faced with significant country market differences, it may adopt this structure to gain manufacturing and marketing experience curve effects within geographic areas served by local units.

Jam production at Bonduelle comes under the new, vertically organized divisional structure   ©ImageState/Alamy

organized divisions corresponding to Bonduelle's four strategically determined product markets: canned vegetables for the mass market under Bonduelle-owned brands, canned vegetables under retail brands, canned vegetables for restaurants and other business clients, and deep-frozen vegetables for the mass market. Each product division is led by a vice-president responsible for the whole of Europe, supervising the local managers who, following a sacred rule of the company, are always locals from the country.

FIGURE 10.12 *Product division structure*

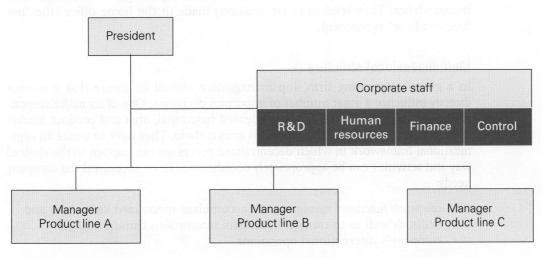

When product lines or brands are more dissimilar than country markets, a global product division structure might be used to gain marketing experience curve effects for each product line across geographic markets.

Advantages Centralization of product market responsibilities in the headquarters hastens the speed and reduces the complexity of decision-making processes. Problems are resolved in a general manner, and evaluation measures are decided on before regional or local units execute the adaptations required by their markets.

The product division structure enables the development of specialized resources. It is most appropriate for conglomerates that organize their business activities along strategic business units, positively discouraging synergies between them. The role of the center is allocating finance as a scarce resource and providing financial control.

The Acer Group, a Taiwan-based PC maker, components manufacturer, and OEM supplier to firms such as Japan's Hitachi, for example, is divided up into different companies, each with its own top manager, personnel system, and salary structure. Individual divisions do not have to buy from others within the group, and if they do, they pay market prices for goods and services. The headquarters gets its revenues from dividends and from charging the divisions for its services.

Companies that are more intent on synergies may also organize their firms by product markets, under conditions where the advantages of an internationally standardized marketing mix are higher than the advantages of adaptation to accommodate regional or local distinctions. To gain active cooperation from managers who are responsible for local units, those units can be assigned a status of "center of competency."

Disadvantages Firms that organize themselves along independent SBU lines may encounter some difficulties in building critical mass to justify investments. SBU managers may be encouraged to establish networks of outsourcing and joint technology development with external partners.

For example, at United Technologies Corp., the U.S. manufacturer of products such as Sikorsky helicopters, Pratt & Whitney jet engines, and Carrier air conditioners, the different business units share several technologies, such as microelectronics, avionics, motion control, and close-loop electrical designs. An excessive corporate focus on the autonomy of the SBUs, however, may be undermining each of these businesses' efforts to develop successful new products based on shared core competences. Sikorsky developed a new generation of lightweight helicopters with a Korean partner, while Pratt & Whitney looked for foreign joint ventures to co-develop and co-produce a new generation of turbofan engines. Thus, the divisions of United Technologies have become open to predatory alliance partners willing to provide financing and markets in exchange for learning and technology transfer.

To take advantage of the marketing know-how, creativity, and skills in local units, extended information, planning, and control systems are needed. But they usually lead to sizeable overhead, and local units may struggle to maintain their independence. They tend to resist decisions made in the home office (the "not invented here" syndrome).

Multidimensional structure

In a globally operating firm, top management should be aware that it cannot directly influence a great number of important decisions. One of its major responsibilities is to identify and develop talented functional, area and product market managers, and to balance the processes among them. They have to create an organizational framework in which decentralized processes can happen in the desired way and activities can be appropriately coordinated. To be successful the company needs:

- *competent functional management* to accumulate specialized know-how and skills, as well as to transfer successful innovations throughout the company's international operations

- *strong geographic area management*, in many cases even further divided into specific customer group management, to detect, analyze, and respond to the needs of different local markets
- product market management with worldwide product responsibilities to achieve the level of international efficiency and integration that is necessary to be an effective global competitor.

A multidimensional structure simultaneously meets the firm's needs for accumulated experience, market responsiveness, and efficiency. Theoretically, the effectiveness of each management group is maintained, and each group is prevented from dominating the others.

Matrix structure The basic challenge is how best to coordinate functions, geographic areas, customer groups, and product lines at each management level, and with the organization as a whole to achieve a balance between international integration and local adaptation of decisions and activities. One approach to resolving this problem is a **matrix structure**, in which functional, area, and product market managers are on the same level in the firm's hierarchy. This forces them to cooperate with each other when making decisions. Dow Chemical is an example of a U.S. company that has adopted a 3D organizational matrix combining six geographic areas, three major functions (research, manufacturing, and marketing), and over 70 products.

Disadvantages of a matrix structure include:

- increased cost
- difficulty of avoiding enduring conflicts
- information overload of corporate managers.

Integrated network The development of a multidimensional organization structure does not necessarily imply that functional, area, and product market management must have the same level of influence on all basic decisions. The company can be regarded as an **integrated network** of interdependent central and local entities, each playing their specific and varying roles depending on the subject of interest. Influence can be determined by assigning responsibility for different sets of activities in the various business units.

Organizational processes

The formal organizational structures of a company are only one element in the struggle for efficient coordination. Formal structures might lose some of their importance in favor of project teams, information networks, and formal as well as informal processes happening inside the given structures. For example, Webasto AG the Stockdorf, Germany-based marketer of sunroofs, heating and air-conditioning systems for passenger cars, buses and trucks has a global organization structure containing business units and central processes (see Figure 10.13).

The champion for R&D, for example:

- receives information about new product development processes in regional units (Europe, Asia, North America)
- takes care that the projects fit the general policy of the firm
- ensures that developments are not duplicated in various locations.

He leads a global team to establish component standards (in order to reduce complexity and increase the number of standardized components without decreasing customer benefits). The champion for purchasing selects the best sources worldwide and reduces the number of suppliers on each continent. Legal, patent, and EDP units have been outsourced.

Control of effectiveness

Having answered the first three of the four basic questions (Which markets to serve? How to behave in those markets? How much of its scarce resources to allocate to what purpose? How to establish and sustain competitive advantages?) an internationally operating organization completes the development of its global core strategy by establishing how the effectiveness of implementing the core strategy is to be controlled. As Chapter 9 emphasized, strong leadership is a must in order for strategies to be implemented. Controlling the effectiveness of implementation actions is an additional reason for the members of an organization to care about implementing the core strategy.

The problem is how to measure effectiveness in a way to avoid extreme emphasis on individual parts of the core strategy. For example, if effectiveness is exclusively controlled by measuring cash flow, personnel will focus on issues such as profits and investments; if it is controlled by EVA (economic value added), personnel will focus on sales volume and capital employed. Human resource development, for example, may become largely secondary. For that reason, the concept of a *scorecard* was developed.

The basic idea underlying scorecards is that the success of a business organization depends on various factors that need to be considered simultaneously. Therefore, organizational effectiveness is not only controlled through one indicator. The balanced scorecard suggested in the literature, for example, considers:

- customer perspective
- internal business process perspective
- innovation and learning perspective
- financial perspective.

FIGURE 10.13 Global structure of Webasto AG

The global organization structure of German Webasto AG contains business units by customers, local subsidiaries, and the following central processes: R&D, purchasing, production, marketing, controlling, personnel management. Each customer is locally served by local subsidiaries. The customer BU manager coordinates customer-related activities worldwide. The central process managers coordinate process-related activities worldwide.

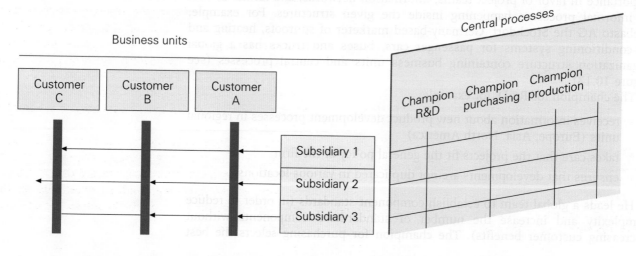

All four are considered essential to the success of a firm. Management has to define measures of effectiveness on each of the four dimensions for each hierarchical level of their organization.

In applying the idea of a scorecard to their strategy implementation management should consider:

- what dimensions are most important for successful implementation of the intended strategic position in the specific business domain of the organization? The perspectives listed earlier may not be equally relevant across various international businesses.

- Are the selected dimensions equally important for the effective implementation of the core strategy?

Based on the strategy of the organization the scorecard may need to be unbalanced. For example, innovation leaders who go for product differentiation may need to emphasize the innovation and learning perspective. By way of contrast, companies that intend to defend their market position by low cost may place less emphasis on the customer and innovation dimensions, but place more on the optimization of internal business processes and financial management.

Summary

To reach the company's intended global strategic position management must determine how much of the available resources are to be allocated to what markets, technologies, organizational units, and processes at what time.

In planning geographic expansion a balanced spread of resources should be obtained. A schedule for international expansion has to be fixed, containing the sequence of market entries and their timing.

The development of a market-entry strategy starts from *positioning the company in the local markets to be served*. The positioning process consists of determining the specific customer segments to be served and making the company or its product attractively distinct to those customers and related stakeholders, always bearing in mind its intended global strategic position. Then, management must *select market-entry modes* that are consistent with:

- intended strategic position
- fixed rules of business behavior
- positioning in each of the country markets to be served.

Market-entry options range from casual exporting to direct foreign investment. They can be classified along two dimensions: direct or indirect approaches and only marketing or both marketing and production.

Each market-entry mode involves trade-offs between market control and degree of risk.

Because of the great number of potential market-entry modes, decision makers have to reduce that number quickly to a manageable amount before a detailed assessment procedure can start. For that purpose, criteria such as objectives formulated in the core strategy, rules of business behavior as well as personnel and financial resources are used. The remaining market-entry modes are critically evaluated for their fit with the intended position of the firm in the local market. Characteristics of the served product market, the product, and the industry are considered for that purpose.

The result is a ranking of feasible market-entry options. For finally deciding which market-entry mode to select criteria from the macro-environment of the local markets are considered.

The developed market-entry strategy is an important contribution to implementing the intended global strategic position of the firm. But implementation will be handicapped without proper *resource allocation to organizational units and processes*. Organizational solutions for international business range from establishing an international marketing manager to global complex structures.

Finally, the *effectiveness of resource allocation* in terms of attaining the intended strategic position must be controlled. For that purpose, a scorecard that translates the core strategy into well-defined objectives on the most important dimensions for business success may be used.

DISCUSSION QUESTIONS

1. What basic options for international expansion exist? What are the internal and external conditions that make each of these options appear an adequate choice?

2. Why do some companies geographically expand their market very quickly after inception? Why do others take a step-by-step approach?

3. How does scheduling the international expansion impact the balance of resource spending? Why is this a relevant issue?

4. Describe the steps to be taken in strategically selecting the entry modes in country markets to be served.

5. Discuss the relationship between the intended strategic global position of a firm, the intended position in a local market, and the selection of the local market-entry mode.

6. What trade-offs are involved in selecting a direct market-entry mode over an indirect one?

7. What trade-offs are involved in deciding to enter a market with marketing activities only or to enter it with marketing and production activities?

8. Take a business organization of your choice and explain why you would use which evaluation criteria in the selection of an entry mode into a new country market.

9. Find three examples of organizational structures of internationally operating companies. What do these structures emphasize with what effect on how these firms operate, and their organizational identity?

10. Try to find practical examples of companies for which controlling the effectiveness of their resource allocation by an unbalanced scorecard may be meaningful. What reasons can you find for this? Discuss.

ADDITIONAL READINGS

Andersen, O. (1997) "Internationalization and market entry mode: a review of theories and conceptual frameworks", *Management International Review*, Special Issue 2, 27–65.

Andersson, U., J. Johanson, and J.-E. Vahlne (1997) "Organic acquisitions in the internationalization process of the business firm", *Management International Review*, Special Issue 2, 67–83.

Ekeledo, I. and K. Sivakumar (2004) "The impact of e-commerce on entry-mode strategies of service firms: a conceptual framework and research propositions", *Journal of International Marketing*, 12(4), 46–70.

Malnight, T.W. (1996) "The transition from decentralized to network-based MNC structures: an evolutionary perspective", *Journal of International Business Studies*, 27(1) 43–65.

Olson, E.M. and St.F. Slater (2002) "The balanced scorecard, competitive strategy, and performance", *Business Horizons*, Indiana University Kelley School of Business.

Taske, D.S. (2003) "Considerations in international intellectual property licensing", *Computer and Internet Lawyer*, 20(8), 10.

Tse, D.K., Y. Pan, and K.Y. Au (1997) "How MNCs choose entry modes and form alliances: the China experience", *Journal of International Business Studies*, 28(4), 779–805.

Welch, D.E. and L.S. Welch (1996) "The internationalization process and networks: a strategic management perspective", *Journal of International Marketing*, 4(3) 11–28.

Useful internet links

A.S. Watson Group   http://www.eu.aswatson.com/

Acer   http://global.acer.com/

Aramco   http://www.saudiaramco.com/

AVL List	http://www.avl.com/
Baker Industries	http://www.bakerindustries.org/
Balzers	http://www.balzers.com/
Berlitz	http://www.berlitz.com/
BMW	http://www.bmw.com/
Bonduelle	http://www.bonduelle.com/
Carrier	http://www.carrier.com/
Cerberus	http://www.cerberusftp.com/
Citroën	http://www.citroen.com/
Club Méditerranée	http://www.clubmed.fr/
Cray Computer	http://www.cray.com/
Daewoo	http://www.daewoo.com/
Delphi Automotive Systems	http://www.delphi.com/
Dow Chemical	http://www.dow.com/
Elk	http://www.elk.at/
FACC	http://www.facc.co.at/e_home
Franchise Help	http://www.franchisehelp.com
Friedrich Grohe	http://www.grohe.com/
H&M	http://www.hm.com/
Hitachi	http://www.hitachi.us/
Ibis	http://www.ibishotel.com/
Master Food	http://www.foodmaster.com/
Nordica	http://www.nordica.com/
Pitney-Bowes	http://www.pb.com/
Polar Electro	http://www.polar.fi/
Pratt & Whitney	http://www.pratt-whitney.com/
Scandic Crown	http://www.scandic-hotels.se/
Selva	http://www.selva.com/
Sielte	http://www.sielte.com/v1/en/index.html
Sikorsky helicopters	http://www.sikorsky.com/sac/Home/0,3170,CLI1_DIV69_ETI541,00.html
Tyrolit	http://www.tyrolit.com/
United Technologies	http://www.utc.com/
Webasto	http://www.webasto.co.uk/home/en/homepage.html
Wild Leitz	http://www.leica.com/
Winterhalter Gastronom	http://www.winterhalter.co.uk/
Yamaha	http://www.yamaha.com/

PART III

BUILDING AND SUSTAINING THE INTENDED GLOBAL POSITION

Top management's basic strategic decisions concerning the intended strategic position of the organization, the rules of business behavior, and the allocation of the firm's resources across businesses and time constitute the general framework for decisions and actions of managers who are responsible for business processes or functions (see Figure III.1). These managers have to develop functional or process-related policies, that is, another set of guidelines, indicating the room to maneuver for managers making operational plans and translating them into actions. Marketing policies, plans, and actions have an important impact on a company's ability to build and sustain its intended global position.

The core of any company's marketing activities is the *development and maintenance of an offer of goods and services* that are attractive to customers and important stakeholders. In most cases material (good) and immaterial (service) parts of the total product (goods and services) delivered are so strongly interrelated that they have to be managed together. Chapter 11 will show that international management of total products is even more demanding than in local business.

International distribution, sales management, and marketing logistics are the subjects of Chapters 12, 13, and 14. They focus on how to ensure that market exchange can occur and customers' orders are executed in the right place at the right time. The international distribution and sales process not only requires that attention be paid to the *choice and management of distribution channels* fitting the intended local market position (Chapter 12), but also that the firm manages salespeople's behavior as this strongly influences *meaning and attractiveness of the company's offer* to all types of potential customer and stakeholder (Chapter 13). Furthermore, the firm must organize the *physical movement of goods and the local provision of services* (Chapter 14).

As one might expect, *communication between a company and its various stakeholders* in an international environment has many hazards for the unwary marketer. Culture, legal regulations, and level of economic development have a major

FIGURE III.1 *International marketing decision process*

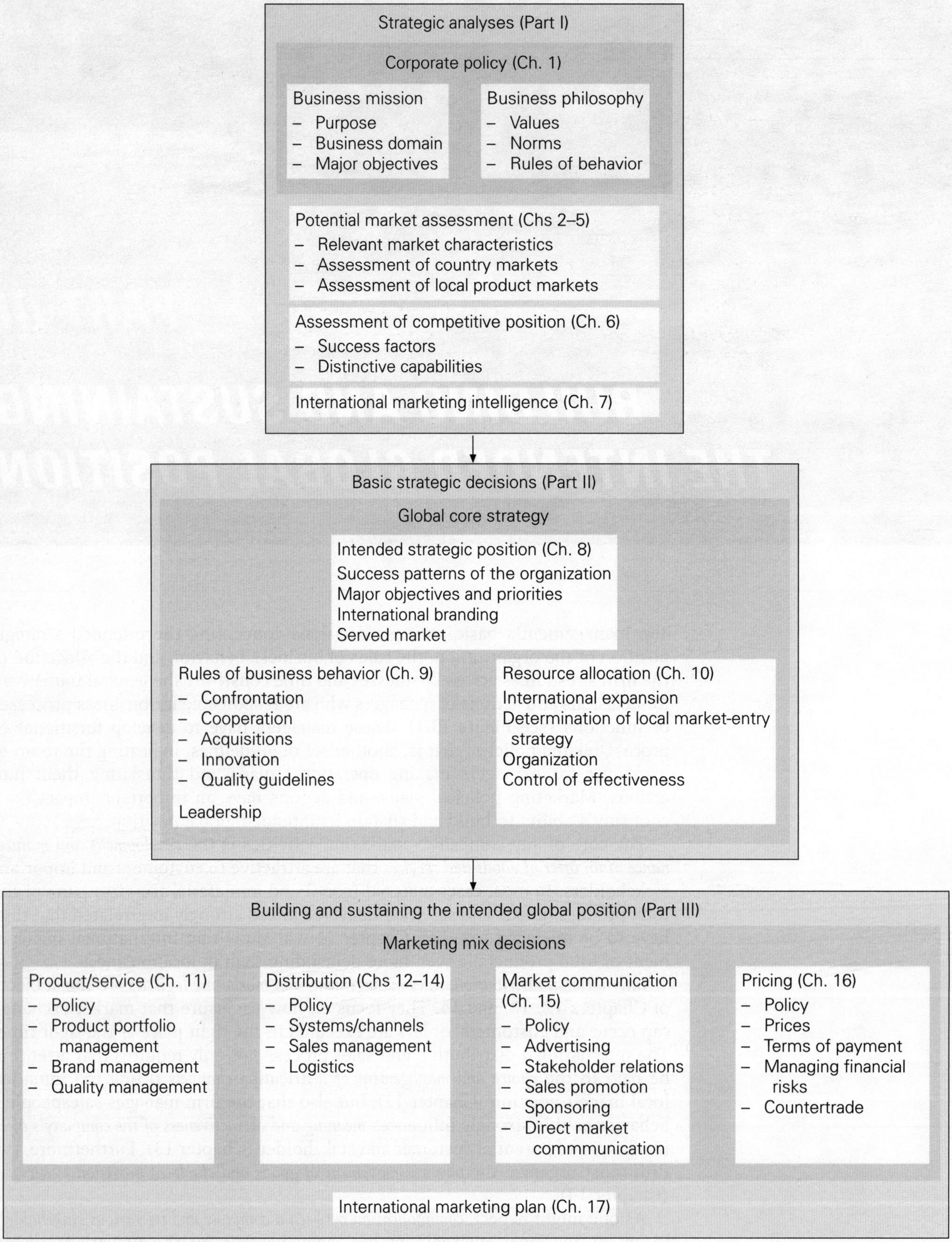

Strategic analyses (Part I)

Corporate policy (Ch. 1)

Business mission
- Purpose
- Business domain
- Major objectives

Business philosophy
- Values
- Norms
- Rules of behavior

Potential market assessment (Chs 2–5)
- Relevant market characteristics
- Assessment of country markets
- Assessment of local product markets

Assessment of competitive position (Ch. 6)
- Success factors
- Distinctive capabilities

International marketing intelligence (Ch. 7)

Basic strategic decisions (Part II)

Global core strategy

Intended strategic position (Ch. 8)
Success patterns of the organization
Major objectives and priorities
International branding
Served market

Rules of business behavior (Ch. 9)
- Confrontation
- Cooperation
- Acquisitions
- Innovation
- Quality guidelines

Leadership

Resource allocation (Ch. 10)
International expansion
Determination of local market-entry
  strategy
Organization
Control of effectiveness

Building and sustaining the intended global position (Part III)

Marketing mix decisions

Product/service (Ch. 11)
- Policy
- Product portfolio management
- Brand management
- Quality management

Distribution (Chs 12–14)
- Policy
- Systems/channels
- Sales management
- Logistics

Market communication (Ch. 15)
- Policy
- Advertising
- Stakeholder relations
- Sales promotion
- Sponsoring
- Direct market commmunication

Pricing (Ch. 16)
- Policy
- Prices
- Terms of payment
- Managing financial risks
- Countertrade

International marketing plan (Ch. 17)

impact on what is suitable in international market communication and what is doomed to failure. Even familiar market communication techniques or media vary considerably across country markets. Chapter 15 discusses the need for a communication policy to integrate the various communication activities of an internationally operating firm. Opportunities for pursuing a highly standardized approach to international market communication are analyzed and contrasted with necessities for local adaptation.

Chapter 16 focuses on an important concern for international marketers: *how to set prices and negotiate terms of payment* that will help to make the company's offers even more attractive to potential customers and provide the firm with sufficient profit. Here again, international marketers face a wider set of issues than domestic marketers. They have to consider a whole range of additional risks that can be covered in various ways but at different costs; and they may be confronted with customers who are very attracted by the company's offer but have no money to pay for it. Countertrade is discussed as a means to resolve such problems.

To apply all available marketing tools in an effective and efficient manner allowing the intended global strategic position to be reached, an *international marketing plan* has to be established. Chapter 17 presents the content of such a plan, and discusses the problems related to its development as well as methods for resolution of those problems. Financial and managerial accounting issues to be considered for a presentation of the international marketing plan to top management or to financial institutions are also covered.

INTERNATIONAL PRODUCT MANAGEMENT

11

Learning objectives

After studying this chapter you will be able to:

- describe the concept of the total product
- explain why a company operating internationally needs a policy governing its international product management
- discuss potential ways of product standardization and adaptation
- describe potential ways of product individualization
- explain the importance of guidelines for an international product portfolio
- discuss the distribution of managerial responsibilities concerning international product management
- explain the importance of a balanced product portfolio to a company's long-term success
- describe the specifics of product innovation processes in firms operating internationally
- explain the importance of choosing an attractive brand name
- discuss the problems of brand protection
- explain the importance of quality assurance for customer satisfaction
- outline the role of packaging in the branding of a product
- explain the relationship between customer satisfaction and quality assurance
- describe the role of quality signaling in the formation of customer expectations
- explain the influence of product management processes on the marketing mix

Chapter outline

International product decisions

The total product
Level of customer integration
Material and immaterial benefits
The product system

International customers
Emotional involvement
Importance for core competence
Meanings

International product policy
Product positioning
Degree of standardization
Product portfolio
Management responsibilities

International product portfolio management
Product lifecycle
Portfolio balance
International product innovation

Product brand management
Choice of brand name
Brand protection
Packaging
Consistency of international product brand management

Product quality management
Customer satisfaction
Quality assurance
Quality signaling

Impact on marketing mix
Pricing
Distribution
Market communication

Summary

INTERNATIONAL MARKETING SPOTLIGHT

Avent: Rolls-Royce of baby products

Avent was born because of the anxieties of a young British entrepreneurial father. Actually, because his first son refused to drink from a traditional baby bottle, Edward Atkin had the idea of creating an anti-colic bottle. This was in 1984. Since then, product lines have been expanded by more than 10 innovations, such as a manual milk pump, a microwave sterilizer, an isolation box, and a pacifier with a luminous ring.

The company has built four modern production sites in the U.K. It owns subsidiaries in the U.S. and in Singapore, employs about 1,000 people, and reaches sales of about €200 million. More than 75% of sales come from international business. As a globally active firm that exports to 70 countries all over the globe, Avent gains market share from its local competitors. With 47% market share Avent is the leader in the babycare segment in its home country.

What have been Avent's success factors so far? A limited number of highly innovative products for higher income parents who want to do the best for their babies and who can pay prices that are about 20% higher than competitors. Perfection in value generation: No new product is launched that is not considered to be the best in its category. And closeness to the customers: Sales representatives gather firsthand information for product innovations from parents who talk about their problems in caring for their loved ones.

The focal question of this chapter is: How can an international marketer develop a bundle of products that allow building and sustaining the intended global strategic position of the firm?

International product decisions

The core of the marketing mix is the bundle of benefits offered by the company to the potential customers via its product. To satisfy the customers those benefits must be attractive and fulfill the customers' expectations. The other elements of the marketing mix – price, distribution, and market communication – must be carefully managed as well, but they cannot compensate for a product that does not fulfill customers' desires. Therefore, positioning decisions are at the heart of product management: Potential customers have to be carefully chosen. Product features as well as processes that are part of the product have to be selected in a way that ensures attractive differentiation recognized by those customers, in comparison to benefits offered by competitors' products.

When a company decides to go international, it must find out whether its products and product lines can be kept unchanged, or if they must be altered, and, if so, to what degree: Changes may be needed in more than the core product. Customer expectations concerning service, warranties, packaging, or width and depth of the product line may be different. The international marketer has to ascertain whether new products need to be developed. The marketer may have to create added features and will manage symbolic features, such as reliability, in a way to offer the most attractive bundle of benefits to customers in all served country markets.

To be able to take the described decisions in an effective way, international marketers must first make sure they know exactly who the customers or decision makers to be targeted are.

That is, the international marketer needs to know its customers closely before taking product management decisions. In a general way the firm's customers have been determined by the intended global strategic position (Chapter 8), which defined the product markets to be served (Figure 11.1). The positioning

FIGURE 11.1   *International marketing decision process*

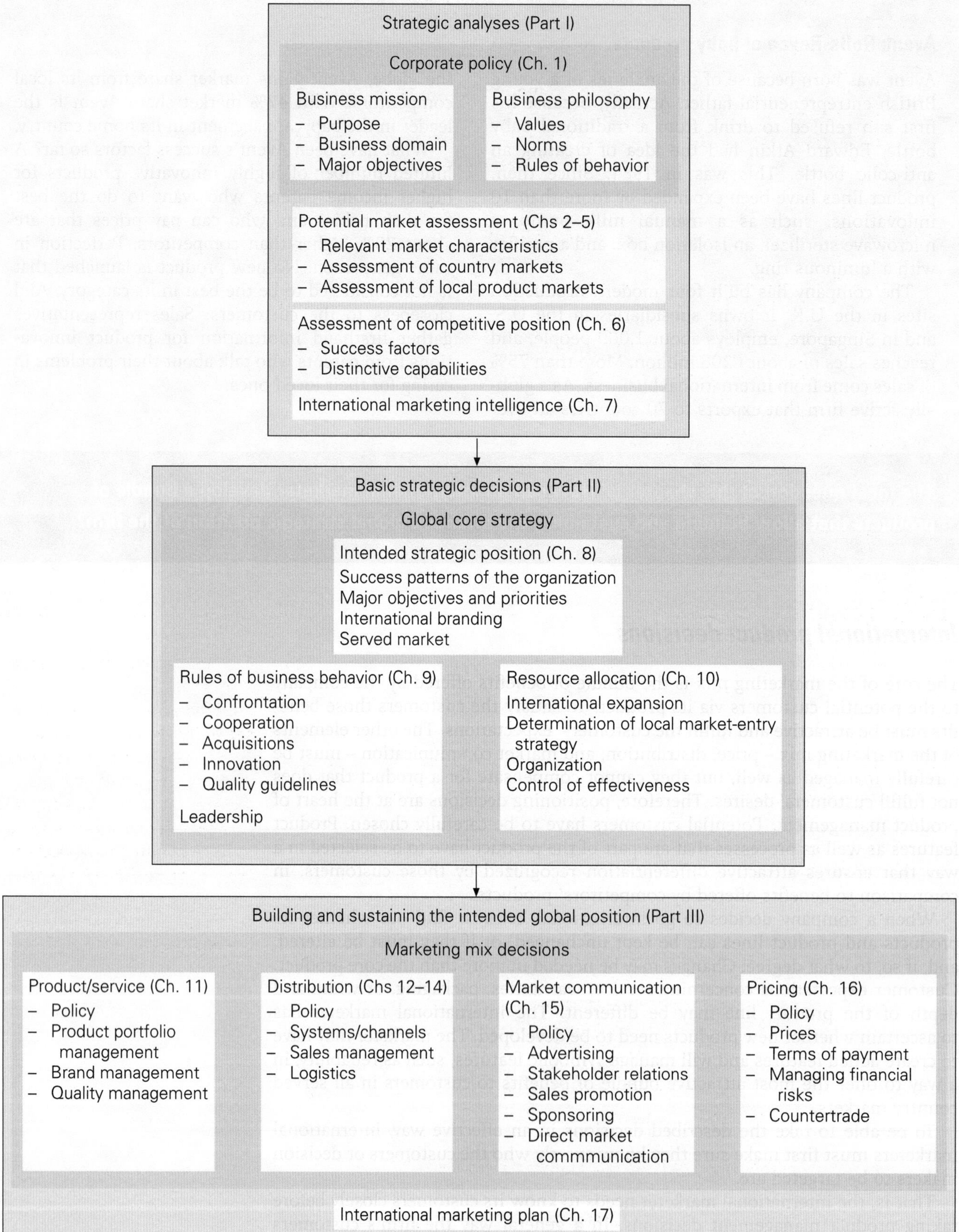

Strategic analyses (Part I)

Corporate policy (Ch. 1)

Business mission
- Purpose
- Business domain
- Major objectives

Business philosophy
- Values
- Norms
- Rules of behavior

Potential market assessment (Chs 2–5)
- Relevant market characteristics
- Assessment of country markets
- Assessment of local product markets

Assessment of competitive position (Ch. 6)
- Success factors
- Distinctive capabilities

International marketing intelligence (Ch. 7)

Basic strategic decisions (Part II)

Global core strategy

Intended strategic position (Ch. 8)
Success patterns of the organization
Major objectives and priorities
International branding
Served market

Rules of business behavior (Ch. 9)
- Confrontation
- Cooperation
- Acquisitions
- Innovation
- Quality guidelines

Leadership

Resource allocation (Ch. 10)
International expansion
Determination of local market-entry
  strategy
Organization
Control of effectiveness

Building and sustaining the intended global position (Part III)

Marketing mix decisions

Product/service (Ch. 11)
- Policy
- Product portfolio
  management
- Brand management
- Quality management

Distribution (Chs 12–14)
- Policy
- Systems/channels
- Sales management
- Logistics

Market communication (Ch. 15)
- Policy
- Advertising
- Stakeholder relations
- Sales promotion
- Sponsoring
- Direct market
  commmunication

Pricing (Ch. 16)
- Policy
- Prices
- Terms of payment
- Managing financial
  risks
- Countertrade

International marketing plan (Ch. 17)

statement of the responsible organizational unit specifies the target customers (Chapter 10). But many organizational units will be responsible for more than one product. Therefore, target customers for each of the products may need to be specified before any marketing mix decisions can be taken. The discussion in this chapter is based on the previously taken decisions and the data gathered for the purpose of taking them. It will focus on how international marketers react to different environments and product-related customer behavior by standardizing part of their total products, adapting or even individualizing them (Figure 11.2).

First, the marketer has to *assess what constitutes its product from the customers' perspective*. For that purpose, a view of the product as a sequence of process steps in which customers are more or less integrated, and as a bundle of material and immaterial results generated by these processes, has proven to be useful (Chapter 9). This view ends the discussion about how to distinguish products from services because every good has immaterial features, such as product information, and to a certain extent involves customers in its development, production, or delivery process. The "total product" perspective opens an integrative view on how to market all kinds of products internationally.

In the following stages, an *international product policy is to be developed*. A firm's product policy statement contains guidelines for:

- product positioning
- intended level of standardization
- product branding
- product portfolio management.

FIGURE 11.2 International product and services management

The international product manager must know how similar potential customers are in the markets to serve. This information helps to determine the appropriate levels of customer integration and immateriality of the firm's products. An international product policy has to be developed. This product policy serves as a guideline for decisions concerning the firm's product portfolio, packaging, and the quality management of the total product.

The general directions given indicate the goals to be achieved by day-to-day operations as well as the limits of decisions and actions to be respected by central as well as local units. The product policy also determines *distribution of responsibilities among managers and management teams* concerning product management issues.

Finally, international product management processes can be executed. The most important processes in international product management are:

- product portfolio management
- brand management
- quality management.

All three cover more than one functional area of the firm, requiring the interfunctional integration of various sub-processes to achieve their goals.

Product portfolio management has multiple goals. Primarily its goal is to supply the markets served by the company with a stream of regularly renewed products that are attractive to customers, competitive compared to other suppliers' products, and profitable to the company.

Brand management tries to achieve and maintain a consistent meaning of the products to customers that positively differentiates them from competitors' products and simplifies customers' decision-making processes in a way that is profitable to the firm.

The goal of quality management is to keep customer satisfaction with the company's products at the highest levels in order to create as many loyal customers as possible and to ensure positive endorsements from them to other potential customers.

The total product

Level of customer integration

As discussed in Chapter 9, all consumer and business/government goods as well as all kinds of services can be positioned on a continuum ranging from highly integrative to highly autonomous according to their value generation processes. Depending on the kind of interaction with the customer, where in the process customers are integrated, how often they are integrated, and to what level of intensity, product management decisions will differ.

If the supplier and the customer of a product need to have physical contact to produce customer value, the product is bound to a certain location. Such products cannot be traded and therefore cannot be exported. Internationalization of business in such cases can only be achieved through international multiplication of self-operated or foreign-operated production sites, such as McDonald's.

Contrariwise, if the contact between marketer and customer may be time- and space-wise decoupled via some intermediary (for example, a retailer) or media (such as a computer), the product can be traded and exported. Banking services, for example, for most of their history were bound to the physical location of a bank and its branch offices. They could only be internationalized by opening up subsidiaries or cooperating closely with local banks. Since then, electronic banking has made banking services independent of specific locations, and therefore exportable.

The parts of value creation and generation processes that take place in the presence of the customers are above their line of visibility. They strongly influence customer perception of product quality and their satisfaction with the product. Some of those parts are locally independent, such as a call center taking orders or treating customer complaints. Invisible parts of value creation or generation processes are all locally independent. They can be performed wherever is best for the supplier, if the parts or elements of the total product produced in a distant location can be physically or virtually transferred to the place of consumption or use. For example, for the consumer of a pizza delivery service, the order-taking process via the phone and the end of the delivery process are above the line of visibility. Where the pizza is made and how it is transported to the customer is up to the producer as long as the delivery time is short enough and the pizza that is delivered looks and tastes good.

Material and immaterial results

In international product management, it is critical to remember that customers may be attracted to a product by both material and immaterial features (see Chapter 9). Customers do not evaluate and choose a mere good. They buy a *bundle of benefits* that they expect to enjoy through the consumption or use of the total product, that is, the combination of material and immaterial features offered by a supplier. Coca-Cola, for example, is more than just a soft drink. In several languages, "Coke is It." This slogan recognizes that coke is more than a physical product. It offers refreshment, enjoyment, entertainment, and represents the "American Way of Life," all of which are immaterial features but are part of the total product.

Customers of an international advertising agency such as U.S.-based Grey Advertising expect the agency to do more than produce international and local campaigns that reach their objectives. They also value personal contacts with a known partner in different parts of the world and the standard application of tools they have experience with. In addition, the name of the agency and its country of origin as well as special references may evoke positive associations in the managers who decide which partner to choose for market communication purposes.

Products conceived as combinations of material and immaterial results of a firm's value generation process are not limited to goods and services. Ideas (which are immaterial only), people, and organizations can also be marketed internationally. For example, social issues such as population control can be marketed in an attempt to change people's ideas about family-planning practices. To increase the attractiveness of population control measures, for example, in many cases material incentives were added to the idea, such as portable radios for people willing to accept surgery. Politicians, such as candidates for General Secretary of the United Nations or the WTO, are internationally marketed by their governments, but also by interested foreign governments. When social organizations such as UNICEF or the Red Cross use marketing techniques for international fund raising, the organizations themselves can often be the products "sold." But in any case, seen from the customer perspective, the offered product consists of a bundle of benefits that can be gained from the product's material and immaterial features.

The product system

Both value creation and value generation processes, as well as their results, interactively influence the benefits customers derive from the total product. The total product can therefore be conceived as a system containing elements as shown in Figure 11.3.

Core product

The core product is the starting point of a potential market transaction. In certain cases, it might be sufficient to provide the core product. For example, when a well-informed person searches for an overview of potential forms of capital investment offered by an international bank, he or she may be satisfied with the information provided by the bank's home page on the internet. In most cases, however, the potential customers expect more than the core product to regard an offer as relevant. The investor might, for example, firmly expect to be personally informed about the choices offered.

Expected features

Potential customers tend to have different expectations depending on their knowledge of and experience with existing offers. Consequently, in international marketing the features expected by potential customers from different country markets vary in composition and importance. Internorm, Europe's second-largest manufacturer of doors and windows based in Austria, for example, found expectations of Spanish customers concerning technical standards such as cold and noise resistance as well as workmanship to be very different from those of its German and Austrian customers. The reasons for those differences in expectations arise not only out of climatic conditions of the countries and the varying style of living; they are also a result of the product offers consumers are acquainted with in their own markets.

Added features

The international marketer must decide how important it is to adapt the firm's product to the expectations in the served markets. The need for adaptation will depend on the customers' willingness to trade off some expected features for unexpected "added" features (see Figure 11.3). When introducing its Lexus model into the U.S., Toyota, for example, offered its potential customers a car that looked a lot like a Mercedes but without the same level of prestige. Toyota not only counteracted this lack with a lower price, they also offered two weeks' trials, and offered to deliver the ordered car to the customer's home and to program the electronically adaptable driver's seat for various family members in advance. All these were added features not expected by but very welcome to the American customers. By way of contrast, when Internorm, the Austrian window producer, tried to convince its potential Spanish customers that higher technical standards and resulting energy savings – also not expected by the customers – would justify a higher price for windows and doors, they failed.

FIGURE 11.3 *Total product system*

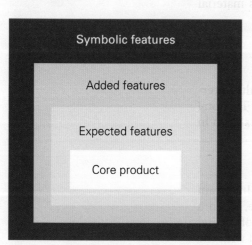

For example: A PC

Brand, country of origin

Free software updates, 24-hour service, free internet provision

CD-ROM drive, basic software, reliability

CPU, screen, board, mouse, processing software, user manual

A total product consists of the core product, additional features expected by the potential customers, added features and symbolic features the supplier can provide to increase the total product's attractiveness, and the processes leading to those features.

International marketers increasingly offer product features added to the features expected by customers in a local market to differentiate their products attractively from competitors. Emenegildo Zegna, the Italian menswear maker, for example, offered clients who buy a Zegna suit an "idea card" that entitled them to all sorts of privileges: once a year for a 2-year period the suit was cleaned and, if needed, repaired; should the suit be stolen or lost, the company promised to replace it at a 50% discount and the client was also entitled to a 50% discount on his son's first Zegna suit.

Symbolic features

When potential customers are affluent relative to the price of a product or when they perceive the offered products as being largely similar, emotional attraction becomes more important in their buying decision. A product's symbolic features can be decisive. Car buyers all over the world, for example, will always watch the price category and will expect certain additional services. But when the decision regarding a price category has been taken, very often symbolic features such as brand, country of origin, status symbol, or the signal of belonging to a specific social group become important. Why would anybody buy an expensive Ferrari were it not for the emotional benefit the purchase produced?

Ferraris have added "symbolic" features
©Richard Naude/Alamy

International customers

An in-depth knowledge of which customers may be interested in the marketer's product and what customers use the product for may be extremely helpful in designing customer value creation and generation processes. For example, Scott Wallace, the owner of Wallace Theater Corp., which runs multiplex cinema screens in 12 states of the U.S., opened a multi-screen cinema on Tutuila Island in American Samoa. He was convinced that his competition was the church. Consumers are not allowed to eat in church. Therefore, at Nu'uuli Place Cinemas they were offered local favorites like Mochi Crunch, a rice cracker, and dried squid chunks as well as nachos, popcorn, and soda.

Emotional involvement

In most cases consumers buy products for their own use or for the use of a family member. Organizational buyers mostly buy for others. Their emotional involvement in the buying process, therefore, is different because it is derived from organizational objectives. Governments and public administrations make their purchases in fields such as defense and public protection, infrastructure, healthcare, education, and tourism to fulfill their public mission. People purchasing for their own use also derive from that mission. Business customers use a product for the production of their company's own product.

Importance for core competence

If a supply is highly important to the core competence of a business customer, the international marketer will need to closely follow the exact specifications of the customer in order to stay in business. If customers consider the supply as less important to their core competence the supplier may take over responsibility for entire parts of the customer's value-added chain. For example, an industrial services firm taking over all maintenance activities for the equipment of an electric generator manufacturer may have full responsibility but also the freedom to do the job its way, whereas a supplier of preformed steel sheets for car-making customers will have to deliver exactly according to technical and logistical specifications.

Meanings

Compared to marketers selling to business firms or public administrations, international consumer product marketers particularly have to watch the meanings of their products. The meaning of a product to its buyers or users may be based on its functionality, on the joy the possession of the product can provide, the personal relationships and social belongingness it can help to express, and the product's ability to represent the identity of the customer.

Each customer constructs the meaning of a product in a situation-specific way depending on personal experiences, social relations, and situational circumstances that seem relevant at the moment. That is, the variety of potential meanings of a marketer's product in international markets is caused by more than just different cultural environments. It is also a result of varying individual product perceptions in different situations. Therefore, the marketer must carefully assess the potential meanings of its product if the firm wants to actively shape its value creation and generation processes and their results, and target them to individuals or specific consumer benefit segments.

International product policy

International product managers must be aware that their customers may be attracted by benefits derived from features at all levels of the product system as well as by the processes that generate those benefits. Depending on culture-dependent preferences, the specifics of the local environment, and competitive offers, potential customers of a product may not only have varying expectations but may also derive different benefits from the same processes and features, or the same benefits from different processes and features of a product. For example, a Vietnamese owner of a Honda motorcycle may be satisfied by the opportunity to buy gasoline bottled in the back of a hut. A Swedish owner of the same bike may expect his gasoline station to tank up, clean, and service the motorcycle while he is buying a soft drink in the shop.

The importance and meaning of processes and features constituting a product from the customers' point of view not only depend on personal predispositions but also on influences from the environment the customers live in. Thus, the variety of product management decisions in international marketing tends to be much broader than it is in local business. The total products of internationally operating firms must be adaptable to local needs.

Flexibility and variety, however, strongly contrast with the desire of most company managers to keep the complexity of their product features and processes low. To avoid unnecessary complexity and resulting cost, an international product policy has to be developed (Figure 11.4). It is based on the intended global strategic position of the firm, a detailed analysis of potential international customers' driving forces, and the current total product. The international product policy provides guidelines concerning:

- product positioning
- degree of product standardization
- product portfolio
- management responsibilities.

Product positioning

A company's international product positioning defines the global differentiation of its products from their major competitors. That is, the central benefit of each product is to be determined independently of the country markets to be served.

For digital cameras the central benefit could be, for example, the instant delivery of the picture; for Cartier watches it could be the social status or the self-confidence transferred to the customer wearing the product.

The local target group(s) and adaptations needed to produce the central benefit do not need to be defined. Even the brand name used locally may be up to the local managers. The U.K.'s Unilever, for example, marketed a product that was variously called Kuschelweich in Germany, Snuggles in the U.S., Huggy in Australia, Coccolino in Italy, and Cajoline in France. But the primarily emotional benefits offered were the same everywhere: security, trust, softness, and affection.

Because of the rising mobility of customers in many countries, such a formulation of product positioning has proven to be more useful than a detailed definition of product features accompanied by total freedom of communicative differentiation. Customers becoming aware of largely varying presentations of "their" product from one country to another do not appreciate such differences.

To provide the central benefit defined in the product positioning statement to individual customers in various country markets, adaptation of product features or of processes, which result in those features, may be needed. Nestlé, for example, used the brand name Bolino to offer its instant soups to young French singles as a snack. In Germany they called the product Maggi 5 Minuten Terrine and positioned it as nutritious and balanced food for 30 to 40 year olds. And in Switzerland the same product was marketed under the brand name Quick Lunch as a fast meal young people can enjoy with their mothers' consent. However, any change in process or the design of a product has an effect on its costs. In many cases, the cost of a product increases with the number and diversity of adaptations to local or even individual particularities. Therefore, the international product manager must define guidelines to what extent the firm's products should be standardized, locally adapted, or even individualized.

FIGURE 11.4 *International product policy*

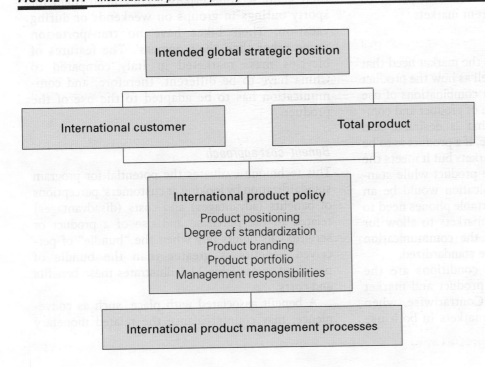

An international product policy is based on the intended global strategic position of the firm as well as the international customers' driving forces, decision-making processes, and product usage.

Degree of standardization

The degree of similarity among a company's international product markets largely determines the extent to which its marketing activities can be the same or similar across country markets, that is, to what extent they can be standardized. Standardization may occur either in marketing programs, that is, the marketing strategies, policies, and activities of a company or in marketing processes, that is, procedures followed by a firm in making marketing decisions, implementing them, and controlling their outcomes. The greatest experience curve effects occur when both programs and processes are standardized.

The Coca-Cola Company has almost totally standardized the marketing program for its flagship brand, Coke. Travelers to all parts of the world readily recognize the product's red and white logo, whatever language is used to identify it. The company's goal is to achieve "one sight, one sound" brand recognition throughout the world. Corporations including McDonald's, Benetton and HILTI have also standardized their marketing programs with considerable success.

Both Procter & Gamble and Nestlé are well known for the high degree of standardization of their marketing processes. Their product concept testing, advertising campaign development, and evaluation of distribution investments, for example, follow stepwise procedures outlined in manuals. Toolbox 11.1 describes some approaches that may be helpful in deciding how much to standardize marketing programs and processes.

TOOLBOX 11.1   Evaluating the potential for program and process standardization

Program standardization

There are several techniques that can be used to evaluate the potential for marketing program standardization. One is the use–need model, which examines the way a product is used in comparison with the need it fulfills. Another is the benefit–cost approach, which analyzes the balance between the customer's perceived benefits and the perceived "costs" of the product in different markets.

Use–need model

The use–need model evaluates the market need that is met by a given product as well as how the product is used (see Figure 11.5). Four combinations of use and need determine the degree of product and communication standardization that is desirable and their related costs. For example, if a product is to be used differently in different markets but it meets the same basic need, adapting the product while standardizing its market communication would be an appropriate decision. Thus, portable phones need to be reengineered for different markets to allow for differences in standards, but the communication theme of "easiest use" could be standardized.

Only when use and need conditions are the same, are fully standardized product and market communication appropriate. Contrariwise, when differences between country markets in both use and need are great, a totally adapted program is needed. For example, an Italian bicycle manufacturer such as Bianchi, which compares the need for bikes and their use in its home market to their need and use in China, will find great differences in both. Italians do not need their bikes as family transport as well as for professional purposes like their Chinese counterparts. They need them for sporty outings in groups on weekends or during vacation. Their bikes have no transportation usage other than their owners'. The features of bicycles mass marketed in Italy compared to China have to be different, therefore, and communication has to be adapted to the use of the product.

Benefit–cost approach

This technique evaluates the potential for program standardization by looking at customers' perceptions of benefits (advantages) and costs (disadvantages) related to the purchase and use of a product or service. Customers buy when the "bundle" of perceived benefits is greater than the bundle of perceived costs. Table 11.1 illustrates these benefits and costs.

A benefit associated with place, such as convenience, may counterbalance the related monetary costs, thereby encouraging a purchase. In societies that value convenience highly, such as the U.S., consumers will pay a higher price to gain convenience; in other societies, such as Pakistan, convenience may be perceived as irrelevant or of low value. A lower price might be more important.

Different perceptions of benefits as well as different perceptions of costs, such as the gain or loss of social prestige through the use of a foreign product, suggest that the company needs to adapt the marketing mix for different consumer groups. By

the same token, if perceived benefits are similar – for example, the sensory benefits of color and style – the company may offer a more standardized marketing mix.

One way to analyze customers' perceptions of benefits and costs related to a product or service is to assess their cognitive structures by the use of the so-called "laddering" technique and to compare to what extent the same benefits and costs are related to the total product by customers in different country markets.

FIGURE 11.5 Use–need model

Use condition

	Same	Different
Same	Same product Same promotion Cost = 1	Adapt product Same promotion Cost = 3
Different	Same product Adapt promotion Cost = 2	Adapt product Adapt promotion Cost = 4

Buyer need

Cost 1 = lowest
Cost 4 = highest

Source: Based on Keegan, W.J. (1969) "Multinational product planning: Strategic alternatives", *Journal of Marketing*, January, pp. 58–62

TABLE 11.1 *Illustrations of perceived benefits and costs*

Type	Customer benefits	Customer costs
Sensory	Appealing appearance, feel, sound, smell, or taste	Unpleasant appearance, feel, sound, smell, or taste
Psychological	Positive state of mind (feeling good, generous, satisfied)	Negative state of mind (feeling bad, guilty)
Place	Attractive, convenient, or comfortable	Unattractive, inconvenient, or uncomfortable
Time	When desired	Time spent in obtaining information, purchasing, or using product
Economic	Potential for resale, enhanced earning power, lower relative financial cost	Higher relative financial costs, high total costs

Source: Adapted from Lovelock, C. and C. Weinberg (1984) *Marketing for Nonprofit Organizations*, New York: John Wiley & Sons, p. 48

Process standardization

In deciding whether to standardize marketing processes, two factors must be considered: (1) sequence of activities, and (2) dynamics and homogeneity of the environments.

Sequence of activities

To gain efficiency effects from process standardization, processes need to be an uninterrupted sequence of foreseeable activities. Routines of behavior, such as physical product quality tests or the calculation of break-even analyses for investments in logistics facilities, can be standardized fairly easily.

If a sequence of activities is adaptive, that is, it is interrupted by purely intellectual steps (considerations) that determine the following activities, their standardization potential is low. The creative processes of research and development, for example, are rather difficult to standardize.

Dynamics and homogeneity of environments

The standardization potential of marketing processes also depends on the dynamics and homogeneity of a firm's environments. A company that specializes in biotechnological problem solutions for their customers, for example, will have difficulties in standardizing its marketing processes because of the dynamic development of its technological environment and the low level of homogeneity in the legal regulations of potential country markets. Where innovative behavior is needed, process standardization is not advisable. Guidelines can be given that indicate a certain sequence of steps be followed and a number of techniques from which to choose. For example, the pre-testing of advertisements can be imposed on sales subsidiaries and a number of approved testing techniques can be determined.

Product standardization

Basically, international marketers have three ways to standardize their products: product extension, the premium prototype approach, and a global common denominator policy.

Product extension This involves the use of the product presentation developed for a single country market in all other served country markets. This policy can be justified if management has good reasons (not ethnocentric reasons or ignorance of the specific conditions in other markets) to consider the reference market to be a lead market for the product category. A lead market is a market that shows how demand in other markets is likely to develop. In the field of information technology products, for example, the U.S. is a lead market for all other countries in the world.

Premium prototype policy When choosing this method of standardization, the marketer identifies the most demanding customers and conditions of product use – which may not be specific to any single country market – and develops an appropriate standard product to meet these conditions. For example, in its effort to cut costs by producing vehicles and parts for markets worldwide instead of making an array of vehicles that are different for each continent, Detroit-based General Motors, which in 1995 had 12 different types of four-cylinder engine alone, decided to adopt a global engine policy. GM invested $1.3 billion to develop a generation of four-cylinder engines for use around the world.

The major problem with such a policy is that many customers may not need the product features of their most demanding peers or may live in environments with lower quality and performance standards. They may be unwilling to pay for a level of performance that seems exaggerated to them. As a consequence the cost savings from standardization may be eaten up by the lower margins.

Global common denominator policy The goal of this method is to define an international product market that contains customers that can be served with a standardized product. Such standardization is possible as long as functional benefits dominate the customers' perceptions, or the product is similarly used across cultural environments. Examples of product categories where functional benefits dominate in most customer segments are PCs, software, camcorders, calculators, and suitcases. SAP, based in Walldorf, Germany, for example, which has a market share of more than one-third of all business administration software sold worldwide, sells standard software packages. Culture box 11.1 gives an example of a consumer product for which a common denominator policy seems applicable.

A global common denominator policy may also work for customer segments containing a large share of highly mobile early adopters who have experienced a product in one country, want to be able to use it in others, and present the product to other customers as highly attractive. This, for instance, may have been the reason for the early success of Club Méditerranée, the French vacation resort company. They started with highly standardized resorts in various parts of the globe, which attracted highly mobile consumers who looked for an enjoyable but predictable vacation environment in a variety of destinations.

Finally, for some products such as pop music, "ethnic" food, beverages, fashion clothes, or luxury items adaptation would be counterproductive. Their major benefit stems from a symbolic value for their consumers, such as modernity, gender equality, status, or membership of a subculture. This symbolic value can only be provided if the product stays largely unadapted. The marketer should not overlook, however, that even for such products some adaptation may be well accepted by local customers. Mexican restaurants in the U.S. or in Europe, for example, are better off serving their food in not exactly the way it would be served in the home country.

Product adaptation

Product standardization does not work everywhere. For example, when Snapple, the U.S. icon beverage of the 1990s, was introduced in Japan in 1994 without any adaptation to suit local tastes, thousands of stores stocked peach-flavored iced tea, pink lemonade, and other Snapple variations. But by the end of 1995 Snapple sales had fallen to 120,000 bottles a month from a monthly 2.4 million bottles just a year earlier. In January 1996 Quaker Oats, the U.S.-based owner of the brand at that time, stopped shipping Snapple drinks to Japan. It had become clear that Japanese consumers loathe some of the very traits of the product: the cloudy

---

CULTURE BOX 11.1

Citibank blitzes Asia

From Bombay to Jakarta, Taipei to Seoul, Bangkok to Manila, "plastic" is proliferating in Asia at a terrific pace. One obvious reason is the growth of disposable income. Less obvious is the growth of independence. A growing number of consumers want to make their own credit decisions at the point of purchase without the hassle of negotiating specific credit availability.

Citibank identified a global consumer who behaves quite similarly wherever s/he is: They dine out, go to concerts and movies, take vacations, and buy consumer durables and clothing. Even though they may not all be westernized, they all have western spending habits. But not the western default habits: Citibank's loss rate on cards in Asia is just half of the 4% industry norm in the U.S.

There is status and prestige in holding plastic. Plastic is a payment instrument, but it is also a lifestyle product. A typical Citibank credit card ad featured a young Asian couple traveling to Paris, Spain, and New Orleans, staying in elegant hotels, driving fancy cars, sipping champagne, and eating sumptuous dinners. Few of Citibank's real-life customers fit the image, but they evidently like to identify with it. In Asia, getting a Citibank card for many consumers is still like gaining admission to a club.

Source: Adapted from Tanzer, A. (1996) "Citibank blitzes Asia", *Forbes*, 6 May, p. 44; www.lafferty.com/advisory/specialistreports/multiclient_2003/study2.asp

appearance of the teas, the sweet fruit juice flavorings – and all that *stuff* floating in the bottles.

Even the most careful determination of the global product market to serve and the choice of a well-defined customer segment often do not help avoid product adaptation to local customer needs and the demands of the macro-environment. For example, Procter & Gamble's Vidal Sassoon shampoos and conditioners contain a single fragrance worldwide, with variations only in the amount: less in Japan, where subtle scents are preferred, and more in Europe. Packages of Ariel detergent look the same all over eastern Europe, but they are printed in 14 languages, including Latvian to Lithuanian.

For the international marketer to enjoy many of the benefits of product standardization and, at the same time, respond to the adaptation demands of local markets, product modification can be applied. A modified product is one where the impact of the changes made in the product's features has a relatively minor influence on the firm's cost situation and marketing efficiency. Basically, there are two product modification policies to choose from: modular modification and the core product approach.

An international marketer who opts for a **modular modification policy** has to develop a standard range of product components, usable worldwide, that can be assembled in a variety of configurations. Such components can be physical products but also immaterial features and processes. Efficiency is likely to be greatest when the physical components are mass produced at single locations, immaterial features and processes are highly standardized, and the number of variants of each is strictly limited. For example, Benton Harbor, U.S.-based Whirlpool Corporation mass produces the physical components of its high-end European Bauknecht brand products, uses pan-European advertising to assure its standardized positioning, but modifies trade marketing activities around promotion and merchandising, and the day-to-day pricing activities with trade partners.

The application of a **core product policy** of international product modification requires the design of a standard core product that can be locally adapted by adding different features or processes. For example, U.S.-based Massey-Fergusson can develop a standard tractor for agricultural use that is designed to operate under various climatic and topographic conditions, which can be equipped additionally with special components adapting the standard product to its specific use. Sixt, the Germany-based international rental car company, as another example, can use the same basic operations system all over the world, specifically adapting the kinds of cars offered to local customers.

Product individualization

Product standardization and product adaptation policies are based on the idea that strategically determined global product markets can be split into well-defined customer segments, which, in turn, can be served with internationally standardized or locally adapted products. However, increasing global competition has made it difficult for many companies located in highly industrialized countries to rely on cost leadership to sell internationally standardized products at a competitive price. Such companies may be forced to improve their competitive market position by increasing the value their products offer to customers. For the individual customer, most additional value comes from an increase in the personal benefits derived from a product. But even products carefully adapted to local conditions represent an average that is offered to the "average" customer of the selected market segment. As a result, there is a gap between the company's offering and what each customer expects.

International product individualization   This seems to be a potential solution. That is, the marketer needs to treat every single customer as a market segment with specific requirements that must be fulfilled. First, the marketer will have to determine the points of common uniqueness, that is, to find out where the potential customers generally differ in their needs, expected benefits, usage, or consumption behavior. To get a complete picture, the product features have to be considered as well as all processes generating customer value. From this analysis, the marketer can decide which features and processes to individualize and at which stage in the value creation and generation process – during product design, production, delivery, or use – to provide the greatest customer value at the lowest possible cost.

Individualization can be achieved in one of the following four ways: adaptive, cosmetic, autonomous or collaborative.

Adaptive individualization This approach may be appropriate when customers want a product to perform in different ways on different occasions. That is, the company offers one standard product that is designed in a way that allows users to alter it themselves. For example, software applications have the built-in technical potential to be adapted to the needs of individual customers by the customers themselves. Carseats, fashion watches, or homeshopping services may accommodate different users having different needs at different times. Customers independently derive their own individual value from the standard product because it allows multiple permutations changing the product's functionality and/or its emotional value.

Because it is the product itself, rather than the supplier that interacts with the customer, adaptive individualization is readily applicable in international marketing. For example, America Online, the U.S. online provider gives its global subscribers the ability to create their own stock portfolios that list only the particular equities and funds they wish to track. In addition, it automatically delivers information from financial publications on the investments in the customers' portfolio, saving them considerable time in searching for information.

Cosmetic individualization When customers in an international product market use a product the same way but differ in the benefits they expect the marketer may choose a policy of **cosmetic individualization**. The company offers a standard core product with a certain number of expected features, which delivers the functional (basic) benefit. Added as well as symbolic product features and the processes generating them are individualized to provide added value. For example, Hertz Corp., the world-leading rental car company based in the U.S., uses standard rental cars in its #1 Club Gold Program. But customers belonging to the program bypass the line at the counter, get shuttle service to the car park, find their name displayed on a screen that directs them to the location of their car, find the trunk of the car open for their luggage, and the heater or air conditioner turned on as the weather demands it.

Efforts to individualize total products with large shares of tangible features and highly autonomous value generation processes in a cosmetic manner will focus near or at the end of the value generation process. For example, the name of the client may be added to a clock face, or a strap chosen by the customer may be mounted to give the watch a personal note. By the same token, when a product is highly integrative and most of its features are immaterial, those processes that involve customers and can make a positive difference from the customers' point of view will be individualized. For example, a bank operating internationally, such as Utrecht (Netherlands)-based Rabobank International, which focuses on corporate, investment and private banking in more than 30 countries in Europe, the Americas and Asia/Australia, will have largely standardized back-office procedures but may design its offices and train its customer contact personnel so that they treat their customers according to their individual expectations.

Autonomous individualization This may be chosen when customers' needs are well known or are at least identifiable and when the customers do not particularly bother with the product because it does not seem important enough to them. Companies such as the Franco-U.K. Sema Group or U.S.-based Electronic Data Systems, both specialists in computer services, for example, take over all hard- and software installation, integration and maintenance activities of their industrial customers. The customers – in the case of Sema they are mainly cellular operators in Europe and Asia – outsource their computer systems activities because they are not part of their core competency. The marketers take over the responsibility of keeping the systems running at a specified level of availability.

The marketer observes the customers' behavior over time without direct information-gathering interactions. The product is individualized according to the determined preferences and usage behavior of each customer within a standard package. The customer may not even be aware of the individualization. For example, the consumption behavior of customers of Ritz-Carlton hotels is observed during each stay. The information is stored in a database, and service is tailored to each customer on the next visit.

Collaborative individualization When customers have to take one-time decisions based on difficult trade-offs between product features, such as comfort for elegance or flexibility for functionality, and when the decisions seem important enough to the customers to exert some effort, international marketers may decide to collaboratively individualize their product.

In this case supplier and customer together determine the features of the total product. The marketer helps the customers to articulate their expectations concerning the product and their problems by using products and services known to the customers. Together they identify the precise total product that fulfills the customer's needs. For example, Chicago-based International Components Corporation, a manufacturer of (battery) chargers, collaborates with its customers in all parts of the globe. In most cases customers approach the company with their product and ask ICC for advice on how to charge it. The company then designs and produces the charger for that product, with a prototype typically available for testing within a few weeks.

Such collaborative individualization has been the rule in most international contractual businesses such as mechanical or software engineering, legal services, or business consulting. A special example is employment services provided by temp agencies. International agencies, such as Netherlands-based Randstad are able to offer international clients an exclusive contract to provide them with the number of qualified personnel they need in all their operating units.

In international consumer product marketing, collaborative individualization has not found many supporters so far. By collaboratively individualizing its products, a company replaces back-end adaptations to local needs and circumstances with front-end specifications on how the most attractive product for the individual consumers should be designed. No inventories of finished products are waiting to find customers. Raw materials or component parts are stocked to be able to react quickly to individual demand. Customer contact personnel are trained to interact sensitively with clients who have strongly differing demands.

For example, Paris Miki, a Japanese eyewear retailer that owns the largest number of eyewear stores in the world, has developed the Mikissimes Custom Designed Eyewear System. The system first takes a digital picture of each customer's face and analyzes its characteristics as well as a set of customer statements concerning the kind of look he or she desires. Then it recommends a distinctive lens size and shape and displays the lenses on the digital image of the consumer's face. The consumer and the optician next jointly adjust the shape and size of the lenses until the customer is pleased with the look. In similar fashion, consumers select the nosebridge, hinges, and arms. Then they receive a photo-quality picture of themselves with the proposed spectacles. Finally, the spectacles are produced in an extremely short space of time.

Collaborative individualization can also take place in the production and delivery stages of a product, for example when customers specify where, when, and how the ordered products should be delivered. This is the case in just-in-time contracts between carmakers such as Italy's Fiat and its suppliers, but also in grocery home delivery services where customers can not only order the products they need but may also indicate when they want them to be delivered.

Product portfolio

The product portfolio of an international marketer contains a certain number of product lines, which are, in turn, characterized by an additional number of product variations. To optimize a company's international product portfolio, the marketer has to formulate rules on the **width** of the portfolio, that is, how many product lines should be offered internationally, and on the **depth** of the portfolio, that is, with how many variations of the total products.

But it is not only the width and depth of an international marketer's product portfolio that strongly influence the firm's success. The right balance may be as important from a long-term perspective. Therefore, guidelines concerning the intended age structure of the portfolio are of great importance.

Age structure

The age structure of a company's products influences its competitiveness and ability to finance operations in the long run. A lack of new products may heavily reduce the attractiveness of the firm's offer to its potential customers. Too many new products at a time may overdraw the financial capacity of a business organization. Management should, therefore, formulate a statement concerning the desired share of new products in the portfolio.

For example, 3M, the St. Paul and Austin, U.S.-based specialist for all kinds of coating and sticking, serving customers in nearly 200 countries, stated that 30% of its annual sales volume must come from products that are not more than 4 years old. In addition, they formulated the rule that 70% of "new products" must be more than simple replacements of current products. As a consequence they register dozens of patents every year and make a substantial part of their annual sales with "first-year" products.

Portfolio width

In most cases a broad product portfolio attracts a higher number of customers than a deep product portfolio by offering various versions of what is basically the same total product. A French marketer of winter sports equipment, such as Salomon, for example, which serves the New Zealand market with alpine skis, cross-country skis, ski poles, ski boots and ski clothes, but also with hiking shoes and equipment has a broader range of customers than a U.S. marketer of snow boards, such as Burton, which initially served the market only with an assortment of boards for different purposes. In the meantime Burton has teamed up with other brands, including Anon eye wear, Gravis footwear, Analog and R.E.D. to increase the width of its portfolio. A product portfolio restricted in width may make it more difficult to attract distribution partners or to run directly owned stores at a profit.

Firms such as the U.K.'s Virgin, in their focus on expansion, develop a tremendously broad portfolio of total products. As Table 11.2 shows, the company has not only taken on British Airways and survived, it also introduced its Virgin Megastores – large record, film, book, and multimedia stores – all over Europe and in the U.S. There are a variety of properties under the Virgin name, such as a bank, vodka, or hotels. But they all have the same essence: They are about innovation and value for money, and there is always an element of fun. Because the concept underlying all Virgin activities migrates across the product categories as well as across country market borders, there is marketing synergy in Virgin's portfolio.

However, too much creativity and an unrestricted range of fields of innovation in most cases reduces the company's focus on core capabilities. Increasing complexity tends to diminish an international marketer's financial success.

Portfolio depth

The number of potential customers is not directly related to the financial success of a firm. A marketer specializing in a small number of product lines but providing a great variation of versions, such as Wolford the Austrian tights, body, swimsuits and underwear maker, may better satisfy the specific needs of an international customer group or may be able to cater specifically to different customer groups in or across countries. A deep product portfolio may ease the positioning of an international marketer in its customers' minds and keep the costs of entering a new market at an acceptable level.

Contrariwise, powerful retailers are increasingly less willing to fill their shelves with a great variety of basically similar products of a supplier. Companies such as Procter & Gamble, therefore, have developed clear guidelines to reduce the depth of their international portfolios in an attempt to reduce costs and improve customer service.

Contribution to attractiveness and meaning

In taking the decision on how broad and deep the company's international product portfolio is going to be, the marketer should bear in mind that the major goal is to provide an attractive customer benefit and to lay the groundwork for the creation of a specific meaning of the firm's offer in the customers' minds. From this point of view, product lines and individual product variations may be analyzed according to their contribution to those goals. Some products that are needed in one country will not be of importance in another. Others that may be needed in a new country market to make the portfolio attractive to local customers may be added by procurement from external sources.

For example, when U.S.-based MCA decided to invest in its first international venture, a theme park in Osaka, Japan, it carefully investigated what kind of entertainment products Japanese customers wanted to buy. In that country, where Disney enjoys an almost religious reverence among consumers, making Tokyo Disneyland the most popular theme park in the world, it was particularly

---

TABLE 11.2 *Virgin's product portfolio*

Virgin Atlantic Airways	Virgin Megastores	In 20 years, Richard Branson has built up a highly diverse product portfolio.
Virgin Bank	Virgin Net	
Virgin Bride	Virgin Power House	
Virgin Cargo	Virgin Radio	
Virgin Cola	Virgin Railways	
Virgin Direct Financial Services	Virgin Records (sold to EMI)	
Virgin Express	Virgie Vie	
Virgin Games	Virgin Vision	
Virgin Holidays	Virgin Vodka	
Virgin Hotels and Pensions		

important to combine the right products in a portfolio of attractions that differentiates itself attractively from Disney.

Management responsibilities

International product management is a complex task involving various functions inside the company as well as outside partners. To produce the best quality from the customers' point of view, all processes needed for the creation and generation of customer value must be closely coordinated and optimized with the intended customer benefit. The marketer has to develop guidelines as to which processes should – in general – take place where in the company and who is responsible, which processes are to be outsourced, and which kinds of external partner are needed to cooperate.

Centralization

Depending on the driving forces of product innovation, research and development activities may be largely centralized, such as in the case of 3M, or the marketer may encourage locally operating business units to drive their own innovation. 3M runs 60 production plants all over the world. It has 30 technology platforms, that is, technological competency centers, and 25 worldwide product divisions. But all product ideas coming from the firm's various local sales organizations are centrally gathered. They are evaluated and, if considered relevant, introduced into the product development process. The only exception is electronics. Because 3M had a hard time finding electronics specialists willing to move to St. Paul, they centralized all innovation processes for this domain in Austin, Texas. The innovation success of 3M and other examples from the computer and pharmaceutical industries, such as Suisse Novartis, which has centralized all its antibiotics development in one location, illustrate that centralization of product development works well in technologically driven product markets.

If a company's success depends on the strength of its brands, centralized brand management has proven to be of great importance. Italian Armani or Prada, Ralph Lauren from the U.S., as well as Paris-based Givenchy, to give some examples, lead their brands very closely from their respective headquarters.

Global teams

In customer-driven product markets, it might be better to anticipate potentials arising from country market-specific differences in a multinational product development team. Procter & Gamble, for example, has had positive experiences with its "Euro Brand Teams" when developing new products for the European market. Such teams consist of people from the most important and the local units most interested in the new product development process.

When Ford Motor Company developed its "global car," marketed in North America as the Contour sedan, the executives of the automaker adopted videoconferencing and CAD/CAM technologies to create a car that would incorporate its best engineering, design, and marketing talent worldwide while also bringing to bear a vision of how a single car design could appeal at once to all major world markets. Rather than creating national product teams or convening elaborate design summits, Ford established a virtual work team to develop the car. In the virtual world, the product development team could transcend the limitations of time and space that characterize management in the physical world. They built and tested prototypes in a simulated computer environment and shared the designs and data with colleagues, 24 hours a day, around the world.

Local champions

Other companies such as W.L. Gore Inc., the U.S. fiber products firm, which has many small operating units all over the highly industrialized and fast-industrializing parts of the world, leave much of their product management activities to the initiative and dedication of local "champions." That is, managers who develop a new product project, regardless of position or function, are encouraged to go and get a budget from their "leader," may build a team of people from all international parts of the firm who are needed for and interested in the project, and take responsibility for its success. If the project is successful, a new operating unit may be constituted that manages the new product internationally.

The pressure to cut project costs and sharply reduce time to market for new products, that is, the cycle time from the product idea to the launch of the product, has led many companies to downsize their central product development groups. Motorola Inc., for example, in its effort to reduce product development cycle time by a factor of 10 in just 2 years, assigned the design of their products to where they are made, to the operating units. Trumpf, the Germany-based marketer of lasers and metal bending machines has established local competence centers for application research in specific technologies in their subsidiaries. Only basic research is carried out in the headquarters.

Outsourcing

The marketer will have to state in its product policy which product management processes or activities are considered as central to the firm's competency and therefore must be kept inside the company.

Some processes of product management may be outsourced to specialized firms, which hold highly specific resources and have acquired in-depth know-how that even a firm operating internationally could hardly build up economically itself. The Fraunhofer Institutes in Germany, for example, take over basic but also applied research projects from international marketers. Graz, Austria-based AVL is the leading developer of car engines in the world. Most new engines of carmakers from all over the world are at least partly developed by this company. Other specialized product management activities, such as searching for a brand name that is internationally acceptable and can be protected, may also be outsourced.

Networking

All processes creating and generating customer value have to be coordinated. For that purpose, close cooperation with selected suppliers, intermediaries, and customers may be required. However, cooperation does not automatically lead to improved use of pooled skills and resources. It has to be built on trusting relationships that need to be developed and maintained. Cooperation can also imply time-consuming communication processes and a drain of information and know-how to competitors. Therefore, the international marketer may wish to specify in its product policy statement how to choose suppliers, intermediaries, and customers with whom to build a network.

International product portfolio management

The most important process of international product management is to develop and maintain a competitive combination of products – a product portfolio – to be offered in the served product markets. That is, customers in those markets consider it as more attractive as offers from competitors and the cash flow generated by the given combination of products assures the long-term success of the firm. Development and maintenance of a successful product portfolio requires answering the following questions:

- Which current products of the company may be marketed internationally? Which products should *not* be offered internationally?
- How can the products to be marketed internationally be bundled into an attractive offer for the different local or regional markets served?

- What additional products are needed to increase the local or regional attractiveness of the current product portfolio? Should they be developed in-house or procured from suppliers?
- When should which product be introduced in which country market? When should products offered in international markets be eliminated?
- How much of the limited resources of time, capital, and capabilities are to be invested in which parts of the product portfolio?

Product lifecycle

For the development and maintenance of an attractive international product portfolio, the marketer needs to consider the international lifecycles of the product categories concerned. But the individual products constituting the portfolio will also be in different stages of their lifecycle, and those stages may vary across the served country markets. The duration of lifecycles will be different across products and so will the duration of their various stages. The shape of the total sales curve will not always follow its theoretically supposed form of an S. And, because of the increasing globalization of many product markets, the difference between the stages of a product's lifecycle across country markets tends to decrease. Nevertheless, the marketer will need to monitor the development of its products in their international markets and consider adequate reactions.

Stages

Because of the high costs of simultaneously introducing a product in more than one country market, lack of production capacities, or lack of personnel capabilities, a company may decide to enter country markets step by step. As a consequence, an internationally marketed product may be in different stages of its lifecycle across the various served country markets. For example, the strategy of New York-based Morgan Stanley, known for its expertise in worldwide underwriting and international mergers and acquisitions, has a strategy to build for the long term in a focused, gradual, and cost-conscious manner. The firm, now active in 28 countries, opens an office only when a specific U.S. business unit, such as asset management or commodity trading, agrees to pay for its startup. Other businesses are then added gradually. As a result, the company's products are in different stages of their lifecycle from Beijing to Bombay to Johannesburg, Geneva or São Paulo.

Such regional differences in the stage of a product's lifecycle may also be due to factors that cannot be influenced by the marketer, such as legal regulations, technical norms, or customers' receptiveness to innovation.

One example is the market for temporary work in Europe. In 1997, the services of temporary work agencies were still illegal in Italy and Greece, while in Germany they faced tough regulatory restrictions. The U.K., France, and the Netherlands stood out as more liberal country markets for temporary labor. But as politicians worried about Europe's continued failure to create new jobs even in periods of economic growth, many governments started reconsidering old labor market tenets and progressively lifting the legal obstacles. As part of a pact to create more jobs, for example, Belgium's labor union, employer, and government representatives agreed to stimulate the use of temporary work.

If the aspiration levels of local customers are in various stages of development, the customers are differently inclined to accept products from other countries. If the degree of mobility in the various local societies varies, different stages of a product's lifecycle in those markets will result. Colorful fashion watchstraps, for example, have been an essential part of French, Italian, and German jewelers' stock for many years. They are in a much more advanced stage of their lifecycle in those countries compared to the U.S., where most customers prefer black or brown watchstraps, or in most Asian countries where metal straps are common.

In any case, differences in the stage of a product's lifecycle across country markets have an impact on the marketing mix to be applied locally and on the resources deployed. Insufficient adaptation of a product to local preferences or norms unnecessarily increases the duration of a product's introduction stage. Kentucky Fried Chicken, for example, took a couple of years before it entered the growth stage in the Japanese market. This was not so much due to the customers' need to learn a new consumption habit. Fast-food stores had existed in Japan long before Kentucky Fried Chicken was founded in the U.S. But the company initially tried to introduce its unchanged model of an American fast-food restaurant and its menu to Japan rather than making necessary adaptations (such as French fries instead of mashed potatoes) to local tastes.

Duration

Product lifecycles are usually longer for industrial products than for consumer products, especially for construction equipment, component parts, raw materials, and maintenance services. Fads and fashion changes, which tend to shorten product lifecycles, are less common for industrial products than for most consumer products. Also, the higher levels of investment required for many industrial products necessitate a longer product lifecycle, so that the firm can recover the costs of research and development.

Nevertheless, in international business there is a general trend toward shortening of product lifecycles. One reason is the sharp increase in global competition, which forces companies to innovate constantly. New or improved products are introduced quickly, in order to stay attractive in the minds of potential customers. (Future issues box 11.1 describes potential problems related to that trend.) Research and development processes are speeded up as companies try to apply their innovations simultaneously in as many products as possible. In addition, to stay cost competitive in globalizing product markets, the production processes of total products are continually shortened and global sourcing tries to minimize procurement expenditures. This, in return, again increases the pressure for innovations on the suppliers' side.

In addition to more intense competition, the number and level of environmental protection regulations have been increasing during the past decade, at least in the most highly industrialized countries. As a result, new or at least improved products, which meet the revised environmental norms had to be developed quickly. The duration of the original lifecycle was shortened.

FUTURE ISSUES BOX 11.1

Second-hand markets for cell phones

In Europe, cell phones are exchanged by their owners on average every 30 months. Considering the hundreds of millions of cell phones in use, old cell phones therefore, represent a major burden on the environment.

Firms such as Greener Solutions, located in the U.K., have been founded to solve that problem. In cooperation with partners such as the Body Shop, pharmacies, or city administrations they collect cell phones no longer used by their owners. Greener Solutions, for example, classifies cell phones in Munich, resets around one-third to function (recycling the rest) and sells them to contract buyers in Africa and Asia. There, they are sold for an average price of €13. Other firms such as OneTwoSold have started online auctions for second-hand phones with impressive success.

Nevertheless, there will be more such initiatives needed, if an ever growing mountain of communication hardware scrap is to be avoided in the future.

Source: Adapted from "Althandys wieder nützlich", *Der Standard*, 6 November 2003, p. 24

Finally, some of the shortening of product lifecycles is due to managers' errors with regard to the positioning of their products. For example, when a marketer of products that are considered attractive by their customers succumbs to the pressure on prices and terms of sale of its intermediaries to grow faster than the competition, or to keep market shares in the short run, the lifecycles of those products are shortened because those decisions place negative pressure on their gross margins. As a result, the need for constant innovation or product changes is growing.

Therefore, product innovation is the most important process in international portfolio management. But it has to be based on a careful consideration of how well the company does and will do with its current products, which ones need to be renewed, and which resources may be spent for what purpose. This is the task of the international product portfolio analysis and determination process.

Portfolio balance

Compared to a local company, the portfolio management of an internationally active firm is complicated by the fact that an international portfolio balance has to be achieved. There always needs to be a sufficiently large number of products (in potentially different country markets), which provide enough cash flow to finance either the development and launch of new or improved products in current markets or the launch of current products in new country markets. In fast growing and globalizing industries, both alternatives will need to be financed. Which products to introduce where and when, and which products to delete from the portfolio must be decided. In addition, the international marketer must determine how much of the available resources to spend on each product, in each of the served or intended country markets.

The goal is to constantly increase the success of the firm or at least to keep it at a level that satisfies the important stakeholders of the firm. For this purpose the products in the portfolio have to be compared across all country markets concerning their current and potential contribution to the company's success. Portfolio analysis has proven to be a useful tool for such comparisons.

Comparison of products

Figure 11.6 shows the potential result of a portfolio analysis comparing a firm's products across country markets. The company's products are evaluated according to two criteria.

Attractiveness of served product markets The attractiveness of served product markets (on the vertical axis) consists of factors such as market growth, intensity of competition, relative market size, or achievable margins.

Relative competitive position The estimation of the products' relative competitive positions (depicted on the horizontal axis) is based on factors expressing the extent to which the features of the total products fit the expectations and aspirations of the stakeholders in their product markets relative to competition. Such factors may be cost and quality, customer services or innovativeness.

Which factors should be used to best "measure" the attractiveness of international product markets and the relative competitive position of the company's products will depend on the business the company is in and must be individually determined by the marketer.

When assessing the relative competitive position of the firm's products, the marketer must not only consider most important competitors' known products, but also products that presently do not exist but are known to be under development or could be developed inside the planning horizon. The size of the circles in the graphic can depict a product's contribution to total profit or cash flow, its share of total sales volume, or its contribution per sales ratio.

Comparison across country markets

Figure 11.7 shows the results of a portfolio analysis in which the competitive positions of a product have been compared across served country markets. One might conclude from this picture that the Japanese market is rather attractive for the product. But the company has not yet been able to develop a sufficiently strong competitive position to take a profit from the attractiveness of this market.

FIGURE 11.6 *Comparison of a company's products across country markets*

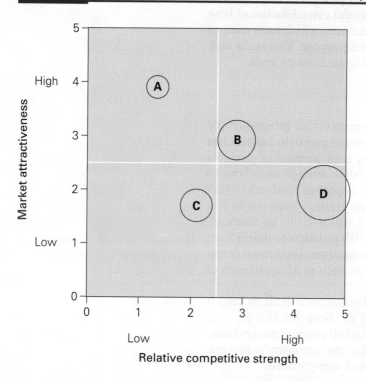

A company operating internationally may compare the position of its products across markets along two dimensions: the attractiveness of the served product markets and the relative strength of each product compared to its major competitors.

A, B, C, D = products of a company
The dimensions of the circles are equivalent to contribution margin relative to turnover

FIGURE 11.7 *Comparison of competitive positions of product A across served country markets*

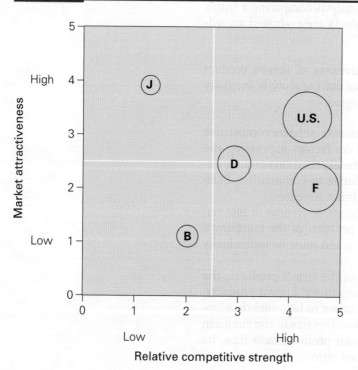

An international marketer may be interested in a comparison of the competitive position of one of its products in each of the differently attractive country markets served.

B = Belgium, D = Germany, F = France, J = Japan,
U.S. = United States of America
The dimensions of the circles are equivalent to contribution margin relative to turnover

If a realistic way of improving this position could be found, the resources needed might be transferred from the German and French markets. But before such a decision is made, the information from both portfolio analyses needs to be linked. Only a total comparison of the competitive positions of all products across all served country markets allows a meaningful decision concerning resource allocation.

Combined comparison

Table 11.3 shows how such an information link can be achieved by portfolio analysis. The vertical axis contains the positions of the company's products in the four quadrants of Figure 11.6. Inside each quadrant are the served country markets. Horizontally, the competitive position of each product is indicated for each country market (compare Figure 11.7). In general, a product with a weak competitive position in a relatively unattractive market (for example, product A in Belgium) represents a drain on the entire company. It might seem plausible to keep a product in a more attractive country market, which at the moment needs more resources than it can provide, such as product A in Japan. But products that are not profitable and do not expect future improvement, for example by outsourcing the production, are to be eliminated. Careful management of a smaller number of products generally allows positive effects of coordination and concentration on a company's profits.

International product innovation

To maintain a balanced international product portfolio, new products have to be continually developed and, together with variations of current products,

TABLE 11.3 Comparison of competitive positions of a company's products across served country markets

Position of product in overall comparison	Position of product in country market				
	?	Star	Cash cow	Dog	Country
?				A	Belgium
	A				Germany
			A		France
	A				Japan
		A			U.S.
Star			B		Belgium
		B			Germany
	B				France
	B				Japan
		B			U.S.
Cash cow		D			Belgium
			D		Germany
				D	France
		D			Japan
			D		U.S.
Dog			C		Belgium
				C	Germany
			C		France
		C			Japan
				C	U.S.

introduced to the markets in a planned way. In international marketing a product can be 'new' in different ways. On the one hand, it can be a real innovation for its global product market. Real innovations are seldom globally successful. This may be due to the varying innovativeness of customers. For example, German, U.K. and European Mediterranean consumers are known to be considerably slower in adopting consumer-durable innovations than Scandinavians. But lack of success may also be due to a lack of corporate information necessary to properly guide adapted product development and market entry.

On the other hand, a "new" product may only be new for a specific country market. Often a company has been successfully marketing a product in some markets before it introduces it in other markets. For example, Coca-Cola introduced Georgia Coffee, a non-carbonated soft drink that tastes of coffee, into the Australian market after having successfully marketed the product in Japan for years.

Finally, a product may only be new to the company itself. In this case most companies find it difficult to establish themselves in markets they do not know well, with products with which they do not have any experience.

New product ideas

To successfully launch a single new product in international markets, several new product ideas are needed. These ideas may be developed with a domestic market perspective, with several different country markets in mind, for global product markets with planned modifications for different regions, or from a global standardization perspective.

Only one in about seven product concepts is a winner. That is, close to half the resources firms spend for product development purposes result in losing products. Some 50% of new products fail at launch. But research has shown that product ideas generated with an international market in mind are generally more successful than product ideas developed for a domestic market only.

To generate a sufficient number of new product ideas, a company may use either internal or external sources (see Figure 11.8). New product ideas may be of a variety of types, including:

- development of a new technology
- a new application of an existing technology
- new solutions for current customer problems
- new product features.

FIGURE 11.8   *Sources for new product ideas in international marketing*

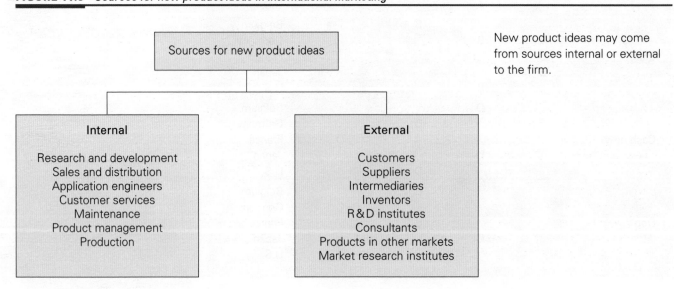

New product ideas may come from sources internal or external to the firm.

An international marketer has access to a greater number and diversity of sources of ideas for new products than a locally operating competitor. For example, the marketer may count on the experience of salespeople, application engineers, and maintenance and customer service personnel operating in various cultural environments with different levels of economic and technological development and different regulatory environments.

Different expectations and aspirations of customers, suppliers, intermediaries, consultants, and inventors located in the country markets served by the firm can be transformed into new product ideas not available to local competitors. Highly successful products of local competitors may be exploited for new product launches in other markets. As Ethics box 11.1 shows, however, there are some limits to be borne in mind in imitating competitors' products and in developing new products based on their ideas.

Because of the great variety of potential sources of new product ideas, the international marketer will have to choose the most valuable ones. Product ideas coming from **lead markets** may receive special attention. Liechtenstein-based HILTI AG, for example, despite its worldwide activities, considers Germany as its lead market for drilling and fixing devices, because the technological level of products needed to be successful in this market is very high compared to most other country markets, including Japan and the U.S. Many international services providers, such as CompuServe, consider the U.S. its lead market. The danger of such focus is twofold: the marketer might not pay attention to innovative ideas coming from "minor" markets or might over-standardize its new products.

The international marketer should not automatically consider its biggest market as the lead market for product innovation ideas. Depending on the served

ETHICS BOX 11.1

Spying, stealing, copying

In a tale reminiscent of a John Le Carré spy novel, a unit of Corange Ltd. of Bermuda sued U.S.-based Johnson & Johnson in June 1996, accusing the medical giant of secretly infiltrating company meetings, stealing confidential documents, and pilfering a secret prototype.

The unit, Boehringer Mannheim Corp., which is based in Indiana, is a rival of J&J in the highly competitive business of making glucose monitors for diabetics. According to the suit, from 1992 to 1994 executives at J&J's LifeScan unit directed workers to surreptitiously attend several Boehringer sales meetings at hotels around the world. The executives, according to the suit, even established awards for J&J employees who did the best spying, including the "Inspector Clouseau Award" and the "Columbo Award."

At a Boehringer meeting in Istanbul, Turkey, a J&J spy allegedly found out about a secret prototype for a new glucose monitor. When LifeScan executives then "challenged" workers to obtain a copy of the prototype, a J&J worker in Germany "illegally obtained" a model and shipped it back to the U.S., the suit charged.

The suit was more surprising because Boehringer admitted two of its people did a little spying of their own – but it insisted it was nothing on the scale of what it was alleging J&J did. Boehringer said once one of its employees, acting on his own initiative, impersonated a doctor while talking to J&J officials at a trade show; on another occasion, a worker took home J&J documents he found in a waiting room.

In a statement, J&J admitted that an internal investigation found that both companies had engaged in unspecified "improper activities" and expressed "regret" that its employees had been involved in such activities. But J&J maintained that its LifeScan unit did not gain any competitive advantage from "information improperly obtained."

Source: Adapted from Langreth, R. (1996) "Rival's suit accuses J&J unit of spying, stealing papers", *Wall Street Journal Europe*, 21–22 June, p. 4

product market, criteria other than size – such as consumer innovativeness, quality expectations, or technological level – may be more important.

In a similar manner, persons, companies, or institutions as sources of new product ideas are not all of similar value to the marketer. Ideas coming from **lead actors**, that is, persons or organizations that may be considered as more innovative or more sensitive concerning the firm's product categories, should be followed more closely. The most sophisticated, demanding and fast moving customers, intermediaries, or media representatives adopt new products first. Less sophisticated people follow their lead after some months. Marketers able to cultivate relationships with lead actors in their industry can therefore pick up new product ideas faster and create a waterfall effect. The Appendix to this chapter contains a guideline on how the internet can be used in that respect.

Moreover, if lead actors are potential customers, they may agree to participate in product development and guarantee a certain sales volume at product launch. For example, Shinko, a Japanese semiconductor packaging manufacturer, used Intel, the world's leading MPU chip producer, as a sponsor company. By working closely with Intel, Shinko was able to meet Intel's packaging design requirements for various chip forms, and became its supplier of choice. When customers such as IBM and Texas Instruments adopted similar technology to Intel's, Shinko was able to provide them with leading-edge materials.

To profit fully from the potentially greater flow of new product ideas in an internationally operating firm, this **flow of ideas must be carefully organized**. Organizational units at different locations led by entrepreneurial people may further local initiatives and diminish central administrative barriers to innovation. To avoid cultural one-sidedness and tunnel vision, such units may be supported by internationally staffed teams of people from all functional areas concerned, which evaluate new product ideas and try to choose the best. Table 11.4 contains a list of criteria that might be used by such a team to evaluate the attractiveness of new product ideas and to select those to be further considered.

Product development

Positively concluded assessment processes of new product ideas result in **product definitions**. The product definition states the goalposts of product development. It determines the intended target market and competitive differen-

---

TABLE 11.4 *Criteria for selection of new product ideas*

> At Exxon Corp.'s Polymers Group the choice of ideas to be considered more closely is based on an investigation of eight key areas:
>
> - strategic fit
> - market attractiveness (existence of need, substantive market)
> - technical feasibility (including manufacturing)
> - supply/entry options
> - competitive advantage (better quality as defined by the customers and/or reduced customer costs, solves customers' problems with competitive products, unique and highly visible benefits)
> - legal/regulatory issues
> - financial attractiveness
> - a solid launch plan.

tiation as well as a list of features and specifications of the new product required to deliver the intended customer benefits.

Based on such a new product definition, a **development project** can be started. Accordingly, development activities are assigned to the members of a cross-functional development team. Under the leadership of a project manager, the team members concurrently work on their assignments. Continuous feedback among the team members who are empowered to take decisions allows the development process to be stopped when insurmountable obstacles of a technical, financial, or marketing nature arise.

The **viability of the new product** will be monitored and discussed throughout product development. For that purpose, milestones are defined at which the project's market, financial, and production viability are checked. Some firms operating internationally have formed new project review teams comprising senior management, which meet regularly to review those projects ready to move on to the next stage. At 3M, for example, a "European Management Committee" decides which new product projects should be further pursued.

While idea assessment may be performed based on checklists, in the product development phase the evaluation process is often based on scoring models. Because the new product and its potential are known with increasing precision, five-point scales can be used where at least the extremes and the median are quantitatively anchored or defined by verbal descriptions. New product projects are cancelled when an individual score or the sum of scores do not reach a pre-specified level. In the case of a positive result, the next step can be started.

An important stage in every product innovation process is **product testing**. For that purpose a prototype (working model, or a sample of the product) that can be tested are developed. As Chapter 7 discussed, product tests can be conducted in laboratories, but preferably are conducted at the sites of cooperating business or administrative customers, or in consumer test markets.

Product brand management

Based on the formulated international product policy the marketer has to take product-related branding decisions. In international marketing some issues such as the choice of an appropriate brand name, the protection of the brand, and packaging adapted to the brand as well as to specific contexts stand out.

Choice of brand name

An essential part of a product brand is its name. If the marketer decides to endow its product with a brand name or to use the company's name as a trademark, the brand name becomes part of the total product. Therefore, the choice of the brand name and its communicative loading with specific meanings is of particular importance. In this choice international marketers are faced with additional problems, compared to their locally operating counterparts.

Gone are the days when corporate executives picked product names at random – such as Germany's Gottlieb Daimler, who named his flagship car Mercedes after the daughter of a client in Argentina. Professional name finders also smile when thinking of the origins of Sweden's IKEA AB, named after furniture maker Ingvar Kamprad from Elmtaryd in the province of Algunazyd.

Pronunciation

If a company entering a new country market keeps its current brand name unchanged without checking its potential, problems with the *pronunciation* of the brand name may occur. For example, most German-speaking customers of Worcester Sauce have difficulties in pronouncing the name properly. The meaning of the brand name in another language may even have negative effects on sales. The name of Soupline, a French detergent, for example, would be inappropriate for markets where English is the dominant language, because – pronounced in English – the brand would be loaded with meanings that are detrimental to the sales of a detergent. A good name is particularly important for products consumers identify with, such as cars. Flop stories abound. Japan's Mitsubishi Motors Corp. had to rename its Pajero model in Spanish-speaking countries because the term describes the process of masturbation. Toyota Motor Corp.'s MR2 model dropped the number from its name in France because the combination sounds like a French swearword.

To avoid problems with pronunciation or the resulting meaning of a brand name, the international marketer may either decide to use different brand names in each country market or language area or try to find a name that can be used throughout its entire international product market.

Strategy box 11.1 describes how Nestlé, a very prominent example, implements the first alternative.

If brand name and company name are the same, which is often the case for business-to-business products and also for many services companies, such difficulties may even be increased. The company cannot easily change its name. If the problem is caused by difficulties in pronouncing the name, as for example Bazar de l'Hôtel de Ville for English-speaking tourists coming to Paris, a simplification or abbreviation of the name can be helpful. In the case of the Parisian department store, the three initials BHV were used.

Meaning

Because communication channels are becoming increasingly international, however, an increasing number of firms want to take advantage of standardizing their brands. They therefore seek brand names that can be used internationally. This

---

STRATEGY BOX 11.1

Nestlé's brand-building machine

Over the decades, Nestlé the world's largest food company, represented a thumping rejection of the one-world, one-brand school of marketing. The company preferred brands to be local and people regional; only technology has gone global. Call it the Roman Empire school of marketing: Colonize as much territory as fast as you can, adapting to native conditions, and then work at holding off the advancing competitors.

Nestlé has poured billions of dollars into local acquisitions – such as Ralston Purina pet foods in the U.S. – and owns some thousand different brands worldwide. Of those brands, only fewer than 1,000 are registered in more than one country, and only 80 are registered in ten.

In the industrially developing world, Nestlé has grown by manipulating ingredients, or processing technology for local conditions, and then putting the appropriate brand name on the resulting product. Sometimes that is a well-known one like Nescafé coffee; generally a local one works fine – for instance Bear Brand condensed milk in Asia. In new markets, Nestlé alights with a mere handful of labels, selected from a basket of six strategic worldwide brands. The idea is to keep complexity low, limit risks, and concentrate the attack. Then the company can allocate marketing budgets into just two or three brands per country to gain big market shares.

Nestlé is the market leader for instant coffee in Australia, France, Japan, and Mexico. In powdered milk Nestlé holds a market share of two-thirds in the Philippines. Already the largest branded food company in Mexico and Thailand, in Brazil where its market share of powdered milk reaches more than half, in Chile where Nestlé has three-quarters of the cookie market, and nearly as much of the soups and sauces market, Nestlé is on its way to becoming the leader in Vietnam and China as well.

was not the case for Rolls-Royce's Silver Mist or Citroën's Evasion models. *Mist* in German means manure and while *evasion* makes French consumers think of freedom and adventure, English speakers tend to think of tax evasion.

A good name must:

- sound appropriate in the languages of the country markets to be served
- spark associations that are both pleasant and express the meaning of the product or its most important benefit.

A good name also has to:

- stand out
- have an emotional impact.

Most international marketers prefer to choose brand names that automatically evoke certain associations in customers' minds. They have to be careful, however, because blunders may occur. Reebok International Ltd., for example, was embarrassed to learn that the designation of its women's running shoe "Incubus" is the name of a mythical demon who preyed on sleeping women.

Otherwise, artificial or technical names must get their meanings attached through costly communication campaigns. Carmakers, for example, increasingly choose real names over the numbers and letters that long marked their models. Perhaps the most revolutionary step in that direction was taken by French Renault when they stopped numbering their models in the manner of R-4 and R-5, and launched, for example, Twingo, Clio, Mégane, and Safrane.

Awareness

Besides pronunciation and semantic problems that have to be resolved in international brand management, current brand awareness needs to be considered. If a brand name has already reached a certain level of awareness in its served markets and evokes meanings that increase the product's attractiveness to current customers, it would not be reasonable to change the name just to standardize branding across country markets. For example, the Austrian cheese manufacturer Rupp had successfully launched the brand Pumuckl for their children's product line in Germany. There, children as well as buying parents knew the figure from a TV series of the same name and liked it. When the firm got ready to launch the same product line in Italy and the U.K., they could not use the same name because in those countries consumers would not only have had difficulties pronouncing the name but did not know the TV series. However, changing the name that was very successful in Germany to allow internationally standardized brand communication would have destroyed the brand equity that had been built up in the German market.

Name-finding agencies

To find an internationally usable name that meets their needs, international marketers may use the services of professional name-finding agencies such as Nomen, a Paris-based agency, which also has subsidiaries in the U.K., Spain, and Italy. For an elaborately designed stereo system by Japanese electronics maker Sony, Nomen sought ideas from painters, rock musicians, actors, and marketing experts who came up with some 2,000 names. The company then checked for ideas in encyclopedias on opera, film, and theatre. Special computer programs scanned the words for possible variations. As a next step, Nomen checked online databanks for overlaps with existing brand names across the globe before presenting a list of 10 names to the client. The whole process took 2 months and ended with the name Scenario.

CDs offer rich pickings for counterfeiters

© doug steley/Alamy

Brand protection

Trademark registration

Developing new international brands demands careful consideration of potential brand names and trademarks. The chosen name or trademark must have the potential to be protected. Chapter 4 discussed the legal aspects of registration and protection of property rights.

Counterfeiting

A major problem for international marketers that have established well-known brands is counterfeiting. Counterfeiting – also discussed in Chapter 4 – causes not only the direct loss of sales but also long-term losses that may be even more serious. For example, counterfeit products are usually of inferior quality, and some such products may even be harmful to their users. For example, Dunhill leather goods are often counterfeited by the use of substances that are not tolerated by the skin. Consumers wearing such fakes may break out in a rash or get allergies. In 2003, according to the Electronic Resellers Association Inc., about 70% of the nearly 200 complaints it received each month involved counterfeit or substandard parts from China. When counterfeit products cease to function properly or cause injury or other problems for their users, the negative image is transferred to the brand that was used in such an unauthorized manner.

As a reaction, some companies join forces to fight brand piracy more effectively. For example, Adidas, Replay, Windsurfing Chiemsee, MCM, Chipie, and BAD & BAD formed an association to fight product piracy, VPM, in Munich, Germany. They exchange know-how on the installation of security mechanisms such as changing the details of product design or construction and information concerning distribution channels members suspected of participating in the counterfeiting network. The Business Software Alliance, representing a group of U.S. software firms, has launched a scheme offering rewards to employees who tip them off about firms using illegal software. Other companies engage private detectives, such as Professional Investigating & Consulting Agency, based in Columbus, Ohio, to investigate cases of counterfeiting.

Packaging

How a consumer product appears to its potential customers may be strongly affected by packaging. Because the package is often the last point at which the marketer has a chance to influence the customer's purchasing decision, it can play a powerful role in promoting the product. Both product delivery and product communication are strongly influenced by elements of the local environments of served country markets. Therefore, packaging deserves particular attention in international marketing.

Legal regulations, available infrastructure, and social and cultural specifics need to be considered. The impact of legal regulations on packaging was discussed in Chapter 4. Because infrastructure mainly influences the physical distribution of a product, its impact on packaging is discussed in Chapter 14. The following section will concentrate on the potential impact of cultural as well as socioeconomic elements on packaging.

Cultural elements

Because packages are the visual surface of a product that customers first come into contact with, they may strongly influence the product's meaning to the customers. For new perfumes or cigarettes to be launched internationally, for example, changing the package color or style may affect sales more than changing the product's name or even ingredients. For highly intangible products, such as legal or cosmetics consulting and restaurant services, the appearance of the location where the service takes place as well as the look of the service providers may serve the purpose of a package: to create a certain meaning of the product to the customer.

Like any perception of meanings, customer reactions to packaging are highly subject to influence by cultural specifics. The design of the package must fit the customers' expectations in size, style, material, and color.

Packages that are the wrong color, such as a black cigarette package in Hong Kong – black is a color of bad luck there – or the wrong size, such as a 2-liter soft drink bottle in the Netherlands – 2-liter bottles are too large for most Dutch refrigerators – can have a negative influence on sales. So can the number of products contained in one package. A U.S. manufacturer of golf balls, for example, which exported its products to Japan, packaged the balls in groups of four. However, when the Japanese word for four is said aloud, it sounds like the word for death. Products grouped in fours, therefore, do not sell well in Japan.

Visuals on packages may also strongly influence local customers' acceptance of a product. The reactions of female consumers to floral designs on soap packages, for example, differ considerably between Hong Kong and the U.S. Consumers in Hong Kong tend to give such designs a low value, whereas Americans associate the same designs with feminine products of neutral value.

Socioeconomic factors

Socioeconomic factors, such as the available family income or family size, may also influence the packaging decisions of international marketers. Multiple packs, which are designed to increase sales because of added convenience, for example, are affected by those factors.

Owing to different family sizes, Pillsbury offers its products in the U.S. mainly in packages for two people whereas their packages sold in less industrially developed markets contain servings for six to eight people.

Even the level of education of the customers targeted in a country market may have an influence on the packaging of a product. Kenya, Malaysia, and Singapore, for example, have introduced standard sizes for cans, bottles, and other food packages to avoid consumer confusion owing to a variety of different sizes and to facilitate price comparisons.

Standardization

International standardization of packaging provides significant sources of cost reduction, such as reduced production, printing, storage, and handling costs, as well as increased speed and quality of physical distribution. For that reason, Bonduelle, the French producer of canned and frozen vegetables, which traditionally had different packaging from one country to another, decided to create the same visual identity for its entire product range all across its European country markets: On packages dominated by a yellow background the name of the company, which is also the brand name, is printed in green below an orange arch which is meant to express the well-being derived from consuming the product.

Multilingual labels, standardized content declarations, internationally used trademarks, or fit with euro-pallets have been used by many companies for the purpose of cost reduction. But full packaging standardization across country markets can only be achieved when:

- the expectations of customers and intermediaries in those markets are not contradictory
- the highest levels of expectations concerning the package's functions can be fulfilled in each market
- cultural differences do not lead to undesirable effects on the product meaning created by the standardized package
- cost limits can be respected.

For example, standardization of toothpaste packaging across Europe is hampered by the fact that many German-speaking customers are demanding non-packaged products. They want to avoid waste of natural resources and environmental pollution through packaging material. By the same token, important shares of customers in the southern and eastern parts of Europe still value expensive-looking "modern" packages, because for those consumers they indicate progress. Both expectations can hardly be satisfied with one standardized packaging concept.

Consistency of international product brand management

To manage a product brand consistently on an international level, the marketer must first make sure that all members of the organization, as well as the personnel of intermediaries who take decisions and act in situations that may influence the meaning of the brand to other stakeholders:

- grasp the essential elements of the brand
- are motivated to act in a way supporting the intended meaning.

Table 11.5 shows a checklist that can be used to systematically monitor the ingredients of a strong product brand. The development of a brand needs perseverance. It also needs patience. Both the use of pricing tools and continual changes in market communication to rapidly increase market shares have proven to be detrimental to a brand's lasting success.

Product quality management

Customer satisfaction

A great number of studies conducted in various parts of the world convincingly show that customer satisfaction with the total product is an important factor of influence on the long-term success of business organizations. Because customers' satisfaction is strongly related to their perception of a product's quality, quality management is a central process of international product management. Customers may experience attractive product quality based on:

- *superior tangible features of the product*, for example, the longest battery life of all the portable phones on the market

---

TABLE 11.5   *Brand report card*

Measures
1   The brand excels at delivering benefits stakeholders truly desire
2   The brand is clearly differentiated from others
3   The brand stays relevant to its stakeholders over time
4   Managers responsible for brand-related decisions and actions understand what the brand should mean to stakeholders
5   The stakeholders' experiences with the brand are consistent
6   Brand-related actions are given proper support over the long run
7   Sources of brand equity are continually monitored

Building a strong brand involves maximizing the scores on all seven measures listed in the brand report card.

Source: Adapted from Keller, K.L. (2000) "The brand report card", *Harvard Business Review*, January–February, p. 149

- *uniqueness of the interaction experience with the supplier* for example, the feeling of being treated like a family member in a small vacation hotel on the Italian island of Sardinia
- *purely symbolic features of the product* for example, the ability to express a certain personal identity by wearing Ferragamo shoes.

As Figure 11.9 shows, customer satisfaction is based on an interaction between customers' expectations concerning the product and their experience with the product. Expectations are influenced by direct as well as indirect (word of mouth, observation) experiences with the product and market communication by the supplier, its competitors and their stakeholders. Product experience is based on the material and immaterial features the marketer provides with its total product, but in the end depends on the degree of fulfillment of customer expectations concerning the product. That is, the quality of a product is defined by its customers.

Marketers have two ways of influencing their customers' quality perceptions. They may use:

- *quality assurance*, that is, they ensure a certain level of performance on each of the material and immaterial features important to the customers
- *quality signaling*, that is, they may try to shape their potential customers' product-related expectations through market communication.

An international marketer will use both ways to be successful.

Because quality perceptions are subjective, they may vary among groups of customers in a country market as well as among country markets. As a consequence, the quality assurance and quality signaling processes of a local company and a company operating internationally are basically the same as far as their objectives and their contents are concerned but in international markets some additional challenges may occur.

Quality assurance

Quality assurance is an ongoing process that runs in parallel with the production of the total product. Depending on the share of material versus immaterial features constituting the product as well as on the level of customer integration in

FIGURE 11.9 *Customer satisfaction*

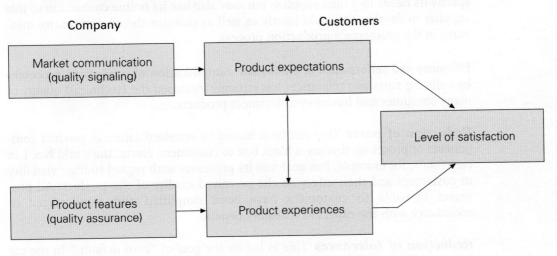

Customer satisfaction with a total product is a result of an interaction between the customer's expectations concerning the product and the customer's experiences with the product. The marketer may influence product experience by quality assurance measures and product expectations by quality signaling.

the production process, quality assurance processes will focus more on material or immaterial aspects of the creation and generation of customer value.

Material features

Quality assurance processes start with the development of a product.

Design quality The number of potential failures can be significantly reduced in advance by an improvement in **design quality**. Webasto AG, the German world leader in car sunroofs, as an example from the industrial products sector, has found that 70% of product costs are determined during the product design and construction phase. They have therefore introduced **FMEA** (failure mode and effect analysis) in all their product development processes. Potential failures are identified and analyzed beforehand in dialogue with major suppliers and customers. The probability of failure occurrence, failure detection, and the resulting costs of such failures are determined.

Products with high FMEA scores are reconstructed to avoid all potential failures right from the beginning. Suppliers are obliged to do the same. And the company cooperates closely with the carmakers it supplies during the startup phase of the use of one of their products in the carmakers' assembly line.

Quality of potential suppliers' products Next, the quality of supplier products needed for the generation of the total product is assessed. In international business it may not be sufficient to exactly specify the features of those supplies in written contracts. Some marketers must first train their suppliers' personnel to increase their level of product-related know-how. A smaller number of suppliers – not more than two per product category supplied – allows the development of long-term relationships that make such investments economically reasonable.

For example, when an international hotel chain such as Marriott Hotels enters a formerly centrally controlled economy, such as Uzbekistan, it might find itself forced to develop a network of suppliers of all the products needed to serve their international customers in the way they expect. Because neither the existing distribution facilities nor the local product quality and reliability come up to the standards of the company, it will have to choose its suppliers carefully, train them accordingly, and make them long-term partners in order to be successful.

Computer online connections between a company and its suppliers may even allow the quality of the supplies to be checked during their production process. For example, when a truck manufacturer such as Sweden's Scania needs a new tube system for an innovative truck model, the company might not only closely specify its needs to a tube supplier, but may also use its online connection to this supplier to develop the mold jointly as well as monitor the quality control measures in the prototype's production process.

Efficiency and performance of production Simplification of production processes by reducing parts and tolerances has strongly increased the (technical) quality of many consumer and business-to-business products.

Reduction of parts This can be achieved by standardization of product components or processes that are a black box to customers. Hertz, the world No. 1 in car rentals, for example, has analyzed its processes with regard to their visibility to customers and their effect on the perceived quality of the product. All processes invisible to customers have been simplified and standardized in accordance with the expected customer benefit.

Reduction of tolerances This is led by the goal of "zero default." In the car industry, for example, PPM (parts per million) is a major quality criterion on which suppliers are measured. It expresses the share of defective parts delivered in a total of 1 million parts. The ppm level accepted by the most important car-makers is 0.1%. To achieve such a level of technical quality, constructive and organizational measures alone are not enough. Company personnel must understand that it is in their own best interest to reach the goal of zero default, and they must be allowed to act as they see fit in their area. If they get increased control over "their" part of the total product's production process, they will be more strongly motivated to continually improve the processes for which they feel responsible. Process oriented (instead of functional) team structures help to increase the understanding of mutual dependence of personnel in the process of generating customer value.

Immaterial features

Quality assurance of the total product is not only achieved through measures concerning the production process of its material elements. Immaterial features of the total product have as much influence on customer satisfaction and therefore also have to be included in total quality management processes. One part of a total product's production process that contains mainly immaterial elements – at least from the customer's perspective – and strongly influences the perceived quality of the product is its distribution.

Distribution Delayed delivery of industrial products, non-availability of consumer products, or negative experiences in personal contacts with the marketer's or its intermediaries' staff may lead to the superior material quality of a product becoming of secondary importance.

In comparison to a locally active firm, the international marketer has to bear the disadvantage that the distribution of its products usually needs to cover much broader areas. International distribution also involves a higher number of personnel as well as intermediaries who have a variety of cultural backgrounds. That is, the number of potential sources of imperfections is multiplied. Only close cooperation and alignment with the members of the firm's distribution channels can help in assuring appropriate quality (see Chapter 12).

Process management Another key to consistent quality experiences for customers are the processes that add up to the total product. There are basically two ways for international marketers to assure the quality of their products via process management. One method is to:

1 map the entire customer value generation process related to a product
2 distinguish phases where the customers are directly involved in the production process from those which are invisible to them
3 divide the entire value generation process into a sequence of small process units that can be more readily standardized.

Each member of personnel directly or indirectly involved in the customer value generation process assumes responsibility for one or more of those process units.

At McDonald's, for example, each staff member plays a predetermined and highly specialized role that is part of the customer service delivery process. Each role can be specifically trained. Such a strict functional division of labor reduces the complexity of each staff member's duty, which, together with the training provided for the narrowly defined job, leads to a reduction of variance in the service provided to the customer, independent of the location of the McDonald's outlet.

The second way to assure the quality of highly intangible and integrative products is to tailor each individual product as much as possible to the specific expectations of the customer.

Instead of offering predetermined bus tours all over Europe, an international tour operator might, for example, only provide the bus and a special consultancy service for customers who want to plan the route and related programs themselves or in cooperation with the tour operator. Such individualization of the product allows increasing customer satisfaction by providing custom-made quality levels of service.

Quality of available personnel Many highly integrative and immaterial products, such as international consultancy or banking, demand high levels of professional as well as social competency from their providers. In addition, if the service provided so far has fully satisfied their customers, demand might grow faster than the capacities of qualified personnel available to the marketer. Company growth has to be brought into line with quality assurance needs.

For example, when Madrid-based Banco Santander, in turning to Latin America as the source of future growth, increased its retail bank business in Chile and Puerto Rico and set up a sizeable investment banking operation in Argentina, it was not able to sufficiently staff retail bank operations in Peru and a financial services unit in Chile with personnel trained in-house.

The capability of a firm to follow its intended path of international growth in such cases may depend on the number of appropriately qualified personnel it can hire and train in the company-specific ways of doing business. If there are not enough candidates available, the choice of partners (franchisees, licensees, joint venture, strategic, or merger partners) or the choice of adequate acquisition objects becomes a critical element of quality assurance. In the case of Banco Santander, for example, it bought two Peruvian retail banks and a controlling interest in Banco Osorno & La Union SA.

In such cases, the international marketer can contribute its know-how, its management techniques, and its planning and control system to the newly acquired unit. But the quality of service experienced by customers will largely depend on the qualifications of the acquired personnel and the personnel development activities set by the marketer.

Quality awareness

Because of the increased complexity of customer value generation processes for companies operating internationally, quality assurance may appear to be more difficult in such firms. Beside considering cultural influences on work discipline, adhering to rules, the importance of precision, or friendliness to customers, the international marketer has to develop a program which creates awareness of the importance of the highest quality for the success of the firm and, therefore, for the job security of personnel throughout the international firm. The distribution of colorful brochures containing leading ideas, norms, and rules will not be sufficient to achieve such awareness. Ongoing organizational and personnel development activities based on an understanding of individuals as exchange partners will be needed.

Quality signaling

When a product's level of immateriality is high, customers cannot visually or physically test a product before buying. They need other cues to assess the attractiveness of the product. Table 11.6 lists some material or immaterial signals informing customers about the quality of the product.

Location and physical outfit

The location in which a product is offered or consumed has an important influence on customers' perception of its potential quality. A Swiss Rado watch offered in a street market in Hong Kong would be considered a fake and could only be sold at a very reduced price, whereas a simple lentil salad with onions served in a five-star restaurant on the Caribbean island of St Barthelemy is considered by some customers as a real treat worth $100. That is, when customers are insecure about the quality of a product they look for external cues to help them develop appropriate expectations. One such signal is location. Rue St Honoré in Paris, for example, is known for its concentration of haute couture shops. New designer brands from Italy, Japan, or the U.K., even from product categories other than fashion, try to establish themselves with a reference shop in this street.

Because a customer's subjective experience with a product is influenced by the environmental setting in which the contact between customer and supplier takes place, a high degree of standardization of this environment contributes to customers having similar quality experiences over time. This is particularly important in international services industries such as restaurants and hotels, but also for the consistent management of customer experiences with global brands. Louis Vuitton customers from Japan, for example, would be very surprised when traveling to Paris if they found a Louis Vuitton shop there that looked completely different from the stores in their home country. At the least, the main visual cues should stimulate a perception of sameness.

Companies internationally offering legal, financial, business, or communication consultancy services may furnish their offices in a way that allows customers to visually experience the quality level of their work. For example, an Austrian information systems consultant firm specializing in CIM software for textile factories buys fabric from their (potential) customers. Well-known fashion designers transform it into fashionable outfits for the firm's personnel. When visiting a customer or receiving a customer at their premises, staff members wear the appropriate clothing, signaling to those customers how much they are willing to focus on their business.

International marketers have to be careful, however, because symbols may have different meanings in different cultural environments. North American customers, for example, partly evaluate the reliability of a potential business partner by the size of their office, whereas in the Netherlands office size is not very important.

Warranties

Warranties are well suited to signaling a marketer's confidence in the functionality of its products. For example, DuoVac, a Canadian producer of central vacuum cleaning systems, offers a 5-year warranty to its international customers and adds a satisfaction guarantee (customers have 12 months to declare if and why they are not satisfied with the product and will get their money back). Such warranties strongly contribute to the attractiveness of the offered products even to

TABLE 11.6 *Material and immaterial signals informing customers about product quality*

Highly immaterial total products need signals indicating the quality of the product to their potential customers. Such signals may come from the:

- location/physical outfit in which the product is offered and consumed
- people offering the product
- warranties given by the supplier concerning product functionality
- references provided by other customers
- country of origin of the product
- local content
- general reputation of the product's supplier

customers who were not familiar with that company before considering a purchase from it.

Warranties are particularly important where customers cannot check the quality of a product before buying it. For example, if a sender of a parcel has no experience of express mail services, such as U.S.-based UPS (United Parcel Service), he or she may hesitate to use such a service. It is more expensive than normal postal services, and who knows if it will really do what it promises. But if the service provider offers a warranty that the parcel will be at the given address within 48 hours or the customer gets his or her money back, the credibility of the offer will be greatly increased.

In international marketing the potential for standardized offers of warranties is limited by differences in the legal systems of the served country markets. Local competitive practices and the level of technology customers in a country market are familiar with also influence the firm's ability to offer similar warranties across markets. But locally adapted warranties may be powerful tools to signal the product quality customers may expect before they buy the product.

Yet, international marketers must not commit their organization to a level of performance that is not realistic. Sometimes it may be necessary to delegate warranty performance to partners in a host market, owing to legal or cultural constraints. Too often, however, such delegation runs the risk of reduced customer satisfaction since those partners may not give the products, repairs or customers' complaints the level of service that the company would provide.

References

Where warranties cannot be given for legal or technical reasons, references might take over their role in diminishing potential customers' perceived risk in buying a product. The number and quality of early references may strongly influence the competitive market position of suppliers in a product market. In international metallurgical engineering, for example, references from properly functioning plants are so important for market success that marketers fight hard to be first with a reference when a new technology is introduced to the market. They even go as far as "buying" a reference, that is, they are ready to lose substantial amounts of money on their first project which implements a new technology on the premises of a well-known customer.

Personal references are important in many consumer and industrial services. For example, when a European personnel manager needs to decide which employment service company to choose for the provision of well-qualified temporary workers, he or she may limit discussions by relying on the big players, such as Adecco, a merger of Switzerland's Adida SA and France's Ecco SA, Manpower, the biggest U.S. firm with headquarters in Brussels from where it coordinates its international expansion, or Randstad Holding NV of the Netherlands. But to ease the business of comparison and to reduce the remaining risk, the manager may partly rely on the experiences of colleagues. Their references are highly informative about the quality of service to expect from the suppliers.

Country of origin

For a customer who has no experience with a product category or is not involved enough to actively consider more complex information, the country of origin may represent an important cue to the quality of a product, in addition to brand name and price. The origin of the product has symbolic value. It arouses specific characteristics attributed to the country.

Customers' associations with a country contain cognitive elements, such as the level of technical or design competence attributed to the country; affective elements, such as the friendliness of people experienced during a vacation in the country or the prestige that can be gained from possessing a product

"Made in . . ."; as well as normative elements, such as "You should not buy a product from a country where human rights are violated."

Quality prejudices Some countries are attributed with high-quality levels concerning specific product categories. Switzerland, for example, is "known" for its watches, the U.K. for its pop music, France for its luxury products, Italy for its fashion design, Germany for its machinery, Japan for its consumer electronics, and the U.S. for its consultants and convenience services. Many such country-related associations have been developed during customers' socialization process. They help consumers as well as business customers to simplify their information-gathering process needed to make a subjectively reasonable decision.

The international marketer should be aware that the characteristics attributed to a country and its products may differ by target customers and situation. Shared history, such as in the case of Austria, the Czech Republic, Croatia, Hungary, Slovakia, and Slovenia, or shared language, such as in France and parts of Belgium and Switzerland, may lead to mutual images that are different from those existing in other countries.

Characteristics attributed to countries may also change over time. For example, for a long time European customers perceived products from Japan as cheap imitations of qualitatively much better products from western highly industrialized countries. Because of Japan's superiority in some areas of technology and management, its products today are associated with high precision, reliable quality, and competitive prices. The same development may take place with products coming from China. In early 2005 Lenovo the Chinese market leader in PCs was allowed to acquire more than 80% of IBM's PC business. The headquarters of the company's PC division will be in New York; and Lenovo procured the rights to use the IBM brand for 5 years.

Country-of-origin-related associations can become an essential part of the meaning of a brand and its attractiveness to potential customers. For example, Barilla, the Italian pasta manufacturer, has managed to use its Italian origin to achieve a high-end image in most European markets that it does not have in the home market. German craftsmanship is a constitutive part of brand perceptions concerning Mercedes. Both McDonald's and Coca-Cola are strongly related to the "American Way of Life," and brands such as Gucci or Armani evoke Italian design competency in the minds of their customers.

Attraction by cultural difference Some products may only be marketed on the basis of their specific cultural background. It is precisely the difference in culture that makes them desirable. When Japanese consumers go to eat a piece of chicken at a Kentucky Fried Chicken outlet in Osaka, for example, they may be buying a bit of the American way of life. Without its specifically American image, this service would just be another way to eat chicken in a whole range of Japanese restaurants. Contrariwise, customers in Europe and the U.S. do not care much about the production sites of their Nike shoes, the Pampers nappies they buy, or the Goodyear tires they use. In those cases, other connotations of the brand are strong enough to determine its meaning to customers.

Ethnocentricity Ethnocentric customers are highly interested in the supposed country of origin of a product or at least the home base of the product's supplier. Products produced in their own country are more highly valued than those produced abroad. Ethnocentric customers in the U.S., for example, when asked to evaluate different brands of car, clearly rate U.S. brands higher than their international competitors. A significantly higher share of French consumers perceives products manufactured in their home country to be superior compared to the evaluations of consumers from other EU member countries.

The return of more nationalistic feelings has led marketers in countries such as Australia, Austria, France, Japan, and the U.S. to make customers explicitly aware of the country of origin of their products. For example, in Austria, local food producers, when confronted with fierce competition from other EU member countries, started a campaign featuring the country as the "food specialty shop" of Europe.

A special problem may arise when the perceived origin of the brand and the country in which the production site is situated are not consistent in customers' minds. Such hybrid products may not be bought because customers perceive increased uncertainty concerning product quality. Figure 11.10 contains a sequence of questions an international marketer should answer before deciding to produce its products in a country that has an image that is different from its brand's perceived origin.

FIGURE 11.10   *Hybrid products?*

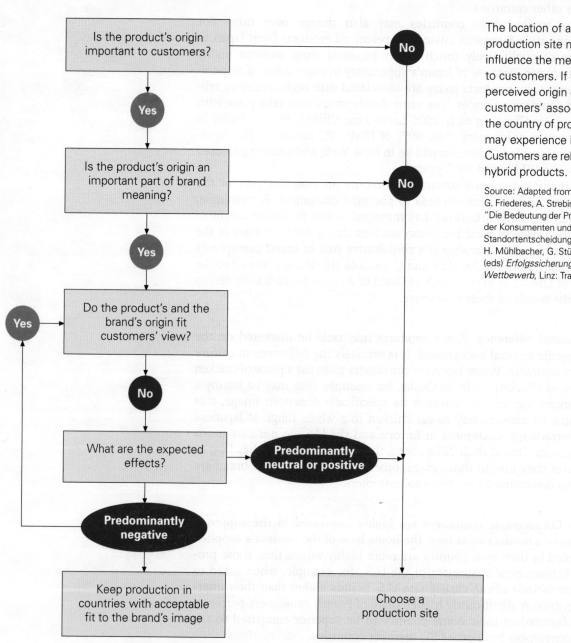

The location of a product's production site may strongly influence the meaning of the brand to customers. If the brand's perceived origin does not fit customers' associations related to the country of production, the brand may experience identity problems. Customers are reluctant to buy such hybrid products.

Source: Adapted from Schweiger, G., G. Friederes, A. Strebinger, and T. Otter (1995) "Die Bedeutung der Produktherkunft aus Sicht der Konsumenten und die Auswirkungen von Standortentscheidung" in G. Schweiger, H. Mühlbacher, G. Stürmer, and R Wödlinger (eds) *Erfolgssicherung in Internationalen Wettbewerb*, Linz: Trauner

When facing ethnocentric customers, a marketer from another country wishing to be successful may choose to become a local supplier through licensing, franchising, joint ventures, or the establishment of a subsidiary, or it must try hard to convince customers through outstanding references, proven better quality, extended warranties, prestigious intermediaries, or significantly lower prices. For example, many of the Korean marketers, such as Samsung or Kia, which had the same country of origin problems as their early Japanese counterparts, have chosen the low-price way to win customers in Europe and the U.S.

Local content

Another potential reaction to customers' ethnocentricity may be to increase the share of locally provided parts of the total product. Unilever, for example, uses locally available oils for the production of their margarine. By doing so, they also increase the goodwill of local politicians and stakeholders in public administration. A more important local content of a product may do more than increase the attractiveness of the marketer's offer. The marketer may also:

- profit from low-priced local supplies
- circumvent import restrictions
- take advantage of country-specific know-how
- develop local business relationships.

But the international marketer should also be aware that local content diminishes its autonomy.

Engineering companies, for example, are often faced with the demand of their international customers that a certain amount of the product's total added value must be produced in the customer's home country. Fulfillment of such a demand leads to additional problems in the organization of the workflow as well as quality assurance problems. It might be difficult to find an appropriate local partner and to meet deadlines set in the contract.

Potential customers may demand a certain amount of local content, such as 10 to 40% of the total product's value, or a specific part of the total product to be produced locally. For example, it is common in Saudi Arabia to prescribe the use of "sponsors," local people who facilitate relations between the international marketer and its Saudi Arabian stakeholders. In Libya, the use of local consultants is obligatory for engineering projects. The reasons for such demands range from forcing some technology transfer and decreasing hard currency payments, to using existing business relations.

In choosing local cooperation partners, mainly information problems arise. Searching on the spot is too expensive for many companies. Information gathering from cooperation partners already active in the country market, banks, chambers of commerce, commercial attachés, or consultants is in most cases less costly and time consuming. But the information received needs to be double-checked for its reliability. If the international marketer has the opportunity to transfer the local content of its product to a firm that can be closely controlled because of capital ownership or contractual agreements, the optimal share of local content may become rather important. The closer elements of the total product are to the core competences of the marketer, however, the less they are suited for local content purposes.

Impact on marketing mix

The product is the key element of the marketing mix. It must provide an attractive benefit to the customer if the entire marketing mix is to be successful.

Pricing

The greater the benefit to the customer and the higher the perceived quality of the product compared to its competitors, the more freedom the marketer has in setting prices. But prices (and customer benefits) are also influenced by the costs of a product. Therefore, the international marketer needs to take care of those costs from the very beginning of the product development process, through the production of the product, to its eventual recycling. Because of their lower sales volume, products exclusively conceived for domestic markets are often less price competitive than their internationally conceived counterparts. By influencing product innovation processes in such a way as to have an international marketing perspective, the marketer can influence the span of maneuver for pricing decisions.

Distribution

Quality management decisions and brand management have an impact on the choice of distribution channels as well as the management of business and personal relationships with intermediaries. The closer the company is to its customers, the better the control over the customer contact personnel and direct customer communication. If available channel members in a country market provide little or no personal selling, the brand must be quickly recognizable. Packaging has to take over an important part of market communication.

Market communication

Communication and distribution mix in the served country markets must be carefully managed to avoid negative surprises for mobile customers who find "their" brands differently positioned in other countries. At least the core of a brand's positioning must remain the same across country markets. Local adaptations to different tastes as well as technical and social norms and varying added features to increase the local attractiveness of a brand must not endanger the internationally shared core meaning of the brand.

The potential for internationally standardized market communication is directly affected by product management. Local brands generally require localized communication, leading to higher budget needs. When the product concept can be easily captured in a symbol, such as Mickey Mouse or the Michelin Man, that makes visual sense in multiple cultures, communication standardization is eased.

Summary

Marketers need to know their customers before taking product management decisions. They have to assess what constitutes their total product seen from the customers' point of view. In international marketing, the processes and features expected by potential customers from different country markets may vary in composition and importance. So do the meanings customers attach to a product.

To avoid unnecessary complexity and the resulting costs, an international product policy has to be developed. It is based on the intended global strategic position of the firm and provides guidelines for all product management processes to be conducted:

- product positioning
- product portfolio management
- brand management
- quality management.

The product policy also determines the distribution of responsibilities among managers and management teams concerning those processes. It is the basis for operative product management decisions.

The goal of product portfolio management is to supply the markets with a stream of regularly renewed products that are attractive to customers, competitive compared to other suppliers' products, and allow the company to make attractive profits as well as to stay financially sound. To achieve this goal, international product management has to develop and maintain a balanced product portfolio.

Each successful launch of a new product in international markets needs several new product ideas to start with. Compared to a locally operating competitor, an international marketer has access to a greater number and diversity of sources of ideas for new products. The international marketer will have to determine the most valuable sources. Ideas coming from lead markets and lead actors in those markets will be the most preferred. Product development needs to be organized in a way that eases the development process.

An essential part of product brand management concerns the name of the product. The choice of the brand name and its communicative loading with specific meanings are of particular importance. Because the loss of a trademark or a brand may have devastating effects on the sales and profits of a firm the marketer must be able to protect the chosen name or trademark.

The packaging of products may strongly contribute to their meanings in the minds of potential customers because packaging is the visual surface of a product. Customer reactions to packaging are highly subject to influence by cultural specifics. The design of the package must fit customers' expectations in size, style, material, and color that reflect socioeconomic as well as cultural influences.

The goal of quality management is to keep customer satisfaction with the company's products at the highest levels in order to have as many loyal customers as possible and to win their positive promotion to other potential customers. To influence their customers' quality perceptions marketers may use quality assurance, which ascertains a given level of performance on each of the material and immaterial features important to the customers. And they may shape the customers' product-related expectations through quality signaling. Both approaches will be used by an international marketer to be successful.

DISCUSSION QUESTIONS

1. Explain why a company operating internationally needs a policy governing its international product management.

2. Search for examples of total consumer products that fit the extremes of high customer integration at a low level of materiality versus high immateriality at a low level of customer integration. How will international product policy decisions differ for those products?

3. How can a company decide the extent of standardization of its products and which standardization policy to choose?

4. Find examples of successful international consumer product individualization and compare them to successful consumer product adaptations. What are the reasons for success?

5. Explain the need for an international product branding policy.

6. What consequences can be expected from the existence of international product portfolio guidelines?

7. Describe different ways of structuring international product development responsibilities and discuss their impact on the product innovations to be expected.

8. How does the product innovation process in an internationally operating firm differ from the product innovation process in a firm with a domestic business focus?

9. Why is quality assurance particularly difficult for an international service provider? Gather some information concerning an example substantiating your points.

10. How may country of origin effects be used in international brand management? Find some recent examples and report on their level of success.

11. In what respects may the packaging of a product influence its meaning to the customers? What would you as an international brand manager do to avoid major packaging mistakes?

ADDITIONAL READINGS

Brentani, U. de and E.J. Kleinschmidt (2004), "Corporate culture and commitment: impact on performance of international new product development programs", *Journal of Product Innovation Management*, 21, 309–33.

Clark, T., D. Rajaratnam, and T. Smith (1996) "Toward a theory of international services: marketing intangibles in a world of nations", *Journal of International Marketing*, 4(2), 9–28.

Francis, J.N.P., J.P.Y. Lam, and J. Walls (2002) "Executive insights: the impact of linguistic differences on international brand name standardization: a comparison of English and Chinese brand names of Fortune-500 companies", *Journal of International Marketing*, 10(1), 98–116.

Green, R.T. and T. Smith (2002) "Executive insights: countering brand counterfeiters", *Journal of International Marketing*, 10(4), 89–106.

Herstatt, C. and E. v. Hippel (1992) "From experience: developing new product concepts via the lead user method: a case study in a 'low-tech' field", *Journal of Product Innovation Management*, 9, 213–21.

Jain, S.C. (1996) "Problems of international protection of intellectual property rights", *Journal of International Marketing*, 4(1), 9–32.

Journal of International Marketing, 10(2), 2002: Special issue on global branding.

Nebenzahl, I.D., E.D. Jaffe, and S.I. Lampert (1997) "Towards a theory of country image effect on product evaluation", *Management International Review*, 37(1), 27–49.

Schuiling, I. and J.-N. Kapferer (2004) "Executive insights: real differences between local and international brands: strategic implications for international marketers", *Journal of International Marketing*, 12(4), 97–112.

Wong, V. (2002) "Antecedents of international new product rollout timeliness", *International Marketing Review*, 19(2/3), 120–32.

Zhou, L. and M.K. Hui (2003) "Symbolic value of foreign products in the Peoples' Republic of China", *Journal of International Marketing*, 11(2), 36–58.

Useful internet links

3M	http://www.3m.com/
Adidas	http://www.adidas.com/
America Online	http://www.aol.com/
Avent	http://www.avent.com/
Banco Santander	http://www.gruposantander.es/
Bauknecht	http://www.bauknecht.de/
Bazar de l'Hôtel de Ville	http://www.bhv.fr/
Boehringer	http://www.Boehringer Mannheim.com
Burton	http://www.burton.com/
Business Software Alliance	http://www.bsa.org/
CompuServe	http://www.compuserve.com/
Electronic Resellers Association	http://www.erai.com/
Ermenegildo Zegna	http://www.zegna.com/
Failure Mode and Effect Analysis Info Centre	http://www.fmeainfocentre.com/
Fraunhofer Institute	http://www.fraunhofer.de/fhg/EN/index.jsp
Givenchy	http://www.givenchy.com/
Grey Advertising	http://www.grey.com
Harvard Business Review	http://harvardbusinessonline.hbsp.harvard.edu/b02/en/hbr/hbr_home.jhtml
Hertz	http://www.hertz.com/
HILTI	http://www.hilti.com/
International Components Corporation	http://www.iccus.com/
Internorm	http://www.internorm.com/english/internormE.html
Johnson & Johnson	http://www.jnj.com/
Marriott Hotels	http://marriott.com/default.mi
Massey-Fergusson	http://www.masseyfergusson.com/
Mitsubishi	http://www.mitsubishi-motors.com/
Morgan Stanley	http://www.morganstanley.com/
Novartis	http://www.novartis.com/
OneTwoSold	http://www.onetwosold.com/
Pillsbury	http://www.pillsbury.com/
Prada	http://www.prada.com/
Professional Investigating & Consulting Agency	http://www.pica.net/
Rabobank International	http://www.rabobank.com/
Ralph Lauren	http://www.polo.com/home/index.jsp
Randstad	http://www.randstad.com/
Red Cross	http://www.icrc.org/
Reebok	http://www.reebok.com/
Replay	http://www.replay.it/
Rolls Royce	http://www.rolls-roycemotorcars.com/
Rupp	http://www.rupp.at/english/index.htm
Salvatore Ferragamo	http://www.ferragamo.com/
SAP	http://www.sap.com/

Scania	http://www.scania.com/
Sixt	http://www.e-sixt.com/
Snapple	http://www.snapple.com/
Texas Instruments	http://www.ti.com/
UNICEF	http://www.unicef.org/
United Nations	http://www.un.org/
Virgin Megastores	http://www.virginmegastores.co.uk/
Wall Street Journal Europe	https://services.wsje.com/home/home1.asp
Wallace Theater	http://www.wallacetheaters.com/
WTO	http://www.wto.org/

Virtual communities concerning product categories or leisure time activities are often virtual meeting places for innovative consumers to discuss opportunities and ideas for new products and their improvement. Members of such communities are particularly interesting sources of new product ideas because of their high product involvement and knowledge as well as their presence on the net.

One option for utilizing the innovative potential of online communities is to create a product-focused community where the same users can participate throughout all stages of the NPD process. The users playfully familiarize with the virtual product from the beginning, get to know the product's use, and give their feedback after virtual presentations and test simulations. Some users may even attain the status of development advisors.

Another approach is to use more than one online community for different NPD stages. This seems to be reasonable assuming that online communities differ in their structure, values, and creativity. Hence, members also differ in their individual characteristics and are more or less suited to contribute to the development task of each process stage. Community members can adopt three roles:

1 source of ideas
2 co-creators
3 users and buyers.

Before selecting one of the approaches marketers must:

● clearly define the objectives of virtual user integration
● formulate their expectation
● structure the development task in a manner that one or more defined development (sub-) task(s) can be selected and delegated to the community members.

When opting for a multi-community approach the international product (development) manager has to follow a sequence of four steps:

● determination of user indicators
● community identification
● virtual interaction design
● user access and motivation.

Determination of user indicators

The profile of user's skills, expertise, and characteristics sought by the marketer depends on the particular development (sub-) task(s) which is (are) assigned to the community members. Consumers with lead user characteristics, for example, are well suited for idea and concept generation whereas a group of consumers which is representative for the users of a specific product segment is better suited for testing activities and sales forecasts. To determine the user's innovation potential personal indicators may be used such as lead user characteristics, domain-specific knowledge regarding product usage, materials, technology, or market, creativity and cognitive style, for example, the ability of divergent thinking, and already invented products.

The level of involvement with the online community and the consumption activity provides another way of valuable categorization:

- tourists lacking strong social ties to the group as well as to the consumption activity
- minglers maintaining strong social ties but not being really into the topic
- devotees, who are highly involved with the activity but not strongly related to the community
- insiders who are strongly associated with the community and highly involved with its central issue.

Community identification

The identification of online communities containing members with the defined user indicators starts with diligent screening. Powerful search engines like google.com or yahoo.com are helpful in identifying the best suited communities. One might begin by entering the product category or activity the new product is related to and start, for example, with screening user groups/newsgroups or topic-related internet sites. Considering a wide variety of options no matter how obvious or abstruse they appear at first sight may lead to useful alternatives.

A pre-selection of most relevant online communities is based on:

- personal impressions
- a quick evaluation of content and design
- information regarding traffic and number of participants.

Before the selected internet pages are examined in more detail it is advisable to briefly check how the producers' intention to integrate community members virtually into new product development is perceived and how the community reacts to external inquiries from producers in general. A first insight may be provided by the netiquette, if available. For a specific project it is best to get in touch with the webmaster asking about her/his opinion and conditions. If the community is administrated by a commercial provider, the announcement of the project will be at a cost. Hence, it is important to get an overview on prices and services offered. The price rates are to be linked to the actual number of community members.

Virtual interaction design

The design of virtual interaction depends on the specific context. Three major dimensions must be considered:

- participants, their expectations and characteristics
- content: what will be exchanged?
- external and internal context.

The interaction has to be rewarding for both marketer and user. Consequently, the design of the virtual interaction has to consider both the objectives of users and marketer by varying the following design parameters:

- *tools*, e.g. toolkit, virtual concept testing, stock market, idea competitions, or open discussion forums
- *incentives*, e.g. notation as co-inventor, supply of proprietary information, monetary compensation
- *intensity*, e.g. number of participants, frequency, and duration
- *communication style*, e.g. formal/informal; one-, bi- or multi-directional, anonymous, autonomy of task performance, level of multimedia richness.

In addition, the virtual interaction design should allow realistic judgment. Abstract ideas and concepts take on shape in the form of virtual products. The presentation of virtual prototypes in real-life situations enables users to evaluate concepts more realistically even though in the early development stages. In addition, the pure functionality of a product has to be combined with emotions and meanings the innovation is intended to communicate. Because users have no experience with a radically new product they must be able to play around with the product features/functions and experience them via a mode of trial and error in a way to make tacit knowledge transferable.

It should also inspire creativity. Innovative problem solutions are created in an environment that stimulates creativity, for example, by presenting various scenarios of the future or some vaguely drafted solutions as catalysts lowering the barrier for brainstorming of new ideas. Participants should be fascinated by the task.

A state of flow should be created. Participants may experience a state of flow when they become totally absorbed in the activity. This may happen when the challenge of the assigned task is congruent to their level of skill, that is, they are challenged to a just manageable extent, and when the task is highly rewarding. Participants are so concentrated that they tend to forget time and space. A state of flow offers an ideal prerequisite for creative ideas and inspires community members to participate again.

Properly offered community functionality enables members to take up, enhance, or just comment on new product ideas and jointly work on them.

Data handling must be pre-specified by the marketer to allow managing and integrating the collected data most effectively in the innovation process.

Clear and transparent regulation – "innoquette" – of legal aspects concerning exploitation rights of generated ideas and protection of data privacy has to be set up to ensure transparent and trustworthy communication. These rules have to be accepted by the participating community members.

User access and motivation

User access consists of getting in touch with the members of online communities and informing them about the part they can play in new product development. Users can be addressed via community postings, banners, pop-ups, short articles on frequently visited websites, online panels, and online communities. Moreover databases and commercial panels can be used to recruit the participants via email, telephone interviews, or postal invitations.

Participants may be attracted through monetary incentives, like awarding bonus points, drawing prizes, or even offering them participation in the success of the new product. But most of the time intrinsic incentives such as the demand for new and better products, curiosity and the fun of exploration, the desire to learn something new, the innovation task itself, the possibility to get exclusive information on innovations, share ideas, get acknowledgment and receive support from the community definitely motivate community members to take part in new product development tasks without any monetary reward.

INTERNATIONAL DISTRIBUTION MANAGEMENT

12

INTERNATIONAL MARKETING SPOTLIGHT

Make your dealers your partners

In the early 1990s many observers predicted that Caterpillar, headquartered in Peoria, Illinois, would join the long list of U.S. corporations that had fallen foul of the Japanese. They focused particularly on the rivalry between Caterpillar and Komatsu. With Komatsu boasting cost advantages of as much as 40% in some product lines and excellent products, observers accepted as a foregone conclusion that Komatsu would fulfill its vow to "encircle Cat" and become the dominant producer in the construction and mining equipment industry. Like many predictions, this one fell short. Despite determined efforts by Komatsu, Hitachi, Kobelco, and other competitors, Caterpillar is still the world's largest manufacturer of construction and mining equipment, diesel and natural gas engines, and industrial gas turbines.

Several factors played a part. They include the high value of Caterpillar's brand name; the excellent quality of products; the high resale value of the machines; a reorganization that made the company leaner and more responsive to customer needs; big investments in manufacturing productivity; faster new product development processes; and the weakening of the dollar relative to the yen. But the biggest reason for Caterpillar's success has been its system of distribution and product support and the close customer relationships it fosters.

The customers know that there is a company called Caterpillar. But the dealers strongly influence the meaning of the firm to the customers. Caterpillar's selected dealers tend to be prominent business leaders in their markets who are deeply involved in community activities. Their reputation and long-term relationships are important because selling Caterpillar's products is a personal business.

Caterpillar helps its dealers finance purchases by customers. It supports dealers in inventory management and control, logistics, equipment

Caterpillar's success is built on sophisticated distribution and product support systems
© Tim Pohl/iStock

management, and maintenance programs. Dealers are involved in programs dealing with product quality, cost reduction, and manufacturing issues. The company also publishes a huge volume of technical material each year and underwrites technical training and support for dealers' personnel.

Caterpillar's top management is convinced that the relationship between a company and its dealers is much more important than the contractual agreements or the techniques and tactics that make the relationship work on the surface. Mutual trust, continuity, and consistency in policies, constant communication, uniform performance standards, and equal consideration of dealers, while recognizing that they are independent and unique in many ways, help the firm to present one face to its customers in more than 200 countries around the world.

Source: Adapted from Fites, D.V. (1996) "Make your dealers your partners", *Harvard Business Review*, March–April, pp. 84–95; www.caterpillar.com/about_cat/index.html 2003

The focal question of this chapter is: **How can international marketers establish and maintain distribution systems that best help to build and sustain their intended global position?**

International distribution decisions

To build and sustain its global strategic position every company must manage distribution, or the flow of products to final customers (see Figure 12.1). In some cases distribution is relatively straightforward. Before the Gulf War, a brewery in Iraq put bottles filled with beer into cases, placed the cases on pallets, and

FIGURE 12.1 *International marketing decision process*

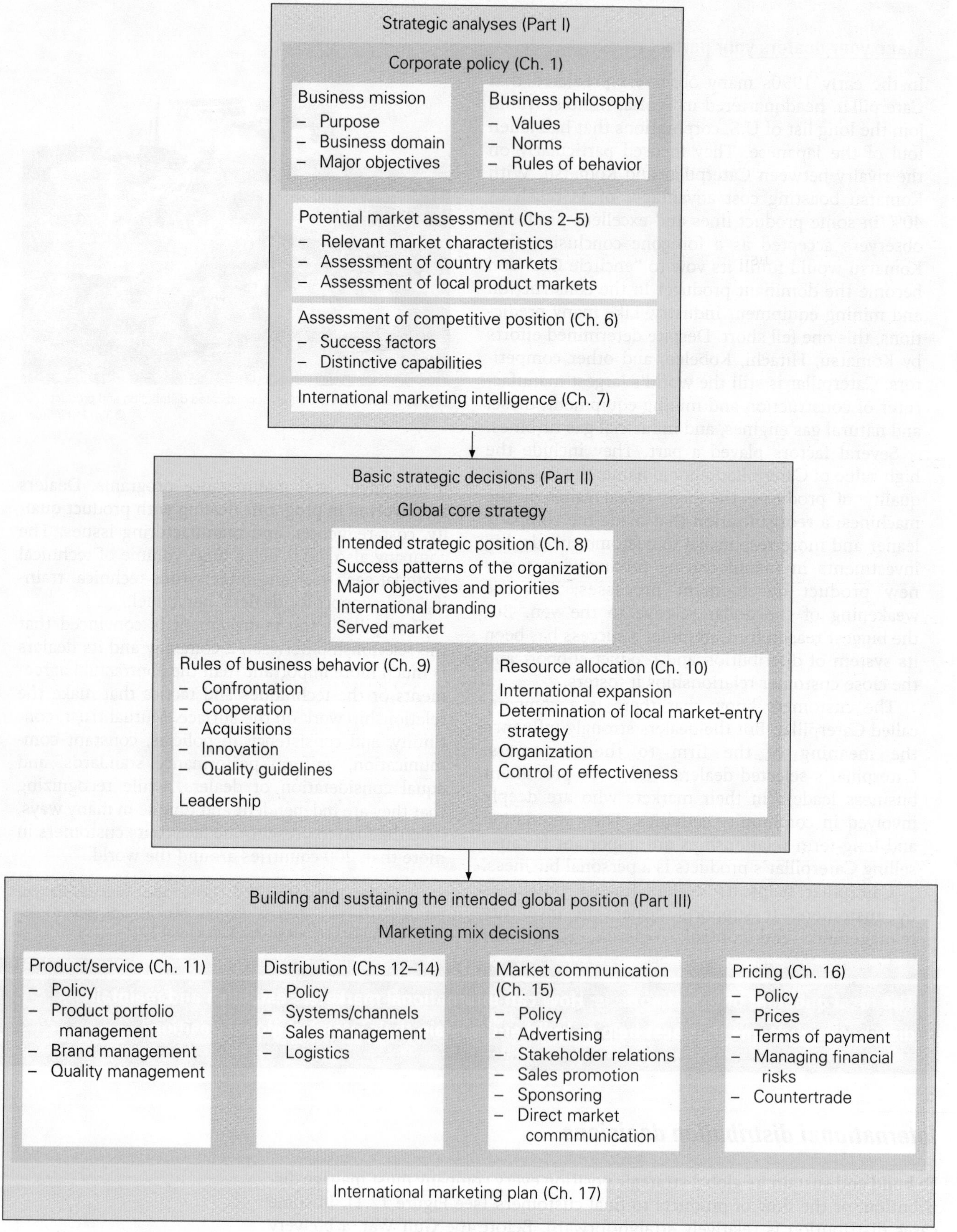

Strategic analyses (Part I)

Corporate policy (Ch. 1)

Business mission
- Purpose
- Business domain
- Major objectives

Business philosophy
- Values
- Norms
- Rules of behavior

Potential market assessment (Chs 2–5)
- Relevant market characteristics
- Assessment of country markets
- Assessment of local product markets

Assessment of competitive position (Ch. 6)
- Success factors
- Distinctive capabilities

International marketing intelligence (Ch. 7)

Basic strategic decisions (Part II)

Global core strategy

Intended strategic position (Ch. 8)
Success patterns of the organization
Major objectives and priorities
International branding
Served market

Rules of business behavior (Ch. 9)
- Confrontation
- Cooperation
- Acquisitions
- Innovation
- Quality guidelines

Leadership

Resource allocation (Ch. 10)
International expansion
Determination of local market-entry
  strategy
Organization
Control of effectiveness

Building and sustaining the intended global position (Part III)

Marketing mix decisions

Product/service (Ch. 11)
- Policy
- Product portfolio
  management
- Brand management
- Quality management

Distribution (Chs 12–14)
- Policy
- Systems/channels
- Sales management
- Logistics

Market communication
(Ch. 15)
- Policy
- Advertising
- Stakeholder relations
- Sales promotion
- Sponsoring
- Direct market
  commmunication

Pricing (Ch. 16)
- Policy
- Prices
- Terms of payment
- Managing financial
  risks
- Countertrade

International marketing plan (Ch. 17)

transported them from the end of the production line to the fence surrounding the company's property. There, customers were waiting impatiently to purchase the product. They climbed to the top of the fence, where the cases were lifted up to them, and money exchanged hands. The firm's distribution system consisted of a forklift and a driver!

The example may seem strange to readers who are familiar with distribution in highly industrialized countries, but it clearly shows that any company's distribution system has two major components: *distribution channels*, that is, the people, organizations or institutions by which goods or services are offered to the customers, including agents, dealers, wholesalers, and retailers; and *the means of physical distribution*, that is, the tools and facilities, including the related information, used by people and organizations to bridge the physical distance between the company and its customers.

An international distribution system shares many characteristics with a domestic one. Both, for example, must:

- make the product available to potential customers
- help inform them about product benefits
- manage distribution partner relationships
- be suited to the company's intended strategic position.

However, designing an international distribution system is more complicated because it must take into account:

- different geographic areas
- varying expectations of distribution partners
- differences in competitive structure
- relevant dimensions of the macro-environment,

such as legal regulations, culture-specific buying habits or the level of economic development. This chapter addresses such factors and others that help determine the best distribution system for goods and services for an international marketing effort.

For the purpose of determining the best distribution system, management has to assess the advantages and disadvantages of different types of systems. It will use various customer and intermediary characteristics to compare alternative distribution channels available in the market. However, *channel selection* is only part of international distribution management. To be successful, international marketers must carefully *manage relationships with the selected channel members*. They need an appropriate organizational structure, as well as a bundle of tools for effective communication, motivation, and control.

This chapter first discusses the need for an *international distribution policy*, that is, the guideline for the *selection of a distribution system and of channel members* described later. The importance of *relationship management* in international distribution channels is highlighted and some tools available to marketing managers are presented.

Chapter 13 will focus on the structure of a company's own salesforce, how to choose and train salespeople for international marketing, and will discuss important issues of how to manage an international salesforce.

The contribution of transportation, packaging, warehousing, and storage to an appropriate level of international customer service will be the focus of Chapter 14.

International distribution policy

Many small and medium-sized companies are so overwhelmed by the complexity of international distribution that they simply conform to existing company procedures (which are likely to be inappropriate for international markets), or take advantage only of opportunities that arise by chance. Even multinational corporations often leave specific distribution decisions to their local offices. In both cases there is a clear need to establish an international distribution policy.

An international distribution policy is a general statement of:

* *goals* that have to be attained by distribution decisions
* *rules of behavior* that are to be met when implementing those decisions.

A company's international distribution policy should reflect its basic strategic decisions. It should help to achieve the intended global position by translating more general goals and objectives into a set of specific distribution guidelines. Those guidelines determine *how the chosen market-entry alternative is to be executed.* They indicate *minimum and maximum levels of capital and personnel* to be committed to achieving a desired level of coverage in each market. They contain *pre-established goals* regarding market share, sales volume, and profit margins for each region, customer group and distribution channel, taking into account the *desired level of company involvement* in the distribution system, and the *desirability of ownership of intermediaries.*

The desirable level of market coverage has to be determined in light of:

* the company's general competitive posture
* long-term market potential
* expected return on investment
* financial strength
* positioning of strategic business units and products
* geographic location of product markets.

For example, mass production companies and manufacturers of specialty items need different levels of market coverage. The mass production company wants intensive distribution, that is, to be represented in as many outlets as possible, because most customers will not be ready to shop for their products. Coca-Cola, BIC razors and Nescafé are examples of products that are distributed in this way. A producer of specialty items, by way of contrast, may choose selective or exclusive distribution. Its customers are either brand loyal or ready to search for the product. Selective distribution may severely limit the number of partners in the distribution channel, cooperating only with channel partners that are well suited to the product's intended position in customers' minds. For example, Patek Philip, a Geneva-based producer of expensive watches, follows a policy of choosing a single renowned specialty shop in every major city to sell its products.

Guidelines concerning the level of the company's involvement in local distribution activities significantly affect the level of market control achieved by the company and the quality of marketing in the targeted areas. The international distribution policy has to ensure that the distribution system of the firm and how it manages the contact points with customers as well as important stakeholders fit the intended brand meaning/positioning. Dallas-based Mary Kay Cosmetics, for example, has a policy of selling directly to its customers through employees known as "beauty consultants." When it started business in China and Russia in 1995, it did not rely on the service quality of local retailing firms, but coordinated all marketing activities through its own people.

Alternative distribution systems

In general, there are two ways to distribute goods:

* directly to the final customer
* indirectly through a more complex system that employs intermediaries.

Producers of industrial goods often sell directly to their customers, using an internal salesforce to initiate and maintain business relationships. Most manufacturers of consumer goods, however, sell to wholesalers or large retailers that may sell to other wholesalers and smaller retailers, which, in turn, sell to the final customer. In either case, distribution often becomes more complex when national boundaries are crossed. This section describes both direct (integrated) and indirect (independent or company-bound) distribution systems.

Integrated distribution

In an integrated distribution system the company's own employees generate sales, administer orders, and deliver products or services. The distribution system is integrated because employees, whatever their title or function within the company, are the agents of distribution.

Several factors determine which members of a firm are most directly involved in generating sales:

- company size
- size of potential market
- level of customers' globalization
- complexity of total product
- hierarchical level of purchase decision maker
- importance of customer services
- available means of contact with customers.

Company size

Compared to large companies, small internationally operating firms have marketing and sales functions that are less specifically assigned to certain people. Distribution activities, therefore, tend to be distributed across all levels of hierarchy.

Size of potential market

When the size of a local market is small, sales will mostly be generated by salespeople, who often report to a regional sales manager. In larger markets, companies that prefer an integrated distribution system tend to establish more complex sales organizations. Liechtenstein's HILTI AG, for example, is dedicated to integrated distribution. Its global distribution system contains regional sales organizations such as Hilti Western Hemisphere, Hilti Latin America and Hilti Asia. In the U.S., customer group-oriented teams, each formed by a territory salesperson, an employee of the national Hilti center and a member of the central customer service unit – both located in Tulsa, Oklahoma – contact and serve their customers. In China, HILTI salespeople sustained by regional distribution centers serve their local customers directly.

Level of customers' globalization

The level of globalization of a firm's customers results in varying members of the firm being involved in business interactions. U.S.-based Xerox, for example, has established a global key account management system. Each global account, that is, firms requiring services in two or more countries, has the focused attention of a senior-level manager, whose responsibilities include working with foreign personnel to ensure delivery of products and services. Xerox also guarantees high-level management attention and support for its global accounts. Top management executives involved in the program not only advise customers on Xerox's services, but also provide input into strategic decisions and participate in sales calls as necessary.

Complexity of total product

Salespeople will handle the entire selling process if the complexity of the total product is low and their customers are simply purchasing agents. The salespeople may report directly to the company's home office, but often visit customers in foreign markets; or they may operate out of subsidiaries or sales offices in different geographic areas. If the purchase decision maker is a powerful person, for example a category purchasing manager of Wal-Mart, the largest retailing firm in the world, yearly listing negotiations will be conducted by a high-level representative of the international marketer.

Hierarchical level of purchase decision maker

Sales of highly complex total products, such as industrial plants or large consulting projects, usually involve higher level members of the supplier organization. Most of the negotiation process is done by teams of functional specialists, but final decision making or at least the signing of contracts is done by members of higher management. For example, when Italy-based Danieli SA offers large metallurgical engineering projects, such as the construction of a new continuous casting plant at the Magnitogorsk steel works in Russia, the specifications and terms of contracts are normally negotiated by specialists in sales, finance, and technology, but the final negotiation and the signing of the contract are done by top management, because they involve important private capital owners, top managers, or high-level public agents in the purchasing organization.

Importance of customer services

Depending on the importance of customer services, such as planning or advice, and the available means of contact with customers in a market, marketers can also sell goods or services directly to the final customer through manufacturer-owned stores or showrooms, or by means of mail-order, telephone or electronic markets. A system of stores owned by the manufacturer is a type of distribution channel that is usually available only to financially strong companies such as LVMH the leading luxury conglomerate in the world. Less well-capitalized firms can choose franchising. This approach may also be used when all other distribution channels are blocked or when the company's marketing strategy is based on direct contact with the final customer.

Available means of contact with customers

Despite the fast development of internet use in all industrially developed as well as emerging countries there are other methods of contact still available.

Mail-order selling This is a distribution system that is still important in international marketing. A number of specialized companies, such as Italian Scala Collections (using the trademark Artigiano) operate internationally. Manufacturers of high-tech industrial products sometimes also still use the mail-order approach. For example, Wild-Leitz, a Swiss-based company specializing in opto-electronics, sends catalogs to customers to sell standard products and spare parts. The physical presence of catalogs serves as a reminder to the potential customers.

Telephone selling This can be used in various ways. Sales clerks or call centers may use the telephone to establish and maintain contact with customers who are never contacted personally. Potential customers may be called to generate leads for the field salesforce. Or current customers may be called to sell products, promote new services, and collect information.

Electronic markets These exist for both consumer and industrial goods and services in highly developed and emerging economies. They have become so important that formerly leading mail-order firms such as GUS (Great Universal

Stores) from England, disposed of their home shopping business. U.S. Amazon.com dominates the electronic book market. The internet is the preferred tool for consumers knowing what they want and going for the convenience of making purchases without leaving home.

As popular examples such as eBay or i-Tunes have shown, computer-based systems provide even rather untrained customers with product offers and information, service, and billing. Some service companies, such as CompuServe, have established addresses, such as Shop@CompuServe that provide less experienced customers with selections of brand name merchants available online, shopping catalogs, and personal buying guides, search facilities by brand and product category as well as simplified "checkout" mechanisms. Even with the increasing array of "facilitating technology" already in place, it still appears, however, that many European customers essentially see electronic markets as supplements to the shops.

In business-to-business markets, the use of the internet as a distribution channel depends on the complexity of the total product. For example, Durst Phototechnik, an Italian marketer of high-tech printers and plotters has a website that allows customers to search for products and services. However, the total product is too complex to be sold via the net. In addition to complexity, email viruses or hacker attacks are a danger to the functioning of distribution through the internet. They can inflict considerable damage in a very short time. For example, the Sobig.F virus reportedly reached 1 million computers in 24 hours.

Independent and company-bound distribution

Independent distribution systems are not directly controlled by the organization. The company uses intermediaries to establish contact with the final customers. Companies that use intermediaries but largely control them are said to have company-bound distribution systems. In domestic as well as international marketing, there are basically two types of intermediary: agents and merchants.

Agents
In domestic marketing they are often called manufacturers' representatives. Agents fully represent the company (also called the principal) in a particular market. They operate in the name of the principal, but they do not take title to the products being distributed, neither do they bear any economic risks.

Merchants
In contrast, merchants do take title to the goods, which they buy, handle, and sell on their own account. In domestic marketing, they are commonly referred to as distributors or wholesalers. Through merchants' activities, time, place, finance, and service utilities are added to the product bundle. A more complete discussion of the types of intermediary that international marketers use is provided in Table 12.1. In most cases the intermediaries in a distribution channel are a mixture of the types described.

Integrated vs independent distribution

Fit with current distribution system
In general, companies tend to develop an international distribution system that reflects their domestic choice. For example, Tissot, a Swiss marketer of watches, may wish to follow a strategy of appealing to a mass market interested in high quality, using as many jewelry stores – which are numerous in Switzerland – as possible supplied from a central warehouse located at the site of the company. Often a similar distribution system does not exist in another country market,

TABLE 12.1 *Types of intermediary*

Representatives establish and maintain relationships with prospective and existing customers in a specified geographic area on behalf of the principal. Representatives do not take physical possession of the product, do not arrange for its shipping or handling, and do not take any credit, market, or exchange risk. A representative does, however, arrange sales between the manufacturer and buyers, and must pass all legal documents to the principal for approval; she or he may not sign them on behalf of the principal. In a continuing relationship the representative may handle only the principal's product lines and complementary lines of other firms. Compensation is in the form of commission.

Brokers and factors are independent agents. They can legally bind the principal to a contract and expose it to risk without taking any risk themselves. **Brokers** are independent individuals or organizations that bring together prospective buyers and sellers to facilitate sales. They often deal in commodities and food products, handling large volumes of merchandise. Normally this is not a continuing relationship and exclusivity is not expected. **Factors**, many of which are banks, perform all normal brokerage functions plus financing. They may finance goods at various stages of the value-added chain. Factors serve to relieve both the seller and buyer of credit risk. The non-continuous relationship between the principal and the factor is also non-exclusive; that is, a factor can serve other sellers as well. Brokers and factors are paid a fee by the seller for services provided.

Distributors have a formalized, continuing relationship with the manufacturer, with exclusive selling rights for a specified geographic area. Distributors take title to (buy) the products they sell to other merchants (wholesalers or retailers), or to industrial customers. Close cooperation between the manufacturer and distributor gives the principal more control over prices, promotional activities, inventory, and service policies than it has when it sells products to a wholesaler.

Dealers have the same function as retailers. But, in addition, they have the same type of continuing relationship with suppliers that distributors have. The major difference between dealers and distributors is that dealers sell the principal's goods directly to final customers. Sometimes, the principal holds an equity share in the dealer's business. In such situations, the principal has considerable control over the relationship and the dealer provides the principal with a great deal of market information. In most cases, dealers have exclusive selling rights for the manufacturer's products in a specified area, and the principal is the dealer's only supplier. Most automobile manufacturers use dealers as their intermediaries. Dealers are also common in the marketing of industrial goods.

Franchising is a special kind of dealership agreement that is well suited to companies with innovative products and fully developed marketing strategies, but insufficient capital to implement those strategies. A franchisee is an individual or organization that is granted the right to conduct business under the franchiser's trade name. The franchiser assists the franchisee in locating, equipping, and designing the business premises. In most cases, franchisees must closely follow the terms of contractual agreements regarding how business is to be conducted. The franchiser is paid a fee or royalties as compensation for fulfilling such functions as management assistance, training, and global marketing. International franchising has become increasingly popular in a number of industries in which standardized services or brand names are especially important to customers. Fashion franchises such as Benetton, Champion, or Escada are found in most developed countries. Fast-food franchises, like McDonald's or Kentucky Fried Chicken, and hotel franchises, like Novotel, Holiday Inn, and the Hilton, are also found throughout the world.

Importers fulfill the same functions as distributors but generally do not have exclusive territorial rights. They may be either wholesalers or retailers, and they may handle the products of many suppliers, sometimes even competing product lines. As a result, the principal has limited control. Distributors, dealers, and importers do not receive direct compensation; their profit is the margin between the buying and selling prices of the products they carry, minus their costs. The margins or discounts offered to merchants vary greatly from one country to another. They depend on the level of competition in a given market, the level of service offered by the intermediary, geographic distance, sales volume, purchasing power, efficiency, and tradition.

however. In such situations management must determine whether a different distribution channel can be used without departing radically from the current pattern of success. For example, an Italian manufacturer of high-fashion, high-priced women's shoes, such as Bruno Magli, considering a new market may find that there are not enough prestigious specialty shops in that market. To achieve sufficient market coverage, the company must look for other outlets. If appropriate alternatives cannot be found, the firm might decide not to enter the market, or it might enter it under a different brand name.

Conditions favoring integrated distribution

The following conditions favor an integrated distribution system.

Specialized product or product use knowledge For example, with complex products such as IBM information technology systems, marketing success depends on specialized product or application knowledge.

High level of service requirements With automobile marketers, a high level of service is necessary, especially after the sale.

Highly differentiated product Specialty steels for example are highly differentiated from competitors' products, or unique. Only company employees may be able to acquire the know-how needed to advise customers adequately.

Product closely related to the company's core business Only employees can ensure close enough contact with customers and intensive sales support when the product is very important to the company's core business.

Strong need to control local marketing practices A member of the distribution system who is a company employee can readily monitor distribution activities and use the authority of the company to influence the behavior of distribution personnel. The company receives firsthand information on what customers expect in terms of delivery time, product modifications, personal contact, and the like if it must ensure that it hires personnel who are sensitive and willing to meet those expectations.

Lack of potential cooperation partners In some regions of the world it may be impossible to find appropriate distribution partners or individuals and firms who are willing to cooperate. In such cases the marketer will be forced to choose an integrated distribution system.

Lower costs and margins Where the existing distribution channels and facilities are so expensive that they would not allow the company to serve the market at a competitive price level, the firm has to do it in an integrated way.

Legal restrictions on foreign investment may prevent marketers from using an integrated distribution system. But there are an additional number of disadvantages that have to be considered in taking an adequate decision (see Table 12.2 for a summary).

Advantages and disadvantages

The major disadvantage of integrated distribution is its potential high cost. Sales managers, salespeople, and physical distribution staff must be hired and trained. The sales organization is likely to lose money during the first few years in a new market, because sales volume will not be sufficient to cover overheads. For these reasons, most companies that are expanding into foreign markets at least initially choose a company-bound or independent distribution system.

When a company competes in a mature product category, direct competition by similar products is likely to be strong. Low costs and prices are crucial to success. In such a situation most companies use non-integrated distribution. As examples from Japan show, however, company-bound distribution systems can be highly successful because they ensure more influence on the marketing behavior of intermediaries. Hitachi KK, one of the biggest firms within the electrical and electronics industry of the world, for example, holds 59% of shares of Hitachi Sales KK. Hitachi Sales KK, is responsible for the communication policy, catalog production, and the management and control of a very great number of wholesalers on three hierarchical levels. The wholesalers are basically financed by the central firm (Hitachi KK), which in a number of cases holds small quantities of their shares. Hitachi KK does not hold any inventory of finished goods. These are delivered to the wholesalers immediately after production. The principal wholesalers might be forced to sell Hitachi products exclusively. Wholesalers on the third level are allowed to sell other branded products to cover their costs.

The tendency to choose independent distribution partners is reinforced by socio-cultural differences between domestic and non-domestic markets. Such a choice may be reasonable, because transferring title to an independent channel member also transfers risk. From the customer's perspective, however, the choice of an independent distribution system may be entirely wrong.

The use of independent distributors reduces the company's opportunities to become familiar with the specific characteristics of the new market, thereby limiting its ability to offer a product that meets the market's needs. Independent distributors may also be a problem because they have considerable freedom to establish local marketing policies. Moreover, independent distributors' loyalty to the manufacturer is likely to be limited, because they may carry a wide range of products, from different manufacturers, and they will favor naturally those products that yield the greatest sales and profits. To overcome these problems, some firms only work with distributors that will focus exclusively on their product lines. This can only be done, however, if the product line is broad enough to generate sufficient sales volume for the distributor, and the profit margins are attractive.

Channel mix

Companies that are successful in international markets generally rely on a mix of different, more or less integrated distribution channels. For example, Warner-Lambert, a U.S.-based manufacturer of razors, chewing gum, and pharmaceutical products, taken over by Pfizer, has succeeded in Japan by using distinct distribution channels for each set of product lines. When entering the market, razors and

TABLE 12.2   *Advantages and disadvantages of integrated vs independent distribution*

	Integrated distribution	Independent distribution	Integrated distribution brings the company into direct contact with its customers, allows close control of local marketing, and helps in avoiding unintentional know-how transfer. Independent distribution can build on existing local distribution systems, relates distribution costs to the level of actual sales, and transfers some risk to distribution partners.
Advantages	Strong influence on local marketing	Transfer of risk	
	Closeness to customers	Cost depending on sales	
	No unintentional know-how transfer	Existing distribution system	
Disadvantages	High fixed cost	Distance from customers	
	No partition of risks	Limited control of local marketing	
	Distribution system needs to be established	Limited loyalty of distributors	

blades were sold through the Hatori trading organization, which, in turn, sold the firm's products through independent wholesalers that provided considerable service to retailers. When Warner-Lambert tried a similar channel for its chewing gum, it failed. Not satisfied with the wholesalers' efforts, the company bypassed them. This change made wholesalers angry and retailers suspicious about the company switching their distribution system. Warner-Lambert then successfully built up its own salesforce to obtain orders from retailers and passed orders back to the wholesalers, resulting in a respectable share of the Japanese chewing gum market. In yet another product market, Warner-Lambert has been manufacturing pharmaceuticals in Japan since 1960, and selling them with great success directly to large drug companies.

International channel evaluation

Making the appropriate choice among the distribution channel options available in foreign markets requires an understanding of the ways in which each might contribute to the goals and objectives of the distribution policy. The marketer must consider a range of customer and intermediary characteristics from which to develop a set of selection criteria, a process that is discussed in this section.

Customer characteristics

An evaluation of distribution methods for a particular region or country market must consider the:

- number of potential customers
- location
- purchasing power
- specific needs
- purchasing habits.

For example, in analyzing the U.S. market, a European manufacturer of furniture fittings would find a considerable concentration of furniture manufacturers in North and South Carolina. It would therefore be likely to choose either an integrated distribution system with a sales office in the Carolinas or an intermediary that is familiar with the major customers and handles complementary product lines.

Differing purchasing habits of potential customers affect distribution decisions. The main reason for these differences is variations in the cultural and economic environments. In great parts of Turkey, Saudi Arabia, and most parts of India, for example, supermarkets are unpopular. Turkish consumers prefer fresh products that have just been harvested, while Saudis require that poultry and meat be slaughtered in a manner known as halal. In India, many people are unable to afford cars or refrigerators. They therefore need to shop at least once a day and buy very small quantities. Culture box 12.1 gives an impression of how such purchasing behavior may change when changes occur in the cultural or economic environment of a country.

Danone yogurt is distributed differently in France and Hong Kong because of the different purchasing habits of customers in those countries. In France, Danone uses self-service discount stores, such as Auchan or Leclerc with spacious fresh food areas and large assortments of general merchandise. These stores, which occupy as much as 250,000-feet^2 of space and have up to 100 checkout counters, serve French consumers as major outlets for dairy products when they do their weekly shopping. It would be impossible for Danone to rely on such outlets in Hong Kong, where the majority of homemakers shop once a day, and buy most of their food in either a street market or an urban shopping mall.

Intermediary characteristics

Functions

Any evaluation of potential distribution partners in a foreign market must be based on an analysis of the responsibilities, or functions, of both the distributing agents and the company itself. The same title may imply different responsibilities, depending on the location. Therefore, the marketer needs to find out what an intermediary's title actually means in each market.

As Table 12.3 shows an intermediary can take over several functions. The following functions are performed to a varying extent. *Physical handling of goods* is especially important for companies with little or no international marketing experience. In addition, intermediaries can provide *assistance in promoting and selling the product*, and *providing services to local customers*. As the example of Caterpillar's dealers shows, intermediaries can help build and maintain the goodwill of government agencies and members of the local community. Intermediaries can also *take over part of the financing* and *bear some of the risk of the distribution process*.

CULTURE BOX 12.1

Malled?

Covering more than 330,000m², SM Megamall in Manila is one of the largest shopping malls in Asia. Other enormous malls are opening across the urbanized areas of the Philippines. From Hong Kong to Jakarta, malls are the places where more and more Asians go – not just to shop, but to eat and be entertained. Asking where the money those customers spend comes from, there are two major factors: First, many Filipinos boost their disposable income by second and third jobs (paying no taxes) and, second, the Philippines have one of the lowest savings rates in Asia.

In Asia, unlike North America, most malls are built in cities, not out of town. Most of the emerging middle classes are found in the cities. The income gap between town and country is particularly pronounced in the Philippines. Although official GDP per capita is only about $1,000, in metropolitan Manila where around 10 million Filipinos live, work, and produce up to 70% of the country's total income, the figure is around $2,500. Many of the people flocking through malls are only window shopping. Part of the appeal is that they are cool and air conditioned. But there are others being flown in on package tours that combine sightseeing in the country, wholesome pleasure, and shopping in some of the malls.

In the U.S., a change in consumer buying habits seems to be emerging. Young people between 13 and 20 – about 30 million people who spend about $60 billion in retail shops a year – tend to increasingly turn their back on shopping malls and to prefer smaller specialty shops located in town centers, such as the award-winning Easton Town Center in Columbus, Ohio. Whereas in the first half of the 1990s U.S. teenagers found it "cool" to "hang around" in shopping malls, in the second half under 50% regarded shopping malls as "hip." This development may be partly due to restrictions on crowding and to increased surveillance by uniformed guards, but it is alarming to shopping mall owners because shopping habits of consumers are largely formed during their teenage years.

In Europe, where town center shopping is the traditional concept, specialty shops and specialty markets (which are bigger) have gained dynamics in their development compared to department stores. Also specialty discount stores at the outskirts of urban agglomerations are considered to have a bright future. And malls are still in with consumers.

Sources: Adapted from MCA Limited, Philippines Special Report, March 2002; Ritchis, B. (2003), "'Town center' concept catches on in Tallahassee, Fla., after national trend", *Knight Ridder Tribune Business News*, Washington, 19 October, p. 1; Special Feature: "WOW Philippines (shopping fiesta)", *Business World*, Manila, 22 October 2003, p. 1

Structure

The structure of a distribution channel is characterized by the number of levels and types of intermediaries in the channel, the number of product lines carried, and the relationships among manufacturers, channel members and government agencies.

Channel length The number of levels and types of intermediary define the length of a distribution channel. The longer the channel, the more expensive the company's products become to the final customers and the less the firm will be able to control or influence the sales contact with end customers. As a rule of thumb, the more economically developed a country, the shorter the distribution channels in that country. In the European Union, for example, there is a trend towards strong concentration of retailing. This trend is leading to: a significant reduction in the number of distributors, the dominance of some retail organizations in most EU markets (in food retailing in Austria, for example, three organizations, Rewe, Spar, and Aldi account for more than 80% of sales), and the formation of voluntary chains of retailers sponsored by distributors, such as Intersport. Headquartered in Bern, Switzerland, Intersport is a voluntary chain of retailers of sporting goods from a great number of countries including Canada, Japan, and the U.S. who have signed partnership contracts and hold shares in the cooperative.

A similar trend towards the vertical integration of wholesaling functions is occurring in Japan: For fashion products in most cases there is only one level of wholesalers. As another Japanese example shows, however, a country's level of economic development is not the only factor that determines the length of distribution channels. The Japanese trade structure for food products is still characterized by a multitude of very small retail shops ("mom and pop" stores in Japan account for more than 50% of retail sales, compared to 3% in the U.S. and 5% in

TABLE 12.3 *Functions potentially performed by intermediaries*

Physical handling of products
Importing the product
Arranging for customs clearance
Providing warehousing facilities
Maintaining a certain inventory level
Performing break-bulk operations
Adapting parts of the product to local needs
Assembling parts
Performing or overseeing delivery

Promotion, sales, and service activities
Obtaining and maintaining a certain level of sales effort
Securing customer service levels
Providing existing customers

Management of business relationships
Building and holding goodwill of business community members
Building and maintaining necessary relationships with government agencies

Financing and risk taking
Providing foreign payment exchange
Financing the distribution process
Assuming certain business risks

Middlemen perform four basic functions. Each of the functions has sub-functions, which would still need to be performed even if the intermediaries were eliminated from the distribution channel.

western Europe) existing in parallel to very large supermarkets, chain stores, and department stores. Up to five levels of wholesalers fill the gap between the manufacturers and the small retailers (see Figure 12.2). The first level, known as primary wholesalers, is split into two groups: Direct transaction wholesalers deliver to the biggest department stores and supermarkets in the most populated areas, while principal wholesalers split bulk goods into smaller units and deliver to secondary wholesalers, who are located in the capitals of the provinces. They hold a gatekeeper function. That is, any manufacturer who wants to get its products widely distributed in Japan has to be accepted by principal wholesalers.

There are two types of secondary wholesaler: Intermediate wholesalers deliver their products to third-level wholesalers, and ultimate wholesalers serve retail shops in their local area; third-level wholesalers serve small local retailers and restaurants conveniently located for customers frequently purchasing small quantities of merchandise, or wholesalers of the next higher level. The ratio of wholesalers to retailers is four times higher in Japan than it is in the U.S. This kind of distribution structure has proven resistant to change so far because high population density creates a shortage of storage space, which, in turn, requires low levels of inventory and frequent deliveries.

Japan's typical structure of a distribution system is even more complex than the structures in many industrially less developed countries. Distribution in the rural areas of the Philippines, for example, is characterized by a sort of wholesaler, called a *bagsakan*, to whom manufacturers sell their products or deliver them on a consignment basis. A bagsakan is usually a person who commands respect in the local area and has access to or possesses significant financial resources. The bagsakan does not deliver to the small retailers, called *sari-sari stores*, in its business area. It is the sari-sari store owners or the sidewalk vendors who pick up the merchandise on either cash or credit terms. Sari-sari stores are

FIGURE 12.2 *Distribution channel structure in the Japanese food industry*

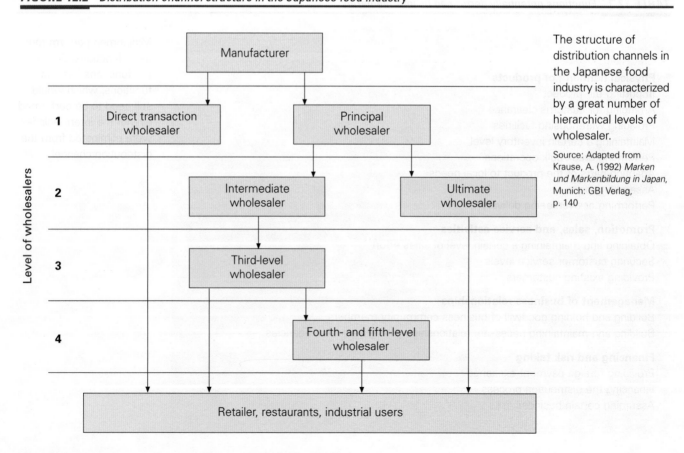

The structure of distribution channels in the Japanese food industry is characterized by a great number of hierarchical levels of wholesaler.

Source: Adapted from Krause, A. (1992) *Marken und Markenbildung in Japan*, Munich: GBI Verlag, p. 140

usually family owned and part of the private homes of their owners; thus, the average size of a store is 2 by 4 meters. Lumped together in this area are the display, stock, and a small workplace, which also serves as an office. Transactions are undertaken through a wide window, with the customer staying outside the store.

In strongly urbanized areas, such as Metro-Manila, sari-sari stores are increasingly replaced by convenience stores, 100–150 meters² in size, offering a wider line-up of products in a supermarket atmosphere that is well lit and air conditioned.

Channel width The **width** of a distribution channel is determined by the number of each type of intermediary in the channel: the larger the number of similar intermediaries in a market, the greater the width of the channel. High channel width should make it easier for a marketer to find distribution partners. As Table 12.4 shows, in Europe the width of distribution channels is very different from one country to another. In Sweden, for example, three retailing organizations control more than 90% of total sales of food in supermarkets. By 2010 the five largest retail companies could account for 30 to 40% of the European market for everyday commodities. In Austria, three retailers control the majority of total sales in home furniture, whereas in Italy the concentration process in retailing has just begun. Future issues box 12.1 shows how the fast economic development may change the retailing environment in China.

Number of product lines carried Intermediaries carry different numbers and assortments of product lines. For example, the Japanese general trading houses, called *sogo shosha*, import and export products ranging from consumer electronics to steel. They ensure supplies of raw materials and energy for their *keiretsu* ("family" of interrelated companies; see Figure 12.2) and sell all its products. Sogo shoshas are also involved in services associated with those products, such as new product development or technology transfer, and in financing big retail outlets. In addition they have built up global information networks linking hundreds of sales offices (Mitsubishi Corp., for example, has 15 offices in the U.S.

TABLE 12.4 *Width of food distribution channels in Europe*

Added market share of the three top supermarket chains in 2004	
Sweden	95%
Norway	86%
Finland	80%
Netherlands	80%
Austria	79%
Switzerland	75%
Denmark	63%
Belgium	62%
Portugal	55%
Ireland	54%
Germany	53%
U.K.	52%
France	44%
Italy	38%
Spain	35%
Greece	25%

Source: Adapted from Szemeliker, L. (2004) "Billa und Spar immer mächtiger", *Der Standard*, 5–6 June, p. 17

alone) "online" by the use of rented satellites. All members of the keiretsu and other firms that belong to the extended network may use those information services. Approximately 50% of Japan's external trade is handled by the 12 largest sogo shoshas. The biggest among them are Itochu, Kanematsu, Marubeni, Mitsubishi, Mitsui & Co., Nichimen, Nissho Iwai, Sumitomo, and Tomen.

The international marketing manager should be aware that intermediaries handling broad product lines have to take resource allocation decisions. They will put more energy into distributing the products of manufacturers with which they have long-established relationships or in which they hold a financial interest.

Networks

A company that seeks to establish a distribution channel in a new market must deal with an existing network of relationships. Because the network is already functioning with products, sellers and buyers, a variety of problems may arise. If, for example, the producer of a competitive product is related to the distributors or retailers, or owns the channels, entry is made more difficult. Typical examples of such networks are the Japanese keiretsu such as Mitsui or Fuyo. These consist of a large number of production companies, distributors, and retailers grouped around a big bank and a general trading house (sogo shosha) mutually holding each other's stock (see Figure 12.3).

Channel ownership by local competitors This can be a major problem for new firms entering the market. For example, in Japan most of the distributors of household electrical appliances are owned by only four manufacturers. A similar situation existed in the cosmetics business where the six largest producers of cosmetics controlled 70% of all cosmetics retailers. Well-known examples are Shiseido Chain Stores or Kanebo Chain Stores. Changes have occurred since. Retailers have included new brands in their offering, and new distribution channels, such as party and door-to-door selling, have been developing.

FUTURE ISSUES BOX 12.1

Hypergrowth for China's hypermarkets

In China, the entire retail sector has been growing at a rate of 7% a year since the late 1990s. It could reach more than $700 billion by 2010.

Although hypermarkets – that is shops of at least 2,500m² in size offering typically an assortment of about 35,000 different food and nonfood items – accounted for only 2% of all Chinese retail sales in 2003, revenues have been growing on average by 64% a year. They are forecast to grow by up to 30% annually through 2010.

In contrast to U.S. or most European hypermarkets, their Chinese counterparts are located in densely populated town areas. Restricted space and constantly increasing prices for land have made operators build multilevel stores. Chinese con-

sumers, even in the prosperous coastal regions, still have far fewer cars than European or U.S. consumers. Therefore, they are shopping more frequently and spending less money on one shopping trip. Thus, shopping carts are smaller. And Wal-Mart offers a shuttle bus service to its customers in Shenzhen.

Prices tend to be 10 to 15% lower compared to supermarkets and department stores. Nevertheless, hypermarkets earn margins up to 3% as opposed to the typical 1% of most locally managed supermarkets. Larger sales volumes enable hypermarket operators, such as Nonggongshong, to negotiate better prices from their suppliers.

Western investors are quite confident concerning future growth. Carrefour opened 31 stores between 1995 and 2003 and plans to open an additional 10 hypermarkets every year.

Source: Adapted from Miu, A. and J. Penhirin (2003) "Hypergrowth for China's hypermarkets", *McKinsey Quarterly*, 2, pp. 14–17

Channel blockage by exclusive contracts Distribution channels may be blocked because competitors have well-established product lines and exclusive contracts with channel members. This is the case in some European beer markets, for example, where manufacturers sign up restaurants as clients for 10 years, offering them large cash advances or financing part of their equipment. Distribution channels may also be quasi-blocked because, like in Japan, local manufacturers finance their intermediaries' inventory, give them cumulative annual rebates, allow the return of all unsold products, and provide all sorts of aids from promotion material, through product and sales training, to sales personnel. Under such circumstances a foreign marketer who wants to enter the distribution system will have a hard time finding intermediaries willing to change their supplier on affordable terms.

For example, in Korea the chaebol appliance manufacturers – Samsung Electronics, LG Electronics and Daewoo Electronics – all have a proprietary network of mom and pop retailers. To get around the chaebol-dominated retail system, U.S.-based Whirlpool joined with two South Korean companies that put its refrigerators in department stores, and with a small number of retailers specializing in imports.

Cartels Competitors may also have divided the market – and hence, the ability to control activity within the channel – among them by forming cartels. Powerful trade associations may have lobbied successfully to restrict channel alternatives or to close them to new entrants. Thus, many European countries protect the owners of small shops by regulating the placement of stores. In Sweden, for instance, town planners decide on the location of retail outlets, so that thinly populated areas, as well as elderly and handicapped customers, will be served. Ethics box 12.1 describes what can happen when no such protection for small retailers exists.

Government control Finally, governments may control access to the channels, in order to control which goods are marketed. Or access may be allowed to one part

---

FIGURE 12.3 *Keiretsu structure*

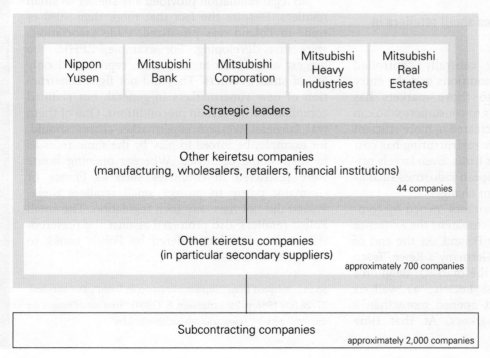

A *keiretsu* is a number of interrelated production companies, wholesalers, and retailers grouped around a major bank and a general trading house. Mitsubishi is the world's biggest keiretsu with sales of more than $270 billion and more than 550,000 personnel. The "strategic leaders" hold shares in more than 1,400 companies, which themselves hold a multitude of shares in other companies.

Source: Adapted from Sydow, J. (1991) "Strategische Netzwerke in Japan", *zfbf*, 43(3), p. 242

of the channel, but effectively barred through regulation or practice from another level, which, of course, limits the channel's usefulness to the marketer. It is imperative, therefore, that the marketer understands the structure of the existing network.

Power relationships

The distribution of power between producers and intermediaries varies from one country to another and from one product market to another. For example, between 1963, when Carrefour's first hypermarket opened at Sainte Geneviéve des Bois near Paris, and the end of the century, the French retailing landscape has seen what some observers call a "commercial revolution." The market share of small food retailers has dropped from 81% in 1963 to about 20% in 2003. Department stores and popular stores encountered great difficulty in maintaining their market shares. The activity level of traditional small retailers of textiles has decreased significantly. At the same time, 800 hypermarkets with a floor space of more than 5,000 meters^2 achieved approximately 35% of food sales and 20% of other goods by the end of the last century. When the 7,000 supermarkets are added, big stores represent more than half the total of food retail sales. Home equipment and DIY retailing have seen the emergence of a new type of store: the specialized supermarket (some well-known names are Bricorama, Conforama, Darty, FNAC). Joint retailers became very important: Leclerc, an association of independent retailers, has a market share of about 12% of retail sales. Such independent retailers run not only most of the supermarkets, but also 250 hypermarkets, that is, more than 30% of the total.

As a result, the concentration of retail purchasing power has dramatically increased. Most French retailers have joined purchasing organizations to improve their position when dealing with manufacturers. This is a reaction to the great

---

ETHICS BOX 12.1

Supermarket boom threatens small retailers in Poland

The opening of formerly centrally controlled economies to free market conditions and the entry of western companies into those markets has improved the supply of goods to consumers who can afford them. Jobs have been created in more efficient companies. But the economic restructuring has cost many more jobs in inefficient firms. Even largely privatized parts of eastern European industries such as retailing encounter significant changes.

The expansion of supermarkets owned by companies from western Europe threatens the existence of small private retailers in Poland. At the end of 1996 big retailers, such as Germany's Rewe, Tesco of the U.K. (now No. 1 in the market), Belgium's Globi, French Auchan and Leclerc, as well as Norway's Rema 1,000, had opened more than a total of 120 big supermarkets. At that time Poland counted 425,000 retail shops, 92% of which had less than 50m^2. There was one shop for 91 inhabitants.

No legal regulation provided any shelter to small retailers. Despite the fact that more than 90% of trade in Poland was privatized, trade associations were just developing. For example, ZPHU, the biggest association at that time, represented only 5% of small retailers. They did not fight construction of new supermarkets in general, but claimed compliance with certain preconditions. One of them was fairness. Western supermarket chains should, for example, be forced to play by the same rules as in their home countries. Whereas opening hours were restricted in countries such as France or Germany, partly to protect small retailers there, Poland did not have any such regulation. The small Polish retailers also protested against the preferential credit conditions offered by Polish banks to foreign companies.

Source: Adapted from "Supermarkt-Boom in Polen", *Der Standard*, 27–28 July 1996, p. 25; Pettersson, B. (2003) "Structural changes for the retail sector", www.sca.com/archive/articles

concentration among the suppliers themselves: One flour supplier has more than 80% market share. Single manufacturers hold about 70% of the cider market, 60% of the market for instant chocolate powder, and more than 50% of the pet food market. The top two French suppliers have more than 60% of the market for cleaning chemicals, mineral waters, and soft drinks, and more than 70% of the market for goods for children, tins, oils, sugar, cereals, and tea. Retail companies buy 30% of their goods from the top 10 manufacturers.

The power relationships between manufacturers and retailers in Japanese distribution channels depend on the degree of brand loyalty and the consumption rate of consumers. For example, TV sets have high brand loyalty and a low consumption rate. They fall into the category where major producers act as "channel captains." Where brand loyalty and the consumption rate are high, such as in the canned food or children's dress markets, intermediaries have a dominant position. In other product markets, such as calculators, bikes or shoes, consumption rate and brand loyalty are rather low. No single distribution channel exists and thus control of the channel is difficult for producers or intermediaries.

The balance of power in emerging economies is still very much in favor of the manufacturer. But concentration tendencies are beginning to take effect. In Mexico, for example, Wal-Mart's acquisition of the country's largest retailer Cifra and the following aggressive path of expansion has caused Mexican competitors Organizacion Soriana, Grupo Gigante, and Comercial Mexicana (which before had acquired a 50% stake in Costco Mexico as well as five Auchan hypermarkets in Mexico City) to form a new alliance in order to reduce purchasing and operating costs by pooling resources.

Power relationships affect a company's ability to control the implementation of marketing mix decisions at each level of the channel. In the U.K., for example, the six largest retail companies represent more than 50% of sales in their sector. Since a limited number of retailers effectively control access to retail outlets, they have enormous power over suppliers' strategies. Smaller suppliers who cannot afford large market communication budgets, for example, may have to give up their own brands and serve powerful retailers as OEM suppliers for their private label products. While Aldi and Lidl, both based in Germany, have 90 to 100% private-label brands, U.K.'s Tesco works with a 45 to 50% share of private labels, and Germany's Metro with 25 to 30%. (Table 12.5 shows the share of private-label brands in various countries in 2004.) Aldi places very tough demands on its suppliers, but is extremely loyal to them if those demands are fulfilled. Manufacturers of branded products may have to provide special programs and support fees before retailers will agree to stock their product. Therefore, such funds would not be available to be spent on consumer advertising or on price reductions.

TABLE 12.5 *Share (%) of private-label brands in various countries*

Switzerland	36	There is still a big difference in the share of private-label brands across highly developed economies.
U.K.	34	
Germany	31	
Netherlands	28	
France	25	
Spain	25	
U.S.	15	
Italy	8	

Source: Fessel-GfK (2004) *Euro Panel*

The creation of international purchasing units has further increased the power of retailers in the purchase relationship. For example, Deuro Buying AG regroups European companies (such as French Carrefour, German Metro, and Spanish Pryca) from 10 different countries. Electronic Partner International, another example, is a cooperation of national retailing groups from nine different EU member countries. The Vianen, Netherlands-based purchasing unit regroups more than 4,000 retailers linked by partnership contracts.

Getting around obstacles

A marketer faced with these kinds of obstacle can find ways to get around them. One possibility is to *choose an innovative distribution channel*. Franchising, mail order, and electronic markets are among the possible alternatives to traditional channels. By signing up franchise partners in Singapore, international retailers headquartered in the U.K., such as the Body Shop, Marks & Spencer and Habitat, have implanted themselves in Singapore, where personal and governmental relationships play an important role in business success.

The marketer can also look for ways to *diversify channels*. One way is to find distribution partners that want to broaden their product lines with complementary products. It is also possible to team up with other distributors or retailers that have been excluded from the distribution networks. In addition, new channels are always being created – specialty discount stores, for instance, or groups of hotels and restaurants – providing new distribution opportunities. It may also be possible to "piggyback" into a new market by using a distribution channel established by a friendly company. For example, to facilitate its entry into Asian markets, a Spanish manufacturer such as Majorica, which produces fashion products from industrially made pearls, uses the distribution channel, consisting of a number of distributors, jewelry stores, department stores, and tax-free shops at airports, established by a cooperating manufacturer of crystal glass.

Other means of circumventing obstacles to market entry include *offering financial incentives* such as higher margins to channel members than are offered by competitors or special bonuses. To build closer ties with their Korean retailers, New York-based Estée Lauder, one of the leading marketers of cosmetics in the U.S., for example, invites local department store executives to New York City each year to meet with Estée Lauder management and visit major retailers. However, companies must be careful not to violate home country legislation, such as the Foreign Corrupt Practices Act in the U.S., which prohibits specific types of payment that may facilitate business activity in international markets.

A company may also consider *buying equity in an intermediary*. In Japan, banks are used for this purpose, because they are closely linked with the large industry groups (keiretsu) through joint ownership and serving as board directors. With their assistance a foreign company can gain an equity share in a Japanese intermediary; in most cases a 10% share will enable the company to become part of an existing distribution network.

Channel member selection

An international marketer can more or less actively govern the process of selecting distribution channel members. Sometimes contacts take place *by accident*, such as during a flight when businesspeople sit next to each other. A considerable number of firms try to find intermediaries in a new country market *by advertisements* in a local newspaper or trade journal soliciting representation. Advertisements have the disadvantage that their response rate is generally low, and they often attract the weakest and most unreliable potential intermediaries. Other more active firms *participate in a local exhibition* and talk to potential intermediaries visiting their exhibits. The relatively low costs of such a search and selection procedure, in most cases, are by far offset by the opportunity cost of the internationally operating firm not knowing its final customers in the country market and, therefore, not having market-related criteria on which to base the choice of distribution partner. In addition, the firm has only very little effective control over its distribution partner's marketing activities, resulting in a "blind approach" concerning local adaptations.

In most cases, a company that wishes to enter a foreign market should take an active role in selecting intermediaries. The firm would be well advised to follow a series of systematic steps in investigating potential distribution partners (see Figure 12.4).

First, the company has to *develop a set of selection criteria* based on its intended global strategic position, the intended local position, and the distribution policy. Then, following those criteria, it has to *gather information on potential intermediaries*. Such information can be obtained from secondary sources, local customers, and experts. Based on the available information, the number of potential channel members is reduced to a *shortlist of attractive candidates* by evaluating them against the selection criteria. Then, the *most attractive-looking candidates are interviewed* on site. First, they are asked whether they are interested in acting as intermediaries for the company. Those that express interest are interviewed, and the interviews are used as a basis for the *selection of appropriate distribution partners*. This active process for selecting channel members will be described in the following.

Selection criteria

Ideally, an intermediary will resemble the most effective members of the company's current distribution channels. Table 12.6 lists some criteria that have proven to be useful in selecting channel members. They are discussed in the following.

FIGURE 12.4 *Channel member selection*

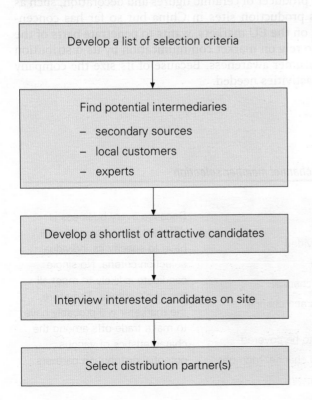

Selection of channel members should be an active process following the steps shown.

Continuity of functions

Depending on the customer needs, an intermediary will have to fulfill various functions.

Storage facilities for products or spare parts help the marketer to reach the customer in time. For example, in order for a manufacturer of diesel engines for vessels to be globally competitive, it needs intermediaries in every big harbor who are able to keep in stock at least those spare parts that are needed most often. Extended stopovers in a harbor because of missing spare parts would not be tolerated by shipping companies because of high quay charges.

In addition, a potential channel member who has *access to appropriate transportation devices* or who can provide *local packaging facilities* may be more attractive as a distribution partner. For example, a producer of frozen food, such as France's Bonduelle, needs local distribution partners that can provide a fleet of trucks equipped to transport their products.

Complementary products and the intermediary's ability to provide *customer services* based on product or product application knowledge may increase the attractiveness of the firm's offer to local customers. For example, if a Vietnamese producer of tableware made from bamboo is searching for intermediaries in Sweden, complementary products such as tablecloths carried by the potential channel member will strongly increase the attractiveness of the supplier's offerings to potential customers. The number of technically trained and experienced personnel available to an intermediary in Argentina, as another example, is crucial to the service level that a manufacturer of machinery, such as Japan's Komatsu, can provide to its local customers.

An intermediary's *production facilities* can increase the speed and flexibility of customer problem solution in a geographically distant market. For example, Douwe Egberts, the Dutch subsidiary of Chicago-based Sara Lee Corp., is one of the world's leading coffee roasters. To be better adapted to local customers' tastes, the firm produces its coffee for the Austrian market through Vienna-based Santora, an intermediary exclusively active in the restaurant business.

Finally, the potential channel member's *market communication activity* can help achieve awareness and build local preference for the marketer's product. For example, when a rather small producer of ceramic figures and decoration, such as Italian Thun, which operates production sites in China but so far has concentrated its marketing activities on the EU markets, wants to penetrate parts of the NAFTA market, it will have to rely on market communication by its distribution partners to achieve some consumer awareness. Because of its size the company cannot afford the promotion activities needed.

TABLE 12.6 *Useful criteria for channel member selection*

- Continuity of functions provided
- Adequate market coverage
- Control of activities within channel
- Compatibility between firm and channel member
- Capital required and costs to be covered
- Distance between firm and channel member

Because every business is different, each company will have to specify its individual selection criteria. No single candidate is likely to meet all the firm's criteria. Therefore, the marketer will probably have to make trade-offs among the characteristics of various potential distribution partners.

Market coverage and control

What market coverage of a local intermediary is adequate to an internationally operating firm strongly depends on the chosen distribution policy. The *size of a potential channel member's sales network* – does it have sales personnel, sales reps or local sales offices and how many?; does it provide access to a multilevel channel of local distribution? – as well as *the intermediary's relations with potential customers*, are indicators of the market coverage the firm can attain by choosing this distribution partner. In Japan, for example, a company should gather information about the distribution network to which a potential channel member belongs. Because of the many levels of intermediaries and the close ties between certain members of a channel, choosing a specific partner can mean opening up a broad distribution system, but also losing the opportunity to get in touch with a whole range of customers.

Sales references help to assess the intermediary's relations. For example, if a distributor of electrical appliances in Spain has been serving El Corte Ingles, the most well-known chain of department stores in that country, it can be considered as a competent partner. However, such references should not be taken only from the potential distribution partner itself. The marketer would be well advised to contact the given references and to countercheck the information received. Nevertheless, some understanding of the cultural background of a local market will be needed to interpret the content of references properly. For example, if a U.S. supplier to a potential intermediary and some of its customers report that a particular firm is timely, financially reliable, and appropriately equipped with technical personnel, they probably mean something different from what a supplier and customer are trying to communicate when they say the same if they are located in Cameroon, India, or Italy.

The importance of a potential channel member's control of local marketing activities increases with the supplier's need to influence final customer contacts. The *relative size* of an intermediary indicates the channel member's potential for control over activities within the channel. If the customers of the intermediary are much bigger in size than the intermediary itself, power relations will be negatively affected. For example, the Swiss producer of WC-Ente, a high-quality cleaning product for sanitary installations, distributes its products in Austria through a small firm called Perolin. This firm is confronted with two chains of supermarkets, which evenly split 70% of the entire market between them. As a result, control over local marketing activities tends to be difficult. Retailers use the very strong position of the brand in consumers' minds to attract customers through low prices. Even the strong brand cannot avoid yearly price negotiations becoming extremely difficult for the distributor.

But it is not only the intermediary's relations with its customers that are important. Depending on the company's product market and the shape of the local macro-environment, *relations with other stakeholders*, such as media, unions, environmentalists or local politicians, may be important. For example, if a producer of genetically manipulated products, such as U.S.-based Monsanto, wants to distribute those products in an environmentally sensitive country such as Switzerland for the first time, it might be much easier to enter the market if the chosen distribution partner has strong relationships with local media and politicians. Otherwise, journalists communicating genetic manipulation as a danger for consumers and their children would provoke resistance from environmentalists, forcing politicians to react in a negative way for the producer.

Compatibility

The compatibility of potential distribution partners has to be checked in terms of reputation and ability to communicate.

The *reputation* of a potential channel member in its local market has to fit the intended positioning of the internationally operating firm or its product. The reputation largely depends on the person(s) representing the intermediary as well as on the positioning of the potential channel member's own product range and the product range it has represented so far. For example, when a company with high-prestige products, such as French Givenchy perfumes, searches for an intermediary in Indonesia, it will first need to find a firm that affluent consumers accept as competent for Givenchy's kind of luxury product. In addition, Givenchy will want to choose a firm owned or managed by a person whose reputation is compatible with its prestigious brand.

Compatibility also means the *ability to communicate* effectively and efficiently with the distribution partner. The company searching for an appropriate channel member will therefore evaluate the information technology available to the different candidates. Denmark's toy maker Lego, for example, might prefer a distributor in São Paulo, Brazil, who is able to communicate in English, can be reached by email 24 hours a day, and who uses an electronic data-processing system compatible with the one used by the company.

Costs

Two kinds of cost are important in selecting a distribution channel.

The capital costs of establishing the channel depend on the size of potential partners and their financial standing. For example, when a Taiwanese bicycle manufacturer enters a distribution agreement with Wal-Mart in the U.S., its capital costs of establishing the channel will be significantly lower.

The costs of maintaining the channel include the direct costs of the firm's integrated distribution channels plus margins, markups, commissions, and other forms of compensation to channel members, whether integrated or independent.

When a luxury sports car manufacturer such as Italy's Ferrari considers distribution in China, for example, it has to calculate the costs of a sales office as well as compensation for Chinese intermediaries. In addition, the costs of the management systems needed to manage the distribution channels have to be considered. These costs will vary over the life of a distribution relationship. In the beginning, travel costs for managers establishing the relationship through know-how and technology transfer may dominate. Later on, the costs of deepening the information links between the supplier and the local channel members may become more important.

Distance

The distance between a marketer and a potential channel member has five dimensions: geographic, social, cultural, technological, and temporal. They must be bridged to develop a close working relationship.

Geographic distance The geographic distance is the physical distance separating the two partners. From a distance point of view, it might seem easier for a Singapore-based Chinese manufacturer to deal with a Malaysian intermediary than with a Chinese located in Hong Kong or in South Africa. An analysis of social and cultural distance may provide another picture.

Social distance This stems from lack of familiarity with the partner's operating methods. Whereas managers of a Chinese manufacturer of dolls are accustomed to working with local distribution partners whose personnel work 7 days a week, they may be highly surprised when confronted with Italian or French potential intermediaries that close down during August because of vacations. But social distance may also be more subtle. If a manufacturer such as Gore, the U.S.-headquartered producer of chemical fibers for consumer and industrial textiles, mainly operating based on individual initiatives and responsibility, is confronted with potential channel members managing their businesses through orders and tight controls, social distance is large. Severe misunderstandings could be the consequence.

Cultural distance This reflects differences in values, norms, and behavior. For example, a U.S. service company, such as Citizen' Bank, which is used to profit and income as primary motivators for business decisions, might have some difficulties in cooperating with Japanese business partners for whom loyalty may be the dominant motivator.

Technological distance This can be described in terms of the competitiveness, compatibility, and quality of product lines currently carried by potential intermediaries, as well as differences in product experience and process technologies.

When Coca-Cola of the U.S. signs up Carlsberg, Denmark's biggest brewing group, as a distributor of Coca-Cola products in Sweden and Norway, for example, the technological distance is very small, because Carlsberg has already acted as a distributor for Coca-Cola in Denmark for many years, through Carlsberg's soft drink subsidiary, Dadeko AS. Contrariwise, when a ship crane manufacturer, such as Austria-based Liebherr, searches for an intermediary who should be able to provide high-level service to international ship companies in Nigeria, the difference in the quality of product lines carried as well as in their way of handling the business may be considerable.

Temporal distance Temporal distance is measured by the length of time between placement of an order and delivery of the product. This time span will be influenced by the closeness of a potential intermediary to the customers. The number of layers of channel members as well as an intermediary's process technology will be crucial for temporal distance.

For example, when a Norwegian producer of canned fish wants to distribute its products in the Netherlands, from a temporal distance point of view the Royal Ahold NV may seem to be an attractive channel partner. The company not only is one of Europe's best performing retailers, but it also holds a 30% market share with its flagship Albert Heijn supermarket chain and other stores, and, in particular, it has invested in sophisticated centralized logistics systems.

Finding potential intermediaries

Knowing which characteristics of potential intermediaries to consider, management can start to search for potential channel members. Major sources of information about potential channel members in a local market are *secondary information sources*, which in most instances are less costly, *local customers*, and *experts in the firm's industry*.

Secondary information sources

The first step in searching for local intermediaries is to locate secondary sources of information. Some of the most valuable sources are listed in Table 12.7. Management should investigate these sources before traveling to a country market to gather firsthand information.

Government agencies, such as registration authorities, will supply specific information for free or for a small fee. As an example, the relevant agencies of the U.S. Department of Commerce are listed in Table 12.8.

Listings of industry members can be obtained from:

- address services
- government sources, such as the U.S. government's Foreign Traders Index
- international institutions, such as the European Union's Business Cooperation Network (BC NET)
- the firm's national chamber of commerce
- trade organizations in the host country
- the home country's trade representative in the host country.

Listings can also be found in:

- telephone directories (yellow page section)
- trade directories.

Such directories are normally organized by geographical criteria and product categories. They are often incomplete and out of date, however.

Local industry or trade journals and magazines contain reports on potential intermediaries as well as on the structure of networks and power relationships in specific local industries. So do industrial reports.

Catalogs from exhibitions and trade fairs can be used to look for intermediaries who are participating. Catalogs from industrial suppliers can supply relevant addresses. Annual reports of potential local customers may provide information concerning their current suppliers. The company's own salesforce may have

TABLE 12.7 *Secondary sources of information on potential distribution channel members*

Government agencies
Reports of international organizations
Trade organizations in the host country
National chamber of commerce
Home country trade representatives in the host country
Banks and insurance companies
Related companies (carriers, forwarding agents, suppliers of complementary goods)
Own salesforce, customers, suppliers, competitors
Annual reports of potential local customers
Industrial reports
Listings of industry members and address services
Industry or trade journals and magazines
Catalogs of exhibitions and trade fairs
Catalogs of industrial suppliers
Consultants

This table illustrates the information sources a company can consult when evaluating potential distribution channel members.

TABLE 12.8 *Services of the U.S. Department of Commerce*

Name	Services
Agent/Distributor Service (ADS)	Contacts up to six middlemen prospects in the countries designated by the firm and determines their interest in corresponding with the firm
Foreign Traders' Index (FTI)	Contains data on more than 150,000 potential middlemen, as well as final customers from 143 countries
New Product Information Service	Provides global publicity for new U.S. products
Trade Opportunities Program (TOP)	Matches the interest of middlemen indicated by the U.S. company with product searches of non-domestic buyers
World Traders' Data Report (WTDR)	Provides general narrative reports on the reliability of the potential middlemen indicated by the firm, as well as a profile of their existing product line(s)

The U.S. Department of Commerce provides many services for international marketers, for relatively small fees.

information on potential intermediaries gathered through personal contacts with personnel from those companies or from other suppliers. Finally, the firm can use specialized consultants to help them find the right local intermediaries.

Before entering into direct contact with any candidate, the marketer may obtain additional information on its business conduct and credit reliability from such sources as banks, insurers, and related companies like carriers or consultants.

Local customers and experts

Using secondary information sources is the cheapest way to find potential intermediaries. But, in most cases, it does not provide enough detailed information about the available distribution partners in a market and how they are perceived by their customers to make a complete choice.

Interviewing final customers in the target market, therefore, is a more expensive but very informative additional means of finding an appropriate channel partner. It helps to discover which distribution channels are preferred and why, and what the customers expect from their suppliers in terms of customer service level. The marketer may also learn the names of reputable intermediaries in this manner.

If interviewing final customers seems to be too slow or too expensive, industry experts such as specialists from the chamber of commerce, specialized journalists, or consultants can be used as information sources. They provide an overview of the industry structure, networks, and power relationships, can give their interpretation of the success factors in local distribution, and can identify the most well known potential intermediaries.

Developing a candidate shortlist

Listing candidates

Using the information gathered from secondary sources, potential local customers and industry experts, management can specify a list of candidates to examine in more detail.

Letter of inquiry

Then the marketer sends a mail to the selected candidates inquiring about their interest in becoming a member of the company's distribution channel. The mail should contain an:

- extensive description of the products to be carried
- an explanation of the firm's general marketing policy and strategy
- a statement of its specific goals in the intermediary's market.

The interested intermediary should be asked to describe the market from its point of view; the description should include:

- major customers and competitors
- an estimate of the firm's potential market share and sales volume within a specified period
- marketing strategy and resources necessary to achieve those objectives.

On-site visits

The answers of the interested intermediaries are compared. The small number of potential channel members that best fulfill the expectations of the company are selected for on-site interviews. On-site visits are the best way to determine a potential partner's requirements and to start an effective working relationship.

Selection of partners

Intermediaries of competitors

Intermediaries used by competitors may seem to be the most attractive potential channel members at first. They are already familiar with the product and the market, and they have an established organization to deal with potential customers. However, there are risks associated with using intermediaries that are serving competitors. First, if an intermediary does not change its alliance, it may *provide competitors with information about the firm's product line*. Second, the intermediary may accept a new product line and maintain the competitor's line simply to *drive the new line out of the market*. And third, the intermediary may *negotiate with a new competitor at any time*.

Intermediaries handling complementary products

For these reasons, it may be safer to choose intermediaries that handle complementary products. They have an established organization, a history of contact with potential customers, technical proficiency, and knowledge of the local market.

The contract

Conventional exports

In cases of conventional exports, the supplier and the channel member operate without contractual commitments. They act strictly as buyers and sellers, and bargain aggressively to establish trade terms for each transaction, each primarily motivated by its own profits and unconcerned about longer term cooperation. The manufacturer frequently renegotiates its export arrangements, and the intermediary obtains products from a variety of suppliers to best adapt to its local business. Such a situation involves higher costs for a company that wants to do international business on a continual basis. It also handicaps an intermediary as it cannot profit from a secured flow of products with fixed quality and stable prices.

Non-contractual agreements

In the past, many firms operating internationally stayed autonomous but coordinated their activities through informal, non-contractual agreements. Owing to ongoing business relations, manufacturer and intermediary understood each other's preferences, capabilities, and expectations. Mutual trust allowed them to informally agree an allocation of functions that made their exchanges more efficient.

Formal contracts

Because of increasing global competition in recent years, suppliers and intermediaries are increasingly being forced to lower their costs further. As a consequence, intermediaries have tried to reduce their number of suppliers, and manufacturers operating internationally have managed to obtain maximum operating economies as well as maximum foreign market impact. Both can be achieved by carefully selecting international business partners and integrating activities on the basis of a formal long-term contract.

The contract drawn up must be reviewed in detail before being signed. Because of differences in legal regulations between different countries, the company wanting to formalize the partnership with a local intermediary should seek the advice of a legal specialist in the intermediary's market. For example, contract termination conditions, including "just causes" of termination (such as deceit, fraud, damage to the other party's interests, or failure to comply with contractual obligations), must be spelled out carefully.

Even with explicit contract specifications, termination of a contract is time consuming, often expensive, and in some cases impossible. In Japan, for example, terminating a contract with a business partner means breaking a strong commitment; it can be very difficult to find another partner. In most European countries, termination, even with "just cause," will cost the firm the equivalent of a year's commission as compensation for the intermediary's efforts to build market share. Thus, it is imperative that the marketer conducts an extremely thorough investigation before signing a contract with a distribution partner.

In some countries formal contracts do not have the same importance they do in other nations, particularly in the U.S. or in Europe. Most channel relationships in Japan or China, for example, do not involve legal contracts. But channel members there are known for working more closely together than counterparts in the U.S. who largely rely on legal contracts.

Managing channel relationships

Distribution as complex exchange

Careful management of relationships with intermediaries is critical to success in international marketing. Distribution can be viewed as a complex exchange system that incorporates many interdependent organizations, each with its own objectives. Only when the interactions satisfy the needs of all partners will the relationships between them remain stable and the marketing objectives of the internationally operating company be achieved. In order to manage its channel relationships in a way that keeps exchanges subjectively balanced, the responsible manager in the internationally operating company needs to analyze the expectations of its distribution partners and fulfill them to the extent that the company's own expectations concerning the relationships are fulfilled. Table 12.9 shows potential mutual expectations of both international marketer and local distribution partners.

Level of uncertainty

The value of cooperation between a manufacturer and its intermediaries within a channel as perceived by the exchange partners is strongly influenced by the *rate of change* and the *level of environmental complexity* faced by the parties involved. The higher the uncertainty, the greater the need to gain information from channel partners and to perform some joint activities. For example, in dynamically evolving markets, such as electronic hardware and computer software markets, most intermediaries are interested in close relationships with major manufacturers providing them with technical, informational, and marketing support.

Ease of replacement

When it is relatively easy for an intermediary to replace a supplier, the intermediary is unlikely to be motivated to form a tight relationship with the supplier. For example, when a procurement manager of Paris-based Printemps, a department store company, can cancel the listing of a no-name supplier of boys' underwear from Thailand and replace it by a cheaper supplier from Guatemala without facing any negative reaction from consumers, the buyer will not place high importance on cultivating that relationship. By the same token, when the supplier is the technology leader in its market or possesses a strong brand, such as U.S.-based Motorola or Nokia from Finland in the cell phone market, intermediaries will be interested in more intensive and potentially exclusive relationships.

Contribution of channel members

The higher the contribution of its channel members to the satisfaction of customer expectations, the more the internationally operating company needs to be concerned about enhancing cooperation with its intermediaries. Organizational structure, motivation, communication, and control can help to manage the channel relationships.

Organization

The company must develop an appropriate organizational structure to manage channel relationships.

Multifunctional integration

Channel relationships can be quite complex; personal contacts between a supplier's and an intermediary's staff may span several levels of the organization and involve employees in the company's sales, service, information technology, design, manufacturing, logistics, and quality-control departments. As an example, Figure 12.5 shows how, in its distribution relationship with Wal-Mart,

TABLE 12.9 *Mutual expectations of international marketer and local distribution partner*

Expectations of company	Expectations of distribution partner	
The distribution partner should	**The supplying partner should**	To keep the relationship balanced and satisfactory for both sides, an international marketer needs to fulfill the expectations of its distribution partners to the extent that its own expectations become satisfied.
• have excellent relations with customers and other important stakeholders	• agree on clear and understandable objectives	
• possess an effective and efficient sales organization	• be ready for joint marketing and service planning	
• provide storage facilities	• provide reliable marketing research data	
• be able to offer added value to customers by delivering entire product systems	• provide realistic gross margins	
• implement the intended position in the market	• have an excellent image	
• help to plan the local budget	• possess latest know-how on the product and its application	
• assist in planning and realizing communication	• provide support through product information and training	
• watch competition and provide latest information on market developments	• provide budgets for market projects	
• deliver in time and corresponding to the order	• have an efficient information system	
• develop and execute market communication plans	• provide performance feedback	
• bear responsibility for local marketing activities and joint realization of projects	• be ready for joint visits to customers	

Procter & Gamble has replaced the traditional transaction between a manufacturer's salesperson and an intermediary's buying agent by multifunctional integration between the retailing and supplying organizations. Teams of both partners representing all functional areas that are directly or indirectly involved in the business exchange work closely together to ensure maximum success for both sides. Channel relationships, therefore, represent a considerable investment of human resources in information exchange, negotiations, transfer of technical knowledge, and social bonding.

Key account management

Because people tend to prefer social relations with partners from the same cultural environment, the company must take care not to allocate too great a share of organizational resources to domestic distribution partners at the expense of building satisfactory relationships with more distant ones. Contrariwise, too much focus on difficult channel relationships might tie up organizational resources that are needed to keep the most cooperative intermediaries satisfied. To avoid those traps, firms confronted with intermediaries handling a large volume of a country's or region's total sales tend to install key account managers who specifically handle the relationships with such major partners. In particular, when channel members become increasingly international themselves, they need to be treated the same in every country market served.

For example, when Rewe, the third-largest retailing organization in Germany and No. 6 in the world, bought the biggest retailer in Austria, the Billa-Merkur Group, all the firms that had supplied both retailers but with different prices and terms of sale experienced trouble. They not only had to accept the lower price for either served country but were forced to pay back the differential amount for the entire business year.

Product category management

If a retailer operating internationally expects a supplier to take over the management of an entire product category, the manufacturer must be prepared for international product category management. That is, it needs the logistics and information systems to properly handle its own and the competitors' product lines in every outlet of the international intermediary.

FIGURE 12.5 *Channel relationship management*

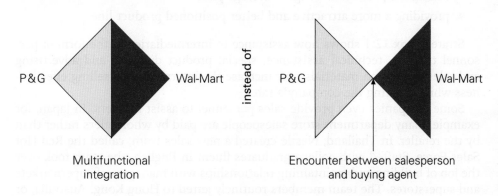

Procter & Gamble replaced the one-to-one encounter between a manufacturer's salesperson and an intermediary's buying agent as the traditional form of channel relationship in consumer goods industries by multifunctional integration between the retailing and supplying organizations. Teams from both partners representing all functional areas that are directly or indirectly involved in the business exchange work closely together to ensure maximum success for both sides.

Systems supply

Similar things may happen to OEM suppliers in industrial businesses. For example, Stuttgart-based Robert Bosch GmbH, a major producer of electrical and braking systems for cars, and the first company which offered ABS (anti-lock braking systems) for cars, was confronted with the demand of its major car manufacturing clients to deliver entire product systems instead of only electronic parts to improve braking systems. To be able to deliver those systems just in time at every site of a customer production plant in Asia, Europe, and North and Latin America, the company acquired 24 brake-making factories in Europe, Latin America, and the U.S. as well as shares of joint ventures in China, India, and Korea from U.S.-based Allied Signal Inc.

Motivation

Financial benefits

The intermediary must be able to make money by handling the product; otherwise it will have little interest in maintaining a relationship with the supplier. Higher margins, larger commissions, or more advantageous credit terms have traditionally served as ways of motivating distribution partners. With increasing speed of new product introductions, however, keeping margins up becomes more and more difficult. Constant innovation compels manufacturers to sell quickly. As an individual PC ages, for example, its value can easily drop 30% in 6 months. Consequently, the main complaint of computer retailers is that profit margins are low. In the U.S. and Japan, big retailers are pleased with gross margins above 10%.

Product turnover

Keeping in mind that margins, commissions, and credit terms are less important to channel members than the amount they derive from the selling process, an international marketer that does not want to sacrifice profits should offer the usual margin percentages and, at the same time, help intermediaries increase the turnover of products through:

- training of sales staff
- provision of sales consultants
- intensive promotion
- attractive product displays
- selling the product at a higher average price
- providing a more attractive and better positioned product line.

Strategy box 12.1 shows how assistance to intermediaries in the form of personnel training, technical assistance, special product displays, and advertising and sales promotion materials may increase the intermediary's selling effectiveness while boosting the company's sales.

Some companies even provide sales personnel to assist retailers. In Japan, for example, many department store salespeople are paid by wholesalers rather than by the retailer. In Thailand, Nestlé created a new sales team, called the Red Hot Sales Force. Staffed with college graduates fluent in English, the team took over the job of building and maintaining relationships with managers of supermarkets and superstores. The team members routinely jetted to Hong Kong, Australia, or the staff-training center in Switzerland for instruction in the latest shelf management techniques. They were supposed to train their customers, the supermarket managers. The hope was to establish solid relationships that will withstand the inevitable competition when it arrives.

Communication

International distribution channels require intensive communication to ensure that the activities of channel members conform to the company's global strategy. Communication efforts may be personal (telephone calls, visits, meetings, training, personnel exchanges) or impersonal (faxes, emails, periodic corporate newsletters, magazines).

Visits play an important role in reinforcing the personal bonds between distribution partners. So do personnel exchanges. These techniques may be used to resolve problems before they escalate and damage trust. For this reason, when Honda entered the U.S. its Japanese managers spent up to 50% of their working time visiting and talking with distributors and dealers in the U.S. International and regional meetings can also be used for transmitting product information, planning, or simply exchanging experiences.

Caterpillar even goes one step further in their management of intermediary relationships. They actively help dealers keep the business in the family. When the principal of a privately held dealership is about 50 years old, the company offers seminars for the family on tax issues and succession planning – both financial and management. These seminars are held two or three times during the principal's active working life to ensure that the next generation is ready. Caterpillar also holds conferences at its headquarters in Peoria, for 15- to 25-year-

The exterior of an Ikea furniture store in Kuwait City with the sign in Arabic

© Planetpix/Alamy

STRATEGY BOX 12.1

We'll provide the shillelaghs

"Guinness is good for you," according to an old U.K. advertising slogan for the black-and-hearty Irish stout. Guinness stout is not to everyone's taste, but enough people love it for it to be a perennial money-maker for its owner, London-based Guinness plc. The company gets about half of its annual revenues from brewing Guinness stout and other beers. Worldwide, sales of Guinness Brewing, Guinness plc's beer arm, have climbed by over 5% a year in the second half of the 1990s.

The key to this strong performance in beer was the growing popularity of ersatz Irish pubs all over the world. These pubs try to create an atmosphere of conviviality and warm welcome for strangers; they feature Irish food and drink and Irish music. There are now some 2,500 of these Irish-themed pubs stretching from Atlanta, Berlin, Moscow, and Paris to Abu Dhabi, Cape Town, Hong Kong, and Tokyo. And this is from virtually nil in the early 1990s.

Guinness does not own pubs. Better than tying up capital in bricks and mortar, Guinness gets what amounts to an override on every Irish pub, for the simple reason that no pub claiming Irish roots can fail to offer Guinness. Even rival brewers like Whitbread plc and Allied Domecq (now Pernod Ricard), opening up Irish pubs, all sell Guinness.

When an entrepreneur or a company such as Gaelic Inns Pte Ltd, for example, a Singapore-based company formed to create Asia Pacific's finest traditional pub chain, wants to start an Irish-style pub, Guinness will be glad to help. It brings the entrepreneur together with an agency that will design the pub, provide the furniture and effects, and fit out the place right down to shillelaghs on the wall. Another agency will help the new pub's owner find Irish bar staff, arrange Irish music and provide food: Recipes like Molly Malone's fish soup and roast stuffed pork loin Limerick style. The company's salespeople train bartenders to use a traditional pouring technique for Guinness.

Gaelic Inns opened Muddy Murphy's in the Orchard Hotel Shopping Arcade, and the outlet became an instant hit with both expatriates and tourists. Today it is also patronized by many Singaporeans.

Encouraging the existing trend costs Guinness almost nothing, save the expense of a few contests (win an Irish pub in Ireland), or sponsoring cartoonists to draw patrons in an Irish pub. Guinness considers itself as the intellectual, not the financial, pub owner.

Source: Adapted from Banks, H. (1996) "We'll provide the shillelaghs", *Forbes*, 8 April, pp. 68, 72; www.gaelicinns.co.sg/corp.htm

old sons and daughters of dealership owners, aiming to introduce them to Caterpillar, to get them interested in the business, and to allow them to meet their peers. The company helps owners arrange jobs inside the Caterpillar organization for their children when they graduate from college, such as a parts salesperson for 2 years, then run the engine business, and next be put in charge of product support.

Control

To control the activities of channel members and avoid conflict, the marketer must ensure that its corporate objectives are clearly communicated to intermediaries. Performance standards based on those objectives may include:

- sales volume per product or product line within a specified period
- inventory level
- market share
- number of accounts per sales territory.

Toolbox 12.1 shows how a marketer, by comparing the levels of market penetration and market coverage reached by its distributors, can control part of the international channel members' goal achievement and clearly communicate some of its objectives.

Attainment of the company's communication objectives is influenced by the promotional efforts of channel members. Those efforts, therefore, must be assessed from the standpoint of their contribution to the desired global corporate branding as well as their contribution to the intermediary's objectives. This assessment should be conducted jointly to avoid differences in interpretation. Visits and international meetings can serve such a control function without being obtrusive.

Impact on marketing mix

Value of total product

International distribution decisions influence product management. They strongly contribute to the value of a product provided to the customer:

TOOLBOX 12.1 Market penetration/market coverage portfolio

Wiberg, a globally operating producer of spices for meat production, based in Salzburg, Austria, uses the kind of portfolio analysis shown in Figure 12.6 to compare the performance of its international distribution partners, and to communicate part of its distribution objectives.

The analysis is based on two dimensions: The level of market penetration in a country market (measured in terms of average sales per outlet) and the level of market coverage (measured in terms of the number of served outlets per 100,000 inhabitants). Intermediaries in countries located in the lower left quadrant must increase the number of outlets they serve as well as the average sales per outlet. Those located in the upper left quadrant have to increase the number of outlets, keeping the average sales per outlet at the current level. Channel members who find their country in the lower right quadrant must increase the average sales per outlet, and those in the upper right field should basically maintain their level of achievement by sensitively dropping outlets with sales below average.

- When a company cannot afford to establish an integrated distribution system and the level of technological sophistication of available distribution partners is relatively low, the firm may be forced to develop products that are easy to handle and with little demand for customer services.

- When the power of intermediaries is high and the resulting pressures on prices are considerable, new products will need to have lower costs of material, production, and handling.

- Brands will not be properly established in a market where strong channel members cannot be found.

- Import agents will not provide the same level of service to final customers as company sales personnel.

Pricing

Pricing is influenced by international distribution decisions. For example, longer distribution channels tend to result in higher prices. The "quality" of a chosen channel strongly influences the market price charged. It is difficult, for example, to charge a premium price for products distributed through discount department stores. Finally, channel control and power relationships affect terms of payment.

A firm selling to an integrated channel member can offer more liberal credit terms, because in most cases it is assuming less risk. A seller with a strong position in an independent channel can dictate more favorable terms of payment, such as payment in advance or an irrevocable letter of credit.

FIGURE 12.6 *Market penetration/market coverage portfolio*

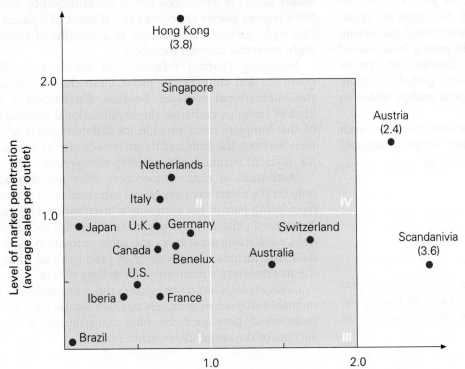

By comparing the levels of market penetration and market coverage reached by its contributors, the international marketer can control part of the international channel member's goal achievement and can clearly communicate some of its objectives.

I = Increase number of outlets and average sales per outlet; II = Increase number of outlets; III = Increase average sales per outlet; IV = Selectively drop outlets below average

Market communication

International distribution decisions also influence market communication:

- The potential for joint advertising and promotional activities depends largely on the nature of the channel members. In fact, marketers may use joint promotional activities to build stronger channel relationships.

- Furthermore, the "quality" of the channel affects the meaning the marketer is able to convey through its promotional campaigns. It is difficult, for example, to be perceived as youthful and modern when using a channel dominated by small, old-fashioned, poorly decorated retail stores.

- Finally, the distribution channel affects the marketer's opportunities for personal contact and communication with customers.

An important role of channels for industrial products and prestige consumer goods is to provide positive personal contact between the marketer and the customer. Thus, the impression conveyed by channel members is very important to the successful marketing of these products.

Summary

Local distribution is a critical step in successful international marketing. If the product cannot be delivered to the market, sales will not occur regardless of the value of the product, the price charged, or the persuasiveness of promotion. Whether the channel is direct or indirect, the international marketing manager has a major challenge in *making local channel decisions* that result in a global distribution system that matches the firm's intended global strategic position and in *managing channel relationships within its distribution system*.

The manager must choose channels that will reach customers effectively and efficiently. Potential channel members must be evaluated concerning:

- functions they perform
- their structure
- their networking ability
- power relations.

Channel members are selected by applying several selection criteria, including *costs* and *multiple types of distance* (geographic, social, cultural, technological, and temporal).

Finding the best intermediaries requires an active search process, not dissimilar to the marketing research process as described in Chapter 7. It starts out with *secondary sources of information* which are enriched by data from *primary sources* as soon as the amount of information to be gathered is restricted to a shortlist of seemingly attractive channel members.

Managing channel relationships across multiple countries and cultures can prove quite challenging to the international manager. Because distribution is a kind of complex exchange the organizational structure of the company must provide for different *power relations* between the firm and its intermediaries as well as for different *intensities of relationship management*.

Motivation of channel members does not depend only on the direct *monetary reward* intermediaries derive from being part of the company's distribution system. *Assistance* in the form of personnel training, technical help, advertising allowances and sales promotion materials may increase the turnover of products and, thus, the intermediary's motivation for selling efforts.

Communication and control systems must be established to enable all channel members to share information and understand how each member contributes to the success of the entire distribution system.

DISCUSSION QUESTIONS

1. Why is international distribution more difficult than domestic distribution, even if the functions performed by a channel of distribution are similar in both situations?

2. What are the advantages and disadvantages of using an integrated distribution system? What choice would you suggest under which conditions?

3. How do the characteristics of the final customers affect the evaluation of international channel options?

4. What influences the length of a distribution channel in a national market, and how does that impact international channel evaluation?

5. Why are intermediary networks of importance to the international marketer, and how should they be taken into consideration?

6. How does distance influence channel member selection? What are your conclusions?

7. What are the advantages and risks to a marketer of discussing a possible partnership with an intermediary that already handles a competitor's product?

8. Describe the process of finalizing the relationship between a marketer and an intermediary. What environmental conditions will have to be considered?

9. What are the major elements in managing international channel relationships, and what potential problems must international marketing managers be prepared to overcome?

ADDITIONAL READINGS

Avlakh, P.S. and M. Kotabe (1997) "Antecedents and performance implications of channel integration in foreign markets", *Journal of International Business Studies*, 28(1), 145–75.

Kim, K. and G.L. Frazier (1996) "A typology of distribution channel systems: a contextual approach", *International Marketing Review*, 13(1), 19–32.

Ojasalo, J. (2001) "Key account management at company and individual levels in business-to-business relationships", *The Journal of Business & Industrial Marketing*, 16(3), 199–216

Pirog, St.F.III, P.A. Schneider, and D.K.K. Lam (1997) "Cohesiveness in Japanese distribution: a socio-cultural framework", *International Marketing Review*, 14(2), 124–34.

Samiee, S., L.S.C. Yip, and S.T.K. Luk (2004) "International marketing in Southeast Asia, retailing trends and opportunities in China", *International Marketing Review*, 21(3), 247–54.

Yip, G.S. and T.L. Madsen (1996) "Global Account management: the new frontier in relationship marketing", *International Marketing Review*, 13(3), 24–42.

Useful internet links

Albert Heijn	http://www.ah.nl/
Aldi	http://www.aldi.com/
Allied Signal Inc	http://www.honeywell.com/
Artigiano	http://www.artigiano.it/
Auchan	http://www.auchan.com/
BIC	http://www.bicworld.com/
Bruno Magli	http://www.brunomagli.com/
Business Cooperation Network	http://www.eu.int/
BusinessWorld	http://www.bworld.com.ph/
Carlsberg	http://www.carlsberg.com/
Carrefour	http://www.carrefour.com/english/homepage/index.jsp

Caterpillar	http://www.cat.com/
Champion	http://www.championusa.com/
Comercial Mexicana	http://www.comercialmexicana.com/
CompuServe Shop	http://www.compuserve.com/
Danieli SA Italy	http://www.danieli.com
Danone	http://www.danone.com/
Douwe Egberts	http://www.douwe-egberts.com/
Durst Phototechnik	http://www.durst-online.com/
eBay	http://www.ebay.com/
El Corte Ingles	http://www.elcorteingles.es/
Escada	http://www.escada.com/
Find Articles	http://www.findarticles.com/
Gaelic Inns Pte	http://www.gaelicinns.com.sg/corp.htm
Great Universal Stores	http://www.gusplc.com/
Grupo Gigante	http://www.grupogigante.com.mx/
Guinness plc	http://www.guinness.com/
Hilton	http://www.hilton.com/
Hitachi	http://www.hitachi.com/
Hitachi KK	http://www.babcock-hitachi.de/en/
Holiday Inn	http://www.holiday-inn.com/
Intersport	http://www.intersport.com/
Itochu	http://www.itochu.com/
i-Tunes	http://www.apple.com/itunes/download/
Kanematsu	http://www.kanematsuusa.com/
Knight Ridder Tribune Business News	http://www.knightridder.com/
Kobelco	http://www.kobelco.co.jp/english/
Komatsu	http://www.komatsu.com/
Lidl	http://www.lidl.co.uk/
Liebherr	http://www.liebherr.com/lh/en/default_lh.asp
LVMH	http://www.lvmh.com/
Majorica	http://www.majorica.com/
Marks & Spencer	http://www.marksandspencer.com/
Marubeni	http://www.marubeni.com/
Mary Kay Cosmetics	http://www.marykay.com/
Metro	http://www.metrogroup.de/servlet/PB/menu/ -1_12_ePRJ-METRODE-TOPLEVEL/index.html
Mitsui	http://www.mitsui.co.jp/tkabz/english/
Monsanto	http://www.monsanto.com/
NAFTA	http://www.nafta-sec-alena.org/DefaultSite/index_e.aspx
Novotel	http://www.novotel.com/
Organizacion Soriana	http://www.soriana.com.mx/
Research and Markets	http://www.researchandmarkets.com/
Rewe	http://www.rewe.de/indexEN.htm
Royal Ahold	http://www.ahold.com/
Tesco	http://www.tesco.com/
Thun Italy	http://www.thun.it/start.html
Tissot	http://www.tissot.ch/
U.S. Department of Commerce	http://www.commerce.gov/trade_opportunities.html
Warner-Lambert	http://www.pfizer.com/
Wild-Leitz	http://www.leica.com/

INTERNATIONAL SALES MANAGEMENT

13

INTERNATIONAL MARKETING SPOTLIGHT

In a global arena, executives need cross-cultural skills

One of the most perplexing issues facing sales managers in an internationally operating company is the diversity of cultures. Effective leadership in one culture can be disastrous in another.

This is why former General Electric Co. CEO Jack Welch told employees: "The Jack Welch of the future cannot be me." Future business leaders will need training to manage across cultures. Training, according to Welch, meant extensive time abroad.

But mere time-in-country is not enough. Sales managers also require in-depth understanding of the cultural values where they do business. They need to know how those values affect relationships with customers, other important stakeholders and sales-force leadership.

Consider the following case that happened some years ago in Southeast Asia. A company owned by nationals held beauty pageants each year to determine the most beautiful female employee. Employees looked forward to the pageants and there was wide participation.

This company was then acquired by a U.S. company, which sent U.S. managers to learn the business. The U.S. managers were opposed to holding the beauty pageant. At the same time, however, they wanted to respect the culture they were in, where such practices were accepted.

Their actions were guided by the fundamental value of respect. First, they met with the leadership of the organization to discuss the cultural clash. The U.S. managers clearly indicated they respected the values of the culture, but they also explained that such pageants would be considered disrespectful in the U.S., and perhaps illegal. Posing the problem in this way made it a "clash of equals": How can we agree on a course of action when cultural values conflict? Through this dialogue, which continued throughout the company at various levels, they reached an agreement to discontinue the event.

While some people disagreed with the decision, they understood it, and continued to be loyal to the company. Other employees, it should be noted, were glad the pageant was discontinued.

A valuable database for learning about dominating values in other cultures is the World Values Survey (www.worldvaluessurvey.org). The World Values Survey covers more than 80 cultures to understand how basic values affect people's attitudes toward economics, gender roles, family values, communal identities, and ethical concerns, among others. The database is continually updated, allowing identification trends. Global sales managers need these data to manage effectively and respectfully.

Jack Welch is right. We need to travel. But we also need to understand what we see when we get there. The World Values Survey provides a tool for managing effectively and respectfully in cultures different from our own.

Source: Adapted from: www.seattle.bizjournals.com/seattle/stories/2004/11/29/editorial3.html?page=1

The focal question of this chapter is: **How can international sales management contribute to building and sustaining the intended strategic position of a business organization?**

International sales management decisions

Every company must manage its sales activities, that is, the establishment, development, and maintenance of relationships with its direct customers. Depending on the decision whether to directly distribute the company's products to the final customers, to use intermediaries for distribution, or to do both to increase the coverage of the market, the customers of an international marketer may be final customers or intermediaries. In any case, proper building and sustaining of relationships with customers is crucial to the success of most international businesses.

Nevertheless, sales management traditionally has been a rather neglected area of international marketing. This is not only due to the fact that marketing and sales activities have been organized in different departments of the firm, and marketing managers perceived sales simply as part of market communication. There is also a widespread understanding that successful sales activities can be easily transferred from the home country of the company to other country markets. However, even in the age of the "global village" customer contact personnel has to consider that people interpret things based on their specific frame of reference, which is strongly influenced by the cultural environment. As a consequence, any attempt to "export" a certain way of thinking, feeling, and acting rather than adapting to the differing environment may lead to problems in building and maintaining business relationships.

Marketers also tend to neglect that potential customers in other country markets often need more information for their buying decision than customers in the home market. Communication problems, such as language barriers or different meanings of verbal and nonverbal communication, which become salient in negotiation and buying behavior, make potential customers feel uncomfortable, not knowing whether they have understood well enough to make the right decision. Potential customers may even consider some of a supplier's "strange behavior" as an expression of doubtful reliability. Information offered by sales support material, such as leaflets or brochures that may be well accepted in the home market of the company, might be considered as insufficient in other markets. The same is true for information offered by the firm via the internet.

Because most often customers want to be convinced of the product and its supplier before they buy, intensive training of customer contact personnel may be needed, covering the product's features, benefits, and proper application per customer segment as well as intercultural communication experience.

Companies doing only some international business tend to consider entering new country markets as a side issue. Instead of appointing the most capable person to manage sales in a new market top management tends to have "somebody" handling that business besides other tasks. Such perspective on international sales leads to sometimes rather strange situations. For example, a company based in the U.K. may appoint three people to take care of sales to the "continent" while a salesforce of 12 people covers the U.K. market.

To acknowledge the importance of sales management for international marketing success, the company has to develop an international sales policy. The sales policy is based on the company's intended global strategic position and international resource allocation. To ensure consistency the sales policy needs to be closely coordinated with product branding, and the distribution, logistics, as well as market communication policies of the firm (see Figure 13.1). Based on the objectives and rules of behavior formulated in the sales policy, sales management can take decisions and actions concerning personal selling, after-sales activities, and the recruitment, selection, and development of the international salesforces. Those issues will be discussed in the following.

International sales policy

To be successful in increasingly competitive global markets international marketers should not leave their sales and after-sales activities to the discretion of the individual members of their salesforce. Consistent building and maintenance of customer relationships across country markets need to be governed by an international sales policy. An **international sales policy** is the guideline for decisions and actions concerning personal selling, after-sales activities and the management of the firm's international salesforce. It contains a set of objectives that have to be attained by sales management decisions and of basic rules of behavior that are to be met when implementing those decisions in sales and sales-related activities.

The firm's international sales policy specifies:

- minimum and maximum levels of capital and personnel to be committed to achieving a desired level of market coverage
- market share, sales volume, and profit margins for each region, customer group, and distribution channel as well as expected return on sales
- how customer relations have to be managed, including after-sales activities such as the handling of customer claims.

A company entering new country markets through merchants can take advantage of the lower costs yet immediate availability of an indirect salesforce. The company sells its products directly to the merchant organization, which then sells the products in the new market. Objectives and rules of behavior specified in the international sales policy in that case will mainly focus on the selection of and relationship management with those business partners.

An international marketer that decides to enter new markets through merchants or independent agents to keep the financial entry risk at a minimum, but plans to involve itself more intensively, for example through the creation of a joint venture or the establishment of sales subsidiaries, if the market proves to be profitable, will formulate a different international sales policy compared to a company that wants to closely control its contacts with final customers. For example, Austria-based Frequentis, the world leader in voice communication systems for air traffic control, built its dynamic growth on the establishment of subsidiaries

FIGURE 13.1 *International sales management decisions*

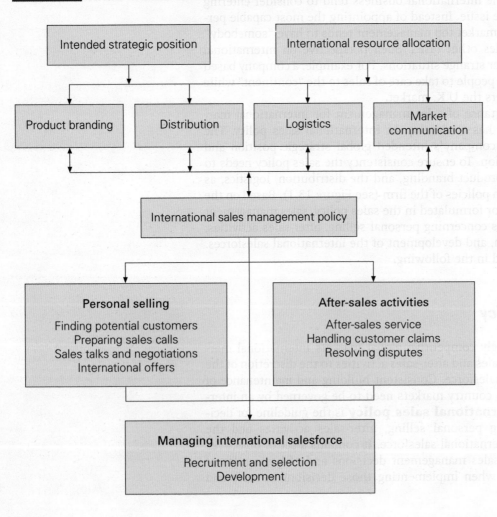

Based on its intended global market position and the general market-entry strategy of the firm, the marketer develops an international sales policy that is closely coordinated with the company's distribution and market communication policies. The international sales policy serves as a guideline for decisions concerning personal selling, after-sales activities, and the management of the international salesforce.

in Australia, Canada, France, Germany, Singapore, Slovakia, the U.K., and the U.S. Additionally, regional offices (e.g. in Cairo and Manila) were founded to ensure close contact with the customers on site. Frequentis's sales policy is governed by the rule: "We are on the spot to be able to meet individual customers' demands immediately and flexibly." Together with joint venture partners and strategic partners the company has formed a worldwide customer-oriented know-how network.

Ethics box 13.1 discusses potential problems that may arise when a company wishes to establish a general code of ethics for all of its customer relations across different country markets.

During most sales activities a substantial amount of personal communication with potential and current customers takes place. To ensure consistency, therefore, the international sales policy of the company must be closely coordinated with the firm's market communication policy. Rules of salespeople behavior in personal contacts with customers and other important stakeholders are based on the intended meaning of the company brand and the position of the firm's products to be reached in the customers' minds. Rules of behavior concerning the selection, training, and motivation of sales personnel give general guidelines on how to contribute to the achievement of the firm's communication objectives through proper management of the international salesforce.

International personal selling

Personal selling is the most effective way to sell in any market. This is true for local or international marketing, as the primary advantage of personal selling in

---

ETHICS BOX 13.1

Cross-national differences in salespeople's ethics?

Internationally operating companies based in the U.S. normally like to have one ethics code that is to be applied in all situations, by all employees. However, there is concern among sales managers that ethical complications may arise when international expansion is ongoing. Specifically, when marketers enter diverse country markets, and use local sales personnel, this may cause problems in terms of the established ethics policy.

A study researched salespeople's ethical views in the computer-related products and services industry in Japan, South Korea, and the U.S. Members of the salesforce were confronted with a variety of situations one after the other, and were asked whether they considered the given situation presented an ethical problem, whether their firm had a policy that addressed the issue, and whether the firm should have such a policy. As might be expected, sales personnel had very different views of what ethical

behavior is, and whether their company should have policies regarding that behavior, on a country-by-country basis.

The results of the research indicate that when employing local personnel as part of a multinational salesforce, sales managers need to evaluate ethical issues that may be found in the target country. Further, just transferring company policies regarding ethical behavior, does not seem to be useful or effective. Contrariwise, automatically adapting to local customs regarding ethical behavior does not work well either.

What may be useful for the international marketer is to develop and clearly communicate throughout the organization an overall principle that must be followed. For example, regarding whether governmental officials should ever be given "fees" for services or not. For specific situations, however, ethical standards of sales policy are more difficult to transfer to culturally and legally diverse country markets.

Source: Based on Dubinsky, A.J. and M.A. Molson (1991) "A cross-national investigation of industrial salespeople's ethical considerations", *Journal of International Business Studies*, 22(4), pp. 651–70

either case is the same, its flexibility. If a potential customer objects to the product or conditions of sale, the salesperson can modify the message or the offer on the spot. The key to success in international personal selling is the matching of seller product, knowledge, and culture, with buyer needs, knowledge, and culture. That is, even more than within a specific country market, international personal selling must be individualized – the "fit" between seller and buyer must be fully understood and carefully managed.

But individualized communication costs money. On a per-contact basis, personal selling is more expensive than other sales techniques, such as catalog sales, selling via the internet, or simply through self-service in a supermarket. Imagine, for example, if Coca-Cola had to employ a door-to-door salesforce in the worldwide country markets in which they sell their products, instead of using intermediaries. Therefore, finding and precisely selecting potential customers to personally sell to is of great importance to international marketers.

The use of personal selling to final customers is usually restricted to situations in which flexibility is required, personalized services are important, and high percontact costs can be justified. Marketers of capital goods such as computer systems or entire plants (which may cost millions of dollars), rely heavily on personal selling. So do marketers of most kinds of service that need to be tailored to the individual customers to satisfy their expectations. In consumer goods markets personal selling is used more selectively; it is used often, for example, in the sale of furniture and cars. In both cases, the customers' personal involvement with the product and the perceived risk incurred with the buying decision is relatively high for most customers. They expect to be personally informed and individually treated. Under similar conditions, personal selling for low-cost consumer goods, such as cosmetics, has also proven effective throughout North America, Europe, and Asia as evidenced by Avon and its salesforces of thousands of people.

Sales costs per successful business transaction can be reduced by carefully selecting potential customers, preparing sales calls, sales talks, and negotiations. A properly formulated offer will also contribute to effective and efficient international personal selling. In the following those points will be further elaborated.

Finding potential customers

The fastest and least expensive way to determine potential customers is to use available internal sources. Those may be the market knowledge of salespeople acquired through experience, and the creativity of company personnel activated by special ways of reasoning. Inquires of potential customers, invitations to tenders, official authorities, such as secretaries of commerce, or private organizations, like trade magazines or the yellow pages, which have been discussed in more detail in Chapter 7, may be further low cost sources of information on potential customers.

Salesforce experience

Market information, for example why customers prefer a certain brand or what they like when using a certain product, is "stored" in the minds of salespeople serving a certain country market. But often the information is not made available to their colleagues simply because no notes have been taken over the years. This knowledge, however, could be of considerable help to define customers in newly served markets, because customers in a worldwide product market may perceive features and benefits of a product or service in similar ways. Therefore, an in-depth investigation of what information has been collected over time by the company's salespeople is advisable. Table 13.1 suggests some questions that are worthwhile asking. Depending on the stage of development of customer relationships in the various served markets such an internal inquiry will produce more or less abundant information.

"Pyramid of acceptance"

Another important source of information about potential customers in new product or country markets is to observe the "pyramid of acceptance" (Figure 13.2). Monitoring the development of many product markets over time shows a recurrent phenomenon. At the beginning of their lifecycles innovative products are only accepted by a small group of pioneers, market volume is small, and product price is high. By the time the product is accepted by a substantial number of customers in the original market segment, it also finds more and more customers in other segments – with maybe different benefits, uses, or applications. This development is accompanied by an increasing international market volume and by decreasing prices.

For example, originally the microprocessor was developed for the ambitious *Apollo* project of the U.S. taking men to the moon for the first time. The quantities sold were low and the product was only accepted by a small group of experts.

TABLE 13.1 *Information to be gathered from salespeople*

• Who are the marketer's best customers at present?	
• What makes the marketer successful there?	
• How has the company identified and addressed new potential customers	
• What are the buying habits of the current customers? Specify concerning: information gathering, search for and assessment of potential suppliers, preparation of an inquiry, people involved in negotiation, decision making, and purchasing	
• What are individual expectations of customer groups as to product, supplier etc.?	
• What are the most important reasons why the company's offer has been accepted or refused by potential customers?	
• What are the customers' expectations as to distribution, pricing, logistics, services, etc.?	
• What economic criteria have been met by the company's product (price/benefit, terms, after sales service, etc.)?	
• What marketing strategies do the competitors apply, where do their limits lie and why?	
• What selling points, what aggressive sales strategies could we derive from our competitors' weaknesses?	
• What new competitors could enter the scene? (substitution products, link-up products, etc.)	

Based on their market experience, salespeople have plenty of information that needs to be gathered, structured, carefully analyzed, and played back to the salesforce to help it do its job.

Considering the cost of developing the microprocessor and the low production quantities the price had to be high. Today, the microprocessor has reached households being installed in video recorders, personal computers, fax and telephones, microwave ovens as well as in children's toys. Every modern automobile has more electronic and computing equipment installed than the former *Apollo* space capsule.

This development is not limited to products: Just-in-time systems originated from the automobile industry and TQM from the aerospace industry. Other products and services also have followed the "law" of the "pyramid of acceptance." Twenty-four-hour service, simpler use of products, lifetime guarantees, increased consumer protection, ergonomic products, and well-designed technical equipment; all these benefits people in industrially developed parts of the world are used to started in one single industry. From there, over the years, they have penetrated many different product markets through varying applications.

Analyzing innovative ideas, technological problem solutions, or services from the point of view of the "pyramid of acceptance" may be the key to new potential customers. It creates an opportunity for the international marketer to be a global pioneer in supplying a product or problem solution developed for a certain group of customers to other product and country markets.

Early adopters

In each market there are potential customers who want to be first in using a new product or service. But not all of those consumers or business organizations are accepted as opinion leaders by other potential customers. Early adopters that other potential customers use as role models who set trends in consumer markets or lead technological changes in industrial markets are of great importance to the international marketer.

For example, Singapore Airlines is a very important customer for aircraft manufacturers. The company has one of the best maintenance and repair facilities and technical staff worldwide and is well known for its outstanding services. If Singapore Airlines accepts a new generation of airplanes it becomes easier for an aircraft marketer to convince other airlines.

In addition to acceptance, *prestige* plays an important role. Being the first airline to put into service a new type of airplane is a well-accepted signal to passengers who become pioneers, excited about the experience to come. As a

---

FIGURE 13.2 *Pyramid of acceptance*

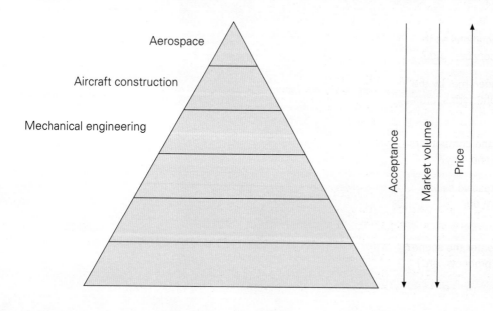

At the beginning of their lifecycle, innovative technologies are only accepted by a small group of pioneers (in one industry), the market volume is small, and the price of the product is high. Over time, these parameters change dramatically.

consequence of this policy, in January 2005 Singapore Airlines was the first airline to order the new Airbus A380 from Airbus Industries in Toulouse. This aircraft provides space for 800 passengers on two levels.

The international marketer entering a market with an idea, product, or service that is new to the market, therefore, has to find out at a very early stage which potential buyers are pioneers and accepted as trendsetters by other customers. Salesforce experience from other product introductions may serve as a valuable source of information concerning such customers to be approached first.

Singapore Airlines was first to order the Airbus A380 © Steve Nichols/Alamy

Inquiries

Quite a number of potential organizational customers take the initiative in searching for a competent supplier that might help solving a problem. The arrival of an inquiry by letter, phone, fax, email, filled-in form, invitation to tender, or as a report of the responsible salesperson provokes a series of steps to be taken:

1 The international marketer has to examine whether it is willing or able to quote. Many companies use databank-based checklists to allow quick examinations of the feasibility and commercial attractiveness of the demanded offers. In case of a negative result the inquiring customer should be given an explanation why the marketer has decided against making an offer, in order to prevent the prospective buyer from never sending an inquiry again. If the decision is positive the marketer has either to prepare the offer immediately or to inform the potential customer of when to expect the offer.

2 Then, the necessary personal capacity to prepare the offer needs to be reserved and a time schedule prepared within the given time limits.

3 If the inquiry is not complete or could give rise to misunderstandings, the marketer has to ask the potential customer for the missing data or a clarification. This can be done either directly or through the salesperson in charge. If the demand of the potential customer cannot be fulfilled in the way specified in the inquiry the international marketer may either:

   – prepare an approximate offer to keep the foot in the door and negotiate changes later, or
   – ask the customer immediately whether an alternative will be accepted.

   Depending on the complexity of the customer's problem to be resolved, the number of potential technical solutions, and the problem specific knowledge of the customer, one or other way may be more successful.

4 If the potential customer has never received any detailed sales literature from the international marketer, an information package should be attached to one of the communications.

To be contacted by a potential customer the international marketer obviously must have left "traces" in the market that enabled the potential customer to find the potential supplier. If the company does not want to rely on chance concerning potential customer inquiries it has to find out which of its market activities has attracted the potential customer's attention. Table 13.2 lists a number of potential attention attractors available to international marketers.

Tenders

When it comes to bigger and therefore more expensive projects governments but also business customers invite potential suppliers to bid. Invitations are published by announcements in relevant newspapers or magazines, by email, over the internet or just by letter. In the European Union, tenders for projects in excess of a certain value and that are launched by public administrations or by companies or institutions that are heavily influenced by government, for example in the sectors of water and energy supply, transportation, or telecommunication have to be

TABLE 13.2 *Potential customer attention attractors*

- Previous product presentations
- Advertisements
- Participation in a fair or exhibition
- Presence in the yellow pages
- Information offered on the company's website
- References given by pleased customers
- Information provided by a commercial representative of the marketer's home country
- Suppliers producing complementary goods
- Databanks
- Price agencies

There is a broad variety of potential customer attention attractors available to international marketers.

TABLE 13.3 *European Union's Tenders Electronic Daily database*

Introduction: Supplement to the Official Journal of the European Union

The *Official Journal of the European Union* (*OJ*) is published each working day in all 20 official languages of the EU. It consists of the following series:

- *OJ L*: Legislation
- *OJ C*: Information and notices
- *OJ S*: Public procurement

The series of the *Official Journal* are published by the Publications Office, the official publishing house of the EU institutions.

All public tenders exceeding specific contract values must be published in the *Supplement to the Official Journal of the European Union* ("S series", "Official Journal S" or "OJ S") and published throughout the EU. The contract value thresholds above which an invitation to tender must be published throughout the EU are laid down in EU Directives. The table provides information on the nature of a contract, the contract value (thresholds), and the relevant EU Directives.

Nature of the contract	Threshold	EU Directive
Public works contracts	€5,000,000	Directive on Public Works Contracts: 93/37/EEC
Service contracts	€200,000	Directive on Service Contracts: 92/50/EEC
Supply contracts	€200,000	Directive on Supply Contracts: 93/36/EEC
Supplies in the water, energy, and transport sectors	€400,000	Sector Directive: 93/38/EEC
Supplies in the telecommunications sector	€600,000	Sector Directive: 93/38/EEC
Public works contracts	€5,000,000	Sector Directive: 93/38/EEC
Contracts coming under GATT regulations	€125,000	

The awarding authorities for tenders are the central government, local or regional authorities, bodies governed by public law, or associations consisting of one or more of these authorities or bodies governed by public law.

Each year supply and public works contracts worth more than €500 billion are published by public authorities in the EU. Each day the *Supplement to the Official Journal* publishes over 650 tenders providing information on:

- public works, supply and service contracts from all EU member states
- supply contracts (for the water, energy, transport, and telecommunication sectors)

published. TED (Tenders Electronic Daily) is the online version of the "Supplement S" of the official journal of the EU, which contains such tenders (Table 13.3).

The number of potential suppliers invited may be limited. One reason may be, for example, that the local government does not want foreign companies to quote. Such restrictions are forbidden in the EU and other free trade areas. Another reason may be that business customers want to limit their relationships to a manageable and efficient small group of long-term suppliers.

Finally, when the project is rather voluminous, complex, or difficult to handle the customer may request potential suppliers to first pass a pre-qualification process. In such a case, the international marketer interested in bidding has to prove its ability to fulfill the kind of project at hand by presenting data concerning, for example, the financial status of the firm, references, engineering ability, machine tools, or production capacity. Only if the marketer passes the pre-qualification is it put on the so called "long list" and is invited to bid. Potential suppliers whose bids are accepted for their (technical) solution are put on a "shortlist."

Marketers having made the shortlist are invited to negotiations.

- public contracts of the EU institutions
- European Development Fund contracts (ACP countries)
- Phare, Tacis, and other contracts from central and eastern Europe
- projects funded by the European Investment Bank (EIB), European Central Bank (ECB), and European Bank for Reconstruction and Development (EBRD)
- contracts from the European Economic Area (Norway, Iceland and Liechtenstein)
- contracts in accordance with the government procurement agreement (GPA) concluded between the United States of America, Japan and Switzerland within the framework of GATT/World Trade Organisation (WTO)
- foundations of European economic interest groupings (EEIG)
- public contracts for food aid
- public contracts for flight services

Since July 1998, the printed edition of the *Official Journal S* has no longer been available. It is now available exclusively in electronic format and is accessible:

- on the internet by accessing the "TED" tender database ("TED internet application", "TED" = tenders electronic daily)
- on a CD-ROM ("OJ S CD-ROM application"), which is available on subscription twice weekly (Wednesdays and Saturdays).

How to obtain EU publications?
Publications for sale, published by the Publications Office, can be obtained through a worldwide network of sales agents.
The list of sales agents can be found on the Office Internet site:
http://www.publications.eu.int/others/sales_agents_en.html
The list is also available on request, by fax, from the Publications Office:
(352) 29 29-42758

How to submit a tender for EU publication?
For information on how to submit a tender for EU publication, please visit the following site:
http://simap.eu.int/EN/pub/src/welcome.htm

Source: European Union,
www.//ted.publications.eu.int/official/GetRecords?Template=TED/static/help/en/ch02.htm#d0e234

Expert interviews

Interviewing experts has proven to be a very efficient method for both gathering firsthand information about and acquiring potential customers. Experts may be decision makers of potential customer organizations, opinion leaders in the relevant industry or customer segment, and users of the product. With experts the international marketer normally can be quite sure to receive information from somebody who is familiar with the product and its application or use. Such experts may be found by:

- contacting the relevant industry associations in order to find out the names of key people
- searching for authors of relevant publications
- looking for people who keep good public relations. Questions like:
  - "What changes does our product need to be accepted in your market?"
  - "Who are our competitors and how do they apply their marketing tools?"
  - "How is the market volume shared between competitors?"

will usually be answered without objections if the expert does not get the impression of being involved in a "camouflaged" sales talk and enjoys talking with a person having a high level of knowledge about the product and the relevant industry in the country market.

Trade fairs, symposia, and articles or advertisements in trade magazines

The firm may play either an active or passive role. An industrial marketer can play an active role, for example, by

- exhibiting the company's goods
- giving a paper at a symposium
- publishing a report on the internet about the advantageous application of the company's products.

In business-to-business marketing, activities may be passive in the sense that the international marketer benefits from the chance to contact a group of potential customers at fairs or symposia. Or the marketer approaches a potential account showing interest in the content of a publication via the author of an article.

Preparing sales calls

Before making the first sales call in a country market the international salesperson has to do a lot of groundwork. Proper preparation before contacting potential customers and starting negotiations should be viewed as a corporate investment. It strongly influences success or failure, yet insufficient attention too often is paid to doing this "homework." U.S. Americans, for example, are trained early to "think on their feet," to expect to be unprepared in effect, and use their persuasive skills to succeed. This might be fairly well received in France where French managers are trained to "operate by the seat of their pants." However, in France, negotiators tend to be more formal, and do not go directly into the agenda at hand, but spend time getting to know the person first. In other cultures such as those found throughout Southeast Asia, thorough preparation is valued very highly. A lack of preparation is considered a strong signal that the potential partner does not take the business under discussion seriously. A business trip should not be considered as a single action but as part of a "project," the individual steps of which need to be carefully managed to be effective and efficient (see Toolbox 13.1).

General preparation

As discussed in Chapter 5, before a salesperson makes any sales contacts with potential customers in a new country market, she or he should review the cultural elements that might influence the establishment of a contact, the negotiation process, and the development of a relationship. When the salesperson contacts a prospective buyer for the first time, discusses a problem to solve, or negotiates a sales contract, the arguments put forward and the silent language used should fit the cultural background of the customer.

In addition, customers expect potential suppliers to be well informed about the specifics of their industry. Therefore, salespeople who are appointed in a country market that is new to them have to get accustomed to the specific characteristics of the economic, political, and legal environments relevant to the company's business. In addition to business-related information some knowledge on trivial things such as who the president of the country is, which party the prime minister represents, the names of the five biggest cities in the country, or milestones in the country's history may be of great help during sales calls. Being well informed about a customer's home country is a sign of interest and politeness that is appreciated all over the world.

Customer database

To carefully choose the most promising potential customers and later, to manage the relationships with current customers in a country market the international marketer will have to gather available information about current and potential customers in a customer database. This database should at least contain basic customer data in forms, such as the one shown in Table 13.4.

A customer database may serve as an important tool for the salesforce when preparing their sales calls. As far as the business side of the contact is concerned

---

TOOLBOX 13.1 Planning an effective and efficient business trip

Beginning with a "plan of action"

- Getting a general idea of all relevant aspects of the project
- Setting targets – defining all steps in the project to be taken
- Setting priorities
- Reserving capacities to fulfill the project
- Preparing a schedule

"You are the tip of the iceberg"

- Defining tasks
- Delegating as much as possible or outsourcing
- Using systematically all help available

"Getting things under control"

- Controlling regularly realization of tasks, schedule, and budget

- Keeping in mind all alternatives and thinking of changing the way of action when needed
- Preventing ill-considered steps or actions

"The business trip is the climax"

- Having all necessary sales tools and information on hand
- Taking advantage of all services offered in the customer's country
- Being prepared for spontaneous contacts

"Harvesting the fruits"

- Noting the results of meetings, and deriving required actions to be taken
- Turning reactions into actions
- Preventing unproductive hours

Source: Adapted from Kornberger, E. (1996) "Effiziente Geschäftsreisen", *Swissexport*, September, pp. 6f

the salesperson can find all up-to-date figures of importance with regard to the customer, including:

TABLE 13.4   *Basic customer data form*

The basic customer data form contains information salespeople should gather about potential customers and should have at hand about current customers.

Basic data on customers		
Name and address of company		
Telephone/fax/email		
Legal form of company		
Year of foundation		
Owners		
CEO		
Most important decision makers		
Headquarters		
Branch offices, subsidiaries, chain stores		
Representatives		
Bank account(s)		
Can be addressed by help of the following persons or companies		
Industry		
Main activities		
Product line (production and/or trade)		
Production sites and procedures		
Contact with other customers and/or influencers		
Customer's customers		
Existing suppliers		
Employees in		Number
	R&D	
	Sales	
	Production	
	Quality control	
	Administration	
	Logistics	
	Purchasing	
	Total	
Selling area in m²		
Equipment		
Total sales		
Realized sales with the customer in 20__ (per type of product)		
Planned sales with the customer in 20__ (per type of product)		
Financial status		
Accounts receivable		
Calendar/appointments		

- total sales
- number of orders placed during the current year
- number and kind of maintenance contracts.

Furthermore, information as to whether there is still an inquiry not answered, how many offers are neither negotiated nor decided, what the issues of previous contacts were, or what has been promised but still not fulfilled by the marketer will be useful in preparing a sales call.

In international sales, language barriers and communication problems result in psychological distance between a prospective buyer and its supplier. The customer tends to perceive greater difficulty in getting in touch with a foreign supplier than with a supplier from the home market. Reliability of both the product and the salesperson, therefore, are even more important for success in international markets than in the home market of an internationally operating firm.

To further a potential customer's perception of reliability a salesperson should at least learn all the information that is available in the customer database by heart. But the salesperson should also try to learn more about the persons to contact than just their name and position – for example, marital status, hobbies, habits, preferences, sectors of interest, or peculiarities of their personality – without violating the person's privacy. With this knowledge it is much easier to find the right words at a given moment, to prevent hurting people without knowing, and to build trust.

Planning sales calls

In international sales the thorough planning and organization of business trips is of great importance.

Bureaucratic hurdles Bureaucratic hurdles, such as the need for an invitation from a resident before one may enter Saudi Arabia, delays of more than 1 month to get a visa for Vietnam (while the salesperson's passport has to stay at the Vietnamese embassy), or complicated testing procedures before a sample of agricultural products may enter the U.S., may cause extended waiting periods and additional costs.

Natural environment and technological resources The cost per hour and per mile of traveling has to be kept as low as possible compared to the number of fruitful sales calls per day. Both are strongly influenced by:

- topography
- climatic conditions
- level of urbanization
- reliability of available infrastructure

of the sales region (discussed in Chapter 3). Different time zones, such as in the U.S. or in Australia may come as a surprise to salespeople acquainted to work in a sales area with one time. Relevant information can be gathered from any country guidebook.

Cultural influences It is not equally easy to get hold of customers all over the world. Some U.K. companies try to hold salespeople off with excuses, such as "Mr. Brown is in a meeting," or "Ms. Hancock is abroad". Different weekends or holiday seasons such as in Islamic countries, and managers of potential customer firms who do not keep their (written) word as to possible presentations, such as in Argentina, may mess up planned sales calls.

The length of discussions heavily influences the potential number of sales calls to be executed by one salesperson. For example, sales talks with Swiss procurement managers tend to be short and precise. In Germany, many purchasing managers even pre-determine the time they are prepared to reserve for negotiations with a salesperson, while their Tunisian counterparts prefer extended sales contacts, which stay rather vague in their content. As was discussed in Chapter 5, punctuality may have different meanings depending on the cultural environment. But extended waiting times may result in higher sales costs per customer contact if they are not planned beforehand.

Customer specifics Customer specifics such as their size, their problem to be resolved, or their product experience may have an impact on the number of business trips needed, their extension and cost.

Size of potential customers For example, a salesperson responsible for internationally operating customers may have to present a product to a team of operations managers in a production plant near Hamburg, Germany, submit the offer to a European purchasing unit in Amsterdam in the Netherlands, and negotiate the contract in the customer's headquarters in Osaka, Japan.

Type of customer problem to be resolved A salesperson wanting to successfully sell to Canada-based Bombardier's aerospace division needs to develop excellent relationships with all functional groups of the customer's organization. All of them must be assured that the supplier is able to master the high complexity of the customer's product and the high security standards of the customers' customers.

Product experience or level of technological know-how of customers For example, a BWT salesperson selling a water treatment installation in Sweden may require much less explanation, provision of infrastructure, and training than selling the same product in Uganda.

Sales manual
The most important tool for an international salesperson in preparing sales calls is the company's sales manual. Table 13.5 suggests the contents of a sales manual.

Company information The first part of the manual serves to inform the potential customers about the supplier and its products. It lists information on:

- international marketer's business domain
- size
- capital structure
- organization
- employees potentially important to the customer.

Product facts describe the reasons why potential customers should consider the marketer's product. They offer an opportunity to identify with customers from the same or a closely related industry that has similar problems and needs. They also relate to the potential customers' experience with products that did not entirely come up to their expectations, and offer an improved solution.

Brochures about individual products or product groups, which preferably should be translated in the customers' language are accompanied by additional *product descriptions* and *sample quotations*. Sample quotations are offers of "average" products. They should help potential customers getting a first impression of the marketer's capabilities.

Lists of suppliers and references The first part of the sales manual also contains a list of suppliers and a list of references.

TABLE 13.5 *Contents of a sales manual*

The sales manual helps salespeople in preparing their sales calls and in negotiating with potential customers. It may also be used for the preparation of international offers.

Information	Details	
Presentation of the company	Legal form of company	Bank account(s)
	Year of foundation	Top management
	Main activities	Headquarters
	Owners	Branch offices, subsidiaries
	Capital stock	Property, rented space
	Size of production and offices, storage capacity	
	Number and education of employees (production, assembling, service, sales, quality insurance, purchasing, etc.)	
	Equipment (machinery, test beds, etc.)	
Organizational structure	Who is responsible for what regarding the customer?	
Names and addresses of sales and service partners	Names, addresses, telephone and fax numbers of people who can be reached 24/7	
Product facts	Description of:	

- the shop, office, or plant of existing customers or of the production process of these customers
- problems those customers wanted to be solved
- previous, obviously not adequate, solutions to these problems
- optimum solution offered and realized by the marketer
- spreading the news

Brochures	Translated in the language of the customers	
(Technical) descriptions	Additional information that is not mentioned in the brochure(s), like dimensions, weight, maximum temperature, advice regarding transportation, storage, handling, maintenance, etc.	
Sample quotations		
Reference list		
List of suppliers		
Spare parts (list/scheme)		
Introductory conditions		
Video films, slides, photos, diskettes, CD-ROMS		
Standards applied		
Certificates		
Operating instructions		
Articles		
Training program		
List of arguments		
Competition comparison chart		
(Technical) questionnaire		
Price list		
Analysis of industries		
Customs tariff numbers (WTO)		
Payoff calculation		
Dictionary of technical terms		
Road map		
Zip code map		

The list of suppliers contains the names of companies that have a good reputation with potential customers. It serves as a demonstration to the potential customers as to how carefully the materials are selected that are used in manufacturing the marketer's products. If the suppliers listed offer their goods and services also in the customers' country market the international marketer may gain additional trust from the prospective buyers.

The reference list is a precious sales tool that should be handled with care. In the hands of competition it could be used efficiently to acquire new customers. Therefore, it is advisable to only hand part of the reference list over to a potential customer, for example, only reference customers in a certain sales area or from the potential customer's industry.

The second part of the sales manual helps the salesperson to prepare the sales call and to provide the potential customers with additional material to substantiate claims made during negotiations.

Treatment of objections Preparing a sales call means that the salesperson has to "sense" any possible objections and to develop counterarguments or alternatives in advance. In international sales where cultural differences between sales staff and the potential customers come into play, the international marketer particularly has to make sure that its salespeople are well prepared to cope with objections of their potential customers. Basic preparation can be achieved by making salespeople analyze the industries belonging to their sales area. This can be done according to the information given in the sales manual about customer groups showing above-average results in country markets served for some time. Salespeople may also analyze the reasons for success of their most important competitors alongside those in established markets. And they may go through the training program contained in the sales manual.

The sales manual also takes care of the fact that customers located in country markets other than the international marketer's headquarters have more potential objections to the marketer and its products than to local suppliers. Some objections are related to weaknesses of the total product compared to its competitors. Therefore, the sales manual contains information on the *standards applied in production*, such as measures of environmental protection, and on *certificates received*, such as an ISO 9000 certificate. It may also contain *articles from trade magazines or scientific reviews* that describe the use or application of the marketer's products in a more neutrally sounding and, therefore, more subjectively reliable way.

Operating instructions for technical products describe the product in more detail than any other sales literature. They provide clues as to outstanding features of the product.

Many objections of customers in international sales are based on emotional reactions rather than rational reasons, including:

- lack of confidence in a foreign company and its representatives
- fear of new products that might not perform in the way that was intended
- a perceived lack of efficient communication with the supplier,
- possible misunderstandings when defining the product and its application
- potential lack of reliable after-sales service.

For example, Inspec Fibres GmbH, an Austrian-based member of the German DEGUSSA Group, selling fibers for technical applications such as high-temperature gas filtration, were surprised to learn from a market survey how much their local clients were influenced by the way the salespersons treated them rather than by the outstanding features of the product.

International salespersons have to anticipate such emotionally based objections from their potential customers. The sales manual supports them by providing *lists of arguments* to be used during sales calls. Experience has shown that customers remember quantified arguments much better than they do mere verbal ones. For example, a salesperson offering a machine tool may praise its high availability as a bald statement of fact. Such verbal descriptions are too abstract to be remembered clearly by customers. By adding that 94.8% of the time the machine tool can be productively used by the customer and showing a record as proof for this claim, high availability becomes a feature of the product that is easily remembered.

The reputation of a salesperson and her reliability perceived by a potential customer is strongly influenced by competence, that is the salesperson's ability to answer questions concerning the product and the offer without having to contact the back office for approval. Therefore, further important aids for the salesforce in preparing a sales call are the price list, the list of spare parts, and the introductory conditions contained in the sales manual. For example, when negotiating the terms of sale, the salesperson can choose between an extended guarantee, a price reduction, a test period, and a return privilege that are contained in the standardized introductory conditions of the manual.

Support material The sales manual may also contain support material to increase the potential customers' trust in the international marketer and its products.

Video films, slides, photographs, or presentations on CD-ROMs or via the internet addressing the marketer's home page showing the manufacturing site of the marketer and the application or use of its products increases credibility. The international marketer may take advantage of the image of its country or of reputable customers. Attention needs to be given, however, that the usage situation shown in the visual material is perceived by the potential customer as closely related to its own situation or to a very desirable state. CD-ROMs may also offer questionnaires customers can fill in in order to facilitate the preparation of inquiries. Through such questionnaires the customer can specify the problem for resolution and the expectations to be fulfilled by the supplier without running the risk of forgetting important details. Language problems are less pronounced, experience with other products can be described, and the infrastructure available at the customer can be detailed.

Customs tariff numbers designated by the WTO or others make it easier for the customer to carry out an import calculation for the entire product or parts of it. They help avoiding import problems or paying too much customs taxes.

A payoff calculation scheme enables a prospective buyer to fill in its own figures. As a consequence, the potential customer tends to have greater trust in the outcome of calculations.

Dictionary of technical terms Finally, the sales manual may support the preparation of sales calls by providing a dictionary of technical terms. Because dictionaries available in bookstores rarely contain the specific vocabulary needed for internationally selling technical goods and services, the international marketer is well advised to develop a collection of technical terms in several languages company salespeople have learned during their discussions with customers and other relevant stakeholders. Such a dictionary assists company personnel and interpreters in their translation jobs. A roadmap and a zip code map that facilitate finding addresses may complete the sales manual.

Sales negotiations

After having carefully planned their sales calls salespersons may start contacting potential customers. In international business a salesperson has to know and to respect the (mostly unwritten) rules of social behavior when getting into personal contact with potential business partners. For example, in the U.K. and Japan, it is important to know and to respect the hierarchical levels of management in a potential customer firm. In Spain, a salesperson should never try to make an appointment during "la siesta," that is between 1.30 pm and 3.30 pm, and she should never expect dinner to start before 10 pm. In Portugal, business partners tend to expect a correctly dressed salesperson (men wearing suits and ties), while their Norwegian counterparts mostly prefer casual or sportive clothing even at dinner.

Starting negotiations

Sales negotiations are viewed and carried out differently from one culture to another. As Chapter 5 illustrated it is important to know how to start a sales talk and how to address negotiation partners.

Bargaining

Bargaining is what most people think of when they think of negotiation – the "give and take" of information and offers. Chapter 5 has shown that bargaining is viewed and carried out differently from one culture to another. A sales technique that has been used effectively in one country market may not be effective in another. Agreement between salesperson and customer may be difficult to reach. Even the very approach to negotiation, whether it is essentially seen as a win–win or a win–lose exercise, is heavily influenced by the businesspeople's cultural backgrounds.

Independent of the cultural environment of a sales negotiation process there are some general rules that an internationally active salesperson should be aware of to be successful.

Check with potential customer regarding mutual understanding of discussed issues
Language problems or the perceived obligation to let the others keep their "face" often make negotiation partners reluctant to ask questions. Salespeople must be aware of making sure that most of what they are trying to communicate is understood and evokes the intended meaning.

Minimize monologues Without listening to the potential customer's opinion salespeople will never find out what this person really wants. When asked questions, the salesperson should answer in short, simple, and few sentences. Otherwise the salesperson risks never being asked again, especially if negotiation takes place in the mother tongue of the salesperson and the business partner has to communicate in a foreign language.

Leave time for potential business partner to take notes After the meeting these notes are the basis for what the interested partner can convey to members of their buying center inside and stakeholders outside the company. The negotiation partners must be furnished with enough and good arguments they can "sell" to those interested others. The benefits the product provides to the potential customer and its stakeholders and the success story of the marketer in its field of competence are key factors in getting the order.

Purchase contract is not negotiated at first meeting The potential customer wants to have sufficient time to learn more about the international marketer, its products, and the given references. Extra time may be needed to check whether the arguments and statements from the salesperson are true. In addition, other people in the company have to be convinced of the advantages of a new supplier. Sometimes, when potential customers are intermediaries, they may want to do some market research concerning the attractiveness of the potential supplier's products. In other cases, when the potential customers have closely regulated ties to their own customers, such as in the aircraft industry, they even may need to ask their own customers for approval of the new supplier or its product. Due to all these requirements of their potential clients, salespeople must find ways to contact prospective customers at regular intervals in order not to be "forgotten."

"Train" customers who are not familiar with the state of the art in the industry Such customers may be provided with information or tools that enable them to evaluate suppliers and products in their particular field. For example, most potential customers of Frequentis, the Austrian supplier of voice communication systems for air traffic control, are not able to follow the technological content closely enough to systematically evaluate products offered by suppliers. Therefore, the company enacts its sales presentations as a kind of training to let the customers learn as much as possible about the equipment and its functioning before they need to take any decision.

Structure of sales talks

Despite all the cultural differences among business manners there are some commonalities salespersons have to respect independent of the country market they serve. Most marketers need to gradually overcome customers' prejudices or lack of confidence in the company and its products. Salespeople, therefore, must express that they are genuinely interested in the customer's problem and in providing the expected customer benefits, and that they are also convinced of their product. They have to carefully treat any objections of the customer and must ask the customer for approval.

Consequently, a promising sales talk should start with an introduction by the salesperson and the company represented. Then the salesperson should thank the potential customer for having been invited to attend the talk and repeat or explain the reason for coming. In this phase, the salesperson will also take the opportunity to present the objective(s) and the topics of the meeting. In the following phase, it may be necessary to create problem awareness on the part of the customer. In this stage the salesperson will ask customers to talk about their current situation and elicit requirements and expectations concerning potential problem solutions. It is essential to agree on issues the customer regards as important. For that purpose and for the presentation of the benefits the company's product is able to provide, the salespersons may use the sales literature contained in the sales manual or equivalent files saved on their notebooks.

Then the issues agreed on are negotiated and the salesperson draws conclusions from the negotiation.

To make sure that the business partner has a similar understanding of the meaning of these conclusions further actions and commitments for both sides need to be fixed. For example, the negotiating parties may agree to writing up a document that organizes proof of claims, prepares the offer, and negotiates with subcontractors.

The salesperson finishes the sales talk by summing up what has been achieved.

All aspects of the negotiation process are summarized in the statement: "Without relationships, you have no deal." Certainly, there are sales talks that will never lead to negotiations; and there are negotiations that will not be concluded with an agreement. But for international marketing to be successful over time, a salesperson must be aware that profit in business mainly depends on repeat business, in consumer as well as organizational markets. In most product markets relationships with customers must be established with a long-term perspective and must be maintained accordingly.

International offer

By presenting an offer the international marketer invites a potential customer to sign a sales contract. Because well-prepared offers may involve substantial costs marketers have to find out the purpose of their offer for the potential customers before quoting.

The offer may serve to get an offer for budgeting purposes or a comparison of prices, as a part of a complete quotation of the potential customer for its own client, or it may represent a real demand.

When the decision to make an offer is taken, the offer may be made verbally or in writing by letter, fax, or email. But whether verbally or in writing, all are equally binding. When preparing a written international offer the marketer has to consider what language to use, legal regulations and local market nuances to respect, product specifications and applications as well as terms of sale and delivery to offer, and for what period of validity the offer is binding.

In addition, the structure of the offer may determine its attractiveness to the customer. After presenting the offer to the customer the salesperson has to ensure an effective follow-up to close the contract.

Preparing the offer

The most convenient solution for the international marketer would be to execute all international correspondence in its own language. Many salespeople from English-speaking countries rely on their customers' ability to read and write their language. They do not consider how much more difficult it is for their customers to express themselves precisely in the way they would like, even if they seem to master the foreign language quite fully.

The best solution for the customers would be to communicate in their language. This possibility is limited, however, by the availability of language skills in the internationally operating firm or of good translators if the language is not one of the more commonly used. Bad translations – in particular of technical and commercial terms – may lead to misunderstandings resulting in reduced attractiveness of the international marketer's offer or in disputes after the contract has been signed. Even professional translators should not be expected to know all the specialist terms included in the original.

To prevent both an offer that does not conform to norms and standards of the customer's country market and possibly substantial fines for disregarding legal regulations, the international marketer must know the business nuances, norms, standards, and legal regulations relevant to its product market before quoting. For example, electrical devices approved in the EU are not automatically approved in Switzerland; and many U.S. customers interpret the delivery term "FOB" (free on board) in a way different from the definition of the incoterms (see Table 14.6).

In preparing an offer the international marketer must also consider that many prospective customers do not clearly define the product and its use when inviting potential suppliers for a bid. Potential suppliers are assumed to know facts that are not mentioned in the inquiry. For example, when an investor sends inquiries for electrical blast furnaces to potential international suppliers those suppliers are assumed to have or that they will acquire additional information about facts such as the existing infrastructure at the construction site, the industrial standards and legal norms to be respected in the country, or the available lifting hoist. In such cases, the international marketer has two possible reactions:

- It may gather the additional information needed to make an offer that is reliable for the customer and minimizes the risk for the marketer. But at the same time the offer may be submitted too late when competitors have already gained an advantage by choosing the alternative reaction.

- The alternative reaction is to present an offer "on the assumption that." This way the international marketer is much faster, but risks offering product features and services the customers are not ready to pay for or overlooking cost drivers that may lead to problems in staying within the offered price.

To decide on one or other way of reacting the international marketer must evaluate what is more important in the specific case: to quickly get in close contact with the customer and to negotiate the details later on, or to make a complete offer to the customer that reduces the marketer's financial risk.

If a potential customer who had never had any contact with the international marketer before has sent an inquiry that specifies the requested product in detail the marketer can assume that those details stem from the potential customer's experience with competitors' products. In such a case, the offer has to state clearly on which points the product substantially differs from the specifications given in the inquiry. It must convince the potential customer that the product offers features that are at least equally or even better suited to fulfill customer expectations and may even provide additional benefits.

If an international inquiry specifies both the requested product and its use or the problem to be resolved by using the product, the marketer may be able to offer the product as specified by the customer. In addition, the marketer may present an alternative for the solution of the described problem that is more competitive than the product demanded by the potential customer. The international marketer should offer both, as the potential customer might have had good reasons, such as existing stock of spare parts, tools, or specifically trained people, to specify the product in the way it did. In any case, a personal check with the customer to clarify the situation is much more advisable than to offer a supposedly "better" solution that does not meet customer requirements.

When an inquiry or the attached terms of purchase do not specify details such as the currency to be used, the place and terms of delivery, or the terms of payment, the international marketer should make the choice. (Chapters 14 and 16 will further elaborate on the factors to be considered in selection terms that are attractive for both business partners.)

Offers may be binding or not.

Not binding offers are rather rare in international business. They only occur when the marketer does not want to commit itself because it cannot entirely control the sequence of events, such as in the case of late or no delivery of substantial parts or services by subcontractors. However, in such a case, the international marketer should state clearly why its offer is not binding. If the marketer does not declare an offer as "not binding" the customer may claim the delivery of what has been offered. The customer may even sue the marketer if it cannot fulfill its commitment.

Structure of an international offer

Both the content and the format of an offer must attract the potential customer's attention. The offer is part of the international marketer's total product. Correct address, clear structure, faultless and pleasingly formatted text, and a transport resistant envelope give the customer an impression of what to expect from the supplier. A clear structure facilitates the potential customer's task to read, understand, and compare the offer with those of competitors. Because this is particularly important in international marketing where language problems may represent a significant obstacle, the structure of an international offer will be described in more detail in the following. To be clear and easily understandable for the potential customer an international offer should have the structure shown in Table 13.6.

Introduction As with sales negotiations, the very first words count. They convey the first impression and should arouse the reader's interest. Referring to the inquiry or another reason for the offer indicates why the potential customer receives the offer. But it also is an occasion to thank the customer for having been considered in the bidding process or for the friendly reception of the salesperson.

When it is the marketer's first offer presented to the potential customer both the company and the personnel serving the customer have to be introduced. Part one of an international marketer's sales manual as it was described earlier may serve as an information platform. By repeating the intended use of the product and by giving reasons for its purchase the international marketer may communicate how well the customer's problem and its expectations have been studied.

Description of the total product The total product should be described considering its features and customer benefits. Depending on what type of product the international marketer is offering, a technical product description may consist of dimensions such as weight, material, function, technical data, mechanical or electrical in- and output, information about required storage space or time, installation, maintenance, physical or online service, repair and spare parts, advises regarding environmental protection and safety, or packaging.

The product description must be complete. It should not leave room for any misunderstandings that could increase the potential customer's doubts about buying from a non-domestic supplier. Therefore, information on the share of local production and how total quality is managed by the international marketer may complete the more product-oriented description.

Guarantees Beside guarantees the marketer has to offer based on legal regulations, there may also be voluntary guarantees aimed at strengthening the com-

---

TABLE 13.6 *Structure of an international offer*

Introduction

- Reason for the offer
- Introduction of the company and the personnel serving the customer
- Intended product use and reasons for purchasing the selected product

Total product

- Description
- Quantity
- Shipment
- Packaging
- Guarantee

Price and terms

- Price/currency
- Terms of payment
- Taxes and customs duties
- Financial commitment
- Delivery time

Period of validity

Reservation of ownership

Order cancellation fee

Attachments

The structure of an international offer largely contributes to the offer being clear and easily understandable for a customer speaking a different language and living in another cultural and regulatory environment.

pany's competitive position. When phrasing a guarantee clause the marketer should take care that an "unlimited" guarantee has not been offered. For example, a special service guarantee for a new computer installation could be limited by a statement such as "The guarantee ends 12 months after startup of the new system, and, at the latest, 18 months after delivery."

Price and terms of sale When indicating the price for the offered product in a certain currency the international marketer should either use the name of the currency in the business language the partners have agreed on or apply the internationally accepted abbreviations for currencies, such as CAD for the Canadian dollar, EUR for the euro, or GBP for the British pound (sterling). Many marketers will not be able to quote in their own currency. In such cases, marketers should use a special clause in their offer, such as a fixed exchange rate, that protects them against negative effects of exchange rate fluctuations (see Chapter 16 for further details).

Fulfilling an order may take a substantial amount of time. If wage increases or rising prices for supplies during that period may threaten the price calculation of the international marketer, a price escalator clause may be used. It normally links the indicated price for the offered product to national or international official indices that can be easily verified by the potential customer and may be certified by official bodies.

In many international business relations the financial commitment of the marketer strongly influences the attractiveness of its offer to the potential customer. By offering a mix of financial assistance through the company itself, a bank recommended by the marketer, and a state-owned institution that supports international business activities, the supplier may substantially increase its attractiveness.

Terms of delivery Who will have to pay what taxes and customs duties mainly depends on the terms of delivery the international marketer is offering. The terms most often used are discussed in Chapter 14.

Delivery time In specifying delivery time the international marketer should never state a fixed date as the date when the prospective buyer will order is unknown. Usual wordings include, for example, "four weeks after receiving the order" or "prompt delivery after having received your down payment."

Period of validity The marketer may also state the period of validity of its offer. If this period is not specified in a written offer it generally ends after a period which consists of two elements: the delivery time of both the offer as well as the goods or services and the time the potential customer usually needs to evaluate the offer and to make a decision. Verbal offers, given personally or by phone, must be accepted or refused immediately if not otherwise agreed.

Risk reduction clauses A reservation of ownership serves to prevent the transfer of title to property when the product is handed over to the customer. Proper wording could be, for example, "Our ownership will not pass over before payment of the full purchase price." Another safety measure for the supplier and the customer is to include a statement concerning an order cancellation fee. Such a statement informs the potential customer under what conditions, for example the payment of a certain percentage of the order value, a placed order may be cancelled.

Attachments Finally, the attractiveness of an offer may be increased by attachments that appeal to all senses of the prospective customer, such as photographs, videos, audio cassettes, diskettes, CD-ROMS, links to the marketer's home page or product samples. However, special care has to be taken that none of those attachments hurts the feelings of the persons involved in the purchasing decision process on the customer side because of sexual, racial, religious, or other cultural reasons.

Follow-up

After the offer has been presented the salesperson takes on an important role in getting the customer's order. As soon as the salesperson can assume that the potential customer has had enough time to read and study the offer as well as to assess and compare it to offers from competitors, follow-up activities may be started. A personal discussion about how the customer evaluates the offer is often carried out via a telephone call, which, in turn, is better than a fax or an email. The problem of international follow-up telephone calls is that talking to someone over the phone requires a much better knowledge of the communication partner's language than a face-to-face discussion where gestures, drawings, or showing and pointing at something help to overcome communication problems. Table 13.7 contains some important questions to be answered as result of a follow-up with a potential customer.

If customers want to postpone their decision or the placing of the order the salesperson has to find out the reason why, the date the customer might be contacted again and, the possibilities for influencing the decision.

In case one of the competitors receives the order, the salesperson should gather information on who has received the order, which part of the company's offer has not met the customer's expectations, and what can be done in the future to come closer to potential customers' expectations.

After-sales activities

Beside personal selling, international sales management is also responsible for an international marketer's after-sales activities. These activities encompass after-sales service, handling customer claims, and resolving disputes with customers.

TABLE 13.7 *Follow-up questions*

• Has the prospective customer understood and appreciated all details of the offer?
• Are further explanations or even a revised offer required?
• Which parts of the offer have to be modified in order to improve the opportunity of receiving the order?
• Who are the competitors and what are their major arguments?
• When will the decision be made?
• Could a personal call of another company member contribute to the decision making by intensifying the salesperson's arguments?
• Is the prospective customer ready to accept the salesperson to negotiate a possible purchase contract? Who else may need to be involved?

During the follow-up of an offer the salesperson should try to get answers to certain important questions.

After-sales service

After-sales service is frequently considered a technical service (installation, maintenance, and repair) of the products sold. However, in order to assure a long-lasting relationship with a satisfied customer, to be allowed to use the customer as a reference, and to encourage positive word of mouth the international marketer has to do more than simply service the products sold. The customer has to be kept satisfied with the product from its purchase to the end of its use or as long as the customer keeps it in its product assortment. For example, a software company not only has to install its product on the customer's computer (or to provide easy installation advice) and to remove bugs from its software. It must also be continually accessible when problems arise, must regularly update the software, inform the customer about new developments that could be of relevance to its product, and may need to offer training for new users.

As a consequence of such extended demand international after-sales service has:

1 To check that customer orders have been fulfilled according to the contract and the expectations of the customers. Shipment may not have been complete, product quality may have been diminished during transportation, delivery time may have been overrun, or the customer might not have received all documents necessary for proper product use, such as the operating manual.

2 Proper functioning of the product must be checked. For example, an international consulting firm specializing in productivity gains of their customers, must offer some follow-ups to check if the changes implemented in the customers' processes have led to the promised results.

3 A system to ensure regular customer contacts needs to be installed. Customers should not hear from the company only when they have a problem with one of its products.

Handling customers' claims

Even total quality management and excellent international after-sales service cannot entirely prevent customer complaints about a product delivered, a service rendered, or the way the customer was treated by the marketer's employees or its intermediaries. There are justified complaints and others where the customer is wrong. Most serious are customer complaints that are combined with a request to either remove the cause for the complaint or to financially compensate the customer for its damages. The international salesperson must be able to handle all cases properly. Certain steps need to be taken in order neither to annoy the customer any further nor to commit their own company in an inadequate way. The greater the cultural distance between the business partners, the more delicate the salesperson's task.

In general, the salesperson:

1 needs to find out what exactly has happened and what has been done already to solve the problem

2 decides on measures to be taken, and – if an organizational customer is concerned – what key persons the customer needs to be kept in touch with

3 may answer the question of how to prevent such things from happening again.

When discussing complaints or claims with a customer there is, of course, high tension between the two business partners. Because of increased emotionality, discussions tend to be less polite. If legal issues come into play, formalities become more important. In any case, intercultural differences play a major role. The salesperson must be closely familiar with the dos and don'ts of interpersonal communication in the customer's culture if insults are to be avoided. Any mishandling of such a situation will lead to even more trouble and to the loss of a customer who will probably herald to other current and potential customers what has happened. Of course, if customer complaints are well treated, customer satisfaction may increase above the level reached before the cause of the complaint arose.

Sensitive handling of customer complaints is highly important for customer satisfaction and the international marketer's word of mouth. Therefore, patient, reliable, and circumspect people with intensive intercultural experience are needed to handle international claims. These complaint managers should also be extremely orderly, since the activities involved in satisfying the customer have to be meticulously organized and realized. Discussions, decisions, and actions should be carefully documented in order to have some proof concerning measures taken, when and by whom in a potential dispute later on.

Resolving disputes

Even the best handling of customer complaints cannot entirely prevent disputes between an international marketer and its customers or other important stakeholders. Like negotiation practices, the processes for recognizing and resolving disputes vary considerably among cultures. As Chapter 5 has shown, different cultures have developed different methods and even different procedures for resolving disputes. In more "cooperative" societies, dispute resolution is achieved through discussion. If an impasse is reached, an arbitrator is called in to settle the dispute. Table 13.8 contains a list of resources for such arbitration processes.

Outside the U.S., arbitration is not only usual, but is also the preferred method of resolving disputes that cannot be eliminated by negotiations. Courts in many countries tend to favor the local business partners interests; and legal processes between a local customer and an internationally operating firm arouse public attention that tends to be mainly negative for the foreign company. Therefore, contrary to U.S. habits, international marketers should avoid resolving disputes in court whenever possible.

Managing the international salesforce

Personal selling is the most effective method of communicating with potential customers. But to ensure the efficiency needed for international success the marketer has to recruit and select the best people for its specific purpose, it has to develop its salesforce, motivate them to reach ambitious goals and compensate them according to their performance.

Recruitment and selection

Searching for sales personnel capable and willing to cope with the challenge of international marketing is a demanding task. The international marketer may employ expatriate personnel, nationals from the country markets to serve, or cosmopolitan employees.

Expatriates

Expatriate personnel are employed by a firm in a country other than their home country. For example, an Italian citizen who works for Olivetti, the Torino-based maker of office equipment, in Spain is an expatriate. Expatriates have the advantage that they are well acquainted with the cultural specifics of the home base. If they have already worked for the company for some time they also know the peculiarities of corporate culture and the products to be sold. Because of this product and process expertise expatriates are frequently used as salespeople for highly technical products.

Expatriates are expensive over the long run – they cost an average of 200% over base salary. Additionally, they often have problems of personal adjustment in the new environment (see Culture box 13.1). Foremost among these, and the ones over which management has the least control, are problems that pertain to the employee's family. Spouses are often unhappy about moving to another country, partly due to limitations on their own career opportunities. Most countries issue a work permit to the firm's employee but make it considerably more

TABLE 13.8 *International arbitration resources*

International marketers may choose from several international arbitration resources when disputes need to be resolved.

International arbitration resources

International Chamber of Commerce (ICC)

The International Chamber of Commerce counsels and arbitrates in Paris. It is controlled by an Administrative Commission constituted by one member of each country whose business organizations are affiliated with the ICC. The commission attempts to counsel a resolution to disputes after a hearing. If that fails, the matter is referred for arbitration to the Court of Arbitration, chosen by the parties and the ICC

American Arbitration Association (AAA)

The American Arbitration Association enables foreign businesses to use arbitration in the U.S. and avoid the complex and costly U.S. legal system. An arbitration may make an award that seems just and equitable under the AAA rules. The association appoints the arbitrator, giving consideration to the parties' preferences and objections

Geneva Conventions on Arbitration

The Geneva Protocol (1923) provides that member nations recognize the validity of arbitration agreements made between parties that are under the jurisdiction of the member nations, irrespective of where the agreement was executed

The Geneva Convention (1927) provides that member nations recognize as binding and enforce under the rules an arbitration award made under an agreement covered by the Geneva Protocol

New York Convention

The New York Convention, created in 1958 by the United Nations Conference on International Arbitration, has no requirement of reciprocity. This means a member nation may apply the convention to awards made in the territory of another member nation, and not its own. However, each member nation must refer parties to a written arbitration agreement. Important member nations include the U.S., Germany, France, Japan, the U.K., and the CIS

UNCITRAL Arbitration Rules

These rules were published by the United Nations Committee on International Trade Law in 1976. They are a model for international arbitration, but are not embodied in a convention

Convention on Settlement of Investment Disputes

This convention provides for the formation of a Center for Settlement of Investment Disputes at the principal office of the Bank of Washington, to settle investment disputes between member nations

Source: Adapted from Walton, A. and M. Vitoria, (1982) *Russell on Arbitration,* 20th edn, (London: Stevens E. Sons; Marshall, E.A. (1983) *The Law of Arbitration,* 3rd edn, London: Sweet and Maxwell

difficult, if not impossible, for the employee's spouse to obtain a work permit. Children also worry about living in a foreign land. They must leave familiar surroundings and friends to attend a new school, sometimes being taught in a foreign language. Music lessons, sports activities, and other hobbies and interests that are important to them may be interrupted. In fact, U.S. companies experience a higher overseas failure rate than do European or Japanese ones. And one of the most important reasons for such failure is family pressures.

Some employees may refuse overseas assignments because of the fear, common among expatriates, that they will be forgotten if they stay away from the home office for several years. Relocation difficulties can represent a major problem to international marketers. When employees from western Europe have been assigned to industrially developing countries, for example, they are frequently provided with additional support for housing, domestic staff, cars, and special educational training for their children. When they return to their home country, they no longer receive this additional compensation package. Often the family and executive react negatively, sensing a loss of status. A further complication is that quite often when given an international assignment, the employee has increased broader responsibility and authority. The return to headquarters, usually with a narrower or less reasonable job, also causes dissatisfaction.

It may first take substantial time for expatriate salespersons to become effective in country markets foreign to them; and repatriation may cause additional problems. As a consequence, with world trade and the number of globally active

CULTURE BOX 13.1

Expatriate salesforce: A tough life in the U.S.

Most Americans think, quite naturally, of expatriates as being Americans living abroad. But as foreign investment and business activity increases in the U.S., so, too, do the number of foreign business people living there. They face the same basic problems adjusting to another culture that Americans do when going abroad.

Asian or European expatriates in the U.S. are isolated from the home culture and (usually) language. The expatriate's family has to adapt to new living conditions, schools, and social systems. For example, one expatriate's wife was shocked when, alone one evening, she opened the door to her home to be confronted by people in face paint and strange clothing, celebrating Hallowe'en. Of more serious concern to the approximately 200,000 Japanese business executives living in the U.S. is whether their children will get the education necessary to prepare them for the notoriously difficult entrance examinations at Japanese universities.

In general, employees' families are not prepared for foreign assignments as extensively as the employees themselves are, despite the fact that

such training is good "people policy" and makes strong economic sense. General Motors, for example, has found that spouses of expatriates have five times greater difficulties in getting accustomed to their new cultural environment than their partners; but the spouses' well-being is very important for the success of the international appointment. Many companies assume that a half-day seminar of general information will suffice to prepare families for foreign assignments. One 4-hour seminar, which excluded children, claimed to prepare U.S. families for a 2-year assignment in Saudi Arabia. The Saudi religious environment and its implications for behavior, including how executives' spouses could expect to be treated socially, were "covered" in a 15-minute talk by an American national who had never been to Saudi Arabia or had any specific training in Saudi customs. In sharp contrast is a 3-day course for NEC executives' wives. The course prepares them for the difficulties of living in the U.S, by offering some language training, information about social customs, and even tips on how to shop successfully in U.S. supermarkets.

Source: Based on O'Reilly, B. (1988) "Japan's uneasy U.S. managers", *Fortune*, 25 April, pp. 10–14; and Stalling, B. (1995) "Der teure Auslandseinsatz scheitert häufig an Integrationsproblemen", *Der Standard*, 25–26 March, p. 16

companies increasing, the proportion of expatriate employees has declined. This switch away from expatriate personnel is due not only to their higher costs, but also to the increased availability of national personnel who are qualified for the job.

Nationals

Nationals are sales employees who are based in their home country. An Australian citizen who sells automatic door systems for railway vehicles of the Austrian-based IFE, a division of Knorr Bremse GmbH, is a national. There is a definite trend toward using nationals in international business. Many economically less developed countries are putting pressure on international marketers to employ nationals. Moreover, as educational systems and training opportunities improve, more qualified national personnel are becoming available.

Because of their lower total cost compared to expatriate salesforces, national salesforces are more attractive for organizational as well as consumer markets. The overwhelming argument in favor of nationals, however, is their superior understanding of the market and their ability to work within its cultural and social norms while pursuing the company's objectives. However, grasping the specific culture of the company may lead to a hostile feeling concerning headquarters.

Cosmopolitan

Cosmopolitan employees are citizens of one country who are employed by a company based in a second country and are working in a third country. A British engineer who works in Indonesia for a business unit of Norwegian Statoil, for example, is a cosmopolitan. This type of employee is more often hired by large multinational firms than by a small company. One advantage of employing a cosmopolitan is similar to that of an expatriate – availability of expertise or knowledge that is otherwise difficult to find. Often such cosmopolitans have a more strongly developed sense of cultural empathy than expatriates, due to their tendency to remain a cosmopolitan employee throughout some considerable proportion of their career.

The increase in world trade, as well as an increase in people's preference to live internationally, has led to an increase in the availability and use of cosmopolitan employees. This trend has been reinforced by the development of educational programs, such as master's degree programs in international business studies offered by cooperating schools in Europe, North and Latin America, and Asia. Such programs are increasingly graduating multilingual, cross-culturally trained, business-knowledgeable future business leaders.

Search profile

For many years the leading criterion for selecting international sales personnel was the ability to speak the language practiced in the company's headquarters. Thus, for example, U.S. firms recruited Arab salespeople and sales managers by first screening them on the basis of their ability to speak English. Although communication between salespeople and management is essential, it is not clear that the ability to speak the company language is the best indicator of the employee's potential for long-term success, even though it may be the easiest standard to apply.

To undertake a more targeted search and to take a more meaningful decision concerning the applicant's qualification for the position to fill, the marketer should define an ideal profile of the salesperson to be recruited. In most cases the salesperson should be:

- an excellent representative of the international marketer
- an expert in solving the target customers' particular problems
- a convincing advocate of the marketer's product who does not "over-commit" the international marketer

● somebody who knows when to withdraw from a project, customer, or market if spending additional resources risks not paying off.

Besides such general features a search profile defines more precise criteria candidates have to meet. Those criteria are based on the potential customers' and other important stakeholders' expectations, and the needs of the international marketer. They may encompass features such as the provision of references (people ready to give confidential information about the candidate), the person's knowledge about the product market, or its readiness to move. Table 13.9 contains a more extensive list of salesperson characteristics to be potentially considered.

Readers following traditional ways of thinking may miss a criterion often applied by international marketers when searching for international sales people: gender. As Future issues box 13.1 tries to show, the importance of gender for success in most international markets has been continually decreasing and should become of minor importance in the future.

Finding qualified salespeople is sometimes a troublesome task. Regardless whether the international marketer has decided to use expatriate, national, or cosmopolitan salespeople the fastest and cheapest way to find the right person may be to look first if there is a person inside the company who matches the search profile right away, or if there is a person inside the company coming close to the search profile who can be further developed by training. If a salesperson has to be sought outside the firm, the marketer can get help from a number of sources listed in Table 13.10.

The most effective way of finding salespeople for international marketing tasks is to ask current or potential customers for relevant hints. This can be done during expert interviews. Sometimes even competitors are of help by not treating their sales personnel the way they expect to be treated.

TABLE 13.9   *Potential search profile for international sales personnel*

Search profile	
● References ● Language skills (speaking/reading/writing) ● Experience as a salesperson (years, positions, size and kind of company, size of orders/projects) ● Knowledge about the product and country market(s) ● Knowledge about the product, its application, or use ● Customers served so far/relationships with important customers ● Relationships with other important stakeholders ● Capacity and motivation ● Additional skills (e.g., managing, repairing and servicing products, engineering, design, etc.) ● Place of residence/readiness to move ● Availability of traveling means ● Availability of communication means	An international marketer's search profile for international sales personnel could contain criteria such as these.

Development of sales personnel

Development programs for international sales personnel generally consist of three elements: training, introduction to the market by a senior salesperson, and improvement of sales planning skills.

Training

To become effective as quickly as possible, newly hired salespeople need to be trained about the company – its intended market position, structure, information system, market communication policy, and actions. Even more important is intensive training concerning the product lines to be sold – their intended

---

FUTURE ISSUES BOX 13.1

Women-owned businesses top 9 million in 1999

Economic clout increases as employment revenues grow

"The increasing number of women-owned businesses and their growing economic impact are changing the business landscape," observed NFWBO's Haber. "Women entrepreneurs are active in the business marketplace accessing capital, buying technology, using the internet to expand their businesses, and establishing retirement plans in much the same way as their male counterparts. However, NFWBO has identified significant differences in how women business owners lead their businesses."

According to NFWBO research women entrepreneurs are more likely than men business owners to place value on business relationships as well as factual information, are more likely than men entrepreneurs to seek out the opinions and input of others, and are more reflective than their male counterparts when making decisions. As women-owned firms continue to increase in numbers and economic strength, it is increasingly valuable for customers, policy makers, and business-to-business marketers to understand and benefit from these similarities and differences.

Source: www.womensbusinessresearch.org/mediacenter/5-11-1999/5-11-1999.htm

Courtesy of the Center for Women's Business Research (www.cfwbr.org)

TABLE 13.10 *Sources of help when searching internationally for salespeople*

The marketer can use a great number of sources when searching for salespersons internationally.

Information sources

- National chamber of commerce
- Chamber of commerce of the country market to serve
- Current and potential customers
- Suppliers
- Suppliers producing complementary goods
- Their customers
- Address services
- Consultants
- Headhunters

positioning in customers' minds, their features, target customer-specific benefits in the country market to be covered, their advantages (and weaknesses) compared to major competitors, as well as their proper application. In addition, salespeople have to be introduced to the sales planning procedures of the company – how to select and acquire potential customers, how to monitor market development, how to make sales forecasts and sales budgets, how to prepare sales calls and traveling, and how to plan promotional activities. They also need adequate knowledge concerning the firm's order processing. This training is traditionally covered by the international marketer's senior personnel or internal trainers.

Most international marketers have realized that their international personnel at all levels need specialized training in how to perform effectively in a foreign environment. Nippon Electronic Corp. (NEC), a Japanese computer company, goes far beyond the norm. Its more than 160 courses help employees prepare for foreign assignments in a wide variety of ways, from polishing their language skills to familiarizing them with business customs of other country markets, and sharpening their negotiating skills.

External trainers are mostly used to improve the sales personnel's approach to customers and internal communication. External trainers are hired to cover subjects such as:

- continual improvement of the salespeople's skills in either the language(s) of the served country market(s) or the company language
- deepening of salespeople's sensibility for differences between the cultural environment of the company's headquarters and the country market(s) they work in
- improving the salespeople's ability to recognize the buying habits of customers in selected country markets
- further raising their negotiating and other communication skills.

For example, international firms such as Swedish-Swiss ABB, U.S.-based AT&T, or Royal Dutch Shell, provide their employees with intercultural sensitivity training through specialized companies before they send their personnel abroad.

General Motors' automobile division has established a worldwide training program for all salespeople in the company and the firm's wholesalers. This program is executed by concern-owned Hughes International's Training Division, and is applied worldwide in the same way. It is typically product market oriented, that is, there are only few minor concessions to local culture and behavior. The program has been carefully designed to fit as many differences as possible and was tested successfully in a train-the-trainer program with participants coming from countries from all over the world for a week.

More recently, "re-entry" training programs have been established to deal with the problem of coming back to the home country. These difficulties are normally more severe for those who have been an expatriate for several years. An inability to readjust to the home culture also results in an increased number of cosmopolitans, employees, and their families choosing to remain outside their home countries.

Introduction to market

The introduction of new salespeople to a market by senior salespersons is probably the most efficient way of getting them acquainted with a new market, its rules, and potential customers. The experience a senior salesperson has collected over the years is rarely written down for the next one to serve the market. Therefore, an excellent way of learning is watching the senior salesperson doing things like making appointments, introducing himself to a new customer, arguing against objections, negotiating prices, or closing contracts.

Beside that business-oriented introduction to the market, some support at the private level for expatriate salespersons and their families to get established in the new environment has proved beneficial. About 30% of all international appointments fail because of insufficient preparation and no proper introduction of employees and their families into their living conditions. Therefore, U.S.-based computer maker Hewlett-Packard, for example, offers its designated expatriates and their families one or two "preview trips" to the host country. Assistance in finding appropriate housing, financial support for moving expenditures, or paying tuition costs for schoolchildren are additional means to ease the introduction of expatriate sales people into a new market.

Planning

In most locally as well as internationally operating companies a disparity exists between procurement, production, and finance managers, on the one side, and sales personnel, on the other, on how accurate the planning of sales figures can and should be. Salespeople do not always understand that without rather precise figures from their side procurement and production cannot plan their level of activity in a way to secure a sufficient flow of products to satisfy customer demand at lowest cost. Neither can finance plan capital investments and liquidity needed to maximize the firm's success. By the same token, people from those other functional areas tend to expect exaggeratedly precise sales forecasts. They appear not to be cognizant of the fact that potential customers rarely guarantee to buy a certain quantity of products on a precise future date. In addition, in international marketing country markets are in different states of economic development and local product markets differ in the stage of the lifecycle they have reached. Therefore, in more mature markets it may be much easier to reach a high level of precision in sales forecasts, while markets in their early stages of development present substantial problems of accuracy.

For example, when Kentucky Fried Chicken first entered the Japanese market its business in the U.S. had already reached a more mature stage of development. Sales figures could be forecasted with great precision in the U.S., whereas in Japan, sales forecasts were based on rough estimates of potential customer frequency and average amounts of money spent by those customers. Because of a lack of knowledge about probable market development and substantial uncertainty in their customers' purchasing behavior many salespeople are reluctant to present precise sales forecasts. They prefer to give "between ... and ..." figures. But nevertheless, they count on the ready availability of the products their customers may need.

A very important part of sales personnel development, therefore, is to strengthen their personal relationships with people from other areas inside the company in order to increase mutual understanding. Training on how to do sales forecasts alone will not be sufficient to achieve the needed level of motivation of sales personnel.

Motivation and compensation

Motivators

Understanding the role of the salesforce in the organization, what motivates people, and the types of stress and concerns the salesforce has, is critical to manage it successfully. A comparison of studies from various country markets with differing cultural environments reveals that the stress sales personnel report is largely similar. However, what motivates those people and how they should be rewarded may still be considerably different.

Motivating salespeople to do their best is one of the most challenging managerial tasks of the international marketer. Economic rewards, such as personal bonuses, are the most effective motivator in North America. But in northern

Europe, where personal income tax rates are substantially higher, non-economic motivators work better. In other, high-context, cultures, economic rewards may not be as effective as social recognition. This is the case in many Asian nations, where sales achievement awards are more likely to be group oriented, and be based on social acknowledgement of achievement, rather than purely economic incentives.

Even in U.S.-based companies high motivation of salespeople cannot be achieved by just offering a high salary and/or commission. Sales managers setting an example to their collaborators, appreciating their salespeople's work in the field, encouraging benchmarking between them, praising them for success, and understanding their failures is a strong motivating factor in all western countries. Caterpillar, for example, uses a variation of the socially visible award structure, an international working vacation, to motivate and train outstanding sales personnel. The best Caterpillar salesperson from each country is invited, together with his or her spouse, to Marbella, Spain, for a vacation combined with further training. This approach appears to be more effective overall than a straight economic reward as it combines an economic recognition (a free vacation including spouse), along with public recognition of employee excellence.

Compensation

The same advantages and disadvantages of using salary versus commission, or some combination of the two, exist internationally as for domestic marketing. Generally, when selling is the individual's primary job, commissions are preferred. But when additional activities (such as gathering customer information or extensive after-sales service) are important, salaries and salary-plus-commission compensation are more popular. However, there are some markets where a commission-only approach is not useful. In highly collective societies (Asian or Arabic, for example), individual efforts and rewards (especially high commissions for the best sales representatives) may not be culturally appropriate. In other cultures, commissions may be interpreted as a signal that the firm is not committed to the employees and is prepared to get rid of them as soon as they fail to perform. Thus, cultural norms should be considered when deciding how to pay sales representatives or branch office employees.

Salespeople may need to be compensated differently depending on their nationality. Central European companies, for example, tend to offer high bonuses to salespeople when they enter a new market. When most potential customers in the market have been reached, the bonuses are reduced. A U.S.-based company might do exactly the opposite. U.S. firms tend to perceive salespeople as entrepreneurs, as self-motivated achievers who want to have more security in the beginning but are interested in receiving larger bonuses after the firm has gained a share of the market.

International sales meetings

International sales meetings are conferences usually held once a year that assemble employed salespeople, agents and merchants cooperating with the firm, people from other functional areas of the company, such as production or finance, and sometimes guest speakers or a moderator from outside. Such international sales meetings may have various objectives.

Learning from reports on local successful problem solutions Participants are invited to report on a subject of their choice. How has a problem been resolved or a target achieved (for example, restructuring the local logistics system to shorten delivery time, improving customer awareness of the company's superior quality, development of a new incentive and sales monitoring system to increase new product introduction endeavors)? Which of the planned and executed marketing activities were particularly successful, which have failed? What are the reasons? Lessons to

be learned by the other participants in the meeting may be drawn in small workshop groups, presented and discussed in the plenary.

Comparison between sales units and intermediaries from all served country markets
Relevant figures, like total sales per number of (potential) customers, share of newly acquired customers, number of sales calls per salesperson, market share, number of orders received per number of sales calls, average value per order, contribution margin per sales, fixed cost, deviation from the budget, number of failures – listed per product group and country market – may be compared. In order to secure a fair comparison, the figures have to be weighed considering differences between sales areas, like customers per square kilometer, market volume and potential, number and size of clients, development stage of the market and infrastructure of the country, price level, competitors, import restrictions, legal restrictions, etc. The "winner of the tournament" then has to present its success story, motivating colleagues to increase their sales efforts, too.

Presentation of new and/or improved products and internal processes to salespeople and intermediaries Many ideas for new products or improvements of internal processes may have come from the served markets through salespeople and intermediaries. They enjoy seeing the impact of their feedback on the company. In addition, the salesforce may be introduced to new technical solutions, applications of a product, new designs, services, or selling methods. As representatives of so many cultures are present at international sales meetings and many different languages may be spoken, misunderstandings may occur. It is advisable, therefore, to organize an unobtrusive test to see what messages the participants have got and what their conclusions from these messages are.

Information concerning strategic and organizational issues Headquarters management may want to present the results of market, competition, and environmental monitoring. Scenarios about the future development of the firm's macro-environment as well as basic assumptions about the development of the firm's product markets during the next planning period may be discussed. Participants may draw first conclusions for their sales budgeting. International sales meetings are also used to announce and discuss organizational changes in the company, to introduce new managers, and to present new acquisitions.

Development of new ideas In creative workshops, new functions and design of the marketer's products, improved methods of selling, applications, efficient sales outlets, better selling arguments, improved service delivery, and internal actions to be taken to improve total quality, information flow, or customer service may be developed.

Whatever objective an international sales meeting specifically is dedicated to, properly organized, the meeting has a highly motivating effect on all participants. The marketer, therefore, has to carefully select

- venue
- date
- topics covered.

Sometimes it might be best to have the meeting at the headquarters, for example, when a new product is presented. Sometimes the meeting should take place at an intermediary to honor its special efforts. For creative purposes, a resort hotel with seminar facilities might be best. And sometimes the location of an important fair may be the right spot. The right date may be before a fair, the end of the financial year of the company, the launch of a new international communication campaign, or a change in top management.

Impact on marketing mix

Value of total product

Sales management also has an impact on customers' perceptions of a firm's total product. Depending on how well the international marketer's salesforce treats customers in pre- and after-sales activities, how much they serve customers as trustworthy consultants in the attempt to continually improve the customers' business, the total product of the marketer is more or less beneficial to its customers.

By the same token, the more complex or quickly changing the international marketer's product the more training of the salesforce is needed to make it an efficient and effective tool in gaining customer interest and trust.

Pricing

If price is defined as all the perceived contributions a customer has to make in a business exchange in order to get a desired product, personal selling significantly influences customers' perception of that price. "Contributions" of customers may start at the point where they are supposed to accept a salesperson they do not know or may even dislike. But the price may also be lowered by close personal relationships between a purchasing manager and the marketer's salesperson. Trust in the business partner not only lowers perceived risks, it also enables purchase decisions to be made based on less search effort. Other suppliers need to be evaluated from time to time, to make sure that product quality and price charged by the preferred supplier are at a competitive level. But a positively valued long-term relationship with a supplier diminishes process costs of the customer. That is, successful relationship management by its salespeople has a significant positive influence on the attractiveness of an international marketer's offers.

Distribution and logistics

International sales management is closely related to distribution and logistics. Depending on whether the marketer has decided to use an integrated or an independent distribution system salespeople have to find potential customers or intermediaries, must make them clients of the company, and establish a relationship with them as business partners. Most activities of channel partner search, motivation, and control described in Chapter 12 are based on contributions of the company's salesforce.

Market communication

Sales management is also closely related to international market communication. Personal selling may be even considered as one of an international marketer's market communication tools. Because personal communication has the strongest impact of all communication tools available to a marketer, the messages sent to potential and current customers through personal contacts have to be closely coordinated with all the other communication efforts of the company. Based on an integrated communication policy the members of the salesforce need to be continually trained in how to behave and what to transmit to the customers. If the company's salesforce – consciously or unconsciously – transmits a message to the customers that does not fit with what the marketer tries to communicate through public relations, advertising, sales promotion, and other activities, a great deal of the firm's communication budget may be lost and potential customers may be confused.

Contrariwise, the international salesforce may be used as an information source on what impact market communication activities have on the target customers. Because of their direct personal contact with the customers, salespeople can report on immediate customer reactions. This is particularly important for customer and intermediary sales promotion activities.

Summary

Building and sustaining positive relationships with target customers is the major task of international sales management. To coordinate diverse sales activities across country markets, the company has first to develop an international sales policy. The sales policy is the guideline for decisions concerning personal selling, after-sales activities, and management of the firm's international salesforce.

The key to success in international personal selling is the matching of seller product, knowledge, and culture, with buyer needs, knowledge, and culture. That is, the "fit" between seller and buyer must be fully understood and carefully managed. But individualized communication is expensive. Therefore, finding and precisely selecting potential customers to personally sell to is of great importance to international marketers. The fastest and least expensive way to determine potential customers is to use available internal sources. Inquiries to potential customers, invitations to tenders, and official authorities or private information providers may be further low-cost sources of information on potential customers.

When potential customers are defined sales costs per successful business transaction can be reduced by carefully preparing sales calls and sales negotiations.

First, the cultural elements that might influence the establishment of a contact, the negotiation process, and the development of a relationship are to be reviewed. A customer database containing available information about current and potential customers as well as the company's sales manual, which contains information concerning the company's products and the customer benefits they provide, help the salesforce in preparing their sales calls.

Thorough planning and organization of business trips can keep the cost per hour and per mile of traveling at an acceptable level compared to the number of successful sales calls per day.

Sales negotiations are viewed and carried out differently from one culture to another. It is important to know how to:

- start a sales talk
- properly address negotiation partners
- react in case of disagreement
- make sure that agreement has been reached.

A properly formulated international offer may strongly contribute to effective and efficient personal selling. The marketer has to consider:

- what language to use
- legal regulations and local market nuances to respect
- product specifications and applications to fulfill
- terms of sale and delivery to offer
- for what period of validity the offer is binding.

In addition, the structure of the offer may determine its attractiveness to the customer. After presenting the offer to the customer the salesperson has to ensure an effective follow-up to close the contract.

After the customer has taken its buying decision an international marketer interested in repeat purchases has to keep this customer satisfied with the product from its purchase to the end of its use or as long as the customer keeps it in its product assortment. A series of after-sales activities from checking if the customer's order has been properly executed to the professional handling of customer complaints and eventual disputes are important tasks of international sales management.

Finally, to ensure effectiveness and efficiency of personal selling, sales management has to recruit and select the best people for its specific purpose. It has to:

- develop the salesforce
- motivate them to reach ambitious goals
- compensate them according to their performance.

Close cooperation with market communication as well as distribution and logistics management will help keep the international marketer's activities focused on reaching the intended global strategic position.

DISCUSSION QUESTIONS

1. How do the distribution policy, the communication policy, and the sales policy of an international marketer relate to one another? Discuss.

2. What tools can a salesperson use to determine the most promising potential customers in a newly served country market? Compare those tools by indicating their specific advantages.

3. What does a salesperson need to do in preparing their first sales calls in a newly served country market?

4. Illustrate the influence of cultural differences on the potential difficulties at the beginning of sales talks. How can an internationally operating firm support its salesforce in adequate preparation to avoid such problems?

5. Explain the reasons why sales negotiations should follow a certain structure independent of the cultural environment in which they take place.

6. Take the example of a company you are familiar with and describe how, in your opinion, an international offer from that company should be structured. Illustrate the points by giving examples.

7. What is the role of salespeople in the handling of international customer complaints? Compare with local complaint handling systems.

8. What can an international marketer do to find the best qualified salespeople for its country markets? Take the example of a firm you are familiar with and discuss the pros and cons of different courses of action.

9. Contact an internationally operating firm and interview them about their international salesforce development activities. Compare with the information gathered by your colleagues. What are your conclusions?

10. What are the major issues of salesforce compensation in general and how are they complicated in an international business environment? Find an example of an internationally operating company and bring it to class for discussion.

ADDITIONAL READINGS

Andaleeb, S.S. and S.F. Anwar (1996) "Factors influencing customer trust in salespersons in a developing country", *Journal of International Marketing*, 4(4), 35–52.

Brengman, M., M. Geuens, B. Weijters, S.M. Smith, and W.R. Swinyard (2005) "Segmenting internet shoppers based on their web-usage-related lifestyle: a cross-cultural validation", *Journal of Business Research*, 58, 79–88.

Dubinsky, A.J., M. Kotabe, C.V. Lim, and W. Wagner (1997) "The impact of values on salespeople's job responses: a cross-national investgation", *Journal of Business Research*, July, 39(3), 195–208.

Harvey, M. (1997) "Dual-career expatriates: expectations, adjustments and satisfaction with international relocation", *Journal of International Business Studies*, 28(3), 627–57.

Laroche, M., L.C. Ueltschy, S. Abe, M. Cleveland, and P. Yannopoulos (2004) "Service quality perceptions and customer satisfaction: evaluating the role of culture", *Journal of International Marketing*, 12(3), 58–85.

Purchase, S. and A. Ward (2003) "ARR model: cross-cultural developments", *International Marketing Review*, 20(2), 161–79

Shankarmahesh M.N., J.B. Ford, and M.S. LaTour (2004) "Determinants of satisfaction in sales negotiations with foreign buyers: perceptions of US export executives", *International Marketing Review*, 21(4/5), 423–46

Sibenius, J. K. (2002) "The hidden challenge of cross-border negotiations", *Harvard Business Review*, March.

Winkler, J. (1999) *Bargaining for Results*, London: William Heinemann Ltd.

Useful internet links

ABB	http://www.abb.com/
Airbus Industries	http://www.airbus.com/
American Arbitration Association (AAA)	http://www.adr.org/
Best Buy	http://www.bestbuy.com/site/index.jsp
Business Journals	http://seattle.bizjournals.com/seattle/
Center for Women's Business Research	http://www.womensbusinessresearch.org/
Degussa	http://www.degussa.de/
Frequentis	http://www.frequentis.com/index.html
General Electric	http://www.ge.com/en/
Geneva Conventions on Arbitration	http://www.eurolegal.org/arbitration/arbconv.htm
IFE	http://www.ife-doors.com/
International Chamber of Commerce (ICC)	http://www.iccwbo.org/
Journal of International Business Studies	http://www.jibs.net/
Knorr Bremse	http://www.knorr-bremse.com/
NEC	http://www.nec.com/
New York Convention	http://www.jus.uio.no/lm/un.arbitration.recognition. and. enforcement.convention.new.york.1958/doc.html
Olivetti	http://www.olivetti.com/
Singapore Airlines	http://www.singaporeair.com/
Statoil	http://www.statoil.com/
Supplement to the Official Journal of the European Union	http://ted.publications.eu.int/official/GetRecords? Template=TED/static/help/en/ch02.htm£d0e234
Tenders Electronic Daily (TED)	http://ted.publications.eu.int/official/
UNCITRAL Arbitration Rules	http://www.uncitral.org/english/
US Small Business Administration – International Sales	http://www.sba.gov/managing/marketing/intlsales.html
World Values Survey	http://www.worldvaluessurvey.org

INTERNATIONAL MARKETING LOGISTICS

Learning objectives

After studying this chapter you will be able to:

- understand the complex interactions between marketing logistics, distribution channel decisions, sales, procurement, and production

- explain what factors influence an international marketer's policy concerning the control of its logistics system

- discuss factors influencing choice of transportation modes

- explain the influence of logistics on product packaging

- illustrate how warehousing decisions and inventory management result in different levels of international customer service

- compare impact of different terms of delivery on the attractiveness of a company's offerings

- explain how a well-managed physical distribution system can become a source of sustainable competitive advantage

Chapter outline

International marketing logistics

International marketing logistics policy

Level of customer service
Integrated vs independent marketing logistics
Choice of logistics partners
Coordination and responsibilities

Operative marketing logistics decisions

Customer service
Transportation
Packaging
Warehousing and storage
Location of customer contact points

Impact on marketing mix

Pricing
Distribution
Market communication
Product management

Summary

INTERNATIONAL MARKETING SPOTLIGHT

International marketing logistics networks

Exel, the British international logistics services provider, has rented a 100,000² meter warehouse in Hirschstetten, Austria, as a product distribution center to take over the responsibility for all warehousing activities of BauMax, the Austrian leader in DIY retailing. This is only one of its many long-term contracts on behalf of major retailers and global manufacturers in the branded consumer goods area.

Large retailing firms and consumer goods manufacturers increasingly tend to outsource the international physical distribution of their products to logistics specialists that organize the order disposition, transportation of products, warehousing and storage, and sometimes even packaging as well as recycling processes to serve their clients' customers at the quality level and time specified. Whereas manufacturers and retailers would have to establish their own international logistics organizations, those specialists can offer international logistics networks of cooperating partners, equipped with modern information management and product-handling tools. Their computer systems determine the optimal transportation routes. Specially designed packaging devices take into account the individual size, nature, and potential spoilage of the goods to be distributed. Highly automated warehouses reduce the fixed costs of manufacturers and retailers.

Exel has grown by an average of 25% a year for the past 18 years. It is the largest distribution business in Canada and Mexico; the principal distributor of frozen food in Austria, Hungary, Poland, and Slovakia; the biggest drinks and fresh produce logistics company in France; the operator of the largest distribution network in sub-Saharan Africa; one of the leaders in consumer goods logistics in China; and the largest distributor of technology, clothing and home and personal care products in Ireland and the U.K.

Source: Adapted from www.exel.com/exel/home

The focal question of this chapter is: How can international marketers establish and maintain distribution logistics systems that best help to build and sustain their intended global position?

International marketing logistics

Besides the establishment and maintenance of customer relationships, a firm's distribution system also exists for the physical distribution of its goods and services. A firm's decisions and actions concerning the physical distribution of its total products, including:

- inventory management
- warehousing
- storage
- shipping and receiving
- transportation
- associated information processes and documentation

are called **marketing logistics**. In international marketing, logistics are increasingly recognized as an important source of potential competitive advantage. As Strategy box 14.1 shows, logistics determine the level of customer service, which is one of the elements of the marketing mix most difficult to imitate.

Factors such as rapid, punctual delivery and reliable supply with products and services of specified quality may outweigh competitive pricing in the international struggle for customers. To provide sustainable competitive advantage, all the marketing logistics activities of an internationally operating company must be organized in a systematic way, based on a marketing logistics policy and integrated with procurement, sales as well as production logistics activities (see Figure 14.1).

Efficient consumer response (ECR) systems, for example, coordinate the flow of goods among manufacturers, transporters, wholesalers, and retailers with the help of an integrated IT system. Cash registers equipped with scanners not only recognize the products bought by a customer and add up the prices, they are also connected to a computer that controls stocks and launches repeat orders when stock falls below pre-specified levels. The manufacturer is connected to the same computer and knows at any time of the day how much of a product needs to be delivered to which retail outlet. Based on this information, production can be continually adapted and purchasing orders made. If the transportation unit is also linked to the information system, marketing logistics are efficiently integrated.

Such integration only makes sense if it is based on general objectives to be reached and basic rules that need to be respected by the parties involved. Therefore, in the following, the contents of an international marketing logistics policy will first be described. Then the operative decisions based on this policy concerning transportation, packaging, warehousing, and storage as well as location will be discussed. The chapter will end with a discussion of some mutual influences of marketing logistics and other marketing mix decisions.

STRATEGY BOX 14.1

Making global connections at Caterpillar

Imagine the following scenario. A part on a Caterpillar machine operating at a copper mine in Chile begins to deteriorate. A district center that continuously monitors the health of all the Caterpillar machines in its area by remotely reading the sensors on each machine automatically spots a problem in the making and sends an electronic alert to the local dealer's field technician through his portable computer. The message tells him the identity and location of the machine and sends his computer the data that sparked the alert and its diagnosis. Then, with the aid of the computer, the technician validates the diagnosis and determines the service or repair required, the cost of labor and parts, and the risks of not performing the work.

The technician's computer also tells him exactly what parts and tools he will need to make the repair. Then, with a touch of a key, the technician ties into Caterpillar's worldwide information system, which links dealers, Caterpillar's parts distribution facilities, Cat's and its suppliers' factories, and the large customers' inventory system. He instantly determines the best sources of the parts and the times

when each source can deliver them to the dealer's drop-off point.

Next, the technician sends a proposal to the customer by computer or phone, and the customer tells him the best time to carry out the repair. With a few more keystrokes, the technician orders the parts. The electronic order instantly goes to the factories or warehouses that can supply the parts in time. At the factory and warehouses, the message triggers the printing of an order ticket and perhaps sets into motion an automated crane that retrieves the parts from a storage rack. Soon the parts are on their way to the dealer's pick-up site.

Within hours of the initial alert, the technician is repairing the machine. An interactive manual on his computer guides him, providing him with the latest best practice procedures for carrying out the repair. The repair completed, the technician closes the work order, prints out an invoice, collects by credit card, and electronically updates the machine's history. That information is added to Caterpillar's database, which helps the company spot any common problems that a particular model might have and thereby continually improve its machines' designs.

The logistics system ties together Caterpillar's factories, distribution centers, dealers, and large customers. The system links some 1,000 locations across 23 time zones and 160 countries.

International marketing logistics policy

The physical distribution of a total product across a variety of international markets necessitates a great number of decisions and activities that, in most cases, are taken and executed by different people (often belonging to different organizations) specializing in certain functions and socialized in various cultural environments. To make sure that the objectives given by the intended global strategic position, the intended positioning of the business unit, and the positioning of the total product(s) are respected by those people, the international marketer or its logistics manager has to develop general guidelines indicating: objectives of marketing logistics and how those objectives should be achieved in general terms. That is, the policy statement indicates:

● level of customer service to achieve

● limits of decisions and actions allowed to reach the given objective (see Table 14.1).

All operative decisions concerning customer service, transportation of goods, physical aspects of packaging, warehousing and storage, as well as the choice of locations have to respect those guidelines.

FIGURE 14.1 *International marketing logistics decisions*

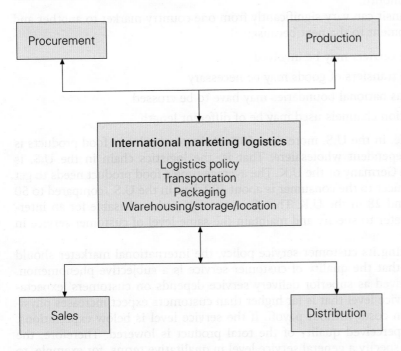

The international marketer first has to develop an international marketing logistics policy to coordinate the various people and organizations involved in the physical distribution process of the firm's products. Based on these guidelines, decisions concerning transportation, physical aspects of packaging, warehousing, storage, and location can be taken. All marketing logistics decisions have to be coordinated with the company's distribution, sales, procurement, and production logistics decisions and actions.

TABLE 14.1 *Contents of an international marketing logistics policy*

● Level of customer service
● Level of ownership of physical distribution devices and facilities
● Selection criteria for logistics partners
● Coordination and responsibilities

The international marketing logistics policy contains objectives and general rules of behavior concerning the level of customer service to be reached and the extent of integration of physical distribution assets. It also lists selection criteria for logistics partners and specifies management responsibilities for marketing logistics functions.

Level of customer service

The level of customer service in marketing logistics is generally measured as: *percentage of properly delivered goods* (the right goods at the quality level indicated in the sales contract), *in a pre-specified period of time* (or at a given point in time).

German Würth Group, the largest wholesaler of fixing and assembly materials in Europe, for example, has defined the customer service goal as delivering 96% of all orders to the customers' premises in 48 hours, exactly according to the customers' orders.

The level of customer service provided by an international marketer in non-domestic markets tends to be lower than that provided in its domestic market, because of factors such as:

- geographic distance
- errors in transmitting and filling orders
- inadequate packaging and preparation for shipment
- transportation problems
- delays in clearing customs.

In Japan, for example, the Japan Harbor Transportation Association controls virtually all traffic by vessels. When a shipping company – foreign or domestic – needs to change a route, a vessel, or a port of call, it has to ask the Harbor Association 6 weeks in advance. If the paperwork is not perfect, approval is delayed for a month.

Time in transit can vary significantly from one country market to another and from one shipment to the next because:

- different carriers may be involved
- multiple transfers of goods may be necessary
- numerous national boundaries may have to be crossed
- distribution channels used may be of different length.

For example, in the U.S. more than 50% of the total sales in food products is made via independent wholesalers. That is, the logistics chain in the U.S. is longer than in Germany or the U.K. The average time a food product needs to get from the producer to the consumer is about 100 days in the U.S., compared to 50 in Germany and 28 in the U.K. Therefore, it may not be advisable for an international marketer to specify and maintain the same level of customer service in all markets.

In formulating its customer service policy, the international marketer should bear in mind that the quality of customer service is a subjective phenomenon. What is perceived as superior delivery service depends on customers' expectations. Any service level that is far higher than customers expect increases physical distribution costs without payoff. If the service level is below expectations, however, the perceived quality of the total product is lowered. Therefore, the company may specify a general service level in qualitative terms, for example, to have the highest customer service level of the industry in each served country market. Based on this general goal, the international logistics manager must adapt the company's physical distribution system to the local service requirements and the capabilities of the competitors in each market.

Integrated vs independent marketing logistics

The physical distribution of a company's products can be executed through transportation devices, warehouses, and storage capacities owned by the company, that is, *integrated marketing logistics*, or through independent service providers, that is, *independent marketing logistics*.

Independent marketing logistics are not directly controlled by the marketer. Companies that use facilitating agencies but largely control them are said to have a company-bound marketing logistics system. There are basically two types of facilitating agency to physically transfer the goods and services of a firm to the final customers, *customhouse brokers* and *freight forwarders*.

Customhouse broker

A customhouse broker serves as an agent for exporters and importers of goods, performing two essential functions:

- facilitating the movement of products through customs
- handling the documentation accompanying international shipments.

Freight forwarder

A freight forwarder provides a broad range of services, including coordination and assistance in planning and all phases of shipment from the company's plant to its markets (see Table 14.2). Compared to the U.S., Australia, and the U.K. where big "industrial" system carriers or contract distributors predominate, Germany still has a great number of middle-sized freight forwarders. In Italy small transportation companies, called *camionisti*, characterize the market. But a trend to concentration can be observed across Europe.

The extent to which companies use integrated physical distribution basically depends on the performance level achieved by service providers specializing in physical distribution compared to company-owned units and their relative costs. The benchmark is the service level expected by the firm's international customers, which has at least to be achieved. If both alternatives, integrated as well as independent marketing logistics, are able to satisfy the customers' expectations, the cost of physical distribution should be minimized.

Take the example of Germany's Liebherr, one of the leading ship and harbor crane producers in the world. They have to serve their customers around the

---

TABLE 14.2 *Services provided by freight forwarders*

Assistance in logistics planning
Quotation of costs, charges, and fees to be covered
Advise on foreign import regulations
Guidance on packaging, marking, and labeling
Preparation of export declarations required by the legal government
Booking of cargo space
Transportation from the firm's premises to the indicated destination
Preparation and processing of airway bills and bills of lading
Preparation of consular documents in the language of the country to which the goods are shipped
Provision for certification of receipt of goods
Provision for warehouse storage
Provision for insurance on request
Preparation of shipping documents and sending them to banks, shippers, or consignees as directed

Source: Adapted from www.ams.usda.gov/tmd/export/freight_forwarding.htm; Stock, J.R. and D.M. Lambert (1983) "Physical distribution management in international marketing", *International Marketing Review*, Autumn, p. 37f

Many activities required to ship a good from one country to another are frequently provided by independent companies, known as freight forwarders. Without these independent companies, small and medium-sized businesses in particular would find it difficult (if not impossible) to be involved in global marketing.

world with spare parts in 48 hours. The company can only use external physical distribution partners where they are fast and reliable enough to fulfill this customer service target. In country markets where such potential partners exist, the relative costs of each alternative will play a major role in the firm's decision.

The decision between integrated, company-bound, and independent marketing logistics systems should be taken considering the more specific factors listed in Table 14.3 and discussed in the following.

Prices and costs

Prices and costs will strongly influence the decision. An international physical distribution system may need large capital investment and a highly developed market information system to function properly. The difference between the *maintenance costs of their own fleet of transportation devices*, the cost of warehouses, the transportation cost, the cost of personnel and the cost of the needed information system versus the *price of the services of an international freight forwarder* often leads companies to decide in favor of an independent physical distribution system. Instead of largely fixed costs service providers have to be paid depending on the level of sales. And because specialized logistics companies serve several clients they are able to invest in the latest equipment, highly trained personnel or latest information systems, which a single manufacturer could hardly afford.

Because the *reliability of the logistics chain* strongly influences the level of service experienced by international customers, however, international marketers might tend to establish company-bound logistics systems through long-term cooperation contracts. They give them a certain influence on the service level of their partners. In addition, via an "open book" policy, such contracts may give cost and price transparency to the marketer without the disadvantage of high fixed costs that characterizes integrated marketing logistics systems.

For example, Fâbrica de Jabón la Corona S.A., the largest producer of laundry detergent in Mexico, has decided to do business in the U.S. by closely cooperating with CaseStack, that offers transportation solutions in all modes, a network of regional warehouses across the U.S., and logistics software. In order to serve its markets, la Corona needs to be able to restock its customers' shelves the next

---

TABLE 14.3 *Factors to be considered in choice of a physical distribution system*

Physical properties	Prices and costs
Goods	Price transparency
Packages	Price sensitivity
Assortment	Cost structure
Way of delivery	Cost variance
Order size and frequency	Level of system development
by sources	Quality
product groups	Potential for rationalization
destinations	Economies of scale and scope
Movements of goods	Availability of alternatives
Number of distribution levels	Potential for cooperation
Number of production sites and	Need for differentiation
sales warehouses	Restrictions
Transportation destinations	

The choice of a physical distribution system depends on the prices and costs of available alternatives, as well as on how the level of physical distribution system development, physical properties of the product to be distributed, order size and frequency, and movements of goods allows the set customer service level to be achieved.

or even the same day. To restock directly from the factory would take 10 days. With the internet tools provided by CaseStack, la Corona can see how much product is available, how much product is being sold every day, and how much inventory is being sent out every day. The manager of international sales can also see when items arrive and in what quantity, and who has picked them up.

Level of system development

Beside prices and costs, the level of development of local physical distribution systems influences the "make or buy" decision in international logistics. In country markets where the level of physical distribution quality, in terms of delivery time or safety of goods, is low and there is a potential for rationalization or economies of scale and scope, integration of the physical distribution function might seem attractive. But if the available means of physical distribution is unfamiliar to the marketer, as for example in some areas of India where goods still are delivered in carts drawn by animals (or, indeed, humans), it may be wiser to rely on experienced local logistical service providers.

Physical properties

Physical properties, such as the kind of goods, packaging needed, selection to be presented to the customers, or the local means of delivery can make it impossible for an international marketer to establish its own logistics system. For example, a Japanese exporter of machinery will not buy ships or airplanes to deliver its products to customers in the U.K. Neither will it buy large containers to transport the product overseas, in order to keep the firm flexible concerning its transportation mode and to avoid unnecessary fixed costs. However, the marketer may sign a contract with an express delivery service that guarantees 48-hour spare parts delivery to all destinations in Europe.

If customers do not buy an individual product but a combination of this product with other products or services that are needed to reach the intended benefit, such as in the case of sanitary equipment, the manufacturer will also opt for independent or company-bound logistics. The same holds if the means of delivery of the product in a country market is very different from what the marketer is used to.

For example, in India or in inland China most razor blades are not sold in big supermarkets such as in the EU or in the U.S. where deliveries can be made by trucks and in bigger loads, but in very small one-room shops that need low-quantity daily delivery because of a lack of storage space. An integrated logistics system would not make much sense under such circumstances.

Order size and frequency

Order size and frequency by sources, product groups, and destinations will also influence the choice of an integrated versus an independent logistics system. If a mechanical engineering firm that constructs steel bridges all over the world wants to make sure that all the parts needed are on the construction site in time and without quality problems, it might decide to use a company-bound logistics systems. This would keep the fixed cost low, allow some price transparency concerning the physical distribution to the international marketer, and give the marketer the security of keeping the construction project on track.

Movement of goods

The movement of goods, that is:

- number of levels of intermediaries in the local distribution channels
- number of production sites and sales warehouses to be serviced
- number and spread of transportation destinations to be covered

is another bundle of factors to be considered. The more levels of intermediaries, sites, and destinations, the greater the tendency to use independent logistics firms.

Taking all these factors into consideration, an international marketing logistics policy may need not to be overly rigid in defining the appropriate physical distribution structure. If the served country markets differ widely in their means of total product delivery, the international logistics policy must allow flexible adaptation. In many cases, marketers will choose a mixture of integrated and independent parts for their distribution system.

Major retailing companies in Europe, such as the German Rewe, are an example: They tend to take over warehousing and storage as well as delivery from producers and to serve their retail outlets through distribution centers where goods of different suppliers are bundled. Handling as well as transportation costs are lowered because of fewer arrivals at the retail units. The central warehouses in the distribution centers hold little or no inventory. They act as transit terminals. This becomes possible because, based on local retail sales, the rhythm of orders is increased and goods are delivered in smaller amounts.

In parallel, more and more major retailers and also consumer goods companies rely on "outsourcing." That is, they leave great parts of the handling of goods to "distributors" or "third-party logistics providers."

Distributors are often the main suppliers, called "category managers," who look after the delivery of an entire product group, including products of competitors.

Third-party logistics providers are mainly business units of big freight forwarders that take over the entire distribution function and add merchandising, debt and credit accounting, cash management, and other services such as mounting, finishing, or the addition of product usage information (see Toolbox 14.1 for an example).

TOOLBOX 14.1 Third-party logistics

Fiege ecm is a third-party logistics provider based in Greven, Germany, that distributes to more than 600 dealers in 75 countries. The Fiege Logistics Center in Mülheim, Germany, is responsible for managing the complete logistics chain for its customers, such as U.S.-based Ingersoll-Rand International Bobcat.

Fiege and its customers agreed on using the SAP R/3 software in combination with an e-commerce system for all information handling and online business requirements.

Every dealer is given password-protected access to the system, including access to all relevant spare parts stock. The dealer can check if an item is in stock. He receives information about the number of pieces per packaging unit, recommended price, net price, and weight per unit of the part. Should a part not be in stock, the Logistics Center orders it from the manufacturer to be sent either to Mülheim or directly to the dealer, based on the customer's needs. As soon as all the order data have been entered, the order is confirmed, and the items are reserved. Orders can be flagged with up to five different categories and priorities, which trigger different delivery speeds.

When an order has been entered, it appears in the SAP screen. Every delivery service provider the ordering dealer has used in the past can be seen and selected. Data from the transport company are transferred into the system so that shipments to anywhere in the world can be monitored.

When the ordered items have been commissioned, packed, and made ready for delivery an address sticker is produced automatically and affixed to the box. The package information is used for printing the necessary shipping documents. All the required documents and trade statistics are automatically sent to the on-site customs office. As soon as the shipment is passed on to a carrier, an invoice is prepared and sent out the next working day.

The customer and the sales department of Fiege's client can track the status of an order at any time using the website by entering the order number, the part number, or the order date.

Source: Adapted from Anonymous (2003) "Outsourcing: a global success story", *Logistics Management*, February, 42(2), pp. E60–62

American and Asian companies have increasingly outsourced their European logistics to specialized service providers in recent years. Only 30 to 40% of U.S. and Japanese manufacturers and almost no Taiwanese and Korean firms operate their own distribution logistics systems in Europe. Many of these logistics providers are located in the Netherlands.

If a company wants to differentiate itself from competitors through its distribution system, it can establish its own physical distribution network. Restrictions on investments in a country may then influence the decision in the direction of a company-bound marketing logistics system.

To allow adaptation and at the same time keep the international marketing logistics system of a company manageable, the minimum requirement for the formulation of a logistics policy is to:

- establish a list of factors to be considered in taking local decisions
- rank them by their importance
- prescribe strategic or environmental considerations.

Choice of logistics partners

To ensure the intended level of customer service, an international marketer opting for an independent or a company-bound logistics system depends heavily on the availability and choice of qualified cooperation partners. The international marketing logistics policy of a firm, therefore, contains the profile of logistics partners to look for. Those partners must not only be reliable, they also need to be ready to participate in decreasing the total costs of logistics.

An international marketer might establish a guideline that only logistics service providers willing to accept cost targets and an open-book policy are to be considered as partners. Such partners are offered long-term contracts that allow them to build up their capacities and customer-specific capabilities without incalculable financial risk.

Coordination and responsibilities

Finally, the international marketing logistics policy also needs to contain some general guidelines concerning:

- roles to be fulfilled inside and outside the company
- coordination of roles between central and local company units
- responsibilities for logistics planning, information, and control.

How important planning and control may be for a firm's international logistics is underlined by the fact that in 2000, because of unreliable freight organization, trucks in Europe were empty for two-thirds of the time they were on the road.

Because logistics can be considered as a horizontal function that concerns or is influenced by decisions from all parts of a company as well as from external partners, most marketing logistics decisions will be taken in cross-functional teams with members from central and local units as well as cooperating firms. Those teams may be led by an internal or external international marketing logistics manager or by varying members of the company depending on the field of experience particularly needed.

Operative marketing logistics decisions

Based on the general guidelines given in the international marketing logistics policy, individual members of the firm can take operative decisions concerning customer service, transportation, packaging, warehousing and storage, as well as choice of locations. The decisions that need to be taken and the factors of influence that need to be considered are described in the following.

Customer service

The marketing logistics manager, working within the framework of the company's basic strategy, must be concerned with minimizing total marketing logistics costs, which reaches a level of 5 to 15% of net profits in European companies, while providing a satisfactory level of customer service.

The level of customer service that a firm can attain is influenced by a broad range of factors from inside and outside the company. For example, while lower levels of inventory may reduce the cost of physical distribution by lowering the capital cost incurred, they may also entail the risk of providing less than satisfactory customer service. Raw materials, parts, or finished products missing from stock may greatly reduce the marketer's ability to react to customer orders in time.

Process coordination

The marketer must consider the entire logistics chain of the company in attempting to achieve the firm's customer service objectives. Close coordination between sales, procurement, production, and physical distribution is needed to ensure a constant level of customer service at reduced cost. It is possible to reach a level of customer service in global product markets that is as high as or even higher than the level maintained in domestic markets. The speed and precision of physical distribution can be augmented by the use of:

- new transportation methods
- improved packaging technology
- advanced methods of preservation
- warehouse merchandising
- direct delivery to the customers' premises
- faster handling of orders through online information systems in a chain of cooperating firms.

Real-time information system

If an international manufacturer and its intermediaries are ready to participate in a real-time information system, POS-scanning data can be used to achieve just-in-time production and delivery, decreasing inventory level, transportation and handling. U.S.-based Levi Strauss, for example, has developed an electronic data interchange system called LeviLink. When a Levi garment is rung up by a cashier at a major retailer, the sales information can be sent electronically to the jeans maker. It uses the information to generate reorders, invoices, or packing slips. The fast delivery based on orders diminishes the risk of wrong distribution of goods to warehouses and retailing outlets where the stock cannot be sold.

Online standards, such as UN/EDIFACT (United Nations Electronic Data Interchange for Administration, Commerce and Transport) that comprises a set of internationally agreed standards, directories, and guidelines for the electronic interchange of data, have been developed to enable communication between the different organizations involved. In Europe, a joint venture between France Telecom, Deutsche Telekom, Digital Equipment, and the Technology Management Group offers an information system called "Euro-Log." It contains modules for electronic data interchange between producers, wholesalers, retailers, banks, and distribution facilitators, the door-to-door management of transport with various transportation modes, and a module for freight management.

Centralization of logistics

There is one basic condition, however, to make such a real-time marketing logistics information system work: The company's logistics function has to be centralized, that is, the physical distribution responsibilities of national sales offices, subsidiaries or intermediaries must be limited to execution functions or even entirely deleted. The Switzerland-based Silver Crystal division of Austrian Swarovski, for example, reduced the responsibilities of its sales offices to building and maintaining customer contacts. The physical distribution of crystal objects is handled out of a single distribution center for each of Europe, North America, and Southeast Asia.

Impact of macro-environment

In country markets with rather complicated import regulations, such as India, some manufacturers establish local production plants in order to achieve a more predictable distribution schedule. Service delivery in global markets is also affected by local differences in available infrastructures. For example, an internationally operating bank such as London-based Barclays Bank must be aware that automatic teller machines are as popular in the U.S. as in western Europe but they are used to deliver many more kinds of banking service. In most parts of Europe, machines are limited to dispensing cash. In some countries they can be used to reload electronic cards with monetary value, called electronic funds transfer, which can then be used to purchase goods and services. And in many parts of Africa, except major cities and more economically developed countries such as South Africa, such a distribution system for banking services does not exist.

Transportation

Based on the company's general policy decision to use either a company-owned, a company-bound, or an independent physical distribution system, the international marketing logistics manager will have to make choices concerning the transportation of its products from the company's premises to the customers. There are different transportation modes available that are more or less suited to the marketer's product and the level of customer service to be achieved. The total costs and the reliability of those transportation modes will also have to be taken into account.

In addition, international transportation of goods is not advisable without proper insurance. The logistics manager will have to consider the trade-off between insurance costs and the risk of losses.

And finally, international transportation often involves extensive paperwork. Because of the specific know-how needed to provide the exact documents to cross borders and to minimize delivery and payment risks, in most cases the marketer will seek the services of an international freight forwarder.

Modes of transportation

Water transportation The most important mode of transportation in international marketing is by water.

Table 14.4 presents an overview of the different types of water transportation available and the services provided. Water transport is advantageous when country markets are characterized by extensive coastlines and heavily populated coastal regions. For example, about half of Australia's population is located in the crescent between Brisbane and Adelaide, which is readily accessible by ocean freight.

Water transportation requires an extensive transportation infrastructure to move goods from the ship to the customer. Port facilities in less industrially developed countries often lack the equipment to handle modern vessels. Even

Shanghai harbor – since 2004 the busiest harbor in the world
© Digital Archive Japan/Alamy

countries with large ports may have an inadequate internal transportation system, with the result that cargoes may remain on vessels or docks for weeks or even months before they can be transported to their final destinations.

Rail transportation This is important in countries where roads are poor or railroad infrastructures are heavily subsidized by the government. All of southeastern Africa, for example, depends on a single railroad line leading from the coast of Mozambique to the mineral-rich inland countries. This line is so important to the economy of the area that the industrialized nations agreed to contribute significantly to the costs of reconstructing the railroad after it was destroyed by rebels during a political coup.

Calls for restrictions on truck shipping in the European Union – a result of pollution, congestion, and noise (see Ethics box 14.1) – have led to the development of mixed transportation modes using roll-on/roll-off railroad cars or special rail containers. The containers are loaded at the shipper's facilities, set on trucks going to the nearest rail terminal, and then loaded onto trains that go as near as possible to their destination. There they are picked up by other trucks to be transported to their final destination. Once the goods have been loaded into the containers, no other handling is required along the entire route.

Truck transportation Trucks can help to overcome problems of inefficient or overloaded port facilities and the lack of adequate railroad lines. For example, Swedish machinery and Austrian fruit juice are trucked to Saudi Arabia, where even the truck may be sold (because it is more economical than supporting an empty return trip) after having discharged its load. Because of the flexibility of truck transportation, this mode of transport has become increasingly popular in Europe. For example, each day more than 5,000 trucks use the Brenner Autobahn (freeway) between Munich and the industrial centers of northern Italy. There,

---

TABLE 14.4 *Types of water transportation and services provided*

Different types of goods use different types of water transportation. Cargo liners carry general cargo over predetermined routes with scheduled times of departure and arrival. Bulk carriers offer contractual services over extended periods of time or for individual trips. Container ships transport containers of standard sizes on regular routes. Tramp vessels are scheduled on demand on irregular routes. Break-bulk ships are traditionally designed ships with their own cranes and cargo-handling equipment (particularly well suited for small ports in industrially less developed countries (LCDs)). Ro/ro ships allow trucks to deposit their containers in the cargo space. Lighter aboard ships (LASH) store barges by crane and lower them at the point of destination.

Type of service	Scheduled services on regular routes		Charter services on individual routes	
Ship	Cargo liners	Container ships	Bulk carriers	Tramp vessels
Cargo	General cargo	Containers	Mass goods	Mass goods
	R/ro cargo			
Contract	Piece good freight contract		Volume freight contract	
	+ Booking	+ Service contract	+ Period/time charter	+ Trip charter
		+ Booking		+ Consecutive trip charter
				+ Period/time charter

Source: Adapted from Gray, H.P. (1982) "International transportation", in I. Walter and T. Murray (eds), *Handbook of International Business*, New York: John Wiley & Sons, pp. 11.3–11.18

close to 10 million tons of freight by truck pass through the freight village of Verona, one of the largest consolidation centers in Europe, every year.

Shipment by air Air shipment reduces transportation time and the need to maintain a large inventory. In many cases airfreight, despite its higher cost, is necessary for successful marketing. For example, Rosenbauer, a European marketer of fire engines, guarantees delivery of essential spare parts within 48 hours all over the world. This could not be done without airfreight.

For air transportation to be efficient, good ground support services are vital. For example, Frankfurt airport is the busiest cargo airport in Europe. Its Cargo City, a major transshipment site for freight used by more than 240 airlines, forwarding agents, and service providers, offers buildings to be leased, distribution and cargo handling services. In addition, Fraport – as it is called – is an air/truck/train/ship port with high-speed train service, direct links to Germany's Autobahn system, access to the inland port on the Rhine, and air links to more international destinations than any other European airport.

Such services tend to be more expensive than the services offered at truck terminals. In addition, in some regions theft and pilferage pose serious problems.

ETHICS BOX 14.1

Marketer's responsibility for environmental protection

With consumers' growing awareness of ecological problems in their environment and the signing of the Kyoto Protocol on the reduction of emissions, two issues have become increasingly important in recent years: Avoiding unnecessary traffic and retro-distribution.

From 1990 to 2001 the number of cars and trucks in the EU grew by 25%. Because of the opening of the formerly centrally controlled economies in eastern Europe and their increasing integration into the EU, the growth rate of road traffic has increased. Freight transport in the EU is expected to grow at least 40% by 2010 compared to the year 2000, with the highest growth expected for the road sector (50%).

Railroad capacities for pan-European transport have not been sufficiently built up in time. The freight rail mode share has declined significantly over the past 30 years. The market shares of passenger and goods railroad traffic were 6 and 8% respectively in 2002. The foreseeable trafficjam on the roads and the resulting CO_2 and NO_2 pollution, which to a significant extent causes the warming of the atmosphere, demand an optimization of vehicles, tours, and loads on the part of responsible marketing logistics managers.

If they are not willing to contribute voluntarily to the reduction of environmental pollution by their own means, they may be forced to adapt to restrictions coming from national governments such as toll payments on the German Autobahn or external regulations of the EU administration. The EU administration has published a White Paper announcing the objective of returning modal shares back to levels existing in 1998. That is, the share of rail traffic is to be increased to 15%.

In a similar way, manufacturers and retailers who are not willing to contribute to the reduction of package waste will be forced to take back, reuse, or recycle an increasing amount of packaging material. In Europe, the European Community Packaging and Packaging Waste Directive, first introduced in late 1994, fixed a minimum recovery of 50–65% of all packaging materials to be achieved by the year 2001. Germany and Switzerland have the most restrictive legislation in the field of packaging. Transportation package material, boxes, and containers, as well as sales package material must be reused or recycled. Even if other European countries so far have less restrictive legislation, international marketers are well advised to rethink their packaging and redistribution systems in advance.

Source: Adapted from European Commission (1999) "Summary report", Brussels; www.fta.co.uk/information/otherissues/eu/020221EUTransportPaper.htm; www.epspackaging.org/ipr.html

The international marketer should ask an international carrier for advice before selecting this transportation mode.

Choosing transportation mode

To decide which transportation modes to use, the international marketer must evaluate existing transportation infrastructures in the geographic areas it wishes to serve. These will differ from one country to another, as will the forms of transportation service available and their cost.

For example, if a Romanian producer of asparagus wants to deliver 90 tons of its produce to Japanese customers, the logistics manager may decide to use the cheapest solution, which is to transport the load to the Romanian port of Constantia by truck and from there to Yokohama by ship. Satellite-driven control of the cooling temperature in the trucks and the ship is able to ensure an undisturbed cold chain until the load's arrival in Japan. There, the length of existing channels of distribution might largely diminish the quality of the product before it arrives at the consumers. Another alternative would be to transport the asparagus by air from Bucharest via Paris to Tokyo. The problem is that there are very few freight flights from the capital of Romania to Paris, and passenger flights can only take about 7 tons of goods (including the passenger's luggage). In addition, the cold chain could be interrupted during the time that the load is waiting in Paris. That leaves the marketer with the alternative of chartering two freight flights with a maximum load of 45 tons from Bucharest to Tokyo. But this would probably be the most expensive solution.

The choice between the basic transportation modes – surface, water, or air – depends on weight, size, form, volume, and value of the products to be transported. The marketer should bear in mind that transportation costs may influence the competitiveness of its total product in a particular market, especially when the price per unit of weight is low (as in the case of many commodities). But for high-value products with high inventory-carrying costs, such as large computers, the total costs of distribution will be lower if a faster, but more expensive, mode of transportation like airfreight is used.

Other factors to be taken into consideration when choosing transportation method include:

- distance to be covered
- total cost
- acceptable transit time
- reliability of the transportation mode.

The reliability of transportation affects the level of "safety" inventory that must be maintained. It is especially important when marketing success depends on precise delivery dates such as in just-in-time delivery to customers in the automotive industry, and when a high unit price makes damage or loss very expensive.

For example, when transports of western European products go to or through Russia, the first problem arises at the border of Belarus. Border controls can take up to 48 hours, making precise delivery dates impossible. Then, once in Russia, the transport needs special guarding during the trip and overnight stops in specially prepared areas if the marketer wants to make sure that its products arrive at their destination. Companies such as Russian Mach have specialized in guarding transports in and through this country. Today, the global positioning system is being used to track the exact position of trucks and railroad cars by satellite.

But theft is also an issue at European ports and U.S. customs locations. Thus, Hutchison Port Holdings, which manages the bulk of container operations at Rotterdam and Felixstowe (the U.K.'s largest port) as well as Hesse-Noord Natie, which operates 80% of the cargo volume at Antwerp, Europe's second-largest port, have equipped their container handling operations with unique software that is integrated with automatic identification technologies and a variety of electronic seals. They digitally lock the containers and transmit real-time alerts about tampering and other events over radio frequencies. One is the standard frequency used by the global total asset visibility network that tracks shipments through more than 700 nodes in 46 countries.

Level of customer service required in a specific market is another important consideration. Transit time and customer service level determine the amount of inventory required in the markets to which goods are being transported. For perishable and seasonal products, and especially for fashion goods, this can be a decisive factor in successful marketing. Fresh flowers exported to the U.S. from Colombia, Israel, and the Netherlands, for example, are highly perishable and are therefore flown to wholesale markets in the U.S. each day.

Ateixo, Spain-based Zara, the fast expanding marketer of fashion, as another example, has adopted the principle of zero inventories. Stores order and receive deliveries twice a week giving their customers good reasons to visit them several times per season. Fabrics coming from Spain, Italy, Turkey, India, or China are cut and colored at a state of the art factory. Based on daily information on what is sold in each Zara store worldwide, product managers decide how many garments to manufacture and which stores will get them. Ten to 15 days after a product has been designed it is shipped to the stores by truck (in Europe) or airfreight (overseas). Some 2 million garments leave the distribution center in Ateixo every week.

Taking all these factors into consideration, the final choice of the transportation service provider often depends on additional services offered by the suppliers (see Culture box 14.1 for an example).

Documentation

The shipment of products in global markets is complicated by the need for extensive documentation. Besides the paperwork needed to document the goods transported, their origin and exact destination, and the details of their transaction, documents also serve the purpose of information and risk reduction for the parties involved. To serve the needs of simplification of administrative work and legal reliability of global business, the International Federation of Freight Forwarding Organizations (FIATA) has developed standardized documents. These documents are particularly important for shipments using a combination

---

CULTURE BOX 14.1

Tracking services of Federal Express and UPS

How much the level of additional services needed to satisfy the expectations of customers in a country market depends on cultural influences is illustrated by the example of the tracking services by Federal Express and UPS.

In the U.S. where "time is money" and many business transactions are based on distrust, Federal Express started allowing individual customers with access to the internet to track packages through the company's site on the worldwide web. Its major competitor, UPS, had to follow suit with the same kind of service. Customers can locate a package in transit by connecting online to the FedEx or UPS site and entering a reference or a tracking number, or by sending an email. Customers can also request software that allows them not only to track their parcels but also to view at any time the entire history of their transaction with FedEx. After the package has been delivered, they can even identify the name of the person who signed for it. U.S. customers perceive this information as an additional value of the service.

Source: Based on www.fedex.com/us/tracking.html; www.ups.com/tracking/tracking.html

of different transportation modes (multi-modal transports) or for shipments of various goods in one load (collective load). The most frequently used documents are listed in Table 14.5.

In addition to these documents, each transportation mode has its specific documents, such as the seaway bill (SWB) or the airway bill (AWB):

- An **export declaration** has to be filled out for statistical purposes of export administration agencies and for fiscal purposes such as the reimbursement of value-added tax.
- The **commercial invoice** is a statement or a bill of the goods sold, describing the content of the transaction in detail.
- A **certificate of origin** is a document specifying the country where the product has mainly been manufactured. It is needed for specifying the applicable tariff.

Country of origin legislation may be more or less rigid, however. For example, if an Italian manufacturer of decoration objects made from clay, such as Bolzano-based Thun, produces the raw objects in a factory in China and does some finishing in Italy, Italian laws allow a specification of origin as "Made in Italy."

Internationally used freight forwarders' documents are the following.

Forwarder's certificate of receipt (FCR) The FCR is an international freight forwarder's takeover and shipment certificate in which the freight forwarder declares that it has taken over a good exactly specified in the document for shipment to a specified receiver or to the receiver's disposition. It serves the purpose of allowing the seller to be able to prove that it has handed over the goods. However, the buyer who receives the FCR from the freight forwarder cannot enforce the handing over of the shipped goods. For this purpose the buyer needs an FBL.

Forwarder's certificate of transport (FCT) In an FCT the freight forwarder certifies that it has taken over the load specified in the document for shipment and indicates its willingness to deliver the goods in accordance with the consignor's orders. By issuing this document the freight forwarder takes over the responsibility for the delivery of the goods to the holder of the FCT at their destination.

TABLE 14.5 Documents most frequently required in international logistics

Document	Purpose	
Export declaration	A form serving the statistical purposes of export administration agencies	Cross-border physical distribution frequently needs extensive documentation for statistical and tariff purposes but also to reduce seller's and buyer's risks in the international transaction.
Commercial invoice	A statement or bill of the goods sold, describing the transaction in detail	
Certificate of origin	A document specifying the exact origin of the product; needed for specifying the applicable tariff	
Freight forwarders' documents	FCR = forwarders' certificate of receipt FCT = forwarders' certificate of transport FWR = FIATA warehouse receipt SDT = shippers' declaration for the transport of dangerous goods FBL = negotiable FIATA combined transport bill of lading	

The FCT is mainly used in cases where the transportation risk remains with the seller until the physical handing over of the goods to the customer. The seller can use the document to demand payment for the goods from the buyer via its bank.

FIATA combined transport bill of lading (FBL) The FIATA combined transport bill of lading (FBL) is a transport document issued by the freight forwarder that is negotiable if the receiver is not *specifically* mentioned in the document and "to order" appears instead. In this document the forwarder takes over the responsibility for the shipped good and its transportation. That is, the freight forwarder in its role as MTO (multi-modal transport operator) is responsible for all carriers used during shipment as well as the handing over of the goods to the customer. A bill of lading should always contain a notification address in case the customer is not present at the point of destination indicated in the document.

In addition to these, export licenses may be required for politically sensitive goods, such as electronic measurement devices. The marketer may also need to fill out a shipper's declaration for the transport of dangerous goods (SDT). This document enables the freight forwarder to identify the goods taken over, to take the needed measures in case of danger, and to clarify responsibilities in case of damage. A consular invoice may be necessary in the country of destination. And many LDCs require foreign exchange licenses (these enable the shipper to collect the price of the goods in hard currency) and import licenses.

In the U.S. most of the documents required for international distribution are coordinated through the **U.S. standard master for international trade**, a master list of documents that improves the flow of international trade by having trading partners use the same documents. However, small and medium-sized companies should seek the assistance of a specialist if they do business in a number of countries or have a large number of items in their product lines. Not only must the necessary documents be filled out, they must also be processed accurately. Errors can cause delayed shipments, higher inventory costs, additional handling and shipping charges, customer dissatisfaction, penalties, and financial losses. In addition, customs procedures, restrictions and requirements differ from one country to another.

Insurance

International transportation regulations, such as:

- Convention Relative au Contrat de Transport International de Marchandises par Route (CMR) for road transportation
- Convention Internationale Concernant le Transport des Marchandises par Chemin de Fer (CIM) for transportation by rail

contain rules concerning the range of liability, the compensation for loss, exceeding the time of delivery, and damage through intention or gross negligence.

Because the amount of compensation stated in these regulations is rather limited, marketers in most cases will need to obtain additional insurance certificates if they have to cover the transportation risk. International insurance companies and freight forwarders will advise them on signing the appropriate contracts for their specific needs.

For example, if the marketer ships its products by container to a harbor that is not deep enough to allow the landing of the container ship, the containers will need to be unloaded at sea onto smaller ships. An insurance contract against "havarie grosse" would cover the risk of loss of the small ship (including its load) taking over the container.

Terms of delivery

The international delivery of goods or services has to be thoroughly negotiated and regulated in the contract of sale between the business partners. The contractual conditions of the sale are called the terms of sale. They contain the terms of payment (to be discussed in Chapter 16) and the terms of delivery. Today, sophisticated international marketers use terms of delivery (and the related logistics costs) as a source of profit. Controlling more aspects of the physical distribution process can make the seller more competitive, because more than the price of the product can be manipulated.

Japanese and Australian companies, for example, typically try to purchase on an "ex works" basis, that is, they are willing to take over the risk and the costs of the entire delivery process from the supplier's premises to their point of destination. This allows them to control all the costs themselves. In the position of the seller, they prefer to take over most of the responsibility and costs for the physical movement of goods until they arrive at the customer's premises.

Incoterms Major difficulties in the negotiation of terms of sale may arise from a lack of knowledge about international logistics. Too often the business partners do not know much about the trade customs in the other country. Different interpretations of terms of delivery already agreed on are a source of continuous trouble. Uncertainty about which country's laws will be applicable to the contract adds to the difficulties. To help avoid such problems, standard terms of delivery have been developed in international trade over the years. These terms were precisely phrased by the International Chamber of Commerce, which is located in Paris. Referred to as incoterms (international commercial terms), their wide usage today is due to international acceptance of their interpretation of the terms of delivery most often applied in international marketing. Following all industrialized countries of Europe, in 1980 the six most important U.S. trade organizations (American Importers' Association, U.S. Chamber of Commerce, Council on International Banking, National Foreign Trade Council, National Committee on International Trade Documentation, U.S. Council of the International Chamber of Commerce) suggested using incoterms instead of the American foreign trade definitions (AFTD) applied until then. In their latest revision, the incoterms 2000 contain 13 types of trade term. They are listed in Table 14.6 in English, German, French, and Italian, together with their abbreviations.

The incoterms regulate the forms of shipment (including destination), the location and point in time of loss and damage risk transfer from the supplier to the customer, as well as the repatriation of costs of shipment (including all additional costs such as for documents or insurance) between the business partners, and the obligations of the buyer and seller concerning the export, transit and import of the merchandise.

FAS, FOB, CFR, CIF, DES, and DEQ are specifically formulated terms for transportation by ship. EXW, FCA, CPT, CIP, DAF, DDU, and DDP are suitable for any transportation mode, including multi-modal transportation. The most important of these incoterms 2000 are discussed in the Appendix to this chapter.

Additions Even when the two parties to the contract agree on the incoterm to use, care must be taken to make sure they are in complete agreement on the specifics. For that reason the following additions in the sales contract are advisable:

- It should be clearly specified how and where the handing over of the merchandise is to happen and who has to carry out the unloading procedure.
- The level and kind of insured risk should be clearly spelled out and be specified concerning its geographic and time coverage. Terms such as "maximum insurance" are to be avoided.
- The exact modes of transport to be used should be listed.
- A "force majeure" clause included in the sales contract is advisable as well as a time-gliding clause, in particular when the marketer takes

responsibility for customs clearance or delivery of the merchandise to a destination far from a harbor in a country with a less developed transportation infrastructure.

UN Convention on International Sales The marketer must be aware that in addition to the explicitly stated use of an incoterm in a sales contract, the UN Convention on International Sales (CIS) is automatically applicable when both buyer and seller have their headquarters in countries that have signed the convention. This convention, which since 1988 has been signed by more than 50 governments including most members of the EU, the members of NAFTA, Russia, and Australia, regulates the signing of international sales contracts concerning goods as well as the resulting rights and obligations of the buyer and the seller.

Packaging

While it may seem that packaging's most important role is to help sell the product, packaging must play several roles and make many contributions if international marketing is to be successful. It must:

- protect the product
- be easy to handle for intermediaries and customers

TABLE 14.6 *Abbreviations and translations of incoterms 2000*

The incoterms 2000, although standardized, have different translations, which the international marketer may need to know in order to manage the terms of sale. The listing of the 13 incoterms here ranks them according to the increasing obligations of the marketer concerning the delivery of its product.

Incoterms	English	German	French	Italian
EXW	Exworks	Ab Werk	À l'usine	Franco fabrica
FCA	Free carrier	Frei Frachtführer	Franco transporteur	Franco trasporto
FAS	Free alongside ship	Frei Längsseite Schiff	Franco lelong bord	Franco sottobordo
FOB	Free on board	Frei an Bord	Franco bord	Franco a bordo
CFR	Cost and freight	Kosten und Fracht	Coûts et fret	Costo e nolo
CIF	Cost, insurance, freight	Kosten, Versicherung Fracht	Coûts, Assurance, Fret	Costo, assicurazione e nolo
CPT	Carriage paid to	Frachtfrei	Port payé jusqu'à	Porto pagato
CIP	Carriage and insurance paid to	Frachtfrei versichert	Port payé assurance comprise	Porto ed assicurazione pagato
DAF	Delivered at frontier	Geliefert Grenze	Rendu frontière	Reso frontiera
DES	Delivered ex ship	Geliefert ab Schiff	Rendu ex ship	Reso ex ship
DEQ	Delivered ex quay	Geliefert ab Kai	Rendu à quai	Reso banchina
DDU	Delivered duty unpaid	Geliefert unverzollt	Rendu droits nonacquittés	Reso nonsdoganato
DDP	Delivered duty paid	Geliefert verzollt	Rendu droits acquittés	Reso sdoganato

Source:"Incoterms 2000™&®*", ICC Publications No. 560(E): ISBN 92.842.1199.9 (EF). Published in its official English version by the International Chamber of Commerce, Paris

Copyright © 1999 International Chamber of Commerce (ICC)

*Incoterms is a trademark of ICC, registered in the European Community and elsewhere.

- be transportable at minimum cost
- meet the legal requirements of the served country markets
- support the company's logistics information system.

Protection

In general, protection is even more important in international shipping than in most domestic markets. The U.S. Carriage of Goods by Sea Act, for example, makes the shipper responsible for appropriate packaging to protect products from damage. The marketer, therefore, must pay special attention to handling characteristics in package design.

The detrimental effects of insufficient packaging are illustrated by the example of Engel, an Austrian manufacturer that sent four truckloads of plastic extruders to Iran, using the pallets (wooden platforms on which several extruders are loaded together) that are normally used in its domestic market. Shortly after the arrival of the merchandise, the marketer received a telex from the customer's bank stating that 90% of the cargo was damaged or did not work. A group of service engineers sent to find out the cause discovered that the customer had neither a forklift nor a crane to use in unloading the trucks. The workers had simply pushed the pallets to the side of the truck and let them fall to the floor; thus the product on the pallet also fell on the floor; a way of unloading not accounted for in the construction of the plastic extruders.

Cargo storage containers play a key role in support of protective packaging
© Pixoi Ltd/Alamy

For consumer goods, packaging also provides protection, a function that is often overshadowed by the promotion function. For example, products destined for consumers in tropical areas need packages that withstand high temperatures combined with high levels of humidity. Goods destined for consumers in mountainous areas must be packaged carefully for transport over winding roads, and, in countries with less developed infrastructures, over rough terrain, sometimes even by pack train instead of trucks.

In international marketing the development of containers plays a major role in fulfilling the protective function of packaging. Containers make it possible to keep the weight of the actual package relatively low. At the same time, the container protects the product against climatic influences, damage during transit, and pilferage. In some important markets of the world, however, packaging in containers is largely unknown. For example, in the early 1990s IBM found out that shipping by rail in China is different from the U.S., where their products got shipped in containers. In China, in many loading stations there were cargo handlers who virtually threw the cartons containing IBM PCs into trains. When Chinese customers complained to IBM that it was selling year-old machines as new, officials were puzzled. But finally, they identified the culprit: Dust had seeped inside each carton despite two layers of plastic sheeting. Another layer ended the complaints.

Today, a large amount of business with China is done by using containers. As there is a huge export volume to the U.S. and the EU, shipping lines are willing to carry empty containers, even at a loss, to China. Because of a shortage of available containers the lines get premium freight rates on Chinese exports. Transit time of container ships between Shanghai and the U.S. is less than a fortnight.

Freight costs

To keep freight costs down, the marketer must use transportation equipment and warehouses as efficiently as possible. This may also require adaptations in package design. For example, high stacks of products in containers or warehouses can be used only when the package is constructed so as to resist pressure.

Handling

When the international marketer serves country markets where its intermediaries or customers possess very different infrastructures to handle the product and its package, such as the highly automated central warehouses of big retail organizations in the U.K. compared to the multilevel distribution channels found in Japan and the small one-room retail outlets that have to be serviced on a daily basis in India, full packaging standardization will be impossible. In Japan, longer channels and smaller retailing outlets often require smaller packages. In India, many intermediaries and shippers handle products by hand, not by machine. Products that are packaged in too large or heavy a container will be difficult to move through the distribution channel. If the shipping containers are too large, the wholesaler will have no choice but to break them down for reshipment or storage, thereby increasing the risk of damage to the product.

Retailers' needs too must be considered. Product packages must be of a suitable size and quantity to be manageable and financially affordable to the retailer. Finally, if consumers do not use cars for shopping, as in many parts of China, packaging must allow the transportation of the product across larger walking or biking distances.

The package size best suited for all country markets served can be approximated by developing packaging systems, that is, a combination of small to large packaging units which fit together. For example, when a Belgian manufacturer of chocolate pralines delivers its products to an importer in Toronto, the use of a container will ease transportation. Packaging the decorative retail boxes into cardboard boxes containing a greater number of retail packages will help the importer to split the entire shipment into smaller units easier to handle for the retailers. If the cardboard boxes can be stapled, that also eases the storage problem for the retailers. Consumers will be pleased by packages that are easy to open but can also be firmly closed again to keep the chocolates fresh.

Support of logistics information system

For logistics optimization purposes such as:

- minimum inventory levels
- shortest transportation routes
- shrinkage
- avoidance of shelf warmers

the product package must contain the information needed by the marketer and all other members of the distribution channel to clearly identify the product.

For example, companies operating internationally in more than 80 countries handle their international orders through an electronic data interchange system called EANCOM. This kind of mailbox system allows the exchange of standardized data by consumer goods manufacturers, customers, freight forwarders, and warehouse firms. Using special data strings of the communication system, orders may be set, changes in orders can be registered as well as any mistakes, the position of goods in the logistics chain may be determined, and inventory may be taken at any time. To make this system work, each package and each pallet transported must be equipped with a code that identifies:

- product
- amount delivered
- destination
- partners involved in production and physical distribution
- when the most recent changes to these data took place.

This last piece of information is of particular importance to the flexibility of the system in reacting to changing market conditions.

The next step in the development of packaging to support logistics information systems is the development of "smart products" as described in Future issues box 14.1. Products or their packages will be equipped with radio frequency identification tags to allow tracking from the time they leave a production line to the time they leave a store.

Warehousing and storage

A company can develop its own warehousing and storage facilities, or this function can be performed by the firm's intermediaries or by specialized companies. Products can be stored at different levels of the distribution channel – in a central or a number of regional distribution centers, at sales offices in various markets, with foreign freight forwarders, or with merchants. The marketer must decide:

- how many warehouses to use
- where to locate them
- how best to manage inventory.

In international logistics these decisions are complicated by the highly complex interrelationships between production sites, warehouses, freight forwarders, carriers, and levels of intermediaries. U.S.-based Caterpillar, for example, maintains 22 parts facilities around the world, with more than 10 million^2 feet of warehouse storage. They service 480,000 line items (different part numbers), of which they stock 320,000. Caterpillar's and its suppliers' factories make the remaining 160,000 on demand. The firm ships 84,000 items per day, or about one per second every day of the year. In addition, the company's dealers, each of whom typically stocks between 40,000 and 50,000 line items, have made huge investments in parts inventories, warehouses, fleets of trucks, and sophisticated information technology.

FUTURE ISSUES BOX 14.1

Auto ID/EPC electronic product codes

In October 1999 the Uniform Code Council, which administers barcode standardization, joined with MIT, Procter & Gamble, and The Gillette Company to found the Auto-ID Center at the Massachusetts Institute of Technology. The mission of this center is to develop next-generation automatic identification systems in collaboration with strategic partners, including both end users and technology providers. Big companies such as Wal-Mart, Johnson & Johnson, Phillips, Westvaco, and International Paper have joined the group. The center has satellite labs at Cambridge University, in Japan, and in Australia.

Radio frequency identification (RFID) is to be adapted to consumer product packaging to allow tracking products from the time they leave a production line to the time they leave a store. Early tests are encouraging. But there are several issues left to be resolved.

Other electronic communication devices such as cordless phones or local wireless networks can interfere with the signals. And although radio tag readers can identify well over 100 tagged items every second from quite a distance, radio waves cannot penetrate metals and liquids.

Retailers will not invest until the product tags are universally readable, as barcodes are today. To reach that goal, retailers, manufacturers and logistics service providers must agree to standards concerning tags and sensors.

Costs are still prohibitive. Starting from 30¢ for an electronic tag they have come down to 10¢, and will go down further with mass production. But while the silicon chips continue to shrink and fall in price, making the attached antennas small and cheap enough is much harder.

Finally, consumer privacy is an issue. The technology in place, it would be easy to combine credit card data with information from the electronic tags to know who bought what, and when, and track the product even after it left the store.

Source: Adapted from Deutsch, C.H. and B.J. Feder (2003) "A radio chip in every consumer product", *New York Times*, 25 February, p. C.1

Number and location of warehouses

In most industrialized countries, modern warehouse facilities are readily available. Specialists like Swiss-based Danzas, a member of the DJL Group, offer customs brokerage, freight forwarding, insurance, packaging, labeling, and transportation services, in addition to warehousing. Similar services are provided by specialist firms in the U.S., such as BDP International. In Japan, in contrast, there are few public warehouses, and demand for those that are available is high, resulting in high costs. In less developed countries, storage facilities are often limited or not available at all. The product may have to be stored in its package or container unprotected, in the open – a possibility that must be considered when designing the package.

Decisions about the number and location of warehouses are influenced by the following factors.

Intended level of customer service The impact of the intended level of customer service is shown by the example of OSRAM GmbH, the No. 3 producer of light bulbs in the world. In 1990 the company had 12 production locations and warehouses for finished goods in all 16 European countries served. To stay competitive OSRAM wanted to reduce costs by reducing its number of warehouses. But even in the light of European unification, the reduction of all warehouses to one centrally located distribution center seemed impossible for one major reason: Customer service at OSRAM is defined as proper delivery of ordered products in 48 hours. This could not be achieved for countries like Finland or Portugal from a warehouse in central Europe or through a central logistics unit managing direct delivery from the production units to the customers. OSRAM decided to have three distribution centers acting as warehouses for related production facilities as well as distribution service centers for a region defined through service demands and not through national boundaries. Products not manufactured in the area of the distribution center are directly delivered on order from the distribution center carrying the product. Where the fixed 48-hour service level cannot be reached with this solution, regional distribution centers are added.

A reduction in the number of warehouses reduces costs, but it does not necessarily reduce the level of customer service in parallel. For example, since 1994 the central warehouse of HILTI U.S. in Tulsa, Oklahoma, besides serving the U.S. market, is the only supplier for the 21 distribution centers of HILTI Canada and HILTI Latin America, logistically managing about 98% of all products sold to customers in those areas. This concentration of warehousing activities has not only led to a decrease in inventory, costs of freight, and storage space required, as well as to a reduction in the number of suppliers, followed by a sharp rise in productivity, but it has also allowed the company to broaden the product range offered and to increase the availability of those products to HILTI's customers.

Customer distribution across served market area Where major customers are concentrated in a certain area, such as the furniture industry in the Carolinas in the U.S. or the leather goods industry in northern Italy, suppliers to those industries will tend to build warehouses (or even production units) close to their customers.

Available infrastructure in a local market More and smaller local warehouses will be needed where the transportation infrastructure does not allow reliable delivery of mostly small amounts of products to customers or intermediaries. For example, the rather poor condition of the infrastructure in the mountainous areas of the Andes does not allow direct delivery to retailers from one central production unit.

Availability of government subsidies, tax breaks, or tariff protection Decision makers may be tempted to invest according to subsidies, tax breaks, or tariff protection.

They should not overlook, however, that such advantages might be offset by controls on exports or imports, fluctuations in exchange rates, insufficient infrastructure, or restrictions on inventory levels due to government policies trying to control hoarding. Thus, the international logistics manager should look at the total picture before making a decision.

Foreign trade zones

Foreign trade zones (FTZs) offer interesting opportunities for international marketing logistics when decisions concerning the location of warehouses have to be taken. FTZs are special areas within a country to which companies may ship products for storage, bulk breaking, labeling, assembling, refining, repackaging, and the like without paying customs duties or taxes. For that reason, for example, a company that has so far delivered its tools and machine parts just in time to customers in the Arabian peninsula by airfreight may decide to build or rent warehouse space in the FTZ of Dubai in the United Arab Emirates. There it can store the products most often needed and may significantly reduce logistics costs by transporting those products to Dubai in containers by ship. Only when the products leave the FTZ to be sold elsewhere in the country do they become subject to local tariffs or taxes. The potential benefits derived from using FTZs are listed in Table 14.7.

There are about 380 free trade zones in the U.S. and many more in another 50 countries such as Brazil, Colombia, Panama, and Uruguay, to name a few in Latin America. Most of the fast developing coastal regions of China are FTZs as well. Usually, foreign trade zones are government owned and supervised by customs agents. They can take the form of real geographical zones, but can also be restricted to free ports, bonded warehouses, or areas restricted to a plant.

Inventory management

When it takes a long time to transport products from the company to its intermediaries or customers, and when delays during transportation are frequent, the company may have large quantities of products in transit at any given time. International marketers must keep more inventory "in the pipeline" than domestic marketers generally do. As a result:

- more working capital is invested in inventory
- capital costs are higher
- there are more accounts receivable.

Inventory control is particularly important under such conditions.

TABLE 14.7 Benefits derived from using foreign trade zones

Decreased working capital

Exemption from paying duties on labor and overhead costs incurred in the FTZ

Lower insurance costs due to customs security requirements

Savings of duties on goods rejected, damaged, or scrapped

Opportunity to stockpile products when quotas are filled or market conditions are sub-optimal

Re-exportation without complicated paperwork

Tariff avoidance if products are exported directly from the FTZ

Products can be assembled, processed, and stored in free trade zones. Companies using such an opportunity can profit from the benefits listed.

Source: "Foreign trade zones: what's in it for the shipper?", *Distribution*, March 1980, pp. 44-7

As discussed earlier, international marketing logistics managers should consider centrally coordinated inventory management, in which an IT system is used to monitor the volume and value of products in transit or stocked in various warehouses. Because products are not sold at the same rate in every country market, an item that is urgently needed in one place may not be selling in another. When computer monitoring is used, fashion products like knitwear or sunglasses, for example, can be shipped directly between two country markets rather than indirectly via the location of the company's headquarters.

A centrally coordinated inventory management is difficult to enforce when distribution channels are not company bound or at least ready to closely cooperate. A distributor's idea of an optimal inventory level is usually based on their market, sales level, and capital needs. The manufacturer will need an integrated information system that allows it to accumulate the sales volumes of all distributors for each product to optimize production runs and shipping activities. In order to balance the different points of view, the manufacturer needs to establish strong relationships with its distributors.

For products that must be delivered over larger distances at very short notice, inventory must be stocked at locations near the final customers if air transportation is too expensive. For that purpose, international logistics service providers often utilize inbound sequencing centers. Such sequencing centers allow for inventory to be kept for only one or two days, available in a few hours to the site of manufacturing or retailing customers, cutting the supplier's inventory holding time from 10 days to 2 hours.

For products with longer order cycles such as the metal-bending machines or laser cutters of Germany's Trumpf, production may follow orders. It is important, however, to consider the purchase patterns of final customers. Not only do the frequency and volume of purchases differ in different markets, but seasonal fluctuations and irregular demand (such as in the fashion industry or for innovative products) complicate the task of the international logistics manager.

Inventory management may differ according to the extent of the company's control over the distribution channels in its various markets. Integrated channels may be fully stocked during periods of high inflation or unfavorable exchange rates, but independent channels will set their own policies. The latter can be influenced by discounts based on order size, order time and frequency, or other characteristics, depending on the firm's objectives. For example, a marketer may offer one free case of the product if the channel member orders 10. Or, if the buying firm changes from ordering every 6 months to every 3, the seller may reward that change with a lower price.

Location of customer contact points

Thus far discussion of international logistics decisions has focused on products dominated by tangible features that can be produced without much customer integration. Such products can be manufactured at a distance from their place of usage or consumption. When the total product contains a high level of immaterial features and/or customers are strongly involved in the value generation process, an essential part of this process will need to be performed close to the customers' homes or premises.

For example, manufacturing elevators is a business without much customer involvement. Therefore, the location of a production site is not of great importance to customers. Five big elevator manufacturers can dominate the world market based on their economies of scale. When it comes to servicing the elevators, however, customers are highly involved. Because stranded people are impatient, engineers must be based within half an hour of every elevator they maintain. As a consequence, a firm that can win service contracts in a small region around its location will be more profitable than one with contracts spread across a larger area. Small local firms can compete with the world's biggest. In such a case the international marketer has to consider the location of its points of customer contact as part of its marketing logistics system.

As discussed in Chapter 11, the choice of location may have a strong influence on the attractiveness and meaning of the marketer's product to its customers. For example, for La Perla, the Bologna, Italy-based maker of fine lingerie, when it came to choosing a Paris location, the rue du Faubourg-Saint-Honoré was by far the most attractive because it is the most prestigious street in Paris. The Faubourg-Saint-Honoré area not only houses famous French names such as Hermès, Guy Laroche, Karl Lagerfeld, and Bernardaud, the oldest and most prestigious Limoges porcelain manufacturer, it has also attracted foreign designers and firms searching for the "right" location for their boutiques and houses: Salvatore Ferragamo, Gianni Versace, Gucci, and Sotheby's, to name but a few.

Other service providers, such as McDonald's, do not look for prestigious locations. For them potential customer traffic is much more important. Therefore, closeness to public transport, recreation areas, or shopping centers are highly attractive characteristics of potential locations for their restaurants. Sweden's furniture retailing giant IKEA, as another example, tends to choose locations outside of big cities. They need lots of space to show their products and provide parking lots for customers, and they need to be easily reachable by supply trucks as well as customers' private cars.

Each service provider operating internationally has to develop its own list of criteria that a potential location has to fulfill in order to be chosen. It will depend on:

- specifics of service provided
- customers expectations concerning service
- meaning of service the provider intends to induce in customers' minds.

Because all three factors are largely influenced by local cultures, many service firms will have to limit their headquarters' influence on location decisions to the establishment of general guidelines and business objectives to achieve.

Impact on marketing mix

Marketing logistics have major interrelationships with the other elements of the marketing mix.

Pricing

In negotiating the terms of sale the final price charged for the total product of an international marketer will be influenced by the logistics costs to be covered. The marketer can use the terms of delivery in a strategic manner to increase the attractiveness of the price to a distribution partner or a business-to-business customer. Marketers selling products with complex after-sales logistics requirements will have to carefully consider the financial consequences when determining the price of their product.

Contrariwise, depending on the price positioning of the product, the marketer will have to adapt its logistics decisions. High-priced luxury goods can be delivered by airfreight, for example, if the customer wants to be served instantaneously.

Distribution

The length and diversity of international distribution channels influence the choice of transportation mode, the packaging of the product, and the number and location of warehouses. Inventory management has to consider the kind of distribution partners available in the local markets. By way of contrast, if the firm's inventory management system, the transportation modes available or the packaging are more flexible, the international marketer has a broader range of distribution partners that can be serviced.

Market communication

Market communication influences the product packaging. For example, mass market customers engage in self-service at the point of purchase (such as a large supermarket). In such cases the package must convey a strong message to the customer. But the package must also be designed to protect the product on the store shelf. The product must be easily handled and stored by intermediaries and customers. Some market communication ideas, therefore, might not be executable in international marketing.

Market communication, in particular public relations, is also influenced by marketing logistics. The way the company transports its products, how much it moves them around over long distances creating more or less traffic, or how it packages the products to be more or less harmful to the environment influences the opportunities of public relations managers to create attractive information concerning the firm's activities.

Product management

Product management is also influenced by international marketing logistics. In international business-to-business markets, for example, a short delivery time and accuracy increasingly become competitive necessities as part of the total product. Both strongly depend on marketing logistics. Warehouses close to important customers, inventory management based on online information systems, and close working relationships with international carriers are needed to fulfill customer service expectations.

Product line management also depends on the firm's logistics capabilities and resources. The faster and the more precise the information about products bought or staying in stock in different parts of the world, the more precise the offer of products that are attractive to the local customers can be.

Summary

Marketing logistics include a firm's decisions and actions concerning the physical distribution of its total products. In international marketing, logistics are increasingly recognized as an important source of potential competitive advantage. To provide sustainable competitive advantage, all marketing logistics activities must be organized in a systematic way, based on a marketing logistics policy and integrated with procurement as well as production logistics and sales activities.

The firm's marketing logistics policy determines the *level of customer service to achieve* and the limits of decisions and actions allowed to reach the given objective. It also contains a basic *decision concerning the dependence or independence of the organizational units* carrying out the physical distribution activities of the company. This decision will be based on considerations concerning:

* prices and costs
* levels of logistics infrastructure development in the served country markets
* physical properties of the merchandise
* order size and frequency
* necessary movement of goods.

If all these factors differ widely from one served country market to another, the international logistics policy must allow flexible adaptation. In many cases internationally operating marketers will choose a mixture of integrated and independent parts for their physical distribution system.

The international marketing logistics policy of a firm further contains the *profile of ideal logistics partners*. Those partners must not only be reliable, but also need to be ready to participate in decreasing the total costs of logistics. Such partners are offered long-term contracts that allow them to build up their capacities and customer-specific capabilities without incalculable financial risk.

Finally, the international marketing logistics policy also needs to contain some:

* general guidelines concerning the roles to be fulfilled inside and outside the company
* information regarding coordination between central and local company units
* responsibilities for logistics planning, information and control.

All operative decisions concerning customer service, transportation of goods, physical aspects of packaging, warehousing and storage, as well as the choice of locations for direct customer contact have to respect the guidelines stated in the firm's logistics policy.

The level of customer service provided by an international marketer in non-domestic markets tends to be lower than that provided in its domestic market. But in global product markets a level of customer service can be reached that is as high as or even higher than the level maintained in domestic markets. The speed and precision of physical distribution can be augmented by:

* use of new transportation methods
* improved packaging technology
* advanced methods of preservation
* warehouse merchandising
* direct delivery to the customers' premises
* faster handling of orders through online information systems in a chain of cooperating firms.

To decide which transportation modes to use, the international marketer must evaluate the transportation infrastructures in the geographic areas it wishes to serve. These will differ from one country to another, as will the forms of transportation services available and their costs.

The choice of transportation modes depends on:

* weight, size, form, volume, and value of the products to be transported
* distance to be covered
* total cost
* acceptable transit time
* reliability of the transportation mode
* level of customer service required in a specific market.

The shipment of products in international markets is complicated by the need for extensive documentation. Besides the paperwork needed to document:

* goods transported
* their origin and exact destination
* details of their transaction

documents also serve the purpose of information and risk reduction for the parties involved.

Packaging, in addition to its promotional role, must:

* protect the product

- be easy to handle for intermediaries and customers
- be transportable at minimum cost
- meet the legal requirements of the served country markets.

In addition, packages must be equipped in a way that supports the company's logistics information system.

An international marketer can build its own warehousing and storage facilities, or this function can be performed by the firm's intermediaries or by specialized companies. Products can be stored at different levels of international distribution channels. The marketer must decide how many warehouses to use, where to locate them, and how best to manage inventory. Evaluations of warehousing and storage alternatives are based on the need to be close to the market and to have minimum inventory and distribution costs while

respecting the obligations coming from the legal and political environments.

When the total product contains a high level of immaterial features and customers are strongly involved in the value generation process, an essential part of this process will need to be performed close to the customers' homes or premises. In such cases the international marketer has to consider the location of its points of customer contact as part of its marketing logistics system. Each internationally operating service provider has to develop its own list of criteria that a potential location has to fulfill in order to be chosen. The criteria will depend on:

- specifics of service provided
- customer expectations concerning service
- meaning of service the provider intends to implant in customers' minds.

DISCUSSION QUESTIONS

1. Contact a firm operating internationally and try to find out what policy they have established concerning their customer service level. What factors of influence did they consider?

2. Under what conditions would you suggest choosing an integrated marketing logistics system?

3. Try to find practical examples of mainly integrated, independent, and company-bound marketing logistics systems. How do the companies using those systems differ in product and country markets served?

4. Discuss the factors that would lead a company operating internationally to centralize its marketing logistics versus factors that would lead to decentralization.

5. Find examples of firms operating internationally that are well known for their high

level of customer service. What do they have in common?

6. Discuss the factors of influence on international transportation decisions.

7. Why is packaging so particularly important in international marketing? What problems need to be resolved?

8. How do warehousing and storage decisions relate to other parts of the marketing mix? Try to find illustrative examples.

9. Contact a firm operating internationally and find out what term(s) of delivery they mainly use and why. What alternative(s) would you consider and why?

10. How is international marketing logistics interrelated with international channel management?

ADDITIONAL READINGS

Gershenhom, A. (2004) "The making of a successful global supply chain", World Trade, 17(12), 19–21.

Lambert, D.M., S.J. Garcia-Dastugue, and K.L. Croxton (2005) "An evaluation of process-oriented supply chain management frameworks", Journal of Business Logistics, 26(1), 25–51.

Smagalla, D. (2004) "Supply-chain culture clash", Sloan Management Review, fall, 46(1), 6.

Useful internet links

BauMax	http://www.baumax.com/
Bernardaud	http://www.bernardaud.fr/
CaseStack	http://www.casestack.com/
Danzas	http://www.us.danzas.com/
Deutsche Telekom	http://www.telekom3.de/en-p/home/cc-startseite.html
Digital Equipment	http://www.digital.com/
EANCOM	http://www.gs1.org/index.php? http://www.ean-int.org/eancom.html&2
Engel	http://www.engel.at/at/Default.asp?LangID=2
Exel	http://www.exel.com/exel/home
Fábrica de Jabón la Corona	http://www.lacorona.com.mx/
Federal Express	http://www.fedex.com/
FIATA	http://www.fiata.com/
Fiege ecm	http://www.fiege.de/english/html/e_logstc.html
France Telecom	http://www.francetelecom.com/
Fraport	http://www.fraport.com/cms/default/rubrik/2/2228.htm
Freight Transport Association	http://www.fta.co.uk/information/otherissues/eu/ 020221EUTransportPaper.htm
Gianni Versace	http://www.versace.com/
Gucci	http://www.gucci.com/
Hermès	http://www.hermes.com/
INCOTERMS	http://www.iccwbo.org/index_incoterms.asp
List free trade zones worldwide	http://www.kishtpc.com/Freetrade%20ZONES.htm
Logistics Management	http://www.manufacturing.net/lm/
New York Times	http://www.nytimes.com/
OSRAM	http://www.osram.com/
Radio frequency identification (RFID)	http://www.rfidjournal.com/
Rosenbauer	http://www.rosenbauer.com/
Sotheby's	http://www.sothebys.com/
UN Convention on International Sales (CIS)	http://www.uncitral.org/english/texts/sales/CISG.htm
Uniform Code Council	http://www.uc-council.org/
United Nations Electronic Data Interchange for Administration, Commerceand Transport	http://www.unece.org/trade/untdid/
UPS United States	http://www.ups.com/tracking/tracking.html
U.S. Carriage of Goods by Sea Act	http://www.cargolaw.com/cogsa.html

APPENDIX: INCOTERMS 2000

The incoterms in their latest version of the year 2000 contain 13 terms of delivery. Those terms refer only to sales contracts. They regulate the obligations of seller and buyer concerning the sharing of delivery costs and the transition of risk from the seller to the buyer. In addition, they determine diverse obligations of both parties, such as customs declarations or procurement of documents. The incoterms do *not* refer to the contract for carriage.

Out of the 13 terms, FAS, FOB, CFR, CIF, DES, and DEQ are specifically formulated terms for transportation by ship. EXW, FCA, CPT, CIP, DAF, DDU, and DDP are suitable for any transportation mode, including multi-modal transportation. Some of these incoterms 2000 are discussed in the following.

Ex works (EXW)

EXW signifies the term of delivery most advantageous to the seller. It puts all the obligations of shipment, including documentation for export, transit and import, onto the buyer. The buyer also bears the risk of merchandise damage or loss as soon as the goods leave the premises of the seller. However, when the seller and buyer agree on using EXW and the marketer – in an act of friendliness – helps the buyer to load the merchandise on the transportation vehicle, the marketer is fully responsible for any damage that might occur.

In considering which incoterm is best to choose from the list of 13 terms, the international marketer should be aware that EXW may increase the "perceived costs," including the psychological price the customer has to pay, to the point where they are greater than the "perceived benefits." In particular, internationally inexperienced customers located on other continents will not be ready to take over the burden of organizing the entire shipment on their own, even if they could rely on the help of international freight forwarders. A substantial number of business opportunities may be lost to competitors who choose terms of sale more convenient to customers.

Free carrier (FCA)

Using the term FCA, the contractual partners agree that the risk and the responsibility of the costs of shipment are to be covered by the buyer as soon as the merchandise has been handed over to the carrier at a specified location, at a specified point in time or during a given time period. The "carrier" is the organization that either ships the goods specified in the sales contract or organizes their shipment (that is, a freight forwarder) through a third party. The seller has to provide merchandise ready for export. That is, the seller has to provide all documents and has to take care of all customs formalities needed to pass the border of its country.

The costs of quality tests as well as volume checks needed for proper handing over of the merchandise to the carrier are to be paid by the seller who is also responsible for packaging the goods in an appropriate way for the mode of transportation indicated by the buyer.

Carriage (and insurance) paid to (CPT/CIP)

Under the term CPT, the seller has to pay all the costs of packaging, shipment, and documentation until the merchandise has reached the location at the time specified in the contract. The risk of merchandise damage or loss is transferred to the buyer when the goods are handed over to the first carrier. Again, the seller has to provide merchandise ready for export and has to inform the buyer about the handing over of the goods to the carrier. The seller has to cover the costs of product tests and packaging needed for appropriate shipment.

When the conditions characterizing CPT are enlarged to include the seller's obligation to insure the merchandise (at a minimum coverage level) against damage and loss during shipment from the time when the goods are handed over to the first carrier until the merchandise is taken over by the customer at the destination specified in the sales contract, the term used is carriage and insurance paid to (CIP).

Delivered at frontier (DAF)

Compared to CPT, the seller using the term DAF additionally has to bear the risk of damage and loss of the merchandise until its arrival at the border location specified in the contract. Because the term does not indicate *which* border, the contract partners are well advised to specify exactly the location from where onwards the risk is to be borne by the buyer. In the interest of the marketer, the location should be the last possible before arriving at the border. If the place indicated in the contract is located across the border, the seller has to take care of all the customs formalities and pay the import duties. Concerning packaging, the marketer should note that it has to provide the kind of packaging appropriate for transportation after the customer has taken over the merchandise, if the marketer was informed about the transportation mode to be used by the customer before signing the contract.

Delivered duty unpaid (DDU)

DDU covers the need of marketers to have a term available that leaves all costs and risks to the seller until the merchandise has been handed over at the location in the buyer's country at the point in time or during the period specified in the sales contract, but that leaves all paperwork needed for import and the import duties to be dealt with by the customer. The customer also has to bear all costs and risks resulting from its failure to clear the merchandise for import in time.

Practical use of this term has shown how important it is to specify the exact location where the merchandise is to be handed over. It is not sufficient, for example, to indicate only the name of a town, such as Birmingham. A precise address will help to avoid problems between the contractual partners. So does a precise indication in the sales contract of who will have to pay value-added tax.

Because of the generally open borders inside the EU, this term is particularly suited for European marketers wanting to maximize the level of service to their international customers located in EU member countries. If there are any special documents needed for importing the merchandise or any dues to pay, the buyer, who knows the specifics of its national legal environment much better than the seller, is responsible for taking care of them.

Delivered duty paid (DDP)

DDP puts the entire burden of the costs and risks involved in the international shipment of goods on the seller. The merchandise must be delivered to the buyer's premises as stipulated in the sales contract. DDP is generally viewed as the least viable term. It requires considerable experience in international shipment on the part of the marketer, even when an international freight forwarder is used. In most cases, therefore, some other term of sale will be used by the business partners, leaving part of the obligations to the buyer.

"Incoterms 2000" should be referred to specifically whenever the terms are used, together with a location; for example: FCA Kuala Lumpur Incoterms 2000.

INTERNATIONAL MARKET COMMUNICATION

15

INTERNATIONAL MARKETING SPOTLIGHT

Häagen-Dazs

British Grand Metropolitan launched Häagen-Dazs in Europe in 1989 despite an economic recession, a tired, stagnant category, and established competitors. Unilever, Nestlé, Mars, and a great number of small but strong local ice cream manufacturers – such as Schöller in Germany, Mövenpick in Switzerland, and Sagit in Italy – advertised extensively, had high levels of name recognition, and controlled the limited freezer space in European supermarkets. In countries such as the U.K., strong private labels held more than 40% of the take-home market. And in addition, Häagen-Dazs was launched at a price 30 to 40% higher than its closest competitors. How did it succeed?

The conventional way to introduce a new product such as Häagen-Dazs is to lead with a major advertising effort. But Grand Met chose a different route. It first opened several ice cream parlors in prominent, affluent locations with heavy foot traffic. The café-like stores, deliberately designed to contrast with the more traditional, sterile ice cream parlors common in the U.S., made a statement about Häagen-Dazs. Additional approaches were pursued to fuel word of mouth communications: branded freezers in food retail stores; sponsorship of cultural events; and a relatively low-budget print media campaign with the theme "The Ultimate Experience in Personal Pleasure."

Linking the brand to arts sponsorship was a particularly savvy move. At one event, the Opera Factory's production of *Don Giovanni* in London, the ice cream was even incorporated into the show. When the Don called for sorbet, he received a container of Häagen-Dazs. A windfall of free publicity began and spread among target consumers.

Grand Met's brand building efforts in Europe were extremely successful. Häagen-Dazs brand awareness in the U.K., for example, reached more than 50% within a few months. Today the brand commands one-third of the market for top-of-the-line ice cream even though it continues to charge a hefty premium over competitive brands.

Source: Adapted from Joachimsthaler, E. and D.A. Aaker (1997) "Building brands without mass media", *Harvard Business Review*, January–February, pp. 39–50

The Häagen-Dazs parlor in London's Covent Garden

© Jeremy Horner/CORBIS

The focal question of this chapter is: **How can international marketers develop a communication platform and implement integrated market communication activities that best help to build and sustain their intended global position?**

International market communication

Visibility to potential customers and important stakeholders is very important for marketing success all over the world. Wherever they live, people tend to react positively to companies and products they know about, even if they have never had personal contact with them. Mere visibility can signal reliability, superior quality, and leadership. In the U.S., for example, many consumers believe that nationally advertised products are better than only locally advertised competitors. When it comes to a buying decision, the products, brands, and service providers that come to the decision makers' minds first have the highest probability of being chosen. Therefore, communicating effectively with its potential and current customers in the served markets is an extremely important task for every international marketer.

Visibility and resulting awareness of customers and stakeholders are important, but not enough. They can be accompanied by negative emotions because of unpleasant experiences or negative word of mouth. Awareness can also be achieved by competitors. In most international markets the marketer will encounter competitors' products that have been on the market for a substantial amount of time and with which customers have extended experience. To make those customers first try the new offer and then change to the new way of satisfying their needs, the international marketer will need to communicate additional benefits of its products to the customers. Therefore, *attractive differentiation from competitive offers* is a second major task of international market communication.

Current and potential customers are not the only audience to be addressed by a company's market communication. In every international market the company serves, there are *other stakeholders* who have an interest in or are concerned by what the company is doing and how it does it. Suppliers, intermediaries, capital owners, legal regulators and administrators, media, unions, or neighbors of the company's production sites all have their specific expectations concerning the company's activities. Depending on the level of satisfaction of those expectations, the local stakeholders will either promote the company, let it work, or use their power to counteract the international marketer's plans and activities. Effective communication with those stakeholders is of crucial importance to their reactions.

The international marketer basically has the same communication tools at its disposal as its local counterparts. However:

- advertising
- public relations
- sales promotion
- sponsoring
- direct communication

need additional international coordination. This chapter, therefore, will first focus on the development of an international market communication policy (Figure 15.1). Based on the determination of the most important stakeholder groups in the company's served market(s) and general market communication objectives a communication platform can be developed. Together with communication guidelines such a platform provides coordination to the market communication activities – international and local – of all organizational units of an internationally operating firm. Coordination or even integration of market communication activities is a prerequisite to achieving the intended global strategic position of the company, the intended position of its business units and products in the stakeholders' minds. Coordination of communication will be an issue that runs through the entire chapter.

Based on the international market communication policy, communication activities aimed at important stakeholders may be planned and executed. The chapter will first discuss international advertising, before it focuses on public relations, sales promotion, sponsoring, and some frequently used tools in international direct market communication. The most important direct communication tool used in the establishment and maintenance of personal relationships with all kinds of company stakeholders, traditionally known as "personal selling," has already been discussed (Chapter 13).

Integrated market communication

The major objective of every marketer in its many different efforts to communicate with the various stakeholders of the company is to achieve the intended strategic position of the company, and the intended position of its business units and its products in the stakeholders' minds. To reach that general objective the marketer needs to counteract the tendency to information overload of its target audiences, ease their processes of recognition and learning, clearly differentiate the firm and its products from competitors, while holding the costs of market communication activities as low as possible.

Examples of internationally successful companies show that those goals can best be reached if all market communication activities are coordinated to achieve consistency. That is, any communicative efforts of the company should be consistent and supportive of its corporate, business unit, or product brand identities (see Strategy box 15.1).

For example, the essence of the Body Shop's brand identity is its profits-with-a-principle philosophy. This philosophy sends a clear message to employees and customers alike. The company opposes testing on animals, helps less industrially developed economies through its "Trade, Not Aid" mission, contributes to rainforest preservation efforts, is active in women's issues, and sets an example for recycling. It participates in "Save the Whales" rallies, advocates for other endangered species, and supports the development of alternative energy sources. These efforts are not ancillary to the Body Shop brand; they are expressions of the brand. And the vision carries right through the customers' in-store experience. A clerk wearing a Body Shop T-shirt bearing a social message greets customers entering a Body Shop. Displayed among the store's goods and tester samples are posters and colorful handouts (printed on recycled paper) that provide information about the products, about social causes the company supports, and about how customers can get involved in rallies, social cause advocacy groups, and the like.

FIGURE 15.1 *International market communication*

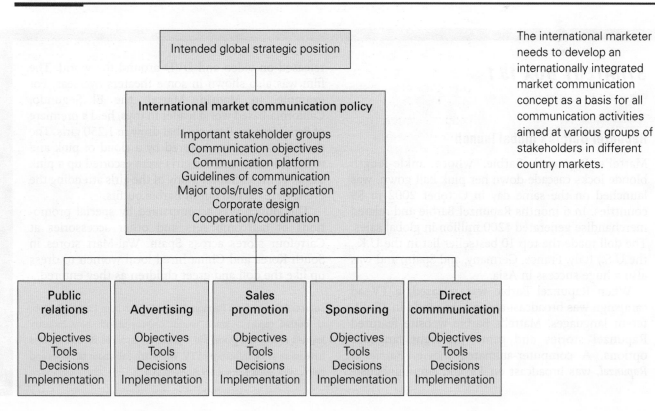

The international marketer needs to develop an internationally integrated market communication concept as a basis for all communication activities aimed at various groups of stakeholders in different country markets.

Market communication policy

To ensure consistency in all communicative activities of the firm, those activities need to be integrated. That is, based on the intended global strategic position, the international marketer has to develop an international market communication policy.

Important stakeholder groups

Such a communication policy development process starts with the determination of the firm's most important stakeholder groups in the product and country markets served. Communication managers need to know:

- what stakeholders they have to address
- how much attention they should pay to which stakeholder group
- how those stakeholders are interrelated.

Communication objectives

For each of the stakeholder groups, general communication objectives have to be fixed. The communication objectives answer the question of what the company needs to achieve by communicating with each of the stakeholder groups in order to reach the intended position in their minds.

For example, what should customers, intermediaries, suppliers, media and administrators perceive in order for the company to be perceived as the quality leader in its market?

International communication platform

The following development of an international communication platform is the centerpiece of an integrated communication policy. The communication platform defines the *central message to be communicated* to all stakeholders of the firm. For example, Avis, the U.S.-based international rental car company, has successfully

---

STRATEGY BOX 15.1

Rapunzel Barbie's global launch

Mattel's Rapunzel Barbie, whose ankle-length blonde locks cascade down her pink ball gown, was launched on the same day in October 2002 in 59 countries. In 6 months Rapunzel Barbie and related merchandise generated $200 million in global sales. The doll made the top 10 bestseller list in the U.K., the U.S., Italy, France, Germany, and Spain, and was also a huge success in Asia.

When Rapunzel Barbie was released, a TV ad campaign was broadcast around the world in 35 different languages. Mattel's Barbie website featured Rapunzel stories and games in eight language options. A computer-animated movie, *Barbie as Rapunzel*, was broadcast on TV and simultaneously released on video and DVD around the world. The film was also shown in some theaters overseas. For example, in Madrid, Mattel, the El Segundo, California-based world leader in toys, held a premiere of *Barbie Princess Rapunzel* that drew in 1,250 girls. The theater was nearly obscured by a cloud of pink and white balloons, and the girls were escorted up a pink carpet to the entrance. Many of the girls attending the event were decked out in Barbie outfits.

The launch was accompanied by special promotions of haircomb sets and other accessories at Carrefour stores across Spain. Wal-Mart stores in South Korea and China hired local women to dress up like the doll and greet children as they entered.

Source: Adapted from Bannon, L. and C. Vitzthum (2003) "A global journal report – small world: one-toy-fits-all: how industry learned to love the global kid – goodbye, Japanese Barbie, blondes have more sales; influence of TV, Wal-Mart – all about fantasies and hair", *Wall Street Journal*, 29 April, p. A.1

chosen the central message "We try harder," and EXXON uses the symbol of a tiger to visually represent its central message to the stakeholders.

This central message needs to be refined into consistent *core messages* for each stakeholder group. For example, "We try harder" may translate into the promise of complete international service for customers and excellent personal relations with media.

To coordinate the transfer of the core messages into a consistent choice of communication tools, the communication platform needs to specify the *major tools* the marketer wants to be applied in its international market communication. The choice will depend on the contribution each communication tool can make to reaching the stated objectives and how those tools can be used in a way that mutually increases the effects of others. For example, when Paris-based Cartier International, the marketer of prestigious jewelry, watches, and accessories, decides to sponsor an international artist, this artist could also be used in testimonial advertisements, and press and other media reports about the artist and his or her sponsored shows could be launched.

Guidelines of communication

In addition, to ensure consistency of the firm's international communication activities, a guideline concerning *corporate design* has to be developed. This guideline determines the logo, sign, color(s), music, size and type of writing, layout of printed matter or even lighting to be used internationally. The example of the Louis Vuitton North America headquarters in New York City shows that even a company's buildings can contribute to the communication of corporate identity. The building, planned by Christian de Portzamparc who won the Pritzker prize (the "Nobel Prize of architecture") in 1994, expresses the extravagance of the firm, by using special materials, different fluorescent front lighting, and a façade that looks entirely different from the neighboring buildings.

Finally, the international marketer has to specify some *rules of cooperation and coordination* concerning the implementation of market communication decisions. Those rules should help to:

The Louis Vuitton building in New York
Source: www.wirednewyork.com/louis_vuitton.htm

- overcome functional differences as well as the creative egoism of organizational subunits at different hierarchical levels
- prevent the dominance of short-term sales goals
- state to what extent and in what role external service providers (such as advertising agencies) are to be involved in the planning and execution of the communication activities.

Coordination of market communication

Not every international marketer needs a high level of coordination of its market communication. The appropriate level of coordination depends on how important an internationally standardized identity is to the success of a company and its products. Total products with widespread international presence that attract highly mobile customers, such as Hilton, need the highest degree of coordination of market communication among country markets to achieve and sustain the intended position in their customers' and other important stakeholders' minds. Coca-Cola changed its highly standardized approach when it was found to be rather insensitive to local markets. In 2000 the company decided to permit local teams to develop advertising to local consumers. Some brands are globally present, such as Windows or Caterpillar, but mainly attract users that are hardly interested in the companies' market communication in other markets. They do not need a high level of international coordination of communication activities.

Some companies operate internationally but market purely local products that do not have any external signs in common, such as the brand name, the logo or the package. Such products do not need any coordination of their communication activities. Potential coordination needs only arise from the goal of achieving the intended general position of the firm in the minds of customers and other important stakeholders.

But even market communication for an entirely localized product may profit from some central coordination. When it comes to cross-market learning, for example, local managers may have an advantage over competitors if they are informed about successful communication activities in other local markets. The level of coordination is restricted to fast and targeted transfer of information.

In any case, when it comes to the implementation of specific local communication activities, local managers or service providers will have to take responsibility. For any of the major communication tools discussed in the following section, therefore, the international marketer will have to decide how they should best be implemented. As a general rule, contradictory company and product communication as well as local communication activities that upset other local activities in neighboring country markets should be avoided; and the transfer of effective campaign designs to other markets should be encouraged.

Advertising

Advertising is the paid communication of company messages through impersonal media. Like local marketers, an internationally operating firm uses advertising mainly to:

- stimulate potential customers' interest in its products
- make those products reach an intended position in the (potential) customers' minds
- continually remind the customers of the benefits to be gained by buying and using the product
- prepare the ground for positive buying decisions by the customers.

Basically, an international marketer has to take the same kinds of decision concerning its advertising activities as local competitors. An *advertising policy* must be developed, *advertising message and media* chosen, and the message implemented in *visual and/or verbal advertising copy*.

When developing an international advertising campaign, the marketer, in addition, has to decide those parts of the campaign to *standardize* across country markets and those parts to *adapt locally*.

Besides influences from cultural differences, the availability of media in the targeted country markets and legal restrictions on advertising in those markets need to be considered. The international marketer also has to decide how much of the advertising planning and execution should be done in-house, rather than in cooperation with or entirely outsourced to one or more advertising agencies. Finally, the implementation of the planned advertising activities across all parts of the internationally operating company needs to be organized.

Standardization vs adaptation

When deliberating over the level of standardization of its international advertising campaigns, a marketer should not only look at the potential cost savings inherent in a high degree of standardization. The intended position of the product to be advertised in the target customers' minds and the psychological processes leading to that positioning must have a more prominent influence on the decision. Standardization may only concern the *content of the advertising message*, leaving advertising copy and media choice to local decision makers. But it may also concern *the media used* as well as *the advertising copy*.

Levels of standardization

Depending on a product's intended position in the customers' minds and the target audience, the optimal level of standardization may range from complete standardization to complete localization. For example, Red Bull uses an entirely standardized campaign worldwide to advertise its energizing drink (Figure 15.2). Television as the medium and the ads – comics drawings and the tagline, "Red Bull gives you wiiings" – are the same all across the served country markets. Only the language used in the soundtrack of the spot is adapted to the countries where the spot is aired. Such a very high degree of standardization is possible because

FIGURE 15.2 *Blueprint of a Red Bull TV commercial*

Red Bull uses the same TV commercials worldwide. Only the text is translated into the local language: Red Bull gives you wiiings!!!

Red Bull verleiht Flüüügel.

the target audience is rather young (and open to international, less local culture-specific appeals) and the positioning is independent of local preferences.

When Guerlain, a subsidiary of the French luxury products group LVMH, launched its perfume "Champs-Elysées," in an endeavor to increase the company's international visibility it used almost as standardized an advertising approach. In a TV spot Sophie Marceau, a French movie star who has a strong attraction for Asian consumers, particularly Japanese, was shown on the globally known Parisian boulevard bearing the product's name. In this case the target group was not so young as to accept culturally "foreign" appeals easily, but the message cues used were simple to interpret and attractive enough to be voluntarily accepted by the target audience.

At the other extreme, Nestlé used an entirely adapted advertising approach when introducing Nescafé to Thailand. Because selling a hot beverage in the tropics seemed to be the marketing equivalent of selling snow to Eskimos, the local managers decided to give up the traditional western taste, aroma, and stimulation message for advertising coffee on TV. Instead, the new ads played on the increasing urban stress, showing a man kicking a taxi door in frustration. The campaign promoted coffee as a way to relax from the pressures of the traffic, the office, and even romance. Within Nestlé, the switch caused a ruckus. The zone manager for Asia stalked out of a screening of the first TV ad of the campaign. But the local group still had authority for Thailand and held firm. Coffee sales in Thailand jumped from $25 million in the first year to $100 million 6 years later, when Nescafé held 80% of the market. An adaptation of the advertising message and copy was needed in this case, because the target audience as well as the intended meaning of the product to those customers was different compared to other parts of the world. The medium could be kept similar because it was available in the country market and reached the targeted audience.

In most cases the level of advertising standardization lies in between the two extremes. When the visual used in an ad transfers similar and acceptable meanings to the target audiences in the served markets, and the media is appropriate in all those markets, only the text of the advertisement may need some adaptation. For example, Wonderbra ads all over Europe used the same series of visuals, but adapted taglines. In the U.K., for example, it read: "Look me in the eyes and tell me that you love me," whereas in France it was: "Regardez-moi dans les yeux … j'ai dit les yeux" (Look into my eyes … I said, into my eyes).

Adaptations of advertising copy

Concerning the psychological processes involved in advertising communication, the international marketer must be aware that a communicator cannot directly transmit any message to its target audience. The communicator can only present informational cues selected in a way that will, hopefully, evoke the intended information in the minds of its target audience. The information itself is produced in the recipients' minds through interpretation of (selectively) received cues. What message the members of the target audience receive by interpreting the cues depends on the cognitions and affects activated by the communicator. What cognitions are evoked depends on the situation as well as the recipients' individual frames of reference that have developed through socialization and individual experience. Effective communication requires that the communicator and the communicants *share some common set of meanings concerning the communication object* or at least that the communicator has enough knowledge about *the cognitive structures of its target audience* as well as *the emotional impact of selected cues on that target audience* to be able to tailor its informational cues specifically (see Figure 15.3). If a shared set of meanings does not exist or cannot be established, the communicator will not be able to transmit its message to the target audience.

People who have been raised in the same cultural environment tend to have at least some common frame of reference. In international marketing the situation is complicated by the fact that very often communicator and recipients have different cultural frames of reference. Because their interpretation is related to personal experiences and socialization, the meanings evoked by pictures are as culture specific as the meanings evoked by words. For example, DIM had great success when advertising their tights brand Diam in France showing a female torero encircled by male minotaurs. French consumers – females and males alike – liked the perceived sexy touch of the message. But in Spain, the firm had to replace the ad in order not to offend Spanish machismo. Therefore, the advertiser must find objects, persons, and contexts by which the intended meanings may be evoked in the target customers' minds.

When the same meaning is to be evoked in the minds of customers from different cultural backgrounds, an adaptation in visuals and text may be needed. For example, Reims-based Moët & Chandon wanted to make their target customers perceive their product as a piece of art comparable to a garment of a famous fashion house, in order to differentiate their champagne from a number of less prestigious brands also produced in the region of France called Champagne. For that purpose the company used print ads in the U.K. that compared their product with a classical garment. In France they also chose print ads but with a baroque garment for comparison, and in Italy they compared their product with a sensuous garment worn by a *signora* (lady).

An international marketer who wants to find out if the same visual and text cues may be used across all or a group of targeted country markets may want to check the correspondence of the meanings of those cues to the target audiences in the served markets. Toolbox 15.1 describes a method serving that purpose.

If the cognitions evoked by an ad in the target audiences across country markets converge satisfactorily, a standardized use of the advertisement is feasible. If not, adaptations in text and/or visuals need to be made (see Culture box 15.1).

Media

The possibility of implementing a more or less standardized advertising copy across country markets also depends on the availability and cost of adequate local media.

Media availability may be restricted in international markets. Whereas in some industrially less developed countries advertising in print media or television is limited to a very small number of available media, in higher industrially

FIGURE 15.3 *Frames of reference influencing international communication effectiveness*

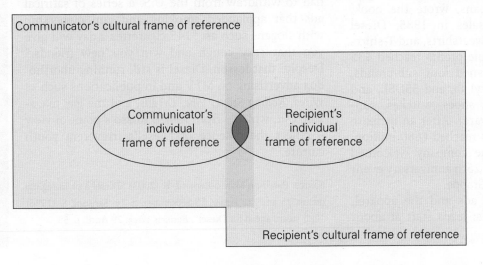

The communicator and the recipient both have their individual frames of reference for the interpretation of informational cues. In international communication those individual frames of reference additionally are embedded in different cultural frames of reference. Effective communication can only occur if there are at least some common meanings concerning the communication object.

developed areas of the world legal restrictions (discussed in Chapter 4), may reduce the number of media available to the marketer. In most countries of the EU, for example, there are limitations on the number and length of television commercials that may be broadcast on public television channels. On these

---

TOOLBOX 15.1   Assessing potential for cue standardization

Association tests can help the international marketer determine the cognitions activated by a word or a picture in an advertisement. Interviewees from the various country markets to be served are invited to spontaneously utter all thoughts that are evoked by a verbal or visual stimulus during a short time span (usually one minute). The aggregation of association paths of individuals from each culture results in culture-specific distributions of associations. The cross-cultural overlap of those distributions can be used as an indicator for the standardization potential of the tested stimulus.

The overlap of culture-specific distributions can be determined by measuring their mutual related-

ness, that is, a measure of convergence among the audiences' cognitive structures. A coefficient of overlap between two distributions of associations can be calculated by summing up the lower frequencies of associations occurring in both distributions and dividing that sum by the total frequency of all associations in both distributions.

Inside a single culture, the meaning of a word or a visual stimulus should be rather homogeneous. Therefore, the intra-cultural split-half overlaps of the respective distributions of associations can be used as a benchmark for a sufficient size of the cross-cultural coefficient.

CULTURE BOX 15.1

Full steam ahead for Diesel

Sumo wrestlers kissing. A row of chimpanzees giving the fascist salute, inflatable naked dolls at a board meeting with a hugely obese CEO. Parents advised that "teaching kids to kill helps them deal directly with reality." When it comes to outrageous advertising, Italy's Renzo Rosso, the owner and CEO of Bassano del Grappa-based Diesel, Europe's hottest marketer of blue jeans, wrote the book. From just $9 million in sales in 1985, Diesel increased its sales of jeans, sweatshirts, and T-shirts to $350 million in 1995, while profits reached $35 million. In 2002, Diesel owned four sub-brands, Diesel, Diesel Kids, DieselStyLab, and 55DSL, and had six licenses (cosmetics, shoes, watches, sunglasses, luggage, and paperware). After an increase of 20% in the last year, sales reached €680 million. And in September 2003 the company welcomed close to 30,000 people to the 25th anniversary event of the brand in Bassano del Grappa.

European teens love the ads and the apparel, which commands high prices: Jeans start at about

$90. Renzo Rosso has widened distribution by opening directly owned Diesel stores. In March 1996, the first Diesel megastore in the U.S., a cavernous two-story showcase replete with a coffee bar and full-time DJ, was inaugurated on New York's Lexington Avenue. The grand opening included mini-skirted models dancing in the windows and an all-night party for 2,000 people.

Diesel's ad tactics tend to be a problem in the U.S., however. Its prankish campaigns have not always had the desired effect among politically correct or puritanical Americans. In 1993, the company had to withdraw from the U.S. a series of satirical ads that applauded smoking and gun ownership with slogans such as: "145 cigarettes a day will give you that sexy cough and win you new friends." Despite that lesson, Diesel is still running unorthodox advertising on MTV and in publications such as *Wired*, *Rolling Stone*, *Vibe*, *Details*, and the gay magazine *Out*, which – from Renzo Rosso's point of view – reflect the essence of Diesel's irreverent youth culture.

Source: Based on Martin-Bernard, F. (2003) "Diesel à plein régime depuis 25 ans", *Le Figaro*, 15 September, p. 16; Sansoni, S. (1996) "Full steam ahead for Diesel", *Business Week*, 29 April, p. 58

channels commercials are normally broadcast in blocks between shows, not within the shows themselves. Only the development of private channels and satellite TV has changed that situation. In Australia only ads that have been produced in Australia or with Australian actors are accepted for airing on broadcast media. In South Africa television time must be purchased 1 year in advance.

Faced with the lack of media traditionally used in their home markets, international advertisers must try other options such as advertising:

- in cinemas
- on public transportation devices
- on trucks and cabs
- on billboards.

Fuji Photo Film of Japan, for example, has replaced the blood-red billboards that once trumpeted the thoughts of Chairman Mao high above Shanghai's famous waterfront, the Bund, by its green logo. In Europe, bus tickets, supermarket till rolls, and phone cards are used to advertise. Polygram Records has promoted new albums on the back of bus tickets in the U.K. Joop! Jeans was one of the more visible companies using advertisements on and in taxi cabs in the EU. In Istanbul, Turkey, public buses are covered completely by advertisements. Pepsi, MasterCard, and M&M/Mars, for example, have found this to be a very cost-effective way of reaching large audiences; and Calvin Klein Cosmetics, as a final example, has used buses, bus shelters, billboards, trams in Italy, and the metro in Paris to launch its fragrance CK: ONE.

Sometimes the problem is too many media choices rather than too few. A country-wide advertising campaign using newspapers in India, for example, would require the purchase of space in about 100 major papers. Because only the relatively well educated buy newspapers in India, the marketer would not only face considerable problems of scheduling and possible overlap, but could still miss an important portion of the target audience.

Besides the lack of traditionally used media, another difficulty encountered in some country markets is the *inability to generate sufficient frequency* of advertising contacts. Frequency is, of course, important in making potential customers aware of the availability of the product, and what the product might do for them. Media in international markets vary considerably in their ability to contact the target audiences as often as the international marketer would like. Legal restrictions on buying advertising time or space, or on the total time and space which may be allocated to advertising, limit the number of times an advertiser may use specific media. However, compared to highly industrialized countries where customers are bombarded by hundreds of advertisements every day, audiences in other markets may not need such high frequency rates to still have effective advertising contacts. There, owing to the relatively low number of ads, the lower frequency might be at least partially offset by the increased likelihood that customers pay more attention to the ads.

Problems of frequency and reach may be overcome in markets where the targeted audiences have access to and use cable media. For example, when media and telecommunications industries were deregulated in Latin American countries, the market started growing very rapidly. Because of the economic crisis that hit in the second half of the 1990s, however, that development came to a halt. Only in 2002 did the Latin American cable market start to grow again. Table 15.1 shows the rather limited and very much concentrated (Argentina, Brazil, Mexico) multi-channel penetration in Latin America at that time.

The number and availability of international media for advertising purposes has grown significantly. MTV, for example, reaches young target groups in more than 70 countries. CNN, as another example, reaches information-conscious customers in all parts of the world. It has regionalized some of its news to become even more internationally attractive. For target audiences of industrial buyers and more highly educated consumers, newspapers and magazines providing international editions may be a potential choice. The *Wall Street Journal* and the *Financial Times*, for example, publish American, Asian, and European editions; so do U.S.-based magazines like *Newsweek*, *Reader's Digest*, and the German *Wirtschaftswoche*.

If all the expected advertising media are available in a country, the international marketer must evaluate the cost/benefit ratio of advertising compared to other elements of the promotional mix. If costs are high compared to the overall market communication budget, then even if advertising would be the first tool to use from the company's market communication policy point of view, it may not be the best choice compared to other options.

International advertising implementation

The success of an international advertising campaign depends on more than the firm's ability to evoke the intended meanings in its customers' minds by choosing the right advertising copy and the appropriate media in accordance with the general market communication objectives of the firm; it also depends on the company's ability to properly organize the production and international insertion process of its advertisements. For that purpose the international marketer needs to:

- establish an internal group of qualified people willing to cooperate internationally
- manage its contacts with external service providers such as advertising agencies.

TABLE 15.1 *Multi-channel penetration in Latin America*

Country	Operator	Subscribers in million
Pan-regional	DirecTV Latin America	1.640
Pan-regional	Sky Latin America	1.570
Argentina	Cablevision	1.400
	Supercanal	0.420
	Teledigital	0.165
Argentina/Paraguay/Uruguay	Multicanal	1.290
Brazil	Net Servicos	1.420
	TVA	0.320
	Canbras	0.176
Chile	VTR	0.446
	Metropolis-Intercom	0.272
Colombia	Cablecentro	0.110
Mexico	Cablevision	0.442
	Megacable	0.430
	Multivision	0.330
	Cablemas	0.300
Peru	Cablemagico	0.340
Venezuela	Intercable	0.340
	Cabletel	0.135
	Supercable	0.120

Latin America's multi-channel penetration has suffered from the effects of economic crisis. Compared to penetration rates in the northern part of the continent, subscriber figures are still small. But growth has been picking up in recent years.

Source: Based on Kagan World Media, March 2002 estimates, www.cablelabs.com/news/newsletter/SPECS/MarApr–2003/story5.html

In-house responsibilities

Many firms operating on an international level feel the necessity to closely coordinate their international advertising activities. Some are establishing the position of worldwide media director to coordinate international activities and to help solve problems like finding sufficient funds for regional buys that cut across many countries' budgets.

When U.S.-based Whirlpool acquired the household appliances business of Philips, they found out that every country subsidiary or sales office had its own advertising agencies and did its own advertising development around individual markets. Whirlpool, in contrast, decided to be the first in the industry to develop a common advertising campaign across Europe. It encountered a lot of initial resistance from the markets, each claiming to be different and needing local adaptation. To overcome these problems Whirlpool established an "International Creative Council," which had members of the marketing or advertising people from the key European markets. That council worked directly with Publicis, the firm's advertising agency. The team members of the agency were also selected from their European network to represent the different country markets. By gathering key people and having experts from local markets involved, the development of the advertising campaign went smoothly and the campaign received immediate approval in all local units of the company.

Advertising agencies

Some international marketers consolidate their company's entire advertising account at one globally operating advertising agency. The coordination requirements of agency clients that operate in increasingly global industries have led major advertising agencies to strengthen their international services. For example, London-based Saatchi & Saatchi has 138 offices in 82 countries. Young & Rubicam has global managing directors and their teams who provide a corporate global perspective for each campaign. The managing director is responsible for all communications with the client. Some globally active agencies have either acquired local agencies (with sometimes questionable success) or established international networks of cooperating partners. London-based WPP Group is currently one of the world's largest networks, consisting of a variety of agencies including Grey Global, Ogilvy & Mather Worldwide, J. Walter Thompson, Red Cell/Batey Ads, Young & Rubicam, and Scall, McCabe & Sloves, each of which also has their own set of subsidiaries. Table 15.2 lists the biggest groups of advertising agencies in the world.

Japan's advertising industry is dominated by two companies: Dentsu and Hakuhodo. They control most domestic billings and growing segments of the world's billings. Dentsu, which alone controls more than 20% of the domestic advertising market, tends to buy blocks of space on TV channels and sell them to advertisers. The company covers every aspect of a client's needs with a "total communications solution" package. Dentsu employs 34,000 people in Japan spread between dozens of national offices and 25 subsidiaries, which include film and video companies, internet-related companies, theme parks and resort companies, real estate, property management, and insurance. Because overseas revenues accounted for just a very small percentage of Dentsu's total turnover, the company has been aggressive in forming capital alliances with global advertising giants. In 2002, for example, Dentsu obtained a 15% stake in France's Publicis Groupe SA.

Smaller Hakuhodo is allied with giant U.S. advertising groups like Interpublic Group and Omnicom Group Inc.. They acquired independent German and U.S. agencies to expand their network in western countries. Hakuhodo employs about 3,500 people in 15 domestic branches and 17 more offices around the world. They have brought Hakuhodo's proprietary online greeting card with sweepstakes technology to the U.S. through a subsidiary called SharedGreetings Inc.

Agency–client relationships

Agency–client relationships vary considerably in different country markets. In many markets relationships with agencies are viewed as long-term personal ties, not simply as contracts that may be ended whenever the client or the agency is displeased. In the U.S. and Europe, it has been common practice to change agencies every few years. Some managers argue that such changes keep the level of creativity of their companies' advertising campaigns high.

But McDonald's, for example, found that changing agencies in Brazil is not only difficult, it can also be harmful to the company's image. When the company switched to a new agency, its former agency generated a great deal of negative publicity, calling McDonald's "paramilitary" and claiming that it had lost money because of the company's actions. In Japan, relationships once formed between a client and its agency are usually long term. After years of working together, the agency becomes almost an integral part of the client company itself. With increasing single sourcing, that is, the concentration of the whole international advertising account in the hands of one single agency, and as a consequence of an increasing understanding that successful market communication needs an integration of all communication tools applied, the Japanese approach to building and maintaining long-term relationships with full service agencies as business partners has growing appeal for many international marketers.

Stakeholder relations

Stakeholder relations are the planned building and maintenance of relations between a company and its stakeholders with the objective of establishing a positively valued position of the company in those stakeholders' perceptions. A stakeholder relations manager designs and executes programs that help earn and maintain stakeholders' understanding and acceptance of the company and its activities. Ethics box 15.1 describes how an internationally operating firm can generate enormous value for a number of its stakeholders and simultaneously can strengthen its competitive position. The ability to influence influential stakeholders is very important in international marketing. The international marketer may define a general goal for its stakeholder relations, such as Coca-Cola's promise that "everyone who is touched by the business of Coca-Cola will

TABLE 15.2 *World's leading advertising agency groups*

The list shows the top advertising groups of the world ranked according to their gross earnings worldwide as well as their total number of client assignments in 2003.

Rank	Advertising group	Headquarters	Worldwide gross income 2003 in billion €	Total number of client assignments 2003
1	Omnicom Group	New York	7.0	1,333
2	WPP Group	London	5.5	2,711
3	Interpublic Group	New York	4.8	2,094
4	Publicis Group	Paris	3.6	1,886
5	Dentsu	Tokyo	2.0	n.a.

Source: Based on *Advertising Age's Global Marketing* 2003 edition, 10 November, p. 16; "Der neue Markenriese in der Werbewelt", *Der Standard*, 24 September, 2004, p. 31

benefit." But depending on the stakeholder group to be addressed, specific objectives will be defined and different stakeholder relations tools applied.

Investor relations

Investor relations activities have the objective of establishing and maintaining the trust of (potential) investors in the way the company is led by its management. The more favorably the financial community views the company, the lower the interest rate the company may be charged when it borrows money to finance its international expansion, and the higher its stocks may be valued. This may be one of the reasons why top management of the giant United Parcel Service of America Inc. (UPS) headquartered in Atlanta, Georgia, was worried that the industry and freight customers around the world regarded the company as a wallflower – while its flashy rival, Federal Express Corp., acted like the belle of the ball. UPS invested billions of dollars to build distribution systems in Europe and Asia where it did not have the kind of corporate identity enjoyed at home. But even in its home market UPS was no more than Big Brown to most customers. To remain competitive in an increasingly global business with very thin margins, the company needed recognition as the kind of dynamic, technologically nimble concern that customers demand and the Wall Street financing required to satisfy them. As one of the company's leading managers put it, however, "until a few years ago, the requirements for being a public-relations person at UPS were how many ways you could say, 'No comment'." These days, UPS is talking. The company

ETHICS BOX 15.1

Cisco Networking Academy

Cisco, the U.S.-based leading producer of networking equipment and routers used to connect computers to the internet, grew rapidly in the last decade of 20th century. But as internet use expanded, customers around the world encountered a chronic shortage of qualified network administrators, which became a severe limiting factor in Cisco's continued growth. Following some private initiatives in schools close to the company's headquarters, company executives began to realize that they could develop a web-based distance-learning curriculum to train and certify students in network administration. The Networking Academy was born.

At the suggestion of the U.S. Department of Education, the company began to target schools located in areas designated by the federal government as among the most economically challenged in the country. Later on, Cisco worked with the United Nations to expand the effort to economically developing countries, where job opportunities are particularly scarce and networking skills rather limited. Cisco has also organized a global database of employment opportunities for academy graduates, creating an efficient job market that benefits the graduates and the regions in which they live, but also Cisco and its IT partners.

Other companies, such as Sun Microsystems, Hewlett-Packard, Adobe Systems, and Panduit, supplemented Cisco's contributions by donating or discounting products and services of their own, such as internet access, computer hardware and software, courses in programming, web design, and cabling.

Since its creation in the late 1990s the program has grown to more than 10,000 academies in about 150 countries. Cisco estimates that half of the academy graduates have found jobs in the IT industry. The company has generated justified pride and enthusiasm among company employees, goodwill among its partners, and loyalty among academy graduates. But as the leading provider of routers, Cisco stands to substantially benefit from its initiative: Through actively engaging others, Cisco does not bear the full cost of the program. And by increasing the skills of its customers the company has strengthened the bases of its served market and significantly enlarged its potential.

Source: Adapted from Porter, M.E. and M.R. Kramer (2002) "The competitive advantage of corporate philanthropy", *Harvard Business Review*, December, pp. 57–68

releases quarterly earnings over a public business wire and opened up to journalists in an effort to build public profile.

The tools most often used in international investor relations are

- financial reports
- documentation concerning the company's strategy, product innovation, and market achievements
- site visits
- "roadshows" for financial analysts as well as major investors.
- websites, which, with the global spread of the internet, have gained a prominent position in investor relations.

Government relations

A company's government relations activities should help to create and maintain a local regulatory and administrative environment that helps the firm to do business. The best basis for satisfactory relationships with local governments and administrations is to *fulfill their rules and regulations*. In addition, *continual information on the latest technological standards* as well as some technology transfer, investments in local infrastructure, and donations or endowments may help to ease market entry as well as ongoing business. Microsoft, for example, learned that being a "good citizen" can be very helpful for developing business in China. When it opened its Beijing office in 1992, the company planned to use its Taiwan operations to supply a Mandarin-language version of Windows designed especially for the mainland's simplified characters. But the Electronics Industry Ministry resented the fact that Microsoft was relying on the mainland's rival for such sophisticated work. Bill Gates got a frosty reception in Beijing when he personally started the launch of P-Win, the Chinese version of Windows, in 1994. The Chinese electronics industry threatened to ban Chinese Windows, and President Jiang Zemin personally admonished Gates, suggesting he spend more time in China and "learn something from 5,000 years of Chinese history." In the meantime, Bill Gates not only took an extended vacation in China, but Microsoft has set up training institutes at the Chinese Academy of Social Sciences, three universities, and more than 70 centers. It employs full-time Chinese instructors, trained in the U.S., who teach computer architecture, networking and client–server applications. In addition, the company has become affiliated with Chinese researchers to develop technology in such areas as interactive television and Chinese handwriting and speech recognition. Windows is now officially "endorsed" by the government.

Not unlike many other relations, personal relationships built on some kind of trust may play a major role in government relations. Large internationally operating firms, therefore, hire lobbyists in the capitals of the most industrially developed countries or regions of the world such as Washington, D.C., Tokyo or Brussels, in order to help ensure favorable treatment in national or trade organization laws. In less democratically developed countries, members of the ruling establishment are paid for their roles as "intermediaries" in making contacts or easing the negotiation of sales contracts.

Media relations

Relations with print or electronic mass media, trade journals, and magazines have the objective of keeping journalists directly informed about developments inside and "around" the company and about its products, and by that means to indirectly inform members of the "general public" who may be interested in that information but cannot be directly reached by the company.

Media relations are mainly cultivated by:

- personal contacts
- press releases
- press conferences
- press events.

Such relations generate "free" exposure in the print and broadcast media, because the marketer does not pay for the media time or space. But obtaining the type of publicity expected requires careful preparation by staff or an outside agency, and that does cost money. When entering a country market for the first time, or when introducing a significantly different product into a market, a company may be able to generate considerable publicity. When the activity is less "newsworthy," it is up to the media relations manager to make it interesting for the media.

Newsworthiness

When Wolford, the Austrian tights manufacturer, introduced its new "Support and Forming Range," ladies' tights and bodices that help women to have slimmer thighs and present their body more attractively, they saved at least an estimated $500,000 of advertising budget by hiring the late Helmuth Newton, one of the most well-known photo artists in the world, to shoot 10 pictures of models wearing those products. The pictures were exclusively (for about 12 days) sent to one major medium per country in western Europe, Hong Kong, Japan, and the U.S., together with a story of how those pictures were taken. The media reported cost free on two to six pages showing the pictures with the new products and the name of Wolford. This way, 8.4 million readers all over the world were exposed to the information. The pictures (including all rights for the entire world for 5 years) had cost the company no more than about $300,000. At the end of the period, exclusive information and pictures were given to other media that were highly interested, and the same pictures were used for packages and displays.

Other ways to make company or product information "newsworthy" include "wrapping" them into special events for selected journalists or for a specifically defined group of target customers. For example, haute couture presentations employing world-famous models are regularly arranged by fashion houses such as French Christian Dior, Italian Ferrucio Ferragamo, or U.S. Donna Karan. Despite their regularity they are spectacular enough to attract journalists from all important fashion media as well as from television channels that report the shows globally. This publicity is very important for the marketers because their main sales do not come from haute couture. All fashion houses have prêt à porter product lines which are sold to the more affluent consumers all over the world, as well as perfume, accessories and other product lines which they sell either themselves or through licensing. The highly emotional cues produced by the media reports about the haute couture presentations strongly influence the meaning of the brands to consumers.

Lack of control

A problem with publicity is that because it is "free," the international marketer loses some control over what is said about the company or product, how it is said, and where it is said. Thus, instead of having the ability to affect reach and frequency directly, a company is at the mercy of the media in terms of how much exposure it receives. Additionally, the media may edit the material in a manner that is not necessarily favorable towards the marketer or its products – 1995, for example, is a year that is burned into the memories of executives at Royal/Dutch Shell Group based in Rotterdam and London. A bad slip in earnings was at least partly provoked by a media campaign in the spring that led to consumer boycotts of the firm's European retail outlets and forced Shell to back down on plans to dump its defunct Brent Spar drilling rig in the North Sea. In the autumn, Shell again got in the line of fire from activists backed by the media who wanted the company to get out of Nigeria following the execution of nine dissidents after what neutral observers called a sham trial. Shell found it difficult to claim the moral high ground in Nigeria. The company had to admit causing some environmental damage, and it had to concede that oil money rarely makes it back to needy communities. But because Nigeria accounted for about 14% of Shell's crude oil production and some $130 million in operating earnings, Shell officials in major capitals around the world used all their personal contacts to dissuade ministers from organizing an oil boycott. Shell also met with stock analysts, assuring them that the Nigerian operation's future was secure.

Crisis management plan

A crisis management plan is essential for successfully dealing with crises provoked by events that the company may consider outside its control. Such a public relations plan should be in place and understood by all personnel concerned, before the crisis hits. For example, *critical media* who will share the public's reaction to the disaster must have been pre-identified. The company will preferably have established good working relationships with these media in advance. Second, *key stakeholder groups* will have been listed. There too, campaigns to regain trust and positive image will need to be undertaken. For example, in the wake of the bovine spongiform encephalitis (BSE) crisis, the supply of meat to the fast-food sector has been shrouded in suspicion. McDonald's France committed itself to a high-quality, safe food policy and strongly asserted its partnership with French agriculture. Following the spectacular dismantling of a McDonald's restaurant in Millau in 2000 by activists of the Small Farmers' Union, McDonald's decided to exhibit at the 2001 Salon de l'Agriculture, the big annual agriculture fair in Paris.

Speed of reaction is also critical. All this depends, of course, on a contingency plan that is fully developed, and shared.

Customer relations

The role of customer relations is to prepare the ground for other communication tools by creating a generally positive perception of the company and its products. In an environment of credibility and trust, advertising messages have a greater chance of being effective and sales personnel have a greater chance of being listened to.

For example, Pfizer, the pharmaceutical giant based in the U.S., has used its treatment for the prevention of trachoma, the major cause of preventable blindness in less economically developed countries, to enhance its long-term business prospects by helping build the infrastructure required to expand its markets. In addition to donating the drugs, Pfizer cooperated with private foundations, world health organizations, and the British government to build up the infrastructure needed to prescribe and distribute the treatment to populations that previously had minimal access to healthcare, much less modern pharmaceuticals. Within 1 year, the incidence of trachoma was reduced by half among the target populations. The final aim is to reach 30 million people.

A company's relations with its customers and intermediaries are strongly influenced by personal contacts as well as by various types of non-personal market communication activities:

- business and research reports
- customer magazines and brochures
- direct mailings

- telephone calls
- documentary films
- teaching materials for schools
- the internet

can be used as media.

More personal contacts may be established during *site visits by customers or intermediaries*. *Receptions and showrooms* as well as *events* also serve the purpose of establishing personal contacts.

The internet provides additional opportunities for international marketers to establish and maintain contacts with customers all around the world. Machinery marketers, such as Italian Durst or U.S.-based Vutech, the two leaders in large photo-quality printers not only have websites presenting their latest technological achievements, they also send out newsletters and application experience reports to their customers. Consumer goods marketers, such as Italian Ferrero, have established chatrooms or even community platforms for consumers wanting to exchange their brand experiences or participate in product development.

Personnel relations

Personnel relations as part of a company's stakeholder relations have a twofold purpose. On the one hand, personnel relations activities should help to develop the intended *corporate identity* in the minds of the company's personnel. People working for the international marketer should feel part of a social entity, different from others in a way that is attractive to them. On the other hand, personnel relations have an objective of *projecting an attractive picture of the company*, its products, and activities to potential members of the workforce outside the firm. They should help to attract personnel with the level of qualification needed to ensure the future success of the firm.

Personnel relations may play a major role in the success of a company. A *brochure* that introduces new members of the organization to the corporate mission, the business domain, and the major objectives of the firm in combination with some personal introduction to the most important "rules of the game" given by a personal coach may help in socializing new entrants. An *international company magazine*, such as *Unilever Magazine* or *HILTI International*, can help make employees all over the globe feel that they are part of an attractive community.

Personal letters explaining special developments, such as new investments or the move of production units to other locations, as well as:

- office outings
- company ceremonies
- financial participation in medical aid and retirement programs

serve the purpose of increasing the commitment of personnel to the company. So do *company visits by family members of personnel*.

Company presentations at schools and universities, participation in the *financing of local infrastructure*, such as kindergartens, ambulance services or housing, or financial involvement in *local research or development programs* may help attracting highly qualified personnel. Companies that directly invest in production sites in China, for example, may find it much easier to get qualified personnel in sufficient numbers when housing can be provided. Computer firms, such as IBM, have invested heavily in local university infrastructures to gain high visibility with students and to be interesting enough to attract the best job applicants.

The international marketer has to bear in mind, however, that the perception of such personnel relations activities by local groups of the company's current and potential personnel is very much culture bound. A company ceremony that might be perfectly appropriate in the U.S. may be rejected as ridiculous in France and be disastrous for the local company's hierarchical structure in Pakistan. A company magazine has a very limited effect in a country where many of the workers in the factory are illiterate.

Implementing international stakeholder relations

A company's stakeholders may vary from one product and country market to another. So do those stakeholders' expectations concerning the company's behavior and outcomes. Effective stakeholder relations activities, therefore, are mostly local in nature. They can be planned and executed in cooperation with local or international public relations agencies. In Europe, the trend of large internationally operating companies is to handle stakeholder relations themselves, with recourse to agencies mainly for backup. At ABB, the Swiss–Swedish energy and construction giant, for example, the company's in-house stakeholder relations managers hire agencies with local market knowledge to ensure a better impact for each campaign.

Coordination of campaigns

Because the number of international media and the international mobility of many members of a company's local stakeholder groups are increasing, internationally operating firms need to coordinate their local stakeholder relations campaigns. A *stakeholder relations policy* must be developed that states some basic guidelines to be followed by local managers and agencies. In addition, the installation of a central stakeholder relations coordinator becomes increasingly important. This person has to initiate and lead the development process of an international stakeholder relations policy. Such a process would bring together managers responsible for stakeholder relations in the most important markets of the firm and local representatives of public relations agencies in those major markets to determine the guidelines to be followed throughout the firm and the major stakeholder relations tools to be used.

The stakeholder relations coordinator also has to:

- ensure the consistency of local stakeholder relations activities
- stimulate the exchange of information and experience about successful campaigns throughout the company
- coach local managers responsible for stakeholder relations through advice, feedback, and training.

Such a coordinator has to develop a *company-wide monitoring system* to compare the effectiveness and efficiency of stakeholder relations activities undertaken.

And finally, this person is the company's stakeholder relations representative in a market communication team that ensures the consistency of the firm's market communications mix.

Agencies

International public relations agencies have followed their clients in the internationalization of business. For example, Hill & Knowlton, one of the world's largest public relations agencies has 70 offices in 38 countries around the globe. Most of those offices, as well as those of the major international competitors, U.S.-based Weber Shandwick a unit of the Interpublic Group of Companies (IPG) and Burson-Marsteller, are concentrated in the more economically developed countries. In the EU, 80% of public relations agencies are small to medium-sized, with fewer than 15 employees. Since the early 1990s cross-border associations of such smaller companies have multiplied. EuroPR, for example, is a network of nine agencies in the U.K., Belgium, Denmark, Finland, France, Germany, Italy, Spain, and Sweden. The constituent companies share a common expertise in information technology, and serve computer, software and communications clients.

Sales promotion

Sales promotion is the catch-all term for short-term market communication decisions and activities that try to gain attention, stimulate interest, and provide motivation of (potential) customers, staff or intermediaries for a company and its products. All sales promotion activities have the general goal of stimulating sales. How important sales promotion activities have become is illustrated by the fact that for many packaged consumer goods companies, sales promotion expenditures have passed advertising to become the largest single cost item besides costs of production.

The variety of sales promotion activities of international marketers and the frequency with which they are offered have increased over time. Table 15.3 lists the sales promotion tools most commonly used in international marketing, their communication targets, specific objectives, and key issues to be considered in choosing among them.

Targets of sales promotion

Sales promotion activities may be directed at one or more of three types of target: customers, staff, or intermediary.

TABLE 15.3 *Sales promotion tools*

Tools	Target group	Objective
Coupons	Customers	Stimulate trial or encourage repeat purchase
Price-offs	Customers	Encourage repeat purchase
Trade allowances	Intermediaries	Build distribution; increase orders
Samples	Customers; intermediaries; staff	Stimulate trial purchase; build distribution; increase orders
In, on, and near packs	Customers	Increase attractiveness/perception of value
Self-liquidating packs	Customers	Stimulate trial or encourage repeat purchase premiums
Continuity premiums	Customers	Encourage repeat purchase
Bonus packs	Customers	Encourage repeat purchase
Contests and sweepstakes	Customers; staff; intermediaries	Stimulate trial purchase; increase orders
Displays	Customers; intermediaries	Attract attention; provide information
Training	Customers; staff; intermediaries	Provide information; improve sales capabilities
Events	Customers; staff; intermediaries	Attract attention; provide information
Trade shows and exhibitions	Customers; staff; intermediaries	Attract attention; provide information; build distribution; stimulate (trial) purchase
Product demonstrations	Customers; intermediaries	Attract attention; provide information; build distribution; stimulate (trial) purchase

The sales promotion tools most often applied in international marketing have different communication target groups and different objectives.

Customer promotions

Sales promotion activities directed towards organizational buyers or consumers are called **customer promotions**. They may try to stimulate the marketer's total sales by *reducing the price* customers have to pay.

Direct price reductions for customers are achieved by the distribution and redemption of coupons or by price-offs. A coupon of Pantène, one of the Procter & Gamble hair-styling brands, for example, is aimed at consumers. Consumers respond differently to coupons, of course, depending on culture, importance of the product, and level of income. North American consumers are the most frequent coupon users in the world. About 80% of key grocery shoppers in Canadian households use coupons when shopping. In the U.S., about 300 billion coupons are distributed to consumers each year. Consumers in Belgium and the U.K. are the EU's most active coupon users, while consumers in Italy and Spain are far more modest in couponing. They get their coupons mainly from in/on-pack promotions, whereas consumers in the U.K. clip most of their coupons from newspapers and magazines. In the U.S., free-standing inserts in print media account for about 80% of coupon distribution, while in-ad couponing represents the majority of all coupons distributed in Canada.

Other customer promotion tools, such as:

- bonus packs
- free samples
- in/on and near packs (coupons or additional products attached to or near the product)
- premiums

all add value to a marketer's product. For example, the Albert Heijn grocery chain in the Netherlands distributes savings stamps based on the total amount of a customer's purchase.

Contests and sweepstakes offer "something for nothing," which has universal appeal. U.K. newspapers, for instance, "give away" thousands of pounds daily in bingo and other contests that may be entered by readers.

Customer promotion may be mainly used to provide information. For example, consumers may be targeted by displays used to draw attention to the marketer's product, to ease the handling of the product portfolio, and to improve product logistics. For example, Austria-based Hirsch Armbänder AG, one of the leading manufacturers of watchstraps in the world, uses a display developed by Mateo Thun, an Italian designer, to present its products to consumers in retail stores. Those free-standing displays not only attract the attention of consumers, they also present the entire product range to interested customers, serve the retailer as storage space, and automatically inform the shop manager about items running out of stock. Care must be taken by the international marketer that the displays it offers to retailers fit their stores and the sales volume handled. In small sari-sari stores in the Philippines, for example, a display that is well suited for Australian supermarkets may be larger than the entire store.

Sales promotion activities providing information may be particularly important in *attracting potential customers' attention* when introducing a new product. When a U.K. manufacturer of pharmaceuticals introduced a new cold remedy in the U.S., for example, it used a promotional gift to attract the attention of medical doctors and to stay in their minds. The gift was a coffee mug with a drawing that showed a doctor and his patient. When hot coffee was poured into the mug the drawing changed. It showed the doctor giving an injection to the patient, an ugly bug trying to escape, and a text that read: "Claforan kills bugs." The sales promotion was a big success. Because the gift had a social value – the transformation of the drawing could be shown to others who did not possess the mug – the message was not only repeated to the members of the target group often enough to stay in their minds, but was also spread to many other people who learned about the existence of the new drug and its major effect.

Sales promotion tools that provide information are particularly important in internationally *marketing technical products* and services to organizational buyers. Product demonstrations during site visits to reference plants are an example of such customer promotion activities for organizational buyers. They allow the potential buyers to evaluate the product in action without risk. In addition, representatives of the potential buying organization get the opportunity to travel at no personal cost, a fact that may be an attractive added value for buyers from less industrially developed countries or less well-capitalized organizations. For example, when a manufacturer of ultra-filtration devices, such as Sweden's Alfa Laval, invites agents from Bulgarian local administrations to visit an installation of the company's product in a customer's car painting plant near Paris, those agents will not only be able to see the Alfa Laval filters in action but might also enjoy an additional day in the capital of France.

Staff promotions

Staff promotion activities are designed to stimulate the marketer's own personnel or an external salesforce. An international sales contest run by U.S.-based Caterpillar, in which the most outstanding members of the distributors' salesforce are rewarded by a trip to the headquarters in Peoria plus a subsequent 10-day vacation on a Caribbean island, is an example of a staff promotion. Issues that influence the international application of staff promotions are similar to those discussed in Chapter 13 for salesforce motivation and compensation.

Intermediary promotions

A company's activities having the purpose of increasing intermediaries' interest in buying and selling larger amounts of the marketer's products are called **intermediary promotions**. Because specialty retailers, mass merchandisers, and buying cooperatives are becoming increasingly transnational in scope, intermediary promotions also have to become more international in design and coverage.

Internationally, intermediaries respond to promotions that have a positive impact on their profit. Therefore, trade allowances are the most common sales promotion tool used by manufacturers to target their retailers. They are especially effective in highly competitive markets or when no single manufacturer has a dominant share of the market. Consumer goods manufacturers should bear in mind, however, that increasing reliance on price promotions to boost short-term local sales results that might seem necessary in country markets with powerful retail organizations tend to:

- reduce brand profitability
- increase contradictory brand communication
- dilute brand franchises with customers.

In Europe, many marketers of branded products complain about consumers' increasing price sensitivity and a tendency to buy exclusively at low (action) prices. In the Italian detergent market, for example, 80% of sales occur as part of a special offer. German retailers report very similar consumer behavior. Many of the marketers concerned overlook the fact that they, together with their retailing partners, in an attempt to increase their sales volume and market share by the continual use of trade allowances and price-offs, have taught their customers to wait for special prices.

Objectives of sales promotion

Sales promotion activities may have the objective of *informing* the target audience about the company's activities and products. They may be undertaken to *encourage trial purchases* by potential customers or to *stimulate repeat purchases*.

Finally, sales promotion also serves the purpose of *building and enlarging distribution*.

Information

Sales promotion activities aimed at potential customers or intermediaries may provide the latest information on company-related developments, such as going public, or on new products. Their interest is to capture attention and transfer the intended information. Some sales promotion activities have an openly stated goal of informing the target audience, an example being when about 90 managers from international computer and software companies, such as IBM, ICL, SAP, and Unisys, meet with 135 managers from eastern European banks at an "international banking forum" in the European Alps. Since the computer and software managers present their latest products and exchange computer application experiences, the information (and sales) purpose is predominant.

Other target groups, and in particular consumers who may be much less involved with a marketer's product, are not necessarily interested in a marketer's information. For them, sales promotion activities with an attention-getting purpose need to be predominantly *entertaining*. Events and theme parks have proved to be successful tools in that respect. For example, German Adidas has developed what it calls *urban culture programs*. The programs include participatory events across Europe such as a streetball challenge and festival, and a track-and-field clinic. Events that draw respectable crowds of people include not only athletics but also fashion shows, music, and other entertainment. Interested partners have joined Adidas in the events: major sports leagues, sports celebrities, other marketers targeting the same youth segment, and media services that cover the events.

The U.K. chocolate manufacturer Cadbury has developed a visitor center called Cadbury World. Visitors can take a journey through the history of chocolate and the history of Cadbury complete with a museum, a restaurant, a partial tour of the packaging plant, and a "chocolate event" store. They learn about the origin of cocoa and chocolate, the life of the Mayan and Aztec Indians, how chocolate reached Europe, and how John Cadbury's empire began and grew. Every year more than 450,000 people visit the park and profit from hundreds of opportunities to sample the company's extensive line of chocolate products. The regional tourist board, hotel chains, and the British Railways Board have publicized the park to promote their own services.

Encouragement of trial purchases

Sales promotion activities are frequently designed to stimulate trial purchases. When other market communication measures, such as advertising, have captured a customer's attention, sales promotion can motivate the customer to try a product by reducing the perceived risk involved. This is the case when the customer is offered a free sample. For example, when Italian wine marketers from the Tuscany area offer free samples to Danish customers in supermarkets, they know that consumers are more likely to buy their wines. On the one hand, consumers have an opportunity to taste the wines before buying, and, on the other, most consumers feel a certain obligation to reciprocate when they have accepted a free offer.

Stimulation of repeat purchases

Other sales promotion activities are designed to convert trial users into regular users. Premium programs, such as free airline miles invented by American

Airlines in 1981, are an example. Mileage programs first started to give an incentive to airline customers to stay loyal. Since then they increasingly include all manner of earth-bound goods and services. First, there were "travel partners," such as hotels, car rentals, and credit cards. Now carriers are selling miles to any company that wants to offer them as a sales incentive. Frequent flier miles are available from lawn services, mortgage firms, investment houses, restaurants, furniture stores, and moving companies. In the U.K., British Airways launched an air miles "club," through which members accumulate points from a variety of merchants, including Shell service stations, NatWest Bank Group credit cards, Wine Rack, P&O European Ferries, Hilton, Marriott, and Hertz. Those points can be exchanged for free British Airways tickets, hotels, cruises, cinema tickets, and other awards.

Building and enlarging distribution

Sales promotion can also be designed to build distribution. For example, *free samples* are used to motivate the salesforce and to induce intermediaries or final customers to increase orders. *Trade shows and exhibitions* are particularly important in international marketing for consumer and industrial goods, even if participation in such shows is increasingly expensive. Trade shows and exhibitions are used to build distribution by meeting potential intermediaries or licensing partners interested in cooperation and by securing the market presence needed to maintain successful relationships with business partners. Exhibitions, such as CeBIT in Hanover (Germany), the enormous annual European information technology exhibition with more than 6,000 exhibitors from more than 60 countries located in 26 halls, most of them the size of airplane hangars, with more than $340,000^2$ meters of floor space and about three-quarters of a million visitors, allow the marketer to present and demonstrate its latest range of products, to announce new product launches and to cultivate its image. For that reason, not only industry giants such as Microsoft or Siemens are represented at this exhibition. Smaller firms, such as Taiwan's Advanced Scientific Corp. are present as well as institutions or regions, such as the island of Mauritius, which tries to attract investors for software production facilities.

Participation in international exhibitions, such as Première Vision, the bi-annual get-together of about 850 European cloth manufacturers with fashion professionals from all over the world at Porte de Versailles in Paris, is a must for all marketers that want to be present in their potential customers' minds. But presence is not enough. Each time, the marketer has to have:

- something new to present
- something that attracts the interest of its customers
- something that makes the company stand out from the crowd of exhibitors.

To illustrate, companies such as Italian Botto or Belgian Ucco Sportswear specialize in high-quality specialty cloth. At exhibitions, the Italian firm continually presents new creations from wool, silk, and cashmere combined with microfibers and Lycra. The Belgian firm concentrates on denim fabrics of the latest fashion and fantasy.

The number and importance of large trade shows and exhibits aimed at consumers has grown, too. The Consumer Electronics Shows, held in Chicago each year, for example, or the yearly Salon d'Automobile in Geneva successfully apply the ideas of industrial trade shows to consumer audiences. At the show, consumers have an opportunity to see and try new products; perhaps more important, manufacturers have an opportunity to *observe consumer responses* to new products and product lines. In addition, interest among magazine and newspaper writers in new products or upcoming new technologies can be aroused, which, in turn, leads to publicity in their media.

Because of the rising costs of participation in exhibitions and trade shows in different parts of the world, the marketer needs to gather available information on:

- focus and size of the show
- kinds of visitor expected
- other exhibitors present
- space and locations available.

When planning a fair, the marketer should consider Ramadan for its Islamic customers.

Choice of sales promotion tools

Several factors affect decisions about which sales promotion tool to use. Some of these factors are universal and must be taken into account regardless of the country market in which the company is operating. Other factors are locally based and therefore have special significance for international marketers.

Fit with market communication objectives

The first factor to be considered is the fit of a sales promotion tool with the general market communication objectives of the firm and the product. For example, when the Italian fashion house Giorgio Armani opens a new "Emporio" store in Paris it may arrange a big event with some celebrities to draw a selected number of fashion magazine writers and potential affluent customers into the newly adapted building. But it will not use price-offs like big retailing chains such as French Casino do when they open a new hypermarket on the outskirts of Paris. As the example shows, the sales promotion tools applied have to fit the communication targets and they need to be in line with other communication activities. Armani, for example, may use the opening of the new store to advertise in the most prestigious fashion magazines, such as *Vogue*. Casino, in contrast, would send out flyers announcing super opening discounts and including coupons to all households in its market.

Level of economic and market development

Depending on the level of economic development in a country market, certain sales promotion tools can be applied more or less well. For example, coupons enjoy widespread use in most economically well-developed countries. In most economically less developed countries they are rarely used because of a lack of appropriate coupon distribution media and a lack of infrastructure for their redemption. In contrast, free samples and product demonstrations are by far the most widely applied tools of internationally operating firms in those countries.

The level of maturity a product market has reached in different country markets is another factor to be considered in the choice of sales promotion tools. Tools to promote customer trials may be more appropriate in markets where the product is new to the customers. For example, when pizza delivery services were introduced in European markets, the service providers used full-value couponing and cross-promotions with established products to make potential customers try their new service. In more mature markets, other sales promotion tools that put more emphasis on customer loyalty, such as customer loyalty premiums or membership of customer clubs, might be more effective.

Costs

The cost considerations associated with a sales promotion campaign include, first, an estimate of *the total cost of the campaign*. Second, international marketers need to estimate the *contribution of the campaign towards reaching the given communi-*

cation objectives. And, finally, they must estimate the contribution of the campaign towards *increasing sales*.

For example, free samples are a much more costly means of attracting new customers than cents-off coupons. But when a product benefit, such as good taste, the perfect functioning of a weaving machine, or the superior service in a new restaurant, is most easily communicated through trial use, the expense of samples may be necessary to make potential customers try the product.

Estimates of sales promotion costs in international marketing are complicated by the likelihood that the cost of the campaign, and contribution to sales, will vary market by market. For example, in the U.S., where contests and sweepstakes are most popular, a contest costs about $3 per thousand entrants, and sweepstakes cost about $350 per thousand entrants. Despite the fact that payoffs or rewards are commonly many times higher than those found in Europe, Asia, Latin America, or Africa, only about 20% of the population generally sends in entries to contests or sweepstakes. As a general rule, the lower the average income of the target group, the lower the reward or prize has to be to stimulate interest.

Intermediary capabilities

The willingness and ability of distributors, wholesalers, and retailers in various country markets to accommodate the special requirements of sales promotion activities is another important issue. Price-off coupons or customer loyalty premiums, for example, must be handled and processed by retailers. Bonus packs and premiums may require flexibility in storage and shelf space so that oversized and oddly shaped products can be accommodated. Local distributors of machinery manufacturers must be ready to install sample machines at potential customers' sites and dismantle them in case of non-purchase.

As we saw in Chapter 12, intermediaries in different countries vary in their capabilities. In country markets with a low literacy rate, for example, many retailers may not have the training or accounting skills necessary to keep track of coupon schemes. In countries where small store sizes predominate, such as in most Southeast Asian countries, the use of promotional tools that occupy store space or slow down checkout traffic is precluded.

Channel power

The importance of the members of a product's value-added chain relative to one another is also a factor to be considered in the choice of sales promotion tools. For example, when a manufacturer has a high degree of channel power because its products are in strong demand, trade allowances typically are not used. The distributor either buys from the manufacturer at the given price or not at all. When large intermediaries, such as Woolworth's in Australia, Ahold in the Netherlands, Carrefour in France, or Wal-Mart in the U.S., have substantial channel power, they can demand large trade allowances and in-store consumer promotions from marketers with rather weak brands or threaten to buy from another manufacturer.

Norms

The degree to which a sales promotion tool is consistent with or violates local legal, cultural or business norms is a factor to be considered carefully in each country market. The potential influence of legal norms on the choice of sales promotion activities was discussed in Chapter 4. The influence of cultural norms may vary significantly among country markets. Coupons, for example, are not widely used in Japan. Japanese consumers are still too embarrassed to be seen at a checkout redeeming them. Likewise, Danish Lego's "Bunny Set" promotion – the toys plus a discounted premium offer, a storage case in the shape of a bunny – failed to impress its intended target of Japanese mothers, even though the same sales promotion had earlier proved very successful in the U.S. Unlike their U.S.

counterparts, who thought the offering was a great bargain, the Japanese mothers considered the on-pack bunny superfluous. They objected to the notion of being forced to waste money on unwanted products.

Point-of-purchase displays work well in countries where self-service is the norm in the industry. But, by placing the product within reach of the customer, such displays violate the service norms of small shopkeepers in many areas of the world. For example, in many countries coffee is still typically sold in small stores where the shopkeeper grinds the coffee beans. An introductory offer of a coffee mug with the purchase of ground coffee is likely to be resisted by retailers, if not by consumers. They would ignore such premiums.

Decision and implementation

In light of the differences in local conditions just described, companies operating internationally have traditionally treated sales promotion as a local affair. Local intermediaries or product, brand, or sales managers have enjoyed great latitude in the formulation and implementation of sales promotion activities. However, because of the growing importance of *sales promotion spending* compared to other market communication activities such as media advertising, and the increasing realization of marketing managers that all market communication decisions and activities need to be *conceptually integrated*, the distribution of responsibilities concerning sales promotion decisions and implementation in the company has become an issue.

The objective of any solution should be to upgrade the performance of local market communication. The impact of sales promotion activities and their contribution to the achievement of the company's communication goals compared to their costs should be maximized. As the discussion of key issues to be considered when choosing sales promotion tools has shown, there are good reasons for leaving sales promotion activities primarily in the hands of local management. But some central coordination may help to improve local practices.

Table 15.4 contains a list of responsibilities a central sales promotion coordination unit or coordinator of an internationally operating firm could take. The central coordination unit would be responsible for:

TABLE 15.4 *Role of an international sales promotion coordinator*

The international sales promotion coordinator's role would be to:

- Lead the development process of guidelines for international sales promotion
- Facilitate the information transfer about successful sales promotion campaigns
- Encourage cross-fertilization of sales promotion ideas and practices among local managers
- Develop and suggest training programs on sales promotion planning, design, and evaluation
- Advise locally responsible managers on solutions to specific promotion problems
- Develop standard systems for comparatively monitoring effectiveness and efficiency of sales promotion activities and performance of local managers

An international sales promotion coordinator could play the role of a coach for local managers who have to implement the international sales promotion policy of the firm.

Source: Adapted from Kashani, K. and J.A. Quelch (1990) "Can sales promotion go global?", *Business Horizons*, May–June, pp. 37–43

- leading the development process of global sales promotion guidelines
- expressing the main objectives to reach
- major tools to apply
- coordinating local sales promotion with other local market communication activities.

The coordination unit would also have to:

- facilitate information transfer about successful sales promotion campaigns among local managers
- encourage cross-fertilization of ideas and practices among the local market representatives
- act as a coach

in terms of suggesting training programs and advising local managers on solutions to specific sales promotion problems. Finally, it would be the coordination unit's responsibility to develop standard systems for comparatively monitoring the effectiveness and efficiency of sales promotion activities and the performance of local managers. Local or locally responsible managers still have to implement the company's sales promotion policy. Implementation means translating the international policy guidelines into *country market-specific objectives* for example, expand shelf space and increase trial purchases; into decisions concerning the *tools* to be used for example, trade allowances and sampling; the *products to be promoted*, the timing and the specific *terms of sales promotion activities*, for example, which intermediaries should get what amount of allowances for what return. Implementation also means the *execution of those decisions*, such as the preparation of the salesforce for their contacts with intermediaries or organizing the production of samples and their distribution to customers at the point of sale or at home.

Sponsoring

Whatever country markets an international marketer is serving, there are many different marketers trying to communicate with their potential customers – whether through advertising appeals in San Francisco or through personal communication in the souk of Marrakesh. To be noticed by its target audiences, an international marketer's communication needs to stand out from others in a positive manner. In highly industrialized economies, advertising appeals, personal selling, and sales promotions have traditionally been used to communicate with customers. Advertising in particular, however, suffers from *commercial information overflow*, which confronts customers. This information overflow results in extremely small probabilities of a firm's commercial messages being recognized and, if recognized, attracting more than very short periods of attention. In addition, the ever increasing number of available media vehicles is focusing on smaller and smaller target groups in order to attract users who change their interests depending on the situation-specific context. The selection of most adequate media to reach the targeted customer segments turns into a nightmare. As a result, most smaller companies cannot afford the advertising budgets needed for a substantial coverage of all attractive potential country markets. Faced with these problems, companies have invented new kinds of communication tool. The currently most important of those in international marketing are sponsoring and direct market communication.

Sponsoring can be defined as the provision of resources (money, people, equipment) by an organization directly to an event, cause, or activity in exchange for a direct association (link) to the event, cause, or activity. Sponsored events may be sports events, such as the Olympic Games in 1996 sponsored by companies such as Coca-Cola, United Parcel Service, and Hilton, or cultural

Advertising messages form a backdrop for the Mens' Downhill at the Hahnenkamm Rennen, Kitzbuhel, Austria

©Walter Luger GEPA-pictures/RED BULL

events, such as Copenhagen, cultural capital of Europe for 1 year sponsored by Danish Lego. Sponsored causes may be social or environmental, such as the construction of a new village for orphans and children from destabilized families by International SOS-Kinderdorf in Brazil, or a Greenpeace campaign against the deforestation of the Amazon river basin.

Objectives of sponsoring

In many companies operating internationally, sponsoring is still understood as a way to achieve *customer awareness*; either directly through providing time and space for advertising messages (for example, when a brand name is shown on the perimeter board of an ice skating rink) or indirectly through media transmissions of events (for example, when the firm's logo on the headband of a ski jump celebrity is shown on television) or through reports about events in the media.

Besides customer awareness, sponsoring presents multiple opportunities to achieve *awareness in other important stakeholders*, such as media or administrators. But more important, sponsoring enables establishment, strengthening, or change in the meanings customers associate with the sponsor and its products.

Just as customers associate celebrities with certain meanings, so too the events, causes, and activities of sponsored organizations are associated with meanings. For example, Hugo Boss, located in the provincial town of Metzingen in southern Germany, was founded in 1923. It was always a producer of high-quality clothing, but not many people knew about it. The company established its current image of exclusivity paired with high quality in large part through effective use of sponsorship. In the early 1970s Hugo Boss sponsored Porsche in Formula 1 races to capitalize on Porsche's strong exclusive image and international presence. Since then, the company has sponsored international tennis, golf, and ski competitions. It has funded exhibitions and artists, and it sponsored *Miami Vice* and *L.A.Law*, both of which featured Hugo Boss garments. The visibility and meanings transferred to the brand paid off quickly. Hugo Boss garments are now sold in 60 countries. More than half its sales come from outside Germany, with a substantial part generated outside Europe.

Decision and implementation

An international marketer interested in the transfer of meanings from a sponsored event or a cause to its company or its product must take care in selecting the most appropriate sponsoring object. The marketer must check

1 The *type of event, cause, or activity considered for sponsoring* must fit the meaning the sponsor wants to achieve in the minds of its customers and important stakeholders. For example, when Dominique Perrin, the CEO of Paris-based Cartier, decides to sponsor an exhibition of art works by César, he will not only consider how much he personally likes those exhibits, but also how well the meanings such an exhibition brings to the minds of the tens of thousands of international visitors fit the meaning that he wants to be transferred to the sponsor, Cartier.

2 The *similarity between the sponsor and the event or cause sponsored* as perceived by the firm's customers may be based on the use of the sponsor's product during the sponsored event, for example, when Castrol sponsors a Formula 1 Grand Prix race, or when spectators of the soccer World Cup stay in rooms of an international hotel chain that sponsors the event.

   Perceived similarity may also be based on the relation between the meaning of the event and the meaning of the sponsor's product, for example, when Coca-Cola sponsored the Voodoo Lounge concert tour of the Rolling Stones around the world such similarity may have been lacking.

3 The *potential media attention to be attracted*. When Red Bull sponsors athletes who reach out for extraordinary achievements, such as jumping into deep mountain holes using a parachute, they do not only consider the meaning transferred to their brand but also the news value for the media in comparison to the cost of the sponsorship.

4 *The involvement of the sponsor's customers with the event or cause* to be sponsored, that is, the personal or social importance they attach to the event or cause, and the involvement with the sponsor's product needs to be considered. If the involvement with the sponsoring object is high, such as for many social or environmental causes, but also for field hockey games in India, rugby in New Zealand, or soccer in Columbia, the sponsor can count on a high level of attention from the target audience. If, in addition, the target audience's involvement with the sponsor or its product is rather low, the transfer of meaning from the sponsored event or cause to the sponsor might be easier. This may have been the case when Eastman Kodak of the U.S. replaced its major competitor, Japan's Fuji Photo Film, as sponsor of widely watched soccer matches in China.

Direct market communication

In industrially developed economies, mass marketing has become increasingly difficult in recent years. More affluent consumers are less loyal, constantly looking for more attractive offers or lower prices. To respond appropriately to this development, the international marketer needs to have close contacts with its potential customers. A more direct market communication than the traditional contact via mass media is needed. In international business-to-business industries competition has grown tremendously. Marketers, therefore, need to be closer to their potential customers, know their problems more precisely, and serve them more individually.

Direct market communication might be a solution. In directly communicating with their customers, international marketers may gain:

- many opportunities for testing new offers
- high flexibility in adapting offers to the specific customer needs
- control of the efficiency of communication spending
- reduced visibility of communication activities for competitors.

These advantages may be gained at relatively limited cost and time. In addition, direct communication contacts may be initiated by potential customers visiting the marketer's home page, calling, or sending an order form.

In direct one-to-one marketing each customer is a particular case getting an individualized offer. Business partners may develop shared management systems, such as logistics information systems, discussed in Chapter 14. Because the most important tool of direct communication, personal selling, has already been discussed in Chapter 13, the following section will focus on direct mailings and electronic direct communication. Both kinds of direct communication replace the personal contact by a visual and verbal contact; hence, the importance of composition, formulation, and presentation of the message, which must convince potential customers and make them take a buying decision, and of the customer order fulfillment process, which must replace personal contacts in building trust. Attractive message composition, formulation, and presentation as well as order fulfillment processes establishing trust are largely complicated by cultural differences in international marketing.

Direct mailings

The traditional approach to direct market communication is direct mailings. In order to be highly efficient such mailings must be based on a well-developed, targeted database.

Customer database

A file of current and potential customers containing their names, postal addresses, phone numbers, email addresses, and socioeconomic profiles needs to be established. This file has to be filled with behavioral data concerning each customer. As the example of Nestlé's Casa Buitoni Club in the U.K. shows, such a database can be established by a creative campaign integrating various market communication tools. Nestlé's strategy was that Buitoni would become a helpful authority on Italian food – a brand and company to which consumers could turn for advice on the many varieties of pasta and their preparation. The first stage of the Buitoni direct marketing effort was designed to strengthen brand awareness and create a core database of consumers interested in getting involved in Italian cooking. Buitoni gave free recipe booklets to anyone who responded to its offers, which were made in the press and through teletext or direct-response television. Brand awareness was further improved by in-store sampling, sponsorship, a roadshow with many sampling activities, and public relations connected to the London Marathon, the most popular running event in the U.K. The integrated communications campaign resulted in a database of more than 200,000 consumers. In the next step the households in the database were invited to join the Casa Buitoni Club. Those responding received an Italian-lifestyle information pack and a full-color quarterly newsletter (with articles about different Italian regions), pasta recipes, and discount vouchers. Membership benefits also included a free phone number for anyone wanting cooking advice or suggestions. In addition, there was the opportunity to sample new products, merchandise offered against proof of purchase, and suggestions on planning pasta feasts. The success of this direct marketing effort has influenced the marketing of Buitoni in other countries, for example, Japan.

Personalized communication can only be achieved if the marketer knows what the customer buys, when, at what price, where (at home or in business), how (order, payment method), why, following what (an offer or another purchase). Based on these data customer reactions may be profiled, customers classified, their value to the company may be determined, customer loyalty measured, and customers selected.

Companies such as Consodata or Calyx-Claritas have created mega-consumer databases for Europe by sending out several million questionnaires to households. These questionnaires contained more than 150 questions concerning:

- socio-demographic data
- purchasing behavior (locations, amounts, frequencies, intentions)
- consumption (types of product, brand, amount, preference)
- equipment (leisure, car, financial, environment)
- lifestyle (leisure and cultural activities, media use, vacation).

International marketers using direct mailings can buy specific database contents, services such as bus mailings, or results of analyses such as a comparison of their own files with the database of the supplier or consumer analyses by regions.

Problems in international direct mailing

The problems an international marketer may encounter in using direct mailings and some solutions to those problems are illustrated by the example of Germany's Neckermann, one of Europe's leading catalog businesses.

In conceiving its 1,400-page catalog of garments and home equipment for the German market, Neckermann bears in mind that some of those pages will be used for its French, Belgian, and Dutch catalogs. In order to avoid too much of a bias in the direction of a local culture, accessories shown in the catalog are limited. In addition, whenever possible, parts of the text are written in English to reduce adaptation costs. The models used to display the garments represent all types of person in the country markets served. Nevertheless, some country-specific adaptations need to be made. First, the catalog itself is differently positioned: in Germany as "the intelligent buy," in the Netherlands as "the thickest catalog," and in France as "the European catalog." The consumers in the served countries also wear different sizes; Germans and Dutch are taller than the French. And some prices need to be changed: Leather goods are used as rather low-priced attention attractors in Germany. In France, they are considered as expensive. Finally, sales promotion regulations vary between the countries. Samples and premiums are governed by very restrictive regulations in Germany compared to France.

The applicability of direct mailing largely depends on:

- high literacy rates in the served country markets
- dependable postal services.

These requirements mean that direct mailing is not appropriate for a large number of markets. In some African countries, for example, it takes longer to send a letter to another city within the country than to send one from the capital overseas. India, by way of contrast, boasts that a letter mailed in India will reach any destination in the country within 3 days. This means that international marketers should give serious consideration to sending direct mail to educated consumers in India.

Electronic direct communication

The rapid development of new electronic media has enlarged the international marketer's opportunities to enter into individual communication contact with its customers. Selling directly through television is an electronic option that originated in the U.S. and has expanded throughout western Europe. Telephone sales are discussed in Chapter 10. Another option is electronic catalogs. France Telecom, for example, has established what is called the Teletel network. By the year 2000 there were 6.5 million minitel videotex terminals installed in French homes, which not only served as an electronic telephone directory but also displayed goods and services that could be ordered directly from the sellers by phone.

Market communication via the internet

The direct communication medium of today is the internet. By the end of the year 2005 there will be an estimated 976 million internauts worldwide. The opportunities to use the internet for market communication purposes are manifold. But most marketers still approach the new media through the static, one-way, mass market broadcast model of traditional media. For advertising purposes, for example, a diverse range of formats, including skyscrapers, embedded messages, banners, buttons, sponsored pages, or text links are used. A somewhat more sophisticated approach is offered by the three market-leading search engines Google, Yahoo!, and MSN Search. There, users are only presented advertising messages that relate to the specific field of interest they use the search engine for. Nevertheless, the results of even this approach are mostly uninspiring applications that fall short of the new medium's potential. Marketers will have to learn how to create entirely new forms of interactions and transactions with customers. To do so they will need to accept a fundamental change in the traditional communication balance of power by giving the consumer more control over their relationship. In an interactive, two-way, addressable world, it is the customer – *not* the marketer – who decides with whom to interact, what to interact about, and how to interact at all.

The internet can dynamically deliver personalized two-way communication with identified users in real time. Customers can search for products and services fulfilling their need, and can order them instantaneously. If customers have reasons to complain they can do it on the home page of the supplier and get an immediate response.

For example, Germany's Erco Leuchten, the world leader for light systems in museums, has a home page containing 150,000 pages and 1.2 million links. The information material on products, projects, and user advice is presented in four languages. Products are demonstrated in various uses. Forms for international tenders are provided in a way to allow their use by all international customers. For example, when Spanish Zara publishes a tender for lighting new shops a Japanese architect must be able to use Erco's information material to successfully offer its services.

The internet can also be used for public relations purposes. For example, Parfums Fabergé, Paris, launched an internet site to accompany *The Shape of Things*, a four-part television program it was sponsoring in the U.K. about design. The world wide web magazine, also entitled *The Shape of Things*, explored European design from various points of view. Although the site's principal aim was to provide an interesting and informative guide to European design, it also provided an obvious opportunity to build Fabergé's brand position – a passion for design – through overt linkage with contemporary design and style leaders.

Beside information delivery and the opportunity to circumvent traditional intermediaries (discussed in Chapter 12), the internet allows the establishment of international customer relationships even for companies that would traditionally be restricted to doing only local business. For example, HotHotHot, a single-store retailer in Pasadena, California, selling hot sauces, chilli mixes and other spicy food, created one of the world wide web's first commercial storefronts. Since the day the retailer's website became operational, HotHotHot received daily orders, creating a steady revenue stream representing a substantial share of total sales. What is more, the site drove store traffic, with online customers from all over the U.S. and Europe stopping by the store when they were in Pasadena, while communication costs on the website amounted to only 5% of online revenue.

E-commerce websites of travel agencies, marketers of consumer electronics, or cultural products invite customers from all parts of the world to exchange their experiences. They publish "web magazines" that mix technical information with evaluations and stakeholder relations material.

A step further is to provide a forum for "missionary customers"; those enthusiastic consumers eager to communicate with their peers concerning a certain brand. Such brand communities, like niketalk, can either be independent of the company or be created and to a certain extent managed by the marketer. Agencies, such as Paris-based Heaven are specialists in facilitating community sites. They provide assistance to interested individuals in the design and the development of sites. Heaven, for example, helped establish and manage communities focused on Microsoft's XBox as well as Thierry Mugler's perfume called Bimen. Future issues box 15.1 gives an example of how dangerous an internet "buzz" can be when it takes a company by surprise.

Problems in using the internet for global communication

One major problem for international marketers in using the internet for global market communication is still a *lack of penetration* in the less economically developed regions of the world. Whereas in 2004 more than 13 million subscribers had signed up for broadband internet access in the U.S. and Canada, for example, in Latin America cable operators had enlisted no more than 400,000 subscribers for high-speed data services. Internet usage in the same year was estimated to reach 30 million, that is, less than 5% of the entire population. With the large income disparities and low telephone penetration rates in most Latin American countries, web penetration is likely to remain low.

FUTURE ISSUES BOX 15.1

Marketing to the digital consumer

The rapid development of interactive media still confronts international marketers with opportunities seemingly difficult to grasp. Most companies have established a website and call it important to their international competitiveness. But at the same time most of the firms fall short of leveraging the full capabilities of interactive media. While most applications provide product information and feature basic email capabilities, a smaller number provide any sort of interactive content. Rather few websites make an effort to seriously collect information about their users, and even fewer provide an opportunity to allow user-to-user communications.

What tremendous influence such user-to-user communications can have on a company's reputation is illustrated by the case of Kryptonite: In September 2004 a young man in Seattle found out by chance that he could open his Kryptonite anti-theft bicycle lock with a simple ballpoint pen. Half-amused half-angry, he decided to inform the members of his favorite "blog" on the internet by adding a video clip showing him opening the anti-theft lock. Very quickly the site filled with comments. Other members possessing the same kind of lock tried to open it with a ballpoint pen and many succeeded. They spread out the news on other sites of the web. In a couple of hours the video reached internet communities focused on cycling, then consumer associations all around the world. Kryptonite faced a serious loss in reputation.

To avoid that risk and even, perhaps, to take advantage of the potential emergence of a "buzz" marketers will need to build some of the more specialized skills in interactive electronic communication, such as audience creation and intelligent agent development. They will need to closely follow and maybe participate in the discussions going on in various communities related to the company's activities.

Source: Adapted from Eudes, Y. (2005), "Les guérilleros du net-marketing", *Le Monde*, 1 February, p. 14

Culture-specific interpretations of contents is another important issue to consider. Even though the internet makes every site globally accessible, it does not make every site interculturally legible. For example, when Lego created the world's first Advent calendar – an illustrated calendar for December that includes 24 small doors, one for each day from the first of the month until Christmas, which can be opened day by day to reveal little surprise pictures – it received thousands of emails of complaint. Mainly Jewish site visitors wanted to know why Lego was suddenly supporting Christmas. For the authors of the calendar, all people from Scandinavia for whom Christmas is a natural part of family life, this came as a surprise. They had not considered they would be insulting the values of customers from other cultural backgrounds.

A great number of *independent players in the distribution channel*, each following its own online communication pattern, can be another major challenge for an international marketer. Scania, one of the world's leading manufacturers of trucks, buses, and engines, operating in about 100 countries, for example, sells through a network of distributors. Because it had developed its individual internet communication approaches, implementing globally coordinated brand communication had been difficult for Scania's headquarters. The company, therefore, developed a communication platform for the internet that provides general guidelines while leaving enough freedom for distribution partners to publish local content. To make the distributors follow the company guidelines, Scania offers a toolkit that incorporates proven implementation techniques plus cost-free training allowing the distributors to develop and launch extensive national sites within weeks.

Impact on marketing mix

International market communication decisions have a major impact on other tools of a company's marketing mix.

Distribution

The communication tools discussed in this chapter all have an impact on distributor and retailer relations as well as on the success potential of personnel selling.

Staff promotion activities may help reinforcing relations with distributors or retailing partners. But because they have a direct impact on the behavior of the partners' personnel, staff promotions need to be closely coordinated with those partners. In general, advertising campaigns are well received by members of distribution channels because they help increase their sales. Direct market communication activities, in contrast, may find distribution partners less enthusiastic, in particular when they end up in e-commerce.

Advertising and sponsoring activities prepare the ground for salespeople contacts with potential customers. Sales promotion campaigns may ease reaching sales goals in a market. Direct market communication, in contrast, may take away business from salespeople. At the extreme, it may even replace them. Again, close coordination between communication and sales management is needed to fully exploit the communication potential of campaigns and to avoid distrust.

Distribution logistics can be strongly supported by stakeholder relations activities. But, by the same token, direct market communication will be reduced to information transfer if distribution logistics managers are not closely involved in its planning and implementation.

Product management

Depending on the sophistication of a marketer's direct market communication activities product development can be influenced in one or all of its stages from information gathering to product testing.

Product quality management has to closely cooperate with advertising in order to avoid over-promising. And brand management needs to take part in the development of the communication platform. Core messages, media selection, sales promotion activities as well as the choice of sponsoring partners can have a strong influence on brand meaning. They need to be coordinated to produce a reinforcing pattern of experiences for stakeholders at all touch points.

Summary

The major objective of an international marketer in its communication with various stakeholders in a multitude of country markets is to achieve the intended strategic position of the company and its products in the stakeholders' minds. Examples of internationally successful companies show that this goal can best be reached if all market communication activities are coordinated in a way to be consistent and supportive of its brand identity.

To ensure consistent market communication the international marketer has to develop a market communication policy. Policy development starts with the *determination of the firm's most important stakeholder groups* in the product and country markets served. For each of those stakeholder groups *general communication objectives* are fixed, and a *communication platform* is developed. The communication platform defines the *central message* to be communicated to all stakeholders of the firm. This central message then is refined into *consistent core messages* for each stakeholder group.

To assure a local choice of communication tools appropriate for message transfer, the *major communication tools* the marketer wants to be applied also have to be determined. An additional *guideline concerning corporate design* defines the elements of all communication activities that have to be kept constant.

Finally, the international marketer has to specify some rules of cooperation with external partners and rules of coordination among internal units for the implementation of market communication decisions.

Based on the international market communication policy, decisions concerning the integrated application of various communication tools can be taken. International advertising is mainly used to:

- stimulate potential customers' interest in the company's products
- make those products reach the intended position in the (potential) customers' minds
- continually remind the customers of the benefits to be gained by buying and using the product
- prepare the ground for positive buying decisions by the customers.

When developing an international advertising campaign, the marketer has to decide which parts of the campaign to standardize across country markets and which parts to adapt locally:

- influences from cultural differences
- the availability of media in the targeted country markets
- legal restrictions on advertising

in those markets need to be considered. The success of an international advertising campaign also depends on the company's ability to properly organize the production and international launching of its advertisements. For that purpose, an internal group of qualified people willing to cooperate across country markets needs to be established and contacts with external service providers such as advertising agencies need to be managed.

Stakeholder relations serve the planned building and maintenance of communicative relations between the company and its stakeholders with the objective of establishing a positively valued meaning of the company in those stakeholders' perceptions.

Sales promotion is the catch-all term for short-term market communication decisions and activities that:

- inform the target audience about the company's activities and products
- encourage trial purchases by potential customers or stimulate repeat purchases
- help to build and enlarge distribution.

Because sales promotion activities are basically local, the international marketer choosing the appropriate tools not only has to consider their fit with the general market communication objectives, but also the:

- level of market development
- costs incurred
- legal restrictions

- intermediary capabilities
- local cultural and business norms.

For international coordination purposes the establishment of a central coordinator seems advisable.

As traditional media have become more expensive, cluttered, and overloaded with commercial messages, sponsoring has increasingly become a cost-effective alternative for international market communication. Sponsoring presents multiple opportunities to achieve awareness of customers and other important stakeholders, such as media or administrators. But more important, sponsoring allows the establishment, strengthening, and change in meanings customers associate with the sponsor's name and with its products. For this reason, the type of event, cause, or activity considered for sponsoring must be carefully chosen to fit the meaning the sponsor wants to achieve with its customers and important stakeholders.

Finally, direct communication through electronic media is a market communication tool that has enormously increased in importance. To stay internationally competitive in the future, marketers will have to use the entire communication potential of interactive electronic media in a creative manner.

DISCUSSION QUESTIONS

1. Discuss the need for internationally coordinated market communication. Why is it that most international marketers are only at the beginning of such market communication coordination?

2. What does it need for an international communicator to establish successful communication with the members of its audience?

3. Find an example of an event creating negative publicity for a firm operating internationally. How did the firm handle this situation? What do you suggest the firm *should* have done?

4. What needs to be checked and how, before an international marketer can decide to standardize its international advertising?

5. Why can companies with rather small international market communication budgets be as successful in communicating with their potential customers as much bigger companies with large advertising budgets? Find examples of what they have done.

6. Why are sales promotion activities mainly local? Find examples, and explain what an international marketer, nevertheless, can do to ensure their international coordination and their fit with the general market communication objectives of the firm.

7. Why can sponsoring be an attractive communication tool for international marketers? What does it need to make sponsoring internationally successful?

8. Compare examples of companies using new electronic media for direct communication with their potential customers and other stakeholders. How do their approaches differ? How internationally sensitive are they?

9. How would you suggest organizing the integrated market communication of a firm operating internationally and why?

Useful internet links

Adidas	http://www.adidas.com/
Adobe	http://www.adobe.com/
Alfa Laval	http://www.alfalaval.com/
Avis	http://www.avis.com/
Botto	http://www.gruppobotto.com/flash/inglese/homepage%20inglese.htm
Buitoni	http://www.buitoni.com/
Business Horizons	http://www.businesshorizons.org/
Business Week	http://www.businessweek.com/
Cadbury	http://www.cadbury.co.uk/
Calvin Klein	http://www.calvinklein.com/
Cartier	http://www.cartier.com/

ADDITIONAL READINGS

Alden, D.L., J.-B.E.M. Steenkamp, R. Batra (1999) "Brand positioning through advertising in Asia, North America, and Europe: the role of global consumer culture", *Journal of Marketing*, January, 63, 75–87.

Griffith, D.A., A. Chandra, and J.K. Ryans Jr. (2003) "Examining the intricacies of promotion standardization: factors influencing advertising message and packaging", *Journal of International Marketing*, 11(3), 30–47.

Harker, D. (1998) "Achieving acceptable advertising: an analysis of advertising regulation in five countries", *International Marketing Review*, 15(2), 101–118.

Joachimsthaler, E. and D.A. Aacker (2003) *Building Brands without Mass Media*, Princeton, N.J.: Harvard Business School Press.

Journal of Business Research, November 1996, 37(3), Special Issue on integrated marketing communications.

Lee, K., G. Qian, J.H. Yu, and Y. Ho (2005) "Trading favors for marketing advantage: evidence from Hong Kong, China, and the United States", *Journal of International Marketing*, 13(1), 1–35.

Castrol	http://www.castrol.com/
CeBIT	http://www.cebit.de/
Christian Dior	http://www.dior.com/
Cisco	http://www.cisco.com/
CNN	http://www.cnn.com/
Consodata	http://www.consodata.com/
Consumer Electronics Show	http://www.cesweb.org/
Dentsu	http://www.dentsu.com/
Diesel	http://www.diesel.com/
Erco Leuchten	http://www.erco.com/
EuroPR	http://www.europrgroup.com/
EXXON	http://www.exxon.com/
Ferrero	http://www.ferrerousa.com/
Financial Times	http://www.ft.com/
Fuji Photo Film	http://www.fujifilm.com/
Google	http://www.google.com/
Häagen-Dazs	http://www.haagen-dazs.com/
Hakuhodo	http://www.hakuhodo.co.jp/english/
Harvard Business Review	http://www.hbsp.harvard.edu/
Hertz	http://www.hertz.com/
Hilton	http://www.hilton.com/
Hirsch	http://www.hirschag.com/
Hugo Boss	http://www.bossshops.com/shops/boss/en/boss_shops_home.html
International Advertising Resource Center	http://www.bgsu.edu/departments/tcom/faculty/ha/intlad1.html
International SOS-Kinderdorf	http://www.sos-kinderdorfinternational.org/
Interpublic Group	http://www.interpublic.com/
Joop!	http://www.joop.com/
Kagan World Media	http://www.kagan.com/

Kryptonite	http://www.kryptonitelock.com/
Lego	http://www.lego.com/
M&M	http://www.mms.com/
MasterCard	http://www.mastercard.com/
Minitel	http://www.minitel.fr/
Moët & Chandon	http://www.moet.com/
Le Monde	http://www.lemonde.fr/
MSN Search	http://search.msn.com/
MTV	http://www.mtv.com/
Neckermann	http://www.neckermann.de/
Newsweek	http://www.newsweek.com/
Niketalk	http://www.niketalk.com/
Omnicom Group Inc	http://www.omnicomgroup.com/
P&O European Ferries	http://www.poferries.com/
Pepsi	http://www.pepsi.com/
Première Vision	http://www.premierevision.fr/en/home/home.php
Rapunzel Barbie	http://www.barbie.com/
Red Bull	http://www.redbull.com/
Salon d'Automobile in Geneva	http://www.salon-auto.ch/fr/pratiques/acces.php
Unisys	http://www.unisys.com/
Vogue	http://www.vogueparis.com
Wall Street Journal	http://www.wsj.com/
Weber Shandwick	http://www.webershandwick.com/
Whirlpool	http://www.whirlpool.com/
Wine Rack	http://www.winerack.com/
Wonderbra	http://www.wonderbra.com/
Woolworth	http://www.woolworths.com.au/
Young & Rubicam	http://www.yr.com/

16

INTERNATIONAL PRICING DECISIONS

Learning objectives

After studying this chapter you will be able to:

- explain the complexity of pricing decisions in international business as compared to national sales

- explain the importance of an international pricing policy for the firm's sales activities

- distinguish the factors that influence the final price charged in a market

- explain their importance and impact on the price

- evaluate risks to be considered and ways to reduce or cover them

- choose payment method best suited to a business deal

- discuss the pros and cons of countertrade

Chapter outline

International pricing decisions

International pricing policy

General rules for price determination

Factors influencing price setting

Costs
Market
Macro-environment
Price escalation

Payment terms

Factors affecting choice
Methods of payment

Managing financial risks

Managing exchange rate risk
Guarantees
Insurance

Countertrade

Barter
Other forms of countertrade
Company and government motives
Concerns about countertrade
Countertrade opportunities

Impact on marketing mix

Summary

INTERNATIONAL MARKETING SPOTLIGHT

Are international prices beyond corporate control?

The changing value of one currency versus the other is but one of the environmental issues that affect the setting of international prices. Generally, the exchange rate between currencies is seen as an uncontrollable variable, one that the organization must accept and one that they have little to no ability to influence. But changes in the U.S. dollar to yen exchange rate, and the different ways Japanese and American carmakers have reacted to those changes, may indicate that although the exchange rate cannot be directly managed, its impact on international prices may be somewhat manageable.

Financial markets can undermine price setting © Pierre Janssen/iStock

Until the mid-1990s, U.S. automakers enjoyed an average price advantage of $3,000 per car over Japanese models, thanks to the yen rising in value against the dollar (about 90 yen to the dollar), making Japanese exports more expensive in the U.S. But in the mid-1990s, that price advantage began rapidly evaporating, as the yen lost value against the dollar, rising to 115 to 130 against the dollar. Worse for U.S. carmakers, North American consumers began to show an even greater interest in the affordability of new cars.

While the yen was very strong, Japanese firms designed lower production cost cars, so they could be profitable at even 80 to 85 yen to the dollar. They also shifted more manufacturing to the U.S. and Mexico, inside the NAFTA market. U.S. automakers fought back by gaining in efficiency, even beginning to export more to Japan as the yen remained high and U.S. companies gained in production efficiencies. Still, in 1997, Japanese car prices were cut by 1.1%, while U.S. companies *increased* their prices by 2.8%. U.S. companies lost even more sales to Japanese companies as a result. This loss was not only a result of the changes in the exchange rate, it was also partially a result of more investment by Japanese companies in design-efficient car models, increasing their spending on product development, and improving their processes in the value-added chain.

The focal question of this chapter is: **How can international marketers determine the monetary and non-monetary assets they want to get in exchange for the benefits they provide to the customers in a way that allows building and sustaining the intended global strategic position of their organization?**

International pricing decisions

Many marketers operating on an international level mention pricing when asked for the most difficult decision in their company's marketing mix. They attribute that difficulty to the increasing level of international competition from firms with different production costs, taxation systems, labor regulations, or other business environments. Low growth in markets also contributes to the price-setting problem. So do different locations on the experience curve owing to the varying size of home markets.

Nevertheless, pricing is a very important tool of every international marketer when it comes to building and sustaining intended strategic position. As Figure 16.1 shows, it determines the attractiveness of a company's offer together with product, distribution, and communication activities. All these other tools will not be much use, however, if customers consider the price they are supposed to pay excessive.

When talking about prices most marketers think in terms of monetary returns. From a customer's perspective, however, the **price** of a product is the sum of all monetary and non-monetary assets the customer has to exchange (or "spend") in order to obtain the benefit(s) provided by the product. As the "costs–benefit model" discussed in Chapter 11 illustrated, customers may perceive that many non-monetary "costs" are associated with a product. Some of those non-monetary costs cannot be influenced by international marketers. Many others are under their control. Some are part of the product design; others are due to the distribution system the marketer has chosen, the logistics and after-sales service available or the positioning of the product offer, and the marketer's communication. Thus, the monetary costs customers have to bear when accepting an offer are only part of the total cost they perceive. But they are highly important to most customers.

Pricing decisions – in the sense of determining the monetary costs to customers – need to be made carefully (see Figure 16.2).

They include:

- *An international pricing policy*. Based on the corporate objectives and the intended positioning the **international pricing policy** determines general rules for setting basic prices and using price reductions, the selection of terms of payment, and the potential use of countertrade.

FIGURE 16.1   *Contribution of pricing to building and sustaining the intended global strategic position*

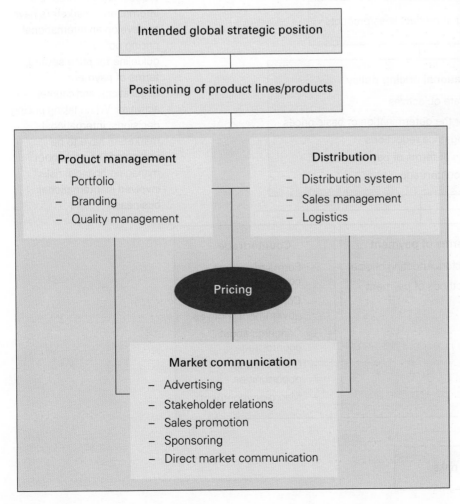

Pricing determines the attractiveness of a company's offer together with product, distribution, and communication activities. All those other tools will be useless, however, if customers consider the price they are supposed to pay as excessive.

- *Price setting.* **Price setting** is the determination of the basic price of a product, the price structure of the entire product line, and the system of rebates, discounts, and refunds the firm will offer in exchange for specific actions. This decision will be strongly influenced by the costs of the company, the intended position of the total product to be offered, the expectations of the most important stakeholders, the pricing of competitors as well as the macro-environment.

- *Terms of payment.* **Terms of payment** are contractual statements fixing the point in time and the circumstances of payment for the products to be delivered. Price setting as well as the choice of terms of payment have to carefully consider and manage the financial risks that are manifold in international business.

- *Potential countertrade.* **Countertrade** is non-monetary and partial monetary exchanges that are of importance in a global business environment characterized by enhanced competition between industrialized and newly industrialized economies, striving for business in

FIGURE 16.2 *International pricing decisions*

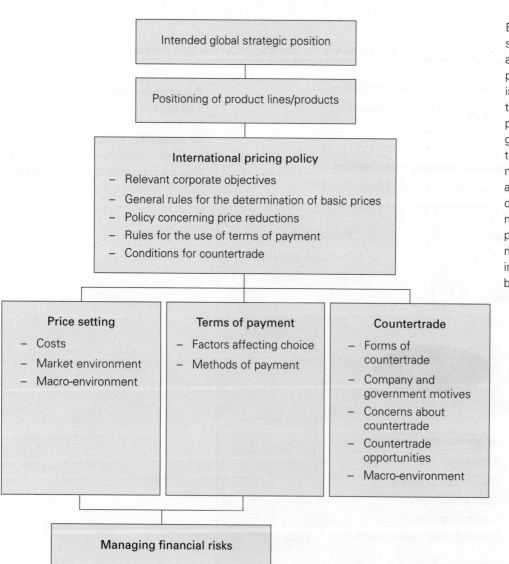

Based on the intended global strategic position of the firm and the positioning of their product lines or products, international marketers have to develop an international pricing policy. It is the guideline for price setting, terms of payment negotiations, and countertrade activities. When taking pricing decisions, international marketers have to be particularly careful about managing financial risks involved in international business.

developing countries plagued by hard currency shortages and huge trade imbalances.

In the following, we discuss the factors influencing those pricing decisions and potential consequences resulting from a marketer's choices.

International pricing policy

International pricing decisions are much more difficult to standardize than product decisions or promotion activities. Competitors in various countries have different cost structures, resulting in different prices. Taxes, duties, government regulations, and political influences vary, as does the purchasing power of the target markets. The distribution channels are of different lengths, and distribution channel members expect margins specific to their markets. Prices set according to local conditions are optimal for the company as a whole, however, only if the pricing decision in one country does not affect profitability in another country. Because local managers tend to maximize goal achievement of the business they are responsible for, international marketers must make sure that the intended global strategic position of the company or the business unit as well as the positioning of its product lines and individual products are the basis for all pricing decisions. For that purpose they need to formulate an international pricing policy.

The pricing policy should *restate corporate objectives* relevant to individual pricing decisions such as expected profit margins, returns on investment, and market shares. It should also state a *general rule of how to determine prices*, including a pricing strategy, such as quick penetration of markets through low prices, skimming of high margins in market niches where the company has a significant competitive advantage, maintaining the competitive position in saturated markets, or concentrating on a market niche which requires a high-priced product versus covering the entire product category market; state the *company policy concerning rebates*, refunds, and discounts given to customers; indicate *preferred terms of payment* available to salespeople in their struggle to get orders, and to be used in specific markets. These terms should be chosen according to company expectations, knowledge of the customers, and the acceptable level of financial risk; specify conditions when *countertrade can be offered* or accepted to gain an order.

General rules for price determination

When defining an international pricing policy, marketers need to formulate general rules concerning the determination of basic prices in all of the business units of their company. They may select from:

- standard pricing policy
- standard formula pricing policy
- price adaptation policy
- strategic pricing policy

Standard pricing

With a standard pricing policy, the marketer charges the same base price for a product in every country market served. A company, for example, may set the price to wholesalers for its fountain pens at $25 each in all markets. Either the customer has to pay for freight, insurance and duties directly, or the company adds a specific amount to the base price.

This is the simplest policy for a company to administer. The task of setting the product price according to the firm's position on the experience curve is also simplified. That is, the price can be set with reference to the company's projected unit costs. But standard pricing is also the least customer-oriented pricing policy, and it does not respond to competitive and environmental factors specific to each market. Products may end up overpriced, or even underpriced. Optimal positioning as well as maximum profitability are achieved only by chance.

Standard formula pricing

With standard formula pricing, the company calculates the price for a product following the same formula in all country markets around the world. There are different ways to establish this formula.

Full-cost pricing **Full-cost pricing** consists of taking the full-cost price calculated for the product (production plus marketing, etc.) in the domestic market and adding the additional costs resulting from international transportation, taxes, tariffs, distribution, and promotion. Often this alternative results in prices that are too high to be competitive in non-domestic markets.

Direct cost plus contribution margin When choosing a **direct cost plus contribution margin formula** the production cost of the product is taken as the basis and additional costs due to the non-domestic marketing process plus a desired profit margin are added. Because of the complexity of the international marketing process, however, additional indirect administrative and marketing costs may arise without being included in the formula. This method, therefore, may lead to prices that do not cover all the costs incurred by the company.

Relevant cost A differential formula or relevant cost formula is the most useful approach in standard formula pricing decisions. The **relevant cost** includes all the incremental costs resulting from a non-domestic business opportunity that would not be incurred otherwise and adds them to the production cost. The manager then compares those costs with the additional revenues from the sale. If a suitable profit results, the price is set.

The biggest disadvantage of all these formulas is the resulting loss in company flexibility to react to differing or changing circumstances in the markets. A given strategic goal, such as high penetration of all served markets, may not be achieved owing to the non-flexible nature of the company's pricing policy.

Price adaptation

Price adaptation as an international policy means that the prices of the company's products are determined in a decentralized manner, according to the local managers' analysis of the various markets. This policy allows extremely flexible reactions to market and competitive developments.

For example, the U.S. is the country with the lowest IKEA prices overall. But some products are less expensive in Europe. For instance, although IKEA products are most expensive in Finland, one specific mattress is 42% less expensive there than in the U.S.

Despite its advantages price adaptation has some major disadvantages.

Difficulty of developing a global strategic position For example, a pen priced at $15 (wholesale) in Italy but $32 in Norway may represent two different market positions, one more prestigious than the other.

Second, if the price differences between markets become too big there is another danger.

Parallel imports Otherwise known as **gray markets** (basically, an import by an unauthorized party). When this occurs, channel members located in low-price markets not under the strict control of the firm may resell the product to market areas with significantly higher prices.

For example, the director of global marketing at the corporate headquarters of a U.S.-based company selling prestigious high-priced liquor under the same established brand name in almost every country around the world received strong complaints from the head of the company's subsidiary in Japan about substantial quantities of the product that had entered the country through unauthorized channels. These imports were traced to the U.S. where they had been sold to a distributor at a highly competitive price. The distributor had sold some of the products to an exporter who shipped the liquor to Japan and made a profit by selling it to local wholesalers at prices below those charged by the liquor manufacturer's own Japanese subsidiary.

Re-imports to the country of manufacture This can happen if prices in the foreign market are significantly lower than in the home market. Henkel, an international marketer of adhesives headquartered in Germany, had such a problem with Belgian re-exporters because prices in Belgium were too low. Other examples such as Kodak film, made in the U.S., imported from Taiwan to Germany illustrate that lateral importation through unauthorized channels may take place.

Depending on the legal regulations in the countries involved, gray markets may be relatively easy to stop but, simultaneously, hard to rule out (see Ethics box 16.1). In EU countries, for example, Articles 85 and 86 of the Treaty of Rome forbid limitations of free trade between and among member states. EU Commission and EU Court rulings have established the legality of all kinds of gray import. For example, the U.K.'s Parker Pen paid a penalty of some $980,000 when it tried to prevent its German distributor, Herlitz, from exporting Parker pens to other European countries.

Distribution channels that are not at all consistent with the firm's strategic positioning can get hold of its products and sell them at prices far below the

ETHICS BOX 16.1

Gray markets

As parallel importing spreads, a growing number of nations will face the question: What does a trademark owner own? The answer to this question largely depends on ethical standards agreed on in different societies.

The U.S. Supreme Court affirmed the Customs Service in: (1) denying imports by a third party when U.S. firms purchase U.S. trademark rights from independent foreign firms; and (2) permitting entry when U.S. firms register U.S. trademarks for goods manufactured abroad by foreign partner firms, incorporated foreign subsidiaries, or unincorporated foreign divisions. The Court disapproved entry when a U.S. trademark owner authorizes an independent foreign manufacturer to use the trademark abroad (KMart Corp. vs Cartier, Inc. et al. (1988), 86 Supreme Court 495).

However, regulations on gray markets may vary considerably from country to country. In Hong Kong and Singapore, there is a flood of parallel imports ranging from small-ticket items, such as soap and batteries, to more expensive goods, such as watches and electronic equipment. Several sole agents have taken parallel importers to court, but so far the courts have ruled in favor of parallel importers, thus granting them a justifiable status.

A European Commission Regulation mandates that auto manufacturers have to deliver a car to every citizen in any country of the EU. Also, each subsidiary of an automaker is required to back its warranty in every country regardless of where the car is purchased. Because this regulation has not led to a leveling of car prices, some car dealers in Europe specialize in offering "Euro-cars," parallel imported from other European countries. The car buyer can order a car from a catalog for delivery in about 3 weeks.

intended level. Silhouette, the Austrian manufacturer of spectacle frames and sunglasses for example, found their leading Titan Minimal Art glasses in Southeast Asia at outlets and price levels they did not consider adequate to their intended market position. The gray market outlets profit from the marketing efforts of the company, but often they do not provide the same level of customer service as the approved intermediaries. Those intermediaries, of course, complain about the unexpected competition. Because customers do not draw a distinction between regular channels of distribution and gray markets, such a development is usually detrimental to the overall business of the company.

Combating gray markets This requires suppliers to obtain accurate and timely information on their existence and magnitude. Data sources such as product serial numbers, warranty cards, and factory rebate programs need to be used. They increase costs but help to track the movement of the product to parallel importers and to assess the magnitude of the problem. To find out the distribution partner who had sold the products to the gray market, Silhouette had to mark the next batches delivered to their distributors in the entire region in a way nobody noticed. Buying their own products from the gray market allowed them to find out that the distributor in Hong Kong had not played to the rules.

A priori avoiding parallel imports This is less costly than combating them after they have happened. Henkel, for example, learning from negative experience, has built a computer model, including cost factors, trade structures, physical distribution costs, and price differences regarded as acceptable, to calculate price differences ("price corridors") between European country markets that will avoid parallel imports. In addition a "European Management Team" including managers of subsidiaries in the most important European markets regularly discusses pricing policy issues.

Strategic pricing

When a company follows a strategic pricing policy it formulates a rule for the determination of local prices depending on the intended strategic position. The absolute minimum of price standardization necessary to attain the intended global strategic position can be achieved through price lines (or price patterns) set by the home office.

Price lines Price lines set the company's prices relative to competitors'. They are followed in each market, but regional or local management can accommodate local costs, customer income levels, distribution margin requirements, and competition. Price lines also allow adaptation of prices to the changing market saturation levels that accompany different stages in the product lifecycle.

Price differentiation among country markets can be achieved without hampering the company's overall pricing policy. HILTI, Liechtenstein's specialist in fastening problems, for example, follows a global high-price strategy based on superior quality and direct distribution. Its products are more expensive than those of all competitors wherever they are sold. Nevertheless, HILTI's prices in Japan are significantly lower than European prices (depending on the exchange rate between the yen and the euro) over all its product lines, because of necessary adaptation to local price levels.

Central coordination Strategic pricing requires central coordination of pricing decisions. The people responsible for local pricing decisions not only have to follow the price lines, but also report to company headquarters their decisions concerning specific prices. The home office, having a general overview of the company's prices and the prices of relevant competitors, will then accept the suggested prices or negotiate with the local managers to come to a mutually acceptable solution. How difficult it may be to find a decision acceptable to all parties involved is illustrated by the variations of average prices in the European detergent market. The average price ratio of concentrated to powder detergents is about 60% in Germany compared to 100% in neighboring Belgium. Product line pricing across markets would not be consistent with prevailing price structures, while too much adaptation would lead to gray markets.

Internal pricing

Products, personnel, capital, rights, and know-how are readily transferred across country boundaries between subsidiaries. As a consequence the company has to determine how it wants to be paid, where, and how much for its deliveries to non-domestic affiliates. It has to establish an internal pricing policy. That is, rules have to be formulated on how to set prices that transfer funds between different parts of the company and allocate resources to specific uses. Those rules are also referred to as intra-company pricing or transfer pricing.

Transfer prices are not necessarily linked to the market value of the items transferred. The rules on what prices to charge and how have to take into account the firm's goals of maximizing and managing profits and of optimizing the development of the company as a whole, the subsidiaries' goals of successful development and earning recognition for their efforts, and the need of the headquarters to determine and compare the performance of its non-domestic business units. For example, if profit is transferred out of a subsidiary, the manager of that subsidiary should be evaluated on criteria other than just how much profit was generated.

Objectives In setting the rules for internal pricing a company's management can have various objectives in mind.

Lowering tax payments The company's tax payments can be lowered by using internal pricing to transfer profits from units in high-tax areas to low-tax areas. Australian companies, for example, are said to move in the region of $2 billion a year to corporate links in low- or no-tax countries, including Singapore and Hong Kong. In Europe, companies locate a sales subsidiary that officially handles their entire international sales activities in a low-tax country, such as Switzerland. That subsidiary purchases the products from the factory at cost and sells them at a profit to customers and affiliates around the world. Physically, the products never touch Swiss soil. They are shipped straight from the factory to the customers' premises.

Even if corporate tax rates are similar between parent and subsidiary countries, differences in tariff rates on the transferred goods are important in the determination of transfer prices. Machine parts, for example, might enjoy lower tariff rates than assembled machines.

Profit transfer The company can transfer profits from countries with foreign exchange restrictions or other economic controls to the unit that is supposed to make profits. This transfer is made possible by charging higher prices than reflect their true cost of production for merchandise, royalty payments on licenses, or payment for services delivered to the local subsidiary.

Other objectives Other objectives of internal pricing include:

- counteracting the influences of currency exchange fluctuations
- reducing the impact of inflation on the company's assets
- subsidizing new subsidiaries while they build market share
- minimizing duties to be paid
- justifying high prices in one area of the world while making profits in another.

For example, some oil companies have justified their high gasoline prices in Europe by claiming they make very low profits, owing to high costs, in Europe. They purchase the gasoline from their own European refineries, which also make low profits. The refineries, however, purchase crude oil from oil transportation companies that are located in low-tax countries. Of course, the transportation companies, which make substantial profits, are also controlled by the oil companies. So are a substantial number of oilwells.

Avoiding intensive tax audits and penalties if irregularities are discovered The internal pricing policy of a firm operating internationally must permit the achievement of corporate objectives while also allowing the company to live in peace with the local tax authorities. IBM, for example, is proud of being a good taxpayer in the countries where it does business.

Methods Internal prices should be easy to determine. For U.S.-based companies, Section 482 of the Internal Revenue Code calls for the determination of transfer prices to meet the basic arm's length standard. This code applies to all allocations of income between U.S. parent companies and their foreign operations, as well as between U.S. operations and their foreign parent companies.

The **arm's length price** is the price that would have resulted from negotiations between independent business partners in a similar transaction. Table 16.1 summarizes the methods fulfilling the demands of that standard. Feeding one of the first five methods listed with reliable data can be a nightmare. There either

TABLE 16.1 *Methods to determine transfer prices meeting the basic arm's length standard*

Method	Description
Comparable/uncontrolled	Compares the internal transfer price charged to the price an independent supplier selling a similar good charges to an independent buyer
Resale price/gross margin	Requires the internal unit selling to another internal unit to compare its gross profit margin to that attained by independent suppliers selling to independent buyers
Cost-plus/gross markup	Requires the internal seller to add a gross profit to the costs of the good sold to an internal buyer that is comparable to the gross profit earned by companies performing similar functions
Comparable profits	Requires the internal seller to compare its profits to those of similar units of internationally operating companies
Profit split	First, allocates profits between business units on the basis of functions performed, assets used, and risks assumed by each unit. Then, compares relative profits with those of uncontrolled internationally operating companies in similar situations
Unspecified	Information is to be provided on prices or profits that the controlled taxpayer could have realized by selecting a realistic alternative to the internal transaction

The internationally operating company having to determine internal transfer prices among its local units may select the method from the following list that provides the most accurate price for its unique situation.

do not exist any comparable independent suppliers, their cost structures are incomparable, or data – in particular on overhead and indirect costs – are extremely difficult to obtain.

Therefore, another method that is easier to administer and is acceptable to local tax authorities has to be selected. One is to *calculate the market price of goods, services or know-how internally transferred*. This approach is well suited to adapting to, and accounting for, local market conditions. The internal price would be the local market price minus the margin necessary for the subsidiary to cover its costs and expected profit margin. The approach is easy to justify to government authorities. It also allows every affiliate to be organized as its own profit center. But it raises the question of what costs to consider in the determination of the price. An international marketer introducing a product new to the local market may have difficulties in justifying the chosen internal price to government authorities. *Activity-based costing* could provide a rationale for cost allocation that may seem acceptable to those authorities.

Factors influencing price setting

In certain cases the marketer has little influence on the price that can be obtained for a product. The mechanisms of supply and demand dictate the price for largely undifferentiated products (such as wheat, copper, coffee, cement, flour, electricity, gas, and crude oil) that are marketed in large quantities on international commodity exchanges. Also, when a government is the customer or the marketer is confronted with strongly restrictive government regulations, the company often has only one alternative: accept the price or lose the customer's business.

However, most manufactured products and many services offer the opportunity of price setting. The marketer analyzes all relevant costs, the market environment, and relevant dimensions of the macro-environment such as economic conditions and governmental influences; sets the price based on these analyses; and then manages price escalation.

Costs

Costs determine a product's lower price limit. In the long run they have to be fully covered for the business to survive. In international pricing decisions, the same basic cost factors apply as in domestic pricing. There are some additional costs, however, that can strongly influence the minimum price of a product when sold in another country.

The costs of doing business, such as information gathering, travel expenses, and support of employees, are usually considerably higher in international than in domestic marketing.

The longer the distribution channel, the *higher the sum of margins and allowances* added for middlemen will be (see Figure 16.3).

Additional packaging and labeling, transportation and inventory-financing costs, as well as additional insurance against damage or loss, also increase the price.

Regardless of whether they are absorbed by the company or passed on to the customer, *taxes, tariffs, and administrative fees* (for documents, for example) add to international costs as well. Turnover taxes (in Japan and other countries) and value-added taxes (most popular in Europe) vary between 2 and 32%.

Market

Market factors that affect the prices of products are customers, competitors, business groups, and the country-specific structure of distribution. It is often a mixture of all those influences that strongly influences price setting by international marketers.

For example, Volkswagen of China, the market leader of carmakers in China with production sites in Shanghai and Changchun decreased the prices for all its models in 2004 by more than 10%. After an increase of 75% in 2003 the growth rate of care sales in China had dropped to 18% in 2004. Price wars among suppliers, less easy access to consumer credits, increasing gasoline prices, and expectations of further price cuts and a broader offer of imported cars after China's full integration into the WTO had made consumers "wait and see."

Customers

The attractiveness of a product to the target customers determines its real value, that is, the theoretical price ceiling in a given market. This price level will be decreased in many cases by the limited purchasing power of customers (especially in LDCs and emerging economies in eastern Europe, Latin America, and Southeast Asia). When prices are negotiated between business partners (for example, marketers and government agencies), the final price also depends on their negotiation skills.

Competition

The prices of competitive products and customer satisfaction with those products strongly influence what customers are willing to pay for the international marketer's product. A company's price setting, therefore, is influenced by the competitive structure of local markets. In the ice cream market of the European Union, for example, only one company – Eskimo, which belongs to Unilever – has achieved a significant presence in all member countries. In Belgium, Germany, Italy, and the Netherlands, local firms play an important role. This means that Eskimo has to deal with varying competitors with different backgrounds and competitive advantages. In Germany, the main competitor has a strong position in the premium segment, whereas in Belgium, the local prime contender has set

FIGURE 16.3 *Cost impact of distribution channel length*

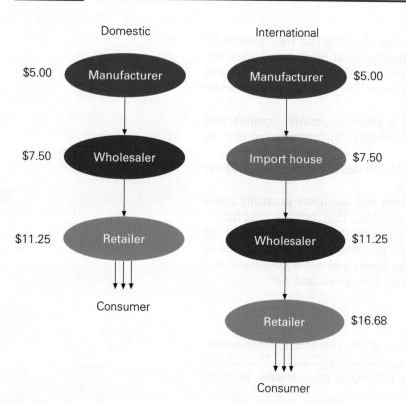

International marketers may face a price escalation effect due to longer distribution channels. This figure illustrates a typical three-member domestic channel and a typical four-member international channel. Assuming each channel member adds 50% to its price to cover costs, taxes, and its own profits, impact on retail price is considerable.

prices in the low to medium range. Eskimo's international price setting has to take these country-specific constellations into account.

Generally speaking, competition has the tendency to lower prices, to a point that may become dangerous to the existence of the firm. Deregulation of the U.S. air travel market, for example, has driven some well-known companies, such as Eastern Airlines or Pan Am, out of business.

Business groups

Companies may try to limit competition by forming one or more business groups. *Industry associations*, for example, gather information about market developments and transactions. They may represent their members in negotiations with governments or unions, as is the case in most European countries. *Loose groups of competitors* may agree on general rules of fair competition. *Cartels* may set prices (as OPEC tries to do), allocate market areas, establish sales volumes (as in the paper industry in some countries), or even constitute a selling unit that distributes profits to the members at the end of the year.

The international marketer has to evaluate the market power of such groups and sometimes join them, when the legal regulations at home and in the local market are appropriate. When the chances of winning are high, some firms choose to fight them.

Distribution

The level of *concentration* in local distribution varies across countries. In the Netherlands, for example, the top two food retailers hold a higher market share than the top seven in Italy. As a result, the potential of international marketers to freely set their prices and to use various above-the-line discounts may differ considerably within similar retail formats (see Strategy box 16.1).

The *importance of retail organization types* also differs between country markets. Watch distribution in Italy and Spain, for example, mainly relies on traditional retailers such as jewelers and watch stores. In Australia, watches are sold in supermarkets and department stores. Such differences not only influence the channel costs to be considered in price setting but also the potential of an international marketer to set prices and freely determine terms of payment.

In addition, the degree of *internationalization of intermediaries* strongly affects a marketer's ability to achieve price differentiation. International retail chains or procurement groups may purchase in the country with the lowest price level or force their suppliers to charge the same (lowest) price in all served country markets.

Macro-environment

Economic conditions

The following economic conditions have the strongest impacts on international pricing decisions: income distribution, growth rates, exchange rates, and inflation.

The *income distribution* of a country market affects the prices at which different groups of customers can afford the company's products.

Growth rates are an index of market maturity. In fast growing, young product markets pricing decisions are often made with the goal of keeping up with the pace or even winning a substantial market share before others. In more mature or stagnant markets, price competition may be fierce when local or regional competitors try to fend off new market entrants who set low prices to attract customers.

For example, when Compaq Computer of Houston, Texas, started selling desktop PCs in Japan for less than half what local manufacturers had been asking, it started a price war. Fujitsu, Japan's biggest computer company, determined not to lose market share, reacted by selling PCs at a loss. It could easily make up the loss with profits from semiconductors and telecom gear. That stirred up market leader NEC Corp., which matched Fujitsu's price cuts, and, in some cases, even undercut them. As a consequence, Compaq boosted its market share in Japan by only 0.1 points, to a puny 3.8%.

The influence of *exchange rates* on prices is illustrated by fluctuations in the value of the U.S. dollar in Europe in 2000–2005. The euro exchanged for one U.S. dollar in early 1999, went down to a value of $0.75 in 2001, but up again to $1.32 in 2005. This means that prices for U.S. products headed for Europe first rose by 25%, and then were cut by nearly half in less than 4 years. Managing such fluctuations will be discussed in the section on methods of payment.

High *inflation* requires periodic price adjustments to cover rising costs. Because inflation rates are not the same in different country markets, the international marketer is confronted with a sometimes complex puzzle of possible price changes and risks. If inflation is high in the country of production, the firm may not be able to adjust prices as necessary, and it may thus be forced to absorb increases in input prices. If inflation is high in the customer's country, the feasibility of increasing prices will depend on:

- customer reaction
- government controls
- additional costs of changing price tags, reprogramming cash registers, and other activities related to price changes.

STRATEGY BOX 16.1

The battle: Manufacturers against retailers

In countries such as Norway, Sweden, or Austria the three largest retailers control about 80% of the food market and even the biggest marketers cannot ignore them. Retailers and manufacturers sit together at the end of every year to negotiate on product ranges (listings) and discounts for the following year. In this situation, a jungle of discount systems may emerge.

At the end of the 1990s, German retailers were offered at least 25 different types of discount, for example, for turnover increases, jubilees, or mergers. These discounts meant that some retailers were able to supply goods a little more cheaply than their competitors.

Because of the wide range of products and the variety of discounts, Procter & Gamble had enormous expenses. More than 100 people were responsible for handling and controlling the complicated order and discount system. They were among the first marketers to try to break it. In 1996 they began negotiations with retailers by announcing that they will cancel all discounts and replace them with a

much simpler system of permanent low manufacturer prices. According to this system, discounts are given based on the amount of goods ordered, continuity of orders, compatibility of data processing systems with those of P&G, and also on the ease of facilities to deliver the ordered goods. To make the system more attractive to retailers, P&G announced a reduction of the variety of its product range: 26% in detergents, 32% in babycare products, 30% in soft drinks, and 15% in bodycare products.

However, first reactions of retailers showed that they did not want to give up the existing system. Rewe, the No. 1 German retailer, removed some P&G brands from the listed products of its more than 2,000 Penny (discount) shops. Edeka, hitherto having ordered more than $600 million worth of goods a year from P&G, threatened to stop ordering P&G's products. Although Procter & Gamble and a minority of retailers believed that the proposed system to be more effective, only the strongest of the firm's brands were able to force the big retailers to keep them listed.

Experience in the U.S. where P&G started the same attempt 5 years earlier, showed that at first, retailers slowed purchases. But by the end of the 1990s the firm's overall volume market share in the U.S. had either held steady or increased for 4 years in a row.

If payment from a customer located in an inflationary market is expected to be delayed (which would lower the real price paid), the inflation rate should be considered in price negotiations.

Culture

Culture box 16.1 gives an example how culture-specific meanings of numbers can have an impact on price setting. In western societies prices that end in the digit 9 such as €2.49 or $19.99 are often used in advertised prices of products and services because they influence price perceptions of consumers who tend to round down such prices. In China the digit 9 has no relevant meaning to consumers. In contrast 4 has a negative connotation (death) and thus, is avoided in setting prices.

Government

Government activities and regulations also influence prices. The effects of exchange rate and balance of payment policies were discussed in Chapter 3. Governments may also impose *price controls* on specific products. These may be:

- price floors
- price ceilings
- restrictions on price changes
- maximum or minimum profit margins.

In some European countries, for example, retailers are forbidden by law to sell products below the price they paid for them. For certain products, the Norwegian government has set margins that may not be undercut by competitors.

Government subsidies can help lower prices to increase marketers' global competitiveness. Such subsidies often depend on the power of lobby groups and other non-economic developments. The U.S. government, for example, is an ardent fighter against subsidies that decrease prices and distort competition in the iron and steel industries. But it heavily subsidizes farmers, allowing them to export grains at prices that cannot be matched by farmers in developing countries.

Frequently, exports of government-subsidized products are viewed in the importing country as *dumping*. In these situations, domestic competitors put

CULTURE BOX 16.1

Superstition and price-ending choice

The Chinese culture's respect for the supernatural leads to numerical digits having traditional, superstitious meanings. Two in particular, the digits 8 and 4, have evaluative connotations that may affect their use in price setting.

The digit 8 in Chinese is pronounced *ba*, similar in pronunciation to *fa*, which means "to become rich" or "enrichment," and to *fu*, which means "lucky." Thus, 8 is not only associated with both prosperity and good luck but also used in a significant amount of price endings.

In contrast, the digit 4 (*si*) is pronounced in exactly the same way as "to die," except for the tone, and thus is associated with death. Chinese businesspeople therefore, avoid this digit at the end of their set prices wherever it is possible.

Although the digit 9 carries a meaning of "being long" that can be interpreted positively as "longevity," this meaning is not considered relevant in commerce. A Beijing marketing executive noted, "no one would want to have their price last forever."

Source: Adapted from Simmons, L.C. and R.M. Schindler (2002) "Cultural superstitions and the price endings used in Chinese advertising", *Journal of International Marketing*, 11(2), 101–111

pressure on their governments to impose a countervailing tariff to make the imported product equivalent in price to the domestically produced one.

Price escalation

The result of all of these factors of influence may be price escalation. Table 16.2 contains an example of how the costs of an exported product, from manufacture to delivery to the first channel member, are calculated. Marketing costs and taxes in the local market have to be added to derive the final customer price. Considering all the additions to the domestic price "ex works" (at the point of production), it is understandable that the consumer price for a Canada-manufactured product sold in Japan may be double the price charged in the domestic market.

In many cases, price escalation effects will prohibit the marketer from successfully entering new country markets. However, there are several approaches to counteract the problem, as is demonstrated by consumer products sold overseas at a lower price than the domestic price (such as Italian wine and shoes sold in the U.S.).

TABLE 16.2 *Example of price calculation for an exported product*

Production cost	$10.00
+ Profit margin (10%)	1.00
Price "ex works"	$11.00
+ Transportation	0.50
+ Transport insurance	0.05
+ Freight-forwarding fee	0.02
+ Handling costs	0.02
Price "FOR/FOT"	$11.59
+ Cost of shipment to boarder	0.20
+ Export support fee	0.03
+ Export administration fees	0.01
Price "delivered at frontier"	$11.83
+ Cost of shipment to port of departure	0.05
Price "freight carriage" (and insurance), port of departure	$11.88
+ Port costs	0.04
Price "free on board", port of departure	$11.92
+ Cost of documents	0.01
+ Cost of bill of lading	0.01
+ Sea freight	0.15
Price "C&F", port of destination	$12.09
+ Freight insurance FPA (free particular average)	0.06
Price "cost, insurance, freight", port of destination	$12.15
= Price "ex ship", port of destination	
+ Port costs	0.10
Price "ex quay" (duties on buyer's account)	$12.25
+ Import duties	1.10
Price "ex quay", port of destination	$13.35
+ Transportation costs	0.70
+ Freight-forwarder costs	0.25
+ Transportation insurance	0.15
Price "delivered, duty paid"	$14.45

In order to export a product, many functions must be performed. Each, of course, must be paid for. This table illustrates how the price to the importer (the price "delivered, duty paid") escalates from the full cost of manufacturing.

The firm may choose to enter markets that are in an early stage of the product's lifecycle, and are therefore less resistant to higher prices. It may position the product (or product line) in a way to avoid direct competition with less expensive competitors. An innovative shortening of the distribution channel, without decreasing the level of customer service, may also reduce costs. This is particularly important when a cumulative turnover tax has to be paid.

Product modifications, such as replacing costly materials and features with less expensive ones, may effectively reduce the costs to be covered. However, the marketer has to take care that this change does not negatively influence the value to the customer.

Assembly of components, production of parts, or production of the entire product either locally or in a third, low-wage country are other possible ways to counteract price escalation. Shipping components to be assembled in the target market may change the tariff rate. Cars exported to Brazil, for example, once rated a lower tariff when the tires were not mounted on them until after their arrival at the docks. Japanese carmakers such as Toyota, Honda, and Nissan have built factories in Ireland, the U.K., and the U.S. to be able to serve the EU and NAFTA markets at competitive prices. European companies, such as VA MCE, an Austrian supplier of mechanical engineering and industrial services, found it necessary to produce goods for the U.S. market in Mexico.

One way to reduce the impact of higher prices on customer demand is to *lease the product*. This is a particularly attractive approach for international marketers of industrial goods, such as machinery, transportation vehicles, or industrial robots. It not only helps overcome the short-term negative effect of a high price, but may also help to lessen the problems of insufficient hard currency or the costs of product maintenance personnel. In fact, the ability to lease, or to provide credit at low interest rates, is a significant marketing tool for international marketers.

The final solution is to *lower the net price*. This can be achieved by constantly increasing the company's productivity, then gaining economies of scale. But it can also be done for a short span of time by diminishing the profit margin. Or the firm can charge only part of the costs. Most or all of the product's R&D (research and development) costs, for example, can be charged to the home market. This approach has to be considered with prudence, however. It not only directly influences the company's profit margin (prices once lowered can seldom be substantially raised later), but may also lead to the filing of dumping charges by local competitors.

The final price for a product should not be set before the business partners negotiate the terms of delivery and the terms of payment. The various terms of delivery available to an international marketer and their consequences for business partners concerning costs and risks to be borne were discussed in Chapter 14. The most frequently applied terms of payment in international marketing are discussed in the following section.

Payment terms

Terms of payment are most often the result of a sales negotiation process. They state the point in time and the circumstances of payment for the goods or services to be delivered. Every marketer wants to get paid as quickly as possible and according to the invoice. Customers want to obtain the merchandise as ordered. A smooth process of exchange is in the interest of both parties, therefore. But many potential payment disputes can disturb the process, especially in international marketing.

Factors affecting choice

The most important determinant of payment terms is the financial risk anticipated by the business partners in the transaction process. Table 16.3 lists the various kinds of financial risk occurring in international marketing as well as their sources, which are discussed in the following.

Financial risk

Financial risk in international payment procedures may arise from various sources.

Business partner reliability A lack of business partner reliability results in payment risk. The level of trust and the strength of the relationship between the two business partners as well as the level of knowledge about the buyer's financial strength or weakness strongly influence the chosen term of payment. Sales subsidiaries normally get their merchandise on an open-account basis. But most Korean companies will not deliver anything to Colombian customers, for example, without having received an irrevocable letter of credit, owing to the higher risks.

Physical distance Another source of financial risk is the distance between the business partners. Distance influences the duration and complication of shipment. It can also reduce the safety and quality of the product; that is, it results in a **product risk** for the customer. A Swiss wholesaler selling blue jeans manufactured in Thailand to an importer in Denmark, therefore, will not pay for the goods before his bank has received and approved the entire set of shipping documents agreed in the terms of payment.

Nature of merchandise The nature of the merchandise may influence the product and the payment risks involved with a contract. If Davidoff, the Belgian marketer of cigars, purchases tobacco from Egypt, for example, it will not pay the invoiced amount before having inspected the quality of the merchandise.

Political or social instability Political or social instability in one or both of the partners' home countries results in **institutional risk**. For example, many companies in Hungary, Poland, and Slovakia involved in business with the former Soviet Union not only lost essential orders but also their base of existence when the USSR was split up into a group of countries, such as Armenia, Azerbaijan, Belarus, Estonia, Kazakhstan, Latvia, and Moldova to name just a few, with no convertible currencies at that time.

Fluctuating exchange rates **Currency risk** arises from fluctuating exchange rates (exchange rate risk) that strongly affect the price of the merchandise and the potential profit, or from currency exchange restrictions. Future issues box

TABLE 16.3 *Sources of financial risk*

Source	Risk	
Business partner reliability	Payment risk	There are a great number of sources and a variety of kinds of financial risk in international marketing.
Physical distance	Product risk	
Nature of merchandise	Product risk	
Political/social instability	Institutional risk	
Fluctuating exchange rates	Currency risk	
Currency exchange restrictions	Currency risk	
Inflation	Inflation risk	
Temporary financing	Interest rate risk	

16.1 shows that governments are concerned with avoiding such fluctuations in order to smooth international trade. Exchange rate risk arises from the need to conduct the international business transaction in at least one foreign currency. The terms of payment state a price in a particular currency. For example, an export from a U.S.-based company to one in the U.K. might be billed at $5,750, payable in 30 days on receipt of the invoice. Thus the importer is assuming the exchange rate risk. If the value of the U.S. dollar increases after the price has been set, the U.K. importer will have to exchange more pounds for dollars, effectively raising the price of the imported product. Of course, if the price of the product is quoted in a foreign currency, the home-country organization bears the exchange rate risk.

Fluctuations in foreign exchange rates can threaten and even eliminate profitability
© Jyothi Joshi/iStock

Currency exchange restrictions Associated with exchange rate risk is the risk that the exchange of currencies might be restricted. A **blocked currency** means that the government does not allow any international transfer of domestic currencies. When selling consumer goods to Belarus, for example, payment must be fixed in a foreign currency, mainly US dollars, euros, or Swiss francs. The payment needs to go from the customer to the local bank managing the supplier's foreign currency account and from there via the country's central bank to the marketer's bank in the home country. Each bank involved in the transfer charges some fee (mostly a percentage of the transferred sum), diminishing the final amount the marketer will find in his account.

FUTURE ISSUES BOX 16.1

One Asian currency?

Ever since Southeast Asian currencies collapsed in 1997–98, threatening the economic development of the region, governments in that part of the world have been looking for ways to make sure it does not happen again. Nevertheless, Asian governments are holding close to $2 trillion in their reserve accounts. Buying U.S. dollars to keep their currencies weak and boost their countries exports, however, leaves them vulnerable to the same problems as at the end of the last century: over-reliance on the U.S. dollar.

One solution that is attracting some attention is giving the region a common currency, making it less dependent on the changes of value of the dollar and the yen. The idea of creating a common currency akin to Europe's successful euro – or at least a regional "trading currency" for bonds that could serve as a precursor to actual monetary union – is not really new. But moves by regional governments and international financial institutions to create a more unified bond market in Asia are raising hopes that the idea could work. Skeptics say that it could never become reality given the differences among the region's diverse economies. Others think that a common currency remains an "ideal," but could be reached in a step-by-step process over an extended period of time.

One suggestion is that the region's biggest countries create a new Asian Bond Corporation, to buy local currency debt from countries such as Japan, Korea, and Thailand. The new entity would then issue bonds denominated in a new "basket currency" – an artificial trading currency based on the value of a weighted average of the currencies in the basket. Because it would be backed by government bonds, such a fund would establish a market price for the combination of the currencies. That could serve as a benchmark to allow companies in the region to easily raise money in neighboring countries, such as bonds in baht to finance operations in Thailand. Foreign exchange risk could be removed.

Many economists believe that a common currency in Southeast Asia remains far fetched. But strengthening the region's bond markets would be a worthy undertaking.

Source: Adapted from Buckman, R. and J. Singer (2003) "Euro for Asia gains in allure: Regional or 'trading' currency might be steadying factor", *Wall Street Journal* (Eastern edition), 3 October, p. C.16

Less severe than blocked currencies are **currency licensing restrictions**. These occur when all foreign exchange transactions must be done through a central bank, or another agency, at the official (and fixed) rate. This system controls the sale or purchase of products by granting or denying a license to sell or buy foreign currency. Taiwan, for example, requires all exporters and importers to buy currencies through its central bank. In most cases, written documentation of the business deal is required before the national bank will become involved. This means that the handling of foreign exchange transactions is somewhat time consuming, resulting in additional costs.

Multiple exchange rates also restrict currencies. In this case, products approved by the local administration are assigned currency exchange rates that facilitate sales by lowering their prices. Non-approved goods are in effect penalized by exchange rates that make their prices higher.

Import deposit requirements influence the real exchange rate by requiring companies selling to a certain country to deposit a specific amount of money with the government or a domestic bank prior to the sale. Once the funds are deposited, a license for foreign currency transfer or permission to sell is granted. Many developing nations use this form of restriction, which effectively increases the amount of money lost while those inactive funds are held as the deposit.

Finally, national banks or administrative bodies may control the quantity of currency that is exchanged. For example, countries may place a quota on the amount of foreign or local currency that may be brought into, or taken out of, the country. Countries with no freely convertible currencies do not allow their citizens to leave the country with more than the equivalent of a few hundred dollars, or less, in the domestic currency. Quantity control effectively influences the volume of products that can be traded, because it changes the price of the product and the costs of marketing support.

When exchange restrictions are lifted, sizeable adjustments in financial markets and trade flows may result. When Poland eliminated its convertibility restrictions, for example, trade flows with former COMECON partners decreased whereas markets for both consumer and industrial goods were opened to more international buyers and sellers.

All kinds of existing currency exchange restriction will be considered when the terms of payment are specified in a sales contract. They mainly complicate the documentation needed before any monetary transaction takes place, or lead to commercial transactions with little or no financial settlement, so-called counter-trade agreements.

Inflation   Inflation directly affects the real buying power of customers in a market and therefore constitutes another source of financial risk. While exchange rate fluctuations are in theory supposed to exactly offset the inflation rate, inflation may, in fact, be greater or even less than the change in currency rates. Devaluation of a currency should increase exports, because export prices will be lower. But this may not occur if the change is overwhelmed by a high inflation rate.

The inflation risk also has a direct effect on international finance. Highly fluctuating inflation rates, for example, influence the price that must be set. But they also have an impact on the value of profits that are transferred back to the parent company. There are also certain asset management decisions that must be made with respect to economies experiencing high inflation. For example, when the Brazilian economy was experiencing 1,000% inflation, Brazilian buyers tried to minimize accounts receivable and maximize accounts payable. This is because the value of the money used to settle accounts decreased daily. Thus prolonging payment meant that the buying company would pay in "cheaper" (less valuable) money.

Temporary financing Setting terms of payment also presents the company with an **interest rate risk**. This risk exists when the inflow and outflow of a currency do not match, and temporary financing is required. This is true either domestically or internationally. An international cash manager has an opportunity to raise money from a wider set of sources than does a domestic manager. At the same time, funds owed internationally are also subject to changing interest rates. If two or more currencies are involved in the debt of a company and interest rates change, the internationally operating firm will be exposed to higher interest rate risks compared to a domestic one.

For example, a U.S.-based seller of cattle to Japan and the U.K. may borrow to finance the costs of the sale and inventory, until an inflow of capital from the buyers occurs. A decision has to be made, including whether to be paid in dollars, yen or pounds sterling and in which country and currency the seller prefers to finance working capital. The loan is subject to interest rate fluctuations. Depending on the fluctuation of interest to be paid or earned in the three countries, the profit of the cattle marketer can vary significantly.

Industry standards and degree of competition

Beside the sources of financial risk discussed earlier, the industry standards and degree of competition may affect the choice of terms of payment. Companies that are in a highly competitive industry (such as the telecommunications, PC, or steel-making industries) or are mass marketers of consumer goods (such as Nestlé, Matsushita, or Whirlpool) may have to accept a higher risk payment form in order to offer a competitive pricing option to their customers.

Market strength and negotiation skills

The market strength of each of the business partners as well as their negotiation skills also determine the terms of payment fixed in a contract. A very strong customer such as Wal-Mart Stores Inc., which had market shares of, for example, 32% of disposable diapers, 26% of toothpaste, and 20% of pet food in the U.S. in 2002 is strong enough to dictate terms of payment to its international suppliers. As described in Chapter 13, superior negotiation skills may help salespeople convince their customers to accept terms of payment that lower the risks for the supplier.

Degree of marketer's customer orientation

The degree of a marketer's customer orientation will also co-determine the preferred terms of payment. The better the marketer understands potential risks perceived by its customers and the more the marketer wants to establish long-lasting business relationships the more it will be able to offer terms of payment which are highly attractive to the customer.

Methods of payment

The methods of payment not only regulate the way goods or services are to be exchanged, but they also represent a financial tool that can be used effectively in a competitive marketing program. Figure 16.4 gives an overview of the parties potentially involved in international payment procedures and their relationships. In addition to the primary business partners, most often their banks will be involved. National regulations and international agreements also affect payment procedures and have to be followed. Third parties, for example investors who buy the financial arrangement (similar to the idea of factoring account receivables) or government-run export banks providing guarantees, may enter the picture. Depending on the parties involved, and the factors that affect choice, the specific method of payment will be selected.

The methods of payment available to the international marketer range from high-credit, high-risk, customer-oriented methods to low-credit, low-risk, producer-oriented methods. Th...

These are discussed in the following section.

Consignment

When a consignment contract exists, the marketer or consignor delivers the products to the customer but retains the title to them until the customer has sold them to a third party or has consumed/used them and paid the marketer. For example, BASF, a German marketer of special chemicals, may have a contract with a customer in Morocco under which the barrels containing the chemicals are stored at the customer's premises, but remain the property of the supplier until they enter the production process. The consignee is assured of having the needed volume of merchandise at each point in the production process and in many cases does not have to pay taxes or duties before using the products.

Efficient use of consignment requires that the marketer be able to control the volume of both the merchandise in stock and consigned merchandise. The major problem with consignment is that the marketer assumes part of the financing of the customer's inventory and absorbs a high credit risk.

Open accounts

This is the payment method most often used in domestic marketing. It offers full credit terms to the customer. Because of the high risk involved in open accounts

---

FIGURE 16.4 *Parties involved in an international payment procedure*

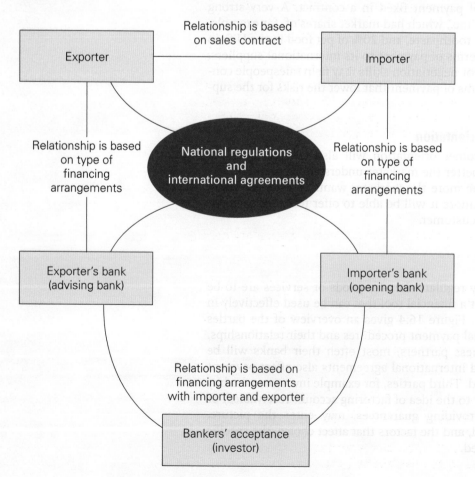

To ensure that the exporter gets paid by the importer, various parties must be involved, and many activities must be completed.

Source: Eng, M. (1982) "Trade financing" in I. Walter and T. Murray (eds) *Handbook of International Business*, New York: John Wiley & Sons, p.137.

Copyright © 1982 John Wiley & Sons, Inc. Reprinted by permission of John Wiley & Sons, Inc.

in international marketing, this alternative is mostly used between production and sales units of companies operating internationally or in cases where long-lasting, reliable business relationships exist.

In Europe many business deals have to be made on an open-account basis, because customers will not accept any other payment method. But even in the European Union open accounts differ as regards the time allowed for payment and in the risk involved across countries. Customers in countries with a Roman cultural background are significantly slower in paying their dues. In France, for example, the usual limits for payment are 90 days in the ice cream market and 60 days for detergents compared to 30 days for both in the Netherlands. Italian customers have a reputation for being extremely slow in paying their open accounts. Ninety days are usually fixed limits, but payments may take twice as long.

Marketers from countries such as Germany or the U.S. who are used to shorter payment times and greater reliability of their customers concerning compliance with contractual terms tend to become very nervous and to threaten their customers with legal actions. Their Italian or French customers will not understand such impatience and change their suppliers if possible.

International marketers who are aware of such cultural differences will gather precise information on the credit reliability of new customers, set their prices accordingly (to cover the higher costs for lost interest), and if they need to be re-financed more quickly, sell their accounts receivable to a bank.

Payment against documents

An alternative method of payment that decreases the risk of the marketer is to make payment dependent on the presentation of documents specified in the sales contract. After shipping the goods to the customer, the marketer presents the documents to its bank. They prove that the goods were sent to the customer as specified in the contract. The bank, in turn, forwards the documents to the bank of the customer for collection of payment. This way the customer is guaranteed that the merchandise has been shipped as stated in the contract before it is paid for. The marketer gains security in that the documents are not handed over to the customer before the customer has agreed to pay for the merchandise.

In most cases, when payment against documents is chosen as the method of payment a draft is used. A draft for payment is an order written by a seller requesting the buyer to pay a specified amount of money at a specified time. Basically, there are three different kinds of draft, which can be negotiated and included in the contract.

Sight draft On presentation of a sight draft the marketer has to be paid immediately.

Time draft With a time draft, payment must be made within a specified time period, usually 30, 60, 90, 120, or 180 days.

Deferred payment Deferred payment means that the marketer is paid by a specific date fixed in the contract. Deferred payment may be negotiated when the merchandise has to pass government examination before it is allowed to enter the country, as is the case with food and drugs exported to the U.S. If the marketer needs to be paid before the fixed time has elapsed, the draft can be sold in a financial market or to the customer's bank at a discount.

The two most popular forms of payment against documents are *documents against payment* (D/P), based on a sight draft, and *documents against acceptance* (D/A), based on a time draft. On receipt of payment from the customer, its bank proceeds as indicated by the marketer. The documents are handed over to the customer and the funds are remitted to the marketer's bank. This bank, in turn, makes them available to the firm. Costs incurred by the marketer for this method of payment are approximately 2% of the sales volume.

Using this method of payment, the seller has no security guarantee to be paid even after having shipped the goods and presented the documents as specified in the contract. If the buyer refuses to pay, the supplier can only be sure of keeping ownership of the goods if the contract states specific documents, such as the bill of lading, that must be presented to get hold of the goods. Even then the situation is difficult for the marketer. The shipped goods have to be sold to another local client or repatriated. Because this is not only rather complicated but sometimes also expensive, the banks involved in the payment procedure should be given an address (of a reliable business partner or a freight forwarder) to be contacted in case of problems. Payment against documents, therefore, is only used as a method of payment when seller and buyer know each other as reliable partners and do not have any doubt concerning each other's willingness and ability to fulfill the contract.

Letter of credit

A letter of credit (L/C) is a written obligation from a bank made at the request of the customer to honor a marketer's drafts or other demands for payment on compliance with conditions specified in the document. Figure 16.5 depicts the entire process. For example, if a Canadian manufacturer of snowmobiles signs a contract with a Finnish customer requiring a letter of credit, the Finnish buyer will ask its bank to prepare a letter of credit in favor of the Canadian supplier. If that bank (the issuing bank) is ready to assume responsibility for payment, it will contact the marketer's bank in Canada. This bank (the advising bank) can either confirm the letter of credit or not, forwarding the letter of credit to the snowmobile manufacturer.

FIGURE 16.5   *Letter of credit process*

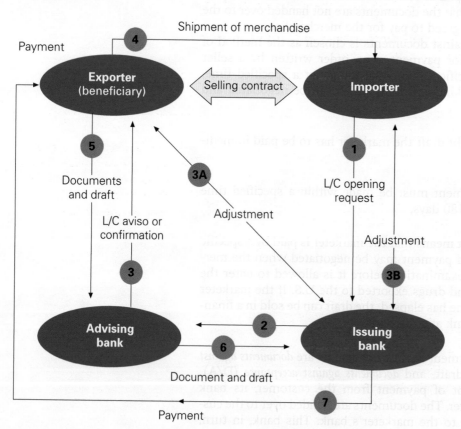

Letters of credit, which reduce international commercial risk, must be managed through a series of steps and involve a variety of organizations.

After receiving the letter of credit, the marketer should carefully review all the points listed in Table 16.4. If there are any discrepancies between the contents of the letter of credit and the sales contract, the marketer should ask the issuing bank and/or the customer for adjustment. It is important to do this before shipping the merchandise, because even an extremely small difference between the contents of the letter of credit and the shipment documents may result in refusal of payment by the issuing bank. For example, the Finnish bank may refuse to meet its obligations because one letter in one word in the documents of the Canadian supplier is different from the letter of credit.

After shipping the merchandise, the Canadian marketer (the beneficiary) presents all the necessary documents and a draft to the advising Canadian bank. The bank reviews and forwards them to the issuing Finnish bank. This bank will closely examine the documents and the draft. If it confirms the information in the letter of credit, the marketer will be paid according to the type of draft, and the customer will receive title to the merchandise.

Depending on the decisions of the two banks involved, the letter of credit may take different forms. An irrevocable letter of credit implies that the issuing bank may irrevocably commit itself to pay the marketer's draft. If the bank keeps its freedom to amend or cancel the credit at any time, the letter of credit is a revocable letter of credit. In practice this form of letter of credit is not common, because it does not provide any security to the marketer and therefore does not justify the cost of the procedure.

Irrevocable letters of credit may be *confirmed* by the advising bank or not. If an irrevocable letter of credit is *unconfirmed*, the advising bank is not obliged to pay the draft. The advising bank will not confirm a letter of credit when the issuing bank (perhaps because of its political/economic environment) represents an unacceptable credit risk. Most banks located in industrialized countries issue lists of countries for which they are not prepared to confirm letters of credit.

Letters of credit must be closely checked for forgeries, which have become more and more sophisticated. For example, the only mistake in a faked letter of credit from Nigeria was that the trunk of the elephant in the bank logo pointed to the left instead of to the right.

Most marketers dealing with unknown customer banks will try to get a confirmed, irrevocable letter of credit. This is the most secure payment method, after

TABLE 16.4 *Points to review in a letter of credit*

1 Name and address must be correct
2 Credit amount must be sufficient to cover shipment agreed in the sales contract, especially if freight and insurance charges are to be paid by the exporter
3 Required documents must be obtainable and in accordance with the sales contract
4 Points of shipment and destination of merchandise must be correctly stated
5 Shipping date must allow sufficient time to dispatch goods from supplier's warehouse to shipping point
6 Expiration of credit must allow sufficient time for presentation of draft and required documents at the banking office where credit expires
7 Description of merchandise and any specifications must agree with terms of sale

To avoid any surprises later on, a marketer should carefully review all points concerning a letter of credit as listed here, before shipping the merchandise.

cash in advance. It ensures that the marketer will be paid by the advising bank, provided all conditions stated in the letter of credit are met, even if the issuing bank will not honor the draft for any reason.

When goods are shipped to a customer on a continuing basis, a *revolving letter of credit* may be issued. In other words, the letter of credit applies to the sale of multiple shipments over an extended period of time. *Back-to-back letters of credit* occur when an intermediary uses an irrevocable letter of credit to ask the advising bank to open a similar letter of credit in favor of the ultimate supplier of the merchandise. A small Swiss trading house may, for example, possess an irrevocable letter of credit for a shipment of electric generators, manufactured by General Electric in the U.S.A., to Ethiopia. Because of the small size of the trading house, GE may not be prepared to do business without an irrevocable letter of credit from the trading house. The trader, therefore, may ask its bank to issue a letter of credit in favor of GE, offering the Ethiopian irrevocable letter of credit as security.

A special form of letters of credit used in raw materials delivery contracts with customers in east Asia and the CIS are the so-called *"red clause letters of credit."* They contain a special clause (printed in red) that allows the advising bank to transfer part or the entire cash equivalent before the supplier presents the documents claimed in the letter of credit. The payment in advance should give the supplier the working capital needed to fulfill its obligations. Any risk of non-delivery is borne by the customer, however.

The cost of a letter of credit can approach 3% of the sales value shown in the invoice. Despite this high cost in comparison to an open account, the marketer will choose to rely on a letter of credit if the customer represents an unknown credit risk; the foreign exchange regulations of the customer's country do not allow simple, direct payments; or transportation costs are high.

Payment in advance

Payment in advance is the most attractive method of payment for the marketer, generating revenue before goods are shipped or services are provided. The customer bears all risks and, in effect, helps finance production of the goods or services. The payment can be made by the customer, its bank, or the marketer's bank at the time the order is placed with the marketer.

Full payment in advance is rarely encountered in international marketing. It may be used when the market position of the supplier is very strong and the customer's credit rating is unsatisfactory or unknown. For example, a company with a very strong brand, such as French Louis Vuitton, can ask its customers in industrializing countries, such as Indonesia, to pay for their orders in advance. And when China opened up its trading policy with western nations, it offered payment in advance for training, by European specialists, of managers at industrial plants.

Partial payment in advance may be negotiated when the size of the order is so large that it overwhelms the supplier's financing capability. For example, customer-specific engineering and/or production involve enormous working capital. When the construction of a steelmill for the site at Ahwaz in southwestern Iran was negotiated between an Iranian delegation and Japanese as well as European engineering firms, the Iranians offered one-third of the project's anticipated dollar volume as payment in advance to indicate their willingness and ability to finance the huge project.

Managing financial risks

Even the most elaborate methods of payment are not able to account for all the financial risks related to an international business contract. An organization engaged in international operations has several options available to help manage financial risk, including not engaging in international trade (hence no risk stemming from that kind of business), and direct foreign investment (to avoid being considered a "foreign" company). Before selecting one of these options, management should evaluate the risks and risk management options in light of the current global financial framework. Sources of funds and the organizations that regulate financial activity help determine the appropriate financial management approach.

Managing exchange rate risk

The exchange rate risk can be assumed by the organization itself, the customer, or it can be transferred to a third party in international financial markets, thus covering exchange rate fluctuations. Markets that buy and sell currencies are made up of commercial banks, central banks, and some individuals and companies. In any case, the exchange risk must be borne by some organization in order for the exchange (sale) to occur.

Choice of currency

One of the two business partners can avoid bearing exchange rate risk through the choice of currency in the business contract. Doing business only in their own currency is an easy solution for companies located in world currency areas such as the U.S. dollar, the euro, the Japanese yen, or the Swiss franc. If business is done with a subsidiary located outside such an area, however, the risk stays with the firm.

Foreign currency account

A company doing regular import and export business in a foreign currency can open a foreign currency account. A French textile company that buys raw materials from Bangladesh and semi-finished products from Malaysia and Vietnam, for example, and sells its branded products to the U.S. may do the entire business on a dollar basis. All the inflows and outflows of dollars accompanying the imports and exports are registered in a foreign currency account, thus covering most of the exchange rate fluctuations.

Spot market

If the company does only irregular business in a foreign currency or is not able to balance the flows of foreign currency, it can rely on the spot market to buy and sell major currencies (blocked currencies do not have a financial market, and financial markets for minor currencies are limited) for its immediate needs. While there are variations within the spot market, its basic usefulness to the company operating internationally lies in the ability to buy or sell foreign currencies at any time.

For example, a Mexican company importing products from Singapore could buy U.S. dollars on the spot market, at the spot rate, when its bill becomes due (assuming the price is quoted in U.S. dollars). But waiting until the bill becomes due means that the Mexican company is incurring a currency exchange risk. If the dollar goes up against the peso between the date of sale and payment, the Mexicans must pay more for the product. If the dollar goes down against the peso, the Mexicans pay less.

Accurate prediction in any market, in particular one subject to political pressures and rapid changes, such as the currency exchange market, is very difficult. Therefore, most businesses do not wish to carry exchange rate risk themselves, as speculation is not their primary business. They may:

- sell their receivables in foreign currency
- take foreign currency credits

- use forward markets
- buy foreign currency options to minimize a potential exchange rate loss.

Selling foreign currency receivables

Accounts receivable in foreign currency can be sold to a bank if the buyer has accepted a draft. Short-term receivables that are due in a certain period of time can be sold to factoring banks that credit the sellers in their own currency and take over payment as well as exchange rate risks. The International Factors Group, for example, contains cooperating factoring banks from 27 countries, including the major OECD members but also Hong Kong, Hungary, Indonesia, Korea, Malaysia, the Philippines, Singapore, Thailand, and Turkey. Long-term receivables might be handed over to a bank through a forfeiting contract. The seller is credited in its own currency (that is, the bank takes over the exchange rate risk) but keeps the payment risk. In any case, the bank will take a certain percentage of the invoiced amount as a discount to cover its costs and risks.

Foreign currency credit

To cover the firm's exchange rate risk, management may take a credit of the same amount, period of validity, and currency as a foreign account receivable. The credit is paid back when the buyer pays its dues. When an Indian producer of software sells its products to the U.K. and finances the working capital needed for that business through a pound sterling loan, it applies this risk minimization tool.

Forward market

A forward, or future, market exists because there is uncertainty as to the future value or exchange rate of a particular currency. It is that uncertainty that prompts the buying and selling of currency exchange risk. This process is usually referred to as **hedging**. For example, a Hungarian exporter of dairy products may sell 5 million forints worth of yogurt and butter to a buyer in Portugal. Assume the current exchange rate of the forint = €30,004 (the Portuguese currency unit). The terms of payment specify payment in euros in 60 days. At the current exchange rate, the Hungarian firm has a collectable in 60 days of €20,000. At the time the agreement is signed, the exporter can sell that amount of euros in the forward market for delivery in 60 days, in effect shifting the exchange rate risk to the buying bank. If the 60-day forward rate is forint 1 = €0.0039, the exporter will receive €19,500. That is, he will incur a loss of 2.5% compared to the 5 million forints fixed in the sales contract. But the exporter knows about this "loss" in advance, and can adjust the price accordingly. Or the exporter may decide that a known 128,205 forint loss is more acceptable than the risk of unknown loss or gain if it does not use the forward market (the bank can minimize its risk by simultaneously buying and selling foreign currencies).

Foreign currency option

Foreign currency credits and hedging are difficult to handle if the cash flow pattern resulting from different foreign accounts receivable is hard to determine exactly. In such cases the internationally operating company can buy foreign currency options. That is, the firm buys the right to buy and sell foreign currency in a time span of generally 3 months. During this time the financial manager of the company can profit from exchange rate fluctuations and limit the risk of losses.

Guarantees

One way to restrict financial risks other than exchange rate fluctuations in international business is to use guarantees. Government-owned or government-directed organizations, such as Hermès and KFW in Germany, COFACE in France or Ex–Im Bank in the U.S., provide financial packages designed to increase exports. Export financing is made available either through direct loans to importers, or by making credit to importers more readily available. In addition, various types of guarantees that protect against different kinds of financial risks are available to exporters and importers through banks.

Bill of lading guarantees

These instruments ensure that the importer or receiver of merchandise will perform as stated in the documents signed by the importer. They cover the shipper against the demand of a third party when the shipper distributes merchandise to the receiver without getting the bill of lading at the same time.

Bid bonds

Also called *participation guarantees* or *tender guarantees*, bid bonds guarantee the prospective buyer that the chosen bidding firm is willing and able to sign a contract according to the offer made.

Payment guarantees

These ensure that the supplier will be paid as stated in the contract with the customer against presentation of the sales documents. Alfred Kärcher GmbH, a German producer of cleaning equipment for private and commercial purposes, for example, contacted one of its international banks to get a payment guarantee when it was signing an initial sales contract with a customer in Latin America. The country risk seemed acceptable and, according to available credit information, the customer was a prominent firm in its country. Nevertheless, Kärcher's treasurer considered the risk unspecified. The company paid a premium for an insurance policy that allowed them not to have to give further securities to the provider.

Insurance

Various types of international financial risk that are not due to exchange rate fluctuations or cannot be covered by guarantees might be covered through insurance. Insurance is available from private agencies, governments, and special organizations. Table 16.5 illustrates some of the insurance alternatives available from a U.S., a U.K., and a typical state scheme.

When private companies provide insurance, they offer the insurance against financial risks in specific countries as a product for sale. The contract value that may be insured, the percentage of the contract that is insurable, and the fees all vary according to the assessment of the risk involved.

State or federal agencies that provide insurance do so to support exports. The Ministry of International Trade and Industry (MITI) in Japan, for example, provides export insurance covering commercial and political risks in a manner similar to that of the FCIA in the U.S. The Overseas Private Investment Corp. (OPIC), as another example, has a traditional role of being an insurer of last resort for U.S. companies investing in overseas projects.

Countertrade

Under certain circumstances, the customer may prefer **countertrade**. This has been defined as a commercial transaction in which provisions are made, in one or a series of related contracts, for payment by deliveries of goods and/or services in addition to, or in place of, financial settlement.

Countertrade has a long history in international trade. Manhattan Island, for example, was sold in such an agreement to settlers from Europe. Today some

10–15% of international trade involves countertrade mainly between industrialized and economically developing countries and a growing amount of south–south business between LDCs.

For example, Indonesia, the People's Republic of China, and Malaysia are big countertrading countries. Thailand and India had high growth rates in countertrade in the 1990s. Even highly industrialized economies (such as Australia, Austria, Belgium, Canada, the Netherlands, New Zealand, Norway, Sweden, and the U.K.) have joined the ranks of countries that use countertrade arrangements for certain kinds of transactions.

In addition to trading companies that specialize in countertrade, many of the biggest companies in the world, such as General Electric or Coca-Cola, were involved in countertrade transactions in the 1990s.

Over the years many different forms of countertrade have developed. **Barter** is the exchange of goods or services without transfers of money in a short timeframe, generally one year or less, formalized in one contract. All the other forms of countertrade are based on two or more separate contracts. They include full or partial monetary compensation, and the contracts are generally for periods longer than 1 year. Three different kinds of barter found in international business and three other forms of countertrade are now discussed.

Barter

Classic barter

In classic barter, both parties function as buyers and sellers in a mutual exchange of products with offsetting values. The exchanged products may be industrial goods, consumer goods, services, or commodities. Bangladesh, for example, has classic barter agreements with eastern European countries, such as Bulgaria, and other LDCs, such as Pakistan. It trades agricultural commodities, textiles, hides, and paper products for industrial equipment, machinery, chemicals, fertilizers, metals, and medicines. Another example is the Malaysian-owned rubber trading company, Sime Darby, which exchanged cocoa beans delivered by Mexican tire manufacturers for Malaysian rubber. Classic barter is relatively rare in international marketing.

TABLE 16.5 *Comparison of risk protection through insurances*

Item	Underwriter		
	AIG/CIGNA (U.S.)	Lloyd's (U.K.)	Typical state scheme (central Europe)
Export embargo	Yes	Yes	Yes
Import embargo	Yes	Yes	Yes
Government buyer non-payment	Yes	Yes	Yes
Exchange transfer	Yes	Yes	Yes
Failure of bank to honor ILC	Yes	No	Yes
Confiscation/expropriation/ nationalization	Yes	Yes	Yes
Contract non-ratification	Yes	Yes	No
Private-buyer non-payment	Yes	No	Yes
Barter	Yes	Yes	No
Kidnap and ransom	AIG only	Yes	No

Although various agencies offer insurance against financial risks, their coverage varies considerably.

Source: J. Schwabe, Schwabe, Ley & Greiner GmbH, Vienna, Austria

Closed-end barter

Closed-end barter differs from classic barter in that one of the business partners already has a buyer at hand for the products to be traded before the contract is signed. Most often it will be the partner located in the more economically developed area. Closed-end barter very much diminishes the risk associated with barter.

Clearing account barter

Clearing account barter is based on bilateral clearing agreements between governments. It has gained importance in economic relationships between LDCs.

Other forms of countertrade

Compensation arrangements

Compensation is used for industrial projects that involve technology or capital transfer from industrialized to developing economies. When plant equipment or turnkey plants are sold to firms in those countries, their governments may sign the contract only if the suppliers are willing to take back the products manufactured by that equipment over an extended period of time (5–10 years) as part of the payment. For example, Dunbee-Combex-Marx, a U.K. toy manufacturer, and China agreed that the firm would furnish toy-making machinery and molds to China in return for a 50% cash down-payment and 50% of the toys made in the Chinese factory. Such contracts are also called buyback arrangements.

Compensation arrangements help the international marketer to insure part of the firm's accounts receivable. Taking into account the costs of selling the products accepted as compensation (or the costs of an international trader who takes over the burden of selling them), the value of those products can be considered as insured payment. Compensation also allows the marketer to set a higher price in international tenders because the customer only needs to pay part of the entire project costs in hard currency. Varying compensation quotas can be used to differentiate the offer from competitors.

Counterpurchase

Counterpurchase is an indirect form of compensation trading. It is characterized by buying and selling agreements that are basically independent of each other. They are either partially or totally paid in cash or in bank credit. Counterpurchase is a form of countertrade, because the supplier in a business deal signs a second contract agreeing to buy products, defined within broad categories, from the customer within a period of time that ranges from 1 to 5 years.

When engineering companies want to do business with firms in Africa, for example, they often have to accept such buying contracts. Because of their lack of hard currencies, many African firms can only buy western technology if the sellers are ready to buy and market their products in exchange. The western companies rely on the services of specialized trading houses to do that job for them.

A special case of counterpurchase is the establishment of **evidence accounts**. These usually occur when an exporter or a trading company in an industrialized country signs a counterpurchase contract with the government of a developing country. In an "umbrella" trade agreement the two parties arrange that two-way trade between the firm – as well as other businesses designated by it – and firms in the developing country be partially or fully balanced over a specified period of time, typically 1 to 5 years. In one such deal, a trading company agreed to buy a large amount of crude oil from Iran at OPEC prices and use the country's bank credit stemming from that deal to pay western companies, in hard currency, for their delivery of industrial as well as consumer products to customers in Iran.

Offsets

Offsets are most common in sizeable weapon delivery contracts, the construction of large power stations, other public infrastructure projects, and industrialization projects between a supplying firm (as general contractor) and a government. They usually combine domestic content, co-production, and technology transfer requirements with long-term counterpurchase arrangements. The marketer is faced with a (government) customer who is ready to sign a contract only if the marketer agrees to counterpurchase goods from the customer country, transfer technological know-how by producing components and equipment in the buyer's country, subcontract compatible components to local manufacturers, or meet other conditions.

In one such case, the Austrian government announced that in exchange for a €4 billion purchase of EADS Euro-fighter aircraft, Austrian firms would not only participate in the production of components for Airbus planes but also be accepted for supply contracts in many other areas such as cars or technological research projects.

Company and government motives

Government initiatives concerning countertrade vary. They range from incentives to the imposition of such agreements as a condition of doing business. Mexico has for some time imposed export performance requirements on imports and investment. Brazil and Indonesia have imposed domestic content requirements on imports and local industrial projects. EU nations are officially neutral concerning private companies' decisions, but most have created public services to advise firms or actively promote countertrade.

Lack of capital

The reasons for countertrade in LDCs are found in the countries' economic development difficulties. Many LDCs experience severe financial bottlenecks due to a combination of credit cuts, balance of payment problems, sluggish exports, and high debts with U.S., European, and Japanese banks. These conditions have left most developing countries with few alternatives other than countertrade to acquire badly needed capital goods and services. As about 40% of industrialized nations' trade is done with LDCs, this is of importance to firms from those nations.

Shortage of hard currency

A second major reason for countertrade agreements is the chronic shortage of hard currency in most LDC firms. They need equipment and technology from higher industrialized markets to enhance their economic development and international competitiveness, but they lack internationally accepted currency to pay for those supplies. Countertrade is often the only way they can obtain those resources.

Lack of competitive skills

The lack of internationally competitive industrial skills is another reason some countries engage in countertrade. Most selling problems in LDCs occur because of their low level of familiarity with basic marketing activities. They do not have enough experience in building an international distribution system, packaging, design, promotion, and after-sales services. Many industrial exports from these countries are not due to active marketing by the manufacturer, but result from the purchasing activities of companies from industrially more developed countries. Those companies bring in product and process technology as well as management know-how, and they use the less developed country's raw material and cheap labor, but they may not transfer much of their technology.

Lack of competitiveness

Another reason for countertrade is that it opens markets to products that would not be bought otherwise, because of global overcapacities or insufficient quality or promotion. Initially, consumer goods from China, for example, might not have found their way to the U.S. consumer without China's requirement that U.S. companies accept countertrade items. Machinery from Romania would also probably not have been sold to western buyers without the imposition of countertrade agreements through the Romanian government or Romanian firms. In the meantime, many companies in those countries have used the experience acquired by countertrade deals to significantly increase their know-how and to become strong competitors in world markets.

Production regulations of cartels

A fifth reason for countertrade is the restrictive production regulations of cartels that have led to overcapacity in some countries' commodity production. The relatively low production quota for crude oil for OPEC members in the 1990s led some of them to use their overproduction in countertrade offers to industrialized countries at official OPEC prices. Nigeria, for example, traded crude oil with many nations in return for tires, paper, gasoline, automobile parts, and vegetable oil, among other products. Trading firms in highly industrialized countries accepted the prices as a means to open up the oil producers' markets to Western products.

Political reasons

Finally, there may also be political reasons for countertrade. Iran, for example, circumvented officially restricted relationships with some of the major western countries by signing countertrade contracts with international trading houses for crude oil and chemicals in return for all kinds of industrial and even consumer goods. Those trading houses, not constrained by any similar political restrictions, were able to deliver the products from sources otherwise not officially available to Iran.

Concerns about countertrade

Most companies located in western industrialized economies have entered the countertrade business with a decided lack of enthusiasm.

Use of traded goods

The major concerns are that the company may have no in-house use for the traded goods, or it may encounter difficulties in reselling them to third parties. This may be due to the type of compensating goods offered by the partners, or possibly their low quality. But it may also be due to a lack of sufficiently trained people in the companies. Coca-Cola, for example, in one of its first countertrade deals, found itself stuck with substandard Chinese honey that could not be sold for 2 years.

Uncertainty and complexity

Another major concern expressed by western companies is the uncertainty and complexity of a countertrade deal. Information from the countertrade partners regarding prices, product quality, and proprietary issues may be hard to obtain. A firm dealing with an indebted country may find, for example, that banks and/ or the IMF have prior claims on the goods offered as part of the countertrade agreement.

Legal and contractual issues can be difficult to deal with. There is the further problem of setting exchange ratios for the goods to be traded. Government instability, red tape, and inefficiency add to the complications. Other concerns include increased costs, negotiation problems, and the possible strengthening of potential competitors.

Countertrade opportunities

Despite these difficulties and constraints, countertrade can be regarded as a possible source of additional service for customers who have exchange problems, rather than as a burden. Countertrade can be a major competitive marketing tool vis-à-vis other firms that may not feel comfortable with such deals. It allows the firm to *take advantage of local tariff laws* that may be stricter for traditional imports than for countertrade goods. It can also be used to open markets and *gain favorable recognition from local administrators*, an important asset later on. General Electric, for example, has successfully used countertrade as a competitive tool, helping it to beat competition for business around the world. Using barter helped GE save a deal the company had made to build turbine generators for nuclear energy generation in Romania. When the country got into a cash flow squeeze, GE agreed to accept one-half of the total contract worth in Romanian industrial products, including railroad cars and ship containers. GE later won a second contract over competitors for nuclear energy equipment, in part due to its flexibility in accepting barter in the first contract.

Traded consumer goods are sometimes difficult to sell, but specialized trading houses have proven to be very successful in finding customers. Countertrade is a way of *developing a market* despite credit difficulties, exchange problems, and currency controls. It increases the company's sales volume, allows fuller use of the firm's productive capacity, and, in some cases, provides a source of economically attractive inputs in the firm's production process.

Impact on marketing mix

International pricing decisions strongly interact with decisions concerning the company's product management, distribution, and promotional goals and efforts. The buyer may use the price of the product to judge its quality, its attractiveness to others, and its general value. That is, in the absence of other cues, especially when the customer has little experience with the product, price will be used as an indicator of the product's technical and social reliability. Thus price may be a major communication tool for the international marketer.

Price can also be used to compete, through a better price–value relationship. When the product quality and design are at least as attractive as those of competitors, the price may nevertheless be set at a lower level to gain market entrance and penetration. The success of Japanese cameras, automobiles, motorcycles, and audio and video products in the U.S. and Europe is a striking example of the concerted use of such a strategy. Korean and Chinese firms have successfully followed the example.

Price also interacts with distribution. High-fashion, high-prestige, high-quality products, which have correspondingly high prices, are not sold through discount outlets. Marketers of these products carefully choose the right distribution channels. By the same token, if the distribution infrastructure in a country market is complicated, with long distribution channels, the price will automatically be higher than in markets with short distribution channels. If a given price is essential for the company's market success, its management will try to establish control over the entire distribution process. The choice of distribution system will follow from this requirement.

Summary

Proper pricing of goods and services is key to success in international marketing. Although a firm should have an international pricing policy, the actual price charged in the marketplace is influenced by many different factors, several of which the firm may influence in a limited way. Determination of that price – whether standard formula, price adaptation, or strategically set – must take these factors into account.

The major factors of influence include the *cost of the good*, which determines the lower price limit, and *market demand*, which sets the upper price limit. The final price usually lies between the two and depends on the company's:

- pricing policy
- competition
- structure, power, and actions of local intermediaries as well as other important stakeholders
- general economic conditions
- local government regulations.

In order to avoid direct price competition and to have a broader range of pricing alternatives, the international marketer must handle the terms of payment in a sophisticated manner. The methods of payment selected are affected by several factors; most importantly:

- risks associated with the sale

- merchandise itself
- industrial and competitive practices.

Alternative terms of payment must be chosen to make the firm's product more attractive to customers and to increase corporate profits.

Even the most sophisticated choice of terms of payment cannot avoid financial risks inherent in international marketing. Therefore, when taking pricing decisions, management has to consider which risks should be taken by the firm and which turned over to agencies, banks, and insurance companies. The cost of such complex risk reduction actions have to be covered by price.

When economic or political factors inhibit the exchange of goods or services strictly for money, various forms of countertrade can be employed. *Barter* is normally a short-term, one-time, countertrade contract. Other forms of countertrade, that are for longer periods of time, or multiple contracts such as *buyback* or *counterpurchase*, permit a more permanent relationship between buyer and seller without necessarily involving money. Companies usually engage in countertrade in order to enter markets that are otherwise blocked to them by governments that are trying to manage severe financial constraints. These deals are so important that no company operating internationally can afford to totally overlook countertrade.

DISCUSSION QUESTIONS

1. Why is pricing probably the most difficult element in the international marketing mix to manage?

2. Which is the best international pricing policy for a corporation: standard, standard formula, price adaptation, or strategic pricing? Why?

3. "Because a price is the market's perception of the product's value, costs really don't matter, especially in international marketing. Another less price-sensitive market can always be found." Do you agree or disagree with that statement, and why?

4. How do government policies affect the international pricing decision?

5. Which of the terms of payment is of greatest advantage to the international marketer? Which

results in the greatest risk being retained by the international marketer? Explain.

6. What factors affect the choice of terms of payment, and what is their effect?

7. When and why would you recommend that an international marketer use an open account as the method of payment?

8. What role does a letter of credit play in international marketing?

9. Will countertrade increase or decrease in importance in the future? Why?

10. Describe how pricing affects the other elements of the international marketing mix. Try to find examples from the trade press.

ADDITIONAL READINGS

Assmus, G. and C. Wiese (1995) "How to address the gray market threat using price coordination", *Sloan Management Review*, spring, 31–41.

Bolton, R.N. and M.B.Matthew (2003) "Price-based global market segmentation for services", *Journal of Marketing*, July, 67, 108–28.

Dolan, R.J. (1995) "How do you know when the price is right?", *Harvard Business Review*, September–October, 174–83.

Paun, D.A. and A. Shoham (1996) "Marketing motives in international countertrade: an empirical examination", *Journal of International Marketing*, 4(3), 29–47

Useful internet links

BASF	http://www.corporate.basf.com/en/
CIS	http://www.cisstat.com/eng/cis.htm
COFACE	http://www.coface.com/
COMECON	http://en.wikipedia.org/wiki/Comecon
Davidoff	http://www.davidoff.com/
Edeka	http://www.edeka.de/EDEKA/Content/DE/Home/index.jsp
Eskimo	http://www.eskimo.at/
Ex–Im Bank	http://www.exim.gov/
FCIA	http://www.fcia.com/
Henkel	http://www.henkel.com/
Herlitz	http://www.herlitz.de/index.php?id=289&L=2
Hermès	http://www.eulerhermes.com/ger/en/index.html
HILTI	http://www.hilti.com/
ifgroup	http://www.ifgroup.com/html/siteplan.htm
IKEA	http://www.ikea.com/
International Factors Group	http://www.ifgroup.com/
Journal of International Marketing	http://www.marketingpower.com/content1055C364.php
Kärcher	http://www.karcher.com/
KFW	http://www.kfw.de/EN/Inhalt.jsp
KMart Corp	http://www.kmartcorp.com/
Ministry of International Trade and Industry (MITI), Malaysia	http://www.miti.gov.my/
OECD	http://www.oecd.org/
OPEC	http://www.opec.org/
Overseas Private Investment Corp. (OPIC)	http://www.opic.gov/
Parker Pen	http://www.parkerpen.com/sanford/consumer/parker/jhtml/index.jhtml
SITPRO (Simplifying International Trade)	http://www.sitpro.org.uk/trade/lettcred.html
Treaty of Rome	http://www.cerebalaw.com/rome.htm
Wall Street Journal	http://www.wsj.com/
WTO	http://www.wto.org/

INTERNATIONAL MARKETING PLAN

17

Learning objectives

After studying this chapter you will be able to:

- summarize international marketing decisions

- explain the hierarchical structure of marketing decisions and plans

- illustrate the content and structure of an international marketing plan

- evaluate marketing and business plans

Chapter outline

International business plan

Hierarchical levels of business plan development
Marketing's contribution to the business plan

International marketing strategy

International product policy
International distribution policy
International sales policy
International logistics policy
International pricing policy
International market communication policy

International marketing plan

Audiences
Structure

International marketing planning manual

Company or business unit international marketing plan
Planning procedure

Summary

INTERNATIONAL MARKETING SPOTLIGHT

A bumpy ride

Michelin's roly-poly Bibendum, Goodyear's winged boot, Firestone's gothic script, and Pirelli's bizarre, loopy "p": Few consumer industries can boast such a wealth of classic trademarks. In North America, which makes up about 40% of the world tire market, wholesalers and retailers have been able to develop their own budget brands. In Europe, which accounts for about one-third of world sales, the advent of budget tires in the 1980s came as a shock to the established companies.

The main tiremakers in Europe had been pursuing a risky pricing policy. For decades, the industry had been convinced that it was worth making losses on tires sold direct to carmakers in order to guarantee profits in the retail market: Drivers tend to replace their tires with an identical set from the same maker. Tire companies therefore compensated for larger losses on tires sold to carmakers by raising their margins on retail sales.

At the end of the 1980s Europe began to be targeted by obscure tiremakers from east Asia, such as Kumho and Hankook of South Korea, and by eastern European firms. Their tires often sold for less than half the price of a premium brand. In Britain, the South Koreans alone have captured roughly 25% of the market; in Germany, the South Korean share is about 10%. Because fixed costs in the tire industry are high, and the largest firms had too much capacity, prices fell by more than 5–10% a year at the end of the 1980s. That hurt still more after rubber prices began rising in 1994. Profits shriveled or disappeared.

Not until the middle of the 1990s did the industry start recovering. Tiremakers have overhauled their business by redefining their strategic positions, revamping their management systems, improving productivity, and adapting their marketing mix. For example, Italian Pirelli, present in Europe and Latin America, decided at the start of 1993 to concentrate on the world market for luxury and speed. The firm has worked hard since to become the supplier of tires fitted in the factory on BMWs, Porsches, and most fancy cars. The world's three biggest tiremakers, each of which have a little under 20% of the market, cannot afford to concentrate all their sales up-market. Instead, they have developed second- and even third-tier brands. Michelin, for example, introduced its "Classic" range of mid-priced tires in 1994. In 1995 it signed a pact with Germany's Continental, part of which was an agreement to introduce Michelin's first budget tire.

Continental, which had no fewer than nine brands in Europe, used to manage each brand separately. In 1994, the firm decided to organize itself by markets instead. Its brands now resemble a portfolio, with Continental and Uniroyal reserved for the top end, from which managers pick a tire suitable for each segment of their market.

Cost cutting and increasing productivity was another important remedy: In 1990, only 1% of Continental's tires were made in Portugal and Slovakia, where labor costs are low. In 1996 that figure had increased to 25%. In the same period, sales per employee had increased by more than one-third. Between 1994 and 1996 Michelin decreased its stocks as a proportion of sales by 25%. The company's strict hierarchy was replaced by 21 decentralized business units, nine of them managing products and the rest providing services for the group.

All this has helped to halt the advance of new tire companies. European tire marketing has become a permanently lower margin, cost-conscious, and more customer-focused business.

Source: Adapted from "Tyres in Europe – A bumpy ride", *The Economist*, 17 February, 1996, pp. 59f.

The focal question of this chapter is: **What content and structure does an international marketing plan need to have, and how does it need to be integrated into an international business plan to fulfill its purpose?**

International business plan

The description of the international marketing decision process given in preceding chapters has illustrated the high complexity and interrelatedness of marketing analyses, decisions, and actions in an international business environment (Figure 17.1). In addition to marketing-specific considerations, an internationally operating firm needs to manage its financial and human resources as well as its production operations in a coordinated way to achieve its major objectives. The most important tool for the coordination of analyses, decisions, and actions is the development of an international business plan.

The business plan of a company presents:

- mission and philosophy driving the firm
- a complete analysis of the business
- objectives
- markets in which the company operates
- competition against which it must establish or sustain its strategic position
- problems that must be overcome in order for the objectives to be reached.

The business plan also contains decisions made by managers on different levels of organizational hierarchy and activities planned to resolve any problems detected. It answers the questions why, what, how, when, where, and whom for each action during the planning period. As such, the business plan is a comprehensive operating manual that management will use to navigate their way to their objectives.

This chapter discusses:

- contribution of marketing to the development of an international business plan
- establishment of an international marketing strategy
- development of an international marketing plan
- potential audiences and structure
- planning procedure necessary for successful implementation.

Hierarchical levels of business plan development

Corporate policy

At the corporate level, the basic task in developing an international business plan is to define or revise the corporate policy and to formalize it in a written statement. As discussed in Chapter 2, a corporate policy statement includes information about the company's mission and business philosophy. The mission states the rationale behind the organization's existence. The business philosophy guides the manner in which relationships inside the company and with business partners as well as other stakeholders are managed (Figure 17.2).

In general, the people dominating an organization define its corporate policy statement. Those dominant people may be the owners or top managers of the firm, but the dominant group may also contain representatives of other important stakeholders, such as investors, creditors, or the labor force. Managers of lower hierarchical levels may be invited to participate in the corporate policy development process in order to generate their commitment for its content.

Core strategy

Based on the corporate policy, a core strategy of the organization needs to be established that defines the scope, shape, and structure of the firm. The formulation

FIGURE 17.1 *International marketing decision process*

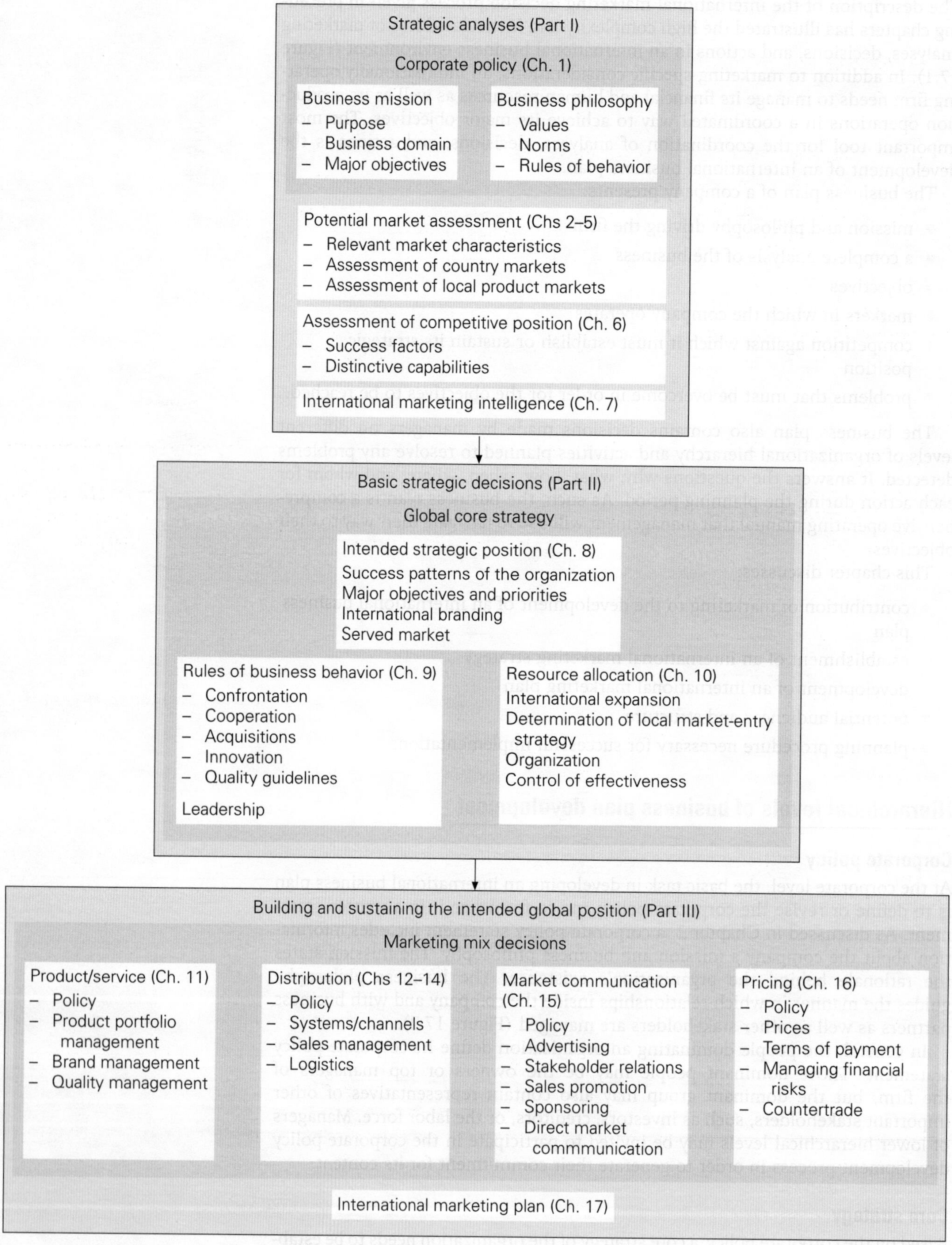

Strategic analyses (Part I)

Corporate policy (Ch. 1)

Business mission
– Purpose
– Business domain
– Major objectives

Business philosophy
– Values
– Norms
– Rules of behavior

Potential market assessment (Chs 2–5)
– Relevant market characteristics
– Assessment of country markets
– Assessment of local product markets

Assessment of competitive position (Ch. 6)
– Success factors
– Distinctive capabilities

International marketing intelligence (Ch. 7)

Basic strategic decisions (Part II)

Global core strategy

Intended strategic position (Ch. 8)
Success patterns of the organization
Major objectives and priorities
International branding
Served market

Rules of business behavior (Ch. 9)
– Confrontation
– Cooperation
– Acquisitions
– Innovation
– Quality guidelines

Leadership

Resource allocation (Ch. 10)
International expansion
Determination of local market-entry
  strategy
Organization
Control of effectiveness

Building and sustaining the intended global position (Part III)

Marketing mix decisions

Product/service (Ch. 11)
– Policy
– Product portfolio
  management
– Brand management
– Quality management

Distribution (Chs 12–14)
– Policy
– Systems/channels
– Sales management
– Logistics

Market communication (Ch. 15)
– Policy
– Advertising
– Stakeholder relations
– Sales promotion
– Sponsoring
– Direct market
  commmunication

Pricing (Ch. 16)
– Policy
– Prices
– Terms of payment
– Managing financial
  risks
– Countertrade

International marketing plan (Ch. 17)

of a core strategy requires careful assessment of the attractiveness of potential markets (discussed in Chapter 2), as well as of the firm's distinctive capabilities and resulting potential competitive advantages (discussed in Chapter 6). The core strategy determines:

- company objectives and their priorities
- portfolio of product and country markets to be served (see Chapter 8)
- rules of behavior to be followed in serving those markets (Chapter 9)
- international allocation of resources available to the firm (Chapter 10).

If the portfolio of the internationally operating company contains more than one clearly defined product market, the next step in developing an international business plan may be to formulate business unit strategies.

Business unit strategy

A business unit strategy focuses on the achievement and maintenance of a strategic position in a specific product market. It is basically developed in the same manner as the firm's core strategy. But its development is the responsibility

---

FIGURE 17.2 *From corporate policy to marketing plan*

The work on an international business plan starts with the development of a corporate policy. Core strategy and business unit strategy are the bases for developing a marketing strategy, which, in turn, lays the ground for the marketing plan.

of managers leading the individual business unit; and the decisions taken are based on a more detailed analysis of customers, competitors, and other important stakeholders as well as the business unit's resources and skills for competing in specific market segments. Smaller companies or firms that focus on an international market niche may not need to distinguish between different business units. In such case, management may go directly from the formulation of their organization's core strategy to the definition of the marketing strategy.

Marketing strategy

The marketing strategy serves the purpose of implementing the core or a business unit strategy. Depending on the size of the firm's business the marketing strategy is formulated by top management or business unit managers. It contains the policies, that is the objectives and basic guidelines that have to be respected by managers who are responsible for specific marketing decisions and actions, such as advertising, sales, product line management, or distribution. Similar to all other strategy statements of the firm, the marketing strategy tells those managers what they are expected to achieve and what courses of action are not appropriate management. The marketing strategy also defines the allocation of resources across marketing sub-processes.

Marketing plan

Finally, a marketing plan can be developed on the basis of the marketing strategy. In an internationally operating firm serving various country markets marketing plans will be developed for each of those markets. Those plans specify the objectives of local marketing management showing how much the local units are able to contribute to the achievement of the overall objectives. The various marketing activities (discussed in Chapters 11–16) needed to reach the local objectives are presented in detail, and the budgets planned for each of the marketing tools and actions are given.

Marketing's contributions to the business plan

As the discussion of the international marketing decision process in this book has shown, marketing orientation, marketing analyses, and marketing techniques may contribute on all hierarchical levels to the development of a comprehensive international business plan.

Contributions to corporate policy

Marketing-oriented top managers or entrepreneurs will promote marketing orientation as the basic perspective from which to look at the company's business. Figure 17.3 shows what parts of corporate policy may be influenced by a marketing orientation, that is by marketing's benefit, exchange, and systems perspectives (discussed in Chapter 1).

The corporate mission statement begins by defining the general purpose of the company – the vision of its founders or top managers. Based on marketing's benefit perspective this vision will be formulated in such a way as to express the central value(s) provided by the company to its customers or to society. For example, Germany's DaimlerChrysler has stated that the firm wants to significantly contribute to the individual mobility of people all over the world.

The systems perspective of marketing-oriented managers will guide the definition of the company's business domain. In addition to the prospective customers the definition will include all major stakeholders of the firm that need to be satisfied to a certain extent in order to provide the organization with the needed resources. For example, a producer of electronic toys, such as Japan's Nintendo, will focus not only on children and their parents as their customers, but they will also be aware that other stakeholders are important for the company's long-term

Research and design

©Comstock Images/Alamy

success. The expectations of electronic component suppliers, toy distributors, educators, and media as well as the company's own labor force and its investors need to be satisfied at least up to a level that makes them refrain from fighting Nintendo's interests.

Marketing's benefit perspective will make sure that the benefits to be provided to the important stakeholders are defined from the stakeholders' points of view. For example, the definition of the Denmark-based manufacturer of plastics Borealis's business domain will not only contain a general description of the customers they plan to serve, such as the producers of packaging material and auto parts, but also of those customers' markets, such as the food industry and the automotive industry. Benefits to be provided to those stakeholders may read for

FIGURE 17.3 *Impact of marketing orientation on corporate policy*

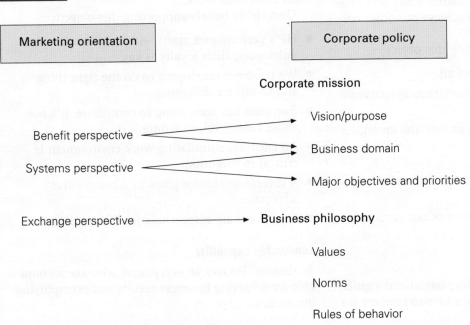

Marketing orientation's benefit, systems, and exchange perspectives impact on the formulation of various parts of corporate policy.

STRATEGY BOX 17.1

HP Invent – corporate objectives

"It is necessary that people work together in unison toward common objectives and avoid working at cross purposes at all levels if the ultimate in efficiency and achievement is to be obtained."

Dave Packard

HPs corporate objectives have guided the company in the conduct of its business since 1957, when first written by co-founders Bill Hewlett and Dave Packard.

Customer loyalty

To provide products, services and solutions of the highest quality and deliver more value to our customers that earns their respect and loyalty.

Underlying beliefs supporting this objective:

- Our continued success is dependent on increasing the loyalty of our customers.
- Listening attentively to customers to truly understand their needs, then delivering solutions that translate into customer success is essential to earn customer loyalty.
- Competitive total cost of ownership, quality, inventiveness, and the way we do business drives customer loyalty.

Profit

To achieve sufficient profit to finance our company growth, create value for our shareholders and provide the resources we need to achieve our other corporate objectives.

Underlying beliefs supporting this objective:

- Profit is the responsibility of all.
- Balance of long-term and short-term objectives is the key to profitability.
- Profit allows us to reinvest in new and emerging business opportunities.
- Profit is highly correlated to generating cash, which brings more flexibility to the business at a lower cost.
- Profit enables the achievement of our corporate objectives.

Market leadership

To grow by continually providing useful and significant products, services and solutions to markets we already serve – and to expand into new areas that build on our technologies, competencies and customer interests.

Underlying beliefs supporting this objective:

- There are more places we can contribute than we will be capable of contributing: We must focus.
- To be average in the marketplace is not good enough, we play to win.
- We must be No. 1 or No. 2 in our chosen fields.

Growth

To view change in the market as an opportunity to grow; to use our profits and our ability to develop and produce innovative products, services and solutions that satisfy emerging customer needs.

Underlying beliefs supporting this objective:

- Growth comes from taking smart risks, based on the state of the industry – that requires both a conviction in studying the trends, but also in inducing change in our industry.
- Our size (and diversity of businesses) gives us ability to weather economic cycles and turn them to our favor.

Employee commitment

To help HP employees share in the company's success that they make possible; to provide people with employment opportunities based on performance; to create with them a safe, exciting and inclusive work environment that values their diversity and recognizes individual contributions; and to help them gain a sense of satisfaction and accomplishment from their work.

Underlying beliefs supporting this objective:

- HP's performance starts with motivated employees; their loyalty is key.
- We trust our employees to do the right thing and to make a difference.
- Everyone has something to contribute: It's not about title, level, or tenure.
- An exciting, stimulating work environment is critical to invention.
- A diverse workforce gives us a competitive advantage.
- Employees are responsible for lifelong learning.

Leadership capability

To develop leaders at every level who are accountable for achieving business results and exemplifying our values.

Underlying beliefs supporting this objective:

- Leaders inspire, foster collaboration and turn vision and strategies into action – with focused, clear goals.
- Effective leaders coach, relay good news and bad, and give feedback that works.
- Leaders demonstrate self-awareness and a willingness to accept feedback and continuously develop.
- Leaders speak with one voice and act to eliminate busy work.
- It is important to measure people on the results they achieve against goals they helped to create.

Global citizenship

Good citizenship is good business. We live up to our responsibility to society by being an economic, intellectual and social asset to each country and community in which we do business.

Underlying beliefs supporting this objective:

- The highest standards of honesty and integrity are critical to developing customer and stakeholder loyalty.
- The betterment of our society is not a job to be left to a few; it is the responsibility to be shared by all.
- This objective is essential to delivering on the brand promise.

Source: www.hp.com/

example "packaging material at low cost, highly attractive to consumers, adapted to the needs of the specific product."

The formulation of the firm's major objectives and their priorities in the corporate mission is also open to influence from marketing orientation. As shown in Strategy box 17.1 objectives may include sales growth rate, return on sales, market share, acceptable level of risk exposure, approach to technology and innovation, image and goodwill, establishment of a specific working climate within the organization, or independence.

Depending on how much the authors of the corporate policy have adopted a systems perspective, the chosen objectives will focus on one stakeholder group's interests or cover the interests of a broader range of important stakeholders. The example described in Ethics box 17.1 may be the starting point for a discussion

ETHICS BOX 17.1

"Tobacco war" in Kenya and Tanzania

While tobacco marketing in Europe and the U.S. becomes more and more restricted, tobacco manufacturers, after having heavily invested in Asian markets, have discovered the African market as a promising business arena. In particular, the countries south of the Sahara with 850 million potential smokers have become a new target.

In one of its 1997 issues medical journal *The Lancet* reported on a "tobacco war" between British-American Tobacco and J.R. Reynolds in Kenya and Tanzania. Philip Morris, the third biggest player in the industry was about to enter the market. Never before had the tobacco industry launched such a

massive advertising campaign in Africa. In 1997, the year when the company agreed to pay millions of dollars to partly compensate for damage their products have caused to the health of the country's population in the U.S., J.R. Reynolds started the construction of a production plant in Dar-es-Salaam, the biggest city in Tanzania. The plant will produce about 4 billion cigarettes a year.

The question may be raised: Should managers do everything that is not explicitly forbidden to raise their shareholders' (and their personal) income? Is it ethically acceptable to pay millions of dollars for admitted damage to the health of the home country's population and to parallel invest in the requirements for creating the same damage elsewhere?

Source: Based on "Tabak-Krieg in Kenya und Tansania", *Der Standard*, 13–14 September, 1997, p. 4

about what focusing on one stakeholder group's interests may do to a company's success in the long run.

Because objectives are not always consistent – a high sales growth rate goal may conflict with a goal restricting the use of foreign capital, for example – the mission statement should indicate which priorities are to be pursued. Here again, the level of systems perspective adopted by the authors of the corporate policy statement becomes important. Shareholder-, customer-, and employee-related objectives must not dominate all other objectives in any case.

Finally, marketing orientation will influence the basic values and norms the company wants its personnel to respect in their internal and external behavior. The more an exchange perspective guides the formulation of business philosophy the more the rules of behavior will emphasize reciprocity, relationship building, trust, and commitment in contrast to individual achievement, competition, exploitation, or control.

Contributions to the core strategy

A global core strategy is based on the assessment of corporate policy's feasibility. As illustrated by Figure 17.4 marketing contributes an essential part of the skills needed to properly conduct the analyses that lay the ground for the development of a core strategy.

Strategic analyses to evaluate the potential of making corporate policy become reality must cover: the *attractiveness of potential country markets*. As Chapters 2–5 and Chapter 7 of this book have shown, marketing provides the skills needed to conduct careful assessments of the economic, cultural, political, and legal environments as well as the specific operating environments of the local product markets; *the competitive position of the organization*. A comparison with major competitors in the most attractive markets will help the firm identify whether it can excel on any of the success factors. Chapter 6 has shown the essential role of marketing know-how in this stage of corporate strategy development.

Relying on the firm's current and potential competitive advantages in attractive markets, management will assess strategic alternatives. It will determine the intended strategic position of the company, that is:

- intended meaning of the brands constituting its brand architecture
- international portfolio of product and country markets to serve
- technologies needed to satisfy the current and potential aspirations of customers and stakeholders in the served markets (Chapter 8).

Closely related to those decisions, management has to determine general rules of behavior concerning:

FIGURE 17.4 *Contribution of marketing skills to core strategy development*

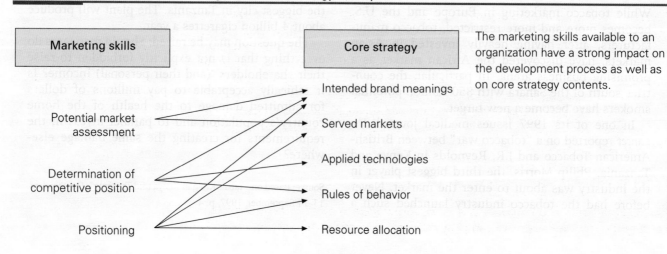

The marketing skills available to an organization have a strong impact on the development process as well as on core strategy contents.

- competition
- innovation
- mergers and acquisitions
- quality.

All these should help in reaching intended strategic position (Chapter 9).

The international allocation of company resources, in particular the general way and the speed in which country markets are entered as well as the spread of resources across organizational units completes the core strategy of the internationally operating company. Chapter 10 has shown that market-entry decisions and the organizational structure of a firm are largely influenced by the level of marketing orientation of top managers and the marketing capabilities available to the company.

Contributions to business unit strategies

Every company, whether operating internationally or only locally, will be positioned in the minds of its customers and other stakeholders. If it does not want that process to be entirely out of its control, the company must define an intended strategic position in every product market it has selected. That is, it must select the customer group(s) to be served and the way it wants to attractively differentiate itself from the most important competitors.

In addition, business unit strategy statements must define the intended strategic position in every individual country market to be served in light of the locally existing customer segments, important stakeholders, and major competitors. Local market-entry decisions will depend on that strategic objective. As a consequence, at the level of business unit strategy development market segmentation and competitive differentiation dominate planning activities. Therefore, at this level a distinction between strategic planning and marketing planning may be rather difficult to make. It only becomes evident when, based on positioning and market-entry decisions, resource allocation decisions have to be made. There, financial considerations, the development and deployment of human resources, as well as operations management considerations, such as outsourcing decisions, alliances, or location decisions, play a substantial part in the planning process.

Based on the intended strategic position in a product market and considering the resource allocation decisions given in the same document, an international marketing strategy may be developed. The following sections focus on this part of an international business plan.

International marketing strategy

An international marketing strategy contains *"basic assumptions,"* that is, a general overview of the served product market(s), their volume, structure, major players, and expected development; general *marketing objectives* of the firm or business unit, such as, to be an early follower in all served product markets or to first enter attractive country markets with the help of distributors that may later be acquired if the market fulfills its promise; and *marketing policies*, such as product branding, product line management, or distribution channel decisions.

Chapters 11 to 16 of this book have discussed the need for such policies in the different sub-areas of the marketing mix. Their purpose is summarized in the following.

International product policy

An international product policy has to be formulated to avoid unnecessary complexity and resulting costs in a company faced with internationally varying customer perceptions of the importance and meaning of features and processes constituting its total product. Such product policy provides a framework inside of which all product management processes of the firm are to be conducted. It lays down:

* general positioning for each product (line)
* intended degree of product standardization
* intended meaning of product brands and their market appearance
* quality standards
* firm's objectives and rules concerning product portfolio management.

International distribution policy

The international distribution policy of the firm determines how its market-entry strategy is to be executed. It contains general objectives regarding market share, sales volume, profit margins, and return on sales, which may be specified by region, customer group, and distribution channel, taking into account the desired level of company involvement in the distribution system, and the desirability of ownership of intermediaries.

Guidelines indicate minimum and maximum levels of capital and personnel to be committed to achieving the intended level of coverage in each market. They also specify rules for:

* selection of intermediaries and customers
* management of relationships with those selected business partners
* selection, training, and motivation of sales personnel.

International sales policy

The international sales policy is a guideline for decisions and actions concerning personal selling, after-sales activities, and the management of the firm's international salesforce. The sales policy specifies:

* minimum and maximum levels of capital and personnel to be committed to achieving a desired level of market coverage
* market share, sales volume, and profit margins for each region, customer group, and distribution channel as well as the expected return on sales
* how customer relations have to be managed, including after-sales activities such as handling customer claims and complaints.

International logistics policy

The international logistics policy of the firm determines:

* level of customer service to be achieved
* selection of integrated or independent marketing logistics systems
* specific conditions when to favor which system.

The logistics policy may also contain:

* profile of logistics partners to look for
* roles in the distribution logistics chain that have to be fulfilled inside or outside the company
* coordination between central and local company units
* responsibilities for logistics planning, information, and control.

International pricing policy

The international pricing policy restates corporate objectives relevant to individual pricing decisions such as expected profit margins, return on sales, and market shares. It also includes the preferred pricing strategy, such as quick penetration of mass markets through low prices where the company has no defendable competitive advantage or skimming of high margins in market niches where the company has a significant competitive advantage.

In order to make sales figures comparable across country markets the pricing policy may state how prices have to be calculated.

The company or business unit policy concerning rebates, refunds, and discounts given to customers is stated as well as the terms of payment available in specific markets to salespeople struggling for orders.

International market communication policy

The international market communication policy of the firm aims to ensure dynamic self-resemblance in all communicative activities across country markets.

General communication objectives for each of the important stakeholder groups are formulated. An *international communication platform* defines the central message to be communicated, which may be specified into consistent core messages for each stakeholder group. To coordinate the transfer of the core messages into a consistent choice of communication tools the communication policy determines the *major communication tools* to be applied internationally. A *guideline concerning corporate design* determines the general formal appearance of every communicative activity of the firm. Finally, the international market communication policy should contain some *rules concerning cooperation and coordination* in implementing market communication decisions that help to avoid conflicts among organizational subunits at different hierarchical levels and regulate the role of external service providers in the planning and execution of communication activities.

The marketing strategy is the basis for more short-term operative considerations such as product development, advertising, or pricing activities contained in what most companies call a marketing plan.

International marketing plan

The marketing plan is the core of an international business plan on its operative level. All marketing plans should start with an overview of strategic decisions relevant for short-term marketing activities, such as the product and country markets to serve, the benefits to provide to the customers in those markets and the way to achieve their satisfaction in attractive contrast to major competitors.

The specific content of a marketing plan will vary depending on the company and the industry it is in. In developing the marketing plan the responsible managers have to additionally consider that varying audiences may be interested in the plan. Accordingly, the content of marketing plans needs to be flexibly presented with differing focus.

The structure of marketing plans may be rather similar across industries and firms. Inside an internationally operating firm marketing plans established by various operational units or close cooperation partners, such as distributors or franchisees, which are faced with different local environments need to be comparable in order to allow the aggregation of data. The following section will discuss *how* marketing plans may need to be adaptable to varying target audiences, what *structure* local marketing plans should have that allow the aggregation of activities and data into an international marketing plan, and how the planning procedure should be *organized* to allow effective and efficient planning.

Audiences

The preparation of a marketing plan is an exercise that must cause marketing managers involved in whatever part of the planning procedure to examine their basic assumptions, going into all details, since these must be justified to third parties. Hindsight is a quality that many marketing people have in abundance but a marketing plan is designed to eliminate the necessity of hindsight as much as possible. When preparing the international marketing plan managers have to consider which target persons or groups they are addressing.

Internal audiences

Internal audiences may be the chief executive officer or the board of directors who take the final decisions or the middle management and staff who need to be convinced of the plan's content to properly implement it. When evaluating a plan, controllers, accountants, and finance managers usually look for a payback within a reasonable period. Although this may seem short sighted it must be recognized that financial personnel are risk averse mostly because of external pressures.

Other arguments are often needed to convince colleagues from the marketing, production, or supply areas to switch to a new process, such as competitor and customer pressures that force quality improvement without raising prices, or increasing market share in parallel with increasing the firm's level of environmental protection. There may also be a works council, a supervisory board, or an advisory board that may want to be informed about the marketing plan. Depending on their specific mission they will be more or less interested in figures or details of particular activities.

External audiences

External audiences for the marketing plan may be capital owners, creditors, private and institutional investors as well as presumptive buyers of the company who are mainly interested in the return on and the risk of their investment.

Shareholders, investors, venture capitalists, and bankers want a marketing plan to contain all information needed by financial analysts to assess the financial consequences of the proposed decisions and planned actions. For them the marketing plan must demonstrate in a rigorous manner that the objectives set are reachable with actions that are commercially viable.

Licensors and licensees, franchisees, potential joint venture and other cooperation partners, by way of contrast, may more strongly focus on the capabilities of their (potential) partner. They are mainly interested in the firm's strengths and weaknesses compared to its major competitors, how the company plans to create or take advantage of market opportunities, and how it plans to fill detected gaps. Finally, national and international subsidizing councils as well as private and public national or international funding institutions may be mainly interested in a sound general concept that promises to provide public benefits.

In any case a marketing plan should be:

- as short as possible
- clearly structured
- consistent
- convincing.

Some of the persons or groups the marketing plan addresses may be more interested in figures, others may focus on the served markets' potential and the marketing activities of the firm to take advantage of that potential. Again others may focus on how the marketing plan was developed (who participated in the process, what assumptions were taken, or how data were gathered), while another audience may just be interested in the outcomes of the process. In any case, it is important to obtain agreement from all the parties involved as to the aims and objectives of the plan and to obtain commitment to its contents.

To be considered convincing by people with such differing preoccupations as the ones just described, an international marketing plan must have a flexible structure. It needs to comprise all required information. But it should allow detailed illustration of just the issues that the specific audience is mainly interested in. For that purpose the information needs to be presentable at different degrees of aggregation.

Structure

Marketing plans are differently conceptualized in the literature. Even institutions like banks, funding organizations, or administrative authorities granting subsidies to firms presenting viable marketing plans, which should have a vital interest in well structured, informative, and plausible marketing plans, have differing requirements and standards concerning those plans.

One explanation for this finding may be that the businesses of companies preparing marketing plans vary greatly in their focus and extent. Small and only locally active firms have rather simply structured marketing plans compared to large, globally operating companies. The more product and country markets a company serves, the more individual marketing plans need to be coordinated and consolidated to produce one single marketing plan for the entire company.

In addition, the legal regulations regarding commercial and tax accounting differ from country to country, making a comparison between marketing plans of various origins difficult. However, for an internationally operating company to optimize the use of its skills and resources across product and country markets, marketing plans established by different organizational units must be able to be equally interpreted. Differences in interpretation of the term "plan" and in the structure of the plan's content have to be overcome for the purpose of making decisions comparable and planned actions based on those decisions acceptable to all persons involved in or concerned by their execution. For that purpose, the following section will suggest a potential structure for local as well as consolidated marketing plans of an internationally operating firm that might be found in the company's international marketing planning manual. An extremely helpful tool is the business plan structure offered by Venture, a joint venture of the Eidgenössische Technische Hochschule, Zurich (ETH) and McKinsey & Company, Switzerland. They offer downloads of fully programmed Excel spreadsheets that the marketer can easily apply.

Marketing plans of local operating units

Table 17.1 shows an example of the potential structure and content of a marketing plan to be developed by all local operating units of an international marketer serving consumer markets. Such operating units may be subsidiaries, sales offices, or distribution partners in a country market. But the structure suggested in Table 17.1 may also be used by sales managers of an exporting firm who need to prepare a marketing plan for the country market or sales region they are responsible for.

Preface The plan starts with a short preface. In this introduction the author(s) of the plan state(s) the reason for presenting the marketing plan, the audience the plan is targeted at, the main assumptions the author(s) had to make (for example, the development of the inflation rate, getting an import license in time, or finding a local supplier), the persons involved in preparing the plan (including a "thank you" to all who cooperated), the time spent, and the decisions the author(s) are expecting.

TABLE 17.1 *Potential structure and content of a local marketing plan*

Following the introduction the most essential contents of a marketing plan are summarized. A description of the actual situation constitutes the basis for the formulation of objectives. The activity plan shows how those objectives are to be reached. The budget figures express the expenses for the planned activities and relate them to expected results.

Table of contents

1 Introduction

2 Executive summary

3 Actual situation

    3.1   Internal situation

        3.1.1   Strategic market position

        3.1.2   Objectives and levels of achievement (e.g., sales, profits, market shares, average prices by product lines, products, sales regions, customer (group)s)

        3.1.3   Marketing mix

        3.1.4   Organization and personnel

        3.1.5   Costs and financial status

    3.2   External situation

        3.2.1   Macro-environment (important dimensions, relevant factors of influence, development)

        3.2.2   Industry (e.g., sales potential, sales volume, structure, profitability, particular events and developments of significance)

        3.2.3   Intermediaries (e.g., structure, business behavior, particular events, developments of significance)

        3.2.4   Customers (e.g., regional distribution, purchasing power, specific characteristics, purchasing behavior, consumption behavior, expectations, segments)

        3.2.5   Competitors (e.g., served customer segments, intended or existing differentiation, competitive strategy, market share, marketing mix, cost structure, financial structure, technical know-how, alliances)

        3.2.6   Other important stakeholders (e.g., media, legislators, trade unions, ecologists)

    3.3   Assessment of internal and external situation

        3.3.1   Strengths and weaknesses

        3.3.2   Opportunities and threats

        3.3.3   Gaps

4 Objectives

    4.1   Intended strategic position

        4.1.1   Target customer segments

        4.1.2   Differentiation from competitors

    4.2   Sales and market share objectives (e.g., by existing customers, new customers, customer segments, sales area, product lines, products)

    4.3   Marketing mix objectives

    4.4   Financial objectives (e.g., profit, free cash flow, return on sales, capital turnover)

    4.5   Activity plan

        4.5.1   Marketing mix

            4.5.1.1   Product management

            4.5.1.2   Distribution and sales management

            4.5.1.3   Pricing

            4.5.1.4   Market communication

        4.5.2   Organization and personnel

            4.5.2.1   Organization

            4.5.2.2   Personnel (e.g., personnel development measures, continuous improvement activities, layoffs)

            4.5.2.3   Monitoring (e.g., marketing research, information system, controlling)

5 Budgets

    5.1   Product management budget

    5.2   Distribution and sales budget

    5.3   Market communication budget

    5.4   Personnel budget

    5.5   Monitoring budget

Executive summary Then the marketing plan summarizes the major results of the analyses undertaken and the conclusions drawn from those results in an executive summary taking no more than a maximum of two pages. The executive summary is the most important part of the marketing plan because people reading the plan tend not to study the rest of the plan if the executive summary is not convincing. Most central decision makers in internationally operating firms suffer from continual information overflow. They are not ready to read more than two pages in order to find out the most important points of a message. As a consequence, marketing managers do not have much room for a lengthy narration. Sentences must be precise and self-explanatory, using an attractive writing style. Furthermore, persuasive headings are needed to gain and keep the audience's attention. They may be also very helpful when the statements made in the executive summary are presented to decision makers with the help of transparencies, slides, or a computer animation.

Actual situation In the following material, readers interested in more detail may find information concerning the actual situation of the organizational unit as it developed during the last 3 to 5 years, as well as the development of the served market(s) during the same period.

Set objectives and the degree of their achievement for example, in terms of products sold in the market, average price, number of customers reached, sales per customer, or market share are described as well as development of the firm's local strategic position, applied marketing mix for example, activities set in trade advertising and related budgets, fairs and exhibitions attended, product launches, key account or merchandising activities, and terms of sale, local organizational structure, and activities in personnel development.

Development of costs related to the activities undertaken, local calculation of prices, and the resulting price list are shown together with the financial situation of the operating unit.

The description of the served market(s) may encompass an overview of the development of macro-environmental dimensions relevant to the international marketer's business, such as import regulations, inflation and currency exchange rates, economic climate, improvements in infrastructure, or changes in values dominating the local society. Further, the marketing plan will describe the development of the local industry the company is part of. First, data on the general development are presented, such as market volume compared to market potential, average price of products sold, shares of differently priced product lines, or the average profitability in the industry. Then, more specific information concerning intermediaries, customers, and competitors is added. The structure of potential and served intermediaries, their relationships with major suppliers (share of company products sold compared to competitors' products), and their business behavior may be of particular interest. Regional distribution, purchasing power, buying and consumption patterns, brand or supplier awareness as well as expectations of customers may be described and used to form customer segments. Major competitors are characterized by features such as their size (in sales, employees, market share, and profitability), competitive behavior, the strategic position they have reached, the marketing mix they apply, their cost structure, financial resources, relationships and alliances, or their market specific know-how.

In addition to the description of past developments in the operating and macro-environments that make the reader understand why the actual situation of the local unit is as has been indicated in the marketing plan, the foreseeable development of those environments (up to the planning horizon) is presented. In preparing that outlook into the future of the business, responsible managers will rely on the basic assumptions given by their company's marketing strategy. Short-term figures such as the development of sales, stock, accounts receivable, or liquidity will partly be based on estimations sourced to field experience of staff and partly on forecasts using more or less sophisticated computer models.

Internal and external developments Assessment of internal and external developments reveals the strengths and weaknesses of the operational unit at date compared to its strengths and weaknesses at the planning horizon if marketing activities are carried on without changes. It also highlights potential opportunities and threats stemming from the fit between the operational unit's current skills and resources and foreseeable developments in the macro-environment. Based on this assessment gaps can be defined that need to be filled in order to make the operating unit properly contribute to the general marketing objectives stated in the company's or business unit's marketing strategy.

For example, if the marketing strategy of a Japanese manufacturer of industrial transportation systems defines the objective of reaching at least a market share that places the firm in the first three ranks of suppliers in every served market and its European subsidiary serving the automotive industry is in danger of slipping from rank four to rank five in its market, there is an evident need to fill this gap between general objectives and actual development with appropriate measures.

Marketing objectives Because the general marketing objectives stated in the marketing strategy and the marketing objectives of the local unit in general do not totally fit in the short run, the marketing objectives of the unit are stated in the marketing plan. Most international marketers find it useful to indicate the local unit's intended strategic position, that is, the customer segments (rank ordered by priority) to be reached during the planning period and the differentiation from competitors to be achieved in those customers' minds; sales and market share objectives by current and new customers, customer segments, and regions; objectives concerning the marketing mix, for example, the objective of increasing market share in a specific customer segment may be supported by the objectives of launching an improved product, increasing distribution intensity, raising the attractiveness of terms of sale to intermediaries, and participating in special target group events; financial objectives, telling the audience what contribution local marketing managers expect to make to the overall profitability of the firm.

Marketing meeting

©Comstock Images/Alamy

Activities The following section of the marketing plan contains the activities to be implemented during the planning period in order to reach the set objectives and to monitor their success. In a marketing plan all marketing activities are described in detail. Organizational measures and personnel development needs to ensure marketing success are indicated as well as activities needed to monitor business development.

Budgets Finally, the marketing plan presents the costs of planned activities and compares them to expected revenues in detailed budgets.

International marketing planning manual

To make sure that all managers and distributors of the company who regularly have to establish marketing plans employ the same structure, the same forms and definitions, the central marketing unit in the international marketer's headquarters may be well advised to develop an *international marketing planning manual*. Such manual serves as a guideline for planners. It prescribes the general structure all marketing plans have to follow. The manual contains the forms to be used, and assures easy consolidation of data. This is important for the establishment of a company or business unit international marketing plan.

Company or business unit international marketing plan

Marketing plans of local units must be consolidated to provide the information needed by senior management in order to agree or disagree with what has been planned. Basically, such a consolidated plan follows the same structure as the marketing plans of the subunits. But it provides information on an aggregated level, that is, activities are reported in less detail.

Introduction and executive summary

As with marketing plans of local units the company or business unit international marketing plan starts with an introduction and an executive summary.

Actual situation

The description of the actual situation starts with an overview of internal preconditions and assumptions that underlie all marketing planning activities (see Table 17.2). First comes a revision of corporate policy and corporate strategy statements as far as they are relevant for marketing decisions and actions, followed by the guidelines for the application of marketing tools stated in the marketing strategy.

An overview of the structure of the firm's or business unit's marketing organization shows to the plan's audiences what functional marketing areas exist, where in the firm's hierarchy they are located, and how they are coordinated by senior management. Regular teams and special taskforces are described as to their purpose, size, and participating members. The same is done for external cooperation partners, such as market research agencies, market communication specialists, new product development or logistics partners.

A flowchart may inform the reader about the sequence of analyses and decisions, the participating organizational units, and the timing of the international marketing decision process. The description of the internal situation continues with marketing achievements of the company or business unit during the reporting period (generally 3 years).

It starts with a comparison of quantitative and qualitative marketing objectives as fixed in the reporting period with the results achieved in the same period. Those results are compared to the objectives stated for the planning period (for example the coming 3 years). Then, the range of products marketed by the company/business unit is described, indicating their specific features, their target groups, their applications, and major benefits provided to the customers. An overview of current customers is given. For the most important customers name, location, products purchased, and sales are indicated. The other customers are grouped depending on their purchasing volumes. If available, average contribution margins achieved per important customer or customer group when provided will further increase the level of information.

TABLE 17.2 *Description of firm's actual marketing situation*

The description of the actual marketing situation includes internal and external information needed to assess the relative strengths and weaknesses of the firm, as well as opportunities and threats it is facing from the macro-environment and to determine strategic gaps to be filled by marketing actions.

Table of contents
  1 Actual situation
  1.1 Corporate policy and strategies
    1.1.1 Corporate policy
      1.1.1.1 Corporate mission
      1.1.1.2 Corporate philosophy
    1.1.2 Corporate strategy
      1.1.2.1 Portfolio strategy
      1.1.2.2 Competitive strategy
      1.1.2.3 Market-entry strategy
    1.1.3 Marketing strategy
      1.1.3.1 Product policy
      1.1.3.2 Distribution policy
      1.1.3.3 Pricing policy
      1.1.3.4 Market communication policy
    1.1.4 Marketing organization
  1.2 Marketing achievements
    1.2.1 Marketing objectives and results

Objectives	Results				Plan	
	2004	2005	2006	2007	2008	2009
1 Quantitative objectives (e.g., sales, market share, ROS, share of new products, customer retention rate, etc.)						
2 Qualitative objectives (e.g., reputation, awareness, customer satisfaction, lasting relationships, etc.)						

    1.2.2 Range of products/industries/applications

Range of products	Description	Features	Target groups	Applications industries	Benefits

    1.2.3 Important customers

Location	Name	Product	Sales 200_

1.2.4 Important suppliers

Location	Name	Product	Value

1.2.5 Other important stakeholders

Stakeholder group	Interests	Actions	Reactions

1.2.6 Major investments realized

Type	Purpose	Location	Value

1.3 Development of external environments
    1.3.1 Macro-environment
        (e.g., political risk, currency exchange rates, legislation, liberalization)
    1.3.2 Industry
        (e.g., total sales volume, structure of supply, average prices, profit margin, emerging markets, technological innovation)
    1.3.3 Customers
        (e.g., structure of intermediaries, emerging intermediaries, customer segments, emerging expectations)
    1.3.4 Competitors
        (e.g., strategic groups, alliances, competitive strategy of major competitors, mergers/acquisitions, new product launches)
    1.3.5 Other important stakeholders
        (e.g., suppliers, investors, creditors, administrators, media)
1.4 Situation assessment
    1.4.1 Strengths and weaknesses
    1.4.2 Opportunities and threats
    1.4.3 Strategic gaps
1.5 Internal marketing objectives and budgets
1.6 Expected results

A list of important suppliers and other important stakeholders indicating their specific interests concerning the company's business as well as the actions set by the firm and the reactions of the stakeholders further enriches the audience's picture of the actual situation. A description of major investments realized in the marketing area finishes the marketing achievements section of the plan. It may contain information on special activities such as the construction of a new warehouse, the opening of new company owned stores, or the installation of a new marketing information system.

Development of external environments The description of the actual situation would not be complete without a presentation of the results of external analyses. The international marketing plan, therefore, contains a section that summarizes information concerning the development of external environments from the marketing plans of the local operating units. Important changes compared to earlier reporting periods and compared to assumptions that were taken for the actual reporting period are specifically highlighted.

Situation assessment

As a conclusion from reported internal and external developments, in the next section of the plan a situation assessment is given. It determines the strengths and weaknesses of the company or business unit compared to its major competitors, focusing on the success factors in each of the served product markets and in the major country markets or regions. Together with the detected opportunities and threats from the international macro-environment of the business, those strengths and weaknesses provide the basis for an analysis of strategic gaps. The international marketing plan enumerates and illustrates the various areas in which the company needs to improve.

For example, setting different transfer prices to distributors and sales offices may have led to price differences in final customer prices that may be considered an invitation for parallel imports. The lack of an efficient customer information system may have led to differing treatment of the subsidiaries of the same globally active customer, resulting in customer complaints, and pressure on prices. A lack of total quality assurance may have caused defective products to be sent back, increasing costs and harming the firm's reputation. Those gaps must at least be partly filled by marketing activities.

International marketing objectives and budgets

The illustration of gaps found as a result of the actual situation analysis leads the audiences of the plan back to the objectives formulated for the planning period. The following section of the international marketing plan entitled "International marketing objectives and budgets" particularly emphasizes sales forecasts for the planning period and budgets needed to realize those sales figures (see Table 17.3). It starts with reminding the audiences of the company's or business unit's intended global strategic position. This is the standard of comparison for all activities budgeted in the following. Any budgeted activity needs to make a contribution to reaching this standard.

Sales forecasts for each local product market stored in a databank allow fast and flexible computation of total sales forecasts for products, product lines, international product markets, country markets, regions, industries, or international key accounts. As Table 17.3 illustrates, information can be sorted, filtered, and combined according to the needs of the user. For example, the international sales forecast for a product market can be determined by adding all sales forecasts for the local product markets to be found in the marketing plans of the local operating units. The firm's forecasted total sales are the result of adding up the forecasts for all different product markets. Total sales in a country market can be determined by adding up all sales forecasts for different product markets in that geographic area. For liquidity planning purposes, a forecast of accounts receivable during the planning period is generated. It is based on the sales forecast and the customers paying habits, as far as the marketer knows of those habits.

The presentation of budget figures starts with a general overview. The total marketing budget is given by types of cost, split into their variable and fixed parts. An overview of expected order backlog and development of stock are added. Audiences interested in more details may directly switch to the presentation of product, marketing tool, and marketing administration budgets.

Product budgets These contain all activities planned for a specific product or product line, indicating their fixed and variable costs and the country where those activities are set. The information needed to establish those budgets again is compiled from the marketing plans of the local operating units (see Figure 17.5).

Marketing tools budgets The same information may be used to establish budgets for each bundle of marketing tools. In the international product management budget, for example, all activities concerning new product development, taking

TABLE 17.3 *Content of "international marketing objectives and budgets"*

The objectives and budgets section of an international marketing plan should contain a summary of the intended global strategic position of the firm/business unit, sales forecasts, and budgets.

1 Intended global strategic position
    1.1 Target markets
        1.1.1 Product markets
        1.1.2 Country markets
        1.1.3 Customer segments
    1.2 Major benefits/competitive differentiation
    1.3 Technologies
2 Sales forecast

    2.1 Sales

Year	Product	Country	Rep	Industry	Number of customers	Number of orders	Units	Price per unit	Sales ($)	Market share
2005	A	U.K.	I	Chemistry	12	14	91			
2006	B	U.K.	II	Steelworks						
2007	D	A	III	Chemistry						
2008	B	F	IV	Food						
2009	E	U.S.	V	Food						
2010	C	NL	IV	Food						
2011										
—	—	—	—	—			—	—	—	

    2.2 Accounts receivable

Product	1st quarter 2006 ($)	2nd quarter 2006 ($)	3rd quarter 2006 ($)	4th quarter 2006 ($)	1st half-year 2007 ($)	2nd half-year 2007 ($)
A accounts receivable – payments + new accounts receivable accounts receivable						
B accounts receivable – payment + new accounts receivable accounts receivable						
Total accounts receivable – payments + new accounts receivable accounts receivable						

3   Budgets

3.1   Overview

3.1.1   Total marketing budget

Type of cost	Fixed costs ($)			Variable costs ($)		
	2005	2006	2007	2005	2006	2007
Total						

3.1.2   Order backlog/sales/bookings

Product	1st quarter 2006 ($)	2nd quarter 2006 ($)	3rd quarter 2006 ($)	4th quarter 2006 ($)	1st half-year 2007 ($)	2nd half-year 2007 ($)
A order backlog						
sales						
bookings						
order backlog						
B order backlog						
sales						
bookings						
order backlog						
Total order backlog						
sales						
bookings						
order backlog						

3.1.3   Development of stock

Product	1st quarter 2006 ($)	2nd quarter 2006 ($)	3rd quarter 2006 ($)	4th quarter 2006 ($)	1st half-year 2007 ($)	2nd half-year 2007 ($)
A stock						
+						
–						
new stock						
B stock						
+						
–						
new stock						
Total stock						
+						
–						
new stock						

3.2   Product budgets

Product A in all countries of the EU, NAFTA, and Latin America

Marketing tool	Decision or action (examples)	Country	Fixed cost ($)	Variable cost per — ($)	Total cost ($)
Product management	Brand (registration and current cost per year)	EU		year	
	Patent (registration and current cost per year)	EU		year	
	New product prototype testing	U.S.		year	
	Packaging (design as fixed cost and price per unit)	EU NAFTA		unit	
	Packaging (design as fixed cost and price per unit)	All countries		unit	
	Warranty	All countries		percentage of sales	
	Service free of charge	Latin America		percentage of sales	
Distribution	Systems/channels Traveling expenses of sales staff	EU NAFTA		percentage of sales or by order	
	Traveling expenses of sales staff	Latin America		percentage of sales or by order	
	Representatives' commission	EU		percentage of sales	
	Representatives' commission	NAFTA		percentage of sales	
	Representatives' commission	Latin America		percentage of sales	
	Training of representatives	All countries			
	Equipment representatives	All countries			
	Sales meetings	All countries			
	Sales office (including rent, furniture, personnel, traveling, stationery, phone, etc.)	U.S.			
	Logistics Warehouse	U.S.			
	Warehouse	Spain			
	Storage fee	Sweden		percentage of sales	

	Transportation (if not considered elsewhere)	NAFTA	
	Transportation (if not considered elsewhere)	Latin America	
	Insurance (if not considered elsewhere)	NAFTA	
		Latin America	
Pricing	Discounts/rebates	EU	percentage of sales
	Discounts/rebates	NAFTA	percentage of sales
	Discounts/rebates	Latin America	percentage of sales
	Action	U.S.	
	Transfer prices	NAFTA	percentage of sales
	Average date of required payment	per country	percentage of sales
	Delcredere	per country	percentage of sales
Marketing communication	Regional radio ad campaign	EU	
	Ads in trade magazines	U.S. Canada	
	Yellow pages	EU per country	
	Yellow pages	NAFTA per country	
	Image brochure	All countries	
	Videotape	All countries	
	Sales manual	per country	
	Press conferences	U.S.	
	Press conferences	Germany	
	Sales promotion activities	France	
	Direct mailing	U.S.	
	Fair	Italy	
	Fair	Brazil	
	Fair	Canada	
	Symposium	U.K.	
	Open house	EU U.S.	

3.3 Marketing tool budgets
    3.3.1 Product management
    3.3.2 Distribution (inc. logistics)
    3.3.3 Pricing
    3.3.4 Market communication
3.4 Marketing administration budget
    3.4.1 Overheads
    3.4.2 Organizational changes

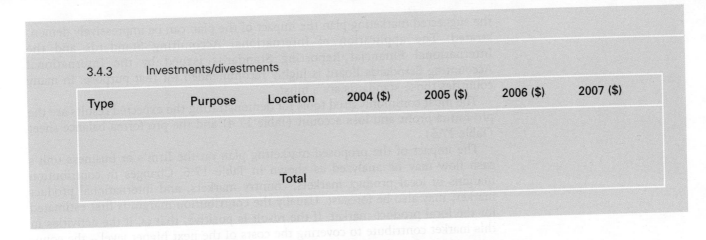

3.4.3 Investments/divestments

Type	Purpose	Location	2004 ($)	2005 ($)	2006 ($)	2007 ($)
		Total				

products off the market, finding brand names, registering patents or brands, warranties, pre- and after-sales services across all served country markets are aggregated to consolidated figures for each category of activity.

Marketing administration budget The marketing administration budget contains all types of overheads, as well as special budgets needed for changes in marketing organization, such as project budgets for the improvement of the reporting system, the preparation of offers, order handling, or the reorganization of warehouses. A final subsection on special investments or divestments, such as the construction of a new warehouse or the outsourcing of logistics, informs senior decision makers about extraordinary expenses planned for the improvement of the firm's marketing effectiveness and efficiency.

Expected results

Having presented the objectives to reach, the activities planned, and the costs of those activities, the international marketing planners need to add an estimation of expected results in order to convince senior decision makers and other interested audiences of how attractive it is to accept or follow their plan. Therefore, a section presenting forecast results based on the previously suggested actions concludes the international marketing plan. By comparing the results to be expected when extrapolating current marketing action with the results forecast for

FIGURE 17.5 *International budgeting hierarchy*

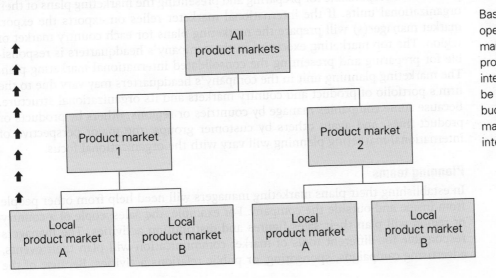

Based on budgets of local operating units concerning marketing activities in their served product markets, budgets for international product markets may be established. Adding those budgets up leads to the total marketing budget of the internationally operating firm.

the suggested marketing plan the impact of the plan can be impressively demonstrated. The application of International Accounting Standards and the International Financial Reporting Standards issued by the International Accounting Standards Board is highly recommended for that purpose. In many countries those standards are a must.

The most commonly used tools for demonstrating the expected results are the pro forma profit and loss account (Table 17.4) and the pro forma balance sheet (Table 17.5).

The impact of the proposed marketing plan on the firm's or business unit's cash flow may be analyzed as shown in Table 17.6. Changes in contribution margins of local product markets, country markets, and international product markets may also be forecast. Usually the contribution margin is first estimated for the local product market. If the result is positive, that is, if the activities in this market contribute to covering the costs of the next higher level – the country market – the estimation procedure continues. Similarly, the country market has to contribute to covering the costs of managing the international product market or business unit, and the latter finally has to contribute to covering the overheads of company management.

Finally, the impact of the proposed marketing plan on the break-even point of local and international product markets as well as country markets may be estimated. Besides break-even analysis, to get an impression of the risk involved with implementing the international marketing plan, a kind of sensitivity analysis of the suggested activities to major changes in the operating and macro-environment can be conducted. Instead of presenting just one single result, the planning team should develop two alternatives that consider significantly different developments of those environments. A more optimistic scenario may be considered as well as a more pessimistic one. In times of economic or other difficulties a company is facing, however, marketing planners may be well advised to probe for the impact of two more negative scenarios, for example by simply reducing sales forecasts by 10 and 20%. In fast growing markets, however, it may make sense to develop alternative plans for market growth rates of 30 and 50%. Most importantly, the international marketer must be intellectually prepared for alternative developments to what seems to be the most realistic current assumption.

Planning procedure

Responsibilities

In general, marketing or sales managers of local operating units and distribution partners are responsible for preparing and presenting the marketing plans of their organizational units. If the international marketer relies on exports the export market manager(s) will prepare the marketing plans for each country market or region. The top marketing executive in the company's headquarters is responsible for preparing and presenting the consolidated international marketing plan. The marketing planning unit in the company's headquarters may vary due to the firm's portfolio of product and country markets and its organizational structure. Because some companies manage by countries or regions, others by products or product lines, and again others by customer groups, the major perspective of international marketing planning will vary with the organizational focus.

Planning teams

In establishing their plans marketing managers will need help from other people from inside and outside the company. For example, the salespeople of a country or region will plan their sales figures and distribution activities. The managers responsible for different tools of market communication will plan their events, advertising campaigns, sponsoring, or public relations activities. Because of the complexity of the planning task, which needs information input and know-how from all across the company's functional areas, inter-functional planning teams may help to assure that all aspects of the planning task are appropriately considered. Under the leadership of the responsible marketing manager at least in certain steps of the planning process (such as the establishment of the profit and loss account) or when preparing certain sections of the marketing plan (for example, the personnel development section) specialists from the functional areas concerned need to be involved. Production, controlling, personnel, procurement, logistics, research and development, or finance managers may contribute their information for pricing, personnel development, or new product development decisions. In addition to the know-how and information those people may provide to increase the quality of marketing planning, the participation of those people in the planning process strongly contributes to its implementation. Culture box 17.1 gives an impression of what problems may arise in intercultural planning teams, but also how much teamwork may contribute to improved planning results and adherence of team members to the decided course of action.

As with any project carried out by a team, it is important to brief the participants in the planning process as to the basic requirements of the plan and to agree on deadlines for the contributors. The team leader may go through the objectives and policies stated in the company's or business unit's marketing

TABLE 17.4 *Pro forma profit and loss account*

Income and expenditures	$* 2006	$** 2006	$* 2007	$** 2007
Sales income				
Cost of goods				
Gross profit				
Expenditure				
Administration				
Rent and rates				
Product management				
Distribution				
Pricing				
Market communication				
Overheads				
Depreciation				
Interest				
Total expenditure				
PBIT (profit before interest and tax)				
Taxation				
Profit after tax				
Gross % (gross profit divided by sales income)				
Total expenditure % (total expenditure divided by sales income)				
ROI % (return on investment)				
Gearing %				

* Result when keeping current action unchanged
** Result when implementing the marketing plan

Source: Adapted from Office for Official Publications of the European Union, Directorate-General XIII (1994) "Preparing a technology business plan", EU: Luxembourg

The pro forma profit and loss account compares incomes and expenditures when marketing action is kept unchanged with incomes and expenditures when the suggested marketing plan is implemented.

TABLE 17.5 *Pro forma balance sheet*

The pro forma balance sheet compares assets and liabilities when marketing action is kept unchanged with assets and liabilities when the suggested marketing plan is implemented.

Assets and liabilities	$*	$**	$*	$**
	2006	2006	2007	2007

Assets

A Called-up share capital not paid
B Fixed assets
I Intangible assets
  1 Development costs
  2 Concessions, patents, licenses, trademarks
  3 Similar rights and assets
  4 Goodwill
  5 Payments on account
II Tangible assets
  1 Land and buildings
  2 Plant and machinery
  3 Fixtures, fittings, tools, and equipment
  4 Payments on account
  5 Assets in course of construction
III Investments
  1 Shares in group companies
  2 Loans to group companies
  3 Shares in related companies
  4 Loans to related companies
  5 Other investments other than loans
  6 Other loans
  7 Own shares
C Current assets
I Stocks
  1 Raw materials and consumables
  2 Work in progress
  3 Finished goods and goods for resale
  4 Payments on account
II Debtors
  1 Trade debtors
  2 Amounts owed group companies
  3 Amounts owed by related companies
  4 Other debtors
  5 Called-up share capital not paid
  6 Prepayments and accrued income
III Investments
  1 Shares in group companies
  2 Own shares
  3 Other investments
IV Cash at bank and in hand
D Prepayments and accrued income

Liabilities

A Capital and reserves
I Called-up share capital
II Share premium account
III Revaluation reserve

IV   Other reserves
     1 Capital redemption reserve
     2 Reserve for own shares
     3 Reserves provided for by the articles of association
     4 Other reserves
V   Profit and loss account
B   Provisions for liabilities and charges
     1 Pensions and similar obligations
     2 Taxation, including deferred taxation
     3 Other provisions
C   Creditors
     1 Debenture loans
     2 Bank loans and overdrafts
     3 Payments received on account
     4 Trade creditors
     5 Bills of exchange payable
     6 Amounts owed to group companies
     7 Amounts owed to related companies
     8 Other creditors including taxation and social security
     9 Accruals and deferred income
D   Accruals and deferred income

  * Result when keeping current action unchanged
  ** Result when implementing the marketing plan

strategy. The basic assumptions concerning the development of the macro-environment and the industry may be discussed with the goal to create some basic shared understanding of what the major issues are that need to be tackled, and what the major objectives are that should be reached. This technique known as "pre-briefing" takes some additional time to get planning activities started. But it has enormous benefits later on resulting in fewer criticisms and internal politics that otherwise might sink a marketing plan at a first presentation.

Updates

Preparing the marketing plan starts where the strategic part of the international marketing decision process ends. The principal results of this decision process – for example, which country markets to serve with which kind of product through which market-entry mode – may be valid for some longer term. They represent the basis from which the more short-term-oriented marketing plan is developed. Because the activities contained in the marketing plan and the figures related to those activities are planned in great detail they are subject to change. Consequently, at least a yearly update of the marketing plan is required. Planned activities and figures must be reviewed at least quarterly in the light of actual developments in all environments of the company. Future issues box 17.1 gives an impression of how much advances in information technology will speed up the rhythm of plan reviews in the coming years. Any discrepancies between the original assumptions and the recorded development, which result in performance figures that deviate from expectations, must be accounted for and the assumptions modified if necessary.

Any of the revisions of marketing plans where inputs like sales, prices, costs, or currency exchange rates may change should have a mid-range planning horizon. The horizon will vary with the company's business domain, but in most cases it is between 2 and 5 years. That is, activities and figures should not only

TABLE 17.6 *Cash flow forecast*

The cash flow forecast compares cash flows when marketing action is kept unchanged with cash flows when the suggested marketing plan is implemented.

Cash flows	$*	$**	$*	$**
	2006	2006	2007	2007
Cash inflows				
Sales				
Capital				
Loans				
Total inflow				
Cash outflows				
Machinery				
Raw material				
Labor				
Rent				
Rates				
Distribution related expenditures				
Market communication				
General overheads				
Administration overheads				
Loan interest				
Total inflow				
Balance brought forward				
Balance carried forward				

* Result when keeping current action unchanged
** Result when implementing the marketing plan

Source: Adapted from Office for Official Publications of the European Union, Directorate-General XIII (1994) "Preparing a technology business plan," EU: Luxembourg

be adjusted for the actual planning period, which, in most cases, extends across 1 year from the point in time of the plan revision. Forecasts for the subsequent periods must also be adjusted in line with the revised assumptions. At least the central figures in the profit and loss account as well as in the pro forma balance sheet for the next 2 to 5 years need to be adjusted. This way the company and its subunits will have rolling marketing plans that are responsive to changes in the business environment.

CULTURE BOX 17.1

Mercedes made in Alabama

Possessing nothing but the proverbial blank sheet of paper, Andreas Renschler, CEO of the Alabama factory of Stuttgart, Germany-based Daimler-Chrysler, set out to "create" his factory in 1993. He very deliberately pieced together a team that included U.S. executives with Detroit auto experience, along with a couple who had worked for Japanese transplants in North America. He drafted a perfectly balanced ticket: Four Germans, four Americans at management's top tier. The plan was to plumb the assembled U.S. automotive talent for fresh insights about how to run a factory. Those with Japanese transplant experience, he hoped, could provide pointers on how a foreign automaker might best go about setting up shop in the U.S.

But the members of the management team hailed from very different manufacturing traditions and possessed vastly different ideas about how to do things. They all spoke different languages – GM-ese, Nissan-ese, Mercedes-ese, as it were. Questions such as how to configure the assembly line set off fierce debates. Progress would probably never have been possible had it not been for one of the headquarters' infrequent directives – a very rigid timeframe that was in place from day one. Thus, the team had no choice but to fight until it came up with blueprints for a factory and plans for hiring a workforce. Despite all the cultural differences, the Vance, Alabama, factory has proven to be a success. The design, a sleek E-shape with interconnected shops, has turned out especially efficient.

Source: Adapted from Martin, J. (1997) "Mercedes: made in Alabama", *Fortune*, 7 July, pp. 150–58.

FUTURE ISSUES BOX 17.1

The marketing plan of the future

The fast development of information technology will have a major impact on the development and update of future marketing plans.

The marketing plan of the future will probably be:

- "instant". Inputs will be made at the customer's office and transferred immediately. All new data at the factory, like change in stock, price increase of a supplier etc. will be instantly considered by the system. This will offer up-to-the-second information to all relevant people inside and outside the company at any given time.
- "online". All data will be collected, computed, and saved at one location, that is the server or network of the marketer's company. As a consequence all relevant people have the same level of information and there is no time lag. Their notebooks will work as terminals.
- "continually rolling". All changes will be considered instantly. This way the marketing plan is kept permanently up to date and adapted

to new facts, for instance, changes in the macro-environment.
- "independent of the location". The next generation of cell phones will offer worldwide use of telephone networks across the globe directly via satellite, putting international marketers in the position of having access to their "home" databank day and night.
- "standardized". Software has been and will be developed that, on the one hand, takes into account all features telecommunication systems and high-end hardware – like dictating directly into a machine – offer and, on the other hand, uses standardized protocols for data transfer like the United Nations' EDIFACT.
- "using more and more external data". Data available in the world wide web concerning the macro-environment, industries, intermediaries, potential customers, competitors, and other important stakeholders may be automatically considered by the computer system by executing updating routines.

Source: Based on Negroponte, N. (1995) *Being Digital*, London: Coronet Books; results of presentations and discussions at European Forum Alpbach, 1995 and 1996, Alpbach, Austria

Summary

The primary objective in preparing an international business plan is to set out a convincing case to secure internal and external financing for the startup, expansion, or continuation of an international business. The business plan must demonstrate in a rigorous manner the commercial viability of the proposed actions. The plan should cover all aspects of the business: from the corporate mission, to the corporate strategy, business unit and functional area strategies, right down to functional area plans.

Marketing orientation and marketing analyses may have a significant impact on the formulation of corporate philosophy and corporate strategy. They influence the basic approach of a company's management to their business and lead their decision-making processes in a way to start from the determination of attractive markets. The influence of marketing orientation and marketing technology leads market choice as well as competitive strategy decisions to be taken based on the skills and resources needed to successfully serve the most attractive markets.

Marketing strategy and plan are the core parts of an international business plan. They encompass the results of analyses, decisions, guidelines, and actions that are based on the basic strategic decisions of senior management and have been discussed in detail throughout this book. Marketing plans should have a flexible structure, comprising all required information, but a different degree of consolidation of each section depending on the audience they are presented to. In any case, a marketing plan should be:

- as short as possible
- clearly structured
- consistent
- convincing.

The international marketing plan usually is based on marketing plans of local operating units or of managers who are responsible for certain international sales areas. All marketing plans should comprise:

- a preface or introduction
- an executive summary
- a description of the actual position of the firm
- results from an analysis of the external environments relevant to the company's business.

This analytical part of the plan is concluded by the determination of the firm's relative marketing strengths and weaknesses, opportunities and threats it is facing from being more or less well adapted to developments in the macro-environment, and strategic gaps that need to be filled in order to keep or make the company successful. Based on that information, marketing planners have to specify marketing objectives for the planning period. Those objectives will be derived from more general objectives stated in the corporate, business unit, and marketing strategy statements. All marketing activities proposed in the following section of the plan have to contribute to reaching the set goals.

The higher the level of plan aggregation the more abstract the content of the plan becomes. That is, marketing plans of locally responsible units describe all planned activities in some detail, whereas the company's or a business unit's international marketing plan mainly contains budget figures that stand for the planned activities.

To convincingly present the proposed marketing actions the marketing plan needs finally to demonstrate how much better off the company will be when it implements the plan. For that purpose, result forecasts for an unchanged course of action are compared to result estimates under the condition that the proposed marketing plan is implemented.

Pro forma profit and loss statements, pro forma balance sheets, cash flow projections, contribution margin estimates, and break-even analyses under both conditions serve the purpose of comparison. An analysis of the sensitivity of those forecast results to changes in the assumed environment helps the final decision makers to get an impression of the risks involved with their decision.

What the real outcomes of international marketing strategies and plans will be nobody can know exactly beforehand. The success of an international marketer will depend not only on the perfection of its analyses, the professionalism of the conclusions drawn, and the motivation of all people involved in the implementation of plans. The marketer will also need a substantial amount of *luck* to become and stay a major player in the international business arena.

DISCUSSION QUESTIONS

1. Why does the international marketing decision process have different hierarchical levels? Explain by using the example of a company you are familiar with.

2. Find the example of two corporate policies on the internet and compare them concerning the visible influence of marketing orientation on their formulation.

3. To what extent does marketing influence the development of a corporate strategy? Find examples for the points you make.

4. Ask a local marketing or sales manager of an internationally operating firm to show you the table of contents of the marketing plan they have to prepare. How does it compare to what was discussed in this chapter?

5. What audiences may be interested in the international marketing plan of a firm? What are they particularly interested in?

6. Along what dimensions should international marketing planning information be structured to be flexibly usable for various audiences?

7. Describe the steps in the process of development of an international marketing plan. Who should be involved in the planning team at what stage?

ADDITIONAL READINGS

Covin, J.G., D.P. Slevin, and R.L. Schultz (1997) "Top management decision sharing and adherence to plans", *Journal of Business Research*, 40, 21–36.

Hooley, G.J., G.E. Greenley, J.W. Cadogan, and J. Fahy (2005) "The performance impact of marketing resources", *Journal of Business Research*, 58, 18–27.

Looser, U. and Schläpfer, B./McKinsey & Company (2002) "The new venture adventure", London: McKinsey & Company.

Schlegelmilch, B.B. and R. Sinkovics (1998) "Viewpoint: marketing in the information age – can we plan for an unpredictable future?", *International Marketing Review*, 15(3), 162–70.

Varadarajan, P.R. and T. Clark (1994) "Delineating the scope of corporate, business, and marketing strategy", *Journal of Business Research*, 31, 93–105.

Webster, F.E. Jr. (1992) "The changing role of marketing in the corporation", *Journal of Marketing*, October, 56, 1–17.

Useful internet links

Daimler-Chrysler	http://www.daimlerchrysler.com/
The Economist	http://www.economist.com/
EDIFACT	http://www.unece.org/trade/untdid/
ETH Zurich	http://www.ethz.ch/index_EN
Firestone	http://www.bridgestone-firestone.com/
Fortune	http://www.fortune.com/
Goodyear	http://www.goodyear.com/
HP Invent	http://www.hp.com/
International Accounting Standards Board	http://www.iasplus.com/index.htm
J.R. Reynolds	http://www.rjrt.com/
The Lancet	http://www.thelancet.com/
McKinsey & Company, Switzerland	http://www.mckinsey.ch/
Michelin	http://www.michelin.com/
Pirelli	http://www.pirelli.com/en_42/tyres/tyres.jhtml?s1=4400002&s2=4400004
Venture	http://www.venture.ch/service_downloads_d.asp

Index